中国教育统计年鉴

EDUCATIONAL STATISTICS YEARBOOK OF CHINA

2017

中华人民共和国
教育部发展规划司

DEPARTMENT OF DEVELOPMENT & PLANNING
MINISTRY OF EDUCATION
THE PEOPLE'S REPUBLIC OF CHINA

图书在版编目（CIP）数据

中国教育统计年鉴 = Educational Statistics Yearbook of China. 2017 : 汉英对照 / 中华人民共和国教育部发展规划司编. -- 北京 : 中国统计出版社, 2018.9

ISBN 978-7-5037-8751-5

Ⅰ. ①中… Ⅱ. ①中… Ⅲ. ①教育统计-统计资料-中国-2017-年鉴-汉、英 Ⅳ. ①G526.6-54

中国版本图书馆 CIP 数据核字（2018）第 266563 号

中国教育统计年鉴—2017

作　　者/ 中华人民共和国教育部发展规划司
责任编辑/ 郭栋　张洁
装帧设计/ 黄晨
出版发行/ 中国统计出版社
地　　址/ 北京市丰台区西三环南路甲 6 号　邮政编码/100073
电　　话/ 邮购（010）63376909　书店（010）68783171
网　　址/ http://www.zgtjcbs.com
印　　刷/ 河北鑫兆源印刷有限公司
经　　销/ 新华书店
开　　本/ 787mm×1092mm　1/16
字　　数/ 1120 千字
印　　张/ 46.75
版　　别/ 2018 年 9 月第 1 版
版　　次/ 2018 年 9 月第 1 次印刷
定　　价/ 220.00 元

如有印装错误，本社发行部负责调换。

《中国教育统计年鉴》
编辑委员会名单

说　　明

《中国教育统计年鉴》（2017）是一本全面反映中华人民共和国教育事业发展情况的资料性年鉴，是由教育部发展规划司根据全国各省、自治区、直辖市教育委员会、教育厅填报的学校基层报表数字整理汇编而成的。教育部教育管理信息中心承担了数据的计算机处理汇总工作。

本年鉴包括以下部分：综合部分、高等教育、中等教育、初等教育、幼儿教育、特殊教育、全国各级各类学校的分布情况、办学条件、科学研究等。

本年鉴是各有关部门研究教育改革和发展的必备资料工具书，是教育界各机关、学校指导部门制定教育计划、指导教育改革必不可少的依据。

本年鉴所列资料，未含台湾省、香港特别行政区和澳门特别行政区的数字；凡未注明年份的均为2017年的数字。

Notes from the Compiler

The Educational Statistics Yearbook of China for 2017 is an informational yearbook com-prehensively reflecting the development of the educational undertaking of the People's Republic of China, and it was compiled by the Department of Development and Planning of Ministry of Education, based on the synthetic statistical returns relating to schools of various types and levels completed by the Educational Commissions (or the Bureaus of Education) of the provincial governnments and the governments of various autonomous regions and municipalities directly under the State Council All data were processed and calculated using Computers by the Educational Management Information Center of Ministry of Education.

The yearbook is composed of the following parts: summary tables, higher education, secondary education, primary education, pre-primary education, special education, geographical distribution of schools by type and level, Physical Facilities, Scientific Research Activities.

The yearbook is a requisite reference for all departments concerned with the study of educational reform and development, and provides indispensable factual information to the educational community (circles), the state organs, and all supervisory bodies of education (schools) engaged in curricular development and the guidance of educational reform.

The yearbook lacks the data of Education Expenditure, Taiwan Province, Hong Kong Special Administrative Region and Macao Special Administrative Region. Data in tables are for 2017, unless otherwise notified.

备　　注

自2011年起，我部对教育事业统计报表进行了全面改革，贯彻实施了国家统计局首次颁布的《统计用城乡划分代码》。新的城乡划分标准，将原来的城市、县镇、农村的三个分类调整为三大类七小类，即城区(含主城区、城乡结合区)、镇区（含镇中心区、镇乡结合区、特殊区域)、乡村（含乡中心区、村庄)。

2017年全国教育事业发展统计公报[1]

2017年，全国教育系统深入学习贯彻习近平总书记系列重要讲话精神和治国理政新理念新思想新战略，全面贯彻党的教育方针，坚持教育为人民服务，为中国共产党治国理政服务，为巩固和发展中国特色社会主义制度服务，为改革开放和社会主义现代化建设服务。紧紧围绕提高教育质量这一战略主题，以立德树人为根本任务、以促进公平为基本要求、以优化结构为主攻方向、以深化改革为根本动力，加快推进教育现代化，教育事业发展取得新进展。

一、学前教育

全国共有幼儿园25.50万所，比上年增加1.51万所，入园儿童1937.95万人，比上年减少15.87万人。在园儿童（包括附设班）4600.14万人，比上年增加186.28万人。幼儿园园长和教师共271.21万人，比上年增加21.33万人。学前教育毛入园率[2] 达到79.6%，比上年提高2.2个百分点。

二、义务教育

全国共有义务教育阶段学校21.89万所，比上年减少1.08万所；招生3313.78万人；在校生1.45亿人；专任教师949.36万人；九年义务教育巩固率[3] 93.8%。

1. 小学

全国共有小学16.70万所，比上年减少1.06万所；招生1766.55万人，比上年增加14.09万人；在校生10093.70万人，比上年增加180.69万人；毕业生1565.90万人，比上年增加58.45万人。小学学龄儿童净入学率[4] 达到99.91%。

小学教职工[5]（不含九年一贯制学校、十二年一贯制学校小学段）564.53万人，比上年增加10.80万人；专任教师594.49万人，比上年增加15.58万人。专任教师学历合格率[6] 99.96%，比上年提高0.02个百分点。生师比16.98∶1。

普通小学（含教学点）校舍建筑面积75088.46万平方米，比上年增加4123.98万平方米。设施设备配备达标的学校比例[7] 情况分别为：体育运动场（馆）面积达标学校比例84.77%，体育器械配备达标学校比例89.99%，音乐器材配备达标学校比例89.60%，美术器材配备达标学校比例89.41%，数学自然实验仪器达标学校比例。

2. 初中

全国共有初中学校5.19万所（含职业初中15所），比上年减少224所。招生1547.22万人，比上年增加60.05万人；在校生4442.06万人，比上年增加112.69万人；毕业生1397.47万人，比上年减少26.40万人。初中阶段毛入学率103.5%，初中毕业生升学率94.9%。

初中教职工（含九年一贯制学校，不含完全中学、十二年一贯制学校初中段）407.81万人，比上年增加8.06万人；专任教师354.87万人，比上年增加6.09万人。初中专任教师学历合格率99.83%，比上年提高0.07个百分点。生师比12.52∶1。

初中校舍建筑面积61006.74万平方米，比上年增加3179.54万平方米。设施设备配备达标的学校比例情况分别为：体育运动场（馆）面积达标学校比例90.35%，体育器械配备达标学校比例93.97%，音乐器材配备达标学校比例93.44%，美术器材配备达标学校比例93.17%，理科实验仪器达标学校比例94.11%。

3. 进城务工人员随迁子女

全国义务教育阶段在校生中进城务工人员随迁子女[8] 共1406.63万人。其中，在小学就读1042.18万人，在初中就读364.45万人。

三、特殊教育

全国共有特殊教育学校2107所，比上年增加27所；特殊教育学校共有专任教师5.60万人，比上年增加0.28万人。

全国共招收特殊教育学生11.08万人，比上年增加1.93万人；在校生57.88万人，比上年增加8.71万人。其中，视力残疾学生3.77万人，听力残疾学生8.98万人，智力残疾学生27.88万人，其他残疾学生14.06万人。特殊教育毕业生6.94万人，比上年增加1.02万人。

普通小学、初中随班就读和附设特教班招收的学生5.66万人，在校生30.40万人，分别占特殊教育招生总数和在校生总数的51.10%和52.52%。

四、高中阶段教育

全国高中阶段教育[9] 共有学校2.46万所，比上年减少93所；招生1382.49万人，比上年减少13.78万人；在校学生3970.99万人，比上年增加0.93万人。高中阶段毛入学率88.3%，比上年提高0.8个百分点。

1. 普通高中

全国普通高中1.36万所，比上年增加172所；招生招生800.05万人，比上年减少2.87万人；在校生2374.55万人，比上年增加7.90万人；毕业生775.73万人，比上年减少16.62万人。

普通高中教职工（含完全中学、十二年一贯制学校）266.51万人，比上年增加7.31万人；专任教师177.40万人，比上年增加4.05万人，生师比13.39∶1，比上年的13.65∶1有所改善；专任教师学历合格率98.15%，比上年提高0.24个百分点。

普通高中共有校舍建筑面积51511.74万平方米，比上年增长2369.43万平方米。普通高中设施设备配备达标的学校比例情况分别为：体育运动场（馆）面积达标学校比例91.14%，体育器械配备达标学校比例92.97%，音乐器材配备达标学校比例91.82%，美术器材配备达标学校比例 91.94%，理科实验仪器达标学校比例 93.15%。

2. 成人高中

全国成人高中 392 所，比上年减少 43 所；在校生 3.94 万人，毕业生 3.90 万人。成人高中教职工 3174 人，专任教师 2421 人。

3. 中等职业教育

全国中等职业教育[10] 共有学校 1.07 万所，比上年减少 222 所。其中，普通中等专业学校 3346 所，比上年减少 52 所；职业高中 3617 所，比上年减少 109 所；技工学校 2490 所，比上年减少 36 所；成人中等专业学校 1218 所，比上年减少 25 所。

中等职业教育招生 582.43 万人，比上年减少 10.91 万人，占高中阶段教育招生总数的 42.13%。其中，普通中专招生 246.25 万人，比上年减少 8.94 万人；职业高中招生 148.40 万人，比上年减少 3.04 万人；技工学校招生 130.91 万人，比上年增加 3.71 万人；成人中专招生 56.88 万人，比上年减少 2.65 万人。

中等职业教育在校生 1592.50 万人，比上年减少 6.52 万人，占高中阶段教育在校生总数的 40.10%。其中，普通中专在校生 712.99 万人，比上年减少 5.13 万人；职业高中在校生 414.06 万人，比上年减少 2.52 万人；技工学校在校生 338.21 万人，比上年增加 15.06 万人；成人中专在校生 127.24 万人，比上年减少 13.92 万人。

中等职业教育毕业生 496.88 万人，比上年减少 36.75 万人。其中，普通中专毕业生 216.99 万人，比上年减少 12.03 万人；职业高中毕业生 128.99 万人，比上年减少 12.88 万人；技工学校毕业生 90.48 万人，比上年减少 2.59 万人；成人中专毕业生 60.41 万人，比上年减少 9.25 万人。

中等职业教育学校共有教职工 107.97 万人，比上年减少 0.64 万人。其中，普通中等专业学校教职工 39.68 万人，比上年减少 4581 人；职业高中教职工 34.38 万人，比上年减少 880 人；技工学校教职工 26.86 万人，比上年增加 3512 人；成人中等专业学校教职工 5.97 万人，比上年减少 3939 人。

中等职业教育学校共有专任教师 83.92 万人，比上年减少 393 人，生师比[11] 19.59∶1，比上年的 19.84∶1 有所改善。其中，普通中等专业学校专任教师 30.16 万人，比上年减少 1120 人；职业高中专任教师 28.61 万人，比上年增加 979 人；技工学校专任教师 19.88 万人，比上年增加 2352 人；成人中等专业学校专任教师 4.48 万人，比上年减少 2437 人。

五、高等教育

全国各类高等教育在学总规模达到 3779 万人，高等教育毛入学率达到 45.7%。全国共有普通高等学校和成人高等学校 2913 所，比上年增加 35 所。其中，普通高等学校 2631 所（含独立学院 265 所），比上年增加 35 所；成人高等学校 282 所，比上年减少 2 所。普通高校中本科院校 1243 所，比上年增加 6 所；高职（专科）院校 1388 所，比上年增加 29 所。全国共有研究生培养机构 815 个，其中，普通高校 578 个，科研机构 237 个。

研究生招生 80.61 万人，比上年增加 13.8 万人，其中，博士生招生 8.39 万人，硕士生招生 72.22 万人。在学研究生 263.86 万人，比上年增加 65.75 万人，其中，在学博士生 36.2 万人，在学硕士生 227.66 万人。毕业研究生 57.8 万人，比上年增加 1.41 万人，其中，毕业博士生 5.8 万人，毕业硕士生 52.0 万人。

普通高等教育本专科共招生 761.49 万人，比上年增加 12.88 万人；在校生 2753.59 万人，比上年增加 57.74 万人；毕业生 735.83 万人，比上年增加 31.65 万人。

成人高等教育本专科共招生 217.53 万人，比上年增加 6.3 万人；在校生 544.14 万人，比上年减少 40.25 万人；毕业生 247.03 万人，比上年增加 2.57 万人。

全国高等教育自学考试学历教育报考 504.10 万人次，取得毕业证书 67.77 万人。

普通高等学校校均规模[12] 10430 人，其中，本科学校 14639 人，高职（专科）学校 6662 人。

普通高等学校教职工 244.3 万人，比上年增加 3.82 万人；专任教师 163.32 万人，比上年增加 3.13 万人。普通高校生师比[13] 为 17.52：1，其中，本科学校 17.42：1，高职（专科）学校 17.74：1。成人高等学校教职工 4.14 万人，比上年减少 1711 人；专任教师 2.4 万人，比上年减少 1224 人。

普通高等学校校舍总建筑面积[14] 95400.32 万平方米，比上年增加 2729.28 万平方米；教学科研仪器设备总值[15] 4514.42 亿元，比上年增加 479.87 亿元。

六、成人培训与扫盲教育

全国接受各种非学历高等教育的学生 927.37 万人次，当年已毕（结）业 980.84 万人次；接受各种非学历中等教育的学生达 4538.30 万人次，当年已毕（结）业 4744.07 万人次。

全国职业技术培训机构 8.92 万所，比上年减少 0.41 万所；教职工 51.50 万人；专任教师 28.96 万人。

全国有成人小学 0.97 万所，在校生 75.42 万人，教职工 1.93 万人，其中，专任教师 1.08 万人；成人初中 506 所，在校生 12.70 万人，教职工 1772 人，其中，专任教师 1367 人。

全国共扫除文盲 28.27 万人，比上年减少 4.85 万人；另有 30.40 万人正在参加扫盲学习，比上年减少 3.02 万人。扫盲教育教职工 1.44 万人，比上年减少 1361 人；专任教师 7546 人，比上年增加 141 人。

七、民办教育

全国共有各级各类民办学校 17.76 万所，比上年增加 6668 所；招生 1721.86 万人，比上年增加 81.63 万人；各类教育在校生达 5120.47 万人，比上年增加 295.10 万人。其中：

民办幼儿园 16.04 万所，比上年增加 6169 所；入园儿童 999.32 万人，比上年增加 34.24 万人；在园儿童 2572.34 万人，比上年增加 134.68 万人。

民办普通小学 6107 所，比上年增加 132 所；招生 137.70 万人，比上年增加 9.94 万人；在校生 814.17 万人，比上年增加 57.84 万人。

民办普通初中 5277 所，比上年增加 192 所；招生 209.09 万人，比上年增加 20.36 万人；在校生 577.68 万人，比上年增加 44.87 万人。

民办普通高中3002所，比上年增加215所；招生111.41万人，比上年增加8.52万人；在校生306.26万人，与上年增加27.18万人。

民办中等职业学校2069所，比上年减少46所；招生78.68万人，比上年增加5.04万人；在校生197.33万人，比上年增加13.19人。另有非学历教育学生24.88万人。

民办高校747所（含独立学院265所），比上年增加5所；招生185.35万人，比上年增加3.52万人；在校生651.31万人，比上年增加17.25万人。其中，硕士研究生在校生1223人，本科在校生404.75万人，高职（专科）在校生246.44万人；另有自考助学班学生、预科生、进修及培训学生43.53万人。民办的其他高等教育机构800所，各类注册学生74.47万人。

另外，还有其他民办培训机构1.95万所，846.80万人次接受了培训。

注释：

［1］各项统计数据均未包括香港特别行政区、澳门特别行政区和台湾省。部分数据因四舍五入的原因，存在着与分项合计不等的情况。

［2］毛入学率，是指某一级教育不分年龄的在校学生总数占该级教育国家规定年龄组人口数的百分比。由于包含非正规年龄组（低龄或超龄）学生，毛入学率可能会超过100%。

［3］九年义务教育巩固率，是指初中毕业班学生数占该年级入小学一年级时学生数的百分比。

［4］小学学龄儿童净入学率，是指小学教育在校学龄人口数占小学教育国家规定年龄组人口总数的百分比，是按各地不同入学年龄和学制分别计算的。

［5］因九年一贯制学校的教职工数计入初中阶段教育，完全中学、十二年一贯制学校的教职工数计入高中阶段教育，而专任教师是按照教育层次进行归类，存在小学教职工数据小于专任教师数据的情况。

［6］专任教师学历合格率，是指某一级教育具有国家规定的最低学历要求的专任教师数占该级教育专任教师总数的百分比。各级教育教师的最低学历要求，参照《中华人民共和国教师法》中的相关规定：取得小学教师资格，应当具备中等师范学校毕业及其以上学历；取得初级中学教师、初级职业学校文化、专业课教师资格，应当具备高等师范专科学校或者其他大学专科毕业及其以上学历；取得高级中学教师资格和中等专业学校、技工学校、职业高中文化课、专业课教师资格，应当具备高等师范院校本科或者其他大学本科毕业及其以上学历。

［7］设施设备配备达标的学校，是指体育运动场（馆）面积、体育器械配备达到《教育部卫生部财政部关于印发国家学校体育卫生条件试行基本标准的通知》（教体艺［2008］5号）的相关标准；音乐器材配备、美术器材配备、数学自然实验仪器、理科实验仪器等达到各省、自治区、直辖市规定的仪器配备相关标准。含普通小学、初中和普通高中。

［8］进城务工人员随迁子女，是指户籍登记在外省（区、市）、本省外县（区）的乡村，随务工父母到输入地的城区、镇区（同住）并接受义务教育的适龄儿童少年。

［9］高中阶段包括普通高中、成人高中、中等职业学校。

［10］中等职业教育包括普通中等专业学校、职业高中、技工学校和成人中等专业学校。

［11］中等职业教育生师比不含技工学校数据。

［12］普通高等学校校均规模，仅含普通本专科在校生，不含分校点数据。

［13］普通高校生师比，不含分校点数据，学生总数为折合学生数。

［14］［15］包括学校产权和非产权独立使用。

目　　录

第一部分　教育事业发展

一、综合部分

各级各类学校校数、教职工、专任教师情况 …… 2
各级各类学历教育学生情况 …… 3
各级各类非学历教育学生情况 …… 4
各级各类民办学校校数、教职工、专任教师情况 …… 5
各级各类民办教育学生情况 …… 6
各级各类学校女学生数 …… 7
各级各类学校女教师、女教职工数 …… 8
各级各类学校少数民族学生数 …… 9
各级各类学校少数民族教师、教职工数 …… 10
各级各类学校校数 …… 11
各级各类学历教育学生数 …… 12
各级各类学历教育招生数 …… 14
各级各类学校教职工数 …… 16
各级各类学校专任教师数 …… 18
高中阶段学生数的构成 …… 20
教育规模 …… 20
小学学龄儿童净入学率 …… 21
各级教育毛入学率 …… 21
各级普通学校毕业生升学率 …… 22
每十万人口各级学校平均在校生数 …… 22
各级普通学校生师比 …… 23
普通高等学校校均规模 …… 23
各级自学考试基本情况 …… 24

二、高等教育

高等教育学校(机构)数 …… 26
普通高等学校校数 …… 27
普通高等学校在校生规模 …… 27
高等教育学校(机构)学生数 …… 28
分举办者研究生数(总计) …… 29
分举办者研究生数(普通高校) …… 29
分举办者研究生数(科研机构) …… 30
分学科研究生数(总计) …… 30
分学科研究生数(普通高校) …… 32

分学科研究生数(科研机构) …… 32
普通高等教育工科分大类本科学生数 …… 34
普通、成人本专科分举办者学生数 …… 35
普通本、专科分性质类别学生数 …… 36
成人本专科分性质类别学生数 …… 38
普通本科分学科学生数 …… 38
普通专科分专业大类学生数 …… 40
成人本科分学科学生数 …… 40
成人专科分专业大类学生数 …… 41
网络本科分学科学生数 …… 42
网络专科分专业大类学生数 …… 43
高等教育学生数变动情况 …… 44
高等教育非学历教育学生情况 …… 44
高等教育学生中其他情况 …… 45
外国留学生情况 …… 46
高等教育学校(机构)教职工情况(总计) …… 48
高等教育学校(机构)教职工情况(普通高校) …… 48
高等教育学校(机构)教职工情况(成人高校) …… 50
研究生指导教师情况(总计) …… 52
研究生指导教师情况(普通高校) …… 52
分学科专任教师数(总计) …… 54
分学科专任教师数(普通高校) …… 55
分学科专任教师数(成人高校) …… 56
分学科专任教师数(民办的其他高等教育机构) …… 57
专任教师、聘请校外教师学历情况(总计) …… 58
专任教师、聘请校外教师学历情况(普通高校) …… 58
专任教师、聘请校外教师学历情况(成人高校) …… 59
专任教师、聘请校外教师学历情况(民办的其他高等教育机构) …… 59
专任教师年龄情况(总计) …… 60
专任教师年龄情况(普通高校) …… 60
专任教师年龄情况(成人高校) …… 61
专任教师年龄情况(民办的其他高等教育机构) …… 61
专任教师、聘请校外教师岗位分类情况(总计) …… 62
专任教师、聘请校外教师岗位分类情况(民办的其他高等教育机构) …… 62
专任教师变动情况(总计) …… 64
专任教师变动情况(民办的其他高等教育机构) …… 64
高等教育资产情况(总计) …… 66
高等教育资产情况(民办的其他高等教育机构) …… 66
高等教育校舍情况(总计) …… 68
高等教育校舍情况(普通高校) …… 69
高等教育校舍情况(成人高校) …… 70
高等教育校舍情况(民办的其他高等教育机构) …… 71

三、中等教育

(一)高中阶段教育

普通高中校数、班数 …… 74
普通高中班额情况 …… 75
普通高中学生数 …… 76
中学学校教职工数(初级中学、九年一贯制学校、职业初中、完全中学、高级中学、十二年一贯制学校) …… 78
普通高中分课程专任教师学历情况 …… 80
普通高中专任教师专业技术职务、年龄结构情况 …… 80
普通高中专任教师变动情况 …… 82
普通高中学生、专任教师政治面貌及其他 …… 82
普通高中办学条件(一) …… 84
普通高中办学条件(二) …… 84
普通高中办学条件(三) …… 86
成人高中基本情况 …… 86
中等职业学校(机构)数 …… 87
中等职业学校分办学类型及举办者的中职学生及教职工情况 …… 88
中等职业学校(机构)各类学生数 …… 90
中等职业学校(机构)各类女学生数 …… 90
中等职业学校(机构)学生分科类情况(总计) …… 92
中等职业学校(机构)学生分科类情况(全日制学生) …… 93
中等职业学校(机构)学生分科类情况(普通中专) …… 94
中等职业学校(机构)学生分科类情况(成人中专) …… 95
中等职业学校(机构)学生分科类情况(职业高中) …… 96
中等职业学校(机构)分年龄学生数 …… 97
中等职业学校(机构)分年龄女学生数 …… 97
中等职业学校(机构)学生变动情况 …… 98
中等职业学校(机构)女学生变动情况 …… 98
中等职业学校(机构)其他学生情况 …… 100
中等职业学校(机构)培训学生情况 …… 100
中等职业学校(机构)外国留学生情况 …… 101
中等职业学校(机构)教职工数(总计) …… 102
中等职业学校(机构)教职工数(普通中专) …… 102
中等职业学校(机构)教职工数(成人中专) …… 104
中等职业学校(机构)教职工数(职业高中) …… 104
中等职业学校(机构)教职工数(其他中等职业教育机构) …… 106
中等职业学校(机构)分科专任教师数(总计) …… 108
中等职业学校(机构)分科专任教师数(普通中专) …… 109
中等职业学校(机构)分科专任教师数(成人中专) …… 110
中等职业学校(机构)分科专任教师数(职业高中) …… 111
中等职业学校(机构)分科专任教师数(其他中等职业教育机构) …… 112
中等职业学校(机构)专任教师、聘请校外教师学历情况(合计) …… 113

中等职业学校(机构)专任教师、聘请校外教师学历情况(普通中专) …… 114
中等职业学校(机构)专任教师、聘请校外教师学历情况(成人中专) …… 115
中等职业学校(机构)专任教师、聘请校外教师学历情况(职业高中) …… 116
中等职业学校(机构)专任教师、聘请校外教师学历情况(其他中等职业教育机构) …… 117
中等职业学校(机构)专任教师分年龄情况 …… 118
中等职业学校(机构)专任教师、聘请校外教师岗位分类情况 …… 120
中等职业学校(机构)专任教师变动情况 …… 122
中等职业学校(机构)资产情况 …… 124
中等职业学校(机构)教职工其他情况 …… 126
中等职业学校(机构)校舍情况(总计) …… 127
中等职业学校(机构)校舍情况(普通中专) …… 128
中等职业学校(机构)校舍情况(成人中专) …… 129
中等职业学校(机构)校舍情况(职业高中) …… 130
中等职业学校(机构)校舍情况(其他中等职业教育机构) …… 131
职业技术培训机构基本情况 …… 132
职业技术培训机构资产情况 …… 134

(二)初中阶段教育

初中阶段校数、班数 …… 136
初中班额情况 …… 137
初中学生数 …… 138
初中阶段学龄人口及在校学生情况 …… 140
初中分课程专任教师学历情况 …… 142
初中专任教师专业技术职务、年龄结构情况 …… 144
初中专任教师变动情况 …… 146
初中学生、专任教师其他情况 …… 148
初中办学条件(一) …… 149
初中办学条件(二) …… 150
初中办学条件(三) …… 150
成人初中基本情况 …… 152

四、初等教育(小学)

小学校数、教学点数及班数 …… 154
小学班额情况 …… 155
小学学生数 …… 156
小学学龄人口入学及在校生情况 …… 158
小学学校教职工数 …… 162
小学分课程专任教师学历情况 …… 164
小学专任教师专业技术职务、年龄结构情况 …… 164
小学专任教师变动情况 …… 166
小学学生、教职工政治面貌及其他 …… 166
小学办学条件(一) …… 168
小学办学条件(二) …… 170
小学办学条件(三) …… 170

成人小学基本情况………………………………………………………………………… 171

五、工读学校

工读学校基本情况………………………………………………………………………… 174

六、特殊教育

特殊教育基本情况………………………………………………………………………… 176
特殊教育学校基本情况……………………………………………………………………… 178
特殊教育学校教职工数……………………………………………………………………… 180
特殊教育学校专任教师学历、专业技术职务情况 ………………………………………… 180
特殊教育专任教师变动情况………………………………………………………………… 180
特殊教育学校办学条件(一) ……………………………………………………………… 182
特殊教育学校办学条件(二) ……………………………………………………………… 182

七、学前教育

幼儿园园数、班数 ………………………………………………………………………… 184
学前教育分年龄幼儿数(总计) …………………………………………………………… 186
学前教育分年龄幼儿数(城区) …………………………………………………………… 187
学前教育分年龄幼儿数(城乡结合区) …………………………………………………… 188
学前教育分年龄幼儿数(镇区) …………………………………………………………… 189
学前教育分年龄学生数(镇乡结合区) …………………………………………………… 190
学前教育分年龄幼儿数(乡村) …………………………………………………………… 191
幼儿园教职工数……………………………………………………………………………… 192
幼儿园园长、专任教师学历、专业技术职务情况…………………………………………… 194
幼儿园教职工政治面貌及其他……………………………………………………………… 196
幼儿园办学条件(一) ……………………………………………………………………… 198
幼儿园办学条件(二) ……………………………………………………………………… 198

八、各级各类学校分布情况

高等教育学校(机构)数 …………………………………………………………………… 200
高等学校(机构)研究生数 ………………………………………………………………… 202
普通高校研究生数…………………………………………………………………………… 204
科研机构研究生数…………………………………………………………………………… 206
高等教育本专科学生数……………………………………………………………………… 208
高等教育普通本专科学生数………………………………………………………………… 210
高等教育成人本专科学生数………………………………………………………………… 212
高等教育网络本科、专科生学生数 ………………………………………………………… 214
综合大学本科、专科生学生数 ……………………………………………………………… 216
高等理工院校本科、专科生学生数 ………………………………………………………… 218
高等农业院校本科、专科生学生数 ………………………………………………………… 220
高等林业院校本科、专科生学生数 ………………………………………………………… 222
高等医药院校本科、专科生学生数 ………………………………………………………… 224
高等师范院校本科、专科生学生数 ………………………………………………………… 226

高等语文院校本科、专科生学生数 …… 228
高等财经院校本科、专科生学生数 …… 230
高等政法院校本科、专科生学生数 …… 232
高等体育院校本科、专科生学生数 …… 234
高等艺术院校本科、专科生学生数 …… 236
高等民族院校本科、专科生学生数 …… 238
高等职业学校本科、专科生学生数 …… 240
广播电视大学本专科学生数 …… 242
职工高等学校本专科学生数 …… 244
教育学院本专科学生数 …… 246
管理干部学院本专科学生数 …… 248
普通高等学校举办函授、业余、脱产分本专科学生数 …… 250
高等教育非学历教育学生情况(总计) …… 252
高等教育非学历教育学生情况(普通高校) …… 254
高等教育非学历教育学生情况(成人高校) …… 256
高等教育非学历教育学生情况(民办的其他高等教育机构) …… 258
外国留学生情况 …… 260
高等教育学校(机构)教职工情况(总计) …… 262
高等教育学校(机构)女教职工情况(总计) …… 264
高等教育学校(机构)教职工情况(普通高校) …… 266
高等教育学校(机构)女教职工情况(普通高校) …… 268
高等教育学校(机构)教职工情况(成人高校) …… 270
高等教育学校(机构)女教职工情况(成人高校) …… 272
高等教育学校(机构)教职工情况(民办的其他高等教育机构) …… 274
高等教育学校(机构)女教职工情况(民办的其他高等教育机构) …… 276
专任教师学历、专业技术职务情况(总计) …… 278
专任教师学历、专业技术职务情况(普通高校) …… 279
专任教师学历、专业技术职务情况(成人高校) …… 280
专任教师学历、专业技术职务情况(民办的其他高等教育机构) …… 281
聘请校外教师学历情况(总计) …… 282
聘请校外教师学历情况(普通高校) …… 283
聘请校外教师学历情况(成人高校) …… 284
聘请校外教师学历情况(民办的其他高等教育机构) …… 285
资产情况(学校产权)(总计) …… 286
资产情况(学校产权)(普通高校) …… 288
资产情况(学校产权)(成人高校) …… 290
资产情况(学校产权)(民办的其他高等教育机构) …… 292
资产情况(非学校产权中独立使用) …… 294
资产情况(非学校产权中独立使用)(普通高校) …… 296
资产情况(非学校产权中独立使用)(成人高校) …… 298
资产情况(非学校产权中独立使用)(民办的其他高等教育机构) …… 300
校舍情况(总计) …… 302
校舍情况(普通高校) …… 303

校舍情况(成人高校) …… 304
校舍情况(民办的其他高等教育机构) …… 305
普通高中校数、班数(总计) …… 306
普通高中校数、班数(城区) …… 307
普通高中校数、班数(城乡结合区) …… 308
普通高中校数、班数(镇区) …… 309
普通高中校数、班数(镇乡结合区) …… 310
普通高中校数、班数(乡村) …… 311
普通高中学生数(总计) …… 312
普通高中学生数(城区) …… 313
普通高中学生数(城乡结合区) …… 314
普通高中学生数(镇区) …… 315
普通高中学生数(镇乡结合区) …… 316
普通高中学生数(乡村) …… 317
普通高中女学生数 …… 318
普通中学教职工数(总计) …… 319
普通中学教职工数(城区) …… 320
普通中学教职工数(城乡结合区) …… 321
普通中学教职工数(镇区) …… 322
普通中学教职工数(镇乡结合区) …… 323
普通中学教职工数(乡村) …… 324
普通中学女教职工数 …… 325
普通中学教职工总数中民办教职工数 …… 326
普通高中专任教师学历、专业技术职务情况(总计) …… 328
普通高中专任教师学历、专业技术职务情况(城区) …… 330
普通高中专任教师学历、专业技术职务情况(城乡结合区) …… 332
普通高中专任教师学历、专业技术职务情况(镇区) …… 334
普通高中专任教师学历、专业技术职务情况(镇乡结合区) …… 336
普通高中专任教师学历、专业技术职务情况(乡村) …… 338
普通高中办学条件(一)(总计) …… 340
普通高中办学条件(一)(城区) …… 342
普通高中办学条件(一)(城乡结合区) …… 344
普通高中办学条件(一)(镇区) …… 346
普通高中办学条件(一)(镇乡结合区) …… 348
普通高中办学条件(一)(乡村) …… 350
普通高中办学条件(二)(总计) …… 352
普通高中办学条件(二)(城区) …… 354
普通高中办学条件(二)(城乡结合区) …… 356
普通高中办学条件(二)(镇区) …… 358
普通高中办学条件(二)(镇乡结合区) …… 360
普通高中办学条件(二)(乡村) …… 362
中等职业学校(机构)数 …… 364
中等职业学校(机构)学生数 …… 366

中等职业学校(机构)女学生数 …… 368
普通中专学生数…… 370
普通中专女学生数…… 372
成人中专学生数…… 374
成人中专女学生数…… 376
职业高中学生数…… 378
职业高中女学生数…… 380
中等职业学校(机构)分年龄学生数 …… 382
中等职业学校(机构)分年龄女学生数 …… 384
中等职业学校(机构)培训结业学生情况 …… 386
中等职业学校(机构)培训注册学生情况 …… 388
中等职业学校(机构)学生数变动情况 …… 390
中等职业学校(机构)女学生数变动情况 …… 392
中等职业学校(机构)外国留学生情况 …… 394
中等职业学校(机构)教职工数 …… 396
中等职业学校(机构)女教职工数 …… 398
普通中等专业学校(机构)教职工数 …… 400
普通中等专业学校(机构)女教职工数 …… 402
成人中等专业学校教职工数…… 404
成人中等专业学校女教职工数…… 406
职业高中学校教职工数…… 408
职业高中学校女教职工数…… 410
其他中等职业教育机构教职工数…… 412
其他中等职业教育机构女教职工数…… 414
中等职业学校(机构)专任教师专业技术职务、学历情况 …… 416
普通中专学校专任教师专业技术职务、学历情况 …… 418
成人中专学校专任教师专业技术职务、学历情况 …… 420
职业高中学校专任教师专业技术职务、学历情况 …… 422
其他中等职业教育机构专任教师专业技术职务、学历情况 …… 424
中等职业学校(机构)资产情况(学校产权) …… 426
中等职业学校(机构)资产情况(非学校产权中独立使用) …… 428
普通中专学校资产情况(学校产权) …… 430
普通中专学校资产情况(非学校产权中独立使用) …… 432
成人中专学校资产情况(学校产权) …… 434
成人中专学校资产情况(非学校产权中独立使用) …… 436
职业高中学校资产情况(学校产权) …… 438
职业高中学校资产情况(非学校产权中独立使用) …… 440
其他中等职业教育机构资产情况(学校产权) …… 442
其他中等职业教育机构资产情况(非学校产权中独立使用) …… 444
中等职业学校(机构)校舍情况 …… 446
普通中专学校校舍情况…… 447
成人中专学校校舍情况…… 448
职业高中学校校舍情况…… 449

其他中等职业教育机构校舍情况 …… 450
职业技术培训机构基本情况(总计) …… 452
职工技术培训学校基本情况 …… 454
农村成人文化技术培训学校基本情况 …… 456
其他培训机构基本情况 …… 458
职业技术培训机构资产情况 …… 460
职工技术培训学校资产情况 …… 462
农村成人文化技术培训学校资产情况 …… 464
其他培训机构资产情况 …… 466
初中校数、班数(总计) …… 468
初中校数、班数(城区) …… 470
初中校数、班数(城乡结合区) …… 472
初中校数、班数(镇区) …… 474
初中校数、班数(镇乡结合区) …… 476
初中校数、班数(乡村) …… 478
初中学生数(总计) …… 480
初中学生数(城区) …… 482
初中学生数(城乡结合区) …… 484
初中学生数(镇区) …… 486
初中学生数(镇乡结合区) …… 488
初中学生数(乡村) …… 490
初中女学生数 …… 492
初中专任教师学历、专业技术职务情况(总计) …… 494
初中专任教师学历、专业技术职务情况(城区) …… 496
初中专任教师学历、专业技术职务情况(城乡结合区) …… 498
初中专任教师学历、专业技术职务情况(镇区) …… 500
初中专任教师学历、专业技术职务情况(镇乡结合区) …… 502
初中专任教师学历、专业技术职务情况(乡村) …… 504
初中办学条件(一)(总计) …… 506
初中办学条件(一)(城区) …… 508
初中办学条件(一)(城乡结合区) …… 510
初中办学条件(一)(镇区) …… 512
初中办学条件(一)(镇乡结合区) …… 514
初中办学条件(一)(乡村) …… 516
初中办学条件(二)(总计) …… 518
初中办学条件(二)(城区) …… 520
初中办学条件(二)(城乡结合区) …… 522
初中办学条件(二)(镇区) …… 524
初中办学条件(二)(镇乡结合区) …… 526
初中办学条件(二)(乡村) …… 528
小学校数、教学点数及班数(总计) …… 530
小学校数、教学点数及班数(城区) …… 532
小学校数、教学点数及班数(城乡结合区) …… 534

小学校数、教学点数及班数(镇区) …… 536
小学校数、教学点数及班数(镇乡结合区) …… 538
小学校数、教学点数及班数(乡村) …… 540
小学学生数(总计) …… 542
小学学生数(城区) …… 544
小学学生数(城乡结合区) …… 546
小学学生数(镇区) …… 548
小学学生数(镇乡结合区) …… 550
小学学生数(乡村) …… 552
五年制小学学生数 …… 554
小学女学生数 …… 556
小学教职工数(总数) …… 558
小学教职工数(城区) …… 559
小学教职工数(城乡结合区) …… 560
小学教职工数(镇区) …… 561
小学教职工数(镇乡结合区) …… 562
小学教职工数(乡村) …… 563
小学教职工总数中民办教职工数 …… 564
小学女教职工数 …… 565
小学专任教师学历、专业技术职务情况(总计) …… 566
小学专任教师学历、专业技术职务情况(城区) …… 568
小学专任教师学历、专业技术职务情况(城乡结合区) …… 570
小学专任教师学历、专业技术职务情况(镇区) …… 572
小学专任教师学历、专业技术职务情况(镇乡结合区) …… 574
小学专任教师学历、专业技术职务情况(乡村) …… 576
小学办学条件(一)(总计) …… 578
小学办学条件(一)(城区) …… 580
小学办学条件(一)(城乡结合区) …… 582
小学办学条件(一)(镇区) …… 584
小学办学条件(一)(镇乡结合区) …… 586
小学办学条件(一)(乡村) …… 588
小学办学条件(二)(总计) …… 590
小学办学条件(二)(城区) …… 592
小学办学条件(二)(城乡结合区) …… 594
小学办学条件(二)(镇区) …… 596
小学办学条件(二)(镇乡结合区) …… 598
小学办学条件(二)(乡村) …… 600
工读学校基本情况 …… 602
特殊教育基本情况(总计) …… 604
特殊教育基本情况(城区) …… 606
特殊教育基本情况(城乡结合区) …… 608
特殊教育基本情况(镇区) …… 610
特殊教育基本情况(镇乡结合区) …… 612

特殊教育基本情况(乡村) …… 614
特殊教育女学生数 …… 616
特殊教育学校教职工数 …… 618
特殊教育学校女教职工数 …… 619
特殊教育学校专任教师学历、专业技术职务情况 …… 620
特殊教育学校办学条件(一) …… 622
特殊教育学校办学条件(二) …… 624
学前教育基本情况(总计) …… 625
学前教育基本情况(城区) …… 626
学前教育基本情况(城乡结合区) …… 627
学前教育基本情况(镇区) …… 628
学前教育基本情况(镇乡结合区) …… 629
学前教育基本情况(乡村) …… 630
学前教育中女幼儿数 …… 631
幼儿园教职工数(总计) …… 632
幼儿园教职工数(城区) …… 633
幼儿园教职工数(城乡结合区) …… 634
幼儿园教职工数(镇区) …… 635
幼儿园教职工数(镇乡结合区) …… 636
幼儿园教职工数(乡村) …… 637
幼儿园女教职工数 …… 638
幼儿园园长、专任教师学历、专业技术职务情况(总计) …… 640
幼儿园园长、专任教师学历、专业技术职务情况(城区) …… 642
幼儿园园长、专任教师学历、专业技术职务情况(城乡结合区) …… 644
幼儿园园长、专任教师学历、专业技术职务情况(镇区) …… 646
幼儿园园长、专任教师学历、专业技术职务情况(镇乡结合区) …… 648
幼儿园园长、专任教师学历、专业技术职务情况(乡村) …… 650
幼儿园校舍及其他情况(总计)(一) …… 652
幼儿园校舍及其他情况(城区)(一) …… 654
幼儿园校舍及其他情况(城乡结合区)(一) …… 656
幼儿园校舍及其他情况(镇区)(一) …… 658
幼儿园校舍及其他情况(镇乡结合区)(一) …… 660
幼儿园校舍及其他情况(乡村)(一) …… 662
幼儿园办学条件(总计)(二) …… 664
幼儿园办学条件(城区)(二) …… 665
幼儿园办学条件(城乡结合区)(二) …… 666
幼儿园办学条件(镇区)(二) …… 667
幼儿园办学条件(镇乡结合区)(二) …… 668
幼儿园办学条件(乡村)(二) …… 669

第二部分　办学条件

一、教育经费

各类学校教育经费来源和支出情况（2016 年）…… 672
各地区教育经费来源和支出情况(2016 年）…… 674

二、教育基本建设投资

教育基本建设投资完成情况(总计）…… 678
教育基本建设投资完成情况…… 680

第三部分　科学研究活动及其他

一、自然科学与技术

全国普通高等学校科技人力情况…… 684
全国普通高等学校科技经费情况…… 686
普通高等学校研究与发展课题、成果情况…… 688

二、社会科学

普通高等学校人文、社会科学人力情况…… 692
普通高等学校人文、社会科学研究与发展经费情况…… 694
普通高等学校人文、社会科学研究与发展课题、成果情况…… 696

附表：

国内生产总值…… 700
分地区国内生产总值(2016 年）…… 701
国家财政收支总额及增长速度…… 702
中央财政和地方财政收支总额…… 703
人口数及构成…… 704
分地区按性别分的 15 岁及以上文盲人口(2016 年）…… 705
分地区按性别和受教育程度分的人口(2016 年）…… 706

CONTENTS

Part Ⅰ

THE DEVELOPMENT OF THE EDUCTIONAL UNDERTAKING

Summary Tables

Number of Schools, Educational Personnel and Full-time Teachers by Type and Level ········· 2
Number of Students of Formal Education by Type and Level ········· 3
Number of Students of Non-formal Education by Type and Level ········· 4
Number of Non-government Schools, Educational Personnel and Full-time Teachers by Type and Level ········· 5
Number of Students of Non-government Education by Type and Level ········· 6
Number of Female Students of Schools by Type and Level ········· 7
Number of Female Educational Personnel and Full-time Teachers of Schools by Type and Level ········· 8
Number of Minority Students of Schools by Type and Level ········· 9
Number of Minority Educational Personnel and Full-time Teachers of Schools by Type and Level ········· 10
Number of School by Type and Level ········· 11
Number of Students of Formal Education by Type and Level ········· 12
Number of Entrants of Formal Education by Type and Level ········· 14
Number of Educational Personnel of School by Type and Level ········· 16
Number of Full-time Teachers of Schools by Type and Level ········· 18
Composition of Students in Senior Secondary Schools ········· 20
Size of Education ········· 20
Net Enrolment Rate of School-age Children in Primary Schools ········· 21
Gross Enrolment Rate of Education by Level ········· 21
Promotion Rate of Graduates of Regular School by Level ········· 22
Number of Enrolment of per 100, 000 Inhabitants by Level ········· 22
Pupil-Teacher Ratio of Regular Schools by Level ········· 23
Average Size of Undergraduate in Regular HEIs ········· 23
Basic Statistics of State-administered Examination for Self-learners by Level ········· 24

Higher Education

Number of Higher Education Institutions ········· 26
Number of Regular Higher Educational Institutions ········· 27
Size of Enrolment of Regular Higher Educational Institutions ········· 27
Number of Students in Higher Education Institutions ········· 28
Number of Enrolment for Master's Degree Programs by Providers (Total) ········· 29
Number of Enrolment for Master's Degree Programs by Providers (Regular HEIs) ········· 29
Number of Enrolment for Master's Degree Programs by Providers (Research Institutes) ········· 30
Number of Postgraduate Students by Academic Field (Total) ········· 30
Number of Postgraduate Students by Academic Field (Regular HEIs) ········· 32

Number of Postgraduate Students by Academic Field (Research Institutes) 32
Number of Engineering Students for Normal Courses of Regular HEIs by Subfield 34
Number of Students for Regular and Adult Programs by Providers in HEIs 35
Number of Undergraduate Students by Type of Courses in Regular HEIs 36
Number of Students for Adult Programs by Type of Schools in HEIs 38
Number of Regular Students for Normal Courses in HEIs by Discipline 38
Number of Regular Students for Short-cycle Courses in HEIs by Discipline 40
Number of Adult Students for Normal Courses in HEIs by Discipline 40
Number of Adult Students for Short-cycle Courses in HEIs by Discipline 41
Number of Web-based Students for Normal Courses in HEIs by Discipline 42
Number of Web-based Students for Short-cycle Courses in HEIs by Discipline 43
Changes in Enrolment of Higher Educations 44
Number of Students of Non-formal Education of Higher Education 44
Other Circumstances of Students in Higher Education 45
Information on International Students 46
Number of Educational Personnel in HEIs (Total) 48
Number of Educational Personnel in HEIs (Regular HEIs) 48
Number of Educational Personnel in HEIs (Adult HEIs) 50
Number of Supervisors of Postgraduate Programs (Total) 52
Number of Supervisors of Postgraduate Programs (Regular HEIs) 52
Number of Full-time Teachers by Field of Study (Total) 54
Number of Full-time Teachers by Field of Study (Regular HEIs) 55
Number of Full-time Teachers by Field of Study (Adult HEIs) 56
Number of Full-time Teachers by Field of Study (Other Non-government HEIs) 57
Number of Academic Qualifications of Full-time and Part-time Teachers in HEIs (Total) 58
Number of Academic Qualifications of Full-time and Part-time Teachers in HEIs (Regular HEIs) 58
Number of Academic Qualifications of Full-time and Part-time Teachers in HEIs (Adult HEIs) 59
Number of Academic Qualifications of Full-time and Part-time Teachers in HEIs (Other Non-government HEIs) 59
Number of Full-time Teachers by Age (Total) 60
Number of Full-time Teachers by Age (Regular HEIs) 60
Number of Full-time Teachers by Age (Adult HEIs) 61
Number of Full-time Teachers by Age (Other Non-government HEIs) 61
Number of Full-time and Part-time Teachers Classified by Teaching Content in HEIs (Total) 62
Data on Academic Qualification of Full-time and Invited Teachers Classified by Teaching Content Invited from Other Institutions 62
Changes of Full-time Teachers in HEIs (Total) 64
Changes of Full-time Teachers in HEIs (Other Non-government HEIs) 64
Condition of Fixed Assets and Teaching Resources in Higher Education (Total) 66
Condition of Fixed Assets and Teaching Resources in Higher Education (Other Non-government HEIs) 66
Condition of School Buildings in Higher Education (Total) 68
Condition of School Buildings in Higher Education (Regular HEIs) 69
Condition of School Buildings in Higher Education (Adult HEIs) 70
Condition of School Buildings in Higher Education (Other Non-government HEIs) 71

Secondary Education

Senior Secondary Education

Number of Regular Senior Secondary Schools and Classes …… 74
Size of Class in Regular Senior Secondary Schools …… 75
Number of Students in Regular Senior Secondary Schools …… 76
Number of Educational Personnel in General Secondary Schools …… 78
Number of Full-time Teachers in Regular Senior Secondary Schools by Subject Taught & Academic Qualifications …… 80
Number of Full-time Teachers in Regular Senior Secondary Schools by Professional Rank and Age …… 80
Changes of Full-time Teachers in Regular Senior Secondary Schools …… 82
Supplementary Information on Students and Full-time Teachers of Regular Senior Secondary Schools …… 82
Condition of School Buildings in Regular Senior Secondary Schools (1) …… 84
Condition of School Buildings in Regular Senior Secondary Schools (2) …… 84
Condition of School Buildings in Regular Senior Secondary Schools (3) …… 86
Basic Statistics of Adult Senior Secondary Schools …… 86
Number of Secondary Vocational Schools …… 87
Number of Students and Educational Personnel of Secondary Vocational Schools by Types and Providers …… 88
Number of Students in Secondary Vocational Schools …… 90
Number of Female Students in Secondary Vocational Schools …… 90
Number of Students by Field of Education in Secondary Vocational Schools (Total) …… 92
Number of Students by Field of Education in Secondary Vocational Schools (Full-time Students) …… 93
Number of Students by Field of Education in Secondary Vocational Schools (Regular SSSs) …… 94
Number of Students by Field of Education in Secondary Vocational Schools (Adult SSSs) …… 95
Number of Students by Field of Education in Secondary Vocational Schools (Vocational High Schools) …… 96
Number of Students by Age in Secondary Vocational Schools …… 97
Number of Female Students by Age in Secondary Vocational Schools …… 97
Changes in Enrolment of Secondary Vocational Schools …… 98
Changes in Female Enrolment of Secondary Vocational Schools …… 98
Supplementary Information on Students in Secondary Vocational Schools …… 100
Number of Trainees in Secondary Vocational Schools …… 100
Number of Foreign Students in Secondary Vocational Schools …… 101
Number of Educational Personnel in Secondary Vocational Schools (Total) …… 102
Number of Educational Personnel in Secondary Vocational Schools (Regular SSSs) …… 102
Number of Educational Personnel in Secondary Vocational Schools (Adult SSSs) …… 104
Number of Educational Personnel in Secondary Vocational Schools (Vocational High Schools) …… 104
Number of Educational Personnel in Secondary Vocational Schools (Other Secondary Vocational Education Institutions) …… 106
Number of Full-time Teachers by Field of Education in Secondary Vocational Schools (Total) …… 108
Number of Full-time Teachers by Field of Education in Secondary Vocational Schools (Regular SSSs) …… 109
Number of Full-time Teachers by Field of Education in Secondary Vocational Schools (Adult SSSs) …… 110
Number of Full-time Teachers by Field of Education in Secondary Vocational Schools (Vocational High Schools) …… 111
Number of Full-time Teachers by Field of Education in Secondary Vocational Schools (Other Secondary Vocational Education Institutions) …… 112

Number of Full-time and Part-time Teachers by Academic Qualifications in Secondary Vocational Schools (Total) ··· 113
Number of Full-time and Part-time Teachers by Academic Qualifications in Secondary Vocational Schools (Regular SSSs) ··· 114
Number of Full-time and Part-time Teachers by Academic Qualifications in Secondary Vocational Schools (Adult SSSs) ··· 115
Number of Full-time and Part-time Teachers by Academic Qualifications in Secondary Vocational Schools (Vocational High Schools) ··· 116
Number of Full-time and Part-time Teachers by Academic Qualifications in Secondary Vocational Schools (Other Secondary Vocational Education Institutions) ··· 117
Number of Full-time Teachers by Age in Secondary Vocational Schools ··· 118
Number of Full-time and Part-time Teachers by Teaching Course in Secondary Vocational Schools ··· 120
Changes of Full-time Teachers in Secondary Vocational Schools ··· 122
Condition of Assets and Teaching Resources in Secondary Vocational Schools ··· 124
Supplementary Information on Educational Personnel in Secondary Vocational Schools ··· 126
Conditions of School Buildings in Secondary Vocational Schools (Total) ··· 127
Conditions of School Buildings in Secondary Vocational Schools (Regular SSSs) ··· 128
Conditions of School Buildings in Secondary Vocational Schools (Adult SSSs) ··· 129
Conditions of School Buildings in Secondary Vocational Schools (Vocational High Schools) ··· 130
Conditions of School Buildings in Secondary Vocational Schools (Other Secondary Vocational Education Institutions) ··· 131
Basic Statistics of Vocational-Technical Training Institutions ··· 132
Condition of Assets and Teaching Resources in Vocational Technical Training Institutions ··· 134

Junior Secondary Education

Number of Schools, Classes in Junior Secondary Education ··· 136
Size of Classes in Junior Secondary Schools ··· 137
Number of Students in Junior Secondary Schools ··· 138
Number of School-age Population and Enrolment of Junior Secondary Schools ··· 140
Number of Full-time Teachers in Junior Secondary Schools by Subject Taught & Academic Qualifications ··· 142
Number of Full-time Teachers in Junior Secondary Schools by Professional Rank and Age ··· 144
Changes of Full-time Teachers in Junior Secondary Schools ··· 146
Other Information on Students and Full-time Teachers of Junior Secondary Schools ··· 148
Condition of School Buildings in Junior Secondary Schools (1) ··· 149
Condition of School Buildings in Junior Secondary Schools (2) ··· 150
Condition of School Buildings in Junior Secondary Schools (3) ··· 150
Basic Statistics of Adult Junior Secondary Schools ··· 152

Primary Education (Primary Schools)

Number of Schools, External Teaching Sites & Classes in Primary Schools ··· 154
Size Classes in Primary Schools ··· 155
Number of Students in Primary Schools ··· 156
Number of Schools-age Population of Primary Schools ··· 158
Number of Educational Personnel in Primary Schools ··· 162
Number of Full-time Teachers in Primary Schools by Subject Taught and Academic Qualifications ··· 164
Number of Full-time Teachers in Primary Schools by Professional Rank and Age ··· 164
Changes of Full-time Teachers in Primary Schools ··· 166

Supplementary Information on Students and Educational Personnel of Primary Schools 166
Condition of School Buildings in Primary Schools (1) 168
Condition of School Buildings in Primary Schools (2) 170
Condition of School Buildings in Primary Schools (3) 170
Basic Statistics of Adult Primary Schools 171

Correctional Work-Study Schools

Basic Statistics of Correctional Work-study Schools 174

Special Education

Basic Statistics of Special Education 176
Basic Statistics of Special Education Schools 178
Number of Educational Personnel in Special Education Schools 180
Number of Full-time Teachers in Special Education Schools by Academic Qualifications and Professional Rank 180
Changes of Full-time Teachers in Special Education Schools 180
Condition of School Buildings in Special Education Schools (1) 182
Condition of School Buildings in Special Education Schools (2) 182

Pre-Primary Education

Number of Kindergartens, Classes in Pre-primary Education 184
Number of Children in Pre-school Education by Age (Total) 186
Number of Children in Pre-primary Education by Age (Urban Area) 187
Number of Children in Pre-school Education by Ages (Urban-rural Transitional Area) 188
Number of Children in Pre-school Education by Ages (Counties & Towns Area) 189
Number of Children in Pre-school Education by Ages (County-town Transitional Area) 190
Number of Children in Pre-school Education by Ages (Rural Area) 191
Number of Educational Personnel in Kindergarten 192
Breakdown of Kindergarten Heads, Full-time Teachers by Academic Qualifications and Professional Rank 194
Supplementary Information on Students and Educational Personnel of Kindergarten 196
Condition of Kindergarten Buildings (1) 198
Condition of Kindergarten Buildings (2) 198

Geographical Distribution of Schools by Type and Level

Number of Higher Education Institutions 200
Number of Postgraduate Students in Higher Education Institutions 202
Number of Postgraduates in Higher Education Institutions 204
Number of Postgraduates in Higher Education Institutions 206
Number of Students Enrolled in Normal and Short-cycle Courses in Higher Education 208
Number of Regular Students Enrolled in Normal and Short-cycle Courses in Higher Education 210
Number of Adult Students Enrolled in Normal and Short-cycle Courses in Higher Education 212
Number of Web-based Students Enrolled in Normal and Short-cycle Courses in Higher Education 214
Number of Students of Comprehensive Universities 216
Number of Students of Institutions of Science & Technology 218
Number of Students of Institutions of Agriculture 220

Number of Students of Institutions of Forestry ······ 222
Number of Students of Institutions of Medicine & Pharmacy ······ 224
Number of Students of Institutions of Languages & Literatures ······ 226
Number of Students of Comprehensive Universities ······ 228
Number of Students of Institutions of Finance & Economies ······ 230
Number of Students of Institutions of Political Science & Law ······ 232
Number of Students of Institutions of Physical Culture ······ 234
Number of Students of Institutions of Art ······ 236
Number of Students of Nationalities Institutions ······ 238
Number of Students of Higher Vocational Colleges ······ 240
Number of Students in Radio/TV Universities ······ 242
Number of Students in Workers' Colleges ······ 244
Number of Students in Educational Colleges ······ 246
Number of Students in Institutes for Administration ······ 248
Number of Students in Correspondence Divisions、Sparetime Schools & Short-cycle Courses for Adults Run by Regular HEIs ······ 250
Number of Students in Non-formal Education of HEIs (Total) ······ 252
Number of Students in Non-formal Education of Regular HEIs ······ 254
Number of Students in Non-formal Education of Adults HEIs ······ 256
Number of Students in Non-formal Education of Other Non-government HEIs ······ 258
Information on Foreign Students ······ 260
Number of Educational Personnel in HEIs (Total) ······ 262
Number of Female Educational Personnel in HEIs (Total) ······ 264
Number of Educational Personnel in Regular HEIs ······ 266
Number of Female Educational Personnel in Regular HEIs ······ 268
Number of Educational Personnel in Adult HEIs ······ 270
Number of Female Educational Personnel in Adult HEIs ······ 272
Number of Educational Personnel in Other Non-government HEIs ······ 274
Number of Female Educational Personnel in Other Non-government HEIs ······ 276
Number of Full-time Teacher by Academic Qualification and Professional Rank (Total) ······ 278
Number of Full-time Teacher by Academic Qualification and Professional Rank (Regular HEIs) ······ 279
Number of Full-time Teacher by Academic Qualification and Professional Rank (Adult HEIs) ······ 280
Number of Full-time Teacher by Academic Qualification and Professional Rank (Other Non-government HEIs) ······ 281
Number of Part-time Teachers by Academic Qualifications (Total) ······ 282
Number of Part-time Teachers by Academic Qualifications (Regular HEIs) ······ 283
Number of Part-time Teachers by Academic Qualifications (Adult HEIs) ······ 284
Number of Part-time Teachers by Academic Qualifications (Other Non-government HEIs) ······ 285
Condition of Assets and Teaching Resources (Owned by HEIs) (Total) ······ 286
Condition of Assets and Teaching Resources (Owned by HEIs) (Regular HEIs) ······ 288
Condition of Assets and Teaching Resources (Owned by HEIs) (Adult HEIs) ······ 290
Condition of Assets and Teaching Resources (Other Non-government HEIs) ······ 292
Condition of Assets and Teaching Resources (Not Owned by HEIs) ······ 294
Condition of Assets and Teaching Resources (Not Owned by HEIs) (Regular HEIs) ······ 296
Condition of Assets and Teaching Resources (Not Owned by HEIs) (Adult HEIs) ······ 298
Condition of Assets and Teaching Resources (Not Owned by HEIs) (Other Non-government HEIs) ······ 300

Conditions of School Buildings (Total) ········ 302
Conditions of School Buildings (Regular HEIs) ········ 303
Conditions of School Buildings (Adult HEIs) ········ 304
Conditions of School Buildings (Other Non-government HEIs) ········ 305
Number of Schools and Classes in Regular Senior Secondary Schools (Total) ········ 306
Number of Schools and Classes in Regular Senior Secondary Schools (Urban Area) ········ 307
Number of Schools and Classes in Regular Senior Secondary Schools (Urban-rural Transitional Area) ········ 308
Number of Schools and Classes in Regular Senior Secondary Schools (Counties & Town Area) ········ 309
Number of Schools and Classes in Regular Senior Secondary Schools (County-town Transitional Area) ········ 310
Number of Schools and Classes in Regular Senior Secondary Schools (Rural Area) ········ 311
Number of Students in Regular Senior Secondary Schools (Total) ········ 312
Number of Students in Senior Secondary Schools (Urban Area) ········ 313
Number of Students in Senior Secondary Schools (Urban-rural Transitional Area) ········ 314
Number of Students in Senior Secondary Schools (Counties & Towns Area) ········ 315
Number of Students in Senior Secondary Schools (County-town Transitional Area) ········ 316
Number of Students in Senior Secondary Schools (Rural Area) ········ 317
Number of Female Students in Regular Senior Secondary Schools ········ 318
Number of Educational Personnel in General Secondary Schools (Total) ········ 319
Number of Educational Personnel in General Secondary Schools (Urban Area) ········ 320
Number of Educational Personnel in General Secondary Schools (Urban-rural Transitional Area) ········ 321
Number of Educational Personnel in General Secondary Schools (Counties & Towns Area) ········ 322
Number of Educational Personnel in General Secondary Schools (County-town Transitional Area) ········ 323
Number of Educational Personnel in General Secondary Schools (Rural Area) ········ 324
Number of Female Educational Personnel in General Secondary Schools ········ 325
Number of General Secondary Schools Educational Personnel Maintained by the Communities ········ 326
Number of Full-time Teachers in Regular Senior Secondary Schools by Academic Qualification and Professional Rank (Total) ········ 328
Number of Full-time Teachers in Regular Senior Secondary Schools by Academic Qualification and Professional Rank (Urban Area) ········ 330
Number of Full-time Teachers in Regular Senior Secondary Schools by Academic Qualification and Professional Rank (Urban-rural Transitional Area) ········ 332
Number of Full-time Teachers in Regular Senior Secondary Schools by Academic Qualification and Professional Rank (Counties & Towns Area) ········ 334
Number of Full-time Teachers in Regular Senior Secondary Schools by Academic Qualification and Professional Rank (County-town Transitional Area) ········ 336
Number of Full-time Teachers in Regular Senior Secondary Schools by Academic Qualification and Professional Rank (Rural Area) ········ 338
Condition of School Buildings in Senior Secondary Schools (1) (Total) ········ 340
Condition of School Buildings in Senior Secondary Schools (1) (Urban Area) ········ 342
Condition of School Buildings in Senior Secondary Schools (1) (Urban-rural Transitional Area) ········ 344
Condition of School Buildings in Senior Secondary Schools (1) (Counties & Towns Area) ········ 346
Condition of School Buildings in Senior Secondary Schools (1) (County-town Transitional Area) ········ 348
Condition of School Buildings in Senior Secondary Schools (1) (Rural Area) ········ 350
Condition of School Buildings in Senior Secondary Schools (2) (Total) ········ 352
Condition of School Buildings in Senior Secondary Schools (2) (Urban Area) ········ 354
Condition of School Buildings in Senior Secondary Schools (2) (Urban-rural Transitional Area) ········ 356

Condition of School Buildings in Senior Secondary Schools (2) (Counties & Towns Area) 358
Condition of School Buildings in Senior Secondary Schools (2) (County-Town Transitional Area) 360
Condition of School Buildings in Senior Secondary Schools (2) (Rural Area) 362
Number of Secondary Vocational Schools 364
Number of Students in Secondary Vocational Schools 366
Number of Female Students in Secondary Vocational Schools 368
Number of Students in Reg. Specialized Secondary Schools 370
Number of Female Students in Reg. Specialized Secondary Schools 372
Number of Students in Adult Specialized Secondary Schools 374
Number of Female Students in Adult Specialized Secondary Schools 376
Number of Students in Vocational High Schools 378
Number of Female Students in Vocational High Schools 380
Number of Students by Age in Secondary Vocational Schools 382
Number of Female Students by Age in Secondary Vocational Schools 384
Number of Graduates in Secondary Vocational Schools 386
Number of Enrolment in Secondary Vocational Schools 388
Changes of Enrolment in Secondary Vocational Schools 390
Changes of Female Enrolment in Secondary Vocational Schools 392
Number of Foreign Students in Secondary Vocational Schools 394
Number of Educational Personnel in Secondary Vocational Schools 396
Number of Female Educational Personnel in Secondary Vocational Schools 398
Number of Educational Personnel in Regular Specialized Secondary Vocational Schools 400
Number of Female Educational Personnel in Regular Specialized Secondary Vocational Schools 402
Number of Educational Personnel in Adult Specialized Secondary Schools 404
Number of Female Educational Personnel in Adult Specialized Secondary Schools 406
Number of Educational Personnel in Secondary Vocational Schools 408
Number of Female Educational Personnel in Vocational High Schools 410
Number of Educational Personnel in Other Secondary Vocational Education Institutions 412
Number of Female Educational Personnel in Other Secondary Vocational Education Institutions 414
Number of Full-time Teachers by Professional Rank and Academic Qualifications in
Secondary Vocational Schools 416
Number of Full-time Teachers by Professional Rank and Academic Qualifications in
Reg. Specialized Secondary Schools 418
Number of Full-time Teachers by Professional Rank and Academic Qualifications in
Adult Specialized Secondary Schools 420
Number of Full-time Teachers by Professional Rank and Academic Qualifications in
Vocational High Schools 422
Number of Full-time Teachers by Professional Rank and Academic Qualifications in
Other Secondary Vocational Education Institutions 424
Condition of Assets and Teaching Resources in Secondary Vocational Schools (Owned by SVSs) 426
Condition of Assets and Teaching Resources in Secondary Vocational Schools
(Institutions) (Not Owned by SVSs) 428
Condition of Assets and Teaching Resources in Regular SSSs (Owned by Regular SSSs) 430
Condition of Assets and Teaching Resources in Regular SSSs (Not Owned by Regular SSSs) 432
Condition of Assets and Teaching Resources in Adult SSSs (Owned by Adult SSSs) 434
Condition of Assets and Teaching Resources in Adult SSSs (Not Owned by Adult SSSs) 436

Condition of Assets and Teaching Resources in Vocational High Schools (Owned by VHSs) 438
Condition of Assets and Teaching Resources in Vocational High Schools (Not Owned by VHSs) 440
Condition of Assets and Teaching Resources in Other Secondary Vocational Education Institutions (Owned by SVSs) 442
Condition of Assets and Teaching Resources in Other Secondary Vocational Education Institutions (Not Owned by SVSs) 444
Conditions of School Buildings in Secondary Vocational Schools (Institutions) 446
Conditions of School Buildings in Regular Specialized Secondary Schools 447
Conditions of School Buildings in Adult Specialized Secondary Schools 448
Conditions of School Buildings in Vocational High Schools 449
Conditions of School Buildings in Other Secondary Vocational Education Institutions 450
Basic Statistics of Vocational Technical Training Institutions (Total) 452
Basic Statistics of Vocational Technical Training Schools 454
Basic Statistics of Technical Training Schools for Peasants 456
Basic Statistics of Others 458
Condition of Assets and Teaching Resources in Vocational Technical Training Institutions 460
Condition of Assets and Teaching Resources in Technical Training Schools 462
Condition of Assets and Teaching Resources in Technical Training Schools for Peasants 464
Condition of Assets and Teaching Resources in Others 466
Number of Schools, Classes of Junior Secondary Schools 468
Number of Schools, Classes of Junior secondary Schools (Urban Area) 470
Number of Schools, Classes of Junior Secondary Schools (Urban-rural Transitional Area) 472
Number of Schools, Classes of Junior Secondary Schools (Counties & Towns Area) 474
Number of Schools, Classes of Junior Secondary Schools (County-town Transitional Area) 476
Number of Schools, Classes of Junior Secondary Schools (Rural Area) 478
Number of Students in Junior Secondary Schools 480
Number of Students in Junior Secondary Schools (Urban Area) 482
Number of Students in Junior Secondary Schools (Urban-rural Transitional Area) 484
Number of Students in Junior Secondary Schools (Counties & Towns Area) 486
Number of Students in Junior Secondary Schools (County-town Transitional Area) 488
Number of Students in Junior Secondary Schools (Rural Area) 490
Number of Female Students in Junior Secondary Schools 492
Number of Full-time Teachers in Junior Secondary Schools by Academic Qualifications and Professional Rank (Total) 494
Number of Full-time Teachers in Junior Secondary Schools by Academic Qualifications and Professional Rank (Urban Area) 496
Number of Full-time Teachers in Junior Secondary Schools by Academic Qualifications and Professional Rank (Urban-rural Transitional Area) 498
Number of Full-time Teachers in Junior Secondary Schools by Academic Qualifications and Professional Rank (Counties & Towns Area) 500
Number of Full-time Teachers in Junior Secondary Schools by Academic Qualifications and Professional Rank (County-town Transitional Area) 502
Number of Full-time Teachers in Junior Secondary Schools by Academic Qualifications and Professional Rank (Rural Area) 504
Condition of School Buildings in Junior Secondary Schools (1) (Total) 506
Condition of School Buildings in Junior Secondary Schools (1) (Urban Area) 508

Condition of School Buildings in Junior Secondary Schools (1) (Urban-rural Transitional Area) ………………… 510
Condition of School Buildings in Junior Secondary Schools (1) (Counties & Towns Area) ………………………… 512
Condition of School Buildings in Junior Secondary Schools (1) (County-town Transitional Area) ………………… 514
Condition of School Buildings in Junior Secondary Schools (1) (Rural Area) ……………………………………… 516
Condition of School Buildings in Junior Secondary Schools (2) (Total) …………………………………………… 518
Condition of School Buildings in Junior Secondary Schools (2) (Urban Area) ……………………………………… 520
Condition of School Buildings in Junior Secondary Schools (2) (Urban-rural Transitional Area) ………………… 522
Condition of School Buildings in Junior Secondary Schools (2) (Counties & Towns Area) ………………………… 524
Condition of School Buildings in Junior Secondary Schools (2) (County-town Transitional Area) ………………… 526
Condition of School Buildings in Junior Secondary Schools (2) (Rural Area) ……………………………………… 528
Number of Schools, External Teaching Sites & Classes in Primary Schools ……………………………………… 530
Number of Schools, External Teaching Sites & Classes in Primary Schools (Urban Area) ………………………… 532
Number of Schools, External Teaching Sites & Classes in Primary Schools (Urban-rural Transitional Area) …… 534
Number of Schools, External Teaching Sites & Classes in Primary Schools (Counties & Towns Area) ………… 536
Number of Schools, External Teaching Sites & Classes in Primary Schools (County-town Transitional Area) …… 538
Number of Schools, External Teaching Sites & Classes in Primary Schools (Rural Area) ………………………… 540
Number of Students in Primary Schools (Total) ……………………………………………………………………… 542
Number of Students in Primary Schools (Urban Area) ……………………………………………………………… 544
Number of Students in Primary Schools (Urban-rural Transitional Area) ………………………………………… 546
Number of Students in Primary Schools (Counties & Towns Area) ………………………………………………… 548
Number of Students in Primary Schools (County-town Transitional Area) ………………………………………… 550
Number of Students in Primary Schools (Rural Area) ……………………………………………………………… 552
Number of Students in 5-year Primary Schools ……………………………………………………………………… 554
Number of Female Students in Primary Schools ……………………………………………………………………… 556
Number of Educational Personnel in Primary Schools (Total) ……………………………………………………… 558
Number of Educational Personnel in Primary Schools (Urban Area) ……………………………………………… 559
Number of Educational Personnel in Primary Schools (Urban-rural Transitional Area) ………………………… 560
Number of Educational Personnel in Primary Schools (Counties & Towns Area) ………………………………… 561
Number of Educational Personnel in Primary Schools (County-town Transitional Area) ………………………… 562
Number of Educational Personnel in Primary Schools (Rural Area) ……………………………………………… 563
Number of Primary Schools Educational Personnel Maintained by the Communities …………………………… 564
Number of Female Educational Personnel in Primary Schools ……………………………………………………… 565
Number of Full-time Teacher in Primary Schools by Academic Qualifications and Professional Rank (Total) ……………………………………………………………………………………… 566
Number of Full-time Teacher in Primary Schools by Academic Qualifications and Professional Rank (Urban Area) ……………………………………………………………………………… 568
Number of Full-time Teacher in Primary Schools by Academic Qualifications and Professional Rank (Urban-rural Transitional Area) ……………………………………………………… 570
Number of Full-time Teacher in Primary Schools by Academic Qualifications and Professional Rank (County & Town Area) ……………………………………………………………………… 572
Number of Full-time Teacher in Primary Schools by Academic Qualifications and Professional Rank (County-town Transitional Area) ………………………………………………………… 574
Number of Full-time Teacher in Primary Schools by Academic Qualifications and Professional Rank (Rural Area) ……………………………………………………………………………… 576
Condition of School Buildings in Primary Schools (1) (Total) ………………………………………………………… 578
Condition of School Buildings in Primary Schools (1) (Urban Area) ………………………………………………… 580

Condition of School Buildings in Primary Schools (1) (Urban-rural Transitional Area) 582
Condition of School Buildings in Primary Schools (1) (Counties & Towns Area) 584
Condition of School Buildings in Primary Schools (1) (County-town Transitional Area) 586
Condition of School Buildings in Primary Schools (1) (Rural Area) 588
Condition of School Buildings in Primary Schools (2) (Total) 590
Condition of School Buildings in Primary Schools (2) (Urban Area) 592
Condition of School Buildings in Primary Schools (2) (Urban-rural Transitional Area) 594
Condition of School Buildings in Primary Schools (2) (Counties & Towns Area) 596
Condition of School Buildings in Primary Schools (2) (County-town Transitional Area) 598
Condition of School Buildings in Primary Schools (2) (Rural Area) 600
Basic Statistics of Correctional Work-study Schools 602
Basic Statistics of Special Education (Total) 604
Basic Statistics of Special Education (Urban Area) 606
Basic Statistics of Special Education (Urban-rural Transitional Area) 608
Basic Statistics of Special Education (Counties & Towns Area) 610
Basic Statistics of Special Education (County-town Transitional Area) 612
Basic Statistics of Special Education (Rural Area) 614
Number of Female Students in Special Education 616
Number of Educational Personnel in Special Education Schools 618
Number of Female Educational Personnel in Special Education Schools 619
Number of Full-time Teachers in Special Education Schools by Academic Qualifications and Professional Rank 620
Condition of School Buildings in Special Education Schools (1) 622
Condition of School Buildings in Special Education Schools (2) 624
Basic Statistics of Pre-primary Education (Total) 625
Basic Statistics of Pre-primary Education (Urban Area) 626
Basic Statistics of Pre-primary Education (Urban-rural Transitional Area) 627
Basic Statistics of Pre-primary Education (Counties & Towns Area) 628
Basic Statistics of Pre-primary Education (County-town Transitional Area) 629
Basic Statistics of Pre-primary Education (Rural Area) 630
Number of Female Children in Pre-primary Education 631
Number of Educational Personnel in Kindergarten (Total) 632
Number of Educational Personnel in Kindergarten (Urban Area) 633
Number of Educational Personnel in Kindergarten (Urban-rural Transitional Area) 634
Number of Educational Personnel in Kindergarten (Counties & Towns Area) 635
Number of Educational Personnel in Kindergarten (County-town Transitional Area) 636
Number of Educational Personnel in Kindergarten (Rural Area) 637
Number of Female Educational Personnel in Kindergarten 638
Number of Kindergarten Heads, Full-time Teachers by Academic Qualifications and Professional Rank (Total) 640
Breakdown of Kindergarten Heads, Full-time Teachers by Academic Qualifications and Profession Rank (Urban Area) 642
Breakdown of Kindergarten Heads, Full-time Teachers by Academic Qualifications and Professional Rank (Urban-rural Transitional Area) 644
Breakdown of Kindergarten Heads, Full-time Teachers by Academic Qualifications and Professional Rank (Counties & Towns Area) 646

Breakdown of Kindergarten Heads, Full-time Teachers by Academic Qualifications and Professional Rank (County-town Transitional Area) 648
Breakdown of Kindergarten Heads, Full-time Teachers by Academic Qualifications and Professional Rank (Rural Area) 650
Statistics of Kindergarten Buildings and Others (Total) (1) 652
Statistics of Kindergarten Buildings and Others (Urban Area) (1) 654
Statistics of Kindergarten Buildings and Others (Urban-rural Transitional Area) (1) 656
Statistics of Kindergarten Buildings and Others (Counties& Towns Area) (1) 658
Statistics of Kindergarten Buildings and Others (Urban-rural Transitional Area) (1) 660
Statistics of Kindergarten Buildings and Others (Rural Area) (1) 662
Statistics of Kindergarten Buildings and Others (Total) (2) 664
Statistics of Kindergarten Buildings and Others (Urban Area) (2) 665
Statistics of Kindergarten Buildings and Others (Urban-rural Transitional Area) (2) 666
Statistics of Kindergarten Buildings and Others (Counties & Towns Area) (2) 667
Statistics of Kindergarten Buildings and Others (County-town Transitional Area) (2) 668
Statistics of Kindergarten Buildings and Others (Rural Area) (2) 669

Part Ⅱ

PHYSICAL FACILITIES

Public Expenditure on Education

Sources of Educational Funds and Expenditure for Education in Various School (2016) 672
Sources of Educational Fund and Expenditure for Education by Region (2016) 674

Capital Construction Investment in the Educational Sector

Data on the Completion of Capital Construction Investment in the Educational Sector (Regional Aggregates) ... 678
Data on the Completion of Capital Construction Investment in the Educational Sector 680

Part Ⅲ

SCIENTIFIC RESEARCH ACTIVITES & OTHER

Natural Science and Technology

Scientific and Technical Manpower in Regular HEIs 684
S & T Expenditure in Regular HEIs 686
Statistics of R & D Projects and Achievements in Regular HEIs 688

Social Science

Professional Manpower in Regular HEIs in the Fields of the Humanities and Social Science 692
Humanities and Social Sciences R & D Expenditure in Regular HEIs 694
Basic Statistics of Humanities and Social Sciences R & D and Achievements in Regular HEIs 696

Appendixes

Gross Domestic Product ······ 700
Gross Domestic Product by Region (2016) ······ 701
Total Government Revenue and Expenditures and Their Increase Rate ······ 702
Total Revenue and Expenditures of Central and Local Governments ······ 703
Population and Its Composition ······ 704
Illiterate Population Aged 15 and Over by Sex and Region (2016) ······ 705
Population by Sex, Educational Level and Region (2016) ······ 706

第一部分
Part I

教育事业发展
THE DEVELOPMENT OF THE EDUCATIONAL UNDERTAKING

一、综合部分
Summary Tables

各级各类学校校数、教职工、专任教师情况
Number of Schools, Educational Personnel and Full-time Teachers by Type and Level

	学校数(所) Schools	教职工数(人) Educational Personnel	专任教师数(人) Full-time Teachers
一、高等教育 Higher Education			
(一)研究生培养机构(不计校数) Institutions Providing Postgraduate Programs	(815)	—	—
1. 普通高校 Regular HEIs	(578)	—	—
2. 科研机构 Research Institutes	(237)	—	—
(二)普通高等学校 Regular HEIs	2631	2442995	1633248
1. 本科院校 HEIs Offering Degree Programs	1243	1772342	1150467
其中:独立学院 of Which: Independent Institutions	265	162330	122151
2. 高职(专科)院校 Higher Vocational Colleges	1388	669521	482070
3. 其他普通高教机构(不计校数) Other Institutions	(24)	1132	711
(三)成人高等学校 Adult HEIs	282	41408	23990
(四)民办的其他高等教育机构 Other Non-government HEIs	(800)	20882	9643
二、中等教育 Secondary Education	**77018**	**7827807**	**6165625**
(一)高中阶段教育 Senior Secondary Education	24618	3747959	2615570
1. 高中 Senior Secondary Schools	13947	2668247	1776374
普通高中 Regular Senior Secondary Schools	13555	2665073	1773953
完全中学 Combined Secondary Schools	5460	1056242	531255
高级中学 Regular High Schools	6780	1331610	1176082
十二年一贯制学校 12-Year Schools	1315	277221	66616
成人高中 Adult High Schools	392	3174	2421
2. 中等职业教育 Secondary Vocational Education	10671	1079712	839196
普通中专 Regular Specialized Secondary Schools	3346	396845	301577
成人中专 Adult Specialized Secondary Schools	1218	59705	44773
职业高中 Vocational High Schools	3617	343767	286053
技工学校 Skilled Workers Schools	2490	268565	198798
其他中职机构(不计校数) Other Secondary Vocational Education Institutions	(312)	10830	7995
(二)初中阶段教育 Junior Secondary Education	52400	4079848	3550055
1. 初中 Junior Secondary Schools	51894	4078076	3548688
初级中学 Regular Junior Secondary Schools	35696	2763493	2519334
九年一贯制学校 9-Year Schools	16183	1314104	551604
十二年一贯制学校 12-Year Schools	—	—	73131
完全中学 Combined Secondary Schools	—	—	404179
职业初中 Vocational Junior Secondary Schools	15	479	440
2. 成人初中 Adult Junior Secondary Schools	506	1772	1367
三、初等教育 Primary Education	**176718**	**5664652**	**5955726**
(一)普通小学 Regular Primary Schools	167009	5645319	5944910
小学 Primary Schools	167009	5645319	5282512
九年一贯制学校 9-Year Schools	—	—	596348
十二年一贯制学校 12-Year Schools	—	—	66050
(二)成人小学 Adult Primary Schools	9709	19333	10816
其中:扫盲班 of Which: Literacy Classes	6587	14366	7546
四、工读学校 Correctional Work-Study Schools	**93**	**2922**	**2177**
五、特殊教育 Special Education Schools	**2107**	**65138**	**55979**
六、学前教育 Pre-school Education Institutions	**254950**	**4192850**	**2432138**

注:1. 完全中学的学校数和教职工数计入高中阶段教育,九年一贯制学校的校数和教职工数计入初中阶段教育,十二年一贯制学校的校数和教职工数计入高中阶段教育。专任教师是按照教育层次进行归类;

2. "( )"内数据为不计校数。

Note: 1. The numbers of complete secondary schools and their educational personnel are calculated into the number of senior secondary education, the numbers of Combined Primary and Lower Secondary Schools and their educational personnel are calculated into the junior secondary education, the numbers of the Combined Primary and Secondary Schools and their educational personnel are calculated into senior secondary education. The full-time teachers are classified by educational level;

2. The data within "( )" are not calculated as the number of schools.

各级各类学历教育学生情况

Number of Students of Formal Education by Type and Level

单位：人
unit: person

	毕业生数 Graduates	招生数 Entrants	在校生数 Enrolment
一、高等教育 Higher Education			
（一）研究生 Postgraduates	578045	806103	2639561
博　士 Doctor's Degree	58032	83878	361997
硕　士 Master's Degree	520013	722225	2277564
（二）普通本专科 Undergraduate in Regular HEIs	7358287	7614893	27535869
本　科 Normal Courses	3841839	4107534	16486320
专　科 Short-cycle Courses	3516448	3507359	11049549
（三）成人本专科 Undergraduate in Adult HEIs	2470370	2175302	5441429
本　科 Normal Courses	1091226	1023981	2589809
专　科 Short-cycle Courses	1379144	1151321	2851620
（四）网络本专科生 Web-based Undergraduates	1777905	2861143	7359267
本　科 Normal Courses	659559	993253	2587338
专　科 Short-cycle Courses	1118346	1867890	4771929
二、中等教育 Secondary Education	**26866428**	**29297060**	**84257502**
（一）高中阶段教育 Senior Secondary Education	12765032	13824851	39709871
1. 高中 Senior Secondary Schools	7796262	8000548	23784903
普通高中 Regular Senior Secondary Schools	7757292	8000548	23745484
完全中学 Combined Secondary Schools	2372222	2477207	7322134
高级中学 Regular High Schools	5125357	5169156	15472730
十二年一贯制学校 12-Year Schools	259713	354185	950620
成人高中 Adult High Schools	38970	—	39419
2. 中等职业教育 Secondary Vocational Education	4968770	5824303	15924968
普通中专 Regular Specialized Secondary Schools	2169933	2462485	7129894
成人中专 Adult Specialized Secondary Schools	604125	568771	1272446
职业高中 Vocational High Schools	1289923	1483979	4140553
技工学校 Skilled Workers Schools	904789	1309068	3382075
（二）初中阶段教育 Junior Secondary Education	14101396	15472209	44547631
1. 初中 Junior Secondary Schools	13974699	15472209	44420630
初级中学 Regular Junior Secondary Schools	9978057	10760883	31215383
九年一贯制学校 9-Year Schools	1916050	2378247	6585126
十二年一贯制学校 12-Year Schools	307082	398065	1075624
完全中学 Combined Secondary Schools	1772477	1934058	5541759
职业初中 Vocational Junior Secondary Schools	1033	956	2738
2. 成人初中 Adult Junior Secondary Schools	126697	—	127001
三、初等教育 Primary Education	**16504019**	**17665544**	**101691216**
（一）普通小学 Regular Primary Schools	15658999	17665544	100936980
小学 Primary Schools	13843045	15688419	89460245
九年一贯制学校 9-Year Schools	1645350	1787919	10384335
十二年一贯制学校 12-Year Schools	170604	189206	1092400
（二）成人小学 Adult Primary Schools	845020	—	754236
其中：扫盲班 of Which: Literacy Classes	282673	—	304043
四、工读学校 Correctional Work-Study Schools	**3311**	**3187**	**6048**
五、特殊教育 Special Education Schools	**69401**	**110843**	**578826**
六、学前教育 Pre-school Education Institutions	**16526663**	**19379530**	**46001393**

注：1. 2017 年起，研究生招生、在校生指标内涵发生变化。招生包含全日制和非全日制研究生；在校生、授予学位数包含全日制、非全日制研究生和在职人员攻读硕士学位学生。下同；
2. 完全中学、九年一贯制学校和十二年一贯制学校的学生数按教育层次分别计入对应教育阶段的学生数中；
3. 特殊教育学生数中包括义务教育阶段随班就读、其他学校附设特教班的学生。

Note: 1. From 2017, the indicators meaning of entrants and enrollment of postgraduate students have changed. The number of entrants includes full-time and part-time postgraduate students. The number of Master's and Doctor's Degree awarded includes full-time, part-time postgraduate students and on-the-job students. Same as below;
2. Number of the students in Combined Secondary Schools, 9-Year Schools, 12-Year Schools are classified by educational level;
3. Number of the Students Followed in the Regular Primary and Middle School in the Special Education.

各级各类非学历教育学生情况

Number of Students of Non-formal Education by Type and Level

单位:人次

unit: person-time

	结业生数 Completers	注册学生数 Enrolment
总计 Total	**57249115**	**54656731**
一、高等教育 Higher Education	**9808395**	**9273706**
(一)研究生课程进修班 Postgraduate Courses	9244	12237
(二)自考助学班 Classes Run by Non-government HEIs for Students Preparing for Self-Taught Higher Education Examinations	116214	230086
(三)普通预科生 College-preparatory Classes	—	45420
(四)进修及培训 In-service Training	9682937	8985963
其中:资格证书培训 of Which: For Certificates of Vocational Qualifications	2234987	2252372
岗位证书培训 For Certificates of Job-related Qualifications	2485345	2188331
二、中等职业教育 Secondary Vocational Education	**47440720**	**45383025**
其中:资格证书培训 of Which: For Certificates of Vocational Qualifications	7637840	7274609
岗位证书培训 For Certificates of Job-related Qualifications	11266732	10550536
(一)中等职业学校 Secondary Vocational Schools	4639952	3318076
其中:资格证书培训 of Which: For Certificates of Vocational Qualifications	1730703	1406190
岗位证书培训 For Certificates of Job-related Qualifications	1547596	1123283
(二)职业技术培训机构 Other Vocational-technical Training Institutions	42800768	42064949
其中:资格证书培训 of Which: For Certificates of Vocational Qualifications	5907137	5868419
岗位证书培训 For Certificates of Job-related Qualifications	9719136	9427253

各级各类民办学校校数、教职工、专任教师情况

Number of Non-government Schools, Educational Personnel and Full-time Teachers by Type and Level

	学校数（所）Schools	教职工数（人）Educational Personnel	专任教师数（人）Full-time Teachers
一、高等教育 Higher Education			
（一）研究生培养机构（不计校数）Institutions Providing Postgraduate Programs	（6）	—	—
1. 普通高校 Regular HEIs	（5）	—	—
2. 科研机构 Research Institutes	（1）	—	—
（二）普通高等学校 Regular HEIs	746	436819	316174
1. 本科院校 HEIs Offering Degree Programs	426	315875	231092
其中：独立学院 of Which：Independent Institutions	265	162330	122151
2. 高职（专科）院校 Higher Vocational Colleges	320	120842	85009
3. 其他普通高教机构（不计校数） Other Institutions	（15）	102	73
（三）成人高等学校 Adult HEIs	1	0	0
（四）民办的其他高等教育机构 Other Non-government HEIs	（800）	20882	9643
二、中等教育 Secondary Education	—	—	—
（一）高中阶段教育 Senior Secondary Education	—	—	—
1. 高中 Senior Secondary Schools	—	—	—
普通高中 Regular Senior Secondary Schools	3002	481324	187498
完全中学 Combined Secondary Schools	1056	177092	71080
高级中学 Regular High Schools	938	83879	66957
十二年一贯制学校 12-Year Schools	1008	220353	49461
成人高中 Adult High Schools	—	—	—
2. 中等职业教育 Secondary Vocational Education	—	—	—
普通中专 Regular Specialized Secondary Schools	831	49661	33765
成人中专 Adult Specialized Secondary Schools	121	9034	5956
职业高中 Vocational High Schools	1117	47212	32256
技工学校 Skilled Workers Schools	—	—	—
其他中职机构（不计校数）Other Secondary Vocational Education Institutions	（40）	1709	1113
（二）初中阶段教育 Junior Secondary Education	—	—	—
1. 初中 Junior Secondary Schools	5277	492558	339069
初级中学 Regular Junior Secondary Schools	1293	116302	93815
九年一贯制学校 9-Year Schools	3983	376251	122747
十二年一贯制学校 12-Year Schools	—	—	54980
完全中学 Combined Secondary Schools	—	—	67523
职业初中 Vocational Junior Secondary Schools	1	5	4
2. 成人初中 Adult Junior Secondary Schools	—	—	—
三、初等教育 Primary Education	—	—	—
（一）普通小学 Regular Primary Schools	6107	277063	420099
小学 Primary Schools	6107	277063	207796
九年一贯制学校 9-Year Schools	—	—	161133
十二年一贯制学校 12-Year Schools	—	—	51170
（二）成人小学 Adult Primary Schools	—	—	—
其中：扫盲班 of Which：Literacy Classes	—	—	—
四、工读学校 Correctional Work-Study Schools	**3**	**160**	**131**
五、特殊教育 Special Education Schools	**66**	**1876**	**1243**
六、学前教育 Pre-school Education Institutions	**160372**	**2764718**	**1510277**
另有：民办培训机构（不计校数）Other Vocational-technical Training Institutions	（21234）	294684	161478

注：1. 完全中学的学校数和教职工数计入高中阶段教育，九年一贯制学校的校数和教职工数计入初中阶段教育，十二年一贯制学校的校数和教职工数计入高中阶段教育。专任教师是按照教育层次进行归类；

2. "（ ）"内数据为不计校数。

Note：1. The numbers of complete secondary schools and their educational personnel are calculated into the number of senior secondary education, the numbers of Combined Primary and Lower Secondary Schools and their educational personnel are calculated into the junior secondary education, the numbers of the Combined Primary and Secondary Schools and their educational personnel are calculated into senior secondary education. The full-time teachers are classified by educational level；

2. The data within "（ ）" are not calculated as the number of schools.

各级各类民办教育学生情况

Number of Students of Non-government Education by Type and Level

单位:人
unit: person

	毕业生数 Graduates	招生数 Entrants	在校生数 Enrolment
一、高等教育 Higher Education			
(一)研究生 Postgraduates	232	747	1223
博 士 Doctor's Degree	—	—	—
硕 士 Master's Degree	232	747	1223
(二)普通本专科 Undergraduate in Regular HEIs	1631582	1753700	6284554
本 科 Normal Courses	921506	1016329	4016810
专 科 Short-cycle Courses	710076	737371	2267744
(三)成人本专科 Undergraduate in Adult HEIs	65548	99038	227301
本 科 Normal Courses	7899	15329	30691
专 科 Short-cycle Courses	57649	83709	196610
(四)另有其他学生 Other Students	—	—	—
1. 民办高校 Non-government HEIs	—	—	435387
2. 民办的其他高等教育机构 Other Non-government	—	—	744657
二、中等教育 Secondary Education	—	—	—
(一)高中阶段教育 Senior Secondary Education	—	—	—
1. 高中 Senior Secondary Schools	—	—	—
普通高中 Regular Senior Secondary Schools	828656	1114094	3062608
完全中学 Combined Secondary Schools	335130	428044	1190888
高级中学 Regular High Schools	297411	400562	1118141
十二年一贯制学校 12-Year Schools	196115	285488	753579
成人高中 Adult High Schools	—	—	—
2. 中等职业教育 Secondary Vocational Education	—	—	—
普通中专 Regular Specialized Secondary Schools	276821	405971	1059542
成人中专 Adult Specialized Secondary Schools	88258	116051	220294
职业高中 Vocational High Schools	197233	264787	693448
技工学校 Skilled Workers Schools	0	0	0
另有其他学生 Other Students	0	0	248807
(二)初中阶段教育 Junior Secondary Education	0	0	0
1. 初中 Junior Secondary Schools	1676066	2090925	5776835
初级中学 Regular Junior Secondary Schools	516303	577780	1669840
九年一贯制学校 9-Year Schools	562515	772545	2071731
十二年一贯制学校 12-Year Schools	243550	322693	865326
完全中学 Combined Secondary Schools	353673	417881	1169881
职业初中 Vocational Junior Secondary Schools	25	26	57
2. 成人初中 Adult Junior Secondary Schools	—	—	—
三、初等教育 Primary Education	—	—	—
(一)普通小学 Regular Primary Schools	1267129	1376977	8141720
小学 Primary Schools	622145	702033	4089909
九年一贯制学校 9-Year Schools	511457	536022	3224259
十二年一贯制学校 12-Year Schools	133527	138922	827552
(二)成人小学 Adult Primary Schools	—	—	—
其中:扫盲班 of Which: Literacy Classes	—	—	—
四、工读学校 Correctional Work-Study Schools	**99**	**256**	**593**
五、特殊教育 Special Education Schools	**1378**	**2891**	**13162**
六、学前教育 Pre-school Education Institutions	**8295846**	**9993192**	**25723434**
另有:民办培训机构(不计校数)Other Vocational-technical Tra	—	—	9014369

注:1. 完全中学、九年一贯制学校和十二年一贯制学校的学生数按教育层次分别计入对应教育阶段的学生数中;
2. 特殊教育学生数中包括义务教育阶段随班就读、其他学校附设特教班的学生;
3. "另有:民办培训机构"包括自考助学班学生、预科生、进修及培训学生数;
4. 民办"硕士在校生数"不包括民办在职人员攻读硕士学位在校生数 714 人。

Note: 1. Number of the students in Combined Secondary Schools, 9-Year Schools, 12-Year Schools are classified by educational level;
2. Number of the Students Followed in the Regular Primary and Middle School in the Special Education;
3. Number of the other Students Followed in the Classes Run by Non-government HEIs for Students Preparing for Self-Taught Examinations Learners, College-preparatory Classes, In-service Training;
4. The number of master s degree students in Non-government HEIs does not include the number of On-the-job Personnel Master's Degree Programs' students in Non-government HEIs(Which is 714).

各级各类学校女学生数
Number of Female Students of Schools by Type and Level

单位:人
unit: person

	总计 Total	男 Male	女学生 Female Students 人数 Number	女学生 Female Students 占学生总数的比重(%) Percentage
一、高等教育 Higher Education				
(一)研究生 Postgraduates	2639561	1361427	1278134	48.42
博　士 Doctor's Degree	361997	219824	142173	39.27
硕　士 Master's Degree	2277564	1141603	1135961	49.88
(二)普通本专科 Undergraduate in Regular HEIs	27535869	13067361	14468508	52.54
本　科 Normal Courses	16486320	7626790	8859530	53.74
专　科 Short-cycle Courses	11049549	5440571	5608978	50.76
(三)成人本专科 Undergraduate in Adult HEIs	5441429	2243173	3198256	58.78
本　科 Normal Courses	2589809	988872	1600937	61.82
专　科 Short-cycle Courses	2851620	1254301	1597319	56.01
(四)网络本专科生 Web-based Undergraduates	7359267	3875471	3483796	47.34
本　科 Normal Courses	2587338	1267280	1320058	51.02
专　科 Short-cycle Courses	4771929	2608191	2163738	45.34
二、中等教育 Secondary Education	**84257502**	**44693954**	**39563548**	**46.96**
(一)高中阶段教育 Senior Secondary Education	39709871	20804759	18905112	47.61
1. 高中 Senior Secondary Schools	23784903	11690066	12094837	50.85
普通高中 Regular Senior Secondary Schools	23745484	11672069	12073415	50.85
完全中学 Combined Secondary Schools	7322134	3648673	3673461	50.17
高级中学 Regular High Schools	15472730	7491296	7981434	51.58
十二年一贯制学校 12-Year Schools	950620	532100	418520	44.03
成人高中 Adult High Schools	39419	17997	21422	54.34
2. 中等职业教育 Secondary Vocational Education	15924968	9114693	6810275	42.76
普通中专 Regular Specialized Secondary Schools	7129894	3618568	3511326	49.25
成人中专 Adult Specialized Secondary Schools	1272446	741061	531385	41.76
职业高中 Vocational High Schools	4140553	2370434	1770119	42.75
技工学校 Skilled Workers Schools	3382075	2384630	997445	29.49
(二)初中阶段教育 Junior Secondary Education	44547631	23889195	20658436	46.37
1. 初中 Junior Secondary Schools	44420630	23822271	20598359	46.37
初级中学 Regular Junior Secondary Schools	31215383	16586209	14629174	46.87
九年一贯制学校 9-Year Schools	6585126	3647326	2937800	44.61
十二年一贯制学校 12-Year Schools	1075624	629574	446050	41.47
完全中学 Combined Secondary Schools	5541759	2957587	2584172	46.63
职业初中 Vocational Junior Secondary Schools	2738	1575	1163	42.48
2. 成人初中 Adult Junior Secondary Schools	127001	66924	60077	47.30
三、初等教育 Primary Education	**101691216**	**54406623**	**47284593**	**46.50**
(一)普通小学 Regular Primary Schools	100936980	54053812	46883168	46.45
小学 Primary Schools	89460245	47722460	41737785	46.66
九年一贯制学校 9-Year Schools	10384335	5695164	4689171	45.16
十二年一贯制学校 12-Year Schools	1092400	636188	456212	41.76
(二)成人小学 Adult Primary Schools	754236	352811	401425	53.22
其中:扫盲班 of Which: Literacy Classes	304043	145606	158437	52.11
四、工读学校 Correctional Work-Study Schools	**6048**	**4973**	**1075**	**17.77**
五、特殊教育 Special Education Schools	**578826**	**371821**	**207005**	**35.76**
六、学前教育 Pre-school Education Institutions	**46001393**	**24510701**	**21490692**	**46.72**

注:1. 完全中学、九年一贯制学校和十二年一贯制学校的学生数按教育层次分别计入对应教育阶段的学生数中;
2. 特殊教育学生数中包括义务教育阶段随班就读、其他学校附设特教班的学生。

Note:1. Number of the students in Combined Secondary Schools, 9-Year Schools, 12-Year Schools are classified by educational level;
2. Number of the Students Followed in the Regular Primary and Middle School in the Special Education.

各级各类学校女教师、女教职工数

Number of Female Educational Personnel and Full-time Teachers of Schools by Type and Level

单位:人

unit: person

	教职工数 Educational Personnel	其中:女教职工 of Which: Female Educational Personnel		专任教师数 Full-time Teachers	其中:女专任教师 of Which: Female Full-time Teachers	
		人数 Number	占教职工总数的比重(%) Percentage		人数 Number	占专任教师总数的比重(%) Percentage
一、高等教育 Higher Education						
(一)研究生培养机构(不计校数) Institutions Providing Postgraduate Programs	—	—	—	—	—	—
1. 普通高校 Regular HEIs	—	—	—	—	—	—
2. 科研机构 Research Institutes	—	—	—	—	—	—
(二)普通高等学校 Regular HEIs	2442995	1195657	48.94	1633248	813837	49.83
1. 本科院校 HEIs Offering Degree Programs	1772342	847801	47.84	1150467	551706	47.95
其中:独立学院 of Which:Independent Institutions	162330	84419	52.00	122151	63393	51.90
2. 高职(专科)院校 Higher Vocational Colleges	669521	347254	51.87	482070	261755	54.30
3. 其他普通高教机构(不计校数) Other Institutions	1132	602	53.18	711	376	52.88
(三)成人高等学校 Adult HEIs	41408	21250	51.32	23990	13279	55.35
(四)民办的其他高等教育机构 Other Non-government HEIs	20882	11116	53.23	9643	5058	52.45
二、中等教育 Secondary Education	**7827807**	**4246542**	**54.25**	**6165625**	—	—
(一)高中阶段教育 Senior Secondary Education	3747959	1981926	52.88	2615570	—	—
1. 高中 Senior Secondary Schools	2668247	1450233	54.35	1776374	942804	53.07
普通高中 Regular Senior Secondary Schools	2665073	1448857	54.36	1773953	941702	53.08
完全中学 Combined Secondary Schools	1056242	579882	54.90	531255	278982	52.51
高级中学 Regular High Schools	1331610	688967	51.74	1176082	626909	53.30
十二年一贯制学校 12-Year Schools	277221	180008	64.93	66616	35811	53.76
成人高中 Adult High Schools	3174	1376	43.35	2421	1102	45.52
2. 中等职业教育 Secondary Vocational Education	1079712	531693	49.24	839196	—	—
普通中专 Regular Specialized Secondary Schools	396845	199549	50.28	301577	161544	53.57
成人中专 Adult Specialized Secondary Schools	59705	29693	49.73	44773	23951	53.49
职业高中 Vocational High Schools	343767	175635	51.09	286053	153938	53.81
技工学校 Skilled Workers Schools	268565	121752	45.33	198798	—	—
其他中职机构(不计校数)Other Secondary Vocational Education Institutions	10830	5064	46.76	7995	4104	51.33
(二)初中阶段教育 Junior Secondary Education	4079848	2264616	55.51	3550055	1975108	55.64
1. 初中 Junior Secondary Schools	4078076	2263788	55.51	3548688	1974445	55.64
初级中学 Regular Junior Secondary Schools	2763493	1462783	52.93	2519334	1377999	54.70
九年一贯制学校 9-Year Schools	1314104	800793	60.94	551604	303942	55.10
十二年一贯制学校 12-Year Schools				73131	46667	63.81
完全中学 Combined Secondary Schools				404179	245635	60.77
职业初中 Vocational Junior Secondary Schools	479	212	44.26	440	202	45.91
2. 成人初中 Adult Junior Secondary Schools	1772	828	46.73	1367	663	48.50
三、初等教育 Primary Education	**5664652**	**3683635**	**65.03**	**5955726**	**3999067**	**67.15**
(一)普通小学 Regular Primary Schools	5645319	3675429	65.11	5944910	3994105	67.19
小学 Primary Schools	5645319	3675429	65.11	5282512	3523118	66.69
九年一贯制学校 9-Year Schools				596348	417657	70.04
十二年一贯制学校 12-Year Schools				66050	53330	80.74
(二)成人小学 Adult Primary Schools	19333	8206	42.45	10816	4962	45.88
其中:扫盲班 of Which: Literacy Classes	14366	5848	40.71	7546	3249	43.06
四、工读学校 Correctional Work-Study Schools	**2922**	**1293**	**44.25**	**2177**	**942**	**43.27**
五、特殊教育 Special Education Schools	**65138**	**45868**	**70.42**	**55979**	**41278**	**73.74**
六、学前教育 Pre-school Education Institutions	**4192850**	**3862781**	**92.13**	**2432138**	**2378291**	**97.79**

注:完全中学的学校数和教职工数计入高中阶段教育,九年一贯制学校的校数和教职工数计入初中阶段教育,十二年一贯制学校的校数和教职工数计入高中阶段教育。专任教师是按照教育层次进行归类。

Note: The numbers of complete secondary schools and their educational personnel are calculated into the number of senior secondary education, the numbers of Combined Primary and Lower Secondary Schools and their educational personnel are calculated into the junior secondary education, the numbers of the Combined Primary and Secondary Schools and their educational personnel are calculated into senior secondary education. The full-time teachers are classified by educational level.

各级各类学校少数民族学生数

Number of Minority Students of Schools by Type and Level

单位：人
unit：person

	总计 Total	少数民族学生 Minority Students	
		人数 Number	占学生总数的比重(%) Percentage
一、高等教育 Higher Education			
(一)研究生 Postgraduates	2639561	127995	4.85
博　士 Doctor's Degree	361997	21761	6.01
硕　士 Master's Degree	2277564	106234	4.66
(二)普通本专科 Undergraduate in Regular HEIs	27535869	2488788	9.04
本　科 Normal Courses	16486320	1509452	9.16
专　科 Short-cycle Courses	11049549	979336	8.86
(三)成人本专科 Undergraduate in Adult HEIs	5441429	495838	9.11
本　科 Normal Courses	2589809	235531	9.09
专　科 Short-cycle Courses	2851620	260307	9.13
(四)网络本专科生 Web-based Undergraduates	7359267	518017	7.04
本　科 Normal Courses	2587338	172013	6.65
专　科 Short-cycle Courses	4771929	346004	7.25
二、中等教育 Secondary Education	—	—	—
(一)高中阶段教育 Senior Secondary Education	—	—	—
1. 高中 Senior Secondary Schools			
普通高中 Regular Senior Secondary Schools	23745484	2509863	10.57
完全中学 Combined Secondary Schools	7322134	726561	9.92
高级中学 Regular High Schools	15472730	1730326	11.18
十二年一贯制学校 12-Year Schools	950620	52976	5.57
成人高中 Adult High Schools	166420	21772	13.08
2. 中等职业教育 Secondary Vocational Education	—	—	—
普通中专 Regular Specialized Secondary Schools	7129894	739296	10.37
成人中专 Adult Specialized Secondary Schools	1272446	124256	9.77
职业高中 Vocational High Schools	4140553	396219	9.57
技工学校 Skilled Workers Schools	—	—	—
(二)初中阶段教育 Junior Secondary Education			
1. 初中 Junior Secondary Schools	44420630	5019853	11.30
初级中学 Regular Junior Secondary Schools	31215383	3779064	12.11
九年一贯制学校 9-Year Schools	6585126	618090	9.39
十二年一贯制学校 12-Year Schools	1075624	63229	5.88
完全中学 Combined Secondary Schools	5541759	558441	10.08
职业初中 Vocational Junior Secondary Schools	2738	1029	37.58
2. 成人初中 Adult Junior Secondary Schools			
三、初等教育 Primary Education	—	—	—
(一)普通小学 Regular Primary Schools	100936980	11759653	11.65
小学 Primary Schools	89460245	10714976	11.98
九年一贯制学校 9-Year Schools	10384335	977478	9.41
十二年一贯制学校 12-Year Schools	1092400	67199	6.15
(二)成人小学 Adult Primary Schools	—	—	—
其中：扫盲班 of Which：Literacy Classes	—	—	—
四、工读学校 Correctional Work-Study Schools	—	—	—
五、特殊教育 Special Education Schools	**578826**	**58782**	**10.16**
六、学前教育 Pre-school Education Institutions	**46001393**	**4846099**	**10.53**

注：少数民族成人高中数据包括成人初中数据。
Note：Data on Minority Students of Adult Junior Secondary Schools are included in the data of Adult High Schools.

各级各类学校少数民族教师、教职工数

Number of Minority Educational Personnel and Full-time Teachers of Schools by Type and Level

单位:人

unit: Person

	教职工数 Educational Personnel	少数民族教职工 Minority Educational Personnel		专任教师数 full-time Teachers	少数民族专任教师 Minority full-time Teachers	
		人数 Number	占教职工总数的比重(%) Percentage		人数 Number	占专任教师总数的比重(%) Percentage
一、高等教育 Higher Education						
(一)研究生培养机构(不计校数)Institutions Providing Postgraduate Programs	—	—	—	—	—	—
1. 普通高校 Regular HEIs	—	—	—	—	—	—
2. 科研机构 Research Institutes	—	—	—	—	—	—
(二)普通高等学校 Regular HEIs	2442995	144623	5.92	1633248	93733	5.74
1. 本科院校 HEIs Offering Degree Programs	1772342	105885	5.97	1150467	66145	5.75
其中:独立学院 of Which:Independent Institutions	162330	7469	4.60	122151	4774	3.91
2. 高职(专科)院校 Higher Vocational Colleges	669521	38686	5.78	482070	27556	5.72
3. 其他普通高教机构(不计校数) Other Institutions	1132	52	4.59	711	32	4.50
(三)成人高等学校 Adult HEIs	41408	2197	5.31	23990	1323	5.51
(四)民办的其他高等教育机构 Other Non-government HEIs	20882	156	0.75	9643	60	0.62
二、中等教育 Secondary Education	—	—	—	—	—	—
(一)高中阶段教育 Senior Secondary Education	—	—	—	—	—	—
1. 高中 Senior Secondary Schools	2670019	215291	8.06	1777741	150073	8.44
普通高中 Regular Senior Secondary Schools	2665073	215235	8.08	1773953	150039	8.46
完全中学 Combined Secondary Schools	1056242	84431	7.99	531255	41520	7.82
高级中学 Regular High Schools	1331610	117193	8.80	1176082	104994	8.93
十二年一贯制学校 12-Year Schools	277221	13611	4.91	66616	3525	5.29
成人高中 Adult High Schools	4946	56	1.13	3788	34	0.90
2. 中等职业教育 Secondary Vocational Education	—	—	—	—	—	—
普通中专 Regular Specialized Secondary Schools	396845	24560	6.19	301577	18737	6.21
成人中专 Adult Specialized Secondary Schools	59705	3014	5.05	44773	2326	5.20
职业高中 Vocational High Schools	343767	19754	5.75	286053	16107	5.63
技工学校 Skilled Workers Schools	—	—	—	—	—	—
其他中职机构(不计校数)Other Secondary Vocational Education Institutions	10830	188	1.74	7995	136	1.70
(二)初中阶段教育 Junior Secondary Education	—	—	—	—	—	—
1. 初中 Junior Secondary Schools	4078076	375187	9.20	3548688	330053	9.30
初级中学 Regular Junior Secondary Schools	2763493	271474	9.82	2519334	247587	9.83
九年一贯制学校 9-Year Schools	1314104	103541	7.88	551604	44766	8.12
十二年一贯制学校 12-Year Schools	—	—	—	73131	4147	5.67
完全中学 Combined Secondary Schools	—	—	—	404179	33397	8.26
职业初中 Vocational Junior Secondary Schools	479	172	35.91	440	156	35.45
2. 成人初中 Adult Junior Secondary Schools	—	—	—	—	—	—
三、初等教育 Primary Education	—	—	—	—	—	—
(一)普通小学 Regular Primary Schools	5645319	613823	10.87	5944910	620042	10.43
小学 Primary Schools	5645319	613823	10.87	5282512	567719	10.75
九年一贯制学校 9-Year Schools	—	—	—	596348	48550	8.14
十二年一贯制学校 12-Year Schools	—	—	—	66050	3773	5.71
(二)成人小学 Adult Primary Schools	19333	3399	17.58	10816	2052	18.97
其中:扫盲班 of Which: Literacy Classes	—	—	—	—	—	—
四、工读学校 Correctional Work-Study Schools	—	—	—	—	—	—
五、特殊教育 Special Education Schools	**65138**	**5525**	**8.48**	**55979**	**4831**	**8.63**
六、学前教育 Pre-school Education Institutions	**4192850**	**303468**	**7.24**	**2432138**	**187898**	**7.73**

注:1. 完全中学的学校数和教职工数计入高中阶段教育,九年一贯制学校的校数和教职工数计入初中阶段教育,十二年一贯制学校的校数和教职工数计入高中阶段教育。专任教师是按照教育层次进行归类;

2. 成人高中少数民族教职工数和专任教师数包括成人初中少数民族教职工数和专任教师数。

Note:1. The numbers of complete secondary schools and their educational personnel are calculated into the number of senior secondary education, the numbers of Combined Primary and Lower Secondary Schools and their educational personnel are calculated into the junior secondary education, the numbers of the Combined Primary and Secondary Schools and their educational personnel are calculated into senior secondary education. The full-time teachers are classified by educational level;

2. The number of Minority Educational Personnel and full-time teachers employed by Adult Junior High Schools is included in that employed by Adult High Schools.

各级各类学校校数

Number of School by Type and Level

单位:所

unit: institution

	2007	2008	2009	2010	2011	2012	2013	2014	2015	2016	2017
一、高等教育 Higher Education											
(一)研究生培养机构(不计校数)Institutions Providing Postgraduate Programs	795	796	796	797	755	811	830	788	792	793	815
1. 普通高校 Regular HEIs	479	479	481	481	481	534	548	571	575	576	578
2. 科研机构 Research Institutes	316	317	315	316	274	277	282	217	217	217	237
(二)普通高等学校 Regular HEIs	1908	2263	2305	2358	2409	2442	2491	2529	2560	2596	2631
1. 本科院校 HEIs Offering Degree Programs	740	1079	1090	1112	1129	1145	1170	1202	1219	1237	1243
2. 高职(专科)院校 Higher Vocational Colleges	1168	1184	1215	1246	309	1297	1321	1327	1341	1359	1388
3. 其他普通高教机构(不计校数) Other Institutions	425	77	74	56	47	36	33	31	28	25	24
(三)成人高等学校 Adult HEIs	413	400	384	365	353	348	297	295	292	284	282
(四)民办的其他高等教育机构 Other Non-government HEIs	906	866	812	836	830	823	802	799	813	813	800
二、中等教育 Secondary Education	**92267**	**90121**	**87639**	**85063**	**83810**	**81662**	**80797**	**79670**	**78421**	**77398**	**77018**
(一)高中阶段教育 Senior Secondary Education	31255	30806	29761	28584	27638	26868	26225	25677	24945	24711	24618
1. 高中 Senior Secondary Schools	16423	15959	15360	14712	14545	14205	13963	13799	13743	13818	13947
普通高中 Regular Senior Secondary Schools	15681	15206	14607	14058	13688	13509	13352	13253	13240	13383	13555
成人高中 Adult High Schools	742	753	753	654	857	696	611	546	503	435	392
2. 中等职业教育 Secondary Vocational Education	14832	14847	14401	13872	13093	12663	12262	11878	11202	10893	10671
普通中专 Regular Specialized Secondary Schools	3801	3846	3789	3938	3753	3681	3577	3536	3456	3398	3346
成人中专 Adult Specialized Secondary Schools	2120	1983	1883	1720	1614	1564	1536	1457	1294	1243	1218
职业高中 Vocational High Schools	5916	5915	5652	5206	4802	4517	4267	4067	3907	3726	3617
技工学校 Skilled Workers Schools	2995	3103	3077	3008	2924	2901	2882	2818	2545	2526	2490
其他中职机构(不计校数)Other Secondary Vocational Education Institutions	2868	2483	2390	2012	642	509	451	402	486	342	312
(二)初中阶段教育 Junior Secondary Education	61012	59315	57878	56479	56172	54794	54572	53993	53476	52687	52400
1. 普通初中 Regular Junior Secondary Schools	59109	57701	56167	54823	54063	53167	52764	52597	52383	52102	51879
2. 职业初中 Vocational Junior Secondary Schools	275	213	153	67	54	49	40	26	22	16	15
2. 成人初中 Adult Junior Secondary Schools	1628	1401	1558	1589	2055	1578	1768	1370	1071	569	506
三、初等教育 Primary Education	**369063**	**349126**	**322094**	**290597**	**271804**	**255400**	**235369**	**219632**	**205283**	**189435**	**176718**
(一)普通小学 Regular Primary Schools	320061	300854	280184	257410	241249	228585	213529	201377	190525	177633	167009
(二)成人小学 Adult Primary Schools	49002	48272	41910	33187	30555	26815	21840	18255	14758	11802	9709
其中:扫盲班 of Which: Literacy Classes	33024	34213	27850	22227	20179	18092	15104	12861	10747	8289	6587
四、工读学校 Correctional Work-Study Schools	**76**	**74**	**72**	**77**	**76**	**79**	**78**	**79**	**86**	**89**	**93**
五、特殊教育 Special Education Schools	**1618**	**1640**	**1672**	**1706**	**1767**	**1853**	**1933**	**2000**	**2053**	**2080**	**2107**
六、学前教育 Pre-school Education Institutions	**129086**	**133722**	**138209**	**150420**	**166750**	**181251**	**198553**	**209881**	**223683**	**239812**	**254950**

	2007	2008	2009
一、高等教育 Higher Education			
(一)研究生(人) Postgraduates (person)	1195047	1283046	1404942
(二)普通本专科 Undergraduate in Regular HEIs	1884.90	2021.02	2144.66
(三)成人本专科 Undergraduate in Adult HEIs	524.16	548.29	541.35
(四)其他各类高等学历教育 Students Enrolled in Other Formal Programs			
1. 在职人员攻读硕士学位 Master's Degree Programs for On-the-job Personnel	34.61	39.38	39.43
2. 网络本专科生 Web-based Undergraduates	310.48	355.90	417.27
二、中等教育 Secondary Education	**10321.60**	**10204.36**	**10130.64**
(一)高中阶段教育 Senior Secondary Education	4527.49	4576.07	4640.91
1. 高中 Senior Secondary Schools	2540.48	2488.99	2445.75
普通高中 Regular Senior Secondary Schools	2522.40	2476.28	2434.28
成人高中 Adult High Schools	18.08	12.70	11.47
2. 中等职业教育 Secondary Vocational Education	1987.01	2087.09	2195.17
普通中专 Regular Specialized Secondary Schools	781.63	817.28	840.43
成人中专 Adult Specialized Secondary Schools	112.98	120.65	160.99
职业高中 Vocational High Schools	725.25	750.32	778.42
技工学校 Skilled Workers Schools	367.15	398.85	415.32
(二)初中阶段教育 Junior Secondary Education	5794.11	5628.29	5489.73
1. 普通初中 Regular Junior Secondary Schools	5720.90	5574.15	5433.64
2. 职业初中 Vocational Junior Secondary Schools	15.30	10.82	7.30
3. 成人初中 Adult Junior Secondary Schools	57.92	43.32	48.79
三、初等教育 Primary Education	**10789.87**	**10566.59**	**10282.29**
(一)普通小学 Regular Primary Schools	10564.00	10331.51	10071.47
(二)成人小学 Adult Primary Schools	225.87	235.08	210.82
其中:扫盲班 of Which: Literacy Classes	103.76	124.96	114.86
四、工读学校 Correctional Work-Study Schools	**0.91**	**0.96**	**0.92**
五、特殊教育 Special Education Schools	**41.93**	**41.74**	**42.81**
六、学前教育 Pre-school Education Institutions	**2348.83**	**2474.96**	**2657.81**

注:2017 年起,硕士研究生在校生数含有在职人员攻读硕士学位学生。
Note: From 2017, the number of On-the-job Personnel of Master's degree Programs are included in the number of enrolment of Master's degree.

教育学生数

Education by Type and Level

单位:万人

unit: 10 thousand persons

2010	2011	2012	2013	2014	2015	2016	2017
1538416	1645845	1719818	1793953	1847689	1911406	1981051	2639561
2231.79	2308.51	2391.32	2468.07	2547.70	2625.30	2695.84	2753.59
536.04	547.50	583.11	626.41	653.12	635.94	584.39	544.14
42.03	46.17	48.99	55.87	59.61	58.75	58.18	0.00
453.14	492.48	570.41	614.64	631.45	628.47	644.93	735.93
10018.58	**9807.85**	**9421.42**	**8858.28**	**8601.54**	**8383.34**	**8327.44**	**8425.75**
4676.25	4686.60	4595.28	4369.92	4170.65	4037.69	3970.06	3970.99
2438.83	2481.28	2481.59	2446.95	2415.37	2380.99	2371.05	2378.49
2427.34	2454.82	2467.17	2435.88	2400.47	2374.40	2366.65	2374.55
11.50	26.45	14.42	11.07	14.90	6.59	4.40	3.94
2237.42	2205.33	2113.69	1922.97	1755.28	1656.70	1599.01	1592.50
877.71	855.21	812.56	772.18	749.14	732.71	718.12	712.99
212.40	238.73	254.27	229.98	194.36	162.67	141.17	127.24
726.33	680.97	623.05	534.22	472.82	439.86	416.57	414.06
420.98	430.42	423.81	386.59	338.97	321.46	323.15	338.21
5342.33	5121.25	4826.14	4488.35	4430.89	4345.65	4357.38	4454.76
5275.91	5064.21	4761.18	4439.07	4383.86	4311.44	4329.00	4441.79
3.42	2.60	1.88	1.05	0.77	0.51	0.37	0.27
63.00	54.45	63.08	48.23	46.26	33.70	28.01	12.70
10135.36	**10094.28**	**9860.23**	**9484.81**	**9567.49**	**9787.00**	**9996.28**	**10169.12**
9940.70	9926.37	9695.90	9360.55	9451.07	9692.18	9913.01	10093.70
194.66	167.92	164.33	124.26	116.43	94.82	83.27	75.42
108.08	74.89	68.91	61.92	45.55	47.48	33.42	30.40
1.07	**0.90**	**1.06**	**0.93**	**0.85**	**0.79**	**0.72**	**0.60**
42.56	**39.87**	**37.88**	**36.81**	**39.49**	**44.22**	**49.17**	**57.88**
2976.67	**3424.45**	**3685.76**	**3894.69**	**4050.71**	**4264.83**	**4413.86**	**4600.14**

各级各类学历
Number of Entrants of Formal

	2007	2008	2009
一、高等教育 Higher Education			
（一）研究生（人） Postgraduates（person）	418612	446422	510953
（二）普通本专科 Undergraduate in Regular HEIs	565.92	607.66	639.49
（三）成人本专科 Undergraduate in Adult HEIs	191.11	202.56	201.48
（四）其他各类高等学历教育 Students Enrolled in Other Formal Programs			
1. 在职人员攻读硕士学位 Master's Degree Programs for On-the-job Personnel	12.69	13.34	11.60
2. 网络本专科生 Web-based Undergraduates	123.44	147.22	162.57
二、中等教育 Secondary Education	**3518.69**	**3508.71**	**3487.31**
（一）高中阶段教育 Senior Secondary Education	1650.19	1649.12	1698.86
1. 高中 Senior Secondary Schools	840.16	837.01	830.34
普通高中 Regular Senior Secondary Schools	840.16	837.01	830.34
成人高中 Adult High Schools			
2. 中等职业教育 Secondary Vocational Education	810.02	812.11	868.52
普通中专 Regular Specialized Secondary Schools	297.29	303.78	311.71
成人中专 Adult Specialized Secondary Schools	52.00	55.83	86.89
职业高中 Vocational High Schools	302.18	290.66	313.17
技工学校 Skilled Workers Schools	158.55	161.84	156.75
（二）初中阶段教育 Junior Secondary Education	1868.50	1859.60	1788.45
1. 普通初中 Regular Junior Secondary Schools	1863.75	1856.17	1786.39
2. 职业初中 Vocational Junior Secondary Schools	4.75	3.43	2.06
3. 成人初中 Adult Junior Secondary Schools			
三、初等教育 Primary Education	**1736.07**	**1695.72**	**1637.80**
（一）普通小学 Regular Primary Schools	1736.07	1695.72	1637.80
（二）成人小学 Adult Primary Schools			
其中：扫盲班 of Which: Literacy Classes			
四、工读学校 Correctional Work-Study Schools	**0.44**	**0.48**	**0.39**
五、特殊教育 Special Education Schools	**6.34**	**6.24**	**6.40**
六、学前教育 Pre-school Education Institutions	**1433.61**	**1482.71**	**1546.86**

教育招生数
Education by Type and Level

单位:万人
unit: 10 thousand persons

2010	2011	2012	2013	2014	2015	2016	2017
538177	560168	589673	611381	621323	645055	667064	806103
661.76	681.50	688.83	699.83	721.40	737.85	748.61	761.49
208.43	218.51	243.96	256.49	265.60	236.75	211.23	217.53
12.49	13.41	14.06	16.76	16.24	12.79	12.94	—
166.37	187.15	196.45	220.07	206.19	203.40	229.61	286.11
3423.24	**3299.38**	**3169.51**	**2993.54**	**2864.18**	**2808.88**	**2883.43**	**2929.71**
1706.66	1664.65	1598.74	1497.45	1416.36	1397.86	1396.26	1382.49
836.24	850.78	844.61	822.70	796.60	796.61	802.92	800.05
836.24	850.78	844.61	822.70	796.60	796.61	802.92	800.05
870.42	813.87	754.13	674.76	619.76	601.25	593.34	582.43
316.61	299.57	277.36	271.47	259.66	259.95	255.18	246.25
116.11	103.96	105.81	86.26	74.16	64.68	59.53	56.88
278.67	246.43	213.90	183.53	161.54	155.20	151.43	148.40
159.02	163.90	157.06	133.50	124.41	121.43	127.20	130.91
1716.58	1634.73	1570.77	1496.09	1447.82	1411.02	1487.17	1547.22
1715.49	1634.01	1570.24	1495.73	1447.58	1410.85	1487.03	1547.13
1.09	0.72	0.53	0.35	0.24	0.18	0.14	0.10
1691.70	**1736.80**	**1714.66**	**1695.36**	**1658.42**	**1729.04**	**1752.47**	**1766.55**
1691.70	1736.80	1714.66	1695.36	1658.42	1729.04	1752.47	1766.55
0.40	**0.57**	**0.45**	**0.39**	**0.35**	**0.38**	**0.33**	**0.32**
6.49	**6.41**	**6.57**	**6.60**	**7.07**	**8.33**	**9.15**	**11.08**
1700.39	**1827.31**	**1911.92**	**1970.03**	**1987.78**	**2008.85**	**1922.09**	**1937.95**

	2007	2008	2009
一、高等教育 Higher Education			
(一)研究生培养机构(不计校数) Institutions Providing Postgraduate Programs			
1. 普通高校 Regular HEIs			
2. 科研机构 Research Institutes			
(二)普通高等学校 Regular HEIs	197.45	205.10	211.15
1. 本科院校 HEIs Offering Degree Programs	129.29	147.39	151.21
2. 高职(专科)院校 Higher Vocational Colleges	54.24	57.07	59.29
3. 其他普通高教机构(不计校数) Other Institutions	13.93	0.65	0.64
(三)成人高等学校 Adult HEIs	13.63	8.99	8.42
(四)民办的其他高等教育机构 Other Non-government HEIs	4.33	4.03	3.81
二、中等教育 Secondary Education	**703.09**	**705.99**	**709.36**
(一)高中阶段教育 Senior Secondary Education	701.29	704.45	708.07
1. 高中 Senior Secondary Schools	581.68	582.23	585.15
普通高中 Regular Senior Secondary Schools	580.97	581.57	584.54
成人高中 Adult High Schools	0.71	0.65	0.61
2. 中等职业教育 Secondary Vocational Education	119.61	122.22	122.92
普通中专 Regular Specialized Secondary Schools	38.85	40.28	41.13
成人中专 Adult Specialized Secondary Schools	10.62	10.33	9.42
职业高中 Vocational High Schools	41.73	42.78	42.56
技工学校 Skilled Workers Schools	24.00	24.88	25.97
其他中职机构(不计校数) Other Secondary Vocational Education Institutions	4.41	3.96	3.84
(二)初中阶段教育 Junior Secondary Education	1.80	1.54	1.28
1. 普通初中 Regular Junior Secondary Schools			
2. 职业初中 Vocational Junior Secondary Schools	1.04	0.76	0.52
3. 成人初中 Adult Junior Secondary Schools	0.76	0.78	0.76
三、初等教育 Primary Education	**622.90**	**623.93**	**621.83**
(一)普通小学 Regular Primary Schools	613.38	613.29	613.55
(二)成人小学 Adult Primary Schools	9.52	10.64	8.27
其中:扫盲班 of Which: Literacy Classes	7.23	8.62	6.16
四、工读学校 Correctional Work-Study Schools	**0.25**	**0.27**	**0.27**
五、特殊教育 Special Education Schools	**4.49**	**4.60**	**4.75**
六、学前教育 Pre-school Education Institutions	**131.72**	**143.42**	**157.08**

教职工数

of School by Type and Level

单位：万人

unit: 10 thousand persons

2010	2011	2012	2013	2014	2015	2016	2017
215.66	220.48	225.44	229.63	233.57	236.93	240.48	244.30
154.80	158.57	162.76	165.75	170.31	172.76	175.06	177.23
60.32	61.47	62.24	63.00	62.50	63.93	65.26	66.95
0.54	0.44	0.43	0.87	0.76	0.25	0.16	0.11
7.71	6.90	6.56	5.64	5.29	5.13	4.31	4.14
3.81	3.48	3.19	2.84	2.63	2.44	2.25	2.09
709.50	**759.89**	**760.79**	**756.91**	**761.55**	**763.01**	**768.16**	**782.78**
708.55	364.57	365.93	363.31	365.11	364.94	368.14	374.80
586.39	243.45	246.99	247.97	251.90	254.76	259.53	266.82
585.93	242.74	246.26	247.36	250.94	254.32	259.19	266.51
0.47	0.71	0.73	0.61	0.96	0.43	0.33	0.32
122.16	121.12	118.94	115.34	113.21	110.18	108.61	107.97
43.50	43.50	43.06	41.93	41.81	40.88	40.14	39.68
8.53	8.13	7.75	7.27	7.34	6.60	6.36	5.97
40.32	40.67	39.43	37.54	36.09	35.28	34.46	34.38
26.49	26.61	26.81	26.94	26.52	26.03	26.51	26.86
3.30	2.20	1.89	1.66	1.45	1.40	1.13	1.08
0.94	395.32	394.86	393.60	396.45	398.07	400.03	407.98
	394.25	393.74	392.77	395.49	397.57	399.70	407.76
0.22	0.17	0.17	0.11	0.08	0.06	0.05	0.05
0.73	0.90	0.95	0.73	0.87	0.44	0.28	0.18
617.56	**565.04**	**559.58**	**553.85**	**552.94**	**551.94**	**556.05**	**566.47**
610.98	558.49	553.85	549.49	548.89	548.94	553.73	564.53
6.58	6.55	5.73	4.36	4.05	2.99	2.32	1.93
5.04	4.95	3.83	3.27	2.61	2.22	1.57	1.44
0.26	**0.26**	**0.27**	**0.27**	**0.28**	**0.30**	**0.29**	**0.29**
4.92	**5.12**	**5.36**	**5.51**	**5.74**	**5.95**	**6.25**	**6.51**
184.93	**220.44**	**249.00**	**282.68**	**314.22**	**349.58**	**381.78**	**419.29**

各级各类学校

Number of Full-time Teachers of

	2007	2008	2009
一、高等教育 Higher Education			
(一)研究生培养机构(不计校数) Institutions Providing Postgraduate Programs			
1. 普通高校 Regular HEIs			
2. 科研机构 Research Institutes			
(二)普通高等学校 Regular HEIs	116.83	123.75	129.52
1. 本科院校 HEIs Offering Degree Programs	71.72	85.60	89.60
2. 高职(专科)院校 Higher Vocational Colleges	35.48	37.71	39.50
3. 其他普通高教机构(不计校数) Other Institutions	9.63	0.43	0.42
(三)成人高等学校 Adult HEIs	8.02	5.32	5.04
(四)民办的其他高等教育机构 Other Non-government HEIs	2.06	1.91	1.79
二、中等教育 Secondary Education	**578.40**	**585.54**	**588.85**
(一)高中阶段教育 Senior Secondary Education	230.68	237.49	236.63
1. 高中 Senior Secondary Schools	144.79	148.01	149.77
普通高中 Regular Senior Secondary Schools	144.31	147.55	149.33
成人高中 Adult High Schools	0.48	0.45	0.44
2. 中等职业教育 Secondary Vocational Education	85.89	89.49	86.86
普通中专 Regular Specialized Secondary Schools	24.90	26.14	27.23
成人中专 Adult Specialized Secondary Schools	6.76	6.66	6.26
职业高中 Vocational High Schools	30.87	31.97	32.15
技工学校 Skilled Workers Schools	20.43	22.07	18.64
其他中职机构(不计校数) Other Secondary Vocational Education Institutions	2.94	2.65	2.58
(二)初中阶段教育 Junior Secondary Education	347.72	348.05	352.23
1. 普通初中 Regular Junior Secondary Schools	346.43	346.90	351.34
2. 职业初中 Vocational Junior Secondary Schools	0.87	0.66	0.46
3. 成人初中 Adult Junior Secondary Schools	0.42	0.50	0.42
三、初等教育 Primary Education	**565.22**	**566.87**	**566.75**
(一)普通小学 Regular Primary Schools	561.26	562.19	563.34
(二)成人小学 Adult Primary Schools	3.96	4.67	3.40
其中:扫盲班 of Which: Literacy Classes	2.79	3.70	2.16
四、工读学校 Correctional Work-Study Schools	**0.17**	**0.17**	**0.17**
五、特殊教育 Special Education Schools	**3.50**	**3.63**	**3.79**
六、学前教育 Pre-school Education Institutions	**82.68**	**89.86**	**98.59**

专任教师数
Schools by Type and Level

单位：万人
unit: 10 thousand persons

2010	2011	2012	2013	2014	2015	2016	2017
134.31	139.27	144.03	149.69	153.45	157.26	160.20	163.32
93.55	97.69	101.40	105.50	109.17	111.64	113.40	115.05
40.41	41.26	42.34	43.66	43.83	45.46	46.69	48.21
0.35	0.31	0.30	0.53	0.46	0.16	0.10	0.07
4.59	4.09	3.94	3.36	3.15	3.02	2.52	2.40
1.78	1.61	1.49	1.34	1.21	1.11	1.03	0.96
592.20	**597.60**	**599.38**	**598.84**	**602.51**	**602.22**	**606.56**	**616.56**
239.22	244.45	248.18	250.16	252.91	254.28	257.56	261.56
152.17	156.26	160.08	163.36	167.07	169.88	173.60	177.64
151.82	155.68	159.50	162.90	166.27	169.54	173.35	177.40
0.35	0.58	0.58	0.46	0.80	0.34	0.25	0.24
87.05	88.19	88.10	86.79	85.84	84.41	83.96	83.92
29.50	30.39	30.56	30.36	30.69	30.43	30.27	30.16
5.70	5.52	5.42	5.20	5.31	4.82	4.72	4.48
30.70	31.55	31.17	30.14	29.33	29.00	28.51	28.61
18.95	19.26	19.69	19.92	19.46	19.16	19.64	19.88
2.20	1.48	1.26	1.17	1.04	0.99	0.82	0.80
352.97	353.15	351.20	348.68	349.60	347.93	349.00	355.01
352.34	352.30	350.28	348.00	348.77	347.51	348.73	354.82
0.20	0.15	0.15	0.10	0.08	0.06	0.05	0.04
0.44	0.70	0.76	0.58	0.76	0.37	0.22	0.14
564.58	**563.86**	**561.58**	**560.73**	**565.56**	**570.08**	**580.15**	**595.57**
561.71	560.49	558.55	558.46	563.39	568.51	578.91	594.49
2.87	3.37	3.03	2.26	2.17	1.57	1.24	1.08
1.95	2.32	1.78	1.54	1.08	1.07	0.74	0.75
0.17	**0.18**	**0.18**	**0.19**	**0.19**	**0.21**	**0.21**	**0.22**
3.97	**4.13**	**4.37**	**4.57**	**4.81**	**5.03**	**5.32**	**5.60**
114.42	**131.56**	**147.92**	**166.35**	**184.41**	**205.10**	**223.21**	**243.21**

高中阶段学生数的构成
Composition of Students in Senior Secondary Schools

	合计 Total	普通高中 Regular Senior Secondary Schools	成人高中 Adult High Schools	中等职业教育 Secondary Vocational Schools				
				小计 Subtotal	中等专业学校 Regular Specialized Secondary Schools	成人中专 Adult Specialized Secondary Schools	职业高中 Vocational High Schools	技工学校 Skilled Worker Schools
学生数(万人) No. of Students (10 thousand persons)								
2007	4527.44	2522.40	18.08	1986.96	781.63	112.98	725.25	367.10
2008	4574.73	2476.28	12.70	2085.74	817.28	120.65	750.32	397.50
2009	4639.85	2434.28	11.47	2194.11	840.43	160.99	778.42	414.26
2010	4676.18	2427.30	11.50	2237.38	877.70	212.40	726.30	420.98
2011	4685.56	2454.82	26.45	2204.28	855.21	238.73	680.97	429.37
2012	4594.29	2467.17	14.42	2112.70	812.56	254.27	623.05	422.82
2013	4369.92	2435.88	11.07	1922.97	772.18	229.98	534.22	386.59
2014	4170.65	2400.47	14.90	1755.28	749.14	194.36	472.82	338.97
2015	4037.69	2374.40	6.59	1656.70	732.71	162.67	439.86	321.46
2016	3970.06	2366.65	4.40	1599.01	718.12	141.17	416.57	323.15
2017	3970.99	2374.55	3.94	1592.50	712.99	127.24	414.06	338.21
比重(%) Percentage								
2007	100.00	55.71	0.40	43.89	17.26	2.50	16.02	8.11
2008	100.00	54.13	0.28	45.59	17.87	2.64	16.40	8.69
2009	100.00	52.46	0.25	47.29	18.11	3.47	16.78	8.93
2010	100.00	51.91	0.25	47.85	18.77	4.54	15.53	9.00
2011	100.00	52.39	0.56	47.04	18.25	5.09	14.53	9.16
2012	100.00	53.70	0.31	45.99	17.69	5.53	13.56	9.20
2013	100.00	55.74	0.25	44.00	17.67	5.26	12.22	8.85
2014	100.00	57.56	0.36	42.09	17.96	4.66	11.34	8.13
2015	100.00	58.81	0.16	41.03	18.15	4.03	10.89	7.96
2016	100.00	59.61	0.11	40.28	18.09	3.56	10.49	8.14
2017	100.00	59.80	0.10	40.10	17.96	3.20	10.43	8.52

教育规模
Size of Education

单位:万人
unit: 10 thousand person

年份 Year	学校数(万所) Schools (10 thousand)	在校生数(万人) Enrolment	教职工数(万人) Educational Personnel	教育人口 Educational Population	教育人口比重(%) Proportion of Education Population
2007	65.54	32187.15	1675.33	33862.48	25.76
2008	57.73	32098.60	1692.30	33790.91	25.57
2009	55.24	32097.31	1715.47	33812.78	25.34
2010	53.06	32215.86	1740.57	33956.43	25.32
2011	52.70	32755.42	1781.52	34536.93	25.63
2012	52.30	32142.44	1809.89	33952.34	25.07
2013	51.95	31813.11	1837.32	33650.43	25.10
2014	51.42	31734.68	1874.02	33608.70	24.70
2015	51.24	31907.15	1915.29	33822.43	25.22
2016	51.17	32294.45	1959.57	34254.02	25.55
2017	51.38	32986.70	2025.87	35012.57	26.11

小学学龄儿童净入学率

Net Enrolment Rate of School-age Children in Primary Schools

单位:%
unit: %

年份 Year	学龄儿童入学率 Net Enrolment Rate of School-age Children		
	全国学龄儿童数(万人) No. of School-age Children (10,000 persons)	已入学学龄儿童数(万人) No. of School-age Children Enrolled (10,000 persons)	净入学率 Net Enrolment Rate
2007	9947. 9	9896. 8	99. 49
2008	9772. 0	9727. 1	99. 54
2009	9606. 6	9548. 6	99. 40
2010	9501. 5	9473. 3	99. 70
2011	9522. 4	9502. 5	99. 79
2012	9296. 8	9282. 7	99. 85
2013	8962. 1	8935. 7	99. 71
2014	9107. 1	9090. 1	99. 81
2015	9368. 2	9356. 7	99. 88
2016	9583. 6	9575. 9	99. 92
2017	9779. 2	9770. 2	99. 91

注:1991 年以前的净入学率是按 7-11 周岁统一计算的;从 1991 年起净入学率是按各地不同入学年龄和学制分别计算的。
Note: Net Enrolment Rate of School-age children before 1991 was calculated on the basis of primary school pupils aged 7-11 enrolled. From 1991 onwards its calculation has taken account of the age of entry and the length of schooling prevailing.

各级教育毛入学率

Gross Enrolment Rate of Education by Level

单位:%
unit: %

年份 Year	学前教育 Pre-school Education Institutions 3-5 周岁 the Age of 3-5	小学 Primary Education 按各地相应学龄计算 According to Provincial Entrant Age Primary Schools Years	初中阶段 Junior Secondary Education 12-14 周岁 the Age of 12-14	高中阶段 Senior Secondary Education 15-17 周岁 the Age of 15-17	高等教育 Higher Education 18-22 周岁 the Age of 18-22
2007	44. 6	106. 2	98. 0	66. 0	23. 0
2008	47. 3	105. 7	98. 5	74. 0	23. 3
2009	50. 9	104. 8	99. 0	79. 2	24. 2
2010	56. 6	104. 6	100. 1	82. 5	26. 5
2011	62. 3	104. 2	100. 1	84. 0	26. 9
2012	64. 5	104. 3	102. 1	85. 0	30. 0
2013	67. 5	104. 4	104. 1	86. 0	34. 5
2014	70. 5	103. 8	103. 5	86. 5	37. 5
2015	75. 0	103. 5	104. 0	87. 0	40. 0
2016	77. 4	104. 4	104. 0	87. 5	42. 7
2017	79. 6	104. 8	103. 5	88. 3	45. 7

各级普通学校毕业生升学率
Promotion Rate of Graduates of Regular School by Level

单位:%
unit: %

年份 Year	小学升初中 Promotion Rate of Primary Schools Graduates	初中升高级中学 Promotion Rate of Junior Secondary Schools Graduates
2007	99.9	80.5
2008	99.7	82.1
2009	99.1	85.6
2010	98.7	87.5
2011	98.3	88.9
2012	98.3	88.4
2013	98.3	91.2
2014	98.0	95.1
2015	98.2	94.1
2016	98.7	93.7
2017	98.8	94.9

每十万人口各级学校平均在校生数
Number of Enrolment of per 100,000 Inhabitants by Level

单位:人
unit: person

年份 Year	普通高校 Higher Educations	高中阶段 Senior Secondary Education	初中阶段 Junior Secondary Education	小学 Primary Education	学前教育 Pre-education
2007	1924	3409	4364	8037	1787
2008	2042	3463	4227	7819	1873
2009	2128	3495	4097	7584	2001
2010	2189	3504	3955	7448	2230
2011	2253	3495	3779	7403	2554
2012	2335	3411	3535	7196	2736
2013	2418	3227	3279	6913	2876
2014	2488	3100	3222	6946	2977
2015	2524	2965	3152	7086	3118
2016	2530	2887	3150	7211	3211
2017	2576	2872	3213	7300	3327

各级普通学校生师比
Pupil-Teacher Ratio of Regular Schools by Level

年份 Year	普通小学 Regular Primary Schools	初中 Junior Secondary Schools	普通高中 Regular Senior Secondary Schools	中等职业学校 Secondary Vocational Schools	普通高校 Regular HEIs		
					全国 Total	本科院校 HEIs Offering Degree Programs	专科院校 Higher Vocational Colleges
2007	18.82	16.52	17.48	23.13	17.28	17.31	17.20
2008	18.38	16.07	16.78	23.32	17.23	17.21	17.27
2009	17.88	15.47	16.30	25.27	17.27	17.23	17.35
2010	17.70	14.98	15.99	25.69	17.33	17.38	17.21
2011	17.71	14.38	15.77	24.97	17.42	17.48	17.28
2012	17.36	13.59	15.47	24.19	17.52	17.65	17.23
2013	16.76	12.76	14.95	22.64	17.53	17.71	17.11
2014	16.78	12.57	14.44	21.34	17.68	17.73	17.57
2015	17.05	12.41	14.01	20.47	17.73	17.69	17.77
2016	17.12	12.41	13.65	19.68	17.07	16.78	17.73
2017	16.98	12.52	13.39	19.59	17.52	17.42	17.74

普通高等学校校均规模
Average Size of Undergraduate in Regular HEIs

单位:人
unit: person

	2007	2008	2009	2010	2011	2012	2013	2014	2015	2016	2017
全国 Total	8571	8679	9086	9298	9446	9675	9814	9995	10197	10342	10430
本科院校 HEIs Offering Degree Programs	14057	12097	12634	13100	13564	13999	14261	14342	14444	14532	14639
高职(专科)院校 Higher Vocational Colleges	5095	5564	5903	5904	5813	5858	5876	6057	6336	6528	6662

注:校均规模为在校生数除以对应校数。
Note: Average Size is the ratio of Total Number of Enrolment to the Total Number of Schools.

各级自学考试基本情况

Basic Statistics of State-administered Examination for Self-learners by Level

	2013		2014		2015		2016		2017	
	上半年 First Half Year	下半年 Second Half Year	上半年 First Half Year	下半年 Second Half Year	上半年 First Half Year	下半年 Second Half Year	上半年 First Half Year	下半年 Second Half Year	上半年 First Half Year	下半年 Second Half Year
毕业生人数 Graduates	403213	331020	382717	391077	345090	394201	347140	330577	274725	277962
本科 Normal Courses	300028	244401	283415	286031	256910	295187	254879	263075	210970	221055
专科 Short-cycle Courses	103185	86619	99302	105046	88180	99014	92261	67502	63755	56907
单科合格科次数 Passed Main-Courses	4504154	3791344	4222633	3587751	3253778	2689573	2855921	2513098	2682435	2504247
本科 Normal Courses	3575846	3048174	3432370	2914833	2625944	2205620	2347555	2067903	2171782	2009382
专科 Short-cycle Courses	928308	743170	790263	672918	627834	483953	508366	445195	510653	494865
报考人数 Applicants	4025917	3637105	3751231	3282469	3151436	2664256	2750218	2290815	2412888	2296550
本科 Normal Courses	3015420	2746375	2857969	2517747	2407814	2046837	2146408	1807546	1917029	1788173
专科 Short-cycle Courses	1010497	890730	893262	764722	743622	617419	603810	483269	495859	508377
首次报考人数 First Time	808792	524943	770737	399823	617209	300789	554570	294099	535775	439351
本科 Normal Courses	617437	385927	622598	320900	511236	236177	456637	220421	434544	316074
专科 Short-cycle Courses	191355	139016	148139	78923	105973	64612	97933	73678	101231	123277
报考科次 Main-Courses be Examined	9318675	8644834	9018778	8048621	7697525	6623765	6786402	5745116	5972349	5926499
本科 Normal Courses	7114731	6645457	6960539	6233502	5927125	5102587	5309048	4586816	4773788	4630705
专科 Short-cycle Courses	2203944	1999377	2058239	1815119	1770400	1521178	1477354	1158300	1198561	1295794
实考人数 Actual Examined	3328968	2840782	2951095	2571533	2505340	2093774	2189452	1789483	2021450	1860619
本科 Normal Courses	2524541	2196518	2309472	2027343	1976240	1667211	1764552	1430793	1612102	1451171
专科 Short-cycle Courses	804427	644264	641623	544190	529100	426563	424900	358690	409348	409448
实考科次 Actual Main-Courses Examined	7356184	6331928	6702844	5916683	5740461	4845721	5025861	4221829	4752930	4560068
本科 Normal Courses	5706255	5008220	5344923	4747604	4613569	3930469	4107894	3427073	3819337	3572982
专科 Short-cycle Courses	1649929	1323708	1357921	1169079	1126892	915252	917967	794756	933593	987086
在档考生人数 Examinees with Study Record	34822706	35016629	35404649	35413395	35685514	35592102	35799532	35763054	35954775	36116164
本科 Normal Courses	13987291	14128817	14468000	14502869	14757195	14698185	14899943	14857289	15010292	15105311
专科 Short-cycle Courses	20697286	20749683	20798520	20772397	20790190	20755788	20761460	20767636	20806354	20872724
其中:新生数 of Which: Current Session	808792	524943	770737	399823	617209	300789	554570	294099	535775	439351
本科 Normal Courses	617437	385927	622598	320900	511236	236177	456637	220421	434544	316074
专科 Short-cycle Courses	191355	139016	148139	78923	105973	64612	97933	73678	101231	123277

二、高等教育
Higher Education

高等教育学校(机构)数

Number of Higher Education Institutions

单位:所
unit: institution

	合计 Total	中央 HEIs under Central Ministries & Agencies			地方 HEIs under Local Auth.				
		小计 Subtotal	教育部 HEIs under MOE	其他部门 HEIs under Other Central Agencies	小计 Subtotal	教育部门 HEIs under MOE	其他部门 Run by Non-ed. Dept.	地方企业 Local Enterprises	民办 Non-government
(一)研究生培养机构 Institutions Providing Postgraduate Programs	815	304	76	228	511	443	61	1	6
1. 普通高校 Regular HEIs	578	110	76	34	468	442	21	0	5
2. 科研机构 Research Institutes	237	194	0	194	43	1	40	1	1
(二)普通高等学校 Regular HEIs	2631	119	76	43	2512	1125	594	47	746
1. 本科院校 HEIs Offering Degree Programs	1243	114	76	38	1129	630	73	0	426
其中:独立学院 of Which: Independent Institutions	265	0	0	0	265	0	0	0	265
2. 高职(专科)院校 Higher Vocational Colleges	1388	5	0	5	1383	495	521	47	320
(三)成人高等学校 Adult HEIs	282	13	1	12	269	92	136	40	1
(四)民办的其他高等教育机构 Other Non-government HEIs	800	0	0	0	800	0	0	0	800

普通高等学校校数

Number of Regular Higher Educational Institutions

单位:所
unit: institution

	合计 Total	本科院校 HEIs Offering Degree Programs	高职(专科)学校 Higher Vocational Colleges	
			小计 Subtotal	其中:高等职业学校 of Which: Tertiary Vocational-technical Colleges
总计 Total	**2631**	**1243**	**1388**	**1254**
综合大学 Comprehensive University	631	305	326	324
理工院校 Natural Sciences & Technology	932	360	572	561
农业院校 Agriculture	81	41	40	40
林业院校 Forestry	19	6	13	13
医药院校 Medicine & Pharmacy	199	107	92	51
师范院校 Teacher Training	229	156	73	5
语文院校 Language & Literature	56	32	24	23
财经院校 Finance & Economics	265	126	139	133
政法院校 Political Science & Law	73	37	36	32
体育院校 Physical Culture	36	16	20	19
艺术院校 Art	92	43	49	49
民族院校 Ethnic Nationality	18	14	4	4

普通高等学校在校生规模

Size of Enrolment of Regular Higher Educational Institutions

单位:所
unit: institution

	学校数 Institutions	300人及以下 300 and under	301-500人 301 to 500	501-1000人 501 to 1000	1001-1500人 1001 to 1500	1501-2000人 1501 to 2000	2001-3000人 2001 to 3000	3001-4000人 3001 to 4000	4001-5000人 4001 to 5000	5001-10000人 5001 to 10000	10001-20000人 10001 to 20000	20001-30000人 20001 to 30000	30001人及以上 30001 and Over
总计 Total	**2631**	**67**	**18**	**47**	**62**	**59**	**125**	**125**	**166**	**822**	**854**	**225**	**61**
综合大学 Comprehensive University	631	18	2	8	10	7	24	21	22	198	222	75	24
理工院校 Natural Sciences & Technology	932	23	8	23	21	26	40	40	62	281	313	74	21
农业院校 Agriculture	81	1	0	0	0	0	4	6	4	22	28	10	6
林业院校 Forestry	19	0	0	0	1	0	1	1	0	10	5	1	0
医药院校 Medicine & Pharmacy	199	1	1	5	4	1	3	12	13	82	73	4	0
师范院校 Teacher Training	229	3	1	2	5	1	7	12	13	55	91	31	8
语文院校 Language & Literature	56	1	2	0	1	3	0	5	5	25	14	0	0
财经院校 Finance & Economics	265	7	1	2	6	6	14	12	12	95	82	26	2
政法院校 Political Science & Law	73	4	0	2	3	4	8	7	19	20	6	0	0
体育院校 Physical Culture	36	7	2	1	2	2	4	2	2	13	1	0	0
艺术院校 Art	92	2	1	4	9	9	19	6	13	17	12	0	0
民族院校 Ethnic Nationality	18	0	0	0	0	0	1	1	1	4	7	4	0

高等教育学校（机构）学生数

Number of Students in Higher Education Institutions

单位：人
unit: person

	毕（结）业生数 Graduates	授予学位数 Degrees Awarded	招生数 Entrants 合计 Total	其中 of Which 应届生 Autumn Session	其中 of Which 春季招生 Spring Session	其中 of Which 预科生转入 Preparatory Students Enrolled	在校生数 Enrolment	预计毕业生数 Estimated Graduates for Next Year
研究生 Postgraduates	578045	682651	806103	511923	—	—	2639561	773025
博　士 Doctor's Degrees	58032	56606	83878	41119	—	—	361997	169022
硕　士 Master's Degrees	520013	626045	722225	470804	—	—	2277564	604003
普通本专科 Undergraduates in Regular HEIs	7358287	3771039	7614893	6784120	3023	44843	27535869	7804685
本　科 Normal Courses	3841839	3771039	4107534	3526135	2707	44086	16486320	4031331
专　科 Short-cycle Courses	3516448	—	3507359	3257985	316	757	11049549	3773354
成人本专科 Undergraduates in Adult HEIs	2470370	156775	2175302	—	—	—	5441429	2282316
本　科 Normal Courses	1091226	156775	1023981	—	—	—	2589809	1018888
专　科 Short-cycle Courses	1379144	—	1151321	—	—	—	2851620	1263428
网络本专科生 Web-based Undergraduates	1777905	55443	2861143	—	1524532	—	7359267	—
本　科 Normal Courses	659559	55443	993253	—	520910	—	2587338	—
专　科 Short-cycle Courses	1118346	—	1867890	—	1003622	—	4771929	—
自考助学班 Class Run by Non-government HEIs for Students Preparing for Self-Taught Higher Education Examinations	61599	—	—	—	—	—	132467	—
普通预科生 College-preparatory Class	—	—	—	—	—	—	45420	—
研究生课程进修班 Postgraduate Courses	9244	—	—	—	—	—	12237	—
进修及培训 In-service Training	8996653	—	—	—	—	—	8338925	—
留学生 Foreign Students	121419	26093	153445	—	40971	—	274809	—

分举办者研究生数(总计)

Number of Enrolment for Master's Degree Programs by Providers (Total)

单位:人
unit: person

	学校(机构)数(所)(Schools)	毕业生数 Graduates			招生数 Entrants			在校生数 Enrolment			预计毕业生数 Estimated Graduates for Next Year		
		合计 Total	博士 Doctor's Degrees	硕士 Master's Degrees	合计 Total	博士 Doctor's Degrees	硕士 Master's Degrees	合计 Total	博士 Doctor's Degrees	硕士 Master's Degrees	合计 Total	博士 Doctor's Degrees	硕士 Master's Degrees
总计 Total	**815**	**578045**	**58032**	**520013**	**806103**	**83878**	**722225**	**2639561**	**361997**	**2277564**	**773025**	**169022**	**604003**
一、中央 Under Central Ministries & Agencies	304	288834	46179	242655	400892	64856	336036	1415059	285091	1129968	412691	131050	281641
1. 教育部 Under MOE	76	231478	34212	197266	322244	48095	274149	1152472	217430	935042	336630	105586	231044
2. 其他部门 Under Other Central Agencies	228	57356	11967	45389	78648	16761	61887	262587	67661	194926	76061	25464	50597
二、地方 Under Local Auth.	511	289211	11853	277358	405211	19022	386189	1224502	76906	1147596	360334	37972	322362
1. 教育部门 Run by Edu. Dept.	443	283624	11777	271847	396960	18813	378147	1200529	76082	1124447	353485	37578	315907
2. 其他部门 Run by Non-ed. Dept.	61	5352	76	5276	7500	209	7291	22026	824	21202	6573	394	6179
3. 地方企业 Run by Local Enterprises	1	3	0	3	4	0	4	10	0	10	3	0	3
4. 民办 Non-government	6	232	0	232	747	0	747	1937	0	1937	273	0	273

注:1. 2017年起,研究生招生、在校生指标内涵发生变化。招生包含全日制和非全日制研究生;在校生、授予学位数包含全日制、非全日制研究生和在职人员攻读硕士学位学生。下同。

Note: 1. From 2017, the indicators meaning of entrants and enrollment of postgraduate students have changed. The number of entrants includes full-time and part-time postgraduate students. The number of Master's and Doctor's Degree awarded includes full-time, part-time postgraduate students and on-the-job students. Same as below.

分举办者研究生数(普通高校)

Number of Enrolment for Master's Degree Programs by Providers (Regular HEIs)

单位:人
unit: person

	学校(机构)数(所)(Schools)	毕业生数 Graduates			招生数 Entrants			在校生数 Enrolment			预计毕业生数 Estimated Graduates for Next Year		
		合计 Total	博士 Doctor's Degrees	硕士 Master's Degrees	合计 Total	博士 Doctor's Degrees	硕士 Master's Degrees	合计 Total	博士 Doctor's Degrees	硕士 Master's Degrees	合计 Total	博士 Doctor's Degrees	硕士 Master's Degrees
总计 Total	**578**	**570296**	**56451**	**513845**	**795938**	**81898**	**714040**	**2608029**	**353922**	**2254107**	**762410**	**165296**	**597114**
一、中央 Under Central Ministries & Agencies	110	282173	44649	237524	392277	62941	329336	1388422	277298	1111124	403320	127443	275877
1. 教育部 Under MOE	76	231478	34212	197266	322244	48095	274149	1152472	217430	935042	336630	105586	231044
2. 其他部门 Under Other Central Agencies	34	50695	10437	40258	70033	14846	55187	235950	59868	176082	66690	21857	44833
二、地方 Under Local Auth.	468	288123	11802	276321	403661	18957	384704	1219607	76624	1142983	359090	37853	321237
1. 教育部门 Run by Edu. Dept.	442	283608	11777	271831	396944	18813	378131	1200483	76082	1124401	353470	37578	315892
2. 其他部门 Run by Non-ed. Dept.	21	4283	25	4258	6156	144	6012	18087	542	17545	5347	275	5072
3. 地方企业 Run by Local Enterprises	0	0	0	0	0	0	0	0	0	0	0	0	0
4. 民办 Non-government	5	232	0	232	561	0	561	1037	0	1037	273	0	273

分举办者
Number of Enrolment for Master's Degree Programs

	学校(机构)数(所)(Schools)	毕业生数 Graduates			招生数 Entrants		
		合计 Total	博士 Doctor's Degrees	硕士 Master's Degrees	合计 Total	博士 Doctor's Degrees	硕士 Master's Degrees
总计 Total	**237**	**7749**	**1581**	**6168**	**10165**	**1980**	**8185**
一、中央 Under Central Ministries & Agencies	194	6661	1530	5131	8615	1915	6700
1. 教育部 Under MOE	0	0	0	0	0	0	0
2. 其他部门 Under Other Central Agencies	194	6661	1530	5131	8615	1915	6700
二、地方 Under Local Auth.	43	1088	51	1037	1550	65	1485
1. 教育部门 Run by Edu. Dept.	1	16	0	16	16	0	16
2. 其他部门 Run by Non-ed. Dept.	40	1069	51	1018	1344	65	1279
3. 地方企业 Run by Local Enterprises	1	3	0	3	4	0	4
4. 民办 Non-government	1	0	0	0	186	0	186

分学科
Number of Postgraduate Students

	毕业生数 Graduates			招生数 Entrants		
	合计 Total	博士 Doctor's Degrees	硕士 Master's Degrees	合计 Total	博士 Doctor's Degrees	硕士 Master's Degrees
总计 Total	**578045**	**58032**	**520013**	**806103**	**83878**	**722225**
其中:女 of Which: Female	299813	22802	277011	423629	35073	388556
学术学位 Academic Degree	340479	55823	284656	401299	81178	320121
专业学位 Professional Degree	237566	2209	235357	404804	2700	402104
哲学 Philosophy	3984	692	3292	4352	914	3438
经济学 Economics	27788	2152	25636	34732	2980	31752
法学 Law	40753	2839	37914	51056	4098	46958
教育学 Education	33932	1028	32904	55115	1585	53530
文学 Literature	31644	1940	29704	35776	2681	33095
历史学 History	5357	731	4626	6142	1092	5050
理学 Science	53133	12208	40925	70081	17481	52600
工学 Engineering	198548	20492	178056	282095	32470	249625
农学 Agriculture	20770	2654	18116	34317	3747	30570
医学 Medicine	66869	9567	57302	86539	11348	75191
军事学 Military Science	203	31	172	92	12	80
管理学 Administrators	76147	3140	73007	120894	4669	116225
艺术学 Art	18917	558	18359	24912	801	24111

注:1. 2017 年起,研究生招生、在校生指标内涵发生变化。招生包含全日制和非全日制研究生;在校生、授予学位数包含全日制、非全日制研究生和在职人员攻读硕士学位学生。下同。

Note: 1. From 2017, the indicators meaning of entrants and enrollment of postgraduate students have changed. The number of entrants includes full-time and part-time postgraduate students. The number of Master's and Doctor's Degree awarded includes full-time, part-time postgraduate students and on-the-job students. Same as below.

研究生数(科研机构)
by Providers (Research Institutes)

单位:人
unit: person

在校生数 Enrolment			预计毕业生数 Estimated Graduates for Next Year		
合计 Total	博士 Doctor's Degrees	硕士 Master's Degrees	合计 Total	博士 Doctor's Degrees	硕士 Master's Degrees
31532	**8075**	**23457**	**10615**	**3726**	**6889**
26637	7793	18844	9371	3607	5764
0	0	0	0	0	0
26637	7793	18844	9371	3607	5764
4895	282	4613	1244	119	1125
46	0	46	15	0	15
3939	282	3657	1226	119	1107
10	0	10	3	0	3
900	0	900	0	0	0

研究生数(总计)
by Academic Field (Total)

单位:人
unit: person

在校生数 Enrolment			预计毕业生数 Estimated Graduates for Next Year		
合计 Total	博士 Doctor's Degrees	硕士 Master's Degrees	合计 Total	博士 Doctor's Degrees	硕士 Master's Degrees
2639561	**361997**	**2277564**	**773025**	**169022**	**604003**
1278134	142173	1135961	379561	64132	315429
1289020	352437	936583	473986	165238	308748
1350541	9560	1340981	299039	3784	295255
14673	4319	10354	5866	2216	3650
89247	14073	75174	34926	7480	27446
153293	18702	134591	49364	9714	39650
180208	6880	173328	41746	3447	38299
99795	12075	87720	38155	6273	31882
19846	5068	14778	7719	2623	5096
216224	68121	148103	74539	28692	45847
1056897	150009	906888	269963	69675	200288
120119	15197	104922	30020	7600	22420
253719	38700	215019	78454	15165	63289
536	144	392	250	99	151
362568	25681	336887	119821	14683	105138
72436	3028	69408	22202	1355	20847

分学科

Number of Postgraduate Students by

	毕业生数 Graduates			招生数 Entrants		
	合计 Total	博士 Doctor's Degrees	硕士 Master's Degrees	合计 Total	博士 Doctor's Degrees	硕士 Master's Degrees
总计 Total	**570296**	**56451**	**513845**	**795938**	**81898**	**714040**
其中:女 of Which: Female	296689	22209	274480	418914	34289	384625
学术学位 Academic Degree	334382	54242	280140	394151	79203	314948
专业学位 Professional Degree	235914	2209	233705	401787	2695	399092
哲学 Philosophy	3836	641	3195	4195	856	3339
经济学 Economics	27079	1959	25120	33849	2731	31118
法学 Law	39818	2648	37170	49760	3827	45933
教育学 Education	33932	1028	32904	55115	1585	53530
文学 Literature	31552	1899	29653	35613	2617	32996
历史学 History	5219	700	4519	5986	1057	4929
理学 Science	52592	12052	40540	69335	17242	52093
工学 Engineering	195922	20057	175865	279167	31958	247209
农学 Agriculture	19919	2432	17487	33133	3512	29621
医学 Medicine	66213	9437	56776	85786	11191	74595
军事学 Military Science	199	31	168	91	12	79
管理学 Administrators	75293	3071	72222	119271	4567	114704
艺术学 Art	18722	496	18226	24637	743	23894

分学科

Number of Postgraduate Students by

	毕业生数 Graduates			招生数 Entrants		
	合计 Total	博士 Doctor's Degrees	硕士 Master's Degrees	合计 Total	博士 Doctor's Degrees	硕士 Master's Degrees
总计 Total	**7749**	**1581**	**6168**	**10165**	**1980**	**8185**
其中:女 of Which: Female	3124	593	2531	4715	784	3931
学术学位 Academic Degree	6097	1581	4516	7148	1975	5173
专业学位 Professional Degree	1652	0	1652	3017	5	3012
哲学 Philosophy	148	51	97	157	58	99
经济学 Economics	709	193	516	883	249	634
法学 Law	935	191	744	1296	271	1025
教育学 Education	0	0	0	0	0	0
文学 Literature	92	41	51	163	64	99
历史学 History	138	31	107	156	35	121
理学 Science	541	156	385	746	239	507
工学 Engineering	2626	435	2191	2928	512	2416
农学 Agriculture	851	222	629	1184	235	949
医学 Medicine	656	130	526	753	157	596
军事学 Military Science	4	0	4	1	0	1
管理学 Administrators	854	69	785	1623	102	1521
艺术学 Art	195	62	133	275	58	217

研究生数(普通高校)
Academic Field (Regular HEIs)

单位:人
unit: person

在校生数 Enrolment			预计毕业生数 Estimated Graduates for Next Year		
合计 Total	博士 Doctor's Degrees	硕士 Master's Degrees	合计 Total	博士 Doctor's Degrees	硕士 Master's Degrees
2608029	**353922**	**2254107**	**762410**	**165296**	**597114**
1264730	139363	1125367	375417	62983	312434
1265876	344372	921504	465401	161512	303889
1342153	9550	1332603	297009	3784	293225
14136	4102	10034	5670	2125	3545
86662	13011	73651	33824	6990	26834
149602	17748	131854	48093	9340	38753
180208	6880	173328	41746	3447	38299
99321	11884	87437	38004	6211	31793
19412	4934	14478	7554	2569	4985
213763	67158	146605	73607	28217	45390
1047357	147414	899943	266380	68359	198021
116061	14355	101706	28996	7213	21783
251428	38220	213208	77746	14981	62765
534	144	390	250	99	151
357905	25241	332664	118562	14471	104091
71640	2831	68809	21978	1274	20704

研究生数(科研机构)
Academic Field (Research Institutes)

单位:人
unit: person

在校生数 Enrolment			预计毕业生数 Estimated Graduates for Next Year		
合计 Total	博士 Doctor's Degrees	硕士 Master's Degrees	合计 Total	博士 Doctor's Degrees	硕士 Master's Degrees
31532	**8075**	**23457**	**10615**	**3726**	**6889**
13404	2810	10594	4144	1149	2995
23144	8065	15079	8585	3726	4859
8388	10	8378	2030	0	2030
537	217	320	196	91	105
2585	1062	1523	1102	490	612
3691	954	2737	1271	374	897
0	0	0	0	0	0
474	191	283	151	62	89
434	134	300	165	54	111
2461	963	1498	932	475	457
9540	2595	6945	3583	1316	2267
4058	842	3216	1024	387	637
2291	480	1811	708	184	524
2	0	2	0	0	0
4663	440	4223	1259	212	1047
796	197	599	224	81	143

普通高等教育工科分大类本科学生数

Number of Engineering Students for Normal Courses of Regular HEIs by Subfield

单位：人
unit: person

	毕业生数(人) Graduates	招生数(人) Entrants	在校生数(人) Enrolment
总计 Total	**1247808**	**1402970**	**5511445**
力学类 Mechanics	4524	4787	19196
机械类 Mechanical Engineering	188771	204915	821665
仪器类 Instrument	18475	16894	73973
材料类 Materials Science	63554	73663	278813
能源动力类 Thermal &Nuclear Energy	23088	27248	104923
电气类 Electric	83289	85561	353689
电子信息类 Electronic Information	161969	179139	700881
自动化类 Automation	47006	52846	206750
计算机类 Computer	206034	289207	1070709
土木类 Civil Engineering	135408	117597	502292
水利类 Hydraulics	12744	13891	55711
测绘类 Survey & Measure	10410	13067	48310
化工与制药类 Chemical Engineering &Pharmaceutics	50970	54997	214028
地质类 Geology	13109	10997	46404
矿业类 Mining Industry	16059	12739	51199
纺织类 Textile	10889	9789	38492
轻工类 Light Industry	8183	7549	31497
交通运输类 Transportation	29556	32772	132547
海洋工程类 Oceanic	2887	3694	13072
航空航天类 Aeronautics & Astronautics	6323	10593	33099
农业工程类 Agriculture Engineering	6767	6315	27581
林业工程类 Forestry Engineering	2625	2759	10176
环境科学与工程类 Environmental Science & Engineering	32750	40852	150283
生物医学工程类 Biomedical Engineering	5248	6865	24816
食品科学与工程类 Food Science & Engineering	35538	42522	163122
建筑类 Architectural	32595	36026	164889
安全科学与工程类 Safety Science & Engineering	9760	10414	40972
生物工程类 Biotechnology	17147	21359	77989
公安技术类 Public Security Technology	6400	8287	30931
其他 Other	5730	5626	23436

普通、成人本专科分举办者学生数

Number of Students for Regular and Adult Programs by Providers in HEIs

单位：人

unit：person

	毕业生数 Graduates			招生数 Entrants			在校生数 Enrolment			预计毕业生数 Estimated Graduates for Next Year		
	合计 Total	本科 Normal Courses	专科 Short-cycle Courses	合计 Total	本科 Normal Courses	专科 Short-cycle Courses	合计 Total	本科 Normal Courses	专科 Short-cycle Courses	合计 Total	本科 Normal Courses	专科 Short-cycle Courses
一、普通本专科 Undergraduate in Regular HEIs	**7358287**	**3841839**	**3516448**	**7614893**	**4107534**	**3507359**	**27535869**	**16486320**	**11049549**	**7804685**	**4031331**	**3773354**
1. 中央院校 HEIs Under Central Ministries & Agencies	441331	424702	16629	466877	450857	16020	1848689	1799422	49267	465185	448196	16989
其中：教育部院校 of Which：Under MOE	324309	321300	3009	341347	339291	2056	1363655	1356944	6711	338373	335746	2627
2. 地方学校 HEIs Under Local Auth.	6916956	3417137	3499819	7148016	3656677	3491339	25687180	14686898	11000282	7339500	3583135	3756365
其中：民办 Non-government	1631582	921506	710076	1753700	1016329	737371	6284554	4016810	2267744	1722972	958053	764919
二、成人本专科 Undergraduate in Adult HEIs	**2470370**	**1091226**	**1379144**	**2175302**	**1023981**	**1151321**	**5441429**	**2589809**	**2851620**	**2282316**	**1018888**	**1263428**
1. 中央院校 HEIs Under Central Ministries & Agencies	258518	158181	100337	206248	126699	79549	534686	346389	188297	238043	148190	89853
其中：教育部院校 of Which：Under MOE	212336	134561	77775	164708	105235	59473	427010	284188	142822	190611	120910	69701
2. 地方学校 HEIs Under Local Auth.	2211852	933045	1278807	1969054	897282	1071772	4906743	2243420	2663323	2044273	870698	1173575
其中：民办 Non-government	65548	7899	57649	99038	15329	83709	227301	30691	196610	77894	11039	66855

普通本、专科分
Number of Undergraduate Students by

	毕业生数 Graduates			招生数 Entrants		
	合计 Total	本科 Normal Courses	专科 Short-cycle Courses	合计 Total	本科 Normal Courses	专科 Short-cycle Courses
总计 Total	**7358287**	**3841839**	**3516448**	**7614893**	**4107534**	**3507359**
其中:女 of Which:Female	3921881	2082178	1839703	4306119	2348669	1957450
一、普通高等学校 Regular HEIs	**7335047**	**3841839**	**3493208**	**7593579**	**4107534**	**3486045**
1. 按类型分 by Type						
本科院校 HEIs Offering Degree Programs	4515422	3832825	682597	4599934	4105993	493941
其中:独立学院 of Which:Independent Institutions	609594	576435	33159	618476	583857	34619
高职(专科)院校 Higher Vocational Colleges	2802510	0	2802510	2990964	0	2990964
其他机构(点)(不计校数) Other Institutions	17115	9014	8101	2681	1541	1140
2. 按性质类型分 by Type of School						
综合大学 Comprehensive Universities	2016499	1073138	943361	2071739	1144392	927347
理工院校 Natural Sciences & Tech.	2634166	1173629	1460537	2735782	1271319	1464463
农业院校 Agriculture	275782	167261	108521	284896	180019	104877
林业院校 Forestry	54614	28153	26461	54159	27518	26641
医药院校 Medicine & Pharmacy	461627	229011	232616	490471	238224	252247
师范院校 Teacher Training	758226	550851	207375	748489	569904	178585
语文院校 Language & Literature	117599	65576	52023	124797	74303	50494
财经院校 Finance & Economics	718952	368148	350804	751636	398088	353548
政法院校 Political Science & Law	100674	50623	50051	103347	50295	53052
体育院校 Physical Culture	32593	24811	7782	36845	27027	9818
艺术院校 Art	101436	55632	45804	123359	65346	58013
民族院校 Ethnic Minorities	62879	55006	7873	68059	61099	6960
二、成人高等学校 Adult HEIs	**23240**	**0**	**23240**	**21314**	**0**	**21314**

性质类别学生数
Type of Courses in Regular HEIs

单位：人
unit: person

在校生数 Enrolment			预计毕业生数 Estimated Graduates for Next Year		
合计 Total	本科 Normal Courses	专科 Short-cycle Courses	合计 Total	本科 Normal Courses	专科 Short-cycle Courses
27535869	**16486320**	**11049549**	**7804685**	**4031331**	**3773354**
14468508	8859530	5608978	3977934	2105152	1872782
27467321	**16486320**	**10981001**	**7780177**	**4031331**	**3748846**
18196099	16471555	1724544	4680799	4026305	654494
2484741	2383463	101278	620635	587283	33352
9246543	0	9246543	3086581	0	3086581
24679	14765	9914	12797	5026	7771
7557531	4592794	2964737	2143590	1124084	1019506
9644376	5074782	4569594	2809249	1254478	1554771
1044413	714015	330398	289376	174431	114945
197407	113572	83835	57394	28745	28649
1821034	1051252	769782	486887	233210	253677
2900191	2285218	614973	787810	569279	218531
453393	291347	162046	126321	69997	56324
2677445	1573434	1104011	761583	386456	375127
354798	198626	156172	101901	49703	52198
136167	106376	29791	35843	25711	10132
422507	250443	172064	115398	58863	56535
258059	234461	23598	64825	56374	8451
68548	**0**	**68548**	**24508**	**0**	**24508**

成人本专科分
Number of Students for Adult Programs

	毕业生数 Graduates			招生数 Entrants		
	合计 Total	本科 Normal Courses	专科 Short-cycle Courses	合计 Total	本科 Normal Courses	专科 Short-cycle Courses
总计 Total	**2470370**	**1091226**	**1379144**	**2175302**	**1023981**	**1151321**
其中:女 of Which:Female	1418857	647942	770915	1274480	638681	635799
一、成人高等学校 Adult HEIs	**141381**	**10032**	**131349**	**137852**	**12266**	**125586**
其中:全脱产 of Which:Full-time	88899	4811	84088	66881	4853	62028
职工高等学校 Workers' Colleges	47788	1637	46151	36922	1687	35235
农民高等学校 Peasants' Colleges	444	0	444	346	0	346
管理干部学院 Institutes for Administration	7562	1004	6558	4304	470	3834
教育学院 Educational Colleges	23223	5105	18118	19294	5822	13472
独立函授学院 Independent Correspondence Colleges	0	0	0	0	0	0
广播电视大学 Radio/TV Universities	62362	2286	60076	76986	4287	72699
其他成人高教机构 Other Adult HEIs	2	0	2	0	0	0
二、普通高等学校 Regular HEIs	**2328989**	**1081194**	**1247795**	**2037450**	**1011715**	**1025735**
函授 Correspondence	1401794	658710	743084	1302001	637775	664226
业余 Spare Time Schools	923640	421409	502231	733835	372905	360930
脱产 Full-time Courses for Adults	3555	1075	2480	1614	1035	579

普通本科分
Number of Regular Students for

	毕业生数 Graduates	招生数 Entrants
总　计 Total	**3841839**	**4107534**
其中:女 of Which:Female	2082178	2348669
哲　学 Philosophy	2108	2723
经济学 Economics	230543	237130
法　学 Law	139048	143055
教育学 Education	141863	165142
文　学 Literature	370471	395437
其中:外语 of Which:Foreign Language	199428	212611
历史学 History	18283	19073
理　学 Science	257768	287868
工　学 Engineering	1247808	1402970
农　学 Agriculture	66641	73352
医　学 Medicine	261636	274537
管理学 Administrators	741061	705786
艺术学 Art	364609	400461
总计中:师范生 of Total:Students Enrolled in Teacher Training Institutions	389612	375089

性质类别学生数
by Type of Schools in HEIs

单位:人
unit: person

在校生数 Enrolment			预计毕业生数 Estimated Graduates for Next Year		
合计 Total	本科 Normal Courses	专科 Short-cycle Courses	合计 Total	本科 Normal Courses	专科 Short-cycle Courses
5441429	**2589809**	**2851620**	**2282316**	**1018888**	**1263428**
3198256	1600937	1597319	1275702	571046	704656
336440	**31761**	**304679**	**159171**	**14140**	**145031**
169491	12116	157375	85631	5637	79994
84830	3902	80928	42260	1930	40330
673	0	673	327	0	327
10519	1712	8807	5554	907	4647
50488	15995	34493	24565	6680	17885
0	0	0	0	0	0
189919	10152	179767	86454	4623	81831
11	0	11	11	0	11
5104989	**2558048**	**2546941**	**2123145**	**1004748**	**1118397**
3072610	1510708	1561902	1280913	600796	680117
2025124	1043774	981350	838718	402864	435854
7255	3566	3689	3514	1088	2426

学科学生数
Normal Courses in HEIs by Discipline

单位:人
unit: person

在校生数 Enrolment	预计毕业生数 Estimated Graduates for Next Year
16486320	**4031331**
8859530	2105152
9666	2302
961507	238318
570397	141987
629323	151092
1535997	368049
814442	190891
74618	18389
1103623	267491
5511445	1347359
283963	69842
1243628	268584
2989829	771768
1572324	386150
1544676	388224

普通专科分专业大类学生数

Number of Regular Students for Short-cycle Courses in HEIs by Discipline

单位:人
unit: person

	毕业生数 Graduates	招生数 Entrants	在校生数 Enrolment	预计毕业生数 Estimated Graduates for Next Year
总计 Total	**3516448**	**3507359**	**11049549**	**3773354**
其中:女 of Which: Female	1839703	1957450	5608978	1872782
农林牧渔大类 Agriculture, Forestry, Husbandry and Fishing	56420	60570	185336	62410
资源环境与安全大类 Resources Environment and Safety	55942	43218	137756	50765
能源动力与材料大类 Energy Power and Material	41181	37081	119951	42364
土木建筑大类 Civil Engineering and Architecture	385930	266671	900876	340082
水利大类 Water Resources	14309	13162	42722	14548
装备制造大类 Equipment Manufacturing	423730	382379	1286520	460101
生物与化工大类 Biology and Chemical Engineering	41968	28506	103623	42240
轻工纺织大类 Light Industry and Textile	17430	17555	52366	17589
食品药品与粮食大类 Food, Medicine and Grain	54742	59024	181599	61382
交通运输大类 Transportation and Communication	173918	233493	661988	202210
电子信息大类 Electronic Information	310889	457623	1258349	377705
医药卫生大类 Medical and Health	419970	450382	1402666	461835
财经商贸大类 Finance, Economics and Business	775258	687966	2306098	831599
旅游大类 Tourism	106866	116039	350421	115909
文化艺术大类 Culture and Arts	170093	164077	519790	182703
新闻传播大类 Journalism and Communication	27321	31050	92263	30715
教育与体育大类 Education and Sport	361951	375891	1203727	398242
公安与司法大类 Public Security and Justice	46750	46390	142112	48670
公共管理与服务大类 Public Administration and Service	31780	36282	101386	32285
总计中:师范生 of the Total: Students Enrolled in Teacher Training Institutions	228521	207971	715186	246999

成人本科分学科学生数

Number of Adult Students for Normal Courses in HEIs by Discipline

单位:人
unit: person

	毕业生数 Graduates	招生数 Entrants	在校生数 Enrolment	预计毕业生数 Estimated Graduates for Next Year
总计 Total	**1091226**	**1023981**	**2589809**	**1018888**
其中: 女 of Which: Female	647942	638681	1600937	571046
哲学 Philosophy	27	0	120	68
经济学 Economics	27016	22039	57231	22959
法学 Law	42643	40362	94610	38456
教育学 Education	70188	93345	193960	71834
文学 Literature	74722	77616	168988	62914
其中:外语 of Which: Foreign Language	18251	14168	35717	14753
历史学 History	1200	1118	2571	990
理学 Science	19789	14289	34288	15298
工学 Engineering	259688	196254	539861	232641
农学 Agriculture	18115	16188	39763	16915
医学 Medicine	284676	301906	788030	292638
管理学 Administrators	278107	248712	630863	249656
艺术学 Art	15055	12152	39524	14519
总计中:师范生 of the Total: Students Enrolled in Teacher Training Institutions	88373	104176	212679	76735

成人专科分专业大类学生数

Number of Adult Students for Short-cycle Courses in HEIs by Discipline

单位:人
unit: person

	毕业生数 Graduates	招生数 Entrants	在校生数 Enrolment	预计毕业生数 Estimated Graduates for Next Year
总计 Total	**1379144**	**1151321**	**2851620**	**1263428**
其中:女 of Which: Female	770915	635799	1597319	704656
农林牧渔大类 Agriculture, Forestry, Husbandry and Fishing	25382	19589	49027	23059
资源环境与安全大类 Resources Environment and Safety	25353	6573	25562	16032
能源动力与材料大类 Energy Power and Material	10448	5403	16415	8756
土木建筑大类 Civil Engineering and Architecture	120447	62474	185894	98736
水利大类 Water Resources	4641	2925	6801	3269
装备制造大类 Equipment Manufacturing	149561	122432	305776	139410
生物与化工大类 Biology and Chemical Engineering	9935	4227	13898	7502
轻工纺织大类 Light Industry and Textile	3529	2141	6238	3368
食品药品与粮食大类 Food, Medicine and Grain	3008	2030	5496	2323
交通运输大类 Transportation and Communication	49420	56440	125431	41629
电子信息大类 Electronic Information	80037	84914	188629	78234
医药卫生大类 Medical and Health	229533	155827	466676	203124
财经商贸大类 Finance, Economics and Business	349793	317660	763487	336201
旅游大类 Tourism	25086	23063	50425	22104
文化艺术大类 Culture and Arts	33026	27361	70228	32992
新闻传播大类 Journalism and Communication	1552	1203	3203	1669
教育与体育大类 Education and Sport	189331	182164	404729	174853
公安与司法大类 Public Security and Justice	17128	17880	37954	15969
公共管理与服务大类 Public Administration and Service	51934	57015	125751	54198
总计中:师范生 of the Total: Students Enrolled in Teacher Training Institutions	107439	95990	214938	94551

网络本科分学科学生数

Number of Web-based Students for Normal Courses in HEIs by Discipline

单位:人
unit: person

	毕业生数 Graduates	招生数 Entrants	在校生数 Enrolment
总计 Total	**659559**	**993253**	**2587338**
其中：女 of Which：Female	345268	505040	1320058
哲学 Philosophy	0	0	0
经济学 Economics	27159	36301	100183
法学 Law	48105	70862	217547
教育学 Education	26816	58591	137513
文学 Literature	31781	53239	142570
其中:外语 of Which:Foreign Language	5019	7550	22857
历史学 History	454	542	1146
理学 Science	5699	9745	20271
工学 Engineering	174982	252841	590165
农学 Agriculture	6593	11445	24974
医学 Medicine	65208	85949	223253
管理学 Administrators	269803	409361	1116464
艺术学 Art	2959	4377	13252
总计中:师范生 of the Total:Students Enrolled in Teacher Training Institutions	16479	33384	72504

网络专科分专业大类学生数

Number of Web-based Students for Short-cycle Courses in HEIs by Discipline

单位:人
unit: person

	毕业生数 Graduates	招生数 Entrants	在校生数 Enrolment
总计 Total	**1118346**	**1867890**	**4771929**
其中:女 of Which: Female	525443	850919	2163738
农林牧渔大类 Agriculture, Forestry, Husbandry and Fishing	35228	52796	173396
资源环境与安全大类 Resources Environment and Safety	13306	9519	24419
能源动力与材料大类 Energy Power and Material	7437	10731	23745
土木建筑大类 Civil Engineering and Architecture	129018	154196	398386
水利大类 Water Resources	5682	8981	24770
装备制造大类 Equipment Manufacturing	80046	129411	345881
生物与化工大类 Biology and Chemical Engineering	3843	4397	11756
轻工纺织大类 Light Industry and Textile	272	377	838
食品药品与粮食大类 Food, Medicine and Grain	1281	2284	5736
交通运输大类 Transportation and Communication	20025	31062	69888
电子信息大类 Electronic Information	44309	116003	264067
医药卫生大类 Medical and Health	57099	78291	212208
财经商贸大类 Finance, Economics and Business	346449	607846	1467741
旅游大类 Tourism	7004	10797	35157
文化艺术大类 Culture and Arts	5523	8926	34067
新闻传播大类 Journalism and Communication	428	850	2599
教育与体育大类 Education and Sport	98020	179808	488051
公安与司法大类 Public Security and Justice	53812	100101	275160
公共管理与服务大类 Public Administration and Service	209564	361514	914064
总计中:师范生 of the Total: Students Enrolled in Teacher Training Institutions	13909	33891	61222

高等教育学生
Changes in Enrolment of

	上学年初报表在校学生数 Enrolment at Beginning of Previous Academic Year	增加学生数 Factors of Increase				
		合计 Total	招生 No. of Students Admitted	复学 Students Resuming Studies	转入 Transfers from Other Inst.	其他 Others
博士研究生 Doctor's Degrees	342027	88505	83878	3096	199	1332
硕士研究生 Master's Degrees	1639024	730572	722225	5644	256	2447
普通本科生 Normal Courses	16129535	4406045	4329995	57684	5950	12416
普通专科生 Short-cycle Courses	10828898	3960567	3891506	35094	4958	29009
成人本科生 Normal Courses Provided by Adult HEIs	2686619	1062112	1023981	13234	11435	13462
成人专科生 Short-cycle Courses Provided by Adult HEIs	3157264	1207531	1151321	9835	13687	32688
网络本科生 Normal Courses Provided by Web-based Programs	2339270	1006177	993253	4288	2105	6531
网络专科生 Short-cycle Courses Provided by Web-based Programs	4110059	2001432	1867890	9376	2628	121538

高等教育非学历教育学生情况
Number of Students of Non-formal Education of Higher Education

单位:人/人次
unit: person/person-time

	结业生数 Completers		注册学生数 Enrolment	
	合计 Total	其中:女 of Which:Female	合计 Total	其中:女 of Which:Female
研究生课程进修班 Postgraduate Courses	9244	5516	12237	7274
自考助学班 Classes Run by Non-government HEIs for Students Preparing for Self-Taught Higher Education Examinations	61599	33327	132467	69870
普通预科生 College-preparatory Classes	—	—	45420	26538
进修及培训 In-service Training	8996653	4095742	8338925	3845007
一个月以内 1 Month Under	5769053	2483927	4970511	2165508
一个月至三个月以内 1 Month to 3 Months Under	1658248	1019775	1659145	1009010
三个月至半年以内 3 Months to 6 Months Under	533608	256390	558708	271711
半年至一年以内 6 Months to 1 Year Under	955178	294563	995551	326850
一年及以上 1 Year and over	80566	41087	155010	71928
总计中:资格证书培训 of the Total: For Certificates of Vocational Qualifications	2107943	929383	2141208	938822
岗位证书培训 For Certificates of Job-related Qualifications	2344467	1040725	2053011	911304
第一产业类培训 Training for First Industry	385473	126032	332223	106702
第二产业类培训 Training for Second Industry	1313180	388055	1244783	369446
第三产业类培训 Training for Third Industry	7298000	3581655	6761919	3368859

数变动情况
Higher Educations

单位:人
unit: person

减少学生数 Factors of Decrease									本学年初报表在校学生数 Enrolment at Beginning of Current Academic Year
合计 Total	毕业 Graduates	结业 Completers of Courses without Formal awards	休学 Suspended	退学 Quitting	开除 Expelled	死亡 Death	转出 Transfers to Other Inst.	其他 Others	
68535	58032	1640	1976	3776	18	42	103	2948	361997
555918	520013	1817	5760	6910	56	136	2223	19003	2277564
4049260	3841839	61969	77616	42955	881	1175	5210	17615	16486320
3739916	3516448	53554	68112	77461	2251	607	1714	19769	11049549
1158922	1091226	5912	12890	25123	12	14	497	23248	2589809
1513175	1379144	14218	21857	53687	10	24	1567	42668	2851620
758109	659559	2943	8564	41086	0	3	1099	44855	2587338
1339562	1118346	2669	33558	54015	0	18	700	130256	4771929

高等教育学生中其他情况
Other Circumstances of Students in Higher Education

单位:人
unit: person

	共产党员 Member of C. P. A	共青团员 Member of C. Y. L	华侨 Overseas Chinese	港澳台 From HK, Macao and Taiwan	少数民族 Minorities	残疾人 Disabled
总计 Total	**2336127**	**28755818**	**3444**	**33194**	**3630638**	**28419**
研究生 Postgraduates	717813	1141923	295	6793	127995	414
博　士 Doctor's Degree	178505	92833	66	2695	21761	49
硕　士 Master's Degree	539308	1049090	229	4098	106234	365
普通本专科 Undergraduates in Regular HEIs	835829	24310008	2228	24228	2488788	23091
本　科 Normal Courses	726229	14888663	1845	23963	1509452	11999
专　科 Short-cycle Courses	109600	9421345	383	265	979336	11092
成人本专科 Undergraduates in Adult HEIs	307968	1814437	920	1782	495838	947
本　科 Normal Courses	213008	789511	883	1051	235531	336
专　科 Short-cycle Courses	94960	1024926	37	731	260307	611
网络本专科生 Web-based Undergraduates	474517	1489450	1	391	518017	3967
本　科 Normal Courses	228970	489595	0	111	172013	1274
专　科 Short-cycle Courses	245547	999855	1	280	346004	2693

	毕(结)业生数 Graduates	授予学位数 Degrees Awarded	招生数 Entrants	
			合计 Total	其中:春季招生 of Which:Spring Term
总计 Total	**121419**	**26093**	**153445**	**40971**
其中:女 of Which:Female	57989	10591	69893	20345
按层次分 by Level of Training	**30396**	**26093**	**58744**	**5871**
博士研究生 Doctor's Degrees	1801	1452	5666	399
硕士研究生 Master's Degrees	9874	8753	16729	1034
本科生 Normal Courses	18181	15888	32357	3926
专科生 Short-cycle Courses	540	—	3992	512
培训 In-service Training	91023	—	94701	35100
分大洲 By Continent				
亚洲 Asia	69578	16987	87983	23182
非洲 Africa	13787	5099	22908	4417
欧洲 Europe	24449	2576	27761	7918
北美洲 North America	9880	941	10457	4159
南美洲 South America	1602	315	2123	535
大洋洲 Australia	2123	175	2213	760
分经费来源 By Sources of Support				
国际组织资助 Aided by IGOs	320	154	410	23
中国政府资助 Aided by Chinese Government	28036	8715	42769	5875
本国政府资助 Aided by Home Government	2127	347	1583	377
学校间交换 Aided by Inter-institutional Exchanges	16834	765	19046	7090
自费 Self-supporting	74102	16112	89637	27606

生情况
International Students

单位:人
unit: person

在校生数 Enrolment					
合计 Total	第一年 1st Year	第二年 2nd Year	第三年 3rd Year	第四年 4th Year	第五年及以上 5th Year and Over
274809	**141497**	**55112**	**34391**	**24157**	**19652**
117487	64179	22784	13561	9459	7504
178271	**56184**	**45775**	**33135**	**23647**	**19530**
18447	5442	4765	3735	2335	2170
39279	16150	13001	6805	2225	1098
114469	30795	26511	21905	19000	16258
6076	3797	1498	690	87	4
96538	85313	9337	1256	510	122
170593	82117	34647	22758	16236	14835
49651	21199	12167	7572	5441	3272
35324	25268	5336	2478	1507	735
12935	8828	1920	978	597	612
3460	2155	628	359	220	98
2846	1930	414	246	156	100
967	402	184	172	168	41
77971	39271	19398	10820	5921	2561
3101	1471	450	485	317	378
20854	17641	2303	625	171	114
171916	82712	32777	22289	17580	16558

高等教育学校(机构)
Number of Educational

	合计 Total	校本部 Educational Personnel			
		小计 Subtotal	专任教师		
			小计 Subtotal	正高级 Senior	副高级 Sub-senior
总计 Total	**2484403**	**2378057**	**1657238**	**210204**	**497670**
其中:女 of Which: Female	1216907	1167291	827116	65298	232647
普通高校 Regular HEIs	2442995	2336980	1633248	208917	490184
成人高校 Adult HEIs	41408	41077	23990	1287	7486

高等教育学校(机构)
Number of Educational

	合计 Total	校本部 Educational Personnel			
		小计 Subtotal	专任教师		
			小计 Subtotal	正高级 Senior	副高级 Sub-senior
总计 Total	**2442995**	**2336980**	**1633248**	**208917**	**490184**
其中:女 of Which: Female	1195657	1146213	813837	64700	228636
分类型:本科院校 by Type:HEIs Offering Degree Programs	1772342	1677918	1150467	187122	366716
其中:独立学院 of Which: Independent Institutions	162330	162038	122151	13300	32456
高职(专科)院校 Higher Vocational Colleges	669521	657930	482070	21731	123247
其他普通高校机构 Other Regular HEIs	1132	1132	711	64	221
分举办者:1. 中央 by Providers:Central Ministries & Agencies	390023	337260	202066	58527	75334
教育部 Under MOE	299927	260644	154597	44491	59251
其他部门 Other Central Agencies	90096	76616	47469	14036	16083
2. 地方 Local Authorities	2052972	1999720	1431182	150390	414850
教育部门 Ed. Dept.	1286465	1240618	881705	109210	273795
其他部门 Non-Ed. Dept.	311227	306162	221564	12310	60564
地方企业 Local Enterprises	18461	18307	11739	292	4010
民办 Non-government	436819	434633	316174	28578	76481

教职工情况(总计)
Personnel in HEIs (Total)

单位:人
unit: person

教职工数 Educational Personnel								
教职工 in Main Campus						科研机构人员 Personnel in Affiliated Research Org.	校办企业职工 Employees in School-run Factories & Farms	其他附设机构人员 Personnel in Others Subsidiary Units
Full-time Teachers			行政人员 Adm. Personnel	教辅人员 Supporting Staff	工勤人员 Workers			
中级 Middle	初级 Junior	未定职级 No-ranking						
654307	**185760**	**109297**	**351495**	**226636**	**142688**	**32823**	**22676**	**50847**
358622	109832	60717	170687	128846	40642	12545	7006	30065
644154	181785	108208	343226	220791	139715	32744	22494	50777
10153	3975	1089	8269	5845	2973	79	182	70

教职工情况(普通高校)
Personnel in HEIs (Regular HEIs)

单位:人
unit: person

教职工数 Educational Personnel								
教职工 in Main Campus						科研机构人员 Personnel in Affiliated Research Org.	校办企业职工 Employees in School-run Factories & Farms	其他附设机构人员 Personnel in Others Subsidiary Units
Full-time Teachers			行政人员 Adm. Personnel	教辅人员 Supporting Staff	工勤人员 Workers			
中级 Middle	初级 Junior	未定职级 No-ranking						
644154	**181785**	**108208**	**343226**	**220791**	**139715**	**32744**	**22494**	**50777**
352854	107537	60110	166933	125546	39897	12495	6906	30043
449207	90089	57333	256296	170727	100428	31688	18979	43757
50361	17523	8511	21776	9724	8387	58	82	152
194635	91608	50849	86739	49909	39212	1056	3515	7020
312	88	26	191	155	75	0	0	0
58994	4553	4658	62607	47772	24815	22633	8890	21240
44305	2852	3698	49524	36384	20139	18395	8056	12832
14689	1701	960	13083	11388	4676	4238	834	8408
585160	177232	103550	280619	173019	114900	10111	13604	29537
367402	83279	48019	175296	115613	68004	8683	10883	26281
92153	38780	17757	42556	24993	17049	801	1476	2788
5186	1612	639	3048	1935	1585	32	84	38
120419	53561	37135	59719	30478	28262	595	1161	430

	合计 Total	校本部 Educational Personnel			
		小计 Subtotal	专任教师		
			小计 Subtotal	正高级 Senior	副高级 Sub-senior
总计 Total	**41408**	**41077**	**23990**	**1287**	**7486**
其中:女 of Which: Female	21250	21078	13279	598	4011
分类型:职工高等学校 by type:Workers' Colleges	15345	15258	9157	243	2880
农民高等学校 Peasants' College	133	133	90	0	14
管理干部学院 Institutes for Administration	5483	5436	3282	409	1068
教育学院 Educational College	5931	5872	3976	184	1346
独立函授学院 Independent Correspondence Colleges	0	0	0	0	0
广播电视大学 Radio/TV Universities	14119	13981	7204	448	2096
其他成人高教机构 Other Adult HEIs Institutions	397	397	281	3	82
分举办者:1. 中央 by Providers:Central Ministries & Agencies	1290	1278	491	50	214
教育部 Under MOE	505	493	149	12	77
其他部门 Other Central Agencies	785	785	342	38	137
2. 地方 Local Authorities	40118	39799	23499	1237	7272
教育部门 Ed. Dept.	19924	19748	11273	613	3411
其他部门 Non-Ed. Dept.	17067	16924	10381	591	3206
地方企业 Local Enterprises	3127	3127	1845	33	655
民办 Non-government	0	0	0	0	0

教职工情况(成人高校)
Personnel in HEIs (Adult HEIs)

单位:人
unit: person

教职工数 Educational Personnel								
教职工 in Main Campus						科研机构人员 Personnel in Affiliated Research Org.	校办企业职工 Employees in School-run Factories & Farms	其他附设机构人员 Personnel in Others Subsidiary Units
Full-time Teachers			行政人员 Adm. Personnel	教辅人员 Supporting Staff	工勤人员 Workers			
中级 Middle	初级 Junior	未定职级 No-ranking						
10153	**3975**	**1089**	**8269**	**5845**	**2973**	**79**	**182**	**70**
5768	2295	607	3754	3300	745	50	100	22
4235	1450	349	2858	1746	1497	2	51	34
41	35	0	19	15	9	0	0	0
1227	405	173	1065	620	469	19	0	28
1575	767	104	859	742	295	16	42	1
0	0	0	0	0	0	0	0	0
2951	1257	452	3389	2702	686	42	89	7
124	61	11	79	20	17	0	0	0
192	25	10	263	277	247	12	0	0
55	0	5	111	211	22	12	0	0
137	25	5	152	66	225	0	0	0
9961	3950	1079	8006	5568	2726	67	182	70
4762	1965	522	4309	3203	963	41	125	10
4374	1703	507	3111	1932	1500	26	57	60
825	282	50	586	433	263	0	0	0
0	0	0	0	0	0	0	0	0

研究生指导
Number of Supervisors

	合计 Total	29岁及以下 29 and Under	30-34岁 30 to 34
总计 Total	**403135**	**1725**	**25900**
其中:女 of Which: Female	126470	665	8243
按专业技术职务分:正高级 by Rank:Senior	191716	96	1865
副高级 Sub-senior	182004	415	12581
中级 Middle	29415	1214	11454
分指导关系:博士导师 by Level of Programs Supervised:Supervisors of Doctoral Programs	20040	21	393
其中:女 of Which: Female	3299	3	69
硕士导师 Supervisors of Master's Degree Programs	307271	1637	23342
其中:女 of Which: Female	108542	644	7791
博士、硕士导师 Supervisors of Doc. & Mas. Degree Programs	75824	67	2165
其中:女 of Which: Female	14629	18	383

研究生指导
Number of Supervisors of

	合计 Total	29岁及以下 29 and Under	30-34岁 30 to 34
总计 Total	**386495**	**1652**	**25490**
其中:女 of Which: Female	123026	654	8130
按专业技术职务分:正高级 by Rank:Senior	180092	44	1826
副高级 Sub-senior	177099	412	12249
中级 Middle	29304	1196	11415
分指导关系:博士导师 by Level of Programs Supervised:Supervisors of Doctoral Programs	17142	12	384
其中:女 of Which: Female	2895	3	67
硕士导师 Supervisors of Master's Degree Programs	294751	1573	22947
其中:女 of Which: Female	105684	633	7680
博士、硕士导师 Supervisors of Doc. & Mas. Degree Programs	74602	67	2159
其中:女 of Which: Female	14447	18	383

教师情况(总计)
of Postgraduate Programs (Total)

单位:人
unit: person

35-39 岁 35 to 39	40-44 岁 40 to 44	45-49 岁 45 to 49	50-54 岁 50 to 54	55-59 岁 55 to 59	60-64 岁 60 to 64	65 岁及以上 65 and Over
70695	**79010**	**77139**	**88140**	**38876**	**15524**	**6126**
24710	28918	27026	24891	8517	2741	759
10602	24920	39644	64054	31042	13923	5570
49402	50131	36150	23613	7645	1563	504
10691	3959	1345	473	189	38	52
1365	2267	3164	5632	3267	2279	1652
224	443	746	905	433	336	140
61116	64980	60337	61340	24896	7562	2061
23014	25748	22948	19982	6450	1566	399
8214	11763	13638	21168	10713	5683	2413
1472	2727	3332	4004	1634	839	220

教师情况(普通高校)
Postgraduate Programs (Regular HEIs)

单位:人
unit: person

35-39 岁 35 to 39	40-44 岁 40 to 44	45-49 岁 45 to 49	50-54 岁 50 to 54	55-59 岁 55 to 59	60-64 岁 60 to 64	65 岁及以上 65 and Over
68511	**75814**	**73523**	**83923**	**36913**	**14895**	**5774**
24151	28127	26184	24151	8244	2652	733
10036	23109	36946	60310	29256	13333	5232
47814	48757	35240	23145	7468	1524	490
10661	3948	1337	468	189	38	52
1282	1978	2650	4681	2699	2015	1441
217	390	649	773	370	300	126
59061	62239	57482	58480	23690	7289	1990
22469	25043	22258	19432	6261	1519	389
8168	11597	13391	20762	10524	5591	2343
1465	2694	3277	3946	1613	833	218

分学科专任教师数(总计)
Number of Full-time Teachers by Field of Study (Total)

单位:人
unit: person

	合计 Total	正高级 Senior	副高级 Sub-Senior	中级 Middle	初级 Junior	未定职级 No-Ranking
总计 Total	**1657238**	**210204**	**497670**	**654307**	**185760**	**109297**
其中:女 of Which: Female	827116	65298	232647	358622	109832	60717
哲学 Philosophy	40215	5386	12223	15294	4450	2862
经济学 Economics	88711	10637	27228	33856	10366	6624
法学 Law	78226	9494	22748	32362	8471	5151
教育学 Education	141306	10993	40369	57673	21366	10905
其中:体育 of which:Sport	65613	4766	20795	26972	9108	3972
文学 Literature	222650	17812	60357	104735	26053	13693
其中:外语 of which:Foreign Language	128321	7490	32706	67091	14206	6828
历史学 History	16986	3128	5404	6182	1340	932
理学 Science	184981	33819	62337	65594	13858	9373
工学 Engineering	455880	63007	146062	175931	43503	27377
其中:计算机 of which:Computer	97043	8570	29628	43852	10131	4862
农学 Agriculture	40140	7825	13302	13638	3144	2231
其中:林学 of Which:Forestry	7160	1153	2375	2516	755	361
医学 Medicine	128137	23961	40455	42326	14489	6906
管理学 Administrators	144575	15394	41014	57962	18473	11732
艺术学 Art	115431	8748	26171	48754	20247	11511

注:不包含民办的其他高等教育机构数据。
Note:Data of Non-government HEIs are not included.

分学科专任教师数(普通高校)
Number of Full-time Teachers by Field of Study (Regular HEIs)

单位:人
unit: person

	合计 Total	正高级 Senior	副高级 Sub-Senior	中级 Middle	初级 Junior	未定职级 No-Ranking
总计 Total	**1633248**	**208917**	**490184**	**644154**	**181785**	**108208**
其中:女 of Which: Female	813837	64700	228636	352854	107537	60110
哲学 Philosophy	39393	5316	11935	14977	4349	2816
经济学 Economics	86451	10431	26455	32936	10087	6542
法学 Law	76770	9355	22295	31758	8280	5082
教育学 Education	138619	10845	39549	56613	20843	10769
其中:体育 of Which:Sport	64733	4750	20597	26559	8888	3939
文学 Literature	218973	17650	59202	103073	25476	13572
其中:外语 of Which:Foreign Language	126697	7439	32204	66297	13969	6788
历史学 History	16679	3103	5277	6066	1304	929
理学 Science	182424	33701	61490	64533	13431	9269
工学 Engineering	449963	62825	144278	173334	42458	27068
其中:计算机 of Which:Computer	94776	8495	28970	42772	9754	4785
农学 Agriculture	39799	7809	13218	13504	3063	2205
其中:林学 of Which:Forestry	7123	1152	2365	2500	746	360
医学 Medicine	127400	23909	40185	42029	14405	6872
管理学 Administrators	142324	15246	40343	57006	18088	11641
艺术学 Art	114453	8727	25957	48325	20001	11443

分学科专任教师数(成人高校)

Number of Full-time Teachers by Field of Study (Adult HEIs)

单位:人
unit: person

	合计 Total	正高级 Senior	副高级 Sub-Senior	中级 Middle	初级 Junior	未定职级 No-Ranking
总计 Total	**23990**	**1287**	**7486**	**10153**	**3975**	**1089**
其中:女 of Which: Female	13279	598	4011	5768	2295	607
哲学 Philosophy	822	70	288	317	101	46
经济学 Economics	2260	206	773	920	279	82
法学 Law	1456	139	453	604	191	69
教育学 Education	2687	148	820	1060	523	136
其中:体育 of Which:Sport	880	16	198	413	220	33
文学 Literature	3677	162	1155	1662	577	121
其中:外语 of Which:Foreign Language	1624	51	502	794	237	40
历史学 History	307	25	127	116	36	3
理学 Science	2557	118	847	1061	427	104
工学 Engineering	5917	182	1784	2597	1045	309
其中:计算机 of Which:Computer	2267	75	658	1080	377	77
农学 Agriculture	341	16	84	134	81	26
其中:林学 of Which:Forestry	37	1	10	16	9	1
医学 Medicine	737	52	270	297	84	34
管理学 Administrators	2251	148	671	956	385	91
艺术学 Art	978	21	214	429	246	68

分学科专任教师数(民办的其他高等教育机构)
Number of Full-time Teachers by Field of Study (Other Non-government HEIs)

单位:人
unit: person

	合计 Total	正高级 Senior	副高级 Sub-Senior	中级 Middle	初级 Junior	未定职级 No-Ranking
总计 Total	**9643**	**730**	**1647**	**3092**	**1545**	**2629**
其中:女 of Which: Female	5058	254	773	1585	894	1552
哲学 Philosophy	290	41	70	98	42	39
经济学 Economics	696	73	206	240	85	92
法学 Law	336	35	93	98	53	57
教育学 Education	1013	78	149	257	195	334
其中:体育 of Which:Sport	367	14	38	108	84	123
文学 Literature	2397	90	301	928	395	683
其中:外语 of Which:Foreign Language	1562	50	149	599	285	479
历史学 History	127	12	30	35	23	27
理学 Science	473	47	120	129	67	110
工学 Engineering	2086	131	313	795	322	525
其中:计算机 of Which:Computer	1202	43	158	501	153	347
农学 Agriculture	63	8	17	12	17	9
其中:林学 of Which:Forestry	18	1	4	5	5	3
医学 Medicine	361	41	79	100	67	74
管理学 Administrators	738	77	145	199	122	195
艺术学 Art	1063	97	124	201	157	484

专任教师、聘请校外教师学历情况(总计)
Number of Academic Qualifications of Full-time and Part-time Teachers in HEIs (Total)

单位:人
unit: person

	合计 Total	博士 Doctor's Degrees	硕士 Master's Degrees	本科 Normal Courses	专科及以下 Short-cycle Courses and Under
1. 专任教师 Full-time Teachers	1657238	398879	602609	637059	18691
其中:女 of Which: Female	827116	144639	354349	321234	6894
正高级 Senior	210204	115439	33245	60396	1124
副高级 Sub-senior	497670	149608	124538	219112	4412
中　级 Middle	654307	116354	295166	236326	6461
初　级 Junior	185760	1759	94684	85995	3322
未定职级 No-ranking	109297	15719	54976	35230	3372
2. 聘请校外教师 Part-time Teachers	521863	76786	161877	255035	28165
其中:女 of Which: Female	203733	19175	71570	104271	8717
外籍教师 Foreign Teachers	18368	9493	4669	4100	106
其他高校教师 Other HEI Teachers	142796	33477	55653	51091	2575
正高级 Senior	90117	39637	21036	28076	1368
副高级 Sub-senior	147006	21680	42832	77295	5199
中　级 Middle	162718	10615	57031	85970	9102
初　级 Junior	46753	602	17501	25339	3311
未定职级 No-ranking	75269	4252	23477	38355	9185

注:不包含民办的其他高等教育机构数据。
Note: Data of Non-government HEIs are not included.

专任教师、聘请校外教师学历情况(普通高校)
Number of Academic Qualifications of Full-time and Part-time Teachers in HEIs (Regular HEIs)

单位:人
unit: person

	合计 Total	博士 Doctor's Degrees	硕士 Master's Degrees	本科 Normal Courses	专科及以下 Short-cycle Courses and Under
1. 专任教师 Full-time Teachers	1633248	397974	596302	621137	17835
其中:女 of Which: Female	813837	144176	350452	312598	6611
正高级 Senior	208917	115235	32923	59637	1122
副高级 Sub-senior	490184	149237	122900	213754	4293
中　级 Middle	644154	116049	292294	229741	6070
初　级 Junior	181785	1753	93650	83288	3094
未定职级 No-ranking	108208	15700	54535	34717	3256
2. 聘请校外教师 Part-time Teachers	487394	76292	154873	229117	27112
其中:女 of Which: Female	186690	19002	68014	91399	8275
外籍教师 Foreign Teachers	18360	9492	4669	4093	106
其他高校教师 Other HEI Teachers	135736	33179	53511	46662	2384
正高级 Senior	88972	39524	20680	27420	1348
副高级 Sub-senior	136680	21456	40928	69258	5038
中　级 Middle	146852	10492	53858	73827	8675
初　级 Junior	41622	584	16431	21524	3083
未定职级 No-ranking	73268	4236	22976	37088	8968

专任教师、聘请校外教师学历情况(成人高校)

Number of Academic Qualifications of Full-time and Part-time Teachers in HEIs (Adult HEIs)

单位:人
unit: person

	合计 Total	博士 Doctor's Degrees	硕士 Master's Degrees	本科 Normal Courses	专科及以下 Short-cycle Courses and Under
1. 专任教师 Full-time Teachers	23990	905	6307	15922	856
其中:女 of Which: Female	13279	463	3897	8636	283
正高级 Senior	1287	204	322	759	2
副高级 Sub-senior	7486	371	1638	5358	119
中　级 Middle	10153	305	2872	6585	391
初　级 Junior	3975	6	1034	2707	228
未定职级 No-ranking	1089	19	441	513	116
2. 聘请校外教师 Part-time Teachers	34469	494	7004	25918	1053
其中:女 of Which: Female	17043	173	3556	12872	442
外籍教师 Foreign Teachers	8	1	0	7	0
其他高校教师 Other HEI Teachers	7060	298	2142	4429	191
正高级 Senior	1145	113	356	656	20
副高级 Sub-senior	10326	224	1904	8037	161
中　级 Middle	15866	123	3173	12143	427
初　级 Junior	5131	18	1070	3815	228
未定职级 No-ranking	2001	16	501	1267	217

专任教师、聘请校外教师学历情况(民办的其他高等教育机构)

Number of Academic Qualifications of Full-time and Part-time Teachers in HEIs (Other Non-government HEIs)

单位:人
unit: person

	合计 Total	博士 Doctor's Degrees	硕士 Master's Degrees	本科 Normal Courses	专科及以下 Short-cycle Courses and Under
1. 专任教师 Full-time Teachers	9643	287	1806	6604	946
其中:女 of Which: Female	5058	84	956	3537	481
正高级 Senior	730	111	205	382	32
副高级 Sub-senior	1647	84	437	1029	97
中　级 Middle	3092	55	572	2263	202
初　级 Junior	1545	6	214	1133	192
未定职级 No-ranking	2629	31	378	1797	423
2. 聘请校外教师 Part-time Teachers	9528	1034	2914	5171	409
其中:女 of Which: Female	3978	292	1210	2295	181
外籍教师 Foreign Teachers	39	1	11	24	3
其他高校教师 Other HEI Teachers	2098	337	788	949	24
正高级 Senior	1471	489	431	522	29
副高级 Sub-senior	2716	380	984	1290	62
中　级 Middle	3213	117	1028	1922	146
初　级 Junior	801	8	203	541	49
未定职级 No-ranking	1327	40	268	896	123

专任教师年龄情况(总计)
Number of Full-time Teachers by Age (Total)

单位:人
unit: person

	合计 Total	29 岁及以下 29 and Under	30-34 岁 30 to 34	35-39 岁 35 to 39	40-44 岁 40 to 44	45-49 岁 45 to 49	50-54 岁 50 to 54	55-59 岁 55 to 59	60-64 岁 60 to 64	65 岁及以上 65 and Over
总计 Total	**1657238**	**197809**	**306899**	**383122**	**249623**	**201418**	**197591**	**82266**	**27272**	**11238**
其中:女 of Which: Female	827116	124188	172348	208555	121135	90546	78743	22541	6975	2085
正高级 Senior	210204	50	1558	10312	26038	43941	70589	35408	16418	5890
副高级 Sub-senior	497670	933	22997	108392	116356	103592	95388	36212	9085	4715
中级 Middle	654307	42137	192695	233654	97503	48716	28468	9059	1559	516
初级 Junior	185760	88258	62342	22224	6608	3437	2005	818	45	23
未定职级 No-ranking	109297	66431	27307	8540	3118	1732	1141	769	165	94

注:不含民办的其他高等教育机构数据。
Note: Data of Non-government HEIs are not included.

专任教师年龄情况(普通高校)
Number of Full-time Teachers by Age (Regular HEIs)

单位:人
unit: person

	合计 Total	29 岁及以下 29 and Under	30-34 岁 30 to 34	35-39 岁 35 to 39	40-44 岁 40 to 44	45-49 岁 45 to 49	50-54 岁 50 to 54	55-59 岁 55 to 59	60-64 岁 60 to 64	65 岁及以上 65 and Over
总计 Total	**1633248**	**194925**	**302533**	**378458**	**245802**	**197969**	**194292**	**80840**	**27205**	**11224**
其中:女 of Which: Female	813837	122339	169732	205805	119014	88677	77056	22169	6960	2085
正高级 Senior	208917	50	1557	10273	25870	43636	70100	35155	16390	5886
副高级 Sub-senior	490184	931	22810	107274	114643	101727	93580	35457	9055	4707
中级 Middle	644154	41667	190036	230674	95825	47622	27574	8692	1550	514
初级 Junior	181785	86529	61045	21763	6390	3294	1916	780	45	23
未定职级 No-ranking	108208	65748	27085	8474	3074	1690	1122	756	165	94

专任教师年龄情况(成人高校)
Number of Full-time Teachers by Age (Adult HEIs)

单位:人
unit: person

	合计 Total	29岁及以下 29 and Under	30-34岁 30 to 34	35-39岁 35 to 39	40-44岁 40 to 44	45-49岁 45 to 49	50-54岁 50 to 54	55-59岁 55 to 59	60-64岁 60 to 64	65岁及以上 65 and Over
总计 Total	**23990**	**2884**	**4366**	**4664**	**3821**	**3449**	**3299**	**1426**	**67**	**14**
其中:女 of Which: Female	13279	1849	2616	2750	2121	1869	1687	372	15	0
正高级 Senior	1287	0	1	39	168	305	489	253	28	4
副高级 Sub-senior	7486	2	187	1118	1713	1865	1808	755	30	8
中级 Middle	10153	470	2659	2980	1678	1094	894	367	9	2
初级 Junior	3975	1729	1297	461	218	143	89	38	0	0
未定职级 No-ranking	1089	683	222	66	44	42	19	13	0	0

专任教师年龄情况(民办的其他高等教育机构)
Number of Full-time Teachers by Age (Other Non-government HEIs)

单位:人
unit: person

	合计 Total	29岁及以下 29 and Under	30-34岁 30 to 34	35-39岁 35 to 39	40-44岁 40 to 44	45-49岁 45 to 49	50-54岁 50 to 54	55-59岁 55 to 59	60-64岁 60 to 64	65岁及以上 65 and Over
总计 Total	**9643**	**2223**	**2053**	**1621**	**1423**	**806**	**591**	**398**	**257**	**271**
其中:女 of Which: Female	5058	1434	1192	856	678	351	248	150	82	67
正高级 Senior	730	3	19	53	74	114	119	114	106	128
副高级 Sub-senior	1647	11	100	218	334	349	284	178	89	84
中级 Middle	3092	437	726	707	712	241	116	59	49	45
初级 Junior	1545	582	510	228	141	32	28	20	4	0
未定职级 No-ranking	2629	1190	698	415	162	70	44	27	9	14

专任教师、聘请校外

Number of Full-time and Part-time

	专任教师中按授课内容分 Full-time Teachers Classified by Teaching Content			
	合计 Total	公共课基础课 Common Required Course	专业课 Special Subjects	
			小计 Subtotal	其中:双师型 of Which: Double-teacher Type
总计 Total	**1588323**	**379820**	**1208503**	**326239**
其中:女 of Which: Female	796292	208580	587712	165819
正高级 Senior	200777	30098	170679	37749
副高级 Sub-senior	480214	107363	372851	125943
中级 Middle	626913	163883	463030	162547
初级 Junior	178468	51284	127184	—
未定职级 No-ranking	101951	27192	74759	—
普通高校 Regular HEIs	**1565342**	**373325**	**1192017**	**321333**
其中:女 of Which: Female	783513	204924	578589	162982
正高级 Senior	199519	29790	169729	37375
副高级 Sub-senior	473051	105444	367607	123954
中级 Middle	617180	161202	455978	160004
初级 Junior	174677	50062	124615	—
未定职级 No-ranking	100915	26827	74088	—
成人高校 Adult HEIs	**22981**	**6495**	**16486**	**4906**
其中:女 of Which: Female	12779	3656	9123	2837
正高级 Senior	1258	308	950	374
副高级 Sub-senior	7163	1919	5244	1989
中级 Middle	9733	2681	7052	2543
初级 Junior	3791	1222	2569	—
未定职级 No-ranking	1036	365	671	—

注:不含民办的其他高等教育机构数据。

Note:Data of Non-government HEIs are not included.

专任教师、聘请校外教师岗位

Data on Academic Qualification of Full-time and Invited Teachers

	专任教师中按授课内容分 Full-time Teachers Classified by Teaching Content			
	合计 Total	公共课基础课 Common Required Course	专业课 Special Subjects	
			小计 Subtotal	其中:双师型 of Which: Double-teacher Type
总计 Total	**9501**	**3384**	**6117**	**908**
其中:女 of Which: Female	4975	1892	3083	434
正高级 Senior	713	222	491	126
副高级 Sub-senior	1619	557	1062	307
中级 Middle	3062	1244	1818	475
初级 Junior	1529	560	969	—
未定职级 No-ranking	2578	801	1777	—

教师岗位分类情况(总计)
Teachers Classified by Teaching Content in HEIs (Total)

单位:人
unit: person

聘请校外教师按授课内容分 Part-time Teachers Classified by Teaching Content				专任教师中不任课人数 Full-time Teachers by Non-teaching				
合计 Total	公共课基础课 Common Required Course	专业课 Special Subjects		合计 Total	进修 In-service	科研 Research	病休 Sick Leave	其他 Others
		小计 Subtotal	其中:双师型 of Which: Double-teacher Type					
521863	**92301**	**429562**	**97419**	**68915**	**23476**	**14013**	**2906**	**28520**
203733	40289	163444	40819	30824	10900	4578	1844	13502
90117	12191	77926	14948	9427	1917	4581	193	2736
147006	24896	122110	38048	17456	7251	3329	692	6184
162718	29339	133379	44423	27394	10754	4807	1414	10419
46753	10214	36539	—	7292	2184	402	438	4268
75269	15661	59608	—	7346	1370	894	169	4913
487394	**80596**	**406798**	**92142**	**67906**	**23415**	**13956**	**2869**	**27666**
186690	34405	152285	38200	30324	10865	4557	1826	13076
88972	11854	77118	14686	9398	1917	4570	192	2719
136680	21329	115351	35975	17133	7233	3304	685	5911
146852	24035	122817	41481	26974	10730	4795	1392	10057
41622	8307	33315	—	7108	2170	393	431	4114
73268	15071	58197	—	7293	1365	894	169	4865
34469	**11705**	**22764**	**5277**	**1009**	**61**	**57**	**37**	**854**
17043	5884	11159	2619	500	35	21	18	426
1145	337	808	262	29	0	11	1	17
10326	3567	6759	2073	323	18	25	7	273
15866	5304	10562	2942	420	24	12	22	362
5131	1907	3224	—	184	14	9	7	154
2001	590	1411	—	53	5	0	0	48

分类情况(民办的其他高等教育机构)
Classified by Teaching Content Invited from Other Institutions

单位:人
unit: person

聘请校外教师按授课内容分 Part-time Teachers Classified by Teaching Content				专任教师中不任课人数 Full-time Teachers by Non-teaching				
合计 Total	公共课基础课 Common Required Course	专业课 Special Subjects		合计 Total	进修 In-service	科研 Research	病休 Sick Leave	其他 Others
		小计 Subtotal	其中:双师型 of Which: Double-teacher Type					
9528	**2933**	**6595**	**1013**	**142**	**35**	**8**	**5**	**94**
3978	1302	2676	417	83	29	2	4	48
1471	420	1051	177	17	2	2	0	13
2716	831	1885	381	28	2	4	1	21
3213	992	2221	455	30	1	0	3	26
801	318	483	—	16	5	1	1	9
1327	372	955	—	51	25	1	0	25

专任教师
Changes of Full-time

	上学年初报表专任教师数 Number of Full-time Teachers at Beginning of Previous Academic Year	增加专任 Factors of			
		合计 Total	录用毕业生 New Recruits from Current Year Graduates		
			小计 Subtotal	其中:of Which:	
				研究生 Completing Doc. & Mas. Deg.	本科 Completing Normal Courses
总计 Total	**1627182**	**119582**	**57056**	**48762**	**3972**
其中:女 of Which: Female	802298	62244	32100	27334	1708
普通高校 Regular HEIs	**1601968**	**118235**	**56639**	**48446**	**3972**
其中:女 of Which: Female	788558	61463	31791	27095	1708
成人高校 Adult HEIs	**25214**	**1347**	**417**	**316**	**0**
其中:女 of Which: Female	13740	781	309	239	0

专任教师
Changes of Full-time Teachers in HEIs

	上学年初报表专任教师数 Number of Full-time Teachers at Beginning of Previous Academic Year	增加专任 Factors of			
		合计 Total	录用毕业生 New Recruits from Current Year Graduates		
			小计 Subtotal	其中:of Which:	
				研究生 Completing Doc. & Mas. Deg.	本科 Completing Normal Courses
总计 Total	**10329**	**1247**	**354**	**48**	**0**
其中:女 of Which: Female	5283	659	237	37	0

变动情况(总计)
Teachers in HEIs (Total)

单位:人
unit:person

教师数 Increase				减少专任教师数 Factors of Decrease				本学年初报表专任教师数 Number of Full-time Teachers at Beginning of Current Academic Year
外单位教师调入 Teachers Recruited from Other Units		校内、外非教师调入 Non-teaching Personnel Changed into Teachers		合计 Total	自然减员 Retired from their Posts during Previous Academic Year	调离教师岗位 Transferred from Teaching to Non-teaching Posts	其他 Others	
小计 Subtotal	其中:高校调入 of Which: fromReg. HEIs	小计 Subtotal	其中:本校调整 of Which: with Change of Status in Their Own Institutions					
29700	**14160**	**32826**	**16394**	**89526**	**27270**	**23218**	**39038**	**1657238**
13692	6035	16452	8490	37426	11096	9593	16737	827116
29211	14039	32385	16091	86955	26731	22785	37439	1633248
13419	5979	16253	8378	36184	10839	9425	15920	813837
489	121	441	303	2571	539	433	1599	23990
273	56	199	112	1242	257	168	817	13279

变动情况(民办的其他高等教育机构)
(Other Non-government HEIs)

单位:人
unit:person

教师数 Increase				减少专任教师数 Factors of Decrease				本学年初报表专任教师数 Number of Full-time Teachers at Beginning of Current Academic Year
外单位教师调入 Teachers Recruited from Other Units		校内、外非教师调入 Non-teaching Personnel Changed into Teachers		合计 Total	自然减员 Retired from Their Posts during Previous Academic Year	调离教师岗位 Transferred from Teaching to Non-teaching Posts	其他 Others	
小计 Subtotal	其中:高校调入 of Which: from Reg. HEIs	小计 Subtotal	其中:本校调整 of Which: with Change of Status in Their Own Institutions					
514	**41**	**379**	**32**	**1933**	**668**	**405**	**860**	**9643**
263	19	159	15	884	268	174	442	5058

高等教育
Condition of Fixed Assets and Teaching

	占地面积(平方米) Areas Occupied (m^2)			图书音像资料情况 Audio-visual ed. Resources	
				图书(万册) Books&Magazines in Libraries (10,000 Volume)	
	合计 Total	其中:绿化用地面积 of Which: Green Areas	其中:运动场地面积 of Which: Sports Areas	合计 Total	当年新增 New Added in Current Year
学校产权 Owned by HEIs	1805535992. 09	590138236. 15	135562439. 60	260505. 13	11880. 60
非学校产权中独立使用 Not Owned by HEIs	242435413. 53	52236681. 47	13888399. 85	6261. 09	780. 85
普通高校 Regular HEIs					
学校产权 Owned by HEIs	1786236448. 50	585505921. 00	133719810. 36	257498. 49	11798. 72
非学校产权中独立使用 Not Owned by HEIs	217250282. 67	46806085. 47	10638277. 55	2287. 62	450. 39
成人高校 Adult HEIs					
学校产权 Owned by HEIs	19299543. 59	4632315. 15	1842629. 24	3006. 64	81. 88
非学校产权中独立使用 Not Owned by HEIs	25185130. 86	5430596. 00	3250122. 30	3973. 47	330. 46

注:不包含民办的其他高等教育机构数据。
Note: Data of Non-government HEIs are not included.

高等教育资产情况
Condition of Fixed Assets and Teaching Resources

	占地面积(平方米) Areas Occupied (m^2)			图书音像资料情况 Audio-visual ed. Resources	
				图书(万册) Books&Magazines in Libraries (10,000 Volume)	
	合计 Total	其中:绿化用地面积 of Which: Green Areas	其中:运动场地面积 of Which: Sports Areas	合计 Total	当年新增 New Added in Current Year
学校产权 Owned by HEIs	5996664. 32	1111260. 26	422611. 86	4157. 49	40. 48
非学校产权中独立使用 Not Owned by HEIs	5612649. 10	693627. 82	519625. 83	189. 29	25. 05

资产情况(总计)
Resources in Higher Education(Total)

计算机数(台) PC (Set)			教室(间) Classroom(Room)		固定资产值(万元) Fixed Assets (10000 yuan)				
合计 Total	其中:教学用计算机 No. of Computers Used for Instruction		合计 Total	其中:网络多媒体教室 of Which: Network Multimedia Classroom	合计 Total	其中:教学、科研仪器设备资产 of Which:Teaching Equipment & Instruments		其中:信息化设备资产值 of Which: Assets of Information Facilities	
	小计 Subtotal	其中:平板电脑 of Which: Tablet PC				小计 Subtotal	当年新增 New Added in Current Year	小计 Subtotal	其中:软件 of Which: Software
12336917	9227205	115170	667619	368207	213524676.88	49812055.73	5992912.85	14251585.04	2813544.34
334849	264891	6632	113018	53928	13511553.08	1025691.37	117525.95	—	—
12145002	9086478	111044	651252	361019	211429828.27	49416383.76	5959808.88	14024426.85	2776856.92
66054	53003	404	83854	40174	11594571.00	536511.11	67610.06	—	—
191915	140727	4126	16367	7188	2094848.60	395671.97	33103.97	227158.19	36687.42
268795	211888	6228	29164	13754	1916982.08	489180.26	49915.88	—	—

(民办的其他高等教育机构)
in Higher Education(Other Non-government HEIs)

计算机数(台) PC (Set)			教室(间) Classroom(Room)		固定资产值(万元) Fixed Assets (10000 yuan)				
合计 Total	其中:教学用计算机 No. of Computers Used for Instruction		合计 Total	其中:网络多媒体教室 of Which: Network Multimedia Classroom	合计 Total	其中:教学、科研仪器设备资产 of Which:Teaching Equipment & Instruments		其中:信息化设备资产值 of Which: Assets of Information Facilities	
	小计 Subtotal	其中:平板电脑 of Which: Tablet PC				小计 Subtotal	当年新增 New Added in Current Year	小计 Subtotal	其中:软件 of Which: Software
62041	50320	2887	4716	1442	1073400.58	81979.44	7571.10	23114.41	4058.26
12280	9873	1362	5585	1752	113474.24	30961.24	2561.02	—	—

高等教育校舍情况(总计)
Condition of School Buildings in Higher Education(Total)

单位:平方米
unit:m^2

	学校产权校舍建筑面积 Floor Area of School Building Owned by HEIs				正在施工校舍建筑面积 Floor Area Under Construction	非学校产权中独立使用校舍建筑面积 Floor Area of School Building Not Owned by HEIs
	合计 Total	其中:危房 of Which: Dilapidated Buildings	其中:当年新增校舍 of Which: New Added in Current Year	其中:被外单位借用 of Which: Floor Space Hired by Other Schools or Units		
总计 Total	**863688901.47**	**1356626.37**	**24701347.79**	**1379978.64**	**60691788.84**	**114850633.09**
一、教学及辅助用房 Buildings for Instruction and Ancillary Uses	**384090179.19**	**520488.96**	**12385121.60**	**420810.08**	**31834187.59**	**52687159.26**
教室 Classroom	137922618.29	182984.74	3162428.36	205736.16	8086952.29	22282318.20
图书馆 Library	46177814.07	42088.75	1615891.16	32789.13	4459755.06	5172854.46
实验室、实习场所 Lab. And Practice Facilities	144812098.81	264302.20	5349705.03	120774.21	11684279.17	19090781.38
专用科研用房 Office Special for Research	21803175.85	11389.01	1022699.42	24562.53	4206971.91	1443181.35
体育馆 Gymnasium	25242571.93	2722.00	1049086.37	23615.15	2636848.56	3354024.63
会堂 Hall	8131900.24	17002.26	185311.26	13332.90	759380.60	1343999.24
二、行政办公用房 Administrative	**48756982.70**	**89649.08**	**1029773.43**	**54826.98**	**2322681.80**	**6637198.37**
三、生活用房 Residential Buildings	**319514258.43**	**548304.17**	**8910737.42**	**632595.69**	**18197116.32**	**53729609.47**
学生宿舍(公寓) Students' Dormitories	236833462.58	303103.07	6384968.51	432841.45	12177310.10	42467265.97
学生食堂 Students' Dining Halls	33829599.42	20555.54	1015054.91	53134.73	1589947.08	5264259.77
教工宿舍(公寓) Apartments for Single	21005063.55	144883.58	967761.91	4374.00	3129715.13	3374787.68
教工食堂 Dining Halls for Teachers, Staff and Workers	1959633.84	2375.00	50004.91	0.00	84491.35	303530.34
生活福利及附属用房 Residential, Welfare and Auxiliary Buildings	25886499.04	77386.98	492947.18	142245.51	1215652.66	2319765.71
四、教工住宅 Residential Quarters for Teachers & Workers	**90473069.03**	**168524.44**	**1506292.38**	**44713.22**	**4886591.28**	**—**
五、其他用房 Other	**20854412.12**	**29659.72**	**869422.96**	**227032.67**	**3451211.85**	**1796665.99**

注:不包含民办的其他高等教育机构数据。
Note:Data of Non-government HEIs are not included.

高等教育校舍情况(普通高校)

Condition of School Buildings in Higher Education (Regular HEIs)

单位:平方米
unit: m^2

	学校产权校舍建筑面积 Floor Area of School Building Owned by HEIs				正在施工校舍建筑面积 Floor Area Under Construction	非学校产权中独立使用校舍建筑面积 Floor Area of School Building Not Owned by HEIs
	合计 Total	其中:危房 of Which: Dilapidated Buildings	其中:当年新增校舍 of Which: New Added in Current Year	其中:被外单位借用 of Which: Floor Space Hired by Other Schools or Units		
总计 Total	**851852684.34**	**1326731.37**	**24555618.08**	**1371877.61**	**59954193.91**	**102150554.49**
一、教学及辅助用房 Buildings for Instruction and Ancillary Uses	**378697276.66**	**515303.96**	**12319475.57**	**420810.08**	**31590540.19**	**45715473.63**
教室 Classroom	135121662.43	179526.74	3131148.04	205736.16	7980876.07	18452097.02
图书馆 Library	45681966.19	40361.75	1594324.90	32789.13	4442564.94	4666021.83
实验室、实习场所 Lab. and Practice Facilities	143402649.57	264302.20	5339818.58	120774.21	11592474.30	17056903.59
专用科研用房 Office Special for Research	21775532.82	11389.01	1022699.42	24562.53	4189949.91	1401031.76
体育馆 Gymnasium	24764766.00	2722.00	1049086.37	23615.15	2628371.37	3049264.29
会堂 Hall	7950699.65	17002.26	182398.26	13332.90	756303.60	1090155.14
二、行政办公用房 Administrative	**47523721.58**	**85598.08**	**1016128.63**	**53198.75**	**2051457.59**	**5428987.52**
三、生活用房 Residential Buildings	**315840662.02**	**528045.17**	**8872477.02**	**627331.69**	**17994997.18**	**49423144.73**
学生宿舍(公寓) Students' Dormitories	234309089.74	282887.07	6365581.61	432841.45	12043167.69	39516216.42
学生食堂 Students' Dining Halls	33349740.36	20555.54	1012053.91	53134.73	1570111.90	4623961.68
教工宿舍(公寓) Apartments for Single	20884195.95	144883.58	957445.11	4374.00	3098515.13	3156626.58
教工食堂 Dining Halls for Teachers, Staff and Workers	1887287.74	2375.00	45108.91	0.00	79533.80	207765.37
生活福利及附属用房 Residential, Welfare and Auxiliary Buildings	25410348.23	77343.98	492287.48	136981.51	1203668.66	1918574.68
四、教工住宅 Residential Quarters for Teachers & Workers	**89248752.34**	**168524.44**	**1506292.38**	**44713.22**	**4886591.28**	—
五、其他用房 Other	**20542271.74**	**29259.72**	**841244.48**	**225823.87**	**3430607.67**	**1582948.61**

高等教育校舍情况(成人高校)

Condition of School Buildings in Higher Education(Adult HEIs)

单位:平方米
unit: m^2

	学校产权校舍建筑面积 Floor Area of School Building Owned by HEIs				正在施工校舍建筑面积 Floor Area Under Construction	非学校产权中独立使用校舍建筑面积 Floor Area of School Building Not Owned by HEIs
	合计 Total	其中:危房 of Which: Dilapidated Buildings	其中:当年新增校舍 of Which: New Added in Current Year	其中:被外单位借用 of Which: Floor Space Hired by Other Schools or Units		
总计 Total	**11836217.13**	**29895.00**	**145729.71**	**8101.03**	**737594.93**	**12700078.60**
一、教学及辅助用房 Buildings for Instruction and Ancillary Uses	**5392902.53**	**5185.00**	**65646.03**	**0**	**243647.40**	**6971685.63**
教室 Classroom	2800955.86	3458.00	31280.32	0	106076.22	3830221.18
图书馆 Library	495847.88	1727.00	21566.26	0	17190.12	506832.63
实验室、实习场所 Lab. and Practice Facilities	1409449.24	0	9886.45	0	91804.87	2033877.79
专用科研用房 Office Special for Research	27643.03	0	0	0	17022.00	42149.59
体育馆 Gymnasium	477805.93	0	0	0	8477.19	304760.34
会堂 Hall	181200.59	0	2913.00	0	3077.00	253844.10
二、行政办公用房 Administrative	**1233261.12**	**4051.00**	**13644.80**	**1628.23**	**271224.21**	**1208210.85**
三、生活用房 Residential Buildings	**3673596.41**	**20259.00**	**38260.40**	**5264.00**	**202119.14**	**4306464.74**
学生宿舍(公寓) Students' Dormitories	2524372.84	20216.00	19386.90	0	134142.41	2951049.55
学生食堂 Students' Dining Halls	479859.06	0	3001.00	0	19835.18	640298.09
教工宿舍(公寓) Apartments for Single	120867.60	0	10316.80	0	31200.00	218161.10
教工食堂 Dining Halls for Teachers, Staff and Workers	72346.10	0	4896.00	0	4957.55	95764.97
生活福利及附属用房 Residential, Welfare and Auxiliary Buildings	476150.81	43.00	659.70	5264.00	11984.00	401191.03
四、教工住宅 Residential Quarters for Teachers & Workers	**1224316.69**	**0**	**0**	**0**	**0**	**—**
五、其他用房 Other	**312140.38**	**400.00**	**28178.48**	**1208.80**	**20604.18**	**213717.38**

高等教育校舍情况(民办的其他高等教育机构)
Condition of School Buildings in Higher Education (Other Non-government HEIs)

单位:平方米
unit: m^2

	学校产权校舍建筑面积 Floor Area of School Building Owned by HEIs				正在施工校舍建筑面积 Floor Area Under Construction	非学校产权中独立使用校舍建筑面积 Floor Area of School Building Not Owned by HEIs
	合计 Total	其中:危房 of Which: Dilapidated Buildings	其中:当年新增校舍 of Which: New Added in Current Year	其中:被外单位借用 of Which: Floor Space Hired by Other Schools or Units		
总计 Total	**2811007.74**	**0**	**85545.20**	**1000.00**	**202692.71**	**2909774.46**
一、教学及辅助用房 Buildings for Instruction and Ancillary Uses	**1357691.82**	**0**	**36420.00**	**1000.00**	**64091.84**	**1409232.06**
教室 Classroom	799481.90	0	10330.00	1000.00	41365.33	923176.24
图书馆 Library	91803.10	0	4790.00	0	22676.51	152147.27
实验室、实习场所 Lab. and Practice Facilities	348570.85	0	200.00	0	50.00	177598.55
专用科研用房 Office Special for Research	5000.00	0	0	0	0	19332.00
体育馆 Gymnasium	71534.00	0	21100.00	0	0	89275.00
会堂 Hall	41301.97	0	0	0	0	47703.00
二、行政办公用房 Administrative	**182883.29**	**0**	**5234.40**	**0**	**16927.01**	**230901.02**
三、生活用房 Residential Buildings	**1131658.98**	**0**	**43220.80**	**0**	**96594.12**	**1247194.18**
学生宿舍(公寓) Students' Dormitories	800866.36	0	22375.80	0	59635.52	980102.30
学生食堂 Students' Dining Halls	155830.28	0	1100.00	0	28662.00	141583.21
教工宿舍(公寓) Apartments for Single	84021.42	0	301.00	0	5610.00	70055.67
教工食堂 Dining Halls for Teachers, Staff and Workers	11493.78	0	53.00	0	200.00	15309.00
生活福利及附属用房 Residential, Welfare and Auxiliary Buildings	79447.14	0	19391.00	0	2486.60	40144.00
四、教工住宅 Residential Quarters for Teachers & Workers	**58721.73**	**0**	**0**	**0**	**0**	**—**
五、其他用房 Other	**80051.92**	**0**	**670.00**	**0**	**25079.74**	**22447.20**

三、中等教育
Secondary Education

(一)高中阶段教育
Senior Secondary Education

普通高中校数、班数
Number of Regular Senior Secondary Schools and Classes

	学校数(所) Schools				班数(个) Classes
	合计 Total	完全中学 Combined Secondary Schools	高级中学 Regular High Schools	十二年一贯制学校 12-Year Schools	
总计 Total	**13555**	**5460**	**6780**	**1315**	**456760**
教育部门办 Run by Ed. Dept.	10385	4349	5771	265	391288
其他部门办 Run by Non-ed. Dept.	160	52	71	37	3295
地方企业办 Run by Local Enterprises	8	3	0	5	120
民办 Non-government	3002	1056	938	1008	62057
城区 Urban Area	6810	2765	3251	794	227141
教育部门办 Run by Ed. Dept.	4950	2112	2667	171	191245
其他部门办 Run by Non-ed. Dept.	77	23	33	21	1585
地方企业办 Run by Local Enterprises	4	2	0	2	49
民办 Non-government	1779	628	551	600	34262
其中:城乡结合区 of Which:Urban-rural Transitional Area	1053	337	520	196	36251
教育部门办 Run by Ed. Dept.	653	229	401	23	28052
其他部门办 Run by Non-ed. Dept.	9	0	6	3	117
地方企业办 Run by Local Enterprises	2	1	0	1	11
民办 Non-government	389	107	113	169	8071
镇区 Counties & Towns Area	6070	2397	3266	407	214223
教育部门办 Run by Ed. Dept.	4982	2009	2896	77	188609
其他部门办 Run by Non-ed. Dept.	75	26	35	14	1541
地方企业办 Run by Local Enterprises	3	1	0	2	71
民办 Non-government	1010	361	335	314	24002
其中:镇乡结合区 of Which: County-town Transitional Area	1486	527	832	127	52863
教育部门办 Run by Ed. Dept.	1129	409	704	16	44542
其他部门办 Run by Non-ed. Dept.	0	0	0	0	0
地方企业办 Run by Local Enterprises	1	0	0	1	6
民办 Non-government	356	118	128	110	8315
乡村 Rural Area	675	298	263	114	15396
教育部门办 Run by Ed. Dept.	453	228	208	17	11434
其他部门办 Run by Non-ed. Dept.	8	3	3	2	169
地方企业办 Run by Local Enterprises	1	0	0	1	0
民办 Non-government	213	67	52	94	3793
总计中:其他学校附设班 of the Total: Classes Attached to Others Schools					1743
独立设置少数民族学校 Inde. Sec. Schools for Minorities	469	257	175	37	13768

普通高中班额情况

Size of Class in Regular Senior Secondary Schools

单位：个
unit: class

	合计 Total	一年级 Grade 1	二年级 Grade 2	三年级 Grade 3
合 计 Total	**456760**	**153425**	**151928**	**151407**
城区：Urban Area				
25 人及以下 Under 25 Persons	5083	1430	1759	1894
26-35 人 Between 26-35	13246	3803	4527	4916
36-45 人 Between 36-45	47196	15615	15641	15940
46-55 人 Between 46-55	108224	38027	35981	34216
56-65 人 Between 56-65	40087	12747	13503	13837
66 人及以上 Over 66 Persons	13305	4235	4373	4697
其中：城乡结合区： of Which: Urban-rural Transitional Area				
25 人及以下 Under 25 Persons	726	233	244	249
26-35 人 Between 26-35	1310	362	442	506
36-45 人 Between 36-45	6614	2299	2133	2182
46-55 人 Between 46-55	18974	6566	6377	6031
56-65 人 Between 56-65	5980	2008	1969	2003
66 人及以上 Over 66 Persons	2647	885	876	886
镇区：Counties&Towns Area				
25 人及以下 Under 25 Persons	1981	557	621	803
26-35 人 Between 26-35	5633	1573	1779	2281
36-45 人 Between 36-45	29753	9739	9492	10522
46-55 人 Between 46-55	95642	32816	31616	31210
56-65 人 Between 56-65	52340	17478	17828	17034
66 人及以上 Over 66 Persons	28874	9964	9699	9211
其中：镇乡结合区： of Which: County-town Transitional Area				
25 人及以下 Under 25 Persons	419	129	125	165
26-35 人 Between 26-35	1291	370	403	518
36-45 人 Between 36-45	7767	2635	2387	2745
46-55 人 Between 46-55	25750	8877	8787	8086
56-65 人 Between 56-65	11830	3958	3979	3893
66 人及以上 Over 66 Persons	5806	2057	1878	1871
乡村：Rural Area				
25 人及以下 Under 25 Persons	331	78	125	128
26-35 人 Between 26-35	759	225	235	299
36-45 人 Between 36-45	2934	1023	958	953
46-55 人 Between 46-55	7486	2759	2427	2300
56-65 人 Between 56-65	2846	992	1008	846
66 人及以上 Over 66 Persons	1040	364	356	320

普通高中
Number of Students in Regular

	毕业生数 Graduates	招生数 Entrants	合计 Total
总 计 Total	**7757292**	**8000548**	**23745484**
其中:女 of Which: Female	3910258	4061922	12073415
少数民族学生 Minority Students	748994	885758	2509863
十二年一贯制学校 12-year Schools	259713	354185	950620
完全中学 Complete Schools	2372222	2477207	7322134
附设普通高中班 Regular Senior School Classes Attached	22685	27414	77745
独立设置少数民族学校 Independent Schools for Minority	209787	248494	708801
残疾人 Schools for Handicapped	5609	6478	19121
随迁子女 Migrant Children	295427	428102	1228842
其中:外省迁入 of Which: from Other Province	79968	143123	382524
本省外县迁入 From Other County	215459	284979	846318
教育部门 Run by Ed. Dept.	6873453	6831371	20516111
其他部门 Run by Non-ed. Dept.	53783	53290	161692
地方企业办 Run by Local Enterprises	1400	1793	5073
民办 Non-government	828656	1114094	3062608
城区 Urban Area	3733722	3786008	11314380
教育部门办 Run by Ed. Dept.	3263755	3177682	9616311
其他部门办 Run by Non-ed. Dept.	26515	24827	77074
地方企业办 Run by Local Enterprises	685	626	1882
民办 Non-government	442767	582873	1619113
其中:城乡结合区 of Which: Urban-rural Transitional Area	592741	627906	1840746
教育部门办 Run by Ed. Dept.	494953	482773	1457785
其他部门办 Run by Non-ed. Dept.	1994	1678	5383
地方企业办 Run by Local Enterprises	150	186	503
民办 Non-government	95644	143269	377075
镇区 Counties & Towns Area	3792139	3936780	11651820
教育部门办 Run by Ed. Dept.	3427456	3450520	10314521
其他部门办 Run by Non-ed. Dept.	24654	25524	76288
地方企业办 Run by Local Enterprises	715	1167	3191
民办 Non-government	339314	459569	1257820
其中:镇乡结合区 of Which: County-town Transitional Area	898492	967771	2832734
教育部门办 Run by Ed. Dept.	792247	811345	2410331
其他部门办 Run by Non-ed. Dept.	0	0	0
地方企业办 Run by Local Enterprises	61	48	168
民办 Non-government	106184	156378	422235
乡村 Rural Area	231431	277760	779284
教育部门办 Run by Ed. Dept.	182242	203169	585279
其他部门办 Run by Non-ed. Dept.	2614	2939	8330
地方企业办 Run by Local Enterprises	0	0	0
民办 Non-government	46575	71652	185675

学生数
Senior Secondary Schools

单位:人
unit: person

在校生数 Enrolment				预计毕业生数 Estimated Graduates for Next Year
其中:女 of Which: Female	一年级 Grade 1	二年级 Grade 2	三年级 Grade 3	
12073415	**8005548**	**7913696**	**7826240**	**7825449**
—	4063957	4027316	3982142	3981544
1353896	886488	832765	790610	790605
418520	354959	314198	281463	281466
3673461	2478235	2439551	2404348	2404264
36502	27492	25801	24452	24452
388876	248672	236926	223203	223203
8004	6500	6259	6362	6350
567700	435294	418821	374727	368228
176688	145429	129960	107135	105519
391012	289865	288861	267592	262709
10624509	6834882	6841226	6840003	6838837
82992	53296	54145	54251	54251
2570	1794	1905	1374	1374
1363344	1115576	1016420	930612	930987
5765683	3788086	3775470	3750824	3750129
5004189	3179573	3214491	3222247	3221177
39516	24833	25613	26628	26628
879	627	642	613	613
721099	583053	534724	501336	501711
921957	628133	612059	600554	600566
754989	482969	486799	488017	488029
2374	1678	1693	2012	2012
232	186	199	118	118
164362	143300	123368	110407	110407
5920699	3939635	3878324	3833861	3833765
5317036	3452107	3433150	3429264	3429168
39222	25524	25658	25106	25106
1691	1167	1263	761	761
562750	460837	418253	378730	378730
1440125	969421	941606	921707	921602
1249809	811806	800045	798480	798375
0	0	0	0	0
90	48	71	49	49
190226	157567	141490	123178	123178
387033	277827	259902	241555	241555
303284	203202	193585	188492	188492
4254	2939	2874	2517	2517
0	0	0	0	0
79495	71686	63443	50546	50546

中学学校教职工数(初级中学、九年一贯制学校、
Number of Educational Personnel in

	教职工数 Educational Personnel			
	合计 Total	专任教师 Full-time Teachers	行政人员 Adm. Personnel	教辅人员 Supporting Staff
总计 Total	**6743149**	**5985039**	**192040**	**267032**
其中:女 of Which: Female	3712645	3387134	55102	137743
少数民族 Minority	590422	532415	12887	21855
教育部门 Run by Ed. Dept.	5704923	5194364	142773	219770
其他部门 Run by Non-ed. Dept.	61907	49828	3464	2798
地方企业办 Run by Local Enterprises	2437	1977	123	75
民办 Non-government	973882	738870	45680	44389
城区 Urban Area	2724686	2379621	95409	122125
教育部门办 Run by Ed. Dept.	2165877	1951895	67435	94043
其他部门办 Run by Non-ed. Dept.	18488	14991	1169	1279
地方企业办 Run by Local Enterprises	1223	954	95	15
民办 Non-government	539098	411781	26710	26788
其中:城乡结合区 of Which:Urban-rural Transitional Area	477284	410725	14694	20871
教育部门办 Run by Ed. Dept.	329395	300303	7993	12765
其他部门办 Run by Non-ed. Dept.	2025	1591	88	178
地方企业办 Run by Local Enterprises	344	234	23	6
民办 Non-government	145520	108597	6590	7922
镇区 Counties & Towns Area	3155322	2827793	73958	118137
教育部门办 Run by Ed. Dept.	2764879	2528544	57007	102992
其他部门办 Run by Non-ed. Dept.	38208	30368	2126	1382
地方企业办 Run by Local Enterprises	972	824	22	60
民办 Non-government	351263	268057	14803	13703
其中:镇乡结合区 of Which: County-town Transitional Area	771662	688438	18613	28550
教育部门办 Run by Ed. Dept.	639099	586462	13036	23429
其他部门办 Run by Non-ed. Dept.	878	755	27	64
地方企业办 Run by Local Enterprises	165	164	0	0
民办 Non-government	131520	101057	5550	5057
乡村 Rural Area	863141	777625	22673	26770
教育部门办 Run by Ed. Dept.	774167	713925	18331	22735
其他部门办 Run by Non-ed. Dept.	5211	4469	169	137
地方企业办 Run by Local Enterprises	242	199	6	0
民办 Non-government	83521	59032	4167	3898

职业初中、完全中学、高级中学、十二年一贯制学校)

General Secondary Schools

单位:人
unit:person

		代课教师 Substitute Teachers	兼任教师 Part-time Teachers
工勤人员 Workers	校办企业职工 Employees in School-run Factories & Farms		
296790	**2248**	**67674**	**16748**
131508	1158	45533	9112
23160	105	3768	1431
147046	970	53646	9730
5804	13	832	99
262	0	22	0
143678	1265	13174	6919
126071	1460	28268	8278
52048	456	24235	4294
1049	0	379	71
159	0	7	0
72815	1004	3647	3913
30700	294	3923	1145
8285	49	2918	381
168	0	50	7
81	0	0	0
22166	245	955	757
134817	617	29099	6433
75879	457	21007	3909
4323	9	428	28
66	0	0	0
54549	151	7664	2496
35844	217	8878	1536
16032	140	6180	654
28	4	2	0
1	0	0	0
19783	73	2696	882
35902	171	10307	2037
19119	57	8404	1527
432	4	25	0
37	0	15	0
16314	110	1863	510

普通高中分课程专
Number of Full-time Teachers in Regular Senior Secondary Schools

	合计 Total	其中:女 of Which: Female	思想品德(政治) Rirtue Education	语文 Language & Literature	数学 Mathe-matics	外语 Foreign Languages 总计 Total	英语 English	日语 Japanese	俄语 Russian	物理 Physics
总　计 Total	**1773953**	**941702**	**110122**	**272218**	**269878**	**263519**	**260954**	**788**	**569**	**154456**
其中:女 of Which:Female	941702	—	61254	167822	117498	199149	197226	654	435	50872
少数民族 Minorities	150039	82571	10156	23795	20944	19047	18726	191	31	12382
研究生毕业 Graduate	158550	104917	11122	24428	22225	25994	25598	178	78	12093
本科毕业 Under-graduate	1582588	825675	97151	243222	243507	233947	231828	594	483	139739
专科毕业 Associate Bachelor	32175	10936	1819	4490	4115	3555	3505	16	8	2609
高中阶段毕业 High School Graduate	615	170	29	75	30	23	23	0	0	14
高中阶段以下毕业 Below High School Graduate	25	4	1	3	1	0	0	0	0	1
城区 Urban Area	890694	505323	54179	134970	135346	133465	132068	548	232	78244
其中:城乡结合区 of Which: Urban-rural Transitional Area	141568	77610	8888	21452	21286	21083	20868	89	25	12192
镇区 Counties & Towns Area	825874	406987	52298	128429	125915	121975	120858	235	332	71530
其中:镇乡结合区 of Which: County-town Transitional Area	204073	104050	13188	31629	30758	29961	29697	44	82	17631
乡村 Rural Area	57385	29392	3645	8819	8617	8079	8028	5	5	4682

普通高中专任教师专业技术
Number of Full-time Teachers in Regular

	合计 Total	其中:女 of Which: Female	24岁及以下 24 and Under	25-29 26 to 29	30-34 30 to 34
总　计 Total	**1773953**	**941702**	**67522**	**250820**	**319235**
其中:女 of Which:Female	941702	—	48632	172490	201625
少数民族 Minorities	150039	82571	7939	29413	28111
中学高级 Senior	491001	196278	19	54	2117
中学一级 1st Grade	645724	336918	126	12450	120666
中学二级 2nd Grade	478858	303526	17023	162647	176498
中学三级 3rd Grade	10546	6212	1637	5026	2201
未定职级 No-ranking	147824	98768	48717	70643	17753
城区 Urban Area	890694	505323	29714	115897	153393
其中:城乡结合区 of Which: Urban-rural Transitional Area	141568	77610	6251	21945	26961
镇区 Counties & Towns Area	825874	406987	33874	123542	155066
其中:镇乡结合区 of Which: County-town Transitional Area	204073	104050	9294	32200	38980
乡村 Rural Area	57385	29392	3934	11381	10776

任教师学历情况

by Subject Taught & Academic Qualifications

单位:人
unit:person

化学 Chemistry	生物 Biology	地理 Geography	历史 History	信息技术 Infor Technology	通用技术 General Technology	体育与健康 Physical Training and Healthy	艺术 Art	音乐 Music	美术 Fine Arts	综合实践活动 Composite Practice	其他 Others	当年不任课 No Teaching Load in Current Year
149898	**115062**	**97676**	**103128**	**41585**	**12448**	**85008**	**2966**	**31601**	**33703**	**3420**	**13130**	**14135**
76003	67881	49792	53788	19317	4276	17461	1675	21731	16338	1525	8236	7084
12271	9803	8484	8919	3744	1021	7334	233	2995	2590	209	4103	2009
14443	14182	8530	11782	2682	606	4145	156	1555	2238	145	1497	727
133182	99399	87483	89741	38008	11310	77969	2659	29161	30488	3049	10554	12019
2257	1472	1647	1584	882	520	2815	143	869	960	206	969	1263
16	9	16	21	13	12	78	8	16	17	17	103	118
0	0	0	0	0	0	1	0	0	0	3	7	8
75652	57667	48827	51460	21000	6617	43649	1315	16076	17190	1608	5903	7526
11819	9345	8023	8346	3337	1085	6795	241	2755	2937	283	885	816
69610	53691	45569	48316	19167	5313	38568	1488	14507	15393	1680	6218	6207
17054	13483	11527	12232	4881	1342	9433	376	3766	4069	374	1237	1132
4636	3704	3280	3352	1418	518	2791	163	1018	1120	132	1009	402

职务、年龄结构情况

Senior Secondary Schools by Professional Rank and Age

单位:人
unit:person

35-39 35 to 39	40-44 40 to 44	45-49 45 to 49	50-54 50 to 54	55-59 55 to 59	60 岁及以上 60 and Over
378096	**272793**	**249304**	**188202**	**45656**	**2325**
210029	132800	107134	65328	3258	406
27104	21212	19598	13729	2872	61
32832	98971	163454	154049	37656	1849
245055	152240	78035	30244	6640	268
93262	19185	6310	2940	940	53
987	316	181	144	49	5
5960	2081	1324	825	371	150
194658	136664	129846	104006	25020	1496
30772	21194	17732	13184	3216	313
172147	128099	113060	79899	19525	662
43700	31739	26236	17336	4329	259
11291	8030	6398	4297	1111	167

普通高中专任
Changes of Full-time Teachers in

	上学年初报表专任教师数 Number of Full-time Teachers at Beginning of Previous Academic Year	增加教师 Factors of Increase				
		合计 Total	录用毕业生 New Recruits from Current Year Graduates		调入 Teachers Recruited from Other Units	校内调整 of Which: with Change of Status in Their Own Institutions
			小计 Subtotal	师范生 Students Enrolled in Teacher Training Institutions		
总　计 Total	**1733459**	**144571**	**60263**	**45502**	**52713**	**22092**
其中:女 of Which: Female	903797	88357	42644	32597	28956	11201
城区 Urban Area	870681	67730	26475	20209	24515	11242
其中:女 of Which: Female	486936	42540	19267	14873	13900	5990
其中:城乡结合区 of Which: Urban-rural Transitional Area	135731	14107	5832	4385	5514	1572
其中:女 of Which: Female	72946	8793	4212	3191	3123	759
镇区 Counties & Towns Area	808204	69059	30507	23005	25384	9736
其中:女 of Which: Female	389528	41324	21185	16150	13608	4640
其中:镇乡结合区 of Which: County-town Transitional Area	197794	18936	8588	6393	7299	2146
其中:女 of Which: Female	98579	11485	6070	4584	3941	1056
乡村 Rural Area	54574	7782	3281	2288	2814	1114
其中:女 of Which: Female	27333	4493	2192	1574	1448	571

普通高中学生、专任教师
Supplementary Information on Students and Full-time

	在校学生中 of Total Students			
	共产党员 Member of C. P. C.	共青团员 Member of C. Y. L.	华侨 Overseas Chinese	港澳台 From H. K, Macao and Taiwan
总　计 Total	**4383**	**16927028**	**1100**	**7087**
其中:女 of Which: Female	1887	8907386	518	3295
城区 Urban Area	2290	8125267	775	6040
其中:女 of Which: Female	1080	4315423	365	2829
其中:城乡结合区 of Which: Urban-rural Transitional Area	453	1322240	200	1578
其中:女 of Which: Female	182	689332	97	710
镇区 Counties & Towns Area	1966	8283979	253	720
其中:女 of Which: Female	761	4322922	119	324
其中:镇乡结合区 of Which: County-town Transitional Area	535	2024310	44	126
其中:女 of Which: Female	245	1060056	18	59
乡村 Rural Area	127	517782	72	327
其中:女 of Which: Female	46	269041	34	142

教师变动情况
Regular Senior Secondary Schools

单位:人
unit:person

	减少教师 Factors of Decrease					本学年初报表专任教师数 Number of Full-time Teachers at Beginning of Current Academic Year
其他 Others	合计 Total	自然减员 Retired from Their Posts during Previous Academic Year	调出 Transferred from Teaching to Non-Teaching Posts	校内调整 of Which: with Change of Status in Their Own Institutions	其他 Others	
9503	**104077**	**14689**	**53137**	**27016**	**9235**	**1773953**
5556	50452	5919	27042	12874	4617	941702
5498	47717	8556	20808	13099	5254	890694
3383	24153	3803	11017	6572	2761	505323
1189	8270	1222	4364	1818	866	141568
699	4129	555	2214	902	458	77610
3432	51389	5564	29490	12787	3548	825874
1891	23865	1851	14586	5780	1648	406987
903	12657	1365	7498	2836	958	204073
418	6014	493	3849	1202	470	104050
573	4971	569	2839	1130	433	57385
282	2434	265	1439	522	208	29392

政治面貌及其他
Teachers of Regular Senior Secondary Schools

单位:人
unit:person

专任教师中 of Total Full-time Teachers			
共产党员 Member of C. P. C.	共青团员 Member of C. Y. L.	民主党派 Member of Non-Communist Part	华侨 Overseas Chinese
595172	**88661**	**31584**	**109**
275063	59208	14655	64
335948	44318	26115	66
172448	30635	12772	39
47322	8335	2077	6
22614	5699	870	4
241628	39332	4906	43
95004	25397	1662	25
57962	9393	1099	10
23051	6057	406	6
17596	5011	563	0
7611	3176	221	0

普通高中

Condition of School Buildings in

	合计 Total	城区 Urban Area	其中:城乡结合区 of Which: Urban-rural Transitional Area
总 计 Total	**515117371.83**	**266620386.71**	**48124332.88**
其中:危房 of Which:Floor Space of Dilapidated Buildings	**3212076.84**	**1294909.53**	**165775.84**
当年新增校舍 New Floor Space Added in Current Year	**21342696.15**	**8940497.77**	**1865957.35**
一、教学及辅助用房 Teaching & Assistant Buildings	**192480843.84**	**103118534.10**	**16976363.46**
教室 Classroom	113760089.28	58629718.79	9611456.00
实验室 Laboratory	32834358.26	17537952.24	2899539.58
图书室 Library	17183958.09	9425753.92	1566335.53
微机室 PC-room	7979431.69	4247512.63	673746.71
语音室 Linguistic	3164142.34	1589978.91	279308.16
体育馆 Gymnasium	17558864.18	11687617.61	1945977.48
二、行政办公用房 Administrative	**41207002.77**	**23151667.04**	**3687286.81**
其中:教师办公室 of Which: for Teachers	23756945.66	13099333.36	2055218.76
三、生活用房 Residential and Welfare	**241670466.83**	**114961018.10**	**23548072.65**
教工宿舍 Apartments for Single	42647664.92	17039845.09	3810282.18
其中:教师周转宿舍 Accommodation for Circulation of Teachers	9789845.07	3676130.14	975364.44
学生宿舍 Students' Dormitories	130728518.06	61825635.08	12968445.79
食堂 Dining Halls	42169475.41	20802039.44	4176684.09
厕所 Toilet	12965708.37	7314059.70	1293550.32
其他 Others	13159100.07	7979438.79	1299110.27
四、其他用房 Rooms for Other Purposes	**39759058.39**	**25389167.47**	**3912609.96**

普通高中

Condition of School Buildings in

	占地面积(平方米) Areas Occupied (m^2)			图书(册) Books & Magazines in Libraries (Volume)	计算机数(台) PC (Set)		
	合计 Total	其中 of Which:			合计 Total	其中:教学用计算机 No. of Computers Used for Instruction	
		绿化用地面积 Green Areas	运动场地面积 Sports Areas			小计 Subtotal	其中:平板电脑 of Which: Tablet PC
合 计 Total	**1018559023.94**	**268973339.01**	**243177686.35**	**922702647**	**5180068**	**4299671**	**254200**
城区 Urban Area	480650439.61	135164757.00	118280350.12	492949539	3033415	2495195	176623
其中:城乡结合区 of Which: Urban-rural Transitional Area	94668113.41	28690372.60	20939009.44	77547263	450062	376838	21340
镇区 Counties & Towns Area	483113234.33	119019821.41	113453856.25	397055654	1963870	1651012	65840
其中:镇乡结合区 of Which: County-town Transitional Area	125183769.66	31599911.94	28049016.96	98122264	493342	419516	19007
乡村 Rural Area	54795350.00	14788760.60	11443479.98	32697454	182783	153464	11737

办学条件(一)
Regular Senior Secondary Schools (1)

单位:平方米
unit: m^2

镇区 Counties & Towns Area	其中:镇乡结合区 of Which: County-town Transitional Area	乡村 Rural Area
224520394.91	**57717789.91**	**23976590.21**
1804798.46	424815.76	112368.85
10760958.19	3533071.24	1641240.19
81563051.84	**20636590.22**	**7799257.90**
50337590.23	12546220.19	4792780.26
14098440.20	3696923.52	1197965.82
7082470.49	1815267.22	675733.68
3422483.59	842356.81	309435.47
1453589.77	386636.53	120573.66
5168477.56	1349185.95	702769.01
16547911.32	**4205469.02**	**1507424.41**
9862761.47	2539845.53	794850.83
114057942.36	**29792543.41**	**12651506.37**
22770075.06	5532381.98	2837744.77
5300235.76	1293825.30	813479.17
62210687.31	16602518.20	6692195.67
19320358.96	5117389.00	2047077.01
5080151.18	1284741.34	571497.49
4676669.85	1255512.89	502991.43
12351489.39	**3083187.26**	**2018401.53**

办学条件(二)
Regular Senior Secondary Schools (2)

教室(间) Classroom(Room)		教室中:普通教室(间) of Which: General Classroom(Room)		固定资产总值(万元)Total Value of Fixed Asset (10,000 yuan)		
合计 Total	其中:网络多媒体教室 of Which: Network Multimedia Classroom	合计 Total	其中:网络多媒体教室 of Which: Network Multimedia Classroom	合计 Total	其中:教学仪器设备资产值 of Which: Total Value of Equip & Instru. 小计 Subtotal	其中:实验设备 of Which: for Experiment
1065685	**704340**	**802602**	**621865**	**83707301.04**	**8854589.85**	**2805597.08**
553310	389083	410587	335130	46561488.10	5550894.53	1583944.87
90616	63156	68248	54871	8696151.95	777490.19	256221.00
466634	288592	358390	263568	33122331.43	3000934.22	1120055.91
117642	72364	90486	65905	8962896.45	774256.37	291370.78
45741	26665	33625	23167	4023481.52	302761.10	101596.30

普通高中办学条件(三)
Condition of School Buildings in Regular Senior Secondary Schools (3)

单位:所
unit:school

	体育运动场(馆)面积达标校数 Schools No: Sprots Areas Reached Standard	体育器械配备达标校数 Schools No: Sports Equip. Reached Standard	音乐器械配备达标校数 Schools No: Musical Instru. Reached Standard	美术器械配备达标校数 Schools No: Fine Arts Instru. Reached Standard	理科实验仪器达标校数 Schools No: Equip. of Natural Sci. Reached Standard	建立校园网校数 Schools No: Campus Networks Set	接入互联网校数 Schools No: Campus Networks Set
合计 Total	**12354**	**12602**	**12446**	**12463**	**12626**	**11977**	**13364**
城区 Urban Area	6230	6403	6354	6372	6408	6278	6711
其中:城乡结合区 of Which: Urban-rural Transitional Area	991	997	993	987	989	965	1037
镇区 Counties & Towns Area	5512	5586	5491	5488	5602	5149	5996
其中:镇乡结合区 of Which: County-town Transitional Area	1357	1378	1352	1347	1369	1273	1465
乡村 Rural Area	612	613	601	603	616	550	657

成人高中
Basic Statistics of Adult

	学校数(所) Schools	教学班(点)(个) External Teaching Sites	毕(结)业生数 Graduates	
			合计 Total	其中:女 of Which: Female
总　计 Total	**392**	**790**	**38970**	**21224**
职工高中 Senior Sec. Schools for Staff & Workers	131	301	18742	10236
农民高中 Senior Sec. Schools for Peasants	261	489	20228	10988

中等职业学校(机构)数
Number of Secondary Vocational Schools

单位:所
unit:institution

	合计 Total	中央 HEIs under Central Ministries& Agencies	地方 Under Local Authorities				
			小计 Subtotal	教育部门 Run by Ed. Dept.	其他部门 Run by other Dept.	地方企业 Run by Local Enterprises	民办 Non-government
中等职业学校 Secondary Vocational Schools	**8181**	**23**	**8158**	**4861**	**1147**	**81**	**2069**
其中:普通中专学校 of Which: Reg. Specialized Sec. Schools	3346	17	3329	1595	862	41	831
成人中专学校 Adults Specialized Sec. Schools	1218	2	1216	938	136	21	121
职业高中学校 Vocational High Schools	3617	4	3613	2328	149	19	1117
其他中等职业教育机构(不计校数) Other Secondary Vocational Education Institutions	312	2	310	179	87	4	40
附设中职班(不计校数) Secondary Vocational Classes Attached	1221	1	1220	590	364	18	248

注:未含技工学校数据(下同)。
Note:Data on Skilled Workers are not included(same as the followings).

基本情况
Senior Secondary Schools

单位:人
unit:person

注册学生数 Enrolment		教职工数 Educational Personnel		专任教师 Full-time Teacher		聘请校外教师 Part-time Teachers
合计 Total	其中:女 of Which: Female	合计 Total	其中:女 of Which: Female	合计 Total	其中:女 of Which: Female	
39419	**21422**	**3174**	**1376**	**2421**	**1102**	**3060**
18262	10119	1192	544	987	432	1071
21157	11303	1982	832	1434	670	1989

中等职业学校分办学类型及

Number of Students and Educational Personnel of Secondary

	合计 Total			中职全日制学生 Full-time Students of SVSs		
	毕业生数 Graduates	招生数 Entrants	在校学生数 Enrolment	毕业生数 Graduates	招生数 Entrants	在校学生数 Enrolment
总　计 Total	**4063981**	**4515235**	**12542893**	**3538416**	**4031201**	**11499626**
其中:女 of Which: Female	1962315	2037673	5812830	1739277	1826714	5373859
分办学类型:普通中专学校 by Type:Reg. Specialized Sec. Schools	1964026	2154433	6146217	1716163	1948901	5633339
成人中专学校 Adults Specialized Sec. Schools	149456	179726	402881	77880	100578	264650
职业高中学校 Vocational High Schools	1498184	1759392	4698566	1320919	1572306	4346315
其他中等职业教育机构 Other Secondary Vocational Education Institutions	61273	56383	165958	46529	45141	129635
附设中职班 Secondary Vocational Classes Attached	391042	365301	1129271	376925	364275	1125687
分举办者:1. 中央 Providers:Central Ministries & Agencies	2709	1633	5987	2709	1633	5987
2. 地方 Local Authorities	4061272	4513602	12536906	3535707	4029568	11493639
教育部门 Under Ed. Dept.	2751645	3002838	8357785	2365539	2646373	7595509
其他部门 Run by Non-ed. Dept.	719662	695616	2117085	643348	638334	1959569
地方企业 Run by Local Enterprises	27653	28339	88752	27114	28033	87756
民办 Non-government	562312	786809	1973284	499706	716828	1850805

举办者的中职学生及教职工情况
Vocational Schools by Types and Providers

单位：人
unit：person

中职非全日制学生 Part-time Students of SVSs			教职工数 Educational Personnel							聘请校外教师 Part-time Teachers
				其中：专任教师 of Which：Full-time Teachers						
毕业生数 Graduates	招生数 Entrants	在校学生数 Enrolment	合计 Total	小计 Subtotal	正高级 Senior	副高级 Sub-senior	中级 Middle	初级 Junior	未定职级 No Rank	
525565	**484034**	**1043267**	**811147**	**640398**	**2552**	**159863**	**252228**	**159561**	**66194**	**92005**
223038	210959	438971	409941	343537	1169	76588	135564	91887	38329	43374
247863	205532	512878	396845	301577	1627	75792	116222	74466	33470	43958
71576	79148	138231	59705	44773	316	13423	18871	8407	3756	20261
177265	187086	352251	343767	286053	575	68700	113980	75087	27711	26394
14744	11242	36323	10830	7995	34	1948	3155	1601	1257	1392
14117	1026	3584								
0	0	0	1804	1142	19	319	514	262	28	140
525565	484034	1043267	809343	639256	2533	159544	251714	159299	66166	91865
386106	356465	762276	566125	474612	952	128658	196232	119134	29636	50471
76314	57282	157516	127917	86655	713	23219	33039	21707	7977	31293
539	306	996	7685	4899	37	1292	1716	1353	501	804
62606	69981	122479	107616	73090	831	6375	20727	17105	28052	9297

中等职业学校(机构)
Number of Students in Secondary

	毕业生数 Graduates		招生数 Entrants		
	合计 Total	其中:获得职业资格证书 of Which: Recipients of Vocational Qualifications	合计 Total	其中:应届毕业 of Which: Graduates of Current Year 小计 Subtotal	其中:初中毕业生 of Which: Junior Secondary School Graduates
一、中职学生总计 Students of SVSs Total	**4063981**	**3218321**	**4515235**	**4091506**	**3988053**
其中:中职全日制学生 of Which: full-time Students of SVSs	3538416	2817470	4031201	3865688	3791914
中职非全日制学生 part-time Students of SVSs	525565	400851	484034	225818	196139
1. 普通中专学生 Students of Regular SSSs	2169933	1613369	2462485	2342257	2290316
2. 成人中专学生 Students of Adult SSSs	604125	465546	568771	301868	268056
3. 职业高中学生 Students of Vocational High Schools	1289923	1139406	1483979	1447381	1429681
二、培训学生 Trainees	**4639952**	—	—	—	—
三、外国留学生 Foreign Students	**1091**	—	—	—	—

注:SSSs=中等专业学校
Note:SSSs=Specialized Secondary Schools

中等职业学校(机构)
Number of Female Students in

	毕业生数 Graduates		招生数 Entrants		
	合计 Total	其中:获得职业资格证书 of Which: Recipients of Vocational Qualifications	合计 Total	其中:应届毕业 of Which: Graduates of Current Year 小计 Subtotal	其中:初中毕业生 of Which: Junior Secondary School Graduates
一、中职学生总计 Students of SVSs Total	**1962315**	**1520489**	**2037673**	**1854141**	**1809236**
其中:中职全日制学生 of Which: full-time Students of SVSs	1739277	1350565	1826714	1754632	1723092
中职非全日制学生 part-time Students of SVSs	223038	169924	210959	99509	86144
1. 普通中专学生 Students of Regular SSSs	1129023	816355	1171045	1117001	1093137
2. 成人中专学生 Students of Adult SSSs	257413	198860	242852	128778	114018
3. 职业高中学生 Students of Vocational High Schools	575879	505274	623776	608362	602081
二、培训学生 Trainees	**2142133**	—	—	—	—
三、外国留学生 Foreign Students	**561**	—	—	—	—

注:SSSs=中等专业学校
Note:SSSs=Specialized Secondary Schools

各类学生数
Vocational Schools

单位：人
unit：person

其中：五年制高职中职段 of Which：5-year Secondary Vocational Education	在校学生数 Enrolment 合计 Total	一年级 Grade 1	二年级 Grade 2	三年级 Grade 3	四年级及以上 Over Grade 4	预计毕业生数 Estimated Graduates for Next Year 合计 Total	其中：五年制高职中职段 of Which：5-year Secondary Vocational Education
466928	**12542893**	**4521553**	**4116171**	**3842756**	**62413**	**4136983**	**423538**
466018	11499626	4037285	3822101	3584246	55994	3655101	423538
910	1043267	484268	294070	258510	6419	481882	0
409469	7129894	2465622	2376403	2239882	47987	2272283	378843
2100	1272446	569013	369312	326792	7329	559016	804
55359	4140553	1486918	1370456	1276082	7097	1305684	43891
—	**3318076**	—	—	—	—	—	—
—	**2673**	—	—	—	—	—	—

各类女学生数
Secondary Vocational Schools

单位：人
unit：person

其中：五年制高职中职段 of Which：5-year Secondary Vocational Education	在校学生数 Enrolment 合计 Total	一年级 Grade 1	二年级 Grade 2	三年级 Grade 3	四年级及以上 Over Grade 4	预计毕业生数 Estimated Graduates for Next Year 合计 Total	其中：五年制高职中职段 of Which：5-year Secondary Vocational Education
234834	**5812830**	**2038443**	**1909984**	**1828381**	**36022**	**1893462**	**224866**
234361	5373859	1827757	1789612	1723537	32953	1694740	224866
473	438971	210686	120372	104844	3069	198722	0
210552	3511326	1171427	1169736	1140673	29490	1112519	205060
862	531385	242541	150833	134679	3332	230052	225
23420	1770119	624475	589415	553029	3200	550891	19581
—	**1561247**	—	—	—	—	—	—
—	**1131**	—	—	—	—	—	—

中等职业学校(机构)学生分科类情况(总计)
Number of Students by Field of Education in Secondary Vocational Schools(Total)

单位:人
unit:person

	毕业生数 Graduates		招生数 Entrants			在校学生数 Enrolment	预计毕业生数 Estimated Graduates for Next Year
	合计 Total	其中:获得职业资格证书 of Which: Recipients of Vocational Qualifications	合计 Total	其中:应届毕业 of Which: Graduates of Current Year 小计 Subtotal	其中:应届毕业 of Which: Graduates of Current Year 其中:初中毕业生 of Which: Junior Secondary School Graduates		
总计 Total	**4063981**	**3218321**	**4515235**	**4091506**	**3988053**	**12542893**	**4136983**
其中:女 of Which: Female	1962315	1520489	2037673	1854141	1809236	5812830	1893462
农林牧渔类 Agriculture, Forestry, Husbandry & Fisheries	327628	253383	272369	193919	184678	791192	303254
资源环境类 Resources & Environment	11620	9561	9201	5831	5622	23912	9695
能源与新能源类 Energy Resources & New ER	14899	12306	11533	10482	10146	34601	12200
土木水利类 Civil Engineering & Water Conservancy	184653	144830	144469	126822	122902	408245	142643
加工制造类 Manufacturing	561121	482122	527249	482762	472531	1541284	546322
石油化工 Petroleum & Chemical Industries	21377	17334	16614	15173	14878	48542	17991
轻纺食品 Light, Textile & Food Industries	38371	33766	36737	28549	27872	91537	36176
交通运输类 Communication & Transport.	410055	340580	522275	488807	480754	1438050	458053
信息技术类 Information Technology	650226	546531	796560	736178	721031	2099578	680515
医药卫生类 Medicine, Pharmaceuticals & Health Care	421861	272558	421440	385997	372897	1285590	421168
休闲保健类 Recreations Services & Make-up Artists	24169	19252	34518	31566	31087	90592	28186
财经商贸类 Finance, Economics, Commerce & Trade	463477	363836	517081	480347	469219	1503893	488946
旅游服务类 Tourist Services	194903	162762	274469	252620	248378	709858	215402
文化艺术类 Culture & Arts	200251	151975	262299	239885	231698	714959	212446
体育与健身 Sports & Body-building	31049	22133	53261	49814	48068	136856	37850
教育类 Educational Services	412827	311677	502199	468659	456075	1345980	427029
司法服务类 Legal Services	13744	5952	19521	17969	16778	49669	15110
公共管理与服务类 Public Administration & Services	48311	39290	54432	43628	42022	129670	46879
其他 Others	33439	28473	39008	32498	31417	98885	37118

中等职业学校(机构)学生分科类情况(全日制学生)

Number of Students by Field of Education in Secondary Vocational Schools(Full-time Students)

单位:人
unit: person

	毕业生数 Graduates		招生数 Entrants			在校学生数 Enrolment	预计毕业生数 Estimated Graduates for Next Year
				其中:应届毕业 of Which: Graduates of Current Year			
	合计 Total	其中:获得职业资格证书 of Which: Recipients of Vocational Qualifications	合计 Total	小计 Subtotal	其中:初中毕业生 of Which: Junior Secondary School Graduates		
总 计 Total	**3538416**	**2817470**	**4031201**	**3865688**	**3791914**	**11499626**	**3655101**
其中:女 of Which: Female	1739277	1350565	1826714	1754632	1723092	5373859	1694740
农林牧渔类 Agriculture, Forestry, Husbandry & Fisheries	199552	159485	170127	151571	146454	529448	192728
资源环境类 Resources & Environment	10152	8658	8934	5583	5374	21698	8037
能源与新能源类 Energy Resources & New ER	14036	11503	10638	10246	9917	32360	11135
土木水利类 Civil Engineering & Water Conservancy	166163	131571	126243	120345	117135	373679	128907
加工制造类 Manufacturing	480974	416581	459559	447966	441803	1383751	473194
石油化工 Petroleum & Chemical Industries	19901	16779	14380	14028	13783	44477	16737
轻纺食品 Light, Textile & Food Industries	29904	25695	27798	24983	24590	76909	27275
交通运输类 Communication & Transport.	374258	311959	491320	474171	467734	1359098	423055
信息技术类 Information Technology	547266	460596	702757	683489	672592	1904964	590798
医药卫生类 Medicine, Pharmaceuticals & Health Care	418020	269802	416825	384511	371844	1277873	419094
休闲保健类 Recreations Services & Make-up Artists	22632	17941	32454	30742	30403	84201	24349
财经商贸类 Finance, Economics, Commerce & Trade	432147	341445	481114	464271	455810	1418758	458579
旅游服务类 Tourist Services	173923	145790	251248	243749	240390	661461	192203
文化艺术类 Culture & Arts	181243	137451	242116	230413	223886	674475	193976
体育与健身 Sports & Body-building	30090	21221	52353	49417	47688	133088	35148
教育类 Educational Services	366670	287780	456694	447972	443041	1289721	384459
司法服务类 Legal Services	12927	5280	18688	17335	16492	47743	14243
公共管理与服务类 Public Administration & Services	32606	25624	39577	37870	36802	105683	34050
其他 Others	25952	22309	28376	27026	26176	80239	27134

中等职业学校(机构)学生分科类情况(普通中专)
Number of Students by Field of Education in Secondary Vocational Schools(Regular SSSs)

单位:人
unit: person

	毕业生数 Graduates		招生数 Entrants			在校学生数 Enrolment	预计毕业生数 Estimated Graduates for Next Year
				其中:应届毕业 of Which: Graduates of Current Year			
	合计 Total	其中:获得职业资格证书 of Which: Recipients of Vocational Qualifications	合计 Total	小计 Subtotal	其中:初中毕业生 of Which: Junior Secondary School Graduates		
总　计 Total	**2169933**	**1613369**	**2462485**	**2342257**	**2290316**	**7129894**	**2272283**
其中:女 of Which: Female	1129023	816355	1171045	1117001	1093137	3511326	1112519
农林牧渔类 Agriculture, Forestry, Husbandry & Fisheries	89209	63240	84745	73360	70421	248394	85084
资源环境类 Resources & Environment	6300	5238	7550	4207	4162	16628	5535
能源与新能源类 Energy Resources & New ER	11630	9202	8619	8274	7965	26589	8953
土木水利类 Civil Engineering & Water Conservancy	121624	91362	90040	85584	83216	268518	93991
加工制造类 Manufacturing	264662	217887	258457	250100	246697	784492	268953
石油化工 Petroleum & Chemical Industries	14900	12288	10514	10191	9972	32109	12027
轻纺食品 Light, Textile & Food Industries	12390	9721	13402	12936	12665	38539	13008
交通运输类 Communication & Transport.	223572	179723	294352	281683	278085	826965	258906
信息技术类 Information Technology	264184	210798	355821	344451	338372	963853	296870
医药卫生类 Medicine, Pharmaceuticals & Health Care	374011	233691	364870	334924	323755	1135415	375615
休闲保健类 Recreations Services & Make-up Artists	11550	8578	17179	16340	16053	45483	13132
财经商贸类 Finance, Economics, Commerce & Trade	282595	209757	300967	287878	281555	907122	298728
旅游服务类 Tourist Services	83155	64964	128019	123463	120925	333101	93423
文化艺术类 Culture & Arts	98211	68443	135986	126329	121048	386891	109384
体育与健身 Sports & Body-building	20018	12676	30734	29401	27783	87449	25086
教育类 Educational Services	258464	193808	320148	314089	310024	916606	276175
司法服务类 Legal Services	7711	2405	8435	8013	7257	22429	7596
公共管理与服务类 Public Administration & Services	14851	10234	17569	16101	15785	49372	16875
其他 Others	10896	9354	15078	14933	14576	39939	12942

中等职业学校(机构)学生分科类情况(成人中专)

Number of Students by Field of Education in Secondary Vocational Schools(Adult SSSs)

单位:人
unit: person

	毕业生数 Graduates		招生数 Entrants			在校学生数 Enrolment	预计毕业生数 Estimated Graduates for Next Year
				其中:应届毕业 of Which: Graduates of Current Year			
	合计 Total	其中:获得职业资格证书 of Which: Recipients of Vocational Qualifications	合计 Total	小计 Subtotal	其中:初中毕业生 of Which: Junior Secondary School Graduates		
总　计 Total	**604125**	**465546**	**568771**	**301868**	**268056**	**1272446**	**559016**
其中:女 of Which: Female	257413	198860	242852	128778	114018	531385	230052
农林牧渔类 Agriculture, Forestry, Husbandry & Fisheries	137554	99941	107827	46392	41768	287061	119865
资源环境类 Resources & Environment	1865	1116	340	320	320	2390	1705
能源与新能源类 Energy Resources & New ER	994	924	1230	550	531	3045	1264
土木水利类 Civil Engineering & Water Conservancy	22496	16758	21758	9511	8730	44428	17339
加工制造类 Manufacturing	88542	73372	73569	40439	36199	176451	80444
石油化工 Petroleum & Chemical Industries	1538	617	2234	1145	1095	4105	1294
轻纺食品 Light, Textile & Food Industries	8550	8145	9330	3719	3430	15295	9235
交通运输类 Communication & Transport.	47859	40014	44635	27829	25855	117119	47749
信息技术类 Information Technology	115886	95764	107300	64706	58769	229008	103654
医药卫生类 Medicine, Pharmaceuticals & Health Care	9976	7331	10770	6089	5391	22854	6492
休闲保健类 Recreations Services & Make-up Artists	1882	1632	2168	926	786	7069	4197
财经商贸类 Finance, Economics, Commerce & Trade	39918	30109	43490	23253	19894	106988	38938
旅游服务类 Tourist Services	24135	19727	27606	13206	12298	60560	27014
文化艺术类 Culture & Arts	22061	17253	23950	13152	11428	49421	21041
体育与健身 Sports & Body-building	3495	3014	11788	9923	9833	22181	5026
教育类 Educational Services	50652	27914	50221	25270	17615	69765	47029
司法服务类 Legal Services	1660	777	3255	2424	2044	6765	2081
公共管理与服务类 Public Administration & Services	17409	14812	16478	7352	6639	28362	14571
其他 Others	7653	6326	10822	5662	5431	19579	10078

中等职业学校(机构)学生分科类情况(职业高中)

Number of Students by Field of Education in Secondary Vocational Schools(Vocational High Schools)

单位:人
unit:person

	毕业生数 Graduates		招生数 Entrants			在校学生数 Enrolment	预计毕业生数 Estimated Graduates for Next Year
				其中:应届毕业 of Which: Graduates of Current Year			
	合计 Total	其中:获得职业资格证书 of Which: Recipients of Vocational Qualifications	合计 Total	小计 Subtotal	其中:初中毕业生 of Which: Junior Secondary School Graduates		
总计 Total	**1289923**	**1139406**	**1483979**	**1447381**	**1429681**	**4140553**	**1305684**
其中:女 of Which: Female	575879	505274	623776	608362	602081	1770119	550891
农林牧渔类 Agriculture, Forestry, Husbandry &Fisheries	100865	90202	79797	74167	72489	255737	98305
资源环境类 Resources & Environment	3455	3207	1311	1304	1140	4894	2455
能源与新能源类 Energy Resources & New ER	2275	2180	1684	1658	1650	4967	1983
土木水利类 Civil Engineering & Water Conservancy	40533	36710	32671	31727	30956	95299	31313
加工制造类 Manufacturing	207917	190863	195223	192223	189635	580341	196925
石油化工 Petroleum & Chemical Industries	4939	4429	3866	3837	3811	12328	4670
轻纺食品 Light, Textile & Food Industries	17431	15900	14005	11894	11777	37703	13933
交通运输类 Communication & Transport.	138624	120843	183288	179295	176814	493966	151398
信息技术类 Information Technology	270156	239969	333439	327021	323890	906717	279991
医药卫生类 Medicine, Pharmaceuticals & Health Care	37874	31536	45800	44984	43751	127321	39061
休闲保健类 Recreations Services & Make-up Artists	10737	9042	15171	14300	14248	38040	10857
财经商贸类 Finance, Economics, Commerce & Trade	140964	123970	172624	169216	167770	489783	151280
旅游服务类 Tourist Services	87613	78071	118844	115951	115155	316197	94965
文化艺术类 Culture & Arts	79979	66279	102363	100404	99222	278647	82021
体育与健身 Sports & Body-building	7536	6443	10739	10490	10452	27226	7738
教育类 Educational Services	103711	89955	131830	129300	128436	359609	103825
司法服务类 Legal Services	4373	2770	7831	7532	7477	20475	5433
公共管理与服务类 Public Administration & Services	16051	14244	20385	20175	19598	51936	15433
其他 Others	14890	12793	13108	11903	11410	39367	14098

中等职业学校(机构)分年龄学生数
Number of Students by Age in Secondary Vocational Schools

单位:人
unit: person

	合计 Total	14岁及以下 14 Years and Under	15岁 15 Years	16岁 16 Years	17岁 17 Years	18岁 18 Years	19岁 19 Years	20岁 20 Years	21岁 21 Years	22岁及以上 22 Years and Over
总　计 Total	**12542893**	**207371**	**2060238**	**3327294**	**3256194**	**1837589**	**679760**	**270206**	**165814**	**738427**
中职全日制学生 Full-time Students of SVSs	11499626	206560	2015658	3249678	3162784	1745791	606496	193812	92822	226025
中职非全日制学生 Part-time Students of SVSs	1043267	811	44580	77616	93410	91798	73264	76394	72992	512402
1. 普通中专学生 Students of Regular SSSs	7129894	133260	1194031	1985334	1964385	1118064	402842	138093	62698	131187
2. 成人中专学生 Students of Adult SSSs	1272446	4148	84517	135430	148764	121104	85992	82045	77203	533243
3. 职业高中学生 Students of High Vocational Schools	4140553	69963	781690	1206530	1143045	598421	190926	50068	25913	73997

中等职业学校(机构)分年龄女学生数
Number of Female Students by Age in Secondary Vocational Schools

单位:人
unit: person

	合计 Total	14岁及以下 14 Years and Under	15岁 15 Years	16岁 16 Years	17岁 17 Years	18岁 18 Years	19岁 19 Years	20岁 20 Years	21岁 21 Years	22岁及以上 22 Years and Over
总计 Total	**5812830**	**106036**	**965843**	**1542961**	**1520585**	**847521**	**311746**	**123545**	**75712**	**318881**
中职全日制学生 Full-time Students of SVSs	5373859	105816	945659	1509787	1481129	807375	281997	92007	45449	104640
中职非全日制学生 Part-time Students of SVSs	438971	220	20184	33174	39456	40146	29749	31538	30263	214241
1. 普通中专学生 Students of Regular SSSs	3511326	71848	591973	971675	971899	545563	196738	69126	32035	60469
2. 成人中专学生 Students of Adult SSSs	531385	1888	36931	57159	61908	50216	33989	33792	32226	223276
3. 职业高中学生 Students of High Vocational Schools	1770119	32300	336939	514127	486778	251742	81019	20627	11451	35136

中等职业学校(机构)
Changes in Enrolment of Secondary

	上学年初报表在校学生数 Enrolment at Beginning of Previous Academic Year	增加学生数 Factors of Increase				
		合计 Total	招生 No. of Students Admitted	复学 Students Resuming Studies	转入 Transfers from Other Inst.	其他 Others
总　计 Total	**12758317**	**4871902**	**4515235**	**8456**	**273235**	**74976**
中职全日制学生 Full-time Students of SVSs	11597566	4346917	4031201	8072	250425	57219
中职非全日制学生 Part-time Students of SVSs	1160751	524985	484034	384	22810	17757
1. 普通中专学生 Students of Regular SSSs	7139551	2653899	2462485	5787	141514	44113
2. 成人中专学生 Students of Adult SSSs	1410655	614808	568771	814	26370	18853
3. 职业高中学生 Students of High Vocational Schools	4208111	1603195	1483979	1855	105351	12010

中等职业学校(机构)
Changes in Female Enrolment of

	上学年初报表在校学生数 Enrolment at Beginning of Previous Academic Year	增加学生数 Factors of Increase				
		合计 Total	招生 No. of Students Admitted	复学 Students Resuming Studies	转入 Transfers from Other Inst.	其他 Others
总　计 Total	**6034231**	**2191723**	**2037673**	**3481**	**115954**	**34615**
中职全日制学生 Full-time Students of SVSs	5550500	1965333	1826714	3341	107759	27519
中职非全日制学生 Part-time Students of SVSs	483731	226390	210959	140	8195	7096
1. 普通中专学生 Students of Regular SSSs	3611351	1261764	1171045	2329	65538	22852
2. 成人中专学生 Students of Adult SSSs	588116	261192	242852	400	10407	7533
3. 职业高中学生 Students of High Vocational Schools	1834764	668767	623776	752	40009	4230

学生变动情况
Vocational Schools

单位:人
unit:person

减少学生数 Factors of Decrease									本学年初报表在校学生数 Total Enrolment at Beginning of Current Academic Year
合计 Total	毕业 Graduates	结业 Completers of Courses without Formal Awards	休学 Suspended	退学 Quitting	开除 Expelled	死亡 Dead	转出 Transfers to Other Inst.	其他 Others	
5087326	**4063981**	**100381**	**22111**	**384258**	**5855**	**380**	**385682**	**124678**	**12542893**
4444857	3538416	45918	19906	360968	5836	378	366035	107400	11499626
642469	525565	54463	2205	23290	19	2	19647	17278	1043267
2663556	2169933	30606	15175	232212	4246	234	145359	65791	7129894
753017	604125	55179	2522	35223	94	14	36522	19338	1272446
1670753	1289923	14596	4414	116823	1515	132	203801	39549	4140553

女学生变动情况
Secondary Vocational Schools

单位:人
unit:person

减少学生数 Factors of Decrease									本学年初报表在校学生数 Total Enrolment at Beginning of Current Academic Year
合计 Total	毕业 Graduates	结业 Completers of Courses Without Formal Awards	休学 Suspended	退学 Quitting	开除 Expelled	死亡 Dead	转出 Transfers to Other Inst.	其他 Others	
2413124	**1962315**	**43478**	**9164**	**160492**	**1833**	**92**	**177579**	**58171**	**5812830**
2141974	1739277	19479	7537	151761	1830	92	169605	52393	5373859
271150	223038	23999	1627	8731	3	0	7974	5778	438971
1361789	1129023	13620	5795	102901	1486	55	75671	33238	3511326
317923	257413	24096	1738	11495	22	5	15858	7296	531385
733412	575879	5762	1631	46096	325	32	86050	17637	1770119

中等职业学校(机构)其他学生情况
Supplementary Information on Students in Secondary Vocational Schools

单位:人
unit: person

	共产党员 Member of C. P. A	共青团员 Member of C. Y. L	华侨 Overseas Chinese	港澳台 From HK, Macao and Taiwan	少数民族 Minorities	残疾人 Disabled
总计 Total	**16399**	**6873530**	**136**	**1561**	**1259771**	**19519**
其中:女 of Which: Female	4218	3392518	61	607	571307	7237
中职全日制学生 Full-time Students of SVSs	6486	6631152	134	1560	1153188	19391
中职非全日制学生 Part-time Students of SVSs	9913	242378	2	1	106583	128
1. 普通中专学生 Students of Regular SSSs	4136	3946222	52	1132	739296	8753
2. 成人中专学生 Students of Adult SSSs	10864	355903	6	35	124256	535
3. 职业高中学生 Students of High Vocational Schools	1399	2571405	78	394	396219	10231

中等职业学校(机构)培训学生情况
Number of Trainees in Secondary Vocational Schools

单位:人次
unit: person-time

	结业生数 Graduates		注册学生数 Enrolment	
	合计 Total	其中:女 of Which: Female	合计 Total	其中:女 of Which: Female
总计 Total	**4639952**	**2142133**	**3318076**	**1561247**
其中:少数民族 of Which: Minority	325197	156763	179744	83486
资格证书培训 For Certificates of Vocational Qualifications	1730703	794226	1406190	652355
岗位证书培训 For Certificates of Job-related Qualifications	1547596	733928	1123283	531661
按产业结构分:第一产业类培训 by Industry: Training for First Industry	777247	333608	487596	201560
第二产业类培训 Training for Second Industry	961125	285300	789264	234888
第三产业类培训 Training for Third Industry	2901580	1523225	2041216	1124799
按培训时间分:一个月以内 by Length of Training: 1 Month Under	2924948	1300902	1834252	837854
一个月至三个月以内 1 Month to 3 Months	822364	411649	643207	319625
三个月至半年以内 3 Months to 6 Months	345118	162892	269540	127909
半年至一年以内 6 Months to 1 Year	341575	171801	282715	140360
一年及以上 1 Year and Over	205947	94889	288362	135499

中等职业学校(机构)外国留学生情况

Number of Foreign Students in Secondary Vocational Schools

单位:人
unit: person

	结业生数 Graduates		注册学生数 Enrolment	
	合计 Total	其中:女 of Which: Female	合计 Total	其中:女 of Which: Female
总　计 Total	**1091**	**561**	**2673**	**1131**
按时间分:by Time				
一个月以内 1 Month Under	530	294	460	251
一个月至三个月以内 1 Month to 3 Months	11	5	97	59
三个月至半年以内 3 Months to 6 Months	31	22	104	58
半年至一年以内 6 Months to 1 Year	89	52	140	103
一年及以上 1 Year and Over	430	188	1872	660
按大洲分:by Continent				
亚洲 Asia	917	473	2374	1010
非洲 Africa	3	1	156	46
欧洲 Europe	67	36	100	52
北美洲 North America	98	45	15	6
南美洲 South America	5	5	22	14
大洋洲 Oceania	1	1	6	3

中等职业学校
Number of Educational Personnel in

	教职工数 Educational		
	合计 Total	校本部 Educational Personnel	
		小计 Subtotal	专任教师 Full-time Teachers
总　计 Total	**811147**	**804848**	**640398**
其中:女 of Which: Female	409941	407021	343537
正高级 Senior	3560	3556	2552
副高级 Sub-senior	183026	182739	159863
中　级 Middle	285906	285254	252228
初　级 Junior	186009	185214	159561
未定职级 No-ranking	152646	148085	66194
总计中:聘任制 of Which:Part-time	187170	185722	144968
其中:女 of Which: Female	96209	95396	77587
正高级 Senior	878	878	633
副高级 Sub-senior	31183	31160	27904
中　级 Middle	58443	58347	52216
初　级 Junior	44242	43919	38182
未定职级 No-ranking	52424	51418	26033

中等职业学校(机构)
Number of Educational Personnel in

	教职工数 Educational		
	合计 Total	校本部 Educational Personne	
		小计 Subtotal	专任教师 Full-time Teachers
总　计 Total	**396845**	**393425**	**301577**
其中:女 of Which: Female	199549	197970	161544
正高级 Senior	2195	2193	1627
副高级 Sub-senior	86273	86186	75792
中　级 Middle	133845	133635	116222
初　级 Junior	90479	89991	74466
未定职级 No-ranking	84053	81420	33470
总计中:聘任制 of Which:Part-time	89139	88059	66467
其中:女 of Which: Female	45868	45270	35575
正高级 Senior	425	425	328
副高级 Sub-senior	13836	13830	12470
中　级 Middle	26194	26133	23207
初　级 Junior	21454	21156	17648
未定职级 No-ranking	27230	26515	12814

(机构)教职工数(总计)
Secondary Vocational Schools (Total)

单位:人
unit:person

Personnel 教职工 in Main Campus: 行政人员 Adm. Personnel	教辅人员 Supporting Staff	工勤人员 Workers	校办企业职工 Employees in School-run Factories & Farms	其他附设机构人员 Personnel in Others Subsidiary Units	聘请校外教师 Part-time Teachers
65681	**49028**	**49741**	**3227**	**3072**	**92005**
24257	24121	15106	1327	1593	43374
860	123	21	0	4	2368
16543	5990	343	24	263	16824
16432	15454	1140	32	620	29104
10544	13933	1176	52	743	13943
21302	13528	47061	3119	1442	29766
15180	12117	13457	509	939	—
6440	6136	5233	217	596	—
214	30	1	0	0	—
2201	989	66	3	20	—
3115	2789	227	4	92	—
2502	2983	252	8	315	—
7148	5326	12911	494	512	—

教职工数(普通中专)
Secondary Vocational Schools (Regular SSSs)

单位:人
unit:person

Personnel 教职工 in Main Campus: 行政人员 Adm. Personnel	教辅人员 Supporting Staff	工勤人员 Workers	校办企业职工 Employees in School-run Factories & Farms	其他附设机构人员 Personnel in Others Subsidiary Units	聘请校外教师 Part-time Teachers
38862	**25007**	**27979**	**1736**	**1684**	**43958**
15404	12761	8261	623	956	22641
475	78	13	0	2	1156
7708	2479	207	19	68	7161
9337	7481	595	19	191	12449
7242	7512	771	43	445	7747
14100	7457	26393	1655	978	15445
8206	6182	7204	314	766	—
3692	3244	2759	107	491	—
85	12	0	0	0	—
978	345	37	3	3	—
1543	1249	134	4	57	—
1587	1764	157	8	290	—
4013	2812	6876	299	416	—

中等职业学校(机构)

Number of Educational Personnel in Secondary

	教职工数 Educational		
	合计 Total	校本部 Educational Personnel	
		小计 Subtotal	专任教师 Full-time Teachers
总　计 Total	**59705**	**58906**	**44773**
其中:女 of Which: Female	29693	29289	23951
正高级 Senior	410	410	316
副高级 Sub-senior	15764	15749	13423
中　级 Middle	22157	22142	18871
初　级 Junior	10495	10487	8407
未定职级 No-ranking	10879	10118	3756
总计中:聘任制 of Which:Part-time	12802	12718	9174
其中:女 of Which: Female	6702	6639	5034
正高级 Senior	82	82	68
副高级 Sub-senior	2208	2208	1892
中　级 Middle	3922	3922	3256
初　级 Junior	2560	2560	2085
未定职级 No-ranking	4030	3946	1873

中等职业学校(机构)

Number of Educational Personnel in Secondary

	教职工数 Educational		
	合计 Total	校本部 Educational Personnel	
		小计 Subtotal	专任教师 Full-time Teachers
总　计 Total	**343767**	**341698**	**286053**
其中:女 of Which: Female	175635	174699	153938
正高级 Senior	902	900	575
副高级 Sub-senior	78559	78374	68700
中　级 Middle	126215	125788	113980
初　级 Junior	82994	82695	75087
未定职级 No-ranking	55097	53941	27711
总计中:聘任制 of Which:Part-time	83088	82804	67708
其中:女 of Which: Female	42508	42356	36019
正高级 Senior	360	360	230
副高级 Sub-senior	14860	14843	13308
中　级 Middle	27704	27669	25199
初　级 Junior	19670	19645	18010
未定职级 No-ranking	20494	20287	10961

教职工数(成人中专)
Vocational Schools (Adult SSSs)

单位:人
unit:person

Personnel 教 职 工 in Main Campus 行政人员 Adm. Personnel	教辅人员 Supporting Staff	工勤人员 Workers	校办企业职工 Employees in School-run Factories & Farms	其他附设机构人员 Personnel in Others Subsidiary Units	聘请校外教师 Part-time Teachers
6105	**4319**	**3709**	**682**	**117**	**20261**
2054	2066	1218	371	33	7177
87	6	1	0	0	878
1756	550	20	0	15	6273
1681	1521	69	0	15	10145
905	1133	42	0	8	2073
1676	1109	3577	682	79	892
1398	1135	1011	78	6	—
538	573	494	60	3	—
14	0	0	0	0	—
180	136	0	0	0	—
302	360	4	0	0	—
229	240	6	0	0	—
673	399	1001	78	6	—

教职工数(职业高中)
Vocational Schools (Vocational High Schools)

单位:人
unit:person

Personnel 教 职 工 in Main Campus 行政人员 Adm. Personnel	教辅人员 Supporting Staff	工勤人员 Workers	校办企业职工 Employees in School-run Factories & Farms	其他附设机构人员 Personnel in Others Subsidiary Units	聘请校外教师 Part-time Teachers
19431	**18877**	**17337**	**809**	**1260**	**26394**
6393	8923	5445	333	603	12858
281	38	6	0	2	303
6670	2893	111	5	180	3047
5100	6249	459	13	414	5942
2191	5075	342	9	290	3903
5189	4622	16419	782	374	13199
5340	4688	5068	117	167	—
2137	2270	1930	50	102	—
112	18	0	0	0	—
1003	505	27	0	17	—
1230	1160	80	0	35	—
618	938	79	0	25	—
2377	2067	4882	117	90	—

中等职业学校(机构)

Number of Educational Personnel in Secondary

	教职工数 Educational		
	合计 Total	校本部 Educational Personnel	
		小计 Subtotal	专任教师 Full-time Teachers
总　计 Total	**10830**	**10819**	**7995**
其中:女 of Which: Female	5064	5063	4104
正高级 Senior	53	53	34
副高级 Sub-senior	2430	2430	1948
中　级 Middle	3689	3689	3155
初　级 Junior	2041	2041	1601
未定职级 No-ranking	2617	2606	1257
总计中:聘任制 of Which:Part-time	2141	2141	1619
其中:女 of Which: Female	1131	1131	959
正高级 Senior	11	11	7
副高级 Sub-senior	279	279	234
中　级 Middle	623	623	554
初　级 Junior	558	558	439
未定职级 No-ranking	670	670	385

教职工数(其他中等职业教育机构)
Vocational Schools (Other Secondary Vocational Education Institutions)

单位:人
unit:person

Personnel 教 职 工 in Main Campus			校办企业职工 Employees in School-run Factories & Farms	其他附设机构人员 Personnel in Others Subsidiary Units	聘请校外教师 Part-time Teachers
行政人员 Adm. Personnel	教辅人员 Supporting Staff	工勤人员 Workers			
1283	**825**	**716**	**0**	**11**	**1392**
406	371	182	0	1	698
17	1	1	0	0	31
409	68	5	0	0	343
314	203	17	0	0	568
206	213	21	0	0	220
337	340	672	0	11	230
236	112	174	0	0	—
73	49	50	0	0	—
3	0	1	0	0	—
40	3	2	0	0	—
40	20	9	0	0	—
68	41	10	0	0	—
85	48	152	0	0	—

中等职业学校(机构)分科专任教师数(总计)
Number of Full-time Teachers by Field of Education in Secondary Vocational Schools(Total)

单位:人
unit:person

	合计 Total	其中:女 of Which: Female	正高级 Senior	副高级 Sub-Senior	中级 Middle	初级 Junior	未定职级 No-ranking
总　计 Total	**640398**	**343537**	**2552**	**159863**	**252228**	**159561**	**66194**
其中:女 of Which: Female	343537	—	1169	76588	135564	91887	38329
文化基础课 General Required Subjects	265472	151625	698	75653	108854	58344	21923
专业课 Specialized Subjects	350740	183238	1795	79715	133910	94516	40804
农林牧渔类 Agriculture, Forestry, Animal Husbandry & Fisheries	18873	8514	159	5902	7732	4051	1029
资源环境类 Resources & Environment	1682	716	8	434	665	432	143
能源与新能源类 Energy Resources & New ER	2219	947	8	633	815	556	207
土木水利类 Civil Engineering & Water Conservancy	11004	5050	52	2572	3823	3220	1337
加工制造类 Manufacturing	46205	17419	201	11444	17416	12482	4662
石油化工类 Petroleum & Chemical Industries	2852	1293	23	902	1058	662	207
轻纺食品类 Light, Textile & Food Industries	4197	2370	14	915	1445	1214	609
交通运输类 Communication & Transport	22259	7539	112	3700	7471	6765	4211
信息技术类 Information Technology	59704	30060	153	12550	25475	15300	6226
医药卫生类 Medicine, Pharmacy & Health Care	24131	16174	405	6091	8973	6048	2614
休闲保健类 Recreation Services & Make-up Artists	1613	949	6	274	598	454	281
财经商贸类 Finance, Economics, Commerce & Trade	38225	25200	138	9572	14439	9856	4220
旅游服务类 Tourist Services	17692	11585	41	3619	6508	5084	2440
文化艺术类 Culture & Arts	33132	21146	235	5457	12058	10572	4810
体育与健身 Sports & Body-building	14680	4127	63	3036	5805	4091	1685
教育类 Educational Services	35370	21745	102	9072	13452	9281	3463
司法服务类 Legal Services	1860	846	12	320	686	384	458
公共管理与服务类 Public Administration & Services	5091	2787	32	981	1873	1404	801
其他 Others	9951	4771	31	2241	3618	2660	1401
实习指导课 Practice Guidance Lessons	24186	8674	59	4495	9464	6701	3467

中等职业学校(机构)分科专任教师数(普通中专)
Number of Full-time Teachers by Field of Education in Secondary Vocational Schools(Regular SSSs)

单位:人
unit:person

	合计 Total	其中:女 of Which: Female	正高级 Senior	副高级 Sub-Senior	中级 Middle	初级 Junior	未定职级 No-ranking
总　计 Total	**301577**	**161544**	**1627**	**75792**	**116222**	**74466**	**33470**
其中:女 of Which: Female	161544	—	792	37012	62230	42285	19225
文化基础课 General Required Subjects	109078	62330	402	31215	44026	23612	9823
专业课 Specialized Subjects	180201	95085	1194	42591	67580	47198	21638
农林牧渔类 Agriculture, Forestry, Animal Husbandry & Fisheries	6637	2892	55	2349	2451	1328	454
资源环境类 Resources & Environment	1009	465	4	303	394	249	59
能源与新能源类 Energy Resources & New ER	1484	612	4	467	534	354	125
土木水利类 Civil Engineering & Water Conservancy	6740	3222	45	1683	2301	1943	768
加工制造类 Manufacturing	24258	9401	143	6269	9118	6239	2489
石油化工类 Petroleum & Chemical Industries	1840	842	21	633	664	416	106
轻纺食品类 Light, Textile & Food Industries	1971	1141	9	455	661	496	350
交通运输类 Communication & Transport	11495	4011	69	1942	3724	3481	2279
信息技术类 Information Technology	27618	13715	88	5953	11787	6701	3089
医药卫生类 Medicine, Pharmacy & Health Care	18585	12740	317	4977	6938	4486	1867
休闲保健类 Recreation Services & Make-up Artists	646	393	4	99	239	182	122
财经商贸类 Finance, Economics, Commerce & Trade	21576	14084	100	5646	8023	5350	2457
旅游服务类 Tourist Services	7492	4737	22	1576	2733	2056	1105
文化艺术类 Culture & Arts	17613	11124	164	3099	6395	5419	2536
体育与健身 Sports & Body-building	8368	2411	55	1969	3282	2311	751
教育类 Educational Services	14892	9248	56	3477	5382	4188	1789
司法服务类 Legal Services	1079	517	10	220	406	216	227
公共管理与服务类 Public Administration & Services	2291	1230	12	412	848	624	395
其他 Others	4607	2300	16	1062	1700	1159	670
实习指导课 Practice Guidance Lessons	12298	4129	31	1986	4616	3656	2009

中等职业学校(机构)分科专任教师数(成人中专)
Number of Full-time Teachers by Field of Education in Secondary Vocational Schools(Adult SSSs)

单位:人
unit:person

	合计 Total	其中:女 of Which: Female	正高级 Senior	副高级 Sub-Senior	中级 Middle	初级 Junior	未定职级 No-ranking
总 计 Total	**44773**	**23951**	**316**	**13423**	**18871**	**8407**	**3756**
其中:女 of Which: Female	23951	—	110	6408	10510	4759	2164
文化基础课 General Required Subjects	23051	13098	88	7451	9862	4000	1650
专业课 Specialized Subjects	19037	9529	218	5047	7888	3978	1906
农林牧渔类 Agriculture, Forestry, Animal Husbandry & Fisheries	4154	1813	86	1004	1992	918	154
资源环境类 Resources & Environment	86	26	1	33	33	14	5
能源与新能源类 Energy Resources & New ER	165	62	2	45	87	24	7
土木水利类 Civil Engineering & Water Conservancy	370	203	1	95	121	90	63
加工制造类 Manufacturing	977	370	9	238	350	250	130
石油化工类 Petroleum & Chemical Industries	23	10	0	3	10	6	4
轻纺食品类 Light, Textile & Food Industries	183	52	0	28	66	73	16
交通运输类 Communication & Transport	957	430	10	87	287	285	288
信息技术类 Information Technology	1520	667	13	301	600	363	243
医药卫生类 Medicine, Pharmacy & Health Care	895	557	39	273	337	195	51
休闲保健类 Recreation Services & Make-up Artists	44	20	0	9	19	11	5
财经商贸类 Finance, Economics, Commerce & Trade	836	493	15	264	317	124	116
旅游服务类 Tourist Services	303	195	1	56	98	78	70
文化艺术类 Culture & Arts	727	421	4	63	217	257	186
体育与健身 Sports & Body-building	492	101	1	39	150	78	224
教育类 Educational Services	6203	3551	21	2293	2813	905	171
司法服务类 Legal Services	54	32	1	10	18	14	11
公共管理与服务类 Public Administration & Services	255	144	11	59	82	44	59
其他 Others	793	382	3	147	291	249	103
实习指导课 Practice Guidance Lessons	2685	1324	10	925	1121	429	200

中等职业学校(机构)分科专任教师数(职业高中)
Number of Full-time Teachers by Field of Education in Secondary Vocational Schools(Vocational High Schools)

单位:人
unit:person

	合计 Total	其中:女 of Which: Female	正高级 Senior	副高级 Sub-Senior	中级 Middle	初级 Junior	未定职级 No-ranking
总计 Total	**286053**	**153938**	**575**	**68700**	**113980**	**75087**	**27711**
其中:女 of Which: Female	153938	—	253	32314	61225	43949	16197
文化基础课 General Required Subjects	129862	74281	199	36112	53598	30043	9910
专业课 Specialized Subjects	147367	76570	360	31081	56824	42506	16596
农林牧渔类 Agriculture, Forestry, Animal Husbandry & Fisheries	7998	3763	18	2506	3267	1787	420
资源环境类 Resources & Environment	555	219	3	89	220	164	79
能源与新能源类 Energy Resources & New ER	568	272	2	120	193	178	75
土木水利类 Civil Engineering & Water Conservancy	3788	1585	6	776	1376	1156	474
加工制造类 Manufacturing	20509	7476	43	4817	7746	5911	1992
石油化工类 Petroleum & Chemical Industries	984	439	2	265	380	240	97
轻纺食品类 Light, Textile & Food Industries	2019	1166	5	428	712	636	238
交通运输类 Communication & Transport	9541	3019	32	1630	3398	2942	1539
信息技术类 Information Technology	30021	15382	52	6197	12853	8125	2794
医药卫生类 Medicine, Pharmacy & Health Care	4220	2683	41	727	1490	1293	669
休闲保健类 Recreation Services & Make-up Artists	917	531	2	166	338	261	150
财经商贸类 Finance, Economics, Commerce & Trade	15408	10341	23	3582	5960	4280	1563
旅游服务类 Tourist Services	9747	6553	18	1969	3626	2900	1234
文化艺术类 Culture & Arts	14525	9427	66	2249	5332	4847	2031
体育与健身 Sports & Body-building	5442	1498	5	927	2253	1618	639
教育类 Educational Services	13540	8515	22	3071	4947	4062	1438
司法服务类 Legal Services	705	286	1	81	255	150	218
公共管理与服务类 Public Administration & Services	2473	1382	9	495	916	723	330
其他 Others	4407	2033	10	986	1562	1233	616
实习指导课 Practice Guidance Lessons	8824	3087	16	1507	3558	2538	1205

中等职业学校(机构)分科专任教师数(其他中等职业教育机构)
Number of Full-time Teachers by Field of Education in Secondary Vocational Schools(Other Secondary Vocational Education Institutions)

单位:人
unit:person

	合计 Total	其中:女 of Which: Female	正高级 Senior	副高级 Sub-Senior	中级 Middle	初级 Junior	未定职级 No-ranking
总计 Total	**7995**	**4104**	**34**	**1948**	**3155**	**1601**	**1257**
其中:女 of Which: Female	4104	—	14	854	1599	894	743
文化基础课 General Required Subjects	3481	1916	9	875	1368	689	540
专业课 Specialized Subjects	4135	2054	23	996	1618	834	664
农林牧渔类 Agriculture, Forestry, Animal Husbandry & Fisheries	84	46	0	43	22	18	1
资源环境类 Resources & Environment	32	6	0	9	18	5	0
能源与新能源类 Energy Resources & New ER	2	1	0	1	1	0	0
土木水利类 Civil Engineering & Water Conservancy	106	40	0	18	25	31	32
加工制造类 Manufacturing	461	172	6	120	202	82	51
石油化工类 Petroleum & Chemical Industries	5	2	0	1	4	0	0
轻纺食品类 Light, Textile & Food Industries	24	11	0	4	6	9	5
交通运输类 Communication & Transport	266	79	1	41	62	57	105
信息技术类 Information Technology	545	296	0	99	235	111	100
医药卫生类 Medicine, Pharmacy & Health Care	431	194	8	114	208	74	27
休闲保健类 Recreation Services & Make-up Artists	6	5	0	0	2	0	4
财经商贸类 Finance, Economics, Commerce & Trade	405	282	0	80	139	102	84
旅游服务类 Tourist Services	150	100	0	18	51	50	31
文化艺术类 Culture & Arts	267	174	1	46	114	49	57
体育与健身 Sports & Body-building	378	117	2	101	120	84	71
教育类 Educational Services	735	431	3	231	310	126	65
司法服务类 Legal Services	22	11	0	9	7	4	2
公共管理与服务类 Public Administration & Services	72	31	0	15	27	13	17
其他 Others	144	56	2	46	65	19	12
实习指导课 Practice Guidance Lessons	379	134	2	77	169	78	53

中等职业学校(机构)专任教师、聘请校外教师学历情况(合计)

Number of Full-time and Part-time Teachers by Academic Qualifications in Secondary Vocational Schools(Total)

单位:人
unit:person

	合计 Total	博士研究生 Doctors	硕士研究生 Masters	本科 Normal Courses	专科 Short-cycle Courses	高中阶段及以下 Below High School Graduate
1. 专任教师 Full-time Teacher	640398	526	48429	537558	51709	2176
其中:女 of Which: Female	343537	239	31051	290383	21262	602
实习指导课教师 Practice Course Teacher	24186	4	917	17964	4886	415
正高级 Senior	2552	79	514	1804	144	11
副高级 Sub-senior	159863	184	12031	141459	6070	119
中　级 Middle	252228	179	20567	212792	18138	552
初　级 Junior	159561	46	9428	134141	15273	673
未定职级 No-ranking	66194	38	5889	47362	12084	821
2. 聘请校外教师 Part-time Teacher	92005	688	7354	67588	15105	1270
其中:女 of Which: Female	43374	333	3942	32845	5945	309
实习指导课教师 Practice Course Teacher	7544	34	526	4882	1872	230
外籍教师 Foreign Teachers Among Part-time Teachers	188	11	24	138	14	1
正高级 Senior	2368	139	531	1472	188	38
副高级 Sub-senior	16824	281	1927	13184	1351	81
中　级 Middle	29104	146	2192	22088	4514	164
初　级 Junior	13943	49	1139	10143	2511	101
未定职级 No-ranking	29766	73	1565	20701	6541	886

中等职业学校(机构)专任教师、聘请校外教师学历情况(普通中专)

Number of Full-time and Part-time Teachers by Academic Qualifications in Secondary Vocational Schools(Regular SSSs)

单位:人
unit: person

	合计 Total	博士研究生 Doctors	硕士研究生 Masters	本科 Normal Courses	专科 Short-cycle Courses	高中阶段及以下 Below High School Graduate
1. 专任教师 Full-time Teacher	301577	352	31747	246737	21390	1351
其中:女 of Which: Female	161544	166	20517	131924	8573	364
实习指导课教师 Practice Course Teacher	12298	0	551	8823	2614	310
正高级 Senior	1627	55	345	1143	74	10
副高级 Sub-senior	75792	130	8008	65340	2235	79
中　级 Middle	116222	124	13529	95030	7234	305
初　级 Junior	74466	20	6199	61589	6250	408
未定职级 No-ranking	33470	23	3666	23635	5597	549
2. 聘请校外教师 Part-time Teacher	43958	373	4786	32884	5232	683
其中:女 of Which: Female	22641	194	2667	17551	2057	172
实习指导课教师 Practice Course Teacher	3472	8	306	2302	731	125
外籍教师 Foreign Teachers Among Part-time Teachers	85	7	11	60	7	0
正高级 Senior	1156	67	230	707	124	28
副高级 Sub-senior	7161	120	1086	5508	408	39
中　级 Middle	12449	104	1457	9713	1080	95
初　级 Junior	7747	44	885	5754	1019	45
未定职级 No-ranking	15445	38	1128	11202	2601	476

中等职业学校(机构)专任教师、聘请校外教师学历情况(成人中专)

Number of Full-time and Part-time Teachers by Academic Qualifications in Secondary Vocational Schools(Adult SSSs)

单位:人
unit: person

	合计 Total	博士研究生 Doctors	硕士研究生 Masters	本科 Normal Courses	专科 Short-cycle Courses	高中阶段及以下 Below High School Graduate
1. 专任教师 Full-time Teacher	44773	42	2183	35451	6959	138
其中:女 of Which: Female	23951	21	1216	19321	3338	55
实习指导课教师 Practice Course Teacher	2685	2	109	1960	608	6
正高级 Senior	316	10	64	224	18	0
副高级 Sub-senior	13423	24	716	11595	1076	12
中　级 Middle	18871	4	812	15025	2954	76
初　级 Junior	8407	3	345	6068	1963	28
未定职级 No-ranking	3756	1	246	2539	948	22
2. 聘请校外教师 Part-time Teacher	20261	99	1209	14831	4033	89
其中:女 of Which: Female	7177	30	518	5078	1512	39
实习指导课教师 Practice Course Teacher	1502	1	120	904	453	24
外籍教师 Foreign Teachers Among Part-time Teachers	6	0	1	3	2	0
正高级 Senior	878	42	234	563	39	0
副高级 Sub-senior	6273	34	494	5041	674	30
中　级 Middle	10145	14	302	7316	2476	37
初　级 Junior	2073	5	94	1314	641	19
未定职级 No-ranking	892	4	85	597	203	3

中等职业学校(机构)专任教师、聘请校外教师学历情况(职业高中)

Number of Full-time and Part-time Teachers by Academic Qualifications in Secondary Vocational Schools(Vocational High Schools)

单位:人
unit: person

	合计 Total	博士研究生 Doctors	硕士研究生 Masters	本科 Normal Courses	专科 Short-cycle Courses	高中阶段及以下 Below High School Graduate
1. 专任教师 Full-time Teacher	286053	107	13658	249077	22562	649
其中:女 of Which: Female	153938	40	8803	135934	8987	174
实习指导课教师 Practice Course Teacher	8824	2	210	6923	1591	98
正高级 Senior	575	14	98	410	52	1
副高级 Sub-senior	68700	26	3114	62851	2681	28
中　级 Middle	113980	34	5864	100241	7675	166
初　级 Junior	75087	20	2719	65245	6873	230
未定职级 No-ranking	27711	13	1863	20330	5281	224
2. 聘请校外教师 Part-time Teacher	26394	215	1141	18833	5718	487
其中:女 of Which: Female	12858	108	636	9711	2309	94
实习指导课教师 Practice Course Teacher	2335	25	95	1483	655	77
外籍教师 Foreign Teachers Among Part-time Teachers	94	4	12	73	4	1
正高级 Senior	303	30	66	178	22	7
副高级 Sub-senior	3047	127	272	2384	253	11
中　级 Middle	5942	27	361	4624	898	32
初　级 Junior	3903	0	104	2929	833	37
未定职级 No-ranking	13199	31	338	8718	3712	400

中等职业学校（机构）专任教师、聘请校外教师学历情况（其他中等职业教育机构）

Number of Full-time and Part-time Teachers by Academic Qualifications in Secondary Vocational Schools (Other Secondary Vocational Education Institutions)

单位：人
unit: person

	合计 Total	博士研究生 Doctors	硕士研究生 Masters	本科 Normal Courses	专科 Short-cycle Courses	高中阶段及以下 Below High School Graduate
1. 专任教师 Full-time Teacher	7995	25	841	6293	798	38
其中：女 of Which: Female	4104	12	515	3204	364	9
实习指导课教师 Practice Course Teacher	379	0	47	258	73	1
正高级 Senior	34	0	7	27	0	0
副高级 Sub-senior	1948	4	193	1673	78	0
中　级 Middle	3155	17	362	2496	275	5
初　级 Junior	1601	3	165	1239	187	7
未定职级 No-ranking	1257	1	114	858	258	26
2. 聘请校外教师 Part-time Teacher	1392	1	218	1040	122	11
其中：女 of Which: Female	698	1	121	505	67	4
实习指导课教师 Practice Course Teacher	235	0	5	193	33	4
外籍教师 Foreign Teachers Among Part-time Teachers	3	0	0	2	1	0
正高级 Senior	31	0	1	24	3	3
副高级 Sub-senior	343	0	75	251	16	1
中　级 Middle	568	1	72	435	60	0
初　级 Junior	220	0	56	146	18	0
未定职级 No-ranking	230	0	14	184	25	7

中等职业学校(机构)

Number of Full-time Teachers by Age in

	合计 Total	29 岁及以下 29 and Under	30-34 岁 30 to 34	35-39 岁 35 to 39
总　计 Total	**640398**	**105870**	**111103**	**116139**
其中:女 of Which: Female	343537	67651	66639	66886
正高级 Senior	2552	0	2	90
副高级 Sub-senior	159863	5	1164	11418
中　级 Middle	252228	7550	43161	69696
初　级 Junior	159561	52740	54434	30517
未定职级 No-ranking	66194	45575	12342	4418
普通中专学校 Regular SSSs	301577	53196	56729	53244
其中:女 of Which: Female	161544	34222	33902	30405
正高级 Senior	1627	0	2	49
副高级 Sub-senior	75792	2	633	5914
中　级 Middle	116222	3946	23976	32599
初　级 Junior	74466	26661	25686	12346
未定职级 No-ranking	33470	22587	6432	2336
成人中专学校 Adult SSSs	44773	5240	5325	6824
其中:女 of Which: Female	23951	3097	2877	4108
正高级 Senior	316	0	0	20
副高级 Sub-senior	13423	0	84	621
中　级 Middle	18871	525	2121	3948
初　级 Junior	8407	2230	2368	1940
未定职级 No-ranking	3756	2485	752	295
职业高中学校 High Vocational Schools	286053	46064	47649	54716
其中:女 of Which: Female	153938	29507	29013	31571
正高级 Senior	575	0	0	21
副高级 Sub-senior	68700	3	424	4748
中　级 Middle	113980	3003	16513	32338
初　级 Junior	75087	23388	25806	15901
未定职级 No-ranking	27711	19670	4906	1708
其他中等职业教育机构 Other Secondary Vocational Education Institutions	7995	1370	1400	1355
其中:女 of Which: Female	4104	825	847	802
正高级 Senior	34	0	0	0
副高级 Sub-senior	1948	0	23	135
中　级 Middle	3155	76	551	811
初　级 Junior	1601	461	574	330
未定职级 No-ranking	1257	833	252	79

专任教师分年龄情况
Secondary Vocational Schools

单位:人
unit:person

40-44 岁 40 to 44	45-49 岁 45 to 49	50-54 岁 50 to 54	55-59 岁 55 to 59	60 岁及以上 60 and over
105683	**101067**	**76027**	**23271**	**1238**
57346	49522	33045	2183	265
213	553	1007	519	168
32349	50963	48732	14608	624
59472	41406	23599	7041	303
11734	6955	2268	884	29
1915	1190	421	219	114
45374	45065	36312	11006	651
23868	21718	16007	1272	150
134	349	660	337	96
14957	23349	23653	6954	330
24061	17670	10664	3153	153
5217	3049	1060	432	15
1005	648	275	130	57
8099	8796	7705	2697	87
4840	5001	3774	239	15
25	64	134	59	14
2114	3892	4842	1825	45
4880	4133	2505	735	24
940	636	215	77	1
140	71	9	1	3
51016	45911	31037	9172	488
28014	22265	12842	629	97
50	130	202	114	58
14919	23151	19621	5589	245
29859	18990	10127	3029	121
5460	3199	963	357	13
728	441	124	83	51
1194	1295	973	396	12
624	538	422	43	3
4	10	11	9	0
359	571	616	240	4
672	613	303	124	5
117	71	30	18	0
42	30	13	5	3

	本学年授课专任教师 Full-time Teacher by Teaching Content			
	合计 Total	文化基础课 Common Required Subject	专业课、实习指导课 Special Subject and Practice Course	
			小计 Subtotal	其中:双师型 of Which:Double-teacher Type
总　计 Total	**631582**	**262154**	**369428**	**192026**
其中:女 of Which: Female	339173	149970	189203	94002
正高级 Senior	2492	687	1805	946
副高级 Sub-senior	157146	74626	82520	51745
中　级 Middle	248764	107484	141280	84346
初　级 Junior	157630	57581	100049	46942
未定职级 No-ranking	65550	21776	43774	8047
普通中专学校 Regular SSSs	298303	107880	190423	102841
其中:女 of Which: Female	160020	61763	98257	50896
正高级 Senior	1588	394	1194	700
副高级 Sub-senior	74935	30860	44075	29282
中　级 Middle	115028	43588	71440	44945
初　级 Junior	73710	23315	50395	23664
未定职级 No-ranking	33042	9723	23319	4250
成人中专学校 Adult SSSs	42332	22396	19936	5026
其中:女 of Which: Female	22549	12732	9817	2342
正高级 Senior	308	86	222	55
副高级 Sub-senior	12452	7234	5218	1334
中　级 Middle	17828	9552	8276	2237
初　级 Junior	8042	3885	4157	1219
未定职级 No-ranking	3702	1639	2063	181
职业高中学校 High Vocational Schools	283038	128462	154576	82335
其中:女 of Which: Female	152538	73589	78949	40031
正高级 Senior	562	198	364	178
副高级 Sub-senior	67822	35666	32156	20597
中　级 Middle	112791	53005	59786	36340
初　级 Junior	74310	29717	44593	21751
未定职级 No-ranking	27553	9876	17677	3469
其他中等职业教育机构 Other Secondary Vocational Education Institutions	7909	3416	4493	1824
其中:女 of Which: Female	4066	1886	2180	733
正高级 Senior	34	9	25	13
副高级 Sub-senior	1937	866	1071	532
中　级 Middle	3117	1339	1778	824
初　级 Junior	1568	664	904	308
未定职级 No-ranking	1253	538	715	147

聘请校外教师岗位分类情况
by Teaching Course in Secondary Vocational Schools

单位：人
unit：person

本学年授课聘请校外教师 Part-time Teacher by Teaching Content				本学年不授课专任教师 Full-time Teacher by Non-teaching			
合计 Total	文化基础课 Common Required Subject	专业课、实习指导课 Special Subject and Practice Course		合计 Total	进修 In-service	病休 Sick-leave	其他 Others
		小计 Subtotal	其中：双师型 of Which: Double-teacher Type				
92005	**23011**	**68994**	**22268**	**8816**	**766**	**931**	**7119**
43374	13265	30109	9336	4364	392	527	3445
2368	452	1916	760	60	6	1	53
16824	3485	13339	5808	2717	210	229	2278
29104	6553	22551	8827	3464	357	386	2721
13943	3859	10084	3026	1931	141	284	1506
29766	8662	21104	3847	644	52	31	561
43958	11485	32473	11115	3274	222	363	2689
22641	6783	15858	5210	1524	87	214	1223
1156	177	979	469	39	4	1	34
7161	1455	5706	2597	857	30	103	724
12449	2896	9553	4082	1194	116	147	931
7747	2102	5645	1802	756	49	89	618
15445	4855	10590	2165	428	23	23	382
20261	4836	15425	4627	2441	314	23	2104
7177	2324	4853	1564	1402	200	10	1192
878	214	664	153	8	2	0	6
6273	1357	4916	1773	971	138	4	829
10145	2311	7834	2317	1043	144	9	890
2073	691	1382	356	365	24	10	331
892	263	629	28	54	6	0	48
26394	6283	20111	6301	3015	219	545	2251
12858	3914	8944	2502	1400	100	303	997
303	56	247	135	13	0	0	13
3047	567	2480	1358	878	40	122	716
5942	1171	4771	2327	1189	94	230	865
3903	976	2927	843	777	62	185	530
13199	3513	9686	1638	158	23	8	127
1392	407	985	225	86	11	0	75
698	244	454	60	38	5	0	33
31	5	26	3	0	0	0	0
343	106	237	80	11	2	0	9
568	175	393	101	38	3	0	35
220	90	130	25	33	6	0	27
230	31	199	16	4	0	0	4

中等职业学校(机构)
Changes of Full-time Teachers in

	上学年初报表专任教师数 Number of Full-time Teachers at Beginning of Previous Academic Year	增加专任 Factors of				
		合计 Total	录用毕业生 New Recruits from Current Year Graduates			外单位 Teachers Recruited
			小计 Subtotal	研究生 Completing Doc,&Mas. Deg. Prog.	本科生 Completing 1st Degree Courses	小计 Subtotal
总　计 Total	**643143**	**49814**	**19266**	**2834**	**14232**	**18331**
其中:女 of Which: Female	339629	28222	12238	2058	9141	9583
普通中专学校 Regular SSSs	302199	23766	9341	1774	6827	7593
其中:女 of Which: Female	159751	13578	6011	1314	4371	3883
成人中专学校 Adult SSSs	47173	3566	879	125	514	1863
其中:女 of Which: Female	24368	2042	607	86	388	979
职业高中学校 High Vocational Schools	285562	21536	8637	874	6610	8595
其中:女 of Which: Female	151303	12136	5394	628	4226	4600
其中等职业教育他机构 Other Secondary Vocational Education Institutions	8209	946	409	61	281	280
其中:女 of Which: Female	4207	466	226	30	156	121

专任教师变动情况
Secondary Vocational Schools

单位:人
unit:person

教师数 Increase				减少专任教师数 Factors of Decrease				本学年初报表专任教师数 Number of Full-time Teachers at Beginning of Current Academic Year
教师调入 from Other Units	非教师调入 Non-teaching Personnel Changed into Teachers		其他 Others	合计 Total	自然减员 Retired from Their Posts during Previous Academic Year	调离教师岗位 Transferred from Teaching to Non-teaching Posts	其他 Others	
其中:中职学校调入 of Which: from Other SVSs	小计 Subtotal	其中:本校调整 of Which: with Change of Status in Their Own Institutions						
7615	**6590**	**4108**	**5627**	**52559**	**11268**	**15245**	**26046**	**640398**
3756	3351	1983	3050	24392	4589	7006	12797	343459
4359	3275	1982	3557	24388	5180	5309	13899	301577
2136	1704	983	1980	11785	2195	2345	7245	161544
263	380	268	444	5966	1120	1358	3488	44773
140	173	118	283	2459	421	596	1442	23951
2975	2741	1712	1563	21045	4822	8364	7859	286053
1472	1380	819	762	9579	1923	3954	3702	153860
18	194	146	63	1160	146	214	800	7995
8	94	63	25	569	50	111	408	4104

	占地面积(平方米) Areas Occupied (m^2)			图书(册) Books (Volume)	
	合计 Total	其中:绿化用地面积 of Which: Green Areas	其中:运动场地面积 of Which: Sports Areas	合计 Total	当年新增 New Added in Current Year
总　计 Total					
学校产权 Owned by SVSs	455609059. 89	108786057. 88	71957633. 32	319803855	14957596
非学校产权中独立使用 Not Owned by SVSs	40771057. 82	7898098. 55	6527340. 45	7203358	433425
普通中专学校 Regular SSSs					
学校产权 Owned by SSSs	238179673. 37	62117241. 11	35392619. 79	174644415	6954896
非学校产权中独立使用 Not Owned by SSSs	21783386. 16	4379689. 63	3440907. 01	3820206	286562
成人中专学校 Adult SSSs					
学校产权 Owned by Adult SSSs	18476087. 77	3222099. 69	2565491. 25	17467190	1124230
非学校产权中独立使用 Not Owned by Adult SSSs	2478308. 55	383452. 75	353630. 32	1551304	39720
职业高中学校 High Vocational Schools					
学校产权 Owned by VHSs	192261195. 57	42160354. 55	33043507. 20	123580072	6786469
非学校产权中独立使用 Not Owned by VHSs	15624360. 41	2974789. 17	2598802. 12	1623546	106143
其他中等职业教育机构 Other Secondary Vocational Education Institutions					
学校产权 Owned by SVSs	6692103. 18	1286362. 53	956015. 08	4112178	92001
非学校产权中独立使用 Not Owned by SVSs	885002. 70	160167. 00	134001. 00	208302	1000

(机构)资产情况
in Secondary Vocational Schools

计算机数(台) PC (Set)			教室中:普通教室(间) of Which: General Classroom (Room)		固定资产值(万元) Fixed Assets (10,000 yuan)		
合计 Total	其中:教学用计算机 No. of Computers Used for Instruction		合计 Total	其中:网络多媒体教室 of Which: Network Multimedia Classroom	合计 Total	其中:教学、实习仪器设备资产值 of which: Teaching Equipment & Instruments	
	小计 Subtotal	其中:平板电脑 of Which: Tablet PC				小计 Subtotal	当年新增 New Added in Current Year
3266672	2682114	111855	396732	189143	33850302. 66	7797421. 54	979289. 10
67335	52523	2832	43325	16486	1559835. 54	182357. 82	28881. 81
1741325	1431639	55191	195839	98660	18983359. 95	4380305. 20	548089. 94
33022	25890	1234	22621	9099	807700. 45	99487. 19	15699. 70
151338	118066	8246	23163	6795	1024557. 75	206053. 89	18752. 63
9145	6604	696	3968	1310	82708. 97	16676. 21	1647. 22
1336003	1102544	47729	171819	81019	13472508. 94	3144519. 52	404342. 02
22752	17929	886	15963	5712	635042. 57	60634. 97	11404. 12
38006	29865	689	5911	2669	369876. 03	66542. 93	8104. 51
2416	2100	16	773	365	34383. 55	5559. 45	130. 77

中等职业学校(机构)教职工其他情况

Supplementary Information on Educational Personnel in Secondary Vocational Schools

单位:人

unit: person

	共产党员 Member of C. P. A	共青团员 Member of C. Y. L	民主党派 Member of Non-Communist Part	华侨 Overseas Chinese	港澳台 From HK, Macao and Taiwan	少数民族 Minorities
总计 Total						
教职工 Educational Personnel	284146	39799	11420	22	22	47516
其中:女 of Which: Female	123822	23621	6267	9	15	24200
专任教师 Full-time Teachers	218848	30843	9743	15	14	37306
其中:女 of Which: Female	102826	19172	5491	7	11	19993
普通中专学校 SSSs						
教职工 Educational Personnel	148366	20775	7001	18	16	24560
其中:女 of Which: Female	67257	12484	3852	7	12	12502
专任教师 Full-time Teachers	110268	15640	5962	11	11	18737
其中:女 of Which: Female	54407	9854	3379	5	9	9989
成人中专学校 Adult SSSs						
教职工 Educational Personnel	23636	2567	561	1	0	3014
其中:女 of Which: Female	9424	1389	313	0	0	1496
专任教师 Full-time Teachers	17964	1728	462	1	0	2326
其中:女 of Which: Female	7697	1009	256	0	0	1239
职业高中学校 High Vocational Schools						
教职工 Educational Personnel	107893	15951	3719	3	6	19754
其中:女 of Which: Female	45463	9492	2019	2	3	10095
专任教师 Full-time Teachers	87539	13086	3198	3	3	16107
其中:女 of Which: Female	39372	8110	1783	2	2	8685
其他中等职业教育机构 Other Secondary Vocational Education Institutions						
教职工 Educational Personnel	4251	506	139	0	0	188
其中:女 of Which: Female	1678	256	83	0	0	107
专任教师 Full-time Teachers	3077	389	121	0	0	136
其中:女 of Which: Female	1350	199	73	0	0	80

中等职业学校(机构)校舍情况(总计)
Conditions of School Buildings in Secondary Vocational Schools(Total)

单位:平方米
unit: m^2

	学校产权校舍建筑面积 Floor Area of School Building Owned by SVSs				正在施工校舍建筑面积 Floor Area Under Construction	非学校产权中独立使用校舍建筑面积 Floor Area of School Building Not Owned by SVSs
	合计 Total	其中:危房 of Which: Dilapidated Buildings	其中:当年新增校舍 of Which: New Added in Current Year	其中:被外单位借用 of Which: Floor Space Hired by Other Schools or Units		
总　计 Total	**212069097.26**	**855697.30**	**6537898.62**	**1012783.28**	**8047020.31**	**21903232.25**
一、教学及辅助用房 Buildings for Instruction and Ancillary Uses	**103214993.10**	**371575.88**	**3528568.71**	**514354.81**	**4831298.75**	**10291496.20**
教室 Classroom	44914792.05	218463.33	1276321.87	369227.78	1477234.87	4858896.22
图书馆 Library	6991640.38	12362.20	182796.57	8505.00	354773.99	731860.06
实验室、实习场所 Lab. And Practice Facilities	42215021.31	119394.25	1821450.72	107774.02	2347839.36	3445742.58
体育馆 Gymnasium	6146928.15	1820.00	175578.57	24684.01	471566.16	894923.45
会堂 Hall	2946611.21	19536.10	72420.98	4164.00	179884.37	360073.89
二、行政办公用房 Administrative	**14383235.43**	**62193.66**	**339955.74**	**77399.22**	**393787.76**	**1347157.40**
三、生活用房 Residential Buildings	**78636399.79**	**324834.63**	**2337648.24**	**365312.44**	**2395201.09**	**9406535.05**
学生宿舍(公寓) Students' Dormitories	52683914.10	218427.71	1673912.94	291781.70	1666472.53	6596622.91
学生食堂 Students' Dining Halls	13273177.01	30983.48	351728.57	33735.46	402458.58	1353665.86
教工宿舍(公寓) Apartments for Single	5699382.07	39914.78	175574.71	22831.68	231680.66	828667.96
教工食堂 Dining Halls for Teachers, Staff and Workers	1076490.01	2228.25	20679.81	792.24	12212.10	115450.69
生活福利及附属用房 Residential, Welfare and Auxiliary Buildings	5903436.60	33280.41	115752.21	16171.36	82377.22	512127.63
四、教工住宅 Residential Quarters for Teachers & Workers	**8907951.33**	**50533.96**	**71551.22**	**7662.00**	**192087.00**	**—**
五、其他用房 Other	**6926517.61**	**46559.17**	**260174.71**	**48054.81**	**234645.71**	**858043.60**

中等职业学校(机构)校舍情况(普通中专)
Conditions of School Buildings in Secondary Vocational Schools(Regular SSSs)

单位:平方米
unit: m^2

	学校产权校舍建筑面积 Floor Area of School Building Owned by SSSs				正在施工校舍建筑面积 Floor Area Under Construction	非学校产权中独立使用校舍建筑面积 Floor Area of School Building Not Owned by SSSs
	合计 Total	其中:危房 of Which: Dilapidated Buildings	其中:当年新增校舍 of Which: New Added in Current Year	其中:被外单位借用 of Which: Floor Space Hired by Other Schools or Units		
总计 Total	**115479473.92**	**457699.93**	**3452789.93**	**575761.62**	**5541585.39**	**12228795.92**
一、教学及辅助用房 Buildings for Instruction and Ancillary Uses	**55439083.42**	**201198.25**	**1772083.64**	**290407.20**	**3170893.54**	**5771925.42**
教室 Classroom	23389251.83	99446.24	643450.65	223503.38	1026658.60	2618378.34
图书馆 Library	3960778.55	7591.00	97756.24	6074.00	268022.11	306431.54
实验室、实习场所 Lab. and Practice Facilities	22536473.97	78487.91	916977.32	38478.81	1406637.87	2023398.70
体育馆 Gymnasium	4034587.00	1571.00	83717.18	21864.01	338950.73	631261.73
会堂 Hall	1517992.07	14102.10	30182.25	487.00	130624.23	192455.11
二、行政办公用房 Administrative	**7471390.89**	**29051.76**	**186626.98**	**38639.48**	**279665.35**	**711364.12**
三、生活用房 Residential Buildings	**43101758.88**	**182171.96**	**1310258.95**	**223440.57**	**1760535.40**	**5242989.63**
学生宿舍(公寓) Students' Dormitories	29693255.26	133002.31	951484.41	194049.70	1175493.85	3785169.17
学生食堂 Students' Dining Halls	7072904.74	14413.45	179347.53	15326.48	302682.69	708943.18
教工宿舍(公寓) Apartments for Single	2773920.45	17459.78	99270.04	6845.00	193835.60	356394.30
教工食堂 Dining Halls for Teachers, Staff and Workers	530306.82	646.25	10208.96	260.06	11405.40	54453.39
生活福利及附属用房 Residential, Welfare and Auxiliary Buildings	3031371.61	16650.17	69948.01	6959.33	77117.86	338029.59
四、教工住宅 Residential Quarters for Teachers & Workers	**6044490.92**	**29471.00**	**45179.22**	**7382.00**	**150881.00**	**—**
五、其他用房 Other	**3422749.81**	**15806.96**	**138641.14**	**15892.37**	**179610.10**	**502516.75**

中等职业学校(机构)校舍情况(成人中专)
Conditions of School Buildings in Secondary Vocational Schools(Adult SSSs)

单位:平方米
unit: m^2

	学校产权校舍建筑面积 Floor Area of School Building Owned by SSSs				正在施工校舍建筑面积 Floor Area Under Construction	非学校产权中独立使用校舍建筑面积 Floor Area of School Building Not Owned by SSSs
	合计 Total	其中:危房 of Which: Dilapidated Buildings	其中:当年新增校舍 of Which: New Added in Current Year	其中:被外单位借用 of Which: Floor Space Hired by Other Schools or Units		
总计 Total	**8719934.84**	**74417.82**	**171093.49**	**91941.71**	**129127.84**	**1619348.51**
一、教学及辅助用房 Buildings for Instruction and Ancillary Uses	**3816095.47**	**30323.00**	**84608.40**	**33275.93**	**74419.65**	**804260.40**
教室 Classroom	2161803.01	25143.00	41731.26	25934.55	39693.65	388514.22
图书馆 Library	319323.54	688.00	5790.85	1218.00	300.00	116675.62
实验室、实习场所 Lab. and Practice Facilities	991460.31	2289.00	33376.69	1820.38	0	243698.20
体育馆 Gymnasium	161620.37	180.00	2194.00	2100.00	11446.00	27307.44
会堂 Hall	181888.24	2023.00	1515.60	2203.00	22980.00	28064.92
二、行政办公用房 Administrative	**1006654.72**	**12219.40**	**11817.12**	**16475.78**	**300.00**	**153563.77**
三、生活用房 Residential Buildings	**3094092.66**	**27715.42**	**52439.94**	**32110.00**	**54218.19**	**606706.05**
学生宿舍(公寓) Students' Dormitories	1988623.60	11138.30	40331.58	23554.00	50674.19	390813.16
学生食堂 Students' Dining Halls	435245.54	1378.00	8823.70	3450.00	3544.00	108149.10
教工宿舍(公寓) Apartments for Single	225832.20	8790.00	0	2800.00	0	75021.90
教工食堂 Dining Halls for Teachers, Staff and Workers	74410.72	750.00	2217.12	360.00	0	11707.04
生活福利及附属用房 Residential, Welfare and Auxiliary Buildings	369980.60	5659.12	1067.54	1946.00	0	21014.85
四、教工住宅 Residential Quarters for Teachers & Workers	**405059.78**	**1828.00**	**2320.00**	**280.00**	**0**	**—**
五、其他用房 Other	**398032.21**	**2332.00**	**19908.03**	**9800.00**	**190.00**	**54818.29**

中等职业学校(机构)校舍情况(职业高中)

Conditions of School Buildings in Secondary Vocational Schools (Vocational High Schools)

单位:平方米
unit: m^2

	学校产权校舍建筑面积 Floor Area of School Building Owned by VHSs				正在施工校舍建筑面积 Floor Area Under Construction	非学校产权中独立使用校舍建筑面积 Floor Area of School Building Not Owned by VHSs
	合计 Total	其中:危房 of Which: Dilapidated Buildings	其中:当年新增校舍 of Which: New Added in Current Year	其中:被外单位借用 of Which: Floor Space Hired by Other Schools or Units		
总计 Total	**84994233.66**	**319072.55**	**2833878.20**	**329086.97**	**2291632.08**	**7628987.93**
一、教学及辅助用房 Buildings for Instruction and Ancillary Uses	**42557932.46**	**139374.63**	**1618739.67**	**181740.08**	**1536630.56**	**3534087.05**
教室 Classroom	18704434.45	93194.09	564599.96	110858.25	382064.62	1759210.66
图书馆 Library	2553222.23	4083.20	78849.48	1213.00	86151.88	296235.90
实验室、实习场所 Lab. and Practice Facilities	18311100.83	38617.34	856596.71	67474.83	923484.49	1126866.68
体育馆 Gymnasium	1794914.32	69.00	80170.39	720.00	121169.43	216451.35
会堂 Hall	1194260.63	3411.00	38523.13	1474.00	23760.14	135322.46
二、行政办公用房 Administrative	**5709544.03**	**20460.50**	**141511.64**	**17418.76**	**113022.41**	**455577.48**
三、生活用房 Residential Buildings	**31414574.01**	**112055.25**	**961949.35**	**107565.69**	**545927.50**	**3379390.42**
学生宿舍(公寓) Students' Dormitories	20326845.73	72295.10	672096.95	74178.00	408684.49	2285290.32
学生食堂 Students' Dining Halls	5594015.10	15192.03	160757.34	13976.98	93831.89	515410.88
教工宿舍(公寓) Apartments for Single	2633510.66	12865.00	76304.67	12346.68	37845.06	384141.76
教工食堂 Dining Halls for Teachers, Staff and Workers	446058.24	832.00	8053.73	0	806.70	48529.66
生活福利及附属用房 Residential, Welfare and Auxiliary Buildings	2414144.28	10871.12	44736.66	7064.03	4759.36	146017.80
四、教工住宅 Residential Quarters for Teachers & Workers	**2317571.01**	**19223.96**	**24052.00**	**0**	**41206.00**	**—**
五、其他用房 Other	**2994612.15**	**27958.21**	**87625.54**	**22362.44**	**54845.61**	**259932.98**

中等职业学校(机构)校舍情况(其他中等职业教育机构)
Conditions of School Buildings in Secondary Vocational Schools (Other Secondary Vocational Education Institutions)

单位:平方米
unit: m^2

	学校产权校舍建筑面积 Floor Area of School Building Owned by SVSs				正在施工校舍建筑面积 Floor Area Under Construction	非学校产权中独立使用校舍建筑面积 Floor Area of School Building Not Owned by SVSs
	合计 Total	其中:危房 of Which: Dilapidated Buildings	其中:当年新增校舍 of Which: New Added in Current Year	其中:被外单位借用 of Which: Floor Space Hired by Other Schools or Units		
总计 Total	**2875454.84**	**4507.00**	**80137.00**	**15992.98**	**84675.00**	**426099.89**
一、教学及辅助用房 Buildings for Instruction and Ancillary Uses	**1401881.75**	**680.00**	**53137.00**	**8931.60**	**49355.00**	**181223.33**
教室 Classroom	659302.76	680.00	26540.00	8931.60	28818.00	92793.00
图书馆 Library	158316.06	0	400.00	0	300.00	12517.00
实验室、实习场所 Lab. and Practice Facilities	375986.20	0	14500.00	0	17717.00	51779.00
体育馆 Gymnasium	155806.46	0	9497.00	0	0	19902.93
会堂 Hall	52470.27	0	2200.00	0	2520.00	4231.40
二、行政办公用房 Administrative	**195645.79**	**462.00**	**0**	**4865.20**	**800.00**	**26652.03**
三、生活用房 Residential Buildings	**1025974.24**	**2892.00**	**13000.00**	**2196.18**	**34520.00**	**177448.95**
学生宿舍(公寓) Students' Dormitories	675189.51	1992.00	10000.00	0	31620.00	135350.26
学生食堂 Students' Dining Halls	171011.63	0	2800.00	982.00	2400.00	21162.70
教工宿舍(公寓) Apartments for Single	66118.76	800.00	0	840.00	0	13110.00
教工食堂 Dining Halls for Teachers, Staff and Workers	25714.23	0	200.00	172.18	0	760.60
生活福利及附属用房 Residential, Welfare and Auxiliary Buildings	87940.11	100.00	0	202.00	500.00	7065.39
四、教工住宅 Residential Quarters for Teachers & Workers	**140829.62**	**11.00**	**0**	**0**	**0**	**—**
五、其他用房 Other	**111123.44**	**462.00**	**14000.00**	**0**	**0**	**40775.58**

	学校数（所）Schools	教学班（点）（个）External Teaching Sites (Classes)	结业生数 合计 Total
总　计 Total	**89211**	**517924**	**42800768**
职工技术培训学校（机构）Vocational-technical Training Schools	2333	33665	2894687
教育部门办 Run by Ed. Dept.	886	15768	1370585
其他部门办 Run by Non-Ed. Dept.	849	13983	1276119
民办 Non-state/private	598	3914	247983
农村成人文化技术培训学校（机构）Technical Training Schools for Peasants	64307	207441	29703643
教育部门办 Run by Ed. Dept.	62236	199338	28541702
其中：县办 of Which：County-run	2034	22787	3364229
乡办 of Which：Township-run	10616	80357	13995031
村办 of Which：Village-run	49586	96194	11182442
其他部门办 Run by Non-Ed. Dept.	1625	6025	970510
民办 Non-government	446	2078	191431
其他培训机构（含社会培训机构）Others	22571	276818	10202438
教育部门办 Run by Ed. Dept.	764	6917	826058
其他部门办 Run by Non-Ed. Dept.	1617	24661	1687342
民办 Non-government	20190	245240	7689038
总计中：少数民族 Total of：Minority	—	—	3033865
培训形式：资格证书培训			
Mode of Training：For Certificates of Vocational Qualifications	—	—	5907137
岗位证书培训 For Certificates of Job-related Qualifications	—	—	9719136
按产业结构分：第一产业类培训 By Industry：Training For first Industry		—	16053496
第二产业类培训 Training for Second Industry	—	—	7437095
第三产业类培训 Training for Third Industry	—	—	19310177
按培训时间分：by Length of Training			
一个月以内 1 Month	—	—	26378554
一个月至三个月以内 1 Month to 3 Months	—	—	7906435
三个月至半年以内 3 Months to 6 Months	—	—	3903915
半年至一年以内 6 Months to 1 Year	—	—	3670086
一年及以上 1 Year and Over	—	—	941778

机构基本情况
Training Institutions

单位：人/人次
unit：person/person-time

Graduates 其中：女 of Which: Female	注册学生数 Enrolment 合计 Total	其中：女 of Which: Female	教职工数 Educational Personnel 合计 Total	其中：专任教师 of Which: Full-time Teacher	聘请校外教师 Part-time Teachers
21272081	**42064949**	**20834989**	**514975**	**289647**	**243592**
1380479	2903058	1367227	60473	46226	16130
724234	1359473	713803	40524	32581	8683
524135	1295898	526182	11382	7952	4684
132110	247687	127242	8567	5693	2763
14712983	28082089	13801071	128491	67702	135077
14094834	27127374	13284582	121973	63589	126392
1635121	3029359	1442578	21079	14063	14642
7055182	13446585	6703469	44028	26669	54822
5404531	10651430	5138535	56866	22857	56928
520440	779721	425565	3740	2413	7698
97709	174994	90924	2778	1700	987
5178619	11079802	5666691	326011	175719	92385
396897	804348	426317	12273	8118	5245
805687	1683766	771165	30399	13516	13777
3976035	8591688	4469209	283339	154085	73363
1425159	3097308	1441360	7930	3781	5495
2795303	5868419	2741948	—	—	—
4764619	9427253	4644930	—	—	—
7772858	15235646	7348399	—	—	—
3492922	7311328	3396904	—	—	—
10006301	19517975	10089686	—	—	—
13280069	24245805	12120011	—	—	—
3709380	8260628	3917085	—	—	—
1957552	4238026	2071871	—	—	—
1857771	3959681	2047861	—	—	—
467309	1360809	678161	—	—	—

职业技术培训机构资产情况

Condition of Assets and Teaching Resources in Vocational Technical Training Institutions

	合 计 Total	职工技术培训学校(机构) Vocational Technical Training Schools (Institutions)	农村成人文化技术培训学校(机构) Technical Training Schools for Peasants	其他培训机构(含社会培训机构) Others
占地面积(平方米) Areas Occupied (m^2)	103581068.28	30562141.45	46577063.56	26441863.27
教学行政用房建筑面积(平方米) Administrative (m^2)	62376001.05	8739859.71	13044852.12	40591289.22
图书(册) Books (Volume)	125186655.00	25188312.00	44001188.00	55997155.00
计算机数(台) PC (Set)	741915.00	178669.00	233830.00	329416.00
其中:教学用计算机 No. of Computers Used for Instruction	617531.00	149777.00	206992.00	260762.00
其中:平板电脑 of Which: Tablet PC	77556.00	10172.00	19418.00	47966.00
教室(间) Classroom (Room)	299090.00	33862.00	108211.00	157017.00
其中:网络多媒体教室 of Which: Network Multimedia Classroom	81527.00	13072.00	23061.00	45394.00
固定资产总值(万元) Fixed Assets (10,000 yuan)	30181304.63	6316791.15	14181307.07	9683206.41
其中:教学、实习仪器设备资产值 of Which: Teaching Equipment &Instruments	8120921.28	397247.07	1155327.13	6568347.09

(二)初中阶段教育
Junior Secondary Education

初中阶段校数、班数
Number of Schools, Classes in Junior Secondary Education

	学校数(所) Schools				班数(个) Classes				
	合计 Total	初级中学 Regular Junior Secondary Schools	九年一贯制学校 9-Year Schools	职业初中 Vocational Junior Secondary Schools	小计 Subtotal	一年级 Grade 1	二年级 Grade 2	三年级 Grade 3	四年级 Grade 4
总　计 Total	**51894**	**35696**	**16183**	**15**	**948200**	**330312**	**312290**	**295441**	**10157**
教育部门 Run by Ed. Dept.	46091	34246	11832	13	820975	284194	270322	257292	9167
其他部门 Run by Non-ed. Dept.	505	156	348	1	5808	1845	1889	1873	201
地方企业办 Run by Local Enterprises	21	1	20	0	243	96	78	69	0
民办 Non-government	5277	1293	3983	1	121174	44177	40001	36207	789
城区 Urban Area	12355	7930	4422	3	336717	117220	110373	102925	6199
教育部门 Run by Ed. Dept.	9734	7299	2433	2	271285	93639	88788	83384	5474
其他部门 Run by Non-ed. Dept.	130	60	69	1	1878	586	624	643	25
地方企业办 Run by Local Enterprises	7	0	7	0	114	42	38	34	0
民办 Non-government	2484	571	1913	0	63440	22953	20923	18864	700
其中:城乡结合区 of Which:Urban-rural Transitional Area	2635	1510	1125	0	56103	20053	18478	16780	792
教育部门 Run by Ed. Dept.	1926	1420	506	0	41305	14474	13508	12589	734
其他部门 Run by Non-ed. Dept.	18	10	8	0	167	52	56	55	4
地方企业办 Run by Local Enterprises	1	0	1	0	24	8	9	7	0
民办 Non-government	690	80	610	0	14607	5519	4905	4129	54
镇区 Counties & Towns Area	24251	18260	5986	5	464182	161859	153362	145844	3117
教育部门 Run by Ed. Dept.	21940	17637	4299	4	413017	143374	136446	130293	2904
其他部门 Run by Non-ed. Dept.	317	83	234	0	3414	1082	1098	1068	166
地方企业办 Run by Local Enterprises	6	0	6	0	95	42	30	23	0
民办 Non-government	1988	540	1447	1	47656	17361	15788	14460	47
其中:镇乡结合区 of Which: County-town Transitional Area	5807	4317	1489	1	112943	39978	37231	34926	808
教育部门 Run by Ed. Dept.	5051	4112	938	1	95415	33446	31433	29754	782
其他部门 Run by Non-ed. Dept.	15	8	7	0	202	79	63	56	4
地方企业办 Run by Local Enterprises	1	0	1	0	16	5	5	6	0
民办 Non-government	740	197	543	0	17310	6448	5730	5110	22
乡村 Rural Area	15288	9506	5775	7	147301	51233	48555	46672	841
教育部门 Run by Ed. Dept.	14417	9310	5100	7	136673	47181	45088	43615	789
其他部门 Run by Non-ed. Dept.	58	13	45	0	516	177	167	162	10
地方企业办 Run by Local Enterprises	8	1	7	0	34	12	10	12	0
民办 Non-government	805	182	623	0	10078	3863	3290	2883	42
总计中:四年制 of the Total:4-Year	—	—	—	—	44739	11779	11841	10963	10156
其他学校附设班 Classes Attached to Others Schools	—	—	—	—	3880	1306	1272	1241	61
独立设置少数民族学校 Inde. Sec. Schools for Minorities	1600	1045	552	3	29899	10256	9806	9794	43

初中班额情况
Size of Classes in Junior Secondary Schools

单位：个
unit: class

	合计 Total	一年级 Grade 1	二年级 Grade 2	三年级 Grade 3	四年级 Grade 4
合 计 Total	**948200**	**330312**	**312290**	**295441**	**10157**
城区：Urban Area					
25 人及以下 Under 25 Persons	11080	2936	3201	3929	1014
26-35 人 Between 26-35	31659	9501	9927	10950	1281
36-45 人 Between 36-45	91907	30581	28994	30874	1458
46-55 人 Between 46-55	159165	61466	52392	43465	1842
56-65 人 Between 56-65	34654	10496	12568	11131	459
66 人及以上 Over 66 Persons	8252	2240	3291	2576	145
其中：城乡结合区：					
of Which: Urban-rural Transitional Area					
25 人及以下 Under 25 Persons	1555	473	473	517	92
26-35 人 Between 26-35	4925	1535	1491	1769	130
36-45 人 Between 36-45	16063	5405	5229	5216	213
46-55 人 Between 46-55	27210	10692	9025	7185	308
56-65 人 Between 56-65	4904	1552	1681	1622	49
66 人及以上 Over 66 Persons	1446	396	579	471	0
镇区：Counties&Towns Area					
25 人及以下 Under 25 Persons	8973	2803	2876	3058	236
26-35 人 Between 26-35	34573	10891	11029	12107	546
36-45 人 Between 36-45	121005	41403	39434	38998	1170
46-55 人 Between 46-55	226450	87281	72117	66058	994
56-65 人 Between 56-65	54698	14816	20496	19260	126
66 人及以上 Over 66 Persons	18483	4665	7410	6363	45
其中：镇乡结合区：					
of Which: County-town Transitional Area					
25 人及以下 Under 25 Persons	2016	669	637	662	48
26-35 人 Between 26-35	7767	2458	2428	2765	116
36-45 人 Between 36-45	29425	10103	9657	9368	297
46-55 人 Between 46-55	55116	21581	17377	15880	278
56-65 人 Between 56-65	13940	3893	5304	4701	42
66 人及以上 Over 66 Persons	4679	1274	1828	1550	27
乡村：Rural Area					
25 人及以下 Under 25 Persons	7937	2594	2526	2714	103
26-35 人 Between 26-35	21827	6998	7174	7423	232
36-45 人 Between 36-45	49623	17151	16519	15653	300
46-55 人 Between 46-55	55024	21047	17418	16374	185
56-65 人 Between 56-65	10042	2752	3767	3502	21
66 人及以上 Over 66 Persons	2848	691	1151	1006	0

初　中
Number of Students in Junior

	毕业生数 Graduates	招生数 Entrants		
			合计 Total	其中:女 of Which: Female
总　计 Total	**13974699**	**15472209**	**44420630**	**20598359**
其中:女 of Which: Female	6517118	7163711	20598359	—
少数民族学生 Minority Students	1578170	1759557	5019853	2397270
四年制 4-Year	413382	476935	1829506	869763
九年一贯制学校 9-Year Schools	1916050	2378247	6585126	2937800
十二年一贯制学校 12-Year Schools	307082	398065	1075624	446050
完全中学 Complete Secondary Schools	1772477	1934058	5541759	2584172
附设普通初中班 Junior Sec. Classes Attached	57632	55523	165386	74498
附设职业初中班 Vocational Junior Sec. Classes Attached	64	35	100	28
独立设置少数民族学校 Inde. Sec. Schools for Minorities	454806	469763	1372944	662889
随迁子女 Migrant Children	1250706	1764308	4922520	2159239
其中:外省迁入 of Which: from Other Province	470119	748140	2013941	871475
本省外县迁入 From Other County	780587	1016168	2908579	1287764
进城务工人员随迁子女 Children of Migrant Workers	943837	1299836	3644540	1607398
其中:外省迁入 of Which: from Other Province	348143	546291	1470075	636994
本省外县迁入 From Other County	595694	753545	2174465	970404
农村留守儿童 Children Left Behind	1444164	1695521	4860813	2264221
教育部门 Run by Ed. Dept.	12224918	13307792	38420927	18090264
其他部门 Run by Non-ed. Dept.	70835	69836	213231	98551
地方企业办 Run by Local Enterprises	2880	3656	9637	4153
民办 Non-government	1676066	2090925	5776835	2405391
城区 Urban Area	4836743	5499957	15671422	7214833
教育部门 Run by Ed. Dept.	3951368	4412054	12646946	5922201
其他部门 Run by Non-ed. Dept.	25281	23567	73774	32722
地方企业办 Run by Local Enterprises	1428	1585	4453	1926
民办 Non-government	858666	1062751	2946249	1257984
其中:城乡结合区 of Which: Urban-rural Transitional Area	772556	937061	2611372	1174389
教育部门 Run by Ed. Dept.	588431	678645	1925416	895096
其他部门 Run by Non-ed. Dept.	2017	1827	5979	2467
地方企业办 Run by Local Enterprises	207	264	869	397
民办 Non-government	181901	256325	679108	276429
镇区 Counties & Towns Area	7058957	7732411	22315114	10381757
教育部门 Run by Ed. Dept.	6325263	6836212	19812549	9353920
其他部门 Run by Non-ed. Dept.	39924	39582	120298	56624
地方企业办 Run by Local Enterprises	1101	1758	4133	1835
民办 Non-government	692669	854859	2378134	969378
其中:镇乡结合区 of Which: County-town Transitional Area	1672711	1917134	5445874	2523266
教育部门 Run by Ed. Dept.	1433003	1598728	4583098	2169220
其他部门 Run by Non-ed. Dept.	2613	3699	8727	4006
地方企业办 Run by Local Enterprises	229	176	591	243
民办 Non-government	236866	314531	853458	349797
乡村 Rural Area	2078999	2239841	6434094	3001769
教育部门 Run by Ed. Dept.	1948287	2059526	5961432	2814143
其他部门 Run by Non-ed. Dept.	5630	6687	19159	9205
地方企业办 Run by Local Enterprises	351	313	1051	392
民办 Non-government	124731	173315	452452	178029

学　生　数
Secondary Schools

单位:人
unit:person

在校生数 Enrolment				预计毕业生数 Estimated Graduates for Next Year
一年级 Grade 1	二年级 Grade 2	三年级 Grade 3	四年级 Grade 4	
15475352	**14780316**	**13757832**	**407130**	**13716736**
7164699	6864436	6376220	193004	6350286
1759801	1662156	1589547	8349	1588989
477093	497057	448226	407130	407130
2378897	2178019	1948505	79705	1941007
398167	356245	316029	5183	315160
1934442	1849499	1729422	28396	1725049
55564	54703	52632	2487	53845
35	32	30	3	3
469889	453098	448497	1460	448390
1769654	1650579	1444854	57433	1413470
750453	676085	559249	28154	543850
1019201	974494	885605	29279	869620
1302439	1220827	1076865	44409	1055467
546842	492985	410835	19413	400321
755597	727842	666030	24996	655146
1696941	1639379	1519866	4627	1510009
13310436	12783294	11956440	370757	11921407
69889	69384	67382	6576	67437
3656	3148	2833	0	2821
2091371	1924490	1731177	29797	1725071
5501470	5202446	4720147	247359	4698121
4413197	4194769	3819394	219586	3801706
23620	24173	24944	1037	25065
1585	1537	1331	0	1319
1063068	981967	874478	26736	870031
937256	869448	771744	32924	768900
678742	636997	578777	30900	576454
1827	1933	2046	173	2080
264	356	249	0	237
256423	230162	190672	1851	190129
7733657	7446673	7006561	128223	6989696
6837383	6612372	6241327	121467	6226316
39582	38906	36655	5155	36537
1758	1312	1063	0	1063
854934	794083	727516	1601	725780
1917406	1813459	1680322	34687	1672969
1598941	1525160	1425237	33760	1418990
3699	2621	2294	113	2287
176	204	211	0	211
314590	285474	252580	814	251481
2240225	2131197	2031124	31548	2028919
2059856	1976153	1895719	29704	1893385
6687	6305	5783	384	5835
313	299	439	0	439
173369	148440	129183	1460	129260

初中阶段学龄人口及在校学生情况

Number of School-age Population and Enrolment of Junior Secondary Schools

单位:人
unit: person

	在校学龄人口数 School-age Population		在校生数 Enrolment					
	合计 Total	其中:女 of Which: Female	合计 Total	其中:女 of Which: Female	一年级 Grade 1	二年级 Grade 2	三年级 Grade 3	四年级 Grade 4
总　计 Total	**39734257**	**18475777**	**44420630**	**20598359**	**15475352**	**14780316**	**13757832**	**407130**
10 岁及以下 Under 10 Years	0	0	16836	9252	15097	1401	338	0
11 岁 11 Years	348773	169432	1029108	519427	998736	26582	3746	44
12 岁 12 Years	10627715	5025246	11219189	5320610	10062885	1111521	44577	206
13 岁 13 Years	14461931	6715481	14461931	6715481	3837099	9560233	1056076	8523
14 岁 14 Years	12766983	5852646	12773271	5855525	474529	3498954	8527338	272450
15 岁 15 Years	1528855	712972	4226391	1881753	68631	498029	3545325	114406
16 岁 16 Years	0	0	580087	246544	12709	64809	492327	10242
17 岁 17 Years	0	0	91513	39505	3944	14156	72239	1174
18 岁及以上 Over 18 Years	0	0	22304	10262	1722	4631	15866	85
城区 Urban Area	14098662	6517189	15671422	7214833	5501470	5202446	4720147	247359
10 岁及以下 Under 10 Years	0	0	5996	3307	5452	471	73	0
11 岁 11 Years	233176	112797	481576	242007	470898	10033	639	6
12 岁 12 Years	4135929	1952663	4285648	2028300	3746836	521979	16675	158
13 岁 13 Years	5152371	2379302	5152371	2379302	1152700	3522832	472822	4017
14 岁 14 Years	4343197	1967240	4346208	1968692	111506	1016315	3037933	180454
15 岁 15 Years	233989	105187	1235973	528053	11186	114873	1052941	56973
16 岁 16 Years	0	0	141467	56299	2033	12590	121671	5173
17 岁 17 Years	0	0	18561	7339	635	2656	14734	536
18 岁及以上 Over 18 Years	0	0	3622	1534	224	697	2659	42
其中:城乡结合区 of Which: Urban-rural Transitional Area	2351067	1063398	2611372	1174389	937256	869448	771744	32924
10 岁及以下 Under 10 Years	0	0	651	371	584	59	8	0
11 岁 11 Years	29671	14463	69720	34322	67912	1705	99	4
12 岁 12 Years	678490	314149	699488	324509	625133	71733	2539	83
13 岁 13 Years	857298	386733	857298	386733	218200	571123	67375	600
14 岁 14 Years	732721	324730	732760	324739	22525	198060	488446	23729
15 岁 15 Years	52887	23323	221161	91745	2259	23520	187671	7711
16 岁 16 Years	0	0	25672	10112	434	2490	22057	691
17 岁 17 Years	0	0	3748	1472	149	605	2896	98
18 岁及以上 Over 18 Years	0	0	874	386	60	153	653	8

初中阶段学龄人口及在校学生情况(续)
Number of School-age Population and Enrolment of Junior Secondary Schools(Cont.)

单位:人
unit: person

	在校学龄人口数 School-age Population		在校生数 Enrolment					
	合计 Total	其中:女 of Which: Female	合计 Total	其中:女 of Which: Female	一年级 Grade 1	二年级 Grade 2	三年级 Grade 3	四年级 Grade 4
镇区 Counties & Towns Area	19932053	9289561	22315114	10381757	7733657	7446673	7006561	128223
10 岁及以下 Under 10 Years	0	0	8075	4405	7192	675	208	0
11 岁 11 Years	95327	46734	428799	217526	412703	13254	2804	38
12 岁 12 Years	5095513	2407300	5436922	2578028	4950086	463627	23167	42
13 岁 13 Years	7249680	3373493	7249680	3373493	2042221	4745406	458082	3971
14 岁 14 Years	6543322	3015340	6546526	3016735	269546	1892782	4309621	74577
15 岁 15 Years	948211	446694	2266105	1027376	42113	285565	1892958	45469
16 岁 16 Years	0	0	318274	137443	6892	35643	272096	3643
17 岁 17 Years	0	0	49048	21347	2032	7298	39260	458
18 岁及以上 Over 18 Years	0	0	11685	5404	872	2423	8365	25
其中:镇乡结合区 of Which: County-town Transitional Area	4898527	2276980	5445874	2523266	1917406	1813459	1680322	34687
10 岁及以下 Under 10 Years	0	0	1900	1022	1640	208	52	0
11 岁 11 Years	29605	14712	107899	54416	104011	3646	208	34
12 岁 12 Years	1337183	627343	1393490	655530	1267957	116780	8735	18
13 岁 13 Years	1782329	828523	1782329	828523	474920	1191034	115281	1094
14 岁 14 Years	1571427	722939	1574040	724068	57296	434374	1059716	22654
15 岁 15 Years	177983	83463	506536	226369	9675	57358	429740	9763
16 岁 16 Years	0	0	66774	27861	1354	8148	56238	1034
17 岁 17 Years	0	0	10920	4608	410	1494	8932	84
18 岁及以上 Over 18 Years	0	0	1986	869	143	417	1420	6
乡村 Rural Area	5703542	2669027	6434094	3001769	2240225	2131197	2031124	31548
10 岁及以下 Under 10 Years	0	0	2765	1540	2453	255	57	0
11 岁 11 Years	20270	9901	118733	59894	115135	3295	303	0
12 岁 12 Years	1396273	665283	1496619	714282	1365963	125915	4735	6
13 岁 13 Years	2059880	962686	2059880	962686	642178	1291995	125172	535
14 岁 14 Years	1880464	870066	1880537	870098	93477	589857	1179784	17419
15 岁 15 Years	346655	161091	724313	326324	15332	97591	599426	11964
16 岁 16 Years	0	0	120346	52802	3784	16576	98560	1426
17 岁 17 Years	0	0	23904	10819	1277	4202	18245	180
18 岁及以上 Over 18 Years	0	0	6997	3324	626	1511	4842	18

初中分课程专任
Number of Full-time Teachers in Junior Secondary

	合计 Total	其中:女 of Which: Female	思想品德(政治) Politics	语文 Language & Literature	数学 Mathem-atics	外语 Foreign Languages 小计 Subtotal	英语 English	日语 Japanese	俄语 Russian	科学 Science	物理 Physics
总　计 Total	**3548688**	**1974445**	**230091**	**627134**	**603769**	**555506**	**553099**	**364**	**172**	**30005**	**239712**
其中:女 of Which:Female	1974445	—	123387	405425	304438	440751	439060	307	143	13783	87701
少数民族 Minorities	330053	176704	23575	60474	53361	42698	42434	114	11	518	22783
研究生毕业 Graduate	92411	69675	6162	16209	13618	17293	17158	51	27	882	5576
本科毕业 Under-graduate	2910727	1694617	185359	532214	502253	478223	476302	274	130	25980	196150
专科毕业 Associate Bachelor	539517	208695	38191	78127	87218	59734	59385	39	15	3092	37760
高中阶段毕业 High School Graduate	5783	1388	368	561	652	241	239	0	0	45	225
高中阶段以下毕业 Below High School Graduate	250	70	11	23	28	15	15	0	0	6	1
城区 Urban Area	1221327	794159	74756	212191	207183	201569	200542	257	110	13220	83156
其中:城乡结合区 of Which: Urban-rural Transitional Area	202316	120952	12715	35623	34304	32658	32543	14	2	2775	13038
镇区 Counties & Towns Area	1752616	905413	116770	312721	299434	271161	270147	99	41	13109	117722
其中:镇乡结合区 of Which: County-town Transitional Area	421670	227455	28325	75321	72330	65690	65423	16	5	3854	27556
乡村 Rural Area	574745	274873	38565	102222	97152	82776	82410	8	21	3676	38834

教师学历情况
Schools by Subject Taught & Academic Qualifications

单位:人
unit:person

化学 Chem-istry	生物 Biology	历史与社会 History and Soliety	地理 Geogr-aphy	历史 History	体育与健康 Physical Training and Healthy	艺术 Art	音乐 Music	美术 Fine Arts	综合实践活动 Comprehensive Practice			其他 Others	当年不任课 No Teaching Load in Current Year
									小计 Subtotal	信息技术 Information Technique	劳动与技术 Skills Teaching		
153246	**147796**	**30454**	**140481**	**183116**	**196829**	**6453**	**95137**	**91457**	**133490**	**93702**	**34884**	**41764**	**42248**
75924	83875	15238	72219	95921	39928	3332	68516	50797	51648	37865	12050	21879	19683
14635	13666	1373	12863	17161	18922	477	9095	7835	11471	8575	2567	11939	7207
4676	4766	802	3533	5409	4829	153	1825	2213	2398	2063	274	1300	767
126552	115884	24446	108390	145144	156217	4471	77159	72541	101946	76343	22185	28584	29214
21900	26894	5119	28266	32269	35177	1789	15938	16436	28441	15110	11940	11424	11742
116	247	84	281	288	581	40	208	261	669	180	461	420	496
2	5	3	11	6	25	0	7	6	36	6	24	36	29
52709	48129	10629	45003	60738	73577	1480	32644	30845	43997	32436	9889	12274	17227
8191	8190	2156	7719	10153	11808	309	5505	5297	7745	5476	1850	1916	2214
74934	74658	14631	71540	92422	93266	3530	46674	45121	66253	44957	18806	19773	18897
17476	18347	3881	17518	22200	21879	936	11133	10802	16203	10892	4700	3992	4227
25603	25009	5194	23938	29956	29986	1443	15819	15491	23240	16309	6189	9717	6124

初中专任教师专业技术

Number of Full-time Teachers in Junior Secondary

	合 计 Total	其中:女 of Which: Female	24 岁及以下 24 and Under	25-29 25 to 29	30-34 30 to 34
总 计 Total	**3548688**	**1974445**	**135551**	**437382**	**529743**
其中:女 of Which:Female	1974445	—	102283	317344	353159
少数民族 Minorities	330053	176704	13509	46744	54571
中学高级 Senior	673946	308002	11	26	1662
中学一级 1st Grade	1495353	774950	548	16576	148422
中学二级 2nd Grade	1018995	643270	25126	259596	329492
中学三级 3rd Grade	35589	21784	4864	16342	7796
未定职级 No-ranking	324805	226439	105002	144842	42371
城区 Urban Area	1221327	794159	45515	144985	180142
其中:城乡结合区 of Which: Urban-rural Transitional Area	202316	120952	9907	26597	30298
镇区 Counties & Towns Area	1752616	905413	62983	204424	259135
其中:镇乡结合区 of Which: County-town Transitional Area	421670	227455	16917	51046	63221
乡村 Rural Area	574745	274873	27053	87973	90466

职务、年龄结构情况
Schools by Professional Rank and Age

单位:人
unit:person

35-39 35 to 39	40-44 40 to 44	45-49 45 to 49	50-54 50 to 54	55-59 55 to 59	60 岁及以上 60 and Over
672121	**678031**	**576647**	**398684**	**118254**	**2275**
395830	356439	276229	166448	6205	508
64065	62566	50139	30887	7487	85
31491	132607	233138	211008	62775	1228
385287	431834	297425	166126	48521	614
235459	105092	40297	18171	5671	91
3579	1330	838	545	287	8
16305	7168	4949	2834	1000	334
230847	225369	211609	146945	34716	1199
37915	38404	32278	21203	5464	250
333444	347793	285142	196159	62714	822
83064	84484	66058	42701	13867	312
107830	104869	79896	55580	20824	254

	上学年初报表专任教师数 Number of Full-time Teachers at Beginning of Previous Academic Year	增加教师 Factors of Increase					
		合计 Total	录用毕业生 New Recruits from Current Year Graduates		调入 Teachers Recruited from Other Units	校内调整 of Which: with Change of Status in Their Own Institutions	其他 Others
			小计 Subtotal	其中:师范生 of Which: Students Enrolled in Teacher Training Institutions			
总　计 Total	**3487789**	**382290**	**106095**	**75366**	**191823**	**59979**	**24393**
其中:女 of Which: Female	1900525	229564	78649	56222	107378	28713	14824
城区 Urban Area	1181237	128643	34770	25991	61276	20359	12238
其中:女 of Which: Female	759443	84225	26329	19818	38184	11568	8144
其中:城乡结合区 of Which: Urban-rural Transitional Area	194635	25930	7425	5757	12492	3268	2745
其中:女 of Which: Female	114477	16052	5381	4225	7195	1754	1722
镇区 Counties & Towns Area	1723601	188548	49495	34940	99986	30099	8968
其中:女 of Which: Female	870918	108156	36492	25834	53683	13107	4874
其中:镇乡结合区 of Which: County-town Transitional Area	409310	50398	13484	9300	27746	6888	2280
其中:女 of Which: Female	214943	30272	10113	6927	15668	3187	1304
乡村 Rural Area	582951	65099	21830	14435	30561	9521	3187
其中:女 of Which: Female	270164	37183	15828	10570	15511	4038	1806

教师变动情况
Junior Secondary Schools

单位：人
unit：person

减少教师 Factors of Decrease					本学年初报表专任教师数 Number of Full-time Teachers at Beginning of Current Academic Year
合计 Total	自然减员 Retired from Their Posts during Previous Academic Year	调出 Transferred from Teaching to Non-Teaching Posts	校内调整 of Which：with Change of Status in Their Own Institutions	其他 Others	
321391	**42991**	**194657**	**61663**	**22080**	**3548688**
155644	15097	100241	28784	11522	1974445
88553	14697	45076	19501	9279	1221327
49509	7133	26179	10746	5451	794159
18249	2253	10169	3660	2167	202316
9577	873	5708	1868	1128	120952
159533	20725	100621	29045	9142	1752616
73661	6110	50426	12737	4388	905413
38038	4756	24648	6416	2218	421670
17760	1404	12447	2777	1132	227455
73305	7569	48960	13117	3659	574745
32474	1854	23636	5301	1683	274873

初中学生、专任教师其他情况
Other Information on Students and Full-time Teachers of Junior Secondary Schools

单位:人
unit: person

	在校学生中 of Total Students			专任教师中 of Total Full-time Teachers			
	共青团员 Member of C. Y. L.	华侨 Overseas Chinese	港澳台 From H. K, Macao and Taiwan	共产党员 Member of C. P. C.	共青团员 Member of C. Y. L.	民主党派 Member of Non-Communist Party	华侨 Overseas Chinese
总计 Total	**8698773**	**2256**	**17437**	**1042330**	**149482**	**24032**	**495**
其中:女 of Which: Female	4422949	1034	7833	438590	106480	14543	260
城区 Urban Area	2317817	1269	13799	401322	62692	20010	109
其中:女 of Which: Female	1190592	577	6402	227828	46633	12736	68
其中:城乡结合区 of Which: Urban-rural Transitional Area	422451	296	2752	59073	12003	1201	21
其中:女 of Which: Female	212031	123	1222	28234	8624	608	12
镇区 Counties & Towns Area	4858371	753	2052	474932	62169	3233	298
其中:女 of Which: Female	2459510	359	915	160746	42985	1472	146
其中:镇乡结合区 of Which: County-town Transitional Area	1175844	231	542	108854	15374	570	12
其中:女 of Which: Female	587792	118	240	36993	10809	261	8
乡村 Rural Area	1522585	234	1586	166076	24621	789	88
其中:女 of Which: Female	772847	98	516	50016	16862	335	46

初中办学条件(一)

Condition of School Buildings in Junior Secondary Schools (1)

单位:平方米
unit: m^2

	合计 Total	城区 Urban Area	其中:城乡结合区 of Which: Urban-rural Transitional Area	镇区 Counties & Towns Area	其中:镇乡结合区 of Which: County-town Transitional Area	乡村 Rural Area
总 计 Total	**610067403.78**	**189434053.11**	**39542593.83**	**304533759.95**	**76698170.40**	**116099590.72**
其中:危房 of Which: Floor Space of Dilapidated Buildings	3922258.47	677966.53	102072.63	2121957.07	462726.69	1122334.87
当年新增校舍 New Floor Space Added in Current Year	33397915.05	9328700.06	2531832.17	16897442.38	4984857.15	7171772.61
一、教学及辅助用房 Teaching & Assistant Buildings	**248326031.15**	**87182865.12**	**17105955.95**	**117227657.05**	**29208437.54**	**43915508.98**
教室 Classroom	168552069.38	56658185.93	11252286.14	81171958.88	20207993.26	30721924.57
实验室 Laboratory	38525205.80	13027733.54	2543775.81	18375154.23	4620341.57	7122318.03
图书室 Library	15224327.83	5632486.56	1049478.88	7055428.35	1807195.18	2536412.92
微机室 PC-room	11202861.55	3608754.75	707637.29	5418559.95	1294914.76	2175546.85
语音室 Linguistic	3807316.64	1271669.04	255363.56	1891340.95	473614.00	644306.65
体育馆 Gymnasium	11014249.95	6984035.30	1297414.27	3315214.69	804378.77	714999.96
二、行政办公用房 Administrative	**52413298.69**	**19906835.78**	**3476851.93**	**23840474.81**	**6053352.06**	**8665988.10**
其中:教师办公室 of Which: for Teachers	31472625.71	11389624.07	1980228.31	14620813.27	3674185.29	5462188.37
三、生活用房 Residential and Welfare	**254748980.67**	**57142939.23**	**14342684.12**	**142270776.98**	**35842955.26**	**55335264.46**
教工宿舍 Apartments for Single	56885870.33	9125806.28	2528430.94	32733847.83	7328460.87	15026216.22
其中:教师周转宿舍 of Which: Accommodation for Circulation of Teachers	16408703.60	1750621.58	469883.90	9568958.77	1976754.02	5089123.25
学生宿舍 Students' Dormitories	110442376.05	20646500.94	5848819.68	65934930.34	17040179.62	23860944.77
食堂 Dining Halls	48719633.76	12502821.99	3071813.41	26196063.68	6884745.23	10020748.09
厕所 Toilet	18689754.66	6605439.61	1356374.66	8739053.73	2267870.29	3345261.32
其他 Others	20011345.87	8262370.41	1537245.43	8666881.40	2321699.25	3082094.06
四、其他用房 Rooms for Other Purposes	**54579093.27**	**25201412.98**	**4617101.83**	**21194851.11**	**5593425.54**	**8182829.18**

初中办学

Condition of School Buildings in

	占地面积(平方米) Areas Occupied(m^2)			图书(册) Books & Magazines in Libraries (Volume)	计算机数 PC
	合计 Total	其中: of Which:			合计 Total
		绿化用地面积 Green Areas	运动场地面积 Sports Areas		
总　计 Total	**1587527312.42**	**324806918.30**	**452776698.57**	**1583181008**	**7874766**
城区 Urban Area	388417231.93	88690609.22	127254964.88	533466382	3008233
其中:城乡结合区 of Which:Urban-rural Transitional Area	90852558.77	21894886.49	27707913.77	103123994	557023
镇区 Counties and Towns Area	829471392.84	166620893.69	230282094.18	773406666	3540479
其中:镇乡结合区 of Which:County-town Transitional Area	201262610.43	39982888.78	55385250.93	191153586	864424
乡村 Rural Area	369638687.65	69495415.39	95239639.51	276307960	1326054

初中办学

Condition of School Buildings in

	体育运动场(馆)面积达标校数 Schools No: Sports Areas Reached Standard	体育器械配备达标校数 Schools No: Sports Equip. Reached Standard
总　计 Total	**46887**	**48765**
城区 Urban Area	11037	11619
其中:城乡结合区 of Which:Urban-rural Transitional Area	2403	2488
镇区 Counties and Towns Area	22205	23017
其中:镇乡结合区 of Which: County-town Transitional Area	5296	5470
乡村 Rural Area	13645	14129

条件(二)
Junior Secondary Schools (2)

(台) (Set)		教室(间) Classroom(Room)		教室中:普通教室(间) of Which: General Classroom (Room)		固定资产总值(万元) Total Value of Fixed Asset (10,000 yuan)		
其中:教学用计算机 No. of Computers Used for Instruction		合计 Total	其中:网络多媒体教室 of Which: Network Multimedia Classroom	合计 Total	其中:网络多媒体教室 of Which: Network Multimedia Classroom	合计 Total	其中:教学仪器设备资产值 of Which: Total Value of Equip & Instru.	
小计 Subtotal	其中:平板电脑 of Which: Tablet PC						小计 Subtotal	其中:实验设备 of Which: for Experiment
6581785	**310168**	**1811140**	**1162310**	**1332705**	**1009840**	**83716576.76**	**10060241.46**	**2960223.07**
2517666	179927	589479	427922	430816	361157	31246934.99	4226520.59	1047706.74
475981	33313	116904	84935	85896	72736	6512817.41	762616.59	224047.78
2974720	97752	860012	537229	638522	474172	39088754.97	4261869.11	1368979.49
737748	27203	214690	135254	161496	119783	10098685.01	1013548.89	332028.15
1089399	32489	361649	197159	263367	174511	13380886.81	1571851.76	543536.84

条件(三)
Junior Secondary Schools (3)

单位:所
unit:school

音乐器械配备达标校数 Schools No: Musical Instru. Reached Standard	美术器械配备达标校数 Schools No: Fine Arts Instru. Reached Standard	理科实验仪器达标校数 Schools No: Equip. of Natural Sci. Reached Standard	建立校园网校数 Schools No: Campus Networks Set	接入互联网校数 Schools No: Internet Access
48491	**48351**	**48840**	**39822**	**51188**
11554	11527	11553	10664	12147
2476	2467	2475	2214	2597
22894	22828	23090	18711	23958
5433	5404	5479	4516	5719
14043	13996	14197	10447	15083

成人初中基本情况

Basic Statistics of Adult Junior Secondary Schools

单位:人(人次)
unit: person

	学校数(所) Schools	教学班(点)(个) External Teaching Sites	毕(结)业生数 Graduates		注册学生数 Enrolment		教职工数 Educational Personnel		专任教师 Full-time Teacher		聘请校外教师 Part-time Teachers
			合计 Total	其中:女 of Which: Female	合计 Total	其中:女 of Which: Female	合计 Total	其中:女 of Which: Female	合计 Total	其中:女 of Which: Female	
总计 Total	**506**	**1174**	**126697**	**58622**	**127001**	**60077**	**1772**	**828**	**1367**	**663**	**1829**
职工初中 Junior Secondary Schools for Staff & workers	24	32	9337	5618	9978	5861	154	62	73	30	300
农民初中 Junior Secondary Schools for Peasants	482	1142	117360	53004	117023	54216	1618	766	1294	633	1529

四、初等教育(小学)
Primary Education
(Primary Schools)

小学校数、教学点数及班数
Number of Schools, External Teaching Sites & Classes in Primary Schools

	学校数(所) Schools	教学点数(个) External Teaching Sites	班数(个) Classes
总　计 Total	**167009**	**102998**	**2683706**
教育部门 Run by Ed. Dept.	160590	102811	2473015
其他部门 Run by Non-ed. Dept.	293	76	10041
地方企业办 Run by Local Enterprises	19	1	480
民办 Non-government	6107	110	200170
城区 Urban Area	27159	1682	765191
教育部门 Run by Ed. Dept.	24926	1675	659143
其他部门 Run by Non-ed. Dept.	102	5	2703
地方企业办 Run by Local Enterprises	8	0	252
民办 Non-government	2123	2	103093
其中:城乡结合区 of Which:Urban-rural Transitional Area	7817	1270	152239
教育部门 Run by Ed. Dept.	7234	1268	120253
其他部门 Run by Non-ed. Dept.	13	2	268
地方企业办 Run by Local Enterprises	3	0	68
民办 Non-government	567	0	31650
镇区 Counties & Towns Area	43798	11023	904980
教育部门 Run by Ed. Dept.	41541	10986	832882
其他部门 Run by Non-ed. Dept.	143	17	6099
地方企业办 Run by Local Enterprises	2	1	108
民办 Non-government	2112	19	65891
其中:镇乡结合区 of Which: County-town Transitional Area	18045	7969	278351
教育部门 Run by Ed. Dept.	17193	7952	253279
其他部门 Run by Non-ed. Dept.	4	3	139
地方企业办 Run by Local Enterprises	0	1	29
民办 Non-government	848	13	24904
乡村 Rural Area	96052	90293	1013535
教育部门 Run by Ed. Dept.	94123	90150	980990
其他部门 Run by Non-ed. Dept.	48	54	1239
地方企业办 Run by Local Enterprises	9	0	120
民办 Non-government	1872	89	31186
总计中:五年制 of the Total: 5-Year	—	—	69541
九年一贯制学校 9-Year Sec. Schools	—	—	252151
十二年一贯制学校 12-Year Sec. Schools	—	—	28305
其他学校附设 Other Primary Schools Attached	—	—	6153
独立设置的少数民族学校 Inde. Sec. Schools for Minorities	6752	—	82428

小学班额情况
Size Classes in Primary Schools

单位:个
unit: class

	合计 Total	一年级 Grade 1	二年级 Grade 2	三年级 Grade 3	四年级 Grade 4	五年级 Grade 5	六年级 Grade 6	复式班 Multiple-grade Classes
合　计 Total	**2683706**	**500671**	**481170**	**456252**	**429804**	**418866**	**387993**	**8950**
城区: Urban Area								
25 人及以下 Under 25 Persons	31998	5962	5799	5397	5289	5059	4453	39
26-35 人 Between 26-35	79369	14352	13805	13173	13020	13131	11887	1
36-45 人 Between 36-45	303742	63936	55747	51201	48227	45099	39528	4
46-55 人 Between 46-55	245367	46699	43015	42224	40675	38920	33834	0
56-65 人 Between 56-65	81222	9741	13124	14118	14382	15685	14172	0
66 人及以上 Over 66 Persons	23493	2067	3651	4065	4204	4924	4582	0
其中:城乡结合区:								
of Which:Urban-rural Transitional Area								
25 人及以下 Under 25 Persons	14673	2750	2739	2536	2417	2264	1939	28
26-35 人 Between 26-35	21609	3785	3646	3566	3564	3672	3375	1
36-45 人 Between 36-45	61177	12679	10938	10281	9684	9187	8408	0
46-55 人 Between 46-55	41556	8124	7594	7243	6610	6376	5609	0
56-65 人 Between 56-65	10424	1412	1803	1984	1773	1685	1767	0
66 人及以上 Over 66 Persons	2800	196	465	511	553	579	496	0
镇区:Counties&Towns Area								
25 人及以下 Under 25 Persons	86828	18493	17010	14660	13908	12138	10038	581
26-35 人 Between 26-35	124462	23408	21246	20894	20425	19947	18520	22
36-45 人 Between 36-45	355630	68210	61599	58816	55850	56148	55002	5
46-55 人 Between 46-55	225719	38963	37780	37597	36175	37526	37678	0
56-65 人 Between 56-65	83657	8813	12823	14755	14644	15847	16775	0
66 人及以上 Over 66 Persons	28684	2218	4464	5099	5070	5772	6061	0
其中:镇乡结合区:								
of Which:County-town Transitional Area								
25 人及以下 Under 25 Persons	49066	10602	9931	8350	7779	6706	5353	345
26-35 人 Between 26-35	50876	9458	8845	8656	8283	8230	7389	15
36-45 人 Between 36-45	101964	19362	17582	17143	16150	15926	15800	1
46-55 人 Between 46-55	53396	9299	8985	8966	8390	8904	8852	0
56-65 人 Between 56-65	17345	1851	2805	3094	3076	3069	3450	0
66 人及以上 Over 66 Persons	5704	470	907	1034	1001	1087	1205	0
乡村:Rural Area								
25 人及以下 Under 25 Persons	453533	103284	95746	77727	67850	55966	45010	7950
26-35 人 Between 26-35	239137	42968	42442	41414	38670	38410	34975	258
36-45 人 Between 36-45	217294	37392	36638	37371	34562	35581	35686	64
46-55 人 Between 46-55	81474	11891	12955	14016	13331	14352	14912	17
56-65 人 Between 56-65	18202	1905	2768	3032	2951	3583	3954	9
66 人及以上 Over 66 Persons	3895	369	558	693	571	778	926	0

小 学
Number of Students

	毕业生数 Graduates	招生数 Entrants			
		合计 Total	其中:受过学前教育 of Which: Those Received the Pre-school Education	合计 Total	其中:女 of Which: Female
总 计 Total	**15658999**	**17665544**	**17430535**	**100936980**	**46883168**
其中:女 of Which: Female	7236807	8241994	8136329	46883168	—
少数民族 Minorities	1748683	2122670	2032932	11759653	5578175
五年制 5-Year	501043	538554	537660	2627358	1237973
九年一贯制学校 9-Year Schools	1645350	1787919	1765646	10384335	4689171
十二年一贯制学校 12-Year Schools	170604	189206	184401	1092400	456212
附设小学班 Primary School Classes	146631	24158	23143	262552	117872
复式班 Morning & Afternoon Shift Classes	2011	29126	27326	92140	44409
小学教学点 External Teaching Sites	370175	1131101	1101733	4428315	2124779
独立设置少数民族学校 Inde. Sec. Schools for Minorities	468132	548118	524677	3112298	1501512
随迁子女 Migrant Children	1831037	2474288	2456046	14052027	6223729
其中:外省迁入 of Which: from Other Province	867828	1162939	1154897	6622828	2907639
本省外县迁入 From Other County	963209	1311349	1301149	7429199	3316090
进城务工人员随迁子女 Children of Migrant Workers	1383431	1809889	1800113	10421804	4633796
其中:外省迁入 of Which: from Other Province	628279	807701	803817	4695084	2062379
本省外县迁入 From Other County	755152	1002188	996296	5726720	2571417
农村留守儿童 Children Left Behind	1506129	1746431	1709924	10644790	4942217
教育部门 Run by Ed. Dept.	14327070	16225151	16007633	92420593	43295290
其他部门 Run by Non-ed. Dept.	61930	60574	59921	357964	169412
地方企业办 Run by Local Enterprises	2870	2842	2787	16703	7412
民办 Non-government	1267129	1376977	1360194	8141720	3411054
城区 Urban Area	5128287	6300296	6252652	34622854	15909940
教育部门 Run by Ed. Dept.	4495574	5511676	5475385	30267363	14039761
其他部门 Run by Non-ed. Dept.	17926	17535	17471	104697	49332
地方企业办 Run by Local Enterprises	1478	1566	1566	9291	4131
民办 Non-government	613309	769519	758230	4241503	1816716
其中:城乡结合区 of Which: Urban-rural Transitional Area	903613	1193192	1180984	6359140	2887869
教育部门 Run by Ed. Dept.	706444	952869	945599	5017749	2322839
其他部门 Run by Non-ed. Dept.	1511	1581	1573	8679	4209
地方企业办 Run by Local Enterprises	314	474	474	2519	1132
民办 Non-government	195344	238268	233338	1330193	559689
镇区 Counties & Towns Area	6222672	6496373	6438675	38560500	17796448
教育部门 Run by Ed. Dept.	5710991	6053066	5999560	35631442	16596881
其他部门 Run by Non-ed. Dept.	37836	35741	35416	212948	100825
地方企业办 Run by Local Enterprises	796	791	758	4380	2050
民办 Non-government	473049	406775	402941	2711730	1096692
其中:镇乡结合区 of Which: County-town Transitional Area	1658287	1856889	1841314	10666030	4921447
教育部门 Run by Ed. Dept.	1485383	1702802	1687755	9647206	4508453
其他部门 Run by Non-ed. Dept.	955	949	948	5311	2399
地方企业办 Run by Local Enterprises	266	206	173	1302	620
民办 Non-government	171683	152932	152438	1012211	409975
乡村 Rural Area	4308040	4868875	4739208	27753626	13176780
教育部门 Run by Ed. Dept.	4120505	4660409	4532688	26521788	12658648
其他部门 Run by Non-ed. Dept.	6168	7298	7034	40319	19255
地方企业办 Run by Local Enterprises	596	485	463	3032	1231
民办 Non-government	180771	200683	199023	1188487	497646

学生数
in Primary Schools

单位：人
unit：person

在校生数 Enrolment						预计毕业生数 Estimated Graduates for Next Year
一年级 Grade 1	二年级 Grade 2	三年级 Grade 3	四年级 Grade 4	五年级 Grade 5	六年级 Grade 6	
17670612	**17465724**	**17199979**	**16418717**	**16519451**	**15662497**	**16179442**
8243724	8118831	7993262	7599330	7659469	7268552	7511508
2123240	2078143	1994518	1895749	1857280	1810723	1820191
538680	532961	522574	516198	516945	0	516945
1788853	1730391	1727476	1687328	1734175	1716112	1795533
189300	173590	178315	179938	183747	187510	193270
23930	22408	24250	24702	41130	126132	126699
29200	32703	13481	8621	5035	3100	3100
1131571	1094420	838012	596256	457516	310540	315499
548466	537814	532679	510954	496429	485956	488882
2478669	2487995	2451467	2334353	2275749	2023794	2121018
1165320	1170146	1156876	1105348	1090159	934979	1003795
1313349	1317849	1294591	1229005	1185590	1088815	1117223
1810870	1832635	1815517	1741712	1702071	1518999	1595477
808155	822294	818185	788862	783749	673839	725555
1002715	1010341	997332	952850	918322	845160	869922
1747238	1820718	1819558	1728379	1777798	1751099	1752532
16229663	16077760	15773306	15025298	15085060	14229506	14708789
60576	60092	58908	58483	62833	57072	62401
2843	2807	2731	2826	2701	2795	2849
1377530	1325065	1365034	1332110	1368857	1373124	1405403
6301277	6073511	5904363	5720553	5635279	4987871	5316915
5512277	5326894	5157717	5006115	4932582	4331778	4634776
17529	16948	16567	17286	18638	17729	17875
1567	1666	1529	1611	1486	1432	1486
769904	728003	728550	695541	682573	636932	662778
1193405	1134350	1098827	1029328	994662	908568	951181
952973	903215	866635	813207	777682	704037	739495
1581	1450	1352	1404	1452	1440	1455
474	592	510	426	316	201	216
238377	229093	230330	214291	215212	202890	210015
6498819	6488373	6489222	6253523	6431941	6398622	6527757
6055546	6049248	6018569	5771756	5905925	5830398	5950934
35749	36388	35634	34654	37299	33224	38146
791	715	737	729	691	717	717
406733	402022	434282	446384	488026	534283	537960
1857238	1832545	1812623	1720958	1730601	1712065	1744382
1703131	1680448	1647044	1553798	1549449	1513336	1543846
949	910	887	800	891	874	879
206	178	209	250	225	234	234
152952	151009	164483	166110	180036	197621	199423
4870516	4903840	4806394	4444641	4452231	4276004	4334770
4661840	4701618	4597020	4247427	4246553	4067330	4123079
7298	6756	6707	6543	6896	6119	6380
485	426	465	486	524	646	646
200893	195040	202202	190185	198258	201909	204665

小学学龄人口入学

Number of Schools-age Population

	在校学龄人口数 School-age Population		招生数 Entrants		
	合计 Total	其中:女 of Which: Female	合计 Total	其中:受过学前教育 of Which: Those Received thePre-school Education	合计 Total
总　计 Total	**97701819**	**45436895**	**17665544**	**17430535**	**100936980**
5 岁及以下 Under 5 Years	0	0	133060	—	133365
6 岁 6 Years	13603253	6408004	14219768	—	14397722
7 岁 7 Years	17255655	8028319	3155088	—	17255655
8 岁 8 Years	17218838	8019020	127770	—	17218838
9 岁 9 Years	16681924	7756333	19439	—	16681924
10 岁 10 Years	16474861	7644873	5316	—	16474861
11 岁 11 Years	15039910	6916986	2074	—	15109049
12 岁 12 Years	1427378	663360	1407	—	3285430
13 岁 13 Years	0	0	850	—	301136
14 岁 14 Years	0	0	384	—	53072
15 岁及以上 Over 15 Years	0	0	388	—	25928
城区 Urban Area	33714845	15516785	6300296	6252652	34622854
5 岁及以下 Under 5 Years	0	0	37600	—	37601
6 岁 6 Years	5268602	2471979	5382800	—	5437769
7 岁 7 Years	6040362	2781784	852274	—	6040362
8 岁 8 Years	5916212	2721577	24546	—	5916212
9 岁 9 Years	5807366	2667375	1846	—	5807366
10 岁 10 Years	5683595	2609340	597	—	5683595
11 岁 11 Years	4830749	2190240	333	—	4866015
12 岁 12 Years	167959	74490	166	—	775808
13 岁 13 Years	0	0	62	—	50113
14 岁 14 Years	0	0	36	—	6134
15 岁及以上 Over 15 Years	0	0	36	—	1879
其中:城乡结合区 of Which: Urban-rural Transitional Area	6182103	2812859	1193192	1180984	6359140
5 岁及以下 Under 5 Years	0	0	6026	—	5964
6 岁 6 Years	983426	456146	1003249	—	1011158
7 岁 7 Years	1124650	513746	177184	—	1124650
8 岁 8 Years	1099406	499171	5574	—	1099406
9 岁 9 Years	1048017	476179	687	—	1048017
10 岁 10 Years	1004202	454196	202	—	1004202
11 岁 11 Years	883374	395917	119	—	889932
12 岁 12 Years	39028	17504	87	—	160774
13 岁 13 Years	0	0	31	—	12634
14 岁 14 Years	0	0	21	—	1925
15 岁及以上 Over 15 Years	0	0	12	—	478

及在校生情况
of Primary Schools

单位：人
unit：person

在校学生数 Enrolment						
其中：女 of Which: Female	一年级 Grade 1	二年级 Grade 2	三年级 Grade 3	四年级 Grade 4	五年级 Grade 5	六年级 Grade 6
46883168	**17670612**	**17465724**	**17199979**	**16418717**	**16519451**	**15662497**
69692	132908	442	15	—	—	—
6796889	14222002	174528	1146	46	—	—
8028319	3158025	13869206	225722	2355	347	—
8019020	128736	3225960	13562592	294923	6326	301
7756333	19337	163872	3187292	12812156	486951	12316
7644873	5124	21957	183644	3062885	12622756	578495
6947295	1929	5033	28184	203735	3114234	11755934
1457486	1164	2141	7217	31485	240490	3002933
128044	614	983	2095	6264	35820	255360
23567	385	509	1012	2104	7116	41946
11650	388	1093	1060	2764	5411	15212
15909940	6301277	6073511	5904363	5720553	5635279	4987871
20607	37527	70	4	—	—	—
2555069	5382770	54490	505	4	—	—
2781784	853403	5117579	68510	646	224	—
2721577	25040	864317	4931267	94131	1383	74
2667375	1677	33629	863469	4748491	157362	2738
2609340	418	2442	35526	834354	4626199	184656
2205361	205	554	3545	38602	803828	4019281
326621	106	211	930	3260	41397	729904
19203	59	103	321	707	3851	45072
2236	36	57	171	211	739	4920
767	36	59	115	147	296	1226
2887869	1193405	1134350	1098827	1029328	994662	908568
3107	5952	11	1	—	—	—
469569	1003119	7989	49	1	—	—
513746	177635	936971	9964	65	15	—
499171	5609	180517	900058	12949	258	15
476179	663	7575	178370	837896	22806	707
454196	178	775	8493	167758	797762	29236
398753	112	265	1060	9261	162534	716700
67740	73	123	500	994	9986	149098
4582	31	66	186	280	997	11074
637	21	42	110	81	222	1449
189	12	16	36	43	82	289

	在校学龄人口数 School-age Population		招生数 Entrants		
	合计 Total	其中:女 of Which: Female	合计 Total	其中:受过学前教育 of Which: Those Received thePre-school Education	合计 Total
镇区 Counties & Towns Area	37270392	17220110	6496373	6438675	38560500
5岁及以下 Under 5 Years	0	0	51606	—	51775
6岁 6 Years	5008586	2346825	5274311	—	5347590
7岁 7 Years	6412599	2964655	1119425	—	6412599
8岁 8 Years	6489427	3005237	41687	—	6489427
9岁 9 Years	6337034	2927856	6407	—	6337034
10岁 10 Years	6375529	2938628	1597	—	6375529
11岁 11 Years	6064382	2769636	535	—	6088428
12岁 12 Years	582835	267273	494	—	1316168
13岁 13 Years	0	0	137	—	114337
14岁 14 Years	0	0	92	—	18364
15岁及以上 Over 15 Years	0	0	82	—	9249
其中:镇乡结合区 of Which: County-town Transitional Area	10338812	4777330	1856889	1841314	10666030
5岁及以下 Under 5 Years	0	0	14593	—	14655
6岁 6 Years	1459314	683124	1506094	—	1525492
7岁 7 Years	1811738	838291	322773	—	1811738
8岁 8 Years	1816533	841960	11586	—	1816533
9岁 9 Years	1747364	806140	1284	—	1747364
10岁 10 Years	1723801	793699	295	—	1723801
11岁 11 Years	1638248	748708	123	—	1643109
12岁 12 Years	141814	65408	60	—	348767
13岁 13 Years	0	0	35	—	28499
14岁 14 Years	0	0	26	—	4411
15岁及以上 Over 15 Years	0	0	20	—	1661
乡村 Rural Area	26716582	12700000	4868875	4739208	27753626
5岁及以下 Under 5 Years	0	0	43854	—	43989
6岁 6 Years	3326065	1589200	3562657	—	3612363
7岁 7 Years	4802694	2281880	1183389	—	4802694
8岁 8 Years	4813199	2292206	61537	—	4813199
9岁 9 Years	4537524	2161102	11186	—	4537524
10岁 10 Years	4415737	2096905	3122	—	4415737
11岁 11 Years	4144779	1957110	1206	—	4154606
12岁 12 Years	676584	321597	747	—	1193454
13岁 13 Years	0	0	651	—	136686
14岁 14 Years	0	0	256	—	28574
15岁及以上 Over 15 Years	0	0	270	—	14800

及在校生情况(续)
of Primary Schools(Cont.)

单位:人
unit:person

在校学生数 Enrolment						
其中:女 of Which: Female	一年级 Grade 1	二年级 Grade 2	三年级 Grade 3	四年级 Grade 4	五年级 Grade 5	六年级 Grade 6
17796448	6498819	6488373	6489222	6253523	6431941	6398622
26938	51623	151	1	—	—	—
2512157	5275765	71548	251	26	—	—
2964655	1120376	5193156	98175	832	60	—
3005237	41890	1158733	5157665	128545	2482	112
2927856	6418	55095	1157981	4899153	212950	5437
2938628	1566	6705	63324	1137466	4908215	258253
2780364	514	1398	8632	73791	1200644	4803449
580235	356	578	2120	10054	91155	1211905
48079	137	190	546	1843	12271	99350
8198	92	135	251	596	2275	15015
4101	82	684	276	1217	1889	5101
4921447	1857238	1832545	1812623	1720958	1730601	1712065
7576	14582	72	1	—	—	—
715337	1506197	19176	107	12	—	—
838291	322995	1463294	25178	254	17	—
841960	11620	332533	1439438	32251	652	39
806140	1286	15073	326855	1351140	50934	2076
793699	295	1780	17591	314675	1327970	61490
750812	122	409	2372	19197	323613	1297396
153076	60	120	782	2523	23683	321599
11909	35	39	169	570	2775	24911
1847	26	31	72	178	638	3466
800	20	18	58	158	319	1088
13176780	4870516	4903840	4806394	4444641	4452231	4276004
22147	43758	221	10	—	—	—
1729663	3563467	48490	390	16	—	—
2281880	1184246	3558471	59037	877	63	—
2292206	61806	1202910	3473660	72247	2461	115
2161102	11242	75148	1165842	3164512	116639	4141
2096905	3140	12810	84794	1091065	3088342	135586
1961570	1210	3081	16007	91342	1109762	2933204
550630	702	1352	4167	18171	107938	1061124
60762	418	690	1228	3714	19698	110938
13133	257	317	590	1297	4102	22011
6782	270	350	669	1400	3226	8885

	教职 Educational			
	合计 Total	专任教师 Full-time Teachers	行政人员 Adm. Personnel	教辅人员 Supporting Staff
总　计 Total	**5645319**	**5282512**	**130187**	**101351**
其中：女 of Which: Female	3675429	3523118	40554	49760
少数民族 Minority	613823	567719	11761	12438
教育部门 Run by Ed. Dept.	5350407	5059984	116651	90144
其他部门 Run by Non-ed. Dept.	17318	14292	774	863
地方企业办 Run by Local Enterprises	531	440	29	25
民办 Non-government	277063	207796	12733	10319
城区 Urban Area	**1712992**	**1598079**	**45831**	**28050**
教育部门办 Run by Ed. Dept.	1575150	1492804	39450	22825
其他部门办 Run by Non-ed. Dept.	5590	4753	276	314
地方企业办 Run by Local Enterprises	350	286	25	25
民办 Non-government	131902	100236	6080	4886
其中：城乡结合区 of Which: Urban-rural Transitional Area	302717	280804	7999	4099
教育部门办 Run by Ed. Dept.	269583	255916	6415	3155
其他部门办 Run by Non-ed. Dept.	666	569	32	19
地方企业办 Run by Local Enterprises	104	96	5	2
民办 Non-government	32364	24223	1547	923
镇区 Counties & Towns Area	**2045891**	**1912510**	**43041**	**40896**
教育部门办 Run by Ed. Dept.	1941561	1835311	38259	36702
其他部门办 Run by Non-ed. Dept.	9616	7773	414	441
地方企业办 Run by Local Enterprises	59	58	1	0
民办 Non-government	94655	69368	4367	3753
其中：镇乡结合区 Of Which: County-town Transitional Area	585414	550699	12080	9476
教育部门办 Run by Ed. Dept.	549704	524567	10374	8099
其他部门办 Run by Non-ed. Dept.	233	220	4	3
地方企业办 Run by Local Enterprises	0	0	0	0
民办 Non-government	35477	25912	1702	1374
乡村 Rural Area	**1886436**	**1771923**	**41315**	**32405**
教育部门办 Run by Ed. Dept.	1833696	1731869	38942	30617
其他部门办 Run by Non-ed. Dept.	2112	1766	84	108
地方企业办 Run by Local Enterprises	122	96	3	0
民办 Non-government	50506	38192	2286	1680

教职工数
Personnel in Primary Schools

单位:人
unit:person

工数 Personnel		代课教师 Substitute Teachers	兼任教师 Part-time Teachers
工勤人员 Workers	校办企业职工 Employees in School-run Factories & Farms		
130933	**336**	**165689**	**24937**
61811	186	127324	16032
21904	1	11791	4137
83511	117	159952	23750
1380	9	123	19
18	19	18	1
46024	191	5596	1167
40827	**205**	**45475**	**6407**
20012	59	44961	5891
247	0	41	6
14	0	18	1
20554	146	455	509
9805	10	7829	919
4091	6	7698	868
46	0	0	0
1	0	18	0
5667	4	113	51
49371	**73**	**47057**	**5855**
31241	48	44325	5415
980	8	50	11
0	0	0	0
17150	17	2682	429
13129	30	16486	1946
6647	17	15717	1723
6	0	20	0
0	0	0	0
6476	13	749	223
40735	**58**	**73157**	**12675**
32258	10	70666	12444
153	1	32	2
4	19	0	0
8320	28	2459	229

小学分课程专任
Number of Full-time Teachers in Primary Schools

	总计 Total	其中:女 of Which: Female	品德与生活(社会) Virtue Education	语文 Language & Literature	数学 Mathematics	外语 Foreign 小计 Subtotal	英语 English	日语 Japanese
总　计 Total	**5944910**	**3994105**	**230611**	**2142326**	**1714269**	**452551**	**450226**	**114**
其中:女 of Which:Female	3994105	—	117902	1660474	1094897	393350	391618	102
少数民族 Minorities	620042	375924	25088	223584	181175	29237	29039	34
研究生毕业 Graduate	56460	47175	1378	19253	10433	8296	8271	6
本科毕业 Under-graduate	3217461	2418863	93422	1202883	872268	324640	323263	78
专科毕业 Associate Bachelor	2389380	1441881	114496	836866	743152	116147	115272	28
高中阶段毕业 High School Graduate	279341	85717	21121	82681	87781	3455	3407	2
高中阶段以下毕业 Below High School Graduate	2268	469	194	643	635	13	13	0

小学专任教师专业
Number of Full-time Teachers in Primary

	合计 Total	其中:女 of Which Female	24岁及以下 24 and Under	25-29 25 to 29	30-34 30 to 34
合　计 Total	**5944910**	**3994105**	**344281**	**896303**	**888798**
女 Female	3994105	—	291604	736801	683771
少数民族 Minorities	620042	375924	31884	89009	101026
中学高级 Senior Secondary	219299	120835	24	49	1078
小学高级 Senior Primary	2763089	1677480	644	24005	195063
小学一级 1st Grade Primary	1902791	1353724	44485	423446	521661
小学二级 2nd Grade Primary	266430	196718	27871	113835	67114
小学三级 3rd Grade Primary	24036	17818	5185	10555	4078
未定职级 No-ranking	769265	627530	266072	324413	99804

教师学历情况
by Subject Taught and Academic Qualifications

单位:人
unit:person

Languages 俄语 Russian	体育 Physical	科学 Science	艺术 Art	音乐 Music	美术 Fine Arts	综合实践活动 Practical Activities 小计 Subtotal	信息技术 Information Technique	劳动与技术 Skills Teaching	其他 Others	当年不任课 No Teaching Load in Current Year
47	**337029**	**205430**	**24503**	**234356**	**219581**	**223137**	**159046**	**54503**	**109427**	**51690**
35	86091	97269	15606	187053	147525	94081	63709	25260	71341	28516
10	32105	20215	2119	22588	19146	21484	14727	5740	31695	11606
1	5292	2139	197	2732	3332	1945	1628	205	921	542
29	179633	92262	10731	142505	125984	109097	85284	19554	42821	21215
14	131150	96392	12058	81492	80091	98778	66305	28003	55415	23343
3	20772	14532	1511	7572	10093	13185	5783	6664	10134	6504
0	182	105	6	55	81	132	46	77	136	86

技术职务、年龄结构情况
Schools by Professional Rank and Age

单位:人
unit:person

35-39 35 to 39	40-44 40 to 44	45-49 45 to 49	50-54 50 to 54	55-59 55 to 59	60岁及以上 60 and Over
1124204	**908378**	**777989**	**689237**	**311462**	**4258**
806291	607374	489584	370419	7459	802
116107	99205	85234	71028	26389	160
13473	42560	68862	68068	24961	224
586555	620647	568812	521261	243261	2841
450606	214140	120718	88812	38434	489
32537	11526	6756	4505	2229	57
1964	898	606	413	313	24
39069	18607	12235	6178	2264	623

小学专任教
Changes of Full-time

	上学年初报表专任教师数 Total Number of Full-time Teachers at Beginning of Previous Academic Year	增加教师 Factors of Increase				
		合计 Total	录用毕业生 New Recruits from Current Year Graduates		调入 Teachers Recruited from Other Units	校内调整 of Which: with Change of Status in Their Own Institutions
			小计 Subtotal	其中:师范生 of Which: Students Enrolled in Teacher Training Institutions		
合　计 Total	**5789178**	**897979**	**220577**	**149584**	**499593**	**118845**
其中:女 of Which: Female	3782708	609989	180869	123187	321986	63023
城区 Urban Area	1766203	249250	65539	47326	128912	24234
其中:女 of Which: Female	1387823	192973	54765	39642	97123	16395
其中:城乡结合区 of Which: Urban-rural Transitional Area	326700	58804	15257	11133	31170	5176
其中:女 of Which: Female	239027	43855	12552	9195	22407	3217
镇区 Counties and Towns Area	2076132	322460	72569	49320	192365	41826
其中:女 of Which: Female	1396468	221586	60092	41105	128113	22229
其中:镇乡结合区 of Which: County-town Transitional Area	593028	97187	20748	13780	59848	12258
其中:女 of Which: Female	392935	66874	17157	11524	39830	6771
乡村 Rural Area	1946843	326269	82469	52938	178316	52785
其中:女 of Which: Female	998417	195430	66012	42440	96750	24399

小学学生、教职工
Supplementary Information on Students and

	在校学生中 of Total In-school Students			教职 of Total	
	共青团员 Member of C. Y. L.	华侨 Overseas Chinese	港澳台 From H. K, Macao and Taiwan	共产党员 Member of C. P. C.	共青团员 Member of C. Y. L.
合　计 Total	**47099**	**11702**	**109673**	**1456884**	**257885**
其中:女 of Which: Female	21976	5449	48670	747832	212537
城区 Urban Area	14838	4002	94820	521561	120923
其中:女 of Which: Female	6418	1869	42094	367062	102886
其中:城乡结合区 of Which: Urban-rural Transitional Area	2381	710	15679	80629	21608
其中:女 of Which: Female	920	321	6833	48099	18129
镇区 Counties and Towns Area	16791	5279	10034	497439	70558
其中:女 of Which: Female	8184	2478	4419	235019	58629
其中:镇乡结合区 of Which: County-town Transitional Area	4350	1589	2900	130352	18764
其中:女 of Which: Female	2080	732	1335	58911	15617
乡村 Rural Area	15470	2421	4819	437884	66404
其中:女 of Which: Female	7374	1102	2157	145751	51022

师变动情况
Teachers in Primary Schools

单位:人
unit:person

其他 Others	减少教师 Factors of Decrease 合计 Total	自然减员 Retired from Their Posts during Previous Academic Year	调出 Transferred from Teaching to Non-Teaching Posts	校内调整 of Which: with Change of Status in Their Own Institutions	其他 Others	本学年初报表专任教师数 Total Number of Full-time Teachers at Beginning of Current Academic Year
58964	**742247**	**139800**	**444798**	**117809**	**39840**	**5944910**
44111	398592	54796	260987	57982	24827	3994105
30565	149774	27475	86157	18622	17520	1865679
24690	101957	17278	60502	11507	12670	1478839
7201	37859	6582	21987	4628	4662	347645
5679	24032	3467	14574	2729	3262	258850
15700	236779	47106	143589	36291	9793	2161813
11152	134225	20342	89241	18869	5773	1483829
4333	76821	14489	48140	11454	2738	613394
3116	42554	5752	29216	6020	1566	417255
12699	355694	65219	215052	62896	12527	1917418
8269	162410	17176	111244	27606	6384	1031437

政治面貌及其他
Educational Personnel of Primary Schools

单位:人
unit:person

工中 Staff & Workers 民主党派 Member of Dem. Parties	华侨 Overseas Chinese	专任教师中 of Total Full-time Teachers 共产党员 Member of C. P. C.	共青团员 Member of C. Y. L.	民主党派 Member of Dem. Parties	华侨 Overseas Chinese
12821	**1651**	**1498301**	**318197**	**13489**	**1721**
9231	1086	798545	263258	9786	1155
9460	203	544632	154960	9966	220
7194	159	391347	131710	7634	173
558	65	86120	31823	661	67
384	50	53791	26655	464	53
1879	552	512531	88225	1981	586
1319	389	252783	73349	1394	416
362	297	132312	24132	404	299
231	208	62740	20165	256	212
1482	896	441138	75012	1542	915
718	538	154415	58199	758	566

	合计 Total	城区 Urban Area
总　计 Total	**750884632.85**	**211376846.26**
其中:危房 of Which: Floor Space of Dilapidated Buildings	5662588.00	952365.83
当年新增校舍 New Floor Space Added in Current Year	47908701.95	11294981.16
一、教学及辅助用房 Teaching & Assistant Buildings	**403879545.49**	**116838555.74**
教室 Classroom	324222890.83	91510431.98
实验室 Laboratory	25299940.35	6778078.82
图书室 Library	21954594.62	5812840.54
微机室 PC-room	17287216.98	4570668.97
语音室 Linguistic	4799138.81	1404182.39
体育馆 Gymnasium	10315763.90	6762353.04
二、行政办公用房 Administrative	**66051830.39**	**21465836.99**
其中:教师办公室 of Which: for Teachers	43522345.80	13108090.90
三、生活用房 Residential and Welfare	**195354138.72**	**37870312.20**
教工宿舍 Apartments for Single	55857902.92	6660974.15
其中:教师周转宿舍 Accommodation for Circulation of Teachers	16430494.74	1101542.36
学生宿舍 Students' Dormitories	40057714.60	4174652.13
食堂 Dining Halls	42173238.80	9050859.72
厕所 Toilet	31671940.74	8937676.74
其他 Others	25593341.66	9046149.46
四、其他用房 Rooms for Other Purposes	**85599118.25**	**35202141.33**

条件(一)
in Primary Schools (1)

单位:平方米
unit:m^2

其中:城乡结合区 of Which: Urban-rural Transitional Area	镇区 Counties and Towns Area	其中:镇乡结合区 of Which: County-town Transitional Area	乡村 Rural Area
42422942.08	**258459618.36**	**78644976.14**	**281048168.23**
153350.97	1429513.32	441118.15	3280708.85
2855980.00	18555078.76	5732332.55	18058642.03
22615677.02	**137897734.86**	**43094930.35**	**149143254.89**
17662447.01	111995975.47	34822973.80	120716483.38
1366836.89	8561689.13	2761012.86	9960172.40
1190100.00	6968051.48	2349089.20	9173702.60
940629.69	5783229.53	1892072.71	6933318.48
283011.35	1898506.77	565301.55	1496449.65
1172652.08	2690282.48	704480.23	863128.38
3778905.37	**22339720.57**	**6872848.33**	**22246272.83**
2338533.98	14578175.22	4589912.78	15836079.68
9138225.79	**72951031.67**	**20491077.74**	**84532794.85**
2127790.14	21242392.49	5667454.90	27954536.28
328347.10	6696370.41	1467785.09	8632581.97
1203744.50	17853113.68	4245788.93	18029948.79
2147908.32	15759345.77	4579284.55	17363033.31
1864984.15	10056838.39	3354941.90	12677425.61
1793798.68	8039341.34	2643607.46	8507850.86
6890133.90	**25271131.26**	**8186119.72**	**25125845.66**

	占地面积(平方米) Areas Occupied(m^2)			图书(册) Books & Magazines in Libraries (Volume)	计算机数(台)	
	合计 Total	其中:of Which:			合计 Total	其中:教学用 of Which: No. of
		绿化用地面积 Green Areas	运动场地面积 Sports Areas			小计 Subtotal
合 计 Total	**2320835702.22**	**406866153.98**	**730141844.20**	**2288550203**	**12521976**	**10634765**
城区 Urban Area	427437771.89	85786179.52	160549584.86	779274125	4527252	3859944
其中:城乡结合区 of Which: Urban-rural Transitional Area	113317011.29	24393514.11	39215324.71	136865920	803503	688065
镇区 Counties and Towns Area	734620971.98	127147549.74	243062037.64	827288037	4188866	3575497
其中:镇乡结合区 of Which: County-town Transitional Area	250396998.72	43516865.50	80716948.61	243863866	1267630	1097128
乡村 Rural Area	1158776958.35	193932424.72	326530221.70	681988041	3805858	3199324

小学办学条件(三)
Condition of School Buildings in Primary Schools (3)

单位:所
unit:school

	体育运动场(馆)面积达标校数 Schools No: Sports Areas Reached Standard	体育器械配备达标校数 Schools No: Sports Equip. Reached Standard	音乐器械配备达标校数 Schools No: Musical Instru. Reached Standard	美术器械配备达标校数 Schools No: Fine Arts Instru. Reached Standard	教学自然实验仪器达标校数 Schools No: Equip. of Natural Sci. Reached Standard	建立校园网校数 Schools No: Campus Networks Set	接入互联网校数 Schools No: Internet Access
合计 Total	**141576**	**150287**	**149634**	**149323**	**149592**	**107537**	**160746**
城区 Urban Area	23364	25575	25537	25482	25348	22445	26648
其中:城乡结合区 Of Which: Urban-rural Transitional Area	6827	7233	7206	7190	7183	5941	7623
镇区 Counties and Towns Area	37902	40431	40322	40230	40256	30522	43004
其中:镇乡结合区 Of Which: County-town Transitional Area	15315	16297	16212	16196	16209	12166	17671
乡村 Rural Area	80310	84281	83775	83611	83988	54570	91094

PC (set)	教室(间)Classroom(Room)		教教室中:普通教室(间)of Which: General Classroom(Room)		固定资产总值(万元) Total Value of Fixed Asset (10,000 yuan)		
计算机 Computers Used for Instruction 其中:平板电脑 of Which: Tablet PC	合计 Total	其中:网络多媒体教室 of Which: Network Multimedia Classroom	合计 Total	其中:网络多媒体教室 of Which: Network Multimedia Classroom	合计 Total	其中:教学仪器设备资产值 of Which: Total Value of Equip & Instru. 小计 Subtotal	其中:实验设备 of Which: for Experiment
507639	**3895067**	**2214031**	**3012904**	**1960374**	**101627639.12**	**14177074.36**	**2793468.45**
296579	974555	739923	734379	628111	35228792.15	5988685.35	939327.06
40479	196321	134184	145747	115232	6757781.32	914887.07	177862.39
124432	1241533	759821	973199	688480	34436461.16	4479600.15	946637.33
37222	413812	229930	320856	206612	10079679.38	1231888.63	288897.95
86628	1678979	714287	1305326	643783	31962385.81	3708788.87	907504.06

成人小学基本情况
Basic Statistics of Adult Primary Schools

单位:人(人次)
unit:person

	学校数(所) Schools	教学班(点)(个) External Teaching Sites	毕(结)业生数 Graduates 合计 Total	其中:女 of Which: Female	注册学生数 Enrolment 合计 Total	其中:女 of Which: Female	教职工数 Educational Personnel 合计 Total	其中:女 of Which: Female	专任教师 Full-time Teacher 合计 Total	其中:女 of Which: Female	聘请校外教师 Part-time Teachers
合计 Total	**9709**	**17942**	**845020**	**466216**	**754236**	**401425**	**19333**	**8206**	**10816**	**4962**	**12635**
其中:少数民族 of Which: Minority	752	2590	81385	42181	79351	40897	3399	1376	2052	939	2227
职工小学 General Primary Schools for Staff & Workers	45	119	12879	7553	2557	1553	303	120	98	53	124
农民小学 General Primary Schools for Peasants	9664	17823	832141	458663	751679	399872	19030	8086	10718	4909	12511
小学班 Primary Classes	3077	6539	549468	302533	447636	241435	4664	2238	3172	1660	3654
扫盲班 Literacy Classes	6587	11284	282673	156130	304043	158437	14366	5848	7546	3249	8857

五、工读学校
Correctional Work-study Schools

工读学校基本情况
Basic Statistics of Correctional Work-study Schools

单位：人
unit：person

	学校数（所）Schools	班数（个）Classes	离校人数 Schools Leavers	入校人数 No. of Persons Enrolled	在校生数 Enrolment	教职工数 Educational Personnel	
						合计 Total	其中专任教师 of Which：Full-time Teachers
合　计 Total	**93**	**312**	**3311**	**3187**	**6048**	**2922**	**2177**
其中：女 of Which：Female	—	—	464	531	1075	1293	942

六、特殊教育

Special Education

	班数（个）Classes	毕业生数 Graduates	招生数 Entrants			小学	
				合计 Total	其中:女 of Which: Female	一年级 Grade 1	二年级 Grade 2
总　计 Total	**24716**	**69401**	**110843**	**578826**	**207005**	**72367**	**73158**
女 Female	—	23005	36854	196343	0	23762	23995
少数民族学生 Minority Students	—	5894	11915	58782	23707	7644	7830
寄宿生 of the Total Boarders	—	—	25141	154083	58723	14466	15549
特殊教育学校中:寄宿生 of the Special Education Schools: Boarders	—	—	16422	117041	44092	13191	13861
职业技术班 Vocational and Technical Classes	—	840	644	3371	1093	31	23
特殊教育学校 Schools for Special Edu.	24093	25004	44372	242659	89067	36473	32809
视力残疾 Visual Impairment	1218	1832	1509	9005	3324	881	930
听力残疾 Hearing Impairment	6347	9517	7696	55607	24030	4585	4709
言语残疾 Speech Disability	351	151	660	2988	1088	639	566
肢体残疾 Extremity Disability	307	157	848	2905	976	750	551
智力残疾 Intellectual Disability	14728	12787	30256	158704	55459	26255	23805
精神残疾 Mental Disability	317	183	890	3733	734	893	610
多重残疾 Multiple Disability	825	377	2513	9717	3456	2470	1638
小学附设特教班 Classes Attached to Primary Schools	539	396	408	2924	1000	455	442
视力残疾 Visual Impairment	8	3	4	10	3	4	2
听力残疾 Hearing Impairment	32	41	31	173	56	23	9
言语残疾 Speech Disability	12	4	7	40	20	5	21
肢体残疾 Extremity Disability	21	7	13	76	36	10	29
智力残疾 Intellectual Disability	420	330	322	2404	842	375	318
精神残疾 Mental Disability	15	5	16	103	13	10	35
多重残疾 Multiple Disability	31	6	15	118	30	28	28
小学随班就读 Followers in Primary Schools	—	22202	28644	216621	76040	28842	35242
视力残疾 Visual Impairment	—	2416	2152	18929	7094	2158	2900
听力残疾 Hearing Impairment	—	2728	3800	24959	9171	3813	4464
言语残疾 Speech Disability	—	1414	1661	10329	3440	1668	1762
肢体残疾 Extremity Disability	—	3278	7120	53394	19075	7166	8130
智力残疾 Intellectual Disability	—	9878	10808	90114	31287	10898	14434
精神残疾 Mental Disability	—	403	1046	7007	1955	1060	1284
多重残疾 Multiple Disability	—	2085	2057	11889	4018	2079	2268
初中附设特教班 Special Classes Attached to Junior High Schools	37	52	69	266	105	28	37
视力残疾 Visual Impairment	0	0	0	0	0	0	0
听力残疾 Hearing Impairment	0	14	0	0	0	0	0
言语残疾 Speech Disability	0	0	0	0	0	0	0
肢体残疾 Extremity Disability	0	0	0	2	0	0	0
智力残疾 Intellectual Disability	35	38	53	242	98	12	35
精神残疾 Mental Disability	1	0	4	10	1	4	2
多重残疾 Multiple Disability	1	0	12	12	6	12	0
初中随班就读 Followers in Junior High Schools	—	18466	27525	84193	30041	—	—
视力残疾 Visual Impairment	—	2529	3076	9804	3833	—	—
听力残疾 Hearing Impairment	—	2009	2949	9041	3335	—	—
言语残疾 Speech Disability	—	1081	1192	3734	1289	—	—
肢体残疾 Extremity Disability	—	3973	9584	29135	10663	—	—
智力残疾 Intellectual Disability	—	6439	8946	27164	9237	—	—
精神残疾 Mental Disability	—	399	677	2087	637	—	—
多重残疾 Multiple Disability	—	2036	1101	3228	1047	—	—
其他学校附设特教班 Special Classes Attached to Other Schools	47	41	229	269	90	18	0
视力残疾 Visual Impairment	0	0	0	0	0	0	0
听力残疾 Hearing Impairment	1	0	1	5	1	5	0
言语残疾 Speech Disability	0	0	0	0	0	0	0
肢体残疾 Extremity Disability	1	0	4	4	2	0	0
智力残疾 Intellectual Disability	39	41	181	214	74	13	0
精神残疾 Mental Disability	0	0	0	0	0	0	0
多重残疾 Multiple Disability	6	0	43	46	13	0	0
城区 Urban Area	13626	26949	35434	201029	71724	24332	23489
其中:城乡结合区 of Which: Urban-rural Transitional Area	2289	4073	6335	35740	12630	4467	4472
镇区 County and Town Area	9718	28727	49689	243519	88099	29480	30127
其中:镇乡结合区 of Which: County-town Transitional Area	3157	6819	13319	66561	23552	8966	9119
乡村 Rural Area	1372	13725	25720	134278	47182	18555	19542

注:总计中含有送教上门毕业生数 3240 人,招生数 9596 人,在校生数 31894 人。

Note: In total, including the student who received delivering education to home, there are 3240 graduates, 9596 entrants and 31894 enrollments.

单位:人
unit: person

在校生数 Enrolment										
阶段 Primary Education				初中阶段 Junior Secondary Education				高中阶段 Senior Secondary Education		
三年级 Grade 3	四年级 Grade 4	五年级 Grade 5	六年级 Grade 6	一年级 Grade 1	二年级 Grade 2	三年级 Grade 3	四年级 Grade 4	一年级 Grade 1	二年级 Grade 2	三年级及以上 Over and Grade 3
74637	**68758**	**68626**	**64976**	**50624**	**48301**	**45227**	**2093**	**3983**	**3008**	**3068**
25378	23475	23547	21700	17326	16746	15594	743	1588	1231	1258
7657	6820	7026	6543	5184	5010	4449	18	249	167	185
16216	16406	17047	17177	18389	17128	15476	420	2294	1739	1776
14065	13805	13841	13271	10921	9507	8383	387	2294	1739	1776
15	56	74	130	163	175	231	53	918	756	746
32412	26997	26161	23880	19741	17269	15822	1280	3774	2976	3065
1005	925	963	872	885	835	648	32	388	299	342
5156	5391	6416	6671	5899	5762	5334	329	1969	1683	1703
523	347	274	243	148	112	98	11	7	9	11
386	241	228	218	191	120	134	4	26	31	25
23189	18689	17117	14780	11886	9821	9141	866	1315	908	932
514	439	354	350	208	160	148	4	26	11	16
1639	965	809	746	524	459	319	34	43	35	36
484	413	538	526	31	24	11	0	0	0	0
2	0	0	2	0	0	0	0	0	0	0
40	32	28	41	0	0	0	0	0	0	0
5	0	7	2	0	0	0	0	0	0	0
8	9	5	10	4	0	1	0	0	0	0
399	339	457	455	27	24	10	0	0	0	0
15	23	9	11	0	0	0	0	0	0	0
15	10	32	5	0	0	0	0	0	0	0
38087	38199	39057	37194	—	—	—	—	—	—	—
3306	3448	3662	3455	—	—	—	—	—	—	—
4546	4294	4065	3777	—	—	—	—	—	—	—
1860	1749	1746	1544	—	—	—	—	—	—	—
9174	9391	9733	9800	—	—	—	—	—	—	—
15877	16146	16884	15875	—	—	—	—	—	—	—
1186	1225	1155	1097	—	—	—	—	—	—	—
2138	1946	1812	1646	—	—	—	—	—	—	—
17	18	38	11	44	64	9	0	0	0	0
0	0	0	0	0	0	0	0	0	0	0
0	0	0	0	0	0	0	0	0	0	0
0	0	0	0	0	0	0	0	0	0	0
1	1	0	0	0	0	0	0	0	0	0
15	15	38	10	44	64	9	0	0	0	0
1	2	0	1	0	0	0	0	0	0	0
0	0	0	0	0	0	0	0	0	0	0
—	—	—	—	27619	28679	27088	807	—	—	—
—	—	—	—	3083	3389	3292	40	—	—	—
—	—	—	—	2955	3141	2894	51	—	—	—
—	—	—	—	1193	1333	1198	10	—	—	—
—	—	—	—	9607	9910	9486	132	—	—	—
—	—	—	—	8986	9076	8547	555	—	—	—
—	—	—	—	688	742	650	7	—	—	—
—	—	—	—	1107	1088	1021	12	—	—	—
0	0	4	0	0	3	0	0	209	32	3
0	0	0	0	0	0	0	0	0	0	0
0	0	0	0	0	0	0	0	0	0	0
0	0	0	0	0	0	0	0	0	0	0
0	0	4	0	0	0	0	0	0	0	0
0	0	0	0	0	0	0	0	166	32	3
0	0	0	0	0	0	0	0	0	0	0
0	0	0	0	0	3	0	0	43	0	0
24222	22627	22557	20744	18030	17341	16977	1646	3474	2756	2834
5095	4281	4219	3881	3001	2775	2658	192	240	237	222
30815	27846	28184	27068	24740	23154	21083	374	344	160	144
9239	8049	7748	7580	5796	5061	4738	133	80	35	17
19600	18285	17885	17164	7854	7806	7167	73	165	92	90

	学校数(所) Schools	班数(个) Classes	毕业生数 Graduates	招生数 Entrants	合计 Total	其中:女 of Which: Female	小学 一年级 Grade 1	二年级 Grade 2
总　计 Total	**2107**	**24093**	**25004**	**44372**	**242659**	**89067**	**36473**	**32809**
女 Female	—	—	9610	16119	89067	—	12961	11505
少数民族学生 Minority Students	—	—	1967	4708	24025	9169	4052	3882
寄宿生 of the Total Boarders	—	—	—	16354	116784	44000	13155	13841
职业技术班 Vocational and Technical Classes	—	—	833	554	3266	1062	31	23
盲人学校 Visual Impairment	29	392	793	664	3782	1345	339	325
聋人学校 Hearing Impairment	415	4861	5064	10123	51351	19797	8605	7050
培智学校 Intellectual Disability	488	4737	5081	7732	45678	15589	6080	5447
其他特殊教育学校 Other Disability	1175	14103	14066	25853	141848	52336	21449	19987
城区 Urban Area	1027	13308	16522	23115	134858	49481	17817	16228
其中:城乡结合区 of Which: Urban-rural Transitional Area	165	2247	2268	3707	22249	7983	2880	2823
镇区 County and Town Area	947	9467	7395	18808	95167	35215	16639	14903
其中:镇乡结合区 of Which: County-town Transitional Area	312	3110	2414	6339	31510	11332	5476	5026
乡村 Rural Area	133	1318	1087	2449	12634	4371	2017	1678

校基本情况
Special Education Schools

单位：人
unit: person

在校生数 Total In-school Students										
阶段 Primary Education				初中阶段 Junior Secondary Education				高中阶段 Senior Secondary Education		
三年级 Grade 3	四年级 Grade 4	五年级 Grade 5	六年级 Grade 6	一年级 Grade 1	二年级 Grade 2	三年级 Grade 3	四年级 Grade 4	一年级 Grade 1	二年级 Grade 2	三年级及以上 Over and Grade 3
32412	**26997**	**26161**	**23880**	**19741**	**17269**	**15822**	**1280**	**3774**	**2976**	**3065**
11887	9755	9817	8849	7319	6584	5929	464	1519	1221	1257
3562	2780	2888	2276	1545	1368	1056	15	249	167	185
14029	13745	13807	13246	10911	9496	8380	387	2272	1739	1776
13	56	74	130	163	175	231	53	829	745	743
285	390	370	397	313	299	292	46	257	220	249
7315	5598	5203	4445	3707	3161	2918	238	1137	913	1061
5539	4996	4967	4535	4182	3818	3703	533	780	501	597
19273	16013	15621	14503	11539	9991	8909	463	1600	1342	1158
15973	14129	14078	12628	12194	11133	10731	1099	3293	2724	2831
3232	2481	2478	2229	1951	1689	1666	137	230	231	222
14587	11374	10726	9874	6567	5342	4339	168	344	160	144
5034	3752	3485	3272	2213	1633	1422	65	80	35	17
1852	1494	1357	1378	980	794	752	13	137	92	90

特殊教育学
Number of Educational Personnel

	教职 Educational		
	合计 Total	专任教师 Full-time Teachers	行政人员 Adm. Personnel
合　计 Total	**65138**	**55979**	**3336**
其中:女 of Which:Female	45868	41278	1599
少数民族 Minorities	5525	4831	289

特殊教育学校专任
Number of Full-time Teachers in Special Education

	合计 Total	按学历分 By Educational Attainment				
		研究生毕业 Graduate	本科毕业 Under-graduate	专科毕业 Associate Bachelor	高中阶段毕业 High School Graduate	高中阶段以下毕业 Below High School Graduate
合　计 Total	**55979**	**1246**	**36624**	**16952**	**1130**	**27**
其中:女 of Which:Female	41278	1005	27482	12141	630	20
受过特教专业培训 Trainee in special Education	41051	1025	27762	11579	672	13

特殊教育专任
Changes of Full-time Teachers in

	上学年初报表专任教师数 Number of Full-time Teachers at Beginning of Previous Academic Year	增加教师 Factors of Increase					
		合计 Total	录用毕业生 New Recruits from Current Year Graduates		调入 Teachers Recruited from Other Units	校内调整 of Which: with Change of Status in Their Own Institutions	其他 Others
			小计 Subtotal	其中:师范生 of Which: Students Enrolled in Teacher Training Institutions			
合　计 Total	**53213**	**5403**	**1990**	**1525**	**2275**	**645**	**493**
其中:女 of Which: Female	39034	4017	1690	1321	1530	409	388

校教职工数
in Special Education Schools

单位：人
unit: person

工 数 Personnel		代课教师 Substitute Teachers	兼任教师 Part-time Teachers
教辅人员 Supporting Staff	工勤人员 Workers		
2346	**3477**	**1546**	**246**
1540	1451	1231	134
133	272	87	23

教师学历、专业技术职务情况
Schools by Academic Qualifications and Professional Rank

单位：人
unit: person

按专业技术职务分 By Professional Rank					
中学高级 Senior Secondary	小学高级 Senior Primary	小学一级 1st Grade Primary	小学二级 2nd Grade Primary	小学三级 3rd Grade Primary	未定职级 No-ranking
6699	**25292**	**15209**	**2579**	**294**	**5906**
4184	18321	11534	2056	243	4940
4601	18158	11543	2043	233	4473

教师变动情况
Special Education Schools

单位：人
unit: person

减少教师 Factors of Decrease					本学年初报表专任教师数 Number of Full-time Teachers at Beginning of Current Academic Year
合计 Total	自然减员 Retired from Their Posts during Previous Academic Year	调出 Transferred from Teaching to Non-Teaching Posts	校内调整 Of Which: with Change of Status in Their Own Institutions	其他 Others	
2637	**921**	**912**	**475**	**329**	**55979**
1773	614	628	291	240	41278

特殊教育学校办学条件(一)
Condition of School Buildings in Special Education Schools(1)

单位:平方米
unit:m^2

	合计 Total
总计 Total	**9717058.62**
其中:危房 of Which : Floor Space of Dilapidated Buildings	89181.36
当年新增校舍 New Added in Current Year	486769.69
一、教学及辅助用房 Teaching & Assistant Buildings	**4419923.74**
教室 Classroom Only	2385152.15
专用教室 Classroom	1524873.41
实验室 Laboratory	179286.05
微机室 PC-room	151695.17
图书室 Library	178916.96
二、行政办公用房 Administrative	**951778.50**
其中:教师办公室 of Which: for Teachers	517054.36
三、生活用房 Residential and Welfare	**2817182.67**
四、其他用房 Rooms for Other Purposes	**1528173.71**

特殊教育学校办学条件(二)
Condition of School Buildings in Special Education Schools (2)

单位:
unit:

	占地面积(平方米) Areas Occupied(m^2)			图书(册) Books & Magazines in Libraries (Volume)
	合计 Total	其中 of Which		
		绿化用地面积 Green Areas	运动场地面积 Sports Areas	
总 计 Total	**20557725.68**	**4453134.04**	**5080937.79**	**9474607**

七、学前教育

Pre-primary Education

幼儿园园数、班数
Number of Kindergartens, Classes in Pre-primary Education

	园数(所) Kindergartens		班数(个) Classes
	合计 Total	其中:少数民族幼儿园 of Which: Minorities	
总计 Total	**254950**	**7659**	**1612901**
教育部门 Run by Ed. Dept.	75553	6951	560117
其他部门办 Run by Non-ed. Dept.	1809	18	21154
地方企业 Run by Local Enterprises	1289	0	10404
事业单位 Run by Public Institutions	3181	47	22153
部队 Run by Army	511	1	3952
集体办 Run by Communities	12235	47	65451
民办 Non-government	160372	595	929670
城区 Urban Area	78961	348	593017
教育部门 Run by Ed. Dept.	10710	186	119203
其他部门办 Run by Non-ed. Dept.	1070	3	12063
地方企业 Run by Local Enterprises	1044	0	8715
事业单位 Run by Public Institutions	1016	15	8394
部队 Run by Army	477	0	3818
集体办 Run by Communities	3989	14	29998
民办 Non-government	60655	130	410826
其中:城乡结合区 of Which: Urban-rural Transitional Area	15577	77	104615
教育部门 Run by Ed. Dept.	2266	61	18744
其他部门办 Run by Non-ed. Dept.	57	0	555
地方企业 Run by Local Enterprises	80	0	598
事业单位 Run by Public Institutions	112	1	612
部队 Run by Army	13	0	82
集体办 Run by Communities	1759	3	10947
民办 Non-government	11290	12	73077

幼儿园园数、班数(续)
Number of Kindergartens, Classes in Pre-primary Education (Cont.)

	园数(所) Kindergartens		班数(个) Classes
	合计 Total	其中:少数民族幼儿园 of Which: Minorities	
镇区 County and Town Area	85807	1312	576473
教育部门 Run by Ed. Dept.	23613	991	203829
其他部门办 Run by Non-ed. Dept.	589	6	5804
地方企业 Run by Local Enterprises	211	0	1501
事业单位 Run by Public Institutions	884	16	6230
部队 Run by Army	13	0	54
集体办 Run by Communities	2521	10	17015
民办 Non-government	57976	289	342040
其中:镇乡结合区 of Which: County-town Transitional Area	25947	362	159294
教育部门 Run by Ed. Dept.	7340	308	55366
其他部门办 Run by Non-ed. Dept.	52	1	724
地方企业 Run by Local Enterprises	40	0	270
事业单位 Run by Public Institutions	249	1	1617
部队 Run by Army	2	0	9
集体办 Run by Communities	1341	4	7460
民办 Non-government	16923	48	93848
乡村 Rural Area	90182	5999	443411
教育部门 Run by Ed. Dept.	41230	5774	237085
其他部门办 Run by Non-ed. Dept.	150	9	3287
地方企业 Run by Local Enterprises	34	0	188
事业单位 Run by Public Institutions	1281	16	7529
部队 Run by Army	21	1	80
集体办 Run by Communities	5725	23	18438
民办 Non-government	41741	176	176804
其中:独立设置幼儿园 of the Total: Inde. Kinder.	0	0	1445327
附设幼儿班 Kinder. Classes Attached to School	0	0	167574

学前教育分年龄幼儿数(总计)

Number of Children in Pre-school Education by Age(Total)

单位:人

unit: person

	入园(班)人数 Entrants	在园(班)人数 Enrolment	离园(班)人数 Leavers
总　计 Total	**19379530**	**46001393**	**16526663**
其中:女 of Which:Female	9125023	21490692	7814108
少数民族 Minorities	2469014	4846099	1826829
残疾人 Disability	11519	27113	32831
教育部门 Run by Ed. Dept.	7976543	16657082	6903336
2岁及以下 2 Years and Under	130352	136591	—
3岁 3 Years	3212286	3464624	—
4岁 4 Years	1736876	5018155	—
5岁 5 Years	2283736	6788309	1247414
6岁及以上 6 Years and Over	613293	1249403	5655922
其他部门 Run by Non-ed. Dept.	311460	698507	251050
2岁及以下 2 Years and Under	16666	17184	—
3岁 3 Years	148417	169223	—
4岁 4 Years	61263	217334	—
5岁 5 Years	60824	246302	41872
6岁及以上 6 Years and Over	24290	48464	209178
地方企业 Run by Local Enterprises	110866	320150	99570
2岁及以下 2 Years and Under	11365	12252	—
3岁 3 Years	71957	91383	—
4岁 4 Years	15145	102638	—
5岁 5 Years	11205	107285	12740
6岁及以上 6 Years and Over	1194	6592	86830
事业单位 Run by Public Institutions	298718	623394	305097
2岁及以下 2 Years and Under	11175	12280	—
3岁 3 Years	94066	117521	—
4岁 4 Years	50334	170151	—
5岁 5 Years	134036	302484	63620
6岁及以上 6 Years and Over	9107	20958	241477
部队 Run by Army	35046	121738	40229
2岁及以下 2 Years and Under	3246	3426	—
3岁 3 Years	26654	33779	—
4岁 4 Years	3173	39797	—
5岁 5 Years	1888	43259	3891
6岁及以上 6 Years and Over	85	1477	36338
集体 Run by Communities	653705	1857088	631535
2岁及以下 2 Years and Under	26324	28307	—
3岁 3 Years	445886	505640	—
4岁 4 Years	97930	606808	—
5岁 5 Years	77132	686388	51931
6岁及以上 6 Years and Over	6433	29945	579604
民办 Non-government	9993192	25723434	8295846
2岁及以下 2 Years and Under	817069	919504	—
3岁 3 Years	4705531	6183945	—
4岁 4 Years	2175794	8105459	—
5岁 5 Years	2013727	9595290	1493244
6岁及以上 6 Years and Over	281071	919236	6802602

注:幼儿数包括:独立设置幼儿园和附设幼儿班的幼儿数,下同。

Note: Data on Independent Set Kindergarten and Attached Preschool are included in the number of Children. The same as below.

学前教育分年龄幼儿数(城区)
Number of Children in Pre-primary Education by Age(Urban Area)

单位:人
unit: person

	入园(班)人数 Entrants	在园(班)人数 Enrolment	离园(班)人数 Leavers
总计 Total	**6439559**	**17068501**	**5391642**
其中:女 of Which:Female	3031151	7957635	2526402
少数民族 Minorities	377014	886015	283673
残疾人 Disability	4263	11019	8558
教育部门 Run by Ed. Dept.	1635203	3965467	1361893
2岁及以下 2 Years and Under	37939	39945	—
3岁 3 Years	1057304	1127419	—
4岁 4 Years	208911	1257749	—
5岁 5 Years	276091	1436198	188006
6岁及以上 6 Years and Over	54958	104156	1173887
其他部门 Run by Non-ed. Dept.	144366	407383	128655
2岁及以下 2 Years and Under	13091	13502	—
3岁 3 Years	103036	118426	—
4岁 4 Years	15384	131097	—
5岁 5 Years	11587	138080	15205
6岁及以上 6 Years and Over	1268	6278	113450
地方企业 Run by Local Enterprises	92257	267949	82283
2岁及以下 2 Years and Under	9893	10727	—
3岁 3 Years	59935	76388	—
4岁 4 Years	12134	85934	—
5岁 5 Years	9269	89420	9839
6岁及以上 6 Years and Over	1026	5480	72444
事业单位 Run by Public Institutions	104272	270422	99245
2岁及以下 2 Years and Under	8599	9251	—
3岁 3 Years	56140	69791	—
4岁 4 Years	12141	81146	—
5岁 5 Years	26186	106824	15832
6岁及以上 6 Years and Over	1206	3410	83413
部队 Run by Army	33723	118414	39246
2岁及以下 2 Years and Under	3181	3341	—
3岁 3 Years	25831	32853	—
4岁 4 Years	2943	38584	—
5岁 5 Years	1693	42197	3791
6岁及以上 6 Years and Over	75	1439	35455
集体 Run by Communities	330243	946005	311082
2岁及以下 2 Years and Under	14630	15827	—
3岁 3 Years	230671	264760	—
4岁 4 Years	45965	309864	—
5岁 5 Years	36558	342712	22193
6岁及以上 6 Years and Over	2419	12842	288889
民办 Non-government	4099495	11092861	3369238
2岁及以下 2 Years and Under	393320	450082	—
3岁 3 Years	2022651	2773422	—
4岁 4 Years	823672	3450371	—
5岁 5 Years	766022	4083940	454544
6岁及以上 6 Years and Over	93830	335046	2914694

学前教育分年龄幼儿数(城乡结合区)
Number of Children in Pre-school Education by Ages (Urban-rural Transitional Area)

单位:人
unit: person

	入园(班)人数 Entrants	在园(班)人数 Enrolment	离园(班)人数 Leavers
总计 Total	**1175733**	**3004454**	**970424**
其中:女 of Which:Female	548085	1385613	444177
少数民族 Minorities	67754	135693	43881
残疾人 Disability	656	1619	1394
教育部门 Run by Ed. Dept.	272256	584435	215188
2岁及以下 2 Years and Under	5598	5817	—
3岁 3 Years	133006	144399	—
4岁 4 Years	47940	177197	—
5岁 5 Years	66862	226629	31987
6岁及以上 6 Years and Over	18850	30393	183201
其他部门 Run by Non-ed. Dept.	6560	18079	5942
2岁及以下 2 Years and Under	217	218	—
3岁 3 Years	4634	5184	—
4岁 4 Years	844	5909	—
5岁 5 Years	673	6336	664
6岁及以上 6 Years and Over	192	432	5278
地方企业 Run by Local Enterprises	7109	17814	5627
2岁及以下 2 Years and Under	398	437	—
3岁 3 Years	4406	5381	—
4岁 4 Years	1068	5674	—
5岁 5 Years	1201	6156	582
6岁及以上 6 Years and Over	36	166	5045
事业单位 Run by Public Institutions	8477	19168	8707
2岁及以下 2 Years and Under	317	385	—
3岁 3 Years	3634	4275	—
4岁 4 Years	864	5218	—
5岁 5 Years	3573	9002	1798
6岁及以上 6 Years and Over	89	288	6909
部队 Run by Army	774	2516	808
2岁及以下 2 Years and Under	84	84	—
3岁 3 Years	517	740	—
4岁 4 Years	66	722	—
5岁 5 Years	94	929	5
6岁及以上 6 Years and Over	13	41	803
集体 Run by Communities	116994	333821	111822
2岁及以下 2 Years and Under	4904	5440	—
3岁 3 Years	75719	89492	—
4岁 4 Years	20209	109954	—
5岁 5 Years	15080	123342	9635
6岁及以上 6 Years and Over	1082	5593	102187
民办 Non-government	763563	2028621	622330
2岁及以下 2 Years and Under	58456	65684	—
3岁 3 Years	368564	490737	—
4岁 4 Years	168796	646144	—
5岁 5 Years	149997	763945	90572
6岁及以上 6 Years and Over	17750	62111	531758

学前教育分年龄幼儿数(镇区)
Number of Children in Pre-school Education by Ages (Counties & Towns Area)

单位:人
unit: person

	入园(班)人数 Entrants	在园(班)人数 Enrolment	离园(班)人数 Leavers
总计 Total	**7500240**	**17575032**	**6435136**
其中:女 of Which:Female	3515359	8180853	3045410
少数民族 Minorities	891856	1867001	706509
残疾人 Disability	4367	9721	11556
教育部门 Run by Ed. Dept.	3127747	6805814	2789995
2岁及以下 2 Years and Under	60576	63257	—
3岁 3 Years	1358321	1471807	—
4岁 4 Years	664114	2072702	—
5岁 5 Years	843772	2772934	551919
6岁及以上 6 Years and Over	200964	425114	2238076
其他部门 Run by Non-ed. Dept.	98026	188440	68691
2岁及以下 2 Years and Under	3131	3232	—
3岁 3 Years	35803	40561	—
4岁 4 Years	28834	60919	—
5岁 5 Years	24315	68930	14260
6岁及以上 6 Years and Over	5943	14798	54431
地方企业 Run by Local Enterprises	16572	47112	15397
2岁及以下 2 Years and Under	1319	1362	—
3岁 3 Years	10981	13627	—
4岁 4 Years	2529	15093	—
5岁 5 Years	1610	16013	2475
6岁及以上 6 Years and Over	133	1017	12922
事业单位 Run by Public Institutions	97736	185306	100185
2岁及以下 2 Years and Under	1656	1989	—
3岁 3 Years	23435	29370	—
4岁 4 Years	17799	47991	—
5岁 5 Years	50527	97485	21106
6岁及以上 6 Years and Over	4319	8471	79079
部队 Run by Army	588	1575	497
2岁及以下 2 Years and Under	26	37	—
3岁 3 Years	328	384	—
4岁 4 Years	124	591	—
5岁 5 Years	108	538	64
6岁及以上 6 Years and Over	2	25	433
集体 Run by Communities	181525	509341	173300
2岁及以下 2 Years and Under	5821	6069	—
3岁 3 Years	124951	136653	—
4岁 4 Years	26307	165996	—
5岁 5 Years	22013	191925	13962
6岁及以上 6 Years and Over	2433	8698	159338
民办 Non-government	3978046	9837444	3287071
2岁及以下 2 Years and Under	304742	338873	—
3岁 3 Years	1776813	2286420	—
4岁 4 Years	909442	3093253	—
5岁 5 Years	858312	3712948	675121
6岁及以上 6 Years and Over	128737	405950	2611950

学前教育分年龄学生数(镇乡结合区)

Number of Children in Pre-school Education by Ages (County-town Transitional Area)

单位:人
unit: person

	入园(班)人数 Entrants	在园(班)人数 Enrolment	离园(班)人数 Leavers
总计 Total	**1976286**	**4615523**	**1716483**
其中:女 of Which:Female	926809	2149238	810753
少数民族 Minorities	176712	351451	134503
残疾人 Disability	1281	2405	2151
教育部门 Run by Ed. Dept.	806234	1681520	731496
2岁及以下 2 Years and Under	12028	12683	—
3岁 3 Years	320486	346227	—
4岁 4 Years	169112	501234	—
5岁 5 Years	244269	713040	147032
6岁及以上 6 Years and Over	60339	108336	584464
其他部门 Run by Non-ed. Dept.	11741	21390	8041
2岁及以下 2 Years and Under	406	410	—
3岁 3 Years	4373	5094	—
4岁 4 Years	2865	6799	—
5岁 5 Years	2955	7827	1107
6岁及以上 6 Years and Over	1142	1260	6934
地方企业 Run by Local Enterprises	2883	8636	2632
2岁及以下 2 Years and Under	170	177	—
3岁 3 Years	2076	2592	—
4岁 4 Years	368	2632	—
5岁 5 Years	258	3101	424
6岁及以上 6 Years and Over	11	134	2208
事业单位 Run by Public Institutions	24363	46431	25680
2岁及以下 2 Years and Under	352	457	—
3岁 3 Years	6524	7642	—
4岁 4 Years	3922	11772	—
5岁 5 Years	12834	24951	5626
6岁及以上 6 Years and Over	731	1609	20054
部队 Run by Army	72	253	56
2岁及以下 2 Years and Under	0	0	—
3岁 3 Years	50	69	—
4岁 4 Years	18	75	—
5岁 5 Years	4	88	0
6岁及以上 6 Years and Over	0	21	56
集体 Run by Communities	77221	211770	72574
2岁及以下 2 Years and Under	2515	2633	—
3岁 3 Years	49389	55161	—
4岁 4 Years	12711	68389	—
5岁 5 Years	11387	81831	7243
6岁及以上 6 Years and Over	1219	3756	65331
民办 Non-government	1053772	2645523	876004
2岁及以下 2 Years and Under	79997	88375	—
3岁 3 Years	487562	624862	—
4岁 4 Years	235884	840840	—
5岁 5 Years	218232	992419	175609
6岁及以上 6 Years and Over	32097	99027	700395

学前教育分年龄幼儿数(乡村)
Number of Children in Pre-school Education by Ages (Rural Area)

单位:人
unit: person

	入园(班)人数 Entrants	在园(班)人数 Enrolment	离园(班)人数 Leavers
总计 Total	**5439731**	**11357860**	**4699885**
其中:女 of Which:Female	2578513	5352204	2242296
少数民族 Minorities	1200144	2093083	836647
残疾人 Disability	2889	6373	12717
教育部门 Run by Ed. Dept.	3213593	5885801	2751448
2 岁及以下 2 Years and Under	31837	33389	—
3 岁 3 Years	796661	865398	—
4 岁 4 Years	863851	1687704	—
5 岁 5 Years	1163873	2579177	507489
6 岁及以上 6 Years and Over	357371	720133	2243959
其他部门 Run by Non-ed. Dept.	69068	102684	53704
2 岁及以下 2 Years and Under	444	450	—
3 岁 3 Years	9578	10236	—
4 岁 4 Years	17045	25318	—
5 岁 5 Years	24922	39292	12407
6 岁及以上 6 Years and Over	17079	27388	41297
地方企业 Run by Local Enterprises	2037	5089	1890
2 岁及以下 2 Years and Under	153	163	—
3 岁 3 Years	1041	1368	—
4 岁 4 Years	482	1611	—
5 岁 5 Years	326	1852	426
6 岁及以上 6 Years and Over	35	95	1464
事业单位 Run by Public Institutions	96710	167666	105667
2 岁及以下 2 Years and Under	920	1040	—
3 岁 3 Years	14491	18360	—
4 岁 4 Years	20394	41014	—
5 岁 5 Years	57323	98175	26682
6 岁及以上 6 Years and Over	3582	9077	78985
部队 Run by Army	735	1749	486
2 岁及以下 2 Years and Under	39	48	—
3 岁 3 Years	495	542	—
4 岁 4 Years	106	622	—
5 岁 5 Years	87	524	36
6 岁及以上 6 Years and Over	8	13	450
集体 Run by Communities	141937	401742	147153
2 岁及以下 2 Years and Under	5873	6411	—
3 岁 3 Years	90264	104227	—
4 岁 4 Years	25658	130948	—
5 岁 5 Years	18561	151751	15776
6 岁及以上 6 Years and Over	1581	8405	131377
民办 Non-government	1915651	4793129	1639537
2 岁及以下 2 Years and Under	119007	130549	—
3 岁 3 Years	906067	1124103	—
4 岁 4 Years	442680	1561835	—
5 岁 5 Years	389393	1798402	363579
6 岁及以上 6 Years and Over	58504	178240	1275958

幼儿园教

Number of Educational Personnel

	教 职 Educational	
	合计 Total	园长 Kindergarten Heads
总 计 Total	**4192850**	**279927**
其中:女 of Which: Female	3862781	252329
少数民族 Minorities	303468	22600
学前教育专业 Pre-primary Education Programmes	1978047	163701
教育部门 Run by Ed. Dept.	1047622	63828
其他部门办 Run by Non-ed. Dept.	72958	3143
地方企业 Run by Local Enterprises	44265	2141
事业单位 Run by Public Institutions	48146	3308
部队 Run by Army	19414	852
集体办 Run by Communities	195727	12012
民办 Non-government	2764718	194643
城区 Urban Area	2069988	110954
教育部门 Run by Ed. Dept.	390763	15407
其他部门办 Run by Non-ed. Dept.	55011	2217
地方企业 Run by Local Enterprises	37401	1783
事业单位 Run by Public Institutions	31784	1579
部队 Run by Army	18846	816
集体办 Run by Communities	109765	5283
民办 Non-government	1426418	83869
其中:城乡结合区 Of Which:Urban-rural Transitional Area	333633	19618
教育部门 Run by Ed. Dept.	44658	2281
其他部门办 Run by Non-ed. Dept.	2523	97
地方企业 Run by Local Enterprises	2564	144
事业单位 Run by Public Institutions	1382	117
部队 Run by Army	372	17
集体办 Run by Communities	38345	2144
民办 Non-government	243789	14818
镇区 County and Town Area	1443717	97107
教育部门 Run by Ed. Dept.	430780	23876
其他部门办 Run by Non-ed. Dept.	15973	790
地方企业 Run by Local Enterprises	6036	308
事业单位 Run by Public Institutions	10174	868
部队 Run by Army	224	15
集体办 Run by Communities	49097	2735
民办 Non-government	931433	68515
其中:镇乡结合区 Of Which:County-town Transitional Area	369634	27797
教育部门 Run by Ed. Dept.	93131	6483
其他部门办 Run by Non-ed. Dept.	1391	91
地方企业 Run by Local Enterprises	1070	50
事业单位 Run by Public Institutions	2552	237
部队 Run by Army	21	2
集体办 Run by Communities	20746	1397
民办 Non-government	250723	19537
乡村 Rural Area	679145	71866
教育部门 Run by Ed. Dept.	226079	24545
其他部门办 Run by Non-ed. Dept.	1974	136
地方企业 Run by Local Enterprises	828	50
事业单位 Run by Public Institutions	6188	861
部队 Run by Army	344	21
集体办 Run by Communities	36865	3994
民办 Non-government	406867	42259

职工数
in Kindergarten

单位:人
unit:person

工　数 Personnel				代课教师 Substitute Teachers	兼任教师 Part-time Teachers
专任教师 Full-time Teachers	保健医 Health Physician	保育员 Caretaker	其他 Other		
2432138	**101341**	**813673**	**565771**	**173360**	**41782**
2378291	92154	796887	343120	162586	34247
187898	3982	58071	30917	16381	10978
1686479	12961	84742	30164	59269	11377
701159	17414	161457	103764	132569	18524
40692	1964	13221	13938	3134	6506
24676	1199	8083	8166	640	48
28808	1174	7781	7075	3091	1368
9805	713	3687	4357	201	23
116721	4363	35638	26993	7306	1014
1510277	74514	583806	401478	26419	14299
1150623	59159	419270	329982	41039	8108
251126	9903	61680	52647	29854	2685
30296	1599	10122	10777	1072	126
20647	1054	6886	7031	483	43
17729	934	5809	5733	1457	360
9472	698	3589	4271	198	23
62049	2896	22306	17231	1282	229
759304	42075	308878	232292	6693	4642
184179	9220	68139	52477	6947	1237
28589	881	7559	5348	4985	428
1492	64	402	468	29	9
1452	70	438	460	30	0
858	25	235	147	255	30
197	14	74	70	0	0
21599	970	7507	6125	533	69
129992	7196	51924	39859	1115	701
876958	29153	273141	167358	80893	16889
297400	5663	65965	37876	63598	6883
9189	340	2789	2865	991	2313
3552	126	1019	1031	156	5
7012	168	1248	878	706	707
145	4	28	32	0	0
31259	876	8340	5887	2782	432
528401	21976	193752	118789	12660	6549
221470	7776	69575	43016	21886	3820
63230	1192	14478	7748	16524	1576
823	35	228	214	188	600
708	17	141	154	20	1
1666	51	377	221	260	109
18	0	1	0	0	0
13178	381	3358	2432	1356	116
141847	6100	50992	32247	3538	1418
404557	13029	121262	68431	51428	16785
152633	1848	33812	13241	39117	8956
1207	25	310	296	1071	4067
477	19	178	104	1	0
4067	72	724	464	928	301
188	11	70	54	3	0
23413	591	4992	3875	3242	353
222572	10463	81176	50397	7066	3108

幼儿园园长、专任教师
Breakdown of Kindergarten Heads, Full-time Teachers

	合计 Total	按学历分 By Educational Attainment				
		研究生毕业 Graduate	本科毕业 Under-graduate	专科毕业 Associate Bachelor	高中阶段毕业 High School Graduate	高中阶段以下毕业 Below High School Graduate
合计 Total	**2712065**	**7253**	**607705**	**1553973**	**497624**	**45510**
园长 Kindergarten Heads	279927	2906	93982	149472	30950	2617
专任教师 Full-time Teachers	2432138	4347	513723	1404501	466674	42893
城区 Urban Area	1261577	5765	340434	739089	167041	9248
园长 Kindergarten Heads	110954	2254	46427	53973	7752	548
专任教师 Full-time Teachers	1150623	3511	294007	685116	159289	8700
其中:城乡结合区	203797	393	38142	126080	36888	2294
of Which: Urban-rural Transitional Area						
园长 Kindergarten Heads	19618	190	7134	10368	1789	137
专任教师 Full-time Teachers	184179	203	31008	115712	35099	2157
镇区 County and Town Area	974065	1191	198377	558848	196904	18745
园长 Kindergarten Heads	97107	511	30642	53879	11238	837
专任教师 Full-time Teachers	876958	680	167735	504969	185666	17908
其中:镇乡结合区	249267	285	41797	142936	58399	5850
of Which: County-town Transitional Area						
园长 Kindergarten Heads	27797	127	7951	15763	3671	285
专任教师 Full-time Teachers	221470	158	33846	127173	54728	5565
乡村 Rural Area	476423	297	68894	256036	133679	17517
园长 Kindergarten Heads	71866	141	16913	41620	11960	1232
专任教师 Full-time Teachers	404557	156	51981	214416	121719	16285

学历、专业技术职务情况
by Academic Qualifications and Professional Rank

单位：人
unit：person

按专业技术职务分 By Professional Rank					
中学高级 Senior Secondary	小学高级 Senior Primary	小学一级 1st Grade Primary	小学二级 2nd Grade Primary	小学三级 3rd Grade Primary	未定职级 No-ranking
22736	**209649**	**297644**	**146776**	**27636**	**2007624**
11485	42232	31038	12094	2522	180556
11251	167417	266606	134682	25114	1827068
12165	99245	144460	66865	13135	925707
6452	16605	13245	5033	1171	68448
5713	82640	131215	61832	11964	857259
844	8272	15670	8495	2516	168000
488	2044	2374	1128	305	13279
356	6228	13296	7367	2211	154721
7876	78778	107903	54760	9131	715617
3688	14733	9281	3622	677	65106
4188	64045	98622	51138	8454	650511
1394	16074	22774	12103	1984	194938
751	3848	2617	1027	181	19373
643	12226	20157	11076	1803	175565
2695	31626	45281	25151	5370	366300
1345	10894	8512	3439	674	47002
1350	20732	36769	21712	4696	319298

	教职工中 of Total Educational Personnel		
	共产党员 Member of C. P. C.	共青团员 Member of C. Y. L.	民主党派 Member of Dem. Parties
合计 Total	**252929**	**648725**	**5281**
其中:女 of Which: Female	219685	634074	4908
城区 Urban Area	132536	390779	3506
其中:女 of Which: Female	121750	383815	3256
其中:城乡结合区 of Which: Urban-rural Transitional Area	13245	59278	508
其中:女 of Which: Female	11640	58265	468
镇区 Counties and Towns Area	83965	183312	1380
其中:女 of Which: Female	71905	179294	1290
其中:镇乡结合区 of Which: County-town Transitional Area	17229	44279	149
其中:女 of Which: Female	14240	43347	137
乡村 Rural Area	36428	74634	395
其中:女 of Which: Female	26030	70965	362

政治面貌及其他
Educational Personnel of Kindergarten

单位:人
unit:person

	专任教师中 of Total Full-time Teachers			
华侨 Overseas Chinese	共产党员 Member of C. P. C.	共青团员 Member of C. Y. L.	民主党派 Member of Dem. Parties	华侨 Overseas Chinese
1992	**171545**	**566006**	**2795**	**1299**
1882	160333	556988	2738	1276
766	89612	344320	1764	485
728	86865	340151	1728	480
127	8492	51512	247	84
120	8105	51040	240	82
850	59993	158421	770	559
809	55391	156296	759	553
198	11525	37758	84	126
189	10539	37335	83	125
376	21940	63265	261	255
345	18077	60541	251	243

幼儿园办学条件(一)
Condition of Kindergarten Buildings (1)

单位:平方米
unit: m^2

	合计 Total	城区 Urban Area	其中:城乡结合区 of Which: Urban-rural Transitional Area	镇区 Counties and Towns Area	其中:镇乡结合区 of Which: County-town Transitional Area	乡村 Rural Area
总计 Total	**320492661.90**	**138887118.67**	**24496136.85**	**118326052.52**	**30652165.29**	**63279490.71**
其中 of Which :						
危房 Floor Space of Dilapi-dated Buildings	671751.82	282792.49	28416.01	248016.46	51071.02	140942.87
当年新增校舍 New Added in Current Year	22258393.93	6360781.51	1343784.58	8684885.70	2470886.75	7212726.72
一、教学及辅助用房 Teaching &Assistant Buildings	**222597552.15**	**95314435.89**	**16496390.88**	**83032955.39**	**21464085.73**	**44250160.87**
活动室 Recreational	129886413.36	55961796.18	9729613.38	48114434.55	12503628.59	25810182.63
洗手间 Toilet	21462826.93	9143377.21	1584583.53	8003467.95	2082885.26	4315981.77
睡眠室 Bedroom	55644243.64	24710135.82	4142988.41	20840275.02	5215814.26	10093832.80
保健室 Health Care Room	6525020.72	2147601.65	407078.77	2566163.80	690331.45	1811255.27
图书室 Reading Room	9079047.50	3351525.03	632126.79	3508614.07	971426.17	2218908.40
二、行政办公用房 Administrative	**21953165.15**	**8696880.87**	**1491112.40**	**8372471.67**	**2189431.78**	**4883812.61**
其中:教师办公室 Of Which: for Teachers	12621817.49	4322189.74	787110.63	5028507.98	1328941.31	3271119.77
三、生活用房 Residential and Welfare	**33366761.11**	**14154771.71**	**2732612.60**	**12107567.25**	**3141439.01**	**7104422.15**
其中:厨房 of Which:Kitchen	15786934.42	6830332.90	1215763.46	5576433.19	1462715.11	3380168.33
四、其他用房 Rooms for Other Purposes	**42575183.49**	**20721030.20**	**3776020.97**	**14813058.21**	**3857208.77**	**7041095.08**

幼儿园办学条件(二)
Condition of Kindergarten Buildings (2)

	占地面积(平方米) Areas Occupied(m^2)			图书(册) Books & Magazines in Libraries (Volume)
	合计 Total	其中 of Which		
		绿化用地面积 Green Areas	运动场地面积 Sports Areas	
总计 Total	**576405517.95**	**99130312.94**	**192234452.68**	**358862257**
城区 Urban Area	196306542.73	34711049.14	68125066.99	160966292
其中:城乡结合区 of Which: Urban-rural Transitional Area	37417807.53	6931831.53	13184196.86	26203416
镇区 Counties and Towns Area	211349688.93	35422042.75	69938769.99	133466581
其中:镇乡结合区 of Which: County-town Transitional Area	58955808.80	9853086.17	19702191.87	34637932
乡村 Rural Area	168749286.29	28997221.05	54170615.70	64429384

八、各级各类学校分布情况
Geographical Distribution of Schools by Type and Level

地　区 Region	普通高校 Regular HEIs		
	合计 Total	其中:中央部门办 of Which: HEIs under Central Ministries & Agencies	本科院校 HEIs Offering Degree Programs
总　计 Total	**2631**	**119**	**1243**
北　京 Beijing	92	38	67
天　津 Tianjin	57	3	30
河　北 Hebei	121	4	61
山　西 Shanxi	80	0	33
内蒙古 Inner Mongolia	53	0	17
辽　宁 Liaoning	115	5	64
吉　林 Jilin	62	2	37
黑龙江 Heilongjiang	81	3	39
上　海 Shanghai	64	10	38
江　苏 Jiangsu	167	10	77
浙　江 Zhejiang	107	2	59
安　徽 Anhui	119	2	45
福　建 Fujian	89	2	37
江　西 Jiangxi	100	0	43
山　东 Shandong	145	3	67
河　南 Henan	134	1	55
湖　北 Hubei	129	8	68
湖　南 Hunan	124	3	51
广　东 Guangdong	151	5	64
广　西 Guangxi	74	0	36
海　南 Hainan	19	0	7
重　庆 Chongqing	65	2	25
四　川 Sichuan	109	6	51
贵　州 Guizhou	70	0	29
云　南 Yunnan	77	1	32
西　藏 Tibet	7	0	4
陕　西 Shaanxi	93	6	55
甘　肃 Gansu	49	2	22
青　海 Qinghai	12	0	4
宁　夏 Ningxia	19	1	8
新　疆 Xinjiang	47	0	18

学校(机构)数
Education Institutions

单位：所
unit: institution

高职(专科)院校 Higher Vocational Colleges	成人高等学校 Adult HEIs 合计 Total	其中:中央部门办 of Which: HEIs under Central Ministries & Agencies	民办的其他高等教育机构 Other Non-government HEIs
1388	**282**	**13**	**800**
25	23	8	65
27	14	0	0
60	6	1	38
47	11	0	45
36	2	0	0
51	19	2	68
25	14	0	14
42	21	0	36
26	14	0	213
90	8	1	0
48	9	0	20
74	6	0	7
52	3	0	0
57	8	0	23
78	11	0	65
79	11	0	51
61	14	0	18
73	12	0	27
87	14	0	30
38	6	0	0
12	1	0	0
40	4	0	6
58	17	1	39
41	3	0	0
45	2	0	0
3	0	0	0
38	15	0	0
27	5	0	35
8	2	0	0
11	1	0	0
29	6	0	0

高等学校(机
Number of Postgraduate Students in

地　区 Region	毕(结)业生数 Graduates 合计 Total	其中:女 of Which: Female	博　士 Doctor's Degree	硕　士 Master's Degree	授予学位数 Degree Awarded	招生数 合计 Total	其中:女 of Which: Female
总　计 Total	**578045**	**299813**	**58032**	**520013**	**682651**	**806103**	**423629**
北　京 Beijing	90482	44363	17933	72549	110758	120265	60787
天　津 Tianjin	16189	9751	1584	14605	17530	23292	13073
河　北 Hebei	12771	7401	423	12348	14537	17162	9450
山　西 Shanxi	8983	5351	450	8533	10968	12143	7177
内蒙古 Inner Mongolia	5635	3529	173	5462	6879	8223	5266
辽　宁 Liaoning	29767	16542	1787	27980	34052	39439	21986
吉　林 Jilin	18717	11149	1798	16919	23103	23095	14076
黑龙江 Heilongjiang	19328	10054	1781	17547	22914	25076	12503
上　海 Shanghai	40982	20951	5567	35415	49889	59519	30903
江　苏 Jiangsu	45799	21679	4467	41332	53687	64455	31668
浙　江 Zhejiang	18717	9321	1826	16891	21893	27368	13889
安　徽 Anhui	16577	7178	1368	15209	16512	22255	9798
福　建 Fujian	11973	6362	779	11194	14205	17620	9509
江　西 Jiangxi	9132	4777	240	8892	11550	13477	7196
山　东 Shandong	24755	14027	1529	23226	29829	35564	19830
河　南 Henan	12933	7260	318	12615	14935	18352	10262
湖　北 Hubei	35047	17162	3895	31152	43605	51320	25403
湖　南 Hunan	19126	9775	1819	17307	22656	27581	14593
广　东 Guangdong	27148	14085	3055	24093	30610	38832	20349
广　西 Guangxi	9044	4695	197	8847	9588	12038	6613
海　南 Hainan	1336	774	50	1286	1550	2266	1277
重　庆 Chongqing	15517	8212	1046	14471	18441	22437	12493
四　川 Sichuan	25776	12402	2226	23550	29117	36776	18275
贵　州 Guizhou	4929	2740	72	4857	5309	7117	4133
云　南 Yunnan	10253	5645	366	9887	12140	14026	8061
西　藏 Tibet	467	289	4	463	465	706	363
陕　西 Shaanxi	29253	14725	2412	26841	36156	40842	20269
甘　肃 Gansu	9152	4681	643	8509	10086	12810	6887
青　海 Qinghai	1051	563	12	1039	1213	1730	1057
宁　夏 Ningxia	1570	958	43	1527	2025	2278	1429
新　疆 Xinjiang	5636	3412	169	5467	6449	8039	5054

注:2017年起,研究生招生、在校生指标内涵发生变化。招生包含全日制和非全日制研究生;在校生、授予学位数包含全日制、非全日制研究生和在职人员攻读硕士学位学生。下同。

Note: From 2017, the indicators meaning of entrants and enrollment of postgraduate students have changed. The number of entrants includes full-time and part-time postgraduate students. The number of Master's and Doctor's Degree awarded includes full-time, part-time postgraduate students and on-the-job students. Same as below.

构)研究生数

Higher Education Institutions

单位:人
unit:person

Entrants		在校生数 Enrolment				预计毕业生数 Estimated Graduates for Next Year			
博士 Doctor's Degree	硕士 Master's Degree	合计 Total	其中:女 of Which: Female	博士 Doctor's Degree	硕士 Master's Degree	合计 Total	其中:女 of Which: Female	博士 Doctor's Degree	硕士 Master's Degree
83878	**722225**	**2639561**	**1278134**	**361997**	**2277564**	**773025**	**379561**	**169022**	**604003**
23866	96399	400225	183274	99889	300336	123613	58353	43456	80157
2433	20859	72037	37095	9473	62564	20485	11468	3934	16551
724	16438	52220	28044	3111	49109	15791	8621	1578	14213
580	11563	37870	20924	2719	35151	11266	6746	1522	9744
339	7884	26790	15892	1558	25232	7546	4644	759	6787
2929	36510	122624	63408	15366	107258	39984	20357	8077	31907
2418	20677	72319	40714	10476	61843	21876	11907	5821	16055
2847	22229	81158	38478	13132	68026	25075	12299	5514	19561
7702	51817	196953	93289	31875	165078	58480	28857	13586	44894
6494	57961	220209	96544	29155	191054	63624	29452	14596	49028
2830	24538	89087	42102	11976	77111	24151	10845	4262	19889
2242	20013	65873	27713	7919	57954	18279	8491	2567	15712
1486	16134	56927	27888	6256	50671	16468	8244	2636	13832
377	13100	40430	20446	1437	38993	11078	5766	702	10376
2312	33252	115692	59821	10060	105632	31805	17259	5088	26717
648	17704	53687	29741	2345	51342	14084	7568	836	13248
5373	45947	185362	82782	24326	161036	50616	23580	13524	37092
2506	25075	99122	47585	12271	86851	30234	13032	7076	23158
3997	34835	119987	58760	15686	104301	37873	18601	7676	30197
390	11648	34504	17994	1382	33122	10610	4660	668	9942
94	2172	7818	4167	313	7505	1980	1067	101	1879
1454	20983	73485	39803	6213	67272	19590	10444	2212	17378
3320	33456	124446	56045	15562	108884	36317	16749	8383	27934
215	6902	22141	11967	750	21391	6100	3362	343	5757
630	13396	44983	23889	2721	42262	12654	6643	1334	11320
34	672	1804	986	94	1710	579	341	33	546
4187	36655	146780	68217	20188	126592	40131	18078	9754	30377
942	11868	39220	19605	3970	35250	12020	5867	2144	9876
65	1665	4813	2856	176	4637	1300	678	64	1236
89	2189	6324	3925	219	6105	1709	1025	59	1650
355	7684	24671	14180	1379	23292	7707	4557	717	6990

普通高校
Number of Postgraduates in

地　区 Region	毕(结)业生数 Graduates				授予学位数 Degree Awarded	招生数	
	合计 Total	其中:女 of Which: Female	博　士 Doctor's Degree	硕　士 Master's Degree		合计 Total	其中:女 of Which: Female
总　计 Total	**570296**	**296689**	**56451**	**513845**	**674137**	**795938**	**418914**
北　京 Beijing	85145	42144	16511	68634	104751	112988	57245
天　津 Tianjin	16182	9750	1584	14598	17523	23279	13071
河　北 Hebei	12742	7394	423	12319	14508	17124	9440
山　西 Shanxi	8910	5311	450	8460	10895	12070	7151
内蒙古 Inner Mongolia	5633	3529	173	5460	6877	8219	5264
辽　宁 Liaoning	29725	16533	1785	27940	34007	39391	21973
吉　林 Jilin	18678	11131	1798	16880	23068	23025	14028
黑龙江 Heilongjiang	19086	9949	1761	17325	22669	24805	12385
上　海 Shanghai	40425	20712	5513	34912	49309	58906	30614
江　苏 Jiangsu	45627	21634	4452	41175	53513	64266	31614
浙　江 Zhejiang	18634	9298	1825	16809	21810	27258	13854
安　徽 Anhui	16570	7177	1368	15202	16505	22248	9797
福　建 Fujian	11888	6308	779	11109	14092	17472	9411
江　西 Jiangxi	9132	4777	240	8892	11550	13471	7195
山　东 Shandong	24704	14003	1529	23175	29759	35510	19804
河　南 Henan	12878	7245	317	12561	14880	18286	10248
湖　北 Hubei	34774	17079	3888	30886	43333	51011	25299
湖　南 Hunan	19073	9753	1818	17255	22603	27491	14556
广　东 Guangdong	27065	14044	3047	24018	30513	38721	20299
广　西 Guangxi	9044	4695	197	8847	9588	12038	6613
海　南 Hainan	1336	774	50	1286	1550	2266	1277
重　庆 Chongqing	15497	8201	1046	14451	18421	22399	12473
四　川 Sichuan	25512	12302	2204	23308	28853	36443	18124
贵　州 Guizhou	4924	2739	72	4852	5304	7109	4132
云　南 Yunnan	10227	5639	364	9863	12114	14001	8056
西　藏 Tibet	467	289	4	463	465	706	363
陕　西 Shaanxi	29056	14680	2391	26665	35951	40628	20214
甘　肃 Gansu	9105	4666	638	8467	10039	12760	6874
青　海 Qinghai	1051	563	12	1039	1213	1730	1057
宁　夏 Ningxia	1570	958	43	1527	2025	2278	1429
新　疆 Xinjiang	5636	3412	169	5467	6449	8039	5054

注:2017 年起,研究生招生、在校生指标内涵发生变化。招生包含全日制和非全日制研究生;在校生、授予学位数包含全日制、非全日制研究生和在职人员攻读硕士学位学生。下同。

Note: From 2017, the indicators meaning of entrants and enrollment of postgraduate students have changed. The number of entrants includes full-time and part-time postgraduate students. The number of Master's and Doctor's Degree awarded includes full-time, part-time postgraduate students and on-the-job students. Same as below.

研究生数
Higher Education Institutions

单位:人
unit:person

Entrants		在校生数 Enrolment				预计毕业生数 Estimated Graduates for Next Year			
博士 Doctor's Degree	硕士 Master's Degree	合计 Total	其中:女 of Which: Female	博士 Doctor's Degree	硕士 Master's Degree	合计 Total	其中:女 of Which: Female	博士 Doctor's Degree	硕士 Master's Degree
81898	**714040**	**2608029**	**1264730**	**353922**	**2254107**	**762410**	**375417**	**165296**	**597114**
22072	90916	377293	173224	92691	284602	115840	55192	40127	75713
2433	20846	72004	37084	9473	62531	20475	11467	3934	16541
724	16400	52121	28018	3111	49010	15759	8612	1578	14181
580	11490	37658	20826	2719	34939	11198	6718	1522	9676
339	7880	26777	15890	1558	25219	7541	4644	759	6782
2924	36467	122477	63364	15350	107127	39936	20342	8070	31866
2418	20607	72134	40591	10476	61658	21833	11882	5821	16012
2823	21982	80333	38147	13007	67326	24801	12211	5460	19341
7642	51264	195106	92440	31613	163493	57793	28549	13445	44348
6473	57793	219604	96374	29042	190562	63399	29397	14531	48868
2829	24429	88758	41988	11970	76788	24077	10825	4259	19818
2242	20006	65852	27711	7919	57933	18273	8491	2567	15706
1486	15986	56535	27648	6256	50279	16369	8183	2636	13733
377	13094	40412	20442	1437	38975	11072	5765	702	10370
2312	33198	115518	59742	10060	105458	31755	17237	5088	26667
645	17641	53497	29695	2334	51163	14016	7549	834	13182
5366	45645	184465	82495	24284	160181	50334	23496	13514	36820
2506	24985	98906	47501	12269	86637	30169	13032	7075	23094
3989	34732	119596	58587	15658	103938	37763	18546	7664	30099
390	11648	34504	17994	1382	33122	10610	4660	668	9942
94	2172	7818	4167	313	7505	1980	1067	101	1879
1454	20945	73381	39755	6213	67168	19562	10433	2212	17350
3294	33149	123477	55648	15434	108043	35987	16621	8331	27656
215	6894	22121	11963	750	21371	6094	3361	343	5751
629	13372	44898	23865	2707	42191	12619	6630	1323	11296
34	672	1804	986	94	1710	579	341	33	546
4164	36464	146106	68059	20083	126023	39894	18052	9726	30168
935	11825	39066	19565	3945	35121	11966	5854	2133	9833
65	1665	4813	2856	176	4637	1300	678	64	1236
89	2189	6324	3925	219	6105	1709	1025	59	1650
355	7684	24671	14180	1379	23292	7707	4557	717	6990

科研机构

Number of Postgraduates in

地　区 Region	毕(结)业生数 Graduates 合计 Total	其中:女 of Which: Female	博　士 Doctor's Degree	硕　士 Master's Degree	授予学位数 Degree Awarded	招生数 合计 Total	其中:女 of Which: Female
总　计 Total	**7749**	**3124**	**1581**	**6168**	**8514**	**10165**	**4715**
北　京 Beijing	5337	2219	1422	3915	6007	7277	3542
天　津 Tianjin	7	1	0	7	7	13	2
河　北 Hebei	29	7	0	29	29	38	10
山　西 Shanxi	73	40	0	73	73	73	26
内蒙古 Inner Mongolia	2	0	0	2	2	4	2
辽　宁 Liaoning	42	9	2	40	45	48	13
吉　林 Jilin	39	18	0	39	35	70	48
黑龙江 Heilongjiang	242	105	20	222	245	271	118
上　海 Shanghai	557	239	54	503	580	613	289
江　苏 Jiangsu	172	45	15	157	174	189	54
浙　江 Zhejiang	83	23	1	82	83	110	35
安　徽 Anhui	7	1	0	7	7	7	1
福　建 Fujian	85	54	0	85	113	148	98
江　西 Jiangxi	0	0	0	0	0	6	1
山　东 Shandong	51	24	0	51	70	54	26
河　南 Henan	55	15	1	54	55	66	14
湖　北 Hubei	273	83	7	266	272	309	104
湖　南 Hunan	53	22	1	52	53	90	37
广　东 Guangdong	83	41	8	75	97	111	50
广　西 Guangxi	0	0	0	0	0	0	0
海　南 Hainan	0	0	0	0	0	0	0
重　庆 Chongqing	20	11	0	20	20	30	20
四　川 Sichuan	264	100	22	242	264	333	151
贵　州 Guizhou	5	1	0	5	5	8	1
云　南 Yunnan	26	6	2	24	26	25	5
西　藏 Tibet	0	0	0	0	0	0	0
陕　西 Shaanxi	197	45	21	176	205	214	55
甘　肃 Gansu	47	15	5	42	47	50	13
青　海 Qinghai	0	0	0	0	0	0	0
宁　夏 Ningxia	0	0	0	0	0	0	0
新　疆 Xinjiang	0	0	0	0	0	0	0

注:2017 年起,研究生招生、在校生指标内涵发生变化。招生包含全日制和非全日制研究生;在校生、授予学位数包含全日制、非全日制研究生和在职人员攻读硕士学位学生。下同。

Note: From 2017, the indicators meaning of entrants and enrollment of postgraduate students have changed. The number of entrants includes full-time and part-time postgraduate students. The number of Master's and Doctor's Degree awarded includes full-time, part-time postgraduate students and on-the-job students. Same as below.

研究生数

Higher Education Institutions

单位:人
unit:person

Entrants		在校生数 Enrolment				预计毕业生数 Estimated Graduates for Next Year			
博士 Doctor's Degree	硕士 Master's Degree	合计 Total	其中:女 of Which: Female	博士 Doctor's Degree	硕士 Master's Degree	合计 Total	其中:女 of Which: Female	博士 Doctor's Degree	硕士 Master's Degree
1980	**8185**	**31532**	**13404**	**8075**	**23457**	**10615**	**4144**	**3726**	**6889**
1794	5483	22932	10050	7198	15734	7773	3161	3329	4444
0	13	33	11	0	33	10	1	0	10
0	38	99	26	0	99	32	9	0	32
0	73	212	98	0	212	68	28	0	68
0	4	13	2	0	13	5	0	0	5
5	43	147	44	16	131	48	15	7	41
0	70	185	123	0	185	43	25	0	43
24	247	825	331	125	700	274	88	54	220
60	553	1847	849	262	1585	687	308	141	546
21	168	605	170	113	492	225	55	65	160
1	109	329	114	6	323	74	20	3	71
0	7	21	2	0	21	6	0	0	6
0	148	392	240	0	392	99	61	0	99
0	6	18	4	0	18	6	1	0	6
0	54	174	79	0	174	50	22	0	50
3	63	190	46	11	179	68	19	2	66
7	302	897	287	42	855	282	84	10	272
0	90	216	84	2	214	65	0	1	64
8	103	391	173	28	363	110	55	12	98
0	0	0	0	0	0	0	0	0	0
0	0	0	0	0	0	0	0	0	0
0	38	104	48	0	104	28	11	0	28
26	307	969	397	128	841	330	128	52	278
0	8	20	4	0	20	6	1	0	6
1	24	85	24	14	71	35	13	11	24
0	0	0	0	0	0	0	0	0	0
23	191	674	158	105	569	237	26	28	209
7	43	154	40	25	129	54	13	11	43
0	0	0	0	0	0	0	0	0	0
0	0	0	0	0	0	0	0	0	0
0	0	0	0	0	0	0	0	0	0

地 区 Region	毕(结)业生数 Graduates 合计 Total	其中:女 of Which: Female	本 科 Normal Courses	专 科 Short-cycle Courses	授予学位数 Degree Awarded	招生数 合计 Total	其中:女 of Which: Female
总 计 Total	**9828657**	**5340738**	**4933065**	**4895592**	**3927814**	**9790195**	**5580599**
北 京 Beijing	225910	120488	162808	63102	129948	212135	111904
天 津 Tianjin	169770	88514	93926	75844	78244	161117	84808
河 北 Hebei	452157	253542	236345	215812	175783	531633	306641
山 西 Shanxi	254777	138299	134515	120262	113928	225502	138805
内蒙古 Inner Mongolia	133955	73552	67462	66493	56287	129540	75963
辽 宁 Liaoning	330555	171923	204564	125991	176709	313902	167636
吉 林 Jilin	241618	131435	150917	90701	114835	222934	122557
黑龙江 Heilongjiang	260486	135353	156608	103878	126884	233820	123926
上 海 Shanghai	181386	100800	119694	61692	95326	181045	99183
江 苏 Jiangsu	662499	341489	345864	316635	270273	655684	363005
浙 江 Zhejiang	385795	219782	185048	200747	153849	352907	214859
安 徽 Anhui	407077	217935	192362	214715	154865	386665	217122
福 建 Fujian	257277	138174	143299	113978	122374	224783	129603
江 西 Jiangxi	354510	180038	146321	208189	135124	322578	178569
山 东 Shandong	850405	469977	409480	440925	260138	706038	421973
河 南 Henan	663326	360953	321465	341861	257078	694407	416995
湖 北 Hubei	490068	245248	254062	236006	211523	471832	242940
湖 南 Hunan	446518	238984	211242	235276	160827	497806	288977
广 东 Guangdong	747762	426587	305658	442104	250712	813271	445575
广 西 Guangxi	307526	174794	127674	179852	98434	374377	220079
海 南 Hainan	56848	32668	27671	29177	23902	56792	33018
重 庆 Chongqing	251894	135993	115984	135910	102713	251972	142117
四 川 Sichuan	543804	311802	220058	323746	181844	549271	318351
贵 州 Guizhou	194445	111723	98018	96427	71843	234490	138068
云 南 Yunnan	243292	142087	124670	118622	95752	269881	180270
西 藏 Tibet	15635	8283	8940	6695	5766	15009	8585
陕 西 Shaanxi	371007	195029	201277	169730	173922	341306	184518
甘 肃 Gansu	155552	76969	85912	69640	69609	155077	83876
青 海 Qinghai	19929	11202	10311	9618	9581	23992	14059
宁 夏 Ningxia	41721	24140	20761	20960	16477	45961	27929
新 疆 Xinjiang	111153	62975	50149	61004	33264	134468	78688

专科学生数
Short-cycle Courses in Higher Education

单位：人
unit：person

Entrants		在校生数 Enrolment				预计毕业生数 Estimated Graduates for Next Year			
本 科 Normal Courses	专 科 Short-cycle Courses	合计 Total	其中：女 of Which：Female	本 科 Normal Courses	专 科 Short-cycle Courses	合计 Total	其中：女 of Which：Female	本 科 Normal Courses	专 科 Short-cycle Courses
5131515	**4658680**	**32977298**	**17666764**	**19076129**	**13901169**	**10087001**	**5253636**	**5050219**	**5036782**
165020	47115	751492	386469	619546	131946	230631	115092	172676	57955
97243	63874	564004	286004	367153	196851	168959	83581	96179	72780
280201	251432	1686634	923636	974798	711836	485390	249758	253874	231516
135270	90232	846356	475756	537046	309310	253968	135457	136134	117834
68319	61221	469454	252983	269513	199941	139208	75646	69549	69659
196210	117692	1128969	579397	777801	351168	348576	171727	216777	131799
147072	75862	758034	403925	547316	210718	223638	121044	147384	76254
153834	79986	831742	429267	581299	250443	252741	132282	158482	94259
124730	56315	649451	346016	467883	181568	194621	99897	128549	66072
367987	287697	2215714	1099157	1335786	879928	717914	336368	373613	344301
184658	168249	1221923	667940	702614	519309	399300	211655	198441	200859
201254	185411	1328469	692150	749116	579353	422189	217654	199033	223156
131822	92961	854397	458782	545388	309009	265158	137162	148203	116955
155165	167413	1188371	603572	598594	589777	368349	188606	150512	217837
353012	353026	2390447	1311680	1252705	1137742	773475	404744	339715	433760
321675	372732	2286843	1254842	1228694	1058149	695244	367639	328556	366688
250402	221430	1580204	784838	956241	623963	469599	226144	249478	220121
238219	259587	1550999	839126	826005	724994	483210	244753	221576	261634
355013	458258	2578878	1403882	1283838	1295040	766668	412380	318614	448054
163460	210917	1118244	634468	562408	555836	346367	187039	149654	196713
30050	26742	199491	112318	117387	82104	56386	30786	28317	28069
121597	130375	866655	470808	476656	389999	264025	146202	119516	144509
268644	280627	1808075	994637	971286	836789	553818	304134	236496	317322
102558	131932	734602	419684	365597	369005	214573	127535	93725	120848
131971	137910	908819	540312	505570	403249	261396	154089	128992	132404
9756	5253	53725	29307	36891	16834	16191	8830	9980	6211
191389	149917	1218930	627641	743843	475087	378196	189879	204129	174067
82847	72230	539290	271126	328097	211193	154534	73201	87349	67185
12309	11683	77676	43170	43353	34323	24131	12601	11971	12160
25789	20172	147449	82160	90052	57397	43486	22965	23361	20125
64039	70429	421961	241711	213653	208308	115060	64786	49384	65676

高等教育普通
Number of Regular Students Enrolled in Normal and

地 区 Region	毕(结)业生数 Graduates				授予学位数 Degree Awarded	招生数	
	合计 Total	其中:女 of Which: Female	本 科 Normal Courses	专 科 Short-cycle Courses		合计 Total	其中:女 of Which: Female
总 计 Total	**7358287**	**3921881**	**3841839**	**3516448**	**3771039**	**7614893**	**4306119**
北 京 Beijing	155444	81947	121362	34082	119482	150511	79469
天 津 Tianjin	139162	72501	79010	60152	77623	138679	72759
河 北 Hebei	329972	183659	170408	159564	168293	365066	212585
山 西 Shanxi	210429	116812	113275	97154	111556	203277	125549
内蒙古 Inner Mongolia	117798	63848	57501	60297	55965	122078	71409
辽 宁 Liaoning	268767	139935	174113	94654	172505	249805	131024
吉 林 Jilin	170059	89825	114984	55075	112174	171239	91879
黑龙江 Heilongjiang	197183	103407	125363	71820	124278	195192	102033
上 海 Shanghai	134207	73167	86945	47262	85166	135592	74580
江 苏 Jiangsu	489522	251657	252892	236630	246299	456629	263131
浙 江 Zhejiang	276580	157090	146131	130449	144446	255635	159098
安 徽 Anhui	322786	167526	152059	170727	150310	307187	168263
福 建 Fujian	204417	108290	121774	82643	120803	200005	114956
江 西 Jiangxi	295985	143102	122575	173410	121204	288453	155685
山 东 Shandong	571220	312850	245517	325703	242100	548479	326068
河 南 Henan	504119	265313	253804	250315	249042	569361	339708
湖 北 Hubei	394897	193300	212847	182050	207659	394100	199399
湖 南 Hunan	332792	175632	162286	170506	158683	357872	205673
广 东 Guangdong	511222	277133	245563	265659	243473	558417	294567
广 西 Guangxi	210666	114851	88932	121734	87376	266945	151550
海 南 Hainan	50370	27277	24871	25499	23551	52162	29325
重 庆 Chongqing	196414	105272	104704	91710	101731	209497	117443
四 川 Sichuan	386145	213032	184269	201876	180585	433030	245593
贵 州 Guizhou	149037	84188	75025	74012	71164	199747	116238
云 南 Yunnan	175254	101953	96365	78889	94580	202091	135586
西 藏 Tibet	9020	4873	5493	3527	5317	9667	5438
陕 西 Shaanxi	305124	162388	172708	132416	170176	284672	154249
甘 肃 Gansu	124786	62762	70242	54544	68391	131489	71780
青 海 Qinghai	14661	7684	7937	6724	7709	19626	11045
宁 夏 Ningxia	31563	17430	17205	14358	16477	34728	20600
新 疆 Xinjiang	78686	43177	35679	43007	32921	103662	59437

本专科学生数
Short-cycle Courses in Higher Education

单位:人
unit:person

Entrants		在校生数 Enrolment				预计毕业生数 Estimated Graduates for Next Year			
本　科 Normal Courses	专　科 Short-cycle Courses	合计 Total	其中:女 of Which: Female	本　科 Normal Courses	专　科 Short-cycle Courses	合计 Total	其中:女 of Which: Female	本　科 Normal Courses	专　科 Short-cycle Courses
4107534	**3507359**	**27535869**	**14468508**	**16486320**	**11049549**	**7804685**	**3977934**	**4031331**	**3773354**
128213	22298	592878	300347	515269	77609	158210	78854	127780	30430
85746	52933	514669	259867	341775	172894	143621	70124	83296	60325
189114	175952	1268873	687557	735827	533046	345777	181005	175493	170284
121102	82175	762974	428477	488394	274580	219074	117548	118607	100467
62360	59718	448092	239778	252161	195931	127958	68624	60747	67211
166287	83518	980995	494432	702417	278578	287960	140418	187254	100706
118321	52918	643872	334516	478823	165049	171105	89164	116748	54357
130031	65161	734166	374508	518129	216037	204845	105284	127718	77127
95073	40519	514917	270817	376152	138765	144227	73113	94853	49374
267396	189233	1767877	872532	1096984	670893	517918	239660	273758	244160
146183	109452	1002346	543677	616276	386070	293532	153032	157909	135623
160385	146802	1147401	578581	649355	498046	342659	170667	157679	184980
119024	80981	750987	396402	497440	253547	215351	108976	127389	87962
134856	153597	1048289	512550	530546	517743	313527	153169	128990	184537
262937	285542	2015345	1085310	1036819	978526	599314	311372	248133	351181
258032	311329	2004662	1078528	1077108	927554	570592	294638	267607	302985
213037	181063	1400918	686702	863408	537510	387197	184846	211687	175510
178349	179523	1273208	677071	703480	569728	357602	177737	169664	187938
276627	281790	1925775	1013351	1105754	820021	549584	280916	267581	282003
117893	149052	866716	470064	456835	409881	228277	112470	103506	124771
28026	24136	185538	100889	110388	75150	52026	27413	26056	25970
112934	96563	746859	402201	453829	293030	208491	110770	110511	97980
225118	207912	1499715	801108	865109	634606	413791	219761	196688	217103
86696	113051	627672	352750	317072	310600	166121	97761	72713	93408
103172	98919	705854	410865	413831	292023	193399	112915	98795	94604
5802	3865	35643	19268	24212	11431	9436	5105	5691	3745
164600	120072	1069374	548877	670588	398786	318079	158580	175165	142914
71604	59885	466185	235003	292521	173664	126452	60963	73670	52782
9857	9769	66974	36050	37502	29472	18440	9068	8651	9789
20432	14296	121051	65816	78519	42532	32609	17343	18912	13697
48327	55335	346044	190614	179797	166247	87511	46638	38080	49431

地区 Region	毕(结)业生数 Graduates				授予学位数 Degree Awarded	招生数	
	合计 Total	其中:女 of Which: Female	本科 Normal Courses	专科 Short-cycle Courses		合计 Total	其中:女 of Which: Female
总计 Total	**2470370**	**1418857**	**1091226**	**1379144**	**156775**	**2175302**	**1274480**
北京 Beijing	70466	38541	41446	29020	10466	61624	32435
天津 Tianjin	30608	16013	14916	15692	621	22438	12049
河北 Hebei	122185	69883	65937	56248	7490	166567	94056
山西 Shanxi	44348	21487	21240	23108	2372	22225	13256
内蒙古 Inner Mongolia	16157	9704	9961	6196	322	7462	4554
辽宁 Liaoning	61788	31988	30451	31337	4204	64097	36612
吉林 Jilin	71559	41610	35933	35626	2661	51695	30678
黑龙江 Heilongjiang	63303	31946	31245	32058	2606	38628	21893
上海 Shanghai	47179	27633	32749	14430	10160	45453	24603
江苏 Jiangsu	172977	89832	92972	80005	23974	199055	99874
浙江 Zhejiang	109215	62692	38917	70298	9403	97272	55761
安徽 Anhui	84291	50409	40303	43988	4555	79478	48859
福建 Fujian	52860	29884	21525	31335	1571	24778	14647
江西 Jiangxi	58525	36936	23746	34779	13920	34125	22884
山东 Shandong	279185	157127	163963	115222	18038	157559	95905
河南 Henan	159207	95640	67661	91546	8036	125046	77287
湖北 Hubei	95171	51948	41215	53956	3864	77732	43541
湖南 Hunan	113726	63352	48956	64770	2144	139934	83304
广东 Guangdong	236540	149454	60095	176445	7239	254854	151008
广西 Guangxi	96860	59943	38742	58118	11058	107432	68529
海南 Hainan	6478	5391	2800	3678	351	4630	3693
重庆 Chongqing	55480	30721	11280	44200	982	42475	24674
四川 Sichuan	157659	98770	35789	121870	1259	116241	72758
贵州 Guizhou	45408	27535	22993	22415	679	34743	21830
云南 Yunnan	68038	40134	28305	39733	1172	67790	44684
西藏 Tibet	6615	3410	3447	3168	449	5342	3147
陕西 Shaanxi	65883	32641	28569	37314	3746	56634	30269
甘肃 Gansu	30766	14207	15670	15096	1218	23588	12096
青海 Qinghai	5268	3518	2374	2894	1872	4366	3014
宁夏 Ningxia	10158	6710	3556	6602	0	11233	7329
新疆 Xinjiang	32467	19798	14470	17997	343	30806	19251

本专科学生数
Short-cycle Courses in Higher Education

单位:人
unit:person

Entrants		在校生数 Enrolment				预计毕业生数 Estimated Graduates for Next Year			
本 科 Normal Courses	专 科 Short-cycle Courses	合计 Total	其中:女 of Which: Female	本 科 Normal Courses	专 科 Short-cycle Courses	合计 Total	其中:女 of Which: Female	本 科 Normal Courses	专 科 Short-cycle Courses
1023981	**1151321**	**5441429**	**3198256**	**2589809**	**2851620**	**2282316**	**1275702**	**1018888**	**1263428**
36807	24817	158614	86122	104277	54337	72421	36238	44896	27525
11497	10941	49335	26137	25378	23957	25338	13457	12883	12455
91087	75480	417761	236079	238971	178790	139613	68753	78381	61232
14168	8057	83382	47279	48652	34730	34894	17909	17527	17367
5959	1503	21362	13205	17352	4010	11250	7022	8802	2448
29923	34174	147974	84965	75384	72590	60616	31309	29523	31093
28751	22944	114162	69409	68493	45669	52533	31880	30636	21897
23803	14825	97576	54759	63170	34406	47896	26998	30764	17132
29657	15796	134534	75199	91731	42803	50394	26784	33696	16698
100591	98464	447837	226625	238802	209035	199996	96708	99855	100141
38475	58797	219577	124263	86338	133239	105768	58623	40532	65236
40869	38609	181068	113569	99761	81307	79530	46987	41354	38176
12798	11980	103410	62380	47948	55462	49807	28186	20814	28993
20309	13816	140082	91022	68048	72034	54822	35437	21522	33300
90075	67484	375102	226370	215886	159216	174161	93372	91582	82579
63643	61403	282181	176314	151586	130595	124652	73001	60949	63703
37365	40367	179286	98136	92833	86453	82402	41298	37791	44611
59870	80064	277791	162055	122525	155266	125608	67016	51912	73696
78386	176468	653103	390531	178084	475019	217084	131464	51033	166051
45567	61865	251528	164404	105573	145955	118090	74569	46148	71942
2024	2606	13953	11429	6999	6954	4360	3373	2261	2099
8663	33812	119796	68607	22827	96969	55534	35432	9005	46529
43526	72715	308360	193529	106177	202183	140027	84373	39808	100219
15862	18881	106930	66934	48525	58405	48452	29774	21012	27440
28799	38991	202965	129447	91739	111226	67997	41174	30197	37800
3954	1388	18082	10039	12679	5403	6755	3725	4289	2466
26789	29845	149556	78764	73255	76301	60117	31299	28964	31153
11243	12345	73105	36123	35576	37529	28082	12238	13679	14403
2452	1914	10702	7120	5851	4851	5691	3533	3320	2371
5357	5876	26398	16344	11533	14865	10877	5622	4449	6428
15712	15094	75917	51097	33856	42061	27549	18148	11304	16245

高等教育网络

Number of Web-based Students Enrolled in Normal and

地　区 Region	毕(结)业生数 Graduates				授予学位数 Degrees Awarded	招生数
	合计 Total	其中:女 of Which: Female	本　科 Normal Courses	专　科 Short-cycle Courses		合计 Total
总　计 Total	**1777905**	**870711**	**659559**	**1118346**	**55443**	**2861143**
北　京 Beijing	933474	471978	290057	643417	21637	1437655
天　津 Tianjin	35230	14986	13768	21462	1023	90871
河　北 Hebei	0	0	0	0	0	0
山　西 Shanxi	0	0	0	0	0	0
内蒙古 Inner Mongolia	0	0	0	0	0	0
辽　宁 Liaoning	84413	38859	46051	38362	5917	139163
吉　林 Jilin	78137	43372	35124	43013	506	95194
黑龙江 Heilongjiang	24215	9360	7945	16270	623	38846
上　海 Shanghai	41863	22952	13200	28663	2541	55068
江　苏 Jiangsu	24469	13000	12312	12157	3288	45117
浙　江 Zhejiang	12386	7811	9413	2973	2704	14194
安　徽 Anhui	109	39	109	0	0	9
福　建 Fujian	23156	12622	11256	11900	665	42715
江　西 Jiangxi	0	0	0	0	0	0
山　东 Shandong	46441	20035	20871	25570	2533	109562
河　南 Henan	34830	18255	14903	19927	1502	62936
湖　北 Hubei	63034	26153	21984	41050	1689	90610
湖　南 Hunan	26737	14977	12718	14019	554	30708
广　东 Guangdong	27764	17592	12101	15663	1142	41362
广　西 Guangxi	0	0	0	0	0	0
海　南 Hainan	0	0	0	0	0	0
重　庆 Chongqing	71410	30647	34602	36808	777	86471
四　川 Sichuan	146426	56810	63507	82919	3725	282599
贵　州 Guizhou	0	0	0	0	0	0
云　南 Yunnan	14069	7604	78	13991	0	4335
西　藏 Tibet	0	0	0	0	0	0
陕　西 Shaanxi	72518	33675	32321	40197	4311	155273
甘　肃 Gansu	17224	9984	7239	9985	306	38455
青　海 Qinghai	0	0	0	0	0	0
宁　夏 Ningxia	0	0	0	0	0	0
新　疆 Xinjiang	0	0	0	0	0	0

本科、专科生学生数
Short-cycle Courses in Higher Education

单位:人
unit:person

Entrants			在校生数 Enrolment			
其中:女 of Which: Female	本 科 Normal Courses	专 科 Short-cycle Courses	合计 Total	其中:女 of Which: Female	本 科 Normal Courses	专 科 Short-cycle Courses
1355959	**993253**	**1867890**	**7359267**	**3483796**	**2587338**	**4771929**
687781	417138	1020517	4386477	2093527	1355591	3030886
42854	33647	57224	159394	70131	63329	96065
0	0	0	0	0	0	0
0	0	0	0	0	0	0
0	0	0	0	0	0	0
62865	71230	67933	320961	144692	174110	146851
59588	43447	51747	247908	146023	116371	131537
14112	12869	25977	73294	26667	25174	48120
31649	20730	34338	123742	67089	41941	81801
23271	19488	25629	87614	45265	44234	43380
8832	10800	3394	39443	23729	29718	9725
2	9	0	1781	566	847	934
24785	19673	23042	85698	46612	41556	44142
0	0	0	0	0	0	0
49739	41330	68232	205011	91320	83150	121861
33936	23681	39255	132489	67295	53737	78752
40200	31721	58889	211630	92024	78404	133226
16817	15255	15453	67357	35973	34169	33188
27316	17674	23688	106976	66612	48775	58201
0	0	0	0	0	0	0
0	0	0	0	0	0	0
36853	39964	46507	159612	59565	71224	88388
101506	100020	182579	484070	187704	180324	303746
0	0	0	0	0	0	0
1841	4	4331	104149	51205	1868	102281
0	0	0	0	0	0	0
71782	61306	93967	280427	123524	109718	170709
20230	13267	25188	81234	44273	33098	48136
0	0	0	0	0	0	0
0	0	0	0	0	0	0
0	0	0	0	0	0	0

综合大学本科、
Number of Students of

地　区 Region	毕(结)业生数 Graduates			招生数 Entrants		
	合计 Total	本　科 Normal Courses	专　科 Short-cycle Courses	合计 Total	本　科 Normal Courses	专　科 Short-cycle Courses
总　计 Total	**2016499**	**1073138**	**943361**	**2071739**	**1144392**	**927347**
北　京 Beijing	19551	16988	2563	17250	15834	1416
天　津 Tianjin	36481	12408	24073	37400	14525	22875
河　北 Hebei	60099	26917	33182	72299	34182	38117
山　西 Shanxi	54847	33055	21792	47528	31021	16507
内蒙古 Inner Mongolia	51069	30588	20481	54107	33159	20948
辽　宁 Liaoning	40235	22010	18225	37110	20212	16898
吉　林 Jilin	29052	26553	2499	29912	26604	3308
黑龙江 Heilongjiang	54467	32237	22230	51988	32743	19245
上　海 Shanghai	15826	15582	244	16531	16423	108
江　苏 Jiangsu	80195	68562	11633	76651	72025	4626
浙　江 Zhejiang	106271	41909	64362	96546	42403	54143
安　徽 Anhui	34375	24843	9532	33770	27222	6548
福　建 Fujian	67202	47166	20036	62819	43484	19335
江　西 Jiangxi	111767	42707	69060	106139	47517	58622
山　东 Shandong	284683	109357	175326	270725	120492	150233
河　南 Henan	71440	59384	12056	74440	58811	15629
湖　北 Hubei	43224	40631	2593	40632	39472	1160
湖　南 Hunan	148932	82487	66445	157836	89317	68519
广　东 Guangdong	245624	104973	140651	267384	114236	153148
广　西 Guangxi	51834	26918	24916	69874	34369	35505
海　南 Hainan	18757	15866	2891	20624	17082	3542
重　庆 Chongqing	50332	30110	20222	53252	31432	21820
四　川 Sichuan	129024	47649	81375	142791	58933	83858
贵　州 Guizhou	49432	19094	30338	67137	20862	46275
云　南 Yunnan	34106	21645	12461	34890	23655	11235
西　藏 Tibet	3632	2055	1577	3658	2137	1521
陕　西 Shaanxi	66157	36235	29922	57874	33750	24124
甘　肃 Gansu	23997	14004	9993	24270	15983	8287
青　海 Qinghai	4880	4050	830	7924	4931	2993
宁　夏 Ningxia	7458	5254	2204	8297	6126	2171
新　疆 Xinjiang	21550	11901	9649	30081	15450	14631

专科生学生数

Comprehensive Universities

单位：人
unit: person

在校生数 Enrolment			预计毕业生数 Estimated Graduates for Next Year		
合计 Total	本　科 Normal Courses	专　科 Short-cycle Courses	合计 Total	本　科 Normal Courses	专　科 Short-cycle Courses
7557531	**4592794**	**2964737**	**2143590**	**1124084**	**1019506**
71904	67468	4436	19603	17450	2153
127510	55358	72152	37337	12966	24371
245051	128282	116769	66196	29015	37181
187662	130337	57325	54170	33181	20989
202140	134457	67683	55716	32585	23131
142233	86142	56091	44311	24932	19379
118370	110136	8234	29299	27161	2138
198811	132572	66239	57766	33368	24398
67328	66806	522	17376	17122	254
323327	297664	25663	85500	74140	11360
371808	179665	192143	114397	46299	68098
131879	108288	23591	34991	25768	9223
248004	185130	62874	70727	48603	22124
394237	185590	208647	121462	45267	76195
978151	468552	509599	291327	111264	180063
294536	247436	47100	80136	62752	17384
168028	163783	4245	42973	41270	1703
577329	353293	224036	159528	85724	73804
907551	461775	445776	265995	113150	152845
229169	135315	93854	56208	30220	25988
77865	66896	10969	19637	15998	3639
190915	126140	64775	52428	31247	21181
476964	224624	252340	136605	51178	85427
202501	73771	128730	55328	16705	38623
133462	91342	42120	36393	20444	15949
13663	8369	5294	3998	2032	1966
228850	138234	90616	70139	35843	34296
90212	63573	26639	25012	15677	9335
27735	19445	8290	6870	4533	2337
30157	23828	6329	8110	5953	2157
100179	58523	41656	24052	12237	11815

地 区 Region	毕(结)业生数 Graduates			招生数 Entrants		
	合计 Total	本 科 Normal Courses	专 科 Short-cycle Courses	合计 Total	本 科 Normal Courses	专 科 Short-cycle Courses
总 计 Total	**2634166**	**1173629**	**1460537**	**2735782**	**1271319**	**1464463**
北 京 Beijing	65167	50644	14523	64020	55686	8334
天 津 Tianjin	53806	30314	23492	53095	33550	19545
河 北 Hebei	129062	61915	67147	143885	68647	75238
山 西 Shanxi	63855	31819	32036	61412	36040	25372
内蒙古 Inner Mongolia	32333	5064	27269	33405	5609	27796
辽 宁 Liaoning	126655	85247	41408	118130	82824	35306
吉 林 Jilin	63370	31620	31750	62545	33451	29094
黑龙江 Heilongjiang	54802	36782	18020	56117	40114	16003
上 海 Shanghai	49910	31111	18799	51739	34287	17452
江 苏 Jiangsu	272991	108115	164876	249594	117036	132558
浙 江 Zhejiang	69301	42531	26770	63722	41961	21761
安 徽 Anhui	137336	46809	90527	129266	51985	77281
福 建 Fujian	60362	33018	27344	61391	34908	26483
江 西 Jiangxi	96567	42991	53576	94694	47108	47586
山 东 Shandong	136658	55175	81483	139010	61465	77545
河 南 Henan	218942	79345	139597	261455	81368	180087
湖 北 Hubei	249285	104112	145173	245486	102829	142657
湖 南 Hunan	92006	36604	55402	100863	40624	60239
广 东 Guangdong	124723	41659	83064	139339	53280	86059
广 西 Guangxi	70262	23897	46365	83780	31810	51970
海 南 Hainan	8436	0	8436	7394	0	7394
重 庆 Chongqing	70815	23676	47139	79326	29957	49369
四 川 Sichuan	124771	60849	63922	140243	72973	67270
贵 州 Guizhou	20270	2800	17470	34625	3436	31189
云 南 Yunnan	33106	9719	23387	43700	10358	33342
西 藏 Tibet	0	0	0	0	0	0
陕 西 Shaanxi	131867	74801	57066	126940	73327	53613
甘 肃 Gansu	43871	17032	26839	48560	17471	31089
青 海 Qinghai	3122	0	3122	3542	0	3542
宁 夏 Ningxia	8813	4844	3969	10052	6249	3803
新 疆 Xinjiang	21702	1136	20566	28452	2966	25486

本科、专科生学生数
Institutions of Science & Technology

单位:人
unit:person

在校生数 Enrolment			预计毕业生数 Estimated Graduates for Next Year		
合计 Total	本科 Normal Courses	专科 Short-cycle Courses	合计 Total	本科 Normal Courses	专科 Short-cycle Courses
9644376	**5074782**	**4569594**	**2809249**	**1254478**	**1554771**
251160	219944	31216	65918	53633	12285
198011	133200	64811	56215	33177	23038
484394	263681	220713	132197	63040	69157
228816	140329	88487	67672	34075	33597
113344	22685	90659	36393	5466	30927
465988	348243	117745	137615	93707	43908
226442	133400	93042	63597	32720	30877
207579	155656	51923	56387	38034	18353
197212	137661	59551	56127	35084	21043
948074	476332	471742	290242	120307	169935
255450	177641	77809	73580	46541	27039
472947	210188	262759	152634	51498	101136
227520	141907	85613	65283	35253	30030
339427	184281	155146	99249	45238	54011
503788	239861	263927	152630	57988	94642
868926	336833	532093	252718	83411	169307
835866	415001	420865	237882	101408	136474
342979	159685	183294	99245	39012	60233
451021	201384	249637	132463	45711	86752
269777	122853	146924	76533	29415	47118
22523	0	22523	7862	0	7862
266577	116087	150490	76851	26507	50344
483362	283984	199378	134637	66781	67856
90364	12169	78195	24772	2999	21773
131224	41184	90040	37447	10214	27233
0	0	0	0	0	0
467563	296996	170567	138493	77475	61018
162045	71259	90786	45545	18340	27205
10123	0	10123	3487	0	3487
35763	23382	12381	9685	5496	4189
86111	8956	77155	25890	1948	23942

地区 Region	毕(结)业生数 Graduates			招生数 Entrants		
	合计 Total	本科 Normal Courses	专科 Short-cycle Courses	合计 Total	本科 Normal Courses	专科 Short-cycle Courses
总计 Total	**275782**	**167261**	**108521**	**284896**	**180019**	**104877**
北京 Beijing	6139	4291	1848	5679	4542	1137
天津 Tianjin	3287	2851	436	2817	2565	252
河北 Hebei	10223	8657	1566	9378	9378	0
山西 Shanxi	10229	9653	576	10208	9614	594
内蒙古 Inner Mongolia	7925	6742	1183	8046	7068	978
辽宁 Liaoning	11801	6393	5408	10668	6185	4483
吉林 Jilin	12292	8901	3391	11859	8948	2911
黑龙江 Heilongjiang	20995	9621	11374	19006	9386	9620
上海 Shanghai	4216	3023	1193	3948	3015	933
江苏 Jiangsu	17696	4272	13424	15792	4289	11503
浙江 Zhejiang	4638	2363	2275	4026	2412	1614
安徽 Anhui	4688	4688	0	4439	4439	0
福建 Fujian	11284	5667	5617	11777	5431	6346
江西 Jiangxi	7602	4750	2852	8478	4851	3627
山东 Shandong	20607	15466	5141	22192	17041	5151
河南 Henan	25393	8246	17147	26724	13080	13644
湖北 Hubei	4426	4426	0	4625	4625	0
湖南 Hunan	9771	6274	3497	10474	6787	3687
广东 Guangdong	20204	20202	2	21443	21443	0
广西 Guangxi	7554	0	7554	10023	0	10023
海南 Hainan	0	0	0	0	0	0
重庆 Chongqing	0	0	0	0	0	0
四川 Sichuan	12043	8198	3845	13467	10033	3434
贵州 Guizhou	0	0	0	2068	0	2068
云南 Yunnan	8888	4399	4489	11106	4659	6447
西藏 Tibet	1415	1151	264	1326	1127	199
陕西 Shaanxi	11331	5322	6009	11587	5197	6390
甘肃 Gansu	8283	4005	4278	7216	4062	3154
青海 Qinghai	978	0	978	730	0	730
宁夏 Ningxia	0	0	0	0	0	0
新疆 Xinjiang	11874	7700	4174	15794	9842	5952

本科、专科生学生数
of Institutions of Agriculture

单位:人
unit:person

在校生数 Enrolment			预计毕业生数 Estimated Graduates for Next Year		
合计 Total	本 科 Normal Courses	专 科 Short-cycle Courses	合计 Total	本 科 Normal Courses	专 科 Short-cycle Courses
1044413	**714015**	**330398**	**289376**	**174431**	**114945**
22508	18196	4312	6149	4508	1641
12165	11204	961	3484	3023	461
37909	37084	825	9777	8976	801
39661	37454	2207	9732	8955	777
31821	28254	3567	8049	6788	1261
41171	26346	14825	12832	7357	5475
46444	35935	10509	12730	8778	3952
70498	37752	32746	21193	9642	11551
15256	11761	3495	3945	2780	1165
57862	17397	40465	18985	4354	14631
16227	9711	6516	4888	2549	2339
18042	18042	0	4559	4559	0
40962	22484	18478	12076	5897	6179
31131	19680	11451	8943	4750	4193
82111	65269	16842	21874	15601	6273
91780	47103	44677	27350	10041	17309
18654	18654	0	4635	4635	0
38346	26849	11497	10400	6630	3770
88905	88904	1	22431	22430	1
26374	0	26374	7815	0	7815
0	0	0	0	0	0
0	0	0	0	0	0
48197	38049	10148	12017	8482	3535
2865	0	2865	451	0	451
36028	19162	16866	9829	4835	4994
5810	5213	597	1380	1183	197
40233	20995	19238	11624	5334	6290
27683	16806	10877	8196	4333	3863
3372	0	3372	1303	0	1303
0	0	0	0	0	0
52398	35711	16687	12729	8011	4718

地区 Region	毕(结)业生数 Graduates			招生数 Entrants		
	合计 Total	本科 Normal Courses	专科 Short-cycle Courses	合计 Total	本科 Normal Courses	专科 Short-cycle Courses
总计 Total	**54614**	**28153**	**26461**	**54159**	**27518**	**26641**
北京 Beijing	3235	3235	0	3351	3351	0
天津 Tianjin	0	0	0	0	0	0
河北 Hebei	0	0	0	0	0	0
山西 Shanxi	1644	0	1644	1010	0	1010
内蒙古 Inner Mongolia	0	0	0	0	0	0
辽宁 Liaoning	1849	0	1849	2029	0	2029
吉林 Jilin	0	0	0	0	0	0
黑龙江 Heilongjiang	8098	4510	3588	8799	4824	3975
上海 Shanghai	0	0	0	0	0	0
江苏 Jiangsu	6849	6849	0	6009	6009	0
浙江 Zhejiang	3581	3581	0	3650	3650	0
安徽 Anhui	1121	0	1121	961	0	961
福建 Fujian	1966	0	1966	2132	0	2132
江西 Jiangxi	3611	0	3611	2665	0	2665
山东 Shandong	0	0	0	0	0	0
河南 Henan	483	0	483	1859	0	1859
湖北 Hubei	3411	0	3411	2942	0	2942
湖南 Hunan	6386	5848	538	6473	5909	564
广东 Guangdong	0	0	0	0	0	0
广西 Guangxi	2441	0	2441	2933	0	2933
海南 Hainan	0	0	0	0	0	0
重庆 Chongqing	0	0	0	0	0	0
四川 Sichuan	0	0	0	0	0	0
贵州 Guizhou	0	0	0	0	0	0
云南 Yunnan	6602	4130	2472	6727	3775	2952
西藏 Tibet	0	0	0	0	0	0
陕西 Shaanxi	0	0	0	0	0	0
甘肃 Gansu	3082	0	3082	2127	0	2127
青海 Qinghai	0	0	0	0	0	0
宁夏 Ningxia	255	0	255	492	0	492
新疆 Xinjiang	0	0	0	0	0	0

本科、专科生学生数
of Institutions of Forestry

单位:人
unit:person

在校生数 Enrolment			预计毕业生数 Estimated Graduates for Next Year		
合计 Total	本 科 Normal Courses	专 科 Short-cycle Courses	合计 Total	本 科 Normal Courses	专 科 Short-cycle Courses
197407	**113572**	**83835**	**57394**	**28745**	**28649**
13233	13233	0	3282	3282	0
0	0	0	0	0	0
0	0	0	0	0	0
3946	0	3946	1618	0	1618
0	0	0	0	0	0
6480	0	6480	2211	0	2211
0	0	0	0	0	0
31407	18973	12434	8649	4472	4177
0	0	0	0	0	0
26530	26530	0	6838	6838	0
14501	14501	0	3776	3776	0
2985	0	2985	1119	0	1119
6702	0	6702	2332	0	2332
9801	0	9801	3959	0	3959
0	0	0	0	0	0
5257	0	5257	1537	0	1537
8744	0	8744	2951	0	2951
25568	23855	1713	6528	5969	559
0	0	0	0	0	0
7954	0	7954	2528	0	2528
0	0	0	0	0	0
0	0	0	0	0	0
0	0	0	0	0	0
0	0	0	0	0	0
24643	16480	8163	7013	4408	2605
0	0	0	0	0	0
0	0	0	0	0	0
8304	0	8304	2760	0	2760
0	0	0	0	0	0
1352	0	1352	293	0	293
0	0	0	0	0	0

地 区 Region	毕(结)业生数 Graduates			招生数 Entrants		
	合计 Total	本 科 Normal Courses	专 科 Short-cycle Courses	合计 Total	本 科 Normal Courses	专 科 Short-cycle Courses
总 计 Total	**461627**	**229011**	**232616**	**490471**	**238224**	**252247**
北 京 Beijing	3846	2161	1685	4611	3361	1250
天 津 Tianjin	8918	4479	4439	8560	4899	3661
河 北 Hebei	30222	11501	18721	33797	11158	22639
山 西 Shanxi	13271	8769	4502	14877	9636	5241
内蒙古 Inner Mongolia	4435	2346	2089	4045	2452	1593
辽 宁 Liaoning	22211	17066	5145	21278	16296	4982
吉 林 Jilin	9621	4026	5595	10937	3685	7252
黑龙江 Heilongjiang	15300	9903	5397	15261	9881	5380
上 海 Shanghai	6013	857	5156	4043	2163	1880
江 苏 Jiangsu	19632	12347	7285	21669	12371	9298
浙 江 Zhejiang	13594	6596	6998	12762	7499	5263
安 徽 Anhui	26995	13191	13804	23867	12660	11207
福 建 Fujian	15983	5231	10752	15355	5365	9990
江 西 Jiangxi	16208	6104	10104	18186	6290	11896
山 东 Shandong	53860	23175	30685	46982	19582	27400
河 南 Henan	31729	11110	20619	38929	9459	29470
湖 北 Hubei	10536	6829	3707	10019	6296	3723
湖 南 Hunan	22168	8647	13521	23610	10046	13564
广 东 Guangdong	23458	16346	7112	27340	18189	9151
广 西 Guangxi	16967	9012	7955	21337	11080	10257
海 南 Hainan	2769	1700	1069	2770	1889	881
重 庆 Chongqing	13253	4723	8530	12933	3804	9129
四 川 Sichuan	20378	11857	8521	23861	14892	8969
贵 州 Guizhou	22253	12486	9767	27820	14364	13456
云 南 Yunnan	15647	6519	9128	20231	7515	12716
西 藏 Tibet	204	204	0	300	260	40
陕 西 Shaanxi	10228	6171	4057	9089	5591	3498
甘 肃 Gansu	4483	1973	2510	7586	3400	4186
青 海 Qinghai	880	0	880	1035	0	1035
宁 夏 Ningxia	1978	1147	831	1673	1137	536
新 疆 Xinjiang	4587	2535	2052	5708	3004	2704

本科、专科生学生数

Institutions of Medicine & Pharmacy

单位:人
unit:person

在校生数 Enrolment			预计毕业生数 Estimated Graduates for Next Year		
合计 Total	本科 Normal Courses	专科 Short-cycle Courses	合计 Total	本科 Normal Courses	专科 Short-cycle Courses
1821034	**1051252**	**769782**	**486887**	**233210**	**253677**
17349	12586	4763	4057	2212	1845
33189	20689	12500	8856	4367	4489
119583	50888	68695	32728	11211	21517
58514	44551	13963	14251	9771	4480
16935	10856	6079	4418	2212	2206
91407	74518	16889	22353	16501	5852
37195	16476	20719	9866	3667	6199
60239	43459	16780	15934	9771	6163
14192	6161	8031	3742	914	2828
81684	54768	26916	20921	12844	8077
51862	32259	19603	14183	6808	7375
94503	56407	38096	25369	12028	13341
54420	24425	29995	16154	5494	10660
66244	29494	36750	20020	6439	13581
182902	88120	94782	54780	21187	33593
134232	51861	82371	38467	12551	25916
40272	29195	11077	10495	6814	3681
85539	41905	43634	23320	8804	14516
96682	72159	24523	25463	17359	8104
76273	48600	27673	18536	10471	8065
10780	7989	2791	2653	1664	989
44421	19048	25373	13334	4602	8732
92869	62927	29942	23076	12796	10280
98564	60331	38233	24719	13645	11074
67255	33474	33781	16896	7105	9791
1394	1274	120	288	249	39
38104	25879	12225	10362	6242	4120
22284	12703	9581	4094	1985	2109
3128	0	3128	976	0	976
6591	4973	1618	1562	993	569
22428	13277	9151	5014	2504	2510

地 区 Region	毕(结)业生数 Graduates			招生数 Entrants		
	合计 Total	本 科 Normal Courses	专 科 Short-cycle Courses	合计 Total	本 科 Normal Courses	专 科 Short-cycle Courses
总 计 Total	**758226**	**550851**	**207375**	**748489**	**569904**	**178585**
北 京 Beijing	5590	5125	465	5271	5271	0
天 津 Tianjin	10416	9735	681	9903	9403	500
河 北 Hebei	52063	35244	16819	51880	37831	14049
山 西 Shanxi	27775	15928	11847	26719	15679	11040
内蒙古 Inner Mongolia	11738	8225	3513	11842	8413	3429
辽 宁 Liaoning	22340	13437	8903	20512	11467	9045
吉 林 Jilin	25661	21357	4304	25833	22145	3688
黑龙江 Heilongjiang	19315	14453	4862	18606	14049	4557
上 海 Shanghai	8376	8274	102	8542	8542	0
江 苏 Jiangsu	49274	31839	17435	38821	32993	5828
浙 江 Zhejiang	24833	22444	2389	23425	21750	1675
安 徽 Anhui	60419	49829	10590	56872	50971	5901
福 建 Fujian	22369	19106	3263	21996	17527	4469
江 西 Jiangxi	28371	16724	11647	29167	18113	11054
山 东 Shandong	23437	17132	6305	22093	19214	2879
河 南 Henan	71953	55002	16951	70759	52514	18245
湖 北 Hubei	24589	15178	9411	28195	16213	11982
湖 南 Hunan	14430	10895	3535	16246	13335	2911
广 东 Guangdong	27556	23226	4330	26748	20588	6160
广 西 Guangxi	23079	15356	7723	28179	19409	8770
海 南 Hainan	6532	3993	2539	6869	5354	1515
重 庆 Chongqing	19699	15162	4537	15075	13561	1514
四 川 Sichuan	50737	30693	20044	50893	38705	12188
贵 州 Guizhou	33909	26133	7776	36184	26926	9258
云 南 Yunnan	26558	17724	8834	27809	20360	7449
西 藏 Tibet	898	0	898	1373	0	1373
陕 西 Shaanxi	29993	22712	7281	28441	21242	7199
甘 肃 Gansu	19196	15427	3769	17930	13802	4128
青 海 Qinghai	2644	2021	623	3593	2567	1026
宁 夏 Ningxia	2448	1446	1002	3026	1930	1096
新 疆 Xinjiang	12028	7031	4997	15687	10030	5657

本科、专科生学生数

Institutions of Languages & Literatures

单位:人
unit:person

在校生数 Enrolment			预计毕业生数 Estimated Graduates for Next Year		
合计 Total	本科 Normal Courses	专科 Short-cycle Courses	合计 Total	本科 Normal Courses	专科 Short-cycle Courses
2900191	**2285218**	**614973**	**787810**	**569279**	**218531**
21428	21144	284	5573	5289	284
41586	39740	1846	10698	10054	644
195187	148121	47066	53869	36987	16882
101104	64801	36303	30060	16693	13367
46255	34757	11498	12780	8948	3832
78463	49312	29151	24588	14336	10252
100462	88815	11647	25161	21387	3774
70600	55869	14731	18737	14127	4610
34826	34822	4	9130	9126	4
164347	134541	29806	49105	33143	15962
98602	92093	6509	26307	24010	2297
233929	205847	28082	62387	51615	10772
86275	73574	12701	23634	19466	4168
104559	69047	35512	28038	16733	11305
87215	72946	14269	23927	17378	6549
280574	221913	58661	76690	56660	20030
102502	63562	38940	27356	15526	11830
62868	49834	13034	16576	11715	4861
104952	91214	13738	27491	24080	3411
99389	73840	25549	25392	17645	7747
27260	19861	7399	7336	4430	2906
69033	58834	10199	20494	15847	4647
188091	142872	45219	48951	31610	17341
132862	101060	31802	35193	24447	10746
108175	79808	28367	29205	18440	10765
3579	0	3579	919	0	919
110168	86169	23999	31027	22897	8130
69430	57822	11608	18497	14899	3598
12116	9098	3018	3201	2120	1081
9310	6628	2682	2243	1610	633
55044	37274	17770	13245	8061	5184

地区 Region	毕(结)业生数 Graduates			招生数 Entrants		
	合计 Total	本科 Normal Courses	专科 Short-cycle Courses	合计 Total	本科 Normal Courses	专科 Short-cycle Courses
总 计 Total	**117599**	**65576**	**52023**	**124797**	**74303**	**50494**
北 京 Beijing	10967	8108	2859	11590	9200	2390
天 津 Tianjin	5020	3527	1493	5079	3576	1503
河 北 Hebei	7943	1654	6289	9586	2111	7475
山 西 Shanxi	6737	994	5743	7248	2343	4905
内蒙古 Inner Mongolia	82	0	82	168	0	168
辽 宁 Liaoning	4941	3474	1467	5532	4493	1039
吉 林 Jilin	5101	5101	0	5387	5387	0
黑龙江 Heilongjiang	2267	2267	0	2361	2361	0
上 海 Shanghai	5665	1464	4201	4298	1549	2749
江 苏 Jiangsu	0	0	0	0	0	0
浙 江 Zhejiang	9233	8598	635	9575	8932	643
安 徽 Anhui	4816	1470	3346	5141	2081	3060
福 建 Fujian	1982	0	1982	2572	0	2572
江 西 Jiangxi	0	0	0	0	0	0
山 东 Shandong	3913	0	3913	1756	0	1756
河 南 Henan	0	0	0	0	0	0
湖 北 Hubei	1999	1986	13	2685	2381	304
湖 南 Hunan	10710	2542	8168	11238	2211	9027
广 东 Guangdong	6817	6817	0	7134	7134	0
广 西 Guangxi	3556	1651	1905	4323	3698	625
海 南 Hainan	1106	0	1106	1392	0	1392
重 庆 Chongqing	6244	6244	0	6632	6632	0
四 川 Sichuan	4914	2538	2376	8050	3135	4915
贵 州 Guizhou	0	0	0	0	0	0
云 南 Yunnan	660	0	660	564	0	564
西 藏 Tibet	0	0	0	0	0	0
陕 西 Shaanxi	10125	7141	2984	9575	7079	2496
甘 肃 Gansu	2801	0	2801	2911	0	2911
青 海 Qinghai	0	0	0	0	0	0
宁 夏 Ningxia	0	0	0	0	0	0
新 疆 Xinjiang	0	0	0	0	0	0

本科、专科生学生数
Comprehensive Universities

单位：人
unit: person

在校生数 Enrolment			预计毕业生数 Estimated Graduates for Next Year		
合计 Total	本科 Normal Courses	专科 Short-cycle Courses	合计 Total	本科 Normal Courses	专科 Short-cycle Courses
453393	**291347**	**162046**	**126321**	**69997**	**56324**
45608	38498	7110	12282	9619	2663
19265	14378	4887	5257	3581	1676
31830	7738	24092	8646	1610	7036
24779	8647	16132	7467	1649	5818
410	0	410	102	0	102
20264	17043	3221	5020	3915	1105
21169	21169	0	5111	5111	0
9269	9269	0	2341	2341	0
16138	6002	10136	5753	1495	4258
0	0	0	0	0	0
38646	36677	1969	9636	8996	640
17687	7813	9874	5190	1691	3499
7843	0	7843	2637	0	2637
0	0	0	0	0	0
8348	0	8348	3778	0	3778
0	0	0	0	0	0
9535	8927	608	1938	1936	2
35633	9262	26371	10909	2487	8422
29037	29037	0	7375	7375	0
14747	11678	3069	3706	2107	1599
4385	0	4385	1682	0	1682
26169	26169	0	6378	6378	0
25263	11506	13757	6857	2390	4467
0	0	0	0	0	0
3580	0	3580	1100	0	1100
0	0	0	0	0	0
35830	27534	8296	10731	7316	3415
7958	0	7958	2425	0	2425
0	0	0	0	0	0
0	0	0	0	0	0
0	0	0	0	0	0

地 区 Region	毕(结)业生数 Graduates			招生数 Entrants		
	合计 Total	本 科 Normal Courses	专 科 Short-cycle Courses	合计 Total	本 科 Normal Courses	专 科 Short-cycle Courses
总 计 Total	**718952**	**368148**	**350804**	**751636**	**398088**	**353548**
北 京 Beijing	21221	14094	7127	18595	14195	4400
天 津 Tianjin	14290	11536	2754	15129	12914	2215
河 北 Hebei	22066	16033	6033	20831	16241	4590
山 西 Shanxi	26075	13057	13018	28160	16241	11919
内蒙古 Inner Mongolia	9330	4536	4794	8536	4694	3842
辽 宁 Liaoning	19338	11205	8133	16453	10221	6232
吉 林 Jilin	13467	10066	3401	13772	10377	3395
黑龙江 Heilongjiang	17239	14286	2953	17541	14950	2591
上 海 Shanghai	33375	18566	14809	35297	20596	14701
江 苏 Jiangsu	29430	11338	18092	33835	12508	21327
浙 江 Zhejiang	36441	14767	21674	34443	14151	20292
安 徽 Anhui	46462	11229	35233	45260	11027	34233
福 建 Fujian	20185	10547	9638	18469	11320	7149
江 西 Jiangxi	24084	8197	15887	22654	9888	12766
山 东 Shandong	34275	15681	18594	31592	15079	16513
河 南 Henan	74030	38776	35254	80301	40456	39845
湖 北 Hubei	33629	22277	11352	35420	23839	11581
湖 南 Hunan	17017	7376	9641	19417	8550	10867
广 东 Guangdong	51217	27402	23815	55313	36066	19247
广 西 Guangxi	19638	4923	14715	23390	6214	17176
海 南 Hainan	11250	3312	7938	11341	3701	7640
重 庆 Chongqing	28146	18170	9976	33716	21142	12574
四 川 Sichuan	16282	5128	11154	20370	5948	14422
贵 州 Guizhou	15056	8127	6929	20354	10683	9671
云 南 Yunnan	36272	22194	14078	42613	22518	20095
西 藏 Tibet	188	79	109	348	152	196
陕 西 Shaanxi	31967	11986	19981	29408	10582	18826
甘 肃 Gansu	9215	9215	0	10061	8531	1530
青 海 Qinghai	0	0	0	0	0	0
宁 夏 Ningxia	3722	0	3722	3713	0	3713
新 疆 Xinjiang	4045	4045	0	5304	5304	0

本科、专科生学生数
Institutions of Finance & Economies

单位：人
unit: person

在校生数 Enrolment			预计毕业生数 Estimated Graduates for Next Year		
合计 Total	本 科 Normal Courses	专 科 Short-cycle Courses	合计 Total	本 科 Normal Courses	专 科 Short-cycle Courses
2677445	**1573434**	**1104011**	**761583**	**386456**	**375127**
74296	58597	15699	21190	14979	6211
57765	49851	7914	14575	11852	2723
83067	65995	17072	22793	16544	6249
101207	61248	39959	28484	14283	14201
31803	18844	12959	9502	4748	4754
66096	42959	23137	20226	11603	8623
52087	41544	10543	13842	10214	3628
67897	58259	9638	17927	14522	3405
129055	80047	49008	36620	19970	16650
112940	49347	63593	32014	11839	20175
126844	59311	67533	38526	15543	22983
153398	42770	110628	48971	10520	38451
66890	45016	21874	18542	11342	7200
78843	38109	40734	23168	9476	13692
119503	62596	56907	36312	15301	21011
282758	163492	119266	79506	40464	39042
125226	93220	32006	33741	22286	11455
65738	32262	33476	18373	7404	10969
203023	138859	64164	55894	32321	23573
73962	24337	49625	21351	5463	15888
37865	15642	22223	11346	3964	7382
116932	80775	36157	30366	18989	11377
65842	21935	43907	19442	4944	14498
65608	39209	26399	18275	9226	9049
147957	90828	57129	41392	23114	18278
910	601	309	181	143	38
102482	43232	59250	32201	12008	20193
37897	35525	2372	9664	9664	0
0	0	0	0	0	0
10530	0	10530	3429	0	3429
19024	19024	0	3730	3730	0

地　区 Region	毕(结)业生数 Graduates 合计 Total	本　科 Normal Courses	专　科 Short-cycle Courses	招生数 Entrants 合计 Total	本　科 Normal Courses	专　科 Short-cycle Courses
总　计 Total	**100674**	**50623**	**50051**	**103347**	**50295**	**53052**
北　京 Beijing	10967	8203	2764	10500	7378	3122
天　津 Tianjin	939	0	939	1081	0	1081
河　北 Hebei	7670	2710	4960	10008	2565	7443
山　西 Shanxi	2655	0	2655	2567	528	2039
内蒙古 Inner Mongolia	398	0	398	451	0	451
辽　宁 Liaoning	4327	2440	1887	3925	2312	1613
吉　林 Jilin	3158	1150	2008	3056	1327	1729
黑龙江 Heilongjiang	1319	0	1319	1944	0	1944
上　海 Shanghai	6188	5297	891	6399	5457	942
江　苏 Jiangsu	2943	2943	0	2841	2841	0
浙　江 Zhejiang	2687	1395	1292	2161	1188	973
安　徽 Anhui	2591	0	2591	3644	0	3644
福　建 Fujian	1039	1039	0	989	989	0
江　西 Jiangxi	3599	1102	2497	3369	1089	2280
山　东 Shandong	6397	3460	2937	6395	3755	2640
河　南 Henan	4990	1941	3049	7282	2344	4938
湖　北 Hubei	4385	917	3468	3963	1058	2905
湖　南 Hunan	3160	1613	1547	3274	1570	1704
广　东 Guangdong	2520	1022	1498	3186	1634	1552
广　西 Guangxi	1467	0	1467	1106	499	607
海　南 Hainan	1520	0	1520	1602	0	1602
重　庆 Chongqing	5018	5018	0	4828	4828	0
四　川 Sichuan	3375	1995	1380	2714	1237	1477
贵　州 Guizhou	1731	0	1731	1531	397	1134
云　南 Yunnan	2493	1469	1024	2268	1133	1135
西　藏 Tibet	277	0	277	267	0	267
陕　西 Shaanxi	6051	3776	2275	5048	3245	1803
甘　肃 Gansu	3557	2632	925	4346	2364	1982
青　海 Qinghai	280	0	280	236	0	236
宁　夏 Ningxia	1086	0	1086	1073	0	1073
新　疆 Xinjiang	1887	501	1386	1293	557	736

本科、专科生学生数
Institutions of Political Science & Law

单位:人
unit:person

在校生数 Enrolment			预计毕业生数 Estimated Graduates for Next Year		
合计 Total	本 科 Normal Courses	专 科 Short-cycle Courses	合计 Total	本 科 Normal Courses	专 科 Short-cycle Courses
354798	**198626**	**156172**	**101901**	**49703**	**52198**
37172	28078	9094	10683	7593	3090
3328	0	3328	1106	0	1106
30097	8823	21274	8916	2523	6393
6698	1027	5671	1780	0	1780
1332	0	1332	432	0	432
13211	8612	4599	3548	2047	1501
10600	5612	4988	2866	1312	1554
4866	0	4866	1722	0	1722
23007	21139	1868	6388	5503	885
11703	11703	0	2969	2969	0
8280	5391	2889	2347	1310	1037
9776	0	9776	2904	0	2904
4904	4904	0	1334	1334	0
11272	4345	6927	3631	1087	2544
23676	14571	9105	6700	3283	3417
22984	8470	14514	6479	1728	4751
13780	4069	9711	4553	921	3632
11593	6535	5058	3605	1919	1686
10641	6286	4355	3054	1421	1633
4006	2381	1625	503	0	503
4690	0	4690	1510	0	1510
19741	19741	0	4979	4979	0
9614	5297	4317	2716	1456	1260
4772	397	4375	1691	0	1691
7869	4641	3228	2396	1236	1160
858	0	858	291	0	291
19753	13447	6306	5724	3555	2169
14536	10492	4044	3738	2805	933
941	0	941	411	0	411
3168	0	3168	1082	0	1082
5930	2665	3265	1843	722	1121

地 区 Region	毕(结)业生数 Graduates			招生数 Entrants		
	合计 Total	本 科 Normal Courses	专 科 Short-cycle Courses	合计 Total	本 科 Normal Courses	专 科 Short-cycle Courses
总 计 Total	**32593**	**24811**	**7782**	**36845**	**27027**	**9818**
北 京 Beijing	2858	2805	53	3176	3109	67
天 津 Tianjin	2574	2334	240	2749	2646	103
河 北 Hebei	1360	1272	88	1639	1550	89
山 西 Shanxi	401	0	401	423	0	423
内蒙古 Inner Mongolia	89	0	89	151	0	151
辽 宁 Liaoning	1969	1844	125	1834	1834	0
吉 林 Jilin	1455	1455	0	2270	1587	683
黑龙江 Heilongjiang	1304	1304	0	2016	1607	409
上 海 Shanghai	1034	981	53	1138	996	142
江 苏 Jiangsu	1509	1509	0	1666	1666	0
浙 江 Zhejiang	255	0	255	122	0	122
安 徽 Anhui	436	0	436	660	0	660
福 建 Fujian	465	0	465	543	0	543
江 西 Jiangxi	0	0	0	0	0	0
山 东 Shandong	1799	1799	0	2134	2134	0
河 南 Henan	1912	0	1912	486	0	486
湖 北 Hubei	3868	3649	219	4288	3972	316
湖 南 Hunan	618	0	618	1198	0	1198
广 东 Guangdong	3180	1621	1559	3189	1627	1562
广 西 Guangxi	472	0	472	1425	0	1425
海 南 Hainan	0	0	0	170	0	170
重 庆 Chongqing	0	0	0	0	0	0
四 川 Sichuan	2163	2163	0	2239	2239	0
贵 州 Guizhou	0	0	0	0	0	0
云 南 Yunnan	676	0	676	1153	0	1153
西 藏 Tibet	0	0	0	0	0	0
陕 西 Shaanxi	2075	2075	0	2060	2060	0
甘 肃 Gansu	0	0	0	0	0	0
青 海 Qinghai	0	0	0	0	0	0
宁 夏 Ningxia	0	0	0	0	0	0
新 疆 Xinjiang	121	0	121	116	0	116

本科、专科生学生数
Institutions of Physical Culture

单位:人
unit:person

在校生数 Enrolment			预计毕业生数 Estimated Graduates for Next Year		
合计 Total	本 科 Normal Courses	专 科 Short-cycle Courses	合计 Total	本 科 Normal Courses	专 科 Short-cycle Courses
136167	**106376**	**29791**	**35843**	**25711**	**10132**
12400	12200	200	3026	2958	68
10466	10234	232	2589	2462	127
5928	5716	212	1410	1313	97
1033	0	1033	475	0	475
464	0	464	159	0	159
7567	7442	125	2070	1948	122
6965	6282	683	1545	1545	0
7442	6064	1378	1920	1441	479
4411	3927	484	1223	1029	194
6791	6791	0	1668	1668	0
651	0	651	280	0	280
1997	0	1997	706	0	706
1772	0	1772	582	0	582
0	0	0	0	0	0
8019	8019	0	1853	1853	0
4142	0	4142	2063	0	2063
16528	15571	957	4033	3735	298
3281	0	3281	888	0	888
11536	6569	4967	3328	1531	1797
3802	0	3802	909	0	909
170	0	170	0	0	0
0	0	0	0	0	0
9413	9413	0	2210	2210	0
0	0	0	0	0	0
2873	0	2873	813	0	813
0	0	0	0	0	0
8148	8148	0	2018	2018	0
0	0	0	0	0	0
0	0	0	0	0	0
0	0	0	0	0	0
368	0	368	75	0	75

地 区 Region	毕(结)业生数 Graduates			招生数 Entrants		
	合计 Total	本 科 Normal Courses	专 科 Short-cycle Courses	合计 Total	本 科 Normal Courses	专 科 Short-cycle Courses
总 计 Total	**101436**	**55632**	**45804**	**123359**	**65346**	**58013**
北 京 Beijing	3185	2990	195	3662	3480	182
天 津 Tianjin	3256	1826	1430	2866	1668	1198
河 北 Hebei	7320	4505	2815	8984	5451	3533
山 西 Shanxi	699	0	699	895	0	895
内蒙古 Inner Mongolia	399	0	399	1327	965	362
辽 宁 Liaoning	9040	6937	2103	8058	6167	1891
吉 林 Jilin	4756	4755	1	4810	4810	0
黑龙江 Heilongjiang	562	0	562	748	116	632
上 海 Shanghai	3604	1790	1814	3657	2045	1612
江 苏 Jiangsu	8698	5118	3580	9751	5658	4093
浙 江 Zhejiang	4652	1947	2705	4337	2237	2100
安 徽 Anhui	988	0	988	899	0	899
福 建 Fujian	1448	0	1448	1962	0	1962
江 西 Jiangxi	951	0	951	1163	0	1163
山 东 Shandong	5287	4272	1015	5600	4175	1425
河 南 Henan	2451	0	2451	5984	0	5984
湖 北 Hubei	4971	2742	2229	5589	2829	2760
湖 南 Hunan	3007	0	3007	3378	0	3378
广 东 Guangdong	5923	2295	3628	7341	2430	4911
广 西 Guangxi	5043	3272	1771	9267	6285	2982
海 南 Hainan	0	0	0	0	0	0
重 庆 Chongqing	2907	1601	1306	3735	1578	2157
四 川 Sichuan	13370	4985	8385	19259	8157	11102
贵 州 Guizhou	0	0	0	0	0	0
云 南 Yunnan	4932	3278	1654	5311	3594	1717
西 藏 Tibet	0	0	0	0	0	0
陕 西 Shaanxi	3015	2489	526	3358	2527	831
甘 肃 Gansu	0	0	0	0	0	0
青 海 Qinghai	0	0	0	0	0	0
宁 夏 Ningxia	80	0	80	191	0	191
新 疆 Xinjiang	892	830	62	1227	1174	53

本科、专科生学生数
Institutions of Art

单位：人
unit：person

在校生数 Enrolment			预计毕业生数 Estimated Graduates for Next Year		
合计 Total	本　科 Normal Courses	专　科 Short-cycle Courses	合计 Total	本　科 Normal Courses	专　科 Short-cycle Courses
422507	**250443**	**172064**	**115398**	**58863**	**56535**
14537	14042	495	3527	3337	190
11331	7121	4210	3451	1814	1637
29467	19499	9968	7560	4274	3286
2670	0	2670	899	0	899
3588	2308	1280	407	0	407
31186	24871	6315	8992	6714	2278
19454	19454	0	4853	4853	0
2411	256	2155	776	0	776
13492	7826	5666	3923	1830	2093
34263	21911	12352	9421	5656	3765
16450	9027	7423	4600	2077	2523
3065	0	3065	1200	0	1200
5379	0	5379	1734	0	1734
3916	0	3916	1369	0	1369
20917	16885	4032	5808	4278	1530
16060	0	16060	4635	0	4635
19707	11463	8244	5627	2835	2792
10595	0	10595	3362	0	3362
22427	9567	12860	6090	2203	3887
27806	21286	6520	6323	4281	2042
0	0	0	0	0	0
13071	7035	6036	3661	1962	1699
63266	29190	34076	17588	5860	11728
0	0	0	0	0	0
19935	14381	5554	5382	3545	1837
0	0	0	0	0	0
12214	9954	2260	3112	2477	635
0	0	0	0	0	0
0	0	0	0	0	0
738	0	738	165	0	165
4562	4367	195	933	867	66

地 区 Region	毕(结)业生数 Graduates			招生数 Entrants		
	合计 Total	本 科 Normal Courses	专 科 Short-cycle Courses	合计 Total	本 科 Normal Courses	专 科 Short-cycle Courses
总 计 Total	**62879**	**55006**	**7873**	**68059**	**61099**	**6960**
北 京 Beijing	2718	2718	0	2806	2806	0
天 津 Tianjin	0	0	0	0	0	0
河 北 Hebei	0	0	0	0	0	0
山 西 Shanxi	0	0	0	0	0	0
内蒙古 Inner Mongolia	0	0	0	0	0	0
辽 宁 Liaoning	4060	4060	0	4276	4276	0
吉 林 Jilin	0	0	0	0	0	0
黑龙江 Heilongjiang	1032	0	1032	709	0	709
上 海 Shanghai	0	0	0	0	0	0
江 苏 Jiangsu	0	0	0	0	0	0
浙 江 Zhejiang	0	0	0	0	0	0
安 徽 Anhui	0	0	0	0	0	0
福 建 Fujian	0	0	0	0	0	0
江 西 Jiangxi	0	0	0	0	0	0
山 东 Shandong	0	0	0	0	0	0
河 南 Henan	0	0	0	0	0	0
湖 北 Hubei	10100	10100	0	9523	9523	0
湖 南 Hunan	4271	0	4271	3865	0	3865
广 东 Guangdong	0	0	0	0	0	0
广 西 Guangxi	4120	3903	217	4827	4529	298
海 南 Hainan	0	0	0	0	0	0
重 庆 Chongqing	0	0	0	0	0	0
四 川 Sichuan	8918	8214	704	9143	8866	277
贵 州 Guizhou	6386	6385	1	10028	10028	0
云 南 Yunnan	5314	5288	26	5719	5605	114
西 藏 Tibet	2406	2004	402	2395	2126	269
陕 西 Shaanxi	0	0	0	0	0	0
甘 肃 Gansu	5954	5954	0	5991	5991	0
青 海 Qinghai	1877	1866	11	2566	2359	207
宁 夏 Ningxia	5723	4514	1209	6211	4990	1221
新 疆 Xinjiang	0	0	0	0	0	0

本科、专科生学生数
Nationalities Institutions

单位:人
unit: person

在校生数 Enrolment			预计毕业生数 Estimated Graduates for Next Year		
合计 Total	本 科 Normal Courses	专 科 Short-cycle Courses	合计 Total	本 科 Normal Courses	专 科 Short-cycle Courses
258059	**234461**	**23598**	**64825**	**56374**	**8451**
11283	11283	0	2920	2920	0
0	0	0	0	0	0
0	0	0	0	0	0
0	0	0	0	0	0
0	0	0	0	0	0
16929	16929	0	4194	4194	0
0	0	0	0	0	0
2472	0	2472	1061	0	1061
0	0	0	0	0	0
0	0	0	0	0	0
0	0	0	0	0	0
0	0	0	0	0	0
0	0	0	0	0	0
0	0	0	0	0	0
0	0	0	0	0	0
0	0	0	0	0	0
39963	39963	0	10321	10321	0
13709	0	13709	4838	0	4838
0	0	0	0	0	0
17343	16545	798	4141	3904	237
0	0	0	0	0	0
0	0	0	0	0	0
36600	35312	1288	9547	8981	566
30136	30135	1	5692	5691	1
22853	22531	322	5533	5454	79
9429	8755	674	2379	2084	295
0	0	0	0	0	0
24341	24341	0	5967	5967	0
9559	8959	600	2192	1998	194
23442	19708	3734	6040	4860	1180
0	0	0	0	0	0

地 区 Region	毕(结)业生数 Graduates			招生数 Entrants		
	合计 Total	本 科 Normal Courses	专 科 Short-cycle Courses	合计 Total	本 科 Normal Courses	专 科 Short-cycle Courses
总 计 Total	**2556588**	**0**	**2556588**	**2719629**	**0**	**2719629**
北 京 Beijing	22678	0	22678	15208	0	15208
天 津 Tianjin	49949	0	49949	45406	0	45406
河 北 Hebei	96023	0	96023	117894	0	117894
山 西 Shanxi	65841	0	65841	58555	0	58555
内蒙古 Inner Mongolia	46819	0	46819	48584	0	48584
辽 宁 Liaoning	70222	0	70222	61331	0	61331
吉 林 Jilin	29431	0	29431	29909	0	29909
黑龙江 Heilongjiang	53224	0	53224	50278	0	50278
上 海 Shanghai	33434	0	33434	31404	0	31404
江 苏 Jiangsu	215591	0	215591	181380	0	181380
浙 江 Zhejiang	115594	0	115594	99262	0	99262
安 徽 Anhui	135526	0	135526	124722	0	124722
福 建 Fujian	66031	0	66031	67343	0	67343
江 西 Jiangxi	101165	0	101165	102896	0	102896
山 东 Shandong	217780	0	217780	198342	0	198342
河 南 Henan	138204	0	138204	204402	0	204402
湖 北 Hubei	143582	0	143582	143424	0	143424
湖 南 Hunan	142372	0	142372	160178	0	160178
广 东 Guangdong	229874	0	229874	257055	0	257055
广 西 Guangxi	77681	0	77681	107263	0	107263
海 南 Hainan	18731	0	18731	18562	0	18562
重 庆 Chongqing	70067	0	70067	83206	0	83206
四 川 Sichuan	131694	0	131694	157618	0	157618
贵 州 Guizhou	52690	0	52690	89642	0	89642
云 南 Yunnan	44830	0	44830	62842	0	62842
西 藏 Tibet	1503	0	1503	1521	0	1521
陕 西 Shaanxi	95994	0	95994	86813	0	86813
甘 肃 Gansu	41819	0	41819	49503	0	49503
青 海 Qinghai	6090	0	6090	8415	0	8415
宁 夏 Ningxia	10332	0	10332	10701	0	10701
新 疆 Xinjiang	31817	0	31817	45970	0	45970

本科、专科生学生数
Higher Vocational Colleges

单位：人
unit: person

在校生数 Enrolment			预计毕业生数 Estimated Graduates for Next Year		
合计 Total	本科 Normal Courses	专科 Short-cycle Courses	合计 Total	本科 Normal Courses	专科 Short-cycle Courses
8411238	**0**	**8411238**	**2813032**	**0**	**2813032**
54310	0	54310	20491	0	20491
147692	0	147692	51123	0	51123
345526	0	345526	105875	0	105875
190659	0	190659	68945	0	68945
156712	0	156712	53125	0	53125
206545	0	206545	75033	0	75033
92714	0	92714	29672	0	29672
163568	0	163568	57775	0	57775
104700	0	104700	36094	0	36094
633271	0	633271	225068	0	225068
348112	0	348112	121490	0	121490
412966	0	412966	152741	0	152741
210882	0	210882	71485	0	71485
331678	0	331678	114347	0	114347
687088	0	687088	249232	0	249232
578189	0	578189	175612	0	175612
425507	0	425507	137805	0	137805
494546	0	494546	159343	0	159343
738779	0	738779	250057	0	250057
284340	0	284340	82168	0	82168
55665	0	55665	18873	0	18873
244737	0	244737	78406	0	78406
461703	0	461703	152128	0	152128
232580	0	232580	66768	0	66768
181704	0	181704	56620	0	56620
5084	0	5084	1836	0	1836
291498	0	291498	103550	0	103550
141478	0	141478	41074	0	41074
25521	0	25521	8422	0	8422
31222	0	31222	10136	0	10136
132262	0	132262	37738	0	37738

地 区 Region	毕(结)业生数 Graduates			招生数 Entrants		
	合计 Total	本 科 Normal Courses	专 科 Short-cycle Courses	合计 Total	本 科 Normal Courses	专 科 Short-cycle Courses
总 计 Total	**62362**	**2286**	**60076**	**76986**	**4287**	**72699**
北 京 Beijing	3	0	3	0	0	0
天 津 Tianjin	101	0	101	2	1	1
河 北 Hebei	3920	40	3880	6475	109	6366
山 西 Shanxi	1064	0	1064	547	0	547
内蒙古 Inner Mongolia	423	0	423	16	0	16
辽 宁 Liaoning	1742	0	1742	1103	0	1103
吉 林 Jilin	697	0	697	83	0	83
黑龙江 Heilongjiang	1412	0	1412	1169	0	1169
上 海 Shanghai	0	0	0	0	0	0
江 苏 Jiangsu	4220	274	3946	10146	990	9156
浙 江 Zhejiang	5217	0	5217	4211	22	4189
安 徽 Anhui	516	176	340	134	40	94
福 建 Fujian	4483	0	4483	2239	113	2126
江 西 Jiangxi	1551	369	1182	1605	425	1180
山 东 Shandong	5205	436	4769	9275	704	8571
河 南 Henan	235	15	220	14	4	10
湖 北 Hubei	1163	260	903	456	106	350
湖 南 Hunan	224	0	224	613	0	613
广 东 Guangdong	3495	46	3449	13117	837	12280
广 西 Guangxi	441	280	161	357	216	141
海 南 Hainan	98	0	98	76	0	76
重 庆 Chongqing	9502	0	9502	8551	0	8551
四 川 Sichuan	5739	280	5459	4040	208	3832
贵 州 Guizhou	1692	0	1692	346	0	346
云 南 Yunnan	3533	43	3490	2777	326	2451
西 藏 Tibet	0	0	0	0	0	0
陕 西 Shaanxi	989	67	922	4659	186	4473
甘 肃 Gansu	1803	0	1803	2958	0	2958
青 海 Qinghai	360	0	360	99	0	99
宁 夏 Ningxia	1371	0	1371	950	0	950
新 疆 Xinjiang	1163	0	1163	968	0	968

本专科学生数
in Radio/TV Universities

单位：人
unit：person

在校生数 Enrolment			预计毕业生数 Estimated Graduates for Next Year		
合计 Total	本科 Normal Courses	专科 Short-cycle Courses	合计 Total	本科 Normal Courses	专科 Short-cycle Courses
189919	**10152**	**179767**	**86454**	**4623**	**81831**
210	0	210	210	0	210
50	1	49	48	0	48
12043	266	11777	4267	110	4157
1229	0	1229	682	0	682
26	0	26	10	0	10
2797	0	2797	1694	0	1694
255	0	255	172	0	172
2336	0	2336	1025	0	1025
0	0	0	0	0	0
19949	1879	18070	9803	889	8914
12513	190	12323	5104	151	4953
919	492	427	412	231	181
8431	196	8235	3528	0	3528
4130	1036	3094	2332	611	1721
20739	1834	18905	11113	781	10332
184	14	170	170	10	160
1319	440	879	699	170	529
980	0	980	316	0	316
23925	1386	22539	4444	549	3895
931	564	367	568	342	226
180	0	180	104	0	104
27939	0	27939	13840	0	13840
15279	715	14564	10961	507	10454
5365	0	5365	4649	0	4649
5809	541	5268	2835	47	2788
0	0	0	0	0	0
11608	598	11010	4159	225	3934
4193	0	4193	1235	0	1235
762	0	762	525	0	525
3336	0	3336	450	0	450
2482	0	2482	1099	0	1099

地区 Region	毕(结)业生数 Graduates			招生数 Entrants		
	合计 Total	本科 Normal Courses	专科 Short-cycle Courses	合计 Total	本科 Normal Courses	专科 Short-cycle Courses
总计 Total	**47788**	**1637**	**46151**	**36922**	**1687**	**35235**
北京 Beijing	4189	146	4043	3807	39	3768
天津 Tianjin	5574	0	5574	3411	0	3411
河北 Hebei	744	0	744	1076	0	1076
山西 Shanxi	3473	684	2789	879	417	462
内蒙古 Inner Mongolia	0	0	0	0	0	0
辽宁 Liaoning	4182	0	4182	5753	0	5753
吉林 Jilin	2954	742	2212	2518	1216	1302
黑龙江 Heilongjiang	1185	0	1185	282	0	282
上海 Shanghai	1487	0	1487	1409	0	1409
江苏 Jiangsu	93	0	93	120	0	120
浙江 Zhejiang	1959	0	1959	878	0	878
安徽 Anhui	617	0	617	1537	0	1537
福建 Fujian	0	0	0	0	0	0
江西 Jiangxi	725	0	725	17	0	17
山东 Shandong	1642	0	1642	470	0	470
河南 Henan	3690	0	3690	2821	0	2821
湖北 Hubei	0	0	0	0	0	0
湖南 Hunan	2570	0	2570	2506	0	2506
广东 Guangdong	2407	0	2407	2706	0	2706
广西 Guangxi	93	0	93	55	0	55
海南 Hainan	0	0	0	0	0	0
重庆 Chongqing	166	0	166	95	0	95
四川 Sichuan	5209	34	5175	3268	14	3254
贵州 Guizhou	116	0	116	5	0	5
云南 Yunnan	63	0	63	0	0	0
西藏 Tibet	0	0	0	0	0	0
陕西 Shaanxi	3691	31	3660	2327	1	2326
甘肃 Gansu	176	0	176	107	0	107
青海 Qinghai	783	0	783	875	0	875
宁夏 Ningxia	0	0	0	0	0	0
新疆 Xinjiang	0	0	0	0	0	0

本专科学生数
in Workers' Colleges

单位：人
unit: person

在校生数 Enrolment			预计毕业生数 Estimated Graduates for Next Year		
合计 Total	本 科 Normal Courses	专 科 Short-cycle Courses	合计 Total	本 科 Normal Courses	专 科 Short-cycle Courses
84830	**3902**	**80928**	**42260**	**1930**	**40330**
8135	182	7953	4054	104	3950
7453	0	7453	4042	0	4042
2256	0	2256	1176	0	1176
4167	1283	2884	2565	624	1941
0	0	0	0	0	0
10803	0	10803	4056	0	4056
5217	2384	2833	2699	1168	1531
1311	0	1311	835	0	835
5080	0	5080	3420	0	3420
218	0	218	98	0	98
2411	0	2411	1366	0	1366
1626	0	1626	89	0	89
0	0	0	0	0	0
341	0	341	321	0	321
1292	0	1292	816	0	816
5669	0	5669	2704	0	2704
0	0	0	0	0	0
5014	0	5014	2338	0	2338
5621	0	5621	2229	0	2229
114	0	114	65	0	65
0	0	0	0	0	0
284	0	284	149	0	149
9062	39	9023	5035	25	5010
33	0	33	28	0	28
184	0	184	156	0	156
0	0	0	0	0	0
6168	14	6154	2682	9	2673
560	0	560	435	0	435
1811	0	1811	902	0	902
0	0	0	0	0	0
0	0	0	0	0	0

地 区 Region	毕(结)业生数 Graduates			招生数 Entrants		
	合计 Total	本 科 Normal Courses	专 科 Short-cycle Courses	合计 Total	本 科 Normal Courses	专 科 Short-cycle Courses
总 计 Total	**23223**	**5105**	**18118**	**19294**	**5822**	**13472**
北 京 Beijing	575	239	336	440	304	136
天 津 Tianjin	0	0	0	0	0	0
河 北 Hebei	0	0	0	0	0	0
山 西 Shanxi	128	0	128	18	0	18
内蒙古 Inner Mongolia	0	0	0	0	0	0
辽 宁 Liaoning	1417	446	971	2053	771	1282
吉 林 Jilin	1346	782	564	367	257	110
黑龙江 Heilongjiang	2655	988	1667	1703	917	786
上 海 Shanghai	0	0	0	0	0	0
江 苏 Jiangsu	1505	0	1505	1500	0	1500
浙 江 Zhejiang	1961	859	1102	2945	599	2346
安 徽 Anhui	0	0	0	0	0	0
福 建 Fujian	3258	946	2312	3932	1578	2354
江 西 Jiangxi	4410	0	4410	135	0	135
山 东 Shandong	3	0	3	0	0	0
河 南 Henan	2105	0	2105	469	0	469
湖 北 Hubei	855	0	855	881	0	881
湖 南 Hunan	267	0	267	486	0	486
广 东 Guangdong	0	0	0	0	0	0
广 西 Guangxi	1451	845	606	3476	1396	2080
海 南 Hainan	0	0	0	0	0	0
重 庆 Chongqing	0	0	0	0	0	0
四 川 Sichuan	0	0	0	0	0	0
贵 州 Guizhou	0	0	0	0	0	0
云 南 Yunnan	0	0	0	0	0	0
西 藏 Tibet	0	0	0	0	0	0
陕 西 Shaanxi	666	0	666	343	0	343
甘 肃 Gansu	0	0	0	0	0	0
青 海 Qinghai	0	0	0	0	0	0
宁 夏 Ningxia	0	0	0	0	0	0
新 疆 Xinjiang	621	0	621	546	0	546

专科学生数
in Educational Colleges

单位：人
unit: person

在校生数 Enrolment			预计毕业生数 Estimated Graduates for Next Year		
合计 Total	本科 Normal Courses	专科 Short-cycle Courses	合计 Total	本科 Normal Courses	专科 Short-cycle Courses
50488	**15995**	**34493**	**24565**	**6680**	**17885**
1724	1036	688	709	263	446
0	0	0	0	0	0
0	0	0	0	0	0
36	0	36	18	0	18
0	0	0	0	0	0
3739	1348	2391	1686	577	1109
756	570	186	344	268	76
4420	2649	1771	2529	1544	985
0	0	0	0	0	0
2903	0	2903	1403	0	1403
6247	2519	3728	2287	936	1351
0	0	0	0	0	0
15517	4939	10578	7115	1702	5413
2391	0	2391	2147	0	2147
2	0	2	2	0	2
1386	0	1386	858	0	858
1737	0	1737	856	0	856
965	0	965	479	0	479
0	0	0	0	0	0
6926	2934	3992	3303	1390	1913
0	0	0	0	0	0
0	0	0	0	0	0
0	0	0	0	0	0
0	0	0	0	0	0
0	0	0	0	0	0
0	0	0	0	0	0
648	0	648	305	0	305
0	0	0	0	0	0
0	0	0	0	0	0
0	0	0	0	0	0
1091	0	1091	524	0	524

地区 Region	毕(结)业生数 Graduates			招生数 Entrants		
	合计 Total	本科 Normal Courses	专科 Short-cycle Courses	合计 Total	本科 Normal Courses	专科 Short-cycle Courses
总计 Total	**7562**	**1004**	**6558**	**4304**	**470**	**3834**
北京 Beijing	1681	111	1570	871	0	871
天津 Tianjin	23	0	23	0	0	0
河北 Hebei	2	0	2	1	0	1
山西 Shanxi	5	0	5	0	0	0
内蒙古 Inner Mongolia	0	0	0	0	0	0
辽宁 Liaoning	117	86	31	41	41	0
吉林 Jilin	507	111	396	246	62	184
黑龙江 Heilongjiang	1886	260	1626	1450	255	1195
上海 Shanghai	297	0	297	175	0	175
江苏 Jiangsu	1565	0	1565	1073	0	1073
浙江 Zhejiang	0	0	0	0	0	0
安徽 Anhui	103	0	103	30	0	30
福建 Fujian	0	0	0	0	0	0
江西 Jiangxi	257	201	56	41	27	14
山东 Shandong	0	0	0	0	0	0
河南 Henan	0	0	0	0	0	0
湖北 Hubei	102	0	102	51	0	51
湖南 Hunan	0	0	0	0	0	0
广东 Guangdong	0	0	0	0	0	0
广西 Guangxi	676	235	441	254	85	169
海南 Hainan	0	0	0	0	0	0
重庆 Chongqing	0	0	0	0	0	0
四川 Sichuan	0	0	0	0	0	0
贵州 Guizhou	0	0	0	0	0	0
云南 Yunnan	0	0	0	0	0	0
西藏 Tibet	0	0	0	0	0	0
陕西 Shaanxi	341	0	341	71	0	71
甘肃 Gansu	0	0	0	0	0	0
青海 Qinghai	0	0	0	0	0	0
宁夏 Ningxia	0	0	0	0	0	0
新疆 Xinjiang	0	0	0	0	0	0

本专科学生数
in Institutes for Administration

单位:人
unit:person

在校生数 Enrolment			预计毕业生数 Estimated Graduates for Next Year		
合计 Total	本 科 Normal Courses	专 科 Short-cycle Courses	合计 Total	本 科 Normal Courses	专 科 Short-cycle Courses
10519	**1712**	**8807**	**5554**	**907**	**4647**
1590	0	1590	719	0	719
6	0	6	6	0	6
12	0	12	2	0	2
0	0	0	0	0	0
0	0	0	0	0	0
171	166	5	91	86	5
528	129	399	282	67	215
2918	520	2398	1468	265	1203
776	0	776	290	0	290
2173	0	2173	1100	0	1100
0	0	0	0	0	0
66	0	66	36	0	36
0	0	0	0	0	0
49	32	17	5	4	1
0	0	0	0	0	0
0	0	0	0	0	0
131	0	131	80	0	80
0	0	0	0	0	0
0	0	0	0	0	0
1809	865	944	1256	485	771
0	0	0	0	0	0
0	0	0	0	0	0
0	0	0	0	0	0
0	0	0	0	0	0
0	0	0	0	0	0
0	0	0	0	0	0
290	0	290	219	0	219
0	0	0	0	0	0
0	0	0	0	0	0
0	0	0	0	0	0
0	0	0	0	0	0

普通高等学校举办函授、业余、

Number of Students in Correspondence Courses for Adults Run

地 区 Region	函授、业余 Divisions of Correspondence and Sparetime Schools							
	毕业生数 Graduates			招生数 Entrants			在校生数 Enrolment	
	合计 Total	本 科 Normal Courses	专 科 Short-cycle Courses	合计 Total	本 科 Normal Courses	专 科 Short-cycle Courses	合计 Total	本 科 Normal Courses
总 计 Total	**2325434**	**1080119**	**1245315**	**2035836**	**1010680**	**1025156**	**5097734**	**2554482**
北 京 Beijing	63997	40929	23068	56506	36464	20042	146955	103059
天 津 Tianjin	24910	14916	9994	19025	11496	7529	41826	25377
河 北 Hebei	116942	65364	51578	158331	90294	68037	400994	236291
山 西 Shanxi	39678	20556	19122	20781	13751	7030	77950	47369
内蒙古 Inner Mongolia	15734	9961	5773	7446	5959	1487	21336	17352
辽 宁 Liaoning	54330	29919	24411	55147	29111	26036	130464	73870
吉 林 Jilin	65611	34298	31313	48135	27216	20919	106733	65410
黑龙江 Heilongjiang	56165	29997	26168	34024	22631	11393	86591	60001
上 海 Shanghai	45395	32749	12646	43869	29657	14212	128678	91731
江 苏 Jiangsu	165271	92605	72666	186216	99601	86615	422592	236923
浙 江 Zhejiang	99724	37868	61856	88890	37687	51203	197259	83028
安 徽 Anhui	83055	40127	42928	77777	40829	36948	178457	99269
福 建 Fujian	45119	20579	24540	18607	11107	7500	79462	42813
江 西 Jiangxi	51260	23076	28184	32327	19857	12470	133171	66980
山 东 Shandong	272335	163527	108808	147814	89371	58443	353069	214052
河 南 Henan	153119	67646	85473	121742	63639	58103	274884	151572
湖 北 Hubei	93050	40954	52096	76344	37259	39085	176099	92393
湖 南 Hunan	110466	48956	61510	136329	59870	76459	270772	122525
广 东 Guangdong	230497	60049	170448	239031	77549	161482	623444	176698
广 西 Guangxi	94198	37382	56816	103290	43870	59420	241748	101210
海 南 Hainan	6380	2800	3580	4554	2024	2530	13773	6999
重 庆 Chongqing	45812	11280	34532	33829	8663	25166	91573	22827
四 川 Sichuan	146711	35475	111236	108933	43304	65629	284019	105423
贵 州 Guizhou	42646	22993	19653	34392	15862	18530	99693	48525
云 南 Yunnan	64442	28262	36180	65013	28473	36540	196972	91198
西 藏 Tibet	6615	3447	3168	5342	3954	1388	18082	12679
陕 西 Shaanxi	60196	28471	31725	49234	26602	22632	130842	72643
甘 肃 Gansu	28787	15670	13117	20523	11243	9280	68280	35576
青 海 Qinghai	4125	2374	1751	3392	2452	940	8129	5851
宁 夏 Ningxia	8787	3556	5231	10283	5357	4926	23062	11533
新 疆 Xinjiang	30077	14333	15744	28710	15528	13182	70825	33305

脱产分本专科学生数
Divisions、Sparetime Schools & Short-cycle by Regular HEIs

单位:人
unit:person

	脱产 Short-cycle Courses for Adults								
	毕业生数 Graduates			招生数 Entrants			在校生数 Enrolment		
专 科 Short-cycle Courses	合计 Total	本 科 Normal Courses	专 科 Short-cycle Courses	合计 Total	本 科 Normal Courses	专 科 Short-cycle Courses	合计 Total	本 科 Normal Courses	专 科 Short-cycle Courses
2543252	**3555**	**1075**	**2480**	**1614**	**1035**	**579**	**7255**	**3566**	**3689**
43896	21	21	0	0	0	0	0	0	0
16449	0	0	0	0	0	0	0	0	0
164703	577	533	44	684	684	0	2456	2414	42
30581	0	0	0	0	0	0	0	0	0
3984	0	0	0	0	0	0	0	0	0
56594	0	0	0	0	0	0	0	0	0
41323	0	0	0	0	0	0	0	0	0
26590	0	0	0	0	0	0	0	0	0
36947	0	0	0	0	0	0	0	0	0
185669	323	93	230	0	0	0	2	0	2
114231	352	190	162	348	167	181	1136	601	535
79188	0	0	0	0	0	0	0	0	0
36649	0	0	0	0	0	0	0	0	0
66191	322	100	222	0	0	0	0	0	0
139017	0	0	0	0	0	0	0	0	0
123312	58	0	58	0	0	0	58	0	58
83706	1	1	0	0	0	0	0	0	0
148247	199	0	199	0	0	0	60	0	60
446746	141	0	141	0	0	0	113	0	113
140538	1	0	1	0	0	0	0	0	0
6774	0	0	0	0	0	0	0	0	0
68746	0	0	0	0	0	0	0	0	0
178596	0	0	0	0	0	0	0	0	0
51168	954	0	954	0	0	0	1839	0	1839
105774	0	0	0	0	0	0	0	0	0
5403	0	0	0	0	0	0	0	0	0
58199	0	0	0	0	0	0	0	0	0
32704	0	0	0	0	0	0	72	0	72
2278	0	0	0	0	0	0	0	0	0
11529	0	0	0	0	0	0	0	0	0
37520	606	137	469	582	184	398	1519	551	968

高等教育非学历

Number of Students in Non-formal

地 区 Region	毕(结)业生数 Graduates												
	自考助学班 Classes Run by Non-government HEIs for Students Preparing for Self-directed State-administrated Examinations	普通预科生 College-preparatory Classes	研究生课程进修班 Postgraduate Courses	进修及培训 In-service Training									
				总计 Total	其中:资格证书培训 of Which: For Certificates of Vocational Qualifications	岗位证书培训 For Certificates of Job-related Qualifications	其中:第一产业类培训 of Which: Training for First Industry	第二产业类培训 Training for Second Industry	第三产业类培训 Training for Third Industry	一个月以内 1 Month under	一个月至三个月以内 1 Month to 3 Months under	三个月至半年以内 3 Months to 6 Months under	半年至一年以内 3 Months to 6 Months under
总 计 Total	**116214**	**—**	**9244**	**9682937**	**2234987**	**2485345**	**419436**	**1395476**	**7868025**	**6099260**	**1726787**	**713677**	**994648**
北 京 Beijing	4745	—	3363	903813	51683	104843	23774	44180	835859	733042	30581	42383	81078
天 津 Tianjin	924	—	179	219033	128358	70858	36179	54884	127970	162103	42217	11538	3014
河 北 Hebei	4716	—	141	116643	17806	32199	2891	50824	62928	86379	22820	4288	1608
山 西 Shanxi	1832	—	0	59896	30256	13505	1218	14175	44503	38216	2971	635	2810
内蒙古 Inner Mongolia	0	—	0	83919	45766	21486	6014	42357	35548	73791	9780	348	0
辽 宁 Liaoning	8485	—	0	284890	64985	184849	7412	137597	139881	185511	36531	5565	57200
吉 林 Jilin	5765	—	0	51319	11755	2857	31598	2127	17594	45077	1202	231	831
黑龙江 Heilongjiang	189	—	63	118457	28517	42162	3532	40225	74700	79314	3708	603	34683
上 海 Shanghai	1689	—	0	1200757	134448	208282	3023	73021	1124713	484123	96719	191023	401632
江 苏 Jiangsu	13981	—	939	595041	227737	209197	58516	174368	362157	464101	76376	32141	17931
浙 江 Zhejiang	6849	—	657	1045697	166990	306553	42363	115139	888195	924075	86966	17293	10185
安 徽 Anhui	776	—	297	315295	50167	41163	4766	16294	294235	92374	6751	5484	205573
福 建 Fujian	956	—	364	251600	55765	170917	9764	7718	234118	77328	95203	3075	74377
江 西 Jiangxi	1990	—	0	69523	19660	32637	4502	15687	49334	53197	6174	9351	244
山 东 Shandong	3323	—	0	425156	159867	143710	17870	109455	297831	335752	59323	16140	7128
河 南 Henan	3035	—	770	329074	193541	84936	7999	24447	296628	270081	30422	19781	3695
湖 北 Hubei	13146	—	0	339053	112421	87723	9182	115933	213938	259988	52315	17256	8804
湖 南 Hunan	10690	—	0	306952	86619	52893	30739	42542	233671	150681	29333	116481	4737
广 东 Guangdong	4266	—	721	1546907	213596	93029	8323	30511	1508073	620382	853335	54760	12071
广 西 Guangxi	7059	—	407	199180	65658	98160	26780	59370	113030	169995	23062	4155	1397
海 南 Hainan	2741	—	0	6831	2595	303	1914	406	4511	3832	2789	0	210
重 庆 Chongqing	2304	—	0	120967	44401	20091	19284	12367	89316	99326	15043	1893	3616
四 川 Sichuan	8432	—	0	442943	104205	192506	27439	89267	326237	294359	55745	38817	45067
贵 州 Guizhou	5014	—	11	146866	60019	35361	2569	19302	124995	105929	5448	11065	4042
云 南 Yunnan	0	—	559	108272	53415	33854	9085	26044	73143	81085	20836	5663	348
西 藏 Tibet	0	—	0	3437	2505	932	932	0	2505	2982	435	20	0
陕 西 Shaanxi	0	—	190	157936	61870	39324	9391	35372	113173	102505	38910	10175	2910
甘 肃 Gansu	2779	—	0	118474	8772	97061	4918	7590	105966	20262	5419	83456	7118
青 海 Qinghai	464	—	0	24673	749	18170	0	11078	13595	23488	1051	134	0
宁 夏 Ningxia	0	—	0	20004	7262	9830	233	11897	7874	16105	1116	0	1466
新 疆 Xinjiang	64	—	583	70329	23599	35954	7226	11299	51804	43877	14206	9923	873

注:包含民办的其他高等教育机构数据。

Note: Data of Non-government HEIs are included.

教育学生情况(总计)
Education of HEIs (Total)

单位:人/人次
unit:person/person-time

一年及以上 1 Year and over	自考助学班 Classes Run by Non-government HEIs for Students Preparing for Self-directed State-administrated Examinations	普通预科生 College-preparatory Classes	研究生课程进修班 Postgraduate Courses	注册学生数 Enrolment — 进修及培训 In-service Training: 总计 Total	其中:资格证书培训 of Which: For Certificates of Vocational Qualifications	岗位证书培训 For Certificates of Job-related Qualifications	其中:第一产业类培训 of Which: Training for First Industry	第二产业类培训 Training for Second Industry	第三产业类培训 Training for Third Industry	一个月以内 1 Month under	一个月至三个月以内 1 Month to 3 Months under	三个月至半年以内 3 Months to 6 Months under	半年至一年以内 3 Months to 6 Months under	一年及以上 1 Year and over
148565	**230086**	**45420**	**12237**	**8985963**	**2252372**	**2188331**	**362754**	**1326784**	**7296425**	**5279933**	**1707445**	**673803**	**1050121**	**274661**
16729	10188	1809	6134	889983	50113	110424	21806	37420	830757	678116	25022	33179	112712	40954
161	3889	743	204	213099	145590	49692	36938	57290	118871	152604	38535	18263	3536	161
1548	7772	665	156	105829	19996	17936	3644	38422	63763	74101	23182	3443	1672	3431
15264	6337	135	0	53255	30148	13091	1765	11311	40179	28130	5100	1277	2728	16020
0	0	1494	0	68064	42331	13438	3612	41248	23204	62730	5026	308	0	0
83	15088	1624	0	256077	63174	168299	6901	129853	119323	163710	35803	5614	50867	83
3978	5931	1581	0	51833	12054	2871	31600	2264	17969	45551	1242	231	831	3978
149	1124	1546	0	97020	27139	34598	2355	35269	59396	58641	2429	1058	34706	186
27260	3690	1113	152	1059802	102739	162333	3774	77178	978850	373918	89173	132793	414379	49539
4492	30417	1381	152	460790	197735	166462	47009	153280	260501	351777	54836	26793	18344	9040
7178	14058	560	576	767616	147186	232794	34041	71999	661576	691089	44621	11455	13534	6917
5113	2508	328	297	320330	55570	40232	5108	16242	298980	94565	6976	5300	206138	7351
1617	6439	1089	490	232612	61873	159795	10689	9256	212667	57955	94336	4039	74293	1989
557	832	1857	0	53378	22596	24907	4585	9102	39691	35800	5773	10926	345	534
6813	5803	579	207	401989	135395	96004	24801	92724	284464	324902	39819	17000	11508	8760
5095	2749	1481	42	329446	202815	79336	7983	26100	295363	267944	35364	21163	4461	514
690	25787	2520	0	349774	128521	87657	9184	129932	210658	256542	60705	19683	11398	1446
5720	15873	2304	0	314926	95430	46271	30055	46041	238830	146009	36111	120686	5602	6518
6359	11117	616	1616	1569851	280732	102620	6611	40055	1523185	588524	889237	72089	13255	6746
571	9704	3886	547	158300	49048	79270	7073	68200	83027	123371	29114	4250	1184	381
0	12518	119	0	32607	6192	878	1914	552	30141	2787	3428	0	1392	25000
1089	3390	1126	0	79486	36631	22195	3259	27138	49089	58685	15799	1929	3073	0
8955	18647	3126	0	452693	111141	198299	21950	92917	337826	272563	69956	42261	44642	23271
20382	11517	4809	464	178543	60798	66175	2631	20004	155908	104624	7787	11105	4072	50955
340	0	3403	929	117194	61965	34539	8809	28306	80079	81987	22249	12268	350	340
0	0	0	0	3442	2510	932	932	0	2510	2987	435	20	0	0
3436	0	905	116	162851	66914	41585	10441	34598	117812	102572	41264	12170	3400	3445
2219	2412	2155	0	121260	10102	94632	5508	5209	110543	18330	5274	83692	9248	4716
0	1450	1045	0	5354	1154	1118	0	1673	3681	5354	0	0	0	0
1317	0	1421	0	21266	8245	9954	432	12606	8228	17130	1130	0	1578	1428
1450	846	0	155	57293	16535	29994	7344	10595	39354	36935	17719	808	873	958

地区 Region	毕(结)业生数 Graduates												
	自考助学班 Classes Run by Non-government HEIs for Students Preparing for Self-directed State-administrated Examinations	普通预科生 College-preparatory Classes	研究生课程进修班 Postgraduate Courses	进修及培训 In-service Training									
				总计 Total	其中:资格证书培训 of Which: For Certificates of Vocational Qualifications	岗位证书培训 For Certificates of Job-related Qualifications	其中:第一产业类培训 of Which: Training for First Industry	第二产业类培训 Training for Second Industry	第三产业类培训 Training for Third Industry	一个月以内 1 Month under	一个月至三个月以内 1 Month to 3 Months under	三个月至半年以内 3 Months to 6 Months under	半年至一年以内 3 Months to 6 Months under
总 计 Total	**58731**	**—**	**9068**	**5795802**	**1746730**	**1806071**	**328125**	**1257050**	**4210627**	**4666023**	**614116**	**302310**	**165184**
北 京 Beijing	413	—	3187	481952	34778	83186	6242	40429	435281	404861	26293	26476	16739
天 津 Tianjin	924	—	179	136447	72613	50475	3925	32163	100359	105202	18028	10150	2906
河 北 Hebei	202	—	141	111124	16216	30484	840	49785	60499	86053	21283	2031	309
山 西 Shanxi	0	—	0	30996	9649	9994	965	11378	18653	29466	1395	0	135
内蒙古 Inner Mongolia	0	—	0	83919	45766	21486	6014	42357	35548	73791	9780	348	0
辽 宁 Liaoning	189	—	0	183636	34259	123544	7412	136589	39635	156304	14934	891	11424
吉 林 Jilin	4751	—	0	47523	9258	2656	31598	1926	13999	42349	1082	231	831
黑龙江 Heilongjiang	53	—	63	76063	26503	35539	2699	36464	36900	70027	3708	527	1652
上 海 Shanghai	0	—	0	247129	74587	102967	2020	21530	223579	172093	41570	21427	3764
江 苏 Jiangsu	13981	—	939	568134	212558	199206	54210	166317	347607	449738	67525	29113	17397
浙 江 Zhejiang	1248	—	657	966440	159276	301855	42303	111942	812195	868796	70919	16763	9392
安 徽 Anhui	636	—	297	82043	28260	27717	2906	13802	65335	65910	4556	2149	7390
福 建 Fujian	956	—	364	95316	55406	15909	8488	7718	79110	76153	8525	3075	5946
江 西 Jiangxi	1669	—	0	66195	19276	32454	4502	15209	46484	53072	4437	7973	156
山 东 Shandong	1457	—	0	312975	125421	93948	10266	90148	212561	252583	44960	8025	4806
河 南 Henan	0	—	770	124072	29143	49478	7112	23818	93142	92404	6314	19220	2552
湖 北 Hubei	6580	—	0	337412	111129	87514	9182	115769	212461	258903	52161	16854	8804
湖 南 Hunan	3224	—	0	192102	85016	45374	27445	40980	123677	144520	28867	13495	3415
广 东 Guangdong	2027	—	721	496724	210543	83725	8223	26693	461808	394291	34743	53067	11371
广 西 Guangxi	7059	—	407	180756	65658	85742	21669	59370	99717	156875	20862	1051	1397
海 南 Hainan	0	—	0	3328	2595	303	1914	406	1008	329	2789	0	210
重 庆 Chongqing	1423	—	0	118408	44246	19391	18609	12102	87697	97672	14993	1843	2811
四 川 Sichuan	4345	—	0	392122	95225	173608	22857	88061	281204	256150	53811	37330	42586
贵 州 Guizhou	5014	—	11	124201	60019	12696	2569	19302	102330	105690	5448	9021	4042
云 南 Yunnan	0	—	559	108272	53415	33854	9085	26044	73143	81085	20836	5663	348
西 藏 Tibet	0	—	0	3437	2505	932	932	0	2505	2982	435	20	0
陕 西 Shaanxi	0	—	190	98226	33225	14579	3281	24884	70061	75616	16400	4375	1469
甘 肃 Gansu	2052	—	0	21443	8172	3501	3398	7590	10455	17685	1089	1135	1430
青 海 Qinghai	464	—	0	24673	749	18170	0	11078	13595	23488	1051	134	0
宁 夏 Ningxia	0	—	0	20004	7262	9830	233	11897	7874	16105	1116	0	1466
新 疆 Xinjiang	64	—	583	60730	14000	35954	7226	11299	42205	35830	14206	9923	436

注:包含民办的其他高等教育机构数据。

Note: Data of Non-government HEIs are included.

教育学生情况(普通高校)
Education of Regular HEIs

单位:人/人次
unit:person/person-time

	注册学生数 Enrolment													
				进修及培训 In-service Training										
一年及以上 1 Year and over	自考助学班 Classes Run by Non-government HEIs for Students Preparing for Self-directed State-administrated Examinations	普通预科生 College-preparatory Classes	研究生课程进修班 Postgraduate Courses	总计 Total	其中:资格证书培训 of Which: For Certificates of Vocational Qualifications	岗位证书培训 For Certificates of Job-related Qualifications	其中:第一产业类培训 of Which: Training for First Industry	第二产业类培训 Training for Second Industry	第三产业类培训 Training for Third Industry	一个月以内 1 Month under	一个月至三个月以内 1 Month to 3 Months under	三个月至半年以内 3 Months to 6 Months under	半年至一年以内 3 Months to 6 Months under	一年及以上 1 Year and over
48169	**119519**	**45420**	**11981**	**5119189**	**1790306**	**1513905**	**277976**	**1201043**	**3640170**	**3931670**	**616332**	**322734**	**187941**	**60512**
7583	675	1809	5878	452969	35682	87634	4811	33711	414447	362654	21523	18500	33853	16439
161	3889	743	204	120415	79189	29867	3925	31227	85263	92458	9094	15614	3088	161
1448	307	665	156	99889	17933	16692	1276	37415	61198	74011	21882	1362	143	2491
0	0	135	0	25199	9068	11714	1010	11095	13094	22894	1614	0	691	0
0	0	1494	0	68064	42331	13438	3612	41248	23204	62730	5026	308	0	0
83	471	1624	0	179010	35855	118551	6901	129683	42426	156110	15654	778	6385	83
3030	4751	1581	0	47822	9557	2656	31600	2049	14173	42648	1082	231	831	3030
149	809	1546	0	60290	25468	33296	2355	34487	23448	55018	2429	982	1675	186
8275	0	1113	152	140231	38467	59610	2020	25017	113194	61042	40772	23298	4105	11014
4361	30417	1381	152	447375	190564	160830	45487	152375	249513	347264	51791	25748	17295	5277
570	3550	560	576	692069	143290	229649	33975	67726	590368	639891	31741	10902	9310	225
2038	2358	328	297	85519	32038	26852	3272	13838	68409	68122	4800	1989	8013	2595
1617	6038	1089	490	77604	61873	4787	10689	9256	57659	57955	7759	4039	5862	1989
557	238	1857	0	51026	22378	24724	4585	9102	37339	35800	4922	9614	156	534
2601	4083	579	207	310927	117568	52178	24050	75279	211598	254025	35280	9877	9083	2662
3582	80	1481	42	124935	38443	43549	7140	25725	92070	90102	11234	20481	3118	0
690	11788	2520	0	347979	127075	87448	9184	129765	209030	255457	60544	19254	11398	1326
1805	10978	2304	0	202792	93977	44201	26961	45319	130512	141445	35747	18900	4330	2370
3252	7275	616	1616	526234	277978	93807	6601	36567	483066	368369	70422	70641	12915	3887
571	9704	3886	547	139326	49048	66849	1412	68200	69714	109704	26914	1143	1184	381
0	0	119	0	7607	6192	878	1914	552	5141	2787	3428	0	1392	0
1089	1651	1126	0	78812	36546	21606	3259	27138	48415	58685	15799	1929	2399	0
2245	5121	3126	0	387088	105684	177659	15003	92203	279882	235691	68347	39094	40904	3052
0	11517	4809	464	125305	60798	12937	2631	20004	102670	104385	7787	9061	4072	0
340	0	3403	929	117194	61965	34539	8809	28306	80079	81987	22249	12268	350	340
0	0	0	0	3442	2510	932	932	0	2510	2987	435	20	0	0
366	0	905	116	99823	36659	15132	3297	23673	72853	74549	18264	4770	1865	375
104	1523	2155	0	19508	9414	824	3489	5209	10810	15827	944	1123	1510	104
0	1450	1045	0	5354	1154	1118	0	1673	3681	5354	0	0	0	0
1317	0	1421	0	21266	8245	9954	432	12606	8228	17130	1130	0	1578	1428
335	846	0	155	54115	13357	29994	7344	10595	36176	34589	17719	808	436	563

地 区 Region	毕(结)业生数 Graduates												
	自考助学班 Classes Run by Non-government HEIs for Students Preparing for Self-directed State-administrated Examinations	普通预科生 College-preparatory Classes	研究生课程进修班 Postgraduate Courses	进修及培训 In-service Training									
				总计 Total	其中:资格证书培训 of Which: For Certificates of Vocational Qualifications	岗位证书培训 For Certificates of Job-related Qualifications	其中:第一产业类培训 of Which: Training for First Industry	第二产业类培训 Training for Second Industry	第三产业类培训 Training for Third Industry	一个月以内 1 Month under	一个月至三个月以内 1 Month to 3 Months under	三个月至半年以内 3 Months to 6 Months under	半年至一年以内 3 Months to 6 Months under
总 计 Total	**2868**	**—**	**0**	**2771985**	**359698**	**538396**	**57348**	**56130**	**2658507**	**1051968**	**1038025**	**230810**	**418785**
北 京 Beijing	0	—	0	364025	12168	19842	0	190	363835	283391	3249	13778	62797
天 津 Tianjin	0	—	0	82586	55745	20383	32254	22721	27611	56901	24189	1388	108
河 北 Hebei	0	—	0	0	0	0	0	0	0	0	0	0	0
山 西 Shanxi	0	—	0	2598	0	2598	0	2598	0	2598	0	0	0
内蒙古 Inner Mongolia	0	—	0	0	0	0	0	0	0	0	0	0	0
辽 宁 Liaoning	0	—	0	101254	30726	61305	0	1008	100246	29207	21597	4674	45776
吉 林 Jilin	0	—	0	2698	2497	201	0	201	2497	2502	0	0	0
黑龙江 Heilongjiang	0	—	0	42394	2014	6623	833	3761	37800	9287	0	76	33031
上 海 Shanghai	0	—	0	99433	14907	32683	394	0	99039	76247	10090	10500	2596
江 苏 Jiangsu	0	—	0	26907	15179	9991	4306	8051	14550	14363	8851	3028	534
浙 江 Zhejiang	127	—	0	69601	2370	3871	0	1610	67991	54539	11083	473	728
安 徽 Anhui	0	—	0	219589	15550	6140	61	78	219450	22656	889	0	196044
福 建 Fujian	0	—	0	156284	359	155008	1276	0	155008	1175	86678	0	68431
江 西 Jiangxi	0	—	0	0	0	0	0	0	0	0	0	0	0
山 东 Shandong	0	—	0	9356	0	0	0	0	9356	9356	0	0	0
河 南 Henan	0	—	0	199412	162695	35050	287	0	199125	176569	22843	0	0
湖 北 Hubei	0	—	0	402	402	0	0	40	362	0	0	402	0
湖 南 Hunan	0	—	0	114850	1603	7519	3294	1562	109994	6161	466	102986	1322
广 东 Guangdong	0	—	0	1035439	1429	8260	0	3418	1032021	216340	818139	960	0
广 西 Guangxi	0	—	0	18424	0	12418	5111	0	13313	13120	2200	3104	0
海 南 Hainan	2741	—	0	3503	0	0	0	0	3503	3503	0	0	0
重 庆 Chongqing	0	—	0	1754	50	0	665	245	844	1654	50	50	0
四 川 Sichuan	0	—	0	36242	3760	15834	1778	159	34305	35285	861	96	0
贵 州 Guizhou	0	—	0	22665	0	22665	0	0	22665	239	0	2044	0
云 南 Yunnan	0	—	0	0	0	0	0	0	0	0	0	0	0
西 藏 Tibet	0	—	0	0	0	0	0	0	0	0	0	0	0
陕 西 Shaanxi	0	—	0	59710	28645	24745	6110	10488	43112	26889	22510	5800	1441
甘 肃 Gansu	0	—	0	93260	0	93260	979	0	92281	1939	4330	81451	5540
青 海 Qinghai	0	—	0	0	0	0	0	0	0	0	0	0	0
宁 夏 Ningxia	0	—	0	0	0	0	0	0	0	0	0	0	0
新 疆 Xinjiang	0	—	0	9599	9599	0	0	0	9599	8047	0	0	437

注:包含民办的其他高等教育机构数据。
Note: Data of Non-government HEIs are included.

教育学生情况(成人高校)

Education of Adults HEIs

单位:人/人次

Unit:person/person-time

	注册学生数 Enrolment													
				进修及培训 In-service Training										
一年及以上 1 Year and over	自考助学班 Classes Run by Non-government HEIs for Students Preparing for Self-directed State-administrated Examinations	普通预科生 College-preparatory Classes	研究生课程进修班 Postgraduate Courses	总计 Total	其中:资格证书培训 of Which: For Certificates of Vocational Qualifications	岗位证书培训 For Certificates of Job-related Qualifications	其中:第一产业类培训 of Which: Training for First Industry	第二产业类培训 Training for Second Industry	第三产业类培训 Training for Third Industry	一个月以内 1 Month under	一个月至三个月以内 1 Month to 3 Months under	三个月至半年以内 3 Months to 6 Months under	半年至一年以内 3 Months to 6 Months under	一年及以上 1 Year and over
32397	**12948**	**0**	**0**	**2791274**	**349387**	**539106**	**54247**	**43740**	**2693287**	**988183**	**1036706**	**235486**	**436401**	**94498**
810	0	0	0	368597	9538	18837	0	0	368597	271846	3077	12105	77376	4193
0	0	0	0	92684	66401	19825	33013	26063	33608	60146	29441	2649	448	0
0	0	0	0	0	0	0	0	0	0	0	0	0	0	0
0	0	0	0	0	0	0	0	0	0	0	0	0	0	0
0	0	0	0	0	0	0	0	0	0	0	0	0	0	0
0	0	0	0	77067	27319	49748	0	170	76897	7600	20149	4836	44482	0
196	0	0	0	2712	2497	215	0	215	2497	2516	0	0	0	196
0	0	0	0	36730	1671	1302	0	782	35948	3623	0	76	33031	0
0	0	0	0	104346	14917	32753	394	0	103952	76241	10675	14834	2596	0
131	0	0	0	13415	7171	5632	1522	905	10988	4513	3045	1045	1049	3763
2778	29	0	0	68927	810	885	0	260	68667	50433	11083	473	4160	2778
0	0	0	0	219589	15550	6140	61	78	219450	22656	889	0	196044	0
0	401	0	0	155008	0	155008	0	0	155008	0	86577	0	68431	0
0	0	0	0	0	0	0	0	0	0	0	0	0	0	0
0	0	0	0	9356	0	0	0	0	9356	9356	0	0	0	0
0	0	0	0	199412	162695	35030	287	0	199125	176569	22843	0	0	0
0	0	0	0	429	429	0	0	43	386	0	0	429	0	0
3915	0	0	0	112134	1453	2070	3094	722	108318	4564	364	101786	1272	4148
0	0	0	0	1035439	1429	8260	0	3418	1032021	216340	818139	960	0	0
0	0	0	0	18974	0	12421	5661	0	13313	13667	2200	3107	0	0
0	12518	0	0	25000	0	0	0	0	25000	0	0	0	0	25000
0	0	0	0	0	0	0	0	0	0	0	0	0	0	0
0	0	0	0	38373	4074	17651	2092	159	36122	35566	894	1913	0	0
20382	0	0	0	53238	0	53238	0	0	53238	239	0	2044	0	50955
0	0	0	0	0	0	0	0	0	0	0	0	0	0	0
0	0	0	0	0	0	0	0	0	0	0	0	0	0	0
3070	0	0	0	63028	30255	26453	7144	10925	44959	28023	23000	7400	1535	3070
0	0	0	0	93638	0	93638	979	0	92659	1939	4330	81829	5540	0
0	0	0	0	0	0	0	0	0	0	0	0	0	0	0
0	0	0	0	0	0	0	0	0	0	0	0	0	0	0
1115	0	0	0	3178	3178	0	0	0	3178	2346	0	0	437	395

高等教育非学历教育
Number of Students in Non-formal Education

地 区 Region	毕(结)业生数 Graduates												
	自考助学班 Classes Run by Non-government HEIs for Students Preparing for Self-directed State-administrated Examinations	普通预科生 College-preparatory Classes	研究生课程进修班 Postgraduate Courses	进修及培训 In-service Training									
				总计 Total	其中:资格证书培训 of Which: For Certificates of Vocational Qualifications	岗位证书培训 For Certificates of Job-related Qualifications	其中:第一产业类培训 of Which: Training for First Industry	第二产业类培训 Training for Second Industry	第三产业类培训 Training for Third Industry	一个月以内 1 Month under	一个月至三个月以内 1 Month to 3 Months under	三个月至半年以内 3 Months to 6 Months under	半年至一年以内 3 Months to 6 Months under
总 计 Total	**54615**	**—**	**0**	**686284**	**127044**	**140878**	**33963**	**82296**	**570025**	**330207**	**68539**	**180069**	**39470**
北 京 Beijing	4332	—	0	57836	4737	1815	17532	3561	36743	44790	1039	2129	1542
天 津 Tianjin	0	—	0	0	0	0	0	0	0	0	0	0	0
河 北 Hebei	4514	—	0	5519	1590	1715	2051	1039	2429	326	1537	2257	1299
山 西 Shanxi	1832	—	0	26302	20607	913	253	199	25850	6152	1576	635	2675
内蒙古 Inner Mongolia	0	—	0	0	0	0	0	0	0	0	0	0	0
辽 宁 Liaoning	8296	—	0	0	0	0	0	0	0	0	0	0	0
吉 林 Jilin	1014	—	0	1098	0	0	0	0	1098	226	120	0	0
黑龙江 Heilongjiang	136	—	0	0	0	0	0	0	0	0	0	0	0
上 海 Shanghai	1689	—	0	425329	43439	72632	609	51491	373229	184721	38952	158608	24063
江 苏 Jiangsu	0	—	0	0	0	0	0	0	0	0	0	0	0
浙 江 Zhejiang	5474	—	0	9656	5344	827	60	1587	8009	740	4964	57	65
安 徽 Anhui	140	—	0	13663	6357	7306	1799	2414	9450	3808	1306	3335	2139
福 建 Fujian	0	—	0	0	0	0	0	0	0	0	0	0	0
江 西 Jiangxi	321	—	0	3328	384	183	0	478	2850	125	1737	1378	88
山 东 Shandong	1866	—	0	102825	34446	49762	7604	19307	75914	73813	14363	8115	2322
河 南 Henan	3035	—	0	5590	1703	408	600	629	4361	1108	1265	561	1143
湖 北 Hubei	6566	—	0	1239	890	209	0	124	1115	1085	154	0	0
湖 南 Hunan	7466	—	0	0	0	0	0	0	0	0	0	0	0
广 东 Guangdong	2239	—	0	14744	1622	1044	100	400	14244	9751	453	733	700
广 西 Guangxi	0	—	0	0	0	0	0	0	0	0	0	0	0
海 南 Hainan	0	—	0	0	0	0	0	0	0	0	0	0	0
重 庆 Chongqing	881	—	0	805	105	700	10	20	775	0	0	0	805
四 川 Sichuan	4087	—	0	14579	5220	3064	2804	1047	10728	2924	1073	1391	2481
贵 州 Guizhou	0	—	0	0	0	0	0	0	0	0	0	0	0
云 南 Yunnan	0	—	0	0	0	0	0	0	0	0	0	0	0
西 藏 Tibet	0	—	0	0	0	0	0	0	0	0	0	0	0
陕 西 Shaanxi	0	—	0	0	0	0	0	0	0	0	0	0	0
甘 肃 Gansu	727	—	0	3771	600	300	541	0	3230	638	0	870	148
青 海 Qinghai	0	—	0	0	0	0	0	0	0	0	0	0	0
宁 夏 Ningxia	0	—	0	0	0	0	0	0	0	0	0	0	0
新 疆 Xinjiang	0	—	0	0	0	0	0	0	0	0	0	0	0

注:包含民办的其他高等教育机构数据。

Note: Data of Non-government HEIs are included.

学生情况(民办的其他高等教育机构)
of Other Non-government HEIs

单位:人/人次
unit:person/person-time

	注册学生数 Enrolment			进修及培训 In-service Training										
一年及以上 1 Year and over	自考助学班 Classes Run by Non-government HEIs for Students Preparing for Self-directed State-administrated Examinations	普通预科生 College-preparatory Classes	研究生课程进修班 Postgraduate Courses	总计 Total	其中:资格证书培训 of Which: For Certificates of Vocational Qualifications	岗位证书培训 For Certificates of Job-related Qualifications	其中:第一产业类培训 of Which: Training for First Industry	第二产业类培训 Training for Second Industry	第三产业类培训 Training for Third Industry	一个月以内 1 Month under	一个月至三个月以内 1 Month to 3 Months under	三个月至半年以内 3 Months to 6 Months under	半年至一年以内 3 Months to 6 Months under	一年及以上 1 Year and over
67999	**97619**	**0**	**0**	**647038**	**111164**	**135320**	**30531**	**82001**	**534506**	**309422**	**48300**	**115095**	**54570**	**119651**
8336	9513	0	0	68417	4893	3953	16995	3709	47713	43616	422	2574	1483	20322
0	0	0	0	0	0	0	0	0	0	0	0	0	0	0
100	7465	0	0	5940	2063	1244	2368	1007	2565	90	1300	2081	1529	940
15264	6337	0	0	28056	21080	1377	755	216	27085	5236	3486	1277	2037	16020
0	0	0	0	0	0	0	0	0	0	0	0	0	0	0
0	14617	0	0	0	0	0	0	0	0	0	0	0	0	0
752	1180	0	0	1299	0	0	0	0	1299	387	160	0	0	752
0	315	0	0	0	0	0	0	0	0	0	0	0	0	0
18985	3690	0	0	386763	47840	69970	1360	52161	333242	185977	31619	94173	36469	38525
0	0	0	0	0	0	0	0	0	0	0	0	0	0	0
3830	10479	0	0	6620	3086	2260	66	4013	2541	765	1797	80	64	3914
3075	150	0	0	15222	7982	7240	1775	2326	11121	3787	1287	3311	2081	4756
0	0	0	0	0	0	0	0	0	0	0	0	0	0	0
0	594	0	0	2352	218	183	0	0	2352	0	851	1312	189	0
4212	1720	0	0	81706	17827	43826	751	17445	63510	61521	4539	7123	2425	6098
1513	2669	0	0	5099	1677	757	556	375	4168	1273	1287	682	1343	514
0	13999	0	0	1366	1017	209	0	124	1242	1085	161	0	0	120
0	4895	0	0	0	0	0	0	0	0	0	0	0	0	0
3107	3842	0	0	8178	1325	553	10	70	8098	3815	676	488	340	2859
0	0	0	0	0	0	0	0	0	0	0	0	0	0	0
0	0	0	0	0	0	0	0	0	0	0	0	0	0	0
0	1739	0	0	674	85	589	0	0	674	0	0	0	674	0
6710	13526	0	0	27232	1383	2989	4855	555	21822	1306	715	1254	3738	20219
0	0	0	0	0	0	0	0	0	0	0	0	0	0	0
0	0	0	0	0	0	0	0	0	0	0	0	0	0	0
0	0	0	0	0	0	0	0	0	0	0	0	0	0	0
0	0	0	0	0	0	0	0	0	0	0	0	0	0	0
2115	889	0	0	8114	688	170	1040	0	7074	564	0	740	2198	4612
0	0	0	0	0	0	0	0	0	0	0	0	0	0	0
0	0	0	0	0	0	0	0	0	0	0	0	0	0	0
0	0	0	0	0	0	0	0	0	0	0	0	0	0	0

地　区 Region	毕(结)业生数 Graduates	授予学位数 Degrees Awarded	招生数 Entrants	
			合计 Total	其中：春季招生 of Which: Spring Term
总　计 Total	**121419**	**26093**	**153445**	**40971**
北　京 Beijing	26012	5682	28578	8575
天　津 Tianjin	5870	858	5973	839
河　北 Hebei	657	426	949	241
山　西 Shanxi	145	4	402	46
内蒙古 Inner Mongolia	604	304	710	47
辽　宁 Liaoning	5610	2171	7269	1867
吉　林 Jilin	2401	575	2788	599
黑龙江 Heilongjiang	3718	800	5110	2262
上　海 Shanghai	16014	2699	19912	6509
江　苏 Jiangsu	9004	1655	16407	3436
浙　江 Zhejiang	7683	1515	11278	3067
安　徽 Anhui	783	294	1245	230
福　建 Fujian	2465	379	2421	419
江　西 Jiangxi	1013	484	1317	220
山　东 Shandong	6328	894	7357	2095
河　南 Henan	1195	248	1690	613
湖　北 Hubei	4549	1578	6255	1044
湖　南 Hunan	1181	358	1807	426
广　东 Guangdong	4319	1358	4588	1086
广　西 Guangxi	3386	595	3593	1655
海　南 Hainan	736	51	1630	287
重　庆 Chongqing	4126	587	4208	997
四　川 Sichuan	2688	631	4321	812
贵　州 Guizhou	953	40	1664	120
云　南 Yunnan	4182	745	3998	1027
西　藏 Tibet	4	0	19	0
陕　西 Shaanxi	4109	631	4961	1666
甘　肃 Gansu	551	211	835	49
青　海 Qinghai	125	7	182	89
宁　夏 Ningxia	101	61	293	50
新　疆 Xinjiang	887	252	1685	598

学生情况
Foreign Students

单位:人
unit:person

在校生数 Enrolment					
合计 Total	第一年 1st Year	第二年 2nd Year	第三年 3rd Year	第四年 4th Year	第五年及以上 5th Year
274809	**141497**	**55112**	**34391**	**24157**	**19652**
42724	22962	8845	5083	3717	2117
9337	5445	1585	977	568	762
3570	914	680	690	634	652
643	423	164	48	8	0
2345	756	465	338	406	380
17730	7184	3845	2680	2248	1773
5463	2798	1190	675	351	449
7538	3627	1388	923	722	878
31997	19987	5537	3358	2010	1105
29184	15265	6005	3546	2039	2329
19898	10214	4103	2588	1782	1211
2835	1263	667	452	286	167
4633	2138	833	770	362	530
3814	1321	580	600	528	785
12941	7284	2353	1367	1193	744
3536	1656	854	379	267	380
14196	5395	3507	2177	1659	1458
3576	1769	600	581	396	230
12958	7012	2167	1589	1130	1060
6626	3453	1411	924	689	149
2354	1549	372	129	146	158
4041	1935	893	591	310	312
7900	4335	1705	791	539	530
2741	1638	535	357	156	55
7805	3850	1802	943	587	623
34	19	15	0	0	0
8343	4427	1740	1042	819	315
1737	871	407	244	170	45
367	193	103	37	18	16
589	220	96	83	60	130
3354	1594	665	429	357	309

地区 Region	教职 Educational					
	合计 Total	校本部 Educational Personnel				
		小计 Subtotal	专任教师 Full-time Teachers			
			小计 Subtotal	正高级 Senior	副高级 Sub-senior	中级 Middle
总　计 Total	**2484403**	**2378057**	**1657238**	**210204**	**497670**	**654307**
北　京 Beijing	145507	127081	71167	19810	25166	22263
天　津 Tianjin	48361	46949	31671	4855	10390	12658
河　北 Hebei	106424	104014	73384	10164	22352	29284
山　西 Shanxi	61192	59109	42042	2847	11068	16986
内蒙古 Inner Mongolia	40018	39308	26629	2830	8580	10375
辽　宁 Liaoning	100276	98297	64515	9209	20854	26853
吉　林 Jilin	65377	63089	41406	6695	13634	15274
黑龙江 Heilongjiang	76239	74012	47479	7594	16644	18314
上　海 Shanghai	75333	70868	44220	8209	14268	17318
江　苏 Jiangsu	169732	161535	113543	15766	39080	46396
浙　江 Zhejiang	93823	89690	63064	9197	19480	26540
安　徽 Anhui	82341	80086	61015	5386	16711	24231
福　建 Fujian	68771	66408	45639	5606	13592	18745
江　西 Jiangxi	80995	78625	57151	5413	14771	22720
山　东 Shandong	155891	150995	111855	11069	32573	48220
河　南 Henan	147254	141992	109553	8852	28365	45328
湖　北 Hubei	132384	126810	84176	11260	27963	31264
湖　南 Hunan	103528	100239	71006	7756	20845	28329
广　东 Guangdong	158770	152239	106890	14037	28909	44009
广　西 Guangxi	68458	61178	44325	4805	11906	17786
海　南 Hainan	14939	14771	9698	1251	2771	3745
重　庆 Chongqing	59606	57867	42429	4963	12219	17473
四　川 Sichuan	123963	118485	85106	9027	22866	32650
贵　州 Guizhou	48468	47839	35398	3343	11164	10422
云　南 Yunnan	53713	52722	39316	4131	10831	14777
西　藏 Tibet	3707	3623	2484	236	807	990
陕　西 Shaanxi	106630	101408	68356	8852	20290	27943
甘　肃 Gansu	41703	38805	28869	3325	9505	11267
青　海 Qinghai	7169	6902	4843	807	1543	1112
宁　夏 Ningxia	11819	11445	8272	1401	2383	2094
新　疆 Xinjiang	32012	31666	21737	1508	6140	8941

注：不含民办的其他高等教育机构数据。

Note: Data of Non-government HEIs is not included.

教职工情况(总计)
Personnel in HEIs(Total)

单位:人
unit: person

工数 Personnel							
教职工 in Main Campus					科研机构人员 Personnel in Affiliated Research Org.	校办企业职工 Employees in School-run Factories & Farms	其他附设机构人员 Personnel in Others Subsidiary Units
初级 Junior	未定职级 No-ranking	行政人员 Adm. Personnel	教辅人员 Supporting Staff	工勤人员 Workers			
185760	**109297**	**351495**	**226636**	**142688**	**32823**	**22676**	**50847**
2270	1658	24907	18200	12807	7752	1196	9478
2209	1559	8197	4756	2325	404	230	778
6505	5079	14307	9354	6969	270	771	1369
7929	3212	7647	5362	4058	577	202	1304
2789	2055	6052	4165	2462	152	148	410
5728	1871	17264	9525	6993	691	577	711
4770	1033	9385	6869	5429	535	198	1555
3435	1492	12335	7747	6451	1156	473	598
2827	1598	13174	9505	3969	1929	1483	1053
8104	4197	24704	14870	8418	2436	1539	4222
3939	3908	15590	8363	2673	1831	738	1564
11147	3540	9007	6078	3986	943	350	962
6023	1673	11655	6609	2505	641	1175	547
8118	6129	7951	9945	3578	448	1507	415
14321	5672	19567	12801	6772	1835	2115	946
19251	7757	14599	9531	8309	407	709	4146
8500	5189	20247	13026	9361	1752	1872	1950
7288	6788	14012	9789	5432	751	1200	1338
7989	11946	23293	14795	7261	3492	783	2256
3493	6335	8640	4751	3462	200	669	6411
1091	840	2268	1527	1278	85	22	61
4678	3096	8207	4424	2807	338	419	982
14913	5650	15887	9555	7937	1114	2434	1930
5990	4479	7009	3596	1836	242	271	116
6162	3415	6649	4022	2735	368	313	310
334	117	586	352	201	25	0	59
7698	3573	16109	10167	6776	1406	921	2895
3509	1263	5188	2572	2176	569	282	2047
755	626	854	761	444	257	0	10
1487	907	1599	937	637	138	0	236
2508	2640	4606	2682	2641	79	79	188

高等教育学校(机构)
Number of Female Educational

地区 Region	教职 Educational					
	合计 Total	校本部 Educational Personnel				
		小计 Subtotal	专任教师 Full-time Teachers			
			小计 Subtotal	正高级 Senior	副高级 Sub-senior	中级 Middle
总　计 Total	**1216907**	**1167291**	**827116**	**65298**	**232647**	**358622**
北　京 Beijing	73485	63507	32427	5205	12487	12548
天　津 Tianjin	24669	23939	16531	1679	5404	7392
河　北 Hebei	57106	56100	42310	4679	12468	17695
山　西 Shanxi	33212	31957	24414	1299	6117	10034
内蒙古 Inner Mongolia	21408	21114	15588	1366	4965	6414
辽　宁 Liaoning	52005	51219	35791	3787	11418	16104
吉　林 Jilin	32846	31773	22916	2910	7412	8990
黑龙江 Heilongjiang	38100	37119	25971	3402	8918	10644
上　海 Shanghai	36973	35322	21235	1799	6796	10040
江　苏 Jiangsu	79030	75472	52310	3666	16762	24834
浙　江 Zhejiang	44318	42854	28825	2324	8183	14124
安　徽 Anhui	35660	34866	26659	1161	6183	11526
福　建 Fujian	33844	32706	22365	1556	6004	10382
江　西 Jiangxi	37297	36460	26705	1605	5742	11377
山　东 Shandong	76095	74482	57854	3425	15246	26959
河　南 Henan	71687	68532	54905	3155	12944	23286
湖　北 Hubei	60903	58452	38403	2630	11739	16270
湖　南 Hunan	50676	49466	35293	2030	9317	15530
广　东 Guangdong	77238	74205	51183	3829	12603	23851
广　西 Guangxi	35637	30742	21970	1555	5344	9613
海　南 Hainan	7749	7665	5065	419	1314	2201
重　庆 Chongqing	28351	27651	20089	1250	5220	9253
四　川 Sichuan	59522	57205	41508	2534	10131	17034
贵　州 Guizhou	24610	24324	18391	1317	5684	5648
云　南 Yunnan	28149	27669	21336	1556	5491	8476
西　藏 Tibet	1844	1798	1289	82	396	551
陕　西 Shaanxi	50125	47890	33167	2490	8877	15152
甘　肃 Gansu	18611	17418	13587	959	4140	5901
青　海 Qinghai	3438	3350	2558	355	820	591
宁　夏 Ningxia	6241	6126	4678	652	1310	1173
新　疆 Xinjiang	16078	15908	11793	622	3212	5009

注:不含民办的其他高等教育机构数据。

Note: Data of Non-government HEIs is not included.

女教职工情况(总计)
Personnel in HEIs(Total)

单位:人
unit: person

工　数 Personnel							
教职工 in Main Campus					科研机构人员 Personnel in Affiliated Research Org.	校办企业职工 Employees in School-run Factories & Farms	其他附设机构人员 Personnel in Others Subsidiary Units
初级 Junior	未定职级 No-ranking	行政人员 Adm. Personnel	教辅人员 Supporting Staff	工勤人员 Workers			
109832	**60717**	**170687**	**128846**	**40642**	**12545**	**7006**	**30065**
1374	813	14640	11676	4764	3384	308	6286
1271	785	4266	2584	558	129	53	548
4233	3235	6498	5462	1830	119	216	671
4977	1987	3229	3265	1049	208	67	980
1653	1190	2535	2482	509	76	47	171
3421	1061	8596	5615	1217	276	128	382
2942	662	4166	3838	853	262	52	759
2104	903	5453	4311	1384	603	89	289
1732	868	7775	5249	1063	782	389	480
4850	2198	12171	8542	2449	811	365	2382
2284	1910	8513	4752	764	583	201	680
5979	1810	3917	3228	1062	256	69	469
3624	799	5890	3656	795	258	544	336
4637	3344	3402	5384	969	187	461	189
8958	3266	7581	7262	1785	563	486	564
11209	4311	6317	5191	2119	144	195	2816
4934	2830	9758	7286	3005	611	791	1049
4347	4069	6779	5876	1518	239	271	700
4437	6463	12135	8285	2602	1279	276	1478
1894	3564	4569	2735	1468	107	245	4543
617	514	1123	916	561	40	3	41
2787	1579	4284	2436	842	97	95	508
8816	2973	7840	4946	2911	448	1116	753
3330	2412	3445	2028	460	98	112	76
3853	1960	3120	2200	1013	149	107	224
201	59	259	210	40	10	0	36
4633	2015	7284	5626	1813	513	232	1490
1927	660	2036	1271	524	145	64	984
406	386	298	423	71	81	0	7
959	584	703	546	199	53	0	62
1443	1507	2105	1565	445	34	24	112

地区 Region	教职 Educational					
	合计 Total	校本部 Educational Personnel				
		小计 Subtotal	专任教师 Full-time Teachers			
			小计 Subtotal	正高级 Senior	副高级 Sub-senior	中级 Middle
总　计 Total	**2442995**	**2336980**	**1633248**	**208917**	**490184**	**644154**
北　京 Beijing	142197	123789	69715	19697	24670	21569
天　津 Tianjin	47143	45731	31060	4810	10134	12424
河　北 Hebei	105505	103101	72890	10132	22206	29121
山　西 Shanxi	59116	57067	40971	2819	10682	16527
内蒙古 Inner Mongolia	39598	38888	26408	2813	8497	10310
辽　宁 Liaoning	97806	95830	63157	9106	20283	26347
吉　林 Jilin	63351	61076	40097	6586	13154	14790
黑龙江 Heilongjiang	73918	71691	46278	7478	16088	17957
上　海 Shanghai	73891	69449	43484	8191	14082	16906
江　苏 Jiangsu	168583	160390	112888	15677	38866	46116
浙　江 Zhejiang	92654	88532	62357	9170	19236	26209
安　徽 Anhui	81266	79039	60429	5355	16550	23915
福　建 Fujian	68302	65939	45398	5576	13494	18653
江　西 Jiangxi	80113	77743	56519	5348	14596	22474
山　东 Shandong	154311	149415	110807	11015	32219	47755
河　南 Henan	145755	140493	108449	8826	28080	44884
湖　北 Hubei	131395	125821	83507	11237	27764	31009
湖　南 Hunan	102318	99032	70249	7736	20578	28015
广　东 Guangdong	154540	148059	104381	13982	28373	42833
广　西 Guangxi	66934	59699	43246	4701	11582	17294
海　南 Hainan	14753	14585	9602	1246	2755	3691
重　庆 Chongqing	58388	56668	41708	4924	11999	17230
四　川 Sichuan	121894	116446	83949	9011	22568	32077
贵　州 Guizhou	47896	47273	35072	3329	11079	10329
云　南 Yunnan	53533	52542	39271	4127	10811	14763
西　藏 Tibet	3707	3623	2484	236	807	990
陕　西 Shaanxi	103994	98800	66930	8802	19909	27235
甘　肃 Gansu	41179	38281	28474	3313	9370	11086
青　海 Qinghai	6911	6644	4671	799	1501	1027
宁　夏 Ningxia	11695	11321	8196	1393	2352	2068
新　疆 Xinjiang	30349	30013	20601	1482	5899	8550

教职工情况(普通高校)
Personnel in Regular HEIs

单位:人
unit: person

工　数 Personnel							
教职工 in Main Campus					科研机构人员 Personnel in Affiliated Research Org.	校办企业职工 Employees in School-run Factories & Farms	其他附设机构人员 Personnel in Others Subsidiary Units
初级 Junior	未定职级 No-ranking	行政人员 Adm. Personnel	教辅人员 Supporting Staff	工勤人员 Workers			
181785	**108208**	**343226**	**220791**	**139715**	**32744**	**22494**	**50777**
2159	1620	24023	17572	12479	7738	1196	9474
2140	1552	7946	4461	2264	404	230	778
6388	5043	14060	9278	6873	264	771	1369
7765	3178	7177	5044	3875	573	187	1289
2740	2048	5976	4076	2428	152	148	410
5572	1849	16768	9152	6753	691	574	711
4566	1001	9106	6575	5298	522	198	1555
3285	1470	11912	7248	6253	1156	473	598
2745	1560	12902	9176	3887	1916	1473	1053
8043	4186	24523	14612	8367	2432	1539	4222
3876	3866	15309	8236	2630	1821	738	1563
11080	3529	8814	5894	3902	943	350	934
6003	1672	11496	6552	2493	641	1175	547
7996	6105	7819	9878	3527	448	1507	415
14162	5656	19293	12631	6684	1835	2115	946
18914	7745	14381	9414	8249	407	709	4146
8314	5183	20042	12943	9329	1752	1872	1950
7188	6732	13766	9654	5363	751	1200	1335
7532	11661	22441	14255	6982	3487	738	2256
3411	6258	8426	4650	3377	197	627	6411
1074	836	2216	1505	1262	85	22	61
4519	3036	7998	4205	2757	338	407	975
14684	5609	15428	9397	7672	1114	2406	1928
5881	4454	6839	3536	1826	236	271	116
6159	3411	6560	3990	2721	368	313	310
334	117	586	352	201	25	0	59
7451	3533	15549	9816	6505	1406	900	2888
3464	1241	5117	2530	2160	569	282	2047
731	613	817	729	427	257	0	10
1481	902	1568	929	628	138	0	236
2128	2542	4368	2501	2543	78	73	185

高等教育学校(机构)
Number of Female Educational

地区 Region	合计 Total	教职 Educational 校本部 Educational Personnel 小计 Subtotal	专任教师 Full-time Teachers 小计 Subtotal	正高级 Senior	副高级 Sub-senior	中级 Middle
总计 Total	**1195657**	**1146213**	**813837**	**64700**	**228636**	**352854**
北京 Beijing	71527	61561	31464	5150	12164	12057
天津 Tianjin	23998	23268	16134	1658	5238	7234
河北 Hebei	56600	55598	41996	4663	12375	17574
山西 Shanxi	32075	30826	23710	1284	5873	9714
内蒙古 Inner Mongolia	21193	20899	15451	1353	4914	6379
辽宁 Liaoning	50731	49946	34988	3732	11043	15804
吉林 Jilin	31733	30669	22127	2834	7132	8692
黑龙江 Heilongjiang	36923	35942	25306	3330	8631	10438
上海 Shanghai	36165	34522	20756	1793	6676	9759
江苏 Jiangsu	78439	74885	51979	3646	16652	24683
浙江 Zhejiang	43731	42273	28439	2312	8058	13935
安徽 Anhui	35175	34391	26393	1154	6110	11386
福建 Fujian	33604	32466	22223	1542	5942	10329
江西 Jiangxi	36895	36058	26390	1577	5658	11267
山东 Shandong	75400	73787	57323	3406	15098	26712
河南 Henan	70912	67757	54296	3142	12805	23042
湖北 Hubei	60438	57987	38073	2620	11658	16143
湖南 Hunan	50122	48912	34929	2019	9191	15375
广东 Guangdong	75012	72020	49838	3804	12333	23202
广西 Guangxi	34836	29975	21377	1515	5180	9323
海南 Hainan	7658	7574	5009	415	1304	2168
重庆 Chongqing	27753	27056	19714	1237	5103	9123
四川 Sichuan	58636	56334	40966	2531	9999	16778
贵州 Guizhou	24297	24016	18200	1307	5633	5600
云南 Yunnan	28058	27578	21308	1554	5479	8467
西藏 Tibet	1844	1798	1289	82	396	551
陕西 Shaanxi	48796	46571	32454	2470	8711	14800
甘肃 Gansu	18381	17188	13403	955	4087	5808
青海 Qinghai	3334	3246	2481	354	795	554
宁夏 Ningxia	6185	6070	4644	647	1298	1161
新疆 Xinjiang	15206	15040	11177	614	3100	4796

女教职工情况(普通高校)
Personnel in Regular HEIs

单位:人
unit: person

工数 Personnel							
教职工 in Main Campus					科研机构人员 Personnel in Affiliated Research Org.	校办企业职工 Employees in School-run Factories & Farms	其他附设机构人员 Personnel in Others Subsidiary Units
		行政人员 Adm. Personnel	教辅人员 Supporting Staff	工勤人员 Workers			
初级 Junior	未定职级 No-ranking						
107537	**60110**	**166933**	**125546**	**39897**	**12495**	**6906**	**30043**
1301	792	14121	11300	4676	3375	308	6283
1224	780	4154	2424	556	129	53	548
4164	3220	6390	5413	1799	115	216	671
4872	1967	3050	3079	987	204	67	978
1617	1188	2514	2431	503	76	47	171
3352	1057	8365	5413	1180	276	127	382
2832	637	4066	3662	814	253	52	759
2016	891	5269	4019	1348	603	89	289
1685	843	7639	5070	1057	776	387	480
4807	2191	12076	8396	2434	807	365	2382
2244	1890	8391	4695	748	577	201	680
5940	1803	3834	3123	1041	256	69	459
3611	799	5824	3626	793	258	544	336
4558	3330	3362	5341	965	187	461	189
8850	3257	7506	7200	1758	563	486	564
11007	4300	6233	5121	2107	144	195	2816
4826	2826	9677	7242	2995	611	791	1049
4300	4044	6686	5799	1498	239	271	700
4192	6307	11696	7983	2503	1277	237	1478
1850	3509	4461	2687	1450	106	212	4543
611	511	1100	904	561	40	3	41
2705	1546	4186	2317	839	97	94	506
8705	2953	7629	4877	2862	448	1103	751
3267	2393	3353	2003	460	93	112	76
3850	1958	3077	2180	1013	149	107	224
201	59	259	210	40	10	0	36
4487	1986	7020	5390	1707	513	225	1487
1906	647	2015	1252	518	145	64	984
394	384	292	407	66	81	0	7
955	583	686	542	198	53	0	62
1208	1459	2002	1440	421	34	20	112

地 区 Region	合计 Total	教职 Educational					
		校本部 Educational Personnel					
		小计 Subtotal	专任教师 Full-time Teachers				
			小计 Subtotal	正高级 Senior	副高级 Sub-senior	中级 Middle
总 计 Total	**41408**	**41077**	**23990**	**1287**	**7486**	**10153**
北 京 Beijing	3310	3292	1452	113	496	694
天 津 Tianjin	1218	1218	611	45	256	234
河 北 Hebei	919	913	494	32	146	163
山 西 Shanxi	2076	2042	1071	28	386	459
内蒙古 Inner Mongolia	420	420	221	17	83	65
辽 宁 Liaoning	2470	2467	1358	103	571	506
吉 林 Jilin	2026	2013	1309	109	480	484
黑龙江 Heilongjiang	2321	2321	1201	116	556	357
上 海 Shanghai	1442	1419	736	18	186	412
江 苏 Jiangsu	1149	1145	655	89	214	280
浙 江 Zhejiang	1169	1158	707	27	244	331
安 徽 Anhui	1075	1047	586	31	161	316
福 建 Fujian	469	469	241	30	98	92
江 西 Jiangxi	882	882	632	65	175	246
山 东 Shandong	1580	1580	1048	54	354	465
河 南 Henan	1499	1499	1104	26	285	444
湖 北 Hubei	989	989	669	23	199	255
湖 南 Hunan	1210	1207	757	20	267	314
广 东 Guangdong	4230	4180	2509	55	536	1176
广 西 Guangxi	1524	1479	1079	104	324	492
海 南 Hainan	186	186	96	5	16	54
重 庆 Chongqing	1218	1199	721	39	220	243
四 川 Sichuan	2069	2039	1157	16	298	573
贵 州 Guizhou	572	566	326	14	85	93
云 南 Yunnan	180	180	45	4	20	14
西 藏 Tibet	0	0	0	0	0	0
陕 西 Shaanxi	2636	2608	1426	50	381	708
甘 肃 Gansu	524	524	395	12	135	181
青 海 Qinghai	258	258	172	8	42	85
宁 夏 Ningxia	124	124	76	8	31	26
新 疆 Xinjiang	1663	1653	1136	26	241	391

教职工情况(成人高校)
Personnel in Adult HEIs

单位:人
unit: person

工　数 Personnel							
教职工 in Main Campus					科研机构人员 Personnel in Affiliated Research Org.	校办企业职工 Employees in School-run Factories & Farms	其他附设机构人员 Personnel in Others Subsidiary Units
		行政人员 Adm. Personnel	教辅人员 Supporting Staff	工勤人员 Workers			
初级 Junior	未定职级 No-ranking						
3975	**1089**	**8269**	**5845**	**2973**	**79**	**182**	**70**
111	38	884	628	328	14	0	4
69	7	251	295	61	0	0	0
117	36	247	76	96	6	0	0
164	34	470	318	183	4	15	15
49	7	76	89	34	0	0	0
156	22	496	373	240	0	3	0
204	32	279	294	131	13	0	0
150	22	423	499	198	0	0	0
82	38	272	329	82	13	10	0
61	11	181	258	51	4	0	0
63	42	281	127	43	10	0	1
67	11	193	184	84	0	0	28
20	1	159	57	12	0	0	0
122	24	132	67	51	0	0	0
159	16	274	170	88	0	0	0
337	12	218	117	60	0	0	0
186	6	205	83	32	0	0	0
100	56	246	135	69	0	0	3
457	285	852	540	279	5	45	0
82	77	214	101	85	3	42	0
17	4	52	22	16	0	0	0
159	60	209	219	50	0	12	7
229	41	459	158	265	0	28	2
109	25	170	60	10	6	0	0
3	4	89	32	14	0	0	0
0	0	0	0	0	0	0	0
247	40	560	351	271	0	21	7
45	22	71	42	16	0	0	0
24	13	37	32	17	0	0	0
6	5	31	8	9	0	0	0
380	98	238	181	98	1	6	3

地 区 Region	合计 Total	校本部 Educational Personnel 小计 Subtotal	专任教师 Full-time Teachers 小计 Subtotal	正高级 Senior	副高级 Sub-senior	中级 Middle
总 计 Total	**21250**	**21078**	**13279**	**598**	**4011**	**5768**
北 京 Beijing	1958	1946	963	55	323	491
天 津 Tianjin	671	671	397	21	166	158
河 北 Hebei	506	502	314	16	93	121
山 西 Shanxi	1137	1131	704	15	244	320
内蒙古 Inner Mongolia	215	215	137	13	51	35
辽 宁 Liaoning	1274	1273	803	55	375	300
吉 林 Jilin	1113	1104	789	76	280	298
黑龙江 Heilongjiang	1177	1177	665	72	287	206
上 海 Shanghai	808	800	479	6	120	281
江 苏 Jiangsu	591	587	331	20	110	151
浙 江 Zhejiang	587	581	386	12	125	189
安 徽 Anhui	485	475	266	7	73	140
福 建 Fujian	240	240	142	14	62	53
江 西 Jiangxi	402	402	315	28	84	110
山 东 Shandong	695	695	531	19	148	247
河 南 Henan	775	775	609	13	139	244
湖 北 Hubei	465	465	330	10	81	127
湖 南 Hunan	554	554	364	11	126	155
广 东 Guangdong	2226	2185	1345	25	270	649
广 西 Guangxi	801	767	593	40	164	290
海 南 Hainan	91	91	56	4	10	33
重 庆 Chongqing	598	595	375	13	117	130
四 川 Sichuan	886	871	542	3	132	276
贵 州 Guizhou	313	308	191	10	51	48
云 南 Yunnan	91	91	28	2	12	9
西 藏 Tibet	0	0	0	0	0	0
陕 西 Shaanxi	1329	1319	713	20	166	352
甘 肃 Gansu	230	230	184	4	53	93
青 海 Qinghai	104	104	77	1	25	37
宁 夏 Ningxia	56	56	34	5	12	12
新 疆 Xinjiang	872	868	616	8	112	213

Top spanning header over columns 2–7: 教 职 Educational

女教职工情况(成人高校)

Personnel in Adult HEIs

单位:人
unit: person

工数 Personnel							
教职工 in Main Campus					科研机构人员 Personnel in Affiliated Research Org.	校办企业职工 Employees in School-run Factories & Farms	其他附设机构人员 Personnel in Others Subsidiary Units
初级 Junior	未定职级 No-ranking	行政人员 Adm. Personnel	教辅人员 Supporting Staff	工勤人员 Workers			
2295	**607**	**3754**	**3300**	**745**	**50**	**100**	**22**
73	21	519	376	88	9	0	3
47	5	112	160	2	0	0	0
69	15	108	49	31	4	0	0
105	20	179	186	62	4	0	2
36	2	21	51	6	0	0	0
69	4	231	202	37	0	1	0
110	25	100	176	39	9	0	0
88	12	184	292	36	0	0	0
47	25	136	179	6	6	2	0
43	7	95	146	15	4	0	0
40	20	122	57	16	6	0	0
39	7	83	105	21	0	0	10
13	0	66	30	2	0	0	0
79	14	40	43	4	0	0	0
108	9	75	62	27	0	0	0
202	11	84	70	12	0	0	0
108	4	81	44	10	0	0	0
47	25	93	77	20	0	0	0
245	156	439	302	99	2	39	0
44	55	108	48	18	1	33	0
6	3	23	12	0	0	0	0
82	33	98	119	3	0	1	2
111	20	211	69	49	0	13	2
63	19	92	25	0	5	0	0
3	2	43	20	0	0	0	0
0	0	0	0	0	0	0	0
146	29	264	236	106	0	7	3
21	13	21	19	6	0	0	0
12	2	6	16	5	0	0	0
4	1	17	4	1	0	0	0
235	48	103	125	24	0	4	0

地 区 Region	教 职 Educational					
	合计 Total	校本部 Educational Personnel				
		小计 Subtotal	专任教师 Full-time Teachers			
			小计 Subtotal	正高级 Senior	副高级 Sub-senior	中级 Middle
总 计 Total	**20882**	**20767**	**9643**	**730**	**1647**	**3092**
北 京 Beijing	3791	3782	1517	143	219	449
天 津 Tianjin	0	0	0	0	0	0
河 北 Hebei	1053	1053	576	75	122	136
山 西 Shanxi	884	884	492	56	108	125
内蒙古 Inner Mongolia	0	0	0	0	0	0
辽 宁 Liaoning	1209	1209	848	50	181	511
吉 林 Jilin	193	193	97	13	28	35
黑龙江 Heilongjiang	77	77	34	2	12	6
上 海 Shanghai	4715	4707	1584	127	235	487
江 苏 Jiangsu	0	0	0	0	0	0
浙 江 Zhejiang	1477	1476	625	16	75	275
安 徽 Anhui	447	447	189	2	12	36
福 建 Fujian	0	0	0	0	0	0
江 西 Jiangxi	221	221	41	2	9	3
山 东 Shandong	2256	2195	1308	100	236	440
河 南 Henan	611	611	314	10	35	95
湖 北 Hubei	556	556	150	21	68	44
湖 南 Hunan	269	268	130	4	27	40
广 东 Guangdong	811	796	373	23	59	107
广 西 Guangxi	0	0	0	0	0	0
海 南 Hainan	0	0	0	0	0	0
重 庆 Chongqing	382	376	237	8	36	75
四 川 Sichuan	1383	1383	813	30	85	167
贵 州 Guizhou	0	0	0	0	0	0
云 南 Yunnan	0	0	0	0	0	0
西 藏 Tibet	0	0	0	0	0	0
陕 西 Shaanxi	0	0	0	0	0	0
甘 肃 Gansu	547	533	315	48	100	61
青 海 Qinghai	0	0	0	0	0	0
宁 夏 Ningxia	0	0	0	0	0	0
新 疆 Xinjiang	0	0	0	0	0	0

教职工情况(民办的其他高等教育机构)
Other Non-government HEIs

单位:人
unit: person

工　数
Personnel

教职工 in Main Campus					科研机构人员 Personnel in Affiliated Research Org.	校办企业职工 Employees in School-run Factories & Farms	其他附设机构人员 Personnel in Others Subsidiary Units
初级 Junior	未定职级 No-ranking	行政人员 Adm. Personnel	教辅人员 Supporting Staff	工勤人员 Workers			
1545	**2629**	**6418**	**2802**	**1904**	**16**	**19**	**80**
137	569	1360	566	339	0	4	5
0	0	0	0	0	0	0	0
116	127	268	111	98	0	0	0
81	122	233	83	76	0	0	0
0	0	0	0	0	0	0	0
101	5	310	36	15	0	0	0
15	6	62	21	13	0	0	0
10	4	19	8	16	0	0	0
220	515	1853	929	341	5	1	2
0	0	0	0	0	0	0	0
141	118	436	219	196	1	0	0
24	115	166	48	44	0	0	0
0	0	0	0	0	0	0	0
9	18	59	53	68	0	0	0
304	228	536	162	189	4	2	55
36	138	116	98	83	0	0	0
16	1	214	121	71	0	0	0
32	27	79	35	24	1	0	0
61	123	187	107	129	5	10	0
0	0	0	0	0	0	0	0
0	0	0	0	0	0	0	0
11	107	88	39	12	0	2	4
182	349	282	119	169	0	0	0
0	0	0	0	0	0	0	0
0	0	0	0	0	0	0	0
0	0	0	0	0	0	0	0
0	0	0	0	0	0	0	0
49	57	150	47	21	0	0	14
0	0	0	0	0	0	0	0
0	0	0	0	0	0	0	0
0	0	0	0	0	0	0	0

高等教育学校(机构)
Number of Female Educational Personnel in

地区 Region	合计 Total	校本部 Educational Personnel					
		小计 Subtotal	专任教师 Full-time Teachers				
			小计 Subtotal	正高级 Senior	副高级 Sub-senior	中级 Middle	
总计 Total	**11116**	**11058**	**5058**	**254**	**773**	**1585**	
北京 Beijing	2000	1996	791	48	116	231	
天津 Tianjin	0	0	0	0	0	0	
河北 Hebei	556	556	339	36	72	86	
山西 Shanxi	432	432	253	12	65	55	
内蒙古 Inner Mongolia	0	0	0	0	0	0	
辽宁 Liaoning	658	658	447	34	98	269	
吉林 Jilin	116	116	53	4	19	20	
黑龙江 Heilongjiang	56	56	28	1	10	3	
上海 Shanghai	2788	2786	824	32	74	246	
江苏 Jiangsu	0	0	0	0	0	0	
浙江 Zhejiang	817	816	355	5	44	160	
安徽 Anhui	205	205	92	0	5	18	
福建 Fujian	0	0	0	0	0	0	
江西 Jiangxi	95	95	20	1	4	2	
山东 Shandong	1081	1044	637	41	104	207	
河南 Henan	331	331	170	2	16	46	
湖北 Hubei	285	285	64	8	27	18	
湖南 Hunan	144	144	81	2	14	26	
广东 Guangdong	390	385	180	8	22	50	
广西 Guangxi	0	0	0	0	0	0	
海南 Hainan	0	0	0	0	0	0	
重庆 Chongqing	172	169	117	0	7	25	
四川 Sichuan	776	776	479	10	38	96	
贵州 Guizhou	0	0	0	0	0	0	
云南 Yunnan	0	0	0	0	0	0	
西藏 Tibet	0	0	0	0	0	0	
陕西 Shaanxi	0	0	0	0	0	0	
甘肃 Gansu	214	208	128	10	38	27	
青海 Qinghai	0	0	0	0	0	0	
宁夏 Ningxia	0	0	0	0	0	0	
新疆 Xinjiang	0	0	0	0	0	0	

Top spanning header: 教职 Educational

女教职工情况(民办的其他高等教育机构)
Other Non-government HEIs

单位:人
unit: person

工数 Personnel							
教职工 in Main Campus					科研机构人员 Personnel in Affiliated Research Org.	校办企业职工 Employees in School-run Factories & Farms	其他附设机构人员 Personnel in Others Subsidiary Units
初级 Junior	未定职级 No-ranking	行政人员 Adm. Personnel	教辅人员 Supporting Staff	工勤人员 Workers			
894	**1552**	**3439**	**1674**	**887**	**3**	**10**	**45**
80	316	696	323	186	0	2	2
0	0	0	0	0	0	0	0
71	74	113	71	33	0	0	0
46	75	115	35	29	0	0	0
0	0	0	0	0	0	0	0
43	3	176	26	9	0	0	0
8	2	41	17	5	0	0	0
10	4	12	8	8	0	0	0
147	325	1156	623	183	1	1	0
0	0	0	0	0	0	0	0
71	75	248	110	103	1	0	0
9	60	74	23	16	0	0	0
0	0	0	0	0	0	0	0
5	8	30	19	26	0	0	0
155	130	245	91	71	1	1	35
17	89	67	56	38	0	0	0
10	1	109	80	32	0	0	0
24	15	37	15	11	0	0	0
37	63	88	62	55	0	5	0
0	0	0	0	0	0	0	0
0	0	0	0	0	0	0	0
6	79	32	14	6	0	1	2
127	208	150	82	65	0	0	0
0	0	0	0	0	0	0	0
0	0	0	0	0	0	0	0
0	0	0	0	0	0	0	0
0	0	0	0	0	0	0	0
28	25	50	19	11	0	0	6
0	0	0	0	0	0	0	0
0	0	0	0	0	0	0	0
0	0	0	0	0	0	0	0

专任教师学历、专业技术职务情况(总计)
Number of Full-time Teacher by Academic Qualification and Professional Rank(Total)

单位:人
unit: person

地区 Region	合计 Total	按学历分 By Academic Qualification				按专业技术职务分 By Professional Rank				
		博士 Doctor's Degrees	硕士 Master's Degrees	本科 Normal Courses	专科及以下 Short-cycle Courses and Under	正高级 Senior	副高级 Sub-Senior	中级 Middle	初级 Junior	未定职级 No-ranking
总计 Total	**1657238**	**398879**	**602609**	**637059**	**18691**	**210204**	**497670**	**654307**	**185760**	**109297**
北京 Beijing	71167	43532	17320	9962	353	19810	25166	22263	2270	1658
天津 Tianjin	31671	10999	10848	9633	191	4855	10390	12658	2209	1559
河北 Hebei	73384	11793	28068	32874	649	10164	22352	29284	6505	5079
山西 Shanxi	42042	6212	16340	18927	563	2847	11068	16986	7929	3212
内蒙古 Inner Mongolia	26629	3557	9611	12960	501	2830	8580	10375	2789	2055
辽宁 Liaoning	64515	16217	23872	23567	859	9209	20854	26853	5728	1871
吉林 Jilin	41406	10277	16161	14544	424	6695	13634	15274	4770	1033
黑龙江 Heilongjiang	47479	11897	17336	17984	262	7594	16644	18314	3435	1492
上海 Shanghai	44220	22996	13444	7374	406	8209	14268	17318	2827	1598
江苏 Jiangsu	113543	37636	37460	37951	496	15766	39080	46396	8104	4197
浙江 Zhejiang	63064	20038	21769	20905	352	9197	19480	26540	3939	3908
安徽 Anhui	61015	10354	26387	23795	479	5386	16711	24231	11147	3540
福建 Fujian	45639	11210	16471	17689	269	5606	13592	18745	6023	1673
江西 Jiangxi	57151	7849	18799	29132	1371	5413	14771	22720	8118	6129
山东 Shandong	111855	23311	40076	47300	1168	11069	32573	48220	14321	5672
河南 Henan	109553	16440	43243	48244	1626	8852	28365	45328	19251	7757
湖北 Hubei	84176	23624	29804	29610	1138	11260	27963	31264	8500	5189
湖南 Hunan	71006	13167	24179	32902	758	7756	20845	28329	7288	6788
广东 Guangdong	106890	26768	38531	40175	1416	14037	28909	44009	7989	11946
广西 Guangxi	44325	5924	20718	17201	482	4805	11906	17786	3493	6335
海南 Hainan	9698	1427	3901	4227	143	1251	2771	3745	1091	840
重庆 Chongqing	42429	9378	17261	15270	520	4963	12219	17473	4678	3096
四川 Sichuan	85106	15601	32599	35527	1379	9027	22866	32650	14913	5650
贵州 Guizhou	35398	4284	12714	17910	490	3343	11164	10422	5990	4479
云南 Yunnan	39316	5690	14495	18501	630	4131	10831	14777	6162	3415
西藏 Tibet	2484	247	1300	916	21	236	807	990	334	117
陕西 Shaanxi	68356	19431	26041	22063	821	8852	20290	27943	7698	3573
甘肃 Gansu	28869	4314	10806	13431	318	3325	9505	11267	3509	1263
青海 Qinghai	4843	606	1310	2815	112	807	1543	1112	755	626
宁夏 Ningxia	8272	1205	3117	3879	71	1401	2383	2094	1487	907
新疆 Xinjiang	21737	2895	8628	9791	423	1508	6140	8941	2508	2640

注:不含民办的其他高等教育机构数据。
Note: Data of Non-government HEIs is not included.

专任教师学历、专业技术职务情况(普通高校)

Number of Full-time Teacher by Academic Qualification and Professional Rank(Regular HEIs)

单位:人
unit:person

地区 Region	合计 Total	按学历分 By Academic Qualification				按专业技术职务分 By Professional Rank				
		博士 Doctor's Degrees	硕士 Master's Degrees	本科 Normal Courses	专科及以下 Short-cycle Courses and Under	正高级 Senior	副高级 Sub-Senior	中级 Middle	初级 Junior	未定职级 No-ranking
总计 Total	**1633248**	**397974**	**596302**	**621137**	**17835**	**208917**	**490184**	**644154**	**181785**	**108208**
北京 Beijing	69715	43194	16770	9411	340	19697	24670	21569	2159	1620
天津 Tianjin	31060	10941	10692	9238	189	4810	10134	12424	2140	1552
河北 Hebei	72890	11791	27904	32548	647	10132	22206	29121	6388	5043
山西 Shanxi	40971	6206	16150	18112	503	2819	10682	16527	7765	3178
内蒙古 Inner Mongolia	26408	3553	9535	12821	499	2813	8497	10310	2740	2048
辽宁 Liaoning	63157	16192	23613	22568	784	9106	20283	26347	5572	1849
吉林 Jilin	40097	10211	15682	13818	386	6586	13154	14790	4566	1001
黑龙江 Heilongjiang	46278	11873	17164	17002	239	7478	16088	17957	3285	1470
上海 Shanghai	43484	22934	13181	6965	404	8191	14082	16906	2745	1560
江苏 Jiangsu	112888	37586	37208	37615	479	15677	38866	46116	8043	4186
浙江 Zhejiang	62357	20019	21566	20425	347	9170	19236	26209	3876	3866
安徽 Anhui	60429	10337	26257	23362	473	5355	16550	23915	11080	3529
福建 Fujian	45398	11183	16390	17558	267	5576	13494	18653	6003	1672
江西 Jiangxi	56519	7837	18638	28678	1366	5348	14596	22474	7996	6105
山东 Shandong	110807	23279	39814	46596	1118	11015	32219	47755	14162	5656
河南 Henan	108449	16439	43092	47311	1607	8826	28080	44884	18914	7745
湖北 Hubei	83507	23621	29570	29180	1136	11237	27764	31009	8314	5183
湖南 Hunan	70249	13163	24089	32293	704	7736	20578	28015	7188	6732
广东 Guangdong	104381	26718	37918	38435	1310	13982	28373	42833	7532	11661
广西 Guangxi	43246	5875	20161	16730	480	4701	11582	17294	3411	6258
海南 Hainan	9602	1427	3878	4154	143	1246	2755	3691	1074	836
重庆 Chongqing	41708	9361	16942	14904	501	4924	11999	17230	4519	3036
四川 Sichuan	83949	15585	32374	34733	1257	9011	22568	32077	14684	5609
贵州 Guizhou	35072	4280	12608	17701	483	3329	11079	10329	5881	4454
云南 Yunnan	39271	5689	14491	18462	629	4127	10811	14763	6159	3411
西藏 Tibet	2484	247	1300	916	21	236	807	990	334	117
陕西 Shaanxi	66930	19426	25736	21054	714	8802	19909	27235	7451	3533
甘肃 Gansu	28474	4313	10733	13144	284	3313	9370	11086	3464	1241
青海 Qinghai	4671	606	1288	2706	71	799	1501	1027	731	613
宁夏 Ningxia	8196	1205	3113	3810	68	1393	2352	2068	1481	902
新疆 Xinjiang	20601	2883	8445	8887	386	1482	5899	8550	2128	2542

专任教师学历、专业技术职务情况(成人高校)
Number of Full-time Teacher by Academic Qualification and Professional Rank(Adult HEIs)

单位:人
unit:person

地 区 Region	合计 Total	按学历分 By Academic Qualification				按专业技术职务分 By Professional Rank				
		博 士 Doctor's Degrees	硕 士 Master's Degrees	本 科 Normal Courses	专科及以下 Short-cycle Courses and Under	正高级 Senior	副高级 Sub-Senior	中 级 Middle	初 级 Junior	未定职级 No-ranking
总 计 Total	**23990**	**905**	**6307**	**15922**	**856**	**1287**	**7486**	**10153**	**3975**	**1089**
北 京 Beijing	1452	338	550	551	13	113	496	694	111	38
天 津 Tianjin	611	58	156	395	2	45	256	234	69	7
河 北 Hebei	494	2	164	326	2	32	146	163	117	36
山 西 Shanxi	1071	6	190	815	60	28	386	459	164	34
内蒙古 Inner Mongolia	221	4	76	139	2	17	83	65	49	7
辽 宁 Liaoning	1358	25	259	999	75	103	571	506	156	22
吉 林 Jilin	1309	66	479	726	38	109	480	484	204	32
黑龙江 Heilongjiang	1201	24	172	982	23	116	556	357	150	22
上 海 Shanghai	736	62	263	409	2	18	186	412	82	38
江 苏 Jiangsu	655	50	252	336	17	89	214	280	61	11
浙 江 Zhejiang	707	19	203	480	5	27	244	331	63	42
安 徽 Anhui	586	17	130	433	6	31	161	316	67	11
福 建 Fujian	241	27	81	131	2	30	98	92	20	1
江 西 Jiangxi	632	12	161	454	5	65	175	246	122	24
山 东 Shandong	1048	32	262	704	50	54	354	465	159	16
河 南 Henan	1104	1	151	933	19	26	285	444	337	12
湖 北 Hubei	669	3	234	430	2	23	199	255	186	6
湖 南 Hunan	757	4	90	609	54	20	267	314	100	56
广 东 Guangdong	2509	50	613	1740	106	55	536	1176	457	285
广 西 Guangxi	1079	49	557	471	2	104	324	492	82	77
海 南 Hainan	96	0	23	73	0	5	16	54	17	4
重 庆 Chongqing	721	17	319	366	19	39	220	243	159	60
四 川 Sichuan	1157	16	225	794	122	16	298	573	229	41
贵 州 Guizhou	326	4	106	209	7	14	85	93	109	25
云 南 Yunnan	45	1	4	39	1	4	20	14	3	4
西 藏 Tibet	0	0	0	0	0	0	0	0	0	0
陕 西 Shaanxi	1426	5	305	1009	107	50	381	708	247	40
甘 肃 Gansu	395	1	73	287	34	12	135	181	45	22
青 海 Qinghai	172	0	22	109	41	8	42	85	24	13
宁 夏 Ningxia	76	0	4	69	3	8	31	26	6	5
新 疆 Xinjiang	1136	12	183	904	37	26	241	391	380	98

专任教师学历、专业技术职务情况(民办的其他高等教育机构)

Number of Full-time Teacher by Academic Qualification and Professional Rank(Other Non-government HEIs)

单位:人
unit:person

地区 Region	合计 Total	按学历分 By Academic Qualification				按专业技术职务分 By Professional Rank				
		博士 Doctor's Degrees	硕士 Master's Degrees	本科 Normal Courses	专科及以下 Short-cycle Courses and Under	正高级 Senior	副高级 Sub-Senior	中级 Middle	初级 Junior	未定职级 No-ranking
总计 Total	**9643**	**287**	**1806**	**6604**	**946**	**730**	**1647**	**3092**	**1545**	**2629**
北京 Beijing	1517	71	317	990	139	143	219	449	137	569
天津 Tianjin	0	0	0	0	0	0	0	0	0	0
河北 Hebei	576	1	152	333	90	75	122	136	116	127
山西 Shanxi	492	21	80	333	58	56	108	125	81	122
内蒙古 Inner Mongolia	0	0	0	0	0	0	0	0	0	0
辽宁 Liaoning	848	0	187	643	18	50	181	511	101	5
吉林 Jilin	97	21	17	56	3	13	28	35	15	6
黑龙江 Heilongjiang	34	0	0	34	0	2	12	6	10	4
上海 Shanghai	1584	85	317	1059	123	127	235	487	220	515
江苏 Jiangsu	0	0	0	0	0	0	0	0	0	0
浙江 Zhejiang	625	14	147	443	21	16	75	275	141	118
安徽 Anhui	189	2	26	155	6	2	12	36	24	115
福建 Fujian	0	0	0	0	0	0	0	0	0	0
江西 Jiangxi	41	1	9	26	5	2	9	3	9	18
山东 Shandong	1308	20	158	893	237	100	236	440	304	228
河南 Henan	314	4	46	243	21	10	35	95	36	138
湖北 Hubei	150	13	54	72	11	21	68	44	16	1
湖南 Hunan	130	2	39	77	12	4	27	40	32	27
广东 Guangdong	373	6	59	265	43	23	59	107	61	123
广西 Guangxi	0	0	0	0	0	0	0	0	0	0
海南 Hainan	0	0	0	0	0	0	0	0	0	0
重庆 Chongqing	237	0	20	178	39	8	36	75	11	107
四川 Sichuan	813	20	99	595	99	30	85	167	182	349
贵州 Guizhou	0	0	0	0	0	0	0	0	0	0
云南 Yunnan	0	0	0	0	0	0	0	0	0	0
西藏 Tibet	0	0	0	0	0	0	0	0	0	0
陕西 Shaanxi	0	0	0	0	0	0	0	0	0	0
甘肃 Gansu	315	6	79	209	21	48	100	61	49	57
青海 Qinghai	0	0	0	0	0	0	0	0	0	0
宁夏 Ningxia	0	0	0	0	0	0	0	0	0	0
新疆 Xinjiang	0	0	0	0	0	0	0	0	0	0

聘请校外教师学历情况(总计)
Number of Part-time Teachers by Academic Qualifications (Total)

单位:人
unit:person

	合计 Total	博士 Doctor's Degrees	硕士 Master's Degrees	本科 Normal Courses	专科及以下 Short-cycle Courses and Under
总 计 Total	**521863**	**76786**	**161877**	**255035**	**28165**
北 京 Beijing	16103	6004	4935	4690	474
天 津 Tianjin	10881	1132	2683	6362	704
河 北 Hebei	16480	1950	5452	8069	1009
山 西 Shanxi	6685	922	2338	3140	285
内蒙古 Inner Mongolia	8123	762	2816	4194	351
辽 宁 Liaoning	17177	2628	5318	8228	1003
吉 林 Jilin	9310	1599	2719	4492	500
黑龙江 Heilongjiang	17373	3046	6053	7755	519
上 海 Shanghai	16338	5214	5083	5539	502
江 苏 Jiangsu	46894	7918	14001	21713	3262
浙 江 Zhejiang	25904	3359	7125	13726	1694
安 徽 Anhui	20331	4017	7551	8271	492
福 建 Fujian	13999	2245	3796	7084	874
江 西 Jiangxi	16994	1404	5481	9246	863
山 东 Shandong	38588	4808	11035	20621	2124
河 南 Henan	28602	2803	10661	14274	864
湖 北 Hubei	28337	4911	9961	12041	1424
湖 南 Hunan	24215	3108	7310	12908	889
广 东 Guangdong	41761	4558	11000	22302	3901
广 西 Guangxi	17108	1203	5873	8893	1139
海 南 Hainan	2963	470	820	1531	142
重 庆 Chongqing	16076	1826	5360	8252	638
四 川 Sichuan	22903	4095	6595	11086	1127
贵 州 Guizhou	9204	920	2591	5214	479
云 南 Yunnan	14392	1372	4542	7477	1001
西 藏 Tibet	194	68	47	69	10
陕 西 Shaanxi	20266	3161	6576	9730	799
甘 肃 Gansu	4175	692	1335	1968	180
青 海 Qinghai	953	17	73	638	225
宁 夏 Ningxia	1488	91	432	872	93
新 疆 Xinjiang	8046	483	2315	4650	598

聘请校外教师学历情况（普通高校）

Number of Part-time Teachers by Academic Qualifications (Regular HEIs)

单位：人
unit: person

	合计 Total	博士 Doctor's Degrees	硕士 Master's Degrees	本科 Normal Courses	专科及以下 Short-cycle Courses and Under
总计 Total	**487394**	**76292**	**154873**	**229117**	**27112**
北京 Beijing	15364	5938	4574	4405	447
天津 Tianjin	9231	1128	2383	5024	696
河北 Hebei	16253	1948	5376	7977	952
山西 Shanxi	6177	911	2197	2800	269
内蒙古 Inner Mongolia	8057	758	2800	4148	351
辽宁 Liaoning	14434	2611	4622	6329	872
吉林 Jilin	8133	1591	2629	3445	468
黑龙江 Heilongjiang	16220	3027	5903	6802	488
上海 Shanghai	15039	5171	4704	4689	475
江苏 Jiangsu	42729	7887	12961	18653	3228
浙江 Zhejiang	22777	3329	6508	11281	1659
安徽 Anhui	20078	4013	7467	8106	492
福建 Fujian	13979	2244	3782	7080	873
江西 Jiangxi	16694	1400	5363	9089	842
山东 Shandong	38144	4805	11002	20216	2121
河南 Henan	26219	2795	10295	12310	819
湖北 Hubei	28213	4896	9914	11979	1424
湖南 Hunan	24131	3108	7293	12844	886
广东 Guangdong	37543	4529	10313	18977	3724
广西 Guangxi	16667	1194	5802	8563	1108
海南 Hainan	2901	469	816	1479	137
重庆 Chongqing	14697	1820	5209	7121	547
四川 Sichuan	21636	4034	6413	10099	1090
贵州 Guizhou	8989	919	2564	5080	426
云南 Yunnan	14392	1372	4542	7477	1001
西藏 Tibet	194	68	47	69	10
陕西 Shaanxi	15791	3045	5335	6766	645
甘肃 Gansu	4059	692	1301	1896	170
青海 Qinghai	913	17	73	616	207
宁夏 Ningxia	1385	91	428	773	93
新疆 Xinjiang	6355	482	2257	3024	592

聘请校外教师学历情况(成人高校)
Number of Part-time Teachers by Academic Qualifications (Adult HEIs)

单位:人
unit:person

	合计 Total	博士 Doctor's Degrees	硕士 Master's Degrees	本科 Normal Courses	专科及以下 Short-cycle Courses and Under
总 计 Total	**34469**	**494**	**7004**	**25918**	**1053**
北 京 Beijing	739	66	361	285	27
天 津 Tianjin	1650	4	300	1338	8
河 北 Hebei	227	2	76	92	57
山 西 Shanxi	508	11	141	340	16
内蒙古 Inner Mongolia	66	4	16	46	0
辽 宁 Liaoning	2743	17	696	1899	131
吉 林 Jilin	1177	8	90	1047	32
黑龙江 Heilongjiang	1153	19	150	953	31
上 海 Shanghai	1299	43	379	850	27
江 苏 Jiangsu	4165	31	1040	3060	34
浙 江 Zhejiang	3127	30	617	2445	35
安 徽 Anhui	253	4	84	165	0
福 建 Fujian	20	1	14	4	1
江 西 Jiangxi	300	4	118	157	21
山 东 Shandong	444	3	33	405	3
河 南 Henan	2383	8	366	1964	45
湖 北 Hubei	124	15	47	62	0
湖 南 Hunan	84	0	17	64	3
广 东 Guangdong	4218	29	687	3325	177
广 西 Guangxi	441	9	71	330	31
海 南 Hainan	62	1	4	52	5
重 庆 Chongqing	1379	6	151	1131	91
四 川 Sichuan	1267	61	182	987	37
贵 州 Guizhou	215	1	27	134	53
云 南 Yunnan	0	0	0	0	0
西 藏 Tibet	0	0	0	0	0
陕 西 Shaanxi	4475	116	1241	2964	154
甘 肃 Gansu	116	0	34	72	10
青 海 Qinghai	40	0	0	22	18
宁 夏 Ningxia	103	0	4	99	0
新 疆 Xinjiang	1691	1	58	1626	6

聘请校外教师学历情况(民办的其他高等教育机构)
Number of Part-time Teachers by Academic Qualifications (Other Non-government HEIs)

单位:人
unit:person

	合计 Total	博士 Doctor's Degrees	硕士 Master's Degrees	本科 Normal Courses	专科及以下 Short-cycle Courses and Under
总　计 Total	**9528**	**1034**	**2914**	**5171**	**409**
北　京 Beijing	1388	126	370	838	54
天　津 Tianjin	0	0	0	0	0
河　北 Hebei	269	6	107	153	3
山　西 Shanxi	401	84	87	199	31
内蒙古 Inner Mongolia	0	0	0	0	0
辽　宁 Liaoning	371	35	130	206	0
吉　林 Jilin	68	19	13	33	3
黑龙江 Heilongjiang	61	0	2	55	4
上　海 Shanghai	3846	599	1071	2044	132
江　苏 Jiangsu	0	0	0	0	0
浙　江 Zhejiang	433	18	167	246	2
安　徽 Anhui	62	4	23	32	3
福　建 Fujian	0	0	0	0	0
江　西 Jiangxi	138	0	25	62	51
山　东 Shandong	697	47	237	325	88
河　南 Henan	152	14	59	73	6
湖　北 Hubei	363	15	183	163	2
湖　南 Hunan	13	0	3	10	0
广　东 Guangdong	354	13	203	134	4
广　西 Guangxi	0	0	0	0	0
海　南 Hainan	0	0	0	0	0
重　庆 Chongqing	141	8	31	101	1
四　川 Sichuan	579	37	123	395	24
贵　州 Guizhou	0	0	0	0	0
云　南 Yunnan	0	0	0	0	0
西　藏 Tibet	0	0	0	0	0
陕　西 Shaanxi	0	0	0	0	0
甘　肃 Gansu	192	9	80	102	1
青　海 Qinghai	0	0	0	0	0
宁　夏 Ningxia	0	0	0	0	0
新　疆 Xinjiang	0	0	0	0	0

地区 Region	占地面积(平方米) Areas Occupied (m^2)			图书(万册) Books & Magazines in Libraries(10,000 Volume)		
	合计 Total	其中:绿化用地面积 of Which: Green Areas	其中:运动场地面积 of Which: Sports Areas	合计 Total	当年新增 New Added in Current Year	合计 Total
总　计 Total	**1805535992.09**	**590138236.15**	**135562439.60**	**260505.13**	**11880.60**	**12336917**
北　京 Beijing	49001403.91	17677233.31	3745231.85	11683.31	343.04	754026
天　津 Tianjin	40245011.97	10812551.81	2772565.04	5262.66	180.17	262475
河　北 Hebei	75598101.22	20387492.28	6810547.76	10773.36	533.06	442932
山　西 Shanxi	36182383.90	9038457.61	3455969.31	5863.99	184.52	234909
内蒙古 Inner Mongolia	35614857.31	9043316.94	3034691.27	3604.36	173.51	187862
辽　宁 Liaoning	68374015.95	21236612.83	5410231.57	9588.22	317.10	508812
吉　林 Jilin	45049587.58	12495092.73	3166608.50	6654.69	314.79	322449
黑龙江 Heilongjiang	60461134.30	14501844.78	4119428.49	7913.93	236.71	354213
上　海 Shanghai	34461117.34	12958300.57	2688668.02	7400.55	226.90	495954
江　苏 Jiangsu	132705221.92	48903234.71	9414496.25	18089.51	781.92	1098172
浙　江 Zhejiang	65557400.15	21186703.43	5935648.94	11267.01	509.06	608158
安　徽 Anhui	74776392.95	23478540.28	5477424.74	9573.26	393.22	419513
福　建 Fujian	49653724.56	17922303.88	3889286.09	7654.63	324.44	353600
江　西 Jiangxi	65878817.23	26558681.80	5305637.79	9774.28	584.63	377805
山　东 Shandong	136727411.79	46530609.55	9604271.94	18059.80	721.23	709099
河　南 Henan	111457945.86	32083019.81	9060173.41	16582.86	955.34	678201
湖　北 Hubei	91874277.57	33962453.26	6921095.27	13783.81	464.18	634510
湖　南 Hunan	75566860.94	24969083.41	5040888.80	11092.24	479.73	456777
广　东 Guangdong	100762460.66	37162726.04	7916393.16	16653.13	825.49	831803
广　西 Guangxi	51060639.98	15436472.08	3374306.43	6568.81	513.54	302490
海　南 Hainan	13190726.27	4135686.27	825682.66	1671.26	88.02	70180
重　庆 Chongqing	51576707.31	18908220.76	3646973.06	6587.92	330.96	317134
四　川 Sichuan	94163917.63	31285614.92	6876338.87	12590.16	580.04	543056
贵　州 Guizhou	44154211.33	16144603.56	2899321.35	5128.06	458.06	205758
云　南 Yunnan	41333904.01	15089785.37	3079994.25	6150.80	319.46	223219
西　藏 Tibet	3510458.76	914480.37	299005.26	399.34	15.45	18603
陕　西 Shaanxi	61194216.74	17471518.64	5036460.67	11212.81	553.84	516959
甘　肃 Gansu	35434069.28	10125813.16	2353228.40	3944.72	230.00	177622
青　海 Qinghai	5679102.14	2149951.33	397966.97	619.27	53.68	28326
宁　夏 Ningxia	12215845.94	4159487.88	807955.87	1130.04	59.79	62616
新　疆 Xinjiang	42074065.59	13408342.78	2195947.61	3226.31	128.71	139684

注:不含民办的其他高等教育机构数据。
Note: Data of Non-government HEIs is not Included.

产权)(总计)
Resources (Owned by HEIs) (Total)

计算机数(台) PC (Set)		教室(间) Classroom(Room)		固定资产值(万元) Fixed Assets (10,000 yuan)				
其中:教学用计算机 No. of Computers Used for Instruction		合计 Total	其中:网络多媒体教室 of Which: Network Multimedia Classroom	合计 Total	其中:教学、科研仪器设备资产 of Which: Teaching Equipment & Instruments		其中:信息化设备资产值 of Which: Assets of Information Facilities	
小计 Subtotal	其中:平板电脑 of Which: Tablet PC				小计 Subtotal	当年新增 New Added in Current Year	小计 Subtotal	其中:软件 of Which: Software
9227205	**115170**	**667619**	**368207**	**213524676.88**	**49812055.73**	**5992912.85**	**14251585.04**	**2813544.34**
438356	9967	20617	14636	17053047.22	5980635.69	616172.38	1546486.48	396138.96
187758	1673	10380	5747	5693208.33	1321426.40	149297.86	335328.46	70170.04
338616	2745	28713	14738	7789937.75	1529178.54	174492.21	434425.34	76817.49
185975	1919	19229	8588	3602878.37	879071.91	81681.72	244664.25	35742.13
153585	1288	13408	7418	3736731.16	783598.12	82176.44	210369.61	45534.33
402232	4888	26783	12089	8116826.15	1794355.70	196099.53	554968.78	99487.52
232569	1435	14693	6755	5105082.86	1348583.85	166751.78	380463.94	56747.90
278235	1000	21593	9350	6682873.59	1590623.07	161900.13	443959.45	80036.77
320259	4469	15638	9931	9918005.46	2937006.98	322990.08	811000.62	183783.54
830808	13537	43485	28619	17477004.72	4149532.58	455515.12	1102368.64	182037.46
459133	5900	25635	18092	10192308.92	2453334.95	293908.02	647212.09	132421.22
332197	2155	28036	13988	6185314.91	1596301.83	238794.87	382562.24	66089.25
262282	1553	16836	9323	6458678.43	1359358.46	205758.75	388674.69	87397.00
302680	3917	26428	13503	6019375.75	1131623.07	154287.18	348398.90	56501.84
548719	4398	47627	25114	12926578.27	2501477.98	318417.56	788568.87	161297.40
558364	8472	46652	23434	9288246.45	2203769.28	295686.66	664608.51	103151.09
453657	3632	36152	19336	10067251.49	2407047.07	266594.95	597259.49	110772.37
335023	7789	34154	19403	7367980.26	1510557.67	196276.45	448535.21	66003.18
651789	12559	24847	18749	13035252.88	3095139.24	431213.07	955637.02	192796.31
257086	3066	15537	8633	4030894.34	1071319.76	172483.90	305737.90	65632.07
53587	412	3517	2383	1411778.03	253239.60	32978.85	81595.03	14308.71
241179	1879	19598	12524	6623127.84	976753.01	131962.43	372236.47	64630.00
401746	3809	32713	19106	9446261.35	2053475.22	201049.43	678638.99	188259.89
164838	1930	21048	10289	3746349.09	626425.71	97860.43	224553.08	37387.89
177903	760	18231	8304	5041988.92	699963.56	99582.80	276610.04	38991.54
14187	102	808	635	299199.29	72526.00	15635.92	29888.34	5622.57
346076	4547	25924	13221	9701185.13	2022865.35	237890.69	585963.99	118492.35
130223	3394	10950	5580	2974069.28	631986.15	85593.36	161464.59	23724.67
21836	304	2473	1082	362090.26	123251.25	30886.02	26022.01	8271.65
45174	316	4109	2094	1024025.67	235594.98	25931.74	81550.79	16812.75
101133	1355	11805	5543	2147124.70	472032.73	53042.53	141831.21	28484.43

资产情况(学校
Condition of Assets and Teaching

地　区 Region	占地面积(平方米) Areas Occupied (m^2)			图书(万册) Books & Magazines in Libraries(10,000 Volume)		
	合计 Total	其中:绿化用地面积 of Which: Green Areas	其中:运动场地面积 of Which: Sports Areas	合计 Total	当年新增 New Added in Current Year	合计 Total
总　计 Total	**1786236448.50**	**585505921.00**	**133719810.36**	**257498.49**	**11798.72**	**12145002**
北　京 Beijing	47594250.49	17388567.21	3668716.85	11458.86	340.26	738347
天　津 Tianjin	39763112.31	10736450.31	2738914.34	5103.41	178.79	255428
河　北 Hebei	75138576.62	20265758.28	6723592.76	10689.50	520.31	437670
山　西 Shanxi	35532881.90	8883151.61	3356227.31	5749.49	183.65	229619
内蒙古 Inner Mongolia	35524307.31	9035456.94	3026691.27	3585.73	173.51	185861
辽　宁 Liaoning	67544975.98	21116292.11	5244338.97	9399.14	315.88	494842
吉　林 Jilin	44314074.87	12438981.38	3101376.11	6550.56	313.22	315986
黑龙江 Heilongjiang	59730492.34	14407911.57	4035903.24	7742.29	235.28	347337
上　海 Shanghai	34018379.87	12894305.01	2660240.70	7285.32	226.44	480328
江　苏 Jiangsu	132134517.92	48771290.71	9356439.25	17994.34	780.15	1089974
浙　江 Zhejiang	65216684.65	21109210.43	5883014.94	11180.31	508.17	600999
安　徽 Anhui	74089981.95	23446767.58	5395744.74	9497.02	391.70	414493
福　建 Fujian	49557376.56	17901135.88	3877664.09	7601.69	323.78	351359
江　西 Jiangxi	65293808.09	26339845.80	5257607.79	9648.23	581.78	369707
山　东 Shandong	135250069.59	46125506.15	9500092.74	17944.20	719.77	703226
河　南 Henan	110793995.79	31943438.56	8976736.55	16444.31	946.17	670002
湖　北 Hubei	91472404.07	33839914.26	6882001.27	13680.52	460.12	631602
湖　南 Hunan	74986177.94	24772842.41	4975027.80	10975.83	477.82	447981
广　东 Guangdong	99876442.05	36840924.67	7872707.16	16571.61	820.34	821987
广　西 Guangxi	50399968.88	15314099.08	3324545.43	6395.32	510.12	294602
海　南 Hainan	13108315.82	4092221.62	823732.66	1661.96	88.02	68960
重　庆 Chongqing	50476719.91	18489571.76	3546583.06	6480.09	321.45	307323
四　川 Sichuan	92759432.70	30996441.63	6686624.87	12478.80	575.16	536391
贵　州 Guizhou	43703478.77	15998539.11	2847657.43	5081.49	456.11	202931
云　南 Yunnan	41280769.23	15076707.37	3078484.25	6144.00	319.46	222280
西　藏 Tibet	3510458.76	914480.37	299005.26	399.34	15.45	18603
陕　西 Shaanxi	59771830.74	17148770.64	4926019.67	11009.19	549.41	508219
甘　肃 Gansu	35347553.48	10112013.16	2341727.40	3901.49	229.32	175589
青　海 Qinghai	5595934.14	2133657.33	377857.97	607.53	53.68	27246
宁　夏 Ningxia	12193368.94	4152687.88	804335.87	1126.74	59.79	61569
新　疆 Xinjiang	40256106.83	12818980.18	2130198.61	3110.20	123.61	134541

产权)(普通高校)
Resources(Owned by HEIs)(Regular HEIs)

计算机数(台) PC (Set)		教室(间) Classroom(Room)		固定资产值(万元) Fixed Assets (10,000 yuan)				
其中:教学用计算机 No. of Computers Used for Instruction		合计 Total	其中:网络多媒体教室 of Which: Network Multimedia Classroom	合计 Total	其中:教学、科研仪器设备资产 of Which:Teaching Equipment & Instruments		其中:信息化设备资产值 of Which: Assets of Information Facilities	
小计 Subtotal	其中:平板电脑 of Which: Tablet PC				小计 Subtotal	当年新增 New Added in Current Year	小计 Subtotal	其中:软件 of Which: Software
9086478	**111044**	**651252**	**361019**	**211429828.27**	**49416383.76**	**5959808.88**	**14024426.85**	**2776856.92**
427360	9838	19572	13939	16726085.27	5949762.77	614328.65	1513416.08	392289.64
183406	1627	9755	5515	5649952.29	1308713.45	147119.65	333224.56	70080.47
335369	2671	28336	14583	7748251.16	1520431.16	174109.97	429302.62	76244.75
181482	1919	18300	8385	3550734.34	865630.21	81354.32	239451.12	35492.45
152232	1222	13291	7365	3727503.60	780968.21	82065.89	208387.36	45482.61
391616	4806	25585	11635	7997217.02	1769579.96	194089.78	546326.33	98311.28
227664	1359	14050	6581	5036405.07	1331523.15	164672.62	373497.50	55074.55
273767	994	20685	9155	6618832.13	1576782.19	159537.82	435205.86	79137.21
309014	4168	14727	9285	9765427.22	2892930.80	321408.12	774822.73	172982.84
825469	13414	43150	28434	17365858.93	4141256.56	455275.22	1093346.55	180513.32
453487	5848	24924	17549	10129937.63	2440816.11	292329.50	635225.20	131343.96
328219	2124	27562	13794	6123864.41	1589067.20	238120.08	372257.20	65142.97
260879	1552	16715	9240	6440402.91	1352654.80	205482.97	384254.24	86752.73
295563	2853	26152	13266	5957047.44	1115046.04	151647.17	337888.85	54994.04
545044	4393	47035	24941	12829366.48	2485200.65	317359.24	784370.54	160226.50
551596	8242	45909	23164	9244773.69	2190288.38	295318.60	660878.74	102524.70
451468	3561	35439	19219	10021628.06	2396889.98	265953.63	593861.04	110434.96
329100	7494	33264	18776	7315777.68	1495350.02	194108.20	444657.12	64747.28
644723	12271	24297	18330	12955514.22	3078468.46	430287.27	943429.79	191833.09
250484	3048	15178	8426	3969736.18	1057550.21	172212.01	300237.34	64863.21
52599	412	3472	2347	1405310.86	250727.80	32341.38	79151.36	13745.99
234250	1794	19028	12170	6487652.24	957824.72	129177.44	362982.72	62988.76
396507	3712	31777	18878	9348997.91	2033765.51	199761.18	672158.36	186750.85
162673	1929	20808	10180	3680347.32	621129.20	97022.39	220400.34	36692.15
177051	758	18144	8291	5020693.05	696887.72	99174.40	274048.61	38419.70
14187	102	808	635	299199.29	72526.00	15635.92	29888.34	5622.57
339774	4266	24718	13012	9614727.65	1995936.41	237022.19	580277.18	117642.55
128355	3388	10814	5511	2946246.07	627317.85	85453.18	158565.27	23537.70
20952	220	2418	1052	356114.26	121751.25	30876.02	25482.01	8241.35
44145	315	4089	2080	1020365.44	233703.21	24808.44	80541.19	16668.97
98043	744	11250	5281	2075858.47	465903.77	51755.66	136890.70	28073.77

地　区 Region	占地面积(平方米) Areas Occupied (m^2)			图书(万册) Books & Magazines in Libraries(10,000 Volume)		
	合计 Total	其中:绿化用地面积 of Which: Green Areas	其中:运动场地面积 of Which: Sports Areas	合计 Total	当年新增 New Added in Current Year	合计 Total
总　计 Total	**19299543.59**	**4632315.15**	**1842629.24**	**3006.64**	**81.88**	**191915**
北　京 Beijing	1407153.42	288666.10	76515.00	224.45	2.78	15679
天　津 Tianjin	481899.66	76101.50	33650.70	159.25	1.38	7047
河　北 Hebei	459524.60	121734.00	86955.00	83.87	12.75	5262
山　西 Shanxi	649502.00	155306.00	99742.00	114.51	0.87	5290
内蒙古 Inner Mongolia	90550.00	7860.00	8000.00	18.63	0	2001
辽　宁 Liaoning	829039.97	120320.72	165892.60	189.08	1.23	13970
吉　林 Jilin	735512.71	56111.35	65232.39	104.14	1.56	6463
黑龙江 Heilongjiang	730641.96	93933.21	83525.25	171.64	1.43	6876
上　海 Shanghai	442737.47	63995.56	28427.32	115.23	0.45	15626
江　苏 Jiangsu	570704.00	131944.00	58057.00	95.17	1.77	8198
浙　江 Zhejiang	340715.50	77493.00	52634.00	86.70	0.89	7159
安　徽 Anhui	686411.00	31772.70	81680.00	76.24	1.52	5020
福　建 Fujian	96348.00	21168.00	11622.00	52.95	0.65	2241
江　西 Jiangxi	585009.14	218836.00	48030.00	126.05	2.85	8098
山　东 Shandong	1477342.20	405103.40	104179.20	115.60	1.47	5873
河　南 Henan	663950.07	139581.25	83436.86	138.56	9.17	8199
湖　北 Hubei	401873.50	122539.00	39094.00	103.29	4.06	2908
湖　南 Hunan	580683.00	196241.00	65861.00	116.41	1.91	8796
广　东 Guangdong	886018.61	321801.37	43686.00	81.52	5.14	9816
广　西 Guangxi	660671.10	122373.00	49761.00	173.49	3.42	7888
海　南 Hainan	82410.45	43464.65	1950.00	9.30	0	1220
重　庆 Chongqing	1099987.40	418649.00	100390.00	107.83	9.51	9811
四　川 Sichuan	1404484.93	289173.29	189714.00	111.37	4.89	6665
贵　州 Guizhou	450732.56	146064.45	51663.92	46.57	1.95	2827
云　南 Yunnan	53134.78	13078.00	1510.00	6.80	0	939
西　藏 Tibet	0	0	0	0	0	0
陕　西 Shaanxi	1422386.00	322748.00	110441.00	203.62	4.43	8740
甘　肃 Gansu	86515.80	13800.00	11501.00	43.23	0.68	2033
青　海 Qinghai	83168.00	16294.00	20109.00	11.74	0	1080
宁　夏 Ningxia	22477.00	6800.00	3620.00	3.30	0	1047
新　疆 Xinjiang	1817958.76	589362.60	65749.00	116.11	5.10	5143

产权)(成人高校)
Resources (Owned by HEIs)(Adult HEIs)

计算机数(台) PC (Set)		教室(间) Classroom(Room)		固定资产值(万元) Fixed Assets (10,000 yuan)				
其中:教学用计算机 No. of Computers Used for Instruction		合计 Total	其中:网络多媒体教室 of Which: Network Multimedia Classroom	合计 Total	其中:教学、科研仪器设备资产 of Which: Teaching Equipment & Instruments		其中:信息化设备资产值 of Which: Assets of Information Facilities	
小计 Subtotal	其中:平板电脑 of Which: Tablet PC				小计 Subtotal	当年新增 New Added in Current Year	小计 Subtotal	其中:软件 of Which: Software
140727	**4126**	**16367**	**7188**	**2094848.60**	**395671.97**	**33103.97**	**227158.19**	**36687.42**
10996	129	1045	697	326961.95	30872.91	1843.73	33070.40	3849.33
4352	46	625	232	43256.04	12712.95	2178.22	2103.90	89.57
3247	74	377	155	41686.58	8747.38	382.23	5122.73	572.74
4493	0	929	203	52144.03	13441.70	327.40	5213.13	249.68
1353	66	117	53	9227.56	2629.91	110.55	1982.25	51.72
10616	82	1198	454	119609.13	24775.74	2009.75	8642.46	1176.23
4905	76	643	174	68677.79	17060.70	2079.16	6966.43	1673.35
4468	6	908	195	64041.46	13840.88	2362.31	8753.59	899.55
11245	301	911	646	152578.24	44076.18	1581.96	36177.89	10800.70
5339	123	335	185	111145.79	8276.02	239.91	9022.08	1524.14
5646	52	711	543	62371.29	12518.85	1578.52	11986.89	1077.26
3978	31	474	194	61450.50	7234.62	674.79	10305.04	946.28
1403	1	121	83	18275.52	6703.66	275.78	4420.45	644.27
7117	1064	276	237	62328.31	16577.03	2640.01	10510.05	1507.80
3675	5	592	173	97211.79	16277.33	1058.33	4198.33	1070.90
6768	230	743	270	43472.76	13480.90	368.06	3729.77	626.39
2189	71	713	117	45623.43	10157.09	641.32	3398.45	337.42
5923	295	890	627	52202.58	15207.65	2168.25	3878.09	1255.90
7066	288	550	419	79738.66	16670.78	925.81	12207.24	963.22
6602	18	359	207	61158.17	13769.54	271.89	5500.56	768.86
988	0	45	36	6467.17	2511.80	637.47	2443.67	562.72
6929	85	570	354	135475.60	18928.29	2784.99	9253.75	1641.24
5239	97	936	228	97263.44	19709.71	1288.25	6480.64	1509.04
2165	1	240	109	66001.77	5296.52	838.05	4152.74	695.74
852	2	87	13	21295.87	3075.84	408.40	2561.43	571.84
0	0	0	0	0	0	0	0	0
6302	281	1206	209	86457.49	26928.94	868.50	5686.81	849.80
1868	6	136	69	27823.21	4668.30	140.18	2899.32	186.97
884	84	55	30	5976.00	1500.00	10.00	540.00	30.30
1029	1	20	14	3660.23	1891.77	1123.30	1009.60	143.78
3090	611	555	262	71266.23	6128.96	1286.87	4940.51	410.66

地　区 Region	占地面积(平方米) Areas Occupied (m²)			图书(万册) Books & Magazines in Libraries(10,000 Volume)		
	合计 Total	其中:绿化用地面积 of Which: Green Areas	其中:运动场地面积 of Which: Sports Areas	合计 Total	当年新增 New Added in Current Year	合计 Total
总　计 Total	**5996664.32**	**1111260.26**	**422611.86**	**4157.49**	**40.48**	**62041**
北　京 Beijing	361846.00	85119.00	13672.00	229.73	0.41	14128
天　津 Tianjin	0	0	0	0	0	0
河　北 Hebei	751617.00	68066.00	30800.00	48.65	2.13	1791
山　西 Shanxi	422636.00	37022.00	35476.00	109.20	6.21	2776
内蒙古 Inner Mongolia	0	0	0	0	0	0
辽　宁 Liaoning	129150.00	24402.00	14900.00	108.10	0	1394
吉　林 Jilin	29086.00	3000.00	10000.00	15.50	0.10	345
黑龙江 Heilongjiang	21942.00	2000.00	5000.00	2.00	0	233
上　海 Shanghai	168133.00	42926.00	21231.00	39.59	2.99	6412
江　苏 Jiangsu	0	0	0	0	0	0
浙　江 Zhejiang	154443.20	87648.00	19385.00	37.77	1.16	3685
安　徽 Anhui	366997.00	81770.00	28044.00	56.00	0.00	7247
福　建 Fujian	0	0	0	0	0	0
江　西 Jiangxi	826793.59	205032.50	76271.00	25.83	0.76	2842
山　东 Shandong	1813610.00	340945.00	95472.00	3235.98	3.36	9081
河　南 Henan	110188.48	8517.18	2781.32	46.46	6.16	1225
湖　北 Hubei	71457.00	21373.00	0	15.30	0.18	1892
湖　南 Hunan	0	0	0	23.60	1.05	935
广　东 Guangdong	218189.83	6500.18	21000.54	42.00	7.90	3283
广　西 Guangxi	0	0	0	0	0	0
海　南 Hainan	0	0	0	0	0	0
重　庆 Chongqing	315672.22	25147.00	12655.00	34.70	0.00	897
四　川 Sichuan	222959.00	71092.40	34450.00	72.26	1.65	3251
贵　州 Guizhou	0	0	0	0	0	0
云　南 Yunnan	0	0	0	0	0	0
西　藏 Tibet	0	0	0	0	0	0
陕　西 Shaanxi	0	0	0	0	0	0
甘　肃 Gansu	11944.00	700.00	1474.00	14.81	6.42	624
青　海 Qinghai	0	0	0	0	0	0
宁　夏 Ningxia	0	0	0	0	0	0
新　疆 Xinjiang	0	0	0	0	0	0

（民办的其他高等教育机构）
Resources (Other Non-government HEIs)

计算机数（台）PC (Set)		教室（间）Classroom (Room)		固定资产值（万元）Fixed Assets (10,000 yuan)				
其中：教学用计算机 No. of Computers Used for Instruction		合计 Total	其中：网络多媒体教室 of Which: Network Multimedia Classroom	合计 Total	其中：教学、科研仪器设备资产 of Which: Teaching Equipment & Instruments		其中：信息化设备资产值 of Which: Assets of Information Facilities	
小计 Subtotal	其中：平板电脑 of Which: Tablet PC				小计 Subtotal	当年新增 New Added in Current Year	小计 Subtotal	其中：软件 of Which: Software
50320	**2887**	**4716**	**1442**	**1073400.58**	**81979.44**	**7571.10**	**23114.41**	**4058.26**
10993	175	969	86	274348.32	21951.27	2301.43	3818.31	135.39
0	0	0	0	0	0	0	0	0
1420	29	101	38	15340.23	2630.26	305.61	737.71	293.87
2275	8	541	68	16397.27	3187.41	128.59	1253.73	214.12
0	0	0	0	0	0	0	0	0
1048	0	532	225	5154.00	2862.00	9.00	43.90	7.40
265	2	90	21	907.30	365.00	16.00	202.00	5.00
192	0	60	0	1108.00	210.00	0	68.71	10.19
5107	543	191	76	19927.87	6685.82	1515.81	1969.80	301.15
0	0	0	0	0	0	0	0	0
2705	298	314	150	524965.78	6955.31	254.00	2347.52	476.16
6922	17	320	218	17300.64	7590.08	112.00	2200.00	153.80
0	0	0	0	0	0	0	0	0
2541	429	172	13	16459.16	1518.16	435.00	1718.67	475.33
6700	321	526	132	47355.37	11008.05	513.95	3452.31	1220.46
1030	142	105	20	4972.41	1022.02	18.06	1346.82	251.75
1477	81	104	36	30906.71	2517.70	11.35	493.45	7.15
668	178	0	0	2820.19	2411.84	1140.98	357.00	101.00
2975	80	190	114	14434.42	2666.67	469.21	594.55	72.50
0	0	0	0	0	0	0	0	0
0	0	0	0	0	0	0	0	0
815	214	218	86	50429.90	1636.52	104.33	1669.70	119.10
2682	176	237	143	29046.71	6337.10	203.73	746.25	200.50
0	0	0	0	0	0	0	0	0
0	0	0	0	0	0	0	0	0
0	0	0	0	0	0	0	0	0
0	0	0	0	0	0	0	0	0
505	194	46	16	1526.31	424.23	32.05	93.99	13.39
0	0	0	0	0	0	0	0	0
0	0	0	0	0	0	0	0	0
0	0	0	0	0	0	0	0	0

资产情况(非学校
Condition of Assets and Teaching

地区 Region	占地面积(平方米) Areas Occupied (m^2)			图书(万册) Books & Magazines in Libraries(10,000 Volume)		
	合计 Total	其中:绿化用地面积 of Which: Green Areas	其中:运动场地面积 of Which: Sports Areas	合计 Total	当年新增 New Added in Current Year	合计 Total
总 计 Total	**242435413.53**	**52236681.47**	**13888399.85**	**6261.09**	**780.85**	**334849**
北 京 Beijing	7013048.76	1734218.53	576023.37	226.10	194.30	229
天 津 Tianjin	2800740.58	204324.00	163906.00	679.86	3.80	9427
河 北 Hebei	6927061.07	631971.72	338341.74	95.37	55.46	2307
山 西 Shanxi	5904879.25	936247.79	497226.22	74.66	0	8350
内蒙古 Inner Mongolia	2945903.96	484597.35	276819.66	24.62	0.30	1488
辽 宁 Liaoning	7857042.23	1446820.35	710883.43	298.80	14.29	17290
吉 林 Jilin	8259322.12	1400076.31	252650.00	49.83	4.66	4853
黑龙江 Heilongjiang	3406661.27	465310.80	284516.00	165.27	0	8178
上 海 Shanghai	5525262.02	1235896.36	296769.28	255.25	10.69	25907
江 苏 Jiangsu	20812014.24	4464232.46	1408192.30	468.96	20.22	38965
浙 江 Zhejiang	10431923.29	2629912.26	673959.93	370.61	12.14	35926
安 徽 Anhui	5002851.24	724123.00	262139.00	191.43	2.00	10820
福 建 Fujian	12592474.39	3231510.48	839057.44	323.79	15.09	6933
江 西 Jiangxi	11340843.92	3370727.12	665053.83	39.26	0.00	229
山 东 Shandong	12232717.80	2680628.57	526320.60	229.17	1.70	5456
河 南 Henan	12275191.33	2272307.96	681130.97	323.10	42.26	15172
湖 北 Hubei	13700251.04	2386238.00	634197.68	363.83	2.30	15223
湖 南 Hunan	9024805.75	1490446.32	285089.37	421.74	5.81	5703
广 东 Guangdong	27353854.66	9181992.99	1855607.96	621.48	17.41	53607
广 西 Guangxi	6798166.06	937449.67	250662.00	132.76	12.81	8790
海 南 Hainan	1845751.32	183357.00	74162.85	9.60	9.60	417
重 庆 Chongqing	2576286.08	154394.37	25140.60	36.08	1.50	9976
四 川 Sichuan	13060632.68	2317466.69	746557.64	108.67	58.00	4439
贵 州 Guizhou	4302075.76	1740600.85	61825.12	282.72	253.14	14793
云 南 Yunnan	6401270.35	1273459.10	241676.86	43.58	23.68	2436
西 藏 Tibet	0	0	0	1.32	0	0
陕 西 Shaanxi	16205423.81	3796237.32	893018.43	200.36	19.46	16828
甘 肃 Gansu	3083800.85	299883.10	112009.51	2.91	0	180
青 海 Qinghai	33333.00	0	0	0	0	369
宁 夏 Ningxia	84000.02	0	0	32.00	0	0
新 疆 Xinjiang	2637824.68	562251.00	255462.06	187.95	0.20	10558

注:不含民办的其他高等教育机构数据。

Note: Data of Non-government HEIs is not Included.

产权中独立使用)
Resources (Not Owned by HEIs)

计算机数(台) PC (Set)		教室(间) Classroom(Room)		固定资产值(万元) Fixed Assets (10,000 yuan)				
其中:教学用计算机 No. of Computers Used for Instruction		合计 Total	其中:网络多媒体教室 of Which: Network Multimedia Classroom	合计 Total	其中:教学、科研仪器设备资产 of Which: Teaching Equipment & Instruments		其中:信息化设备资产值 of Which: Assets of Information Facilities	
小计 Subtotal	其中:平板电脑 of Which: Tablet PC				小计 Subtotal	当年新增 New Added in Current Year	小计 Subtotal	其中:软件 of Which: Software
264891	**6632**	**113018**	**53928**	**13511553.08**	**1025691.37**	**117525.95**	**—**	**—**
180	0	1502	850	265108.62	22255.36	52.00	—	—
8181	0	2186	1486	244006.36	16289.98	741.54	—	—
1983	0	1141	353	220704.90	19816.19	3659.61	—	—
7067	0	2372	1061	157477.41	13325.27	80.00	—	—
1277	0	1115	451	191748.52	1304.55	131.00	—	—
13193	312	5811	2254	813631.45	49576.33	4170.18	—	—
3991	265	3410	1031	184262.95	6798.42	540.59	—	—
6622	0	2335	1357	93485.28	18629.37	801.58	—	—
22002	3366	3816	2689	446876.56	84041.13	13918.26	—	—
30116	317	9486	5648	1039644.79	146857.73	13610.96	—	—
26062	312	4599	3141	1173672.46	62260.80	720.36	—	—
9154	0	3215	1286	234446.11	20121.35	11.30	—	—
6214	1	4926	2624	577897.24	44839.08	3129.05	—	—
226	0	2938	1027	228068.15	26553.90	5718.20	—	—
4076	0	5311	1820	767708.42	26761.17	7105.37	—	—
12899	399	5380	2557	571037.63	34640.47	11200.39	—	—
12165	120	6715	1468	746678.54	47539.99	491.85	—	—
4879	53	4118	1711	552132.80	38098.08	2314.24	—	—
43426	599	14406	9078	2555624.08	91661.34	5364.85	—	—
4657	237	3218	1736	221075.71	19493.99	1466.86	—	—
259	0	253	118	174080.31	2968.60	2380.27	—	—
7211	263	1479	707	185183.31	17987.14	1761.86	—	—
3541	41	6250	3625	977220.45	112944.04	14076.04	—	—
12111	191	2018	490	258631.71	44689.72	20156.55	—	—
2156	14	3884	1668	335547.49	10438.37	970.94	—	—
0	0	0	0	608.50	0	0	—	—
12554	30	7573	3010	156637.08	24361.09	681.00	—	—
120	80	220	93	73888.02	4373.42	60.00	—	—
300	0	13	13	3652.00	995.00	8.00	—	—
0	0	27	2	7556.00	0	0	—	—
8269	32	3301	574	53260.21	16069.47	2203.09	—	—

资产情况(非学校产权
Condition of Assets and Teaching

地区 Region	占地面积(平方米) Areas Occupied (m^2)			图书(万册) Books & Magazines in Libraries(10,000 Volume)		
	合计 Total	其中:绿化用地面积 of Which: Green Areas	其中:运动场地面积 of Which: Sports Areas	合计 Total	当年新增 New Added in Current Year	合计 Total
总　计 Total	**217250282.7**	**46806085.47**	**10638277.55**	**2287.62**	**450.39**	**66054**
北　京 Beijing	6997545.76	1734218.53	576023.37	223.9	194.3	179
天　津 Tianjin	2216619.58	163643	60897	14.43	0.1	734
河　北 Hebei	6927061.07	631971.72	338341.74	95.37	55.46	2307
山　西 Shanxi	5789430.25	925647.79	476066.22	38.68	0	4736
内蒙古 Inner Mongolia	2945903.96	484597.35	276819.66	24.62	0.3	1488
辽　宁 Liaoning	5242266.71	929650.4	367783.45	30.68	0	1182
吉　林 Jilin	7837686.12	1292764.31	156561	4.56	4.56	901
黑龙江 Heilongjiang	2449773.27	366722.8	55966	1.8	0	128
上　海 Shanghai	4782314.05	1095077.34	243358.96	40.7	1.58	2565
江　苏 Jiangsu	17103141.41	3371644.17	857869.17	72.18	10.97	2027
浙　江 Zhejiang	7364358.29	1614896.26	303158.93	71.21	3.11	1343
安　徽 Anhui	3334374.24	507761	160335	96.18	2	2200
福　建 Fujian	12592474.39	3231510.48	839057.44	323.79	15.09	6933
江　西 Jiangxi	11237283.92	3340727.12	624053.83	39.26	0	229
山　东 Shandong	12232717.8	2680628.57	526320.6	229.17	1.7	5456
河　南 Henan	11833924.33	2160188.96	647547.97	119.23	42.26	6993
湖　北 Hubei	11825504.04	2046491	441124.68	82.2	2.1	3134
湖　南 Hunan	8928409.75	1456746.32	283089.37	404.76	5.81	4973
广　东 Guangdong	23716897.26	8079675.94	1184512.6	90.45	6.95	1063
广　西 Guangxi	6643064.06	914468.67	224834	65.51	12.81	5838
海　南 Hainan	1845751.32	183357	74162.85	9.6	9.6	417
重　庆 Chongqing	1908756.17	154394.37	25140.6	1.47	0	191
四　川 Sichuan	12871784.35	2252026.86	704740.74	108.67	58	4321
贵　州 Guizhou	3227591.86	1726190.6	57831.94	19.38	0	2452
云　南 Yunnan	6401270.35	1273459.1	241676.86	43.58	23.68	2436
西　藏 Tibet	0	0	0	1.32	0	0
陕　西 Shaanxi	14944883.81	3546742.71	754357	0	0	127
甘　肃 Gansu	3042241.85	285883.1	106209.51	2.91	0	180
青　海 Qinghai	33333	0	0	0	0	0
宁　夏 Ningxia	84000.02	0	0	32	0	0
新　疆 Xinjiang	889919.68	355000	30437.06	0	0	1521

中独立使用)(普通高校)
Resources (Not Owned by HEIs)(Regular HEIs)

计算机数(台) PC (Set)		教室(间) Classroom(Room)		固定资产值(万元) Fixed Assets (10,000 yuan)				
其中:教学用计算机 No. of Computers Used for Instruction		合计 Total	其中:网络多媒体教室 of Which: Network Multimedia Classroom	合计 Total	其中:教学、科研仪器设备资产 of Which: Teaching Equipment & Instruments		其中:信息化设备资产值 of Which: Assets of Information Facilities	
小计 Subtotal	其中:平板电脑 of Which: Tablet PC				小计 Subtotal	当年新增 New Added in Current Year	小计 Subtotal	其中:软件 of Which: Software
53003	**404**	**83854**	**40174**	**11594571.00**	**536511.11**	**67610.06**	**—**	**—**
176	0	1487	847	265068.62	22250.36	52.00	—	—
600	0	1113	461	218843.80	6889.87	181.54	—	—
1983	0	1141	353	220704.90	19816.19	3659.61	—	—
4348	0	2145	984	144960.75	10927.86	80.00	—	—
1277	0	1115	451	191748.52	1304.55	131.00	—	—
884	7	3740	1364	713184.75	16308.16	1414.76	—	—
851	0	3078	948	159405.24	899.36	285.96	—	—
115	0	1301	404	51931.56	8810.12	801.58	—	—
2142	43	1872	1299	209647.12	15263.50	2792.54	—	—
1713	0	6585	3849	663280.32	30516.71	4935.78	—	—
440	15	1926	1207	879003.26	11400.86	611.49	—	—
1995	0	1682	651	165403.72	6738.35	11.30	—	—
6214	1	4926	2624	577897.24	44839.08	3129.05	—	—
226	0	2863	997	222968.15	26553.90	5718.20	—	—
4076	0	5311	1820	767708.42	26761.17	7105.37	—	—
6279	39	4459	2261	524229.70	23161.98	10736.37	—	—
2761	0	4163	1251	678036.72	29031.46	491.85	—	—
4149	53	4014	1649	546923.90	36264.73	2180.94	—	—
956	0	9815	6351	2273661.62	11856.92	881.00	—	—
2308	64	2765	1634	191634.60	14470.98	1446.86	—	—
259	0	253	118	174080.31	2968.60	2380.27	—	—
143	4	794	370	146927.97	5443.75	1149.27	—	—
3429	41	6234	3622	976037.19	112944.04	14076.04	—	—
2059	11	1109	162	81648.48	21444.64	740.35	—	—
2156	14	3884	1668	335547.49	10438.37	970.94	—	—
0	0	0	0	608.50	0	0	—	—
90	0	5507	2519	120986.90	12120.62	600.00	—	—
120	80	220	93	73888.02	4373.42	60.00	—	—
0	0	13	13	986.00	8.00	8.00	—	—
0	0	27	2	7556.00	0	0	—	—
1254	32	312	202	10061.21	2703.55	978.00	—	—

地 区 Region	占地面积(平方米) Areas Occupied (m^2)			图书(万册) Books & Magazines in Libraries(10,000 Volume)		
	合计 Total	其中:绿化用地面积 of Which: Green Areas	其中:运动场地面积 of Which: Sports Areas	合计 Total	当年新增 New Added in Current Year	合计 Total
总 计 Total	**25185130.86**	**5430596**	**3250122.3**	**3973.47**	**330.45**	**268795**
北 京 Beijing	15503	0	0	2.2	0	50
天 津 Tianjin	584121	40681	103009	665.43	3.7	8693
河 北 Hebei	0	0	0	0	0	0
山 西 Shanxi	115449	10600	21160	35.98	0	3614
内蒙古 Inner Mongolia	0	0	0	0	0	0
辽 宁 Liaoning	2614775.52	517169.95	343099.98	268.12	14.29	16108
吉 林 Jilin	421636	107312	96089	45.27	0.1	3952
黑龙江 Heilongjiang	956888	98588	228550	163.47	0	8050
上 海 Shanghai	742947.97	140819.02	53410.32	214.55	9.12	23342
江 苏 Jiangsu	3708872.83	1092588.29	550323.13	396.78	9.25	36938
浙 江 Zhejiang	3067565	1015016	370801	299.4	9.03	34583
安 徽 Anhui	1668477	216362	101804	95.25	0	8620
福 建 Fujian	0	0	0	0	0	0
江 西 Jiangxi	103560	30000	41000	0	0	0
山 东 Shandong	0	0	0	0	0	0
河 南 Henan	441267	112119	33583	203.87	0	8179
湖 北 Hubei	1874747	339747	193073	281.63	0.2	12089
湖 南 Hunan	96396	33700	2000	16.98	0	730
广 东 Guangdong	3636957.4	1102317.05	671095.36	531.04	10.47	52544
广 西 Guangxi	155102	22981	25828	67.25	0	2952
海 南 Hainan	0	0	0	0	0	0
重 庆 Chongqing	667529.91	0	0	34.61	1.5	9785
四 川 Sichuan	188848.33	65439.83	41816.9	0	0	118
贵 州 Guizhou	1074483.9	14410.25	3993.18	263.34	253.14	12341
云 南 Yunnan	0	0	0	0	0	0
西 藏 Tibet	0	0	0	0	0	0
陕 西 Shaanxi	1260540	249494.61	138661.43	200.36	19.46	16701
甘 肃 Gansu	41559	14000	5800	0	0	0
青 海 Qinghai	0	0	0	0	0	369
宁 夏 Ningxia	0	0	0	0	0	0
新 疆 Xinjiang	1747905	207251	225025	187.95	0.2	9037

中独立使用)(成人高校)
Resources (Not Owned by HEIs) (Adult HEIs)

计算机数(台) PC (Set)		教室(间) Classroom(Room)		固定资产值(万元) Fixed Assets (10,000 yuan)				
其中:教学用计算机 No. of Computers Used for Instruction		合计 Total	其中:网络多媒体教室 of Which: Network Multimedia Classroom	合计 Total	其中:教学、科研仪器设备资产 of Which: Teaching Equipment & Instruments		其中:信息化设备资产值 of Which: Assets of Information Facilities	
小计 Subtotal	其中:平板电脑 of Which: Tablet PC				小计 Subtotal	当年新增 New Added in Current Year	小计 Subtotal	其中:软件 of Which: Software
211888	**6228**	**29164**	**13754**	**1916982.08**	**489180.26**	**49915.88**	**—**	**—**
4	0	15	3	40.00	5.00	0	—	—
7581	0	1073	1025	25162.56	9400.11	560.00	—	—
0	0	0	0	0	0	0	—	—
2719	0	227	77	12516.66	2397.41	0	—	—
0	0	0	0	0	0	0	—	—
12309	305	2071	890	100446.70	33268.17	2755.42	—	—
3140	265	332	83	24857.72	5899.06	254.63	—	—
6507	0	1034	953	41553.72	9819.25	0	—	—
19860	3323	1944	1390	237229.44	68777.63	11125.72	—	—
28403	317	2901	1799	376364.47	116341.03	8675.19	—	—
25622	297	2673	1934	294669.20	50859.94	108.87	—	—
7159	0	1533	635	69042.39	13383.00	0	—	—
0	0	0	0	0	0	0	—	—
0	0	75	30	5100.00	0	0	—	—
0	0	0	0	0	0	0	—	—
6620	360	921	296	46807.93	11478.49	464.02	—	—
9404	120	2552	217	68641.82	18508.53	0	—	—
730	0	104	62	5208.90	1833.35	133.30	—	—
42470	599	4591	2727	281962.46	79804.42	4483.85	—	—
2349	173	453	102	29441.11	5023.01	20.00	—	—
0	0	0	0	0	0	0	—	—
7068	259	685	337	38255.34	12543.39	612.59	—	—
112	0	16	3	1183.26	0	0	—	—
10052	180	909	328	176983.23	23245.08	19416.20	—	—
0	0	0	0	0	0	0	—	—
0	0	0	0	0	0	0	—	—
12464	30	2066	491	35650.18	12240.47	81.00	—	—
0	0	0	0	0	0	0	—	—
300	0	0	0	2666.00	987.00	0	—	—
0	0	0	0	0	0	0	—	—
7015	0	2989	372	43199.00	13365.92	1225.09	—	—

地 区 Region	占地面积(平方米) Areas Occupied (m^2)			图书(万册) Books & Magazines in Libraries(10,000 Volume)		
	合计 Total	其中:绿化用地面积 of Which: Green Areas	其中:运动场地面积 of Which: Sports Areas	合计 Total	当年新增 New Added in Current Year	合计 Total
总 计 Total	**5612649.1**	**693627.82**	**519625.83**	**189.29**	**25.05**	**12280**
北 京 Beijing	1043011.48	292266	221110	6.36	3.7	661
天 津 Tianjin	0	0	0	0	0	0
河 北 Hebei	178099.98	20349.99	10099.99	4.2	1.2	657
山 西 Shanxi	398119	69287	26434	41.51	5.51	531
内蒙古 Inner Mongolia	0	0	0	0	0	0
辽 宁 Liaoning	64026	5860	7750	3.5	0	2412
吉 林 Jilin	29000	3000	10000	1	1	242
黑龙江 Heilongjiang	11000	370	1500	0	0	0
上 海 Shanghai	257855.23	23305	18626	57.88	6.92	3956
江 苏 Jiangsu	0	0	0	0	0	0
浙 江 Zhejiang	243347	60208	29298	16.07	0	1687
安 徽 Anhui	148070	20000	10000	6.7	0	0
福 建 Fujian	0	0	0	0	0	0
江 西 Jiangxi	1443688	10710	10200	0	0	37
山 东 Shandong	260671.52	38910	43625	23.04	0.2	290
河 南 Henan	241709.71	27407.33	35399.84	8	4	297
湖 北 Hubei	111997	11540	7790	1.5	0	85
湖 南 Hunan	302630	8800	7100	1	0	0
广 东 Guangdong	294018.4	45361.5	32043	3.8	1.02	747
广 西 Guangxi	0	0	0	0	0	0
海 南 Hainan	0	0	0	0	0	0
重 庆 Chongqing	20024	0	4005	0	0	0
四 川 Sichuan	539821.9	53305	38195	12.98	1.5	515
贵 州 Guizhou	0	0	0	0	0	0
云 南 Yunnan	0	0	0	0	0	0
西 藏 Tibet	0	0	0	0	0	0
陕 西 Shaanxi	0	0	0	0	0	0
甘 肃 Gansu	25559.88	2948	6450	1.75	0	163
青 海 Qinghai	0	0	0	0	0	0
宁 夏 Ningxia	0	0	0	0	0	0
新 疆 Xinjiang	0	0	0	0	0	0

中独立使用)(民办的其他高等教育机构)
(Not Owned by HEIs)(Other Non-government HEIs)

计算机数(台) PC (Set)		教室(间) Classroom(Room)		固定资产值(万元) Fixed Assets (10,000 yuan)				
其中:教学用计算机 No. of Computers Used for Instruction		合计 Total	其中:网络多媒体教室 of Which: Network Multimedia Classroom	合计 Total	其中:教学、科研仪器设备资产 of Which: Teaching Equipment & Instruments		其中:信息化设备资产值 of Which: Assets of Information Facilities	
小计 Subtotal	其中:平板电脑 of Which: Tablet PC				小计 Subtotal	当年新增 New Added in Current Year	小计 Subtotal	其中:软件 of Which: Software
9873	**1362**	**5585**	**1752**	**113474.24**	**30961.24**	**2561.02**	**—**	**—**
420	177	743	316	19097.95	2970.09	281.88	—	—
0	0	0	0	0	0	0	—	—
603	1	180	49	1533.83	958.93	258.9	—	—
443	16	418	130	4646.02	557.11	51.02	—	—
0	0	0	0	0	0	0	—	—
2021	0	333	137	4614.1	1913.2	8	—	—
230	0	31	22	1200	376	376	—	—
0	0	146	3	0	0	0	—	—
3346	436	1566	386	8289.55	3408.22	727.55	—	—
0	0	0	0	0	0	0	—	—
1371	560	354	63	25836.03	4510.88	415.14	—	—
0	0	77	29	3882	21	12	—	—
0	0	0	0	0	0	0	—	—
28	0	86	8	1316.2	144.2	136	—	—
179	43	510	165	12319.67	1899.27	7.17	—	—
69	7	237	157	8575.34	1601.97	33.26	—	—
85	0	165	44	2610.75	366.7	5.6	—	—
0	0	87	41	0	0	0	—	—
537	0	263	79	2838.14	1414.07	155	—	—
0	0	0	0	0	0	0	—	—
0	0	0	0	0	0	0	—	—
0	0	8	8	38	22	2	—	—
435	105	313	88	15618.86	10485	67.9	—	—
0	0	0	0	0	0	0	—	—
0	0	0	0	0	0	0	—	—
0	0	0	0	0	0	0	—	—
0	0	0	0	0	0	0	—	—
106	17	68	27	1057.8	312.6	23.6	—	—
0	0	0	0	0	0	0	—	—
0	0	0	0	0	0	0	—	—
0	0	0	0	0	0	0	—	—

校舍情况（总计）
Conditions of School Buildings (Total)

单位：平方米
unit：m²

地　区 Region	学校产权校舍建筑面积 Floor Area of School Building Owned by HEIs				正在施工校舍建筑面积 Floor Area Under Construction	非学校产权中独立使用建筑面积 Floor Area of School Building Not Owned by HEIs
	合计 Total	其中：危房 of Which：Dilapidated Buildings	其中：当年新增校舍 of Which：New Added in Current Year	其中：被外单位借用 of Which：Floor Space Hired by Other Schools or Units		
总　计 Total	**863688901.47**	**1356626.37**	**24701347.79**	**1379978.64**	**60691788.84**	**114850633.09**
北　京 Beijing	41170757.69	114273.26	483516.04	134465.70	2908352.69	1970040.85
天　津 Tianjin	16761307.30	2499.00	458998.25	0	2395443.39	1571096.84
河　北 Hebei	36585955.55	0	873421.80	0	1729863.53	1907460.91
山　西 Shanxi	21271664.98	17693.23	199101.74	9598.27	1319933.52	2537605.35
内蒙古 Inner Mongolia	13976143.56	6689.00	487133.41	1212.36	860933.74	894463.75
辽　宁 Liaoning	32038268.32	46532.57	661499.27	1510.00	1800271.36	5001256.77
吉　林 Jilin	18868002.99	0	96803.65	0	1090371.30	2936984.24
黑龙江 Heilongjiang	27345604.76	16516.00	412917.15	2130.00	805734.85	1798723.57
上　海 Shanghai	21799458.36	0	514921.01	281668.91	1509450.15	3571361.13
江　苏 Jiangsu	58465035.61	55418.35	1248796.47	275756.09	3882231.12	10054061.17
浙　江 Zhejiang	32880560.42	1320.41	1218273.08	218346.52	4034929.41	7338476.74
安　徽 Anhui	34529280.05	77735.73	1146279.85	30502.35	1903525.33	2299652.70
福　建 Fujian	20417977.98	21943.00	244195.81	1966.40	1958420.42	6517980.28
江　西 Jiangxi	31675914.33	32747.30	492718.78	141823.20	1125665.85	3521211.95
山　东 Shandong	58424328.95	320503.43	1014376.70	18272.00	3514305.21	6203358.72
河　南 Henan	59776612.39	78285.00	2764685.35	87112.50	3050204.94	5435551.30
湖　北 Hubei	48683359.55	29834.98	667273.92	53248.95	2571675.53	6303331.64
湖　南 Hunan	35473818.80	109121.45	973652.74	0	2070204.60	4096980.27
广　东 Guangdong	43992515.97	18608.30	1837675.61	1104.00	1579586.72	16362078.30
广　西 Guangxi	23278814.97	89141.58	1566426.79	13673.00	2190341.74	3320598.43
海　南 Hainan	5354612.37	23951.61	4878.00	1478.00	415771.65	1185190.26
重　庆 Chongqing	24615852.50	13261.29	805367.19	0	892583.68	1660712.89
四　川 Sichuan	39598618.81	37148.85	1226771.75	21537.63	4029367.72	6775938.55
贵　州 Guizhou	23063558.47	5522.40	1640683.33	11182.76	2288005.20	1544671.00
云　南 Yunnan	16483280.60	112005.87	519236.97	67125.00	2413703.88	3309635.21
西　藏 Tibet	1286916.75	6602.00	18710.52	6265.00	174030.39	0
陕　西 Shaanxi	39666689.25	14627.95	1548244.88	0	4401856.09	5038932.63
甘　肃 Gansu	16252286.01	36340.40	616530.82	0	1575387.44	761697.76
青　海 Qinghai	2684669.53	5753.00	385877.00	0	139313.20	19124.00
宁　夏 Ningxia	4155986.69	0	197889.43	0	114667.20	54055.00
新　疆 Xinjiang	13111047.96	62550.41	374490.48	0	1945656.99	858400.88

注：不含民办的其他高等教育机构数据。
Note：Data of Non-government HEIs is not included.

校舍情况(普通高校)
Conditions of School Buildings (Regular HEIs)

单位:平方米
unit: m^2

地 区 Region	学校产权校舍建筑面积 Floor Area of School Building Owned by HEIs				正在施工校舍建筑面积 Floor Area Under Construction	非学校产权中独立使用建筑面积 Floor Area of School Building Not Owned by HEIs
	合计 Total	其中:危房 of Which: Dilapidated Buildings	其中:当年新增校舍 of Which: New Added in Current Year	其中:被外单位借用 of Which: Floor Space Hired by Other Schools or Units		
总 计 Total	**851852684.34**	**1326731.37**	**24555618.08**	**1371877.61**	**59954193.91**	**102150554.49**
北 京 Beijing	40248622.40	114273.26	477222.04	134465.70	2908352.69	1961012.85
天 津 Tianjin	16458575.05	2499.00	447647.25	0	2395443.39	1050403.84
河 北 Hebei	36263210.55	0	873421.80	0	1727005.53	1907460.91
山 西 Shanxi	20671962.30	17693.23	199101.74	9598.27	1319933.52	2496772.35
内蒙古 Inner Mongolia	13890643.67	6689.00	487133.41	1212.36	860933.74	894463.75
辽 宁 Liaoning	31452223.69	46532.57	657511.87	1510.00	1779620.86	3888449.98
吉 林 Jilin	18466716.33	0	96803.65	0	831119.70	2697406.35
黑龙江 Heilongjiang	26835102.70	16516.00	412917.15	2130.00	805720.85	1348183.57
上 海 Shanghai	21336208.24	0	514921.01	275045.88	1504953.15	2813216.53
江 苏 Jiangsu	58121664.61	55418.35	1248796.47	275756.09	3882231.12	8026645.32
浙 江 Zhejiang	32576757.96	1320.41	1183133.60	218346.52	3957149.41	5555422.71
安 徽 Anhui	34134848.23	77735.73	1136131.03	30502.35	1873268.33	1891899.70
福 建 Fujian	20314292.98	21943.00	244195.81	1966.40	1958420.42	6517980.28
江 西 Jiangxi	31368155.25	32747.30	492718.78	141823.20	1120866.30	3469909.95
山 东 Shandong	57848185.95	320503.43	1014376.70	18272.00	3456303.21	6203358.72
河 南 Henan	59206422.28	78285.00	2764685.35	87112.50	3050204.94	5206680.50
湖 北 Hubei	48386679.55	29834.98	667273.92	53248.95	2571675.53	5480960.64
湖 南 Hunan	35035199.80	108721.45	964812.74	0	1889310.60	4048457.27
广 东 Guangdong	43606955.11	18608.30	1837675.61	1104.00	1579586.72	14488549.79
广 西 Guangxi	22829218.89	61369.58	1566426.79	13673.00	2126837.74	3187115.43
海 南 Hainan	5275584.21	23951.61	4878.00	0	415771.65	1185190.26
重 庆 Chongqing	24055442.25	13261.29	776732.13	0	892583.68	1269955.83
四 川 Sichuan	38780911.45	37105.85	1197693.80	21537.63	4011323.44	6764717.75
贵 州 Guizhou	22809233.10	5522.40	1640329.33	11182.76	2288005.20	795595.55
云 南 Yunnan	16431535.60	112005.87	519236.97	67125.00	2413703.88	3309635.21
西 藏 Tibet	1286916.75	6602.00	18710.52	6265.00	174030.39	0
陕 西 Shaanxi	38715017.85	12947.95	1548244.88	0	4401856.09	4484390.81
甘 肃 Gansu	16130360.55	36340.40	616530.82	0	1575387.44	761697.76
青 海 Qinghai	2652814.53	5753.00	385877.00	0	139313.20	19124.00
宁 夏 Ningxia	4127115.69	0	197889.43	0	114667.20	54055.00
新 疆 Xinjiang	12536106.82	62550.41	362588.48	0	1928613.99	371841.88

校舍情况(成人高校)
Conditions of School Buildings (Adult HEIs)

单位:平方米
unit: m^2

地区 Region	学校产权校舍建筑面积 Floor Area of School Building Owned by HEIs				正在施工校舍建筑面积 Floor Area Under Construction	非学校产权中独立使用建筑面积 Floor Area of School Building Not Owned by HEIs
	合计 Total	其中:危房 of Which: Dilapidated Buildings	其中:当年新增校舍 of Which: New Added in Current Year	其中:被外单位借用 of Which: Floor Space Hired by Other Schools or Units		
总　计 Total	**11836217.13**	**29895.00**	**145729.71**	**8101.03**	**737594.93**	**12700078.60**
北　京 Beijing	922135.29	0	6294.00	0	0	9028.00
天　津 Tianjin	302732.25	0	11351.00	0	0	520693.00
河　北 Hebei	322745.00	0	0	0	2858.00	0
山　西 Shanxi	599702.68	0	0	0	0	40833.00
内蒙古 Inner Mongolia	85499.89	0	0	0	0	0
辽　宁 Liaoning	586044.63	0	3987.40	0	20650.50	1112806.79
吉　林 Jilin	401286.66	0	0	0	259251.60	239577.89
黑龙江 Heilongjiang	510502.06	0	0	0	14.00	450540.00
上　海 Shanghai	463250.12	0	0	6623.03	4497.00	758144.60
江　苏 Jiangsu	343371.00	0	0	0	0	2027415.85
浙　江 Zhejiang	303802.46	0	35139.48	0	77780.00	1783054.03
安　徽 Anhui	394431.82	0	10148.82	0	30257.00	407753.00
福　建 Fujian	103685.00	0	0	0	0	0
江　西 Jiangxi	307759.08	0	0	0	4799.55	51302.00
山　东 Shandong	576143.00	0	0	0	58002.00	0
河　南 Henan	570190.11	0	0	0	0	228870.80
湖　北 Hubei	296680.00	0	0	0	0	822371.00
湖　南 Hunan	438619.00	400.00	8840.00	0	180894.00	48523.00
广　东 Guangdong	385560.86	0	0	0	0	1873528.51
广　西 Guangxi	449596.08	27772.00	0	0	63504.00	133483.00
海　南 Hainan	79028.16	0	0	1478.00	0	0
重　庆 Chongqing	560410.25	0	28635.06	0	0	390757.06
四　川 Sichuan	817707.36	43.00	29077.95	0	18044.28	11220.80
贵　州 Guizhou	254325.37	0	354.00	0	0	749075.45
云　南 Yunnan	51745.00	0	0	0	0	0
西　藏 Tibet	0	0	0	0	0	0
陕　西 Shaanxi	951671.40	1680.00	0	0	0	554541.82
甘　肃 Gansu	121925.46	0	0	0	0	0
青　海 Qinghai	31855.00	0	0	0	0	0
宁　夏 Ningxia	28871.00	0	0	0	0	0
新　疆 Xinjiang	574941.14	0	11902.00	0	17043.00	486559.00

校舍情况(民办的其他高等教育机构)
Conditions of School Buildings (Other Non-government HEIs)

单位:平方米
unit: m^2

地 区 Region	学校产权校舍建筑面积 Floor Area of School Building Owned by HEIs				正在施工校舍建筑面积 Floor Area Under Construction	非学校产权中独立使用建筑面积 Floor Area of School Building Not Owned by HEIs
	合计 Total	其中:危房 of Which: Dilapidated Buildings	其中:当年新增校舍 of Which: New Added in Current Year	其中:被外单位借用 of Which: Floor Space Hired by Other Schools or Units		
总 计 Total	**2811007.74**	**0**	**85545.20**	**1000.00**	**202692.71**	**2909774.46**
北 京 Beijing	495168.53	0	9600.00	0	0	987342.26
天 津 Tianjin	0	0	0	0	0	0
河 北 Hebei	61491.62	0	5992.20	0	6309.42	55578.25
山 西 Shanxi	256295.00	0	1	0	0	93018.00
内蒙古 Inner Mongolia	0	0	0	0	0	0
辽 宁 Liaoning	171823.00	0	0	0	0	106734.00
吉 林 Jilin	32200.00	0	0	0	0	48222.00
黑龙江 Heilongjiang	10651.00	0	0	0	0	9800.00
上 海 Shanghai	60493.00	0	0	1000.00	1480.00	330154.10
江 苏 Jiangsu	0	0	0	0	0	0
浙 江 Zhejiang	279880.00	0	0	0	0	224485.00
安 徽 Anhui	195058.00	0	0	0	0	42612.00
福 建 Fujian	0	0	0	0	0	0
江 西 Jiangxi	159381.06	0	34370.00	0	98166.69	39719.00
山 东 Shandong	373910.48	0	0	0	0	244552.49
河 南 Henan	156645.18	0	182.00	0	0	109789.38
湖 北 Hubei	48065.00	0	0	0	0	155868.00
湖 南 Hunan	0	0	0	0	0	52383.00
广 东 Guangdong	72338.83	0	0	0	0	182702.20
广 西 Guangxi	0	0	0	0	0	0
海 南 Hainan	0	0	0	0	0	0
重 庆 Chongqing	220987.89	0	35400.00	0	92686.60	15534.00
四 川 Sichuan	194081.15	0	0	0	0	187597.90
贵 州 Guizhou	0	0	0	0	0	0
云 南 Yunnan	0	0	0	0	0	0
西 藏 Tibet	0	0	0	0	0	0
陕 西 Shaanxi	0	0	0	0	0	0
甘 肃 Gansu	22538.00	0	0	0	4050.00	23682.88
青 海 Qinghai	0	0	0	0	0	0
宁 夏 Ningxia	0	0	0	0	0	0
新 疆 Xinjiang	0	0	0	0	0	0

普通高中校数、班数(总计)
Number of Schools and Classes in Regular Senior Secondary Schools(Total)

地　区 Region	学校数(所) Schools				班数(个) Classes			
	合计 Total	完全中学 Combined Secondary Schools	高级中学 Regular High Schools	十二年一贯制学校 12-Year Schools	合计 Total	一年级 Grade 1	二年级 Grade 2	三年级 Grade 3
总　计 Total	**13555**	**5460**	**6780**	**1315**	**456760**	**153425**	**151928**	**151407**
北　京 Beijing	304	180	37	87	5157	1627	1697	1833
天　津 Tianjin	187	105	71	11	3913	1286	1305	1322
河　北 Hebei	630	209	367	54	22895	8061	7604	7230
山　西 Shanxi	505	211	250	44	14772	4784	4970	5018
内蒙古 Inner Mongolia	293	115	153	25	9530	3162	3190	3178
辽　宁 Liaoning	418	59	332	27	13439	4528	4467	4444
吉　林 Jilin	244	65	167	12	8173	2770	2730	2673
黑龙江 Heilongjiang	371	87	261	23	10900	3641	3664	3595
上　海 Shanghai	258	94	138	26	4717	1569	1565	1583
江　苏 Jiangsu	564	104	411	49	21109	6925	7055	7129
浙　江 Zhejiang	580	78	460	42	18454	6198	6156	6100
安　徽 Anhui	662	301	287	74	21426	7024	7146	7256
福　建 Fujian	534	421	83	30	13345	4371	4511	4463
江　西 Jiangxi	475	243	150	82	17214	5911	5696	5607
山　东 Shandong	592	101	433	58	32652	11222	10890	10540
河　南 Henan	813	156	569	88	32551	11241	10815	10495
湖　北 Hubei	532	77	407	48	15551	5088	5182	5281
湖　南 Hunan	608	210	322	76	20056	6965	6681	6410
广　东 Guangdong	1030	560	340	130	38055	12240	12715	13100
广　西 Guangxi	460	183	261	16	15942	5573	5347	5022
海　南 Hainan	116	79	14	23	3411	1141	1137	1133
重　庆 Chongqing	255	218	35	2	10870	3589	3557	3724
四　川 Sichuan	754	525	154	75	26033	8625	8542	8866
贵　州 Guizhou	451	167	237	47	18110	6249	5955	5906
云　南 Yunnan	509	333	147	29	14891	5237	4936	4718
西　藏 Tibet	34	5	26	3	1206	410	394	402
陕　西 Shaanxi	473	197	235	41	14577	4718	4775	5084
甘　肃 Gansu	384	158	210	16	11112	3576	3685	3851
青　海 Qinghai	101	37	45	19	2373	800	810	763
宁　夏 Ningxia	63	20	43	0	2740	912	889	939
新　疆 Xinjiang	355	162	135	58	11586	3982	3862	3742

普通高中校数、班数(城区)
Number of Schools and Classes in Regular Senior Secondary Schools(Urban Area)

地区 Region	学校数(所) Schools				班数(个) Classes			
	合计 Total	完全中学 Combined Secondary Schools	高级中学 Regular High Schools	十二年一贯制学校 12-Year Schools	合计 Total	一年级 Grade 1	二年级 Grade 2	三年级 Grade 3
总　计 Total	**6810**	**2765**	**3251**	**794**	**227141**	**75857**	**75784**	**75500**
北　京 Beijing	274	164	34	76	4876	1541	1619	1716
天　津 Tianjin	155	104	41	10	3258	1068	1092	1098
河　北 Hebei	280	122	136	22	9862	3448	3259	3155
山　西 Shanxi	243	148	71	24	6487	2111	2190	2186
内蒙古 Inner Mongolia	150	61	76	13	4877	1615	1638	1624
辽　宁 Liaoning	317	52	242	23	9743	3270	3237	3236
吉　林 Jilin	149	34	107	8	5511	1851	1830	1830
黑龙江 Heilongjiang	210	47	146	17	6394	2102	2161	2131
上　海 Shanghai	230	85	121	24	4227	1403	1402	1422
江　苏 Jiangsu	325	58	236	31	12186	3981	4120	4085
浙　江 Zhejiang	322	49	240	33	10684	3620	3565	3499
安　徽 Anhui	221	98	95	28	7545	2462	2545	2538
福　建 Fujian	208	153	37	18	6142	2040	2075	2027
江　西 Jiangxi	199	116	42	41	6744	2299	2249	2196
山　东 Shandong	324	63	234	27	17794	6079	5930	5785
河　南 Henan	327	81	216	30	12244	4184	4103	3957
湖　北 Hubei	324	52	237	35	9630	3160	3214	3256
湖　南 Hunan	230	91	104	35	7397	2544	2465	2388
广　东 Guangdong	648	307	237	104	26350	8596	8819	8935
广　西 Guangxi	200	77	112	11	6624	2290	2225	2109
海　南 Hainan	65	44	9	12	2096	692	696	708
重　庆 Chongqing	136	114	21	1	6171	2038	2022	2111
四　川 Sichuan	285	184	54	47	10998	3607	3616	3775
贵　州 Guizhou	161	56	80	25	6057	2108	1984	1965
云　南 Yunnan	220	141	57	22	5563	1922	1859	1782
西　藏 Tibet	15	1	11	3	537	180	178	179
陕　西 Shaanxi	239	130	79	30	6253	2040	2064	2149
甘　肃 Gansu	124	46	72	6	3466	1149	1149	1168
青　海 Qinghai	39	10	22	7	869	293	301	275
宁　夏 Ningxia	36	11	25	0	1687	565	545	577
新　疆 Xinjiang	154	66	57	31	4869	1599	1632	1638

普通高中校数、班数(城乡结合区)
Number of Schools and Classes in Regular Senior Secondary Schools (Urban-rural Transitional Area)

地 区 Region	学校数(所) Schools				班数(个) Classes			
	合计 Total	完全中学 Combined Secondary Schools	高级中学 Regular High Schools	十二年一贯制学校 12-Year Schools	合计 Total	一年级 Grade 1	二年级 Grade 2	三年级 Grade 3
总 计 Total	**1053**	**337**	**520**	**196**	**36251**	**12353**	**12041**	**11857**
北 京 Beijing	24	8	5	11	317	102	102	113
天 津 Tianjin	12	5	6	1	318	109	104	105
河 北 Hebei	57	14	35	8	2264	834	719	711
山 西 Shanxi	30	14	12	4	817	274	275	268
内蒙古 Inner Mongolia	8	2	6	0	216	69	70	77
辽 宁 Liaoning	29	4	23	2	1114	372	361	381
吉 林 Jilin	10	3	6	1	209	72	71	66
黑龙江 Heilongjiang	15	3	11	1	351	118	120	113
上 海 Shanghai	14	2	8	4	246	85	80	81
江 苏 Jiangsu	34	6	24	4	1401	453	471	477
浙 江 Zhejiang	86	10	66	10	2656	913	887	856
安 徽 Anhui	43	19	19	5	1332	420	451	461
福 建 Fujian	29	19	3	7	794	265	273	256
江 西 Jiangxi	15	5	4	6	548	192	177	179
山 东 Shandong	87	16	61	10	4813	1643	1619	1551
河 南 Henan	61	6	43	12	2196	799	726	671
湖 北 Hubei	51	9	28	14	1493	512	493	488
湖 南 Hunan	30	9	14	7	933	314	309	310
广 东 Guangdong	191	76	74	41	7618	2502	2563	2553
广 西 Guangxi	33	12	17	4	1257	439	418	400
海 南 Hainan	8	5	2	1	208	69	68	71
重 庆 Chongqing	7	4	3	0	350	120	113	117
四 川 Sichuan	36	17	4	15	1013	343	335	335
贵 州 Guizhou	31	9	12	10	1033	373	341	319
云 南 Yunnan	59	37	12	10	1549	558	504	487
西 藏 Tibet	0	0	0	0	0	0	0	0
陕 西 Shaanxi	23	10	10	3	554	176	178	200
甘 肃 Gansu	6	4	2	0	77	30	25	22
青 海 Qinghai	6	2	4	0	140	46	47	47
宁 夏 Ningxia	3	2	1	0	77	30	23	24
新 疆 Xinjiang	15	5	5	5	357	121	118	118

普通高中校数、班数(镇区)

Number of Schools and Classes in Regular Senior Secondary Schools(Counties & Town Area)

地 区 Region	学校数(所) Schools				班数(个) Classes			
	合计 Total	完全中学 Combined Secondary Schools	高级中学 Regular High Schools	十二年一贯制学校 12-Year Schools	合计 Total	一年级 Grade 1	二年级 Grade 2	三年级 Grade 3
总 计 Total	**6070**	**2397**	**3266**	**407**	**214223**	**72127**	**71035**	**71061**
北 京 Beijing	13	8	2	3	117	33	27	57
天 津 Tianjin	28	1	26	1	577	192	187	198
河 北 Hebei	322	81	217	24	12221	4298	4089	3834
山 西 Shanxi	218	44	159	15	7304	2331	2455	2518
内蒙古 Inner Mongolia	133	49	75	9	4489	1490	1500	1499
辽 宁 Liaoning	90	5	82	3	3360	1132	1125	1103
吉 林 Jilin	86	28	56	2	2558	878	858	822
黑龙江 Heilongjiang	154	39	110	5	4324	1477	1436	1411
上 海 Shanghai	22	5	15	2	420	141	139	140
江 苏 Jiangsu	235	44	173	18	8761	2890	2880	2991
浙 江 Zhejiang	221	21	193	7	6920	2292	2306	2322
安 徽 Anhui	405	188	179	38	13153	4331	4355	4467
福 建 Fujian	285	230	45	10	6615	2135	2237	2243
江 西 Jiangxi	252	116	103	33	10101	3490	3326	3285
山 东 Shandong	250	36	191	23	14476	4994	4831	4651
河 南 Henan	451	70	326	55	19539	6750	6460	6329
湖 北 Hubei	187	23	152	12	5446	1773	1810	1863
湖 南 Hunan	345	110	198	37	11876	4139	3954	3783
广 东 Guangdong	316	217	85	14	9837	3049	3277	3511
广 西 Guangxi	235	94	137	4	8323	2913	2795	2615
海 南 Hainan	40	29	4	7	1097	363	360	374
重 庆 Chongqing	109	95	14	0	4313	1420	1411	1482
四 川 Sichuan	441	322	98	21	14590	4867	4773	4950
贵 州 Guizhou	265	99	150	16	11581	3958	3821	3802
云 南 Yunnan	255	171	80	4	8596	3033	2837	2726
西 藏 Tibet	6	1	5	0	192	57	65	70
陕 西 Shaanxi	221	62	149	10	8011	2581	2605	2825
甘 肃 Gansu	240	102	132	6	7237	2293	2399	2545
青 海 Qinghai	56	25	20	11	1365	460	462	443
宁 夏 Ningxia	27	9	18	0	1053	347	344	362
新 疆 Xinjiang	162	73	72	17	5771	2020	1911	1840

普通高中校数、班数(镇乡结合区)
Number of Schools and Classes in Regular Senior Secondary Schools(County-town Transitional Area)

地区 Region	学校数(所) Schools				班数(个) Classes			
	合计 Total	完全中学 Combined Secondary Schools	高级中学 Regular High Schools	十二年一贯制学校 12-Year Schools	合计 Total	一年级 Grade 1	二年级 Grade 2	三年级 Grade 3
总 计 Total	**1486**	**527**	**832**	**127**	**52863**	**18026**	**17559**	**17278**
北 京 Beijing	6	3	2	1	55	15	10	30
天 津 Tianjin	16	0	16	0	373	126	121	126
河 北 Hebei	136	43	83	10	5148	1827	1713	1608
山 西 Shanxi	82	15	59	8	2635	836	884	915
内蒙古 Inner Mongolia	13	3	9	1	408	139	135	134
辽 宁 Liaoning	12	3	8	1	305	105	106	94
吉 林 Jilin	4	2	2	0	142	47	53	42
黑龙江 Heilongjiang	15	4	10	1	450	151	148	151
上 海 Shanghai	5	2	2	1	69	22	23	24
江 苏 Jiangsu	57	10	43	4	2197	703	718	776
浙 江 Zhejiang	68	6	59	3	2185	734	720	731
安 徽 Anhui	75	34	29	12	2136	713	705	718
福 建 Fujian	74	61	9	4	1681	550	578	553
江 西 Jiangxi	45	20	17	8	1513	532	526	455
山 东 Shandong	110	18	80	12	6333	2210	2120	2003
河 南 Henan	151	22	111	18	5923	2085	1959	1879
湖 北 Hubei	44	5	36	3	1194	400	399	395
湖 南 Hunan	69	22	37	10	2244	792	749	703
广 东 Guangdong	117	77	36	4	4226	1327	1400	1499
广 西 Guangxi	32	13	18	1	969	363	329	277
海 南 Hainan	11	8	1	2	305	102	101	102
重 庆 Chongqing	18	17	1	0	932	299	301	332
四 川 Sichuan	56	29	19	8	1641	580	511	550
贵 州 Guizhou	62	25	30	7	2328	809	763	756
云 南 Yunnan	70	43	26	1	2486	897	815	774
西 藏 Tibet	0	0	0	0	0	0	0	0
陕 西 Shaanxi	58	15	38	5	2069	674	697	698
甘 肃 Gansu	46	17	29	0	1524	499	507	518
青 海 Qinghai	10	4	6	0	381	128	133	120
宁 夏 Ningxia	3	0	3	0	102	34	33	35
新 疆 Xinjiang	21	6	13	2	909	327	302	280

普通高中校数、班数(乡村)
Number of Schools and Classes in Regular Senior Secondary Schools(Rural Area)

地区 Region	学校数(所) Schools				班数(个) Classes			
	合计 Total	完全中学 Combined Secondary Schools	高级中学 Regular High Schools	十二年一贯制学校 12-Year Schools	合计 Total	一年级 Grade 1	二年级 Grade 2	三年级 Grade 3
总　计 Total	**675**	**298**	**263**	**114**	**15396**	**5441**	**5109**	**4846**
北　京 Beijing	17	8	1	8	164	53	51	60
天　津 Tianjin	4	0	4	0	78	26	26	26
河　北 Hebei	28	6	14	8	812	315	256	241
山　西 Shanxi	44	19	20	5	981	342	325	314
内蒙古 Inner Mongolia	10	5	2	3	164	57	52	55
辽　宁 Liaoning	11	2	8	1	336	126	105	105
吉　林 Jilin	9	3	4	2	104	41	42	21
黑龙江 Heilongjiang	7	1	5	1	182	62	67	53
上　海 Shanghai	6	4	2	0	70	25	24	21
江　苏 Jiangsu	4	2	2	0	162	54	55	53
浙　江 Zhejiang	37	8	27	2	850	286	285	279
安　徽 Anhui	36	15	13	8	728	231	246	251
福　建 Fujian	41	38	1	2	588	196	199	193
江　西 Jiangxi	24	11	5	8	369	122	121	126
山　东 Shandong	18	2	8	8	382	149	129	104
河　南 Henan	35	5	27	3	768	307	252	209
湖　北 Hubei	21	2	18	1	475	155	158	162
湖　南 Hunan	33	9	20	4	783	282	262	239
广　东 Guangdong	66	36	18	12	1868	595	619	654
广　西 Guangxi	25	12	12	1	995	370	327	298
海　南 Hainan	11	6	1	4	218	86	81	51
重　庆 Chongqing	10	9	0	1	386	131	124	131
四　川 Sichuan	28	19	2	7	445	151	153	141
贵　州 Guizhou	25	12	7	6	472	183	150	139
云　南 Yunnan	34	21	10	3	732	282	240	210
西　藏 Tibet	13	3	10	0	477	173	151	153
陕　西 Shaanxi	13	5	7	1	313	97	106	110
甘　肃 Gansu	20	10	6	4	409	134	137	138
青　海 Qinghai	6	2	3	1	139	47	47	45
宁　夏 Ningxia	0	0	0	0	0	0	0	0
新　疆 Xinjiang	39	23	6	10	946	363	319	264

普通高中学生数(总计)
Number of Students in Regular Senior Secondary Schools (Total)

单位:人
unit: person

地 区 Region	毕业生数 Graduates	招生数 Entrants	在校生数 Enrolment					预计毕业生数 Estimated Graduates for Next Year
			合计 Total	其中:女 of Which: Female	一年级 Grade 1	二年级 Grade 2	三年级 Grade 3	
总 计 Total	**7757292**	**8000548**	**23745484**	**12073415**	**8005548**	**7913696**	**7826240**	**7825449**
北 京 Beijing	49685	53755	163977	83900	54068	53980	55929	55929
天 津 Tianjin	55239	54984	163601	84898	54993	54665	53943	53943
河 北 Hebei	376969	457055	1291375	681788	457055	432318	402002	402002
山 西 Shanxi	260270	227416	719683	377521	227426	244463	247794	247794
内蒙古 Inner Mongolia	153262	143632	435827	229123	143632	145584	146611	146611
辽 宁 Liaoning	202502	213683	629623	331714	213712	209095	206816	206816
吉 林 Jilin	130110	141705	413783	218085	141705	138633	133445	133445
黑龙江 Heilongjiang	181619	189010	556496	292090	189010	186206	181280	181280
上 海 Shanghai	51344	53276	158924	83142	53800	52978	52146	52146
江 苏 Jiangsu	317594	314573	943365	458506	314765	315592	313008	313008
浙 江 Zhejiang	246221	259298	773353	396482	259319	258352	255682	255682
安 徽 Anhui	376695	352692	1084974	512084	353548	361854	369572	369572
福 建 Fujian	196523	208867	637102	325606	208948	216179	211975	211975
江 西 Jiangxi	301912	334383	966977	432045	334733	323028	309216	309216
山 东 Shandong	553774	550056	1654861	854374	550060	554614	550187	550187
河 南 Henan	631394	709731	2054919	1042648	709991	682795	662133	662133
湖 北 Hubei	289536	271228	819413	391182	271272	272891	275250	275250
湖 南 Hunan	344076	398100	1146267	562400	398108	383529	364630	364630
广 东 Guangdong	676686	611384	1892669	929764	611753	633794	647122	645959
广 西 Guangxi	281761	350724	974811	525632	350775	327125	296911	296977
海 南 Hainan	56105	56627	171077	83443	56638	57297	57142	57448
重 庆 Chongqing	210874	201279	601804	309945	201494	195839	204471	204471
四 川 Sichuan	490317	464671	1412959	724463	464843	465495	482621	482621
贵 州 Guizhou	323440	348498	1011043	528648	348508	330755	331780	331780
云 南 Yunnan	252177	297919	834140	466431	298107	278364	257669	257669
西 藏 Tibet	18339	20587	58758	31691	20608	19043	19107	19107
陕 西 Shaanxi	266982	243804	756647	371612	244405	248438	263804	263804
甘 肃 Gansu	208113	182636	577281	286972	182636	192357	202288	202288
青 海 Qinghai	38284	42437	123865	65055	43020	41543	39302	39302
宁 夏 Ningxia	53632	49189	148837	80416	49207	47284	52346	52346
新 疆 Xinjiang	161857	197349	567073	311755	197409	189606	180058	180058

普通高中学生数(城区)
Number of Students in Senior Secondary Schools (Urban Area)

单位:人
unit: person

地 区 Region	毕业生数 Graduates	招生数 Entrants	在校生数 Enrolment					预计毕业生数 Estimated Graduates for Next Year
			合计 Total	其中:女 of Which: Female	一年级 Grade 1	二年级 Grade 2	三年级 Grade 3	
总 计 Total	**3733722**	**3786008**	**11314380**	**5765683**	**3788086**	**3775470**	**3750824**	**3750129**
北 京 Beijing	47033	50991	155492	79680	51302	51457	52733	52733
天 津 Tianjin	45386	45078	134290	69523	45087	44980	44223	44223
河 北 Hebei	161930	188673	538488	285697	188673	179526	170289	170289
山 西 Shanxi	112047	99060	313001	164938	99063	106887	107051	107051
内蒙古 Inner Mongolia	77944	73980	224416	119175	73980	74852	75584	75584
辽 宁 Liaoning	143026	150347	444879	232946	150364	147339	147176	147176
吉 林 Jilin	89239	94503	278401	147324	94503	92584	91314	91314
黑龙江 Heilongjiang	104990	107203	318940	166809	107203	107095	104642	104642
上 海 Shanghai	45773	47406	141587	74090	47859	47188	46540	46540
江 苏 Jiangsu	176067	179330	538786	266674	179415	181903	177468	177468
浙 江 Zhejiang	140862	152015	448619	228348	152024	149608	146987	146987
安 徽 Anhui	129704	122163	373772	179002	122227	125695	125850	125850
福 建 Fujian	91334	99261	298850	153662	99278	101131	98441	98441
江 西 Jiangxi	117134	127434	371000	166428	127533	123930	119537	119537
山 东 Shandong	299748	293095	880990	458199	293095	294415	293480	293480
河 南 Henan	226811	245884	721304	372235	245899	240636	234769	234769
湖 北 Hubei	175490	165373	498096	239278	165380	165513	167203	167203
湖 南 Hunan	123657	138379	404170	196735	138379	135143	130648	130648
广 东 Guangdong	452773	426030	1302442	637900	426391	437012	439039	437972
广 西 Guangxi	115185	136160	387644	208454	136195	130490	120959	121025
海 南 Hainan	35147	34346	104456	49613	34341	34681	35434	35740
重 庆 Chongqing	116195	110082	334168	173705	110121	109891	114156	114156
四 川 Sichuan	207608	189969	582394	298684	190025	191124	201245	201245
贵 州 Guizhou	106555	112144	323742	168783	112144	104619	106979	106979
云 南 Yunnan	91949	104074	298160	168111	104115	99928	94117	94117
西 藏 Tibet	8680	8917	26206	14378	8934	8597	8675	8675
陕 西 Shaanxi	108117	102464	316970	157235	102499	104513	109958	109958
甘 肃 Gansu	61198	58179	178728	88744	58179	59665	60884	60884
青 海 Qinghai	14096	14612	43858	22702	15007	15040	13811	13811
宁 夏 Ningxia	32470	30878	93271	50025	30878	29747	32646	32646
新 疆 Xinjiang	75574	77978	237260	126606	77993	80281	78986	78986

普通高中学生数(城乡结合区)
Number of Students in Senior Secondary Schools (Urban-rural Transitional Area)

单位:人
unit:person

地 区 Region	毕业生数 Graduates	招生数 Entrants	在校生数 Enrolment					预计毕业生数 Estimated Graduates for Next Year
			合计 Total	其中:女 of Which: Female	一年级 Grade 1	二年级 Grade 2	三年级 Grade 3	
总 计 Total	**592741**	**627906**	**1840746**	**921957**	**628133**	**612059**	**600554**	**600566**
北 京 Beijing	2823	3277	9393	4888	3282	2790	3321	3321
天 津 Tianjin	4897	4832	14242	7736	4832	4797	4613	4613
河 北 Hebei	39274	46939	127104	65416	46939	40987	39178	39178
山 西 Shanxi	13745	11789	37293	19920	11789	12791	12713	12713
内蒙古 Inner Mongolia	3315	2886	9422	4665	2886	3130	3406	3406
辽 宁 Liaoning	17741	18006	53632	27510	18009	17415	18208	18208
吉 林 Jilin	3179	3787	10626	5281	3787	3565	3274	3274
黑龙江 Heilongjiang	5339	5556	16260	8073	5556	5563	5141	5141
上 海 Shanghai	2506	2989	8701	4777	3072	2817	2812	2812
江 苏 Jiangsu	20553	20780	63497	30342	20815	21291	21391	21391
浙 江 Zhejiang	32721	38224	111234	55610	38226	37039	35969	35969
安 徽 Anhui	21246	20816	62526	29988	20816	20699	21011	21011
福 建 Fujian	11128	12818	38966	19510	12820	13459	12687	12687
江 西 Jiangxi	8670	10223	30442	13153	10228	10024	10190	10190
山 东 Shandong	79576	80311	241201	121628	80311	81233	79657	79657
河 南 Henan	40168	47752	132392	66581	47752	43377	41263	41263
湖 北 Hubei	28525	27772	80844	39011	27772	26716	26356	26356
湖 南 Hunan	15772	17193	52699	25178	17193	17641	17865	17865
广 东 Guangdong	131359	127392	383648	184833	127424	128815	127409	127421
广 西 Guangxi	21679	25599	73059	39200	25599	24560	22900	22900
海 南 Hainan	4069	3730	11245	5187	3730	3838	3677	3677
重 庆 Chongqing	5951	6850	19503	9494	6850	6317	6336	6336
四 川 Sichuan	15321	16301	48269	25391	16301	15990	15978	15978
贵 州 Guizhou	15296	20230	55786	29022	20230	18198	17358	17358
云 南 Yunnan	27917	32139	88864	48750	32166	29352	27346	27346
西 藏 Tibet	0	0	0	0	0	0	0	0
陕 西 Shaanxi	9638	8598	27695	13745	8605	8970	10120	10120
甘 肃 Gansu	1308	1460	3838	1848	1460	1264	1114	1114
青 海 Qinghai	2548	2216	6832	3509	2242	2291	2299	2299
宁 夏 Ningxia	1304	1510	3891	2127	1510	1171	1210	1210
新 疆 Xinjiang	5173	5931	17642	9584	5931	5959	5752	5752

普通高中学生数(镇区)
Number of Students in Senior Secondary Schools (Counties & Towns Area)

单位:人
unit:person

地 区 Region	毕业生数 Graduates	招生数 Entrants	在校生数 Enrolment 合计 Total	其中:女 of Which: Female	一年级 Grade 1	二年级 Grade 2	三年级 Grade 3	预计毕业生数 Estimated Graduates for Next Year
总 计 Total	**3792139**	**3936780**	**11651820**	**5920699**	**3939635**	**3878324**	**3833861**	**3833765**
北 京 Beijing	1229	843	2973	1394	844	777	1352	1352
天 津 Tianjin	8717	8735	25937	13640	8735	8596	8606	8606
河 北 Hebei	202555	250706	706509	372366	250706	238145	217658	217658
山 西 Shanxi	131783	112500	359509	188981	112505	121464	125540	125540
内蒙古 Inner Mongolia	73048	66994	203769	106060	66994	68309	68466	68466
辽 宁 Liaoning	54337	57204	168399	90420	57216	56565	54618	54618
吉 林 Jilin	40547	45317	130801	68891	45317	44087	41397	41397
黑龙江 Heilongjiang	73952	78531	227944	120371	78531	75605	73808	73808
上 海 Shanghai	4894	5108	15173	7911	5176	5075	4922	4922
江 苏 Jiangsu	139015	132671	396864	188087	132778	131145	132941	132941
浙 江 Zhejiang	94335	95494	290019	150728	95506	97284	97229	97229
安 徽 Anhui	235158	219272	674476	316403	220064	223368	231044	231044
福 建 Fujian	97992	100891	312279	160143	100952	106209	105118	105118
江 西 Jiangxi	179086	201004	578879	259496	201223	193229	184427	184427
山 东 Shandong	249877	249857	755217	387593	249861	253588	251768	251768
河 南 Henan	392179	445680	1287272	647624	445925	427116	414231	414231
湖 北 Hubei	106219	98286	297857	141549	98323	99375	100159	100159
湖 南 Hunan	207935	243033	696723	344189	243041	232860	220822	220822
广 东 Guangdong	189742	155510	498136	246921	155515	166359	176262	176166
广 西 Guangxi	150900	192598	529509	287200	192611	177547	159351	159351
海 南 Hainan	18473	18264	55891	28670	18270	18572	19049	19049
重 庆 Chongqing	87258	83822	246220	125761	83995	79211	83014	83014
四 川 Sichuan	276908	267496	809366	414915	267612	267065	274689	274689
贵 州 Guizhou	210473	226955	662144	346986	226965	218001	217178	217178
云 南 Yunnan	149894	178538	497231	276852	178684	165839	152708	152708
西 藏 Tibet	3276	2891	9185	4972	2895	3075	3215	3215
陕 西 Shaanxi	153332	136562	424436	207194	137126	138746	148564	148564
甘 肃 Gansu	139430	117156	376223	187511	117156	125205	133862	133862
青 海 Qinghai	22412	25211	72786	38513	25397	24146	23243	23243
宁 夏 Ningxia	21162	18311	55566	30391	18329	17537	19700	19700
新 疆 Xinjiang	76021	101340	284527	158967	101383	94224	88920	88920

普通高中学生数(镇乡结合区)
Number of Students in Senior Secondary Schools (County-town Transitional Area)

单位:人
unit:person

地 区 Region	毕业生数 Graduates	招生数 Entrants	在校生数 Enrolment 合计 Total	其中:女 of Which: Female	一年级 Grade 1	二年级 Grade 2	三年级 Grade 3	预计毕业生数 Estimated Graduates for Next Year
总 计 Total	**898492**	**967771**	**2832734**	**1440125**	**969421**	**941606**	**921707**	**921602**
北 京 Beijing	558	311	1078	533	311	300	467	467
天 津 Tianjin	5510	5682	16847	8901	5682	5645	5520	5520
河 北 Hebei	83892	107665	300194	157080	107665	99825	92704	92704
山 西 Shanxi	46686	39764	127207	66035	39764	43076	44367	44367
内蒙古 Inner Mongolia	6631	6365	18737	9179	6365	6301	6071	6071
辽 宁 Liaoning	4148	5277	14838	7736	5277	5192	4369	4369
吉 林 Jilin	1870	2267	6573	3503	2267	2368	1938	1938
黑龙江 Heilongjiang	6923	7557	23105	11990	7557	7873	7675	7675
上 海 Shanghai	970	794	2586	1352	796	867	923	923
江 苏 Jiangsu	36575	31767	97803	46460	31771	32120	33912	33912
浙 江 Zhejiang	30974	31075	92867	48396	31077	30734	31056	31056
安 徽 Anhui	34627	35151	106471	50253	35836	34910	35725	35725
福 建 Fujian	23395	25705	78559	39390	25717	27080	25762	25762
江 西 Jiangxi	26144	30954	87198	38329	30971	29952	26275	26275
山 东 Shandong	105890	111281	329205	169038	111285	110577	107343	107343
河 南 Henan	111699	131952	373745	189596	131952	122910	118883	118883
湖 北 Hubei	24136	23150	68653	33438	23171	23128	22354	22354
湖 南 Hunan	38902	47708	134846	66764	47708	44810	42328	42328
广 东 Guangdong	77720	67851	214508	105829	67853	71104	75551	75446
广 西 Guangxi	14468	22878	58626	29880	22878	19761	15987	15987
海 南 Hainan	4976	5176	15346	8124	5179	5140	5027	5027
重 庆 Chongqing	19609	18335	55147	28877	18471	17341	19335	19335
四 川 Sichuan	28355	27800	80978	42070	27803	25675	27500	27500
贵 州 Guizhou	39701	44283	127894	66198	44288	41475	42131	42131
云 南 Yunnan	39839	50853	138410	77920	50904	45863	41643	41643
西 藏 Tibet	0	0	0	0	0	0	0	0
陕 西 Shaanxi	36422	35066	109273	51942	35588	36743	36942	36942
甘 肃 Gansu	28412	24969	78318	39628	24969	26275	27074	27074
青 海 Qinghai	6531	7144	21408	11174	7315	7285	6808	6808
宁 夏 Ningxia	2043	2037	6015	3281	2037	1896	2082	2082
新 疆 Xinjiang	10886	16954	46299	27229	16964	15380	13955	13955

普通高中学生数(乡村)
Number of Students in Senior Secondary Schools (Rural Area)

单位:人
unit: person

地区 Region	毕业生数 Graduates	招生数 Entrants	在校生数 Enrolment 合计 Total	其中:女 of Which: Female	一年级 Grade 1	二年级 Grade 2	三年级 Grade 3	预计毕业生数 Estimated Graduates for Next Year
总 计 Total	**231431**	**277760**	**779284**	**387033**	**277827**	**259902**	**241555**	**241555**
北 京 Beijing	1423	1921	5512	2826	1922	1746	1844	1844
天 津 Tianjin	1136	1171	3374	1735	1171	1089	1114	1114
河 北 Hebei	12484	17676	46378	23725	17676	14647	14055	14055
山 西 Shanxi	16440	15856	47173	23602	15858	16112	15203	15203
内蒙古 Inner Mongolia	2270	2658	7642	3888	2658	2423	2561	2561
辽 宁 Liaoning	5139	6132	16345	8348	6132	5191	5022	5022
吉 林 Jilin	324	1885	4581	1870	1885	1962	734	734
黑龙江 Heilongjiang	2677	3276	9612	4910	3276	3506	2830	2830
上 海 Shanghai	677	762	2164	1141	765	715	684	684
江 苏 Jiangsu	2512	2572	7715	3745	2572	2544	2599	2599
浙 江 Zhejiang	11024	11789	34715	17406	11789	11460	11466	11466
安 徽 Anhui	11833	11257	36726	16679	11257	12791	12678	12678
福 建 Fujian	7197	8715	25973	11801	8718	8839	8416	8416
江 西 Jiangxi	5692	5945	17098	6121	5977	5869	5252	5252
山 东 Shandong	4149	7104	18654	8582	7104	6611	4939	4939
河 南 Henan	12404	18167	46343	22789	18167	15043	13133	13133
湖 北 Hubei	7827	7569	23460	10355	7569	8003	7888	7888
湖 南 Hunan	12484	16688	45374	21476	16688	15526	13160	13160
广 东 Guangdong	34171	29844	92091	44943	29847	30423	31821	31821
广 西 Guangxi	15676	21966	57658	29978	21969	19088	16601	16601
海 南 Hainan	2485	4017	10730	5160	4027	4044	2659	2659
重 庆 Chongqing	7421	7375	21416	10479	7378	6737	7301	7301
四 川 Sichuan	5801	7206	21199	10864	7206	7306	6687	6687
贵 州 Guizhou	6412	9399	25157	12879	9399	8135	7623	7623
云 南 Yunnan	10334	15307	38749	21468	15308	12597	10844	10844
西 藏 Tibet	6383	8779	23367	12341	8779	7371	7217	7217
陕 西 Shaanxi	5533	4778	15241	7183	4780	5179	5282	5282
甘 肃 Gansu	7485	7301	22330	10717	7301	7487	7542	7542
青 海 Qinghai	1776	2614	7221	3840	2616	2357	2248	2248
宁 夏 Ningxia	0	0	0	0	0	0	0	0
新 疆 Xinjiang	10262	18031	45286	26182	18033	15101	12152	12152

普通高中女学生数
Number of Female Students in Regular Senior Secondary Schools

单位：人
unit：person

地　区 Region	毕业生数 Graduates	招生数 Entrants	在校生数 Enrolment 合计 Total	在校生数 Enrolment 一年级 Grade 1	在校生数 Enrolment 二年级 Grade 2	在校生数 Enrolment 三年级 Grade 3	预计毕业生数 Estimated Graduates for Next Year
总　计 Total	**3910258**	**4061922**	**12073415**	**4063957**	**4027316**	**3982142**	**3981544**
北　京 Beijing	26301	27670	83900	27829	27177	28894	28894
天　津 Tianjin	28746	28597	84898	28600	28580	27718	27718
河　北 Hebei	197710	241767	681788	241767	227781	212240	212240
山　西 Shanxi	136095	119347	377521	119352	127564	130605	130605
内蒙古 Inner Mongolia	79988	75001	229123	75001	76628	77494	77494
辽　宁 Liaoning	106128	112674	331714	112685	109807	109222	109222
吉　林 Jilin	67485	74467	218085	74467	73283	70335	70335
黑龙江 Heilongjiang	95174	98348	292090	98348	97562	96180	96180
上　海 Shanghai	27002	27800	83142	28063	27759	27320	27320
江　苏 Jiangsu	153763	152560	458506	152628	154341	151537	151537
浙　江 Zhejiang	126710	132473	396482	132484	132535	131463	131463
安　徽 Anhui	175889	167070	512084	167448	171239	173397	173397
福　建 Fujian	99946	105740	325606	105769	110790	109047	109047
江　西 Jiangxi	132072	149130	432045	149230	144921	137894	137894
山　东 Shandong	282104	283440	854374	283442	286208	284724	284724
河　南 Henan	318239	358891	1042648	359019	347408	336221	336221
湖　北 Hubei	133642	129985	391182	129997	130139	131046	131046
湖　南 Hunan	170618	192831	562400	192832	188693	180875	180875
广　东 Guangdong	331168	299633	929764	299728	310681	319355	318668
广　西 Guangxi	152101	186980	525632	186999	176716	161917	161917
海　南 Hainan	26913	27925	83443	27932	28045	27466	27555
重　庆 Chongqing	108254	102685	309945	102793	100956	106196	106196
四　川 Sichuan	250718	238152	724463	238220	239022	247221	247221
贵　州 Guizhou	166090	181949	528648	181956	173299	173393	173393
云　南 Yunnan	137605	167707	466431	167758	156389	142284	142284
西　藏 Tibet	10362	11141	31691	11151	10218	10322	10322
陕　西 Shaanxi	130716	119873	371612	120106	122883	128623	128623
甘　肃 Gansu	101748	91696	286972	91696	94763	100513	100513
青　海 Qinghai	19984	22242	65055	22481	22089	20485	20485
宁　夏 Ningxia	27998	26731	80416	26734	25442	28240	28240
新　疆 Xinjiang	88989	107417	311755	107442	104398	99915	99915

普通中学教职工数(总计)
Number of Educational Personnel in General Secondary Schools (Total)

单位:人
unit: person

地区 Region	教职工数 Educational Personnel						代课教师 Substitute Teachers	兼任教师 Part-time Teachers
	合计 Total	专任教师 Full-time Teachers	行政人员 Adm. Personnel	教辅人员 Supporting Staff	工勤人员 Workers	校办企业职工 Employees in School-run Factories & Farms		
总 计 Total	**6743149**	**5985039**	**192040**	**267032**	**296790**	**2248**	**67674**	**16748**
北 京 Beijing	86966	66635	7123	9514	3638	56	0	1180
天 津 Tianjin	54283	45939	3555	3593	1185	11	288	479
河 北 Hebei	348659	305676	11777	16682	14378	146	3292	327
山 西 Shanxi	220769	187836	5974	12631	14259	69	8132	1052
内蒙古 Inner Mongolia	131690	102894	6551	13915	8323	7	945	86
辽 宁 Liaoning	203494	176466	17755	5412	3845	16	58	85
吉 林 Jilin	133216	108671	7730	13125	3621	69	682	386
黑龙江 Heilongjiang	178931	150643	9280	10964	8043	1	1624	210
上 海 Shanghai	84172	67833	5891	6257	4156	35	322	283
江 苏 Jiangsu	353638	313611	7185	16194	16439	209	2622	148
浙 江 Zhejiang	249243	222385	5589	9459	11512	298	0	434
安 徽 Anhui	297780	264060	7092	9253	17345	30	3909	995
福 建 Fujian	179489	159515	5070	7845	6990	69	2002	154
江 西 Jiangxi	210049	200470	1567	2890	5065	57	654	838
山 东 Shandong	502004	455113	9547	22512	14781	51	2969	515
河 南 Henan	514076	462146	13391	13286	25248	5	17468	1308
湖 北 Hubei	244964	213770	6770	11475	12829	120	3171	743
湖 南 Hunan	313347	285312	7176	10218	10609	32	3134	572
广 东 Guangdong	593806	520388	15977	20270	36747	424	288	668
广 西 Guangxi	216934	195029	3368	7297	11155	85	1144	1231
海 南 Hainan	54144	46432	1292	1370	4893	157	1102	344
重 庆 Chongqing	132388	121746	2824	3536	4209	73	917	183
四 川 Sichuan	396986	364248	7127	9106	16478	27	4027	1165
贵 州 Guizhou	222933	204290	4163	3286	11130	64	124	1231
云 南 Yunnan	211987	194254	2636	3773	11214	110	8	830
西 藏 Tibet	16063	15515	135	120	293	0	7	1
陕 西 Shaanxi	197886	172287	9653	8902	7033	11	1830	112
甘 肃 Gansu	149536	139943	2429	4201	2961	2	1781	820
青 海 Qinghai	32288	30564	267	300	1149	8	718	91
宁 夏 Ningxia	35178	33243	336	914	685	0	568	70
新 疆 Xinjiang	176250	158125	2810	8732	6577	6	3888	207

普通中学教职工数(城区)
Number of Educational Personnel in General Secondary Schools (Urban Area)

单位:人
unit:person

地 区 Region	教职工数 Educational Personnel						代课教师 Substitute Teachers	兼任教师 Part-time Teachers
	合计 Total	专任教师 Full-time Teachers	行政人员 Adm. Personnel	教辅人员 Supporting Staff	工勤人员 Workers	校办企业职工 Employees in School-run Factories & Farms		
总 计 Total	**2724686**	**2379621**	**95409**	**122125**	**126071**	**1460**	**28268**	**8278**
北 京 Beijing	74053	57314	5892	7696	3095	56	0	1166
天 津 Tianjin	41332	34563	2742	3022	994	11	244	467
河 北 Hebei	115459	100891	3971	5687	4793	117	1584	125
山 西 Shanxi	79651	67019	2929	4198	5458	47	3681	797
内蒙古 Inner Mongolia	53064	43250	3536	4370	1905	3	466	23
辽 宁 Liaoning	113020	97928	10052	2873	2155	12	14	77
吉 林 Jilin	59312	49138	2974	5262	1869	69	430	243
黑龙江 Heilongjiang	81153	69477	4281	4910	2484	1	544	153
上 海 Shanghai	71453	57943	4823	5496	3156	35	292	230
江 苏 Jiangsu	177387	158326	3789	8112	7094	66	1465	71
浙 江 Zhejiang	135008	119158	3367	5326	6868	289	0	281
安 徽 Anhui	75631	67101	1970	2485	4069	6	1824	483
福 建 Fujian	69199	61457	2035	2664	2997	46	1309	92
江 西 Jiangxi	64982	61372	803	1033	1760	14	146	309
山 东 Shandong	220864	198975	4785	10689	6383	32	1862	343
河 南 Henan	143857	128679	5275	3901	5997	5	4857	345
湖 北 Hubei	116058	100052	3919	5389	6624	74	1888	202
湖 南 Hunan	88032	78157	2416	3772	3680	7	939	187
广 东 Guangdong	366735	314599	9279	15113	27387	357	262	497
广 西 Guangxi	67819	59754	1401	2812	3795	57	397	437
海 南 Hainan	25291	20975	750	780	2748	38	832	164
重 庆 Chongqing	61415	55654	1632	2006	2116	7	404	70
四 川 Sichuan	123230	108905	2945	4706	6672	2	1418	278
贵 州 Guizhou	56939	51375	1410	1178	2966	10	54	343
云 南 Yunnan	55055	49139	1314	1520	2993	89	3	297
西 藏 Tibet	5073	4821	56	38	158	0	0	0
陕 西 Shaanxi	70270	60103	4820	2866	2479	2	322	96
甘 肃 Gansu	35639	32716	924	981	1016	2	630	446
青 海 Qinghai	9440	8911	115	120	290	4	184	37
宁 夏 Ningxia	14999	14137	200	360	302	0	326	8
新 疆 Xinjiang	53266	47732	1004	2760	1768	2	1891	11

普通中学教职工数(城乡结合区)
Number of Educational Personnel in General Secondary Schools (Urban-rural Transitional Area)

单位:人
unit:person

地 区 Region	教职工数 Educational Personnel						代课教师 Substitute Teachers	兼任教师 Part-time Teachers
	合计 Total	专任教师 Full-time Teachers	行政人员 Adm. Personnel	教辅人员 Supporting Staff	工勤人员 Workers	校办企业职工 Employees in School-run Factories & Farms		
总 计 Total	**477284**	**410725**	**14694**	**20871**	**30700**	**294**	**3923**	**1145**
北 京 Beijing	7378	4796	742	1049	791	0	0	32
天 津 Tianjin	3299	2865	231	163	40	0	35	2
河 北 Hebei	28387	25055	821	1134	1333	44	253	26
山 西 Shanxi	9602	7631	321	614	1027	9	497	85
内蒙古 Inner Mongolia	1398	1083	63	154	98	0	31	0
辽 宁 Liaoning	10581	9375	780	190	234	2	2	1
吉 林 Jilin	2423	1911	173	270	67	2	22	1
黑龙江 Heilongjiang	6071	4864	330	508	369	0	15	11
上 海 Shanghai	5828	4994	360	260	209	5	40	2
江 苏 Jiangsu	21886	19257	469	1134	1026	0	135	4
浙 江 Zhejiang	34955	29786	1015	1341	2813	0	0	80
安 徽 Anhui	12351	10730	356	452	813	0	407	293
福 建 Fujian	10642	8926	365	441	896	14	113	4
江 西 Jiangxi	6660	6396	81	73	106	4	20	89
山 东 Shandong	61701	55025	1407	3100	2142	27	703	55
河 南 Henan	24846	22120	800	535	1391	0	802	30
湖 北 Hubei	18398	15103	569	851	1874	1	117	38
湖 南 Hunan	11723	10453	292	552	424	2	82	14
广 东 Guangdong	119891	101256	3375	4826	10382	52	32	103
广 西 Guangxi	12425	11203	160	403	621	38	126	46
海 南 Hainan	2348	1996	36	111	205	0	36	58
重 庆 Chongqing	4894	4415	89	95	295	0	23	9
四 川 Sichuan	15706	12600	505	1368	1233	0	88	14
贵 州 Guizhou	9789	8737	246	215	585	6	21	23
云 南 Yunnan	15109	13266	377	290	1088	88	0	107
西 藏 Tibet	0	0	0	0	0	0	0	0
陕 西 Shaanxi	7956	6629	550	505	272	0	7	0
甘 肃 Gansu	2218	2092	38	44	44	0	137	0
青 海 Qinghai	1780	1741	11	13	15	0	22	11
宁 夏 Ningxia	1115	1092	7	3	13	0	14	0
新 疆 Xinjiang	5924	5328	125	177	294	0	143	7

普通中学教职工数(镇区)

Number of Educational Personnel in General Secondary Schools (Counties & Towns Area)

单位:人
unit:person

地区 Region	教职工数 Educational Personnel						代课教师 Substitute Teachers	兼任教师 Part-time Teachers
	合计 Total	专任教师 Full-time Teachers	行政人员 Adm. Personnel	教辅人员 Supporting Staff	工勤人员 Workers	校办企业职工 Employees in School-run Factories & Farms		
总　计 Total	**3155322**	**2827793**	**73958**	**118137**	**134817**	**617**	**29099**	**6433**
北　京 Beijing	7154	5073	705	1067	309	0	0	8
天　津 Tianjin	9190	8041	551	445	153	0	33	12
河　北 Hebei	185625	161882	6091	9672	7951	29	1354	181
山　西 Shanxi	107352	92777	2128	6238	6191	18	3422	200
内蒙古 Inner Mongolia	69669	53098	2565	8396	5606	4	421	42
辽　宁 Liaoning	69241	59954	5839	2032	1413	3	29	2
吉　林 Jilin	49667	40263	2966	5213	1225	0	203	91
黑龙江 Heilongjiang	73084	60766	3681	4047	4590	0	667	41
上　海 Shanghai	10367	8191	862	568	746	0	21	50
江　苏 Jiangsu	162401	143398	3084	7433	8347	139	1124	77
浙　江 Zhejiang	93760	84771	1755	3438	3787	9	0	149
安　徽 Anhui	167279	147395	4005	5312	10543	24	1699	283
福　建 Fujian	84421	75345	2186	4081	2788	21	437	47
江　西 Jiangxi	110941	106429	435	1577	2475	25	393	444
山　东 Shandong	244975	223538	4115	10223	7080	19	929	131
河　南 Henan	286522	256185	6501	7756	16080	0	9981	895
湖　北 Hubei	102185	89940	2236	5009	4959	41	976	434
湖　南 Hunan	169383	154713	3493	5595	5557	25	1383	362
广　东 Guangdong	175456	161185	4928	3963	5358	22	22	77
广　西 Guangxi	124352	112789	1638	3851	6056	18	650	690
海　南 Hainan	24343	21677	410	483	1692	81	182	155
重　庆 Chongqing	60813	56745	1000	1336	1670	62	249	41
四　川 Sichuan	207745	193349	2902	3692	7777	25	1488	595
贵　州 Guizhou	137198	126207	2157	1859	6943	32	69	724
云　南 Yunnan	109820	101205	915	1924	5769	7	5	233
西　藏 Tibet	7075	6930	23	36	86	0	7	1
陕　西 Shaanxi	113240	99719	4151	5342	4019	9	1455	14
甘　肃 Gansu	83457	77850	1174	2893	1540	0	486	224
青　海 Qinghai	16626	15820	131	138	533	4	417	19
宁　夏 Ningxia	15300	14379	103	516	302	0	144	60
新　疆 Xinjiang	76681	68179	1228	4002	3272	0	853	151

普通中学教职工数(镇乡结合区)

Number of Educational Personnel in General Secondary Schools (County-town Transitional Area)

单位:人
unit:person

地 区 Region	教职工数 Educational Personnel						代课教师 Substitute Teachers	兼任教师 Part-time Teachers
	合计 Total	专任教师 Full-time Teachers	行政人员 Adm. Personnel	教辅人员 Supporting Staff	工勤人员 Workers	校办企业职工 Employees in School-run Factories & Farms		
总 计 Total	**771662**	**688438**	**18613**	**28550**	**35844**	**217**	**8878**	**1536**
北 京 Beijing	2828	1878	383	447	120	0	0	0
天 津 Tianjin	4416	3890	262	208	56	0	4	12
河 北 Hebei	80988	70645	2650	3807	3885	1	801	49
山 西 Shanxi	33672	28784	704	1996	2178	10	1156	89
内蒙古 Inner Mongolia	6785	4930	251	1126	478	0	16	0
辽 宁 Liaoning	7893	6947	610	218	117	1	2	0
吉 林 Jilin	4610	3666	332	519	93	0	25	2
黑龙江 Heilongjiang	6140	5316	238	362	224	0	23	0
上 海 Shanghai	2443	1875	189	183	196	0	9	39
江 苏 Jiangsu	40112	35483	763	1935	1908	23	524	3
浙 江 Zhejiang	29380	26540	608	1073	1153	6	0	98
安 徽 Anhui	33231	28286	960	1067	2918	0	627	179
福 建 Fujian	22687	19987	768	1014	907	11	111	31
江 西 Jiangxi	18239	17238	113	310	567	11	153	79
山 东 Shandong	96649	88313	1501	3931	2885	19	419	15
河 南 Henan	93966	82659	2435	2316	6556	0	3096	256
湖 北 Hubei	23412	20579	469	1058	1295	11	167	107
湖 南 Hunan	35483	32795	681	972	1035	0	367	140
广 东 Guangdong	57815	52902	1621	1283	1999	10	8	33
广 西 Guangxi	22379	20450	295	579	1055	0	89	118
海 南 Hainan	3298	2820	76	56	270	76	26	15
重 庆 Chongqing	10646	9882	186	287	286	5	58	18
四 川 Sichuan	28676	25961	632	662	1396	25	166	98
贵 州 Guizhou	23598	21575	478	307	1238	0	12	108
云 南 Yunnan	24513	22401	211	627	1272	2	4	39
西 藏 Tibet	651	639	4	0	8	0	4	0
陕 西 Shaanxi	23953	20974	849	1048	1080	2	693	0
甘 肃 Gansu	16467	15359	181	650	277	0	70	6
青 海 Qinghai	4204	4119	13	11	57	4	69	2
宁 夏 Ningxia	1602	1552	15	22	13	0	24	0
新 疆 Xinjiang	10926	9993	135	476	322	0	155	0

普通中学教职工数(乡村)

Number of Educational Personnel in General Secondary Schools(Rural Area)

单位:人
unit:person

地 区 Region	教职工数 Educational Personnel						代课教师 Substitute Teachers	兼任教师 Part-time Teachers
	合计 Total	专任教师 Full-time Teachers	行政人员 Adm. Personnel	教辅人员 Supporting Staff	工勤人员 Workers	校办企业职工 Employees in School-run Factories & Farms		
总 计 Total	**863141**	**777625**	**22673**	**26770**	**35902**	**171**	**10307**	**2037**
北 京 Beijing	5759	4248	526	751	234	0	0	6
天 津 Tianjin	3761	3335	262	126	38	0	11	0
河 北 Hebei	47575	42903	1715	1323	1634	0	354	21
山 西 Shanxi	33766	28040	917	2195	2610	4	1029	55
内蒙古 Inner Mongolia	8957	6546	450	1149	812	0	58	21
辽 宁 Liaoning	21233	18584	1864	507	277	1	15	6
吉 林 Jilin	24237	19270	1790	2650	527	0	49	52
黑龙江 Heilongjiang	24694	20400	1318	2007	969	0	413	16
上 海 Shanghai	2352	1699	206	193	254	0	9	3
江 苏 Jiangsu	13850	11887	312	649	998	4	33	0
浙 江 Zhejiang	20475	18456	467	695	857	0	0	4
安 徽 Anhui	54870	49564	1117	1456	2733	0	386	229
福 建 Fujian	25869	22713	849	1100	1205	2	256	15
江 西 Jiangxi	34126	32669	329	280	830	18	115	85
山 东 Shandong	36165	32600	647	1600	1318	0	178	41
河 南 Henan	83697	77282	1615	1629	3171	0	2630	68
湖 北 Hubei	26721	23778	615	1077	1246	5	307	107
湖 南 Hunan	55932	52442	1267	851	1372	0	812	23
广 东 Guangdong	51615	44604	1770	1194	4002	45	4	94
广 西 Guangxi	24763	22486	329	634	1304	10	97	104
海 南 Hainan	4510	3780	132	107	453	38	88	25
重 庆 Chongqing	10160	9347	192	194	423	4	264	72
四 川 Sichuan	66011	61994	1280	708	2029	0	1121	292
贵 州 Guizhou	28796	26708	596	249	1221	22	1	164
云 南 Yunnan	47112	43910	407	329	2452	14	0	300
西 藏 Tibet	3915	3764	56	46	49	0	0	0
陕 西 Shaanxi	14376	12465	682	694	535	0	53	2
甘 肃 Gansu	30440	29377	331	327	405	0	665	150
青 海 Qinghai	6222	5833	21	42	326	0	117	35
宁 夏 Ningxia	4879	4727	33	38	81	0	98	2
新 疆 Xinjiang	46303	42214	578	1970	1537	4	1144	45

普通中学女教职工数
Number of Female Educational Personnel in General Secondary Schools

单位：人
unit：person

地 区 Region	教职工数 Educational Personnel						代课教师 Substitute Teachers	兼任教师 Part-time Teachers
	合计 Total	专任教师 Full-time Teachers	行政人员 Adm. Personnel	教辅人员 Supporting Staff	工勤人员 Workers	校办企业职工 Employees in School-run Factories & Farms		
总 计 Total	**3712645**	**3387134**	**55102**	**137743**	**131508**	**1158**	**45533**	**9112**
北 京 Beijing	62471	50779	3943	6391	1344	14	0	831
天 津 Tianjin	36411	32594	1429	2112	274	2	211	343
河 北 Hebei	230650	212162	2863	9219	6348	58	2516	166
山 西 Shanxi	140685	125657	1698	6516	6794	20	5615	628
内蒙古 Inner Mongolia	78575	67453	2061	6770	2290	1	590	44
辽 宁 Liaoning	132554	121890	6562	3503	594	5	55	50
吉 林 Jilin	83069	73303	2060	6516	1179	11	454	197
黑龙江 Heilongjiang	109825	98567	3038	5438	2782	0	1127	104
上 海 Shanghai	58916	49550	3141	4452	1756	17	208	186
江 苏 Jiangsu	182664	167677	1527	6884	6498	78	1745	50
浙 江 Zhejiang	145022	131555	1723	5240	6287	217	0	241
安 徽 Anhui	128705	114358	1446	4162	8721	18	2072	468
福 建 Fujian	86389	78294	1248	3813	2986	48	1333	72
江 西 Jiangxi	97906	93679	565	1476	2158	28	415	482
山 东 Shandong	270655	254216	2188	8892	5331	28	2021	316
河 南 Henan	305742	282655	3875	6649	12563	0	12505	785
湖 北 Hubei	109774	97582	1493	4726	5933	40	1988	307
湖 南 Hunan	158967	148069	1128	5273	4477	20	2163	233
广 东 Guangdong	342125	307372	3434	12755	18319	245	206	370
广 西 Guangxi	117452	106692	970	4096	5644	50	782	672
海 南 Hainan	28588	24759	441	797	2506	85	802	188
重 庆 Chongqing	65314	61484	773	1721	1285	51	599	91
四 川 Sichuan	199557	185785	1737	5076	6937	22	2805	552
贵 州 Guizhou	102267	93269	856	1700	6405	37	63	577
云 南 Yunnan	108360	99974	771	1972	5587	56	7	519
西 藏 Tibet	8267	8002	56	70	139	0	5	0
陕 西 Shaanxi	108905	99290	2767	4323	2524	1	1092	71
甘 肃 Gansu	64072	61173	307	1748	843	1	855	365
青 海 Qinghai	17498	16686	70	145	593	4	416	28
宁 夏 Ningxia	19242	18466	75	475	226	0	385	52
新 疆 Xinjiang	112018	104142	857	4833	2185	1	2498	124

普通中学教职工总

Number of General Secondary Schools Educational

地 区 Region	教职工数		
	合计 Total	专任教师 Full-time Teachers	行政人员 Adm. Personnel
总 计 Total	**973882**	**738870**	**45680**
北 京 Beijing	12469	7433	1763
天 津 Tianjin	3596	2592	383
河 北 Hebei	58964	46629	2647
山 西 Shanxi	47844	34287	2067
内蒙古 Inner Mongolia	5660	4189	526
辽 宁 Liaoning	11887	10134	1129
吉 林 Jilin	10775	8358	584
黑龙江 Heilongjiang	8103	6076	556
上 海 Shanghai	12079	9055	912
江 苏 Jiangsu	52996	41848	1856
浙 江 Zhejiang	62628	48678	2281
安 徽 Anhui	66709	48460	3189
福 建 Fujian	23475	17460	1252
江 西 Jiangxi	22027	17237	884
山 东 Shandong	66093	53859	2595
河 南 Henan	109780	83710	5551
湖 北 Hubei	31151	22137	1407
湖 南 Hunan	37558	29842	1396
广 东 Guangdong	165838	126726	5425
广 西 Guangxi	20294	14305	1086
海 南 Hainan	10919	7009	661
重 庆 Chongqing	10962	8232	604
四 川 Sichuan	48202	34653	2183
贵 州 Guizhou	28270	21405	1347
云 南 Yunnan	16224	12642	1011
西 藏 Tibet	110	87	7
陕 西 Shaanxi	20614	15316	1823
甘 肃 Gansu	4267	3250	283
青 海 Qinghai	544	358	58
宁 夏 Ningxia	1298	1066	76
新 疆 Xinjiang	2546	1837	138

数中民办教职工数

Personnel Maintained by the Communities

单位：人
unit：person

Educational Personnel				
教辅人员 Supporting Staff	工勤人员 Workers	校办企业职工 Employees in School-run Factories & Farms	代课教师 Substitute Teachers	兼任教师 Part-time Teachers
44389	**143678**	**1265**	**13174**	**6919**
1407	1844	22	0	67
310	311	0	157	448
2342	7341	5	0	209
2124	9358	8	2733	744
237	708	0	31	12
373	244	7	0	52
611	1203	19	98	11
327	1144	0	0	23
1250	844	18	0	208
2411	6856	25	44	39
3016	8383	270	0	371
3148	11892	20	1428	746
1146	3551	66	25	102
1246	2611	49	380	613
2554	7057	28	533	156
3303	17212	4	7203	712
1452	6121	34	13	326
1858	4442	20	45	291
7271	26036	380	7	226
1058	3776	69	11	347
386	2814	49	0	1
492	1623	11	217	92
3173	8168	25	0	67
1013	4472	33	55	154
461	2009	101	0	369
5	11	0	0	0
975	2500	0	0	51
235	497	2	141	443
8	120	0	3	28
56	100	0	0	7
141	430	0	50	4

地　区 Region	合计 Total	其中：女 of Which: Female	按学历分 By Academic Qualification			
			研究生毕业 Graduate	本科毕业 Under-graduate	专科毕业 Associate Bachelor	高中阶段毕业 High School Graduate
总　计 Total	**1773953**	**941702**	**158550**	**1582588**	**32175**	**615**
北　京 Beijing	21452	15391	6061	15368	22	1
天　津 Tianjin	16504	11706	2752	13658	93	1
河　北 Hebei	94430	61579	7793	84474	2147	16
山　西 Shanxi	63941	39923	6012	56472	1446	11
内蒙古 Inner Mongolia	35652	21811	4339	30639	673	1
辽　宁 Liaoning	51346	35175	5280	45443	575	43
吉　林 Jilin	29934	19596	2767	26892	272	3
黑龙江 Heilongjiang	42452	27561	2937	38984	524	7
上　海 Shanghai	17937	11891	3893	14028	15	1
江　苏 Jiangsu	94719	46564	14951	79364	399	5
浙　江 Zhejiang	69608	36867	6698	62570	337	3
安　徽 Anhui	77998	31284	5339	71357	1295	7
福　建 Fujian	50720	24607	3209	46466	1034	11
江　西 Jiangxi	55727	24007	4653	47678	3334	57
山　东 Shandong	134446	71214	14072	119131	1182	55
河　南 Henan	124687	67401	11326	110322	2977	62
湖　北 Hubei	65929	26788	5023	59382	1426	95
湖　南 Hunan	75802	33434	4351	69769	1635	47
广　东 Guangdong	151435	82749	17218	132738	1471	8
广　西 Guangxi	55988	31095	3726	50945	1291	22
海　南 Hainan	13328	7357	735	12234	356	3
重　庆 Chongqing	39436	19407	2852	35931	626	27
四　川 Sichuan	97461	45644	5314	89974	2162	11
贵　州 Guizhou	64094	29839	2503	60021	1533	37
云　南 Yunnan	56573	29132	2509	53090	948	25
西　藏 Tibet	5187	2691	300	4807	80	0
陕　西 Shaanxi	57297	30695	6047	50653	589	8
甘　肃 Gansu	45386	18644	3053	40374	1919	39
青　海 Qinghai	9093	4711	449	8230	414	0
宁　夏 Ningxia	10904	5848	820	9923	160	1
新　疆 Xinjiang	44487	27091	1568	41671	1240	8

专业技术职务情况(总计)
Schools by Academic Qualification and Professional Rank(Total)

单位:人
unit: person

	按专业技术职务分 By Professional Rank				
高中阶段毕业以下 Below High School Graduate	中学高级 Senior Secondary	中学一级 1st Grade	中学二级 2nd Grade	中学三级 3rd Grade	未定职级 No-ranking
25	**491001**	**645724**	**478858**	**10546**	**147824**
0	8421	6676	4734	35	1586
0	6168	7049	2625	28	634
0	23728	38668	22123	1137	8774
0	12653	19640	22984	703	7961
0	11611	12582	8176	0	3283
5	20891	18204	8121	229	3901
0	8504	12091	6802	100	2437
0	13882	17237	9742	94	1497
0	5459	7888	3626	15	949
0	36593	37141	17064	10	3911
0	23763	24652	15106	200	5887
0	23417	27172	18094	957	8358
0	15880	19378	13241	76	2145
5	20471	16820	12111	473	5852
6	28652	50613	42953	559	11669
0	27640	41447	43778	996	10826
3	22018	27150	13528	570	2663
0	22247	28836	17639	477	6603
0	33985	63650	40284	769	12747
4	11851	21837	15398	918	5984
0	3607	4496	4085	90	1050
0	9754	14110	13647	69	1856
0	29877	36101	26049	217	5217
0	13929	18711	22201	624	8629
1	17114	17309	16785	70	5295
0	770	1805	1774	95	743
0	13728	20602	18731	221	4015
1	9278	16952	16623	242	2291
0	2440	2875	2345	441	992
0	2994	3227	3775	51	857
0	9676	10805	14714	80	9212

普通高中专任教师学历、
Number of Full-time Teachers in Regular Senior Secondary Schools by

地 区 Region	合计 Total	其中:女 of Which: Female	按学历分 By Academic Qualification			
			研究生毕业 Graduate	本科毕业 Under-graduate	专科毕业 Associate Bachelor	高中阶段毕业 High School Graduate
总 计 Total	**890694**	**505323**	**106342**	**773219**	**10981**	**148**
北 京 Beijing	20004	14441	5519	14462	22	1
天 津 Tianjin	13778	9967	2569	11145	64	0
河 北 Hebei	41719	28074	3973	36571	1165	10
山 西 Shanxi	27769	18061	3058	24238	472	1
内蒙古 Inner Mongolia	18468	11586	2742	15456	269	1
辽 宁 Liaoning	37585	26290	4365	32888	311	20
吉 林 Jilin	19901	13263	2163	17528	207	3
黑龙江 Heilongjiang	25348	16804	2118	22931	295	4
上 海 Shanghai	16130	10792	3645	12471	13	1
江 苏 Jiangsu	54663	28517	10452	44007	199	5
浙 江 Zhejiang	40288	21876	4554	35588	144	2
安 徽 Anhui	26874	11979	2335	24127	410	2
福 建 Fujian	22755	12765	2207	20263	282	3
江 西 Jiangxi	22575	10650	2689	18883	996	7
山 东 Shandong	75271	42055	9016	65730	508	17
河 南 Henan	46837	26466	5784	40408	636	9
湖 北 Hubei	41106	18117	4022	36486	586	10
湖 南 Hunan	28458	13493	2361	25616	470	11
广 东 Guangdong	102930	57768	14056	88126	745	3
广 西 Guangxi	23914	13979	2504	21082	325	2
海 南 Hainan	8088	4602	510	7389	187	2
重 庆 Chongqing	23260	11780	2365	20644	237	14
四 川 Sichuan	41827	20350	3437	37702	682	6
贵 州 Guizhou	21579	11294	1468	19734	372	5
云 南 Yunnan	21468	11721	1597	19647	219	5
西 藏 Tibet	2292	1163	190	2082	20	0
陕 西 Shaanxi	23854	13928	3444	20111	298	1
甘 肃 Gansu	13339	6307	1318	11685	333	3
青 海 Qinghai	3266	1780	182	2975	109	0
宁 夏 Ningxia	6710	3753	653	5969	88	0
新 疆 Xinjiang	18638	11702	1046	17275	317	0

专业技术职务情况(城区)

Academic Qualification and Professional Rank(Urban Area)

单位:人
unit: person

	按专业技术职务分 By Professional Rank				
高中阶段毕业以下 Below High School Graduate	中学高级 Senior Secondary	中学一级 1st Grade	中学二级 2nd Grade	中学三级 3rd Grade	未定职级 No-ranking
4	**273307**	**331813**	**211947**	**4302**	**69325**
0	8110	6279	4354	34	1227
0	5384	5909	2003	24	458
0	11336	17717	8804	531	3331
0	6071	8849	8774	106	3969
0	6615	6113	3901	0	1839
1	15613	13283	5393	156	3140
0	5773	7839	4460	63	1766
0	8971	10673	4961	28	715
0	5005	7097	3194	15	819
0	22580	21393	8326	7	2357
0	14407	14075	8028	109	3669
0	8510	9761	5556	224	2823
0	7305	8331	5815	40	1264
0	8945	6525	4906	153	2046
0	16583	29023	23181	291	6193
0	11866	16600	14516	318	3537
2	15171	15870	7923	358	1784
0	9131	10964	5732	149	2482
0	25985	42822	24811	476	8836
1	5556	9070	6384	333	2571
0	2370	2784	2165	46	723
0	6337	8553	7272	7	1091
0	13979	15795	9962	115	1976
0	5733	6553	6478	169	2646
0	6927	6623	5400	31	2487
0	528	987	623	37	117
0	6364	8463	6906	96	2025
0	3628	5212	3724	107	668
0	918	967	818	223	340
0	2108	2034	1976	29	563
0	5498	5649	5601	27	1863

普通高中专任教师学历、
Number of Full-time Teachers in Regular Senior Secondary Schools by

地　区 Region	合计 Total	其中:女 of Which: Female	按学历分 By Academic Qualification			
			研究生毕业 Graduate	本科毕业 Under-graduate	专科毕业 Associate Bachelor	高中阶段毕业 High School Graduate
总　计 Total	**141568**	**77610**	**14830**	**124663**	**2049**	**26**
北　京 Beijing	1234	823	359	872	3	0
天　津 Tianjin	1387	989	220	1154	13	0
河　北 Hebei	9498	6392	844	8276	377	1
山　西 Shanxi	3466	2090	367	2939	159	1
内蒙古 Inner Mongolia	773	492	88	671	14	0
辽　宁 Liaoning	4208	2859	381	3793	32	2
吉　林 Jilin	864	562	38	807	19	0
黑龙江 Heilongjiang	1456	934	149	1291	15	1
上　海 Shanghai	1033	700	243	788	2	0
江　苏 Jiangsu	6289	3030	921	5343	25	0
浙　江 Zhejiang	9738	5375	977	8715	46	0
安　徽 Anhui	4650	1900	381	4209	60	0
福　建 Fujian	2977	1611	249	2688	39	1
江　西 Jiangxi	1741	744	149	1487	101	4
山　东 Shandong	19733	10963	2250	17360	119	4
河　南 Henan	8406	4762	1101	7154	150	1
湖　北 Hubei	6399	2561	524	5792	82	1
湖　南 Hunan	3700	1659	283	3327	86	4
广　东 Guangdong	29433	15985	3552	25558	321	2
广　西 Guangxi	4441	2593	337	4032	72	0
海　南 Hainan	828	463	47	766	15	0
重　庆 Chongqing	1205	547	71	1102	32	0
四　川 Sichuan	3768	1770	408	3308	52	0
贵　州 Guizhou	3558	1878	211	3295	52	0
云　南 Yunnan	6126	3289	285	5751	86	4
西　藏 Tibet	0	0	0	0	0	0
陕　西 Shaanxi	2082	1173	272	1788	22	0
甘　肃 Gansu	344	177	30	304	10	0
青　海 Qinghai	581	303	16	550	15	0
宁　夏 Ningxia	344	163	17	325	2	0
新　疆 Xinjiang	1306	823	60	1218	28	0

专业技术职务情况(城乡结合区)

Academic Qualification and Professional Rank(Urban-rural Transitional Area)

单位:人

unit: person

	按专业技术职务分 By Professional Rank				
高中阶段毕业以下 Below High School Graduate	中学高级 Senior Secondary	中学一级 1st Grade	中学二级 2nd Grade	中学三级 3rd Grade	未定职级 No-ranking
0	**35624**	**51022**	**38528**	**967**	**15427**
0	388	341	348	0	157
0	503	600	224	0	60
0	2394	3890	2083	58	1073
0	598	1022	1189	29	628
0	267	274	129	0	103
0	1714	1385	593	48	468
0	278	386	151	0	49
0	574	510	312	0	60
0	348	388	217	4	76
0	2279	2420	1206	0	384
0	2812	3258	2500	54	1114
0	1407	1550	782	51	860
0	958	977	731	25	286
0	582	504	400	38	217
0	3645	6648	6986	209	2245
0	1696	2696	2971	44	999
0	2190	2462	1330	81	336
0	1087	1507	739	35	332
0	6087	12482	7859	184	2821
0	862	1583	1467	18	511
0	136	232	375	0	85
0	188	406	571	0	40
0	1073	1330	1123	3	239
0	803	957	1189	7	602
0	1760	1732	1526	15	1093
0	0	0	0	0	0
0	482	686	680	9	225
0	38	99	144	1	62
0	151	197	128	37	68
0	111	134	72	0	27
0	213	366	503	17	207

普通高中专任教师学历、

Number of Full-time Teachers in Regular Senior Secondary Schools by

地 区 Region	合计 Total	其中:女 of Which: Female	按学历分 By Academic Qualification			
			研究生毕业 Graduate	本科毕业 Under-graduate	专科毕业 Associate Bachelor	高中阶段毕业 High School Graduate
总 计 Total	**825874**	**406987**	**47745**	**757934**	**19724**	**450**
北 京 Beijing	627	427	313	314	0	0
天 津 Tianjin	2414	1542	166	2220	27	1
河 北 Hebei	49506	31506	3393	45211	896	6
山 西 Shanxi	32280	19499	2455	29000	817	8
内蒙古 Inner Mongolia	16656	9909	1561	14725	370	0
辽 宁 Liaoning	12509	8079	842	11415	225	23
吉 林 Jilin	9606	6095	580	8973	53	0
黑龙江 Heilongjiang	16388	10296	798	15364	223	3
上 海 Shanghai	1601	972	226	1375	0	0
江 苏 Jiangsu	39469	17797	4450	34819	200	0
浙 江 Zhejiang	26220	13481	1831	24221	167	1
安 徽 Anhui	48296	18223	2846	44626	819	5
福 建 Fujian	25793	10940	897	24168	720	8
江 西 Jiangxi	32469	13100	1945	28188	2282	49
山 东 Shandong	57507	28302	4877	51923	664	37
河 南 Henan	74986	39307	5232	67449	2252	53
湖 北 Hubei	22851	7970	875	21143	747	85
湖 南 Hunan	44652	18808	1897	41623	1098	34
广 东 Guangdong	40910	21246	2352	37877	676	5
广 西 Guangxi	29159	15551	1092	27256	792	16
海 南 Hainan	4398	2271	141	4092	164	1
重 庆 Chongqing	14903	7018	437	14115	340	11
四 川 Sichuan	53865	24411	1769	50666	1425	5
贵 州 Guizhou	40860	17779	914	38829	1086	31
云 南 Yunnan	32542	16064	820	31004	697	20
西 藏 Tibet	822	420	33	772	17	0
陕 西 Shaanxi	32150	16162	2531	29331	282	6
甘 肃 Gansu	30509	11709	1635	27308	1531	34
青 海 Qinghai	5356	2696	236	4836	284	0
宁 夏 Ningxia	4194	2095	167	3954	72	1
新 疆 Xinjiang	22376	13312	434	21137	798	7

专业技术职务情况（镇区）

Academic Qualification and Professional Rank（Counties & Towns Area）

单位：人

unit：person

	按专业技术职务分 By Professional Rank				
高中阶段毕业以下 Below High School Graduate	中学高级 Senior Secondary	中学一级 1st Grade	中学二级 2nd Grade	中学三级 3rd Grade	未定职级 No-ranking
21	**206122**	**294679**	**250214**	**5570**	**69289**
0	75	139	149	1	263
0	689	989	575	4	157
0	11756	19641	12643	565	4901
0	6067	9840	12945	504	2924
0	4855	6261	4177	0	1363
4	4852	4477	2534	72	574
0	2666	4081	2248	13	598
0	4726	6376	4529	65	692
0	389	713	403	0	96
0	13813	15504	8606	3	1543
0	8530	9484	6288	21	1897
0	14345	16560	11674	659	5058
0	8082	10203	6740	34	734
5	11395	10190	7108	311	3465
6	11832	21063	19248	253	5111
0	15265	24016	28299	673	6733
1	6344	10519	5052	174	762
0	12426	16827	11221	280	3898
0	6550	17509	13499	236	3116
3	5705	11673	8367	532	2882
0	1003	1465	1691	36	203
0	3138	5191	5875	61	638
0	15408	19628	15586	102	3141
0	7879	11780	15198	434	5569
1	9720	10008	10386	37	2391
0	56	215	343	28	180
0	7086	11629	11350	123	1962
1	5385	11162	12403	100	1459
0	1415	1747	1435	185	574
0	886	1193	1799	22	294
0	3784	4596	7843	42	6111

普通高中专任教师学历、
Number of Full-time Teachers in Regular Senior Secondary Schools by

地　区 Region	合计 Total	其中:女 of Which: Female	按学历分 By Academic Qualification			
			研究生毕业 Graduate	本科毕业 Under-graduate	专科毕业 Associate Bachelor	高中阶段毕业 High School Graduate
总　计 Total	**204073**	**104050**	**12637**	**186475**	**4882**	**76**
北　京 Beijing	357	239	186	171	0	0
天　津 Tianjin	1546	983	104	1422	20	0
河　北 Hebei	20385	13023	1487	18514	380	4
山　西 Shanxi	11250	6857	674	10270	301	5
内蒙古 Inner Mongolia	1613	895	154	1435	24	0
辽　宁 Liaoning	1108	689	117	959	31	1
吉　林 Jilin	502	306	106	392	4	0
黑龙江 Heilongjiang	1503	925	78	1418	7	0
上　海 Shanghai	236	145	31	205	0	0
江　苏 Jiangsu	9792	4570	1187	8537	68	0
浙　江 Zhejiang	8296	4324	535	7703	58	0
安　徽 Anhui	7437	2779	375	6880	180	2
福　建 Fujian	6256	2623	165	5885	202	4
江　西 Jiangxi	4629	1978	232	4031	360	6
山　东 Shandong	25160	12247	2072	22884	194	7
河　南 Henan	22845	12310	1612	20134	1079	20
湖　北 Hubei	4770	1627	145	4540	82	3
湖　南 Hunan	8517	3662	411	7758	346	2
广　东 Guangdong	16727	8807	883	15625	217	2
广　西 Guangxi	3200	1796	73	3017	107	3
海　南 Hainan	1194	665	49	1125	20	0
重　庆 Chongqing	3116	1474	122	2961	31	2
四　川 Sichuan	6258	3082	324	5804	130	0
贵　州 Guizhou	7957	3468	169	7565	218	5
云　南 Yunnan	9489	4964	234	9071	181	3
西　藏 Tibet	0	0	0	0	0	0
陕　西 Shaanxi	8239	4232	610	7520	106	3
甘　肃 Gansu	6338	2438	388	5647	299	4
青　海 Qinghai	1576	784	49	1434	93	0
宁　夏 Ningxia	410	210	9	397	4	0
新　疆 Xinjiang	3367	1948	56	3171	140	0

专业技术职务情况(镇乡结合区)
Academic Qualification and Professional Rank(County-town Transitional Area)

单位:人
unit: person

高中阶段毕业以下 Below High School Graduate	按专业技术职务分 By Professional Rank				
	中学高级 Senior Secondary	中学一级 1st Grade	中学二级 2nd Grade	中学三级 3rd Grade	未定职级 No-ranking
3	**46392**	**71723**	**63980**	**2038**	**19940**
0	46	70	47	0	194
0	453	623	378	0	92
0	4699	8052	4980	277	2377
0	2096	3328	4300	341	1185
0	498	558	400	0	157
0	375	423	225	3	82
0	178	213	109	0	2
0	513	516	405	37	32
0	59	119	40	0	18
0	3351	3701	2409	0	331
0	2537	2954	2244	4	557
0	2071	2487	1719	249	911
0	1760	2382	1776	13	325
0	1276	1146	1082	138	987
3	5169	9370	8602	63	1956
0	4487	7287	8166	248	2657
0	1357	2093	1042	55	223
0	2257	3198	2174	53	835
0	2601	7257	5473	132	1264
0	478	1189	1052	91	390
0	222	325	591	25	31
0	622	1014	1302	12	166
0	1622	2290	1843	5	498
0	1261	2104	2943	145	1504
0	2746	2854	3180	9	700
0	0	0	0	0	0
0	1838	2754	2940	44	663
0	1015	2236	2644	49	394
0	403	544	481	23	125
0	70	132	184	6	18
0	332	504	1249	16	1266

普通高中专任教师学历、
Number of Full-time Teachers in Regular Senior Secondary Schools by

地　区 Region	合计 Total	其中:女 of Which: Female	按学历分 By Academic Qualification			
			研究生毕业 Graduate	本科毕业 Under- graduate	专科毕业 Associate Bachelor	高中阶段毕业 High School Graduate
总　计 Total	**57385**	**29392**	**4463**	**51435**	**1470**	**17**
北　京 Beijing	821	523	229	592	0	0
天　津 Tianjin	312	197	17	293	2	0
河　北 Hebei	3205	1999	427	2692	86	0
山　西 Shanxi	3892	2363	499	3234	157	2
内蒙古 Inner Mongolia	528	316	36	458	34	0
辽　宁 Liaoning	1252	806	73	1140	39	0
吉　林 Jilin	427	238	24	391	12	0
黑龙江 Heilongjiang	716	461	21	689	6	0
上　海 Shanghai	206	127	22	182	2	0
江　苏 Jiangsu	587	250	49	538	0	0
浙　江 Zhejiang	3100	1510	313	2761	26	0
安　徽 Anhui	2828	1082	158	2604	66	0
福　建 Fujian	2172	902	105	2035	32	0
江　西 Jiangxi	683	257	19	607	56	1
山　东 Shandong	1668	857	179	1478	10	1
河　南 Henan	2864	1628	310	2465	89	0
湖　北 Hubei	1972	701	126	1753	93	0
湖　南 Hunan	2692	1133	93	2530	67	2
广　东 Guangdong	7595	3735	810	6735	50	0
广　西 Guangxi	2915	1565	130	2607	174	4
海　南 Hainan	842	484	84	753	5	0
重　庆 Chongqing	1273	609	50	1172	49	2
四　川 Sichuan	1769	883	108	1606	55	0
贵　州 Guizhou	1655	766	121	1458	75	1
云　南 Yunnan	2563	1347	92	2439	32	0
西　藏 Tibet	2073	1108	77	1953	43	0
陕　西 Shaanxi	1293	605	72	1211	9	1
甘　肃 Gansu	1538	628	100	1381	55	2
青　海 Qinghai	471	235	31	419	21	0
宁　夏 Ningxia	0	0	0	0	0	0
新　疆 Xinjiang	3473	2077	88	3259	125	1

专业技术职务情况(乡村)
Academic Qualification and Professional Rank(Rural Area)

单位:人
unit: person

	按专业技术职务分 By Professional Rank				
高中阶段毕业以下 Below High School Graduate	中学高级 Senior Secondary	中学一级 1st Grade	中学二级 2nd Grade	中学三级 3rd Grade	未定职级 No-ranking
0	**11572**	**19232**	**16697**	**674**	**9210**
0	236	258	231	0	96
0	95	151	47	0	19
0	636	1310	676	41	542
0	515	951	1265	93	1068
0	141	208	98	0	81
0	426	444	194	1	187
0	65	171	94	24	73
0	185	188	252	1	90
0	65	78	29	0	34
0	200	244	132	0	11
0	826	1093	790	70	321
0	562	851	864	74	477
0	493	844	686	2	147
0	131	105	97	9	341
0	237	527	524	15	365
0	509	831	963	5	556
0	503	761	553	38	117
0	690	1045	686	48	223
0	1450	3319	1974	57	795
0	590	1094	647	53	531
0	234	247	229	8	124
0	279	366	500	1	127
0	490	678	501	0	100
0	317	378	525	21	414
0	467	678	999	2	417
0	186	603	808	30	446
0	278	510	475	2	28
0	265	578	496	35	164
0	107	161	92	33	78
0	0	0	0	0	0
0	394	560	1270	11	1238

普通高中办学
Condition of School Buildings in Senior

地　区 Region	校舍建筑面积 Floor Space	教学及辅助用房 Teaching & Assistant Buildings							行政办公用房 Administrative	
		合计 Total	其中： of Which：						合计 Total	其中：教师办公室 of Which: for Teachers
			教室 Classroom	实验室 Laboratory	图书室 Library	微机室 PC-room	语音室 Linguistic	体育馆 Gymnasium		
总　计 Total	**515117371.83**	**192480843.84**	**113760089.28**	**32834358.26**	**17183958.09**	**7979431.69**	**3164142.34**	**17558864.18**	**41207002.77**	**23756945.66**
北　京 Beijing	9870093.57	3477576.03	1864157.83	578308.08	284361.21	140712.36	27463.48	582573.07	985428.93	494083.11
天　津 Tianjin	4891817.97	1829183.15	970814.86	319766.16	165710.97	74221.40	28393.13	270276.63	621231.46	371806.25
河　北 Hebei	24127145.79	8945461.48	5239004.22	1798232.51	908730.10	386678.69	151351.61	461464.35	1942169.19	1281709.89
山　西 Shanxi	17672176.16	6247789.00	3801211.32	1095236.26	604476.32	247097.52	93744.16	406023.42	1464033.92	905671.58
内蒙古 Inner Mongolia	9740807.80	4059326.00	2433193.84	623271.59	326372.17	133994.85	63852.27	478641.28	896839.14	612667.96
辽　宁 Liaoning	11077512.10	3951836.32	2100680.90	562721.87	389924.91	188182.85	71594.41	638731.38	1067293.28	598603.04
吉　林 Jilin	5921760.42	2081085.17	1204725.74	281645.20	159756.30	97671.93	45871.63	291414.37	617136.21	356064.69
黑龙江 Heilongjiang	8520975.99	3315080.28	1904736.90	499935.94	222787.02	140171.56	62747.02	484701.84	960062.61	574856.68
上　海 Shanghai	7104194.31	2963145.26	1316361.16	634939.99	288228.14	121958.23	37352.72	564305.02	753536.10	332497.77
江　苏 Jiangsu	28986992.57	12337002.89	5903366.35	2404836.26	1506393.68	713604.88	255338.84	1553462.88	2718648.72	1550377.31
浙　江 Zhejiang	24948740.24	9431913.11	4664721.03	1737425.09	1042458.93	318079.30	123090.27	1546138.49	1918944.40	1118340.70
安　徽 Anhui	25390682.32	9283265.66	5798962.90	1551162.43	793579.08	402732.86	135878.97	600949.42	1787646.28	976010.30
福　建 Fujian	19135093.95	7996041.83	4224551.15	1777544.91	904982.94	254426.48	77875.47	756660.88	1408193.84	666350.87
江　西 Jiangxi	18055138.80	7235260.22	4655836.20	1028139.91	651936.50	301036.91	116915.33	481395.37	1482387.33	683960.58
山　东 Shandong	32106632.31	10916160.18	5748351.92	2275555.84	1110625.94	570352.47	311227.96	900046.05	3035465.24	1719973.12
河　南 Henan	30510479.60	10453974.04	7097088.35	1592720.98	854692.04	388513.81	144226.80	376732.06	2613589.69	1738321.41
湖　北 Hubei	18502118.22	5913159.21	3501347.22	1042233.78	495322.72	232373.46	121622.22	520259.81	1497161.13	841373.35
湖　南 Hunan	24317472.79	8177680.36	4569515.38	1319221.34	808293.16	318847.61	153905.14	1007897.73	1547276.61	889536.26
广　东 Guangdong	50613508.00	20235049.59	12577890.66	3110290.82	1499837.24	746087.73	319121.26	1981821.88	3462319.03	1909468.75
广　西 Guangxi	16972692.24	6045986.85	3896709.42	929149.89	512631.96	222188.97	97941.63	387364.98	920919.49	595534.02
海　南 Hainan	5150703.88	1945709.81	1286844.60	272624.10	161344.94	62695.44	17906.60	144294.13	251932.99	138818.78
重　庆 Chongqing	13831394.72	5235484.09	3469107.88	751583.71	362943.45	182586.70	72317.60	396944.75	907381.28	444878.76
四　川 Sichuan	29818031.51	11586736.78	7880499.79	1636307.77	754795.76	465238.03	167838.72	682056.71	1832131.50	1094718.46
贵　州 Guizhou	17650451.03	5716373.39	3455715.27	983923.40	509489.94	205722.45	88190.64	473331.69	1295476.86	698523.72
云　南 Yunnan	18131459.12	6692912.60	4067098.05	1085506.30	596899.77	327479.15	123210.66	492718.67	1160714.40	648000.42
西　藏 Tibet	1352485.84	431835.68	244597.00	69923.94	41112.12	12863.93	9278.99	54059.70	81172.18	53025.67
陕　西 Shaanxi	14325019.70	5258036.75	3196384.99	1021353.28	431340.09	240720.71	115819.75	252417.93	1424069.29	876685.00
甘　肃 Gansu	9457328.79	3641755.74	2365592.63	644855.46	270956.35	177641.89	51603.70	131105.71	929667.89	631873.66
青　海 Qinghai	2501324.56	926071.36	519892.91	195540.49	82324.58	34147.33	12548.66	81617.39	202680.99	131648.81
宁　夏 Ningxia	2733248.79	1177332.85	630278.20	259129.97	100202.08	64232.55	26574.80	96915.25	302255.40	208504.36
新　疆 Xinjiang	11699888.74	4972618.16	3170850.61	751270.99	341447.68	207169.64	39337.90	462541.34	1119237.39	613060.38

条件(一)(总计)
Secondary Schools (1) (Total)

单位:平方米
unit: m^2

生活用房 Residential and Welfare							其他用房 Rooms for Other Purposes	校舍面积中 of the Floor Space	
合计 Total	教工宿舍 Apartments for Single		学生宿舍 Students' Dormitories	食堂 Dining Halls	厕所 Toilet	其他 Others		危房面积 Floor Space of Dilapidated Buildings	当年新增校舍 New Floor Space Added in Current Year
	小计 Subtotal	其中:教师周转宿舍 of Which: Accommodation for Circulation of Teachers							
241670466.83	**42647664.92**	**9789845.07**	**130728518.06**	**42169475.41**	**12965708.37**	**13159100.07**	**39759058.39**	**3212076.84**	**21342696.15**
2941588.24	398589.17	72026.54	1166924.09	628016.51	331202.69	416855.78	2465500.37	0	236214.99
1598718.33	154688.10	29805.11	670763.02	338982.55	180739.01	253545.65	842685.03	0	200327.66
11729756.75	1440978.73	298094.82	6946173.79	2244265.17	479366.02	618973.04	1509758.37	5300.01	1877059.43
8257123.80	1243823.74	118382.94	4498082.18	1621445.12	470073.05	423699.71	1703229.44	176440.17	188478.14
3964554.77	215203.90	58104.14	2373494.71	825442.54	276980.36	273433.26	820087.89	0	365089.55
4811659.70	250487.17	47078.99	2615606.03	1099926.56	357801.66	487838.28	1246722.80	7710.00	576494.93
2488573.63	80879.04	4811.01	1320044.71	558098.85	214946.00	314605.03	734965.41	1441.00	91671.99
3316049.03	116170.56	29159.15	1888448.89	669945.87	223127.48	418356.23	929784.07	39720.30	152162.04
2395182.56	130906.41	15749.00	1108372.07	465844.15	278933.01	411126.92	992330.39	0	85430.08
11989334.94	1664960.43	256086.04	6371181.27	2516447.24	676970.05	759775.95	1942006.02	0	517503.56
11455876.66	1490264.23	242607.01	6501899.71	2298008.20	667216.43	498488.09	2142006.07	0	1142967.37
12793689.23	2555280.31	426933.31	6921241.80	2203374.30	583141.58	530651.24	1526081.15	52831.51	665025.21
7935502.63	1990942.60	341276.33	3971563.27	1213820.96	390767.24	368408.56	1795355.65	76631.00	674008.36
8306945.86	1474993.90	319928.59	4591172.10	1452903.24	460602.35	327274.27	1030545.39	141025.74	1368645.75
15643719.44	1937248.49	440176.07	8789365.20	3267356.67	876359.73	773389.35	2511287.45	35829.40	1057994.09
15927080.93	2538046.56	391238.16	9383286.98	2846352.46	688829.87	470565.06	1515834.94	42949.00	695324.84
10032309.42	3018582.53	469360.15	4669399.01	1498110.79	357452.80	488764.29	1059488.46	128008.84	545997.90
12808361.14	3786235.32	844492.39	5858488.91	2031339.32	505479.76	626817.83	1784154.68	160678.32	952056.42
22339710.61	5058178.32	855354.48	11555945.51	3221718.02	1341167.66	1162701.10	4576428.77	41301.00	786075.35
9493783.11	2398024.68	624699.04	5222252.66	1233206.44	333025.78	307273.55	512002.79	226321.70	1002510.41
2706313.14	834468.31	298389.24	1261875.96	361360.03	122070.20	126538.64	246747.94	22147.30	73433.56
6830174.75	1456845.38	304861.99	3757197.74	1046907.23	282850.92	286373.48	858354.60	35133.95	203003.66
14949150.33	2723963.76	889449.69	8651247.35	2449009.55	699292.98	425636.69	1450012.90	97290.41	1859107.84
9367100.92	1670832.20	923369.22	5462099.60	1405526.54	462343.62	366298.96	1271499.86	1857.00	2276539.44
9139378.65	1307628.92	491560.08	5173864.67	1505339.11	452202.17	700343.78	1138453.47	918651.55	1431973.23
780763.80	247503.40	180105.66	350684.35	120364.38	20348.25	41863.42	58714.18	3209.60	85892.70
6674632.42	1287636.67	246184.35	3575063.69	1060236.66	409992.39	341703.01	968281.24	13246.80	864909.50
3902377.22	509335.63	149378.90	2120390.89	619645.21	299273.71	353731.78	983527.94	984352.24	537162.17
1096610.97	152299.21	104438.27	583244.65	200954.87	70423.61	89688.63	275961.24	0	140727.20
1088960.43	45647.06	8942.00	678309.48	231267.84	85509.10	48226.95	164700.11	0	132737.80
4905483.42	467020.19	307802.40	2690833.77	934259.03	367218.89	446151.54	702549.77	0	556170.98

普通高中办学
Condition of School Buildings in

地　区 Region	校舍建筑面积 Floor Space	教学及辅助用房 Teaching & Assistant Buildings							行政办公用房 Administrative	
		合计 Total	其中: of Which:						合计 Total	其中: 教师办公室 of Which: for Teachers
			教室 Classroom	实验室 Laboratory	图书室 Library	微机室 PC-room	语音室 Linguistic	体育馆 Gymnasium		
总　计 Total	**266620386.71**	**103118534.10**	**58629718.79**	**17537952.24**	**9425753.92**	**4247512.63**	**1589978.91**	**11687617.61**	**23151667.04**	**13099333.36**
北　京 Beijing	8848119.84	3152137.20	1702853.84	507350.25	256329.79	126973.85	23302.88	535326.59	913122.66	462417.89
天　津 Tianjin	4307797.42	1653364.73	863694.17	278828.17	156594.95	68309.76	25220.91	260716.77	571347.56	343912.15
河　北 Hebei	10804597.61	4169104.15	2361601.57	809040.83	470461.55	194904.96	70283.70	262811.54	967820.59	668904.21
山　西 Shanxi	8117626.92	2902863.78	1779518.84	484555.55	272572.16	107651.58	34787.14	223778.51	760242.06	466083.88
内蒙古 Inner Mongolia	4898943.85	2096562.28	1254625.54	301800.69	177040.65	65453.24	38895.17	258746.99	476809.86	341278.55
辽　宁 Liaoning	7933070.99	2862999.72	1500576.11	393851.31	293234.93	143147.28	48799.16	483390.93	780561.08	444729.27
吉　林 Jilin	3817132.85	1378881.57	757997.38	203330.94	109097.39	63477.86	26289.64	218688.36	417374.16	239584.34
黑龙江 Heilongjiang	5015017.42	2044495.94	1148394.87	308851.41	141700.46	84170.82	38994.77	322383.61	587293.39	330770.16
上　海 Shanghai	6331735.14	2667600.79	1211113.92	565167.01	256957.59	108867.21	35315.33	490179.73	667982.50	299333.74
江　苏 Jiangsu	16908199.12	7191882.41	3444100.56	1364091.42	875168.24	405010.86	110781.97	992729.36	1648832.50	926058.46
浙　江 Zhejiang	15762162.59	5960629.13	2910536.03	1059274.59	668592.81	199549.81	79381.75	1043294.14	1249336.05	695582.98
安　徽 Anhui	8129512.43	3289274.52	1967772.34	584517.89	281877.33	142917.61	50318.13	261871.22	660244.34	357863.72
福　建 Fujian	8647898.35	3759790.75	1897711.45	842319.96	443659.92	115017.81	29863.81	431217.80	722739.93	353923.52
江　西 Jiangxi	7607938.70	3267909.57	1995930.02	476813.93	286600.22	149221.72	57230.01	302113.67	664959.25	317576.78
山　东 Shandong	17554313.76	6165965.88	3179110.53	1327628.12	644564.56	331715.88	144521.71	538425.08	1810342.40	1008023.12
河　南 Henan	11879586.09	4256756.04	2787934.97	717159.91	341654.00	147228.14	59174.42	203604.60	1090425.40	674061.78
湖　北 Hubei	11293449.42	3933928.46	2295803.08	694580.86	330551.68	152399.53	72481.10	388112.21	994407.65	547352.74
湖　南 Hunan	9787995.29	3680538.74	1948504.37	600081.36	354048.46	136659.20	69698.83	571546.52	620670.53	342289.33
广　东 Guangdong	35193622.97	13872495.25	8373305.33	2101458.65	1087780.94	498423.72	200104.64	1611421.97	2533893.66	1375319.23
广　西 Guangxi	7729826.14	2984475.66	1785786.14	475173.62	266849.73	119649.89	58801.87	278214.41	455677.16	276088.39
海　南 Hainan	3034129.58	1132106.62	751524.08	173825.46	92596.54	38788.44	9061.60	66310.50	169878.03	97167.40
重　庆 Chongqing	7968010.58	3209487.32	2035962.73	448194.03	251309.23	115113.01	50504.48	308403.84	566409.45	278351.60
四　川 Sichuan	13582642.50	5484892.59	3611171.09	773183.65	374605.94	211606.62	79600.03	434725.26	919243.59	535397.17
贵　州 Guizhou	5764179.97	1859735.28	1048062.25	323496.22	162062.10	69314.75	26341.66	230458.30	507762.84	269344.55
云　南 Yunnan	7874390.98	2872242.47	1600062.14	449172.49	268452.32	132791.14	44666.20	377098.18	569463.04	315256.65
西　藏 Tibet	524150.43	177125.05	99144.02	33712.99	14670.59	4676.55	4262.65	20658.25	33709.58	26990.19
陕　西 Shaanxi	6535482.36	2502128.74	1553325.15	453549.43	199787.91	119223.94	50372.57	125869.74	692700.83	430698.99
甘　肃 Gansu	2977086.04	1219495.20	755082.05	214301.66	94234.77	54093.86	24008.34	77774.52	331471.00	213754.30
青　海 Qinghai	969067.16	349766.04	185026.98	76909.61	32042.31	13055.63	3972.00	38759.51	83843.34	46367.51
宁　夏 Ningxia	1729127.97	760636.69	402703.09	166301.75	68449.98	38317.75	11655.64	73208.48	196058.32	131307.93
新　疆 Xinjiang	5093572.24	2259261.53	1420784.15	329428.48	152204.87	89780.21	11286.80	255777.02	487044.29	283542.83

条件(一)(城区)
Senior Secondary Schools (1) (Urban Area)

单位:平方米
unit: m^2

生活用房 Residential and Welfare							其他用房 Rooms for Other Purposes	校舍面积中 of the Floor Space	
合计 Total	教工宿舍 Apartments for Single		学生宿舍 Students' Dormitories	食堂 Dining Halls	厕所 Toilet	其他 Others		危房面积 Floor Space of Dilapidated Buildings	当年新增校舍 New Floor Space Added in Current Year
	小计 Subtotal	其中:教师周转宿舍 of Which: Accommodation for Circulation of Teachers							
114961018.10	**17039845.09**	**3676130.14**	**61825635.08**	**20802039.44**	**7314059.70**	**7979438.79**	**25389167.47**	**1294909.53**	**8940497.77**
2495637.44	340043.55	69931.54	939226.00	540190.82	301263.39	374913.68	2287222.54	0	205097.17
1299300.86	119710.36	25132.11	503802.30	288390.99	160423.39	226973.82	783784.27	0	122893.59
4875295.38	530815.32	135914.50	2845900.97	931167.85	222804.60	344606.64	792377.49	0	681075.65
3488253.28	543773.76	39044.85	1856986.91	656983.25	230320.22	200189.14	966267.80	69031.17	99984.14
1862677.71	102091.13	33434.14	1109502.63	379808.08	149410.53	121865.34	462894.00	0	229819.37
3314555.84	174507.44	39917.01	1728062.26	738500.10	272603.64	400882.40	974954.35	7710.00	316347.50
1538704.15	53599.61	2619.00	735761.04	357672.20	140806.46	250864.84	482172.97	1441.00	72850.99
1914243.78	69407.14	6322.65	1005109.50	386610.89	137793.89	315322.36	468984.31	22379.30	17843.44
2088610.31	103517.10	12577.00	944485.44	410942.54	250443.08	379222.15	907541.54	0	85430.08
6675485.30	560147.13	94447.33	3692865.90	1469648.12	451090.51	501733.64	1391998.91	0	444007.93
7069070.01	873584.47	160575.50	4024324.60	1395993.68	417232.76	357934.50	1483127.40	0	805322.33
3608882.41	452609.51	80334.61	2101080.20	639679.06	199878.79	215634.85	571111.16	4933.55	136288.91
3170987.37	612335.83	136629.24	1680970.57	497047.95	181424.04	199208.98	994380.30	50544.00	329086.73
3144753.45	530426.32	98510.70	1676688.88	592945.07	223773.95	120919.23	530316.43	67726.94	345519.20
8121604.62	749998.09	215756.91	4595468.78	1774512.27	513040.11	488585.37	1456400.86	4333.40	402376.28
5696663.94	799180.22	109299.83	3365307.04	1062289.43	290162.65	179724.60	835740.71	20728.49	160264.09
5748667.09	1613733.46	206282.64	2703850.68	889609.70	225674.96	315798.29	616446.22	52655.84	359943.80
4633160.48	1196052.72	288741.07	2126373.03	791719.76	224356.62	294658.35	853625.54	21758.32	356247.30
15163902.51	2987185.13	548828.69	7992899.64	2323249.47	1023260.95	837307.32	3623331.55	34245.00	534042.57
4066454.40	847878.79	224580.20	2314143.13	533202.41	170129.16	201100.91	223218.92	110508.00	298304.89
1618860.22	505497.27	133036.20	753270.43	207485.39	71661.53	80945.60	113284.71	15334.30	56303.10
3563472.91	606763.06	107591.13	2053964.99	547424.36	178727.02	176593.48	628640.90	15046.00	131439.83
6354777.58	870146.48	287122.67	3830068.34	1114823.97	340365.87	199372.92	823728.74	19814.00	735753.74
2875467.08	488328.61	238045.34	1650406.78	463434.15	173330.78	99966.76	521214.77	0	511090.77
3688150.36	461865.94	124532.65	1961838.70	573196.10	205954.63	485294.99	744535.11	384063.55	570097.53
282903.15	84476.44	66359.44	132829.67	50185.23	9100.55	6311.26	30412.65	3209.60	11641.50
2654371.01	447161.59	75392.87	1398388.03	410951.20	228944.11	168926.08	686281.78	13246.80	440045.67
1011918.36	109197.11	18989.07	518466.43	170069.69	93419.16	120765.97	414201.48	376200.27	192515.64
345561.36	30556.80	18214.08	195066.61	56379.12	24476.02	39082.81	189896.42	0	50541.38
659451.33	22167.02	8582.00	387480.40	158781.04	61701.81	29321.06	112981.63	0	72567.00
1929174.41	153087.69	69385.17	1001045.20	389145.55	140484.52	245411.45	418092.01	0	165755.65

普通高中办学
Condition of School Buildings in Senior Secondary

地 区 Region	校舍建筑面积 Floor Space	教学及辅助用房 Teaching & Assistant Buildings							行政办公用房 Administrative	
		合计 Total	其中：of Which：						合计 Total	其中：教师办公室 of Which：for Teachers
			教室 Classroom	实验室 Laboratory	图书室 Library	微机室 PC-room	语音室 Linguistic	体育馆 Gymnasium		
总 计 Total	**48124332.88**	**16976363.46**	**9611456.00**	**2899539.58**	**1566335.53**	**673746.71**	**279308.16**	**1945977.48**	**3687286.81**	**2055218.76**
北 京 Beijing	739673.54	270363.03	102259.01	28916.66	17612.51	6857.71	2547.35	112169.79	51814.84	29803.98
天 津 Tianjin	309027.52	113673.52	64303.52	15478.00	9137.00	4554.00	802.00	19399.00	23321.00	10088.00
河 北 Hebei	2689220.77	934653.08	517810.46	170474.60	120044.36	43605.61	16285.20	66432.85	185033.29	129332.24
山 西 Shanxi	1107353.58	355588.68	240479.64	50374.00	32579.24	8279.32	2430.48	21446.00	87391.64	54070.24
内蒙古 Inner Mongolia	199759.20	77081.14	39412.46	14338.15	4465.34	3042.49	10692.57	5130.13	20783.45	12468.78
辽 宁 Liaoning	847068.34	287658.04	153476.61	31332.16	27563.58	10424.48	4664.00	60197.21	66644.21	35967.39
吉 林 Jilin	191539.48	51107.12	33109.63	7573.29	3192.47	2763.47	1230.26	3238.00	19921.19	11471.46
黑龙江 Heilongjiang	369173.00	130369.00	68587.00	17656.00	11743.00	5813.00	3888.00	22682.00	34750.00	16814.16
上 海 Shanghai	658014.91	236287.94	124463.12	24585.03	28104.45	8140.60	5025.45	45969.29	68785.83	27573.42
江 苏 Jiangsu	1957738.54	792220.07	422211.67	143128.05	79579.03	41005.04	11073.16	95223.12	190674.65	90354.24
浙 江 Zhejiang	4236807.64	1512794.45	740450.59	280132.91	159024.48	48030.99	16367.69	268787.79	302233.96	170171.75
安 徽 Anhui	1919530.75	695880.38	413833.92	129341.01	63658.60	26954.81	10341.36	51750.68	133271.02	60998.84
福 建 Fujian	1374113.12	507839.32	248095.86	112081.32	71412.18	14685.31	5385.89	56178.76	78622.17	43490.33
江 西 Jiangxi	630431.99	227191.52	140388.11	33816.79	21006.92	15052.70	3702.00	13225.00	34342.02	18089.80
山 东 Shandong	5168117.68	1715569.49	844563.31	386081.03	162412.23	91607.74	47833.23	183071.95	468242.47	272283.59
河 南 Henan	2334344.32	725426.04	467693.74	123001.62	70679.69	26676.34	6986.64	30388.01	187582.90	128678.45
湖 北 Hubei	2217482.25	758269.93	436121.06	106145.21	52578.10	33472.96	18263.60	111689.00	187146.69	86731.48
湖 南 Hunan	1401807.76	509805.44	262859.28	89203.00	62746.14	13069.00	8192.00	73736.02	90851.20	49045.20
广 东 Guangdong	10604417.64	3949780.55	2378781.06	646052.41	312781.79	144217.35	61896.82	406051.12	751069.94	423168.83
广 西 Guangxi	1421765.17	482716.46	325307.54	59572.15	40418.83	19212.63	9232.23	28973.08	82810.52	50294.22
海 南 Hainan	265985.67	91084.77	56536.64	14794.83	7106.60	1967.60	474.60	10204.50	15391.83	7412.10
重 庆 Chongqing	346365.54	99891.02	74565.14	14303.10	3149.24	4093.30	920.24	2860.00	14400.60	9740.20
四 川 Sichuan	1813680.74	606001.42	396620.03	96903.83	40371.09	23611.38	7108.86	41386.23	130208.52	58336.94
贵 州 Guizhou	1211685.57	392423.09	214009.46	70504.56	39755.36	13706.06	9198.70	45248.95	122341.71	71314.45
云 南 Yunnan	2415608.13	780790.49	409364.37	135243.28	77245.91	38084.10	8189.03	112663.80	198653.38	95996.29
西 藏 Tibet	0	0	0	0	0	0	0	0	0	0
陕 西 Shaanxi	667943.18	241700.86	167933.73	30384.77	18356.76	9778.80	3259.80	11987.00	55454.17	34405.74
甘 肃 Gansu	239371.86	113764.00	70455.00	13535.00	2845.00	3085.00	1653.00	22191.00	15500.00	8854.00
青 海 Qinghai	121850.08	49133.10	28528.30	10948.60	4085.40	1679.80	511.00	3380.00	14204.39	7696.42
宁 夏 Ningxia	187360.00	79848.00	50519.00	16430.00	5670.00	3434.00	697.00	3098.00	18045.00	16342.00
新 疆 Xinjiang	477094.91	187451.51	118716.74	27208.22	17010.23	6841.12	456.00	17219.20	37794.22	24224.22

条件(一)(城乡结合区)
Schools (1) (Urban-rural Transitional Area)

单位:平方米
unit: m^2

生活用房 Residential and Welfare							其他用房 Rooms for Other Purposes	校舍面积中 of the Floor Space	
合计 Total	教工宿舍 Apartments for Single: 小计 Subtotal	教工宿舍 Apartments for Single: 其中:教师周转宿舍 of Which: Accommodation for Circulation of Teachers	学生宿舍 Students' Dormitories	食堂 Dining Halls	厕所 Toilet	其他 Others		危房面积 Floor Space of Dilapidated Buildings	当年新增校舍 New Floor Space Added in Current Year
23548072. 65	**3810282. 18**	**975364. 44**	**12968445. 79**	**4176684. 09**	**1293550. 32**	**1299110. 27**	**3912609. 96**	**165775. 84**	**1865957. 35**
311963. 85	47548. 30	2855. 00	156477. 15	57120. 20	26327. 08	24491. 12	105531. 82	0	34429. 50
109038. 00	6462. 00	2234. 00	54472. 00	26263. 00	10910. 00	10931. 00	62995. 00	0	117. 00
1366992. 90	186269. 52	71955. 92	809609. 28	248541. 67	53682. 86	68889. 57	202541. 50	0	99629. 61
581209. 78	103203. 07	100. 00	318683. 62	117969. 74	26567. 35	14786. 00	83163. 48	16074. 00	20840. 00
87566. 40	1393. 00	0	54848. 43	19106. 71	7042. 26	5176. 00	14328. 21	0	7084. 00
392793. 33	15424. 09	3385. 01	215554. 32	79224. 14	29212. 14	53378. 64	99972. 76	0	4992. 02
72411. 83	1415. 00	0	31138. 10	13069. 06	5785. 62	21004. 05	48099. 34	0	2472. 00
161049. 00	17979. 50	2392. 00	77649. 00	30263. 50	9691. 00	25466. 00	43005. 00	0	0
292422. 67	18649. 00	118. 00	171244. 52	45521. 42	33130. 97	23876. 76	60518. 47	0	0
836912. 83	66484. 61	18029. 41	488256. 21	200925. 80	43385. 95	37860. 26	137930. 99	0	10153. 80
2109182. 78	307639. 38	53430. 78	1214295. 87	384624. 65	111803. 72	90819. 16	312596. 45	0	203544. 83
964217. 16	106819. 87	38966. 60	559312. 57	175347. 54	49039. 27	73697. 91	126162. 19	0	27148. 61
598436. 55	120148. 00	15253. 00	336973. 23	92488. 71	22558. 30	26268. 31	189215. 08	0	62754. 90
304826. 73	40488. 58	0	175037. 25	64015. 32	15445. 20	9840. 38	64071. 72	0	89929. 00
2566825. 93	254148. 84	115965. 60	1463276. 67	518247. 53	151736. 13	179416. 76	417479. 79	0	139199. 59
1301291. 14	201778. 86	37432. 88	748365. 01	253364. 17	55896. 27	41886. 83	120044. 24	0	47438. 12
1204740. 87	308293. 74	56033. 00	563351. 72	201526. 39	43899. 89	87669. 13	67324. 76	6594. 84	10675. 00
685003. 12	155761. 40	31409. 20	349961. 40	122139. 52	28306. 80	28834. 00	116148. 00	60. 00	52020. 80
4845018. 96	1023959. 02	195934. 62	2549480. 77	740958. 39	331270. 15	199350. 63	1058548. 19	0	87725. 89
824027. 89	191575. 36	86800. 87	443574. 21	127327. 32	45743. 00	15808. 00	32210. 30	70238. 00	64193. 40
152754. 12	55706. 82	11211. 70	69341. 50	18988. 27	7012. 53	1705. 00	6754. 95	0	5977. 50
192682. 69	5825. 00	1550. 00	141551. 96	29007. 13	14076. 60	2222. 00	39391. 23	15046. 00	0
1005284. 82	131412. 68	53449. 50	622142. 13	189657. 48	37191. 32	24881. 21	72185. 98	0	159046. 00
594858. 09	126865. 34	89261. 14	309295. 32	103335. 90	28413. 34	26948. 19	102062. 68	0	139717. 80
1232901. 09	201939. 98	58112. 60	636793. 85	191512. 95	55832. 47	146821. 84	203263. 17	48163. 00	259030. 47
0	0	0	0	0	0	0	0	0	0
333437. 93	72373. 61	4466. 00	176264. 15	47969. 79	20509. 75	16320. 63	37350. 22	0	108823. 08
91399. 66	7886. 00	2700. 00	62201. 50	16206. 26	4137. 90	968. 00	18708. 20	9600. 00	127107. 60
47476. 20	8350. 00	8155. 00	25102. 00	6824. 00	3193. 20	4007. 00	11036. 39	0	0
71506. 00	4693. 00	900. 00	34056. 00	14529. 00	9448. 00	8780. 00	17961. 00	0	57103. 00
209840. 33	19788. 61	13262. 61	110136. 05	40608. 53	12301. 25	27005. 89	42008. 85	0	44803. 83

普通高中办学

Condition of School Buildings in Senior Secondary

地 区 Region	校舍建筑面积 Floor Space	教学及辅助用房 Teaching & Assistant Buildings							行政办公用房 Administrative	
		合计 Total	其中：of Which：						合计 Total	其中：教师办公室 of Which：for Teachers
			教室 Classroom	实验室 Laboratory	图书室 Library	微机室 PC-room	语音室 Linguistic	体育馆 Gymnasium		
总 计 Total	**224520394.91**	**81563051.84**	**50337590.23**	**14098440.20**	**7082470.49**	**3422483.59**	**1453589.77**	**5168477.56**	**16547911.32**	**9862761.47**
北 京 Beijing	451949.66	142044.00	75179.40	29595.60	11458.00	7448.00	2971.00	15392.00	27461.60	14019.00
天 津 Tianjin	511514.55	154343.42	94043.69	35169.99	7676.02	5093.64	2800.22	9559.86	42554.90	25685.10
河 北 Hebei	12202345.55	4440516.77	2650688.37	947351.14	408697.19	180216.80	75138.19	178425.08	908421.22	573489.27
山 西 Shanxi	7944599.96	2851419.00	1717697.87	530927.38	280456.16	120677.94	50936.02	150723.63	603249.99	379501.70
内蒙古 Inner Mongolia	4538387.01	1861951.18	1116713.89	309123.53	136205.78	65520.30	23954.62	210433.06	403734.18	263008.98
辽 宁 Liaoning	2712057.50	970319.96	539769.33	152536.84	85810.45	35966.82	18737.02	137499.50	258920.68	139673.15
吉 林 Jilin	1960875.06	661578.60	418690.36	74532.26	46613.91	31714.07	17301.99	72726.01	190324.05	112095.35
黑龙江 Heilongjiang	3329874.05	1209842.22	721701.28	182518.37	76937.56	52746.53	21446.25	154492.23	359260.96	233431.26
上 海 Shanghai	628491.62	242240.47	88680.24	62524.98	22155.55	11437.02	1537.39	55905.29	78523.60	27733.03
江 苏 Jiangsu	11851787.29	5060328.01	2422967.83	1023476.83	615246.23	303006.11	143447.49	552183.52	1060305.51	619864.74
浙 江 Zhejiang	7965267.48	3047623.18	1545636.30	598455.20	333181.57	103284.98	39623.24	427441.89	587678.89	367049.51
安 徽 Anhui	16000849.90	5633637.16	3591128.37	917309.56	476950.31	243949.42	79019.65	325279.85	1050450.71	583549.57
福 建 Fujian	9149989.34	3770845.72	2052415.87	832132.47	409493.88	123419.40	44206.24	309177.86	618055.23	285202.78
江 西 Jiangxi	9826101.12	3792067.62	2518016.90	541312.48	360170.53	147255.44	56767.57	168544.70	780337.55	346231.08
山 东 Shandong	13611367.67	4465354.44	2421248.82	899624.85	429805.53	230043.45	162969.52	321662.27	1166438.40	681919.18
河 南 Henan	17641358.48	5901357.09	4097969.51	842279.86	489794.70	228056.02	81350.54	161906.46	1448337.42	1015423.35
湖 北 Hubei	6473881.69	1803515.82	1094867.14	318782.69	144292.34	74433.93	47780.12	123359.60	459599.48	274971.61
湖 南 Hunan	13622381.30	4244542.22	2447859.61	682747.98	438794.70	174854.41	80362.31	419923.21	876507.68	529168.53
广 东 Guangdong	12403759.86	5286158.45	3538802.48	843629.50	339783.96	201065.49	93484.98	269392.04	735566.61	427437.07
广 西 Guangxi	8351943.82	2768165.54	1912605.18	407275.00	227102.33	93351.20	35404.26	92427.57	416905.79	286997.23
海 南 Hainan	1545259.82	646311.98	448862.31	68586.64	55575.40	19725.00	7539.00	46023.63	62866.96	33918.16
重 庆 Chongqing	5417328.74	1873434.81	1318506.74	282926.18	102161.53	62400.94	19679.95	87759.47	312761.11	153721.80
四 川 Sichuan	15167713.07	5804919.71	4075408.69	816210.56	358692.75	240843.95	85549.31	228214.45	863146.88	535104.88
贵 州 Guizhou	10828720.15	3524120.37	2232367.17	608094.49	318204.81	120295.57	52543.08	192615.25	727377.83	405928.15
云 南 Yunnan	8960409.27	3359678.06	2168779.70	570861.89	291694.83	174795.16	71655.50	81890.98	494588.06	279628.97
西 藏 Tibet	215582.11	53948.64	31730.48	7118.42	3649.20	2811.39	1219.39	7419.76	17010.36	7046.42
陕 西 Shaanxi	7431894.68	2619438.78	1569324.23	549930.80	224846.04	116622.54	63870.98	94844.19	702929.54	435460.93
甘 肃 Gansu	6027098.75	2226762.52	1482174.86	402115.70	167601.48	111133.93	26028.36	37708.19	562850.47	400094.66
青 海 Qinghai	1364035.09	522323.02	306828.63	109303.88	38796.27	20201.70	8311.66	38880.88	111479.35	79601.00
宁 夏 Ningxia	1004120.82	416696.16	227575.11	92828.22	31752.10	25914.80	14919.16	23706.77	106197.08	77196.43
新 疆 Xinjiang	5379449.50	2207566.92	1409349.87	359156.91	148869.38	94197.64	23034.76	172958.36	514069.23	268608.58

条件(一)(镇区)
Schools (1) (Counties & Towns Area)

单位:平方米
unit: m^2

生活用房 Residential and Welfare							其他用房 Rooms for Other Purposes	校舍面积中 of the Floor Space	
合计 Total	教工宿舍 Apartments for Single 小计 Subtotal	其中:教师周转宿舍 of Which: Accommodation for Circulation of Teachers	学生宿舍 Students' Dormitories	食堂 Dining Halls	厕所 Toilet	其他 Others		危房面积 Floor Space of Dilapidated Buildings	当年新增校舍 New Floor Space Added in Current Year
114057942.36	**22770075.06**	**5300235.76**	**62210687.31**	**19320358.96**	**5080151.18**	**4676669.85**	**12351489.39**	**1804798.46**	**10760958.19**
210075.06	21929.00	945.00	110464.32	42732.66	13843.08	21106.00	72369.00	0	18234.00
257959.47	28314.74	4673.00	148870.72	44458.56	17956.62	18358.83	56656.76	0	77434.07
6260955.03	767238.67	141151.29	3779849.02	1236020.65	238482.33	239364.36	592452.53	5300.01	1122402.74
3983700.97	595142.53	49989.09	2213820.92	787440.12	192445.83	194851.57	506230.00	107409.00	48139.00
1972616.76	94560.29	21870.00	1194113.68	419537.94	117258.66	147146.19	300084.89	0	119775.24
1300259.00	61821.54	5821.60	766005.02	321019.53	71596.58	79816.33	182557.86	0	158292.74
868408.97	6767.01	1992.01	542514.58	188424.65	70198.54	60504.19	240563.44	0	18821.00
1316243.28	42819.10	22836.50	830141.05	266629.76	77323.31	99330.06	444527.59	15046.00	109316.60
233749.95	18378.31	2181.00	130740.33	39339.61	22798.93	22492.77	73977.60	0	0
5193995.06	1084196.62	161638.71	2612734.71	1027556.00	221925.08	247582.65	537158.71	0	73495.63
3794498.57	517673.36	66978.51	2166824.73	778268.28	213712.64	118019.56	535466.84	0	323734.64
8439184.32	1910374.57	316223.15	4429954.19	1454723.31	360598.96	283533.29	877577.71	45511.96	430628.86
4115002.58	1161651.42	170792.67	2006331.41	607552.87	185570.30	153896.58	646085.81	26087.00	306249.68
4808907.83	870215.29	207332.86	2708774.41	807012.93	223061.40	199843.80	444788.12	73116.76	996631.64
7060015.28	1144571.48	223137.16	3922240.36	1397142.97	333085.58	262974.89	919559.55	31496.00	655617.81
9647384.83	1652225.63	279492.73	5660509.63	1671728.65	381154.12	281766.80	644279.14	21650.00	428576.39
3874345.83	1288617.97	239546.41	1755100.33	559553.69	121108.84	149965.00	336420.56	75353.00	181360.10
7617901.26	2398733.60	527695.32	3472648.28	1163784.56	266999.34	315735.48	883430.14	134208.00	588731.12
5654427.89	1673168.61	202805.20	2803484.97	685347.52	246651.36	245775.43	727606.91	0	194097.78
4901078.25	1405876.29	326465.06	2617378.92	632136.17	145777.23	99909.64	265794.24	110119.00	607769.32
797531.88	269943.04	111860.04	364762.53	103282.64	29052.67	30491.00	38549.00	6813.00	17125.46
3013665.29	802586.91	181883.86	1543953.09	464021.80	95443.56	107659.93	217467.53	20087.95	68355.83
7933694.06	1686437.69	534072.36	4452197.47	1241846.50	340560.94	212651.46	565952.42	77235.41	1083402.77
5890896.52	1087359.75	640455.39	3451498.03	842516.47	257419.91	252102.36	686325.43	1857.00	1330522.50
4770118.90	685419.40	302854.35	2859897.20	819919.20	213079.25	191803.85	336024.25	477953.00	718402.72
118653.02	54087.32	37092.32	46200.08	15908.50	2158.12	299.00	25970.09	0	6563.88
3835255.03	775190.08	169655.18	2094757.13	625413.13	171006.29	168888.40	274271.33	0	410531.33
2680781.80	349896.18	122419.83	1489523.09	419028.72	194453.10	227880.71	556703.96	575555.37	291412.83
653239.51	98062.01	68602.79	333475.34	128474.75	44719.59	48507.82	76993.21	0	84928.82
429509.10	23480.04	360.00	290829.08	72486.80	23807.29	18905.89	51718.48	0	60170.80
2423887.06	193336.61	157412.37	1411092.69	457050.02	186901.73	175506.01	233926.29	0	230232.89

普通高中办学
Condition of School Buildings in Senior

地 区 Region	校舍建筑面积 Floor Space	教学及辅助用房 Teaching & Assistant Buildings							行政办公用房 Administrative	
		合计 Total	其中: of Which:						合计 Total	其中: 教师办公室 of Which: for Teachers
			教室 Classroom	实验室 Laboratory	图书室 Library	微机室 PC-room	语音室 Linguistic	体育馆 Gymnasium		
总 计 Total	**57717789.91**	**20636590.22**	**12546220.19**	**3696923.52**	**1815267.22**	**842356.81**	**386636.53**	**1349185.95**	**4205469.02**	**2539845.53**
北 京 Beijing	221104.00	61974.00	25474.00	18979.00	7574.00	3887.00	706.00	5354.00	12432.00	6579.00
天 津 Tianjin	309531.95	86296.82	50451.79	21993.69	4547.42	3126.44	1612.62	4564.86	25042.70	16206.10
河 北 Hebei	5113549.52	1729724.77	1049105.78	388919.52	147694.25	70135.34	25900.96	47968.92	373246.95	237278.25
山 西 Shanxi	2977292.14	1136221.34	670729.46	212483.81	89951.89	49681.28	24566.90	88808.00	240270.89	151452.09
内蒙古 Inner Mongolia	492310.75	210340.50	114727.15	36675.44	15701.67	5702.24	399.00	37135.00	24483.28	16534.48
辽 宁 Liaoning	356418.74	135592.97	65069.87	28366.49	16457.76	7559.36	3104.43	15035.06	26274.46	10371.00
吉 林 Jilin	258527.21	83926.46	48084.42	8219.08	1499.25	2605.15	442.27	23076.29	20011.47	12229.95
黑龙江 Heilongjiang	396966.56	172763.26	107773.76	28942.69	10716.48	5227.57	2709.76	17393.00	43515.02	28129.16
上 海 Shanghai	165195.96	62075.05	28568.10	18681.48	4620.84	1966.70	283.39	7954.54	16216.30	6467.73
江 苏 Jiangsu	2840068.27	1274588.32	651210.05	255750.43	129047.49	66781.54	29108.68	142690.13	223958.04	124383.02
浙 江 Zhejiang	2620230.30	966138.30	485038.56	190864.51	110054.40	37196.84	17282.40	125701.59	194557.36	112631.79
安 徽 Anhui	2725533.15	893715.86	612785.81	137903.05	53901.85	40083.14	13762.01	35280.00	215756.55	107778.08
福 建 Fujian	2331088.89	883297.23	492843.23	196909.89	104102.64	25597.10	8148.53	55695.84	149983.83	76048.76
江 西 Jiangxi	1605817.83	565656.12	375730.68	73219.43	54151.52	23936.17	11968.30	26650.02	97970.37	53644.82
山 东 Shandong	6367565.09	2070648.21	1125501.74	409328.91	208928.84	106352.73	74953.16	145582.83	509874.87	300439.67
河 南 Henan	5597666.81	1820755.27	1316924.52	238297.21	138262.75	57268.74	16569.19	53432.86	462055.17	320896.95
湖 北 Hubei	1506376.97	411992.82	246938.21	72300.97	37559.00	16092.00	16322.64	22780.00	98266.35	56473.00
湖 南 Hunan	2709084.49	833838.00	448861.80	166195.80	94100.60	39195.40	14475.60	71008.80	213733.62	151497.12
广 东 Guangdong	4693198.17	2100270.44	1361841.60	307378.50	157623.14	83568.90	35817.80	154040.50	311774.90	187575.80
广 西 Guangxi	1172947.15	439078.14	307579.63	54570.48	39381.22	12667.46	4148.00	20731.35	52882.47	32797.56
海 南 Hainan	447265.74	174635.90	120878.86	18544.64	16423.40	5868.00	880.00	12041.00	14050.96	7679.16
重 庆 Chongqing	1189507.80	422447.97	279370.31	68864.34	24029.85	13061.22	6608.25	30514.00	62734.29	27495.66
四 川 Sichuan	1946734.13	731347.28	454605.63	130841.80	49522.32	28036.50	11953.03	56388.00	105804.46	68999.00
贵 州 Guizhou	2500311.41	756534.99	477983.80	128888.03	74816.37	21532.29	19255.08	34059.42	175991.38	108321.36
云 南 Yunnan	2705018.61	996989.04	624839.09	175595.75	99448.15	49592.17	15078.56	32435.32	143383.72	90427.33
西 藏 Tibet	0	0	0	0	0	0	0	0	0	0
陕 西 Shaanxi	2155733.85	738414.01	442958.63	149639.63	52622.04	31802.48	19094.32	42296.91	190045.98	100626.21
甘 肃 Gansu	1222459.32	466987.91	301066.80	89281.62	42294.23	20870.53	5148.83	8325.90	101569.35	73123.27
青 海 Qinghai	303533.17	94314.76	57824.44	24239.54	5777.18	3946.00	1552.60	975.00	21272.56	13746.88
宁 夏 Ningxia	98298.11	42087.92	24914.01	8226.01	1863.02	1910.02	1884.01	3290.85	16108.18	12923.18
新 疆 Xinjiang	688453.82	273936.56	176538.46	36821.78	22593.65	7106.50	2900.21	27975.96	62201.54	27089.15

条件(一)(镇乡结合区)

Secondary Schools (1) (County-town Transitional Area)

单位:平方米
unit: m²

生活用房 Residential and Welfare							其他用房 Rooms for Other Purposes	校舍面积中 of the Floor Space	
合计 Total	教工宿舍 Apartments for Single		学生宿舍 Students' Dormitories	食堂 Dining Halls	厕所 Toilet	其他 Others		危房面积 Floor Space of Dilapidated Buildings	当年新增校舍 New Floor Space Added in Current Year
	小计 Subtotal	其中:教师周转宿舍 of Which: Accommodation for Circulation of Teachers							
29792543.41	**5532381.98**	**1293825.30**	**16602518.20**	**5117389.00**	**1284741.34**	**1255512.89**	**3083187.26**	**424815.76**	**3533071.24**
118924.00	12518.00	0	61632.00	23249.00	5649.00	15876.00	27774.00	0	0
159003.67	21389.94	4673.00	83560.72	30582.56	13244.62	10225.83	39188.76	0	37803.07
2758043.72	340938.10	70967.97	1676360.82	532564.20	103202.32	104978.28	252534.08	0	783432.79
1436086.57	195291.62	24856.60	836422.55	266574.35	68346.81	69451.24	164713.34	73372.00	40730.00
217726.58	14384.00	1440.00	120731.00	48167.00	7353.58	27091.00	39760.39	0	6079.00
172126.66	13208.32	200.00	103381.53	37616.72	14341.45	3578.64	22424.65	0	5086.39
108307.56	935.00	0	64441.83	22606.94	12877.64	7446.15	46281.72	0	3843.00
147920.94	3035.00	1159.00	103739.26	30301.51	5343.14	5502.03	32767.34	0	0
61059.81	1863.00	0	41808.39	8122.61	6204.53	3061.28	25844.80	0	0
1202234.11	247115.89	38182.00	578350.23	234003.48	55639.15	87125.36	139287.80	0	18015.71
1262798.59	159568.92	28565.00	723052.25	257402.40	70802.66	51972.36	196736.05	0	114638.78
1444190.23	319877.56	38561.00	733525.80	287805.45	57456.59	45524.83	171870.51	20618.96	173707.71
1130284.38	332746.20	53118.40	567978.26	167105.44	48786.48	13668.00	167523.45	0	26931.00
904498.64	126422.49	14112.54	550539.93	147849.89	26980.38	52705.95	37692.70	10671.00	114352.38
3352729.19	553350.90	68126.73	1898186.11	624889.51	135505.41	140797.26	434312.82	11293.00	319662.54
3148193.84	491384.12	99883.60	1925515.45	538142.23	112218.60	80933.44	166662.53	14047.00	144888.83
905733.81	240984.91	87173.61	456137.89	136861.51	29438.50	42311.00	90383.99	14749.00	91358.17
1478787.67	436067.80	130964.80	672617.65	233368.00	68860.64	67873.58	182725.20	50583.00	159514.64
2031343.48	584290.11	90362.00	1008877.80	243864.30	104334.40	89976.87	249809.35	0	106886.61
661615.14	154782.65	36061.65	402395.92	83689.56	14624.01	6123.00	19371.40	0	109690.79
255975.88	75076.04	52290.04	118903.53	31525.64	11431.67	19039.00	2603.00	4186.00	6555.46
679449.54	230197.79	53374.92	329683.16	97281.78	12015.37	10271.44	24876.00	0	7426.59
1041188.48	233814.71	81436.37	572387.37	168871.76	51585.00	14529.64	68393.91	0	242292.07
1438943.87	242062.50	141039.26	864915.61	216615.27	50154.20	65196.29	128841.17	0	556310.79
1421159.39	198911.34	76915.71	818678.08	254329.55	69381.49	79858.93	143486.46	122596.00	372484.36
0	0	0	0	0	0	0	0	0	0
1161165.53	196288.08	25300.88	654150.96	199230.80	51430.65	60065.04	66108.33	0	34291.06
577548.27	63067.62	39681.94	331273.17	93383.30	37610.98	52213.20	76353.79	102699.80	10886.54
165259.74	26074.82	20733.78	83721.00	31279.90	11771.18	12412.84	22686.11	0	6256.00
37960.01	1835.05	0	26058.11	6802.71	2155.14	1109.00	2142.00	0	7620.32
312284.11	14899.50	14644.50	193491.82	63301.63	25995.75	14595.41	40031.61	0	32326.64

地 区 Region	校舍建筑面积 Floor Space	教学及辅助用房 Teaching & Assistant Buildings							行政办公用房 Administrative	
		合计 Total	其中: of Which:						合计 Total	其中:教师办公室 of Which: for Teachers
			教室 Classroom	实验室 Laboratory	图书室 Library	微机室 PC-room	语音室 Linguistic	体育馆 Gymnasium		
总 计 Total	**23976590.21**	**7799257.90**	**4792780.26**	**1197965.82**	**675733.68**	**309435.47**	**120573.66**	**702769.01**	**1507424.41**	**794850.83**
北 京 Beijing	570024.07	183394.83	86124.59	41362.23	16573.42	6290.51	1189.60	31854.48	44844.67	17646.22
天 津 Tianjin	72506.00	21475.00	13077.00	5768.00	1440.00	818.00	372.00	0	7329.00	2209.00
河 北 Hebei	1120202.63	335840.56	226714.28	41840.54	29571.36	11556.93	5929.72	20227.73	65927.38	39316.41
山 西 Shanxi	1609949.28	493506.22	303994.61	79753.33	51448.00	18768.00	8021.00	31521.28	100541.87	60086.00
内蒙古 Inner Mongolia	303476.94	100812.54	61854.41	12347.37	13125.74	3021.31	1002.48	9461.23	16295.10	8380.43
辽 宁 Liaoning	432383.61	118516.64	60335.46	16333.72	10879.53	9068.75	4058.23	17840.95	27811.52	14200.62
吉 林 Jilin	143752.51	40625.00	28038.00	3782.00	4045.00	2480.00	2280.00	0	9438.00	4385.00
黑龙江 Heilongjiang	176084.52	60742.12	34640.75	8566.16	4149.00	3254.21	2306.00	7826.00	13508.26	10655.26
上 海 Shanghai	143967.55	53304.00	16567.00	7248.00	9115.00	1654.00	500.00	18220.00	7030.00	5431.00
江 苏 Jiangsu	227006.16	84792.47	36297.96	17268.01	15979.21	5587.91	1109.38	8550.00	9510.71	4454.11
浙 江 Zhejiang	1221310.17	423660.80	208548.70	79695.30	40684.55	15244.51	4085.28	75402.46	81929.46	55708.21
安 徽 Anhui	1260319.99	360353.98	240062.19	49334.98	34751.44	15865.83	6541.19	13798.35	76951.23	34597.01
福 建 Fujian	1337206.26	465405.36	274423.83	103092.48	51829.14	15989.27	3805.42	16265.22	67398.68	27224.57
江 西 Jiangxi	621098.98	175283.03	141889.28	10013.50	5165.75	4559.75	2917.75	10737.00	37090.53	20152.72
山 东 Shandong	940950.88	284839.86	147992.57	48302.87	36255.85	8593.14	3736.73	39958.70	58684.44	30030.82
河 南 Henan	989535.03	295860.91	211183.87	33281.21	23243.34	13229.65	3701.84	11221.00	74826.87	48836.28
湖 北 Hubei	734787.11	175714.93	110677.00	28870.23	20478.70	5540.00	1361.00	8788.00	43154.00	19049.00
湖 南 Hunan	907096.20	252599.40	173151.40	36392.00	15450.00	7334.00	3844.00	16428.00	50098.40	18078.40
广 东 Guangdong	3016125.17	1076395.89	665782.85	165202.67	72272.34	46598.52	25531.64	101007.87	192858.76	106712.45
广 西 Guangxi	890922.28	293345.65	198318.10	46701.27	18679.90	9187.88	3735.50	16723.00	48336.54	32448.40
海 南 Hainan	571314.48	167291.21	86458.21	30212.00	13173.00	4182.00	1306.00	31960.00	19188.00	7733.22
重 庆 Chongqing	446055.40	152561.96	114638.41	20463.50	9472.69	5072.75	2133.17	781.44	28210.72	12805.36
四 川 Sichuan	1067675.94	296924.48	193920.01	46913.56	21497.07	12787.46	2689.38	19117.00	49741.03	24216.41
贵 州 Guizhou	1057550.91	332517.74	175285.85	52332.69	29223.03	16112.13	9305.90	50258.14	60336.19	23251.02
云 南 Yunnan	1296658.87	460992.07	298256.21	65471.92	36752.62	19892.85	6888.96	33729.51	96663.30	53114.80
西 藏 Tibet	612753.30	200761.99	113722.50	29092.53	22792.33	5375.99	3796.95	25981.69	30452.24	18989.06
陕 西 Shaanxi	357642.66	136469.23	73735.61	17873.05	6706.14	4874.23	1576.20	31704.00	28438.92	10525.08
甘 肃 Gansu	453144.00	195498.02	128335.72	28438.10	9120.10	12414.10	1567.00	15623.00	35346.42	18024.70
青 海 Qinghai	168222.31	53982.30	28037.30	9327.00	11486.00	890.00	265.00	3977.00	7358.30	5680.30
宁 夏 Ningxia	0	0	0	0	0	0	0	0	0	0
新 疆 Xinjiang	1226867.00	505789.71	340716.59	62685.60	40373.43	23191.79	5016.34	33805.96	118123.87	60908.97

条件(一)(乡村)
Secondary Schools (1) (Rural Area)

单位:平方米
unit: m^2

生活用房 Residential and Welfare							其他用房 Rooms for Other Purposes	校舍面积中 of the Floor Space	
合计 Total	教工宿舍 Apartments for Single: 小计 Subtotal	教工宿舍 Apartments for Single: 其中:教师周转宿舍 of Which: Accommodation for Circulation of Teachers	学生宿舍 Students' Dormitories	食堂 Dining Halls	厕所 Toilet	其他 Others		危房面积 Floor Space of Dilapidated Buildings	当年新增校舍 New Floor Space Added in Current Year
12651506.37	**2837744.77**	**813479.17**	**6692195.67**	**2047077.01**	**571497.49**	**502991.43**	**2018401.53**	**112368.85**	**1641240.19**
235875.74	36616.62	1150.00	117233.77	45093.03	16096.22	20836.10	105908.83	0	12883.82
41458.00	6663.00	0	18090.00	6133.00	2359.00	8213.00	2244.00	0	0
593506.34	142924.74	21029.03	320423.80	77076.67	18079.09	35002.04	124928.35	0	73581.04
785169.55	104907.45	29349.00	427274.35	177021.75	47307.00	28659.00	230731.64	0	40355.00
129260.30	18552.48	2800.00	69878.40	26096.52	10311.17	4421.73	57109.00	0	15494.94
196844.86	14158.19	1340.38	121538.75	40406.93	13601.44	7139.55	89210.59	0	101854.69
81460.51	20512.42	200.00	41769.09	12002.00	3941.00	3236.00	12229.00	0	0
85561.97	3944.32	0	53198.34	16705.22	8010.28	3703.81	16272.17	2295.00	25002.00
72822.30	9011.00	991.00	33146.30	15562.00	5691.00	9412.00	10811.25	0	0
119854.58	20616.68	0	65580.66	19243.12	3954.46	10459.66	12848.40	0	0
592308.08	99006.40	15053.00	310750.38	123746.24	36271.03	22534.03	123411.83	0	13910.40
745622.50	192296.23	30375.55	390207.41	108971.93	22663.83	31483.10	77392.28	2386.00	98107.44
649512.68	216955.35	33854.42	284261.29	109220.14	23772.90	15303.00	154889.54	0	38671.95
353284.58	74352.29	14085.03	205708.81	52945.24	13767.00	6511.24	55440.84	182.04	26494.91
462099.54	42678.92	1282.00	271656.06	95701.43	30234.04	21829.09	135327.04	0	0
583032.16	86640.71	2445.60	357470.31	112334.38	17513.10	9073.66	35815.09	570.51	106484.36
409296.50	116231.10	23531.10	210448.00	48947.40	10669.00	23001.00	106621.68	0	4694.00
557299.40	191449.00	28056.00	259467.60	75835.00	14123.80	16424.00	47099.00	4712.00	7078.00
1521380.21	397824.58	103720.59	759560.90	213121.03	71255.35	79618.35	225490.31	7056.00	57935.00
526250.46	144269.60	73653.78	290730.61	67867.86	17119.39	6263.00	22989.63	5694.70	96436.20
289921.04	59028.00	53493.00	143843.00	50592.00	21356.00	15102.04	94914.23	0	5.00
253036.55	47495.41	15387.00	159279.66	35461.07	8680.34	2120.07	12246.17	0	3208.00
660678.69	167379.59	68254.66	368981.54	92339.08	18366.17	13612.31	60331.74	241.00	39951.33
600737.32	95143.84	44868.49	360194.79	99575.92	31592.93	14229.84	63959.66	0	434926.17
681109.39	160343.58	64173.08	352128.77	112223.81	33168.29	23244.94	57894.11	56635.00	143472.98
379207.63	108939.64	76653.90	171654.60	54270.65	9089.58	35253.16	2331.44	0	67687.32
185006.38	65285.00	1136.30	81918.53	23872.33	10041.99	3888.53	7728.13	0	14332.50
209677.06	50242.34	7970.00	112401.37	30546.80	11401.45	5085.10	12622.50	32596.60	53233.70
97810.10	23680.40	17621.40	54702.70	16101.00	1228.00	2098.00	9071.61	0	5257.00
0	0	0	0	0	0	0	0	0	0
552421.95	120595.89	81004.86	278695.88	88063.46	39832.64	25234.08	50531.47	0	160182.44

地 区 Region	占地面积(平方米) Areas of School Sites(m^2)			图书(册) Books & Magazines in Libraries (Volume)	
	合计 Total	其中: of Which:			合计 Total
		绿化用地面积 Green Areas	运动场地面积 Sports Areas		
总 计 Total	**1018559023.94**	**268973339.01**	**243177686.35**	**922702647**	**5180068**
北 京 Beijing	14714774.08	3144770.35	4443770.85	19920904	208361
天 津 Tianjin	9129094.94	1534437.94	2521013.86	12044004	68225
河 北 Hebei	48480432.10	9690221.88	11369187.05	44190160	222524
山 西 Shanxi	34143101.07	6367440.40	7470556.24	24663373	151481
内蒙古 Inner Mongolia	22905929.41	4365544.26	5815816.52	14233078	90866
辽 宁 Liaoning	23617311.55	4243347.72	6273923.58	16426463	126814
吉 林 Jilin	12658922.66	2620950.03	3869656.35	11503941	62786
黑龙江 Heilongjiang	20935775.65	3093062.11	5197820.61	10353554	90513
上 海 Shanghai	10557957.27	3546076.46	2434016.80	14833469	129770
江 苏 Jiangsu	54351903.55	19292991.90	12205374.93	52546482	315371
浙 江 Zhejiang	46523278.97	15296045.50	10623672.99	43080113	261620
安 徽 Anhui	52341519.11	13249018.53	10692223.18	33746204	220636
福 建 Fujian	36750640.95	10150824.44	9898798.40	46127431	203313
江 西 Jiangxi	39948430.91	11538155.83	9530901.31	35700485	168858
山 东 Shandong	68112181.60	19661723.44	15478177.65	59452545	328334
河 南 Henan	61969250.10	12846021.67	12035673.00	35193838	186747
湖 北 Hubei	38250621.54	11451139.00	7474274.72	20994889	121613
湖 南 Hunan	47075277.61	13645978.68	9290874.72	34230369	173600
广 东 Guangdong	91403261.43	29602267.23	22495130.13	116884921	655713
广 西 Guangxi	31434382.64	8496378.30	7326704.50	29312572	125144
海 南 Hainan	10353770.06	2778161.52	2197136.19	8221842	47667
重 庆 Chongqing	22446293.22	6610831.70	6360361.29	20412695	124163
四 川 Sichuan	53122057.03	12219944.88	17542421.94	64959407	309215
贵 州 Guizhou	35508896.75	9599700.04	9156740.32	35885513	148876
云 南 Yunnan	40650881.67	12023705.08	8544748.10	31875786	176672
西 藏 Tibet	3696113.26	739083.24	600483.65	1651769	8518
陕 西 Shaanxi	25587509.63	5527707.26	6932262.06	37282350	176556
甘 肃 Gansu	19024190.39	3744092.84	5320483.86	18925545	99686
青 海 Qinghai	5923149.14	1234917.01	1475619.69	5536105	29234
宁 夏 Ningxia	7842145.22	2450024.11	1534180.24	5609371	34885
新 疆 Xinjiang	29099970.43	8208775.66	7065681.62	16903469	112307

学条件(二)(总计)
Secondary Schools (2) (Total)

计算机数(台) PC (Set)		教室(间) Classroom(Room)		教室中:普通教室(间) of Which: General Classroom(Room)		固定资产总值(万元) Total Value of Fixed Asset (10,000 yuan)		
其中:教学用计算机 No. of Computers Used for Instruction		合计 Total	其中:网络多媒体教室 of Which: Network Multimedia Classroom	合计 Total	其中:网络多媒体教室 of Which: Network Multimedia Classroom	合计 Total	其中:教学仪器设备资产值 of Which: Total Value of Equip & Instru.	
小计 Subtotal	其中:平板电脑 of Which: Tablet PC						小计 Subtotal	其中:实验设备 of Which: for Experiment
4299671	**254200**	**1065685**	**704340**	**802602**	**621865**	**83707301.04**	**8854589.85**	**2805597.08**
182507	17710	24768	21397	15910	14921	2532631.96	686647.80	116251.25
57411	2556	11035	8564	7707	6640	813598.04	112140.85	26617.39
208479	13282	51726	35113	42459	33110	3187791.58	284306.73	108572.83
121533	4895	34703	22474	26156	20322	2599015.88	237029.79	101601.61
71534	2652	18480	13500	13629	12095	2052699.41	186488.84	67226.37
93503	10012	25216	14740	19850	13221	1692638.52	191510.62	69970.44
46943	1954	17806	8215	12877	7447	978111.79	101145.33	36999.21
66175	3298	23464	11935	15679	10748	1312432.42	153870.63	45759.83
101200	7418	16067	12101	9949	8622	1993765.50	293269.29	70645.11
271368	13250	55603	37772	35568	30095	6179603.09	541692.13	174444.85
222737	11033	40322	31955	27054	25548	4437150.72	485868.31	131477.17
181913	17506	49822	29128	40838	27244	3599685.17	303631.50	117660.89
161692	4380	41504	29669	27062	24967	2894740.49	373827.05	117333.78
138415	8280	43132	26927	36105	25755	2282858.04	239229.12	80890.46
277815	10081	65257	46339	48622	41326	5581872.25	482891.09	145056.17
153893	13785	60810	33566	51597	31795	3462657.74	249201.97	97412.34
98798	7331	33616	18168	25637	16774	2903883.40	240880.56	96600.23
140830	8231	49036	27751	37835	26439	3774327.98	331267.29	122571.40
543532	46729	95757	77298	72714	66807	8106616.57	969422.72	293162.90
94374	7708	27447	17676	23945	16889	1821093.06	211198.77	78603.15
39008	1997	9148	6408	7286	5868	930768.70	109252.40	33051.61
103460	6854	25211	21423	19791	18420	1881987.67	176949.93	44769.09
262498	9687	65307	40371	54064	37089	4821202.61	637729.27	207840.64
127084	8332	35436	24456	27825	22640	3272300.68	259645.93	95971.86
145421	2991	43804	22400	32813	20721	3043457.70	234553.87	57739.64
6200	94	1934	1253	1654	1186	292843.83	14641.47	4989.77
156623	5387	33091	24814	26120	21768	2507122.76	324661.40	132820.47
86492	2452	26306	14842	15059	12570	1624810.32	144270.20	46099.99
24517	1647	6073	2905	4225	2654	501703.65	40348.06	16009.38
29998	329	5537	3916	4028	3479	608669.70	58500.94	19983.32
83718	2339	28267	17264	18544	14705	2015259.82	178516.01	47463.92

普通高中办

Condition of School Buildings in Senior

地　区 Region	占地面积(平方米) Areas of School Sites(m^2)			图书(册) Books & Magazines in Libraries (Volume)	
	合计 Total	其中： of Which：			合计 Total
		绿化用地面积 Green Areas	运动场地面积 Sports Areas		
总　计 Total	**480650439.61**	**135164757.00**	**118280350.12**	**492949539**	**3033415**
北　京 Beijing	12388328.23	2459967.85	3894944.40	18877264	196969
天　津 Tianjin	7615257.02	1296424.48	2091779.16	10478430	62402
河　北 Hebei	19731519.89	4040618.07	4655234.59	21072968	109771
山　西 Shanxi	13856823.38	2676533.38	3397578.06	12708025	82976
内蒙古 Inner Mongolia	10193286.63	2155476.77	2611644.31	7848655	49231
辽　宁 Liaoning	16710067.56	3053588.84	4539211.57	12905765	101015
吉　林 Jilin	7098459.78	1496381.89	2326276.54	7235983	41261
黑龙江 Heilongjiang	10984176.01	1769589.31	3026864.23	6298113	56609
上　海 Shanghai	9117788.96	3052776.86	2112304.53	13647669	119591
江　苏 Jiangsu	30791396.37	11417365.99	6787382.38	30546371	198309
浙　江 Zhejiang	27601882.37	9269162.27	6304845.21	25492636	162144
安　徽 Anhui	15494092.32	4251023.88	3344392.79	11772611	84901
福　建 Fujian	14131583.38	4002460.03	3849945.91	20936933	104032
江　西 Jiangxi	14587417.43	4390301.52	3496023.88	15047186	77571
山　东 Shandong	36991398.75	11263582.85	8578449.30	34306598	195959
河　南 Henan	22375524.20	5028652.43	4828752.63	16191047	87642
湖　北 Hubei	23278093.49	7624542.49	4710444.87	13240383	81769
湖　南 Hunan	16528636.22	5134580.21	3541067.88	12593375	75931
广　东 Guangdong	55904704.96	18687117.81	14053410.68	78963407	464673
广　西 Guangxi	13125589.66	4045496.39	3116722.81	13599287	65817
海　南 Hainan	5292770.64	1386898.60	1138488.95	4401192	27700
重　庆 Chongqing	12100376.05	3661541.80	3431784.72	11791825	76631
四　川 Sichuan	22025435.24	5562080.92	7034931.24	28034630	148753
贵　州 Guizhou	11461047.37	3262925.25	3241452.12	10795426	54573
云　南 Yunnan	15425872.87	5120234.99	3109285.28	13310787	79265
西　藏 Tibet	1499190.10	278767.50	266714.27	673222	4192
陕　西 Shaanxi	11059186.49	2340177.12	3082239.38	19044732	95153
甘　肃 Gansu	5523648.60	1313421.78	1505894.09	7102010	37890
青　海 Qinghai	1927535.35	548294.74	416949.63	2111226	11680
宁　夏 Ningxia	4560187.20	1451617.27	892790.57	3369420	22258
新　疆 Xinjiang	11269163.09	3123153.71	2892544.14	8552363	56747

学条件(二)(城区)
Secondary Schools (2) (Urban Area)

计算机数(台) PC (Set)		教室(间) Classroom(Room)		教室中:普通教室(间) of Which: General Classroom(Room)		固定资产总值(万元) Total Value of Fixed Asset (10,000 yuan)		
其中:教学用计算机 No. of Computers Used for Instruction		合计 Total	其中:网络多媒体教室 of Which: Network Multimedia Classroom	合计 Total	其中:网络多媒体教室 of Which: Network Multimedia Classroom	合计 Total	其中:教学仪器设备资产值 of Which: Total Value of Equip & Instru.	
小计 Subtotal	其中:平板电脑 of Which: Tablet PC						小计 Subtotal	其中:实验设备 of Which: for Experiment
2495195	**176623**	**553310**	**389083**	**410587**	**335130**	**46561488.10**	**5550894.53**	**1583944.87**
172658	16737	22638	19819	14471	13724	2435441.17	657597.94	111554.10
52711	2245	9902	7694	6892	5936	750759.80	103227.39	23216.21
103203	8102	22983	16578	19008	15644	1493573.16	144581.63	49470.02
65898	2866	17377	11363	12930	10404	1194891.36	128522.46	53605.22
38389	1835	9395	7117	7196	6406	1028857.75	104961.44	32777.16
75658	8301	18129	11299	14036	9980	1231592.02	145515.68	51439.57
31645	1581	11617	5800	8323	5323	655717.85	71662.56	26671.24
41548	2742	14301	7521	9349	6642	782559.42	102729.99	27673.35
93891	6825	14611	11084	9025	7850	1781251.21	272425.09	65367.39
169113	11295	32543	23226	20562	18065	4065777.56	366071.71	109896.92
135216	8549	25308	20118	16859	15897	2863916.55	303048.20	82688.98
69011	12105	17260	10313	14039	9433	1096277.95	116940.37	43793.65
82271	3060	18838	13894	12516	11448	1481033.28	200881.03	57172.02
61790	4766	18410	12029	15204	11375	1048265.08	119434.28	41448.85
162022	5880	36128	26013	26180	22716	3222017.06	298272.53	83326.32
71015	7357	23514	13753	19271	12912	1360387.90	116949.38	42746.18
66286	5319	21384	11707	16364	10869	1855201.74	163856.08	65411.31
61103	4959	20604	12718	16435	12076	1736343.16	149262.85	50822.18
380443	32060	65009	54332	49502	46265	6012827.11	753796.09	201959.72
47427	4565	12575	7979	10633	7515	906790.64	115619.04	36657.64
23383	1782	5453	4049	4447	3707	465011.38	65504.27	20214.92
62700	4544	14784	12429	11731	10708	1219623.22	109438.82	24818.42
128820	6843	28849	19888	23800	18224	2484692.21	326798.35	100327.11
46224	5954	11173	8042	9058	7394	840360.62	96072.06	28234.39
63804	1679	17449	10332	12533	9337	1240030.52	130314.60	25197.75
3038	35	830	565	746	548	89730.07	7680.40	2915.67
82771	1893	16448	12486	12320	10400	1202729.00	185895.92	66195.81
32285	1016	8068	4925	4962	4208	521281.18	50209.43	14957.96
9716	522	2128	986	1564	899	202444.00	16566.28	6502.22
19037	205	3529	2471	2464	2153	399099.18	34955.16	13155.81
42119	1001	12073	8553	8167	7072	893004.97	92103.47	23726.76

地区 Region	占地面积(平方米) Areas of School Sites(m^2)			图书(册) Books & Magazines in Libraries (Volume)	
	合计 Total	其中: of Which:			合计 Total
		绿化用地面积 Green Areas	运动场地面积 Sports Areas		
总　计 Total	**94668113.41**	**28690372.60**	**20939009.44**	**77547263**	**450062**
北　京 Beijing	2037444.82	338121.39	426598.46	883694	7924
天　津 Tianjin	658147.30	113772.00	206632.00	802226	4392
河　北 Hebei	5207622.20	1259850.98	1091805.15	3728962	18777
山　西 Shanxi	2195980.10	395676.00	511502.60	1294959	9597
内蒙古 Inner Mongolia	564894.00	85014.00	132931.00	279548	1559
辽　宁 Liaoning	1969835.67	388814.56	481324.17	1235142	9092
吉　林 Jilin	569335.12	160342.12	162910.12	293934	1285
黑龙江 Heilongjiang	808050.00	150828.00	170563.00	509383	4118
上　海 Shanghai	1125126.98	488595.84	200316.90	730920	7679
江　苏 Jiangsu	3943705.88	1393042.29	776091.68	3621428	19929
浙　江 Zhejiang	7271179.22	2365906.93	1569340.26	5978510	37116
安　徽 Anhui	3845995.97	1024793.04	747178.76	2137951	15113
福　建 Fujian	2527471.90	695966.12	680778.15	2795937	12060
江　西 Jiangxi	1432759.46	471816.70	264369.00	1332090	5339
山　东 Shandong	11508363.28	3913777.19	2520392.12	8705299	49010
河　南 Henan	5478017.97	1100492.09	991539.45	2244229	14266
湖　北 Hubei	4719620.25	1729030.00	901797.56	2403833	14278
湖　南 Hunan	3076704.32	921332.68	583647.58	1704514	9197
广　东 Guangdong	18798899.83	6754200.54	4414386.23	22979492	130686
广　西 Guangxi	2226280.32	595797.48	587549.75	2177222	11020
海　南 Hainan	706864.06	216387.00	150430.70	389010	2540
重　庆 Chongqing	721290.94	148874.17	166620.00	442512	3078
四　川 Sichuan	3027160.12	814205.91	983761.73	3148993	18776
贵　州 Guizhou	2111925.90	611139.44	501354.88	1847308	9065
云　南 Yunnan	4663181.44	1611658.93	808432.64	3174974	18461
西　藏 Tibet	0	0	0	0	0
陕　西 Shaanxi	1254297.06	252009.97	339191.78	1457114	6342
甘　肃 Gansu	360700.46	68600.10	74513.38	266651	1545
青　海 Qinghai	263491.00	81503.00	49977.00	329723	1828
宁　夏 Ningxia	431102.60	132308.90	90393.20	188668	1315
新　疆 Xinjiang	1162665.24	406315.23	352680.19	463037	4675

条件(二)(城乡结合区)
Schools (2) (Urban-rural Transitional Area)

计算机数(台) PC (Set)		教室(间) Classroom(Room)		教室中:普通教室(间) of Which: General Classroom(Room)		固定资产总值(万元) Total Value of Fixed Asset (10,000 yuan)		
其中:教学用计算机 No. of Computers Used for Instruction		合计 Total	其中:网络多媒体教室 of Which: Network Multimedia Classroom	合计 Total	其中:网络多媒体教室 of Which: Network Multimedia Classroom	合计 Total	其中:教学仪器设备资产值 of Which: Total Value of Equip & Instru.	
小计 Subtotal	其中:平板电脑 of Which: Tablet PC						小计 Subtotal	其中:实验设备 of Which: for Experiment
376838	**21340**	**90616**	**63156**	**68248**	**54871**	**8696151.95**	**777490.19**	**256221.00**
6633	422	1475	1105	1068	828	160166.11	24909.29	3417.66
3441	10	797	536	586	420	52723.00	7210.85	1521.46
17837	559	5227	3785	4520	3621	393157.14	27302.09	9980.87
8032	99	2275	1621	1626	1385	162796.61	10356.19	4837.56
1098	0	380	246	261	217	41053.19	3339.65	640.32
7092	469	2086	1161	1599	1038	132733.99	14143.56	7157.66
941	10	452	108	329	104	17024.20	2173.00	762.74
2575	248	814	463	502	447	53483.04	6123.52	2224.15
5391	516	1460	855	1021	716	101633.14	17148.48	3062.01
17469	932	3797	2413	2294	1916	574651.30	38570.69	13769.41
30647	1225	6670	5259	4269	3997	856760.09	77986.71	23271.46
12082	980	3796	2116	2972	1959	258979.12	22623.93	9346.27
9831	422	2657	1750	1708	1404	172593.22	24647.86	8864.28
4496	78	1252	764	1097	729	108980.98	10576.07	1843.22
42429	973	10059	7191	7293	6056	1022035.57	71153.99	22546.24
11699	841	4166	2601	3574	2487	296053.32	19645.71	7644.47
11241	338	4032	2002	3031	1874	437493.53	30351.18	13489.77
7380	281	2810	1811	2433	1763	213518.95	14036.96	5888.96
112807	9444	18998	16277	14787	14135	1976057.41	194762.53	60556.27
8070	966	2226	1488	2007	1399	199715.24	23562.43	5752.57
2308	212	446	376	391	359	64020.20	5813.90	2888.00
2463	104	821	720	709	664	50679.26	3679.43	670.02
16052	733	3304	2145	2603	1858	383938.01	49867.12	16532.15
7487	180	2060	1485	1712	1322	184600.83	21760.90	7605.29
14311	1065	4622	2767	3550	2443	446789.91	27901.87	8448.45
0	0	0	0	0	0	0	0	0
5598	221	1487	861	1024	734	96126.67	13743.91	8250.41
1220	0	628	227	213	194	69491.21	2607.90	866.07
1552	3	335	148	222	135	38322.50	2036.03	1694.16
1295	9	424	183	245	145	48912.16	3705.68	966.73
3361	0	1060	692	602	522	81662.05	5748.75	1722.35

普通高中办学

Condition of School Buildings in Senior Secondary

地 区 Region	占地面积(平方米) Areas of School Sites(m^2)			图书(册) Books & Magazines in Libraries (Volume)	
	合计 Total	其中: of Which:			合计 Total
		绿化用地面积 Green Areas	运动场地面积 Sports Areas		
总 计 Total	**483113234.33**	**119019821.41**	**113453856.25**	**397055654**	**1963870**
北 京 Beijing	998492.00	253771.30	250548.00	419136	5010
天 津 Tianjin	1336013.92	201442.46	372516.70	1373810	5267
河 北 Hebei	26321478.72	5057208.65	6320229.59	21667242	104334
山 西 Shanxi	16946733.09	3097944.02	3328873.90	10370673	59973
内蒙古 Inner Mongolia	12059320.67	2118007.10	3021856.30	6071273	39526
辽 宁 Liaoning	5995629.71	998096.53	1537735.00	3121038	23146
吉 林 Jilin	4905317.88	1035333.14	1454141.21	4062535	20550
黑龙江 Heilongjiang	9447499.64	1269817.80	2061979.38	3854791	32640
上 海 Shanghai	1121796.70	402924.60	254395.60	1034650	8482
江 苏 Jiangsu	23040839.52	7693671.53	5278148.46	21599907	114872
浙 江 Zhejiang	16486148.32	5319420.30	3774959.04	15717148	88071
安 徽 Anhui	34138799.10	8363346.31	6864520.03	20689662	128048
福 建 Fujian	19578286.76	5404601.93	5285218.74	22464828	89350
江 西 Jiangxi	23334790.49	6650695.31	5584017.13	20070509	87455
山 东 Shandong	29075941.85	7844491.59	6642209.35	24365174	125596
河 南 Henan	37077344.67	7453134.53	6815712.44	18089190	93370
湖 北 Hubei	13632047.05	3505098.51	2562805.85	7097712	35736
湖 南 Hunan	28681137.26	8027485.47	5383576.84	20643397	92609
广 东 Guangdong	27762016.63	7857413.31	6743597.21	32495186	156363
广 西 Guangxi	16526314.96	3993772.79	3850694.01	14697108	52861
海 南 Hainan	3702362.64	933705.00	828219.24	3198935	15716
重 庆 Chongqing	9392058.16	2648668.90	2674749.57	8014851	43911
四 川 Sichuan	29140155.83	6045028.03	9972127.50	35324207	151582
贵 州 Guizhou	22001863.08	5700169.15	5541734.04	23190415	89630
云 南 Yunnan	21965969.26	6003950.31	4854782.04	16860725	88644
西 藏 Tibet	739529.57	131266.00	97815.00	317488	1404
陕 西 Shaanxi	13779143.83	3054736.59	3670912.15	17553394	78612
甘 肃 Gansu	12573961.49	2220368.05	3578889.77	10998188	57749
青 海 Qinghai	3510488.79	574678.27	966992.06	3168771	16370
宁 夏 Ningxia	3281958.02	998406.84	641389.67	2239951	12627
新 疆 Xinjiang	14559794.72	4161167.09	3238510.43	6283760	44366

条件(二)(镇区)
Schools (2) (Counties & Towns Area)

计算机数(台) PC (Set)		教室(间) Classroom(Room)		教室中:普通教室(间) of Which: General Classroom(Room)		固定资产总值(万元) Total Value of Fixed Asset (10,000 yuan)		
其中:教学用计算机 No. of Computers Used for Instruction		合计 Total	其中:网络多媒体教室 of Which: Network Multimedia Classroom	合计 Total	其中:网络多媒体教室 of Which: Network Multimedia Classroom	合计 Total	其中:教学仪器设备资产值 of Which: Total Value of Equip & Instru.	
小计 Subtotal	其中:平板电脑 of Which: Tablet PC						小计 Subtotal	其中:实验设备 of Which:for Experiment
1651012	**65840**	**466634**	**288592**	**358390**	**263568**	**33122331.43**	**3000934.22**	**1120055.91**
4295	364	990	747	675	555	37675.84	10077.52	1729.67
4254	311	996	766	733	647	55059.99	8309.26	3168.96
97638	5013	26163	16996	21599	16250	1623883.34	131839.02	56169.93
48851	1341	14735	9659	11442	8795	1104008.24	85833.82	36501.80
31417	797	8641	6142	6069	5461	979047.55	79251.24	33598.81
15607	1522	6263	3055	5144	2896	381036.14	41120.03	17111.50
14682	373	5799	2298	4268	2012	297809.77	28154.42	9796.22
23686	556	8761	4166	6088	3887	502412.72	49473.06	17162.75
6010	538	1193	851	716	636	161310.54	16485.59	4450.76
100280	1955	22650	14331	14697	11831	2049571.57	169912.66	63076.45
77884	2223	13214	10393	9029	8528	1380839.55	165226.34	43504.28
106693	5113	30296	17549	24987	16679	2315350.83	171775.17	69873.37
71003	1249	20014	14020	12930	12058	1168494.79	154164.28	54117.73
73431	3372	23205	14164	19638	13667	1167040.23	114491.25	37737.84
109704	3914	27430	19353	21170	17766	2127093.46	174152.26	59136.95
78251	5634	35558	18777	30753	17900	2007182.83	126187.73	52297.46
29016	1720	11210	5887	8525	5398	950640.24	65168.00	27585.44
76007	3137	26275	14266	19784	13638	1957756.59	173672.62	69029.91
133303	10090	25493	19063	19187	17099	1560943.29	175135.13	77266.73
42190	2504	13443	8741	11985	8432	791803.43	82795.72	35370.60
12302	152	2832	1901	2278	1773	323874.70	32940.01	9123.11
37463	1550	9658	8337	7411	7109	620301.58	63123.79	19257.67
126036	2638	34421	19067	28643	17630	2199357.49	293960.76	102237.02
76899	2059	22471	15418	17456	14411	2143359.44	154737.26	63707.90
74103	1309	23174	11222	17764	10590	1535563.87	94482.89	28869.94
1016	0	268	122	245	122	38405.05	1499.00	734.00
71296	3352	15975	11962	13323	11035	1265896.33	134557.48	64687.55
50765	1071	16869	9265	9440	7814	971991.16	86415.29	28364.84
13880	1038	3633	1813	2409	1657	256977.72	21748.64	8190.55
10961	124	2008	1445	1564	1326	209570.52	23545.77	6827.51
32089	821	12996	6816	8438	5966	938072.63	70698.19	19368.66

地　区 Region	占地面积(平方米) Areas of School Sites(m^2)			图书(册) Books & Magazines in Libraries (Volume)	
	合计 Total	其中: of Which:			合计 Total
		绿化用地面积 Green Areas	运动场地面积 Sports Areas		
总　计 Total	**125183769.66**	**31599911.94**	**28049016.96**	**98122264**	**493342**
北　京 Beijing	450566.00	106204.00	132614.00	217048	2302
天　津 Tianjin	843164.92	137039.46	234675.70	885742	3477
河　北 Hebei	11127937.55	2111785.40	2749944.71	9862820	44433
山　西 Shanxi	6468237.89	1306379.61	1142853.29	3920749	22601
内蒙古 Inner Mongolia	1184060.00	252608.00	298203.00	461222	3009
辽　宁 Liaoning	784681.36	125909.99	129180.48	376191	2243
吉　林 Jilin	508158.25	165217.15	104801.03	487295	2278
黑龙江 Heilongjiang	1073856.61	82560.25	197018.00	355192	3603
上　海 Shanghai	297708.10	86773.60	47788.60	215675	1493
江　苏 Jiangsu	5592137.97	1798597.12	1341910.28	5553928	30703
浙　江 Zhejiang	5586255.89	1732243.61	1110289.27	4927110	26296
安　徽 Anhui	6332894.15	1428958.74	1164722.65	3300298	19476
福　建 Fujian	5180062.73	1449886.95	1404003.67	5482123	21117
江　西 Jiangxi	3787946.19	1021948.53	813938.62	2731522	12338
山　东 Shandong	13466491.46	3773531.94	3211509.25	10762021	54830
河　南 Henan	12468483.69	2703210.44	2208636.91	5230301	30180
湖　北 Hubei	3329949.00	835127.04	595533.00	1592197	7526
湖　南 Hunan	5635592.72	1519037.53	1085863.25	4438563	18434
广　东 Guangdong	10026620.75	3148303.00	2434216.24	12954772	63725
广　西 Guangxi	2216733.77	595959.01	458688.40	1423864	6276
海　南 Hainan	1056355.59	237326.00	205125.24	889120	5493
重　庆 Chongqing	2168132.09	716408.14	530347.88	1523735	8151
四　川 Sichuan	3933686.27	919429.90	1217922.50	3569734	20002
贵　州 Guizhou	5081616.07	1266620.97	1441770.37	4318854	16406
云　南 Yunnan	6900529.38	1798071.65	1320313.00	4388402	25781
西　藏 Tibet	0	0	0	0	0
陕　西 Shaanxi	3994958.91	933668.37	1112841.63	4818402	21516
甘　肃 Gansu	2717762.94	526132.03	701914.40	2136320	10462
青　海 Qinghai	778756.30	166975.00	180016.40	649568	3830
宁　夏 Ningxia	422045.61	103255.10	80385.51	196109	852
新　疆 Xinjiang	1768387.50	550743.41	391989.68	453387	4509

条件(二)(镇乡结合区)
Schools (2) (County-Town Transitional Area)

计算机数(台) PC (set)		教室(间) Classroom(Room)		教室中:普通教室(间) of Which: General Classroom(Room)		固定资产总值(万元) Total Value of Fixed Asset (10,000 yuan)		
其中:教学用计算机 No. of Computers Used for Instruction		合计 Total	其中:网络多媒体教室 of Which: Network Multimedia Classroom	合计 Total	其中:网络多媒体教室 of Which: Network Multimedia Classroom	合计 Total	其中:教学仪器设备资产值 of Which: Total Value of Equip & Instru.	
小计 Subtotal	其中:平板电脑 of Which: Tablet PC						小计 Subtotal	其中:实验设备 of Which: for Experiment
419516	**19007**	**117642**	**72364**	**90486**	**65905**	**8962896.45**	**774256.37**	**291370.78**
1882	123	451	333	348	272	9442.96	4946.12	1061.72
2749	22	555	459	423	397	38945.46	4928.23	2344.32
41898	2479	11226	6993	9666	6754	705166.56	56213.04	23970.71
17802	291	5711	3545	4138	3140	383270.82	33078.71	13740.81
2354	112	798	543	581	495	78459.45	7489.34	2362.91
1452	0	628	318	582	304	79798.33	10361.72	6355.07
1414	116	523	39	428	37	25747.06	3449.98	528.47
2407	145	1160	447	618	417	65577.78	6517.80	2265.50
1185	26	320	198	180	139	47435.33	5957.61	2434.80
26218	861	5944	3866	3706	3119	555613.34	41998.21	14772.88
23003	227	3907	3101	2898	2635	473901.47	53222.04	10639.14
16758	247	5240	2550	4387	2406	390750.69	22542.87	8814.55
17147	145	5410	3677	3454	3180	325544.61	37315.72	14708.12
10849	259	3701	2136	3011	1987	189233.21	20350.69	6417.54
48730	2369	12620	9251	9749	8430	933476.49	86730.69	31137.33
25269	1205	11288	5468	9697	5239	641718.53	42829.67	16518.95
5819	107	2443	1084	1825	1028	229778.08	15219.75	5377.77
14263	601	5300	2666	4095	2468	402398.62	29654.34	12460.08
55176	6941	10026	7228	7453	6592	678267.24	70751.73	33079.89
4657	409	1550	1151	1423	1115	132264.68	7838.95	4563.03
3230	7	642	504	593	486	74033.12	6953.78	1629.00
6770	124	1888	1659	1568	1522	129192.63	12510.08	3470.95
16642	805	4260	2255	3320	1938	370999.51	50828.99	16671.77
15054	4	4907	3377	3908	3186	556496.60	36915.03	14796.84
20543	512	6946	3338	5314	3105	545761.10	30551.83	9647.21
0	0	0	0	0	0	0	0	0
19694	578	4298	3043	3459	2835	437971.76	43062.65	22299.29
8975	135	3374	1966	1925	1609	230322.55	17768.54	4926.43
3319	76	692	376	527	350	63262.37	3878.86	1691.54
839	0	192	112	158	110	26332.00	1705.33	1075.34
3418	81	1642	681	1052	610	141734.08	8684.04	1608.81

地　区 Region	占地面积(平方米) Areas of School Sites(m^2)			图书(册) Books & Magazines in Libraries (Volume)	合计 Total
	合计 Total	其中：of Which：			
		绿化用地面积 Green Areas	运动场地面积 Sports Areas		
总　计 Total	**54795350.00**	**14788760.60**	**11443479.98**	**32697454**	**182783**
北　京 Beijing	1327953.85	431031.20	298278.45	624504	6382
天　津 Tianjin	177824.00	36571.00	56718.00	191764	556
河　北 Hebei	2427433.49	592395.16	393722.87	1449950	8419
山　西 Shanxi	3339544.60	592963.00	744104.28	1584675	8532
内蒙古 Inner Mongolia	653322.11	92060.39	182315.91	313150	2109
辽　宁 Liaoning	911614.28	191662.35	196977.01	399660	2653
吉　林 Jilin	655145.00	89235.00	89238.60	205423	975
黑龙江 Heilongjiang	504100.00	53655.00	108977.00	200650	1264
上　海 Shanghai	318371.61	90375.00	67316.67	151150	1697
江　苏 Jiangsu	519667.66	181954.38	139844.09	400204	2190
浙　江 Zhejiang	2435248.28	707462.93	543868.74	1870329	11405
安　徽 Anhui	2708627.69	634648.34	483310.36	1283931	7687
福　建 Fujian	3040770.81	743762.48	763633.75	2725670	9931
江　西 Jiangxi	2026222.99	497159.00	450860.30	582790	3832
山　东 Shandong	2044841.00	553649.00	257519.00	780773	6779
河　南 Henan	2516381.23	364234.71	391207.93	913601	5735
湖　北 Hubei	1340481.00	321498.00	201024.00	656794	4108
湖　南 Hunan	1865504.13	483913.00	366230.00	993597	5060
广　东 Guangdong	7736539.84	3057736.11	1698122.24	5426328	34677
广　西 Guangxi	1782478.02	457109.12	359287.68	1016177	6466
海　南 Hainan	1358636.78	457557.92	230428.00	621715	4251
重　庆 Chongqing	953859.01	300621.00	253827.00	606019	3621
四　川 Sichuan	1956465.96	612835.93	535363.20	1600570	8880
贵　州 Guizhou	2045986.30	636605.64	373554.16	1899672	4673
云　南 Yunnan	3259039.54	899519.78	580680.78	1704274	8763
西　藏 Tibet	1457393.59	329049.74	235954.38	661059	2922
陕　西 Shaanxi	749179.31	132793.55	179110.53	684224	2791
甘　肃 Gansu	926580.30	210303.01	235700.00	825347	4047
青　海 Qinghai	485125.00	111944.00	91678.00	256108	1184
宁　夏 Ningxia	0	0	0	0	0
新　疆 Xinjiang	3271012.62	924454.86	934627.05	2067346	11194

条件(二)(乡村)
Secondary Schools (2) (Rural Area)

计算机数(台) PC (Set)：其中:教学用计算机 No. of Computers Used for Instruction：小计 Subtotal	计算机数(台) PC (Set)：其中:教学用计算机：其中:平板电脑 of Which: Tablet PC	教室(间) Classroom (Room)：合计 Total	教室(间) Classroom (Room)：其中:网络多媒体教室 of Which: Network Multimedia Classroom	教室中:普通教室(间) of Which: General Classroom (Room)：合计 Total	教室中:普通教室(间)：其中:网络多媒体教室 of Which: Network Multimedia Classroom	固定资产总值(万元) Total Value of Fixed Asset (10,000 yuan)：合计 Total	固定资产总值(万元)：其中:教学仪器设备资产值 of Which: Total Value of Equip & Instru.：小计 Subtotal	固定资产总值(万元)：其中:教学仪器设备资产值：其中:实验设备 of Which: for Experiment
153464	**11737**	**45741**	**26665**	**33625**	**23167**	**4023481.52**	**302761.10**	**101596.30**
5554	609	1140	831	764	642	59514.94	18972.35	2967.48
446	0	137	104	82	57	7778.25	604.20	232.23
7638	167	2580	1539	1852	1216	70335.08	7886.08	2932.88
6784	688	2591	1452	1784	1123	300116.28	22673.51	11494.60
1728	20	444	241	364	228	44794.10	2276.15	850.40
2238	189	824	386	670	345	80010.36	4874.91	1419.36
616	0	390	117	286	112	24584.17	1328.35	531.74
941	0	402	248	242	219	27460.27	1667.57	923.74
1299	55	263	166	208	136	51203.75	4358.61	826.96
1975	0	410	215	309	199	64253.97	5707.76	1471.49
9637	261	1800	1444	1166	1123	192394.63	17593.77	5283.91
6209	288	2266	1266	1812	1132	188056.39	14915.96	3993.87
8418	71	2652	1755	1616	1461	245212.42	18781.74	6044.03
3194	142	1517	734	1263	713	67552.74	5303.59	1703.77
6089	287	1699	973	1272	844	232761.73	10466.30	2592.89
4627	794	1738	1036	1573	983	95087.02	6064.85	2368.70
3496	292	1022	574	748	507	98041.42	11856.48	3603.47
3720	135	2157	767	1616	725	80228.23	8331.82	2719.31
29786	4579	5255	3903	4025	3443	532846.17	40491.50	13936.45
4757	639	1429	956	1327	942	122498.99	12784.01	6574.91
3323	63	863	458	561	388	141882.62	10808.12	3713.58
3297	760	769	657	649	603	42062.87	4387.32	693.00
7642	206	2037	1416	1621	1235	137152.91	16970.15	5276.51
3961	319	1792	996	1311	835	288580.62	8836.60	4029.57
7514	3	3181	846	2516	794	267863.30	9756.39	3671.94
2146	59	836	566	663	516	164708.71	5462.07	1340.10
2556	142	668	366	477	333	38497.42	4207.99	1937.11
3442	365	1369	652	657	548	131537.99	7645.48	2777.19
921	87	312	106	252	98	42281.92	2033.14	1316.60
0	0	0	0	0	0	0	0	0
9510	517	3198	1895	1939	1667	184182.22	15714.35	4368.51

地区 Region	合计 Total	其中：中央部门办 of Which: HEIs under Central Ministries & Agencies	其中：地方公办 of Which: HEIs under Local Auth.	其中：民办 of Which: Non-government	小计 Subtotal	其中：中央部门办 of Which: HEIs under Central Ministries & Agencies	其中：地方公办 of Which: HEIs under Local Auth.
	中等职业学校				普通中专学校 Reg. Specialized Sec. Schools		
总 计 Total	**8181**	**23**	**6089**	**2069**	**3346**	**17**	**2498**
北 京 Beijing	89	7	61	21	30	6	23
天 津 Tianjin	73	0	66	7	38	0	37
河 北 Hebei	609	2	442	165	247	2	104
山 西 Shanxi	449	0	350	99	92	0	79
内蒙古 Inner Mongolia	248	0	182	66	76	0	35
辽 宁 Liaoning	288	0	201	87	105	0	95
吉 林 Jilin	274	1	205	68	43	0	39
黑龙江 Heilongjiang	237	0	184	53	82	0	40
上 海 Shanghai	94	2	88	4	57	2	54
江 苏 Jiangsu	228	0	203	25	161	0	144
浙 江 Zhejiang	251	0	208	43	46	0	40
安 徽 Anhui	359	0	251	108	147	0	119
福 建 Fujian	184	0	152	32	184	0	152
江 西 Jiangxi	366	1	252	113	73	1	56
山 东 Shandong	401	1	301	99	237	0	181
河 南 Henan	640	2	452	186	153	1	130
湖 北 Hubei	289	2	224	63	218	2	172
湖 南 Hunan	467	0	282	185	34	0	32
广 东 Guangdong	459	0	343	116	337	0	242
广 西 Guangxi	271	0	207	64	271	0	207
海 南 Hainan	79	0	45	34	31	0	25
重 庆 Chongqing	132	0	110	22	26	0	22
四 川 Sichuan	436	0	248	188	215	0	72
贵 州 Guizhou	192	0	145	47	66	0	60
云 南 Yunnan	374	2	332	40	82	1	68
西 藏 Tibet	11	0	11	0	11	0	11
陕 西 Shaanxi	245	0	154	91	32	0	30
甘 肃 Gansu	209	0	181	28	117	0	110
青 海 Qinghai	39	0	33	6	35	0	30
宁 夏 Ningxia	28	0	22	6	13	0	7
新 疆 Xinjiang	160	3	154	3	87	2	82

校(机构)数
Vocational Schools

单位:人
unit: institution

Secondary Vocational Schools

	成人中专学校 Adults Specialized Sec. Schools				职业高中学校 Vocational High Schools			
其中:民办 of Which: Non-government	小计 Subtotal	其中:中央部门办 of Which: HEIs under Central Ministries & Agencies	其中:地方公办 of Which: HEIs under Local Auth.	其中:民办 of Which: Non-government	小计 Subtotal	其中:中央部门办 of Which: HEIs under Central Ministries & Agencies	其中:地方公办 of Which: HEIs under Local Auth.	其中:民办 of Which: Non-government
831	**1218**	**2**	**1095**	**121**	**3617**	**4**	**2496**	**1117**
1	11	1	9	1	48	0	29	19
1	18	0	18	0	17	0	11	6
141	164	0	157	7	198	0	181	17
13	119	0	119	0	238	0	152	86
41	60	0	60	0	112	0	87	25
10	1	0	1	0	182	0	105	77
4	75	0	75	0	156	1	91	64
42	40	0	37	3	115	0	107	8
1	12	0	10	2	25	0	24	1
17	15	0	14	1	52	0	45	7
6	20	0	17	3	185	0	151	34
28	41	0	35	6	171	0	97	74
32	0	0	0	0	0	0	0	0
16	87	0	87	0	206	0	109	97
56	35	0	25	10	129	1	95	33
22	173	0	117	56	314	1	205	108
44	10	0	7	3	61	0	45	16
2	88	0	72	16	345	0	178	167
95	6	0	6	0	116	0	95	21
64	0	0	0	0	0	0	0	0
6	1	0	1	0	47	0	19	28
4	43	0	40	3	63	0	48	15
143	20	0	12	8	201	0	164	37
6	7	0	7	0	119	0	78	41
13	129	1	128	0	163	0	136	27
0	0	0	0	0	0	0	0	0
2	3	0	3	0	210	0	121	89
7	20	0	18	2	72	0	53	19
5	2	0	2	0	2	0	1	1
6	2	0	2	0	13	0	13	0
3	16	0	16	0	57	1	56	0

地　区 Region	毕业生数 Graduates		招生数 Entrants			
	合计 Total	其中:获得职业资格证书 of Which: Recipients of Vocational Qualifications	合计 Total	其中:应届毕业 of Which: Graduates of Current Year 小计 Subtotal	其中:初中毕业生 of Which: Junior Secondary School Graduates	其中:五年制高职中职段 of Which: 5-year Secondary Vocational Education
总　计 Total	**4063981**	**3218321**	**4515235**	**4091506**	**3988053**	**466928**
北　京 Beijing	28981	18042	19422	17329	16907	6801
天　津 Tianjin	29111	23553	30316	27511	26882	4643
河　北 Hebei	220087	160310	287128	244910	233487	11576
山　西 Shanxi	111375	97569	109692	100535	96357	15021
内蒙古 Inner Mongolia	67326	46608	67913	61830	60742	8975
辽　宁 Liaoning	96048	62861	103382	91401	88892	9730
吉　林 Jilin	38899	24218	44566	39731	39151	12445
黑龙江 Heilongjiang	74655	51633	64975	52356	48180	3396
上　海 Shanghai	36722	31136	34212	32075	31940	6662
江　苏 Jiangsu	216521	196727	225970	210657	207883	55907
浙　江 Zhejiang	158960	155182	184672	182240	182109	33420
安　徽 Anhui	279668	247163	287852	251124	242447	23877
福　建 Fujian	117763	109951	116477	104173	102533	8243
江　西 Jiangxi	105534	52639	112030	105729	105391	14722
山　东 Shandong	248347	206220	261190	252121	249855	62135
河　南 Henan	318726	249485	420404	366985	357090	36762
湖　北 Hubei	114889	94647	127224	123716	123007	8536
湖　南 Hunan	194901	159209	250215	242724	240693	24565
广　东 Guangdong	342297	232485	322267	303178	291880	6415
广　西 Guangxi	199722	131593	252803	199019	190321	17849
海　南 Hainan	33989	16128	45413	38713	38054	2991
重　庆 Chongqing	94965	78360	109163	106053	105427	14553
四　川 Sichuan	353490	329562	349331	298778	287629	6975
贵　州 Guizhou	158978	122463	183061	168104	165551	5672
云　南 Yunnan	144267	103555	187900	179197	176759	46801
西　藏 Tibet	5599	509	7462	7441	6693	0
陕　西 Shaanxi	95895	75713	98383	93028	88412	10493
甘　肃 Gansu	67833	60848	73230	69220	68692	1872
青　海 Qinghai	19455	12851	28004	18625	17562	833
宁　夏 Ningxia	24660	19452	25067	24173	24004	889
新　疆 Xinjiang	64318	47649	85511	78830	73523	4169

(机构)学生数
Secondary Vocational Schools

单位:人
unit: person

在校学生数 Enrolment					预计毕业生数 Estimated Graduates for Next Year	
合计 Total	一年级 Grade 1	二年级 Grade 2	三年级 Grade 3	四年级及以上 Grade 4 and over	合计 Total	其中:五年制高职中职段 of Which: 5-year Secondary Vocational Education
12542893	**4521553**	**4116171**	**3842756**	**62413**	**4136983**	**423538**
74511	19451	22467	24178	8415	26723	6079
98415	30322	35435	32251	407	35298	4990
706167	287141	224736	193068	1222	238023	9368
329291	109711	102969	114287	2324	120429	14888
192620	67932	64601	59449	638	63667	11528
314385	103392	104908	99982	6103	103030	7456
131774	44572	45241	41630	331	43109	6836
203828	64975	70083	66896	1874	71991	3188
106110	34416	34241	34672	2781	35449	5278
651464	226051	214342	206066	5005	217140	53513
531910	184730	179740	164777	2663	173074	27992
760672	287852	249565	218033	5222	270241	21888
345500	116503	120437	108349	211	115281	8879
344343	117561	117230	108415	1137	106846	24709
793357	261192	273559	257091	1515	262529	60132
1065231	420404	339032	304384	1411	323173	34673
371206	127250	121120	119235	3601	121541	9465
686467	250258	235416	194241	6552	209108	28448
993850	321447	327724	343488	1191	331896	5561
686797	252728	227989	205044	1036	211948	10785
118819	45389	38475	34302	653	33406	1768
308252	109155	99006	99706	385	99575	8998
860013	349451	258134	251808	620	334289	6703
503118	182707	160875	159536	0	164982	5406
501015	187904	166187	146400	524	148670	25698
19300	7462	6740	5098	0	5285	0
262136	98466	82950	80276	444	86998	11049
193859	73306	63253	55680	1620	64082	855
75047	28005	23358	21726	1958	21859	1399
74742	25077	24995	24617	53	24998	2241
238694	86743	81363	68071	2517	72343	3765

地 区 Region	毕业生数 Graduates		招生数 Entrants			
	合计 Total	其中:获得职业资格证书 of Which: Recipients of Vocational Qualifications	合计 Total	其中:应届毕业 of Which: Graduates of Current Year 小计 Subtotal	其中:应届毕业 of Which: Graduates of Current Year 其中:初中毕业生 of Which: Junior Secondary School Graduates	其中:五年制高职中职段 of Which: 5-year Secondary Vocational Education
总 计 Total	**1962315**	**1520489**	**2037673**	**1854141**	**1809236**	**234834**
北 京 Beijing	14567	8777	8751	7505	7262	2649
天 津 Tianjin	12368	9914	12444	11421	11219	1621
河 北 Hebei	105562	74564	129244	108295	102700	6546
山 西 Shanxi	55132	46050	49840	45512	44074	8378
内蒙古 Inner Mongolia	29406	19720	28998	26732	26159	3731
辽 宁 Liaoning	42427	25303	44636	40002	38878	5080
吉 林 Jilin	18454	11124	19593	17417	17191	5350
黑龙江 Heilongjiang	33529	24758	27819	23379	21854	2139
上 海 Shanghai	15739	12163	13738	12873	12838	3171
江 苏 Jiangsu	104978	92500	103686	97133	96362	29554
浙 江 Zhejiang	72004	70025	81198	80044	80010	15278
安 徽 Anhui	133524	116591	134922	118834	115238	13381
福 建 Fujian	49561	46150	49806	45060	44411	3657
江 西 Jiangxi	58637	28090	56649	53332	53186	8261
山 东 Shandong	116457	95768	119097	114714	113620	30826
河 南 Henan	158666	122759	190677	165788	160245	15480
湖 北 Hubei	53858	43476	55949	54506	54153	4621
湖 南 Hunan	96970	76426	114828	112129	111263	12855
广 东 Guangdong	170556	112650	140472	132002	126916	3058
广 西 Guangxi	86693	55646	103036	83682	80854	7593
海 南 Hainan	15636	6734	19189	16414	16189	1609
重 庆 Chongqing	44276	37088	46744	45229	44774	7179
四 川 Sichuan	175154	160012	163178	139605	134352	4047
贵 州 Guizhou	83642	64706	92322	85649	84861	3923
云 南 Yunnan	75601	52227	87694	84361	83179	26328
西 藏 Tibet	2657	185	3120	3103	2877	0
陕 西 Shaanxi	47883	36049	43431	40790	39351	5034
甘 肃 Gansu	37995	34085	37444	35484	35277	1073
青 海 Qinghai	8529	5257	11236	8152	7812	348
宁 夏 Ningxia	13217	10617	11848	11555	11433	610
新 疆 Xinjiang	28637	21075	36084	33439	30698	1454

(机构)女学生数
Secondary Vocational Schools

单位:人
unit:person

在校学生数 Enrolment					预计毕业生数 Estimated Graduates for Next Year	
合计 Total	一年级 Grade 1	二年级 Grade 2	三年级 Grade 3	四年级及以上 Grade 4 and over	合计 Total	其中:五年制高职中职段 of Which: 5-year Secondary Vocational Education
5812830	**2038443**	**1909984**	**1828381**	**36022**	**1893462**	**224866**
35189	8638	10740	11419	4392	12552	2819
39225	12441	13839	12690	255	13893	1802
324954	129335	103052	91996	571	110373	5931
157300	49828	49690	56734	1048	57544	8717
82891	29002	28016	25540	333	26963	4991
137343	44641	44699	42860	5143	43082	4384
59887	19597	21109	18911	270	19015	3182
87942	27676	29256	29905	1105	29126	1758
42466	13763	13676	14243	784	14531	2434
303923	103570	98842	97909	3602	99776	28786
235179	81219	79593	73658	709	75815	12810
355713	134922	116733	101304	2754	120780	13346
150429	49818	52810	47647	154	47763	3892
179313	58583	60527	59588	615	57964	16505
369365	119098	128223	121256	788	124126	30687
504203	190677	160958	152061	507	150909	16242
165375	55910	54500	52963	2002	51826	5212
324286	114854	111016	94473	3943	96846	15296
454364	139830	149771	163912	851	149069	2794
289333	103131	98243	87187	772	86246	5260
52686	19185	17479	15675	347	11864	1050
137512	46733	44009	46406	364	43600	4966
417361	163254	124729	128943	435	165833	4092
259239	91187	84554	83498	0	82091	4195
244291	87695	81075	75127	394	75371	14542
8509	3120	3065	2324	0	2388	0
121264	43427	38383	39165	289	39795	5567
102004	37460	33474	30275	795	32916	467
31438	11217	10223	9296	702	8226	616
36998	11853	12679	12434	32	12524	1111
102848	36779	35021	28982	2066	30655	1412

地区 Region	毕业生数 Graduates		招生数 Entrants			
	合计 Total	其中:获得职业资格证书 of Which: Recipients of Vocational Qualifications	合计 Total	其中:应届毕业 of Which: Graduates of Current Year		其中:五年制高职中职段 of Which:5-year Secondary Vocational Education
				小计 Subtotal	其中:初中毕业生 of Which:Junior Secondary School Graduates	
总　计 Total	**2169933**	**1613369**	**2462485**	**2342257**	**2290316**	**409469**
北　京 Beijing	13493	8521	11013	10689	10276	5408
天　津 Tianjin	18300	16300	20276	19679	19423	3816
河　北 Hebei	95965	71802	143859	133880	130060	11576
山　西 Shanxi	46371	38901	41963	37900	35450	12823
内蒙古 Inner Mongolia	36128	21852	33874	32184	31918	8975
辽　宁 Liaoning	51468	33438	53810	48731	46983	9730
吉　林 Jilin	15794	9887	17306	14979	14672	7438
黑龙江 Heilongjiang	36222	20427	33442	28742	27258	3396
上　海 Shanghai	23734	20062	21887	21665	21628	5635
江　苏 Jiangsu	159484	142199	168920	167438	167210	54698
浙　江 Zhejiang	28002	27310	30179	30099	30096	9183
安　徽 Anhui	88500	75222	122603	120188	119357	23877
福　建 Fujian	68868	64073	99692	98060	97739	8243
江　西 Jiangxi	67684	31026	61604	57897	57640	13657
山　东 Shandong	176150	140669	187147	182276	180691	57998
河　南 Henan	211386	148457	260230	244055	237463	36097
湖　北 Hubei	84564	67126	94336	91532	91054	7123
湖　南 Hunan	66518	43309	61612	60350	59668	23434
广　东 Guangdong	269848	180237	257224	240052	229604	4527
广　西 Guangxi	125553	91850	189114	178787	173703	17849
海　南 Hainan	21168	10090	26646	22608	22147	2900
重　庆 Chongqing	26223	17722	30311	29091	28665	7992
四　川 Sichuan	136514	118476	131238	126411	121866	6614
贵　州 Guizhou	65849	47287	72428	67723	67358	5123
云　南 Yunnan	91361	61459	119158	113102	110885	44653
西　藏 Tibet	5563	507	7441	7420	6672	0
陕　西 Shaanxi	22889	13560	19524	19021	18592	9741
甘　肃 Gansu	44608	38971	48442	47061	46671	1072
青　海 Qinghai	12650	9123	17907	16276	15774	833
宁　夏 Ningxia	15395	12133	14739	14306	14143	889
新　疆 Xinjiang	43681	31373	64560	60055	55650	4169

学生数
Specialized Secondary Schools

单位:人
unit:person

在校学生数 Enrolment					预计毕业生数 Estimated Graduates for Next Year	
合计 Total	一年级 Grade 1	二年级 Grade 2	三年级 Grade 3	四年级及以上 Grade 4 and over	合计 Total	其中:五年制高职中职段 of Which: 5-year Secondary Vocational Education
7129894	**2465622**	**2376403**	**2239882**	**47987**	**2272283**	**378843**
40983	11032	11194	11433	7324	13054	4808
68230	20281	24484	23058	407	23255	4030
385155	143872	131781	108313	1189	110615	9368
125485	41974	39936	41579	1996	46132	12116
102514	33874	35201	32801	638	34726	11528
160249	53816	52048	48975	5410	51053	7456
51527	17306	18231	15769	221	15873	4361
101317	33442	34967	31618	1290	33690	3188
71205	22042	22713	23680	2770	23797	4482
503438	168999	166922	162798	4719	162636	52086
94537	30193	32640	31111	593	31206	7235
338817	122603	112267	99473	4474	101834	21888
280805	99718	96857	84019	211	84396	8879
203941	64280	68229	70307	1125	68557	24314
571833	187149	196818	186498	1368	189239	57808
726815	260230	241831	223343	1411	228694	34006
273847	94362	89240	86644	3601	88679	8203
185846	61650	62548	59887	1761	62744	27531
792845	256227	259676	275751	1191	268855	4304
498171	189049	167902	140184	1036	143466	10785
70932	26622	23345	20754	211	19981	1716
85270	30312	28160	26413	385	26282	4944
393948	131357	131564	130419	608	130469	6365
207934	72074	66814	69046	0	70845	4995
321223	119162	105686	95855	520	97342	23661
19253	7441	6714	5098	0	5259	0
57457	19605	17989	19419	444	19301	10535
135463	48512	45093	41426	432	42036	846
49819	17908	16802	14889	220	15099	1399
43845	14749	14294	14749	53	14468	2241
167190	65781	54457	44573	2379	48700	3765

地区 Region	毕业生数 Graduates		招生数 Entrants			
	合计 Total	其中:获得职业资格证书 of Which: Recipients of Vocational Qualifications	合计 Total	其中:应届毕业 of Which: Graduates of Current Year		其中:五年制高职中职段 of Which:5-year Secondary Vocational Education
				小计 Subtotal	其中:初中毕业生 of Which:Junior Secondary School Graduates	
总　计 Total	**1129023**	**816355**	**1171045**	**1117001**	**1093137**	**210552**
北　京 Beijing	6059	4057	5121	4972	4733	2004
天　津 Tianjin	7543	6718	8032	7891	7734	1247
河　北 Hebei	45266	32941	63835	59235	57741	6546
山　西 Shanxi	25832	19562	20732	18995	18287	7571
内蒙古 Inner Mongolia	15919	8757	14124	13622	13547	3731
辽　宁 Liaoning	23485	13250	24740	22540	21737	5080
吉　林 Jilin	8111	4363	8230	7341	7251	3530
黑龙江 Heilongjiang	18588	11861	17125	15039	14472	2139
上　海 Shanghai	10215	7714	8855	8724	8724	2622
江　苏 Jiangsu	77155	66078	78252	77477	77431	29082
浙　江 Zhejiang	15252	14814	16427	16366	16366	5040
安　徽 Anhui	49638	40894	60788	59831	59585	13381
福　建 Fujian	32684	30502	43097	42417	42273	3657
江　西 Jiangxi	41654	18382	34805	32592	32487	7703
山　东 Shandong	86507	68910	88657	86197	85406	29241
河　南 Henan	112258	79091	124657	116915	113333	15358
湖　北 Hubei	39866	30975	42370	41152	40911	4058
湖　南 Hunan	41315	26365	34093	33477	33032	12333
广　东 Guangdong	140890	91574	116087	108463	103631	2689
广　西 Guangxi	58736	39421	81181	77162	75120	7593
海　南 Hainan	10794	4519	12179	10429	10316	1557
重　庆 Chongqing	14242	10805	15022	14338	13975	4059
四　川 Sichuan	80555	67891	70020	67380	64994	3956
贵　州 Guizhou	37859	27300	39458	37003	36918	3565
云　南 Yunnan	53914	36072	62002	59377	58273	25251
西　藏 Tibet	2644	184	3114	3097	2871	0
陕　西 Shaanxi	12637	6806	9006	8856	8585	4524
甘　肃 Gansu	25635	22154	25132	24511	24355	623
青　海 Qinghai	5751	3930	7891	7363	7186	348
宁　夏 Ningxia	8363	6657	7127	7021	6901	610
新　疆 Xinjiang	19656	13808	28886	27218	24962	1454

女学生数
Specialized Secondary Schools

单位:人
unit:person

在校学生数 Enrolment					预计毕业生数 Estimated Graduates for Next Year	
合计 Total	一年级 Grade 1	二年级 Grade 2	三年级 Grade 3	四年级及以上 Grade 4 and over	合计 Total	其中:五年制高职中职段 of Which: 5-year Secondary Vocational Education
3511326	**1171427**	**1169736**	**1140673**	**29490**	**1112519**	**205060**
19248	5006	5359	4982	3901	5879	2081
25991	8028	9117	8591	255	8776	1347
179351	63926	61838	53028	559	51560	5931
67086	20735	21942	23474	935	23975	7499
43154	14124	14499	14198	333	14516	4991
75346	24745	23411	22669	4521	22712	4384
25297	8230	9104	7793	170	7861	2304
51735	17125	17175	16652	783	16342	1758
28745	8888	8989	10093	775	10180	2024
237775	78193	78486	77680	3416	75935	28223
50670	16430	17659	16340	241	16297	3808
172026	60788	56796	51735	2707	52739	13346
123715	43109	42597	37855	154	36725	3892
117788	35755	38707	42723	603	41032	16274
276006	88658	95831	90794	723	92444	29845
364236	124657	121449	117623	507	112160	16124
124849	42336	41043	39468	2002	38572	4718
109761	34122	36835	37520	1284	37364	14794
376558	115361	123321	137025	851	125002	2600
222664	81447	76709	63736	772	62672	5260
34441	12175	11645	10454	167	7125	1023
44076	15023	14307	14382	364	11966	3164
219071	70095	71972	76579	425	76074	3934
116418	38617	37307	40494	0	40180	3784
174820	62003	57291	55133	393	55358	13135
8490	3114	3052	2324	0	2375	0
28544	9001	9153	10101	289	9781	5218
72797	25138	24506	22812	341	22095	460
22384	7872	7653	6800	59	5664	616
21909	7132	7356	7389	32	7357	1111
76375	29594	24627	20226	1928	21801	1412

地 区 Region	毕业生数 Graduates		招生数 Entrants			
	合计 Total	其中：获得职业资格证书 of Which: Recipients of Vocational Qualifications	合计 Total	其中：应届毕业 of Which: Graduates of Current Year		其中：五年制高职中职段 of Which: 5-year Secondary Vocational Education
				小计 Subtotal	其中：初中毕业生 of Which: Junior Secondary School Graduates	
总 计 Total	**604125**	**465546**	**568771**	**301868**	**268056**	**2100**
北 京 Beijing	9965	4850	5612	3846	3837	0
天 津 Tianjin	2767	228	2246	218	189	0
河 北 Hebei	51587	24974	51978	21919	15229	0
山 西 Shanxi	2668	0	3086	0	0	0
内蒙古 Inner Mongolia	3324	2618	4393	994	600	0
辽 宁 Liaoning	7140	3715	5471	177	158	0
吉 林 Jilin	4119	804	4610	3270	3270	0
黑龙江 Heilongjiang	17427	12472	11159	5929	3577	0
上 海 Shanghai	6017	4641	5454	3542	3444	0
江 苏 Jiangsu	22476	20012	23935	11615	9070	0
浙 江 Zhejiang	7871	6213	9449	7951	7909	0
安 徽 Anhui	101076	87404	100206	66531	60892	0
福 建 Fujian	48895	45878	16785	6113	4794	0
江 西 Jiangxi	3118	1342	1971	1763	1763	0
山 东 Shandong	17766	14612	9126	7202	7092	599
河 南 Henan	23003	21323	70075	34226	31113	91
湖 北 Hubei	3478	2832	1639	1329	1316	50
湖 南 Hunan	20566	19034	27365	22643	22045	110
广 东 Guangdong	4851	2528	3137	2209	2206	0
广 西 Guangxi	74169	39743	63689	20232	16618	0
海 南 Hainan	2570	139	2481	0	0	0
重 庆 Chongqing	5716	4965	5487	5121	5101	450
四 川 Sichuan	113777	109152	95823	51547	45811	0
贵 州 Guizhou	26232	18732	22014	14559	14153	0
云 南 Yunnan	1162	825	1251	134	134	0
西 藏 Tibet	36	2	21	21	21	0
陕 西 Shaanxi	146	131	547	547	547	0
甘 肃 Gansu	10677	10068	7147	4893	4858	800
青 海 Qinghai	6589	3519	9712	2031	1470	0
宁 夏 Ningxia	1307	89	662	218	214	0
新 疆 Xinjiang	3630	2701	2240	1088	625	0

学生数

Specialized Secondary Schools

单位：人
unit：person

在校学生数 Enrolment					预计毕业生数 Estimated Graduates for Next Year	
合计 Total	一年级 Grade 1	二年级 Grade 2	三年级 Grade 3	四年级及以上 Grade 4 and over	合计 Total	其中：五年制高职中职段 of Which：5-year Secondary Vocational Education
1272446	**569013**	**369312**	**326792**	**7329**	**559016**	**804**
22040	5612	7998	7855	575	8365	0
4900	2246	2553	101	0	2579	0
71356	51978	9962	9383	33	51090	0
8712	3086	2602	3024	0	3024	0
7251	4393	1855	1003	0	3152	0
25550	5471	9603	10476	0	10536	0
10317	4610	2677	3030	0	4339	0
40808	11159	14018	15631	0	18065	0
15168	5460	4901	4807	0	5465	0
58766	23935	20748	13931	152	23372	0
21731	9449	9758	2524	0	9379	0
229023	100206	76129	52088	600	96806	0
64695	16785	23580	24330	0	30885	0
8688	2255	3547	2886	0	2887	0
32425	9126	11575	11724	0	12035	361
93078	70075	15435	7568	0	17733	200
5306	1639	1871	1796	0	2064	0
70740	27365	23243	17010	3122	20739	0
11846	3097	3957	4792	0	5451	0
188626	63679	60087	64860	0	68482	0
7479	2481	2424	2574	0	2574	0
19413	5478	4175	9760	0	9760	243
131598	95823	16550	19225	0	101429	0
64241	22014	21040	21187	0	24834	0
1931	1251	402	278	0	843	0
47	21	26	0	0	26	0
926	547	194	185	0	626	0
12599	7147	2700	1633	1119	8767	0
24194	9712	6191	6563	1728	6452	0
2333	662	1248	423	0	1085	0
16659	2251	8263	6145	0	6172	0

地 区 Region	毕业生数 Graduates 合计 Total	毕业生数 Graduates 其中:获得职业资格证书 of Which: Recipients of Vocational Qualifications	招生数 Entrants 合计 Total	其中:应届毕业 of Which: Graduates of Current Year 小计 Subtotal	其中:应届毕业 其中:初中毕业生 of Which: Junior Secondary School Graduates	其中:五年制高职中职段 of Which: 5-year Secondary Vocational Education
总 计 Total	**257413**	**198860**	**242852**	**128778**	**114018**	**862**
北 京 Beijing	5717	2331	2466	1370	1366	0
天 津 Tianjin	1084	72	874	63	63	0
河 北 Hebei	26208	12484	26932	11195	7309	0
山 西 Shanxi	1145	0	1447	0	0	0
内蒙古 Inner Mongolia	1466	1280	1960	625	299	0
辽 宁 Liaoning	2600	1422	1771	51	48	0
吉 林 Jilin	1494	381	1794	1259	1259	0
黑龙江 Heilongjiang	6620	5390	3267	1894	1152	0
上 海 Shanghai	2584	1707	1952	1219	1184	0
江 苏 Jiangsu	10126	8730	10319	5390	4665	0
浙 江 Zhejiang	3028	2262	3319	2485	2465	0
安 徽 Anhui	43874	38034	45385	30436	27900	0
福 建 Fujian	16877	15648	6709	2643	2138	0
江 西 Jiangxi	1632	762	555	422	422	0
山 东 Shandong	7144	5838	3756	2974	2933	125
河 南 Henan	8673	7964	28292	11678	9782	55
湖 北 Hubei	2995	2405	721	610	610	28
湖 南 Hunan	9393	8700	12790	11224	11062	23
广 东 Guangdong	1407	735	929	566	566	0
广 西 Guangxi	27957	16225	21855	6520	5734	0
海 南 Hainan	849	73	979	0	0	0
重 庆 Chongqing	2569	2087	2746	2515	2499	181
四 川 Sichuan	50573	48732	43001	22669	20068	0
贵 州 Guizhou	11207	7952	10136	6995	6890	0
云 南 Yunnan	329	265	440	115	115	0
西 藏 Tibet	13	1	6	6	6	0
陕 西 Shaanxi	89	80	199	199	199	0
甘 肃 Gansu	5252	5101	3618	2406	2402	450
青 海 Qinghai	2700	1256	3180	651	488	0
宁 夏 Ningxia	578	52	269	85	85	0
新 疆 Xinjiang	1230	891	1185	513	309	0

女学生数
Specialized Secondary Schools

单位:人
unit:person

在校学生数 Enrolment					预计毕业生数 Estimated Graduates for Next Year	
合计 Total	一年级 Grade 1	二年级 Grade 2	三年级 Grade 3	四年级及以上 Grade 4 and over	合计 Total	其中:五年制高职中职段 of Which: 5-year Secondary Vocational Education
531385	**242541**	**150833**	**134679**	**3332**	**230052**	**225**
10464	2463	3875	4001	125	3947	0
1873	874	991	8	0	985	0
36594	26932	4830	4820	12	25645	0
4377	1447	1410	1520	0	1520	0
3408	1960	960	488	0	1599	0
8645	1771	3509	3365	0	3333	0
3943	1794	924	1225	0	1589	0
13769	3130	4380	6259	0	5761	0
5262	1938	1767	1557	0	1756	0
26465	10319	9249	6758	139	9521	0
8204	3319	3727	1158	0	3689	0
98256	45385	32514	20357	0	37212	0
26714	6709	10213	9792	0	11038	0
3773	612	1448	1713	0	1714	0
14438	3756	5034	5648	0	5769	85
35341	28292	4701	2348	0	6971	65
2451	721	762	968	0	894	0
33273	12790	10512	7952	2019	9973	0
3899	907	1328	1664	0	1678	0
66669	21684	21534	23451	0	23574	0
2841	979	882	980	0	980	0
9385	2737	1743	4905	0	4905	75
58574	43001	7024	8549	0	45958	0
28818	10136	9375	9307	0	10212	0
780	440	215	125	0	270	0
19	6	13	0	0	13	0
407	199	106	102	0	250	0
5670	3618	892	756	404	4231	0
8570	3180	2372	2385	633	2401	0
1186	269	644	273	0	396	0
7317	1173	3899	2245	0	2268	0

地 区 Region	毕业生数 Graduates		招生数 Entrants			
	合计 Total	其中:获得职业资格证书 of Which: Recipients of Vocational Qualifications	合计 Total	其中:应届毕业 of Which: Graduates of Current Year		其中:五年制高职中职段 of Which:5-year Secondary Vocational Education
				小计 Subtotal	其中:初中毕业生 of Which:Junior Secondary School Graduates	
总 计 Total	**1289923**	**1139406**	**1483979**	**1447381**	**1429681**	**55359**
北 京 Beijing	5523	4671	2797	2794	2794	1393
天 津 Tianjin	8044	7025	7794	7614	7270	827
河 北 Hebei	72535	63534	91291	89111	88198	0
山 西 Shanxi	62336	58668	64643	62635	60907	2198
内蒙古 Inner Mongolia	27874	22138	29646	28652	28224	0
辽 宁 Liaoning	37440	25708	44101	42493	41751	0
吉 林 Jilin	18986	13527	22650	21482	21209	5007
黑龙江 Heilongjiang	21006	18734	20374	17685	17345	0
上 海 Shanghai	6971	6433	6871	6868	6868	1027
江 苏 Jiangsu	34561	34516	33115	31604	31603	1209
浙 江 Zhejiang	123087	121659	145044	144190	144104	24237
安 徽 Anhui	90092	84537	65043	64405	62198	0
福 建 Fujian	0	0	0	0	0	0
江 西 Jiangxi	34732	20271	48455	46069	45988	1065
山 东 Shandong	54431	50939	64917	62643	62072	3538
河 南 Henan	84337	79705	90099	88704	88514	574
湖 北 Hubei	26847	24689	31249	30855	30637	1363
湖 南 Hunan	107817	96866	161238	159731	158980	1021
广 东 Guangdong	67598	49720	61906	60917	60070	1888
广 西 Guangxi	0	0	0	0	0	0
海 南 Hainan	10251	5899	16286	16105	15907	91
重 庆 Chongqing	63026	55673	73365	71841	71661	6111
四 川 Sichuan	103199	101934	122270	120820	119952	361
贵 州 Guizhou	66897	56444	88619	85822	84040	549
云 南 Yunnan	51744	41271	67491	65961	65740	2148
西 藏 Tibet	0	0	0	0	0	0
陕 西 Shaanxi	72860	62022	78312	73460	69273	752
甘 肃 Gansu	12548	11809	17641	17266	17163	0
青 海 Qinghai	216	209	385	318	318	0
宁 夏 Ningxia	7958	7230	9666	9649	9647	0
新 疆 Xinjiang	17007	13575	18711	17687	17248	0

学生数
Vocational High Schools

单位:人
unit:person

在校学生数 Enrolment					预计毕业生数 Estimated Graduates for Next Year	
合计 Total	一年级 Grade 1	二年级 Grade 2	三年级 Grade 3	四年级及以上 Grade 4 and over	合计 Total	其中:五年制高职中职段 of Which: 5-year Secondary Vocational Education
4140553	**1486918**	**1370456**	**1276082**	**7097**	**1305684**	**43891**
11488	2807	3275	4890	516	5304	1271
25285	7795	8398	9092	0	9464	960
249656	91291	82993	75372	0	76318	0
195094	64651	60431	69684	328	71273	2772
82855	29665	27545	25645	0	25789	0
128586	44105	43257	40531	693	41441	0
69930	22656	24333	22831	110	22897	2475
61703	20374	21098	19647	584	20236	0
19737	6914	6627	6185	11	6187	796
89260	33117	26672	29337	134	31132	1427
415642	145088	137342	131142	2070	132489	20757
192832	65043	61169	66472	148	71601	0
0	0	0	0	0	0	0
131714	51026	45454	35222	12	35402	395
189099	64917	65166	58869	147	61255	1963
245338	90099	81766	73473	0	76746	467
92053	31249	30009	30795	0	30798	1262
429881	161243	149625	117344	1669	125625	917
189159	62123	64091	62945	0	57590	1257
0	0	0	0	0	0	0
40408	16286	12706	10974	442	10851	52
203569	73365	66671	63533	0	63533	3811
334467	122271	110020	102164	12	102391	338
230943	88619	73021	69303	0	69303	411
177861	67491	60099	50267	4	50485	2037
0	0	0	0	0	0	0
203753	78314	64767	60672	0	67071	514
45797	17647	15460	12621	69	13279	9
1034	385	365	274	10	308	0
28564	9666	9453	9445	0	9445	0
54845	18711	18643	17353	138	17471	0

地 区 Region	毕业生数 Graduates		招生数 Entrants			
	合计 Total	其中:获得职业资格证书 of Which: Recipients of Vocational Qualifications	合计 Total	其中:应届毕业 of Which: Graduates of Current Year 小计 Subtotal	其中:初中毕业生 of Which: Junior Secondary School Graduates	其中:五年制高职中职段 of Which: 5-year Secondary Vocational Education
总 计 Total	**575879**	**505274**	**623776**	**608362**	**602081**	**23420**
北 京 Beijing	2791	2389	1164	1163	1163	645
天 津 Tianjin	3741	3124	3538	3467	3422	374
河 北 Hebei	34088	29139	38477	37865	37650	0
山 西 Shanxi	28155	26488	27661	26517	25787	807
内蒙古 Inner Mongolia	12021	9683	12914	12485	12313	0
辽 宁 Liaoning	16342	10631	18125	17411	17093	0
吉 林 Jilin	8849	6380	9569	8817	8681	1820
黑龙江 Heilongjiang	8321	7507	7427	6446	6230	0
上 海 Shanghai	2940	2742	2931	2930	2930	549
江 苏 Jiangsu	17697	17692	15115	14266	14266	472
浙 江 Zhejiang	53724	52949	61452	61193	61179	10238
安 徽 Anhui	40012	37663	28749	28567	27753	0
福 建 Fujian	0	0	0	0	0	0
江 西 Jiangxi	15351	8946	21289	20318	20277	558
山 东 Shandong	22806	21020	26684	25543	25281	1460
河 南 Henan	37735	35704	37728	37195	37130	67
湖 北 Hubei	10997	10096	12858	12744	12632	535
湖 南 Hunan	46262	41361	67945	67428	67169	499
广 东 Guangdong	28259	20341	23456	22973	22719	369
广 西 Guangxi	0	0	0	0	0	0
海 南 Hainan	3993	2142	6031	5985	5873	52
重 庆 Chongqing	27465	24196	28976	28376	28300	2939
四 川 Sichuan	44026	43389	50157	49556	49290	91
贵 州 Guizhou	34576	29454	42728	41651	41053	358
云 南 Yunnan	21358	15890	25252	24869	24791	1077
西 藏 Tibet	0	0	0	0	0	0
陕 西 Shaanxi	35157	29163	34226	31735	30567	510
甘 肃 Gansu	7108	6830	8694	8567	8520	0
青 海 Qinghai	78	71	165	138	138	0
宁 夏 Ningxia	4276	3908	4452	4449	4447	0
新 疆 Xinjiang	7751	6376	6013	5708	5427	0

女学生数
Vocational High Schools

单位:人
unit:person

在校学生数 Enrolment					预计毕业生数 Estimated Graduates for Next Year	
合计 Total	一年级 Grade 1	二年级 Grade 2	三年级 Grade 3	四年级及以上 Grade 4 and over	合计 Total	其中:五年制高职中职段 of Which: 5-year Secondary Vocational Education
1770119	**624475**	**589415**	**553029**	**3200**	**550891**	**19581**
5477	1169	1506	2436	366	2726	738
11361	3539	3731	4091	0	4132	455
109009	38477	36384	34148	0	33168	0
85837	27646	26338	31740	113	32049	1218
36329	12918	12557	10854	0	10848	0
53352	18125	17779	16826	622	17037	0
30647	9573	11081	9893	100	9565	878
22438	7421	7701	6994	322	7023	0
8459	2937	2920	2593	9	2595	410
39683	15058	11107	13471	47	14320	563
176305	61470	58207	56160	468	55829	9002
85431	28749	27423	29212	47	30829	0
0	0	0	0	0	0	0
57752	22216	20372	15152	12	15218	231
78921	26684	27358	24814	65	25913	757
104626	37728	34808	32090	0	31778	53
38075	12853	12695	12527	0	12360	494
181252	67942	63669	49001	640	49509	502
73907	23562	25122	25223	0	22389	194
0	0	0	0	0	0	0
15404	6031	4952	4241	180	3759	27
84051	28973	27959	27119	0	26729	1727
139716	50158	45733	43815	10	43801	158
114003	42434	37872	33697	0	31699	411
68691	25252	23569	19869	1	19743	1407
0	0	0	0	0	0	0
92313	34227	29124	28962	0	29764	349
23537	8704	8076	6707	50	6590	7
484	165	198	111	10	161	0
13903	4452	4679	4772	0	4771	0
19156	6012	6495	6511	138	6586	0

中等职业学校(机构)
Number of Students by Age in

地 区 Region	合计 Total	14 岁及以下 14 Years and Under	15 岁 15 Years	16 岁 16 Years	17 岁 17 Years
总 计 Total	**12542893**	**207371**	**2060238**	**3327294**	**3256194**
北 京 Beijing	74511	2460	10675	17855	20596
天 津 Tianjin	98415	757	10843	27700	29776
河 北 Hebei	706167	7134	125298	192961	185599
山 西 Shanxi	329291	6974	60190	89144	90123
内蒙古 Inner Mongolia	192620	1776	24890	47405	52720
辽 宁 Liaoning	314385	6702	49759	81019	78926
吉 林 Jilin	131774	2052	19172	32565	35386
黑龙江 Heilongjiang	203828	2648	22068	39493	43122
上 海 Shanghai	106110	1907	18208	28651	31281
江 苏 Jiangsu	651464	6530	115360	176897	183780
浙 江 Zhejiang	531910	2690	109179	166254	161039
安 徽 Anhui	760672	6016	125139	176782	178110
福 建 Fujian	345500	4925	56108	88235	81220
江 西 Jiangxi	344343	21110	82543	102921	82364
山 东 Shandong	793357	11065	152952	240072	229367
河 南 Henan	1065231	12255	194566	294368	265654
湖 北 Hubei	371206	11393	79029	108229	101150
湖 南 Hunan	686467	22821	174323	216441	163763
广 东 Guangdong	993850	16533	126170	255159	273834
广 西 Guangxi	686797	7875	71421	140446	143817
海 南 Hainan	118819	2382	14025	27768	26578
重 庆 Chongqing	308252	7433	54685	90600	80327
四 川 Sichuan	860013	15143	147363	223431	225534
贵 州 Guizhou	503118	4389	47819	119858	127735
云 南 Yunnan	501015	8359	62598	134582	144738
西 藏 Tibet	19300	1130	2481	4337	4836
陕 西 Shaanxi	262136	4229	44219	73793	72096
甘 肃 Gansu	193859	2746	25616	50333	49517
青 海 Qinghai	75047	642	4605	13435	16039
宁 夏 Ningxia	74742	975	7365	18423	21135
新 疆 Xinjiang	238694	4320	21569	48137	56032

分年龄学生数
Secondary Vocational Schools

单位:人
unit: person

18岁 18 Years	19岁 19 Years	20岁 20 Years	21岁 21 Years	22岁及以上 22 Years and Over
1837589	**679760**	**270206**	**165814**	**738427**
11961	3409	758	297	6500
20654	2926	1562	1506	2691
98945	29142	9408	5078	52602
44679	12008	3702	1609	20862
34195	14355	3898	1808	11573
41867	14816	3630	2195	35471
19385	8903	3667	2428	8216
30322	15535	7127	5691	37822
17221	4431	1051	273	3087
87280	24785	7787	4900	44145
68057	13246	2965	2810	5670
101651	53554	40564	26266	52590
41986	13379	5337	6573	47737
30659	9495	3182	1535	10534
101928	25012	8158	4751	20052
142447	56642	22491	10845	65963
47166	12864	4139	1239	5997
64420	16784	4552	6184	17179
188233	72789	24387	12391	24354
107178	47379	23728	20073	124880
17930	8075	2290	993	18778
47920	15654	4474	2161	4998
130635	50888	23606	15463	27950
95166	50168	20227	10729	27027
95898	34125	9868	3363	7484
3193	1625	761	425	512
42404	14896	4028	1488	4983
33216	14451	5374	2741	9865
11970	6281	3527	2504	16044
15414	6308	2242	950	1930
43609	25835	11716	6545	20931

地 区 Region	合计 Total	14岁及以下 14 Years and Under	15岁 15 Years	16岁 16 Years	17岁 17 Years
总 计 Total	**5812830**	**106036**	**965843**	**1542961**	**1520585**
北 京 Beijing	35189	1416	5015	8399	9185
天 津 Tianjin	39225	414	4462	11464	11622
河 北 Hebei	324954	3269	57687	88440	83814
山 西 Shanxi	157300	3202	29099	43160	43674
内蒙古 Inner Mongolia	82891	938	11289	20487	23016
辽 宁 Liaoning	137343	4276	22725	35653	35853
吉 林 Jilin	59887	1167	8328	14505	16284
黑龙江 Heilongjiang	87942	1486	10309	18138	19558
上 海 Shanghai	42466	756	7838	11406	13063
江 苏 Jiangsu	303923	2768	55225	82830	86618
浙 江 Zhejiang	235179	1369	50184	74470	72033
安 徽 Anhui	355713	3150	62741	84870	82152
福 建 Fujian	150429	1953	25231	39129	36341
江 西 Jiangxi	179313	11605	42083	53111	43504
山 东 Shandong	369365	5756	71204	112407	105286
河 南 Henan	504203	6286	89751	135987	126026
湖 北 Hubei	165375	5413	35782	47067	44714
湖 南 Hunan	324286	12771	84944	102247	75164
广 东 Guangdong	454364	8268	56673	113837	127477
广 西 Guangxi	289333	3755	31044	62518	66179
海 南 Hainan	52686	1089	6417	12040	11595
重 庆 Chongqing	137512	3715	23878	39591	36237
四 川 Sichuan	417361	7709	70718	107329	109980
贵 州 Guizhou	259239	2300	25023	61252	65674
云 南 Yunnan	244291	4105	29943	64772	72001
西 藏 Tibet	8509	491	1158	1962	2125
陕 西 Shaanxi	121264	2198	19859	34277	33879
甘 肃 Gansu	102004	1548	12630	26341	26821
青 海 Qinghai	31438	331	2053	6485	6948
宁 夏 Ningxia	36998	484	3454	9142	10622
新 疆 Xinjiang	102848	2048	9096	19645	23140

分年龄女学生数
Secondary Vocational Schools

单位:人
unit:person

18岁 18 Years	19岁 19 Years	20岁 20 Years	21岁 21 Years	22岁及以上 22 Years and Over
847521	**311746**	**123545**	**75712**	**318881**
5138	1303	267	94	4372
7883	1123	566	592	1099
45993	12660	4236	2407	26448
21238	4999	1412	540	9976
14666	5855	1509	793	4338
18169	6052	1371	829	12415
8765	4526	1781	1139	3392
13321	6587	3045	2241	13257
6219	1593	365	145	1081
39323	10954	3233	1999	20973
28099	5334	985	983	1722
47062	23175	17289	12498	22776
18695	5283	2136	2341	19320
15895	4759	1599	762	5995
47456	12022	3450	2072	9712
67581	28302	11306	5663	33301
20732	5942	1995	681	3049
28794	7341	1870	2502	8653
87094	34091	12286	6206	8432
44780	19466	9979	8022	43590
8048	3185	1038	404	8870
20855	7161	2135	1050	2890
63145	25296	12053	7922	13209
50837	25958	9998	5242	12955
47320	16074	4636	1741	3699
1370	697	320	168	218
19780	6844	1746	587	2094
18177	7825	2907	1369	4386
5004	2594	1243	966	5814
7491	2982	1205	515	1103
18591	11763	5584	3239	9742

地 区 Region	结业生数 合计 Total	其中:女 of Which: Female	其中:少数民族 of Which: Minority	其中:资格证书培训 of Which: Vocational Qualifications Training	其中:岗位证书培训 of Which:Job-Certificate Training	其中:第一产业类培训 By Industry: Training for First Industry
总 计 Total	**4639952**	**2142133**	**325197**	**1730703**	**1547596**	**777247**
北 京 Beijing	53652	24905	1747	18137	11171	1406
天 津 Tianjin	34376	12785	549	26970	3898	1111
河 北 Hebei	210041	116521	25202	49408	50314	61242
山 西 Shanxi	74425	44481	17	26719	25214	12104
内蒙古 Inner Mongolia	82682	42658	8782	27874	41488	5109
辽 宁 Liaoning	224398	42647	12133	36245	38840	13240
吉 林 Jilin	11720	4151	329	4193	5068	1272
黑龙江 Heilongjiang	126391	45754	626	15713	15876	84235
上 海 Shanghai	71199	30264	47	22233	26154	250
江 苏 Jiangsu	326199	142591	377	154856	135117	37226
浙 江 Zhejiang	358670	141178	1845	156693	148893	44357
安 徽 Anhui	297859	129210	247	115714	96477	54360
福 建 Fujian	255257	139351	1287	64030	177307	15536
江 西 Jiangxi	65759	43306	25	23687	30849	25723
山 东 Shandong	241089	96761	1837	109389	73210	32461
河 南 Henan	333629	178996	1861	65713	173184	43911
湖 北 Hubei	66399	28847	6294	32837	13368	8689
湖 南 Hunan	323582	173293	14265	94155	63949	33141
广 东 Guangdong	261394	125292	4267	138039	104238	19562
广 西 Guangxi	138816	60083	49539	65755	33235	34914
海 南 Hainan	23825	10533	1283	7063	6930	11070
重 庆 Chongqing	81011	36921	10186	36331	11113	13450
四 川 Sichuan	172784	86623	10769	109953	42938	29810
贵 州 Guizhou	117697	52801	26515	61171	32394	23923
云 南 Yunnan	335285	174738	94381	143572	107285	66526
西 藏 Tibet	8022	1764	7094	3957	1696	337
陕 西 Shaanxi	148668	71024	483	39532	25997	37774
甘 肃 Gansu	64621	32631	3601	38904	8516	10652
青 海 Qinghai	41073	11970	6253	6712	16885	17073
宁 夏 Ningxia	23099	8415	5391	12496	6665	12545
新 疆 Xinjiang	66330	31637	27965	22652	19327	24238

培训结业学生情况
Secondary Vocational Schools

单位：人
unit: person

Graduates

其中：第二产业类培训 of Which: Training for Second Industry	其中：第三产业类培训 of Which: Training for Third Industry	一个月以内 1 Month Under	一个月至三个月以内 1 Month to 3 Months	三个月至半年以内 3 Months to 6 Months	半年至一年以内 6 Months to 1 Year	一年及以上 1 Year and Over
961125	**2901580**	**2924948**	**822364**	**345118**	**341575**	**205947**
12789	39457	43801	3985	1587	2565	1714
10455	22810	14400	11682	3195	749	4350
28712	120087	119557	27583	31907	17562	13432
11220	51101	42468	7460	12448	10670	1379
26730	50843	61630	3409	4890	8428	4325
33755	177403	188081	20716	8086	5671	1844
3927	6521	8770	882	108	1960	0
10522	31634	115474	5409	1679	855	2974
19964	50985	38061	20325	8257	2545	2011
134240	154733	167405	78342	24671	37011	18770
99047	215266	253198	34348	33267	20269	17588
90601	152898	174574	65124	29719	22662	5780
18968	220753	62838	96531	11721	77378	6789
8580	31456	36035	20530	2351	4017	2826
61858	146770	179977	44007	9012	1489	6604
53249	236469	240196	43607	18983	24933	5910
11437	46273	31418	13250	4523	8719	8489
40368	250073	223979	44269	21251	21701	12382
67686	174146	145613	61983	18456	23860	11482
28887	75015	92209	34197	4489	1961	5960
2241	10514	15385	6293	1086	557	504
21075	46486	51166	12452	8041	2996	6356
47050	95924	82093	32878	14500	13804	29509
32724	61050	83148	15462	13881	3240	1966
21426	247333	216918	61127	31147	12675	13418
1909	5776	4227	1967	313	1515	0
20751	90143	110190	20995	11281	2755	3447
11669	42300	37834	4605	9618	4181	8383
12981	11019	32121	6723	0	1924	305
3642	6912	15433	1967	223	852	4624
12662	29430	36749	20256	4428	2071	2826

地区 Region	结业生数 合计 Total	其中:女 of Which: Female	其中:少数民族 of Which: Minority	其中:资格证书培训 of Which: Vocational Qualifications Training	其中:岗位证书培训 of Which: Job-Certificate Training	其中:第一产业类培训 By Industry: Training for First Industry
总 计 Total	**3318076**	**1561247**	**179744**	**1406190**	**1123283**	**487596**
北 京 Beijing	31697	11635	258	9213	12265	346
天 津 Tianjin	28236	9492	339	23430	2386	63
河 北 Hebei	109022	61973	1484	45204	16183	27554
山 西 Shanxi	45191	26754	12	23528	13943	7314
内蒙古 Inner Mongolia	60428	27737	5765	17371	29064	2367
辽 宁 Liaoning	44573	13117	4815	22060	12861	3084
吉 林 Jilin	8780	3180	393	2714	3694	1327
黑龙江 Heilongjiang	92711	35943	365	8594	7866	70282
上 海 Shanghai	50781	17442	100	22429	17357	408
江 苏 Jiangsu	246729	107561	213	124608	97754	24908
浙 江 Zhejiang	372711	146410	1837	163477	147883	49028
安 徽 Anhui	300045	131629	255	114111	99970	56556
福 建 Fujian	223831	131202	767	52411	165431	7698
江 西 Jiangxi	43933	25909	21	22942	12706	12747
山 东 Shandong	153070	71510	1840	72811	34701	19496
河 南 Henan	181334	91381	1431	40607	104760	16259
湖 北 Hubei	50237	22214	7999	21004	11040	8428
湖 南 Hunan	329780	177845	16034	96516	62741	33007
广 东 Guangdong	218841	101242	4721	147922	57765	6645
广 西 Guangxi	84299	39434	34689	46763	17700	20547
海 南 Hainan	13093	4946	1218	3554	6941	452
重 庆 Chongqing	46795	22396	2550	28768	8398	2507
四 川 Sichuan	194545	98117	12161	121790	57073	28146
贵 州 Guizhou	94284	44985	22021	47316	28296	22675
云 南 Yunnan	135013	64338	33758	48633	61245	24962
西 藏 Tibet	8247	1879	7791	4385	1708	337
陕 西 Shaanxi	71339	34998	483	23448	19118	16213
甘 肃 Gansu	32451	15525	1554	25703	3753	7162
青 海 Qinghai	4914	1577	1227	2753	198	0
宁 夏 Ningxia	20093	7738	4271	9389	6785	12858
新 疆 Xinjiang	21073	11138	9372	12736	1698	4220

培训注册学生情况
Secondary Vocational Schools

单位:人
unit:person

Graduates

其中:第二产业类培训 of Which: Training for Second Industry	其中:第三产业类培训 of Which: Training for Third Industry	一个月以内 1 Month Under	一个月至三个月以内 1 Month to 3 Months	三个月至半年以内 3 Months to 6 Months	半年至一年以内 6 Months to 1 Year	一年及以上 1 Year and Over
789264	**2041216**	**1834252**	**643207**	**269540**	**282715**	**288362**
13277	18074	26928	1870	972	278	1649
10899	17274	14318	10577	398	2892	51
20067	61401	29420	10585	26133	7607	35277
7567	30310	24005	4520	7193	7735	1738
25784	32277	52568	1016	928	3886	2030
25089	16400	27170	11837	2204	2104	1258
1768	5685	6389	1015	103	1273	0
4279	18150	85153	1973	371	210	5004
20719	29654	22293	13389	8207	2874	4018
112358	109463	130188	55186	14858	29343	17154
104437	219246	255419	34506	30816	25870	26100
91394	152095	174538	66453	30368	22736	5950
14549	201584	29750	94653	9336	79197	10895
8397	22789	31291	5938	1837	510	4357
26763	106811	104961	27176	10459	4584	5890
42633	122442	129096	23033	14253	4593	10359
8146	33663	20389	10947	1248	5879	11774
41854	254919	221714	41821	22732	22332	21181
52776	159420	82443	72702	20105	19846	23745
11160	52592	38244	31163	5248	2156	7488
2931	9710	2615	7099	2016	1015	348
9280	35008	19998	8542	6662	1484	10109
64809	101590	85293	35016	12975	16153	45108
26140	45469	63373	12339	12592	3307	2673
10470	99581	78110	25063	14071	4861	12908
1909	6001	4321	1755	331	1840	0
11171	43955	38981	18962	8310	1815	3271
9089	16200	11430	5170	4395	4902	6554
1166	3748	1363	2078	0	0	1473
3667	3568	14800	2375	254	919	1745
4716	12137	7691	4448	165	514	8255

地 区 Region	上学年初报表在校学生数 Enrolment at Beginning of Previous Academic Year	增加学生数 Factors of Increase			
		合计 Total	招 生 No. of Students Admitted	复 学 Students Resuming Studies	转 入 Transfers from Other Inst.
总 计 Total	**12758317**	**4871902**	**4515235**	**8456**	**273235**
北 京 Beijing	85780	23014	19422	158	2069
天 津 Tianjin	101055	31585	30316	177	608
河 北 Hebei	657852	302672	287128	108	14701
山 西 Shanxi	337947	113042	109692	211	2391
内蒙古 Inner Mongolia	202672	72796	67913	67	4512
辽 宁 Liaoning	318885	108509	103382	150	3290
吉 林 Jilin	129856	46294	44566	20	736
黑龙江 Heilongjiang	215729	72093	64975	22	584
上 海 Shanghai	112013	34992	34212	220	356
江 苏 Jiangsu	652499	248639	225970	375	21455
浙 江 Zhejiang	520695	194699	184672	195	8360
安 徽 Anhui	781809	336446	287852	129	40969
福 建 Fujian	380533	135586	116477	384	7259
江 西 Jiangxi	361692	120264	112030	20	2276
山 东 Shandong	809826	276666	261190	442	15010
河 南 Henan	1015766	453201	420404	848	28324
湖 北 Hubei	375637	137872	127224	313	9358
湖 南 Hunan	660887	278223	250215	838	21898
广 东 Guangdong	1065745	380388	322267	275	53712
广 西 Guangxi	698572	256202	252803	318	2473
海 南 Hainan	115032	45911	45413	26	290
重 庆 Chongqing	311632	109687	109163	167	215
四 川 Sichuan	914426	361165	349331	1709	7697
贵 州 Guizhou	550922	195445	183061	108	4033
云 南 Yunnan	486248	193005	187900	305	3664
西 藏 Tibet	18157	7510	7462	18	25
陕 西 Shaanxi	277832	106034	98383	166	2178
甘 肃 Gansu	210710	77267	73230	169	3606
青 海 Qinghai	74057	30966	28004	0	2458
宁 夏 Ningxia	78743	25633	25067	91	450
新 疆 Xinjiang	235108	96096	85511	427	8278

学生数变动情况
Secondary Vocational Schools

单位:人
unit:person

	减少学生数 Factors of Decrease									本学年初报表在校学生数 Enrolment at Beginning of Current Academic Year
其他 Others	合计 Total	毕业 Graduates	结业 Completers of Courses without Formal Awards	休学 Suspended	退学 Quitting	开除 Expelled	死亡 Death	转出 Transfers to Other Inst.	其他 Others	
74976	**5087326**	**4063981**	**100381**	**22111**	**384258**	**5855**	**380**	**385682**	**124678**	**12542893**
1365	34283	28981	360	226	2966	54	7	1537	152	74511
484	34225	29111	4	40	3068	13	1	250	1738	98415
735	254357	220087	5008	325	15132	104	7	12394	1300	706167
748	121698	111375	811	331	5478	16	1	2683	1003	329291
304	82848	67326	870	99	5615	191	6	7049	1692	192620
1687	113009	96048	676	268	9700	99	5	2967	3246	314385
972	44376	38899	5	71	3209	96	1	2095	0	131774
6512	83994	74655	119	23	3307	1	2	5790	97	203828
204	40895	36722	240	283	2835	0	6	493	316	106110
839	249674	216521	335	1309	11446	144	13	19288	618	651464
1472	183484	158960	1247	1540	7919	67	16	11872	1863	531910
7496	357583	279668	1338	113	8200	65	4	59641	8554	760672
11466	170619	117763	23237	2147	14691	388	9	7333	5051	345500
5938	137613	105534	1	204	9855	16	14	16989	5000	344343
24	293135	248347	1689	355	19971	85	11	22635	42	793357
3625	403736	318726	6792	2843	32119	624	4	39099	3529	1065231
977	142303	114889	855	841	7709	165	16	13263	4565	371206
5272	252643	194901	4244	1402	16923	305	23	27727	7118	686467
4134	452283	342297	7300	1046	32744	244	32	55458	13162	993850
608	267977	199722	14132	2048	33869	460	28	5232	12486	686797
182	42124	33989	71	109	5844	83	11	1143	874	118819
142	113067	94965	328	487	14753	242	28	656	1608	308252
2428	415578	353490	7669	3113	26902	464	32	17356	6552	860013
8243	243249	158978	15236	1222	30748	390	18	17790	18867	503118
1136	178238	144267	399	532	22509	448	31	4311	5741	501015
5	6367	5599	0	3	581	10	0	53	121	19300
5307	121730	95895	2757	414	6328	97	2	9044	7193	262136
262	94118	67833	2565	257	9852	112	3	8279	5217	193859
504	29976	19455	411	51	4000	45	2	2527	3485	75047
25	29634	24660	25	91	3538	39	2	594	685	74742
1880	92510	64318	1657	318	12447	788	45	10134	2803	238694

地 区 Region	上学年初报表在校学生数 Enrolment at Beginning of Previous Academic Year	增加学生数 Factors of Increase			
		合计 Total	招 生 No. of Students Admitted	复 学 Students Resuming Studies	转 入 Transfers from Other Inst.
总 计 Total	**6034231**	**2191723**	**2037673**	**3481**	**115954**
北 京 Beijing	41332	10643	8751	70	912
天 津 Tianjin	40890	12820	12444	10	236
河 北 Hebei	311692	135458	129244	34	5852
山 西 Shanxi	165945	51074	49840	157	940
内蒙古 Inner Mongolia	87362	31200	28998	26	2064
辽 宁 Liaoning	140195	47043	44636	66	1588
吉 林 Jilin	60640	20473	19593	8	364
黑龙江 Heilongjiang	95592	30032	27819	0	100
上 海 Shanghai	45298	14113	13738	85	129
江 苏 Jiangsu	310934	114115	103686	166	9634
浙 江 Zhejiang	231194	85341	81198	66	3505
安 徽 Anhui	368508	156034	134922	56	17092
福 建 Fujian	165522	56665	49806	149	1935
江 西 Jiangxi	192658	60579	56649	7	1809
山 东 Shandong	379253	125135	119097	132	5896
河 南 Henan	494363	206166	190677	233	13394
湖 北 Hubei	171032	59057	55949	133	2722
湖 南 Hunan	319896	128751	114828	441	11128
广 东 Guangdong	505578	162319	140472	126	19953
广 西 Guangxi	299324	105196	103036	185	1839
海 南 Hainan	51543	19423	19189	10	147
重 庆 Chongqing	141901	46943	46744	55	99
四 川 Sichuan	454105	167821	163178	820	3160
贵 州 Guizhou	284525	101138	92322	67	2156
云 南 Yunnan	246068	89996	87694	87	1534
西 藏 Tibet	8445	3137	3120	2	10
陕 西 Shaanxi	134176	46481	43431	58	1015
甘 肃 Gansu	112617	39162	37444	21	1657
青 海 Qinghai	30869	12995	11236	0	1628
宁 夏 Ningxia	40350	12065	11848	51	165
新 疆 Xinjiang	102424	40348	36084	160	3291

女学生数变动情况

Secondary Vocational Schools

单位：人
unit: person

其他 Others	减少学生数 Factors of Decrease 合计 Total	毕业 Graduates	结业 Completers of Courses without Formal Awards	休学 Suspended	退学 Quitting	开除 Expelled	死亡 Death	转出 Transfers to Other Inst.	其他 Others	本学年初报表在校学生数 Enrolment at Beginning of Current Academic Year
34615	**2413124**	**1962315**	**43478**	**9164**	**160492**	**1833**	**92**	**177579**	**58171**	**5812830**
910	16786	14567	93	86	1469	4	3	427	137	35189
130	14485	12368	0	26	1283	2	0	141	665	39225
328	122196	105562	2563	184	6723	7	1	6588	568	324954
137	59719	55132	396	95	2154	4	1	1362	575	157300
112	35671	29406	336	12	2271	75	3	3259	309	82891
753	49895	42427	143	144	4175	34	1	1608	1363	137343
508	21226	18454	5	39	1599	48	1	1080	0	59887
2113	37682	33529	42	8	1329	0	1	2712	61	87942
161	16945	15739	54	92	817	0	2	207	34	42466
629	121126	104978	147	364	4988	52	4	10227	366	303923
572	81356	72004	504	601	3034	25	6	4602	580	235179
3964	168829	133524	1018	41	3941	24	0	26765	3516	355713
4775	71758	49561	11187	608	5420	120	2	3191	1669	150429
2114	73924	58637	0	59	4271	1	5	8428	2523	179313
10	135023	116457	890	86	8572	37	2	8971	8	369365
1862	196326	158666	3367	1800	10969	295	0	19146	2083	504203
253	64714	53858	356	254	3106	79	3	4649	2409	165375
2354	124361	96970	1242	692	7678	61	3	15401	2314	324286
1768	213533	170556	3341	444	12105	39	7	21061	5980	454364
136	115187	86693	5101	757	14602	129	5	2608	5292	289333
77	18280	15636	25	57	1970	24	2	297	269	52686
45	51332	44276	97	159	5606	59	7	475	653	137512
663	204565	175154	2915	1472	12050	110	8	8613	4243	417361
6593	126424	83642	6562	360	14524	116	6	9551	11663	259239
681	91773	75601	157	138	10319	121	6	2189	3242	244291
5	3073	2657	0	0	269	2	0	33	112	8509
1977	59393	47883	1221	200	2801	20	1	4494	2773	121264
40	49775	37995	610	146	4238	20	0	4329	2437	102004
131	12426	8529	130	18	1645	12	1	844	1247	31438
1	15417	13217	14	41	1371	24	1	394	355	36998
813	39924	28637	962	181	5193	289	10	3927	725	102848

地　区 Region	结业生数				
	合计 Total	其中:女 of Which: Female	按时间分		
			一个月以内 1 Month Under	一个月至三个月以内 1 Month to 3 Months	三个月至半年以内 3 Months to 6 Months
总　计 Total	**1091**	**561**	**530**	**11**	**31**
北　京 Beijing	239	103	162	9	25
天　津 Tianjin	0	0	0	0	0
河　北 Hebei	1	0	0	0	0
山　西 Shanxi	0	0	0	0	0
内蒙古 Inner Mongolia	9	3	0	0	0
辽　宁 Liaoning	3	0	0	0	0
吉　林 Jilin	0	0	0	0	0
黑龙江 Heilongjiang	0	0	0	0	0
上　海 Shanghai	5	3	0	0	0
江　苏 Jiangsu	0	0	0	0	0
浙　江 Zhejiang	0	0	0	0	0
安　徽 Anhui	0	0	0	0	0
福　建 Fujian	1	1	0	0	0
江　西 Jiangxi	0	0	0	0	0
山　东 Shandong	11	4	0	0	0
河　南 Henan	0	0	0	0	0
湖　北 Hubei	0	0	0	0	0
湖　南 Hunan	0	0	0	0	0
广　东 Guangdong	231	110	46	0	0
广　西 Guangxi	429	269	315	2	6
海　南 Hainan	0	0	0	0	0
重　庆 Chongqing	0	0	0	0	0
四　川 Sichuan	0	0	0	0	0
贵　州 Guizhou	0	0	0	0	0
云　南 Yunnan	150	64	7	0	0
西　藏 Tibet	0	0	0	0	0
陕　西 Shaanxi	0	0	0	0	0
甘　肃 Gansu	0	0	0	0	0
青　海 Qinghai	0	0	0	0	0
宁　夏 Ningxia	12	4	0	0	0
新　疆 Xinjiang	0	0	0	0	0

外国留学生情况
Secondary Vocational Schools

单位：人
unit: person

Graduates							
by Time		按大洲分 by Continent					
半年至一年以内 6 Months to 1 Year	一年及以上 1 Year and Over	亚洲 Asia	非洲 Africa	欧洲 Europe	北美洲 North America	南美洲 South America	大洋洲 Australia
89	**430**	**917**	**3**	**67**	**98**	**5**	**1**
6	37	187	0	20	27	5	0
0	0	0	0	0	0	0	0
1	0	0	0	1	0	0	0
0	0	0	0	0	0	0	0
0	9	9	0	0	0	0	0
0	3	2	0	1	0	0	0
0	0	0	0	0	0	0	0
0	0	0	0	0	0	0	0
4	1	1	0	4	0	0	0
0	0	0	0	0	0	0	0
0	0	0	0	0	0	0	0
0	0	0	0	0	0	0	0
0	1	1	0	0	0	0	0
0	0	0	0	0	0	0	0
0	11	11	0	0	0	0	0
0	0	0	0	0	0	0	0
0	0	0	0	0	0	0	0
0	0	0	0	0	0	0	0
30	155	185	3	41	1	0	1
48	58	359	0	0	70	0	0
0	0	0	0	0	0	0	0
0	0	0	0	0	0	0	0
0	0	0	0	0	0	0	0
0	0	0	0	0	0	0	0
0	143	150	0	0	0	0	0
0	0	0	0	0	0	0	0
0	0	0	0	0	0	0	0
0	0	0	0	0	0	0	0
0	0	0	0	0	0	0	0
0	12	12	0	0	0	0	0
0	0	0	0	0	0	0	0

中等职业学校

Number of Educational Personnel in

地 区 Region	教职工数 Educational		
	合计 Total	校本部教职工 Educational	
		小计 Subtotal	专任教师 Full-time Teachers
总 计 Total	**811147**	**804848**	**640398**
北 京 Beijing	9824	9689	6338
天 津 Tianjin	8421	8356	6108
河 北 Hebei	58789	58537	46119
山 西 Shanxi	31852	31766	25196
内蒙古 Inner Mongolia	18480	18434	13736
辽 宁 Liaoning	27464	27391	20582
吉 林 Jilin	17724	17717	13459
黑龙江 Heilongjiang	19349	19291	14090
上 海 Shanghai	12289	12221	8125
江 苏 Jiangsu	50288	50116	42317
浙 江 Zhejiang	38324	38266	33925
安 徽 Anhui	33157	33007	27804
福 建 Fujian	19813	19794	16479
江 西 Jiangxi	17235	16587	12514
山 东 Shandong	60408	59856	48659
河 南 Henan	62705	61872	49755
湖 北 Hubei	26595	26124	20211
湖 南 Hunan	34447	34397	27001
广 东 Guangdong	58112	57871	45197
广 西 Guangxi	28095	27390	20942
海 南 Hainan	6378	6373	4421
重 庆 Chongqing	18156	17942	14932
四 川 Sichuan	48804	48015	38340
贵 州 Guizhou	21839	21644	18181
云 南 Yunnan	26342	26280	21680
西 藏 Tibet	1631	1631	1520
陕 西 Shaanxi	18671	18590	13962
甘 肃 Gansu	16659	16494	13787
青 海 Qinghai	3041	2967	2433
宁 夏 Ningxia	3482	3475	2752
新 疆 Xinjiang	12773	12755	9833

(机构)教职工数

Secondary Vocational Schools

单位:人
unit: person

Personnel					
Personnel in Main Campus			校办企业职工 Employees in School-run Factories & Farms	其他附设机构人员 Personnel in Others Subsidiary Units	聘请校外教师 Part-time Teachers
行政人员 Adm. Personnel	教辅人员 Supporting Staff	工勤人员 Workers			
65681	**49028**	**49741**	**3227**	**3072**	**92005**
1636	934	781	21	114	1078
1300	512	436	30	35	1003
4887	4120	3411	72	180	2326
2628	1953	1989	15	71	4631
1799	1783	1116	44	2	1360
3369	1504	1936	45	28	3053
1903	1651	704	0	7	1599
2226	1392	1583	41	17	2612
1831	1293	972	15	53	1170
2391	2648	2760	139	33	5606
1278	1848	1215	16	42	4195
2099	1324	1780	106	44	5430
1370	1121	824	9	10	2224
1386	1670	1017	562	86	1744
4120	4116	2961	384	168	4239
5029	3637	3451	674	159	8773
2459	1714	1740	418	53	1607
3182	2108	2106	23	27	3338
4926	3668	4080	26	215	4809
2685	1749	2014	121	584	3680
784	370	798	3	2	764
1331	733	946	155	59	2896
3262	2339	4074	71	718	3712
1541	701	1221	53	142	7159
1394	1102	2104	5	57	5498
68	5	38	0	0	86
2137	1366	1125	45	36	694
908	792	1007	57	108	1930
202	81	251	74	0	1690
301	193	229	3	4	584
1249	601	1072	0	18	2515

中等职业学校

Number of Female Educational Personnel in

地　区 Region	教职工数 Educational		
	合计 Total	校本部教职工 Educational	
		小计 Subtotal	专任教师 Full-time Teachers
总　计 Total	**409941**	**407021**	**343537**
北　京 Beijing	6131	6086	4520
天　津 Tianjin	5054	5022	4037
河　北 Hebei	33916	33790	28983
山　西 Shanxi	17949	17908	15419
内蒙古 Inner Mongolia	9801	9793	8092
辽　宁 Liaoning	15676	15633	13004
吉　林 Jilin	10266	10266	8524
黑龙江 Heilongjiang	10108	10089	8120
上　海 Shanghai	6928	6911	5157
江　苏 Jiangsu	25645	25597	22801
浙　江 Zhejiang	20995	20972	19061
安　徽 Anhui	13051	12962	11299
福　建 Fujian	10032	10026	8653
江　西 Jiangxi	7728	7418	5699
山　东 Shandong	28298	28096	24502
河　南 Henan	31251	30829	26569
湖　北 Hubei	11273	11134	8968
湖　南 Hunan	16367	16337	13642
广　东 Guangdong	29943	29834	24191
广　西 Guangxi	14151	13646	10770
海　南 Hainan	3010	3005	2190
重　庆 Chongqing	9107	9041	7867
四　川 Sichuan	23526	23210	19253
贵　州 Guizhou	10444	10335	8982
云　南 Yunnan	12953	12907	11049
西　藏 Tibet	775	775	738
陕　西 Shaanxi	9012	8973	7314
甘　肃 Gansu	6798	6714	5933
青　海 Qinghai	1291	1262	1108
宁　夏 Ningxia	1737	1737	1457
新　疆 Xinjiang	6725	6713	5635

(机构)女教职工数
Secondary Vocational Schools

单位:人
unit: person

Personnel					
Personnel in Main Campus			校办企业职工 Employees in School-run Factories & Farms	其他附设机构人员 Personnel in Others Subsidiary Units	聘请校外教师 Part-time Teachers
行政人员 Adm. Personnel	教辅人员 Supporting Staff	工勤人员 Workers			
24257	**24121**	**15106**	**1327**	**1593**	**43374**
859	530	177	5	40	602
597	296	92	1	31	564
1785	2020	1002	39	87	1296
882	1043	564	2	39	1949
565	792	344	7	1	761
1333	810	486	31	12	1542
735	854	153	0	0	701
862	711	396	14	5	937
916	688	150	2	15	448
886	1298	612	45	3	2642
493	955	463	7	16	1811
633	526	504	73	16	2186
547	593	233	1	5	1050
545	823	351	298	12	947
1215	1765	614	111	91	2269
1634	1696	930	348	74	4213
854	796	516	119	20	828
1000	971	724	15	15	1813
1959	2069	1615	13	96	2306
1096	937	843	61	444	1504
313	190	312	3	2	281
524	353	297	28	38	1618
1324	1092	1541	16	300	2028
605	298	450	22	87	3037
532	577	749	4	42	2313
18	4	15	0	0	28
688	630	341	13	26	299
194	325	262	20	64	1115
42	29	83	29	0	701
105	101	74	0	0	360
516	349	213	0	12	1225

普通中等专业学校
Number of Educational Personnel in Regular

地 区 Region	教职工数 Educational		
	合计 Total	校本部教职工 Educational	
		小计 Subtotal	专任教师 Full-time Teachers
总 计 Total	**396845**	**393425**	**301577**
北 京 Beijing	3315	3197	1857
天 津 Tianjin	5774	5709	4133
河 北 Hebei	19691	19514	13587
山 西 Shanxi	10887	10862	7691
内蒙古 Inner Mongolia	5704	5700	3920
辽 宁 Liaoning	14046	14003	10480
吉 林 Jilin	4154	4154	3202
黑龙江 Heilongjiang	7956	7918	5068
上 海 Shanghai	8396	8346	5236
江 苏 Jiangsu	35655	35569	30272
浙 江 Zhejiang	6956	6909	5995
安 徽 Anhui	18172	18122	15214
福 建 Fujian	19813	19794	16479
江 西 Jiangxi	6467	6372	4502
山 东 Shandong	36977	36566	29320
河 南 Henan	20319	19883	15322
湖 北 Hubei	20248	19807	14897
湖 南 Hunan	3928	3922	3029
广 东 Guangdong	42185	42068	31617
广 西 Guangxi	28095	27390	20942
海 南 Hainan	3701	3701	2362
重 庆 Chongqing	3857	3828	2831
四 川 Sichuan	22792	22595	16270
贵 州 Guizhou	8243	8208	6520
云 南 Yunnan	10125	10076	7789
西 藏 Tibet	1631	1631	1520
陕 西 Shaanxi	3367	3355	2278
甘 肃 Gansu	11412	11328	9307
青 海 Qinghai	2649	2575	2126
宁 夏 Ningxia	1714	1707	1191
新 疆 Xinjiang	8616	8616	6620

(机构)教职工数

Specialized Secondary Vocational Schools

单位:人
unit: person

Personnel					
Personnel in Main Campus			校办企业职工 Employees in School-run Factories & Farms	其他附设机构人员 Personnel in Others Subsidiary Units	聘请校外教师 Part-time Teachers
行政人员 Adm. Personnel	教辅人员 Supporting Staff	工勤人员 Workers			
38862	**25007**	**27979**	**1736**	**1684**	**43958**
771	292	277	5	113	409
979	276	321	30	35	480
2627	1586	1714	31	146	958
1533	724	914	0	25	1165
883	465	432	3	1	812
1746	673	1104	27	16	1027
546	193	213	0	0	72
1103	754	993	34	4	1031
1530	851	729	15	35	844
1717	1827	1753	83	3	3346
256	418	240	11	36	829
1241	690	977	14	36	3093
1370	1121	824	9	10	2224
665	800	405	27	68	1200
2773	2628	1845	312	99	3134
1995	1155	1411	348	88	2671
2078	1411	1421	398	43	1249
475	186	232	1	5	546
4216	2757	3478	24	93	4345
2685	1749	2014	121	584	3680
583	260	496	0	0	560
481	244	272	29	0	712
2353	1596	2376	66	131	1824
892	352	444	21	14	1588
830	533	924	1	48	2393
68	5	38	0	0	86
532	274	271	3	9	134
669	620	732	46	38	1722
172	70	207	74	0	850
220	112	184	3	4	201
873	385	738	0	0	773

普通中等专业学校

Number of Female Educational Personnel in Regular

地 区 Region	教职工数 Educational		
	合计 Total	校本部教职工 Educational	
		小计 Subtotal	专任教师 Full-time Teachers
总 计 Total	**199549**	**197970**	**161544**
北 京 Beijing	1842	1802	1242
天 津 Tianjin	3292	3260	2630
河 北 Hebei	10633	10546	8043
山 西 Shanxi	5771	5753	4604
内蒙古 Inner Mongolia	3086	3085	2365
辽 宁 Liaoning	8171	8143	6774
吉 林 Jilin	2413	2413	2054
黑龙江 Heilongjiang	4273	4258	3040
上 海 Shanghai	4530	4520	3224
江 苏 Jiangsu	18731	18705	16647
浙 江 Zhejiang	3955	3937	3500
安 徽 Anhui	7590	7569	6638
福 建 Fujian	10032	10026	8653
江 西 Jiangxi	3129	3122	2291
山 东 Shandong	17200	17057	14752
河 南 Henan	10325	10095	8436
湖 北 Hubei	8475	8342	6512
湖 南 Hunan	1946	1941	1601
广 东 Guangdong	21692	21636	17032
广 西 Guangxi	14151	13646	10770
海 南 Hainan	1763	1763	1202
重 庆 Chongqing	1971	1945	1507
四 川 Sichuan	11229	11168	8460
贵 州 Guizhou	4215	4206	3545
云 南 Yunnan	5437	5400	4458
西 藏 Tibet	775	775	738
陕 西 Shaanxi	1591	1583	1207
甘 肃 Gansu	4693	4665	4090
青 海 Qinghai	1129	1100	976
宁 夏 Ningxia	905	905	691
新 疆 Xinjiang	4604	4604	3862

(机构)女教职工数
Specialized Secondary Vocational Schools

单位:人
unit:person

Personnel					
Personnel in Main Campus			校办企业职工 Employees in School-run Factories & Farms	其他附设机构人员 Personnel in Others Subsidiary Units	聘请校外教师 Part-time Teachers
行政人员 Adm. Personnel	教辅人员 Supporting Staff	工勤人员 Workers			
15404	**12761**	**8261**	**623**	**956**	**22641**
374	135	51	1	39	244
431	145	54	1	31	333
1190	805	508	15	72	557
536	431	182	0	18	661
357	253	110	0	1	420
695	409	265	20	8	576
195	121	43	0	0	48
518	404	296	12	3	554
766	423	107	2	8	335
726	897	435	23	3	1632
118	224	95	6	12	439
385	301	245	7	14	1501
547	593	233	1	5	1050
256	438	137	5	2	677
786	1117	402	76	67	1671
693	639	327	179	51	1596
727	686	417	118	15	628
194	88	58	0	5	299
1736	1507	1361	13	43	2069
1096	937	843	61	444	1504
228	130	203	0	0	188
211	128	99	26	0	371
1055	736	917	14	47	1075
396	161	104	3	6	767
359	322	261	0	37	1261
18	4	15	0	0	28
190	124	62	2	6	60
142	256	177	9	19	1010
38	26	60	29	0	482
86	69	59	0	0	112
355	252	135	0	0	493

成人中等专业
Number of Educational Personnel in Adult

地 区 Region	教职工数 Educational		
	合计 Total	校本部教职工 Educational	
		小计 Subtotal	专任教师 Full-time Teachers
总 计 Total	**59705**	**58906**	**44773**
北 京 Beijing	565	565	308
天 津 Tianjin	525	525	255
河 北 Hebei	8179	8155	6469
山 西 Shanxi	3719	3716	3157
内蒙古 Inner Mongolia	2153	2112	1682
辽 宁 Liaoning	499	499	395
吉 林 Jilin	4423	4416	3632
黑龙江 Heilongjiang	2260	2258	1661
上 海 Shanghai	255	255	115
江 苏 Jiangsu	1719	1709	887
浙 江 Zhejiang	1104	1104	655
安 徽 Anhui	1333	1252	1042
福 建 Fujian	0	0	0
江 西 Jiangxi	2314	1783	1609
山 东 Shandong	2982	2982	2435
河 南 Henan	11502	11426	8399
湖 北 Hubei	296	296	185
湖 南 Hunan	3905	3903	2868
广 东 Guangdong	281	281	248
广 西 Guangxi	0	0	0
海 南 Hainan	22	22	20
重 庆 Chongqing	2483	2483	1906
四 川 Sichuan	2269	2269	1411
贵 州 Guizhou	1571	1556	1203
云 南 Yunnan	3183	3181	2698
西 藏 Tibet	0	0	0
陕 西 Shaanxi	191	191	103
甘 肃 Gansu	473	468	378
青 海 Qinghai	382	382	301
宁 夏 Ningxia	131	131	71
新 疆 Xinjiang	986	986	680

学校教职工数
Specialized Secondary Schools

单位:人
unit: person

Personnel					聘请校外教师 Part-time Teachers
Personnel in Main Campus			校办企业职工 Employees in School-run Factories & Farms	其他附设机构人员 Personnel in Others Subsidiary Units	
行政人员 Adm. Personnel	教辅人员 Supporting Staff	工勤人员 Workers			
6105	**4319**	**3709**	**682**	**117**	**20261**
170	34	53	0	0	380
136	104	30	0	0	489
712	648	326	0	24	93
221	175	163	3	0	2203
152	172	106	41	0	1
75	22	7	0	0	1061
364	305	115	0	7	802
414	104	79	2	0	1039
56	58	26	0	0	86
241	260	321	5	5	1432
174	254	21	0	0	822
78	76	56	81	0	440
0	0	0	0	0	0
57	74	43	531	0	10
209	143	195	0	0	161
1383	976	668	19	57	4180
57	44	10	0	0	10
441	273	321	0	2	261
1	29	3	0	0	32
0	0	0	0	0	0
0	1	1	0	0	0
275	154	148	0	0	102
217	143	498	0	0	175
184	85	84	0	15	2145
145	80	258	0	2	1950
0	0	0	0	0	0
61	16	11	0	0	2
46	15	29	0	5	56
30	11	40	0	0	816
30	14	16	0	0	41
176	49	81	0	0	1472

Number of Female Educational Personnel

地 区 Region	教职工数 Educational		
	合计 Total	校本部教职工 Educational	
		小计 Subtotal	专任教师 Full-time Teachers
总 计 Total	**29693**	**29289**	**23951**
北 京 Beijing	306	306	195
天 津 Tianjin	271	271	129
河 北 Hebei	4754	4745	4100
山 西 Shanxi	2198	2197	1945
内蒙古 Inner Mongolia	1131	1124	984
辽 宁 Liaoning	269	269	223
吉 林 Jilin	2657	2657	2335
黑龙江 Heilongjiang	879	877	706
上 海 Shanghai	120	120	64
江 苏 Jiangsu	533	533	354
浙 江 Zhejiang	404	404	263
安 徽 Anhui	585	525	457
福 建 Fujian	0	0	0
江 西 Jiangxi	1084	794	740
山 东 Shandong	1419	1419	1206
河 南 Henan	5742	5711	4559
湖 北 Hubei	158	158	103
湖 南 Hunan	1649	1647	1292
广 东 Guangdong	108	108	89
广 西 Guangxi	0	0	0
海 南 Hainan	4	4	3
重 庆 Chongqing	1154	1154	915
四 川 Sichuan	1235	1235	806
贵 州 Guizhou	576	576	463
云 南 Yunnan	1428	1428	1240
西 藏 Tibet	0	0	0
陕 西 Shaanxi	119	119	66
甘 肃 Gansu	154	152	139
青 海 Qinghai	155	155	127
宁 夏 Ningxia	45	45	27
新 疆 Xinjiang	556	556	421

校女教职工数
in Adult Specialized Secondary Schools

单位:人
unit:person

Personnel					
Personnel in Main Campus			校办企业职工 Employees in School-run Factories & Farms	其他附设机构人员 Personnel in Others Subsidiary Units	聘请校外教师 Part-time Teachers
行政人员 Adm. Personnel	教辅人员 Supporting Staff	工勤人员 Workers			
2054	**2066**	**1218**	**371**	**33**	**7177**
85	13	13	0	0	191
64	63	15	0	0	211
208	343	94	0	9	55
73	102	77	1	0	558
40	85	15	7	0	0
33	11	2	0	0	445
147	160	15	0	0	292
96	56	19	2	0	122
23	24	9	0	0	31
54	110	15	0	0	647
67	66	8	0	0	251
20	29	19	60	0	161
0	0	0	0	0	0
16	30	8	290	0	2
66	88	59	0	0	76
463	471	218	11	20	1672
30	23	2	0	0	4
111	107	137	0	2	114
0	19	0	0	0	12
0	0	0	0	0	0
0	1	0	0	0	0
108	81	50	0	0	60
92	76	261	0	0	105
58	33	22	0	0	683
44	28	116	0	0	592
0	0	0	0	0	0
38	13	2	0	0	2
5	4	4	0	2	24
4	3	21	0	0	210
6	8	4	0	0	29
103	19	13	0	0	628

地 区 Region	教职工数 Educational		
	合计 Total	校本部教职工 Educational	
		小计 Subtotal	专任教师 Full-time Teachers
总 计 Total	**343767**	**341698**	**286053**
北 京 Beijing	5944	5927	4173
天 津 Tianjin	2122	2122	1720
河 北 Hebei	30226	30175	25481
山 西 Shanxi	16976	16918	14150
内蒙古 Inner Mongolia	10623	10622	8134
辽 宁 Liaoning	12919	12889	9707
吉 林 Jilin	8988	8988	6557
黑龙江 Heilongjiang	8708	8694	7102
上 海 Shanghai	3638	3620	2774
江 苏 Jiangsu	10805	10735	9581
浙 江 Zhejiang	29579	29568	26815
安 徽 Anhui	12111	12092	10374
福 建 Fujian	0	0	0
江 西 Jiangxi	8454	8432	6403
山 东 Shandong	19868	19727	16473
河 南 Henan	29508	29188	25046
湖 北 Hubei	5872	5842	5011
湖 南 Hunan	26313	26271	20839
广 东 Guangdong	14543	14419	12476
广 西 Guangxi	0	0	0
海 南 Hainan	2655	2650	2039
重 庆 Chongqing	11673	11488	10088
四 川 Sichuan	23397	22805	20388
贵 州 Guizhou	11914	11769	10369
云 南 Yunnan	12361	12350	10745
西 藏 Tibet	0	0	0
陕 西 Shaanxi	15113	15044	11581
甘 肃 Gansu	4756	4680	4084
青 海 Qinghai	10	10	6
宁 夏 Ningxia	1520	1520	1404
新 疆 Xinjiang	3171	3153	2533

校教职工数
Secondary Vocational Schools

单位:人
unit:person

Personnel					
Personnel in Main Campus			校办企业职工 Employees in School-run Factories & Farms	其他附设机构人员 Personnel in Others Subsidiary Units	聘请校外教师 Part-time Teachers
行政人员 Adm. Personnel	教辅人员 Supporting Staff	工勤人员 Workers			
19431	**18877**	**17337**	**809**	**1260**	**26394**
695	608	451	16	1	289
185	132	85	0	0	34
1480	1877	1337	41	10	1158
851	1037	880	12	46	1232
764	1146	578	0	1	547
1548	809	825	18	12	965
949	1128	354	0	0	708
617	496	479	5	9	305
245	384	217	0	18	240
216	403	535	51	19	654
755	1109	889	5	6	2429
593	448	677	11	8	1661
0	0	0	0	0	0
664	796	569	4	18	534
1074	1318	862	72	69	885
1463	1377	1302	307	13	1879
313	235	283	20	10	348
2256	1629	1547	22	20	2499
584	815	544	2	122	360
0	0	0	0	0	0
201	109	301	3	2	204
557	335	508	126	59	2082
672	575	1170	5	587	1707
443	264	693	32	113	3416
341	384	880	4	7	1103
0	0	0	0	0	0
1544	1076	843	42	27	558
193	157	246	11	65	72
0	0	4	0	0	24
28	63	25	0	0	231
200	167	253	0	18	270

Number of Female Educational Personnel

地区 Region	教职工数 Educational		
	合计 Total	校本部教职工 Educational	
		小计 Subtotal	专任教师 Full-time Teachers
总计 Total	**175635**	**174699**	**153938**
北京 Beijing	3983	3978	3083
天津 Tianjin	1491	1491	1278
河北 Hebei	18136	18106	16473
山西 Shanxi	9866	9844	8773
内蒙古 Inner Mongolia	5584	5584	4743
辽宁 Liaoning	7236	7221	6007
吉林 Jilin	5117	5117	4087
黑龙江 Heilongjiang	4770	4769	4261
上海 Shanghai	2278	2271	1869
江苏 Jiangsu	5395	5373	4990
浙江 Zhejiang	16279	16274	15034
安徽 Anhui	4390	4382	3820
福建 Fujian	0	0	0
江西 Jiangxi	3515	3502	2668
山东 Shandong	9445	9386	8352
河南 Henan	14450	14289	12967
湖北 Hubei	2552	2546	2286
湖南 Hunan	12627	12604	10622
广东 Guangdong	7563	7510	6577
广西 Guangxi	0	0	0
海南 Hainan	1243	1238	985
重庆 Chongqing	5895	5855	5373
四川 Sichuan	10910	10655	9862
贵州 Guizhou	5583	5483	4914
云南 Yunnan	5792	5783	5135
西藏 Tibet	0	0	0
陕西 Shaanxi	7302	7271	6041
甘肃 Gansu	1941	1887	1694
青海 Qinghai	7	7	5
宁夏 Ningxia	720	720	687
新疆 Xinjiang	1565	1553	1352

女教职工数
in Vocational High Schools

单位:人
unit:person

Personnel					
Personnel in Main Campus			校办企业职工 Employees in School-run Factories & Farms	其他附设机构人员 Personnel in Others Subsidiary Units	聘请校外教师 Part-time Teachers
行政人员 Adm. Personnel	教辅人员 Supporting Staff	工勤人员 Workers			
6393	**8923**	**5445**	**333**	**603**	**12858**
400	382	113	4	1	167
102	88	23	0	0	20
367	870	396	24	6	600
266	506	299	1	21	714
168	454	219	0	0	341
605	390	219	11	4	521
371	568	91	0	0	349
208	228	72	0	1	164
127	241	34	0	7	82
36	216	131	22	0	284
275	632	333	1	4	1050
169	161	232	6	2	434
0	0	0	0	0	0
273	355	206	3	10	268
344	547	143	35	24	495
444	520	358	158	3	911
90	83	87	1	5	196
690	766	526	15	8	1382
187	502	244	0	53	173
0	0	0	0	0	0
85	59	109	3	2	93
202	144	136	2	38	1187
167	269	357	2	253	848
141	104	324	19	81	1583
109	182	357	4	5	437
0	0	0	0	0	0
460	493	277	11	20	237
47	65	81	11	43	53
0	0	2	0	0	9
2	20	11	0	0	156
58	78	65	0	12	104

地 区 Region	教职工数 Educational		
	合计 Total	校本部教职工 Educational	
		小计 Subtotal	专任教师 Full-time Teachers
总 计 Total	**10830**	**10819**	**7995**
北 京 Beijing	0	0	0
天 津 Tianjin	0	0	0
河 北 Hebei	693	693	582
山 西 Shanxi	270	270	198
内蒙古 Inner Mongolia	0	0	0
辽 宁 Liaoning	0	0	0
吉 林 Jilin	159	159	68
黑龙江 Heilongjiang	425	421	259
上 海 Shanghai	0	0	0
江 苏 Jiangsu	2109	2103	1577
浙 江 Zhejiang	685	685	460
安 徽 Anhui	1541	1541	1174
福 建 Fujian	0	0	0
江 西 Jiangxi	0	0	0
山 东 Shandong	581	581	431
河 南 Henan	1376	1375	988
湖 北 Hubei	179	179	118
湖 南 Hunan	301	301	265
广 东 Guangdong	1103	1103	856
广 西 Guangxi	0	0	0
海 南 Hainan	0	0	0
重 庆 Chongqing	143	143	107
四 川 Sichuan	346	346	271
贵 州 Guizhou	111	111	89
云 南 Yunnan	673	673	448
西 藏 Tibet	0	0	0
陕 西 Shaanxi	0	0	0
甘 肃 Gansu	18	18	18
青 海 Qinghai	0	0	0
宁 夏 Ningxia	117	117	86
新 疆 Xinjiang	0	0	0

育机构教职工数
Secondary Vocational Education Institutions

单位：人
unit: person

Personnel					
Personnel in Main Campus			校办企业职工 Employees in School-run Factories & Farms	其他附设机构人员 Personnel in Others Subsidiary Units	聘请校外教师 Part-time Teachers
行政人员 Adm. Personnel	教辅人员 Supporting Staff	工勤人员 Workers			
1283	**825**	**716**	**0**	**11**	**1392**
0	0	0	0	0	0
0	0	0	0	0	0
68	9	34	0	0	117
23	17	32	0	0	31
0	0	0	0	0	0
0	0	0	0	0	0
44	25	22	0	0	17
92	38	32	0	4	237
0	0	0	0	0	0
217	158	151	0	6	174
93	67	65	0	0	115
187	110	70	0	0	236
0	0	0	0	0	0
0	0	0	0	0	0
64	27	59	0	0	59
188	129	70	0	1	43
11	24	26	0	0	0
10	20	6	0	0	32
125	67	55	0	0	72
0	0	0	0	0	0
0	0	0	0	0	0
18	0	18	0	0	0
20	25	30	0	0	6
22	0	0	0	0	10
78	105	42	0	0	52
0	0	0	0	0	0
0	0	0	0	0	0
0	0	0	0	0	80
0	0	0	0	0	0
23	4	4	0	0	111
0	0	0	0	0	0

Number of Female Educational Personnel in Other

地 区 Region	教职工数 Educational		
	合计 Total	校本部教职工 Educational	
		小计 Subtotal	专任教师 Full-time Teachers
总 计 Total	**5064**	**5063**	**4104**
北 京 Beijing	0	0	0
天 津 Tianjin	0	0	0
河 北 Hebei	393	393	367
山 西 Shanxi	114	114	97
内蒙古 Inner Mongolia	0	0	0
辽 宁 Liaoning	0	0	0
吉 林 Jilin	79	79	48
黑龙江 Heilongjiang	186	185	113
上 海 Shanghai	0	0	0
江 苏 Jiangsu	986	986	810
浙 江 Zhejiang	357	357	264
安 徽 Anhui	486	486	384
福 建 Fujian	0	0	0
江 西 Jiangxi	0	0	0
山 东 Shandong	234	234	192
河 南 Henan	734	734	607
湖 北 Hubei	88	88	67
湖 南 Hunan	145	145	127
广 东 Guangdong	580	580	493
广 西 Guangxi	0	0	0
海 南 Hainan	0	0	0
重 庆 Chongqing	87	87	72
四 川 Sichuan	152	152	125
贵 州 Guizhou	70	70	60
云 南 Yunnan	296	296	216
西 藏 Tibet	0	0	0
陕 西 Shaanxi	0	0	0
甘 肃 Gansu	10	10	10
青 海 Qinghai	0	0	0
宁 夏 Ningxia	67	67	52
新 疆 Xinjiang	0	0	0

机构女教职工数
Secondary Vocational Education Institutions

单位:人
unit:person

Personnel					
Personnel in Main Campus			校办企业职工 Employees in School-run Factories & Farms	其他附设机构人员 Personnel in Others Subsidiary Units	聘请校外教师 Part-time Teachers
行政人员 Adm. Personnel	教辅人员 Supporting Staff	工勤人员 Workers			
406	**371**	**182**	**0**	**1**	**698**
0	0	0	0	0	0
0	0	0	0	0	0
20	2	4	0	0	84
7	4	6	0	0	16
0	0	0	0	0	0
0	0	0	0	0	0
22	5	4	0	0	12
40	23	9	0	1	97
0	0	0	0	0	0
70	75	31	0	0	79
33	33	27	0	0	71
59	35	8	0	0	90
0	0	0	0	0	0
0	0	0	0	0	0
19	13	10	0	0	27
34	66	27	0	0	34
7	4	10	0	0	0
5	10	3	0	0	18
36	41	10	0	0	52
0	0	0	0	0	0
0	0	0	0	0	0
3	0	12	0	0	0
10	11	6	0	0	0
10	0	0	0	0	4
20	45	15	0	0	23
0	0	0	0	0	0
0	0	0	0	0	0
0	0	0	0	0	28
0	0	0	0	0	0
11	4	0	0	0	63
0	0	0	0	0	0

中等职业学校(机构)专任教

Number of Full-time Teachers by Professional Rank

地 区 Region	合计 Total	按专业技术职务分 By Professional Rank			
		正高级 Senior	副高级 Sub-Senior	中级 Middle	初级 Junior
总 计 Total	**640398**	**2552**	**159863**	**252228**	**159561**
北 京 Beijing	6338	39	1966	2532	1405
天 津 Tianjin	6108	11	2294	2516	1074
河 北 Hebei	46119	128	12935	20034	9160
山 西 Shanxi	25196	45	4639	9596	8403
内蒙古 Inner Mongolia	13736	34	4221	5357	2837
辽 宁 Liaoning	20582	655	7041	8178	3180
吉 林 Jilin	13459	57	4256	5935	2417
黑龙江 Heilongjiang	14090	75	4790	5434	2688
上 海 Shanghai	8125	30	1753	4117	1957
江 苏 Jiangsu	42317	168	13453	17265	8532
浙 江 Zhejiang	33925	57	9318	12577	9255
安 徽 Anhui	27804	40	7643	10848	6525
福 建 Fujian	16479	24	4125	6663	4371
江 西 Jiangxi	12514	49	3655	4151	2425
山 东 Shandong	48659	169	12411	19639	11956
河 南 Henan	49755	155	10670	20671	14080
湖 北 Hubei	20211	75	5109	8889	4724
湖 南 Hunan	27001	87	5790	10849	6291
广 东 Guangdong	45197	59	7862	19892	10745
广 西 Guangxi	20942	81	3607	8221	5688
海 南 Hainan	4421	18	784	1416	1363
重 庆 Chongqing	14932	112	3717	5128	4601
四 川 Sichuan	38340	200	8970	13084	11044
贵 州 Guizhou	18181	53	2967	5436	6290
云 南 Yunnan	21680	32	7034	7391	4720
西 藏 Tibet	1520	0	160	516	396
陕 西 Shaanxi	13962	66	2805	5644	4097
甘 肃 Gansu	13787	25	2621	5414	4765
青 海 Qinghai	2433	1	687	859	642
宁 夏 Ningxia	2752	3	595	776	892
新 疆 Xinjiang	9833	4	1985	3200	3038

师专业技术职务、学历情况
and Academic Qualifications in Secondary Vocational Schools

单位：人
unit: person

	按学历分 By Academic Qualifications				
未定职级 No-ranking	博士研究生 Doctor's Degrees	硕士研究生 Master's Degrees	本科 Normal Courses	专科 Short-cycle Courses	高中阶段及以下 Below High School Graduate
66194	**526**	**48429**	**537558**	**51709**	**2176**
396	42	913	5207	151	25
213	3	857	5029	207	12
3862	19	2162	39713	4126	99
2513	8	1401	21115	2560	112
1287	19	944	11369	1382	22
1528	14	1629	17662	1218	59
794	10	720	11595	1085	49
1103	2	723	12473	871	21
268	40	1463	6365	209	48
2899	57	7144	34092	994	30
2718	7	2637	30313	956	12
2748	12	1467	24698	1597	30
1296	5	960	14487	961	66
2234	2	526	9538	2307	141
4484	38	4019	41589	2872	141
4179	35	4186	40670	4809	55
1414	13	1090	17240	1756	112
3984	37	1194	22419	3247	104
6639	40	4866	37107	2880	304
3345	26	2027	16681	2024	184
840	21	205	3687	444	64
1374	6	1243	12589	1049	45
5042	36	1452	31732	5074	46
3435	9	1007	14968	2102	95
2503	3	1149	18164	2202	162
448	0	98	1343	79	0
1350	8	910	11612	1393	39
962	9	639	11791	1313	35
244	0	76	1894	452	11
486	2	246	2353	147	4
1606	3	476	8063	1242	49

普通中专学校专任教师

Number of Full-time Teachers by Professional Rank and Academic

地 区 Region	合计 Total	按专业技术职务分 By Professional Rank			
		正高级 Senior	副高级 Sub-Senior	中级 Middle	初级 Junior
总 计 Total	**301577**	**1627**	**75792**	**116222**	**74466**
北 京 Beijing	1857	29	480	808	436
天 津 Tianjin	4133	10	1493	1631	822
河 北 Hebei	13587	92	3538	5091	2685
山 西 Shanxi	7691	12	2193	3141	1805
内蒙古 Inner Mongolia	3920	26	1153	1429	775
辽 宁 Liaoning	10480	448	3685	4399	1519
吉 林 Jilin	3202	19	1299	1220	580
黑龙江 Heilongjiang	5068	45	1590	1541	1069
上 海 Shanghai	5236	30	1221	2489	1300
江 苏 Jiangsu	30272	141	9566	12801	5806
浙 江 Zhejiang	5995	27	1627	2153	1759
安 徽 Anhui	15214	20	4604	5513	3712
福 建 Fujian	16479	24	4125	6663	4371
江 西 Jiangxi	4502	38	1056	1526	1137
山 东 Shandong	29320	98	7603	11660	7141
河 南 Henan	15322	83	4038	6196	3964
湖 北 Hubei	14897	62	3876	6418	3504
湖 南 Hunan	3029	16	1015	1008	659
广 东 Guangdong	31617	51	4964	13354	8008
广 西 Guangxi	20942	81	3607	8221	5688
海 南 Hainan	2362	3	498	750	739
重 庆 Chongqing	2831	29	697	868	770
四 川 Sichuan	16270	165	3104	5228	4894
贵 州 Guizhou	6520	15	1192	1764	2481
云 南 Yunnan	7789	10	2462	2212	1849
西 藏 Tibet	1520	0	160	516	396
陕 西 Shaanxi	2278	38	735	850	525
甘 肃 Gansu	9307	15	1956	3715	3185
青 海 Qinghai	2126	0	639	709	549
宁 夏 Ningxia	1191	0	227	215	345
新 疆 Xinjiang	6620	0	1389	2133	1993

专业技术职务、学历情况
Qualifications in Reg. Specialized Secondary Schools

单位:人
unit:person

	按学历分 By Academic Qualification				
未定职级 No-ranking	博士研究生 Doctor's Degree	硕士研究生 Master's Degree	本科 Normal Courses	专科 Short-cycle Courses	高中阶段及以下 Below High School Graduate
33470	**352**	**31747**	**246737**	**21390**	**1351**
104	36	515	1209	77	20
177	3	667	3306	147	10
2181	12	1147	10547	1798	83
540	6	905	6281	458	41
537	18	537	2921	424	20
429	8	1186	8836	422	28
84	3	348	2681	163	7
823	1	514	4256	293	4
196	37	1163	3799	191	46
1958	32	5973	23674	575	18
429	6	726	5114	146	3
1365	6	939	13408	850	11
1296	5	960	14487	961	66
745	1	397	3499	561	44
2818	34	2841	24679	1675	91
1041	19	2232	12190	847	34
1037	9	826	12634	1334	94
331	1	296	2485	232	15
5240	37	2981	25945	2368	286
3345	26	2027	16681	2024	184
372	3	125	2041	152	41
467	3	367	2168	274	19
2879	31	892	12654	2658	35
1068	0	728	5276	469	47
1256	2	799	6483	482	23
448	0	98	1343	79	0
130	4	410	1692	164	8
436	5	517	8129	631	25
229	0	76	1674	365	11
404	2	131	999	55	4
1105	2	424	5646	515	33

成人中专学校专任教师

Number of Full-time Teachers by Professional Rank and Academic

地　区 Region	合计 Total	按专业技术职务分 By Professional Rank			
		正高级 Senior	副高级 Sub-Senior	中级 Middle	初级 Junior
总　计 Total	**44773**	**316**	**13423**	**18871**	**8407**
北　京 Beijing	308	1	65	136	70
天　津 Tianjin	255	0	94	112	44
河　北 Hebei	6469	25	2518	3030	767
山　西 Shanxi	3157	7	443	1507	1118
内蒙古 Inner Mongolia	1682	2	913	600	150
辽　宁 Liaoning	395	40	110	187	56
吉　林 Jilin	3632	7	1313	1812	462
黑龙江 Heilongjiang	1661	24	624	677	253
上　海 Shanghai	115	0	14	80	16
江　苏 Jiangsu	887	0	163	352	231
浙　江 Zhejiang	655	11	216	285	84
安　徽 Anhui	1042	2	219	401	325
福　建 Fujian	0	0	0	0	0
江　西 Jiangxi	1609	0	946	527	110
山　东 Shandong	2435	60	829	879	505
河　南 Henan	8399	39	1651	3345	1717
湖　北 Hubei	185	12	44	59	62
湖　南 Hunan	2868	10	734	1294	518
广　东 Guangdong	248	0	32	111	74
广　西 Guangxi	0	0	0	0	0
海　南 Hainan	20	0	9	5	6
重　庆 Chongqing	1906	40	803	681	215
四　川 Sichuan	1411	12	78	165	622
贵　州 Guizhou	1203	8	167	702	262
云　南 Yunnan	2698	9	1068	1209	387
西　藏 Tibet	0	0	0	0	0
陕　西 Shaanxi	103	0	28	37	27
甘　肃 Gansu	378	0	96	187	81
青　海 Qinghai	301	1	43	149	93
宁　夏 Ningxia	71	3	26	34	8
新　疆 Xinjiang	680	3	177	308	144

专业技术职务、学历情况
Qualifications in Adult Specialized Secondary Schools

单位:人
unit:person

	按学历分 By Academic Qualification				
未定职级 No-ranking	博士研究生 Doctor's Degree	硕士研究生 Master's Degree	本科 Normal Courses	专科 Short-cycle Courses	高中阶段及以下 Below High School Graduate
3756	**42**	**2183**	**35451**	**6959**	**138**
36	3	22	276	6	1
5	0	19	199	36	1
129	6	192	5296	974	1
82	0	22	2452	667	16
17	0	49	1392	241	0
2	0	14	288	91	2
38	2	91	3009	516	14
83	1	35	1472	144	9
5	2	18	93	2	0
141	0	62	729	90	6
59	0	70	494	91	0
95	6	46	943	47	0
0	0	0	0	0	0
26	0	28	1290	278	13
162	1	179	2022	233	0
1647	14	669	6062	1650	4
8	1	5	142	37	0
312	0	65	2265	511	27
31	0	66	144	38	0
0	0	0	0	0	0
0	0	0	17	3	0
167	2	266	1531	103	4
534	0	74	1167	168	2
64	2	58	860	280	3
25	1	86	2157	422	32
0	0	0	0	0	0
11	0	8	89	6	0
14	0	11	285	80	2
15	0	0	217	84	0
0	0	7	55	9	0
48	1	21	505	152	1

职业高中学校专任教师

Number of Full-time Teachers by Professional Rank and

地　区 Region	合计 Total	按专业技术职务分 By Professional Rank			
		正高级 Senior	副高级 Sub-Senior	中级 Middle	初级 Junior
总　计 Total	**286053**	**575**	**68700**	**113980**	**75087**
北　京 Beijing	4173	9	1421	1588	899
天　津 Tianjin	1720	1	707	773	208
河　北 Hebei	25481	11	6676	11648	5633
山　西 Shanxi	14150	26	1952	4865	5419
内蒙古 Inner Mongolia	8134	6	2155	3328	1912
辽　宁 Liaoning	9707	167	3246	3592	1605
吉　林 Jilin	6557	28	1630	2877	1357
黑龙江 Heilongjiang	7102	5	2442	3115	1351
上　海 Shanghai	2774	0	518	1548	641
江　苏 Jiangsu	9581	19	3257	3512	2213
浙　江 Zhejiang	26815	18	7385	9967	7300
安　徽 Anhui	10374	18	2515	4384	2250
福　建 Fujian	0	0	0	0	0
江　西 Jiangxi	6403	11	1653	2098	1178
山　东 Shandong	16473	11	3886	6930	4219
河　南 Henan	25046	29	4799	10748	8097
湖　北 Hubei	5011	1	1151	2369	1151
湖　南 Hunan	20839	61	3965	8437	5059
广　东 Guangdong	12476	0	2679	6035	2534
广　西 Guangxi	0	0	0	0	0
海　南 Hainan	2039	15	277	661	618
重　庆 Chongqing	10088	39	2211	3537	3572
四　川 Sichuan	20388	20	5743	7576	5442
贵　州 Guizhou	10369	30	1600	2929	3514
云　南 Yunnan	10745	11	3494	3953	2450
西　藏 Tibet	0	0	0	0	0
陕　西 Shaanxi	11581	28	2042	4757	3545
甘　肃 Gansu	4084	10	569	1494	1499
青　海 Qinghai	6	0	5	1	0
宁　夏 Ningxia	1404	0	303	499	520
新　疆 Xinjiang	2533	1	419	759	901

专业技术职务、学历情况
Academic Qualifications in Vocational High Schools

单位:人
unit:person

	按学历分 By Academic Qualification				
未定职级 No-ranking	博士研究生 Doctor's Degree	硕士研究生 Master's Degree	本科 Normal Courses	专科 Short-cycle Courses	高中阶段及以下 Below High School Graduate
27711	**107**	**13658**	**249077**	**22562**	**649**
256	3	376	3722	68	4
31	0	171	1524	24	1
1513	1	777	23378	1310	15
1888	2	473	12239	1388	48
733	1	358	7056	717	2
1097	6	429	8538	705	29
665	5	281	5871	372	28
189	0	164	6500	430	8
67	1	282	2473	16	2
580	2	850	8441	283	5
2145	1	1828	24297	681	8
1207	0	313	9472	570	19
0	0	0	0	0	0
1463	1	101	4749	1468	84
1427	3	986	14547	887	50
1373	2	1148	21628	2251	17
339	3	238	4388	369	13
3317	36	827	17422	2493	61
1228	1	1742	10328	388	17
0	0	0	0	0	0
468	18	80	1629	289	23
729	1	610	8801	654	22
1607	5	476	17698	2200	9
2296	7	219	8765	1333	45
837	0	240	9240	1180	85
0	0	0	0	0	0
1209	4	492	9831	1223	31
512	4	93	3377	602	8
0	0	0	3	3	0
82	0	73	1248	83	0
453	0	31	1912	575	15

地 区 Region	合计 Total	按专业技术职务分 By Professional Rank			
		正高级 Senior	副高级 Sub-Senior	中级 Middle	初级 Junior
总 计 Total	**7995**	**34**	**1948**	**3155**	**1601**
北 京 Beijing	0	0	0	0	0
天 津 Tianjin	0	0	0	0	0
河 北 Hebei	582	0	203	265	75
山 西 Shanxi	198	0	51	83	61
内蒙古 Inner Mongolia	0	0	0	0	0
辽 宁 Liaoning	0	0	0	0	0
吉 林 Jilin	68	3	14	26	18
黑龙江 Heilongjiang	259	1	134	101	15
上 海 Shanghai	0	0	0	0	0
江 苏 Jiangsu	1577	8	467	600	282
浙 江 Zhejiang	460	1	90	172	112
安 徽 Anhui	1174	0	305	550	238
福 建 Fujian	0	0	0	0	0
江 西 Jiangxi	0	0	0	0	0
山 东 Shandong	431	0	93	170	91
河 南 Henan	988	4	182	382	302
湖 北 Hubei	118	0	38	43	7
湖 南 Hunan	265	0	76	110	55
广 东 Guangdong	856	8	187	392	129
广 西 Guangxi	0	0	0	0	0
海 南 Hainan	0	0	0	0	0
重 庆 Chongqing	107	4	6	42	44
四 川 Sichuan	271	3	45	115	86
贵 州 Guizhou	89	0	8	41	33
云 南 Yunnan	448	2	10	17	34
西 藏 Tibet	0	0	0	0	0
陕 西 Shaanxi	0	0	0	0	0
甘 肃 Gansu	18	0	0	18	0
青 海 Qinghai	0	0	0	0	0
宁 夏 Ningxia	86	0	39	28	19
新 疆 Xinjiang	0	0	0	0	0

师专业技术职务、学历情况
Qualifications in Other Secondary Vocational Education Institutions

单位：人
unit: person

	按学历分 By Academic Qualification				
未定职级 No-ranking	博士研究生 Doctor's Degree	硕士研究生 Master's Degree	本科 Normal Courses	专科 Short-cycle Courses	高中阶段及以下 Below High School Graduate
1257	**25**	**841**	**6293**	**798**	**38**
0	0	0	0	0	0
0	0	0	0	0	0
39	0	46	492	44	0
3	0	1	143	47	7
0	0	0	0	0	0
0	0	0	0	0	0
7	0	0	34	34	0
8	0	10	245	4	0
0	0	0	0	0	0
220	23	259	1248	46	1
85	0	13	408	38	1
81	0	169	875	130	0
0	0	0	0	0	0
0	0	0	0	0	0
77	0	13	341	77	0
118	0	137	790	61	0
30	0	21	76	16	5
24	0	6	247	11	1
140	2	77	690	86	1
0	0	0	0	0	0
0	0	0	0	0	0
11	0	0	89	18	0
22	0	10	213	48	0
7	0	2	67	20	0
385	0	24	284	118	22
0	0	0	0	0	0
0	0	0	0	0	0
0	0	18	0	0	0
0	0	0	0	0	0
0	0	35	51	0	0
0	0	0	0	0	0

中等职业学校(机构)

Condition of Assets and Teaching Resources in Secondary

地区 Region	占地面积(平方米) Areas Occupied(m^2) 合计 Total	其中:绿化用地面积 of Which: Green Areas	其中:运动场地面积 of Which: Sports Areas	图书(册) Books(Volume) 合计 Total	当年新增 New Added in Current Year
总　计 Total	**455609059.89**	**108786057.88**	**71957633.32**	**319803855**	**14957596**
北　京 Beijing	4276423.00	967937.45	944035.74	4968370	48572
天　津 Tianjin	3519744.77	605384.01	533092.46	3662189	189957
河　北 Hebei	23594443.51	4012537.78	4636478.51	19517680	1070834
山　西 Shanxi	15286144.53	2817952.35	2154019.18	10434378	475310
内蒙古 Inner Mongolia	10385359.59	1838010.06	1931464.00	5683796	184509
辽　宁 Liaoning	11137652.29	1687928.62	2421403.78	8294824	147427
吉　林 Jilin	6280770.55	1177989.74	1274629.92	4809008	124137
黑龙江 Heilongjiang	8663350.80	1354777.45	1574098.39	3958334	152260
上　海 Shanghai	3629039.60	1187747.90	729935.10	6310119	143105
江　苏 Jiangsu	31984985.67	9974217.82	4724446.09	23121096	648025
浙　江 Zhejiang	19698230.12	6026356.78	3838676.10	16365504	939328
安　徽 Anhui	33144765.42	7433680.92	4131268.60	24396459	866414
福　建 Fujian	11572510.85	3211924.35	2088313.25	9636173	275758
江　西 Jiangxi	14218527.00	3755654.00	2060290.00	8105054	479016
山　东 Shandong	34737169.12	9194028.44	5507053.19	23324054	1309002
河　南 Henan	30948058.50	5676123.97	4237798.99	21075766	747119
湖　北 Hubei	14693413.62	3931591.57	2429601.34	9951638	190194
湖　南 Hunan	19285690.20	4965266.78	2801750.75	12289041	807852
广　东 Guangdong	26991249.21	7994004.08	4821561.57	26329622	1188862
广　西 Guangxi	19389859.72	5005810.61	2427157.82	14119881	168748
海　南 Hainan	3085624.68	591990.22	432152.00	2004745	131163
重　庆 Chongqing	11296958.30	2928925.40	1686423.02	7705089	460322
四　川 Sichuan	20991082.05	5148565.12	4223484.40	17042113	1565526
贵　州 Guizhou	16252051.45	4247203.11	2510843.96	8916695	1176377
云　南 Yunnan	16892603.68	3813148.54	2077844.39	8538941	362305
西　藏 Tibet	1600584.80	300430.60	132702.58	446625	888
陕　西 Shaanxi	12678161.41	2050591.01	1717803.94	8231661	587992
甘　肃 Gansu	8174784.75	1634681.15	1397718.55	4239896	148651
青　海 Qinghai	2559731.12	584845.79	375066.00	1345294	81370
宁　夏 Ningxia	4972042.06	1601853.32	435710.48	1219137	81899
新　疆 Xinjiang	13668047.52	3064898.94	1700809.22	3760673	204674

资产情况(学校产权)
Vocational Schools(Owned by SVSs)

计算机数(台) PC(Set)			教室(间) Classroom(Room)		固定资产值(万元) Fixed Assets(10,000 yuan)		
合计 Total	其中:教学用计算机 No. of Computers Used for Instruction		合计 Total	其中:网络多媒体教室 of Which: Network Multimedia Classroom	合计 Total	其中:教学、实习仪器设备资产值 of Which:Teaching Equipment & Instruments	
	小计 Subtotal	其中:平板电脑 of Which: Tablet PC				小计 Subtotal	当年新增 New Added in Current Year
3266672	**2682114**	**111855**	**396732**	**189143**	**33850302.66**	**7797421.54**	**979289.10**
56450	47883	2349	5251	3264	777006.91	311461.62	27570.76
38432	29380	1006	3611	1556	294853.68	98306.05	8222.54
177993	146709	8163	24692	9945	1421941.47	307811.72	40152.40
94399	75135	4024	13841	5143	914537.34	199910.94	30442.64
51815	40950	789	6812	3074	787558.12	164125.68	25813.32
101249	79884	2621	10715	4863	1029307.62	224815.20	28722.26
45611	33598	1820	6215	2126	392692.16	118110.38	19973.04
52591	42573	1753	6746	2615	479098.73	122315.92	17349.74
93738	71526	2941	5894	3817	1218282.09	388977.39	71830.05
250248	209946	5655	27023	17798	3312342.87	646147.06	61445.03
193025	163704	4585	17483	13039	1819429.33	487955.05	67679.39
147320	124079	2036	26057	9534	1851885.11	345751.21	31598.31
104280	86642	4050	9307	6196	815750.43	255013.38	30057.62
81496	66197	2684	10120	4253	662289.98	153286.34	19539.73
225082	182849	9197	32049	14899	2549051.45	531365.35	67779.28
196800	159444	11240	30685	11214	1586699.62	335481.73	40115.28
105349	85829	3125	13644	5566	992966.62	202064.74	24621.12
142010	114954	10381	17233	8099	1312995.67	258311.38	39418.44
332042	280557	6864	24174	16385	2536289.94	746391.93	84872.32
121263	102791	7921	11587	5496	1078620.53	356143.78	42880.16
25695	21352	181	2055	1277	321108.24	79460.80	16144.59
88207	74050	3413	9747	6123	1004759.47	199177.17	19794.66
164241	136888	3967	25820	10174	1875728.49	369460.51	48578.34
87416	72712	2480	11127	6226	1009131.22	206353.62	27903.50
95902	79831	1263	13550	4970	1262432.26	183751.04	26880.89
5243	3904	62	705	114	149498.16	21675.79	2167.02
65779	52706	2078	9947	3527	681980.16	142353.59	14904.36
46938	36516	2155	7239	2796	483162.57	97669.26	7358.20
16014	12088	368	2233	946	304077.64	58625.44	9418.38
15899	13493	116	2948	1305	204511.61	53225.43	6597.53
44145	33944	2568	8222	2803	720313.17	131922.02	19458.19

地 区 Region	占地面积(平方米) Areas Occupied(m^2)			图书(册) Books(Volume)	
	合计 Total	其中:绿化用地面积 of Which: Green Areas	其中:运动场地面积 of Which: Sports Areas	合计 Total	当年新增 New Added in Current Year
总 计 Total	**40771057.82**	**7898098.55**	**6527340.45**	**7203358**	**433425**
北 京 Beijing	487048.00	39223.45	54845.66	10500	1000
天 津 Tianjin	305821.66	42000.00	53126.00	54302	500
河 北 Hebei	3417720.58	303014.82	494969.05	179743	40500
山 西 Shanxi	1021972.14	154593.73	220870.86	607978	0
内蒙古 Inner Mongolia	1103201.41	207180.23	251260.27	24613	1195
辽 宁 Liaoning	1226966.86	183666.00	240147.00	107327	3750
吉 林 Jilin	506518.21	70360.00	143159.00	101300	1000
黑龙江 Heilongjiang	694041.64	80002.12	143490.28	477727	19806
上 海 Shanghai	270304.37	34000.00	33136.80	0	0
江 苏 Jiangsu	984017.36	298616.99	133867.28	39110	850
浙 江 Zhejiang	1075093.40	161253.65	199945.00	168934	30200
安 徽 Anhui	1326756.18	194170.89	116109.39	277492	100
福 建 Fujian	865474.19	292670.74	134791.02	16300	0
江 西 Jiangxi	2763162.00	716186.00	452150.00	160158	11687
山 东 Shandong	2882268.00	607543.30	372182.00	627917	20496
河 南 Henan	2556451.98	411306.92	372238.00	841937	23268
湖 北 Hubei	722674.81	133986.00	97670.00	105495	5300
湖 南 Hunan	1544927.15	316710.13	239432.08	71214	4812
广 东 Guangdong	3884906.43	839058.50	732809.19	368494	6887
广 西 Guangxi	2820704.40	632038.65	277400.66	685890	2860
海 南 Hainan	299828.80	43772.00	22834.00	4500	4500
重 庆 Chongqing	930879.09	213594.00	82786.00	12400	0
四 川 Sichuan	4149262.29	802262.79	731255.04	635834	140759
贵 州 Guizhou	1162041.25	243681.00	205426.00	269900	17700
云 南 Yunnan	1271434.34	290553.00	186184.00	92912	1700
西 藏 Tibet	0	0	0	0	0
陕 西 Shaanxi	1275949.45	358753.24	290496.87	590200	77670
甘 肃 Gansu	963323.44	191286.00	238681.00	581938	16885
青 海 Qinghai	5340.00	0	0	2000	0
宁 夏 Ningxia	155910.73	7295.00	5678.00	0	0
新 疆 Xinjiang	97057.66	29319.40	400.00	87243	0

况(非学校产权中独立使用)
Vocational Schools(Institutions)(Not Owned by SVSs)

计算机数(台) PC(Set)			教室(间) Classroom(Room)		固定资产值(万元) Fixed Assets(10,000 yuan)		
合计 Total	其中:教学用计算机 No. of Computers Used for Instruction		合计 Total	其中:网络多媒体教室 of Which: Network Multimedia Classroom	合计 Total	其中:教学、实习仪器设备资产值 of Which: Teaching Equipment & Instruments	
	小计 Subtotal	其中:平板电脑 of Which: Tablet PC				小计 Subtotal	当年新增 New Added in Current Year
67335	**52523**	**2832**	**43325**	**16486**	**1559835. 54**	**182357. 82**	**28881. 81**
186	84	18	471	196	3080. 48	248. 70	0
350	307	43	536	109	17978. 74	595. 10	4. 50
4501	3689	287	2819	808	89235. 56	16288. 03	6109. 02
1895	1215	32	1101	241	30940. 82	4451. 79	336. 46
839	753	10	610	170	12983. 76	1578. 40	155. 10
1624	1197	110	2333	738	137120. 99	6418. 67	477. 54
2241	1574	2	912	246	22242. 67	1589. 50	773. 00
4354	3753	76	1132	297	38172. 73	7657. 32	357. 03
145	117	7	465	247	15149. 68	3849. 95	1100. 33
1619	1410	0	577	251	24983. 91	2604. 22	189. 92
1209	1095	2	1159	742	63257. 41	7536. 34	638. 37
911	651	0	1330	434	70185. 76	5515. 95	911. 88
260	120	0	708	351	39857. 13	1607. 81	70. 00
2837	2229	222	1640	525	93422. 83	5123. 55	689. 63
3523	2744	225	2871	998	119927. 24	14228. 68	1462. 14
9507	7450	617	3152	926	73749. 32	15210. 20	1587. 92
830	650	65	490	143	23058. 35	3518. 28	296. 08
1792	1487	105	1939	962	65660. 79	8984. 50	2409. 64
5561	4031	30	4958	2471	90523. 31	8679. 49	1020. 74
2007	1560	0	2376	1256	25262. 58	5093. 12	828. 85
456	390	40	326	62	12318. 57	284. 40	95. 20
1159	1098	161	583	295	36371. 57	2815. 21	143. 54
7406	5443	50	5107	1593	165528. 74	24442. 25	7038. 56
1515	1398	141	1146	453	55939. 04	5455. 14	700. 68
1555	1357	0	1964	946	111247. 90	3798. 55	234. 00
0	0	0	0	0	0	0	0
3289	1954	23	1251	277	31259. 34	6381. 54	756. 51
5481	4498	562	1097	704	82417. 99	16808. 97	235. 86
7	0	0	50	2	5. 00	2. 00	0
0	0	0	80	11	131. 44	24. 10	0
276	269	4	142	32	7821. 89	1566. 07	259. 31

地 区 Region	占地面积(平方米) Areas Occupied(m^2)			图书(册) Books(Volume)	
	合计 Total	其中:绿化用地面积 of Which: Green Areas	其中:运动场地面积 of Which: Sports Areas	合计 Total	当年新增 New Added in Current Year
总 计 Total	**238179673.37**	**62117241.11**	**35392619.79**	**174644415**	**6954896**
北 京 Beijing	1480063.88	392837.08	326120.87	1441589	8670
天 津 Tianjin	2784368.58	492369.01	406944.46	2516475	113329
河 北 Hebei	7453309.18	1487580.96	1499427.57	7229548	335540
山 西 Shanxi	6074863.00	1155006.00	735360.00	5523270	67964
内蒙古 Inner Mongolia	3473235.99	817144.00	548733.00	2091009	75527
辽 宁 Liaoning	5300105.07	988642.62	1139774.52	4976427	93292
吉 林 Jilin	2484013.67	486204.01	429876.82	1495372	14854
黑龙江 Heilongjiang	3179503.40	584569.27	541215.70	2250224	32434
上 海 Shanghai	2362803.60	792545.00	463791.10	4375393	109672
江 苏 Jiangsu	20981622.72	7232072.62	3416876.97	16631059	466962
浙 江 Zhejiang	4034480.30	1271833.87	698306.34	2902445	75011
安 徽 Anhui	18589546.99	4608527.83	2289158.33	13621469	515894
福 建 Fujian	11572510.85	3211924.35	2088313.25	9636173	275758
江 西 Jiangxi	6050217.00	2005529.00	737159.00	3376743	240117
山 东 Shandong	24284345.22	6250237.41	3440817.78	15008902	1040192
河 南 Henan	11305537.13	2237037.38	1660086.55	8453875	158366
湖 北 Hubei	12032794.66	3307203.95	1928211.50	8016960	154766
湖 南 Hunan	2418880.00	640599.20	430506.00	1947503	32430
广 东 Guangdong	20170503.80	5930790.75	3243943.23	19577690	1043031
广 西 Guangxi	19389859.72	5005810.61	2427157.82	14119881	168748
海 南 Hainan	1804929.68	324109.22	244926.00	1557205	105920
重 庆 Chongqing	2699141.90	850350.01	361213.93	1879680	41468
四 川 Sichuan	9018245.08	2380018.85	1498770.88	8592781	905165
贵 州 Guizhou	7328748.84	2139874.78	928853.78	3335991	266974
云 南 Yunnan	8011240.54	1837653.01	815594.98	4344392	218993
西 藏 Tibet	1600584.80	300430.60	132702.58	446625	888
陕 西 Shaanxi	2794986.47	561861.68	322915.42	1567552	80097
甘 肃 Gansu	6056119.35	1254334.94	953782.14	3212600	121803
青 海 Qinghai	2512525.12	581821.79	372166.00	1231507	81370
宁 夏 Ningxia	2500784.83	877756.00	188433.05	464503	16342
新 疆 Xinjiang	8429802.00	2110565.31	1121480.22	2819572	93319

情况(学校产权)
in Regular SSSs(Owned by Regular SSSs)

计算机数(台) PC(Set)			教室(间) Classroom(Room)		固定资产值(万元) Fixed Assets(10,000 yuan)		
合计 Total	其中:教学用计算机 No. of Computers Used for Instruction		合计 Total	其中:网络多媒体教室 of Which: Network Multimedia Classroom	合计 Total	其中:教学、实习仪器设备资产值 of Which:Teaching Equipment & Instruments	
	小计 Subtotal	其中:平板电脑 of Which: Tablet PC				小计 Subtotal	当年新增 New Added in Current Year
1741325	**1431639**	**55191**	**195839**	**98660**	**18983359.95**	**4380305.20**	**548089.94**
18352	15472	502	1464	930	271506.39	92994.74	7750.38
28086	21801	937	2854	1216	250662.70	73917.22	6237.83
66059	54163	2528	7908	2979	508583.27	104975.53	9266.30
39698	31852	2387	5017	2182	360072.21	96874.15	12011.07
20601	16441	537	1790	781	300407.52	66463.97	10644.00
55959	43513	1452	5296	2549	612199.23	136129.63	21220.47
14795	11248	675	1806	755	123876.81	45162.75	8774.59
23898	19946	1108	2226	1164	244209.17	58530.25	5366.19
61539	46302	2253	3927	2420	892293.51	285512.10	60908.00
195232	163520	4851	18022	13771	2522032.50	510589.83	46953.73
35825	30403	412	3101	2325	334331.50	93732.19	10445.62
89714	75744	1177	14061	5663	1126862.56	212245.70	23002.02
104280	86642	4050	9307	6196	815750.43	255013.38	30057.62
35248	28281	612	3412	1854	317275.70	81455.84	8101.86
137667	112946	6760	21929	9540	1868624.34	323261.84	45726.75
79560	63367	2142	11422	4114	691589.60	152752.88	17671.87
81357	66802	2324	10639	4270	807709.51	162128.63	18226.85
17874	14705	1251	2434	1206	137779.49	30685.60	6143.76
226431	190550	3706	17859	12023	1816944.61	527233.22	59320.14
121263	102791	7921	11587	5496	1078620.53	356143.78	42880.16
17106	14501	179	1270	943	228601.27	60794.54	13295.59
19486	16686	323	2019	1144	249583.70	40955.63	3134.30
69216	56401	1959	10357	4163	837913.57	152573.99	21753.38
36791	31384	636	4388	2558	305905.23	79112.96	8259.70
41387	35153	499	5797	2287	778840.96	86988.52	16693.54
5243	3904	62	705	114	149498.16	21675.79	2167.02
12409	10231	218	1647	489	128101.71	28698.57	1131.57
32470	25727	1174	4488	1863	361022.90	71113.22	5242.31
15541	11621	328	2162	945	300888.44	58207.84	9409.68
6400	5293	91	1531	574	92799.43	23144.60	3244.62
31838	24249	2137	5414	2146	468873.00	91236.31	13049.00

普通中专学校资产情况
Condition of Assets and Teaching Resources in

地区 Region	占地面积(平方米) Areas Occupied(m^2)			图书(册) Books(Volume)	
	合计 Total	其中:绿化用地面积 of Which: Green Areas	其中:运动场地面积 of Which: Sports Areas	合计 Total	当年新增 New Added in Current Year
总 计 Total	**21783386.16**	**4379689.63**	**3440907.01**	**3820206**	**286562**
北 京 Beijing	34091.00	2100.00	4000.00	0	0
天 津 Tianjin	225511.22	40000.00	33160.00	20000	0
河 北 Hebei	2861367.56	252889.76	354544.01	152000	38400
山 西 Shanxi	360441.00	73780.00	72249.00	0	0
内蒙古 Inner Mongolia	898367.00	194573.00	194983.00	10850	895
辽 宁 Liaoning	461025.00	72530.00	59813.00	33300	1000
吉 林 Jilin	38125.20	520.00	17200.00	0	0
黑龙江 Heilongjiang	503698.64	68096.12	115546.28	340344	11006
上 海 Shanghai	247937.37	27570.00	28468.80	0	0
江 苏 Jiangsu	839317.36	198316.99	121867.28	39110	850
浙 江 Zhejiang	121677.00	32026.00	19271.00	50000	30000
安 徽 Anhui	552011.60	146348.00	52833.00	175100	0
福 建 Fujian	865474.19	292670.74	134791.02	16300	0
江 西 Jiangxi	792258.00	239689.00	113915.00	61356	208
山 东 Shandong	1144223.00	332616.30	161822.00	407883	20396
河 南 Henan	538014.00	106149.00	100809.00	302590	10280
湖 北 Hubei	509738.00	89875.00	71685.00	97495	300
湖 南 Hunan	61405.00	17412.00	12993.00	0	0
广 东 Guangdong	2486066.61	438524.58	494982.52	306075	6573
广 西 Guangxi	2820704.40	632038.65	277400.66	685890	2860
海 南 Hainan	103962.80	14700.00	4792.00	4500	4500
重 庆 Chongqing	113680.80	46289.00	34542.00	0	0
四 川 Sichuan	3614905.73	707295.09	577347.64	448061	140259
贵 州 Guizhou	65476.80	4544.00	35327.80	9100	2200
云 南 Yunnan	306559.00	89865.00	55660.00	3296	0
西 藏 Tibet	0	0	0	0	0
陕 西 Shaanxi	215419.31	74409.00	79784.00	0	0
甘 肃 Gansu	806699.44	174914.00	205442.00	571956	16835
青 海 Qinghai	5340.00	0	0	0	0
宁 夏 Ningxia	155376.73	7295.00	5678.00	0	0
新 疆 Xinjiang	34512.40	2653.40	0	85000	0

(非学校产权中独立使用)
Regular SSSs (Not Owned by Regular SSSs)

计算机数(台) PC(Set)			教室(间) Classroom(Room)		固定资产值(万元) Fixed Assets(10,000 yuan)		
合计 Total	其中:教学用计算机 No. of Computers Used for Instruction		合计 Total	其中:网络多媒体教室 of Which: Network Multimedia Classroom	合计 Total	其中:教学、实习仪器设备资产值 of Which:Teaching Equipment & Instruments	
	小计 Subtotal	其中:平板电脑 of Which: Tablet PC				小计 Subtotal	当年新增 New Added in Current Year
33022	**25890**	**1234**	**22621**	**9099**	**807700.45**	**99487.19**	**15699.70**
0	0	0	145	9	953.68	0	0
0	0	0	176	35	13633.95	0	0
3757	3071	274	2208	596	68927.25	12024.73	3330.04
0	0	0	172	21	3733.79	453.00	6.00
375	372	0	455	117	8770.44	1286.50	142.10
405	218	0	1143	530	63278.86	2006.27	169.52
0	0	0	77	55	8840.41	20.00	0
2800	2518	62	912	220	24910.58	5845.42	200.57
133	109	0	414	229	14335.40	3123.80	497.00
1459	1260	0	290	124	15296.25	1784.15	1.50
0	0	0	155	81	4297.00	2605.00	240.00
448	368	0	700	263	55021.25	3434.62	816.88
260	120	0	708	351	39857.13	1607.81	70.00
453	302	20	439	111	16056.46	859.72	0
1983	1565	140	1077	477	38422.86	6372.31	1380.05
2781	2429	0	469	128	14315.77	4394.30	393.00
750	600	65	224	53	16585.77	3082.70	80.00
0	0	0	24	24	1600.00	120.00	0
2600	1410	30	3712	1625	54541.31	7251.49	936.74
2007	1560	0	2376	1256	25262.58	5093.12	828.85
180	140	40	35	17	1679.34	53.20	40.20
89	70	0	248	51	5528.45	552.70	55.00
5571	3755	24	4225	1234	136936.23	19083.33	5909.44
725	660	10	123	88	3440.00	292.28	15.00
829	727	0	970	682	89439.97	1015.25	32.00
0	0	0	0	0	0	0	0
3	3	3	37	9	763.01	115.12	100.00
5230	4453	562	930	671	77848.61	16003.00	215.86
0	0	0	0	0	0	0	0
0	0	0	80	11	128.24	22.10	0
184	180	4	97	31	3295.85	985.27	239.94

地区 Region	占地面积(平方米) Areas Occupied(m^2)			图书(册) Books(Volume)	
	合计 Total	其中:绿化用地面积 of Which: Green Areas	其中:运动场地面积 of Which: Sports Areas	合计 Total	当年新增 New Added in Current Year
总计 Total	**18476087.77**	**3222099.69**	**2565491.25**	**17467190**	**1124230**
北京 Beijing	191706.00	50280.00	13000.00	127507	2686
天津 Tianjin	51989.76	4380.00	6044.00	115669	2560
河北 Hebei	1269644.10	131241.20	233241.80	2103236	215260
山西 Shanxi	382642.90	40822.23	47220.16	475877	1426
内蒙古 Inner Mongolia	674435.90	75413.06	73765.00	741723	32731
辽宁 Liaoning	46171.00	4008.00	14287.00	159760	2505
吉林 Jilin	559279.93	93018.55	142742.85	1206611	26204
黑龙江 Heilongjiang	515367.06	74296.00	158639.00	244287	37350
上海 Shanghai	35855.00	13460.00	3810.00	48999	0
江苏 Jiangsu	2091887.44	181784.00	66496.40	623056	50002
浙江 Zhejiang	290747.00	64492.24	42731.00	490862	125790
安徽 Anhui	734969.00	76845.00	85792.00	800426	37382
福建 Fujian	0	0	0	0	0
江西 Jiangxi	729327.00	196395.00	92590.00	625128	5760
山东 Shandong	837551.90	234097.01	140272.12	981869	20570
河南 Henan	3749750.07	542669.12	498027.56	3225229	264750
湖北 Hubei	195241.11	60948.00	37226.00	195937	0
湖南 Hunan	2559857.11	749596.01	303245.00	1221874	20158
广东 Guangdong	175635.00	71038.00	36475.00	174621	500
广西 Guangxi	0	0	0	0	0
海南 Hainan	17507.00	3018.00	3782.00	0	0
重庆 Chongqing	634183.89	147871.20	136370.72	997173	166228
四川 Sichuan	831034.76	85757.55	210180.23	801022	22805
贵州 Guizhou	384516.00	49055.00	31410.00	672928	35100
云南 Yunnan	887202.79	185071.00	107751.00	850912	11217
西藏 Tibet	0	0	0	0	0
陕西 Shaanxi	27974.01	1846.00	4400.00	56321	0
甘肃 Gansu	157491.04	29417.52	24504.41	90371	160
青海 Qinghai	23563.00	910.00	1200.00	111287	0
宁夏 Ningxia	7470.00	335.00	740.00	54836	580
新疆 Xinjiang	413088.00	54035.00	49548.00	269669	42506

产情况(学校产权)
in Adult SSSs(Owned by Adult SSSs)

计算机数(台) PC(Set)			教室(间) Classroom(Room)		固定资产值(万元) Fixed Assets(10,000 yuan)		
合计 Total	其中:教学用计算机 No. of Computers Used for Instruction		合计 Total	其中:网络多媒体教室 of Which: Network Multimedia Classroom	合计 Total	其中:教学、实习仪器设备资产值 of Which:Teaching Equipment & Instruments	
	小计 Subtotal	其中:平板电脑 of Which: Tablet PC				小计 Subtotal	当年新增 New Added in Current Year
151338	**118066**	**8246**	**23163**	**6795**	**1024557. 75**	**206053. 89**	**18752. 63**
2340	1904	63	313	206	12740. 51	3510. 60	7. 35
1877	1532	27	117	33	5285. 02	2220. 05	280. 40
18046	14223	1425	2392	652	84304. 70	17325. 29	1390. 20
5243	3907	87	682	120	16075. 00	3549. 39	357. 57
4459	3222	63	506	117	23290. 36	4047. 41	593. 62
828	535	141	88	8	7118. 15	1631. 40	5. 00
7103	4124	87	765	190	37824. 82	8824. 82	693. 82
3264	2653	13	625	192	26156. 41	4126. 56	1415. 62
1148	960	0	104	65	11265. 05	4419. 26	198. 53
4134	3328	141	1151	235	61695. 03	8659. 79	743. 14
4688	3832	442	1127	234	30114. 15	7495. 87	1971. 21
3376	2812	44	865	211	54243. 37	7369. 07	183. 56
0	0	0	0	0	0	0	0
4421	3133	121	823	195	36678. 80	5653. 23	1153. 96
8936	6781	592	1288	486	51715. 22	15167. 20	276. 70
25916	20931	2413	4578	1383	198700. 68	35956. 15	2351. 18
1745	1514	201	250	58	15565. 42	2655. 26	223. 84
15701	13527	1150	2153	431	99077. 88	20516. 56	935. 14
1932	1628	258	212	165	10386. 00	4939. 00	1031. 00
0	0	0	0	0	0	0	0
180	160	0	20	2	563. 00	169. 00	0
13040	10161	400	1452	661	96316. 59	15966. 75	1296. 85
5499	4749	178	1042	381	41415. 59	10418. 04	1596. 30
3981	2867	55	622	181	25069. 35	9291. 95	1086. 00
7545	5791	80	1207	248	52828. 80	7264. 32	440. 60
0	0	0	0	0	0	0	0
640	469	0	233	175	2340. 36	362. 00	3. 54
2353	814	67	139	23	5606. 18	2104. 43	56. 85
427	427	0	50	0	2157. 00	350. 00	0
1006	987	25	31	12	619. 86	246. 60	0
1510	1095	173	328	131	15404. 46	1813. 88	460. 64

地　区 Region	占地面积(平方米) Areas Occupied(m²)			图书(册) Books(Volume)	
	合计 Total	其中:绿化用地面积 of Which: Green Areas	其中:运动场地面积 of Which: Sports Areas	合计 Total	当年新增 New Added in Current Year
总　计 Total	**2478308.55**	**383452.75**	**353630.32**	**1551304**	**39720**
北　京 Beijing	55644.00	6100.00	6850.00	6500	0
天　津 Tianjin	11678.44	200.00	1500.00	8500	0
河　北 Hebei	92523.91	7255.00	10367.30	19243	0
山　西 Shanxi	53842.00	3302.00	15540.00	519158	0
内蒙古 Inner Mongolia	9077.60	360.00	1360.00	5210	0
辽　宁 Liaoning	55679.00	1600.00	12000.00	30700	2000
吉　林 Jilin	38182.01	1700.00	9829.00	0	0
黑龙江 Heilongjiang	10675.00	300.00	3193.00	73383	8300
上　海 Shanghai	2419.00	130.00	240.00	0	0
江　苏 Jiangsu	14500.00	300.00	1800.00	0	0
浙　江 Zhejiang	158300.00	39133.00	22452.00	80500	0
安　徽 Anhui	43259.00	2470.00	4600.00	0	0
福　建 Fujian	0	0	0	0	0
江　西 Jiangxi	114314.00	7060.00	50264.00	6000	200
山　东 Shandong	335956.00	56991.00	33520.00	39006	0
河　南 Henan	881413.48	165064.25	98069.62	389911	12308
湖　北 Hubei	0	0	0	0	0
湖　南 Hunan	88146.35	14746.80	16935.00	4512	412
广　东 Guangdong	0	0	0	0	0
广　西 Guangxi	0	0	0	0	0
海　南 Hainan	0	0	0	0	0
重　庆 Chongqing	167272.00	12770.00	16980.00	2400	0
四　川 Sichuan	131532.50	11350.70	10120.40	100265	0
贵　州 Guizhou	186630.00	50000.00	32960.00	200000	15000
云　南 Yunnan	26185.00	2620.00	5050.00	64016	1500
西　藏 Tibet	0	0	0	0	0
陕　西 Shaanxi	0	0	0	0	0
甘　肃 Gansu	0	0	0	0	0
青　海 Qinghai	0	0	0	2000	0
宁　夏 Ningxia	534.00	0	0	0	0
新　疆 Xinjiang	545.26	0	0	0	0

(非学校产权中独立使用)
in Adult SSSs(Not Owned by Adult SSSs)

计算机数(台) PC(Set)			教室(间) Classroom(Room)		固定资产值(万元) Fixed Assets(10,000 yuan)		
合计 Total	其中:教学用计算机 No. of Computers Used for Instruction 小计 Subtotal	其中:平板电脑 of Which: Tablet PC	合计 Total	其中:网络多媒体教室 of Which: Network Multimedia Classroom	合计 Total	其中:教学、实习仪器设备资产值 of Which: Teaching Equipment & Instruments 小计 Subtotal	当年新增 New Added in Current Year
9145	**6604**	**696**	**3968**	**1310**	**82708.97**	**16676.21**	**1647.22**
136	44	18	104	32	890.80	118.70	0
175	135	40	69	0	490.30	170.20	0
540	475	13	227	92	3278.38	909.18	142.38
734	186	0	177	17	3568.74	1441.50	1.50
178	148	10	28	11	969.00	104.00	13.00
413	323	92	35	4	501.00	218.00	4.00
0	0	0	120	11	1667.10	30.00	10.00
142	71	6	51	17	1015.55	54.00	6.46
2	1	0	21	12	7.30	4.30	4.30
160	150	0	71	27	938.65	378.07	108.42
892	802	0	159	129	10562.29	1541.00	7.00
0	0	0	72	8	574.80	42.00	2.00
0	0	0	0	0	0	0	0
94	18	0	70	15	967.30	114.37	10.00
330	207	49	421	92	8415.60	213.24	2.18
4459	3289	461	1769	536	28863.09	8237.74	1045.20
0	0	0	0	0	0	0	0
190	180	0	167	58	8757.63	715.75	112.11
0	0	0	0	0	0	0	0
0	0	0	0	0	0	0	0
0	0	0	0	0	0	0	0
38	5	1	31	25	2997.80	556.20	31.30
379	330	6	239	212	4933.18	1281.94	0
0	0	0	53	6	1750.00	130.00	130.00
276	240	0	34	4	1274.39	369.40	0
0	0	0	0	0	0	0	0
0	0	0	0	0	0	0	0
0	0	0	0	0	0	0	0
7	0	0	50	2	5.00	2.00	0
0	0	0	0	0	3.20	2.00	0
0	0	0	0	0	277.87	42.63	17.37

地 区 Region	占地面积(平方米) Areas Occupied(m^2)			图书(册) Books(Volume)	
	合计 Total	其中:绿化用地面积 of Which: Green Areas	其中:运动场地面积 of Which: Sports Areas	合计 Total	当年新增 New Added in Current Year
总 计 Total	**192261195.57**	**42160354.55**	**33043507.20**	**123580072**	**6786469**
北 京 Beijing	2604653.12	524820.37	604914.87	3399274	37216
天 津 Tianjin	683386.43	108635.00	120104.00	1030045	74068
河 北 Hebei	14350025.63	2355045.12	2770975.64	9740365	517034
山 西 Shanxi	8638648.63	1618951.32	1335199.02	4419231	403420
内蒙古 Inner Mongolia	6237687.70	945453.00	1308966.00	2851064	76251
辽 宁 Liaoning	5791376.22	695278.00	1267342.26	3158637	51630
吉 林 Jilin	3207476.69	597767.18	696009.61	2074975	83079
黑龙江 Heilongjiang	4927180.00	685012.06	870943.56	1461323	82476
上 海 Shanghai	1230381.00	381742.90	262334.00	1885727	33433
江 苏 Jiangsu	6474492.08	2052658.60	965199.86	4772715	103213
浙 江 Zhejiang	15186395.07	4654469.34	3049957.76	12852183	710136
安 徽 Anhui	12335278.38	2486304.09	1599053.27	9341389	309088
福 建 Fujian	0	0	0	0	0
江 西 Jiangxi	7438983.00	1553730.00	1230541.00	4103183	233139
山 东 Shandong	9453837.95	2677701.02	1894045.93	7214519	247370
河 南 Henan	15470769.24	2820405.47	2031405.27	9132280	317777
湖 北 Hubei	2409872.85	552909.62	449113.84	1688121	34128
湖 南 Hunan	14151512.09	3548441.57	2043585.75	8995502	754004
广 东 Guangdong	6294235.95	1887745.15	1472822.00	5801794	142911
广 西 Guangxi	0	0	0	0	0
海 南 Hainan	1263188.00	264863.00	183444.00	447540	25243
重 庆 Chongqing	7864075.51	1924959.19	1179135.73	4802536	252026
四 川 Sichuan	10915032.71	2607232.72	2497417.29	7530356	630729
贵 州 Guizhou	8480386.93	2053073.33	1533515.18	4881166	871603
云 南 Yunnan	7972304.35	1784424.53	1143709.41	3196625	128345
西 藏 Tibet	0	0	0	0	0
陕 西 Shaanxi	9855200.93	1486883.33	1390488.52	6607788	507895
甘 肃 Gansu	1961174.36	350928.69	419432.00	936925	26688
青 海 Qinghai	23643.00	2114.00	1700.00	2500	0
宁 夏 Ningxia	2214840.23	638507.32	192370.43	580877	64718
新 疆 Xinjiang	4825157.52	900298.63	529781.00	671432	68849

产情况(学校产权)

Vocational High Schools(Owned by VHSs)

计算机数(台) PC(Set)			教室(间) Classroom(Room)		固定资产值(万元) Fixed Assets(10,000 yuan)		
合计 Total	其中:教学用计算机 No. of Computers Used for Instruction		合计 Total	其中:网络多媒体教室 of Which: Network Multimedia Classroom	合计 Total	其中:教学、实习仪器设备资产值 of Which:Teaching Equipment & Instruments	
	小计 Subtotal	其中:平板电脑 of Which: Tablet PC				小计 Subtotal	当年新增 New Added in Current Year
1336003	**1102544**	**47729**	**171819**	**81019**	**13472508. 94**	**3144519. 52**	**404342. 02**
35758	30507	1784	3474	2128	492760. 01	214956. 28	19813. 04
8469	6047	42	640	307	38905. 96	22168. 77	1704. 31
91992	76724	4125	13849	6121	799019. 17	183358. 94	29449. 34
49265	39248	1538	7983	2838	535926. 82	99082. 01	18044. 39
26755	21287	189	4516	2176	463860. 25	93614. 29	14575. 69
44462	35836	1028	5331	2306	409990. 24	87054. 17	7496. 79
23533	18086	1058	3612	1180	229873. 17	63980. 39	10504. 63
25288	19865	626	3865	1241	207315. 93	59380. 91	10561. 73
31051	24264	688	1863	1332	314723. 53	99046. 03	10723. 51
42159	36572	589	6052	2906	640980. 26	110672. 81	13164. 32
149515	127097	3731	12943	10210	1431370. 57	381168. 30	53416. 44
48453	40832	706	10086	3296	616280. 87	112873. 71	6473. 08
0	0	0	0	0	0	0	0
41827	34783	1951	5885	2204	308335. 48	66177. 26	10283. 91
77452	62530	1843	8620	4794	616461. 12	191789. 66	21716. 23
86914	71774	6451	14143	5400	648427. 16	140007. 90	19127. 44
21820	17168	552	2680	1230	162215. 79	36016. 85	6170. 43
107277	85963	7950	12502	6375	1050633. 30	203696. 44	32028. 54
97653	83235	2829	5607	3974	670558. 36	208378. 31	23622. 35
0	0	0	0	0	0	0	0
8409	6691	2	765	332	91943. 97	18497. 26	2849. 00
55297	46858	2690	6189	4250	654458. 54	141336. 05	15288. 51
87740	74247	1820	14147	5551	983763. 68	203332. 82	24840. 99
46562	38394	1781	6087	3475	670804. 64	117361. 71	18462. 80
45090	37433	684	6506	2432	426688. 31	87905. 53	9358. 28
0	0	0	0	0	0	0	0
52730	42006	1860	8067	2863	551538. 09	113293. 02	13769. 25
12115	9975	914	2612	910	116533. 49	24451. 61	2059. 04
46	40	40	21	1	1032. 20	67. 60	8. 70
7574	6482	0	1294	661	102072. 32	25979. 03	2880. 71
10797	8600	258	2480	526	236035. 71	38871. 84	5948. 55

地　区 Region	占地面积(平方米) Areas Occupied(m^2)			图书(册) Books(Volume)	
	合计 Total	其中:绿化用地面积 of Which: Green Areas	其中:运动场地面积 of Which: Sports Areas	合计 Total	当年新增 New Added in Current Year
总　计 Total	**15624360.41**	**2974789.17**	**2598802.12**	**1623546**	**106143**
北　京 Beijing	397313.00	31023.45	43995.66	4000	1000
天　津 Tianjin	68632.00	1800.00	18466.00	25802	500
河　北 Hebei	459303.11	42870.06	130057.74	8500	2100
山　西 Shanxi	595344.14	76511.73	132081.86	88820	0
内蒙古 Inner Mongolia	195756.81	12247.23	54917.27	8553	300
辽　宁 Liaoning	710262.86	109536.00	168334.00	43327	750
吉　林 Jilin	430211.00	68140.00	116130.00	101300	1000
黑龙江 Heilongjiang	166572.00	11400.00	17100.00	13000	0
上　海 Shanghai	19948.00	6300.00	4428.00	0	0
江　苏 Jiangsu	130000.00	100000.00	10000.00	0	0
浙　江 Zhejiang	633005.30	66497.65	124446.00	10000	0
安　徽 Anhui	730385.58	44852.89	58676.39	102392	100
福　建 Fujian	0	0	0	0	0
江　西 Jiangxi	1856590.00	469437.00	287971.00	92802	11279
山　东 Shandong	1172668.00	189228.00	122018.00	62760	0
河　南 Henan	1132851.50	139908.67	171359.38	149436	680
湖　北 Hubei	201800.81	39100.00	23800.00	8000	5000
湖　南 Hunan	1387683.80	284551.33	208190.08	66702	4400
广　东 Guangdong	1211384.82	333833.92	232446.67	62419	314
广　西 Guangxi	0	0	0	0	0
海　南 Hainan	195866.00	29072.00	18042.00	0	0
重　庆 Chongqing	640202.69	153435.00	29764.00	10000	0
四　川 Sichuan	402824.06	83617.00	143787.00	87508	500
贵　州 Guizhou	909934.45	189137.00	137138.20	60800	500
云　南 Yunnan	696666.34	164908.00	101301.00	15000	0
西　藏 Tibet	0	0	0	0	0
陕　西 Shaanxi	1060530.14	284344.24	210712.87	590200	77670
甘　肃 Gansu	156624.00	16372.00	33239.00	9982	50
青　海 Qinghai	0	0	0	0	0
宁　夏 Ningxia	0	0	0	0	0
新　疆 Xinjiang	62000.00	26666.00	400.00	2243	0

(非学校产权中独立使用)
Vocational High Schools(Not Owned by VHSs)

计算机数(台) PC(Set)			教室(间) Classroom(Room)		固定资产值(万元) Fixed Assets(10,000 yuan)		
合计 Total	其中:教学用计算机 No. of Computers Used for Instruction		合计 Total	其中:网络多媒体教室 of Which: Network Multimedia Classroom	合计 Total	其中:教学、实习仪器设备资产值 of Which: Teaching Equipment & Instruments	
	小计 Subtotal	其中:平板电脑 of Which: Tablet PC				小计 Subtotal	当年新增 New Added in Current Year
22752	**17929**	**886**	**15963**	**5712**	**635042.57**	**60634.97**	**11404.12**
50	40	0	222	155	1236.00	130.00	0
175	172	3	291	74	3854.50	424.90	4.50
204	143	0	356	92	16544.73	3354.11	2636.60
1161	1029	32	735	203	23275.55	2478.26	279.60
286	233	0	127	42	3244.32	187.90	0
806	656	18	1155	204	73341.13	4194.41	304.02
2241	1574	2	715	180	11735.16	1539.50	763.00
313	240	8	142	33	5918.40	563.40	150.00
10	7	7	30	6	806.98	721.85	599.03
0	0	0	216	100	8749.00	442.00	80.00
105	90	2	733	493	38559.12	2842.34	391.37
463	283	0	532	151	11369.71	1990.33	93.00
0	0	0	0	0	0	0	0
2290	1909	202	1131	399	76399.07	4149.46	679.63
473	367	20	1155	387	62795.27	4374.91	23.00
2237	1702	156	901	253	30331.42	2501.17	137.72
80	50	0	249	80	5402.58	378.58	205.08
1522	1227	105	1738	870	54664.16	8128.75	2297.53
2803	2463	0	1236	843	35982.00	1428.00	84.00
0	0	0	0	0	0	0	0
276	250	0	291	45	10639.23	231.20	55.00
1032	1023	160	289	209	27745.32	1706.31	57.24
1456	1358	20	643	147	23659.32	4076.97	1129.12
790	738	131	970	359	50749.04	5032.86	555.68
350	290	0	680	85	18726.68	2147.20	200.50
0	0	0	0	0	0	0	0
3286	1951	20	1214	268	30496.33	6266.42	656.51
251	45	0	167	33	4569.38	805.97	20.00
0	0	0	0	0	0	0	0
0	0	0	0	0	0	0	0
92	89	0	45	1	4248.17	538.17	2.00

地 区 Region	占地面积(平方米) Areas Occupied(m^2)			图书(册) Books(Volume)	
	合计 Total	其中:绿化用地面积 of Which: Green Areas	其中:运动场地面积 of Which: Sports Areas	合计 Total	当年新增 New Added in Current Year
总 计 Total	**6692103.18**	**1286362.53**	**956015.08**	**4112178**	**92001**
北 京 Beijing	0	0	0	0	0
天 津 Tianjin	0	0	0	0	0
河 北 Hebei	521464.60	38670.50	132833.50	444531	3000
山 西 Shanxi	189990.00	3172.80	36240.00	16000	2500
内蒙古 Inner Mongolia	0	0	0	0	0
辽 宁 Liaoning	0	0	0	0	0
吉 林 Jilin	30000.26	1000.00	6000.64	32050	0
黑龙江 Heilongjiang	41300.34	10900.12	3300.13	2500	0
上 海 Shanghai	0	0	0	0	0
江 苏 Jiangsu	2436983.43	507702.60	275872.86	1094266	27848
浙 江 Zhejiang	186607.75	35561.33	47681.00	120014	28391
安 徽 Anhui	1484971.05	262004.00	157265.00	633175	4050
福 建 Fujian	0	0	0	0	0
江 西 Jiangxi	0	0	0	0	0
山 东 Shandong	161434.05	31993.00	31917.36	118764	870
河 南 Henan	422002.06	76012.00	48279.61	264382	6226
湖 北 Hubei	55505.00	10530.00	15050.00	50620	1300
湖 南 Hunan	155441.00	26630.00	24414.00	124162	1260
广 东 Guangdong	350874.46	104430.18	68321.34	775517	2420
广 西 Guangxi	0	0	0	0	0
海 南 Hainan	0	0	0	0	0
重 庆 Chongqing	99557.00	5745.00	9702.64	25700	600
四 川 Sichuan	226769.50	75556.00	17116.00	117954	6827
贵 州 Guizhou	58399.68	5200.00	17065.00	26610	2700
云 南 Yunnan	21856.00	6000.00	10789.00	147012	3750
西 藏 Tibet	0	0	0	0	0
陕 西 Shaanxi	0	0	0	0	0
甘 肃 Gansu	0	0	0	0	0
青 海 Qinghai	0	0	0	0	0
宁 夏 Ningxia	248947.00	85255.00	54167.00	118921	259
新 疆 Xinjiang	0	0	0	0	0

资产情况(学校产权)
Secondary Vocational Education Institutions(Owned by SVSs)

计算机数(台) PC(Set)			教室(间) Classroom(Room)		固定资产值(万元) Fixed Assets(10,000 yuan)		
合计 Total	其中:教学用计算机 No. of Computers Used for Instruction		合计 Total	其中:网络多媒体教室 of Which: Network Multimedia Classroom	合计 Total	其中:教学、实习仪器设备资产值 of Which: Teaching Equipment & Instruments	
	小计 Subtotal	其中:平板电脑 of Which: Tablet PC				小计 Subtotal	当年新增 New Added in Current Year
38006	**29865**	**689**	**5911**	**2669**	**369876.03**	**66542.93**	**8104.51**
0	0	0	0	0	0	0	0
0	0	0	0	0	0	0	0
1896	1599	85	543	193	30034.33	2151.96	46.55
193	128	12	159	3	2463.30	405.40	29.60
0	0	0	0	0	0	0	0
0	0	0	0	0	0	0	0
180	140	0	32	1	1117.36	142.42	0
141	109	6	30	18	1417.22	278.20	6.20
0	0	0	0	0	0	0	0
8723	6526	74	1798	886	87635.08	16224.64	583.84
2997	2372	0	312	270	23613.11	5558.69	1846.12
5777	4691	109	1045	364	54498.31	13262.73	1939.65
0	0	0	0	0	0	0	0
0	0	0	0	0	0	0	0
1027	592	2	212	79	12250.77	1146.64	59.60
4410	3372	234	542	317	47982.19	6764.80	964.79
427	345	48	75	8	7475.90	1264.00	0.00
1158	759	30	144	87	25505.00	3412.78	311.00
6026	5144	71	496	223	38400.97	5841.40	898.83
0	0	0	0	0	0	0	0
0	0	0	0	0	0	0	0
384	345	0	87	68	4400.64	918.74	75.00
1786	1491	10	274	79	12635.65	3135.66	387.66
82	67	8	30	12	7352.00	587.00	95.00
1880	1454	0	40	3	4074.19	1592.67	388.47
0	0	0	0	0	0	0	0
0	0	0	0	0	0	0	0
0	0	0	0	0	0	0	0
0	0	0	0	0	0	0	0
919	731	0	92	58	9020.00	3855.20	472.20
0	0	0	0	0	0	0	0

地 区 Region	占地面积(平方米) Areas Occupied(m^2)			图书(册) Books(Volume)	
	合计 Total	其中:绿化用地面积 of Which: Green Areas	其中:运动场地面积 of Which: Sports Areas	合计 Total	当年新增 New Added in Current Year
总 计 Total	**885002.70**	**160167.00**	**134001.00**	**208302**	**1000**
北 京 Beijing	0	0	0	0	0
天 津 Tianjin	0	0	0	0	0
河 北 Hebei	4526.00	0	0	0	0
山 西 Shanxi	12345.00	1000.00	1000.00	0	0
内蒙古 Inner Mongolia	0	0	0	0	0
辽 宁 Liaoning	0	0	0	0	0
吉 林 Jilin	0	0	0	0	0
黑龙江 Heilongjiang	13096.00	206.00	7651.00	51000	500
上 海 Shanghai	0	0	0	0	0
江 苏 Jiangsu	200.00	0	200.00	0	0
浙 江 Zhejiang	162111.10	23597.00	33776.00	28434	200
安 徽 Anhui	1100.00	500.00	0	0	0
福 建 Fujian	0	0	0	0	0
江 西 Jiangxi	0	0	0	0	0
山 东 Shandong	229421.00	28708.00	54822.00	118268	100
河 南 Henan	4173.00	185.00	2000.00	0	0
湖 北 Hubei	11136.00	5011.00	2185.00	0	0
湖 南 Hunan	7692.00	0	1314.00	0	0
广 东 Guangdong	187455.00	66700.00	5380.00	0	0
广 西 Guangxi	0	0	0	0	0
海 南 Hainan	0	0	0	0	0
重 庆 Chongqing	9723.60	1100.00	1500.00	0	0
四 川 Sichuan	0	0	0	0	0
贵 州 Guizhou	0	0	0	0	0
云 南 Yunnan	242024.00	33160.00	24173.00	10600	200
西 藏 Tibet	0	0	0	0	0
陕 西 Shaanxi	0	0	0	0	0
甘 肃 Gansu	0	0	0	0	0
青 海 Qinghai	0	0	0	0	0
宁 夏 Ningxia	0	0	0	0	0
新 疆 Xinjiang	0	0	0	0	0

况(非学校产权中独立使用)
Vocational Education Institutions(Not Owned by SVSs)

计算机数(台) PC(Set)			教室(间) Classroom(Room)		固定资产值(万元) Fixed Assets(10,000 yuan)		
合计 Total	其中:教学用计算机 No. of Computers Used for Instruction		合计 Total	其中:网络多媒体教室 of Which: Network Multimedia Classroom	合计 Total	其中:教学、实习仪器设备资产值 of Which:Teaching Equipment & Instruments	
	小计 Subtotal	其中:平板电脑 of Which: Tablet PC				小计 Subtotal	当年新增 New Added in Current Year
2416	**2100**	**16**	**773**	**365**	**34383.55**	**5559.45**	**130.77**
0	0	0	0	0	0	0	0
0	0	0	0	0	0	0	0
0	0	0	28	28	485.20	0	0
0	0	0	17	0	362.74	79.03	49.36
0	0	0	0	0	0	0	0
0	0	0	0	0	0	0	0
0	0	0	0	0	0	0	0
1099	924	0	27	27	6328.20	1194.50	0
0	0	0	0	0	0	0	0
0	0	0	0	0	0	0	0
212	203	0	112	39	9839.00	548.00	0
0	0	0	26	12	3220.00	49.00	0
0	0	0	0	0	0	0	0
0	0	0	0	0	0	0	0
737	605	16	218	42	10293.51	3268.22	56.91
30	30	0	13	9	239.04	77.00	12.00
0	0	0	17	10	1070.00	57.00	11.00
80	80	0	10	10	639.00	20.00	0
158	158	0	10	3	0	0	0
0	0	0	0	0	0	0	0
0	0	0	0	0	0	0	0
0	0	0	15	10	100.00	0	0
0	0	0	0	0	0	0	0
0	0	0	0	0	0	0	0
100	100	0	280	175	1806.86	266.70	1.50
0	0	0	0	0	0	0	0
0	0	0	0	0	0	0	0
0	0	0	0	0	0	0	0
0	0	0	0	0	0	0	0
0	0	0	0	0	0	0	0
0	0	0	0	0	0	0	0

中等职业学校(机构)校舍情况

Conditions of School Buildings in Secondary Vocational Schools(Institutions)

单位:平方米
unit:m^2

地　区 Region	学校产权校舍建筑面积 Floor Area of School Building Owned by SVSs				正在施工校舍建筑面积 Floor Area Under Construction	非学校产权中独立使用校舍建筑面积 Floor Area of School Building Not Owned by SVSs
	合计 Total	其中:危房 of Which: Dilapidated Buildings	其中:当年新增 of Which: New Added in Current Year	其中:被外单位借用 of Which: Floor Space Hired by Other Schools or Units		
总　计 Total	**212069097.26**	**855697.30**	**6537898.62**	**1012783.28**	**8047020.31**	**21903232.25**
北　京 Beijing	2486314.39	9403.20	33205.30	56256.81	37215.63	196869.20
天　津 Tianjin	1731191.95	0	21021.00	260.80	4694.00	177835.65
河　北 Hebei	10567612.35	27429.18	181760.10	83610.46	229164.43	1391321.43
山　西 Shanxi	7271496.63	67762.80	159344.53	5621.00	188125.06	571878.41
内蒙古 Inner Mongolia	3594374.85	25488.00	88481.72	1203.00	143505.07	295182.01
辽　宁 Liaoning	5192948.35	4430.00	49515.55	6949.00	80864.52	1074829.19
吉　林 Jilin	2530802.28	3513.00	65684.98	4392.80	40891.00	408525.65
黑龙江 Heilongjiang	2952586.02	1350.00	72697.24	3000.00	58551.46	373041.78
上　海 Shanghai	2862165.74	0	17821.00	1400.00	29878.00	224534.19
江　苏 Jiangsu	16246247.58	0	190739.96	17093.00	227657.91	365782.32
浙　江 Zhejiang	10844414.50	0	698613.94	22105.00	299100.34	726489.22
安　徽 Anhui	15503768.11	10925.00	408663.79	13674.80	632601.83	769691.83
福　建 Fujian	5259020.41	33508.00	138006.89	9673.00	346414.56	493704.93
江　西 Jiangxi	5327284.04	10450.32	275839.02	37542.11	113135.09	931900.68
山　东 Shandong	15989598.91	0	891173.38	27037.55	679596.34	1190891.36
河　南 Henan	14994596.79	21364.20	204897.36	39913.80	654385.09	1368901.32
湖　北 Hubei	8078618.03	10225.00	119592.61	86924.00	108883.59	345691.49
湖　南 Hunan	8682743.35	9996.61	181627.70	1370.00	301262.22	1058850.96
广　东 Guangdong	13929598.10	35675.96	183284.28	92837.26	250501.78	2772669.64
广　西 Guangxi	8074436.63	6694.00	332112.94	59814.11	583862.76	1296904.84
海　南 Hainan	1710153.02	19842.90	25152.43	45324.00	56621.47	197194.20
重　庆 Chongqing	6651726.02	0	160167.29	29792.00	217117.00	322433.86
四　川 Sichuan	11430597.16	17700.50	461420.05	63912.00	400030.29	2476236.48
贵　州 Guizhou	7508004.34	8035.95	336921.33	19189.16	1020153.57	757285.50
云　南 Yunnan	6169565.54	268999.90	455755.08	209809.00	525067.92	829626.18
西　藏 Tibet	540863.75	2485.94	53076.30	3594.00	2480.00	0
陕　西 Shaanxi	5200724.61	24337.00	131119.10	6469.00	120128.08	688238.86
甘　肃 Gansu	3575014.61	189666.83	57168.76	6409.00	405165.93	485996.05
青　海 Qinghai	1102896.02	0	106487.32	12433.62	54530.53	21366.00
宁　夏 Ningxia	1504879.03	25885.00	118354.80	13618.00	61748.60	34671.00
新　疆 Xinjiang	4554854.15	20528.01	318192.87	31555.00	173686.24	54688.02

普通中专学校校舍情况
Conditions of School Buildings in Regular Specialized Secondary Schools

单位：平方米
unit：m^2

地 区 Region	学校产权校舍建筑面积 Floor Area of School Building Owned by SVSs				正在施工校舍建筑面积 Floor Area Under Construction	非学校产权中独立使用校舍建筑面积 Floor Area of School Building Not Owned by SVSs
	合计 Total	其中：危房 of Which: Dilapidated Buildings	其中：当年新增 of Which: New Added in Current Year	其中：被外单位借用 of Which: Floor Space Hired by Other Schools or Units		
总 计 Total	**115479473.92**	**457699.93**	**3452789.93**	**575761.62**	**5541585.39**	**12228795.92**
北 京 Beijing	900659.31	9403.20	972.30	283.00	37215.63	32612.00
天 津 Tianjin	1360143.10	0	21021.00	140.80	4694.00	84454.65
河 北 Hebei	4061096.02	11002.74	70353.32	13142.12	83052.54	1114688.76
山 西 Shanxi	3380947.67	34747.00	13082.69	3179.00	69841.87	114035.00
内蒙古 Inner Mongolia	1270303.85	0	0	0	41030.00	233647.70
辽 宁 Liaoning	2678758.12	1442.00	43913.55	6949.00	33054.78	630835.00
吉 林 Jilin	872811.52	0	2933.00	0	0	81817.15
黑龙江 Heilongjiang	1334926.44	0	28211.28	0	26514.23	304211.78
上 海 Shanghai	1927201.14	0	9780.00	0	29878.00	213498.19
江 苏 Jiangsu	11729641.23	0	72355.96	8393.00	183195.97	293125.32
浙 江 Zhejiang	2078993.75	0	92374.00	9822.00	41500.00	140350.53
安 徽 Anhui	8740236.41	10925.00	259440.59	4510.00	534891.73	497104.29
福 建 Fujian	5259020.41	33508.00	138006.89	9673.00	346414.56	493704.93
江 西 Jiangxi	2417978.28	3606.90	146549.16	0	38582.68	224917.65
山 东 Shandong	11251746.86	0	738786.71	11887.37	429281.60	510982.22
河 南 Henan	6297070.42	15104.20	74125.50	3260.00	477331.32	351335.44
湖 北 Hubei	6548840.62	10225.00	85042.61	85215.00	106383.59	244311.00
湖 南 Hunan	1373034.32	4797.00	11200.00	0	126897.72	75876.00
广 东 Guangdong	10307305.86	20922.96	179257.28	43866.60	179423.18	2086150.06
广 西 Guangxi	8074436.63	6694.00	332112.94	59814.11	583862.76	1296904.84
海 南 Hainan	1240294.42	7293.90	25152.43	32705.00	46521.47	26701.20
重 庆 Chongqing	1407188.52	0	94015.35	0	7107.00	125173.20
四 川 Sichuan	5110381.54	3351.50	229234.85	56180.00	250122.20	2060980.21
贵 州 Guizhou	3142112.82	8035.95	128311.28	0	758982.84	57392.00
云 南 Yunnan	3027123.18	89774.80	240632.47	175214.00	426373.00	415350.04
西 藏 Tibet	540863.75	2485.94	53076.30	3594.00	2480.00	0
陕 西 Shaanxi	1414129.11	11313.00	0	0	33169.65	12270.31
甘 肃 Gansu	2685408.87	132090.83	33878.04	0	381183.36	432563.05
青 海 Qinghai	1068678.02	0	106487.32	12433.62	54530.53	0
宁 夏 Ningxia	822168.10	25885.00	73708.00	10038.00	58673.60	34641.00
新 疆 Xinjiang	3155973.63	15091.01	148775.11	25462.00	149395.58	39162.40

成人中专学校校舍情况

Conditions of School Buildings in Adult Specialized Secondary Schools

单位:平方米
unit: m^2

地　区 Region	学校产权校舍建筑面积 Floor Area of School Building Owned by SVSs				正在施工校舍建筑面积 Floor Area Under Construction	非学校产权中独立使用校舍建筑面积 Floor Area of School Building Not Owned by SVSs
	合计 Total	其中:危房 of Which: Dilapidated Buildings	其中:当年新增 of Which: New Added in Current Year	其中:被外单位借用 of Which: Floor Space Hired by Other Schools or Units		
总　计 Total	**8719934.84**	**74417.82**	**171093.49**	**91941.71**	**129127.84**	**1619348.51**
北　京 Beijing	110341.00	0	0	45018.00	0	44789.01
天　津 Tianjin	23270.05	0	0	120.00	0	15654.00
河　北 Hebei	568657.93	953.12	1710.02	12145.91	0	135610.00
山　西 Shanxi	162079.14	10307.00	2287.00	260.00	600.00	40119.00
内蒙古 Inner Mongolia	153984.70	0	5059.90	0	13736.00	11458.00
辽　宁 Liaoning	22927.00	0	0	0	0	31820.00
吉　林 Jilin	290220.11	3513.00	1516.00	0	0	29245.00
黑龙江 Heilongjiang	233792.00	1350.00	2345.00	0	0	12650.00
上　海 Shanghai	39363.44	0	989.00	0	0	1940.00
江　苏 Jiangsu	436705.23	0	0	0	0	18060.00
浙　江 Zhejiang	229994.50	0	57589.50	0	0	80195.94
安　徽 Anhui	389820.00	0	4803.00	0	0	73338.00
福　建 Fujian	0	0	0	0	0	0
江　西 Jiangxi	256235.04	4137.30	6600.68	1494.00	3705.58	19144.00
山　东 Shandong	454325.40	0	7271.60	8580.00	0	131096.00
河　南 Henan	2151274.60	260.00	27320.95	5778.80	104272.26	583068.19
湖　北 Hubei	95363.26	0	0	1709.00	2500.00	0
湖　南 Hunan	929044.39	0	5184.00	0	190.00	58490.91
广　东 Guangdong	80415.00	0	2227.00	5071.00	0	0
广　西 Guangxi	0	0	0	0	0	0
海　南 Hainan	11349.00	11349.00	0	0	0	0
重　庆 Chongqing	601185.07	0	0	0	0	48180.00
四　川 Sichuan	570539.32	0	20321.82	0	0	129716.50
贵　州 Guizhou	329014.00	0	11755.00	0	0	117848.00
云　南 Yunnan	332987.28	39664.40	14113.02	10265.00	4124.00	14984.70
西　藏 Tibet	0	0	0	0	0	0
陕　西 Shaanxi	35952.01	0	0	0	0	0
甘　肃 Gansu	59932.63	2884.00	0	0	0	0
青　海 Qinghai	24600.00	0	0	0	0	21366.00
宁　夏 Ningxia	7325.00	0	0	0	0	30.00
新　疆 Xinjiang	119237.74	0	0	1500.00	0	545.26

职业高中学校校舍情况
Conditions of School Buildings in Vocational High Schools

单位：平方米
unit：m^2

地 区 Region	学校产权校舍建筑面积 Floor Area of School Building Owned by SVSs 合计 Total	其中：危房 of Which：Dilapidated Buildings	其中：当年新增 of Which：New Added in Current Year	其中：被外单位借用 of Which：Floor Space Hired by Other Schools or Units	正在施工校舍建筑面积 Floor Area Under Construction	非学校产权中独立使用校舍建筑面积 Floor Area of School Building Not Owned by SVSs
总　计 Total	**84994233.66**	**319072.55**	**2833878.20**	**329086.97**	**2291632.08**	**7628987.93**
北　京 Beijing	1475314.08	0	32233.00	10955.81	0	119468.19
天　津 Tianjin	347778.80	0	0	0	0	77727.00
河　北 Hebei	5774340.08	15473.32	108476.76	58322.43	146111.89	136496.67
山　西 Shanxi	3675535.82	22708.80	143974.84	2182.00	117683.19	405379.41
内蒙古 Inner Mongolia	2170086.30	25488.00	83421.82	1203.00	88739.07	50076.31
辽　宁 Liaoning	2491263.23	2988.00	5602.00	0	47809.74	412174.19
吉　林 Jilin	1344770.14	0	61235.98	4392.80	40891.00	297463.50
黑龙江 Heilongjiang	1373559.34	0	42140.96	3000.00	32037.23	47285.00
上　海 Shanghai	895601.16	0	7052.00	1400.00	0	9096.00
江　苏 Jiangsu	3252609.72	0	95064.00	2800.00	8461.94	52507.00
浙　江 Zhejiang	8357171.15	0	548650.44	12283.00	256140.34	428776.86
安　徽 Anhui	5844779.63	0	117720.20	4500.00	97710.10	179987.54
福　建 Fujian	0	0	0	0	0	0
江　西 Jiangxi	2653070.72	2706.12	122689.18	36048.11	70846.83	687839.03
山　东 Shandong	4218291.94	0	145115.07	3494.00	245132.74	454089.14
河　南 Henan	6313059.38	6000.00	103450.91	29893.00	72781.51	432271.69
湖　北 Hubei	1377027.15	0	34550.00	0	0	94935.49
湖　南 Hunan	6294495.64	5199.61	165243.70	920.00	174174.50	918106.05
广　东 Guangdong	3223576.00	14753.00	1800.00	42979.66	71078.60	640618.58
广　西 Guangxi	0	0	0	0	0	0
海　南 Hainan	458509.60	1200.00	0	12619.00	10100.00	170493.00
重　庆 Chongqing	4568584.07	0	52151.94	29792.00	210010.00	145747.66
四　川 Sichuan	5619299.80	9842.00	197363.38	7732.00	110950.09	285539.77
贵　州 Guizhou	4010126.52	0	196458.05	19189.16	261170.73	582045.50
云　南 Yunnan	2797587.08	139560.70	201009.59	24330.00	94570.92	256482.44
西　藏 Tibet	0	0	0	0	0	0
陕　西 Shaanxi	3750643.49	13024.00	131119.10	6469.00	86958.43	675968.55
甘　肃 Gansu	829673.11	54692.00	23290.72	6409.00	23982.57	53433.00
青　海 Qinghai	9618.00	0	0	0	0	0
宁　夏 Ningxia	588218.93	0	44646.80	3580.00	0	0
新　疆 Xinjiang	1279642.78	5437.00	169417.76	4593.00	24290.66	14980.36

地 区 Region	学校产权校舍 Floor Area of School 合计 Total	其中:危房 of Which: Dilapidated Buildings
总 计 Total	**2875454.84**	**4507.00**
北 京 Beijing	0	0
天 津 Tianjin	0	0
河 北 Hebei	163518.32	0
山 西 Shanxi	52934.00	0
内蒙古 Inner Mongolia	0	0
辽 宁 Liaoning	0	0
吉 林 Jilin	23000.51	0
黑龙江 Heilongjiang	10308.24	0
上 海 Shanghai	0	0
江 苏 Jiangsu	827291.40	0
浙 江 Zhejiang	178255.10	0
安 徽 Anhui	528932.07	0
福 建 Fujian	0	0
江 西 Jiangxi	0	0
山 东 Shandong	65234.71	0
河 南 Henan	233192.39	0
湖 北 Hubei	57387.00	0
湖 南 Hunan	86169.00	0
广 东 Guangdong	318301.24	0
广 西 Guangxi	0	0
海 南 Hainan	0	0
重 庆 Chongqing	74768.36	0
四 川 Sichuan	130376.50	4507.00
贵 州 Guizhou	26751.00	0
云 南 Yunnan	11868.00	0
西 藏 Tibet	0	0
陕 西 Shaanxi	0	0
甘 肃 Gansu	0	0
青 海 Qinghai	0	0
宁 夏 Ningxia	87167.00	0
新 疆 Xinjiang	0	0

教育机构校舍情况
Secondary Vocational Education Institutions

单位:平方米
unit: m^2

建筑面积 Building Owned by SVSs 其中:当年新增 of Which: New Added in Current Year	其中:被外单位借用 of Which: Floor Space Hired by Other Schools or Units	正在施工校舍建筑面积 Floor Area Under Construction	非学校产权中独立使用校舍建筑面积 Floor Area of School Building Not Owned by SVSs
80137.00	**15992.98**	**84675.00**	**426099.89**
0	0	0	0
0	0	0	0
1220.00	0	0	4526.00
0	0	0	12345.00
0	0	0	0
0	0	0	0
0	0	0	0
0	0	0	8895.00
0	0	0	0
23320.00	5900.00	36000.00	2090.00
0	0	1460.00	77165.89
26700.00	4664.80	0	19262.00
0	0	0	0
0	0	0	0
0	3076.18	5182.00	94724.00
0	982.00	0	2226.00
0	0	0	6445.00
0	450.00	0	6378.00
0	920.00	0	45901.00
0	0	0	0
0	0	0	0
14000.00	0	0	3333.00
14500.00	0	38958.00	0
397.00	0	0	0
0	0	0	142809.00
0	0	0	0
0	0	0	0
0	0	0	0
0	0	0	0
0	0	3075.00	0
0	0	0	0

职业技术培训机构
Basic Statistics of Vocational Technical

地　区 Region	学校数(所) Schools	教学班(点)(个) External Teaching Sites(Class)	结业生数 Graduates	
			计 Total	其中:女 of Which:Female
总　计 Total	**89211**	**517924**	**42800768**	**21272081**
北　京 Beijing	3308	38898	2634921	1324043
天　津 Tianjin	2844	24790	1114642	507708
河　北 Hebei	4059	16703	1374488	687974
山　西 Shanxi	2883	14201	1873989	834106
内蒙古 Inner Mongolia	642	2092	119934	58541
辽　宁 Liaoning	7248	47049	1311167	642359
吉　林 Jilin	2158	6996	165705	76165
黑龙江 Heilongjiang	1392	5282	383043	191743
上　海 Shanghai	689	20193	1743765	988661
江　苏 Jiangsu	8996	77061	7429475	3595807
浙　江 Zhejiang	4040	56581	3436862	1777373
安　徽 Anhui	283	3933	214590	103934
福　建 Fujian	1839	14533	789584	418987
江　西 Jiangxi	74	332	22231	11281
山　东 Shandong	3764	17896	1509430	716580
河　南 Henan	7088	15098	2160723	1005922
湖　北 Hubei	558	2743	228842	115021
湖　南 Hunan	1003	4308	325338	149846
广　东 Guangdong	2225	38843	2642903	1353568
广　西 Guangxi	44	275	19270	7914
海　南 Hainan	245	2057	49835	33480
重　庆 Chongqing	3805	24505	1535140	804359
四　川 Sichuan	4486	14407	2490832	1298408
贵　州 Guizhou	5084	10062	1337112	684105
云　南 Yunnan	9228	27186	4863495	2412850
西　藏 Tibet	0	0	0	0
陕　西 Shaanxi	6672	17515	1274395	662653
甘　肃 Gansu	1960	4489	333219	161711
青　海 Qinghai	648	823	46014	28209
宁　夏 Ningxia	22	208	39481	19000
新　疆 Xinjiang	1924	8865	1330343	599773

基本情况(总计)
Training Institutions(Total)

单位:人/人次
unit:person/person-time

注册学生数 Enrolment		教职工数 Educational Personnel		聘请校外教师 Part-time Teachers
计 Total	其中:女 of Which:Female	计 Total	其中:专任教师 of Which:Full-time Teacher	
42064949	**20834989**	**514975**	**289647**	**243592**
2754909	1372022	104399	33762	17245
907652	394858	9567	4041	6484
1064044	463958	18125	12301	7484
1967036	877848	17737	12203	7581
122296	60054	4127	3161	1151
1669877	844367	50443	30952	10564
266991	124496	9678	6032	1595
315652	156428	11776	8153	1745
1818331	1047537	16097	8281	8587
6652021	3193799	48719	32361	46833
3265023	1685262	23723	17313	26943
229680	111855	2531	2152	4301
750442	393661	11568	5897	6814
17999	8826	458	353	73
1384212	667295	27275	19623	9934
2072566	958458	14758	8816	10255
240464	124458	5216	3742	1027
386069	178138	6039	4379	1025
2749411	1398896	30591	18739	11452
13636	5405	321	272	188
51020	33826	943	199	721
1424946	744254	11294	6018	5985
2448347	1275820	17800	11509	9370
1354921	684732	14646	5605	6295
4582672	2263290	10694	5354	16348
0	0	0	0	0
1447560	758875	33036	19541	16040
341195	169703	7551	5465	2878
39923	24845	480	291	435
42957	21645	251	195	30
1683097	790378	5132	2937	4209

地 区 Region	学校数(所) Schools	教学班(点)(个) External Teaching Sites(Class)	结业生数 Graduates	
			计 Total	其中:女 of Which:Female
总 计 Total	**2333**	**33665**	**2894687**	**1380479**
北 京 Beijing	26	455	31439	14135
天 津 Tianjin	9	244	7999	4281
河 北 Hebei	58	713	47830	24847
山 西 Shanxi	191	6726	835313	314626
内蒙古 Inner Mongolia	28	304	38466	20265
辽 宁 Liaoning	88	542	47956	27978
吉 林 Jilin	74	1796	30744	15262
黑龙江 Heilongjiang	44	284	13700	5351
上 海 Shanghai	20	621	130670	87996
江 苏 Jiangsu	598	7988	427971	207737
浙 江 Zhejiang	101	1889	160529	70940
安 徽 Anhui	36	455	68941	30582
福 建 Fujian	79	1530	186933	111289
江 西 Jiangxi	24	228	15175	7718
山 东 Shandong	22	576	44167	15355
河 南 Henan	149	1402	56343	28609
湖 北 Hubei	24	651	37890	23511
湖 南 Hunan	79	733	43183	19679
广 东 Guangdong	126	1117	57772	30234
广 西 Guangxi	6	144	1861	890
海 南 Hainan	28	185	9710	6760
重 庆 Chongqing	101	518	46743	25792
四 川 Sichuan	133	2098	294766	144092
贵 州 Guizhou	15	189	24766	11936
云 南 Yunnan	51	160	34563	19600
西 藏 Tibet	0	0	0	0
陕 西 Shaanxi	109	1425	161611	92093
甘 肃 Gansu	97	462	31270	17033
青 海 Qinghai	3	71	128	70
宁 夏 Ningxia	2	34	2760	538
新 疆 Xinjiang	12	125	3488	1280

学校基本情况
Technical Training Schools

单位:人/人次
unit:person/person-time

注册学生数 Enrolment		教职工数 Educational Personnel		聘请校外教师 Part-time Teachers
计 Total	其中:女 of Which:Female	计 Total	其中:专任教师 of Which:Full-time Teacher	
2903058	**1367227**	**60473**	**46226**	**16130**
22406	9542	500	294	202
11898	6169	429	383	63
47116	23609	4547	3772	240
838881	315450	3165	1966	1325
35825	18523	1258	1136	227
45485	24392	1216	981	296
39232	20312	1410	847	95
26477	9170	2402	1778	150
138192	95102	1286	984	341
405988	180885	11095	8668	5469
154402	70231	3464	2835	2006
71756	33668	907	804	516
159368	94844	1919	1708	882
10940	5263	321	253	19
42895	14205	2715	1990	122
50517	25609	2245	1758	545
50018	32538	1875	1437	172
63071	28401	2947	2366	90
65085	34047	1699	1040	691
3163	1364	190	167	12
10895	7106	247	183	39
38429	20430	1368	919	72
319986	159051	5748	4310	1075
21432	10222	845	712	229
34959	19965	526	412	211
0	0	0	0	0
152323	86470	2803	2037	654
32456	17111	2513	1851	198
319	160	38	7	60
2886	581	64	63	0
6658	2807	731	565	129

地　区 Region	学校数(所) Schools	教学班(点)(个) External Teaching Sites(Class)	结业生数 Graduates	
			计 Total	其中:女 of Which:Female
总　计 Total	**64307**	**207441**	**29703643**	**14712983**
北　京 Beijing	1908	9112	935612	544332
天　津 Tianjin	2474	6058	422725	206253
河　北 Hebei	3329	9646	1225202	613573
山　西 Shanxi	1820	4220	689537	341015
内蒙古 Inner Mongolia	446	932	54545	24888
辽　宁 Liaoning	1284	3907	544516	250151
吉　林 Jilin	785	851	74043	30346
黑龙江 Heilongjiang	816	2465	223479	113047
上　海 Shanghai	108	5289	480400	280635
江　苏 Jiangsu	6447	24968	5173772	2459474
浙　江 Zhejiang	2332	26452	2766333	1440284
安　徽 Anhui	179	3025	136137	68566
福　建 Fujian	1393	4207	420554	195775
江　西 Jiangxi	39	89	6584	3332
山　东 Shandong	2432	9796	1063038	495288
河　南 Henan	6625	12613	1898023	884931
湖　北 Hubei	422	1037	154921	74197
湖　南 Hunan	691	2140	227912	103023
广　东 Guangdong	591	11672	1896693	943829
广　西 Guangxi	24	31	4780	2066
海　南 Hainan	217	1872	40125	26720
重　庆 Chongqing	3292	9964	1210741	622280
四　川 Sichuan	4021	10175	2041531	1070680
贵　州 Guizhou	4456	7072	1166346	595860
云　南 Yunnan	8532	24269	4577188	2257859
西　藏 Tibet	0	0	0	0
陕　西 Shaanxi	5678	7806	808150	403608
甘　肃 Gansu	1651	2083	203118	91130
青　海 Qinghai	635	687	42349	26388
宁　夏 Ningxia	3	24	1180	311
新　疆 Xinjiang	1677	4979	1214109	543142

培训学校基本情况
Training Schools for Peasants

单位:人/人次
unit:person/person-time

注册学生数 Enrolment		教职工数 Educational Personnel		聘请校外教师 Part-time Teachers
计 Total	其中:女 of Which:Female	计 Total	其中:专任教师 of Which:Full-time Teacher	
28082089	**13801071**	**128491**	**67702**	**135077**
722072	409795	1263	556	2685
304714	151627	1024	586	2452
872525	367713	5596	3154	6296
766462	362625	2946	1409	2998
60375	27418	1602	1233	691
637545	300991	2830	1231	1568
111445	49300	2435	965	1035
223801	112005	4184	2386	1345
410280	238937	998	669	1550
4391070	2078693	15341	9687	24528
2606662	1355729	7958	5444	19873
142160	70691	738	680	3516
420897	196982	3951	540	4072
6589	3334	73	41	48
963376	450426	9057	6192	5615
1819719	838973	10361	5672	8832
150424	72603	1511	1072	541
253432	117630	1497	690	706
1865274	921707	5832	3502	3647
2970	890	48	48	102
40125	26720	696	16	682
1190916	617773	3095	1525	3446
1993205	1048365	8541	4732	6797
1177792	595290	9822	2539	4852
4333460	2125546	7094	3052	13604
0	0	0	0	0
838485	427427	15854	7919	7554
203462	92077	2325	1265	2368
36089	22952	395	245	337
1200	321	9	9	0
1535563	716531	1415	643	3337

地 区 Region	学校数(所) Schools	教学班(点)(个) External Teaching Sites(Class)	结业生数 Graduates	
			计 Total	其中:女 of Which:Female
总 计 Total	**22571**	**276818**	**10202438**	**5178619**
北 京 Beijing	1374	29331	1667870	765576
天 津 Tianjin	361	18488	683918	297174
河 北 Hebei	672	6344	101456	49554
山 西 Shanxi	872	3255	349139	178465
内蒙古 Inner Mongolia	168	856	26923	13388
辽 宁 Liaoning	5876	42600	718695	364230
吉 林 Jilin	1299	4349	60918	30557
黑龙江 Heilongjiang	532	2533	145864	73345
上 海 Shanghai	561	14283	1132695	620030
江 苏 Jiangsu	1951	44105	1827732	928596
浙 江 Zhejiang	1607	28240	510000	266149
安 徽 Anhui	68	453	9512	4786
福 建 Fujian	367	8796	182097	111923
江 西 Jiangxi	11	15	472	231
山 东 Shandong	1310	7524	402225	205937
河 南 Henan	314	1083	206357	92382
湖 北 Hubei	112	1055	36031	17313
湖 南 Hunan	233	1435	54243	27144
广 东 Guangdong	1508	26054	688438	379505
广 西 Guangxi	14	100	12629	4958
海 南 Hainan	0	0	0	0
重 庆 Chongqing	412	14023	277656	156287
四 川 Sichuan	332	2134	154535	83636
贵 州 Guizhou	613	2801	146000	76309
云 南 Yunnan	645	2757	251744	135391
西 藏 Tibet	0	0	0	0
陕 西 Shaanxi	885	8284	304634	166952
甘 肃 Gansu	212	1944	98831	53548
青 海 Qinghai	10	65	3537	1751
宁 夏 Ningxia	17	150	35541	18151
新 疆 Xinjiang	235	3761	112746	55351

构基本情况
of Others

单位：人/人次
unit：person/person-time

注册学生数 Enrolment		教职工数 Educational Personnel		聘请校外教师 Part-time Teachers
计 Total	其中：女 of Which：Female	计 Total	其中：专任教师 of Which：Full-time Teacher	
11079802	**5666691**	**326011**	**175719**	**92385**
2010431	952685	102636	32912	14358
591040	237062	8114	3072	3969
144403	72636	7982	5375	948
361693	199773	11626	8828	3258
26096	14113	1267	792	233
986847	518984	46397	28740	8700
116314	54884	5833	4220	465
65374	35253	5190	3989	250
1269859	713498	13813	6628	6696
1854963	934221	22283	14006	16836
503959	259302	12301	9034	5064
15764	7496	886	668	269
170177	101835	5698	3649	1860
470	229	64	59	6
377941	202664	15503	11441	4197
202330	93876	2152	1386	878
40022	19317	1830	1233	314
69566	32107	1595	1323	229
819052	443142	23060	14197	7114
7503	3151	83	57	74
0	0	0	0	0
195601	106051	6831	3574	2467
135156	68404	3511	2467	1498
155697	79220	3979	2354	1214
214253	117779	3074	1890	2533
0	0	0	0	0
456752	244978	14379	9585	7832
105277	60515	2713	2349	312
3515	1733	47	39	38
38871	20743	178	123	30
140876	71040	2986	1729	743

地　区 Region	占地面积(平方米) Area of School Sites(m^2)	教学行政用房建筑面积(平方米) Administrative (m^2)	图书(册) Books(Volume)
总　计 Total	**103581068.28**	**62376001.05**	**125186655**
北　京 Beijing	4559364.92	29254856.67	35610437
天　津 Tianjin	1388154.07	604643.77	1494925
河　北 Hebei	5665230.28	1875154.69	4104538
山　西 Shanxi	2763508.08	1394906.20	6515618
内蒙古 Inner Mongolia	965688.80	200489.35	860501
辽　宁 Liaoning	4871271.07	2115604.56	3842940
吉　林 Jilin	2038500.50	568244.25	1064662
黑龙江 Heilongjiang	3930298.00	944304.32	1768843
上　海 Shanghai	1825035.00	1317270.00	3172535
江　苏 Jiangsu	15139870.08	5819348.31	12302081
浙　江 Zhejiang	9140685.59	3281905.14	7965765
安　徽 Anhui	2260618.62	359565.28	887779
福　建 Fujian	808886.55	683233.39	1871934
江　西 Jiangxi	374289.00	70472.00	207862
山　东 Shandong	4995524.40	1631573.93	5071905
河　南 Henan	5111265.28	1728190.84	4537214
湖　北 Hubei	3815696.70	936908.80	1690191
湖　南 Hunan	4771476.30	541783.60	2196700
广　东 Guangdong	4783877.00	2085467.00	6031582
广　西 Guangxi	424322.00	88159.00	201833
海　南 Hainan	242279.00	106530.00	192915
重　庆 Chongqing	1174003.98	552050.22	1848226
四　川 Sichuan	2985209.61	1340179.81	4512761
贵　州 Guizhou	3746390.69	1127067.53	2927375
云　南 Yunnan	2864431.73	789323.73	2163583
西　藏 Tibet	0	0	0
陕　西 Shaanxi	5573212.02	1327232.79	4151240
甘　肃 Gansu	2729997.47	685135.99	1342269
青　海 Qinghai	774138.00	54012.70	367857
宁　夏 Ningxia	191256.00	22642.00	42811
新　疆 Xinjiang	3666587.54	869745.18	6237773

机构资产情况
in Vocational Technical Training Institutions

计算机数(台) PC(Set)			教室(间) Classroom(Room)		固定资产总值(万元) Fixed Assets(10,000 yuan)	
合计 Total	其中:教学用计算机 No. of Computers Used for Instruction: 小计 Subtotal	其中:平板电脑 of Which: Tablet PC	合计 Total	其中:网络多媒体教室 of Which: Network Multimedia Classroom	合计 Total	其中:教学、实习仪器设备资产值 of Which: Teaching Equipment & Instruments
741915	**617531**	**77556**	**299090**	**81527**	**30181304.63**	**8120921.28**
74055	54974	17921	32349	6386	265909.68	107052.93
15989	13748	1627	5101	982	42274.19	10558.90
29527	25772	2279	9167	2451	170260.46	46853.10
35625	30315	1130	7685	3434	142699.18	59243.96
4004	3438	98	15208	160	45356.90	12277.00
43351	34925	8648	28216	7084	345419.43	76229.66
8479	7073	690	9043	1465	89058.97	17430.77
11504	8805	451	5232	930	83137.86	31758.91
40522	28793	4316	7571	2945	191711.00	69075.00
99195	86422	15968	39971	12016	1811315.72	722558.18
71445	65195	4584	16857	7283	395313.20	102098.94
5734	5109	235	2036	648	48513.52	11034.33
16396	13382	1147	3823	932	4804987.66	15124.57
1604	1449	180	199	41	12880.00	1861.00
35421	32198	3119	13082	4455	275694.42	74725.31
16585	14655	1725	22038	6515	123999.71	26028.15
17263	15604	461	3173	993	88009.51	24537.06
15462	11688	586	3432	879	124002.06	24870.34
71214	58483	5488	20640	8055	19210588.00	5565602.00
2408	1648	24	238	75	85016.25	44827.67
906	830	72	410	164	11335.10	1299.73
14733	10697	1645	6855	2158	43938.81	12582.56
31442	27044	738	9202	1367	166690.64	35502.06
17751	15060	431	6651	2723	138054.66	31600.40
10868	9606	347	6453	1398	77738.06	14333.93
0	0	0	0	0	0	0
27005	21378	2241	15501	3153	1188219.43	929715.92
11787	9202	257	3196	1397	107046.75	24906.91
667	594	0	783	18	4921.19	1063.55
592	487	46	180	103	3899.02	1479.76
10381	8957	1102	4798	1317	83313.26	24688.67

地 区 Region	占地面积(平方米) Area of School Sites(m^2)	教学行政用房 建筑面积(平方米) Administrative (m^2)	图书(册) Books(Volume)
总 计 Total	**30562141.45**	**8739859.71**	**25188312**
北 京 Beijing	152199.44	93088.30	78918
天 津 Tianjin	202664.00	64260.00	285582
河 北 Hebei	2229133.88	941908.50	1975303
山 西 Shanxi	1150590.38	509369.30	2383649
内蒙古 Inner Mongolia	646457.00	119728.00	564121
辽 宁 Liaoning	633522.00	223583.00	402857
吉 林 Jilin	578368.00	210504.00	288304
黑龙江 Heilongjiang	804662.32	235650.02	424354
上 海 Shanghai	187971.00	268253.00	663320
江 苏 Jiangsu	3022724.01	1050221.00	3209278
浙 江 Zhejiang	2844569.37	588669.01	1743260
安 徽 Anhui	630978.30	69608.00	364360
福 建 Fujian	306409.91	201436.57	675667
江 西 Jiangxi	263388.00	52102.00	142262
山 东 Shandong	1528452.86	400693.00	651168
河 南 Henan	1969916.65	489422.82	1113431
湖 北 Hubei	977871.50	328652.20	1038100
湖 南 Hunan	3375112.30	402537.00	1453888
广 东 Guangdong	180918.00	82697.00	290081
广 西 Guangxi	410242.00	73451.00	170263
海 南 Hainan	205589.00	66680.00	106165
重 庆 Chongqing	42581.00	36334.00	226532
四 川 Sichuan	1208735.71	571899.87	1091649
贵 州 Guizhou	1359914.05	562125.28	835124
云 南 Yunnan	660596.90	102012.00	169898
西 藏 Tibet	0	0	0
陕 西 Shaanxi	1790109.86	465744.52	1870807
甘 肃 Gansu	1321005.43	316152.47	629074
青 海 Qinghai	130331.00	24541.70	77249
宁 夏 Ningxia	64900.00	2240.00	29420
新 疆 Xinjiang	1682227.58	186296.15	2234228

学校资产情况
Resources in Technical Training Schools

计算机数(台) PC(Set)			教室(间) Classroom(Room)		固定资产总值(万元) Fixed Assets(10,000 yuan)	
合计 Total	其中:教学用计算机 No. of Computers Used for Instruction		合计 Total	其中:网络多媒体教室 of Which: Network Multimedia Classroom	合计 Total	其中:教学、实习仪器设备资产值 of Which: Teaching Equipment & Instruments
	小计 Subtotal	其中:平板电脑 of Which: Tablet PC				
178669	**149777**	**10172**	**33862**	**13072**	**6316791.15**	**397247.07**
2629	1991	113	666	322	16438.66	10003.70
1792	1370	303	250	71	17496.11	2395.07
12764	10720	403	1848	747	85292.61	22274.80
9940	9858	36	633	531	90540.44	34832.99
2508	2032	6	294	42	20991.60	7056.00
4108	3558	351	1306	371	23860.22	6834.47
1447	1119	12	1152	71	16961.60	3602.00
4945	3590	206	771	226	39697.63	11412.50
6010	3786	240	257	132	64305.00	18089.00
24682	22685	4086	7804	2603	221440.72	58913.43
18096	16991	183	2140	1652	137126.15	39365.78
2225	1966	42	287	177	13670.00	2332.00
5866	4041	155	510	224	4769811.26	6673.11
1390	1241	82	158	36	11161.00	1580.00
7921	7084	648	1163	618	112227.51	30968.51
7208	6112	130	3859	1328	53458.34	11811.29
6038	5261	265	1136	356	37255.17	11727.17
12224	8734	532	1394	682	108496.34	21144.70
3473	2917	403	694	301	104217.00	4630.00
1235	705	0	147	41	10868.25	2934.67
726	650	42	192	96	9985.10	949.73
1952	1677	320	386	183	4844.50	1659.55
9737	8259	505	1938	438	68878.70	14550.24
6765	5568	62	1113	472	74660.52	19743.69
1978	1708	22	386	167	14277.29	2687.70
0	0	0	0	0	0	0
10499	7587	489	1887	612	80889.68	20565.86
6643	5150	114	953	364	66556.22	16437.93
256	236	0	62	3	4227.37	839.05
325	267	0	49	49	2178.00	859.00
3287	2914	422	427	157	34978.14	10373.13

地 区 Region	占地面积(平方米) Area of School Sites(m^2)	教学行政用房 建筑面积(平方米) Administrative (m^2)	图书(册) Books(Volume)
总 计 Total	**46577063.56**	**13044852.12**	**44001188**
北 京 Beijing	1418230.00	346664.00	1583516
天 津 Tianjin	350225.31	135010.90	455784
河 北 Hebei	2547117.93	636326.26	1617246
山 西 Shanxi	745861.00	231683.00	1398259
内蒙古 Inner Mongolia	220019.80	62228.35	221730
辽 宁 Liaoning	1281525.00	430716.00	884828
吉 林 Jilin	1096282.00	110076.00	246028
黑龙江 Heilongjiang	2810446.00	442091.00	1081039
上 海 Shanghai	415907.00	206796.00	498015
江 苏 Jiangsu	6415800.58	2342226.69	6504403
浙 江 Zhejiang	4462917.25	1826736.61	5325704
安 徽 Anhui	1451510.52	247861.68	348627
福 建 Fujian	189569.21	137530.05	412823
江 西 Jiangxi	51713.00	7624.00	37142
山 东 Shandong	2568900.99	676833.44	3310103
河 南 Henan	2508161.51	1033849.02	3126114
湖 北 Hubei	2457485.50	452250.90	374598
湖 南 Hunan	1273604.00	94570.00	546725
广 东 Guangdong	2663907.00	829220.00	3160222
广 西 Guangxi	11570.00	7848.00	26250
海 南 Hainan	36690.00	39850.00	86750
重 庆 Chongqing	490327.30	255393.97	1054411
四 川 Sichuan	1326544.89	470756.92	2726435
贵 州 Guizhou	2173715.16	415429.77	1421574
云 南 Yunnan	1846864.23	472941.73	1655617
西 藏 Tibet	0	0	0
陕 西 Shaanxi	3154881.25	466702.59	1685438
甘 肃 Gansu	543210.13	108551.24	361232
青 海 Qinghai	625607.00	29151.00	290608
宁 夏 Ningxia	11080.00	1582.00	1580
新 疆 Xinjiang	1427390.00	526351.00	3558387

培训学校资产情况
in Technical Training Schools for Peasants

计算机数(台) PC(Set)			教室(间) Classroom(Room)		固定资产总值(万元) Fixed Assets(10,000 yuan)	
合计 Total	其中:教学用计算机 No. of Computers Used for Instruction 小计 Subtotal	其中:平板电脑 of Which: Tablet PC	合计 Total	其中:网络多媒体教室 of Which: Network Multimedia Classroom	合计 Total	其中:教学、实习仪器设备资产值 of Which: Teaching Equipment & Instruments
233830	**206992**	**19418**	**108211**	**23061**	**14181307.07**	**1155327.13**
8771	7452	345	1302	411	28188.35	10470.11
2920	2661	155	1278	161	6952.05	1874.89
7151	6580	213	2558	579	48706.80	8953.79
4739	3461	535	1971	321	9529.45	2835.87
603	556	24	14693	8	4638.70	1251.40
5589	4942	358	3177	846	43405.58	4172.98
1400	1114	19	1451	500	24563.28	4510.63
3025	2667	10	1190	277	8047.98	2211.75
9384	7217	1161	1066	494	28503.00	12909.00
40017	34612	7993	19910	4223	407576.04	53741.47
34729	32202	2838	6448	2283	182097.93	40377.98
1751	1603	93	1189	213	17862.00	3446.00
3256	3074	596	569	244	12787.79	2576.52
22	22	0	21	0	599.00	107.00
14377	13836	1436	5574	2384	87204.42	22918.94
5047	4580	589	13937	3698	46026.73	9429.41
8701	8496	12	1183	401	25012.43	5277.26
2336	2110	16	1048	69	8067.72	2140.64
30717	27353	1913	4792	1826	12885590.00	894791.00
932	744	16	29	22	49020.00	20305.00
180	180	30	218	68	1350.00	350.00
5092	3505	336	2364	465	16944.12	3100.17
16990	14842	93	5295	513	69636.96	15305.31
7359	6515	45	3110	716	49085.80	6067.77
5499	5006	175	4117	645	47757.64	6288.88
0	0	0	0	0	0	0
8548	7804	79	6109	877	36623.66	9161.67
1516	1078	76	642	315	7931.51	2506.53
401	358	0	713	15	555.82	195.50
0	0	0	0	0	58.00	55.00
2778	2422	262	2257	487	26984.30	7994.65

地　区 Region	占地面积(平方米) Area of School Sites(m^2)	教学行政用房 建筑面积(平方米) Administrative (m^2)	图书(册) Books(Volume)
总　计 Total	**26441863.27**	**40591289.22**	**55997155**
北　京 Beijing	2988935.48	28815104.37	33948003
天　津 Tianjin	835264.76	405372.87	753559
河　北 Hebei	888978.47	296919.93	511989
山　西 Shanxi	867056.70	653853.90	2733710
内蒙古 Inner Mongolia	99212.00	18533.00	74650
辽　宁 Liaoning	2956224.07	1461305.56	2555255
吉　林 Jilin	363850.50	247664.25	530330
黑龙江 Heilongjiang	315189.68	266563.30	263450
上　海 Shanghai	1221157.00	842221.00	2011200
江　苏 Jiangsu	5701345.49	2426900.62	2588400
浙　江 Zhejiang	1833198.97	866499.52	896801
安　徽 Anhui	178129.80	42095.60	174792
福　建 Fujian	312907.43	344266.77	783444
江　西 Jiangxi	59188.00	10746.00	28458
山　东 Shandong	898170.55	554047.49	1110634
河　南 Henan	633187.12	204919.00	297669
湖　北 Hubei	380339.70	156005.70	277493
湖　南 Hunan	122760.00	44676.60	196087
广　东 Guangdong	1939052.00	1173550.00	2581279
广　西 Guangxi	2510.00	6860.00	5320
海　南 Hainan	0	0	0
重　庆 Chongqing	641095.68	260322.25	567283
四　川 Sichuan	449929.01	297523.02	694677
贵　州 Guizhou	212761.48	149512.48	670677
云　南 Yunnan	356970.60	214370.00	338068
西　藏 Tibet	0	0	0
陕　西 Shaanxi	628220.91	394785.68	594995
甘　肃 Gansu	865781.91	260432.28	351963
青　海 Qinghai	18200.00	320.00	0
宁　夏 Ningxia	115276.00	18820.00	11811
新　疆 Xinjiang	556969.96	157098.03	445158

构资产情况
Teaching Resources in Others

计算机数(台) PC(Set)			教室(间) Classroom(Room)		固定资产总值(万元) Fixed Assets(10,000 yuan)	
合计 Total	其中:教学用计算机 No. of Computers Used for Instruction		合计 Total	其中:网络多媒体教室 of Which: Network Multimedia Classroom	合计 Total	其中:教学、实习仪器设备资产值 of Which: Teaching Equipment & Instruments
	小计 Subtotal	其中:平板电脑 of Which: Tablet PC				
329416	**260762**	**47966**	**157017**	**45394**	**9683206.41**	**6568347.09**
62655	45531	17463	30381	5653	221282.67	86579.12
11277	9717	1169	3573	750	17826.03	6288.93
9612	8472	1663	4761	1125	36261.05	15624.51
20946	16996	559	5081	2582	42629.29	21575.10
893	850	68	221	110	19726.60	3969.60
33654	26425	7939	23733	5867	278153.63	65222.21
5632	4840	659	6440	894	47534.09	9318.14
3534	2548	235	3271	427	35392.24	18134.66
25128	17790	2915	6248	2319	98903.00	38077.00
34496	29125	3889	12257	5190	1182298.96	609903.28
18620	16002	1563	8269	3348	76089.12	22355.18
1758	1540	100	560	258	16981.52	5256.33
7274	6267	396	2744	464	22388.61	5874.95
192	186	98	20	5	1120.00	174.00
13123	11278	1035	6345	1453	76262.49	20837.86
4330	3963	1006	4242	1489	24514.65	4787.45
2524	1847	184	854	236	25741.91	7532.63
902	844	38	990	128	7438.00	1585.00
37024	28213	3172	15154	5928	6220781.00	4666181.00
241	199	8	62	12	25128.00	21588.00
0	0	0	0	0	0	0
7689	5515	989	4105	1510	22150.19	7822.84
4715	3943	140	1969	416	28174.98	5646.51
3627	2977	324	2428	1535	14308.34	5788.95
3391	2892	150	1950	586	15703.13	5357.35
0	0	0	0	0	0	0
7958	5987	1673	7505	1664	1070706.09	899988.40
3628	2974	67	1601	718	32559.02	5962.45
10	0	0	8	0	138.00	29.00
267	220	46	131	54	1663.02	565.76
4316	3621	418	2114	673	21350.81	6320.88

地　区 Region	学校数(所) Schools			
	合计 Total	初级中学 Regular Junior Secondary Schools	九年一贯制学校 9-Year Schools	职业初中 Vocational Junior Secondary Schools
总　计 Total	**51894**	**35696**	**16183**	**15**
北　京 Beijing	345	224	121	0
天　津 Tianjin	338	293	45	0
河　北 Hebei	2375	1854	521	0
山　西 Shanxi	1835	1314	521	0
内蒙古 Inner Mongolia	683	463	220	0
辽　宁 Liaoning	1522	989	533	0
吉　林 Jilin	1172	817	350	5
黑龙江 Heilongjiang	1429	904	525	0
上　海 Shanghai	560	369	191	0
江　苏 Jiangsu	2148	1644	504	0
浙　江 Zhejiang	1735	1262	473	0
安　徽 Anhui	2810	1850	960	0
福　建 Fujian	1240	1041	199	0
江　西 Jiangxi	2140	1422	718	0
山　东 Shandong	2968	2148	820	0
河　南 Henan	4515	3590	925	0
湖　北 Hubei	2041	1532	509	0
湖　南 Hunan	3304	2103	1201	0
广　东 Guangdong	3536	2038	1498	0
广　西 Guangxi	1757	1500	257	0
海　南 Hainan	397	207	190	0
重　庆 Chongqing	863	684	179	0
四　川 Sichuan	3722	1729	1990	3
贵　州 Guizhou	2048	1499	544	5
云　南 Yunnan	1668	1426	240	2
西　藏 Tibet	98	94	4	0
陕　西 Shaanxi	1621	1112	509	0
甘　肃 Gansu	1468	882	586	0
青　海 Qinghai	270	99	171	0
宁　夏 Ningxia	247	168	79	0
新　疆 Xinjiang	1039	439	600	0

班数(总计)
Junior Secondary Schools

班数(个) Classes				
合计 Total	一年级 Grade 1	二年级 Grade 2	三年级 Grade 3	四年级 Grade 4
948200	**330312**	**312290**	**295441**	**10157**
9313	3295	3047	2947	24
6949	2403	2148	2117	281
49806	18561	16279	14966	0
24588	8390	8319	7879	0
14562	5067	4742	4716	37
23382	8128	7741	7513	0
15003	5317	5169	4517	0
21761	6630	6585	6157	2389
12818	3447	3366	3068	2937
47242	16912	15769	14550	11
38168	13262	12775	12075	56
45666	15977	15353	14336	0
26586	9307	8847	8432	0
38160	13839	12763	11558	0
68832	23360	21551	19804	4117
82035	28817	27377	25558	283
31241	11062	10479	9679	21
44515	15639	14869	14007	0
78010	27455	26039	24515	1
36663	13017	12141	11505	0
6925	2473	2276	2176	0
21160	7401	7043	6716	0
53657	18950	17794	16913	0
37103	12424	12191	12488	0
36829	13055	11996	11778	0
2728	912	892	924	0
23112	7850	7747	7515	0
19938	6667	6621	6650	0
4415	1488	1461	1466	0
5625	1955	1850	1820	0
21408	7252	7060	7096	0

地 区 Region	学校数(所) Schools			
	合计 Total	初级中学 Regular Junior Secondary Schools	九年一贯制学校 9-Year Schools	职业初中 Vocational Junior Secondary Schools
总 计 Total	**12355**	**7930**	**4422**	**3**
北 京 Beijing	218	129	89	0
天 津 Tianjin	169	141	28	0
河 北 Hebei	413	307	106	0
山 西 Shanxi	325	237	88	0
内蒙古 Inner Mongolia	195	152	43	0
辽 宁 Liaoning	638	488	150	0
吉 林 Jilin	275	206	66	3
黑龙江 Heilongjiang	408	298	110	0
上 海 Shanghai	443	300	143	0
江 苏 Jiangsu	829	639	190	0
浙 江 Zhejiang	707	498	209	0
安 徽 Anhui	362	247	115	0
福 建 Fujian	233	171	62	0
江 西 Jiangxi	282	132	150	0
山 东 Shandong	945	614	331	0
河 南 Henan	788	565	223	0
湖 北 Hubei	591	423	168	0
湖 南 Hunan	401	248	153	0
广 东 Guangdong	1616	706	910	0
广 西 Guangxi	341	198	143	0
海 南 Hainan	96	31	65	0
重 庆 Chongqing	200	154	46	0
四 川 Sichuan	458	224	234	0
贵 州 Guizhou	398	201	197	0
云 南 Yunnan	214	126	88	0
西 藏 Tibet	20	18	2	0
陕 西 Shaanxi	328	224	104	0
甘 肃 Gansu	156	91	65	0
青 海 Qinghai	51	25	26	0
宁 夏 Ningxia	59	56	3	0
新 疆 Xinjiang	196	81	115	0

班数(城区)
Secondary Schools(Urban Area)

班数(个)Classes				
合计 Total	一年级 Grade 1	二年级 Grade 2	三年级 Grade 3	四年级 Grade 4
336717	**117220**	**110373**	**102925**	**6199**
7848	2779	2570	2475	24
4711	1665	1495	1459	92
13486	5072	4451	3963	0
8365	2920	2833	2612	0
5862	2041	1902	1885	34
12561	4388	4204	3969	0
6276	2222	2180	1874	0
9331	2786	2768	2601	1176
10958	2934	2875	2629	2520
23155	8237	7718	7189	11
18920	6616	6303	5945	56
10237	3528	3429	3280	0
10206	3620	3409	3177	0
9552	3458	3202	2892	0
27141	9218	8323	7482	2118
19347	6762	6415	6003	167
12782	4492	4306	3984	0
11350	4046	3799	3505	0
43021	15385	14358	13277	1
8574	3057	2853	2664	0
2898	1014	968	916	0
8630	3089	2874	2667	0
14545	5095	4876	4574	0
7443	2561	2464	2418	0
6882	2469	2258	2155	0
535	184	177	174	0
8397	2895	2822	2680	0
4322	1488	1442	1392	0
1239	421	407	411	0
2155	753	707	695	0
5988	2025	1985	1978	0

地 区 Region	学校数(所) Schools			
	合计 Total	初级中学 Regular Junior Secondary Schools	九年一贯制学校 9-Year Schools	职业初中 Vocational Junior Secondary Schools
总 计 Total	**2635**	**1510**	**1125**	**0**
北 京 Beijing	38	29	9	0
天 津 Tianjin	18	14	4	0
河 北 Hebei	135	95	40	0
山 西 Shanxi	48	38	10	0
内蒙古 Inner Mongolia	5	4	1	0
辽 宁 Liaoning	64	47	17	0
吉 林 Jilin	19	11	8	0
黑龙江 Heilongjiang	38	27	11	0
上 海 Shanghai	36	21	15	0
江 苏 Jiangsu	128	87	41	0
浙 江 Zhejiang	194	122	72	0
安 徽 Anhui	70	42	28	0
福 建 Fujian	56	42	14	0
江 西 Jiangxi	54	26	28	0
山 东 Shandong	303	184	119	0
河 南 Henan	189	127	62	0
湖 北 Hubei	90	59	31	0
湖 南 Hunan	77	44	33	0
广 东 Guangdong	614	235	379	0
广 西 Guangxi	66	39	27	0
海 南 Hainan	10	4	6	0
重 庆 Chongqing	31	26	5	0
四 川 Sichuan	79	37	42	0
贵 州 Guizhou	79	35	44	0
云 南 Yunnan	57	41	16	0
西 藏 Tibet	0	0	0	0
陕 西 Shaanxi	75	47	28	0
甘 肃 Gansu	16	3	13	0
青 海 Qinghai	11	3	8	0
宁 夏 Ningxia	6	6	0	0
新 疆 Xinjiang	29	15	14	0

数(城乡结合区)
Schools(Urban-rural Transitional Area)

班数(个) Classes				
合计 Total	一年级 Grade 1	二年级 Grade 2	三年级 Grade 3	四年级 Grade 4
56103	**20053**	**18478**	**16780**	**792**
737	253	246	238	0
362	130	112	112	8
3423	1309	1136	978	0
943	337	319	287	0
83	31	25	27	0
1034	363	334	337	0
177	59	64	54	0
542	156	155	155	76
888	256	242	206	184
2767	979	932	856	0
4454	1554	1508	1392	0
1447	512	475	460	0
1453	534	479	440	0
1038	402	337	299	0
7429	2592	2309	2005	523
2975	1073	1003	899	0
1793	662	622	509	0
1468	535	482	451	0
13338	4855	4474	4008	1
1579	562	522	495	0
270	92	92	86	0
880	320	278	282	0
1640	575	553	512	0
1246	446	410	390	0
1756	645	576	535	0
0	0	0	0	0
836	295	274	267	0
312	106	108	98	0
230	76	78	76	0
232	88	74	70	0
771	256	259	256	0

地 区 Region	学校数(所) Schools			
	合计 Total	初级中学 Regular Junior Secondary Schools	九年一贯制学校 9-Year Schools	职业初中 Vocational Junior Secondary Schools
总 计 Total	**24251**	**18260**	**5986**	**5**
北 京 Beijing	65	45	20	0
天 津 Tianjin	102	92	10	0
河 北 Hebei	1177	923	254	0
山 西 Shanxi	811	640	171	0
内蒙古 Inner Mongolia	379	275	104	0
辽 宁 Liaoning	581	343	238	0
吉 林 Jilin	477	351	124	2
黑龙江 Heilongjiang	611	407	204	0
上 海 Shanghai	92	54	38	0
江 苏 Jiangsu	1130	875	255	0
浙 江 Zhejiang	738	594	144	0
安 徽 Anhui	1251	898	353	0
福 建 Fujian	526	481	45	0
江 西 Jiangxi	982	717	265	0
山 东 Shandong	1595	1230	365	0
河 南 Henan	2166	1706	460	0
湖 北 Hubei	978	798	180	0
湖 南 Hunan	1611	1134	477	0
广 东 Guangdong	1329	991	338	0
广 西 Guangxi	1012	943	69	0
海 南 Hainan	243	148	95	0
重 庆 Chongqing	489	415	74	0
四 川 Sichuan	1797	1118	679	0
贵 州 Guizhou	1094	924	168	2
云 南 Yunnan	721	666	54	1
西 藏 Tibet	63	61	2	0
陕 西 Shaanxi	1032	719	313	0
甘 肃 Gansu	606	444	162	0
青 海 Qinghai	106	47	59	0
宁 夏 Ningxia	101	77	24	0
新 疆 Xinjiang	386	144	242	0

班数(镇区)
Secondary Schools(Counties & Towns Area)

班数(个) Classes				
合计 Total	一年级 Grade 1	二年级 Grade 2	三年级 Grade 3	四年级 Grade 4
464182	**161859**	**153362**	**145844**	**3117**
846	299	273	274	0
1488	495	433	450	110
27114	10051	8859	8204	0
12232	4150	4139	3943	0
7862	2727	2575	2557	3
8113	2804	2657	2652	0
5892	2090	2020	1782	0
9324	2900	2875	2684	865
1486	409	387	353	337
22051	7924	7390	6737	0
15702	5432	5272	4998	0
25467	8979	8561	7927	0
12022	4193	3984	3845	0
20524	7513	6863	6148	0
35330	11968	11219	10450	1693
45005	15777	15062	14078	88
14317	5085	4803	4408	21
24013	8458	8000	7555	0
27528	9467	9200	8861	0
22787	8059	7535	7193	0
3488	1246	1135	1107	0
10725	3699	3572	3454	0
30010	10647	9905	9458	0
23433	7801	7683	7949	0
18979	6712	6177	6090	0
1698	560	549	589	0
12868	4340	4312	4216	0
10549	3516	3514	3519	0
2257	771	744	742	0
2592	899	857	836	0
8480	2888	2807	2785	0

初中校数、班数
Number of Schools, Classes of Junior Secondary

地　区 Region	学校数(所) Schools			
	合计 Total	初级中学 Regular Junior Secondary Schools	九年一贯制学校 9-Year Schools	职业初中 Vocational Junior Secondary Schools
总　计 Total	**5807**	**4317**	**1489**	**1**
北　京 Beijing	22	17	5	0
天　津 Tianjin	44	41	3	0
河　北 Hebei	490	383	107	0
山　西 Shanxi	199	144	55	0
内蒙古 Inner Mongolia	39	26	13	0
辽　宁 Liaoning	72	40	32	0
吉　林 Jilin	52	35	17	0
黑龙江 Heilongjiang	56	45	11	0
上　海 Shanghai	23	14	9	0
江　苏 Jiangsu	321	261	60	0
浙　江 Zhejiang	230	184	46	0
安　徽 Anhui	294	199	95	0
福　建 Fujian	149	135	14	0
江　西 Jiangxi	219	154	65	0
山　东 Shandong	591	439	152	0
河　南 Henan	745	551	194	0
湖　北 Hubei	236	183	53	0
湖　南 Hunan	382	275	107	0
广　东 Guangdong	386	272	114	0
广　西 Guangxi	204	192	12	0
海　南 Hainan	14	5	9	0
重　庆 Chongqing	75	66	9	0
四　川 Sichuan	292	164	128	0
贵　州 Guizhou	160	117	43	0
云　南 Yunnan	123	109	13	1
西　藏 Tibet	5	5	0	0
陕　西 Shaanxi	180	137	43	0
甘　肃 Gansu	111	72	39	0
青　海 Qinghai	31	9	22	0
宁　夏 Ningxia	14	12	2	0
新　疆 Xinjiang	48	31	17	0

(镇乡结合区)
Schools(County-town Transitional Area)

班数(个) Classes				
合计 Total	一年级 Grade 1	二年级 Grade 2	三年级 Grade 3	四年级 Grade 4
112943	**39978**	**37231**	**34926**	**808**
291	100	92	99	0
621	209	178	183	51
12449	4660	4074	3715	0
3720	1281	1271	1168	0
640	223	206	211	0
979	337	327	315	0
569	206	190	173	0
903	275	281	256	91
352	97	90	83	82
5313	1925	1765	1623	0
4901	1724	1640	1537	0
5439	1954	1828	1657	0
3408	1198	1119	1091	0
3432	1266	1150	1016	0
13504	4671	4244	4012	577
14472	5215	4846	4404	7
3351	1206	1121	1024	0
5322	1888	1767	1667	0
8332	2886	2779	2667	0
4617	1612	1538	1467	0
369	133	123	113	0
1792	623	594	575	0
3845	1384	1281	1180	0
3726	1245	1225	1256	0
3634	1310	1191	1133	0
206	69	61	76	0
2600	873	870	857	0
2072	693	688	691	0
487	167	160	160	0
287	99	102	86	0
1310	449	430	431	0

初中校数、
Number of Schools, Classes of Junior

地　区 Region	学校数(所) Schools			
	合计 Total	初级中学 Regular Junior Secondary Schools	九年一贯制学校 9-Year Schools	职业初中 Vocational Junior Secondary Schools
总　计 Total	**15288**	**9506**	**5775**	**7**
北　京 Beijing	62	50	12	0
天　津 Tianjin	67	60	7	0
河　北 Hebei	785	624	161	0
山　西 Shanxi	699	437	262	0
内蒙古 Inner Mongolia	109	36	73	0
辽　宁 Liaoning	303	158	145	0
吉　林 Jilin	420	260	160	0
黑龙江 Heilongjiang	410	199	211	0
上　海 Shanghai	25	15	10	0
江　苏 Jiangsu	189	130	59	0
浙　江 Zhejiang	290	170	120	0
安　徽 Anhui	1197	705	492	0
福　建 Fujian	481	389	92	0
江　西 Jiangxi	876	573	303	0
山　东 Shandong	428	304	124	0
河　南 Henan	1561	1319	242	0
湖　北 Hubei	472	311	161	0
湖　南 Hunan	1292	721	571	0
广　东 Guangdong	591	341	250	0
广　西 Guangxi	404	359	45	0
海　南 Hainan	58	28	30	0
重　庆 Chongqing	174	115	59	0
四　川 Sichuan	1467	387	1077	3
贵　州 Guizhou	556	374	179	3
云　南 Yunnan	733	634	98	1
西　藏 Tibet	15	15	0	0
陕　西 Shaanxi	261	169	92	0
甘　肃 Gansu	706	347	359	0
青　海 Qinghai	113	27	86	0
宁　夏 Ningxia	87	35	52	0
新　疆 Xinjiang	457	214	243	0

班数(乡村)
Secondary Schools(Rural Area)

班数(个) Classes				
合计 Total	一年级 Grade 1	二年级 Grade 2	三年级 Grade 3	四年级 Grade 4
147301	**51233**	**48555**	**46672**	**841**
619	217	204	198	0
750	243	220	208	79
9206	3438	2969	2799	0
3991	1320	1347	1324	0
838	299	265	274	0
2708	936	880	892	0
2835	1005	969	861	0
3106	944	942	872	348
374	104	104	86	80
2036	751	661	624	0
3546	1214	1200	1132	0
9962	3470	3363	3129	0
4358	1494	1454	1410	0
8084	2868	2698	2518	0
6361	2174	2009	1872	306
17683	6278	5900	5477	28
4142	1485	1370	1287	0
9152	3135	3070	2947	0
7461	2603	2481	2377	0
5302	1901	1753	1648	0
539	213	173	153	0
1805	613	597	595	0
9102	3208	3013	2881	0
6227	2062	2044	2121	0
10968	3874	3561	3533	0
495	168	166	161	0
1847	615	613	619	0
5067	1663	1665	1739	0
919	296	310	313	0
878	303	286	289	0
6940	2339	2268	2333	0

初中学生

Number of Students in

地 区 Region	毕业生数 Graduates	招生数 Entrants	在校生数 Enrolment	
			合计 Total	其中:女 of Which:Female
总 计 Total	**13974699**	**15472209**	**44420630**	**20598359**
北 京 Beijing	82433	103263	266404	125243
天 津 Tianjin	85760	94747	262243	121683
河 北 Hebei	809376	965029	2600675	1224513
山 西 Shanxi	381332	369661	1082430	518546
内蒙古 Inner Mongolia	214631	224753	618655	296012
辽 宁 Liaoning	351861	341100	963450	456139
吉 林 Jilin	204311	221942	618704	294819
黑龙江 Heilongjiang	275946	276022	903983	434462
上 海 Shanghai	89901	120561	411712	194769
江 苏 Jiangsu	612498	757691	2086934	952837
浙 江 Zhejiang	478932	556892	1558460	728929
安 徽 Anhui	617011	702202	2021627	911054
福 建 Fujian	360858	432692	1215717	560070
江 西 Jiangxi	566603	686308	1910421	844779
山 东 Shandong	960401	1093836	3293601	1533374
河 南 Henan	1322926	1494458	4291617	1937765
湖 北 Hubei	444035	526205	1487131	675969
湖 南 Hunan	732605	791540	2296294	1048983
广 东 Guangdong	1114551	1266817	3561001	1601717
广 西 Guangxi	637407	712207	2034632	960539
海 南 Hainan	105107	121338	333342	149527
重 庆 Chongqing	317673	347162	990403	465947
四 川 Sichuan	803508	870815	2491364	1191115
贵 州 Guizhou	657859	600480	1829870	853229
云 南 Yunnan	605422	633890	1872808	891470
西 藏 Tibet	38038	41960	124571	60560
陕 西 Shaanxi	347995	356082	1049654	486472
甘 肃 Gansu	298107	285600	856127	404442
青 海 Qinghai	68199	70462	205814	99834
宁 夏 Ningxia	88852	97652	279180	135523
新 疆 Xinjiang	300561	308842	901806	438038

数(总计)
Junior Secondary Schools

单位:人
unit:person

一年级 Grade 1	二年级 Grade 2	三年级 Grade 3	四年级 Grade 4	预计毕业生数 Estimated Graduates for Next Year
15475352	**14780316**	**13757832**	**407130**	**13716736**
103371	86977	75301	755	75127
94748	80242	77520	9733	77288
965029	863540	772106	0	772106
369685	373497	339248	0	339248
224753	196386	196154	1362	195802
341123	318601	303726	0	303726
221944	216941	179819	0	179819
276022	276273	253171	98517	244668
120719	112217	93497	85279	85279
757691	700686	628098	459	628183
556892	527642	471892	2034	472025
702222	680878	638527	0	638527
432776	407130	375811	0	375811
686765	644321	579335	0	579335
1093836	1048273	957580	193912	934559
1494459	1438616	1344314	14228	1343517
526241	505199	454840	851	454901
791540	780053	724701	0	724701
1267684	1195647	1097670	0	1097670
712226	681626	640780	0	640702
121761	109534	102047	0	102047
347244	331248	311911	0	311911
870818	837502	783044	0	783044
600494	600768	628608	0	628608
634312	625939	612557	0	612557
41960	40825	41786	0	41786
356240	356312	337102	0	337102
285600	287151	283376	0	283376
70554	67504	67756	0	67756
97755	92390	89035	0	89035
308888	296398	296520	0	296520

初中学生
Number of Students in Junior

地 区 Region	毕业生数 Graduates	招生数 Entrants	在校生数 Enrolment	
			合计 Total	其中:女 of Which:Female
总 计 Total	**4836743**	**5499957**	**15671422**	**7214833**
北 京 Beijing	69970	88138	227393	107005
天 津 Tianjin	59829	66394	179789	83802
河 北 Hebei	233260	277192	738329	347895
山 西 Shanxi	134181	135716	384856	185642
内蒙古 Inner Mongolia	93316	95665	262142	124973
辽 宁 Liaoning	189770	187077	519628	245068
吉 林 Jilin	96588	100184	281681	132651
黑龙江 Heilongjiang	126590	120522	409233	195708
上 海 Shanghai	78372	103291	356373	168711
江 苏 Jiangsu	308526	371085	1032286	473571
浙 江 Zhejiang	237738	278419	775584	362259
安 徽 Anhui	150831	161205	471914	209856
福 建 Fujian	143186	179528	497622	226738
江 西 Jiangxi	143237	176487	490289	210841
山 东 Shandong	373673	435673	1320251	612432
河 南 Henan	319222	358150	1036126	458669
湖 北 Hubei	186696	216945	617505	277845
湖 南 Hunan	185075	210172	599563	270275
广 东 Guangdong	589741	722289	1988834	877768
广 西 Guangxi	136607	162832	458854	211094
海 南 Hainan	47929	52615	147771	63877
重 庆 Chongqing	125759	145312	404724	192287
四 川 Sichuan	221901	240348	692182	332630
贵 州 Guizhou	122274	121279	359464	165805
云 南 Yunnan	110634	121636	344907	166588
西 藏 Tibet	7183	8449	24159	11883
陕 西 Shaanxi	128078	138352	399606	184817
甘 肃 Gansu	70362	71551	208540	96946
青 海 Qinghai	20174	21252	60659	29395
宁 夏 Ningxia	36422	39799	112872	54366
新 疆 Xinjiang	89619	92400	268286	133436

数(城区)

Secondary Schools(Urban Area)

单位:人
unit:person

一年级 Grade 1	二年级 Grade 2	三年级 Grade 3	四年级 Grade 4	预计毕业生数 Estimated Graduates for Next Year
5501470	**5202446**	**4720147**	**247359**	**4698121**
88229	74243	64166	755	63992
66395	56038	53910	3446	53695
277192	250727	210410	0	210410
135720	133128	116008	0	116008
95665	81711	83483	1283	83114
187079	176319	156230	0	156230
100186	99488	82007	0	82007
120522	123578	113310	51823	107616
103413	97619	81260	74081	74081
371085	347197	313545	459	313630
278419	261296	233835	2034	233968
161205	159791	150918	0	150918
179537	167568	150517	0	150517
176598	165849	147842	0	147842
435673	410580	369667	104331	361697
358151	345358	323470	9147	322905
216959	211105	189441	0	189441
210172	203905	185486	0	185486
723116	668584	597134	0	597134
162836	154086	141932	0	141854
52815	49240	45716	0	45716
145338	135318	124068	0	124068
240349	235664	216169	0	216169
121284	119282	118898	0	118898
121647	114955	108305	0	108305
8449	8065	7645	0	7645
138387	135971	125248	0	125248
71551	70558	66431	0	66431
21269	19624	19766	0	19766
39816	37328	35728	0	35728
92413	88271	87602	0	87602

初中学生数

Number of Students in Junior Secondary

地　区 Region	毕业生数 Graduates	招生数 Entrants	在校生数 Enrolment	
			合计 Total	其中:女 of Which:Female
总　计 Total	**772556**	**937061**	**2611372**	**1174389**
北　京 Beijing	6549	7608	20453	9560
天　津 Tianjin	4813	5130	13687	6392
河　北 Hebei	57911	72284	194329	89712
山　西 Shanxi	14480	14606	41317	19193
内蒙古 Inner Mongolia	1009	1336	3307	1531
辽　宁 Liaoning	15124	15301	43191	20630
吉　林 Jilin	2315	2334	6774	3087
黑龙江 Heilongjiang	6894	5838	21681	10391
上　海 Shanghai	5465	9158	28423	13199
江　苏 Jiangsu	35272	43161	121078	54342
浙　江 Zhejiang	52773	64615	180191	81915
安　徽 Anhui	20087	23116	64955	28176
福　建 Fujian	18885	25634	68494	30762
江　西 Jiangxi	14922	19441	50628	21582
山　东 Shandong	97906	119747	352405	161823
河　南 Henan	46081	53954	149835	64204
湖　北 Hubei	22839	31791	85195	37077
湖　南 Hunan	22257	27150	74162	33092
广　东 Guangdong	179917	229835	620948	268159
广　西 Guangxi	26389	30446	86038	39339
海　南 Hainan	4385	4925	14076	6048
重　庆 Chongqing	13975	15061	41754	19056
四　川 Sichuan	22645	25654	72123	33855
贵　州 Guizhou	19006	20798	60527	27373
云　南 Yunnan	27393	31352	88465	42231
西　藏 Tibet	0	0	0	0
陕　西 Shaanxi	11261	11662	34020	15377
甘　肃 Gansu	4266	4925	14108	6613
青　海 Qinghai	3687	3755	11275	5580
宁　夏 Ningxia	3594	4802	13046	6196
新　疆 Xinjiang	10456	11642	34887	17894

(城乡结合区)
Schools(Urban-rural Transitional Area)

单位:人
unit:person

一年级 Grade 1	二年级 Grade 2	三年级 Grade 3	四年级 Grade 4	预计毕业生数 Estimated Graduates for Next Year
937256	**869448**	**771744**	**32924**	**768900**
7613	6909	5931	0	5931
5131	4317	3949	290	3974
72284	66397	55648	0	55648
14606	14055	12656	0	12656
1336	912	1059	0	1059
15301	14369	13521	0	13521
2334	2499	1941	0	1941
5838	6286	6257	3300	5651
9183	7734	6249	5257	5257
43161	41061	36856	0	36856
64615	61938	53638	0	53638
23116	21520	20319	0	20319
25636	22891	19967	0	19967
19443	16647	14538	0	14538
119747	110568	98013	24077	96820
53954	50104	45777	0	45777
31793	29802	23600	0	23600
27150	24453	22559	0	22559
229926	209760	181262	0	181262
30446	28790	26802	0	26724
4965	4890	4221	0	4221
15061	13130	13563	0	13563
25654	24545	21924	0	21924
20798	20193	19536	0	19536
31355	29834	27276	0	27276
0	0	0	0	0
11679	11387	10954	0	10954
4925	4812	4371	0	4371
3762	3741	3772	0	3772
4802	4214	4030	0	4030
11642	11690	11555	0	11555

地　区 Region	毕业生数 Graduates	招生数 Entrants	在校生数 Enrolment 合计 Total	在校生数 Enrolment 其中:女 of Which:Female
总　计 Total	**7058957**	**7732411**	**22315114**	**10381757**
北　京 Beijing	7196	9047	23164	10799
天　津 Tianjin	18002	19422	55795	25798
河　北 Hebei	443886	525743	1429555	674650
山　西 Shanxi	194348	187296	556641	266517
内蒙古 Inner Mongolia	111123	117966	326356	156867
辽　宁 Liaoning	125350	118380	341860	162405
吉　林 Jilin	76061	85119	236607	113876
黑龙江 Heilongjiang	116081	121261	382855	184279
上　海 Shanghai	9611	13928	45052	21178
江　苏 Jiangsu	280357	355532	972722	441353
浙　江 Zhejiang	199838	231036	649903	305252
安　徽 Anhui	341898	399445	1143507	511691
福　建 Fujian	165044	192339	545295	252790
江　西 Jiangxi	309780	380055	1055983	464909
山　东 Shandong	502875	561666	1688378	788624
河　南 Henan	737288	832368	2400588	1083916
湖　北 Hubei	201644	242165	683979	314011
湖　南 Hunan	405727	437361	1273612	582299
广　东 Guangdong	418706	433448	1254252	579361
广　西 Guangxi	413041	449313	1295217	618838
海　南 Hainan	51024	59873	163359	75717
重　庆 Chongqing	165072	174895	506097	237379
四　川 Sichuan	457013	497129	1420415	680399
贵　州 Guizhou	420812	383790	1177240	549709
云　南 Yunnan	319523	330021	987425	473339
西　藏 Tibet	23889	25463	77255	37113
陕　西 Shaanxi	194210	194400	579678	269222
甘　肃 Gansu	158649	152077	456701	215426
青　海 Qinghai	35104	36775	106671	51998
宁　夏 Ningxia	40547	44573	128667	62652
新　疆 Xinjiang	115258	120525	350285	169390

数(镇区)

Schools(Counties & Towns Area)

单位:人
unit:person

一年级 Grade 1	二年级 Grade 2	三年级 Grade 3	四年级 Grade 4	预计毕业生数 Estimated Graduates for Next Year
7733657	**7446673**	**7006561**	**128223**	**6989696**
9054	7552	6558	0	6558
19422	16232	16399	3742	16439
525743	472734	431078	0	431078
187309	192518	176814	0	176814
117966	105288	103023	79	103040
118401	109817	113642	0	113642
85119	82694	68794	0	68794
121261	118749	108920	33925	106363
13951	11824	10025	9252	9252
355532	326725	290465	0	290465
231036	220916	197951	0	197951
399457	383820	360230	0	360230
192407	182225	170663	0	170663
380317	356843	318823	0	318823
561666	546586	503767	76359	490475
832368	807676	756529	4015	756168
242181	232063	208884	851	208945
437361	432713	403538	0	403538
433446	420850	399956	0	399956
449324	434277	411616	0	411616
60060	53041	50258	0	50258
174943	169602	161552	0	161552
497131	475984	447300	0	447300
383795	386220	407225	0	407225
330310	331018	326097	0	326097
25463	24915	26877	0	26877
194512	196965	188201	0	188201
152077	153352	151272	0	151272
36843	35005	34823	0	34823
44647	42906	41114	0	41114
120555	115563	114167	0	114167

初中学生数

Number of Students in Junior Secondary

地 区 Region	毕业生数 Graduates	招生数 Entrants	在校生数 Enrolment 合计 Total	在校生数 Enrolment 其中:女 of Which:Female
总 计 Total	**1672711**	**1917134**	**5445874**	**2523266**
北 京 Beijing	2071	2532	6613	3088
天 津 Tianjin	7250	8160	23347	10928
河 北 Hebei	196537	241211	652299	310053
山 西 Shanxi	60066	60180	176689	83390
内蒙古 Inner Mongolia	8988	9119	25631	12125
辽 宁 Liaoning	15020	13920	39583	18630
吉 林 Jilin	6685	7999	21799	10684
黑龙江 Heilongjiang	11154	11559	37186	17905
上 海 Shanghai	2342	3332	10797	5158
江 苏 Jiangsu	66053	83767	227837	103556
浙 江 Zhejiang	61313	73652	203367	94164
安 徽 Anhui	70225	85551	240277	106106
福 建 Fujian	47303	54836	154572	70240
江 西 Jiangxi	49335	63045	170871	76466
山 东 Shandong	188494	217715	645318	300240
河 南 Henan	221100	270209	755259	337999
湖 北 Hubei	46022	58037	161396	74297
湖 南 Hunan	89301	97466	279924	127890
广 东 Guangdong	124554	133274	380694	177412
广 西 Guangxi	83785	92355	266681	128305
海 南 Hainan	5259	6740	18397	8528
重 庆 Chongqing	26946	29852	85073	40085
四 川 Sichuan	53327	63012	176341	84212
贵 州 Guizhou	63727	60329	184400	84542
云 南 Yunnan	60923	64078	189631	92119
西 藏 Tibet	2586	3171	9841	4725
陕 西 Shaanxi	40158	39335	118881	54129
甘 肃 Gansu	31422	30363	90503	41727
青 海 Qinghai	7456	8128	23223	11118
宁 夏 Ningxia	4048	5114	14534	7276
新 疆 Xinjiang	19261	19093	54910	26169

(镇乡结合区)
Schools(County-town Transitional Area)

单位:人
unit:person

一年级 Grade 1	二年级 Grade 2	三年级 Grade 3	四年级 Grade 4	预计毕业生数 Estimated Graduates for Next Year
1917406	**1813459**	**1680322**	**34687**	**1672969**
2537	2118	1958	0	1958
8160	6680	6722	1785	6750
241211	217225	193863	0	193863
60180	62026	54483	0	54483
9119	8384	8128	0	8128
13920	12714	12949	0	12949
7999	7314	6486	0	6486
11559	11382	10427	3818	10063
3333	2778	2401	2285	2285
83767	75901	68169	0	68169
73652	68944	60771	0	60771
85551	80735	73991	0	73991
54874	51128	48570	0	48570
63127	57404	50340	0	50340
217715	206718	194356	26529	187558
270209	254279	230501	270	230398
58038	54623	48735	0	48735
97466	93959	88499	0	88499
133257	127051	120386	0	120386
92355	90420	83906	0	83906
6790	6115	5492	0	5492
29852	28101	27120	0	27120
63014	59331	53996	0	53996
60331	60521	63548	0	63548
64171	63861	61599	0	61599
3171	2946	3724	0	3724
39338	40333	39210	0	39210
30363	30214	29926	0	29926
8133	7493	7597	0	7597
5119	5130	4285	0	4285
19095	17631	18184	0	18184

地区 Region	毕业生数 Graduates	招生数 Entrants	在校生数 Enrolment 合计 Total	其中:女 of Which:Female
总计 Total	**2078999**	**2239841**	**6434094**	**3001769**
北京 Beijing	5267	6078	15847	7439
天津 Tianjin	7929	8931	26659	12083
河北 Hebei	132230	162094	432791	201968
山西 Shanxi	52803	46649	140933	66387
内蒙古 Inner Mongolia	10192	11122	30157	14172
辽宁 Liaoning	36741	35643	101962	48666
吉林 Jilin	31662	36639	100416	48292
黑龙江 Heilongjiang	33275	34239	111895	54475
上海 Shanghai	1918	3342	10287	4880
江苏 Jiangsu	23615	31074	81926	37913
浙江 Zhejiang	41356	47437	132973	61418
安徽 Anhui	124282	141552	406206	189507
福建 Fujian	52628	60825	172800	80542
江西 Jiangxi	113586	129766	364149	169029
山东 Shandong	83853	96497	284972	132318
河南 Henan	266416	303940	854903	395180
湖北 Hubei	55695	67095	185647	84113
湖南 Hunan	141803	144007	423119	196409
广东 Guangdong	106104	111080	317915	144588
广西 Guangxi	87759	100062	280561	130607
海南 Hainan	6154	8850	22212	9933
重庆 Chongqing	26842	26955	79582	36281
四川 Sichuan	124594	133338	378767	178086
贵州 Guizhou	114773	95411	293166	137715
云南 Yunnan	175265	182233	540476	251543
西藏 Tibet	6966	8048	23157	11564
陕西 Shaanxi	25707	23330	70370	32433
甘肃 Gansu	69096	61972	190886	92070
青海 Qinghai	12921	12435	38484	18441
宁夏 Ningxia	11883	13280	37641	18505
新疆 Xinjiang	95684	95917	283235	135212

数(乡村)
Secondary Schools(Rural Area)

单位:人
unit:person

一年级 Grade 1	二年级 Grade 2	三年级 Grade 3	四年级 Grade 4	预计毕业生数 Estimated Graduates for Next Year
2240225	**2131197**	**2031124**	**31548**	**2028919**
6088	5182	4577	0	4577
8931	7972	7211	2545	7154
162094	140079	130618	0	130618
46656	47851	46426	0	46426
11122	9387	9648	0	9648
35643	32465	33854	0	33854
36639	34759	29018	0	29018
34239	33946	30941	12769	30689
3355	2774	2212	1946	1946
31074	26764	24088	0	24088
47437	45430	40106	0	40106
141560	137267	127379	0	127379
60832	57337	54631	0	54631
129850	121629	112670	0	112670
96497	91107	84146	13222	82387
303940	285582	264315	1066	264444
67101	62031	56515	0	56515
144007	143435	135677	0	135677
111122	106213	100580	0	100580
100066	93263	87232	0	87232
8886	7253	6073	0	6073
26963	26328	26291	0	26291
133338	125854	119575	0	119575
95415	95266	102485	0	102485
182355	179966	178155	0	178155
8048	7845	7264	0	7264
23341	23376	23653	0	23653
61972	63241	65673	0	65673
12442	12875	13167	0	13167
13292	12156	12193	0	12193
95920	92564	94751	0	94751

初中女
Number of Female Students

地　区 Region	毕业生数 Graduates	招生数 Entrants	在校生数 Enrolment 合计 Total	 一年级 Grade 1
总　计 Total	**6517118**	**7163711**	**20598359**	**7164699**
北　京 Beijing	38965	48589	125243	48624
天　津 Tianjin	39955	44011	121683	44011
河　北 Hebei	381403	455513	1224513	455513
山　西 Shanxi	182393	178220	518546	178224
内蒙古 Inner Mongolia	103953	107195	296012	107195
辽　宁 Liaoning	167358	160750	456139	160751
吉　林 Jilin	98283	105567	294819	105567
黑龙江 Heilongjiang	132948	132620	434462	132620
上　海 Shanghai	43208	56787	194769	56836
江　苏 Jiangsu	281160	343628	952837	343628
浙　江 Zhejiang	224875	259570	728929	259570
安　徽 Anhui	282500	316400	911054	316404
福　建 Fujian	165930	199063	560070	199084
江　西 Jiangxi	251535	306021	844779	306137
山　东 Shandong	450931	504545	1533374	504545
河　南 Henan	603469	676923	1937765	676924
湖　北 Hubei	199326	239935	675969	239948
湖　南 Hunan	333585	363559	1048983	363559
广　东 Guangdong	497290	572465	1601717	572836
广　西 Guangxi	303182	333111	960539	333119
海　南 Hainan	47054	54552	149527	54636
重　庆 Chongqing	150397	163771	465947	163800
四　川 Sichuan	384082	414743	1191115	414744
贵　州 Guizhou	312029	277373	853229	277375
云　南 Yunnan	295793	298434	891470	298540
西　藏 Tibet	18646	20406	60560	20406
陕　西 Shaanxi	161664	165519	486472	165583
甘　肃 Gansu	142211	134104	404442	134104
青　海 Qinghai	33242	33928	99834	33956
宁　夏 Ningxia	43740	47000	135523	47033
新　疆 Xinjiang	146011	149409	438038	149427

学生数
in Junior Secondary Schools

单位:人
unit:person

二年级 Grade 2	三年级 Grade 3	四年级 Grade 4	预计毕业生数 Estimated Graduates for Next Year
6864436	**6376220**	**193004**	**6350286**
41322	34956	341	34855
37661	35568	4443	35359
410154	358846	0	358846
179660	160662	0	160661
94847	93323	647	93140
154162	141226	0	141226
103687	85565	0	85565
133743	121390	46709	116537
52955	44379	40599	40599
320791	288198	220	288244
246950	221429	980	221512
306200	288450	0	288450
187672	173314	0	173314
283977	254665	0	254665
488446	448070	92313	434905
648450	606026	6365	605644
229783	205851	387	205856
355105	330319	0	330319
538775	490106	0	486751
322368	305052	0	305013
49054	45837	0	45837
155678	146469	0	146469
400737	375634	0	375634
280172	295682	0	295682
298162	294768	0	294768
19950	20204	0	20204
165888	155001	0	155001
135958	134380	0	134380
32856	33022	0	33022
44724	43766	0	43766
144549	144062	0	144062

初中专任教师学历、专业
Number of Full-time Teachers in Junior Secondary Schools

地　区 Region	合计 Total	其中:女 of Which:Female	按学历分 By Educational Attainment		
			研究生毕业 Graduate	本科毕业 Undergraduate	专科毕业 Associate Bachelor
总　计 Total	**3548688**	**1974445**	**92411**	**2910727**	**539517**
北　京 Beijing	34451	26434	6065	28085	294
天　津 Tianjin	26869	18809	2347	23552	927
河　北 Hebei	187549	131201	3932	157993	25490
山　西 Shanxi	108283	72871	1948	85604	20361
内蒙古 Inner Mongolia	57604	38714	2372	48916	6313
辽　宁 Liaoning	99482	68298	3223	84675	11410
吉　林 Jilin	64637	43615	1939	54997	7652
黑龙江 Heilongjiang	89672	58184	1240	75394	12905
上　海 Shanghai	39276	29047	4590	34240	443
江　苏 Jiangsu	181859	95730	9045	165519	7220
浙　江 Zhejiang	124699	73596	3994	115015	5632
安　徽 Anhui	155495	64195	2277	126921	26248
福　建 Fujian	99880	47301	2227	85762	11784
江　西 Jiangxi	120568	52216	1601	88086	30688
山　东 Shandong	275893	150906	9616	233535	32313
河　南 Henan	299006	184050	5863	225660	66278
湖　北 Hubei	129034	58601	2799	94944	30669
湖　南 Hunan	171593	89353	3653	130659	36939
广　东 Guangdong	279821	156636	8316	234990	36405
广　西 Guangxi	129756	68386	1564	103181	24539
海　南 Hainan	25932	12532	269	20621	4967
重　庆 Chongqing	76209	38282	1864	67455	6731
四　川 Sichuan	201344	100249	2843	155765	42677
贵　州 Guizhou	127528	55662	791	102191	24246
云　南 Yunnan	128970	65068	1414	109017	18048
西　藏 Tibet	10042	5107	170	8693	1152
陕　西 Shaanxi	99994	58269	3452	86600	9867
甘　肃 Gansu	81032	35120	1250	66178	13416
青　海 Qinghai	16074	8836	373	13032	2656
宁　夏 Ningxia	20171	11286	390	18121	1648
新　疆 Xinjiang	85965	55891	984	65326	19599

技术职务情况(总计)

by Academic Qualifications and Professional Rank(Total)

单位:人
unit:person

		按专业技术职务分 By Professional Rank				
高中阶段毕业 High School Graduate	高中阶段毕业以下 Below High School Graduate	中学高级 Senior Secondary	中学一级 1st Grade	中学二级 2nd Grade	中学三级 3rd Grade	未定职级 No-ranking
5783	**250**	**673946**	**1495353**	**1018995**	**35589**	**324805**
7	0	8633	12366	10648	128	2676
43	0	8845	12883	4174	36	931
102	32	34667	82711	45292	2548	22331
365	5	11423	35478	46600	1553	13229
3	0	18549	23448	10773	0	4834
145	29	47504	35598	11440	510	4430
48	1	12161	27683	19769	297	4727
131	2	22851	43434	19816	369	3202
3	0	4557	20185	12234	85	2215
75	0	47233	86622	37576	64	10364
58	0	30126	55862	30166	249	8296
47	2	26717	58269	46742	2423	21344
102	5	20914	43004	30309	480	5173
183	10	35585	43369	28056	1101	12457
412	17	39204	120633	88240	1435	26381
1205	0	51259	114015	94524	4712	34496
596	26	26140	67171	27127	1994	6602
323	19	21954	81193	46747	1478	20221
84	26	32604	137611	67979	4458	37169
444	28	16281	66843	31301	1923	13408
74	1	4766	9839	9537	82	1708
154	5	11352	32110	27978	350	4419
59	0	34522	82110	68648	1643	14421
289	11	20161	47762	41022	1926	16657
468	23	40140	42877	36483	1552	7918
27	0	863	4284	3448	350	1097
74	1	12907	38853	40706	940	6588
182	6	8902	30425	37377	892	3436
13	0	3546	6074	4306	569	1579
11	1	4018	6643	7598	131	1781
56	0	15562	25998	32379	1311	10715

初中专任教师学历、专

Number of Full-time Teachers in Junior Secondary Schools by

地 区 Region	合计 Total	其中:女 of Which:Female	按学历分 By Educational Attainment		
			研究生毕业 Graduate	本科毕业 Undergraduate	专科毕业 Associate Bachelor
总 计 Total	**1221327**	**794159**	**67278**	**1049240**	**104004**
北 京 Beijing	28301	22296	5423	22675	196
天 津 Tianjin	18582	14318	2227	15873	462
河 北 Hebei	52829	40281	2209	45676	4938
山 西 Shanxi	34628	25194	1175	29528	3896
内蒙古 Inner Mongolia	22312	16075	1603	18749	1958
辽 宁 Liaoning	52208	39411	2637	45704	3821
吉 林 Jilin	25476	18979	1178	22401	1890
黑龙江 Heilongjiang	39418	28326	1040	33981	4374
上 海 Shanghai	33343	25221	4014	28998	330
江 苏 Jiangsu	87105	52713	6655	78163	2266
浙 江 Zhejiang	61863	39353	2819	56785	2247
安 徽 Anhui	34384	17985	1049	29164	4154
福 建 Fujian	34011	21116	1727	29846	2416
江 西 Jiangxi	29880	16590	1045	23821	4981
山 东 Shandong	104262	65766	6200	91474	6522
河 南 Henan	70950	47880	3071	57644	10120
湖 北 Hubei	49985	27054	2316	39727	7848
湖 南 Hunan	41497	25667	2578	33978	4908
广 东 Guangdong	145595	90375	7495	124733	13345
广 西 Guangxi	30181	19659	1208	25281	3653
海 南 Hainan	9885	5885	166	8407	1301
重 庆 Chongqing	30317	17664	1577	27122	1585
四 川 Sichuan	52309	31427	1956	45296	5038
贵 州 Guizhou	25088	14918	463	21249	3304
云 南 Yunnan	23954	14971	1021	21020	1888
西 藏 Tibet	2286	1337	66	1991	223
陕 西 Shaanxi	30814	20908	2549	26484	1772
甘 肃 Gansu	16454	9287	715	13895	1843
青 海 Qinghai	4479	2859	146	3795	533
宁 夏 Ningxia	7375	4738	242	6755	374
新 疆 Xinjiang	21556	15906	708	19025	1818

业技术职务情况(城区)

Academic Qualifications and Professional Rank(Urban Area)

单位:人
unit:person

高中阶段毕业 High School Graduate	高中阶段毕业以下 Below High School Graduate	按专业技术职务分 By Professional Rank				
		中学高级 Senior Secondary	中学一级 1st Grade	中学二级 2nd Grade	中学三级 3rd Grade	未定职级 No-ranking
754	**51**	**271447**	**509522**	**314659**	**8169**	**117530**
7	0	7298	10198	8630	95	2080
20	0	6306	8472	3074	24	706
6	0	11353	23857	10367	550	6702
29	0	5440	12361	12466	276	4085
2	0	7907	7846	4322	0	2237
36	10	24503	19134	5550	160	2861
7	0	5713	11187	7075	30	1471
23	0	12313	18312	7276	133	1384
1	0	4022	17272	10197	63	1789
21	0	25119	39770	16893	18	5305
12	0	16716	26592	14048	112	4395
15	2	6573	12398	10020	587	4806
18	4	7083	13424	10561	151	2792
30	3	9806	10337	6615	197	2925
64	2	16245	44828	31965	496	10728
115	0	15183	27426	21371	765	6205
84	10	13486	23193	10031	525	2750
28	5	6188	19059	10402	288	5560
21	1	21168	63659	32994	1659	26115
34	5	5165	13844	7187	449	3536
11	0	1960	3400	3355	32	1138
32	1	5130	13184	10361	100	1542
19	0	10092	21259	17670	226	3062
66	6	4464	8912	7084	425	4203
23	2	6679	8509	5988	74	2704
6	0	353	1106	671	38	118
9	0	4617	11379	11852	234	2732
1	0	2932	6863	5941	112	606
5	0	1058	1734	1164	188	335
4	0	1650	2642	2395	105	583
5	0	4925	7365	7134	57	2075

初中专任教师学历、专业技
Number of Full-time Teachers in Junior Secondary Schools by Academic

地　区 Region	合计 Total	其中:女 of Which:Female	按学历分 By Educational Attainment		
			研究生毕业 Graduate	本科毕业 Undergraduate	专科毕业 Associate Bachelor
总　计 Total	**202316**	**120952**	**7457**	**171357**	**23310**
北　京 Beijing	2536	1850	348	2140	47
天　津 Tianjin	1282	899	116	1122	41
河　北 Hebei	12685	9551	334	10467	1882
山　西 Shanxi	3801	2649	99	3107	580
内蒙古 Inner Mongolia	304	227	30	255	19
辽　宁 Liaoning	4235	3035	233	3636	361
吉　林 Jilin	882	611	24	756	98
黑龙江 Heilongjiang	2911	2011	38	2385	479
上　海 Shanghai	2767	1971	350	2382	35
江　苏 Jiangsu	10442	5661	501	9624	315
浙　江 Zhejiang	14212	8481	491	13039	678
安　徽 Anhui	4952	2168	80	4096	776
福　建 Fujian	5074	2608	151	4460	461
江　西 Jiangxi	3271	1637	84	2507	678
山　东 Shandong	29201	17342	1287	25543	2349
河　南 Henan	10907	7263	324	8466	2074
湖　北 Hubei	6951	3557	173	5283	1481
湖　南 Hunan	5495	3118	327	4361	795
广　东 Guangdong	44811	25816	1602	37671	5529
广　西 Guangxi	5717	3575	109	4588	1011
海　南 Hainan	967	497	9	817	140
重　庆 Chongqing	3097	1502	72	2703	317
四　川 Sichuan	5993	3509	188	5230	575
贵　州 Guizhou	4079	2069	64	3323	678
云　南 Yunnan	6188	3543	144	5361	677
西　藏 Tibet	0	0	0	0	0
陕　西 Shaanxi	3665	2183	153	3230	282
甘　肃 Gansu	1175	547	41	961	173
青　海 Qinghai	835	459	16	654	163
宁　夏 Ningxia	748	460	11	702	33
新　疆 Xinjiang	3133	2153	58	2488	583

术职务情况(城乡结合区)

Qualifications and Professional Rank(Urban-rural Transitional Area)

单位:人
unit:person

		按专业技术职务分 By Professional Rank				
高中阶段毕业 High School Graduate	高中阶段毕业以下 Below High School Graduate	中学高级 Senior Secondary	中学一级 1st Grade	中学二级 2nd Grade	中学三级 3rd Grade	未定职级 No-ranking
185	**7**	**34291**	**83582**	**53434**	**2066**	**28943**
1	0	521	907	778	5	325
3	0	399	588	244	0	51
2	0	2225	5514	2756	78	2112
15	0	389	1181	1328	57	846
0	0	97	107	77	0	23
3	2	2138	1374	380	18	325
4	0	178	359	265	1	79
9	0	949	1355	551	34	22
0	0	329	1262	968	9	199
2	0	2589	4832	2283	0	738
4	0	3067	6366	3336	30	1413
0	0	790	1545	1533	178	906
2	0	1104	1909	1390	35	636
2	0	878	1102	804	15	472
20	2	3849	12156	9635	101	3460
43	0	1867	4111	3199	126	1604
14	0	1389	3240	1649	164	509
9	3	691	2576	1259	53	916
9	0	4280	19382	10008	639	10502
9	0	958	2843	1252	99	565
1	0	153	349	366	2	97
5	0	430	1278	1190	55	144
0	0	958	2321	2029	65	620
14	0	582	1473	1135	194	695
6	0	1936	2068	1457	30	697
0	0	0	0	0	0	0
0	0	477	1340	1530	22	296
0	0	157	488	432	0	98
2	0	178	395	203	24	35
2	0	144	213	280	1	110
4	0	589	948	1117	31	448

初中专任教师学历、专
Number of Full-time Teachers in Junior Secondary Schools by Academic

地 区 Region	合计 Total	其中:女 of Which:Female	按学历分 By Educational Attainment		
			研究生毕业 Graduate	本科毕业 Undergraduate	专科毕业 Associate Bachelor
总 计 Total	**1752616**	**905413**	**19820**	**1416314**	**312922**
北 京 Beijing	3380	2307	392	2933	55
天 津 Tianjin	5447	3027	87	5054	294
河 北 Hebei	99843	68887	1360	83478	14904
山 西 Shanxi	54335	36118	516	41753	11893
内蒙古 Inner Mongolia	31729	20479	674	27151	3903
辽 宁 Liaoning	35610	21911	346	29413	5756
吉 林 Jilin	25628	16638	646	21275	3685
黑龙江 Heilongjiang	36609	22578	162	30454	5931
上 海 Shanghai	4799	3071	429	4269	99
江 苏 Jiangsu	86287	39398	2220	79581	4440
浙 江 Zhejiang	51141	28036	941	47493	2671
安 徽 Anhui	84757	34141	969	69121	14657
福 建 Fujian	47606	19879	363	40503	6680
江 西 Jiangxi	64506	26307	467	46027	17900
山 东 Shandong	145628	73295	2926	120430	21983
河 南 Henan	160095	98610	2072	118596	38751
湖 北 Hubei	61150	24902	365	42742	17621
湖 南 Hunan	92543	46598	867	70116	21359
广 东 Guangdong	105821	51916	502	87312	17927
广 西 Guangxi	81285	40398	298	64322	16333
海 南 Hainan	13944	5713	61	10628	3202
重 庆 Chongqing	39402	17648	248	34702	4367
四 川 Sichuan	113598	53453	725	85938	26902
贵 州 Guizhou	80990	32485	256	64114	16455
云 南 Yunnan	66392	32257	258	55716	10137
西 藏 Tibet	6065	2949	77	5292	677
陕 西 Shaanxi	59663	32725	761	51937	6907
甘 肃 Gansu	42801	18223	377	34893	7427
青 海 Qinghai	8212	4489	183	6573	1448
宁 夏 Ningxia	9434	4932	95	8424	911
新 疆 Xinjiang	33916	22043	177	26074	7647

业技术职务情况(镇区)

Qualifications and Professional Rank(Counties & Towns Area)

单位:人
unit:person

高中阶段毕业 High School Graduate	高中阶段毕业以下 Below High School Graduate	按专业技术职务分 By Professional Rank 中学高级 Senior Secondary	中学一级 1st Grade	中学二级 2nd Grade	中学三级 3rd Grade	未定职级 No-ranking
3415	**145**	**310142**	**758234**	**518470**	**18862**	**146908**
0	0	729	1231	1053	21	346
12	0	1667	2840	773	11	156
69	32	17594	43638	25761	1408	11442
170	3	4768	17424	25089	795	6259
1	0	9725	14266	5619	0	2119
81	14	17662	12417	4156	254	1121
22	0	4529	10888	8076	152	1983
62	0	8002	18448	8813	180	1166
2	0	422	2435	1630	10	302
46	0	20336	42574	18696	45	4636
36	0	11395	23709	12861	118	3058
10	0	14176	31336	25207	1383	12655
59	1	10015	21536	13996	261	1798
108	4	19175	24526	14502	578	5725
279	10	19809	64379	47247	760	13433
676	0	25436	60178	51657	2807	20017
408	14	9850	34344	13018	1167	2771
192	9	11257	44875	25568	808	10035
55	25	9453	59761	27520	2079	7008
319	13	9371	43891	19788	1134	7101
52	1	2499	5716	5331	47	351
82	3	5528	16572	15137	230	1935
33	0	18976	47238	38684	959	7741
162	3	13127	32057	25624	1048	9134
269	12	22866	22735	17316	716	2759
19	0	407	2415	2198	253	792
58	0	7252	23606	24895	551	3359
104	0	4245	16164	20651	357	1384
8	0	1758	3111	2202	297	844
3	1	1804	3169	3637	22	802
18	0	6309	10755	11765	411	4676

初中专任教师学历、专业技
Number of Full-time Teachers in Junior Secondary Schools by Academic

地　区 Region	合计 Total	其中：女 of Which: Female	按学历分 By Educational Attainment 研究生毕业 Graduate	 本科毕业 Undergraduate	 专科毕业 Associate Bachelor
总　计 Total	**421670**	**227455**	**5626**	**340982**	**74153**
北　京 Beijing	1182	793	148	1022	12
天　津 Tianjin	2307	1355	32	2120	146
河　北 Hebei	45174	31339	673	37409	7021
山　西 Shanxi	15381	10772	161	11706	3464
内蒙古 Inner Mongolia	2783	1756	35	2313	435
辽　宁 Liaoning	4270	2698	30	3479	750
吉　林 Jilin	2686	1695	168	2109	400
黑龙江 Heilongjiang	3437	2059	24	2796	606
上　海 Shanghai	1145	736	78	1038	28
江　苏 Jiangsu	21233	9787	466	19695	1058
浙　江 Zhejiang	15722	8580	343	14561	810
安　徽 Anhui	17925	7175	235	14355	3331
福　建 Fujian	13161	5596	72	11348	1728
江　西 Jiangxi	10613	4283	41	7193	3364
山　东 Shandong	54962	28255	1121	45976	7756
河　南 Henan	50607	32141	793	37097	12523
湖　北 Hubei	14093	5702	57	9932	3973
湖　南 Hunan	20494	10256	186	15536	4731
广　东 Guangdong	31049	16061	189	25593	5257
广　西 Guangxi	16813	8514	62	13277	3403
海　南 Hainan	1347	662	18	1136	191
重　庆 Chongqing	6419	2834	53	5695	650
四　川 Sichuan	15412	7455	211	11534	3659
贵　州 Guizhou	12298	5105	79	9812	2359
云　南 Yunnan	12434	6451	52	10623	1725
西　藏 Tibet	639	299	2	584	53
陕　西 Shaanxi	11587	6488	190	9964	1425
甘　肃 Gansu	8070	3547	53	6596	1411
青　海 Qinghai	1682	867	30	1366	283
宁　夏 Ningxia	1086	560	3	976	106
新　疆 Xinjiang	5659	3634	21	4141	1495

术职务情况(镇乡结合区)

Qualifications and Professional Rank(County-town Transitional Area)

单位:人
unit:person

高中阶段毕业 High School Graduate	高中阶段毕业以下 Below High School Graduate	按专业技术职务分 By Professional Rank				
		中学高级 Senior Secondary	中学一级 1st Grade	中学二级 2nd Grade	中学三级 3rd Grade	未定职级 No-ranking
854	**55**	**67711**	**180226**	**125072**	**4996**	**43665**
0	0	265	422	352	1	142
9	0	734	1208	286	11	68
39	32	7514	19101	12386	590	5583
50	0	1257	4614	6508	384	2618
0	0	974	1250	417	0	142
11	0	1852	1626	458	34	300
9	0	547	1152	706	7	274
11	0	820	1709	754	46	108
1	0	107	566	363	2	107
14	0	5155	10243	4823	4	1008
8	0	3308	7216	4111	51	1036
4	0	2773	6042	4974	501	3635
13	0	2662	5724	4030	97	648
14	1	2735	3936	2350	139	1453
108	1	7230	23573	17997	335	5827
194	0	7359	18443	16116	825	7864
123	8	2170	7885	3177	223	638
35	6	2489	10027	5690	120	2168
10	0	2830	16647	7912	575	3085
71	0	1922	9244	4251	182	1214
1	1	204	506	588	3	46
19	2	845	2615	2542	24	393
8	0	2206	6527	5312	101	1266
48	0	1577	4902	3862	216	1741
31	3	4347	4588	3048	86	365
0	0	55	270	213	60	41
8	0	1406	4533	4741	139	768
10	0	845	2979	3927	75	244
3	0	422	631	431	95	103
0	1	193	372	407	7	107
2	0	908	1675	2340	63	673

初中专任教师学历、专业

Number of Full-time Teachers in Junior Secondary Schools by

地　区 Region	合计 Total	其中：女 of Which：Female	按学历分 By Educational Attainment		
			研究生毕业 Graduate	本科毕业 Undergraduate	专科毕业 Associate Bachelor
总　计 Total	**574745**	**274873**	**5313**	**445173**	**122591**
北　京 Beijing	2770	1831	250	2477	43
天　津 Tianjin	2840	1464	33	2625	171
河　北 Hebei	34877	22033	363	28839	5648
山　西 Shanxi	19320	11559	257	14323	4572
内蒙古 Inner Mongolia	3563	2160	95	3016	452
辽　宁 Liaoning	11664	6976	240	9558	1833
吉　林 Jilin	13533	7998	115	11321	2077
黑龙江 Heilongjiang	13645	7280	38	10959	2600
上　海 Shanghai	1134	755	147	973	14
江　苏 Jiangsu	8467	3619	170	7775	514
浙　江 Zhejiang	11695	6207	234	10737	714
安　徽 Anhui	36354	12069	259	28636	7437
福　建 Fujian	18263	6306	137	15413	2688
江　西 Jiangxi	26182	9319	89	18238	7807
山　东 Shandong	26003	11845	490	21631	3808
河　南 Henan	67961	37560	720	49420	17407
湖　北 Hubei	17899	6645	118	12475	5200
湖　南 Hunan	37553	17088	208	26565	10672
广　东 Guangdong	28405	14345	319	22945	5133
广　西 Guangxi	18290	8329	58	13578	4553
海　南 Hainan	2103	934	42	1586	464
重　庆 Chongqing	6490	2970	39	5631	779
四　川 Sichuan	35437	15369	162	24531	10737
贵　州 Guizhou	21450	8259	72	16828	4487
云　南 Yunnan	38624	17840	135	32281	6023
西　藏 Tibet	1691	821	27	1410	252
陕　西 Shaanxi	9517	4636	142	8179	1188
甘　肃 Gansu	21777	7610	158	17390	4146
青　海 Qinghai	3383	1488	44	2664	675
宁　夏 Ningxia	3362	1616	53	2942	363
新　疆 Xinjiang	30493	17942	99	20227	10134

技术职务情况(乡村)
Academic Qualifications and Professional Rank(Rural Area)

单位:人
unit:person

		按专业技术职务分 By Professional Rank				
高中阶段毕业 High School Graduate	高中阶段毕业以下 Below High School Graduate	中学高级 Senior Secondary	中学一级 1st Grade	中学二级 2nd Grade	中学三级 3rd Grade	未定职级 No-ranking
1614	**54**	**92357**	**227597**	**185866**	**8558**	**60367**
0	0	606	937	965	12	250
11	0	872	1571	327	1	69
27	0	5720	15216	9164	590	4187
166	2	1215	5693	9045	482	2885
0	0	917	1336	832	0	478
28	5	5339	4047	1734	96	448
19	1	1919	5608	4618	115	1273
46	2	2536	6674	3727	56	652
0	0	113	478	407	12	124
8	0	1778	4278	1987	1	423
10	0	2015	5561	3257	19	843
22	0	5968	14535	11515	453	3883
25	0	3816	8044	5752	68	583
45	3	6604	8506	6939	326	3807
69	5	3150	11426	9028	179	2220
414	0	10640	26411	21496	1140	8274
104	2	2804	9634	4078	302	1081
103	5	4509	17259	10777	382	4626
8	0	1983	14191	7465	720	4046
91	10	1745	9108	4326	340	2771
11	0	307	723	851	3	219
40	1	694	2354	2480	20	942
7	0	5454	13613	12294	458	3618
61	2	2570	6793	8314	453	3320
176	9	10595	11633	13179	762	2455
2	0	103	763	579	59	187
7	1	1038	3868	3959	155	497
77	6	1725	7398	10785	423	1446
0	0	730	1229	940	84	400
4	0	564	832	1566	4	396
33	0	4328	7878	13480	843	3964

初中办学条

Condition of School Buildings in

地 区 Region	校舍建筑面积 Floor Space	教学及辅助用房 Teaching & Assistant Buildings							行政办公用房 Administrative	
		合计 Total	其中：of Which：						合计 Total	其中：教师办公室 of Which：for Teachers
			教室 Classroom	实验室 Laboratory	图书室 Library	微机室 PC-room	语音室 Linguistic	体育馆 Gymnasium		
总 计 Total	**610067403.78**	**248326031.15**	**168552069.38**	**38525205.80**	**15224327.83**	**11202861.55**	**3807316.64**	**11014249.95**	**52413298.69**	**31472625.71**
北 京 Beijing	4220523.64	1709199.47	1059476.88	302143.11	101554.60	78107.11	9895.98	158021.79	557608.37	267117.20
天 津 Tianjin	2798901.88	1335901.58	900405.09	194459.28	82939.25	51601.47	23126.80	83369.69	414244.80	252027.71
河 北 Hebei	27895471.84	11595258.49	7872430.85	2100476.39	713453.80	519328.37	163590.58	225978.50	2177670.45	1485482.91
山 西 Shanxi	15650063.51	5584401.11	3967947.55	794240.95	361536.92	275425.14	85817.74	99432.81	1584034.87	1058825.24
内蒙古 Inner Mongolia	9841701.81	4431947.52	2852746.13	606233.85	255337.99	184231.46	59566.21	473831.88	1040632.39	674550.89
辽 宁 Liaoning	14691541.21	6401031.81	4209888.04	968584.15	349107.92	332370.94	137393.59	403687.17	1856177.95	1073307.35
吉 林 Jilin	8355435.09	3793883.35	2519689.01	589285.78	248839.54	217076.89	99066.48	119925.65	970329.71	626346.85
黑龙江 Heilongjiang	11100344.23	5119327.82	3489681.83	825015.64	216388.93	206321.14	117335.50	264584.78	1388020.17	897175.07
上 海 Shanghai	7646617.59	3737353.96	1995415.99	768592.52	259256.89	167498.16	52772.47	493817.93	946772.73	464787.61
江 苏 Jiangsu	36729060.98	17258816.51	10301706.18	3062393.71	1484573.97	910820.06	286323.04	1212999.55	3831244.99	2024848.07
浙 江 Zhejiang	30130305.49	12896450.50	7925478.83	1799764.82	855600.79	522314.12	156555.61	1636736.33	2653743.87	1467770.54
安 徽 Anhui	27662772.48	12428754.74	9031506.31	1656944.16	681982.88	595365.55	166272.12	296683.72	2355421.02	1421315.97
福 建 Fujian	12594283.98	5063052.34	3202069.55	996906.93	388578.71	201240.64	45771.91	228484.60	1068476.03	498638.24
江 西 Jiangxi	21404002.30	8439759.51	6064666.88	1118333.91	493521.41	355001.69	135693.39	272542.23	1825449.60	988484.07
山 东 Shandong	48120707.09	19252979.37	11867483.20	3844889.28	1457315.65	912951.79	312629.16	857710.29	4833652.93	2722241.91
河 南 Henan	51332024.49	18141278.33	13570503.07	2446287.19	940769.67	740487.64	235306.02	207924.74	4913764.92	3270277.73
湖 北 Hubei	25165660.35	8785592.39	6086684.41	1293177.47	515074.87	429443.75	182001.67	279210.22	1895060.07	1138946.97
湖 南 Hunan	33182776.19	12429597.53	8494278.23	1857361.81	780765.86	537984.66	265666.21	493540.76	2359166.78	1539666.27
广 东 Guangdong	55099720.40	24746101.07	17207171.17	3340414.18	1339417.95	883561.96	410439.75	1565096.06	3741325.18	2223123.19
广 西 Guangxi	24189452.58	9176431.60	6727302.79	1349192.96	459619.57	348352.94	76993.90	214969.44	1078158.00	724758.54
海 南 Hainan	4267558.14	1728369.13	1302176.76	218466.28	98077.42	67050.16	24358.97	18239.54	220995.30	139793.44
重 庆 Chongqing	11774970.99	4322740.68	3180716.94	630354.29	199757.59	159019.59	37866.85	115025.42	867801.83	471976.06
四 川 Sichuan	34261706.74	14648892.02	10593917.97	2171161.52	812295.90	645009.46	177542.32	248964.85	2217787.25	1382526.28
贵 州 Guizhou	22497641.14	7525543.03	5395412.18	1063448.52	441610.58	360022.62	82410.41	182638.72	1425756.22	826989.94
云 南 Yunnan	20289087.40	7127557.29	4916014.62	1133281.97	439500.29	413846.75	100304.05	124609.61	1144474.19	660719.56
西 藏 Tibet	2167701.07	648607.89	472972.24	76617.78	24525.52	28544.67	10378.08	35569.60	123582.15	97141.57
陕 西 Shaanxi	14835139.20	5678466.68	3707430.10	956382.60	380171.76	319587.54	194397.98	120496.70	1664917.66	1113025.62
甘 肃 Gansu	11616794.34	4816861.73	3343486.07	785806.96	307575.34	262864.44	48065.63	69063.29	1138185.47	781975.69
青 海 Qinghai	3441262.66	1383372.54	870535.24	217435.48	97909.41	66238.33	23910.72	107343.36	266690.58	164938.08
宁 夏 Ningxia	3442711.68	1608704.26	1019444.49	336877.55	91274.40	93521.63	15258.79	52327.40	326292.22	202303.54
新 疆 Xinjiang	13661463.29	6509796.90	4403430.78	1020674.76	345992.45	317670.88	70604.71	351423.32	1525860.99	811543.60

件(一)(总计)
Junior Secondary Schools (1) (Total)

单位:平方米
unit: m²

生活用房 Residential and Welfare							其他用房 Rooms for Other Purposes	校舍面积中 of the Floor Space	
合计 Total	教工宿舍 Apartments for Single		学生宿舍 Students' Dormitories	食堂 Dining Halls	厕所 Toilet	其他 Others		危房面积 Floor Space of Dilapidated Buildings	当年新增校舍 New Floor Space Added in Current Year
	小计 Subtotal	其中:教师周转宿舍 of Which: Accommodation for Circulation of Teachers							
254748980.67	**56885870.33**	**16408703.60**	**110442376.05**	**48719633.76**	**18689754.66**	**20011345.87**	**54579093.27**	**3922258.47**	**33397915.05**
988341.74	136075.77	8335.21	188671.43	257538.26	187652.37	218403.91	965374.06	300.00	120363.31
503892.94	46360.01	12741.41	41956.77	123036.12	117884.37	174655.67	544862.56	0	161706.36
11749615.78	1348348.70	414178.23	6299646.78	2373972.90	773285.98	954361.42	2372927.12	3850.01	2553843.33
6533770.54	1047038.70	146544.00	3126274.11	1270908.98	488770.29	600778.46	1947856.99	51600.10	519495.97
3497482.06	240376.23	130920.20	1808640.65	747899.55	360970.44	339595.19	871639.84	0	410250.75
3948484.94	177908.60	70168.30	1228681.84	1195699.18	529359.68	816835.64	2485846.51	25285.00	597175.06
2385578.97	103807.79	60863.24	853755.64	645766.78	297350.73	484898.03	1205643.06	740.00	353758.46
2925816.98	121450.49	73752.69	1099451.74	592623.64	398461.48	713829.63	1667179.26	53349.71	452453.68
1560212.93	46851.39	6386.98	131846.75	552182.86	326481.64	502850.29	1402277.97	0	238862.34
12232075.16	1645595.21	275413.57	4321524.12	3546111.45	1090907.96	1627936.42	3406924.32	0	1161367.52
11158174.65	1745898.70	254991.34	4282974.24	2913075.14	960083.17	1256143.40	3421936.47	0	1517213.15
10767166.55	2650550.27	792902.85	4606553.90	2080467.99	778677.92	650916.47	2111430.17	50204.00	1233879.96
4949160.67	1730168.13	278020.75	1691931.58	815007.90	357225.21	354827.85	1513594.94	98384.80	317438.05
9587718.86	2484376.88	665724.68	4145416.63	1771318.81	631337.10	555269.44	1551074.33	120403.80	1819753.91
18107014.31	2537598.11	693383.77	7823284.34	4215454.98	1723918.94	1806757.94	5927060.48	2430.00	3952538.97
25009249.08	4229090.42	878386.59	12801585.87	5031557.58	1705166.31	1241848.90	3267732.16	80148.18	2604988.42
12545894.21	4927381.26	962702.01	4382069.43	1879027.64	601544.20	755871.68	1939113.68	103312.00	928102.55
15992142.97	5424248.96	1536508.44	5878599.25	2754228.09	871577.66	1063489.01	2401868.91	240462.00	1263371.62
20533891.16	6590947.61	988333.53	7675785.63	2859368.09	1601755.34	1806034.49	6078402.99	23599.82	1442890.66
13342562.92	3764215.51	1222288.55	6952744.09	1869891.50	491161.50	264550.32	592300.06	343998.42	1714291.11
2138970.93	831393.40	283362.68	873673.15	275413.26	110487.33	48003.79	179222.78	38528.00	126629.18
5668417.20	1273484.71	359924.37	2878724.87	992742.24	288364.13	235101.25	916011.28	58888.42	327413.68
15541630.85	4382583.31	1817811.58	6691774.14	2670191.50	1039186.12	757895.78	1853396.62	91285.12	2688310.83
12149416.72	2511835.88	1547070.30	6666658.90	1745071.12	711210.10	514640.72	1396925.17	295.00	2230566.51
11148103.53	2573732.56	1029285.33	5588227.98	1948678.42	554329.84	483134.73	868952.39	1585627.84	1427843.94
1353551.43	511508.52	446925.17	588352.56	148323.55	28370.72	76996.08	41959.60	0	75508.53
6175358.47	1742752.57	345334.33	2344252.15	1087875.89	520439.83	480038.03	1316396.39	3162.05	1027710.65
4683064.01	910746.98	335203.49	2005499.09	832355.47	432838.04	501624.43	978683.13	941185.20	816981.83
1402743.80	254902.31	161635.43	590131.46	269448.85	119377.59	168883.59	388455.74	0	153288.82
1248802.78	170597.51	82022.71	604531.15	242182.68	136870.40	94621.04	258912.42	5219.00	146976.07
4920673.53	724043.84	527581.87	2269155.81	1012213.34	454708.27	460552.27	705131.87	0	1012939.83

初中办学条
Condition of School Buildings in Junior

地 区 Region	校舍建筑面积 Floor Space	教学及辅助用房 Teaching & Assistant Buildings							行政办公用房 Administrative	
		合计 Total	其中: of Which:						合计 Total	其中:教师办公室 of Which: for Teachers
			教室 Classroom	实验室 Laboratory	图书室 Library	微机室 PC-room	语音室 Linguistic	体育馆 Gymnasium		
总 计 Total	**189434053.11**	**87182865.12**	**56658185.93**	**13027733.54**	**5632486.56**	**3608754.75**	**1271669.04**	**6984035.30**	**19906835.78**	**11389624.07**
北 京 Beijing	2819828.00	1210799.54	759476.57	190990.14	73324.61	53825.45	6292.33	126890.44	375966.76	181987.79
天 津 Tianjin	1827226.97	825384.61	526017.06	121815.40	57576.05	31093.37	12671.00	76211.73	265297.12	161899.65
河 北 Hebei	6071254.10	2839712.69	1902834.92	486503.46	194570.74	120834.49	33952.26	101016.82	636554.53	433343.25
山 西 Shanxi	3516641.66	1463852.81	992894.58	224609.00	107510.18	67135.61	24539.96	47163.48	440295.60	283237.40
内蒙古 Inner Mongolia	3122013.42	1710443.19	1122551.77	224776.75	100457.47	61296.72	14809.97	186550.51	395745.77	244608.63
辽 宁 Liaoning	7156389.99	3105269.88	1929951.13	452973.71	175369.93	149398.47	66329.51	331247.13	946033.92	502914.04
吉 林 Jilin	2953953.35	1472520.38	986215.81	192973.32	89760.76	73396.79	34919.11	95254.59	383569.17	227422.34
黑龙江 Heilongjiang	4077387.92	1939909.74	1269908.43	274743.76	81018.94	75254.30	46108.21	192876.10	593074.30	353744.77
上 海 Shanghai	6121935.27	2996752.66	1603418.77	604593.23	200844.61	132623.79	46240.07	409032.19	762090.47	371609.29
江 苏 Jiangsu	17486273.29	8481901.05	4849235.68	1517170.32	778699.86	396915.38	116232.03	823647.78	2066484.50	1049227.31
浙 江 Zhejiang	14871324.99	6714320.90	3982962.32	890732.27	470814.00	258751.17	81263.57	1029797.57	1406270.08	768938.66
安 徽 Anhui	5227259.60	2712579.21	1902065.60	361073.42	145132.10	119221.64	31460.18	153626.27	613784.67	359476.41
福 建 Fujian	3638481.83	1638783.83	1006983.52	281503.20	135869.17	57617.04	17137.54	139673.36	352998.60	168458.99
江 西 Jiangxi	4169602.09	1997194.02	1402051.37	221162.47	113407.66	72486.85	32963.45	155122.22	422115.62	236043.92
山 东 Shandong	17806355.97	7844287.34	4748725.02	1460671.36	579397.03	371382.37	129426.70	554684.86	2137694.33	1161334.46
河 南 Henan	10686647.62	4507897.38	3238822.90	675517.34	245592.65	179696.55	55950.30	112317.64	1350723.41	851720.08
湖 北 Hubei	7925610.38	3381108.44	2333368.89	486047.07	191619.34	146584.59	54423.97	169064.58	823028.08	483465.05
湖 南 Hunan	6044361.49	2549203.75	1645639.56	350340.65	163470.16	96578.43	46341.22	246833.73	487287.86	295691.83
广 东 Guangdong	29555299.74	13917392.22	9426383.41	1812952.74	786924.90	475920.46	217162.74	1198047.97	2129222.85	1269410.39
广 西 Guangxi	4612660.98	2216307.97	1581855.02	290470.65	114208.55	79703.21	22151.22	127919.32	341229.67	210551.65
海 南 Hainan	1149879.50	511016.40	401607.44	49479.43	28079.39	17513.95	7112.19	7224.00	66660.42	43235.62
重 庆 Chongqing	3787691.27	1643225.02	1206102.93	205083.39	76610.57	54814.60	13919.73	86693.80	350620.92	179235.90
四 川 Sichuan	6797998.80	3332586.82	2368720.34	445296.49	185549.65	133034.91	47534.58	152450.85	569035.30	347878.49
贵 州 Guizhou	4029324.61	1578802.01	1067855.94	236583.89	111431.81	66648.58	18096.52	78185.27	394588.65	231291.68
云 南 Yunnan	2940244.97	1230647.21	822749.72	166657.56	90793.70	64006.68	19703.06	66736.49	249859.59	137137.34
西 藏 Tibet	395828.38	126250.45	87981.21	18927.71	4073.03	5289.25	2410.25	7569.00	34268.39	28423.39
陕 西 Shaanxi	3660016.56	1530729.09	1028621.84	228413.96	93185.34	74795.58	35523.27	70189.10	447045.37	308325.16
甘 肃 Gansu	1853916.23	951930.63	641820.96	146348.04	70019.33	43810.71	10403.39	39528.20	229027.15	152701.40
青 海 Qinghai	772111.30	350913.70	218020.17	54862.32	29108.66	18153.88	6733.60	24035.07	81938.23	43431.62
宁 夏 Ningxia	995650.91	528608.63	329879.50	107220.69	28989.86	27009.14	4490.64	31018.80	108521.18	66545.15
新 疆 Xinjiang	3360881.92	1872533.55	1273463.55	247239.80	109076.51	83960.79	15366.47	143426.43	445803.27	236332.41

件(一)(城区)

Secondary Schools (1)(Urban Area)

单位:平方米
unit: m^2

生活用房 Residential and Welfare: 合计 Total	生活用房 Residential and Welfare: 教工宿舍 Apartments for Single: 小计 Subtotal	生活用房 Residential and Welfare: 教工宿舍 Apartments for Single: 其中:教师周转宿舍 of Which: Accommodation for Circulation of Teachers	生活用房 Residential and Welfare: 学生宿舍 Students' Dormitories	生活用房 Residential and Welfare: 食堂 Dining Halls	生活用房 Residential and Welfare: 厕所 Toilet	生活用房 Residential and Welfare: 其他 Others	其他用房 Rooms for Other Purposes	校舍面积中 of the Floor Space: 危房面积 Floor Space of Dilapidated Buildings	校舍面积中 of the Floor Space: 当年新增校舍 New Floor Space Added in Current Year
57142939.23	**9125806.28**	**1750621.58**	**20646500.94**	**12502821.99**	**6605439.61**	**8262370.41**	**25201412.98**	**677966.53**	**9328700.06**
554540.54	61868.52	4778.26	90218.21	155958.70	125618.72	120876.39	678521.16	300.00	117467.82
329911.41	17601.49	4836.00	40207.57	87069.66	75295.09	109737.60	406633.83	0	104233.18
1872742.48	123621.78	15038.91	893515.77	339959.53	177777.67	337867.73	722244.40	2437.99	533263.03
1029026.37	158166.70	21211.78	405301.17	184942.11	110166.61	170449.78	583466.88	4091.00	114904.70
648121.79	35787.29	240.00	280368.04	134900.59	119807.70	77258.17	367702.67	0	179866.84
1549531.27	58132.37	12388.80	293821.03	472340.32	272148.80	453088.75	1555554.92	9112.00	255937.93
662543.53	15672.71	177.00	168710.64	185160.86	113289.37	179709.95	435320.27	0	71825.08
769564.29	14880.37	2904.94	169921.68	120103.68	162518.55	302140.01	774839.59	17725.00	122734.79
1214299.68	26252.29	1149.55	94659.86	413717.28	257780.57	421889.68	1148792.46	0	121948.44
4846078.10	405517.12	72876.58	1416675.77	1611034.65	546424.25	866426.31	2091809.64	0	579790.32
4756688.53	575848.30	96317.13	1627005.10	1401856.23	479401.68	672577.22	1994045.48	0	823960.44
1220403.53	154767.08	10739.01	431393.15	242575.53	184208.71	207459.06	680492.19	2715.00	221816.20
996802.37	238501.88	54923.97	308709.78	198744.69	128721.48	122124.54	649897.03	6473.80	112282.25
1229184.48	200172.55	52144.85	341829.41	307338.37	158516.52	221327.63	521107.97	7164.00	236654.26
5052595.03	604776.07	148616.51	1774911.22	1277961.87	684077.33	710868.54	2771779.27	0	1466583.73
3883501.07	484420.39	68616.30	1912659.11	736500.71	385304.83	364616.03	944525.76	29488.73	379583.25
2707197.71	852860.96	149357.15	826694.77	460947.70	226396.66	340297.62	1014276.15	25420.00	382536.70
2411128.57	572432.88	134208.63	929299.68	518347.74	189487.77	201560.50	596741.31	41028.00	255370.01
9600807.01	2452262.46	337268.75	3516731.00	1525245.84	973229.02	1133338.69	3907877.66	5866.00	1039912.63
1855779.67	425699.46	118942.56	957066.05	272130.07	133744.45	67139.64	199343.67	28136.00	230626.36
497058.41	206409.05	42878.95	170756.69	58927.00	36447.67	24518.00	75144.27	8700.00	30672.00
1344963.55	118587.17	28861.65	695984.54	299889.59	111454.31	119047.94	448881.78	7500.63	130516.90
2336952.20	353680.94	69502.81	1048158.27	497029.59	246467.08	191616.32	559424.48	1959.00	454422.20
1559289.19	264713.58	81209.28	738274.93	246367.12	163879.14	146054.42	496644.76	0	501171.39
1154618.33	228740.45	67760.84	468400.13	205304.37	108249.39	143923.99	305119.84	262653.78	156694.13
225094.52	91161.59	71102.59	74755.24	20362.91	5188.22	33626.56	10215.02	0	14608.99
1154251.73	237408.65	23704.52	347405.94	208918.41	154102.28	206416.45	527990.37	791.00	297009.85
435301.03	41618.96	12601.30	145151.34	62189.87	84110.42	102230.44	237657.42	216404.60	92945.99
168828.13	27944.44	12070.00	35064.00	26374.50	35400.54	44044.65	170431.24	0	31963.36
249914.35	14909.96	710.11	114190.08	49802.10	41675.33	29336.88	108606.75	0	44450.39
826220.36	61388.82	33482.85	328660.77	180820.40	114549.45	140800.92	216324.74	0	222946.90

初中办学条件
Condition of School Buildings in Junior Secondary

地区 Region	校舍建筑面积 Floor Space	教学及辅助用房 Teaching & Assistant Buildings							行政办公用房 Administrative	
		合计 Total	其中: of Which:						合计 Total	其中:教师办公室 of Which: for Teachers
			教室 Classroom	实验室 Laboratory	图书室 Library	微机室 PC-room	语音室 Linguistic	体育馆 Gymnasium		
总　计 Total	**39542593.83**	**17105955.95**	**11252286.14**	**2543775.81**	**1049478.88**	**707637.29**	**255363.56**	**1297414.27**	**3476851.93**	**1980228.31**
北　京 Beijing	381531.89	161807.12	99737.38	24924.51	9165.58	6992.70	256.00	20730.95	47188.83	23225.28
天　津 Tianjin	180894.26	75972.55	51103.82	10945.50	3141.42	2529.50	1537.50	6714.81	23018.14	11177.80
河　北 Hebei	1928816.34	891090.17	607508.65	153664.14	53299.15	36750.63	11168.22	28699.38	153427.19	112086.24
山　西 Shanxi	410422.43	137704.68	94268.92	19375.05	9973.90	6208.48	1593.00	6285.33	40088.13	30322.63
内蒙古 Inner Mongolia	99855.00	36468.00	14199.00	8774.00	3180.00	1357.00	348.00	8610.00	13245.00	6077.00
辽　宁 Liaoning	780147.99	283352.82	165701.76	49329.56	15284.37	12988.61	4179.34	35869.18	81041.81	47439.24
吉　林 Jilin	102830.01	46102.10	33521.02	6574.02	2338.02	2505.02	1164.02	0	16037.02	9504.02
黑龙江 Heilongjiang	341776.51	136876.04	80066.57	20456.92	6092.93	4456.47	2569.15	23234.00	34249.28	18532.18
上　海 Shanghai	608557.81	286564.90	149165.90	60654.98	22552.78	11949.42	6247.85	35993.97	74934.05	30774.56
江　苏 Jiangsu	2182502.58	1022999.79	621589.73	189272.87	80404.13	50276.98	13064.21	68391.87	272846.62	138669.92
浙　江 Zhejiang	3707923.58	1687377.35	1048752.56	204771.85	114436.86	63551.95	20784.69	235079.44	314374.63	169792.44
安　徽 Anhui	671982.13	358662.06	266193.54	40235.53	18702.42	15827.55	3542.02	14161.00	72066.68	43093.71
福　建 Fujian	734788.61	302729.00	195604.80	48504.03	23205.03	11213.03	3714.04	20488.07	63116.26	38042.30
江　西 Jiangxi	821811.96	310086.01	220755.05	26814.11	17723.01	9970.54	5009.30	29814.00	68598.20	28359.89
山　东 Shandong	5937855.65	2465148.13	1436766.82	461605.12	193894.39	117914.36	47750.75	207216.69	592648.61	341555.44
河　南 Henan	2237880.07	750621.53	520991.46	118554.46	47992.82	37178.47	10693.15	15211.17	235416.26	139233.27
湖　北 Hubei	1094130.67	413942.21	284203.85	50136.11	23221.39	17529.46	5004.00	33847.40	99696.32	47475.00
湖　南 Hunan	845544.12	354445.47	240605.78	47382.16	18411.59	15363.61	8969.10	23713.23	66838.88	43395.81
广　东 Guangdong	10708436.53	4999115.00	3452714.74	670400.92	253673.62	179022.69	74232.63	369070.40	731011.26	428284.10
广　西 Guangxi	912093.05	393442.30	285921.20	54175.06	17987.68	12469.89	3112.84	19775.63	49769.23	27694.85
海　南 Hainan	121557.10	47486.10	39341.00	2976.80	3073.00	1493.30	96.00	506.00	5617.00	2930.00
重　庆 Chongqing	527820.10	202505.55	161309.50	20470.47	9115.41	5219.11	1763.26	4627.80	35489.62	20619.11
四　川 Sichuan	905635.81	459770.90	317086.02	57566.04	27677.22	21479.63	8759.04	27202.95	67627.71	38878.53
贵　州 Guizhou	893153.10	290231.04	200522.38	40524.11	12144.44	11384.85	3625.56	22029.70	65834.42	30522.61
云　南 Yunnan	794759.78	309563.12	201183.14	46872.00	21282.90	17213.16	6784.00	16227.92	61184.74	33331.70
西　藏 Tibet	0	0	0	0	0	0	0	0	0	0
陕　西 Shaanxi	665998.72	223856.98	145024.01	39712.39	15389.08	12526.57	6530.93	4674.00	87775.14	57824.74
甘　肃 Gansu	189157.18	93207.00	63761.00	14021.00	9891.00	4601.00	389.00	544.00	21204.00	13787.00
青　海 Qinghai	174505.63	78901.10	56474.30	9775.60	5047.00	3278.20	520.40	3805.60	16720.40	10843.20
宁　夏 Ningxia	113318.64	53361.06	37636.76	9506.23	1503.92	2134.15	180.00	2400.00	10170.46	5516.57
新　疆 Xinjiang	466906.58	232565.87	160575.48	35800.27	9673.82	12250.96	1775.56	12489.78	55616.04	31239.17

(一)(城乡结合区)
Schools (1)(Urban-rural Transitional Area)

单位:平方米
unit: m^2

生活用房 Residential and Welfare							其他用房 Rooms for Other Purposes	校舍面积中 of the Floor Space	
合计 Total	教工宿舍 Apartments for Single: 小计 Subtotal	其中:教师周转宿舍 of Which: Accommodation for Circulation of Teachers	学生宿舍 Students' Dormitories	食堂 Dining Halls	厕所 Toilet	其他 Others		危房面积 Floor Space of Dilapidated Buildings	当年新增校舍 New Floor Space Added in Current Year
14342684.12	**2528430.94**	**469883.90**	**5848819.68**	**3071813.41**	**1356374.66**	**1537245.43**	**4617101.83**	**102072.63**	**2531832.17**
96133.24	12406.15	2224.00	17722.40	22462.96	19559.98	23981.75	76402.70	0	14305.73
25432.22	3096.30	1661.00	1590.00	9008.59	6173.83	5563.50	56471.35	0	0
704977.18	44555.60	8851.06	387542.99	140324.91	60696.48	71857.20	179321.80	0	268141.11
158298.11	17927.99	922.00	82711.19	29880.91	10646.25	17131.77	74331.51	0	47917.00
25394.00	1661.00	0	12042.00	7681.00	3240.00	770.00	24748.00	0	0
241141.46	17291.23	6905.23	62325.47	66142.72	29823.38	65558.66	174611.90	0	36939.73
32294.87	845.01	0	11107.02	7707.02	4373.02	8262.80	8396.02	0	0
85200.96	636.00	50.00	26394.00	15925.00	12668.33	29577.63	85450.23	3240.00	1798.00
149043.18	4341.68	0	30110.15	55118.47	27278.09	32194.79	98015.68	0	0
728559.40	75430.40	22188.96	257039.06	250369.30	63243.99	82476.65	158096.77	0	71794.21
1328185.28	176249.14	13254.95	521619.76	375242.42	114598.51	140475.45	377986.32	0	101078.36
193696.18	43219.12	4300.01	66560.39	49300.34	23196.31	11420.02	47557.21	0	14028.50
263247.12	53254.03	6588.00	105906.01	50565.06	25540.94	27981.08	105696.23	0	45961.78
369760.82	55967.88	22364.00	95529.72	72279.86	20251.76	125731.60	73366.93	0	41026.48
1931373.04	211851.05	64249.83	791007.22	502072.87	227577.81	198864.09	948685.87	0	644249.06
1040156.80	122356.40	18171.39	551438.43	215355.27	75115.63	75891.07	211685.48	0	124905.07
491103.81	155864.00	34500.00	194349.35	78383.44	29773.02	32734.00	89388.33	0	30135.00
353408.29	72000.99	21824.80	150626.92	75220.98	24324.56	31234.84	70851.48	2766.00	19521.00
3625786.14	1014418.90	120089.85	1304608.45	561955.96	365797.73	379005.10	1352524.13	997.00	470457.91
437581.19	80424.09	46784.00	249075.69	71434.04	22118.60	14528.77	31300.33	5817.00	46264.54
66071.00	18789.00	6010.00	28855.00	9220.00	4455.00	4752.00	2383.00	0	12612.00
265547.42	40952.87	3628.00	140940.88	59047.69	17813.65	6792.33	24277.51	3443.63	71242.94
328343.85	63575.44	6923.68	130199.97	72410.23	34365.54	27792.67	49893.35	906.00	58537.44
449184.79	56811.65	24920.30	249949.65	78921.96	33934.77	29566.76	87902.85	0	261878.64
375181.40	96394.68	19321.96	157641.80	71026.39	26975.33	23143.20	48830.52	74197.00	11376.77
0	0	0	0	0	0	0	0	0	0
262538.68	64961.36	3388.12	84237.85	50803.22	29154.03	33382.22	91827.92	791.00	86857.35
69389.18	2591.00	780.00	37199.00	11297.00	10405.85	7896.33	5357.00	9915.00	820.00
50610.22	8330.00	1575.00	10767.00	16602.30	9184.92	5726.00	28273.91	0	27703.00
34072.45	320.00	0	15666.68	7909.78	3218.86	6957.13	15714.67	0	4561.00
160971.84	11907.98	8407.76	74055.63	38143.72	20868.49	15996.02	17752.83	0	17719.55

初中办学条

Condition of School Buildings in Junior

地　区 Region	校舍建筑面积 Floor Space	教学及辅助用房 Teaching & Assistant Buildings							行政办公用房 Administrative	
		合计 Total	其中： of Which:						合计 Total	其中：教师办公室 of Which: for Teachers
			教室 Classroom	实验室 Laboratory	图书室 Library	微机室 PC-room	语音室 Linguistic	体育馆 Gymnasium		
总　计 Total	**304533759.95**	**117227657.05**	**81171958.88**	**18375154.23**	**7055428.35**	**5418559.95**	**1891340.95**	**3315214.69**	**23840474.81**	**14620813.27**
北　京 Beijing	759996.71	266079.60	157743.17	59462.81	15303.59	13931.39	2040.65	17597.99	93957.20	41348.68
天　津 Tianjin	645235.17	341071.22	255221.92	44344.67	16286.09	13461.79	6202.79	5553.96	97811.33	57156.19
河　北 Hebei	15679821.79	6232903.14	4299555.67	1111111.85	360678.56	280715.90	91953.63	88887.53	1093408.90	746013.90
山　西 Shanxi	8486155.27	3027610.19	2216469.70	407536.62	180132.49	142730.35	45109.70	35631.33	798445.17	539060.95
内蒙古 Inner Mongolia	5761862.39	2350908.79	1488390.37	331992.49	136895.84	106670.58	40682.78	246276.73	557361.85	370033.49
辽　宁 Liaoning	5494666.92	2400906.82	1678862.67	369806.59	128038.36	132083.13	50918.01	41198.06	680231.47	415750.43
吉　林 Jilin	3464016.33	1488046.85	1007290.38	230746.17	97687.96	87687.48	39963.80	24671.06	362382.35	239901.44
黑龙江 Heilongjiang	4917511.19	2216143.51	1542403.35	377555.51	92788.09	88823.52	50707.95	63865.09	572160.76	380415.03
上　海 Shanghai	1226994.32	594546.24	313757.22	137522.29	45287.28	28759.37	4729.40	64490.68	145621.26	74521.32
江　苏 Jiangsu	17331927.41	7896317.63	4891284.77	1396390.63	636003.99	460204.14	149285.34	363148.76	1601724.69	883563.02
浙　江 Zhejiang	12169099.88	4974062.48	3137343.47	737453.93	310748.58	209305.27	60352.61	518858.62	1003573.12	558275.10
安　徽 Anhui	14464024.46	6359061.43	4712363.01	806728.96	337425.95	290611.05	93979.01	117953.45	1172720.70	693136.19
福　建 Fujian	5404675.30	2166072.95	1401103.69	442830.15	158687.48	85818.77	16780.30	60852.56	430726.63	197105.15
江　西 Jiangxi	11388296.19	4367974.60	3175212.81	577955.46	263950.31	187461.25	72289.48	91105.29	995354.29	547523.27
山　东 Shandong	25398581.47	9623323.24	5960849.89	2015724.00	762350.61	455098.02	158760.14	270540.58	2299871.66	1322610.96
河　南 Henan	28058016.33	9441462.37	7209825.73	1189267.56	475598.03	365963.66	129234.90	71572.49	2455124.10	1649777.67
湖　北 Hubei	12841364.90	4010957.25	2779286.01	588770.32	238933.20	208492.69	101329.79	94145.24	806106.73	493048.89
湖　南 Hunan	18015223.87	6660551.74	4548427.04	1016300.38	430195.19	297806.25	150942.85	216880.03	1211074.37	813714.27
广　东 Guangdong	19308781.04	8061464.51	5780929.84	1157001.65	420186.77	300163.00	147012.15	256171.10	1188120.32	702399.21
广　西 Guangxi	15506950.56	5515088.88	4095420.52	827471.86	272482.70	209696.28	40359.40	69658.12	598255.63	416104.69
海　南 Hainan	2655727.01	1039874.05	773505.64	143484.85	58585.03	41985.21	14416.78	7896.54	128805.88	80625.82
重　庆 Chongqing	6409965.93	2205886.98	1628505.86	358494.54	99800.87	85451.69	18485.47	15148.55	414660.64	242670.44
四　川 Sichuan	18618416.85	7626700.07	5539441.33	1145255.17	424066.48	338556.79	89413.12	89967.18	1174944.23	736605.02
贵　州 Guizhou	14213292.13	4523569.90	3265615.03	626896.90	257872.28	221890.88	51619.10	99675.71	824799.16	468414.55
云　南 Yunnan	10289593.99	3498473.51	2430536.02	557463.42	208888.19	204591.99	52030.86	44963.03	558441.63	320944.92
西　藏 Tibet	1425013.32	412310.04	296980.41	48455.67	17359.34	19264.81	7074.21	23175.60	77937.37	57855.93
陕　西 Shaanxi	9403231.63	3535767.84	2296311.79	613309.15	242258.49	204936.90	132327.51	46624.00	1017916.51	683931.18
甘　肃 Gansu	6055029.87	2382452.95	1647758.84	396734.38	152345.31	134336.28	26482.55	24795.59	564521.12	380626.90
青　海 Qinghai	1610911.92	628561.44	391887.44	96419.88	43461.46	28894.12	9376.32	58522.22	108736.71	67658.35
宁　夏 Ningxia	1677672.73	728207.08	473315.94	148413.62	41478.67	44867.15	7263.97	12867.73	159471.57	100033.86
新　疆 Xinjiang	5851703.07	2651299.75	1776359.35	414252.75	129651.16	128300.24	30216.38	172519.87	646207.46	339986.45

件(一)(镇区)
Secondary Schools (1)(Counties & Towns Area)

单位:平方米
unit: m^2

生活用房 Residential and Welfare							其他用房 Rooms for Other Purposes	校舍面积中 of the Floor Space	
合计 Total	教工宿舍 Apartments for Single		学生宿舍 Students' Dormitories	食堂 Dining Halls	厕所 Toilet	其他 Others		危房面积 Floor Space of Dilapidated Buildings	当年新增校舍 New Floor Space Added in Current Year
	小计 Subtotal	其中:教师周转宿舍 of Which: Accommodation for Circulation of Teachers							
142270776.98	**32733847.83**	**9568958.77**	**65934930.34**	**26196063.68**	**8739053.73**	**8666881.40**	**21194851.11**	**2121957.07**	**16897442.38**
245034.39	35461.13	1724.95	42603.22	52935.27	37808.31	76226.46	154925.52	0	2027.49
123889.84	19704.51	6514.40	1749.20	26523.02	29781.75	46131.36	82462.78	0	31141.25
7215608.73	800325.56	247195.26	4066355.34	1482275.30	424223.92	442428.61	1137901.02	1000.01	1376403.34
3787280.40	549685.11	69443.62	1945684.41	738313.58	264402.35	289194.95	872819.51	34906.10	305797.29
2433626.39	151349.68	91293.87	1320470.21	530128.47	206264.16	225413.87	419965.36	0	172650.55
1816251.49	77922.80	36736.85	767631.66	529044.91	182817.87	258834.25	597277.14	8713.00	172030.62
1092036.75	50392.21	32387.12	421140.59	287865.16	118308.25	214330.54	521550.38	740.00	232990.79
1467442.33	59989.44	37588.30	652628.66	309536.27	164036.85	281251.11	661764.59	33020.71	187952.84
267350.19	16341.10	5237.43	23739.89	112526.52	54713.07	60029.61	219476.63	0	97255.40
6625126.08	1085657.62	171206.19	2592819.19	1757741.15	488958.72	699949.40	1208759.01	0	475348.22
5127582.43	899819.23	137009.75	2135793.50	1220192.20	389403.79	482373.71	1063881.85	0	571790.54
5995564.74	1437804.85	408501.29	2730281.15	1155333.21	375295.86	296849.67	936677.59	31745.00	691615.20
2312515.79	840012.97	135575.25	821724.60	353734.68	140486.24	156557.30	495359.93	62912.00	167763.04
5277618.12	1390889.26	344516.60	2415491.76	927649.83	325235.08	218352.19	747349.18	70864.30	1020883.78
10872535.93	1582754.24	432431.84	5030669.95	2442326.99	863201.38	953583.37	2602850.64	2430.00	2015464.99
14472478.49	2376866.64	466668.99	7659956.52	2912092.16	906592.48	616970.69	1688951.37	34003.74	1553094.25
7340111.24	3075009.32	557967.38	2649630.69	1047230.18	278075.01	290166.04	684189.68	73722.00	384453.56
9000660.11	3074295.14	878387.80	3403401.72	1518443.37	453324.82	551195.06	1142937.65	117221.00	759951.16
8482453.22	3212969.51	519346.78	3301452.85	1024214.43	448601.65	495214.78	1576742.99	2950.82	163564.93
9100051.56	2623396.95	817306.71	4791068.99	1260017.80	282580.14	142987.68	293554.49	264031.20	1132063.00
1397661.57	537870.59	209776.73	592533.46	186713.26	62175.66	18368.60	89385.51	26272.00	88595.50
3479125.77	917577.58	243880.33	1769463.36	562209.98	140450.21	89424.64	310292.54	37291.68	180387.40
8940818.36	2385761.26	1038658.75	4120806.46	1512539.96	534396.75	387313.93	875954.19	58281.00	1411640.44
8108950.52	1647614.41	1029798.05	4572329.05	1158716.80	430435.61	299854.65	755972.55	0	1418476.28
5877270.10	1322575.65	529874.56	3022410.45	1030459.49	272632.55	229191.96	355408.75	795292.55	760962.70
906928.09	347512.28	319600.03	402469.12	100844.42	20120.75	35981.52	27837.82	0	55615.54
4206294.70	1232663.79	273741.22	1696164.42	742280.68	305906.84	229278.97	643252.58	1664.39	675422.78
2591621.29	493812.36	192442.13	1142468.80	465069.12	217544.37	272726.64	516434.51	459784.57	407294.49
756322.41	127898.13	87378.03	355330.53	150158.12	46174.37	76761.26	117291.36	0	63308.23
694862.06	82829.18	42638.18	375970.24	134248.48	68796.30	33017.86	95132.02	5111.00	55645.70
2255703.89	277085.33	204130.38	1110690.35	464698.87	206308.62	196920.72	298491.97	0	265851.08

初中办学条件
Condition of School Buildings in Junior

地 区 Region	校舍建筑面积 Floor Space	教学及辅助用房 Teaching & Assistant Buildings 合计 Total	其中: of Which: 教室 Classroom	实验室 Laboratory	图书室 Library	微机室 PC-room	语音室 Linguistic	体育馆 Gymnasium	行政办公用房 Administrative 合计 Total	其中:教师办公室 of Which: for Teachers
总 计 Total	**76698170.40**	**29208437.54**	**20207993.26**	**4620341.57**	**1807195.18**	**1294914.76**	**473614.00**	**804378.77**	**6053352.06**	**3674185.29**
北 京 Beijing	250177.74	77715.41	42049.50	22601.88	3522.55	4438.26	881.65	4221.57	30528.17	14188.87
天 津 Tianjin	259351.49	142104.49	109122.55	17470.07	7144.69	5538.59	2478.59	350.00	36589.49	20886.71
河 北 Hebei	7308744.48	2777528.38	1924044.65	483482.22	163461.34	127461.02	41725.46	37353.69	486295.52	334991.20
山 西 Shanxi	2427591.97	880738.14	645976.66	114237.96	53855.76	39467.41	14324.67	12875.68	219651.40	142536.76
内蒙古 Inner Mongolia	554778.55	226886.82	150471.66	33809.22	13225.46	10302.98	2171.00	16906.50	48502.18	33571.81
辽 宁 Liaoning	681250.55	292351.28	203331.83	47093.93	13442.05	15412.73	5101.74	7969.00	77977.60	53480.14
吉 林 Jilin	356564.00	138438.93	97612.19	18663.47	9864.56	8094.61	2148.10	2056.00	39627.29	26691.13
黑龙江 Heilongjiang	392737.86	183407.42	136156.48	27854.84	6409.58	6182.22	2894.30	3910.00	53892.13	39425.45
上 海 Shanghai	320546.49	153491.65	87564.64	30419.65	9317.71	6657.18	751.00	18781.47	39447.45	17589.22
江 苏 Jiangsu	4280304.35	1935771.12	1167328.74	388656.34	146520.52	106659.14	35630.16	90976.22	431544.56	218944.46
浙 江 Zhejiang	3681209.60	1500906.48	971340.36	222956.79	93606.83	65042.18	20688.44	127271.88	302535.76	170045.41
安 徽 Anhui	3351609.93	1388191.59	1035515.77	182266.97	68993.08	57513.20	21233.57	22669.00	256039.50	155565.83
福 建 Fujian	1509158.76	621873.23	389639.15	129557.67	52773.52	21690.77	5149.32	23062.80	124160.50	53351.83
江 西 Jiangxi	2259476.16	806624.32	586544.74	112859.31	41468.02	30856.60	10921.44	23974.21	171139.96	100657.11
山 东 Shandong	9958784.98	3745115.90	2276792.93	785855.02	329995.08	174108.80	70855.83	107508.24	887527.28	518816.35
河 南 Henan	10131519.96	3399929.12	2592972.17	426808.54	166676.69	127013.79	49241.99	37215.94	890497.08	577244.79
湖 北 Hubei	3253578.45	963800.99	686148.52	129004.26	59383.26	52336.47	25276.48	11652.00	210810.92	126145.69
湖 南 Hunan	4213556.32	1510084.64	1006535.38	230521.87	105929.43	69912.94	34795.92	62389.10	285357.87	191041.76
广 东 Guangdong	5599630.10	2548176.97	1885238.89	319801.88	126229.00	85470.08	46550.82	84886.30	397523.20	215015.61
广 西 Guangxi	3149963.65	1157905.79	881922.84	153365.12	55755.67	43658.05	7634.39	15569.72	123417.23	89057.49
海 南 Hainan	185080.44	66768.67	48129.69	7355.25	4888.15	2799.04	748.00	2848.54	8824.72	5957.36
重 庆 Chongqing	1136676.84	398196.30	295569.86	61562.59	15302.43	14110.08	3404.21	8247.13	74592.80	39998.09
四 川 Sichuan	2819773.19	1181070.37	848358.80	180904.25	65769.14	56709.88	13030.74	16297.56	196534.64	116035.42
贵 州 Guizhou	2225021.73	683671.48	479517.01	98311.44	43996.64	35123.68	8944.72	17777.99	113224.11	73178.69
云 南 Yunnan	1805068.28	669492.68	473722.25	98238.97	37838.80	35009.49	8235.31	16447.86	95686.89	57874.06
西 藏 Tibet	160566.26	44366.84	34529.84	4784.00	1278.00	1623.00	917.00	1235.00	10972.36	7189.36
陕 西 Shaanxi	1776241.39	653057.57	423207.63	112256.65	43940.88	38059.12	24402.29	11191.00	194167.69	125975.41
甘 肃 Gansu	1269756.66	495225.44	340262.24	81849.80	33132.06	26626.32	7475.92	5879.10	110141.43	76223.35
青 海 Qinghai	401305.37	160886.79	107963.03	24378.94	11702.85	7452.97	2727.00	6662.00	30841.85	19324.46
宁 夏 Ningxia	191358.62	82805.32	53661.14	20667.09	3749.08	3960.01	768.00	0	18067.03	10323.14
新 疆 Xinjiang	786786.23	321853.41	226762.12	52745.58	18022.35	15624.15	2505.94	6193.27	87233.45	42858.33

(一)(镇乡结合区)
Secondary Schools (1)(County-town Transitional Area)

单位:平方米
unit: m²

生活用房 Residential and Welfare							其他用房 Rooms for Other Purposes	校舍面积中 of the Floor Space	
合计 Total	教工宿舍 Apartments for Single		学生宿舍 Students' Dormitories	食堂 Dining Halls	厕所 Toilet	其他 Others		危房面积 Floor Space of Dilapidated Buildings	当年新增校舍 New Floor Space Added in Current Year
	小计 Subtotal	其中:教师周转宿舍 of Which: Accommodation for Circulation of Teachers							
35842955.26	**7328460.87**	**1976754.02**	**17040179.62**	**6884745.23**	**2267870.29**	**2321699.25**	**5593425.54**	**462726.69**	**4984857.15**
87186.46	10666.81	18.00	12636.07	18814.36	10563.49	34505.73	54747.70	0	1576.49
43484.63	5876.41	805.40	600.00	10393.03	11379.93	15235.26	37172.88	0	18529.25
3536798.41	388193.57	97662.75	2011581.00	714246.95	196199.98	226576.91	508122.17	1000.01	783102.51
1090585.43	160360.73	17362.94	586645.10	213495.96	71346.30	58737.34	236617.00	13479.00	62317.59
256974.15	19541.68	8696.68	151892.50	49585.24	18908.42	17046.31	22415.40	0	8747.85
216320.23	9259.61	1939.05	86301.97	60682.74	23033.33	37042.58	94601.44	0	34690.18
113557.18	7805.03	4005.00	39165.20	34071.89	15601.08	16913.98	64940.60	0	51317.13
130725.41	4441.00	3448.00	60597.14	23385.68	14875.62	27425.97	24712.90	0	3050.90
65308.68	3156.67	775.00	5508.89	29855.40	11872.71	14915.01	62298.71	0	14509.00
1577109.65	287083.83	47292.18	555223.36	440915.16	113953.00	179934.30	335879.02	0	109069.05
1547941.38	246574.74	35177.70	685469.34	367564.38	111209.04	137123.88	329825.98	0	147862.27
1461976.26	341564.29	108839.70	681788.24	288711.69	91624.29	58287.75	245402.58	4153.00	154946.20
644065.71	243979.21	27888.00	221097.41	97647.18	41238.09	40103.82	119059.32	25930.00	37486.55
1169862.56	273797.10	82324.09	573650.15	212068.93	71573.68	38772.70	111849.32	10061.00	175195.99
4285238.54	578245.07	156545.75	1911386.19	952239.98	328870.05	514497.25	1040903.26	0	1000850.29
5210231.77	750212.73	156053.29	2852853.49	1074204.49	338240.74	194720.32	630861.99	8483.20	675413.90
1910027.73	768389.21	142270.31	727136.16	265789.72	74282.68	74429.96	168938.81	0	89858.00
2163006.17	684772.66	241868.38	889992.31	376604.70	103885.66	107750.84	255107.64	51526.00	249684.63
2138311.21	710550.36	84642.91	818644.10	302314.43	156226.50	150575.82	515618.72	1220.00	59234.72
1816210.62	465072.46	146105.75	1000068.08	260957.06	59643.75	30469.27	52430.01	94646.00	278949.16
99499.01	28581.48	7892.00	43596.53	13991.00	8660.00	4670.00	9988.04	0	20947.37
627741.50	153860.13	55495.94	330365.56	105607.03	25876.15	12032.63	36146.24	11039.68	80979.28
1315013.23	322010.29	136065.57	610829.92	241881.98	85792.82	54498.22	127154.95	10648.00	282061.68
1271503.22	241215.85	154187.24	710517.28	183262.24	69450.45	67057.40	156622.92	0	251376.30
961162.42	170802.37	67317.37	512936.83	177624.43	56511.34	43287.45	78726.29	161560.50	125520.91
99602.49	34324.55	34324.55	48912.08	12946.90	1611.22	1807.74	5624.57	0	6077.20
813534.67	236232.12	61363.90	337222.47	143059.83	56996.42	40023.83	115481.46	0	162812.56
578440.92	95804.04	36516.49	256670.00	104512.39	49472.83	71981.66	85948.87	68980.30	41264.52
178401.82	26655.08	18360.08	89130.08	28608.55	11693.99	22314.12	31174.91	0	11260.36
88902.13	13878.35	9079.32	52362.46	15022.25	4695.01	2944.06	1584.14	0	10838.00
344231.67	45553.44	32430.68	175399.71	64679.66	32581.72	26017.14	33467.70	0	35327.31

地　区 Region	校舍建筑面积 Floor Space	教学及辅助用房 Teaching & Assistant Buildings							行政办公用房 Administrative	
		合计 Total	其中：of Which：						合计 Total	其中：教师办公室 of Which：for Teachers
			教室 Classroom	实验室 Laboratory	图书室 Library	微机室 PC-room	语音室 Linguistic	体育馆 Gymnasium		
总　计 Total	**116099590.72**	**43915508.98**	**30721924.57**	**7122318.03**	**2536412.92**	**2175546.85**	**644306.65**	**714999.96**	**8665988.10**	**5462188.37**
北　京 Beijing	640698.93	232320.33	142257.14	51690.16	12926.40	10350.27	1563.00	13533.36	87684.41	43780.73
天　津 Tianjin	326439.74	169445.75	119166.11	28299.21	9077.11	7046.31	4253.01	1604.00	51136.35	32971.87
河　北 Hebei	6144395.95	2522642.66	1670040.26	502861.08	158204.50	117777.98	37684.69	36074.15	447707.02	306125.76
山　西 Shanxi	3647266.58	1092938.11	758583.27	162095.33	73894.25	65559.18	16168.08	16638.00	345294.10	236526.89
内蒙古 Inner Mongolia	957826.00	370595.54	241803.99	49464.61	17984.68	16264.16	4073.46	41004.64	87524.77	59908.77
辽　宁 Liaoning	2040484.30	894855.11	601074.24	145803.85	45699.63	50889.34	20146.07	31241.98	229912.56	154642.88
吉　林 Jilin	1937465.41	833316.12	526182.82	165566.29	61390.82	55992.62	24183.57	0.00	224378.19	159023.07
黑龙江 Heilongjiang	2105445.12	963274.57	677370.05	172716.37	42581.90	42243.32	20519.34	7843.59	222785.11	163015.27
上　海 Shanghai	297688.00	146055.06	78240.00	26477.00	13125.00	6115.00	1803.00	20295.06	39061.00	18657.00
江　苏 Jiangsu	1910860.28	880597.83	561185.73	148832.76	69870.12	53700.54	20805.67	26203.01	163035.80	92057.74
浙　江 Zhejiang	3089880.62	1208067.12	805173.04	171578.62	74038.21	54257.68	14939.43	88080.14	243900.67	140556.78
安　徽 Anhui	7971488.42	3357114.10	2417077.70	489141.78	199424.83	185532.86	40832.93	25104.00	568915.65	368703.37
福　建 Fujian	3551126.85	1258195.56	793982.34	272573.58	94022.06	57804.83	11854.07	27958.68	284750.80	133074.10
江　西 Jiangxi	5846104.02	2074590.89	1487402.70	319215.98	116163.44	95053.59	30440.46	26314.72	407979.69	204916.88
山　东 Shandong	4915769.65	1785368.79	1157908.29	368493.92	115568.01	86471.40	24442.32	32484.85	396086.94	238296.49
河　南 Henan	12587360.54	4191918.58	3121854.44	581502.29	219578.99	194827.43	50120.82	24034.61	1107917.41	768779.98
湖　北 Hubei	4398685.07	1393526.70	974029.51	218360.08	84522.33	74366.47	26247.91	16000.40	265925.26	162433.03
湖　南 Hunan	9123190.83	3219842.04	2300211.63	490720.78	187100.51	143599.98	68382.14	29827.00	660804.55	430260.17
广　东 Guangdong	6235639.62	2767244.34	1999857.92	370459.79	132306.28	107478.50	46264.86	110876.99	423982.01	251313.59
广　西 Guangxi	4069841.04	1445034.75	1050027.25	231250.45	72928.32	58953.45	14483.28	17392.00	138672.70	98102.20
海　南 Hainan	461951.63	177478.68	127063.68	25502.00	11413.00	7551.00	2830.00	3119.00	25529.00	15932.00
重　庆 Chongqing	1577313.79	473628.68	346108.15	66776.36	23346.15	18753.30	5461.65	13183.07	102520.27	50069.72
四　川 Sichuan	8845291.09	3689605.13	2685756.30	580609.86	202679.77	173417.76	40594.62	6546.82	473807.72	298042.77
贵　州 Guizhou	4255024.40	1423171.12	1061941.21	199967.73	72306.49	71483.16	12694.79	4777.74	206368.41	127283.71
云　南 Yunnan	7059248.44	2398436.57	1662728.88	409160.99	139818.40	145248.08	28570.13	12910.09	336172.97	202637.30
西　藏 Tibet	346859.37	110047.40	88010.62	9234.40	3093.15	3990.61	893.62	4825.00	11376.39	10862.25
陕　西 Shaanxi	1771891.01	611969.75	382496.47	114659.49	44727.93	39855.06	26547.20	3683.60	199955.78	120769.28
甘　肃 Gansu	3707848.24	1482478.15	1053906.27	242724.54	85210.70	84717.45	11179.69	4739.50	344637.20	248647.39
青　海 Qinghai	1058239.44	403897.40	260627.63	66153.28	25339.29	19190.33	7800.80	24786.07	76015.64	53848.11
宁　夏 Ningxia	769388.04	351888.55	216249.05	81243.24	20805.87	21645.34	3504.18	8440.87	58299.47	35724.53
新　疆 Xinjiang	4448878.30	1985963.60	1353607.88	359182.21	107264.78	105409.85	25021.86	35477.02	433850.26	235224.74

件(一)(乡村)
Secondary Schools (1)(Rural Area)

单位:平方米
unit: m²

生活用房 Residential and Welfare							其他用房 Rooms for Other Purposes	校舍面积中 of the Floor Space	
合计 Total	教工宿舍 Apartments for Single		学生宿舍 Students' Dormitories	食堂 Dining Halls	厕所 Toilet	其他 Others		危房面积 Floor Space of Dilapidated Buildings	当年新增校舍 New Floor Space Added in Current Year
	小计 Subtotal	其中:教师周转宿舍 of Which: Accommodation for Circulation of Teachers							
55335264.46	**15026216.22**	**5089123.25**	**23860944.77**	**10020748.09**	**3345261.32**	**3082094.06**	**8182829.18**	**1122334.87**	**7171772.61**
188766.81	38746.12	1832.00	55850.00	48644.29	24225.34	21301.06	131927.38	0.00	868.00
50091.69	9054.01	1391.01	0.00	9443.44	12807.53	18786.71	55765.95	0.00	26331.93
2661264.57	424401.36	151944.06	1339775.67	551738.07	171284.39	174065.08	512781.70	412.01	644176.96
1717463.77	339186.89	55888.60	775288.53	347653.29	114201.33	141133.73	491570.60	12603.00	98793.98
415733.88	53239.26	39386.33	207802.40	82870.49	34898.58	36923.15	83971.81	0.00	57733.36
582702.18	41853.43	21042.65	167229.15	194313.95	74393.01	104912.64	333014.45	7460.00	169206.51
630998.69	37742.87	28299.12	263904.41	172740.76	65753.11	90857.54	248772.41	0.00	48942.59
688810.36	46580.68	33259.45	276901.40	162983.69	71906.08	130438.51	230575.08	2604.00	141766.05
78563.06	4258.00	0.00	13447.00	25939.06	13988.00	20931.00	34008.88	0.00	19658.50
760870.98	154420.47	31330.80	312029.16	177335.65	55524.99	61560.71	106355.67	0.00	106228.98
1273903.69	270231.17	21664.46	520175.64	291026.71	91277.70	101192.47	364009.14	0.00	121462.17
3551198.28	1057978.34	373662.55	1444879.60	682559.25	219173.35	146607.74	494260.39	15744.00	320448.56
1639842.51	651653.28	87521.53	561497.20	262528.53	88017.49	76146.01	368337.98	28999.00	37392.76
3080916.26	893315.07	269063.23	1388095.46	536330.61	147585.50	115589.62	282617.18	42375.50	562215.87
2181883.35	350067.80	112335.42	1017703.17	495166.12	176640.23	142306.03	552430.57	0.00	470490.25
6653269.52	1367803.39	343101.30	3228970.24	1382964.71	413269.00	260262.18	634255.03	16655.71	672310.92
2498585.26	999510.98	255377.48	905743.97	370849.76	97072.53	125408.02	240647.85	4170.00	161112.29
4580354.29	1777520.94	523912.01	1545897.85	717436.98	228765.07	310733.45	662189.95	82213.00	248050.45
2450630.93	925715.64	131718.00	857601.78	309907.82	179924.67	177481.02	593782.34	14783.00	239413.10
2386731.69	715119.10	286039.28	1204609.05	337743.63	74836.91	54423.00	99401.90	51831.22	351601.75
244250.95	87113.76	30707.00	110383.00	29773.00	11864.00	5117.19	14693.00	3556.00	7361.68
844327.88	237319.96	87182.39	413276.97	130642.67	36459.61	26628.67	156836.96	14096.11	16509.38
4263860.29	1643141.11	709650.02	1522809.41	660621.95	258322.29	178965.53	418017.95	31045.12	822248.19
2481177.01	599507.89	436062.97	1356054.92	339987.20	116895.35	68731.65	144307.86	295.00	310918.84
4116215.10	1022416.46	431649.93	2097417.40	712914.56	173447.90	110018.78	208423.80	527681.51	510187.11
221528.82	72834.65	56222.55	111128.20	27116.22	3061.75	7388.00	3906.76	0.00	5284.00
814812.04	272680.13	47888.59	300681.79	136676.80	60430.71	44342.61	145153.44	706.66	55278.02
1656141.69	375315.66	130160.06	717878.95	305096.48	131183.25	126667.35	224591.20	264996.03	316741.35
477593.26	99059.74	62187.40	199736.93	92916.23	37802.68	48077.68	100733.14	0.00	58017.23
304026.37	72858.37	38674.42	114370.83	58132.10	26398.77	32266.30	55173.65	108.00	46879.98
1838749.28	385569.69	289968.64	829804.69	366694.07	133850.20	122830.63	190315.16	0.00	524141.85

初中办学条

Condition of School Buildings in

地区 Region	占地面积(平方米) Areas of School Sites(m^2) 合计 Total	其中: of Which: 绿化用地面积 Green Areas	运动场地面积 Sports Areas	图书(册) Books & Magazines in Libraries (Volume)	计算机数(台) PC (Set) 合计 Total	其中:教学用计算机 No. of Computers Used for Instruction 小计 Subtotal	其中:平板电脑 of Which: Tablet PC
总计 Total	**1587527312.42**	**324806918.30**	**452776698.57**	**1583181008**	**7874766**	**6581785**	**310168**
北京 Beijing	9924663.62	1915086.27	3525082.02	10159897	101353	86990	6909
天津 Tianjin	8832619.47	1098558.57	3348374.50	10319460	49112	42118	2596
河北 Hebei	77527722.56	9579606.67	24438536.44	101168065	359284	346281	11418
山西 Shanxi	38481673.52	4938745.53	9722662.52	33301764	210214	166255	2894
内蒙古 Inner Mongolia	33417261.30	5650349.91	8665179.31	19557061	127610	91490	2859
辽宁 Liaoning	45897075.02	6167965.19	18882427.03	51886202	298684	228890	11971
吉林 Jilin	31653852.42	6895227.35	9433777.55	26949510	120620	93428	2239
黑龙江 Heilongjiang	42255459.69	5721587.06	12079228.44	27293146	171835	135876	3762
上海 Shanghai	13708035.71	4290984.72	4011687.61	25693458	177736	142149	11889
江苏 Jiangsu	92153794.78	26712928.51	26548832.86	89460386	523886	454757	16553
浙江 Zhejiang	62233700.01	16997828.79	18847581.62	75782038	477160	422663	23946
安徽 Anhui	84769142.44	13919351.25	19872565.59	59791892	353984	284563	7945
福建 Fujian	32525828.88	8271299.11	8491977.81	30587367	153757	121421	4335
江西 Jiangxi	59554355.13	11805438.86	18426953.37	49715145	201122	159920	6764
山东 Shandong	137735478.61	30828147.37	41141011.59	144126533	718169	626021	19307
河南 Henan	125685634.57	17207321.63	30705745.65	123898107	477386	399897	29777
湖北 Hubei	64554717.14	21222431.41	15000554.40	62933324	241186	201388	14026
湖南 Hunan	89165412.17	15680752.69	18689005.88	73397492	270218	230627	6004
广东 Guangdong	120519109.44	32216605.50	36671818.55	135371107	860589	713300	76668
广西 Guangxi	53077286.04	9252132.56	15907152.51	75889156	218168	168191	5853
海南 Hainan	16322861.99	3587866.64	3144979.12	9311285	46817	40759	1019
重庆 Chongqing	21518501.71	4603186.70	6355997.61	18782961	113084	92883	4373
四川 Sichuan	72256366.15	12826023.83	27213776.34	79408500	416734	340996	11271
贵州 Guizhou	55628482.51	12521575.04	18348691.43	67404516	257752	230459	5330
云南 Yunnan	54735851.45	12055708.71	13997671.97	52845965	246529	203213	1568
西藏 Tibet	6213220.86	801231.85	1041779.38	3196283	18907	11676	390
陕西 Shaanxi	35919086.78	5736798.53	9507488.13	47779884	215249	193276	6480
甘肃 Gansu	31137726.50	5024103.77	8978374.39	29296701	160002	135841	4647
青海 Qinghai	8701143.25	1182911.55	2209252.98	9446799	49019	37119	1892
宁夏 Ningxia	11017623.08	2407277.66	3491960.37	8809799	59281	46029	943
新疆 Xinjiang	50403625.62	13687885.07	14076571.60	29617205	179319	133309	4540

件(二)(总计)
Junior Secondary Schools (2)(Total)

教室(间) Classroom(Room)		教室中:普通教室(间) of Which: General Classroom(Room)		固定资产总值(万元) Total Value of Fixed Asset (10,000 yuan)		
合计 Total	其中:网络多媒体教室 of Which: Network Multimedia Classroom	合计 Total	其中:网络多媒体教室 of Which: Network Multimedia Classroom	合计 Total	其中:教学仪器设备资产值 of Which: Total Value of Equip & Instru. 小计 Subtotal	其中:实验设备 of Which: for Experiment
1811140	**1162310**	**1332705**	**1009840**	**83716576.76**	**10060241.46**	**2960223.07**
14854	12075	8733	7869	1073102.42	306300.90	35871.42
10447	7259	7387	6190	451637.56	66330.76	16081.95
90079	56894	70756	53777	3223516.29	344858.01	137571.63
45547	26811	33769	24278	2040704.29	187936.23	64653.60
27050	19944	16513	15608	1739556.47	209529.48	54038.66
55999	32462	41446	27741	1945263.99	364052.45	109959.86
39465	15789	28061	14062	1135144.82	172214.53	57161.39
47491	25664	30685	22007	1611922.92	262875.49	73342.76
26111	21046	17555	15337	1911539.86	308412.66	66822.00
105725	74808	69665	59116	6843751.08	675807.50	194643.84
75623	64133	53143	51420	4840337.74	651336.54	131134.13
88764	54699	68335	50462	3681687.28	372311.76	119464.91
35377	24479	21679	19895	1614756.59	225054.35	65567.87
66522	38733	51436	36183	2135492.57	259390.40	74437.24
145922	111943	99001	90428	7280433.69	712152.71	181523.51
148275	82020	125186	77091	5403819.17	489588.26	172986.06
64292	38305	47793	35473	2805548.03	320579.48	119155.68
100381	39715	74615	37259	3746321.99	422209.00	148725.79
147228	119094	112535	102902	7420294.86	1058418.72	341343.08
51246	36650	41271	34527	2388745.57	326050.32	100348.05
10284	6059	7919	5533	619538.35	87031.14	27351.68
29136	23806	19640	18011	1582825.94	147889.88	36009.69
109742	56552	86832	50841	4623644.77	704643.42	214589.23
64051	44260	48282	40182	2847565.98	270923.72	80074.34
57263	31197	44211	28816	3115573.16	249228.70	72316.61
4136	2062	3110	1966	391074.78	19524.14	5860.37
43752	28200	33831	25183	2013055.57	239049.38	97681.85
40043	24978	25304	21693	1802066.18	190508.73	56182.93
10539	5509	7325	4961	653354.31	50006.50	14937.93
10329	7421	6994	6147	611563.58	106395.02	32686.60
45467	29743	29693	24882	2162736.97	259631.29	57698.41

地 区 Region	占地面积(平方米) Areas of School Sites(m^2)			图书(册) Books & Magazines in Libraries (Volume)	计算机数(台) PC (Set)		
	合计 Total	其中: of Which:			合计 Total	其中:教学用计算机 No. of Computers Used for Instruction	
		绿化用地面积 Green Areas	运动场地面积 Sports Areas			小计 Subtotal	其中:平板电脑 of Which: Tablet PC
总 计 Total	**388417231.93**	**88690609.22**	**127254964.88**	**533466382**	**3008233**	**2517666**	**179927**
北 京 Beijing	5503700.54	871392.76	2199575.54	7507550	75082	65478	5939
天 津 Tianjin	4299150.29	572069.16	1545588.20	6159350	31348	26307	2293
河 北 Hebei	13136138.44	2074376.55	4648843.22	23353939	96677	92988	2766
山 西 Shanxi	7305481.20	997660.27	2256850.12	9212899	53305	42194	444
内蒙古 Inner Mongolia	7324593.27	1190053.27	2466336.95	7307987	44853	33512	1236
辽 宁 Liaoning	17240560.57	2349705.48	7580162.98	25968288	155387	118239	5617
吉 林 Jilin	6338166.95	1075827.37	2784055.58	11047139	49295	38890	1890
黑龙江 Heilongjiang	10018046.25	1235687.55	3702693.43	10994853	75499	60930	3073
上 海 Shanghai	9759734.55	2878026.87	2887433.84	20833028	147289	118405	10330
江 苏 Jiangsu	35518871.01	10861292.63	11183182.61	41366144	262049	229097	11713
浙 江 Zhejiang	27330911.45	7900931.85	8586259.31	36858636	237622	213806	14597
安 徽 Anhui	11649296.56	2293877.60	3438817.46	12772815	79106	62434	3887
福 建 Fujian	7099634.84	1695636.84	2230422.16	10480238	56505	44421	2764
江 西 Jiangxi	9458249.07	2008593.23	2982082.66	11130435	49409	39172	2279
山 东 Shandong	43360184.43	10065988.57	13850553.60	57184843	303980	263262	13823
河 南 Henan	22407586.64	3560047.20	6445986.08	28579551	128645	106010	9394
湖 北 Hubei	17459015.94	5395729.60	4827768.16	24566218	102167	84310	9667
湖 南 Hunan	12921648.17	2807739.03	3255853.51	13966247	60001	49785	1674
广 东 Guangdong	50490828.43	13642892.66	16850401.59	75559512	498134	414188	55849
广 西 Guangxi	9204291.99	1931705.50	3203297.34	16309571	57292	42460	3083
海 南 Hainan	2090526.99	456698.00	643670.84	2890573	14659	12405	555
重 庆 Chongqing	6423972.40	1496501.64	1901019.65	6344429	39372	32135	2515
四 川 Sichuan	12753317.63	2773909.53	5032776.62	17428657	101207	86715	6253
贵 州 Guizhou	7808770.09	1615362.98	3066018.72	12571089	54409	48400	1800
云 南 Yunnan	6378441.24	1825699.54	1917696.94	8162457	41890	33999	430
西 藏 Tibet	1220547.95	177345.33	195331.53	602504	3750	2382	165
陕 西 Shaanxi	7076151.05	1232382.82	2131544.14	13214520	63886	55592	2265
甘 肃 Gansu	3927856.53	649150.74	1466958.72	6189145	36945	32083	1544
青 海 Qinghai	1664791.75	252067.52	426349.65	2687900	14942	9914	245
宁 夏 Ningxia	3066815.18	716827.44	997244.35	3007694	20084	15931	306
新 疆 Xinjiang	8179950.53	2085429.69	2550189.38	9208171	53444	42222	1531

件(二)(城区)
Secondary Schools (2)(Urban Area)

教室(间) Classroom(Room)		教室中:普通教室(间) of Which: General Classroom(Room)		固定资产总值(万元) Total Value of Fixed Asset (10,000 yuan)		
					其中:教学仪器设备资产值 of Which: Total Value of Equip & Instru.	
合计 Total	其中:网络多媒体教室 of Which: Network Multimedia Classroom	合计 Total	其中:网络多媒体教室 of Which: Network Multimedia Classroom	合计 Total	小计 Subtotal	其中:实验设备 of Which: for Experiment
589479	**427922**	**430816**	**361157**	**31246934.99**	**4226520.59**	**1047706.74**
10555	8887	6455	5916	779698.27	222772.77	25615.24
5952	4586	4393	3838	320475.27	45566.41	8645.80
19347	13765	15279	12756	715366.76	90315.43	28826.24
10837	6873	8099	6240	532228.98	56569.85	15859.80
9492	7080	5976	5653	513832.55	70695.69	17859.07
26057	17141	18674	14250	1002038.62	199733.47	53636.97
14301	7422	10542	6738	469322.30	75793.37	18996.68
16746	10009	11159	8660	541391.81	105990.27	22519.56
21151	16851	14234	12329	1518373.85	254327.00	51181.83
49187	37553	31690	28753	3753343.66	360004.73	91382.50
37794	32332	26741	25670	2659043.05	343728.07	63999.23
17436	11434	13062	10240	856306.13	90720.84	25819.23
11224	8588	7434	6958	580427.23	90993.80	20825.84
14452	9491	11702	8819	494224.91	66005.84	16717.31
56956	44037	38338	35851	3151956.62	322938.31	69064.80
32860	21297	26990	19488	1324050.34	142683.40	44323.36
23911	15962	18023	14609	1064440.95	139982.26	48546.07
19509	10535	15274	9911	911166.50	102057.65	33678.97
83762	71120	65541	60896	4537508.15	718410.04	207180.45
13110	8572	10441	7858	538858.85	81891.31	22792.62
3171	1958	2783	1840	148037.30	31698.71	8519.45
9602	7548	6813	6084	728220.85	60628.90	14281.19
22603	14459	17839	12890	1103035.42	181007.45	46022.73
13372	8834	10272	7733	612401.10	65890.64	15186.44
9568	5418	7393	4898	486407.16	52299.78	12416.63
799	403	602	393	75528.32	3885.36	898.87
11677	8305	8438	7129	595080.74	74139.03	24261.93
7223	5035	5190	4511	316658.61	45746.48	9711.65
2174	1463	1652	1315	153853.03	13246.73	3615.44
3100	2430	2116	1991	195310.77	35137.46	10680.36
11551	8534	7671	6940	568346.90	81659.56	14640.47

初中办学条件
Condition of School Buildings in Junior Secondary

地 区 Region	占地面积(平方米) Areas of School Sites(m^2) 合计 Total	其中: of Which: 绿化用地面积 Green Areas	运动场地面积 Sports Areas	图书(册) Books & Magazines in Libraries (Volume)	计算机数(台) PC (Set) 合计 Total	其中:教学用计算机 No. of Computers Used for Instruction 小计 Subtotal	其中:平板电脑 of Which: Tablet PC
总 计 Total	**90852558.77**	**21894886.49**	**27707913.77**	**103123994**	**557023**	**475981**	**33313**
北 京 Beijing	1061100.79	165475.24	433836.56	998455	9535	8123	1224
天 津 Tianjin	519658.50	61883.17	182257.01	584938	2820	2195	86
河 北 Hebei	4444011.74	737334.38	1539727.67	7280828	27513	26787	572
山 西 Shanxi	1073520.94	164200.23	295102.35	914803	5642	4244	178
内蒙古 Inner Mongolia	242719.00	31923.00	63332.00	122897	926	757	0
辽 宁 Liaoning	2076569.94	334043.82	822121.48	2119889	13190	10203	526
吉 林 Jilin	374118.27	87823.00	85348.00	252518	1204	897	0
黑龙江 Heilongjiang	1067463.32	130230.15	347240.00	698121	5735	4272	300
上 海 Shanghai	1202301.16	425656.85	350388.01	1891958	12182	10316	516
江 苏 Jiangsu	5489342.81	1670173.81	1651292.19	5532959	31519	26883	701
浙 江 Zhejiang	7683534.80	2151642.46	2330853.88	9793477	58110	52313	2020
安 徽 Anhui	2035847.78	321079.33	564901.62	1640952	9913	8099	195
福 建 Fujian	1811722.97	417219.14	494481.21	1786577	8139	6736	85
江 西 Jiangxi	1958662.44	461069.41	541166.09	1585477	6465	5071	121
山 东 Shandong	16118187.03	3883283.31	4786889.32	15873905	78621	69262	2738
河 南 Henan	5399080.22	874415.71	1378467.12	4505061	19970	17236	722
湖 北 Hubei	2671776.50	855668.01	696331.68	2767606	10619	8577	518
湖 南 Hunan	2373038.85	479599.71	570748.40	2015323	7960	6792	222
广 东 Guangdong	20068319.85	5471493.04	6618081.04	27505989	177694	149724	20794
广 西 Guangxi	1790053.94	448462.88	588683.54	3049686	9214	7044	187
海 南 Hainan	352240.80	45316.00	76660.00	290585	1170	1086	42
重 庆 Chongqing	1221954.52	278898.95	277299.10	902144	4622	3839	341
四 川 Sichuan	1984060.63	533714.39	735344.79	2318355	12733	11136	641
贵 州 Guizhou	1841747.55	423365.74	669837.24	2108454	8574	7321	173
云 南 Yunnan	1876587.53	526332.66	531580.66	2305788	9382	8113	0
西 藏 Tibet	0.00	0.00	0.00	0	0	0	0
陕 西 Shaanxi	1470719.99	302833.54	366640.25	1851855	9477	7344	113
甘 肃 Gansu	448934.88	70544.60	151514.50	627729	3467	2996	92
青 海 Qinghai	383529.40	56045.60	96049.40	509830	2567	1885	153
宁 夏 Ningxia	413459.24	171837.16	134091.98	287361	1795	1460	1
新 疆 Xinjiang	1398293.38	313321.20	327646.68	1000474	6265	5270	52

(二)(城乡结合区)
Schools (2)(Urban-rural Transitional Area)

教室(间) Classroom(Room)		教室中:普通教室(间) of Which: General Classroom(Room)		固定资产总值(万元) Total Value of Fixed Asset (10,000 yuan)		
					其中:教学仪器设备资产值 of Which: Total Value of Equip & Instru.	
合计 Total	其中:网络多媒体教室 of Which: Network Multimedia Classroom	合计 Total	其中:网络多媒体教室 of Which: Network Multimedia Classroom	合计 Total	小计 Subtotal	其中:实验设备 of Which: for Experiment
116904	**84935**	**85896**	**72736**	**6512817.41**	**762616.59**	**224047.78**
1419	1152	767	694	80472.70	26182.46	3329.01
534	375	399	343	36985.89	2950.33	681.40
6336	4419	4948	4136	266787.06	24323.68	9490.65
1165	664	742	597	65655.45	4763.06	1407.04
160	111	113	95	16759.81	559.58	279.21
2525	1429	1694	1160	137005.23	19543.03	7202.70
531	201	354	177	12158.62	1641.20	686.78
1184	706	753	596	38429.97	8738.71	2823.41
1916	1440	1230	1067	128447.27	18315.84	3175.81
6434	4741	4123	3676	521232.04	44698.56	14998.83
9998	8446	7274	6962	693427.19	90917.58	19022.42
2434	1568	2015	1452	111132.08	10525.72	3324.48
2089	1399	1258	1153	116248.22	14615.62	3942.95
2256	1325	1735	1247	100967.79	9507.52	2964.08
17346	12933	11327	10470	1097421.15	84968.56	22852.04
6079	3520	4815	3164	252537.28	23338.78	7624.32
3001	1842	2279	1707	139915.87	13988.99	5535.19
2840	1382	2086	1251	141065.93	14406.28	4732.52
31626	26499	25062	23123	1647914.32	245854.48	80588.64
2330	1661	1931	1592	123404.15	14558.11	4683.70
261	179	207	166	24198.10	2338.61	923.60
1451	1116	960	942	80513.91	7685.79	2185.05
3077	1922	2470	1787	135511.52	22084.79	6304.41
2488	1495	1901	1353	139233.14	7967.12	2466.75
2281	1235	1938	1150	137929.20	18203.78	4517.65
0	0	0	0	0.00	0.00	0.00
1948	1203	1283	969	96388.15	10060.79	3817.74
729	500	551	453	39962.44	3786.49	1121.33
548	256	393	249	29812.41	2517.41	801.04
307	241	212	204	15223.16	3128.74	631.26
1611	975	1076	801	86077.35	10444.96	1933.77

地区 Region	占地面积(平方米) Areas of School Sites(m^2) 合计 Total	其中: of Which: 绿化用地面积 Green Areas	运动场地面积 Sports Areas	图书(册) Books & Magazines in Libraries (Volume)	计算机数(台) PC (Set) 合计 Total	其中:教学用计算机 No. of Computers Used for Instruction 小计 Subtotal	其中:平板电脑 of Which: Tablet PC
总　计 Total	**829471392.84**	**166620893.69**	**230282094.18**	**773406666**	**3540479**	**2974720**	**97752**
北　京 Beijing	2099304.55	529691.43	665710.28	1500911	14913	12165	770
天　津 Tianjin	2883279.07	332578.10	1140015.09	2774192	11321	10039	161
河　北 Hebei	43222877.26	4910092.71	13344408.69	56684826	188366	181572	5887
山　西 Shanxi	20074480.54	2522386.26	5237816.32	18162500	111176	90244	1839
内蒙古 Inner Mongolia	20902793.33	3466956.15	5176358.42	10706159	70342	49870	1370
辽　宁 Liaoning	20081712.77	2651753.37	7981425.68	18991213	102319	79602	4135
吉　林 Jilin	13835867.48	3030280.71	4050288.45	10434569	44839	35165	232
黑龙江 Heilongjiang	20996919.46	3036587.53	5968044.18	11951195	68678	53440	407
上　海 Shanghai	3165023.26	1106994.15	903358.73	4069683	25041	19385	1206
江　苏 Jiangsu	49584236.28	13879424.33	13552530.83	43197648	234076	201817	4429
浙　江 Zhejiang	27005467.79	7106282.02	8074861.98	31078185	192399	168002	7841
安　徽 Anhui	43507479.59	7117557.61	10421292.82	30599414	175011	143027	3017
福　建 Fujian	14814381.57	3853987.14	3877656.39	12965665	60026	48427	918
江　西 Jiangxi	31939878.78	6519955.74	9936048.10	26556476	101954	81777	3168
山　东 Shandong	76631994.46	16636278.34	22441483.29	72945158	346626	304602	4784
河　南 Henan	66095479.45	8869722.33	15928530.16	65797130	240695	203625	14019
湖　北 Hubei	34418397.56	11674884.23	7566192.50	28882287	99323	84565	3178
湖　南 Hunan	49239611.95	8614370.67	10212791.93	39839451	137296	117596	3547
广　东 Guangdong	51509807.49	13731590.53	14852087.20	44373048	271956	224145	14821
广　西 Guangxi	34037698.23	5613336.83	9652565.94	48077969	126378	98062	2176
海　南 Hainan	12053638.84	2695978.64	2139842.28	5605102	27307	24151	310
重　庆 Chongqing	12079906.28	2541456.93	3640702.57	10358322	59892	49401	1624
四　川 Sichuan	40039721.61	7386461.01	14588426.36	42178976	214138	172847	4501
贵　州 Guizhou	36295538.37	8339610.53	11517406.17	42203165	157462	141037	2889
云　南 Yunnan	28018510.09	5902861.72	7134212.37	26585760	120723	99066	634
西　藏 Tibet	4096760.98	541259.24	691830.88	2050908	12177	7702	224
陕　西 Shaanxi	23670420.72	3701408.16	6163318.52	30251375	130008	119411	3579
甘　肃 Gansu	15362402.30	2548858.84	4593657.87	14502897	75973	64463	2074
青　海 Qinghai	4260266.02	557607.63	1141120.73	4164130	20833	17082	1240
宁　夏 Ningxia	5184049.14	1103450.25	1632714.78	3986989	25949	20437	451
新　疆 Xinjiang	22363487.62	6097230.56	6055394.67	11931363	73282	51996	2321

件(二)(镇区)
Secondary Schools (2)(Counties & Towns Area)

教室(间) Classroom(Room)		教室中:普通教室(间) of Which: General Classroom(Room)		固定资产总值(万元) Total Value of Fixed Asset (10,000 yuan)		
合计 Total	其中:网络多媒体教室 of Which: Network Multimedia Classroom	合计 Total	其中:网络多媒体教室 of Which: Network Multimedia Classroom	合计 Total	其中:教学仪器设备资产值 of Which: Total Value of Equip & Instru. 小计 Subtotal	其中:实验设备 of Which: for Experiment
860012	**537229**	**638522**	**474172**	**39088754.97**	**4261869.11**	**1368979.49**
2303	1797	1256	1118	157288.95	49290.00	5519.26
2785	1692	1943	1505	87820.77	13080.78	4082.26
49352	30873	38984	29376	1848208.57	185327.23	77445.58
23484	14159	17887	12975	1067969.49	97715.43	36005.41
14609	10860	8897	8468	1043758.84	115758.18	29856.81
21600	10837	16482	9599	683254.02	116268.35	39642.24
15720	5498	11170	4842	432152.00	64142.28	24738.46
20705	11475	13187	9737	793670.68	117027.43	35928.34
3993	3391	2710	2440	328788.55	43657.52	12574.50
50367	33571	33904	27443	2862670.37	280677.70	91952.16
29713	25045	20777	20268	1757389.40	248369.91	52639.38
45676	27463	35654	25572	1919692.64	184214.04	60281.49
14676	10021	9042	8293	634148.57	86060.28	27923.71
34245	20003	26641	18801	1131589.13	128599.46	35917.56
74225	56902	50746	45888	3420682.79	330894.01	94904.54
78363	43388	67752	41400	2942604.92	239830.94	86892.46
29437	16515	21733	15410	1302738.69	133425.89	51598.53
52329	20596	38701	19394	2048901.26	223074.10	79664.38
45925	35112	34366	30740	2156709.80	251744.35	98896.20
30160	22317	24316	21241	1453288.59	192045.16	59822.02
5948	3489	4330	3156	402544.83	47522.49	15497.31
15806	13205	10403	9734	691588.18	71408.43	17553.63
55648	28381	43790	25639	2556032.07	353335.46	108610.59
37722	26818	28305	24500	1785385.92	154224.90	48251.81
27995	15487	21687	14383	1579498.26	112769.61	33008.16
2635	1282	2000	1206	258371.99	12689.04	3813.94
26999	17047	21707	15611	1223134.13	143232.94	63587.69
19488	12267	11851	10473	968177.38	91052.39	26719.35
4840	2427	3374	2239	310675.75	24503.93	7359.76
4660	3272	3116	2747	283908.28	49248.82	13895.85
18604	12039	11811	9974	956110.17	100678.06	24396.09

初中办学条件
Condition of School Buildings in Junior Secondary

地 区 Region	占地面积(平方米) Areas of School Sites(m^2)			图书(册) Books & Magazines in Libraries (Volume)	计算机数(台) PC (Set)		
	合计 Total	其中: of Which: 绿化用地面积 Green Areas	运动场地面积 Sports Areas		合计 Total	其中:教学用计算机 No. of Computers Used for Instruction 小计 Subtotal	其中:平板电脑 of Which: Tablet PC
总 计 Total	**201262610.43**	**39982888.78**	**55385250.93**	**191153586**	**864424**	**737748**	**27203**
北 京 Beijing	648172.73	148778.41	216367.01	444154	4967	4212	335
天 津 Tianjin	1086776.26	130754.55	456396.81	1167402	4584	4021	89
河 北 Hebei	19389727.50	2040134.99	5866418.60	25022571	80813	77992	2396
山 西 Shanxi	5372288.50	600909.14	1398296.25	4998989	29231	23897	624
内蒙古 Inner Mongolia	2175263.25	458391.70	483162.00	944590	6031	4016	100
辽 宁 Liaoning	2453087.36	336838.97	976859.20	2292874	12610	9542	1056
吉 林 Jilin	1360768.74	324601.51	341269.48	924063	4534	3498	77
黑龙江 Heilongjiang	1699937.06	228839.15	459389.00	994108	5230	4344	91
上 海 Shanghai	837490.80	296954.00	242931.13	980776	6016	4942	327
江 苏 Jiangsu	12060021.97	3343781.22	3274302.45	10788571	58012	49599	1666
浙 江 Zhejiang	8480227.72	2111872.80	2454056.47	9453948	58918	52425	2479
安 徽 Anhui	10305911.28	1709712.61	2314227.69	6310374	36767	29142	503
福 建 Fujian	4285758.87	1010016.94	1213348.02	3625044	16252	13647	197
江 西 Jiangxi	6459437.97	1394181.51	1957810.07	4607508	19051	14593	477
山 东 Shandong	28506417.51	6377786.35	8525392.25	27158814	130119	113475	2204
河 南 Henan	23057518.61	3176376.16	5441360.85	20801244	80581	67690	4761
湖 北 Hubei	8520995.68	2862450.26	1899577.27	6891977	24242	20616	476
湖 南 Hunan	11782662.69	2135041.84	2365221.93	9284460	30903	26662	641
广 东 Guangdong	13566034.62	3466496.05	4216482.16	13614734	83053	69597	4807
广 西 Guangxi	7515339.23	1211138.84	1960752.33	10083352	27033	21197	360
海 南 Hainan	601000.45	132177.58	131316.10	343578	1840	1653	0
重 庆 Chongqing	2105423.41	386812.63	654849.47	1540068	8842	7294	287
四 川 Sichuan	6336789.20	1317975.91	2195778.01	5807634	32405	25793	316
贵 州 Guizhou	5534956.02	1256421.84	1751007.37	6584295	23517	21914	303
云 南 Yunnan	4757132.09	1160139.59	1327653.99	4884748	22186	17905	270
西 藏 Tibet	372373.00	46337.00	45515.80	227874	1370	688	0
陕 西 Shaanxi	4497488.38	814257.24	1136119.76	5304795	23332	21505	438
甘 肃 Gansu	3278415.63	589301.60	917716.57	2959334	15124	13139	387
青 海 Qinghai	988451.70	114706.45	276008.83	1201263	5414	4687	688
宁 夏 Ningxia	597112.71	63908.40	199719.61	432267	2883	2219	50
新 疆 Xinjiang	2629629.49	735793.54	685944.45	1478177	8564	5844	798

(二)(镇乡结合区)
Schools (2)(County-town Transitional Area)

教室(间) Classroom(Room)		教室中:普通教室(间) of Which: General Classroom(Room)		固定资产总值(万元) Total Value of Fixed Asset (10,000 yuan)		
					其中:教学仪器设备资产值 of Which: Total Value of Equip & Instru.	
合计 Total	其中:网络多媒体教室 of Which: Network Multimedia Classroom	合计 Total	其中:网络多媒体教室 of Which: Network Multimedia Classroom	合计 Total	小计 Subtotal	其中:实验设备 of Which: for Experiment
214690	**135254**	**161496**	**119783**	**10098685.01**	**1013548.89**	**332028.15**
686	520	366	347	55142.55	16226.19	1357.75
1188	615	813	548	33841.39	5323.82	1576.36
22565	13734	18150	13217	823862.70	81999.59	35034.62
6772	4175	5218	3854	264620.74	28297.16	10797.48
1378	1048	819	764	95122.61	8076.80	2538.79
2577	1397	1996	1193	101833.73	14733.36	5064.20
1423	611	1026	535	60621.93	6264.94	2376.98
1715	913	1067	783	47960.25	7918.72	2375.36
1057	934	710	663	95402.94	12055.25	3434.64
12102	8308	7854	6586	733000.88	68127.56	22052.19
9245	7935	6689	6504	563601.10	78235.17	15468.22
10263	5762	8037	5366	437437.69	38181.01	12142.37
4169	2733	2550	2315	186511.19	24366.97	8550.29
6506	3464	5057	3221	252333.92	25434.10	6999.55
28596	21521	19563	17539	1332858.15	129028.94	37902.92
27596	15328	23562	14608	1145587.06	85588.62	29345.26
7428	4150	5602	3929	328602.06	34659.97	13542.79
11747	4376	8792	4132	509366.20	52280.59	19160.87
14513	11250	11032	9766	678473.74	80674.93	33420.84
6304	4794	5220	4596	310892.92	40061.00	13320.91
335	226	274	208	32597.84	2804.03	968.08
2705	2053	1855	1594	142951.61	11324.34	2508.05
8666	4280	6781	3729	458015.75	54923.79	16559.52
5969	4185	4552	3868	389237.15	23479.56	8436.96
5371	2949	3965	2741	334164.73	20345.28	6588.06
269	155	229	152	29092.17	1177.40	317.40
5065	2818	4205	2564	251328.19	24960.97	10313.60
3847	2326	2345	2039	202474.52	15752.13	5370.43
1605	797	1095	773	79453.68	7207.79	1848.75
535	351	367	311	27908.53	4606.80	864.08
2493	1546	1705	1338	94387.12	9432.14	1790.84

地 区 Region	占地面积(平方米) Areas of School Sites(m^2) 合计 Total	其中: of Which: 绿化用地面积 Green Areas	运动场地面积 Sports Areas	图书(册) Books & Magazines in Libraries (Volume)	计算机数(台) PC (Set) 合计 Total	其中:教学用计算机 No. of Computers Used for Instruction 小计 Subtotal	其中:平板电脑 of Which: Tablet PC
总 计 Total	**369638687.65**	**69495415.39**	**95239639.51**	**276307960**	**1326054**	**1089399**	**32489**
北 京 Beijing	2321658.53	514002.08	659796.20	1151436	11358	9347	200
天 津 Tianjin	1650190.11	193911.31	662771.21	1385918	6443	5772	142
河 北 Hebei	21168706.86	2595137.41	6445284.53	21129300	74241	71721	2765
山 西 Shanxi	11101711.78	1418699.00	2227996.08	5926365	45733	33817	611
内蒙古 Inner Mongolia	5189874.70	993340.49	1022483.94	1542915	12415	8108	253
辽 宁 Liaoning	8574801.68	1166506.34	3320838.37	6926701	40978	31049	2219
吉 林 Jilin	11479817.99	2789119.27	2599433.52	5467802	26486	19373	117
黑龙江 Heilongjiang	11240493.98	1449311.98	2408490.83	4347098	27658	21506	282
上 海 Shanghai	783277.90	305963.70	220895.04	790747	5406	4359	353
江 苏 Jiangsu	7050687.49	1972211.55	1813119.42	4896594	27761	23843	411
浙 江 Zhejiang	7897320.77	1990614.92	2186460.33	7845217	47139	40855	1508
安 徽 Anhui	29612366.29	4507916.04	6012455.31	16419663	99867	79102	1041
福 建 Fujian	10611812.47	2721675.13	2383899.26	7141464	37226	28573	653
江 西 Jiangxi	18156227.28	3276889.89	5508822.61	12028234	49759	38971	1317
山 东 Shandong	17743299.72	4125880.46	4848974.70	13996532	67563	58157	700
河 南 Henan	37182568.48	4777552.10	8331229.41	29521426	108046	90262	6364
湖 北 Hubei	12677303.64	4151817.58	2606593.74	9484819	39696	32513	1181
湖 南 Hunan	27004152.05	4258642.99	5220360.44	19591794	72921	63246	783
广 东 Guangdong	18518473.52	4842122.31	4969329.76	15438547	90499	74967	5998
广 西 Guangxi	9835295.82	1707090.23	3051289.23	11501616	34498	27669	594
海 南 Hainan	2178696.16	435190.00	361466.00	815610	4851	4203	154
重 庆 Chongqing	3014623.03	565228.13	814275.39	2080210	13820	11347	234
四 川 Sichuan	19463326.91	2665653.29	7592573.36	19800867	101389	81434	517
贵 州 Guizhou	11524174.05	2566601.53	3765266.54	12630262	45881	41022	641
云 南 Yunnan	20338900.12	4327147.45	4945762.66	18097748	83916	70148	504
西 藏 Tibet	895911.93	82627.28	154616.97	542871	2980	1592	1
陕 西 Shaanxi	5172515.01	803007.55	1212625.47	4313989	21355	18273	636
甘 肃 Gansu	11847467.67	1826094.19	2917757.80	8604659	47084	39295	1029
青 海 Qinghai	2776085.48	373236.40	641782.60	2594769	13244	10123	407
宁 夏 Ningxia	2766758.76	586999.97	862001.24	1815116	13248	9661	186
新 疆 Xinjiang	19860187.47	5505224.82	5470987.55	8477671	52593	39091	688

件(二)(乡村)
Secondary Schools (2) (Rural Area)

教室(间) Classroom(Room)		教室中:普通教室(间) of Which: General Classroom(Room)		固定资产总值(万元) Total Value of Fixed Asset (10,000 yuan)		
					其中:教学仪器设备资产值 of Which: Total Value of Equip & Instru.	
合计 Total	其中:网络多媒体教室 of Which: Network Multimedia Classroom	合计 Total	其中:网络多媒体教室 of Which: Network Multimedia Classroom	合计 Total	小计 Subtotal	其中:实验设备 of Which: for Experiment
361649	**197159**	**263367**	**174511**	**13380886.81**	**1571851.76**	**543536.84**
1996	1391	1022	835	136115.20	34238.13	4736.92
1710	981	1051	847	43341.52	7683.57	3353.89
21380	12256	16493	11645	659940.96	69215.35	31299.80
11226	5779	7783	5063	440505.83	33650.95	12788.39
2949	2004	1640	1487	181965.08	23075.62	6322.78
8342	4484	6290	3892	259971.35	48050.63	16680.65
9444	2869	6349	2482	233670.53	32278.87	13426.25
10040	4180	6339	3610	276860.43	39857.78	14894.86
967	804	611	568	64377.46	10428.13	3065.67
6171	3684	4071	2920	227737.05	35125.07	11309.19
8116	6756	5625	5482	423905.30	59238.56	14495.52
25652	15802	19619	14650	905688.51	97376.88	33364.18
9477	5870	5203	4644	400180.79	48000.27	16818.32
17825	9239	13093	8563	509678.53	64785.10	21802.37
14741	11004	9917	8689	707794.28	58320.39	17554.17
37052	17335	30444	16203	1137163.91	107073.93	41770.24
10944	5828	8037	5454	438368.39	47171.33	19011.08
28543	8584	20640	7954	786254.23	97077.25	35382.44
17541	12862	12628	11266	726076.91	88264.33	35266.43
7976	5761	6514	5428	396598.12	52113.85	17733.40
1165	612	806	537	68956.22	7809.94	3334.92
3728	3053	2424	2193	163016.90	15852.55	4174.87
31491	13712	25203	12312	964577.28	170300.51	59955.91
12957	8608	9705	7949	449778.97	50808.18	16636.09
19700	10292	15131	9535	1049667.74	84159.31	26891.82
702	377	508	367	57174.47	2949.74	1147.56
5076	2848	3686	2443	194840.70	21677.42	9832.23
13332	7676	8263	6709	517230.19	53709.86	19751.93
3525	1619	2299	1407	188825.53	12255.85	3962.73
2569	1719	1762	1409	132344.54	22008.73	8110.40
15312	9170	10211	7968	638279.90	77293.68	18661.85

小学校数、教学点
Number of Schools, External Teaching

地　区 Region	学校数(所) Schools	教学点数(个) External Teaching Sites	合计 Total	一年级 Grade 1
总　计 Total	**167009**	**102998**	**2683706**	**500671**
北　京 Beijing	984	0	26399	4604
天　津 Tianjin	857	0	17811	3201
河　北 Hebei	11697	6967	163587	31767
山　西 Shanxi	5646	3238	72699	12586
内蒙古 Inner Mongolia	1658	809	35502	6176
辽　宁 Liaoning	3634	543	54571	8916
吉　林 Jilin	4153	401	40346	6581
黑龙江 Heilongjiang	1537	1702	40766	6955
上　海 Shanghai	741	0	21383	4428
江　苏 Jiangsu	4075	917	126792	22593
浙　江 Zhejiang	3286	134	92656	16173
安　徽 Anhui	8108	5073	127254	23587
福　建 Fujian	5190	2121	77440	14231
江　西 Jiangxi	7760	8850	119885	23190
山　东 Shandong	9738	1899	170289	32642
河　南 Henan	20372	12945	267776	50950
湖　北 Hubei	5378	3619	89406	17055
湖　南 Hunan	7757	7837	124580	25039
广　东 Guangdong	10258	6103	238924	45614
广　西 Guangxi	8454	11586	126041	24568
海　南 Hainan	1388	1040	21562	4157
重　庆 Chongqing	2954	1582	52826	8870
四　川 Sichuan	5721	8446	137768	24829
贵　州 Guizhou	7113	3698	93939	17764
云　南 Yunnan	11186	3601	107657	19637
西　藏 Tibet	806	191	8613	1618
陕　西 Shaanxi	4752	2328	66561	12581
甘　肃 Gansu	6172	5128	70545	13173
青　海 Qinghai	758	867	12555	2609
宁　夏 Ningxia	1353	552	15237	2803
新　疆 Xinjiang	3523	821	62336	11774

数及班数(总计)
Sites & Classes in Primary Schools

班数(个)
Classes

二年级 Grade 2	三年级 Grade 3	四年级 Grade 4	五年级 Grade 5	六年级 Grade 6	复式班 Multiple-grade Classes
481170	**456252**	**429804**	**418866**	**387993**	**8950**
4358	4342	4467	4513	4115	0
3157	3051	3029	2957	2416	0
30270	27367	25063	24293	24277	550
12533	12121	11348	11616	11594	901
6330	5911	5834	5695	5528	28
8974	9111	9205	9330	9035	0
6849	6804	6415	6779	6918	0
7428	7292	6927	7528	4636	0
4332	4181	4178	4264	0	0
22054	21583	20959	20455	19148	0
15658	15567	15243	15226	14785	4
22498	21555	20488	20143	18425	558
13594	13166	12813	12085	11398	153
21846	20139	18362	18555	16754	1039
30380	29581	29126	27521	21039	0
49199	46232	42172	40746	38188	289
16015	15271	14099	13463	13133	370
23283	20767	18936	18384	17574	597
44071	42110	37874	36057	33174	24
23083	20929	19553	18578	17670	1660
3918	3686	3391	3230	3178	2
8914	8641	8893	9032	8473	3
23887	23110	22303	21986	21438	215
17171	15901	14621	13768	14489	225
18997	18227	17406	16696	16440	254
1551	1436	1350	1335	1322	1
11950	11003	10518	10094	9713	702
12651	11745	10743	10777	10167	1289
2391	2007	1899	1850	1760	39
2687	2538	2433	2403	2326	47
11141	10878	10156	9507	8880	0

小学校数、教学点
Number of Schools, External Teaching Sites

地　区 Region	学校数(所) Schools	教学点数(个) External Teaching Sites	合计 Total	一年级 Grade 1
总　计 Total	**27159**	**1682**	**765191**	**142757**
北　京 Beijing	635	0	21927	3837
天　津 Tianjin	426	0	12170	2226
河　北 Hebei	1461	154	29959	5733
山　西 Shanxi	869	59	19170	3494
内蒙古 Inner Mongolia	457	4	12157	2086
辽　宁 Liaoning	1089	13	26770	4600
吉　林 Jilin	501	3	12897	2202
黑龙江 Heilongjiang	581	35	15434	2879
上　海 Shanghai	605	0	18267	3803
江　苏 Jiangsu	1437	38	54720	10255
浙　江 Zhejiang	1133	2	44558	8107
安　徽 Anhui	784	52	21514	4017
福　建 Fujian	1076	39	26032	4626
江　西 Jiangxi	755	162	21892	3874
山　东 Shandong	1954	51	54977	11206
河　南 Henan	1831	228	43279	7837
湖　北 Hubei	1145	90	29547	5373
湖　南 Hunan	1103	121	26492	5103
广　东 Guangdong	3457	222	119419	22518
广　西 Guangxi	878	109	21053	4047
海　南 Hainan	205	12	6208	1204
重　庆 Chongqing	648	14	19020	3469
四　川 Sichuan	838	88	30486	5756
贵　州 Guizhou	711	38	15650	3001
云　南 Yunnan	701	66	14431	2707
西　藏 Tibet	32	0	1036	191
陕　西 Shaanxi	909	61	19226	3735
甘　肃 Gansu	376	12	9106	1678
青　海 Qinghai	90	5	2269	405
宁　夏 Ningxia	165	1	3941	718
新　疆 Xinjiang	307	3	11584	2070

数及班数(城区)

& Classes in Primary Schools (Urban Area)

班数(个)
Classes

二年级 Grade 2	三年级 Grade 3	四年级 Grade 4	五年级 Grade 5	六年级 Grade 6	复式班 Multiple-grade Classes
135141	**130178**	**125797**	**122818**	**108456**	**44**
3631	3620	3751	3735	3353	0
2169	2057	2026	1960	1732	0
5299	5071	4733	4556	4566	1
3366	3285	3068	3064	2891	2
2142	2037	2045	1999	1848	0
4436	4471	4487	4543	4233	0
2209	2169	2013	2190	2114	0
2902	2820	2633	2846	1354	0
3708	3582	3569	3605	0	0
9664	9245	8927	8637	7992	0
7686	7511	7332	7148	6774	0
3737	3610	3526	3488	3134	2
4496	4505	4421	4139	3843	2
3739	3640	3510	3631	3486	12
9980	9303	9418	9063	6007	0
7597	7342	6989	6923	6589	2
5124	5034	4785	4637	4593	1
4766	4446	4125	4091	3955	6
21422	20604	19312	18407	17150	6
3771	3520	3378	3278	3056	3
1078	1050	1003	951	922	0
3300	3137	3190	3123	2801	0
5270	5061	4990	4843	4562	4
2812	2684	2495	2315	2342	1
2491	2425	2377	2253	2177	1
186	168	167	169	155	0
3507	3243	3117	2907	2717	0
1573	1509	1455	1472	1418	1
385	376	373	369	361	0
681	656	641	630	615	0
2014	1997	1941	1846	1716	0

小学校数、教学点数
Number of Schools, External Teaching Sites &

地　区 Region	学校数(所) Schools	教学点数(个) External Teaching Sites	合计 Total	一年级 Grade 1
总　计 Total	**7817**	**1270**	**152239**	**28946**
北　京 Beijing	90	0	1884	330
天　津 Tianjin	76	0	1344	249
河　北 Hebei	660	144	8877	1741
山　西 Shanxi	234	37	2766	523
内蒙古 Inner Mongolia	31	2	291	55
辽　宁 Liaoning	172	10	2489	414
吉　林 Jilin	86	3	748	131
黑龙江 Heilongjiang	45	19	873	159
上　海 Shanghai	71	0	1891	386
江　苏 Jiangsu	242	21	6516	1230
浙　江 Zhejiang	358	2	12154	2128
安　徽 Anhui	213	39	3325	627
福　建 Fujian	385	24	5784	1093
江　西 Jiangxi	290	124	4192	756
山　东 Shandong	758	45	15755	3152
河　南 Henan	661	164	9578	1743
湖　北 Hubei	268	53	4333	804
湖　南 Hunan	244	95	3385	690
广　东 Guangdong	1461	188	41600	7999
广　西 Guangxi	295	94	4741	936
海　南 Hainan	48	8	681	130
重　庆 Chongqing	107	9	1829	324
四　川 Sichuan	130	55	4213	806
贵　州 Guizhou	201	29	2842	547
云　南 Yunnan	295	51	4186	804
西　藏 Tibet	1	0	15	3
陕　西 Shaanxi	252	37	3142	642
甘　肃 Gansu	61	9	889	175
青　海 Qinghai	12	5	253	47
宁　夏 Ningxia	18	0	237	44
新　疆 Xinjiang	52	3	1426	278

及班数(城乡结合区)

Classes in Primary Schools (Urban-rural Transitional Area)

班数(个) Classes					
二年级 Grade 2	三年级 Grade 3	四年级 Grade 4	五年级 Grade 5	六年级 Grade 6	复式班 Multiple-grade Classes
27185	**26121**	**24601**	**23763**	**21594**	**29**
301	302	328	326	297	0
246	237	237	204	171	0
1579	1488	1389	1320	1359	1
489	474	423	430	425	2
55	49	49	43	40	0
406	416	425	411	417	0
134	135	116	117	115	0
157	158	149	165	85	0
383	372	371	379	0	0
1166	1101	1053	1014	952	0
2049	2029	1995	2005	1948	0
569	568	542	529	488	2
1042	1009	959	879	801	1
733	723	677	686	612	5
2833	2708	2677	2548	1837	0
1707	1648	1536	1512	1431	1
763	746	676	671	672	1
631	566	515	498	479	6
7620	7254	6562	6290	5875	0
862	816	751	709	664	3
122	113	109	106	101	0
290	289	303	324	299	0
730	706	685	657	625	4
505	492	444	417	436	1
725	704	684	644	624	1
3	3	2	2	2	0
577	522	495	460	446	0
156	143	136	142	136	1
43	41	41	41	40	0
42	38	36	37	40	0
267	271	236	197	177	0

小学校数、教学点
Number of Schools, External Teaching Sites &

地　区 Region	学校数(所) Schools	教学点数(个) External Teaching Sites	合计 Total	一年级 Grade 1
总　计 Total	**43798**	**11023**	**904980**	**160105**
北　京 Beijing	105	0	1938	340
天　津 Tianjin	135	0	2296	395
河　北 Hebei	3374	939	58111	10672
山　西 Shanxi	1552	169	25019	4347
内蒙古 Inner Mongolia	681	49	16131	2663
辽　宁 Liaoning	641	21	13520	2103
吉　林 Jilin	583	21	12179	1983
黑龙江 Heilongjiang	583	102	15147	2486
上　海 Shanghai	93	0	2437	495
江　苏 Jiangsu	1567	150	53914	9208
浙　江 Zhejiang	1077	14	32760	5572
安　徽 Anhui	2121	622	48589	8717
福　建 Fujian	1576	106	27563	4826
江　西 Jiangxi	1999	1059	44060	7562
山　东 Shandong	2842	314	62242	11771
河　南 Henan	5177	1724	90464	16007
湖　北 Hubei	1558	375	31722	5649
湖　南 Hunan	2577	1015	50944	9356
广　东 Guangdong	2400	628	59199	10617
广　西 Guangxi	1929	1433	36695	6707
海　南 Hainan	398	123	7735	1352
重　庆 Chongqing	942	149	20129	3125
四　川 Sichuan	2126	620	55645	9580
贵　州 Guizhou	1989	328	35642	6422
云　南 Yunnan	1631	265	24769	4318
西　藏 Tibet	141	4	2302	394
陕　西 Shaanxi	1938	466	29731	5520
甘　肃 Gansu	1121	214	18839	3421
青　海 Qinghai	179	35	4300	749
宁　夏 Ningxia	222	32	4248	733
新　疆 Xinjiang	541	46	16710	3015

数及班数(镇区)
Classes in Primary Schools (Counties & Towns Area)

班数(个) Classes					
二年级 Grade 2	三年级 Grade 3	四年级 Grade 4	五年级 Grade 5	六年级 Grade 6	复式班 Multiple-grade Classes
154922	**151821**	**146072**	**147378**	**144074**	**608**
317	313	316	330	322	0
402	399	402	401	297	0
10109	9890	9129	9085	9213	13
4273	4197	3906	4080	4188	28
2785	2703	2687	2646	2636	11
2188	2215	2266	2331	2417	0
2050	2043	1918	2029	2156	0
2685	2647	2518	2792	2019	0
487	473	469	513	0	0
9157	9139	8945	8910	8555	0
5451	5486	5387	5467	5397	0
8334	8175	7894	7956	7479	34
4720	4707	4655	4427	4226	2
7173	7096	6841	7596	7662	130
10814	10762	10688	10121	8086	0
15569	15265	14226	14541	14846	10
5473	5463	5095	5020	4981	41
8855	8588	7977	8065	8072	31
10397	9918	9415	9374	9476	2
6250	5887	5804	5986	5959	102
1295	1281	1274	1252	1281	0
3251	3277	3450	3603	3423	0
9305	9288	9170	9173	9125	4
6191	5961	5640	5438	5975	15
4128	4028	3964	4075	4239	17
390	367	380	376	395	0
5251	4887	4698	4650	4593	132
3269	3149	2854	3051	3062	33
735	692	702	705	717	0
713	692	679	712	716	3
2905	2833	2723	2673	2561	0

地　区 Region	学校数(所) Schools	教学点数(个) External Teaching Sites		
			合计 Total	一年级 Grade 1
总　计 Total	**18045**	**7969**	**278351**	**51042**
北　京 Beijing	33	0	534	91
天　津 Tianjin	69	0	1101	188
河　北 Hebei	2169	813	31718	6006
山　西 Shanxi	672	117	8354	1439
内蒙古 Inner Mongolia	69	14	1431	230
辽　宁 Liaoning	162	12	2065	299
吉　林 Jilin	124	19	1400	238
黑龙江 Heilongjiang	68	41	1551	241
上　海 Shanghai	24	0	586	114
江　苏 Jiangsu	654	109	15710	2662
浙　江 Zhejiang	392	7	11010	1869
安　徽 Anhui	730	388	11450	2041
福　建 Fujian	716	68	8858	1598
江　西 Jiangxi	920	813	12361	2328
山　东 Shandong	1509	251	27426	5259
河　南 Henan	2783	1394	36909	6875
湖　北 Hubei	595	255	8638	1610
湖　南 Hunan	945	606	13690	2609
广　东 Guangdong	1305	513	24707	4553
广　西 Guangxi	862	1112	12668	2486
海　南 Hainan	97	65	1262	233
重　庆 Chongqing	225	91	3523	553
四　川 Sichuan	373	476	9006	1589
贵　州 Guizhou	628	207	7936	1455
云　南 Yunnan	639	138	6928	1223
西　藏 Tibet	6	0	158	27
陕　西 Shaanxi	634	248	7689	1424
甘　肃 Gansu	379	141	4832	910
青　海 Qinghai	54	30	1132	207
宁　夏 Ningxia	59	21	705	123
新　疆 Xinjiang	150	20	3013	562

及班数(镇乡结合区)
Classes in Primary Schools (County-town Transitional Area)

班数(个) Classes					
二年级 Grade 2	三年级 Grade 3	四年级 Grade 4	五年级 Grade 5	六年级 Grade 6	复式班 Multiple-grade Classes
49055	**47243**	**44679**	**43922**	**42049**	**361**
86	83	87	96	91	0
198	192	195	189	139	0
5692	5359	4911	4854	4885	11
1424	1395	1317	1361	1397	21
251	235	236	236	243	0
323	339	353	371	380	0
236	229	231	234	232	0
259	267	263	289	232	0
119	112	117	124	0	0
2696	2716	2622	2552	2462	0
1832	1845	1803	1850	1811	0
1979	1945	1859	1860	1752	14
1553	1519	1476	1404	1307	1
2179	2069	1917	1953	1813	102
4825	4755	4645	4369	3573	0
6561	6325	5863	5693	5582	10
1529	1481	1368	1331	1295	24
2474	2298	2126	2101	2064	18
4470	4244	3910	3852	3676	2
2295	2114	2002	1880	1821	70
221	213	201	196	198	0
591	556	595	618	610	0
1534	1503	1464	1466	1450	0
1398	1345	1233	1199	1296	10
1195	1160	1124	1110	1113	3
29	28	27	22	25	0
1377	1276	1225	1187	1149	51
872	808	727	754	739	22
198	188	181	186	172	0
113	109	108	123	127	2
546	535	493	462	415	0

小学校数、教学点

Number of Schools, External Teaching Sites &

地 区 Region	学校数(所) Schools	教学点数(个) External Teaching Sites	合计 Total	一年级 Grade 1
总 计 Total	**96052**	**90293**	**1013535**	**197809**
北 京 Beijing	244	0	2534	427
天 津 Tianjin	296	0	3345	580
河 北 Hebei	6862	5874	75517	15362
山 西 Shanxi	3225	3010	28510	4745
内蒙古 Inner Mongolia	520	756	7214	1427
辽 宁 Liaoning	1904	509	14281	2213
吉 林 Jilin	3069	377	15270	2396
黑龙江 Heilongjiang	373	1565	10185	1590
上 海 Shanghai	43	0	679	130
江 苏 Jiangsu	1071	729	18158	3130
浙 江 Zhejiang	1076	118	15338	2494
安 徽 Anhui	5203	4399	57151	10853
福 建 Fujian	2538	1976	23845	4779
江 西 Jiangxi	5006	7629	53933	11754
山 东 Shandong	4942	1534	53070	9665
河 南 Henan	13364	10993	134033	27106
湖 北 Hubei	2675	3154	28137	6033
湖 南 Hunan	4077	6701	47144	10580
广 东 Guangdong	4401	5253	60306	12479
广 西 Guangxi	5647	10044	68293	13814
海 南 Hainan	785	905	7619	1601
重 庆 Chongqing	1364	1419	13677	2276
四 川 Sichuan	2757	7738	51637	9493
贵 州 Guizhou	4413	3332	42647	8341
云 南 Yunnan	8854	3270	68457	12612
西 藏 Tibet	633	187	5275	1033
陕 西 Shaanxi	1905	1801	17604	3326
甘 肃 Gansu	4675	4902	42600	8074
青 海 Qinghai	489	827	5986	1455
宁 夏 Ningxia	966	519	7048	1352
新 疆 Xinjiang	2675	772	34042	6689

数及班数(乡村)
Classes in Primary Schools (Rural Area)

班数(个) Classes					
二年级 Grade 2	三年级 Grade 3	四年级 Grade 4	五年级 Grade 5	六年级 Grade 6	复式班 Multiple-grade Classes
191107	**174253**	**157935**	**148670**	**135463**	**8298**
410	409	400	448	440	0
586	595	601	596	387	0
14862	12406	11201	10652	10498	536
4894	4639	4374	4472	4515	871
1403	1171	1102	1050	1044	17
2350	2425	2452	2456	2385	0
2590	2592	2484	2560	2648	0
1841	1825	1776	1890	1263	0
137	126	140	146	0	0
3233	3199	3087	2908	2601	0
2521	2570	2524	2611	2614	4
10427	9770	9068	8699	7812	522
4378	3954	3737	3519	3329	149
10934	9403	8011	7328	5606	897
9586	9516	9020	8337	6946	0
26033	23625	20957	19282	16753	277
5418	4774	4219	3806	3559	328
9662	7733	6834	6228	5547	560
12252	11588	9147	8276	6548	16
13062	11522	10371	9314	8655	1555
1545	1355	1114	1027	975	2
2363	2227	2253	2306	2249	3
9312	8761	8143	7970	7751	207
8168	7256	6486	6015	6172	209
12378	11774	11065	10368	10024	236
975	901	803	790	772	1
3192	2873	2703	2537	2403	570
7809	7087	6434	6254	5687	1255
1271	939	824	776	682	39
1293	1190	1113	1061	995	44
6222	6048	5492	4988	4603	0

小学学生
Number of Students in

地　区 Region	毕业生数 Graduates	招生数 Entrants		在校生数 Enrolment	
		合计 Total	其中:受过学前教育 of Which: Those Received the Pre-school Education	合计 Total	其中:女 of Which: Female
总　计 Total	**15658999**	**17665544**	**17430535**	**100936980**	**46883168**
北　京 Beijing	125938	157559	157390	875849	412510
天　津 Tianjin	98503	117656	117089	648049	302537
河　北 Hebei	976942	1134496	1134479	6372170	2968546
山　西 Shanxi	374969	379249	374956	2281194	1093757
内蒙古 Inner Mongolia	225839	215879	215554	1325442	633580
辽　宁 Liaoning	341438	300722	300453	1945975	924880
吉　林 Jilin	223741	189407	188644	1228205	585568
黑龙江 Heilongjiang	278965	221026	219096	1376526	661704
上　海 Shanghai	143115	163701	163627	784896	367567
江　苏 Jiangsu	773664	953228	951102	5402074	2478488
浙　江 Zhejiang	585621	613134	613061	3540079	1628318
安　徽 Anhui	691268	769781	769106	4405178	2017434
福　建 Fujian	438238	533958	531958	3070865	1404586
江　西 Jiangxi	678400	676913	647458	4228966	1908676
山　东 Shandong	1109648	1269806	1269806	7084730	3228869
河　南 Henan	1503121	1723796	1722896	9820554	4517305
湖　北 Hubei	524455	624961	618177	3545680	1611744
湖　南 Hunan	781279	884161	884094	5116575	2370993
广　东 Guangdong	1319106	1743657	1704544	9419581	4297597
广　西 Guangxi	713555	837008	824188	4637548	2163776
海　南 Hainan	122661	142730	140760	809483	362485
重　庆 Chongqing	336536	326026	322585	2099536	996577
四　川 Sichuan	869517	911391	899440	5518361	2648104
贵　州 Guizhou	595600	650473	629938	3620770	1690658
云　南 Yunnan	645496	634773	573308	3752041	1781320
西　藏 Tibet	45601	58283	45012	315122	153862
陕　西 Shaanxi	359973	480513	479371	2523085	1185713
甘　肃 Gansu	294669	336255	327571	1855722	877443
青　海 Qinghai	72761	84977	77731	465091	226131
宁　夏 Ningxia	99430	96628	95488	581350	277274
新　疆 Xinjiang	308950	433397	431653	2286283	1105166

数(总计)
Primary Schools(Total)

单位:人
unit: person

一年级 Grade 1	二年级 Grade 2	三年级 Grade 3	四年级 Grade 4	五年级 Grade 5	六年级 Grade 6	预计毕业生数 Estimated Graduates for Next Year
17670612	**17465724**	**17199979**	**16418717**	**16519451**	**15662497**	**16179442**
157658	145402	145522	148522	151458	127287	128698
117683	115754	111324	110024	105821	87443	100281
1134302	1114688	1100714	1001018	1002211	1019237	1019237
379267	384463	378623	349568	387863	401410	401410
215879	226775	221869	221657	223619	215643	217123
300734	312990	324154	330222	346791	331084	331084
189407	204818	205359	189629	212558	226434	226434
221026	246215	247476	227305	268395	166109	278378
163829	160817	153964	154509	151777	0	151777
953228	935453	923462	893881	879880	816170	816432
613135	593689	592248	586213	585397	569397	571593
769859	738492	744547	726517	743852	681911	681911
534423	530073	533590	525084	490341	457354	457354
679329	683471	697346	674487	761500	732833	732833
1269806	1242268	1251419	1254012	1171210	896015	1114010
1723810	1705980	1682895	1535877	1581322	1590670	1606445
624735	616978	617604	575799	557849	552715	553656
884162	889637	872705	804199	833860	832012	832012
1744575	1704320	1636403	1503736	1455447	1375100	1375100
836779	810328	766263	743344	749481	731353	731353
143070	138536	137852	133528	128225	128272	128272
326116	334994	336661	364650	380132	356983	356983
911392	919651	921719	915265	931665	918669	918669
650516	643104	616755	568675	537331	604389	604389
634929	644043	633406	608862	611221	619580	619580
58286	55590	51902	50401	50454	48489	48489
480754	458100	416226	399960	392033	376012	376012
336261	324662	309698	281309	303660	300132	300133
85323	80952	76025	74224	73861	74706	74706
96735	96517	93987	92146	100070	101895	101895
433604	406964	398261	374094	350167	323193	323193

小学学生
Number of Students in Primary

地　区 Region	毕业生数 Graduates	招生数 Entrants 合计 Total	其中:受过学前教育 of Which: Those Received the Pre-school Education	在校生数 Enrolment 合计 Total	其中:女 of Which: Female
总　计 Total	**5128287**	**6300296**	**6252652**	**34622854**	**15909940**
北　京 Beijing	105999	136107	135946	752970	354815
天　津 Tianjin	66931	86421	85856	464538	217294
河　北 Hebei	224894	271853	271841	1478354	686189
山　西 Shanxi	127521	148887	146988	848149	404892
内蒙古 Inner Mongolia	89839	89715	89611	538131	258208
辽　宁 Liaoning	180323	188091	187980	1128955	536207
吉　林 Jilin	86962	87228	87001	524582	248031
黑龙江 Heilongjiang	117335	110951	110031	630141	301599
上　海 Shanghai	119335	141471	141401	674304	316971
江　苏 Jiangsu	346893	452320	450942	2428691	1108057
浙　江 Zhejiang	278002	322083	322043	1767299	810235
安　徽 Anhui	145108	170163	169995	954231	429782
福　建 Fujian	173461	219028	218155	1245393	565545
江　西 Jiangxi	160030	171313	162662	1021802	452864
山　东 Shandong	386987	480629	480629	2518781	1151538
河　南 Henan	322678	384647	384439	2171044	980019
湖　北 Hubei	200923	247024	244834	1387044	622588
湖　南 Hunan	191536	240190	240171	1329693	605947
广　东 Guangdong	736722	998261	977293	5372837	2403557
广　西 Guangxi	146862	196156	195247	1051929	476907
海　南 Hainan	44853	56880	56659	313341	133850
重　庆 Chongqing	118708	152644	150516	861705	412062
四　川 Sichuan	208187	259536	259432	1437617	687179
贵　州 Guizhou	108544	138227	136614	736316	339345
云　南 Yunnan	107843	124622	124103	693101	328544
西　藏 Tibet	6838	9189	9106	49484	24163
陕　西 Shaanxi	126970	185700	184898	950834	444334
甘　肃 Gansu	67538	80409	80181	440375	204558
青　海 Qinghai	19413	21254	20529	119600	56880
宁　夏 Ningxia	32430	35359	35239	204967	96508
新　疆 Xinjiang	78622	93938	92310	526646	251272

数(城区)
Schools (Urban Area)

单位:人
unit: person

一年级 Grade 1	二年级 Grade 2	三年级 Grade 3	四年级 Grade 4	五年级 Grade 5	六年级 Grade 6	预计毕业生数 Estimated Graduates for Next Year
6301277	**6073511**	**5904363**	**5720553**	**5635279**	**4987871**	**5316915**
136174	125546	125881	128693	129659	107017	108428
86444	84041	78939	77399	73229	64486	68712
271854	257734	250570	233495	230970	233731	233731
148872	147882	142744	131577	139832	137242	137242
89715	91713	89960	90678	92518	83547	84973
188096	185004	190355	188957	198767	177776	177776
87228	89560	87724	79893	91098	89079	89079
110951	116136	115391	106120	122266	59277	122479
141562	138026	132293	132946	129477	0	129477
452320	428319	410985	397992	387310	351765	352027
322084	304091	296120	292219	285014	267771	269967
170172	158755	159864	159928	162760	142752	142752
219160	214737	217406	214213	198088	181789	181789
171434	170264	169740	164558	174827	170979	170979
480629	451634	435408	445948	425279	279883	397305
384649	379692	368108	348755	351338	338502	347924
246721	240579	238790	227461	218452	215041	215041
240190	233622	223577	209682	214100	208522	208522
998925	962139	932717	872146	833444	773466	773466
196159	186201	176524	170579	167453	155013	155013
56882	54281	54346	52336	48764	46732	46732
152671	145989	140963	147347	145672	129063	129063
259537	248083	240234	239666	233412	216685	216685
138246	132431	125724	117698	107974	114243	114243
124629	120055	117984	116291	109368	104774	104774
9189	9172	7870	7993	7966	7294	7294
185733	174591	158287	154222	145145	132856	132856
80412	77482	72458	69813	72031	68179	68179
21263	20239	19470	19606	19819	19203	19203
35391	34363	33337	33883	34551	33442	33442
93985	91150	90594	88459	84696	77762	77762

小学学生数
Number of Students in Primary

地　区 Region	毕业生数 Graduates	招生数 Entrants 合计 Total	其中:受过学前教育 of Which: Those Received the Pre-school Education	在校生数 Enrolment 合计 Total	其中:女 of Which: Female
总　计 Total	**903613**	**1193192**	**1180984**	**6359140**	**2887869**
北　京 Beijing	9142	9919	9919	56829	25865
天　津 Tianjin	6669	9027	9027	48714	22666
河　北 Hebei	55337	70724	70724	371432	171652
山　西 Shanxi	13853	18340	18039	98571	47353
内蒙古 Inner Mongolia	1373	1833	1755	9523	4663
辽　宁 Liaoning	15283	14875	14873	91899	43411
吉　林 Jilin	3683	3949	3945	23077	10941
黑龙江 Heilongjiang	5933	5135	5133	29841	14269
上　海 Shanghai	15078	14412	14410	70940	31817
江　苏 Jiangsu	37986	52690	52688	279076	125090
浙　江 Zhejiang	73270	83257	83241	472473	210706
安　徽 Anhui	18941	23503	23503	127171	57714
福　建 Fujian	30913	48334	48102	252540	115631
江　西 Jiangxi	24501	26714	24914	158582	70892
山　东 Shandong	98156	128523	128523	666808	304197
河　南 Henan	56065	69906	69836	391522	176982
湖　北 Hubei	26274	34049	33549	185380	81880
湖　南 Hunan	19555	26637	26637	137681	63974
广　东 Guangdong	244106	348187	340189	1829126	812355
广　西 Guangxi	29137	42777	42706	220383	101041
海　南 Hainan	3697	5355	5355	28046	12417
重　庆 Chongqing	11023	12789	12729	74831	35291
四　川 Sichuan	24745	33688	33663	178094	84524
贵　州 Guizhou	17941	22959	22602	120876	56393
云　南 Yunnan	27720	33936	33611	182396	86398
西　藏 Tibet	50	105	105	521	239
陕　西 Shaanxi	16757	27512	27498	130150	61373
甘　肃 Gansu	5065	7514	7360	35635	16526
青　海 Qinghai	1979	2091	1897	11571	5520
宁　夏 Ningxia	1505	1975	1974	11119	5261
新　疆 Xinjiang	7876	12477	12477	64333	30828

（城乡结合区）

Schools (Urban-rural Transitional Area)

单位：人
unit: person

一年级 Grade 1	二年级 Grade 2	三年级 Grade 3	四年级 Grade 4	五年级 Grade 5	六年级 Grade 6	预计毕业生数 Estimated Graduates for Next Year
1193405	**1134350**	**1098827**	**1029328**	**994662**	**908568**	**951181**
9931	8941	9198	9966	9907	8886	8886
9029	9019	8606	8743	7269	6048	6647
70725	65298	62873	57877	55499	59160	59160
18325	17982	17119	14374	15434	15337	15337
1833	1887	1716	1538	1405	1144	1256
14876	15053	15575	15905	15331	15159	15159
3949	4194	4216	3478	3573	3667	3667
5135	5039	5427	4954	5878	3408	6036
14420	14616	14159	13888	13857	0	13857
52690	49814	47723	45095	43463	40291	40291
83257	79664	79021	77676	77706	75149	75149
23507	21110	21834	20981	20939	18800	18800
48345	46264	44814	42279	37544	33294	33294
26739	26400	26984	25536	27030	25893	25893
128523	119522	116170	116168	108574	77851	103268
69906	68955	67403	61995	62528	60735	60735
34057	32532	32543	29141	28641	28466	28466
26637	25629	23280	20774	20682	20679	20679
348310	335566	321227	288339	277044	258640	258640
42779	40277	37732	34812	33497	31286	31286
5355	5020	4742	4571	4315	4043	4043
12791	11501	11853	12637	13593	12456	12456
33689	30467	29514	29303	28271	26850	26850
22961	21598	20940	19040	17239	19098	19098
33938	31367	31088	30363	28112	27528	27528
105	108	100	72	79	57	57
27523	24289	21382	20438	18967	17551	17551
7514	6448	5506	5265	5637	5265	5265
2092	1994	1809	1849	1899	1928	1928
1979	1868	1764	1664	1907	1937	1937
12485	11928	12509	10607	8842	7962	7962

小学学生
Number of Students in Primary

地　区 Region	毕业生数 Graduates	招生数 Entrants		在校生数 Enrolment	
		合计 Total	其中:受过学前教育 of Which: Those Received the Pre-school Education	合计 Total	其中:女 of Which: Female
总　计 Total	**6222672**	**6496373**	**6438675**	**38560500**	**17796448**
北　京 Beijing	9534	10540	10540	58638	27655
天　津 Tianjin	13510	13603	13603	79959	37141
河　北 Hebei	396947	439360	439360	2539876	1169912
山　西 Shanxi	159824	160265	158568	960589	457961
内蒙古 Inner Mongolia	106896	98595	98510	617934	295666
辽　宁 Liaoning	97175	69842	69785	499570	236699
吉　林 Jilin	80691	67733	67437	441339	210916
黑龙江 Heilongjiang	115670	84116	83387	555327	266866
上　海 Shanghai	18244	17678	17676	87265	40003
江　苏 Jiangsu	339435	394433	393879	2321417	1062918
浙　江 Zhejiang	219765	212708	212696	1277042	588998
安　徽 Anhui	309698	333030	332820	1951911	878899
福　建 Fujian	175460	206964	206570	1206539	548006
江　西 Jiangxi	340873	299589	289319	1960562	870321
山　东 Shandong	427176	481464	481464	2731127	1230382
河　南 Henan	638027	651477	651193	3882353	1752671
湖　北 Hubei	205853	231915	229795	1357390	619034
湖　南 Hunan	390635	404911	404905	2466916	1137249
广　东 Guangdong	374903	418682	409551	2371466	1096193
广　西 Guangxi	268898	288953	286537	1660135	764373
海　南 Hainan	54313	56947	56057	339414	154098
重　庆 Chongqing	150745	127966	127235	883921	417444
四　川 Sichuan	412397	414847	410617	2579964	1239804
贵　州 Guizhou	268075	287464	281403	1634653	753261
云　南 Yunnan	187054	170793	160888	1043503	495268
西　藏 Tibet	14076	15647	12480	92290	45087
陕　西 Shaanxi	175762	225335	225252	1208343	566950
甘　肃 Gansu	113674	131094	129701	724143	338085
青　海 Qinghai	31159	31888	29077	187135	91431
宁　夏 Ningxia	32631	31981	31898	193702	91799
新　疆 Xinjiang	93572	116553	116472	646077	311358

数(镇区)
Schools (Counties & Towns Area)

单位:人
unit: person

一年级 Grade 1	二年级 Grade 2	三年级 Grade 3	四年级 Grade 4	五年级 Grade 5	六年级 Grade 6	预计毕业生数 Estimated Graduates for Next Year
6498819	**6488373**	**6489222**	**6253523**	**6431941**	**6398622**	**6527757**
10553	9615	9338	9501	10175	9456	9456
13604	13914	13868	14025	13943	10605	13542
439165	431154	438319	402128	408219	420891	420891
160288	160841	158408	145423	162856	172773	172773
98595	104704	103383	103224	104220	103808	103862
69846	78688	81260	85494	89661	94621	94621
67733	73975	73842	67931	75346	82512	82512
84116	97401	97320	88754	106882	80854	113590
17711	17928	17346	16831	17449	0	17449
394433	394086	395867	384099	384763	368169	368169
212708	210010	212749	212087	214947	214541	214541
333062	322229	327448	321766	333064	314342	314342
207182	206931	208840	206602	193499	183485	183485
300993	300629	315680	308626	362153	372481	372481
481464	472551	481124	482504	449473	364011	433918
651485	646861	653836	603767	640696	685708	690818
231967	232333	237110	220689	217257	218034	218975
404912	415002	420818	393043	412451	420690	420690
418810	415106	395172	375720	377222	389436	389436
288974	277320	265616	265658	280663	281904	281904
57189	55986	56561	56622	55809	57247	57247
128008	136808	140413	154890	165342	158460	158460
414847	424393	431817	429543	439350	440014	440014
287468	283307	276623	258552	248030	280673	280673
170821	173973	171689	166674	175919	184427	184427
15649	15275	14721	15478	15381	15786	15786
225472	216472	197898	189348	191212	187941	187941
131094	125483	121085	107840	118485	120156	120157
32024	31209	30056	30762	30535	32549	32549
32015	32259	31374	30658	33272	34124	34124
116631	111930	109641	105284	103667	98924	98924

小学学生数
Number of Students in Primary Schools

地 区 Region	毕业生数 Graduates	招生数 Entrants		在校生数 Enrolment	
		合计 Total	其中:受过学前教育 of Which: Those Received the Pre-school Education	合计 Total	其中:女 of Which: Female
总 计 Total	**1658287**	**1856889**	**1841314**	**10666030**	**4921447**
北 京 Beijing	2546	2727	2727	15606	7363
天 津 Tianjin	6383	6373	6373	38468	17963
河 北 Hebei	196106	231022	231022	1291625	595544
山 西 Shanxi	46342	47359	46773	284389	136064
内蒙古 Inner Mongolia	9349	8296	8288	53073	24689
辽 宁 Liaoning	12925	8300	8296	64501	30324
吉 林 Jilin	7380	7104	7093	42819	20645
黑龙江 Heilongjiang	11480	7364	7364	51823	24949
上 海 Shanghai	4353	4165	4163	21115	9616
江 苏 Jiangsu	94440	107201	107090	637661	292016
浙 江 Zhejiang	70420	71368	71366	426573	194745
安 徽 Anhui	62162	65697	65655	389898	177056
福 建 Fujian	48282	63536	63483	351161	161006
江 西 Jiangxi	70781	67664	64950	427180	195053
山 东 Shandong	178851	206318	206318	1152566	518404
河 南 Henan	211086	236184	236067	1360341	617067
湖 北 Hubei	47647	57803	57179	331533	151460
湖 南 Hunan	88325	97968	97963	572888	266794
广 东 Guangdong	137873	169185	164814	931918	433158
广 西 Guangxi	72193	87714	87027	470598	219310
海 南 Hainan	7134	7966	7953	46240	20612
重 庆 Chongqing	24502	20194	20135	140580	66028
四 川 Sichuan	55465	59448	58766	359412	172157
贵 州 Guizhou	54953	57347	56077	321009	149725
云 南 Yunnan	44688	42590	39982	251930	119367
西 藏 Tibet	975	1261	875	7576	3784
陕 西 Shaanxi	40026	51007	50993	274357	129222
甘 肃 Gansu	24034	29832	29424	157478	74083
青 海 Qinghai	7612	8339	7554	47558	23151
宁 夏 Ningxia	4814	4049	4036	27531	13274
新 疆 Xinjiang	15160	21508	21508	116623	56818

(镇乡结合区)
(County-town Transitional Area)

单位:人
unit: person

一年级 Grade 1	二年级 Grade 2	三年级 Grade 3	四年级 Grade 4	五年级 Grade 5	六年级 Grade 6	预计毕业生数 Estimated Graduates for Next Year
1857238	**1832545**	**1812623**	**1720958**	**1730601**	**1712065**	**1744382**
2733	2474	2394	2577	2853	2575	2575
6374	6797	6806	6840	6594	5057	6464
231023	224692	222194	201799	203149	208768	208768
47362	46923	46209	43595	48780	51520	51520
8296	9173	8832	8719	8787	9266	9302
8300	9660	10293	11393	12149	12706	12706
7104	6876	6906	6779	7515	7639	7639
7364	8391	8778	8288	10347	8655	10979
4169	4352	4110	4129	4355	0	4355
107201	108814	110925	106690	104046	99985	99985
71368	70072	71515	70651	71487	71480	71480
65700	64937	65264	63949	66149	63899	63899
63591	62119	61384	59156	54472	50439	50439
67823	68279	69475	66283	77734	77586	77586
206318	200816	203693	202262	184781	154696	178552
236189	230245	231921	213680	217380	230926	231264
57816	57656	57877	53352	52868	51964	51964
97968	99032	96490	89958	94098	95342	95342
169209	167824	158643	146264	145426	144552	144552
87718	82782	77709	75546	73771	73072	73072
7993	7549	7694	7661	7430	7913	7913
20196	22181	21736	24235	25910	26322	26322
59448	58955	59239	58683	61151	61936	61936
57347	55956	54182	49727	48626	55171	55171
42595	43217	41977	40020	41522	42599	42599
1261	1292	1391	1349	1084	1199	1199
51020	50223	45625	43245	42540	41704	41704
29832	27924	26139	23208	25120	25255	25256
8354	8021	7982	7691	7565	7945	7945
4051	4436	4204	4091	5240	5509	5509
21515	20877	21036	19138	17672	16385	16385

小学学生
Number of Students in Primary

地区 Region	毕业生数 Graduates	招生数 Entrants		在校生数 Enrolment	
		合计 Total	其中:受过学前教育 of Which: Those Received the Pre-school Education	合计 Total	其中:女 of Which: Female
总　计 Total	**4308040**	**4868875**	**4739208**	**27753626**	**13176780**
北　京 Beijing	10405	10912	10904	64241	30040
天　津 Tianjin	18062	17632	17630	103552	48102
河　北 Hebei	355101	423283	423278	2353940	1112445
山　西 Shanxi	87624	70097	69400	472456	230904
内蒙古 Inner Mongolia	29104	27569	27433	169377	79706
辽　宁 Liaoning	63940	42789	42688	317450	151974
吉　林 Jilin	56088	34446	34206	262284	126621
黑龙江 Heilongjiang	45960	25959	25678	191058	93239
上　海 Shanghai	5536	4552	4550	23327	10593
江　苏 Jiangsu	87336	106475	106281	651966	307513
浙　江 Zhejiang	87854	78343	78322	495738	229085
安　徽 Anhui	236462	266588	266291	1499036	708753
福　建 Fujian	89317	107966	107233	618933	291035
江　西 Jiangxi	177497	206011	195477	1246602	585491
山　东 Shandong	295485	307713	307713	1834822	846949
河　南 Henan	542416	687672	687264	3767157	1784615
湖　北 Hubei	117679	146022	143548	801246	370122
湖　南 Hunan	199108	239060	239018	1319966	627797
广　东 Guangdong	207481	326714	317700	1675278	797847
广　西 Guangxi	297795	351899	342404	1925484	922496
海　南 Hainan	23495	28903	28044	156728	74537
重　庆 Chongqing	67083	45416	44834	353910	167071
四　川 Sichuan	248933	237008	229391	1500780	721121
贵　州 Guizhou	218981	224782	211921	1249801	598052
云　南 Yunnan	350599	339358	288317	2015437	957508
西　藏 Tibet	24687	33447	23426	173348	84612
陕　西 Shaanxi	57241	69478	69221	363908	174429
甘　肃 Gansu	113457	124752	117689	691204	334800
青　海 Qinghai	22189	31835	28125	158356	77820
宁　夏 Ningxia	34369	29288	28351	182681	88967
新　疆 Xinjiang	136756	222906	222871	1113560	542536

数(乡村)
Schools (Rural Area)

单位:人
unit: person

一年级 Grade 1	二年级 Grade 2	三年级 Grade 3	四年级 Grade 4	五年级 Grade 5	六年级 Grade 6	预计毕业生数 Estimated Graduates for Next Year
4870516	**4903840**	**4806394**	**4444641**	**4452231**	**4276004**	**4334770**
10931	10241	10303	10328	11624	10814	10814
17635	17799	18517	18600	18649	12352	18027
423283	425800	411825	365395	363022	364615	364615
70107	75740	77471	72568	85175	91395	91395
27569	30358	28526	27755	26881	28288	28288
42792	49298	52539	55771	58363	58687	58687
34446	41283	43793	41805	46114	54843	54843
25959	32678	34765	32431	39247	25978	42309
4556	4863	4325	4732	4851	0	4851
106475	113048	116610	111790	107807	96236	96236
78343	79588	83379	81907	85436	87085	87085
266625	257508	257235	244823	248028	224817	224817
108081	108405	107344	104269	98754	92080	92080
206902	212578	211926	201303	224520	189373	189373
307713	318083	334887	325560	296458	252121	282787
687676	679427	660951	583355	589288	566460	567703
146047	144066	141704	127649	122140	119640	119640
239060	241013	228310	201474	207309	202800	202800
326840	327075	308514	255870	244781	212198	212198
351646	346807	324123	307107	301365	294436	294436
28999	28269	26945	24570	23652	24293	24293
45437	52197	55285	62413	69118	69460	69460
237008	247175	249668	246056	258903	261970	261970
224802	227366	214408	192425	181327	209473	209473
339479	350015	343733	325897	325934	330379	330379
33448	31143	29311	26930	27107	25409	25409
69549	67037	60041	56390	55676	55215	55215
124755	121697	116155	103656	113144	111797	111797
32036	29504	26499	23856	23507	22954	22954
29329	29895	29276	27605	32247	34329	34329
222988	203884	198026	180351	161804	146507	146507

五年制小
Number of Students in

地 区 Region	招生数 Entrants		在校生数 Enrolment	
	合计 Total	其中:受过学前教育 of Which: Received the Pre-school Education	合计 Total	其中:女 of Which: Female
总 计 Total	**538554**	**537660**	**2627358**	**1237973**
北 京 Beijing	1655	1655	7554	3618
天 津 Tianjin	13372	13372	67004	31328
河 北 Hebei	65	65	135	72
山 西 Shanxi	0	0	0	0
内蒙古 Inner Mongolia	1839	1838	8770	4136
辽 宁 Liaoning	0	0	0	0
吉 林 Jilin	0	0	0	0
黑龙江 Heilongjiang	96817	96001	519018	248754
上 海 Shanghai	163701	163627	784896	367567
江 苏 Jiangsu	0	0	494	403
浙 江 Zhejiang	2684	2684	12210	5771
安 徽 Anhui	0	0	0	0
福 建 Fujian	0	0	0	0
江 西 Jiangxi	0	0	0	0
山 东 Shandong	237851	237851	1131296	533338
河 南 Henan	19467	19466	91053	40568
湖 北 Hubei	853	853	4506	2220
湖 南 Hunan	0	0	0	0
广 东 Guangdong	2	2	0	0
广 西 Guangxi	248	246	418	195
海 南 Hainan	0	0	0	0
重 庆 Chongqing	0	0	0	0
四 川 Sichuan	0	0	0	0
贵 州 Guizhou	0	0	0	0
云 南 Yunnan	0	0	0	0
西 藏 Tibet	0	0	0	0
陕 西 Shaanxi	0	0	0	0
甘 肃 Gansu	0	0	4	3
青 海 Qinghai	0	0	0	0
宁 夏 Ningxia	0	0	0	0
新 疆 Xinjiang	0	0	0	0

学学生数

5-year Primary Schools

单位:人
unit: person

一年级 Grade 1	二年级 Grade 2	三年级 Grade 3	四年级 Grade 4	五年级 Grade 5
538680	**532961**	**522574**	**516198**	**516945**
1655	1506	1552	1430	1411
13372	13755	13795	13244	12838
65	70	0	0	0
0	0	0	0	0
1839	1775	1808	1868	1480
0	0	0	0	0
0	0	0	0	0
96817	106901	106148	96883	112269
163829	160817	153964	154509	151777
0	0	0	232	262
2684	2488	2411	2431	2196
0	0	0	0	0
0	0	0	0	0
0	0	0	0	0
237851	225418	222373	227659	217995
19467	19161	19646	17004	15775
853	900	874	938	941
0	0	0	0	0
0	0	0	0	0
248	170	0	0	0
0	0	0	0	0
0	0	0	0	0
0	0	0	0	0
0	0	0	0	0
0	0	0	0	0
0	0	0	0	0
0	0	0	0	0
0	0	3	0	1
0	0	0	0	0
0	0	0	0	0
0	0	0	0	0

小学女
Number of Female Students

地　区 Region	毕业生数 Graduates	招生数 Entrants		在校生数 Enrolment	
		合计 Total	其中:受过学前教育 of Which: Those Received the Pre-school Education	合计 Total	一年级 Grade 1
总　计 Total	**7236807**	**8241994**	**8136329**	**46883168**	**8243724**
北　京 Beijing	58525	75382	75296	412510	75405
天　津 Tianjin	45567	55292	55032	302537	55302
河　北 Hebei	457537	528534	528532	2968546	528463
山　西 Shanxi	179271	182116	180199	1093757	182125
内蒙古 Inner Mongolia	107484	103349	103244	633580	103349
辽　宁 Liaoning	160552	144067	144006	924880	144075
吉　林 Jilin	106856	90973	90701	585568	90973
黑龙江 Heilongjiang	133959	106881	105986	661704	106881
上　海 Shanghai	66422	77100	77070	367567	77145
江　苏 Jiangsu	348408	440403	440306	2478488	440403
浙　江 Zhejiang	271592	282512	282491	1628318	282513
安　徽 Anhui	312113	354892	354683	2017434	354918
福　建 Fujian	201601	243459	242595	1404586	243604
江　西 Jiangxi	303279	307290	294089	1908676	308269
山　东 Shandong	512846	578331	578331	3228869	578331
河　南 Henan	680733	803703	803481	4517305	803707
湖　北 Hubei	240028	285353	282782	1611744	285233
湖　南 Hunan	358905	410365	410349	2370993	410365
广　东 Guangdong	594167	801963	785736	4297597	802278
广　西 Guangxi	332631	390604	384676	2163776	390482
海　南 Hainan	55104	64394	63546	362485	64413
重　庆 Chongqing	158983	155845	154436	996577	155879
四　川 Sichuan	413280	439301	432943	2648104	439301
贵　州 Guizhou	274178	304438	295430	1690658	304449
云　南 Yunnan	302992	302974	273937	1781320	303029
西　藏 Tibet	22277	28509	22126	153862	28512
陕　西 Shaanxi	167211	227148	226653	1185713	227254
甘　肃 Gansu	138478	160151	156062	877443	160152
青　海 Qinghai	35123	41259	37586	226131	41398
宁　夏 Ningxia	47556	46385	45830	277274	46415
新　疆 Xinjiang	149149	209021	208195	1105166	209101

学生数
in Primary Schools

单位:人
unit: person

二年级 Grade 2	三年级 Grade 3	四年级 Grade 4	五年级 Grade 5	六年级 Grade 6	预计毕业生数 Estimated Graduates for Next Year
8118831	**7993262**	**7599330**	**7659469**	**7268552**	**7511508**
68827	68929	69873	70780	58696	59384
54198	51889	50921	49346	40881	46916
518484	512205	465786	465850	477758	477758
184616	182410	166794	185053	192759	192729
107665	105831	106128	106987	103620	104274
147548	154884	155633	165419	157321	157321
98561	97904	88686	101287	108157	108157
118421	119681	107574	129020	80127	134226
75469	71989	72134	70830	0	70830
430335	424259	408668	402711	372112	372248
271213	272727	269786	269409	262670	263727
337327	341353	334052	341307	308477	308477
242035	243855	240049	224355	210688	210690
308915	315934	303339	341811	330408	330408
563673	568434	570450	537128	410853	513956
790276	776425	701361	720591	724945	731946
279116	281309	261820	252855	251411	251867
412609	403590	372124	386041	386264	386264
778502	747885	682513	661177	625242	624168
377264	356581	346160	350460	342829	342828
62179	61243	59918	57163	57569	57569
159001	159014	172496	180800	169387	169387
442773	442926	437254	445189	440661	440661
301463	288570	266124	249314	280738	280738
307582	300427	287696	290128	292458	292458
27308	25243	24527	24684	23588	23588
216339	195030	187461	183405	176224	176224
153898	147121	131037	143194	142041	142041
39435	37134	35923	35925	36316	36316
46136	45162	43285	47719	48557	48557
197663	193318	179758	169531	155795	155795

小学教职工数(总数)
Number of Educational Personnel in Primary Schools (Total)

单位：人
unit: person

地区 Region	教职工数 Educational Personnel						代课教师 Substitute Teachers	兼任教师 Part-time Teachers
	合计 Total	专任教师 Full-time Teachers	行政人员 Adm. Personnel	教辅人员 Supporting Staff	工勤人员 Workers	校办企业职工 Employees in School-run Factories &Farms		
总　计 Total	**5645319**	**5282512**	**130187**	**101351**	**130933**	**336**	**165689**	**24937**
北　京 Beijing	60904	53782	3684	2392	1046	0	0	1017
天　津 Tianjin	45059	40457	3066	953	583	0	685	119
河　北 Hebei	367402	342180	13080	5307	6817	18	10750	712
山　西 Shanxi	170956	153445	3663	8107	5709	32	9398	429
内蒙古 Inner Mongolia	117298	90015	5026	13051	9204	2	1578	71
辽　宁 Liaoning	130123	114568	11856	2687	1010	2	398	53
吉　林 Jilin	110771	94305	6358	8388	1720	0	632	90
黑龙江 Heilongjiang	111146	95968	5263	6572	3333	10	1315	143
上　海 Shanghai	52253	44077	3556	2251	2360	9	511	85
江　苏 Jiangsu	278076	263183	4468	5699	4663	63	11673	388
浙　江 Zhejiang	185188	177049	2774	2174	3186	5	0	320
安　徽 Anhui	222981	214411	2682	2509	3379	0	5748	922
福　建 Fujian	167482	159952	2914	2495	2105	16	12344	288
江　西 Jiangxi	205167	202815	382	642	1320	8	3503	519
山　东 Shandong	391838	377103	4427	5363	4922	23	6771	524
河　南 Henan	517706	488568	9092	5037	15009	0	34880	1568
湖　北 Hubei	196951	184497	3503	4246	4686	19	10345	646
湖　南 Hunan	235374	227970	2816	1774	2812	2	10430	441
广　东 Guangdong	451390	418656	14810	4467	13409	48	397	1247
广　西 Guangxi	250648	237848	3597	2604	6557	42	6921	3986
海　南 Hainan	45647	42618	644	411	1953	21	1615	1029
重　庆 Chongqing	123840	119169	2156	693	1810	12	2895	560
四　川 Sichuan	272219	259573	4527	2103	6016	0	14111	2361
贵　州 Guizhou	202859	189393	3583	1057	8825	1	91	2565
云　南 Yunnan	229197	218558	2602	1240	6796	1	117	3564
西　藏 Tibet	20315	20143	38	44	90	0	392	0
陕　西 Shaanxi	157442	144065	5942	2953	4482	0	2444	7
甘　肃 Gansu	131554	128437	990	1110	1016	1	7334	874
青　海 Qinghai	23287	21922	118	96	1151	0	2187	42
宁　夏 Ningxia	32552	32071	116	89	276	0	1334	151
新　疆 Xinjiang	137694	125714	2454	4837	4688	1	4890	216

小学教职工数(城区)

Number of Educational Personnel in Primary Schools (Urban Area)

单位:人

unit: person

地区 Region	教职工数 Educational Personnel						代课教师 Substitute Teachers	兼任教师 Part-time Teachers
	合计 Total	专任教师 Full-time Teachers	行政人员 Adm. Personnel	教辅人员 Supporting Staff	工勤人员 Workers	校办企业职工 Employees in School-run Factories &Farms		
总计 Total	**1712992**	**1598079**	**45831**	**28050**	**40827**	**205**	**45475**	**6407**
北京 Beijing	49018	43945	2670	1733	670	0	0	1004
天津 Tianjin	32452	28824	2286	844	498	0	323	114
河北 Hebei	76305	71088	2148	1207	1844	18	1251	19
山西 Shanxi	47327	43203	1236	1307	1551	30	2560	131
内蒙古 Inner Mongolia	32959	29733	1469	1257	498	2	848	22
辽宁 Liaoning	68072	59848	6368	1306	548	2	43	19
吉林 Jilin	36183	31780	1830	2067	506	0	239	22
黑龙江 Heilongjiang	43226	38384	2147	1639	1056	0	274	61
上海 Shanghai	44117	37738	2804	1818	1748	9	455	58
江苏 Jiangsu	126058	120196	2027	1896	1930	9	5713	141
浙江 Zhejiang	87088	83026	1169	899	1990	4	0	117
安徽 Anhui	43338	42117	421	223	577	0	2298	217
福建 Fujian	57648	54884	870	628	1252	14	5407	15
江西 Jiangxi	40896	40459	93	79	265	0	125	12
山东 Shandong	127176	121370	1891	1994	1919	2	2525	238
河南 Henan	99030	93419	1734	1017	2860	0	7812	400
湖北 Hubei	66552	62233	1789	1017	1500	13	4099	194
湖南 Hunan	59911	58249	562	425	673	2	2682	300
广东 Guangdong	224564	205924	5799	3065	9736	40	366	811
广西 Guangxi	49535	46657	503	526	1807	42	457	1053
海南 Hainan	12730	11697	200	178	640	15	997	600
重庆 Chongqing	45062	43266	816	313	664	3	1199	234
四川 Sichuan	65223	61250	1027	699	2247	0	3043	253
贵州 Guizhou	33519	32086	486	237	710	0	16	95
云南 Yunnan	33117	31752	412	219	734	0	7	196
西藏 Tibet	3041	2958	27	20	36	0	0	0
陕西 Shaanxi	48337	43606	2323	780	1628	0	293	0
甘肃 Gansu	21880	21392	197	98	193	0	15	65
青海 Qinghai	5110	5042	13	6	49	0	433	0
宁夏 Ningxia	10273	10178	24	12	59	0	407	15
新疆 Xinjiang	23245	21775	490	541	439	0	1588	1

小学教职工数(城乡结合区)
Number of Educational Personnel in Primary Schools (Urban-rural Transitional Area)

单位:人
unit: person

地 区 Region	教职工数 Educational Personnel						代课教师 Substitute Teachers	兼任教师 Part-time Teachers
	合计 Total	专任教师 Full-time Teachers	行政人员 Adm. Personnel	教辅人员 Supporting Staff	工勤人员 Workers	校办企业职工 Employees in School-run Factories &Farms		
总 计 Total	**302717**	**280804**	**7999**	**4099**	**9805**	**10**	**7829**	**919**
北 京 Beijing	3827	3282	307	120	118	0	0	44
天 津 Tianjin	3327	2949	249	102	27	0	152	4
河 北 Hebei	19679	18226	711	210	532	0	330	10
山 西 Shanxi	6422	5866	150	215	191	0	468	44
内蒙古 Inner Mongolia	868	761	46	35	26	0	25	0
辽 宁 Liaoning	6492	5790	544	109	49	0	33	3
吉 林 Jilin	2366	2037	146	135	48	0	20	0
黑龙江 Heilongjiang	3092	2597	195	167	133	0	29	2
上 海 Shanghai	3965	3285	244	103	333	0	43	2
江 苏 Jiangsu	14004	13122	291	292	299	0	830	27
浙 江 Zhejiang	21345	20192	330	230	589	4	0	5
安 徽 Anhui	5854	5629	61	75	89	0	197	7
福 建 Fujian	11678	11233	160	76	209	0	1331	4
江 西 Jiangxi	6876	6824	12	9	31	0	56	5
山 东 Shandong	35887	34152	553	685	497	0	1098	12
河 南 Henan	19748	18596	333	167	652	0	1243	38
湖 北 Hubei	9303	8456	196	216	435	0	448	26
湖 南 Hunan	6487	6331	93	13	50	0	358	16
广 东 Guangdong	69457	62632	2265	631	3923	6	32	187
广 西 Guangxi	10218	9749	103	67	299	0	74	188
海 南 Hainan	1427	1361	18	5	43	0	52	132
重 庆 Chongqing	4226	3971	87	31	137	0	15	0
四 川 Sichuan	7831	7239	164	123	305	0	428	33
贵 州 Guizhou	5378	5134	80	7	157	0	2	28
云 南 Yunnan	9348	8978	101	60	209	0	0	102
西 藏 Tibet	40	40	0	0	0	0	0	0
陕 西 Shaanxi	8128	7171	491	152	314	0	101	0
甘 肃 Gansu	1805	1756	16	19	14	0	0	0
青 海 Qinghai	299	295	2	0	2	0	26	0
宁 夏 Ningxia	581	580	0	0	1	0	30	0
新 疆 Xinjiang	2759	2570	51	45	93	0	408	0

小学教职工数(镇区)

Number of Educational Personnel in Primary Schools (Counties & Towns Area)

单位:人
unit: person

地区 Region	教职工数 Educational Personnel						代课教师 Substitute Teachers	兼任教师 Part-time Teachers
	合计 Total	专任教师 Full-time Teachers	行政人员 Adm. Personnel	教辅人员 Supporting Staff	工勤人员 Workers	校办企业职工 Employees in School-run Factories &Farms		
总　计 Total	**2045891**	**1912510**	**43041**	**40896**	**49371**	**73**	**47057**	**5855**
北　京 Beijing	5048	3967	537	354	190	0	0	0
天　津 Tianjin	5050	4690	269	53	38	0	144	2
河　北 Hebei	135734	125585	4511	2346	3292	0	3311	330
山　西 Shanxi	64669	58543	1175	2712	2237	2	2871	99
内蒙古 Inner Mongolia	58401	42770	2433	7922	5276	0	498	18
辽　宁 Liaoning	33128	28996	3111	733	288	0	45	11
吉　林 Jilin	36690	30764	2247	3102	577	0	123	16
黑龙江 Heilongjiang	42031	35878	1841	2684	1618	10	634	32
上　海 Shanghai	6199	4941	551	330	377	0	41	18
江　苏 Jiangsu	116673	109543	1819	3153	2121	37	4233	158
浙　江 Zhejiang	68346	65457	1110	897	881	1	0	178
安　徽 Anhui	88720	85146	1137	805	1632	0	1076	195
福　建 Fujian	66578	63451	1504	1088	535	0	3415	168
江　西 Jiangxi	86893	85897	183	296	514	3	1016	234
山　东 Shandong	146194	140488	1432	2176	2096	2	2267	109
河　南 Henan	182202	170366	3292	1817	6727	0	11905	375
湖　北 Hubei	72747	68691	794	1574	1682	6	2403	258
湖　南 Hunan	105560	101810	1307	950	1493	0	3360	69
广　东 Guangdong	118087	111261	4047	897	1879	3	22	176
广　西 Guangxi	85785	80769	1314	1301	2401	0	1263	982
海　南 Hainan	18071	16718	261	188	898	6	227	181
重　庆 Chongqing	50148	48429	804	183	731	1	826	162
四　川 Sichuan	124352	119812	1680	708	2152	0	3352	601
贵　州 Guizhou	85514	80033	1454	498	3528	1	35	790
云　南 Yunnan	62767	59297	858	563	2048	1	31	359
西　藏 Tibet	6152	6101	5	7	39	0	115	0
陕　西 Shaanxi	73681	67991	2250	1511	1929	0	1186	0
甘　肃 Gansu	45363	43996	451	511	405	0	1202	163
青　海 Qinghai	8591	8149	57	43	342	0	438	34
宁　夏 Ningxia	10463	10256	50	60	97	0	305	37
新　疆 Xinjiang	36054	32715	557	1434	1348	0	713	100

小学教职工数(镇乡结合区)
Number of Educational Personnel in Primary Schools (County-town Transitional Area)

单位:人
unit: person

地 区 Region	教职工数 Educational Personnel 合计 Total	专任教师 Full-time Teachers	行政人员 Adm. Personnel	教辅人员 Supporting Staff	工勤人员 Workers	校办企业职工 Employees in School-run Factories &Farms	代课教师 Substitute Teachers	兼任教师 Part-time Teachers
总 计 Total	**585414**	**550699**	**12080**	**9476**	**13129**	**30**	**16486**	**1946**
北 京 Beijing	1380	1084	130	100	66	0	0	0
天 津 Tianjin	2352	2191	132	15	14	0	69	0
河 北 Hebei	71368	65927	2427	1106	1908	0	1945	258
山 西 Shanxi	19703	17929	345	839	588	2	920	1
内蒙古 Inner Mongolia	5428	4054	219	871	284	0	42	0
辽 宁 Liaoning	4747	4019	571	120	37	0	17	0
吉 林 Jilin	4342	3403	282	536	121	0	8	1
黑龙江 Heilongjiang	4874	4208	196	371	99	0	71	5
上 海 Shanghai	1420	1099	119	102	100	0	2	0
江 苏 Jiangsu	34652	32170	612	1140	712	18	1385	79
浙 江 Zhejiang	22397	21396	379	274	348	0	0	118
安 徽 Anhui	19869	19070	257	122	420	0	439	55
福 建 Fujian	18634	17984	251	243	156	0	1667	37
江 西 Jiangxi	20834	20513	54	82	185	0	330	89
山 东 Shandong	62873	60529	552	809	983	0	1123	95
河 南 Henan	69297	64867	1326	638	2466	0	3934	203
湖 北 Hubei	19171	18006	200	449	516	0	842	66
湖 南 Hunan	25964	25253	287	146	278	0	1121	23
广 东 Guangdong	47839	44996	1815	322	703	3	17	81
广 西 Guangxi	25040	23958	337	233	512	0	602	467
海 南 Hainan	2929	2677	44	24	178	6	80	25
重 庆 Chongqing	8971	8596	162	39	174	0	194	8
四 川 Sichuan	18452	17656	295	115	386	0	595	94
贵 州 Guizhou	16905	15863	310	85	646	1	0	115
云 南 Yunnan	15996	15449	178	64	305	0	24	61
西 藏 Tibet	427	425	0	0	2	0	7	0
陕 西 Shaanxi	18226	17107	430	200	489	0	285	0
甘 肃 Gansu	10638	10345	60	126	107	0	436	32
青 海 Qinghai	1781	1749	3	12	17	0	85	4
宁 夏 Ningxia	1635	1617	5	6	7	0	25	16
新 疆 Xinjiang	7270	6559	102	287	322	0	221	13

小学教职工数(乡村)
Number of Educational Personnel in Primary Schools (Rural Area)

单位:人
unit: person

地 区 Region	教职工数 Educational Personnel 合计 Total	专任教师 Full-time Teachers	行政人员 Adm. Personnel	教辅人员 Supporting Staff	工勤人员 Workers	校办企业职工 Employees in School-run Factories &Farms	代课教师 Substitute Teachers	兼任教师 Part-time Teachers
总 计 Total	**1886436**	**1771923**	**41315**	**32405**	**40735**	**58**	**73157**	**12675**
北 京 Beijing	6838	5870	477	305	186	0	0	13
天 津 Tianjin	7557	6943	511	56	47	0	218	3
河 北 Hebei	155363	145507	6421	1754	1681	0	6188	363
山 西 Shanxi	58960	51699	1252	4088	1921	0	3967	199
内蒙古 Inner Mongolia	25938	17512	1124	3872	3430	0	232	31
辽 宁 Liaoning	28923	25724	2377	648	174	0	310	23
吉 林 Jilin	37898	31761	2281	3219	637	0	270	52
黑龙江 Heilongjiang	25889	21706	1275	2249	659	0	407	50
上 海 Shanghai	1937	1398	201	103	235	0	15	9
江 苏 Jiangsu	35345	33444	622	650	612	17	1727	89
浙 江 Zhejiang	29754	28566	495	378	315	0	0	25
安 徽 Anhui	90923	87148	1124	1481	1170	0	2374	510
福 建 Fujian	43256	41617	540	779	318	2	3522	105
江 西 Jiangxi	77378	76459	106	267	541	5	2362	273
山 东 Shandong	118468	115245	1104	1193	907	19	1979	177
河 南 Henan	236474	224783	4066	2203	5422	0	15163	793
湖 北 Hubei	57652	53573	920	1655	1504	0	3843	194
湖 南 Hunan	69903	67911	947	399	646	0	4388	72
广 东 Guangdong	108739	101471	4964	505	1794	5	9	260
广 西 Guangxi	115328	110422	1780	777	2349	0	5201	1951
海 南 Hainan	14846	14203	183	45	415	0	391	248
重 庆 Chongqing	28630	27474	536	197	415	8	870	164
四 川 Sichuan	82644	78511	1820	696	1617	0	7716	1507
贵 州 Guizhou	83826	77274	1643	322	4587	0	40	1680
云 南 Yunnan	133313	127509	1332	458	4014	0	79	3009
西 藏 Tibet	11122	11084	6	17	15	0	277	0
陕 西 Shaanxi	35424	32468	1369	662	925	0	965	7
甘 肃 Gansu	64311	63049	342	501	418	1	6117	646
青 海 Qinghai	9586	8731	48	47	760	0	1316	8
宁 夏 Ningxia	11816	11637	42	17	120	0	622	99
新 疆 Xinjiang	78395	71224	1407	2862	2901	1	2589	115

小学教职工总数中民办教职工数

Number of Primary Schools Educational Personnel Maintained by the Communities

单位：人
unit: person

地区 Region	教职工数 Educational Personnel						代课教师 Substitute Teachers	兼任教师 Part-time Teachers
	合计 Total	专任教师 Full-time Teachers	行政人员 Adm. Personnel	教辅人员 Supporting Staff	工勤人员 Workers	校办企业职工 Employees in School-run Factories &Farms		
总计 Total	**277063**	**207796**	**12733**	**10319**	**46024**	**191**	**5596**	**1167**
北京 Beijing	2190	1662	196	108	224	0	0	0
天津 Tianjin	1006	759	99	30	118	0	0	39
河北 Hebei	27337	20467	1468	1237	4147	18	0	99
山西 Shanxi	10603	6957	502	650	2464	30	481	63
内蒙古 Inner Mongolia	1194	829	119	47	199	0	0	6
辽宁 Liaoning	1088	916	92	40	40	0	0	10
吉林 Jilin	1795	1439	105	62	189	0	0	0
黑龙江 Heilongjiang	433	333	32	17	51	0	0	0
上海 Shanghai	6193	4704	458	246	785	0	0	14
江苏 Jiangsu	11922	9451	434	371	1646	20	2	5
浙江 Zhejiang	13818	11130	384	456	1844	4	0	135
安徽 Anhui	10719	7844	436	311	2128	0	50	12
福建 Fujian	4779	3615	196	90	862	16	16	0
江西 Jiangxi	1959	1570	51	114	216	8	31	30
山东 Shandong	19720	15665	789	827	2437	2	87	33
河南 Henan	63069	45821	2948	2487	11813	0	4709	536
湖北 Hubei	5107	3419	228	265	1192	3	0	72
湖南 Hunan	7193	5488	272	476	957	0	8	0
广东 Guangdong	48234	37122	1766	1369	7950	27	11	33
广西 Guangxi	5980	4215	349	169	1205	42	48	8
海南 Hainan	2802	1741	161	41	839	20	0	2
重庆 Chongqing	3313	2589	190	128	406	0	99	7
四川 Sichuan	8330	5762	333	263	1972	0	0	10
贵州 Guizhou	5257	4104	251	185	716	1	15	0
云南 Yunnan	2721	2305	157	15	244	0	0	13
西藏 Tibet	85	74	7	0	4	0	0	0
陕西 Shaanxi	9253	7134	651	257	1211	0	1	0
甘肃 Gansu	159	137	11	2	9	0	0	25
青海 Qinghai	53	33	1	0	19	0	10	0
宁夏 Ningxia	383	246	19	37	81	0	0	0
新疆 Xinjiang	368	265	28	19	56	0	28	15

小学女教职工数
Number of Female Educational Personnel in Primary Schools

单位：人
unit: person

地区 Region	教职工数 Educational Personnel						代课教师 Substitute Teachers	兼任教师 Part-time Teachers
	合计 Total	专任教师 Full-time Teachers	行政人员 Adm. Personnel	教辅人员 Supporting Staff	工勤人员 Workers	校办企业职工 Employees in School-run Factories &Farms		
总　计 Total	**3675429**	**3523118**	**40554**	**49760**	**61811**	**186**	**127324**	**16032**
北　京 Beijing	47607	43642	2089	1554	322	0	0	803
天　津 Tianjin	32943	30548	1610	608	177	0	590	92
河　北 Hebei	275868	266316	3443	2612	3479	18	9390	489
山　西 Shanxi	128426	120202	1150	3977	3065	32	8240	316
内蒙古 Inner Mongolia	74675	65438	1707	5164	2366	0	1120	29
辽　宁 Liaoning	95035	86978	6042	1796	219	0	382	45
吉　林 Jilin	75217	68521	2378	3927	391	0	502	42
黑龙江 Heilongjiang	73747	67560	2332	2977	872	6	1025	96
上　海 Shanghai	41892	36876	2258	1612	1139	7	357	65
江　苏 Jiangsu	185184	179708	1185	2215	2052	24	9362	226
浙　江 Zhejiang	134246	130500	639	1193	1911	3	0	215
安　徽 Anhui	126297	123069	416	945	1867	0	4116	397
福　建 Fujian	110598	108050	641	1015	883	9	10467	187
江　西 Jiangxi	129794	128734	91	423	541	5	2919	363
山　东 Shandong	238577	233236	1165	2190	1978	8	5375	340
河　南 Henan	352428	338694	2503	2838	8393	0	28825	1087
湖　北 Hubei	113973	108427	1127	2161	2255	3	7308	378
湖　南 Hunan	155802	152928	637	1027	1209	1	8221	364
广　东 Guangdong	310457	297745	2938	3107	6638	29	305	1003
广　西 Guangxi	161973	156269	806	1256	3618	24	5426	2632
海　南 Hainan	24188	22845	141	219	977	6	1176	749
重　庆 Chongqing	74763	73353	478	364	560	8	2239	315
四　川 Sichuan	167268	162581	875	1228	2584	0	9633	1246
贵　州 Guizhou	105599	98829	522	482	5765	1	64	1719
云　南 Yunnan	125617	120662	464	481	4009	1	91	2119
西　藏 Tibet	11168	11087	10	29	42	0	190	0
陕　西 Shaanxi	104344	99546	1758	1460	1580	0	1600	7
甘　肃 Gansu	68004	67268	138	327	271	0	3252	511
青　海 Qinghai	13166	12491	26	43	606	0	1267	22
宁　夏 Ningxia	21659	21418	25	62	154	0	1001	58
新　疆 Xinjiang	94914	89597	960	2468	1888	1	2881	117

小学专任教师学历、专业

Number of Full-time Teacher in Primary Schools by

地 区 Region	合计 Total	其中:女 of Which: Female	按学历分 By Educational Attainment			
			研究生毕业 Graduate	本科毕业 Under-graduate	专科毕业 Associate Bachelor	高中阶段毕业 High School Graduate
总 计 Total	**5944910**	**3994105**	**56460**	**3217461**	**2389380**	**279341**
北 京 Beijing	64514	52596	4523	54755	4910	315
天 津 Tianjin	43023	32627	2123	32023	7853	1018
河 北 Hebei	365877	285698	2132	186181	166932	10591
山 西 Shanxi	169057	133065	881	90723	70316	7102
内蒙古 Inner Mongolia	99653	72366	1056	62978	33435	2184
辽 宁 Liaoning	140206	105395	2548	75488	57219	4834
吉 林 Jilin	108405	78613	1290	66526	35047	5539
黑龙江 Heilongjiang	114487	80382	480	57217	51529	5224
上 海 Shanghai	54697	45488	3094	41459	9773	370
江 苏 Jiangsu	300216	205091	5668	236698	53147	4702
浙 江 Zhejiang	205127	151592	3060	156032	43168	2858
安 徽 Anhui	244978	141948	1205	123127	109998	10647
福 建 Fujian	168867	114436	990	84575	69628	13632
江 西 Jiangxi	226990	146190	561	109914	98799	17584
山 东 Shandong	421877	265332	7320	259755	131218	23531
河 南 Henan	527021	369898	2693	255168	240442	28707
湖 北 Hubei	203304	120620	1921	94730	91962	14593
湖 南 Hunan	265887	178210	1667	126235	124091	13782
广 东 Guangdong	507788	365732	5556	296699	192383	13108
广 西 Guangxi	247133	163480	934	101016	124677	20252
海 南 Hainan	49790	27715	123	14670	30401	4568
重 庆 Chongqing	125270	77148	1195	65394	54944	3706
四 川 Sichuan	325016	202473	1584	137274	170783	15360
贵 州 Guizhou	202061	106597	204	88822	99453	13190
云 南 Yunnan	227269	126436	706	102933	107299	15660
西 藏 Tibet	20429	11291	39	9411	10515	443
陕 西 Shaanxi	159061	109872	1642	100833	53367	3208
甘 肃 Gansu	141962	74677	619	82096	47518	11669
青 海 Qinghai	27319	15630	212	15342	10810	940
宁 夏 Ningxia	34239	22750	124	19722	13074	1315
新 疆 Xinjiang	153387	110757	310	69665	74689	8709

技术职务情况(总计)

Academic Qualifications and Professional Rank (Total)

单位:人
unit: person

	按专业技术职务分 By Professional Rank					
高中阶段毕业以下 Below High School Graduate	中学高级 Senior Secondary	小学高级 Senior Primary	小学一级 1st Grade Primary	小学二级 2nd Grade Primary	小学三级 3rd Grade Primary	未定职级 No-ranking
2268	**219299**	**2763089**	**1902791**	**266430**	**24036**	**769265**
11	2905	29642	21921	1385	3	8658
6	2651	26911	9544	693	19	3205
41	10389	156716	134158	12548	1674	50392
35	1069	62709	78839	6276	895	19269
0	22690	46271	18308	2603	0	9781
117	15947	97388	16598	1581	262	8430
3	7955	54914	33852	3005	88	8591
37	11648	62743	34738	1286	52	4020
1	1174	24968	21591	1397	60	5507
1	16890	161206	78139	10720	12	33249
9	8323	103371	67429	2113	184	23707
1	4349	115006	76248	12340	549	36486
42	3001	91321	47580	8109	576	18280
132	6619	101556	65409	13920	2123	37363
53	14379	164821	162998	19633	1249	58797
11	13839	223418	182185	23930	30	83619
98	6701	118283	49766	10562	1791	16201
112	6432	127887	80282	10601	510	40175
42	3924	244677	113527	25341	5163	115156
254	3669	137692	60689	10198	1752	33133
28	377	22962	19046	2624	5	4776
31	4985	55474	51540	3428	296	9547
15	17283	130114	131593	11154	1505	33367
392	1956	105559	55721	14837	1310	22678
671	12292	104691	73420	20224	947	15695
21	807	7272	7094	2039	803	2414
11	2127	58872	69290	9229	344	19199
60	2884	53067	66715	7023	531	11742
15	2210	13981	6609	1257	220	3042
4	2466	14127	11362	1749	29	4506
14	7358	45470	56600	14625	1054	28280

小学专任教师学历、专业
Number of Full-time Teacher in Primary Schools by

地 区 Region	合计 Total	其中:女 of Which: Female	按学历分 By Educational Attainment			
			研究生毕业 Graduate	本科毕业 Under-graduate	专科毕业 Associate Bachelor	高中阶段毕业 High School Graduate
总 计 Total	**1865679**	**1478839**	**42615**	**1284883**	**508553**	**29454**
北 京 Beijing	52954	44431	3848	45251	3675	177
天 津 Tianjin	31027	25568	1980	23212	5335	494
河 北 Hebei	77431	66865	1109	51368	24153	794
山 西 Shanxi	47825	41280	483	31501	15117	721
内蒙古 Inner Mongolia	32203	26229	702	24370	6885	246
辽 宁 Liaoning	67983	56426	2089	42796	21898	1173
吉 林 Jilin	35541	29943	755	26263	7883	640
黑龙江 Heilongjiang	43095	35001	384	26622	14826	1259
上 海 Shanghai	46208	39506	2748	35479	7708	272
江 苏 Jiangsu	136754	105835	4470	112805	18015	1463
浙 江 Zhejiang	100033	78381	2445	78962	17923	702
安 徽 Anhui	47960	34723	584	29560	16683	1132
福 建 Fujian	59575	48166	842	40310	16848	1570
江 西 Jiangxi	49376	38294	368	31939	15959	1103
山 东 Shandong	140812	106201	4724	107534	26226	2324
河 南 Henan	104311	86054	1400	66661	34237	2013
湖 北 Hubei	71194	52395	1620	41867	25557	2148
湖 南 Hunan	66451	52795	1228	42514	21680	1020
广 东 Guangdong	271998	214014	5137	183616	80596	2631
广 西 Guangxi	52316	43095	722	31682	18289	1595
海 南 Hainan	14699	10749	69	6551	7621	458
重 庆 Chongqing	45343	33015	1032	29840	13908	559
四 川 Sichuan	76019	57874	1243	45984	27776	1016
贵 州 Guizhou	36794	27761	112	20407	14911	1345
云 南 Yunnan	35469	26772	509	23294	10760	895
西 藏 Tibet	3201	2224	22	1740	1355	80
陕 西 Shaanxi	49041	39801	1287	35969	11460	324
甘 肃 Gansu	24315	17954	389	15959	7485	481
青 海 Qinghai	6208	4687	97	4226	1791	89
宁 夏 Ningxia	10230	8177	76	6972	3043	138
新 疆 Xinjiang	29313	24623	141	19629	8950	592

技术职务情况(城区)
Academic Qualifications and Professional Rank (Urban Area)

单位:人
unit: person

高中阶段毕业以下 Below High School Graduate	按专业技术职务分 By Professional Rank					
	中学高级 Senior Secondary	小学高级 Senior Primary	小学一级 1st Grade Primary	小学二级 2nd Grade Primary	小学三级 3rd Grade Primary	未定职级 No-ranking
174	**78418**	**880244**	**561482**	**63015**	**6533**	**275987**
3	2503	24550	18006	1135	3	6757
6	1848	19210	6994	431	18	2526
7	2610	38053	25346	2135	218	9069
3	364	20090	19999	1236	127	6009
0	7589	14091	5908	936	0	3679
27	6304	49623	6980	454	52	4570
0	3179	19219	10324	682	47	2090
4	5475	24345	11301	470	17	1487
1	1045	21423	18226	1087	56	4371
1	8732	71378	36069	4145	4	16426
1	5104	49877	30639	981	135	13297
1	1087	23290	16324	1723	170	5366
5	1350	27080	19577	2493	153	8922
7	2177	24487	14456	1665	257	6334
4	4885	54886	54477	4907	346	21311
0	3296	47720	35886	4424	10	12975
2	3173	41641	17095	2858	561	5866
9	1703	33198	18462	1967	268	10853
18	2841	111071	58132	14101	2887	82966
28	1080	25974	12097	2138	411	10616
0	203	5835	4944	1102	0	2615
4	1841	20183	19598	835	56	2830
0	3660	32203	32093	1304	202	6557
19	324	16145	10300	1935	189	7901
11	1867	15838	10978	1600	28	5158
4	251	1405	1032	204	39	270
1	652	17605	19299	2739	87	8659
1	874	11092	10422	705	28	1194
5	374	3063	1826	222	12	711
1	486	4657	3367	489	9	1222
1	1541	11012	11325	1912	143	3380

小学专任教师学历、专业

Number of Full-time Teacher in Primary Schools by Academic

地区 Region	合计 Total	其中:女 of Which: Female	按学历分 By Educational Attainment			
			研究生毕业 Graduate	本科毕业 Under-graduate	专科毕业 Associate Bachelor	高中阶段毕业 High School Graduate
总 计 Total	**347645**	**258850**	**5169**	**221227**	**112883**	**8307**
北 京 Beijing	4308	3455	256	3330	655	67
天 津 Tianjin	3145	2304	161	2375	528	81
河 北 Hebei	21098	17782	208	12086	8505	292
山 西 Shanxi	6230	5148	36	3843	2256	95
内蒙古 Inner Mongolia	767	583	15	566	182	4
辽 宁 Liaoning	6722	5241	193	3859	2492	174
吉 林 Jilin	2202	1734	29	1533	600	40
黑龙江 Heilongjiang	3094	2423	16	1723	1223	132
上 海 Shanghai	4479	3512	187	3195	1043	54
江 苏 Jiangsu	15648	10914	343	11975	3038	292
浙 江 Zhejiang	26028	19473	364	19010	6365	289
安 徽 Anhui	6757	4252	40	3633	2797	286
福 建 Fujian	12108	9254	91	7927	3526	563
江 西 Jiangxi	8208	5780	32	4613	3126	437
山 东 Shandong	40243	27741	1001	29070	9084	1086
河 南 Henan	21403	16854	201	12370	8093	739
湖 北 Hubei	10209	6596	109	5359	4273	468
湖 南 Hunan	7589	5631	135	4470	2754	224
广 东 Guangdong	89644	68279	1162	57345	30086	1037
广 西 Guangxi	10794	8419	115	5787	4373	507
海 南 Hainan	1562	1015	1	476	972	113
重 庆 Chongqing	4084	2697	34	2120	1842	87
四 川 Sichuan	10078	7402	164	6225	3509	180
贵 州 Guizhou	6234	4207	25	3211	2685	306
云 南 Yunnan	9930	6930	45	5594	3828	459
西 藏 Tibet	40	24	0	24	14	2
陕 西 Shaanxi	8053	5940	163	5500	2310	80
甘 肃 Gansu	2329	1642	23	1398	844	64
青 海 Qinghai	620	397	6	355	251	8
宁 夏 Ningxia	580	427	7	365	201	7
新 疆 Xinjiang	3459	2794	7	1890	1428	134

技术职务情况(城乡结合区)
Qualifications and Professional Rank (Urban-rural Transitional Area)

单位:人
unit: person

	按专业技术职务分 By Professional Rank					
高中阶段毕业以下 Below High School Graduate	中学高级 Senior Secondary	小学高级 Senior Primary	小学一级 1st Grade Primary	小学二级 2nd Grade Primary	小学三级 3rd Grade Primary	未定职级 No-ranking
59	**9440**	**147458**	**101320**	**14614**	**2065**	**72748**
0	121	1649	1175	154	3	1206
0	170	2010	787	15	0	163
7	631	9211	7307	740	95	3114
0	37	2450	2831	241	35	636
0	130	303	175	37	0	122
4	838	4826	635	38	2	383
0	169	1181	729	19	5	99
0	447	1670	904	31	2	40
0	42	1352	1674	205	10	1196
0	834	7691	4131	821	0	2171
0	778	11640	8413	312	25	4860
1	141	3395	2256	232	5	728
1	149	5318	3926	585	59	2071
0	231	3860	2572	305	47	1193
2	1386	15358	14949	1463	134	6953
0	589	9318	7265	970	6	3255
0	338	5611	2524	631	137	968
6	193	3622	2178	249	27	1320
14	596	32492	17328	4958	1167	33103
12	173	5461	2531	379	77	2173
0	14	732	469	111	0	236
1	146	1778	1686	150	3	321
0	326	3596	4146	244	72	1694
7	50	2953	1725	391	49	1066
4	557	4843	2979	346	7	1198
0	2	29	6	0	0	3
0	103	2823	3324	431	11	1361
0	46	870	1156	91	1	165
0	35	317	186	10	0	72
0	29	194	160	65	0	132
0	139	905	1193	390	86	746

地　区 Region	合计 Total	其中:女 of Which: Female	按学历分 By Educational Attainment			
			研究生毕业 Graduate	本科毕业 Under-graduate	专科毕业 Associate Bachelor	高中阶段毕业 High School Graduate
总　计 Total	**2161813**	**1483829**	**8549**	**1122782**	**938102**	**91889**
北　京 Beijing	5033	3661	378	4055	513	85
天　津 Tianjin	4870	3139	74	3666	952	178
河　北 Hebei	138118	112992	559	70964	63066	3514
山　西 Shanxi	64705	53912	158	34421	27862	2249
内蒙古 Inner Mongolia	47483	34761	237	28384	17786	1076
辽　宁 Liaoning	40831	28896	217	19159	19557	1845
吉　林 Jilin	35793	26052	385	21881	11911	1615
黑龙江 Heilongjiang	43647	30485	65	20375	21299	1897
上　海 Shanghai	6732	4695	231	4727	1695	79
江　苏 Jiangsu	127185	81248	994	100017	24121	2053
浙　江 Zhejiang	72867	51795	415	53783	17352	1312
安　徽 Anhui	99488	61723	406	50777	44707	3598
福　建 Fujian	65397	44037	89	28478	31506	5314
江　西 Jiangxi	95351	65435	128	46499	42897	5810
山　东 Shandong	160891	103215	1669	94741	56051	8412
河　南 Henan	191470	147853	626	92673	89877	8294
湖　北 Hubei	74630	43969	187	32350	36778	5265
湖　南 Hunan	119328	82036	316	52912	60499	5549
广　东 Guangdong	125715	88107	262	64344	56861	4243
广　西 Guangxi	83114	59754	127	35361	42537	5056
海　南 Hainan	20053	11190	39	5339	12786	1887
重　庆 Chongqing	50869	30479	107	23401	25773	1573
四　川 Sichuan	145698	92028	251	56560	82373	6507
贵　州 Guizhou	84390	48548	49	35890	43484	4907
云　南 Yunnan	61568	39017	73	27434	30570	3394
西　藏 Tibet	6144	3595	7	2959	3019	151
陕　西 Shaanxi	75897	52599	267	47297	26957	1374
甘　肃 Gansu	48536	29914	66	29786	16123	2557
青　海 Qinghai	10401	6546	51	5956	4177	216
宁　夏 Ningxia	11007	7922	22	6353	4293	337
新　疆 Xinjiang	44602	34226	94	22240	20720	1542

技术职务情况(镇区)

Qualifications and Professional Rank (County & Town Area)

单位:人
unit: person

高中阶段毕业以下 Below High School Graduate	按专业技术职务分 By Professional Rank					
	中学高级 Senior Secondary	小学高级 Senior Primary	小学一级 1st Grade Primary	小学二级 2nd Grade Primary	小学三级 3rd Grade Primary	未定职级 No-ranking
491	**87381**	**1033327**	**702342**	**88918**	**6879**	**242966**
2	194	2032	1657	128	0	1022
0	331	3120	1084	77	0	258
15	3762	57151	51786	4945	606	19868
15	353	23082	31477	2467	299	7027
0	10889	23319	8461	1006	0	3808
53	5635	27751	5037	562	102	1744
1	2755	17730	11314	959	17	3018
11	4152	23827	13766	440	13	1449
0	109	2985	2741	168	3	726
0	7178	69815	32582	4840	8	12762
5	2644	38151	24476	759	30	6807
0	1839	46920	29827	5013	243	15646
10	1186	38976	16505	2975	169	5586
17	3219	44473	28376	5513	706	13064
18	6096	60409	62467	7829	535	23555
0	5255	77024	66185	9318	12	33676
50	2419	44303	18267	4004	694	4943
52	2954	58234	37739	4637	165	15599
5	698	71998	28939	5899	1321	16860
33	1623	50590	18633	2732	411	9125
2	117	10500	7338	811	2	1285
15	2298	23003	20484	1287	91	3706
7	8868	60543	59324	3608	309	13046
60	1007	49365	22044	4797	289	6888
97	4338	33362	18519	3594	189	1566
8	300	2355	2138	576	175	600
2	1177	28631	34845	4245	170	6829
4	1153	18234	24799	1804	83	2463
1	983	5393	2503	460	74	988
2	847	4452	4065	475	1	1167
6	3002	15599	14964	2990	162	7885

小学专任教师学历、专业技

Number of Full-time Teacher in Primary Schools by Academic

地 区 Region	合计 Total	其中:女 of Which: Female	按学历分 By Educational Attainment			
			研究生毕业 Graduate	本科毕业 Under-graduate	专科毕业 Associate Bachelor	高中阶段毕业 High School Graduate
总 计 Total	**613394**	**417255**	**2433**	**310082**	**270552**	**30185**
北 京 Beijing	1423	999	104	1117	180	22
天 津 Tianjin	2228	1435	37	1605	505	81
河 北 Hebei	71013	57874	236	33439	35307	2024
山 西 Shanxi	20082	16710	33	10452	8838	744
内蒙古 Inner Mongolia	4588	3281	10	2640	1791	147
辽 宁 Liaoning	5588	4035	19	2603	2746	215
吉 林 Jilin	3881	2832	62	2354	1318	147
黑龙江 Heilongjiang	4584	2995	6	1892	2400	286
上 海 Shanghai	1593	1129	63	1072	443	15
江 苏 Jiangsu	36628	23210	280	27932	7779	637
浙 江 Zhejiang	23918	17101	122	17635	5746	413
安 徽 Anhui	21994	12553	72	10381	10510	1031
福 建 Fujian	18554	12209	36	8166	8571	1777
江 西 Jiangxi	22509	14320	27	9884	10609	1981
山 东 Shandong	68720	42191	597	39038	25080	3994
河 南 Henan	74074	54441	262	34916	35068	3828
湖 北 Hubei	19722	10396	34	8062	9839	1764
湖 南 Hunan	29037	19346	63	13128	14342	1498
广 东 Guangdong	50122	35568	159	25239	22985	1736
广 西 Guangxi	24395	17061	27	9254	13074	2030
海 南 Hainan	2956	1577	2	859	1790	305
重 庆 Chongqing	8943	5245	21	3886	4739	295
四 川 Sichuan	21947	13262	50	8117	12577	1202
贵 州 Guizhou	17183	9162	5	6937	8979	1232
云 南 Yunnan	15927	10186	15	6408	8398	1098
西 藏 Tibet	425	280	0	191	226	8
陕 西 Shaanxi	18255	12643	49	10795	7001	409
甘 肃 Gansu	11296	6743	13	6708	3825	750
青 海 Qinghai	2610	1609	19	1421	1112	58
宁 夏 Ningxia	1673	1150	2	837	772	61
新 疆 Xinjiang	7526	5712	8	3114	4002	397

术职务情况(镇乡结合区)

Qualifications and Professional Rank (County-town Transitional Area)

单位:人
unit: person

	按专业技术职务分 By Professional Rank					
高中阶段毕业以下 Below High School Graduate	中学高级 Senior Secondary	小学高级 Senior Primary	小学一级 1st Grade Primary	小学二级 2nd Grade Primary	小学三级 3rd Grade Primary	未定职级 No-ranking
142	**18858**	**283983**	**204006**	**26200**	**2153**	**78194**
0	42	549	422	29	0	381
0	131	1403	543	21	0	130
7	1704	28557	26920	2782	269	10781
15	120	7225	9934	733	78	1992
0	1253	2242	728	72	0	293
5	780	3659	778	47	11	313
0	349	1679	1361	81	0	411
0	391	2482	1528	36	0	147
0	33	622	610	48	0	280
0	1875	19269	10030	1537	0	3917
2	638	11606	8631	311	11	2721
0	387	9869	6716	1196	68	3758
4	265	10599	5024	977	51	1638
8	598	9787	6790	1410	170	3754
11	2499	26044	26438	3471	307	9961
0	1940	29828	25107	3565	1	13633
23	572	11467	4920	1066	180	1517
6	680	14254	9209	1055	7	3832
3	258	27740	11126	2415	603	7980
10	355	15434	5692	741	90	2083
0	25	1382	1182	105	0	262
2	353	3825	3555	276	34	900
1	1116	9172	8813	607	68	2171
30	132	10396	4529	914	66	1146
8	1071	9105	4880	644	1	226
0	22	177	163	32	16	15
1	190	6816	8663	1053	50	1483
0	212	4308	5812	426	14	524
0	283	1440	616	72	10	189
1	172	725	556	50	0	170
5	412	2322	2730	428	48	1586

地 区 Region	合计 Total	其中:女 of Which: Female	按学历分 By Educational Attainment 研究生毕业 Graduate	本科毕业 Under-graduate	专科毕业 Associate Bachelor	高中阶段毕业 High School Graduate
总 计 Total	**1917418**	**1031437**	**5296**	**809796**	**942725**	**157998**
北 京 Beijing	6527	4504	297	5449	722	53
天 津 Tianjin	7126	3920	69	5145	1566	346
河 北 Hebei	150328	105841	464	63849	79713	6283
山 西 Shanxi	56527	37873	240	24801	27337	4132
内蒙古 Inner Mongolia	19967	11376	117	10224	8764	862
辽 宁 Liaoning	31392	20073	242	13533	15764	1816
吉 林 Jilin	37071	22618	150	18382	15253	3284
黑龙江 Heilongjiang	27745	14896	31	10220	15404	2068
上 海 Shanghai	1757	1287	115	1253	370	19
江 苏 Jiangsu	36277	18008	204	23876	11011	1186
浙 江 Zhejiang	32227	21416	200	23287	7893	844
安 徽 Anhui	97530	45502	215	42790	48608	5917
福 建 Fujian	43895	22233	59	15787	21274	6748
江 西 Jiangxi	82263	42461	65	31476	39943	10671
山 东 Shandong	120174	55916	927	57480	48941	12795
河 南 Henan	231240	135991	667	95834	116328	18400
湖 北 Hubei	57480	24256	114	20513	29627	7180
湖 南 Hunan	80108	43379	123	30809	41912	7213
广 东 Guangdong	110075	63611	157	48739	54926	6234
广 西 Guangxi	111703	60631	85	33973	63851	13601
海 南 Hainan	15038	5776	15	2780	9994	2223
重 庆 Chongqing	29058	13654	56	12153	15263	1574
四 川 Sichuan	103299	52571	90	34730	60634	7837
贵 州 Guizhou	80877	30288	43	32525	41058	6938
云 南 Yunnan	130232	60647	124	52205	65969	11371
西 藏 Tibet	11084	5472	10	4712	6141	212
陕 西 Shaanxi	34123	17472	88	17567	14950	1510
甘 肃 Gansu	69111	26809	164	36351	23910	8631
青 海 Qinghai	10710	4397	64	5160	4842	635
宁 夏 Ningxia	13002	6651	26	6397	5738	840
新 疆 Xinjiang	79472	51908	75	27796	45019	6575

业技术职务情况(乡村)
Academic Qualifications and Professional Rank (Rural Area)

单位:人
unit: person

	按专业技术职务分 By Professional Rank					
高中阶段毕业以下 Below High School Graduate	中学高级 Senior Secondary	小学高级 Senior Primary	小学一级 1st Grade Primary	小学二级 2nd Grade Primary	小学三级 3rd Grade Primary	未定职级 No-ranking
1603	**53500**	**849518**	**638967**	**114497**	**10624**	**250312**
6	208	3060	2258	122	0	879
0	472	4581	1466	185	1	421
19	4017	61512	57026	5468	850	21455
17	352	19537	27363	2573	469	6233
0	4212	8861	3939	661	0	2294
37	4008	20014	4581	565	108	2116
2	2021	17965	12214	1364	24	3483
22	2021	14571	9671	376	22	1084
0	20	560	624	142	1	410
0	980	20013	9488	1735	0	4061
3	575	15343	12314	373	19	3603
0	1423	44796	30097	5604	136	15474
27	465	25265	11498	2641	254	3772
108	1223	32596	22577	6742	1160	17965
31	3398	49526	46054	6897	368	13931
11	5288	98674	80114	10188	8	36968
46	1109	32339	14404	3700	536	5392
51	1775	36455	24081	3997	77	13723
19	385	61608	26456	5341	955	15330
193	966	61128	29959	5328	930	13392
26	57	6627	6764	711	3	876
12	846	12288	11458	1306	149	3011
8	4755	37368	40176	6242	994	13764
313	625	40049	23377	8105	832	7889
563	6087	55491	43923	15030	730	8971
9	256	3512	3924	1259	589	1544
8	298	12636	15146	2245	87	3711
55	857	23741	31494	4514	420	8085
9	853	5525	2280	575	134	1343
1	1133	5018	3930	785	19	2117
7	2815	18859	30311	9723	749	17015

地区 Region	校舍建筑面积 Floor Space	教学及辅助用房 Teaching & Assistant Buildings							行政办公用房 Administrative	
		合计 Total	其中: of Which:						合计 Total	其中:教师办公室 of Which: for Teachers
			教室 Classroom	实验室 Laboratory	图书室 Library	微机室 PC-room	语音室 Linguistic	体育馆 Gymnasium		
总　计 Total	**750884632.85**	**403879545.49**	**324222890.83**	**25299940.35**	**21954594.62**	**17287216.98**	**4799138.81**	**10315763.90**	**66051830.39**	**43522345.80**
北　京 Beijing	7271855.05	3361199.28	2602565.79	213252.31	181499.62	146731.16	14255.46	202894.94	863965.93	450372.05
天　津 Tianjin	4634250.83	2495880.26	2006318.55	101072.88	122534.15	99104.38	41237.28	125613.02	607527.01	394820.86
河　北 Hebei	42205329.61	24723936.50	19926904.22	1696492.20	1449891.51	1169543.70	290102.88	191001.99	3530966.11	2494240.35
山　西 Shanxi	19003974.68	9097562.96	7424014.49	524860.24	512711.67	436675.30	110980.53	88320.73	2160020.66	1591186.93
内蒙古 Inner Mongolia	12909411.41	6631937.90	5266099.29	323902.53	306793.58	260729.94	81359.61	393052.95	1329102.37	911275.92
辽　宁 Liaoning	12566859.48	6645191.37	5212099.76	393196.40	351878.40	326980.04	107518.30	253518.47	1340429.47	863489.70
吉　林 Jilin	9421479.91	5340392.29	4161403.96	381698.70	341767.78	289132.50	94548.87	71840.48	1000024.69	680280.86
黑龙江 Heilongjiang	9383255.19	5195405.00	4132714.84	369166.69	206286.80	204309.32	100896.95	182030.40	1077807.29	715114.51
上　海 Shanghai	5814351.03	3117216.77	2057413.11	363124.54	203307.05	135483.56	38442.72	319445.79	762847.53	393026.75
江　苏 Jiangsu	39408866.11	22992057.71	17145387.06	1639584.31	1411144.47	1107160.24	260368.51	1428413.12	4088700.28	2185231.93
浙　江 Zhejiang	32317525.34	16726436.46	12370476.48	1089505.75	870394.49	632545.46	166924.00	1596590.28	2911229.29	1652599.07
安　徽 Anhui	30300788.94	19307572.97	15526230.45	1286287.43	1108247.36	957261.74	211881.43	217664.56	2658774.40	1817977.67
福　建 Fujian	23686492.33	12506088.10	10085797.57	722080.80	698585.54	504441.55	96866.34	398316.30	1734836.94	1033239.89
江　西 Jiangxi	29378310.12	16588845.07	13986441.80	776018.97	826142.79	591552.64	182266.43	226422.44	2558568.11	1588433.26
山　东 Shandong	47713956.94	25612987.36	19337080.51	2334610.62	1710474.56	1348282.26	344079.90	538459.51	4723678.46	2905491.11
河　南 Henan	66415933.15	36649244.48	30879819.61	1931821.74	1917230.96	1419101.87	352279.54	148990.76	7654373.84	5739918.45
湖　北 Hubei	29711134.77	14611147.86	11546030.59	1074346.80	808987.45	682607.78	223744.77	275430.47	2217377.57	1408689.35
湖　南 Hunan	36817608.77	18377250.66	14669485.64	1406923.89	979425.28	630735.91	296160.24	394519.70	3052876.93	2205092.37
广　东 Guangdong	68881485.56	37536917.25	30291021.67	1741146.41	1852201.80	1408588.79	527929.88	1716028.70	4909630.58	3278823.16
广　西 Guangxi	38097005.88	22895309.00	19897226.33	1026225.02	990368.36	638129.52	112018.87	231340.90	1917468.54	1511632.12
海　南 Hainan	6088764.28	3253688.57	2803400.53	137539.47	149494.74	101872.13	38752.00	22629.70	369707.23	262429.08
重　庆 Chongqing	19513349.86	9911256.46	8277438.29	589970.55	383251.69	318070.41	66741.18	275784.34	1631544.09	974608.90
四　川 Sichuan	36658601.62	20237566.89	16871240.51	1192944.40	966504.62	785081.33	211411.24	210384.79	2467293.89	1654673.53
贵　州 Guizhou	26915947.06	12352764.20	10212542.16	755967.82	682401.84	515312.09	94195.94	92344.35	1889802.30	1168576.45
云　南 Yunnan	33828262.68	15922776.53	12763939.32	1042207.50	958919.53	847994.74	169922.57	139792.87	1839175.09	1209625.89
西　藏 Tibet	4412678.73	1439733.91	1141840.05	76861.01	70929.37	73215.91	19766.27	57121.30	277388.51	216465.73
陕　西 Shaanxi	19429756.57	9695871.95	7294300.95	689144.06	662402.04	584527.47	345231.25	120266.18	2291340.51	1552660.62
甘　肃 Gansu	14791478.94	8100293.89	6609044.87	481498.25	497742.06	394008.84	65445.70	52554.17	1678567.85	1241753.40
青　海 Qinghai	4257553.84	1793494.74	1291894.28	112151.68	137227.54	99657.86	33377.03	119186.35	312865.66	208665.59
宁　夏 Ningxia	4621957.58	2606348.13	2057730.70	205352.38	138812.87	141853.43	26075.76	36522.99	474743.75	297921.45
新　疆 Xinjiang	14426406.59	8153170.97	6374987.45	620985.00	457034.70	436525.11	74357.36	189281.35	1719195.51	914028.85

条件(一)(总计)
in Primary Schools(1)(Total)

单位:平方米
unit: m^2

生活用房 Residential and Welfare							其他用房 Rooms for Other Purposes	校舍面积中 of the Floor Space	
合计 Total	教工宿舍 Apartments for Single 小计 Subtotal	其中:教师周转宿舍 of Which: Accommodation for Circulation of Teachers	学生宿舍 Students' Dormitories	食堂 Dining Halls	厕所 Toilet	其他 Others		危房面积 Floor Space of Dilapidated Buildings	当年新增校舍 New Floor Space Added in Current Year
195354138.72	**55857902.92**	**16430494.74**	**40057714.60**	**42173238.80**	**31671940.74**	**25593341.66**	**85599118.25**	**5662588.00**	**47908701.95**
1199905.70	113405.51	10949.15	73046.66	326974.90	334525.13	351953.50	1846784.14	0.00	256258.85
728577.44	34226.52	3233.76	6175.00	127917.77	248105.58	312152.57	802266.12	0.00	161523.73
8655112.25	1140943.60	239799.09	2441314.11	1466218.61	1824695.89	1781940.04	5295314.75	12749.02	3939985.96
4797727.55	938701.11	123674.88	1338666.45	851271.13	817168.74	851920.12	2948663.51	82634.47	448498.36
3782583.02	358377.65	211661.14	1557337.48	759850.57	597329.44	509687.88	1165788.12	0.00	550686.67
2145592.80	92985.17	33895.84	188565.38	651794.62	557761.51	654486.12	2435645.84	27095.18	760493.51
1549442.22	65609.59	26468.69	164335.07	371036.47	429991.57	518469.52	1531620.71	3339.00	263546.67
1655159.80	62983.69	28109.39	307957.00	264476.47	407589.54	612153.10	1454883.10	27620.35	412781.40
1039415.72	14561.97	2266.00	12123.17	408138.32	268072.17	336520.09	894871.01	0.00	89842.58
7596840.89	885432.79	177890.16	563271.90	2934776.68	1514489.02	1698870.50	4731267.23	0.00	1411272.34
7882056.38	1742379.08	203214.96	719027.44	2851362.17	1240152.14	1329135.55	4797803.21	0.00	1959201.87
5560126.61	1461107.65	329642.48	594479.76	1589330.87	1273492.37	641715.96	2774314.96	73658.77	1845807.66
5267040.52	2330548.41	297005.44	568941.68	609394.10	1018469.38	739686.95	4178526.77	126476.00	861787.62
7527703.62	2899361.57	898325.58	997798.65	1687596.34	1265154.41	677792.65	2703193.32	174568.64	2561138.71
8632948.65	1127040.32	294060.82	1016047.04	2314447.23	2486861.18	1688552.88	8744342.47	259.00	5129767.60
16485471.14	3273278.49	583592.92	4159682.24	3704200.60	3524644.35	1823665.46	5626843.69	68497.98	3696098.99
10136767.60	4114963.51	845782.25	1976550.24	2009976.07	1021156.90	1014120.88	2745841.74	103458.56	1335997.77
11604382.25	3953713.75	993357.02	1974404.05	2759781.94	1404275.33	1512207.18	3783098.93	290503.20	1648986.37
15967307.49	7230725.12	919170.39	2083361.43	1673913.75	2497699.96	2481607.23	10467630.24	28470.88	1448592.27
11229122.79	4476910.61	1669439.05	2643409.78	1933334.33	1355615.07	819853.00	2055105.55	652852.35	3517494.80
2091647.56	1251387.14	444003.66	379016.99	171420.23	187431.44	102391.76	373720.92	30555.86	297457.79
5537369.92	2132844.80	603216.73	760156.55	1264330.66	687302.66	692735.25	2433179.39	83613.96	438273.01
11836664.22	4137405.84	1892754.03	2800861.87	2578438.96	1495598.59	824358.96	2117076.62	127157.05	3619025.75
10325417.83	3185318.64	2103731.32	3477465.77	1840985.22	1131033.70	690614.50	2347962.73	300.00	2662589.25
14199439.00	3779869.00	1317509.37	5150559.73	3221900.07	1228835.76	818274.44	1866872.06	2492180.68	2869787.02
2591001.77	1074673.08	882935.06	868844.72	423984.44	91282.11	132217.42	104554.54	7025.60	433868.27
5411783.50	1566250.87	251836.82	1124724.64	1168635.78	920386.54	631785.67	2030760.61	12807.00	1971485.09
3728262.92	1128740.24	197791.13	499631.99	711820.33	853559.21	534511.15	1284354.28	1233528.01	1374703.48
1653791.86	383691.11	235793.34	622000.72	270530.74	161067.93	216501.36	497401.58	0.00	307517.37
1001054.24	252191.39	117906.10	79605.11	234093.02	267636.79	167527.93	539811.46	3236.44	406386.41
3534421.46	648274.70	491478.17	908351.98	991306.41	560556.33	425932.04	1019618.65	0.00	1227844.78

地区 Region	校舍建筑面积 Floor Space	教学及辅助用房 Teaching & Assistant Buildings							行政办公用房 Administrative	
		合计 Total	其中：of Which：						合计 Total	其中：教师办公室 of Which: for Teachers
			教室 Classroom	实验室 Laboratory	图书室 Library	微机室 PC-room	语音室 Linguistic	体育馆 Gymnasium		
总　计 Total	**211376846.26**	**116838555.74**	**91510431.98**	**6778078.82**	**5812840.54**	**4570668.97**	**1404182.39**	**6762353.04**	**21465836.99**	**13108090.90**
北　京 Beijing	5718697.18	2670168.72	2090211.00	145162.96	140623.45	110372.88	11306.26	172492.17	684546.02	363459.25
天　津 Tianjin	3141348.64	1597795.88	1266237.89	55669.96	76317.64	59964.80	22220.57	117385.02	428424.23	278407.62
河　北 Hebei	7650888.31	4489015.59	3692359.04	254024.81	224369.96	181345.33	50122.95	86793.50	757899.54	541794.56
山　西 Shanxi	4857509.74	2505330.70	2072012.18	121113.39	124454.27	103025.58	34876.33	49848.95	607548.80	412466.79
内蒙古 Inner Mongolia	3838120.44	2478189.20	2016867.50	95789.66	94705.46	80476.85	23761.06	166588.67	428349.98	285572.20
辽　宁 Liaoning	6618874.38	3439301.83	2679616.17	174072.45	168218.96	152247.92	54188.16	210958.17	740349.43	442446.22
吉　林 Jilin	3123231.46	1874185.08	1482803.62	111973.70	105640.00	86448.17	35142.13	52177.46	335451.31	208372.28
黑龙江 Heilongjiang	3640181.58	2016233.53	1560299.35	116665.34	73705.05	76943.24	45480.71	143139.84	476108.04	277768.08
上　海 Shanghai	4860688.90	2631546.91	1729354.55	311591.42	170014.44	113947.11	33595.85	273043.54	634015.12	332196.65
江　苏 Jiangsu	19398385.45	10747784.91	7767911.07	729842.64	679173.69	455928.98	104869.21	1010059.32	2147357.64	1110999.18
浙　江 Zhejiang	15486664.46	8137972.96	5806387.91	490830.09	434675.69	283446.25	86933.46	1035699.56	1417609.93	786652.38
安　徽 Anhui	5620727.21	3564656.35	2903560.83	183167.35	156760.71	158262.66	32213.76	130691.04	621861.75	393042.45
福　建 Fujian	7134463.19	3755925.57	2920514.53	233312.27	216936.24	143808.98	35762.75	205590.80	576318.69	321120.12
江　西 Jiangxi	4983191.10	2888541.95	2382772.62	132310.34	129370.91	99843.04	30828.48	113416.56	507187.58	290412.78
山　东 Shandong	15276881.23	8003142.96	6013901.57	695038.33	475557.71	350985.08	109775.96	357884.31	1673618.95	967997.91
河　南 Henan	10868555.73	5985296.53	5132494.97	253736.04	246522.57	198226.42	61871.04	92445.49	1426102.38	982890.36
湖　北 Hubei	8045651.81	4456936.50	3528906.64	295353.67	222001.86	193224.55	66094.36	151355.42	794535.00	503407.64
湖　南 Hunan	7524198.37	3839080.69	2959443.02	250946.40	186727.10	134168.89	62427.87	245367.41	679361.57	463086.61
广　东 Guangdong	31335929.00	17020202.72	13458707.58	792306.32	755142.14	602909.54	200980.08	1210157.06	2174137.05	1410691.36
广　西 Guangxi	5820847.24	3844143.82	3260129.31	149506.62	157490.58	115888.04	19724.26	141405.01	416806.30	314551.82
海　南 Hainan	1352771.80	798323.23	690455.47	31272.52	31798.54	23988.80	10602.90	10205.00	94033.24	64408.80
重　庆 Chongqing	7429607.71	4073275.40	3293236.01	241162.52	150961.97	126910.22	35636.07	225368.61	749622.20	441690.32
四　川 Sichuan	7920822.30	5033465.76	4047896.33	321307.89	240306.79	204056.49	70331.21	149567.05	698861.98	459270.05
贵　州 Guizhou	3759691.97	1937507.51	1566584.39	100694.49	96692.81	82407.16	24569.83	66558.83	400645.74	242143.70
云　南 Yunnan	3778112.91	2150723.84	1723973.15	112635.01	105808.93	103789.79	31732.89	72784.07	348552.77	216869.84
西　藏 Tibet	353700.38	165196.62	146393.22	4514.50	3945.20	5811.20	2993.50	1539.00	45677.65	30563.89
陕　西 Shaanxi	5118187.99	2658309.33	2089352.17	145917.04	149428.74	131730.83	64557.38	77323.17	661018.05	423771.63
甘　肃 Gansu	2053461.25	1220884.88	1020292.51	48362.18	52288.62	51484.34	11718.93	36738.30	255930.18	173251.61
青　海 Qinghai	666712.73	338545.80	240964.14	23899.28	19780.68	20640.36	7293.54	25967.80	80830.69	46054.68
宁　夏 Ningxia	1257159.36	754323.22	599699.60	51562.23	37397.28	37498.28	7689.22	20476.61	169320.18	101692.68
新　疆 Xinjiang	2741582.44	1762547.75	1367093.64	104337.40	86022.55	80887.19	14881.67	109325.30	433755.00	221037.44

条件(一)(城区)
in Primary Schools (1)(Urban Area)

单位:平方米
unit: m^2

生活用房 Residential and Welfare							其他用房 Rooms for Other Purposes	校舍面积中 of the Floor Space	
合计 Total	教工宿舍 Apartments for Single		学生宿舍 Students' Dormitories	食堂 Dining Halls	厕所 Toilet	其他 Others		危房面积 Floor Space of Dilapidated Buildings	当年新增校舍 New Floor Space Added in Current Year
	小计 Subtotal	其中:教师周转宿舍 of Which: Accommodation for Circulation of Teachers							
37870312. 20	**6660974. 15**	**1101542. 36**	**4174652. 13**	**9050859. 72**	**8937676. 74**	**9046149. 46**	**35202141. 33**	**952365. 83**	**11294981. 16**
827988. 85	52020. 45	5515. 55	35913. 95	242952. 89	257640. 94	239460. 62	1535993. 59	0. 00	228579. 10
492578. 96	10583. 00	355. 00	6025. 00	105291. 77	169331. 05	201348. 14	622549. 57	0. 00	136660. 85
1130956. 92	70743. 17	8205. 53	215350. 94	137450. 31	306836. 12	400576. 38	1273016. 26	5748. 00	663028. 91
775644. 05	102071. 34	12407. 86	140711. 79	85924. 97	209887. 33	237048. 62	968986. 19	20079. 26	161068. 65
533122. 63	44536. 49	19120. 25	107300. 00	67864. 11	169987. 07	143434. 96	398458. 63	0. 00	148954. 94
983335. 02	12780. 22	1889. 02	57689. 16	286619. 31	278941. 66	347304. 67	1455888. 10	9091. 00	379539. 37
389767. 69	4058. 15	292. 12	15809. 51	104805. 99	123561. 37	141532. 67	523827. 38	1800. 00	85970. 31
467362. 61	5736. 40	550. 00	24304. 75	41224. 18	151663. 79	244433. 49	680477. 40	9739. 00	156613. 94
859903. 54	8715. 97	1461. 00	12123. 17	324231. 66	221929. 39	292903. 35	735223. 33	0. 00	74011. 99
3602939. 71	171385. 60	23601. 01	170481. 03	1520080. 50	763570. 73	977421. 85	2900303. 19	0. 00	874806. 44
3350907. 65	418631. 93	38855. 87	329132. 23	1345075. 25	583262. 86	674805. 38	2580173. 92	0. 00	977145. 12
602071. 41	75334. 56	13367. 56	44567. 00	106764. 40	242669. 72	132735. 73	832137. 70	15636. 00	294369. 24
990941. 79	268927. 17	33670. 21	30616. 95	128152. 41	321534. 23	241711. 03	1811277. 14	20627. 00	382649. 70
770235. 69	193756. 43	59397. 15	24179. 80	169046. 02	224147. 14	159106. 30	817225. 88	24081. 70	348701. 34
2575426. 58	223053. 50	49417. 99	294524. 90	648703. 30	720412. 89	688731. 99	3024692. 74	259. 00	1262777. 12
1951974. 01	359934. 77	59472. 64	415629. 87	310327. 80	487920. 59	378160. 98	1505182. 81	12286. 74	378446. 58
1733077. 53	601496. 14	73602. 63	173733. 30	361248. 68	289546. 91	307052. 50	1061102. 78	17735. 00	398851. 94
1738530. 47	378451. 18	73383. 55	222104. 29	441213. 50	296203. 01	400558. 49	1267225. 64	18516. 00	371406. 16
6312226. 21	2107620. 10	240463. 08	838689. 33	904009. 06	1227461. 17	1234446. 55	5829363. 02	12047. 88	875544. 85
1117004. 19	311268. 68	68843. 59	203487. 38	179020. 27	262420. 73	160807. 13	442892. 93	39287. 59	550410. 25
343448. 93	188295. 47	65407. 47	43352. 78	25270. 44	50678. 68	35851. 56	116966. 40	2301. 00	51912. 61
1390853. 02	222398. 28	37990. 80	115445. 31	457021. 66	284050. 00	311937. 77	1215857. 09	19779. 70	285889. 48
1531400. 63	252754. 74	55775. 64	287746. 49	427309. 11	345348. 87	218241. 42	657093. 93	11060. 00	751531. 02
737787. 35	117531. 53	42552. 80	109183. 26	163219. 63	186555. 75	161297. 18	683751. 37	0. 00	405485. 68
746176. 24	162043. 60	30794. 29	84133. 42	148717. 27	160965. 88	190316. 07	532660. 06	403588. 00	245850. 63
136217. 91	81535. 33	68995. 14	18016. 00	19383. 56	6475. 74	10807. 28	6608. 20	3124. 80	28026. 02
1002941. 37	176026. 99	10874. 51	120321. 27	208871. 83	263680. 48	234040. 80	795919. 24	9143. 00	437500. 97
254203. 35	16330. 91	1858. 70	9981. 72	20508. 68	111603. 62	95778. 42	322442. 84	295046. 16	153691. 27
95395. 03	3082. 71	60. 00	8514. 40	7092. 46	34542. 31	42163. 15	151941. 21	0. 00	28291. 41
126917. 85	5628. 50	679. 69	560. 00	6785. 71	72330. 69	41612. 95	206598. 11	1389. 00	93152. 88
298975. 01	14240. 84	2681. 71	15023. 13	56672. 99	112516. 02	100522. 03	246304. 68	0. 00	64112. 39

小学办学

Condition of School Buildings in Primary

地　区 Region	校舍建筑面积 Floor Space	教学及辅助用房 Teaching & Assistant Buildings							行政办公用房 Administrative	
		合计 Total	其中：of Which：教室 Classroom	实验室 Laboratory	图书室 Library	微机室 PC-room	语音室 Linguistic	体育馆 Gymnasium	合计 Total	其中：教师办公室 of Which：for Teachers
总　计 Total	**42422942.08**	**22615677.02**	**17662447.01**	**1366836.89**	**1190100.00**	**940629.69**	**283011.35**	**1172652.08**	**3778905.37**	**2338533.98**
北　京 Beijing	495195.22	259322.34	203253.49	14391.19	14182.49	12729.40	2138.98	12626.79	57289.78	29345.22
天　津 Tianjin	405421.83	190669.32	148070.93	8416.11	9090.32	8085.92	3601.83	13404.21	48840.44	32755.49
河　北 Hebei	2188395.82	1264053.15	1025462.18	84120.67	69453.78	60751.72	13014.35	11250.45	194182.36	138823.42
山　西 Shanxi	736726.76	343203.54	278699.40	20228.68	19964.72	16960.29	3503.35	3847.10	106714.36	68423.76
内蒙古 Inner Mongolia	125316.59	70672.46	59520.66	2504.19	3084.88	2780.73	650.00	2132.00	14073.00	7634.89
辽　宁 Liaoning	720493.24	358879.52	278757.25	20490.22	17909.26	16499.18	6192.23	19031.38	67067.66	44555.49
吉　林 Jilin	249369.35	108330.11	82234.86	7076.55	6275.17	5724.53	1708.00	5311.00	31081.59	18259.61
黑龙江 Heilongjiang	273905.30	128546.13	96330.78	9275.16	6578.93	6435.41	4085.41	5840.44	31058.43	19614.21
上　海 Shanghai	482915.43	252463.04	175887.56	19831.16	15201.82	11225.57	3357.83	26959.10	65151.19	31461.24
江　苏 Jiangsu	2318974.16	1247177.38	887066.61	85525.36	86471.26	62634.83	12938.46	112540.86	231795.64	113802.25
浙　江 Zhejiang	3883974.15	2014461.44	1448055.83	105720.25	109256.03	70966.12	20655.83	259807.38	327209.71	172068.67
安　徽 Anhui	819838.30	504404.54	413764.47	31156.24	23467.55	22564.10	4461.18	8991.00	81524.44	53247.27
福　建 Fujian	1713773.97	919653.88	726340.75	55592.41	53639.82	38348.40	9686.07	36046.43	121073.49	72840.59
江　西 Jiangxi	860001.73	518381.08	433734.40	33589.59	22754.45	20124.64	5139.00	3039.00	80070.16	48620.13
山　东 Shandong	4740317.66	2428145.62	1816691.38	216356.91	147251.69	110820.73	41829.54	95195.37	477257.94	278688.39
河　南 Henan	2386653.11	1299589.88	1099743.65	59950.03	59788.38	49781.98	11914.73	18411.11	285844.89	204772.64
湖　北 Hubei	1294477.10	655717.54	516083.28	47539.38	38927.75	29380.93	11246.72	12539.48	111069.26	67967.68
湖　南 Hunan	1076250.13	524406.00	399434.07	34755.92	29113.13	21275.78	9722.66	30104.44	96962.33	65761.61
广　东 Guangdong	10456523.32	5621029.67	4431832.23	263903.33	252132.44	204162.24	67373.62	401625.81	720289.15	465316.56
广　西 Guangxi	1445834.00	918475.00	765867.83	53077.58	40259.44	27224.76	4938.38	27107.01	87429.34	68446.00
海　南 Hainan	192238.38	105919.18	88939.08	6353.00	5829.86	3404.24	1248.00	145.00	11532.36	8397.36
重　庆 Chongqing	786225.98	373847.35	302143.30	26441.42	16045.55	13621.03	3907.70	11688.35	63439.82	41250.23
四　川 Sichuan	1117090.04	649344.83	519718.02	43753.65	32299.79	27290.65	9657.12	16625.60	96683.62	53926.85
贵　州 Guizhou	729139.91	355105.16	288279.03	21628.94	19090.98	16233.53	3575.92	6296.76	66078.67	40680.80
云　南 Yunnan	1206518.38	656206.90	513449.97	39891.23	42086.76	35527.55	10150.04	15101.35	97071.24	57148.35
西　藏 Tibet	9908.00	3787.00	1646.00	169.00	72.00	441.00	0.00	1459.00	1154.00	639.00
陕　西 Shaanxi	1080654.71	475614.46	359577.30	33729.07	31823.14	27653.49	12389.00	10442.46	127773.42	86463.56
甘　肃 Gansu	191516.86	110459.03	92109.48	5197.08	6036.05	5685.04	1368.38	63.00	22203.76	14327.09
青　海 Qinghai	41460.25	19217.44	15125.49	1278.09	1120.57	1067.65	521.38	104.26	5397.47	3287.52
宁　夏 Ningxia	80053.92	45808.66	36811.05	3694.87	2417.87	2780.87	104.00	0.00	11202.56	6135.26
新　疆 Xinjiang	313778.48	192785.37	157816.68	11199.61	8474.12	8447.38	1931.64	4915.94	40383.29	23872.84

条件(一)(城乡结合区)
Schools (1)(Urban-rural Transitional Area)

单位:平方米
unit: m^2

生活用房 Residential and Welfare							其他用房 Rooms for Other Purposes	校舍面积中 of the Floor Space	
合计 Total	教工宿舍 Apartments for Single		学生宿舍 Students' Dormitories	食堂 Dining Halls	厕所 Toilet	其他 Others		危房面积 Floor Space of Dilapidated Buildings	当年新增校舍 New Floor Space Added in Current Year
	小计 Subtotal	其中:教师周转宿舍 of Which: Accommodation for Circulation of Teachers							
9138225.79	**2127790.14**	**328347.10**	**1203744.50**	**2147908.32**	**1864984.15**	**1793798.68**	**6890133.90**	**153350.97**	**2855980.00**
77362.36	9765.38	789.00	225.00	18636.40	22299.46	26436.12	101220.74	0.00	77004.52
73087.32	457.00	169.00	0.00	20669.83	21117.45	30843.04	92824.75	0.00	22629.66
406528.14	37284.85	2998.07	105710.83	53207.88	102386.38	107938.20	323632.17	0.00	203560.80
115247.27	18867.26	1216.18	15499.00	15800.84	32752.26	32327.91	171561.59	0.00	53630.70
25497.96	2685.75	193.00	7511.75	3375.36	5491.58	6433.52	15073.17	0.00	328.00
120648.30	2666.00	50.00	4148.00	36828.68	35707.24	41298.38	173897.76	0.00	48283.06
43941.52	105.00	20.00	2196.00	8820.01	11006.00	21814.51	66016.13	0.00	9387.00
43218.98	562.92	130.00	3130.00	4704.79	10677.40	24143.87	71081.76	0.00	502.00
86656.92	2435.00	340.00	0.00	38421.76	21426.97	24373.19	78644.28	0.00	19263.00
458697.59	44622.03	2800.16	37712.84	204323.10	90731.48	81308.14	381303.55	0.00	63141.95
982131.15	159519.24	14798.71	137245.86	392865.77	143595.20	148905.08	560171.85	0.00	263754.77
123159.35	21514.56	3626.56	6248.00	20885.67	39057.12	35454.00	110749.97	2518.00	72297.00
284864.01	93341.62	11340.59	3763.00	30074.52	89548.65	68136.22	388182.59	672.00	157189.39
157456.67	41632.62	18604.12	8083.80	44689.54	42788.48	20262.23	104093.82	2408.70	46712.32
1021529.24	103456.13	23170.60	157466.00	255636.57	247567.14	257403.40	813384.86	0.00	530086.32
493018.11	82253.19	13522.61	123134.02	96467.53	118250.73	72912.64	308200.23	1768.12	98178.58
376282.99	114742.92	22526.92	82481.80	76626.71	49420.21	53011.35	151407.31	12364.00	68194.44
295069.71	65445.64	15390.94	40102.49	87419.23	43131.92	58970.43	159812.09	12566.00	68570.10
2198269.85	924852.80	86798.92	183737.38	294952.82	411176.55	383550.30	1916934.65	3984.00	231040.64
316604.17	91711.54	30237.46	62871.49	54695.56	64267.45	43058.13	123325.49	9660.75	160271.47
55763.68	30530.00	15610.00	9699.76	6836.00	6786.96	1910.96	19023.16	216.00	8507.00
182729.95	28776.91	3411.00	21171.33	64667.81	32315.87	35798.03	166208.86	4640.70	68173.34
286710.92	59190.39	19904.97	68240.96	85538.00	51458.70	22282.87	84350.67	418.00	156436.29
201195.86	27078.88	13238.90	37245.94	54835.93	35768.51	46266.60	106760.22	0.00	121098.18
334204.39	91965.51	18759.08	40162.47	82917.47	48943.12	70215.82	119035.85	75959.00	113174.50
4967.00	2057.00	2057.00	1624.00	586.00	357.00	343.00	0.00	0.00	0.00
265900.00	59622.40	4324.71	34370.98	67976.59	54446.77	49483.26	211366.83	525.00	159268.52
40671.19	5864.60	721.90	7623.80	8225.07	11558.27	7399.45	18182.88	25650.70	23963.39
10603.33	0.00	0.00	1999.00	793.90	1663.60	6146.83	6242.01	0.00	522.00
12746.36	1005.00	0.00	0.00	704.00	4610.36	6427.00	10296.34	0.00	0.00
43461.50	3778.00	1596.70	339.00	15724.98	14675.32	8944.20	37148.32	0.00	10811.06

地区 Region	校舍建筑面积 Floor Space	教学及辅助用房 Teaching & Assistant Buildings							行政办公用房 Administrative	
		合计 Total	其中: of Which:						合计 Total	其中:教师办公室 of Which: for Teachers
			教室 Classroom	实验室 Laboratory	图书室 Library	微机室 PC-room	语音室 Linguistic	体育馆 Gymnasium		
总　计 Total	**258459618.36**	**137897734.86**	**111995975.47**	**8561689.13**	**6968051.48**	**5783229.53**	**1898506.77**	**2690282.48**	**22339720.57**	**14578175.22**
北　京 Beijing	691832.23	278024.45	207011.73	19317.58	16396.57	13814.57	1978.20	19505.80	70703.85	37033.98
天　津 Tianjin	582247.11	356073.32	295548.34	14676.43	18539.49	13913.83	6561.23	6834.00	67183.25	45984.72
河　北 Hebei	15035419.98	8525860.73	6908434.51	566131.90	466837.46	392182.67	116228.13	76046.06	1257804.92	874078.84
山　西 Shanxi	6628863.83	3388939.55	2823535.23	177756.83	170639.32	143250.26	45092.22	28665.69	723085.88	533343.83
内蒙古 Inner Mongolia	6278918.86	3069242.51	2394596.54	156132.63	143680.98	126883.72	45330.45	202618.19	623663.49	420114.32
辽　宁 Liaoning	2875576.81	1502608.98	1225606.02	82989.25	69979.79	72992.43	28084.20	22957.29	302787.15	203012.84
吉　林 Jilin	2873081.57	1663988.16	1334140.81	100463.42	96111.26	80403.09	36781.02	16088.56	278562.35	187591.94
黑龙江 Heilongjiang	3364343.24	1884306.45	1537269.89	139613.26	66538.08	69351.39	38368.33	33165.50	355864.32	255348.53
上　海 Shanghai	716200.24	361277.11	245859.05	38871.44	25550.29	15729.03	3494.57	31772.73	92483.83	44472.86
江　苏 Jiangsu	15469550.03	9209179.91	7004053.95	692672.38	535126.89	463394.13	121232.37	392700.19	1544518.94	829998.10
浙　江 Zhejiang	11330459.16	5943375.96	4477147.04	429885.46	294849.03	234218.51	56326.85	450949.07	1047115.38	600483.61
安　徽 Anhui	11588248.45	7478717.22	6162189.20	448912.09	363285.76	333288.92	89684.73	81356.52	1004798.54	646831.05
福　建 Fujian	8472135.71	4760060.30	3931975.26	231229.83	239034.95	173704.23	36026.32	148089.71	646304.99	372787.96
江　西 Jiangxi	11694781.07	6485042.71	5507415.76	294307.59	281869.09	221119.44	84263.07	96067.76	1101458.77	628167.62
山　东 Shandong	17311683.59	9055660.75	6869876.69	835585.29	601081.12	459348.97	135908.79	153859.89	1686368.34	1045309.84
河　南 Henan	22131215.25	11612911.12	9871352.86	581638.93	549025.33	436333.85	128389.14	46171.01	2476026.93	1800814.16
湖　北 Hubei	10718807.13	5169718.32	4132039.26	377980.93	249355.58	225622.87	88284.63	96435.05	725656.23	468776.38
湖　南 Hunan	15110147.78	7455506.23	5896158.07	644222.72	395675.93	273523.99	135957.63	109967.89	1166942.06	824082.31
广　东 Guangdong	17600688.96	9799089.85	8147587.19	410432.06	431662.53	356619.49	172136.60	280651.98	1235047.90	836586.08
广　西 Guangxi	12051200.56	6908618.05	6068444.47	302907.58	268300.94	185494.86	33720.25	49749.95	580380.94	448683.18
海　南 Hainan	2405301.15	1253581.20	1084930.51	50949.52	53996.59	40650.30	14662.02	8392.26	138400.35	96487.86
重　庆 Chongqing	7260420.52	3646239.34	3124883.69	206183.93	131526.97	118056.78	25203.15	40384.82	545976.45	330869.38
四　川 Sichuan	15042763.46	8426952.73	7081224.80	485974.87	379449.14	329214.14	93363.04	57726.74	988117.02	658192.49
贵　州 Guizhou	11010013.57	4740358.78	3957332.65	276691.35	237880.78	202325.37	47008.05	19120.58	775563.57	461870.35
云　南 Yunnan	8235725.94	3842906.40	3119204.32	236747.78	211865.91	195204.82	46065.56	33818.01	589906.38	379468.38
西　藏 Tibet	1266498.41	398799.61	307596.91	21007.78	18381.41	20956.42	4765.25	26091.84	71992.42	57666.77
陕　西 Shaanxi	8931063.86	4476348.64	3367915.33	326400.36	303128.36	266467.24	178280.34	34157.01	976686.74	673982.61
甘　肃 Gansu	4840345.98	2636189.43	2117852.12	172875.97	160124.93	135899.68	37038.19	12398.54	536791.28	386257.51
青　海 Qinghai	1607429.73	638974.16	452273.80	39178.85	46482.50	36379.62	14587.90	50071.49	112737.69	75378.61
宁　夏 Ningxia	1412910.87	805157.70	644632.91	58182.38	36989.62	41868.88	10064.53	13419.38	160422.50	100851.93
新　疆 Xinjiang	3921743.31	2124025.19	1697886.56	141768.74	104684.88	105016.03	23620.01	51048.97	456368.11	253647.18

条件(一)(镇区)
Primary Schools (1) (Counties & Towns Area)

单位:平方米
unit: m²

生活用房 Residential and Welfare							其他用房 Rooms for Other Purposes	校舍面积中 of the Floor Space	
合计 Total	教工宿舍 Apartments for Single		学生宿舍 Students' Dormitories	食堂 Dining Halls	厕所 Toilet	其他 Others		危房面积 Floor Space of Dilapidated Buildings	当年新增校舍 New Floor Space Added in Current Year
	小计 Subtotal	其中:教师周转宿舍 of Which: Accommodation for Circulation of Teachers							
72951031.67	**21242392.49**	**6696370.41**	**17853113.68**	**15759345.77**	**10056838.39**	**8039341.34**	**25271131.26**	**1429513.32**	**18555078.76**
183530.63	25462.70	1438.00	16087.25	42645.60	34517.77	64817.31	159573.30	0.00	18971.60
89747.90	7164.81	935.76	150.00	11868.50	30152.89	40411.70	69242.64	0.00	7962.76
3466966.28	410615.00	90256.68	1154298.14	626459.30	625993.78	649600.06	1784788.05	0.00	1523361.34
1716919.11	306217.64	50806.28	570668.00	320937.59	263377.80	255718.08	799919.29	34227.00	177948.51
2070393.47	156594.49	93954.69	954440.43	456110.46	278551.23	224696.86	515619.39	0.00	277440.54
619187.38	34406.74	16052.43	90441.69	228071.48	116939.10	149328.37	450993.30	4960.88	179884.31
553425.69	24491.72	15668.20	93746.17	166538.62	111210.65	157438.53	377105.37	0.00	79761.87
690399.09	23754.85	12385.52	195703.38	134657.16	138208.54	198075.16	433773.38	3563.26	145519.13
133200.17	4711.00	445.00	0.00	56987.60	34021.09	37480.48	129239.13	0.00	15830.59
3184799.76	543100.02	118581.42	337124.08	1204653.35	555653.88	544268.43	1531051.42	0.00	394010.40
2892092.41	748793.46	111012.90	236825.82	1014642.60	447570.48	444260.05	1447875.41	0.00	776482.10
2192085.65	609901.89	147910.34	325862.15	592581.54	426162.09	237577.98	912647.04	19931.00	748124.56
1970984.37	862922.39	134906.12	311165.56	223577.62	348759.19	224559.61	1094786.05	37529.00	300755.36
2997062.92	1107954.68	344949.62	586099.67	624085.22	447640.89	231282.46	1111216.67	63457.80	1313438.28
3566656.59	524574.51	143434.12	541825.68	1060857.54	889732.52	549666.34	3002997.91	0.00	2243157.86
6186152.93	1131524.90	176961.06	1991297.59	1379154.83	1077957.54	606218.07	1856124.27	21305.33	1373981.44
4059379.56	1781559.18	373955.10	852574.16	771917.38	315249.98	338078.86	764053.02	39836.56	519845.77
5217533.51	1880047.91	537451.10	1054332.26	1221140.38	509111.47	552901.49	1270165.98	106866.20	895115.43
4555406.30	2173319.46	362846.02	857287.26	425523.24	549092.03	550184.31	2011144.91	4369.00	353382.99
4043301.19	1650766.53	598502.98	1100829.22	696090.71	371286.56	224328.17	518900.38	183630.80	1199576.01
907701.60	475221.95	180021.45	239907.21	93516.84	64289.94	34765.66	105618.00	4862.00	94066.71
2320564.90	1045667.16	310643.81	332975.66	478496.88	233674.88	229750.32	747639.83	27218.55	80391.43
4885467.69	1779460.39	864139.45	1207961.63	1050893.40	546209.00	300943.27	742226.02	58603.25	1555537.14
4519737.97	1297123.89	874357.31	1747502.71	744042.10	443997.65	287071.62	974353.25	300.00	1320302.65
3213358.73	843806.99	350097.68	1130011.38	739797.64	283833.53	215909.19	589554.43	524925.20	711454.86
765282.84	320768.88	261552.23	266617.97	121395.53	19801.15	36699.31	30423.54	1044.00	114162.03
2673260.92	810111.39	174652.76	701635.48	559441.71	368696.93	233375.41	804767.56	2728.00	1012133.01
1227234.88	313461.11	92537.78	225893.05	261194.62	238036.78	188649.32	440130.39	290105.05	518115.36
683995.07	126186.92	90696.62	308969.72	118326.56	53473.53	77038.34	171722.81	0.00	93872.73
284461.38	62183.75	38512.04	33990.96	68207.28	82114.79	37964.60	162869.29	50.44	202130.18
1080740.78	160516.18	126705.94	386889.40	265532.49	151520.73	116281.98	260609.23	0.00	308361.81

小学办学条件
Condition of School Buildings in Primary

地 区 Region	校舍建筑面积 Floor Space	教学及辅助用房 Teaching & Assistant Buildings 合计 Total	其中：of Which： 教室 Classroom	实验室 Laboratory	图书室 Library	微机室 PC-room	语音室 Linguistic	体育馆 Gymnasium	行政办公用房 Administrative 合计 Total	其中：教师办公室 of Which：for Teachers
总 计 Total	**78644976.14**	**43094930.35**	**34822973.80**	**2761012.86**	**2349089.20**	**1892072.71**	**565301.55**	**704480.23**	**6872848.33**	**4589912.78**
北 京 Beijing	162572.59	68236.91	53394.16	5027.56	3869.18	3405.08	146.00	2394.93	18094.21	9168.64
天 津 Tianjin	272667.80	172635.66	145431.32	7671.82	7735.48	6734.82	3080.22	1982.00	33305.78	22161.01
河 北 Hebei	8157185.24	4700787.47	3780188.26	321370.03	276225.87	228431.48	61497.44	33074.39	653274.02	447359.45
山 西 Shanxi	2184203.86	1123021.29	913905.81	66785.22	63689.36	54988.95	16412.70	7239.25	249355.07	180602.80
内蒙古 Inner Mongolia	561679.51	260198.27	208236.33	12883.85	14120.42	11367.17	3194.50	10396.00	55783.48	35008.32
辽 宁 Liaoning	454916.59	238799.25	187441.47	15355.37	12829.04	12132.72	4052.65	6988.00	43581.10	27252.62
吉 林 Jilin	341611.56	180630.46	148548.54	11385.30	8921.90	7980.72	2434.00	1360.00	36943.46	25517.82
黑龙江 Heilongjiang	418550.55	219887.59	173948.60	15840.51	9493.06	10093.98	4543.00	5968.44	42129.06	31566.16
上 海 Shanghai	143131.82	75266.95	52627.78	9205.20	5246.05	3138.06	526.80	4523.06	20471.96	9221.43
江 苏 Jiangsu	4587265.76	2797375.43	2189792.28	190262.89	149249.15	138880.77	29793.93	99396.41	465049.48	247288.57
浙 江 Zhejiang	3715819.74	1976624.90	1503981.09	140595.52	97137.45	75893.04	20890.83	138126.97	346514.22	206916.22
安 徽 Anhui	2742615.95	1760983.12	1435404.45	118647.68	98469.77	83610.65	19335.57	5515.00	232419.24	162822.95
福 建 Fujian	2688023.76	1509289.91	1231154.11	85375.29	81591.50	62115.66	11410.29	37643.06	187334.76	111100.46
江 西 Jiangxi	3213925.62	1765171.95	1497839.49	78236.63	91131.44	67218.65	22746.73	7999.01	278571.41	171719.92
山 东 Shandong	7926122.47	4189469.65	3144459.05	386222.14	285939.52	225889.22	67504.74	79454.98	754404.15	470684.37
河 南 Henan	9172603.71	4932272.41	4150852.38	256087.08	262710.16	190879.37	49743.08	22000.34	1076393.09	807352.57
湖 北 Hubei	3120551.56	1439749.84	1145489.48	116010.98	77255.33	67751.37	19873.28	13369.40	200353.72	125323.52
湖 南 Hunan	4241403.67	2098920.98	1673045.81	166145.78	113907.58	78392.51	36851.65	30577.65	353500.51	255129.69
广 东 Guangdong	7537344.05	4334731.67	3572326.34	192023.60	198241.86	165669.77	67622.67	138847.43	539268.49	370295.76
广 西 Guangxi	3715095.34	2346047.77	2065141.30	100384.95	95800.42	62982.21	12592.59	9146.30	176592.20	145246.26
海 南 Hainan	416982.60	217642.81	191237.89	8464.54	10655.84	5955.54	1166.50	162.50	25282.72	16778.24
重 庆 Chongqing	1292469.35	651042.39	557180.32	38816.62	24264.10	19368.94	4213.95	7198.46	100821.93	57061.55
四 川 Sichuan	2441976.60	1336471.77	1117131.12	82333.33	61187.31	51454.06	11764.83	12601.12	155392.89	107131.38
贵 州 Guizhou	2164630.43	1030133.04	857819.66	63153.22	54986.59	42649.46	8075.62	3448.49	144086.53	93093.62
云 南 Yunnan	2117449.35	1085792.17	877223.14	70707.01	64062.35	56277.88	11230.79	6291.00	149121.07	103638.16
西 藏 Tibet	68867.64	22418.00	19292.00	486.00	1098.00	1302.00	240.00	0.00	7324.34	5533.94
陕 西 Shaanxi	2277601.28	1206470.33	879298.40	99153.62	89443.59	80686.39	51290.22	6598.11	248898.60	170596.17
甘 肃 Gansu	1227169.08	679725.87	519587.03	51354.14	50604.87	40987.93	15267.90	1924.00	140117.60	96648.44
青 海 Qinghai	331647.86	139541.04	106644.82	9274.24	9573.21	7457.87	2004.00	4586.90	24940.73	15182.34
宁 夏 Ningxia	274107.73	143180.40	111918.38	10771.31	7330.24	7838.32	2200.37	3121.78	27622.47	14493.40
新 疆 Xinjiang	674783.07	392411.05	312432.99	30981.43	22318.56	20538.12	3594.70	2545.25	85900.04	48017.00

（一）（镇乡结合区）

Schools (1) (County-town Transitional Area)

单位：平方米
unit: m^2

生活用房 Residential and Welfare							其他用房 Rooms for Other Purposes	校舍面积中 of the Floor Space	
合计 Total	教工宿舍 Apartments for Single		学生宿舍 Students' Dormitories	食堂 Dining Halls	厕所 Toilet	其他 Others		危房面积 Floor Space of Dilapidated Buildings	当年新增校舍 New Floor Space Added in Current Year
	小计 Subtotal	其中：教师周转宿舍 of Which: Accommodation for Circulation of Teachers							
20491077.74	**5667454.90**	**1467785.09**	**4245788.93**	**4579284.55**	**3354941.90**	**2643607.46**	**8186119.72**	**441118.15**	**5732332.55**
51805.27	5662.48	0.00	4532.68	9338.91	8053.05	24218.15	24436.20	0.00	3185.28
38946.36	4371.12	398.00	150.00	7141.90	13352.64	13930.70	27780.00	0.00	5373.76
1828304.29	216305.49	37103.99	602262.99	317217.11	356897.04	335621.66	974819.46	0.00	848829.49
517324.31	90347.26	15434.00	150838.24	99328.57	88675.33	88134.91	294503.19	835.00	73521.02
189386.79	15618.11	8604.61	78110.25	45803.59	31468.74	18386.10	56310.97	0.00	10545.87
105142.39	4276.36	1595.03	22572.00	33467.78	20458.38	24367.87	67393.85	0.00	15445.64
78065.75	4370.00	1634.00	14540.00	20802.07	14049.32	24304.36	45971.89	0.00	3213.00
90975.74	1981.44	738.48	25770.42	16549.15	18904.98	27769.75	65558.16	534.00	18754.41
29175.44	1439.00	0.00	0.00	12022.12	6362.40	9351.92	18217.47	0.00	4970.00
944356.50	192812.86	43080.99	56092.47	333018.46	176681.30	185751.41	380484.35	0.00	128386.16
889321.97	226527.17	25242.69	63255.58	335317.33	141991.12	122230.77	503358.65	0.00	311407.47
545397.70	143137.12	30584.19	65109.68	155348.86	111855.47	69946.57	203815.89	6990.00	116186.40
580171.76	284797.83	32930.71	46042.04	56012.19	116164.91	77154.79	411227.33	6207.00	107661.05
912139.98	329466.72	101926.85	167615.64	199652.46	136015.73	79389.43	258042.28	9053.55	298407.44
1581235.81	212453.42	59421.22	217257.95	483483.02	424218.16	243823.26	1401012.86	0.00	1136559.78
2427553.34	398967.49	53062.14	695803.55	553006.66	493466.42	286309.22	736384.87	7696.95	491473.17
1272867.86	534372.98	127277.44	285125.00	252703.04	102834.44	97832.40	207580.14	11267.56	113033.39
1412935.05	501235.93	152760.45	232477.94	356282.70	147388.63	175549.85	376047.13	50970.20	294095.20
1773612.31	821000.06	121204.18	243920.74	169848.87	257681.31	281161.33	889731.58	2732.00	89403.39
987045.80	374976.69	141594.80	215319.98	177121.77	139332.48	80294.88	205409.57	81070.80	378106.88
149401.71	83938.21	19760.90	32758.36	11323.14	13363.60	8018.40	24655.36	1732.00	16118.76
430002.27	184909.35	39709.78	66631.86	96501.41	44535.59	37424.06	110602.76	5442.53	2942.86
830817.60	263470.78	130029.77	216007.62	190927.04	92294.27	68117.89	119294.34	6804.00	320006.14
817393.66	236264.40	147702.51	287465.42	154117.88	91953.27	47592.69	173017.20	300.00	235302.12
719637.48	183908.93	55797.54	204205.22	196734.72	79552.33	55236.28	162898.63	159246.33	179755.33
38382.45	18447.30	16287.30	11658.58	4191.30	1307.80	2777.47	742.85	0.00	5300.00
608290.26	191793.39	35554.94	116962.29	136460.78	106952.68	56121.12	213942.09	1564.00	245607.92
292819.70	62937.69	13241.27	34798.78	62360.98	68749.93	63972.32	114505.91	88652.23	108855.10
122820.91	29935.17	20583.93	42011.71	22101.53	10704.77	18067.73	44345.18	0.00	12394.15
71007.18	22503.92	13192.93	8235.00	19391.22	13389.86	7487.18	32297.68	20.00	77143.50
154740.10	25226.23	21330.45	38256.94	51707.99	26285.95	13262.99	41731.88	0.00	80347.87

地 区 Region	校舍建筑面积 Floor Space	教学及辅助用房 Teaching & Assistant Buildings							行政办公用房 Administrative	
		合计 Total	其中: of Which:						合计 Total	其中:教师办公室 of Which: for Teachers
			教室 Classroom	实验室 Laboratory	图书室 Library	微机室 PC-room	语音室 Linguistic	体育馆 Gymnasium		
总 计 Total	**281048168.23**	**149143254.89**	**120716483.38**	**9960172.40**	**9173702.60**	**6933318.48**	**1496449.65**	**863128.38**	**22246272.83**	**15836079.68**
北 京 Beijing	861325.64	413006.11	305343.06	48771.77	24479.60	22543.71	971.00	10896.97	108716.06	49878.82
天 津 Tianjin	910655.08	542011.06	444532.32	30726.49	27677.02	25225.75	12455.48	1394.00	111919.53	70428.52
河 北 Hebei	19519021.32	11709060.18	9326110.67	876335.49	758684.09	596015.70	123751.80	28162.43	1515261.65	1078366.95
山 西 Shanxi	7517601.11	3203292.71	2528467.08	225990.02	217618.08	190399.46	31011.98	9806.09	829385.98	645376.31
内蒙古 Inner Mongolia	2792372.11	1084506.19	854635.25	71980.24	68407.14	53369.37	12268.10	23846.09	277088.90	205589.40
辽 宁 Liaoning	3072408.29	1703280.56	1306877.57	136134.70	113679.65	101739.69	25245.94	19603.01	297292.89	218030.64
吉 林 Jilin	3425166.88	1802219.05	1344459.53	169261.58	140016.52	122281.24	22625.72	3574.46	386011.03	284316.64
黑龙江 Heilongjiang	2378730.37	1294865.02	1035145.60	112888.09	66043.67	58014.69	17047.91	5725.06	245834.93	181997.90
上 海 Shanghai	237461.89	124392.75	82199.51	12661.68	7742.32	5807.42	1352.30	14629.52	36348.58	16357.24
江 苏 Jiangsu	4540930.63	3035092.89	2373422.04	217069.29	196843.89	187837.13	34266.93	25653.61	396823.70	244234.65
浙 江 Zhejiang	5500401.72	2645087.54	2086941.53	168790.20	140869.77	114880.70	23663.69	109941.65	446503.98	265463.08
安 徽 Anhui	13091813.28	8264199.40	6460480.42	654207.99	588200.89	465710.16	89982.94	5617.00	1032114.11	778104.17
福 建 Fujian	8079893.43	3990102.23	3233307.78	257538.70	242614.35	186928.34	25077.27	44635.79	512213.26	339331.81
江 西 Jiangxi	12700337.95	7215260.41	6096253.42	349401.04	414902.79	270590.16	67174.88	16938.12	949921.76	669852.86
山 东 Shandong	15125392.12	8554183.65	6453302.25	803987.00	633835.73	537948.21	98395.15	26715.31	1363691.17	892183.36
河 南 Henan	33416162.17	19051036.83	15875971.78	1096446.77	1121683.06	784541.60	162019.36	10374.26	3752244.53	2956213.93
湖 北 Hubei	10946675.83	4984493.04	3885084.69	401012.20	337630.01	263760.36	69365.78	27640.00	697186.34	436505.33
湖 南 Hunan	14183262.62	7082663.74	5813884.55	511754.77	397022.25	223043.03	97774.74	39184.40	1206573.30	917923.45
广 东 Guangdong	19944867.60	10717624.68	8684726.90	538408.03	665397.13	449059.76	154813.20	225219.66	1500445.63	1031545.72
广 西 Guangxi	20224958.08	12142547.13	10568652.55	573810.82	564576.84	336746.62	58574.36	40185.94	920281.30	748397.12
海 南 Hainan	2330691.33	1201784.14	1028014.55	55317.43	63699.61	37233.03	13487.08	4032.44	137273.64	101532.42
重 庆 Chongqing	4823321.63	2191741.72	1859318.59	142624.10	100762.75	73103.41	5901.96	10030.91	335945.44	202049.20
四 川 Sichuan	13695015.86	6777148.40	5742119.38	385661.64	346748.69	251810.70	47716.99	3091.00	780314.89	537210.99
贵 州 Guizhou	12146241.52	5674897.91	4688625.12	378581.98	347828.25	230579.56	22618.06	6664.94	713592.99	464562.40
云 南 Yunnan	21814423.83	9929146.29	7920761.85	692824.71	641244.69	549000.13	92124.12	33190.79	900715.94	613287.67
西 藏 Tibet	2792479.94	875737.68	687849.92	51338.73	48602.76	46448.29	12007.52	29490.46	159718.44	128235.07
陕 西 Shaanxi	5380504.72	2561213.98	1837033.45	216826.66	209844.94	186329.40	102393.53	8786.00	653635.72	454906.38
甘 肃 Gansu	7897671.71	4243219.58	3470900.24	260260.10	285328.51	206624.82	16688.58	3417.33	885846.39	682244.28
青 海 Qinghai	1983411.38	815974.78	598656.34	49073.55	70964.36	42637.88	11495.59	43147.06	119297.28	87232.30
宁 夏 Ningxia	1951887.35	1046867.21	813398.19	95607.77	64425.97	62486.27	8322.01	2627.00	145001.07	95376.84
新 疆 Xinjiang	7763080.84	4266598.03	3310007.25	374878.86	266327.27	250621.89	35855.68	28907.08	829072.40	439344.23

条件(一)(乡村)
Primary Schools (1)(Rural Area)

单位:平方米
unit: m^2

生活用房 Residential and Welfare							其他用房 Rooms for Other Purposes	校舍面积中 of the Floor Space	
合计 Total	教工宿舍 Apartments for Single		学生宿舍 Students' Dormitories	食堂 Dining Halls	厕所 Toilet	其他 Others		危房面积 Floor Space of Dilapidated Buildings	当年新增校舍 New Floor Space Added in Current Year
	小计 Subtotal	其中:教师周转宿舍 of Which: Accommodation for Circulation of Teachers							
84532794.85	27954536.28	8632581.97	18029948.79	17363033.31	12677425.61	8507850.86	25125845.66	3280708.85	18058642.03
188386.22	35922.36	3995.60	21045.46	41376.41	42366.42	47675.57	151217.25	0.00	8708.15
146250.58	16478.71	1943.00	0.00	10757.50	48621.64	70392.73	110473.91	0.00	16900.12
4057189.05	659585.43	141336.88	1071665.03	702309.00	891865.99	731763.60	2237510.44	7001.02	1753595.71
2305164.39	530412.13	60460.74	627286.66	444408.57	343903.61	359153.42	1179758.03	28328.21	109481.20
1179066.92	157246.67	98586.20	495597.05	235876.00	148791.14	141556.06	251710.10	0.00	124291.19
543070.40	45798.21	15954.39	40434.53	137103.83	161880.75	157853.08	528764.44	13043.30	201069.83
606248.84	37059.72	10508.37	54779.39	99691.86	195219.55	219498.32	630687.96	1539.00	97814.49
497398.10	33492.44	15173.87	87948.87	88595.13	117717.21	169644.45	340632.32	14318.09	110648.33
46312.01	1135.00	360.00	0.00	26919.06	12121.69	6136.26	30408.55	0.00	0.00
809101.42	170947.17	35707.73	55666.79	210042.83	195264.41	177180.22	299912.62	0.00	142455.50
1639056.32	574953.69	53346.19	153069.39	491644.32	209318.80	210070.12	769753.88	0.00	205574.65
2765969.55	775871.20	168364.58	224050.61	889984.93	604660.56	271402.25	1029530.22	38091.77	803313.86
2305114.36	1198698.85	128429.11	227159.17	257664.07	348175.96	273416.31	1272463.58	68320.00	178382.56
3760405.01	1597650.46	493978.81	387519.18	894465.10	593366.38	287403.89	774750.77	87029.14	898999.09
2490865.48	379412.31	101208.71	179696.46	604886.39	876715.77	450154.55	2716651.82	0.00	1623832.62
8347344.20	1781818.82	347159.22	1752754.78	2014717.97	1958766.22	839286.41	2265536.61	34905.91	1943670.97
4344310.51	1731908.19	398224.52	950242.78	876810.01	416360.01	368989.52	920685.94	45887.00	417300.06
4648318.27	1695214.66	382522.37	697967.50	1097428.06	598960.85	558747.20	1245707.31	165121.00	382464.78
5099674.98	2949785.56	315861.29	387384.84	344381.45	721146.76	696976.37	2627122.31	12054.00	219664.43
6068817.41	2514875.40	1002092.48	1339093.18	1058223.35	721907.78	434717.70	1093312.24	429933.96	1767508.54
840497.03	587869.72	198574.74	95757.00	52632.95	72462.82	31774.54	151136.52	23392.86	151478.47
1825952.00	864779.36	254582.12	311735.58	328812.12	169577.78	151047.16	469682.47	36615.71	71992.10
5419795.90	2105190.71	972838.94	1305153.75	1100236.45	604040.72	305174.27	717756.67	57493.80	1311957.59
5067892.51	1770663.22	1186821.21	1620779.80	933723.49	500480.30	242245.70	689858.11	0.00	936800.92
10239904.03	2774018.41	936617.40	3936414.93	2333385.16	784036.35	412049.18	744657.57	1563667.48	1912481.53
1689501.02	672368.87	552387.69	584210.75	283205.35	65005.22	84710.83	67522.80	2856.80	291680.22
1735581.21	580112.49	66309.55	302767.89	400322.24	288009.13	164369.46	430073.81	936.00	521851.11
2246824.69	798948.22	103394.65	263757.22	430117.03	503918.81	250083.41	521781.05	648376.80	702896.85
874401.76	254421.48	145036.72	304516.60	145111.72	73052.09	97299.87	173737.56	0.00	185353.23
589675.01	184379.14	78714.37	45054.15	159100.03	113191.31	87950.38	170344.06	1797.00	111103.35
2154705.67	473517.68	362090.52	506439.45	669100.93	296519.58	209128.03	512704.74	0.00	855370.58

地 区 Region	占地面积(平方米) Areas of School Sites(m^2)			图书(册) Books & Magazines in Libraries (Volume)	计算机数(台) PC (Set)		
	合计 Total	其中: of Which:			合计 Total	其中:教学用计算机 No. of Computers Used for Instruction	
		绿化用地面积 Green Areas	运动场地面积 Sports Areas			小计 Subtotal	其中:平板电脑 of Which: Tablet PC
总 计 Total	**2320835702.22**	**406866153.98**	**730141844.20**	**2288550203**	**12521976**	**10634765**	**507639**
北 京 Beijing	14397211.98	2371381.75	5529567.51	27949854	248947	216188	25561
天 津 Tianjin	12697774.40	1504105.53	4932786.42	20810048	107488	92888	4762
河 北 Hebei	157946521.30	15737825.70	53607299.13	170745780	816076	794127	24732
山 西 Shanxi	56310477.12	6814906.02	15781930.08	46557764	358523	287081	6454
内蒙古 Inner Mongolia	55184289.54	8391418.90	13541820.42	26030084	202993	150908	4358
辽 宁 Liaoning	46721639.54	5040362.22	21296994.71	55938273	332973	273203	15526
吉 林 Jilin	54739938.04	11341801.70	13670283.58	35088885	152791	125788	3416
黑龙江 Heilongjiang	43236107.85	5662327.38	14770966.63	22972281	173957	138375	4289
上 海 Shanghai	10193736.73	2867816.40	3141115.31	26415296	179691	141005	13522
江 苏 Jiangsu	109186240.60	29094042.23	34195716.69	132063139	770833	676017	26301
浙 江 Zhejiang	69086151.75	16128471.01	23012871.23	105734424	696556	625540	48042
安 徽 Anhui	107269548.95	15094262.09	29137826.11	77384700	590808	495489	13828
福 建 Fujian	54173143.60	10738274.02	18965872.67	78249909	400829	331716	8313
江 西 Jiangxi	83954629.17	12317653.83	31007070.99	67072330	276081	210547	8492
山 东 Shandong	174114213.42	35016500.93	64626793.99	196378997	1092079	963279	24172
河 南 Henan	214439554.11	26457861.28	56397028.78	185868979	730196	615438	41739
湖 北 Hubei	94107776.58	29316600.47	23425590.65	94369954	399180	345752	24275
湖 南 Hunan	102988833.53	14776870.91	24116627.23	104835944	358077	307059	8014
广 东 Guangdong	179313142.54	41090398.88	63143200.60	204009045	1413462	1176341	118293
广 西 Guangxi	106346654.41	15170307.40	41637551.38	128622932	431450	335613	7956
海 南 Hainan	30917997.12	6532025.44	5791286.26	13967820	84282	71999	2972
重 庆 Chongqing	41942957.16	7130428.19	13010865.55	33008624	276251	231767	8899
四 川 Sichuan	83979056.54	11568016.75	34530590.53	85534034	541333	447358	18977
贵 州 Guizhou	72364282.48	14622878.76	26895591.04	83274998	345253	301854	13478
云 南 Yunnan	97964453.21	16877494.27	25853836.30	88396273	426632	339961	2020
西 藏 Tibet	16365891.19	1855959.79	2824360.66	5254634	51793	36639	1263
陕 西 Shaanxi	55331398.77	7904789.77	16511542.19	79678219	416245	378843	9851
甘 肃 Gansu	60829031.00	9370519.33	17076328.57	37694807	245288	210079	7620
青 海 Qinghai	15806870.77	2041041.68	3417801.94	11110020	66815	54236	3767
宁 夏 Ningxia	20183054.60	3669786.31	6496800.12	12179187	101501	79635	2469
新 疆 Xinjiang	78743124.22	20360025.04	21793926.93	31352969	233593	180040	4278

条件(二)(总计)
in Primary Schools (2)(Total)

教室(间) Classroom(Room)		教室中:普通教室(间) of Which: General Classroom(Room)		固定资产总值(万元) Total Value of Fixed Asset (10,000 yuan)		
合计 Total	其中:网络多媒体教室 of Which: Network Multimedia Classroom	合计 Total	其中:网络多媒体教室 of Which: Network Multimedia Classroom	合计 Total	其中:教学仪器设备资产值 of Which: Total Value of Equip & Instru.	
					小计 Subtotal	其中:实验设备 of Which: For Experiment
3895067	**2214031**	**3012904**	**1960374**	**101627639. 12**	**14177074. 36**	**2793468. 45**
34459	30340	23848	22315	2011994. 17	731300. 43	58392. 11
24599	19126	18922	16619	777659. 67	127346. 15	15550. 84
271066	144960	218210	137648	4494775. 22	584343. 66	186403. 82
106450	57392	81129	52838	2369867. 24	286421. 94	59995. 98
53226	37342	36271	30962	2240893. 45	311232. 16	42353. 60
77185	39883	58044	34093	1506231. 34	348195. 02	59492. 35
66816	21842	51658	19936	1213679. 84	219976. 02	45039. 12
58813	29973	40835	25978	1229567. 06	231175. 47	38216. 24
26774	23508	19334	17915	1536108. 18	297768. 21	50057. 24
179493	130002	126848	104130	7370147. 79	865262. 28	175095. 78
121344	107636	86485	85143	5230658. 43	849848. 93	121862. 21
173944	108958	140434	103270	4006233. 09	542203. 96	116981. 61
122414	81873	84348	71771	3273611. 62	560325. 99	92518. 37
179115	83258	138842	78258	2880288. 77	397369. 43	72606. 68
257373	200741	178859	161253	7792169. 82	875724. 98	163938. 89
404163	149674	350555	141400	6116887. 59	675221. 63	175773. 26
132974	72913	106163	68042	3219531. 99	438130. 04	126859. 05
188515	58335	148844	54067	3935574. 57	449141. 36	119633. 42
293863	219275	222625	193830	8918216. 26	1397953. 96	311642. 52
189111	90517	150739	85402	4235576. 80	638814. 34	121471. 57
26458	11311	20647	10464	957496. 72	116979. 24	24915. 97
80667	64466	56010	50469	2255215. 20	290752. 95	33113. 89
185808	78462	157968	71248	5372082. 28	855079. 23	183466. 89
137793	88831	106916	83143	2971469. 30	368515. 95	73268. 84
172515	75443	140168	70436	5626438. 21	485267. 46	85517. 94
12611	5165	9958	4758	1151310. 63	48187. 46	8493. 47
98204	59300	78108	53558	2723015. 61	376125. 24	104376. 44
97874	54634	74656	51146	2128409. 01	279310. 66	50602. 99
18277	7545	13488	6623	858603. 09	52408. 72	7915. 65
24551	15648	17540	13305	896070. 08	160968. 30	29585. 32
78612	45678	54452	40354	2327856. 09	315723. 19	38326. 40

地 区 Region	占地面积(平方米) Areas of School Sites(m^2) 合计 Total	其中: of Which: 绿化用地面积 Green Areas	运动场地面积 Sports Areas	图书(册) Books & Magazines in Libraries (Volume)	计算机数(台) PC (Set) 合计 Total	其中:教学用计算机 No. of Computers Used for Instruction 小计 Subtotal	其中:平板电脑 of Which: Tablet PC
总 计 Total	**427437771.89**	**85786179.52**	**160549584.86**	**779274125**	**4527252**	**3859944**	**296579**
北 京 Beijing	9072613.73	1368506.27	3602958.62	22849880	205231	179147	23780
天 津 Tianjin	6409250.91	791090.06	2391240.75	14618532	75184	63697	4015
河 北 Hebei	19117194.11	2123665.82	7041149.34	38167832	179304	174736	6796
山 西 Shanxi	9972288.64	1350407.68	3463842.10	15877500	100275	83870	2925
内蒙古 Inner Mongolia	8671708.92	1228128.20	3338934.49	10514561	71608	57962	1886
辽 宁 Liaoning	15377619.72	1742699.31	7922096.33	33582851	198688	165057	8636
吉 林 Jilin	6745466.56	813042.46	3288938.04	14583431	61682	51851	2424
黑龙江 Heilongjiang	8252174.07	954031.50	3808525.21	10769451	86820	70457	3537
上 海 Shanghai	8004910.88	2180576.93	2471778.69	22528207	156193	122487	12304
江 苏 Jiangsu	39319059.14	10883850.01	13626343.71	60022884	372302	327419	18352
浙 江 Zhejiang	28355453.20	7103174.81	9856427.01	49089156	323083	294666	23968
安 徽 Anhui	11887935.67	2015855.12	4108355.59	17115125	128067	104115	7103
福 建 Fujian	12046634.80	2522087.01	4696324.66	31313067	148315	124397	4718
江 西 Jiangxi	10270013.42	1768979.29	4077722.04	14502906	69806	53175	3395
山 东 Shandong	37894639.37	7886445.63	15166356.42	66486276	351253	310041	19154
河 南 Henan	21861652.98	2877998.89	7273606.71	38448757	167176	139967	9101
湖 北 Hubei	18256590.40	5642432.20	5362322.48	34874847	153554	131650	18630
湖 南 Hunan	15591083.21	2925307.48	4509981.18	27662723	103585	86068	3457
广 东 Guangdong	57506002.78	14254893.47	22152049.48	105575808	710553	593435	75852
广 西 Guangxi	10591620.54	1789256.44	4713224.54	28186943	93864	66050	2903
海 南 Hainan	2772596.41	551618.64	817768.99	4941885	26199	22050	1205
重 庆 Chongqing	13167912.29	2495873.75	4199343.26	13517672	114165	95169	6345
四 川 Sichuan	13732234.26	2381399.16	6540364.06	22901769	173027	152958	14876
贵 州 Guizhou	7375068.70	1355622.76	3482949.41	14828186	75518	66735	9909
云 南 Yunnan	8231828.86	2027120.55	2779061.64	14460195	76391	61308	702
西 藏 Tibet	900222.59	154985.22	185294.65	720288	5549	3596	64
陕 西 Shaanxi	10735378.61	1674791.82	3613782.21	27388196	142569	128567	3859
甘 肃 Gansu	4025146.81	578707.31	1675540.04	7834550	51784	45606	2490
青 海 Qinghai	1378642.95	246770.15	474528.72	3257993	18502	14262	1537
宁 夏 Ningxia	3778025.83	798388.58	1569744.87	4209151	30570	24139	1542
新 疆 Xinjiang	6136801.53	1298473.00	2339029.62	8443503	56435	45307	1114

条件(二)(城区)
Primary Schools (2)(Urban Area)

教室(间) Classroom(Room)		教室中:普通教室(间) of Which: General Classroom(Room)		固定资产总值(万元) Total Value of Fixed Asset (10,000 yuan)		
					其中:教学仪器设备资产值 of Which: Total Value of Equip & Instru.	
合计 Total	其中:网络多媒体教室 of Which: Network Multimedia Classroom	合计 Total	其中:网络多媒体教室 of Which: Network Multimedia Classroom	合计 Total	小计 Subtotal	其中:实验设备 of Which: For Experiment
974555	**739923**	**734379**	**628111**	**35228792.15**	**5988685.35**	**939327.06**
27350	24695	19297	18349	1689759.60	618333.44	48689.62
15579	13591	12461	11743	542189.90	96481.71	8091.66
43162	29740	33886	27287	841560.75	157228.61	39723.36
25149	17599	19320	16063	651916.16	99203.15	16675.57
17194	13401	11932	11262	623586.06	109312.24	12900.59
35607	25833	26788	21761	881324.03	228180.49	31902.57
19261	10236	15686	9414	513517.34	97552.40	15086.76
21093	14484	14862	12464	486972.86	116289.69	13105.54
22607	20125	16393	15354	1339349.66	260562.39	40692.36
78758	64065	53632	49574	4125705.46	475688.57	83170.35
55808	50465	39655	38964	2817309.80	420785.48	55821.90
27190	19550	21658	17831	863307.75	129011.88	18816.86
35019	28012	25664	23939	1208227.13	229480.20	28454.90
26698	16805	21196	15473	603463.26	89015.08	13671.12
75116	60773	52270	49430	2980823.29	355599.82	53740.21
54173	34182	44970	31210	1164262.97	155534.18	31558.24
37350	27199	29480	24431	1120802.49	194250.55	47220.36
35793	20748	28796	18720	1197181.42	143596.64	30630.38
122939	104543	95528	90150	4637370.72	884993.44	178727.67
26916	18876	21327	17212	847148.95	142951.47	21850.95
5806	3848	4953	3611	251496.93	41536.11	7918.44
27065	23399	19478	18750	1089840.03	136728.33	13394.03
36544	24998	29307	21873	1367432.83	290129.67	51149.03
19616	14793	15130	13133	548547.11	78316.17	9037.23
21022	12381	16218	11132	582122.94	80921.04	11043.57
1348	906	1021	838	97436.79	5143.95	906.06
25904	19511	19186	16622	950613.47	141061.10	30776.47
11723	8301	8469	7483	334178.34	65600.47	6923.61
2932	2149	2083	1767	147476.41	13485.02	1750.78
6315	4781	4557	4049	250020.06	52111.81	9421.96
13518	9934	9176	8222	473847.64	79600.26	6474.90

地 区 Region	占地面积(平方米) Areas of School Sites(m^2) 合计 Total	其中: of Which: 绿化用地面积 Green Areas	运动场地面积 Sports Areas	图书(册) Books & Magazines in Libraries (Volume)	计算机数(台) PC (Set) 合计 Total	其中:教学用计算机 No. of Computers Used for Instruction 小计 Subtotal	其中:平板电脑 of Which: Tablet PC
总 计 Total	**113317011.29**	**24393514.11**	**39215324.71**	**136865920**	**803503**	**688065**	**40479**
北 京 Beijing	1335578.33	207720.53	558463.44	1888835	13691	11596	718
天 津 Tianjin	1165817.56	154345.83	446301.68	1777397	8430	6856	305
河 北 Hebei	7544218.60	831046.11	2765934.81	9027614	47236	45798	1315
山 西 Shanxi	2106664.21	299880.89	625364.75	2113897	14330	11182	362
内蒙古 Inner Mongolia	451479.22	66841.05	123407.65	230257	1849	1398	0
辽 宁 Liaoning	2470161.03	327987.11	1102284.21	2781794	16747	14254	937
吉 林 Jilin	1078225.44	181881.03	351020.02	675170	3904	2819	12
黑龙江 Heilongjiang	974980.30	139446.44	359352.05	532813	5079	3696	178
上 海 Shanghai	940007.46	249621.00	286597.00	2199529	11081	8551	472
江 苏 Jiangsu	5946756.55	1793742.32	1885317.91	6668723	39183	34257	1207
浙 江 Zhejiang	8325679.00	2039280.37	2771907.72	12117858	78626	71694	3605
安 徽 Anhui	2665625.38	455847.63	715047.47	2015080	15687	13206	363
福 建 Fujian	4031444.46	822973.14	1394979.22	6406323	30895	26246	411
江 西 Jiangxi	2530017.66	389190.02	1012072.91	2254263	9876	7756	178
山 东 Shandong	15171052.50	3311148.64	5726603.15	17512670	97956	86825	1940
河 南 Henan	6965162.07	950932.39	2059292.22	7156193	32786	28097	1830
湖 北 Hubei	4047940.20	1365409.81	1042129.09	4394809	19984	16513	1383
湖 南 Hunan	3085451.66	618647.47	703109.28	2994983	12797	10465	231
广 东 Guangdong	24903561.89	6748001.71	8978897.39	32633149	225816	189392	21095
广 西 Guangxi	3130680.19	498720.11	1360889.66	5809478	19612	14424	277
海 南 Hainan	787729.02	147695.50	155359.00	490733	3122	2540	111
重 庆 Chongqing	1573808.21	270720.88	480239.36	1067228	9942	7993	255
四 川 Sichuan	2390888.60	479317.02	1017059.72	2573124	19939	18008	862
贵 州 Guizhou	1693339.19	362619.66	751339.76	2319206	12229	10723	1496
云 南 Yunnan	3176932.33	724457.04	1018348.49	3755509	18829	15270	27
西 藏 Tibet	24299.00	2000.00	7459.00	9150	115	50	0
陕 西 Shaanxi	2781923.97	510756.83	889767.27	3957148	23088	19805	631
甘 肃 Gansu	579145.81	100616.12	185379.51	525580	3691	3221	65
青 海 Qinghai	136843.70	20951.04	39721.20	181189	982	604	0
宁 夏 Ningxia	311386.67	74901.81	110667.95	207910	1716	1364	0
新 疆 Xinjiang	990211.08	246814.61	291011.82	588308	4285	3462	213

(二)(城乡结合区)
Schools (2)(Urban-rural Transitional Area)

教室(间) Classroom(Room)		教室中:普通教室(间) of Which: General Classroom(Room)		固定资产总值(万元) Total Value of Fixed Asset (10,000 yuan)		
					其中:教学仪器设备资产值 of Which: Total Value of Equip & Instru.	
合计 Total	其中:网络多媒体教室 of Which: Network Multimedia Classroom	合计 Total	其中:网络多媒体教室 of Which: Network Multimedia Classroom	合计 Total	小计 Subtotal	其中:实验设备 of Which: For Experiment
196321	**134184**	**145747**	**115232**	**6757781. 32**	**914887. 07**	**177862. 39**
2610	1985	1849	1497	98951. 34	40134. 97	4764. 17
1876	1474	1436	1256	79799. 39	9303. 44	955. 30
13619	7730	10713	7219	244780. 62	35316. 57	10704. 41
4039	2468	3025	2299	88347. 29	11060. 24	2208. 74
589	333	354	281	25509. 72	2533. 34	531. 27
4047	2067	2873	1718	110075. 43	21387. 89	4176. 27
1373	667	1067	606	34610. 97	5576. 95	698. 80
1468	872	857	688	33548. 71	5815. 29	1094. 71
2181	1777	1736	1443	81731. 74	15375. 63	3501. 98
9277	6501	6453	5056	570430. 24	44767. 98	6995. 66
14211	12652	10178	10000	705892. 06	100932. 05	13911. 38
4328	2779	3435	2607	131727. 64	13893. 44	2860. 52
8986	6237	6244	5466	245123. 98	44052. 52	6051. 21
5762	2706	4248	2520	87604. 89	12999. 49	1969. 06
22943	17844	15278	14342	900794. 77	82109. 70	15055. 77
12811	6706	10126	6035	235203. 06	29632. 03	7205. 61
5792	3518	4485	3250	201238. 81	23554. 24	6628. 16
4940	2144	3922	1979	193805. 11	16100. 68	3705. 98
41275	33181	31416	28838	1490085. 57	254576. 63	60555. 88
6747	4008	5259	3699	203673. 47	31772. 28	5654. 80
839	385	677	368	38275. 93	4674. 23	765. 31
2972	2370	1955	1796	91370. 48	9689. 81	1506. 28
4894	2948	3940	2627	201900. 33	36676. 81	6427. 47
3890	2680	2935	2396	112268. 44	11276. 45	1779. 96
6591	3024	5381	2830	214611. 06	18306. 20	2636. 88
15	15	15	15	2425. 40	108. 00	6. 40
4916	3142	3468	2662	224716. 33	19359. 28	3759. 92
1083	605	752	552	34585. 82	4277. 27	477. 11
210	119	151	98	8356. 58	667. 91	99. 87
393	291	298	252	16197. 70	2614. 98	416. 91
1644	956	1221	837	50138. 47	6340. 77	756. 62

地 区 Region	占地面积(平方米) Areas of School Sites(m^2)			图书(册) Books & Magazines in Libraries (Volume)	计算机数(台) PC (Set)		
	合计 Total	其中: of Which:			合计 Total	其中:教学用计算机 No. of Computers Used for Instruction	
		绿化用地面积 Green Areas	运动场地面积 Sports Areas			小计 Subtotal	其中:平板电脑 of Which: Tablet PC
总 计 Total	**734620971.98**	**127147549.74**	**243062037.64**	**827288037**	**4188866**	**3575497**	**124432**
北 京 Beijing	1713092.10	388137.63	625821.91	2020659	17755	15377	975
天 津 Tianjin	2257530.17	229013.20	938565.01	2633512	12502	11376	360
河 北 Hebei	50410600.51	5097120.96	16832451.21	63731124	286098	278793	8385
山 西 Shanxi	16874018.85	1928855.37	5517654.24	18888257	132724	109847	2044
内蒙古 Inner Mongolia	22964069.31	3417633.69	6215857.97	12208226	96649	68852	1398
辽 宁 Liaoning	10951544.71	1062124.11	4846729.46	12131053	69240	54843	4298
吉 林 Jilin	10958851.15	1979319.17	4137430.15	12240382	48473	40982	872
黑龙江 Heilongjiang	12404117.97	1565883.01	4395813.19	8704876	59243	47177	506
上 海 Shanghai	1558725.85	480755.24	483751.25	2978679	17503	14037	1106
江 苏 Jiangsu	47338211.09	12653787.06	14329736.33	55000967	304233	266147	6524
浙 江 Zhejiang	25932158.60	5869394.72	8615146.42	39420704	258509	231224	20106
安 徽 Anhui	35282736.25	4832042.81	11278033.62	31945912	232507	198902	4049
福 建 Fujian	18409310.35	3590152.16	6959724.50	29614903	143527	116625	2465
江 西 Jiangxi	31140268.23	4642040.86	11922086.65	29694926	117310	88227	2740
山 东 Shandong	60657404.74	12250002.23	22257567.52	71923478	356533	314258	2993
河 南 Henan	60586684.54	7202715.96	16409243.80	65181445	255251	217072	14773
湖 北 Hubei	32099466.61	10028620.25	8608430.61	35342973	130138	114263	2800
湖 南 Hunan	40970002.44	5647597.99	9802826.58	47998100	148967	129802	3604
广 东 Guangdong	48165025.31	10213608.93	17860700.03	52137533	355396	297005	23885
广 西 Guangxi	28431885.10	3926557.93	11021783.21	46021034	127297	98702	2000
海 南 Hainan	8847504.56	1706070.94	2186017.91	5530525	32083	28694	693
重 庆 Chongqing	16195501.27	2564775.73	5229516.80	13315113	103867	89588	1827
四 川 Sichuan	32032864.39	4477379.83	14182832.01	39090769	227830	185358	3647
贵 州 Guizhou	28243944.69	5442953.66	10701126.28	35949560	141470	124819	2370
云 南 Yunnan	21793602.40	4107180.19	6620978.33	23483619	108389	82944	670
西 藏 Tibet	4333257.50	535255.64	739573.20	1571627	13834	9801	385
陕 西 Shaanxi	23538625.82	3251503.60	7619941.87	37875928	191979	179405	4351
甘 肃 Gansu	14591042.96	2212188.72	5072537.96	13622952	85430	73604	2048
青 海 Qinghai	4603786.28	672502.09	1185688.12	4152856	22230	18532	967
宁 夏 Ningxia	5020026.85	893235.26	1795645.94	3865464	30528	23857	680
新 疆 Xinjiang	16315111.38	4279140.80	4668825.56	9010881	61371	45384	911

条件(二)(镇区)
Schools (2)(Counties & Towns Area)

教室(间) Classroom(Room)		教室中:普通教室(间) of Which: General Classroom(Room)		固定资产总值(万元) Total Value of Fixed Asset (10,000 yuan)		
合计 Total	其中:网络多媒体教室 of Which: Network Multimedia Classroom	合计 Total	其中:网络多媒体教室 of Which: Network Multimedia Classroom	合计 Total	其中:教学仪器设备资产值 of Which: Total Value of Equip & Instru. 小计 Subtotal	其中:实验设备 of Which: For Experiment
1241533	**759821**	**973199**	**688480**	**34436461.16**	**4479600.15**	**946637.33**
2866	2154	1864	1575	129785.21	47855.55	3948.10
3432	2231	2490	2026	92109.16	13495.80	3325.03
88695	51084	71959	48873	1735577.34	202119.23	65662.27
34203	21608	26896	20083	812894.49	108552.73	21988.14
23041	17350	15744	14420	1170023.68	145986.71	20808.59
17645	8050	13301	7284	337196.13	65067.24	13935.35
18445	6742	14825	6177	374336.98	72391.98	14334.79
20144	11306	14142	10028	495332.29	82668.47	16940.81
3145	2575	2190	1930	143458.11	29010.29	7164.42
72214	51842	52464	43376	2685500.91	315581.27	70990.44
43477	38519	31791	31392	1702895.95	304157.59	44852.07
61096	39683	50023	37863	1570758.86	217060.88	45942.13
41674	29744	29295	26562	1193952.65	200757.89	36701.81
61106	35172	48333	33303	1170397.83	165531.29	27017.04
89313	69780	64143	57847	2709964.43	283596.97	55116.13
121438	53316	106841	51267	2222015.70	227553.43	58770.34
44690	25317	36125	24251	1082878.18	136200.84	44343.36
70803	24939	56807	23779	1604858.34	190714.07	53756.79
73713	55147	57791	50531	2140813.18	272192.15	69796.76
51575	30777	41596	29436	1332001.57	200374.88	35465.65
9043	4331	6900	3917	370722.34	44606.36	9302.75
29358	24301	20472	19313	775502.17	101513.99	11488.93
70831	34716	59683	32345	2214813.98	360275.09	78312.14
48437	35619	38407	33711	1311663.98	147054.66	26200.83
38960	20251	31292	19074	1398708.08	117519.65	18592.98
3143	1541	2539	1463	308061.44	13845.61	2078.66
42288	26204	34962	24510	1204259.66	171473.37	53250.23
25908	16539	18671	15311	773866.00	96214.45	15389.04
5836	2835	4180	2521	308664.07	19420.37	3443.42
6610	4590	4583	3924	310682.28	51016.00	8509.50
18404	11558	12890	10388	752766.16	75791.33	9208.80

小学办学条件
Condition of School Buildings in Primary

地 区 Region	占地面积(平方米) Areas of School Sites(m^2)			图书(册) Books & Magazines in Libraries (Volume)	计算机数(台) PC (Set)		
	合计 Total	其中: of Which:			合计 Total	其中:教学用计算机 No. of Computers Used for Instruction	
		绿化用地面积 Green Areas	运动场地面积 Sports Areas			小计 Subtotal	其中:平板电脑 of Which: Tablet PC
总 计 Total	**250396998.72**	**43516865.50**	**80716948.61**	**243863866**	**1267630**	**1097128**	**37222**
北 京 Beijing	457533.05	103114.00	172491.00	636003	5234	4408	212
天 津 Tianjin	1103076.26	114640.87	462246.00	1228922	5876	5323	48
河 北 Hebei	29641681.09	2912229.76	9987021.84	32887766	150896	146997	3372
山 西 Shanxi	5888047.24	711650.01	1913454.31	5565096	43249	35205	967
内蒙古 Inner Mongolia	2234693.08	388066.10	557996.30	970387	9088	5868	176
辽 宁 Liaoning	1993928.97	223931.71	822986.98	1665665	9987	7669	503
吉 林 Jilin	1928796.01	375730.53	522955.55	1043210	5118	3895	8
黑龙江 Heilongjiang	1721352.56	290586.62	529040.33	944406	7070	5727	3
上 海 Shanghai	328532.90	94728.71	110548.00	612915	3593	2921	208
江 苏 Jiangsu	15384190.19	4077965.14	4584382.63	16835159	91343	78763	2136
浙 江 Zhejiang	8648524.09	1910736.15	2928306.11	12762316	82320	75099	4368
安 徽 Anhui	10143184.11	1529624.70	2769320.58	6803853	50890	43598	678
福 建 Fujian	6938556.45	1310502.43	2498322.51	8167683	43129	36400	609
江 西 Jiangxi	9593899.80	1465258.37	3562746.29	6694204	26218	19758	780
山 东 Shandong	29688031.20	5926422.29	11024978.91	31248431	166868	146353	951
河 南 Henan	29054519.85	3688354.92	7584283.91	23923405	95906	79619	5426
湖 北 Hubei	10354549.04	3240684.67	2590882.80	9121522	34462	30375	756
湖 南 Hunan	13014891.67	1845652.15	2908654.17	11952496	40855	35946	743
广 东 Guangdong	21725418.03	4728188.84	7802601.50	21250650	156065	131243	11349
广 西 Guangxi	10879532.45	1554179.82	4240092.24	12878245	38396	31388	686
海 南 Hainan	2233273.02	450932.00	427185.40	768401	4581	3943	216
重 庆 Chongqing	3021373.71	497147.13	926963.67	2207032	16953	14723	238
四 川 Sichuan	6008232.65	896659.81	2459956.82	5426639	33052	26648	338
贵 州 Guizhou	6137751.71	1263595.98	2425137.61	7103554	28404	25514	517
云 南 Yunnan	5918017.51	1065655.28	1796168.22	5828821	28136	21490	291
西 藏 Tibet	203220.57	14327.00	45885.00	131514	962	636	0
陕 西 Shaanxi	6790177.31	1008396.10	2159528.79	9144019	47990	44690	786
甘 肃 Gansu	4376958.64	669301.55	1438113.32	3099948	20008	16951	278
青 海 Qinghai	815654.37	117788.60	191804.10	838761	5474	4188	244
宁 夏 Ningxia	1015310.29	162847.14	322343.77	598180	4833	3930	67
新 疆 Xinjiang	3154090.90	877967.12	950549.95	1524663	10674	7860	268

(二)(镇乡结合区)
Schools (2)(County-town Transitional Area)

教室(间) Classroom(Room)		教室中:普通教室(间) of Which: General Classroom(Room)		固定资产总值(万元) Total Value of Fixed Asset (10,000 yuan)		
					其中:教学仪器设备资产值 of Which: Total Value of Equip & Instru.	
合计 Total	其中:网络多媒体教室 of Which: Network Multimedia Classroom	合计 Total	其中:网络多媒体教室 of Which: Network Multimedia Classroom	合计 Total	小计 Subtotal	其中:实验设备 of Which: For Experiment
413812	**229930**	**320856**	**206612**	**10079679.38**	**1231888.63**	**288897.95**
774	584	529	414	33571.58	12428.37	1247.13
1709	1054	1197	946	38776.67	5166.13	1610.01
51051	26990	41436	25982	903302.88	104607.01	35450.92
11855	6839	8943	6369	249823.24	32667.02	7837.30
2109	1492	1411	1220	93700.80	11869.45	1355.15
2855	1111	2140	993	48141.87	8773.77	2147.31
2212	584	1734	541	37502.26	6333.21	1274.17
2358	1257	1621	1110	60498.53	8913.23	1893.53
658	587	481	453	43631.16	6263.26	1672.37
22935	14998	16117	12330	777334.48	89423.06	21420.47
14552	12911	10690	10560	574531.73	100210.38	14268.90
15509	9397	12674	8915	384745.27	45420.40	11986.71
14126	9390	9661	8412	364322.37	57413.51	10827.25
19251	8706	14514	8153	315450.18	40000.02	6920.91
41507	32138	28828	25940	1296381.92	127199.23	26762.75
54254	19616	46927	18636	904216.04	86626.00	24590.99
13412	6738	10494	6394	324024.60	36737.56	12888.43
21195	6306	17181	5937	428038.91	49470.35	14490.49
33079	23443	24864	21311	850028.87	112451.13	29458.51
19519	8947	15614	8553	417007.25	60703.64	11743.48
1727	620	1310	553	64840.86	7820.38	1897.91
5645	4368	3907	3449	160160.53	16426.34	1949.28
12236	4800	10417	4322	360020.21	50599.70	11055.90
11490	7474	8837	7028	266305.02	29217.35	6355.17
11776	5322	9329	4960	361184.39	32550.28	5928.60
182	105	161	101	16451.86	1123.77	230.80
12198	6485	10106	6011	301396.92	43403.83	14626.92
6962	4125	5030	3829	192766.60	20962.47	3644.18
1535	540	1074	507	66718.39	5135.79	795.08
1290	816	855	694	54785.78	7668.88	982.43
3851	2187	2774	1989	90018.18	14303.07	1584.89

小学办学
Condition of School Buildings in

地区 Region	占地面积(平方米) Areas of School Sites(m^2) 合计 Total	其中: of Which: 绿化用地面积 Green Areas	其中: of Which: 运动场地面积 Sports Areas	图书(册) Books & Magazines in Libraries (Volume)	计算机数(台) PC (Set) 合计 Total	其中:教学用计算机 No. of Computers Used for Instruction 小计 Subtotal	其中:平板电脑 of Which: Tablet PC
总　计 Total	**1158776958.35**	**193932424.72**	**326530221.70**	**681988041**	**3805858**	**3199324**	**86628**
北　京 Beijing	3611506.15	614737.85	1300786.98	3079315	25961	21664	806
天　津 Tianjin	4030993.32	484002.27	1602980.66	3558004	19802	17815	387
河　北 Hebei	88418726.68	8517038.92	29733698.58	68846824	350674	340598	9551
山　西 Shanxi	29464169.63	3535642.97	6800433.74	11792007	125524	93364	1485
内蒙古 Inner Mongolia	23548511.31	3745657.01	3987027.96	3307297	34736	24094	1074
辽　宁 Liaoning	20392475.11	2235538.80	8528168.92	10224369	65045	53303	2592
吉　林 Jilin	37035620.33	8549440.07	6243915.39	8265072	42636	32955	120
黑龙江 Heilongjiang	22579815.81	3142412.87	6566628.23	3497954	27894	20741	246
上　海 Shanghai	630100.00	206484.23	185585.37	908410	5995	4481	112
江　苏 Jiangsu	22528970.37	5556405.16	6239636.65	17039288	94298	82451	1425
浙　江 Zhejiang	14798539.95	3155901.48	4541297.80	17224564	114964	99650	3968
安　徽 Anhui	60098877.03	8246364.16	13751436.90	28323663	230234	192472	2676
福　建 Fujian	23717198.45	4626034.85	7309823.51	17321939	108987	90694	1130
江　西 Jiangxi	42544347.52	5906633.68	15007262.30	22874498	88965	69145	2357
山　东 Shandong	75562169.31	14880053.07	27202870.05	57969243	384293	338980	2025
河　南 Henan	131991216.59	16377146.43	32714178.27	82238777	307769	258399	17865
湖　北 Hubei	43751719.57	13645548.02	9454837.56	24152134	115488	99839	2845
湖　南 Hunan	46427747.88	6203965.44	9803819.47	29175121	105525	91189	953
广　东 Guangdong	73642114.45	16621896.48	23130451.09	46295704	347513	285901	18556
广　西 Guangxi	67323148.77	9454493.03	25902543.63	54414955	210289	170861	3053
海　南 Hainan	19297896.15	4274335.86	2787499.36	3495410	26000	21255	1074
重　庆 Chongqing	12579543.60	2069778.71	3582005.49	6175839	58219	47010	727
四　川 Sichuan	38213957.89	4709237.76	13807394.46	23541496	140476	109042	454
贵　州 Guizhou	36745269.09	7824302.34	12711515.35	32497252	128265	110300	1199
云　南 Yunnan	67939021.95	10743193.53	16453796.33	50452459	241852	195709	648
西　藏 Tibet	11132411.10	1165718.93	1899492.81	2962719	32410	23242	814
陕　西 Shaanxi	21057394.34	2978494.35	5277818.11	14414095	81697	70871	1641
甘　肃 Gansu	42212841.23	6579623.30	10328250.57	16237305	108074	90869	3082
青　海 Qinghai	9824441.54	1121769.44	1757585.10	3699171	26083	21442	1263
宁　夏 Ningxia	11385001.92	1978162.47	3131409.31	4104572	40403	31639	247
新　疆 Xinjiang	56291211.31	14782411.24	14786071.75	13898585	115787	89349	2253

条件(二)(乡村)
Primary Schools (2)(Rural Area)

教室(间) Classroom(Room)		教室中:普通教室(间) of Which: General Classroom(Room)		固定资产总值(万元) Total Value of Fixed Asset (10,000 yuan)		
合计 Total	其中:网络多媒体教室 of Which: Network Multimedia Classroom	合计 Total	其中:网络多媒体教室 of Which: Network Multimedia Classroom	合计 Total	其中:教学仪器设备资产值 of Which: Total Value of Equip & Instru. 小计 Subtotal	其中:实验设备 of Which: For Experiment
1678979	**714287**	**1305326**	**643783**	**31962385.81**	**3708788.87**	**907504.06**
4243	3491	2687	2391	192449.36	65111.43	5754.39
5588	3304	3971	2850	143360.61	17368.65	4134.16
139209	64136	112365	61488	1917637.13	224995.82	81018.19
47098	18185	34913	16692	905056.59	78666.07	21332.27
12991	6591	8595	5280	447283.71	55933.21	8644.42
23933	6000	17955	5048	287711.19	54947.29	13654.42
29110	4864	21147	4345	325825.51	50031.63	15617.57
17576	4183	11831	3486	247261.91	32217.31	8169.89
1022	808	751	631	53300.41	8195.53	2200.45
28521	14095	20752	11180	558941.41	73992.43	20934.99
22059	18652	15039	14787	710452.69	124905.86	21188.24
85658	49725	68753	47576	1572166.49	196131.20	52222.62
45721	24117	29389	21270	871431.83	130087.90	27361.67
91311	31281	69313	29482	1106427.67	142823.06	31918.52
92944	70188	62446	53976	2101382.10	236528.19	55082.55
228552	62176	198744	58923	2730608.92	292134.02	85444.68
50934	20397	40558	19360	1015851.32	107678.65	35295.33
81919	12648	63241	11568	1133534.82	114830.65	35246.25
97211	59585	69306	53149	2140032.36	240768.37	63118.09
110620	40864	87816	38754	2056426.28	295487.99	64154.97
11609	3132	8794	2936	335277.45	30836.77	7694.78
24244	16766	16060	12406	389872.99	52510.64	8230.93
78433	18748	68978	17030	1789835.48	204674.48	54005.72
69740	38419	53379	36299	1111258.21	143145.12	38030.78
112533	42811	92658	40230	3645607.19	286826.78	55881.38
8120	2718	6398	2457	745812.40	29197.90	5508.74
30012	13585	23960	12426	568142.48	63590.76	20349.73
60243	29794	47516	28352	1020364.68	117495.74	28290.34
9509	2561	7225	2335	402462.61	19503.34	2721.46
11626	6277	8400	5332	335367.74	57840.49	11653.86
46690	24186	32386	21744	1101242.28	160331.60	22642.70

地 区 Region	学校数（所）Schools	班数（个）Classes	离校人数 Schools Leavers
总 计 Total	**93**	**312**	**3311**
北 京 Beijing	6	31	250
天 津 Tianjin	3	0	0
河 北 Hebei	0	0	0
山 西 Shanxi	1	9	88
内蒙古 Inner Mongolia	0	0	0
辽 宁 Liaoning	10	18	184
吉 林 Jilin	3	11	40
黑龙江 Heilongjiang	1	3	0
上 海 Shanghai	12	68	331
江 苏 Jiangsu	0	0	0
浙 江 Zhejiang	2	16	144
安 徽 Anhui	3	0	0
福 建 Fujian	0	0	0
江 西 Jiangxi	2	10	208
山 东 Shandong	0	0	0
河 南 Henan	3	12	48
湖 北 Hubei	2	8	54
湖 南 Hunan	2	9	0
广 东 Guangdong	3	27	103
广 西 Guangxi	3	0	0
海 南 Hainan	0	0	0
重 庆 Chongqing	2	1	68
四 川 Sichuan	9	28	423
贵 州 Guizhou	18	35	813
云 南 Yunnan	2	7	58
西 藏 Tibet	0	0	0
陕 西 Shaanxi	1	3	14
甘 肃 Gansu	0	0	0
青 海 Qinghai	0	0	0
宁 夏 Ningxia	0	0	0
新 疆 Xinjiang	5	16	485

基本情况
Work-study Schools

单位:人
unit: person

入校人数 No. of Persons Enrolled	在校生数 Enrolment	教职工数 Educational Personnel	
		合计 Total	其中:专任教师 of Which: Full-time Teachers
3187	**6048**	**2922**	**2177**
224	618	270	204
0	0	74	57
0	0	0	0
120	170	76	63
0	0	0	0
236	487	321	234
74	203	110	53
15	33	20	18
409	749	454	364
0	0	0	0
171	315	76	63
0	0	50	34
0	0	0	0
210	350	52	47
0	0	0	0
40	175	65	56
38	106	46	39
35	263	89	77
264	401	235	203
13	13	34	24
0	0	0	0
32	32	26	24
257	473	223	170
808	1043	316	256
78	150	61	55
0	0	0	0
15	27	43	33
0	0	0	0
0	0	0	0
0	0	0	0
148	440	281	103

地　区 Region	学校数（所） Schools	班数（个） Classes	毕业生数 Graduates	招生数 Entrants	在校生数				
					合计 Total	其中：女 of Which: Female	小学阶段		
							一年级 Grade 1	二年级 Grade 2	三年级 Grade 3
总　计 Total	**2107**	**24716**	**69401**	**110843**	**578826**	**207005**	**72367**	**73158**	**74637**
北　京 Beijing	21	316	1545	907	6440	2279	416	524	608
天　津 Tianjin	20	271	325	549	3987	1364	540	403	343
河　北 Hebei	161	1491	1693	3124	17112	6187	2221	1990	2214
山　西 Shanxi	73	814	1662	2508	12684	5027	1401	1523	1504
内蒙古 Inner Mongolia	44	538	1129	2324	11094	4174	1834	1366	1559
辽　宁 Liaoning	75	824	989	1654	11226	3723	1416	1235	1209
吉　林 Jilin	50	581	780	1466	8797	3129	1020	1047	1169
黑龙江 Heilongjiang	73	973	1292	2780	12375	4355	2214	1796	1305
上　海 Shanghai	30	465	1684	1192	7409	2596	355	359	539
江　苏 Jiangsu	101	1325	3630	4267	27512	9445	2982	3182	3716
浙　江 Zhejiang	86	1005	2910	3069	18532	6531	1456	1712	1858
安　徽 Anhui	72	966	1634	4983	27354	9584	3640	3778	5251
福　建 Fujian	71	1002	4010	4067	25099	8559	2337	2666	3214
江　西 Jiangxi	89	910	4206	5966	30330	10933	4010	3907	3804
山　东 Shandong	147	1868	4044	5375	28501	9925	4077	3571	3396
河　南 Henan	148	1458	2127	6509	30672	10835	4871	4967	4381
湖　北 Hubei	84	768	1278	2294	13953	4765	1636	1890	1786
湖　南 Hunan	79	870	3070	6295	31192	10717	4516	4393	4066
广　东 Guangdong	133	1862	4254	8893	44084	13833	5890	5354	6072
广　西 Guangxi	79	998	1758	4573	22080	7325	3267	3311	2893
海　南 Hainan	7	102	313	548	2556	851	233	323	298
重　庆 Chongqing	36	415	2162	3348	18585	6750	2034	2204	2388
四　川 Sichuan	127	1363	9557	10361	53461	20171	5895	7246	6385
贵　州 Guizhou	76	1057	2407	5269	25840	9552	3408	3824	3893
云　南 Yunnan	64	793	6007	7358	34075	13525	3875	3796	3603
西　藏 Tibet	5	68	271	769	4050	1784	466	498	462
陕　西 Shaanxi	58	525	1411	3226	14683	5432	2207	1979	2017
甘　肃 Gansu	41	439	1232	2531	13492	4881	1447	1650	1613
青　海 Qinghai	16	138	414	1173	5061	2037	667	899	651
宁　夏 Ningxia	13	160	555	1009	5319	2060	648	473	969
新　疆 Xinjiang	28	351	1052	2456	11271	4676	1388	1292	1471

基本情况(总计)
Special Education(Total)

单位:人
unit: person

Enrolment

Primary Education			初中阶段 Junior Secondary Education				高中阶段 Senior Secondary Education		
四年级 Grade 4	五年级 Grade 5	六年级 Grade 6	一年级 Grade 1	二年级 Grade 2	三年级 Grade 3	四年级 Grade 4	一年级 Grade 1	二年级 Grade 2	三年级及以上 Over Grade 3
68758	**68626**	**64976**	**50624**	**48301**	**45227**	**2093**	**3983**	**3008**	**3068**
745	808	934	639	725	863	40	38	43	57
505	418	432	308	340	250	12	152	78	206
2008	2135	1989	1755	1330	1091	44	78	139	118
1569	1528	1455	1142	1087	1037	0	173	139	126
1241	1222	1277	867	787	748	21	46	36	90
1171	1229	1267	1017	1023	990	18	273	207	171
904	1039	1043	801	775	762	35	73	81	48
1236	1404	798	1035	1015	973	316	106	90	87
689	785	0	935	1021	1078	990	373	121	164
3344	3464	3323	2265	2087	2283	8	311	270	277
2034	2196	2704	2070	2024	1877	0	300	173	128
3460	2962	2710	1806	1786	1536	0	118	96	211
3230	3273	3440	2180	2114	2275	33	122	115	100
4029	4267	3471	2454	2216	1925	0	100	67	80
3298	3065	2671	2637	2394	2132	470	287	252	251
3628	3406	3062	2363	2067	1678	33	109	60	47
1714	1719	1521	1293	1111	1049	50	72	86	26
3765	3641	3162	2436	2732	2361	0	62	37	21
5262	4792	4535	3719	3432	3791	14	450	382	391
2744	2699	2752	1569	1492	1250	1	42	25	35
350	345	307	210	210	176	0	46	29	29
2418	2518	2259	1615	1518	1414	0	102	71	44
6503	6462	6745	4875	4753	4215	0	185	114	83
2938	2767	3077	2096	1980	1591	0	111	87	68
3559	4099	4141	3740	3667	3550	0	19	13	13
512	571	454	367	332	352	0	18	11	7
1846	1694	1627	1213	1128	897	8	22	22	23
1572	1647	1574	1278	1314	1238	0	59	55	45
535	539	497	430	377	431	0	17	8	10
639	555	590	479	397	429	0	41	52	47
1310	1377	1159	1030	1067	985	0	78	49	65

地　区 Region	学校数（所）Schools	班数（个）Classes	毕业生数 Graduates	招生数 Entrants	在校生数				
					合计 Total	其中：女 of Which: Female	小学阶段		
							一年级 Grade 1	二年级 Grade 2	三年级 Grade 3
总　计 Total	**1027**	**13626**	**26949**	**35434**	**201029**	**71724**	**24332**	**23489**	**24222**
北　京 Beijing	17	269	1309	783	5379	1880	357	425	501
天　津 Tianjin	20	271	271	479	3622	1239	508	359	296
河　北 Hebei	54	601	808	999	6745	2492	754	722	846
山　西 Shanxi	31	388	764	1092	4769	1892	590	494	505
内蒙古 Inner Mongolia	18	283	384	715	3989	1503	592	564	568
辽　宁 Liaoning	57	659	724	1049	7778	2604	973	790	836
吉　林 Jilin	35	447	454	792	4813	1664	589	614	672
黑龙江 Heilongjiang	38	540	580	1248	6113	2153	966	865	779
上　海 Shanghai	27	414	1367	966	6184	2142	332	320	448
江　苏 Jiangsu	77	976	2092	2295	15397	5353	1669	1677	1940
浙　江 Zhejiang	50	610	1409	1461	8660	3054	712	829	862
安　徽 Anhui	23	381	558	935	5945	2070	682	704	1154
福　建 Fujian	35	536	1446	1418	8513	2938	890	838	1123
江　西 Jiangxi	28	340	1000	1227	6749	2388	802	822	793
山　东 Shandong	82	1099	2125	2632	13870	4912	1988	1658	1440
河　南 Henan	60	632	906	1472	7931	2916	1072	1125	1016
湖　北 Hubei	45	462	742	976	6657	2327	705	930	776
湖　南 Hunan	28	375	644	1169	7247	2500	1127	1064	797
广　东 Guangdong	88	1447	2772	4144	21719	6941	2813	2785	2730
广　西 Guangxi	27	394	592	1188	5629	1885	873	746	734
海　南 Hainan	3	68	192	215	987	339	75	111	91
重　庆 Chongqing	21	252	777	1095	6111	2418	666	619	819
四　川 Sichuan	50	600	1766	1800	10969	4168	1097	1421	1346
贵　州 Guizhou	25	396	608	1169	5353	2038	705	698	832
云　南 Yunnan	23	364	1175	1394	6527	2652	824	689	746
西　藏 Tibet	2	24	34	123	650	295	135	99	54
陕　西 Shaanxi	22	237	355	841	3861	1567	626	509	485
甘　肃 Gansu	14	220	449	549	3109	1187	363	298	364
青　海 Qinghai	5	59	117	257	1160	452	169	244	108
宁　夏 Ningxia	6	84	173	366	1621	649	252	133	180
新　疆 Xinjiang	16	198	356	585	2672	1106	426	337	381

情况(城区)
Education (Urban Area)

单位:人
unit: person

Enrolment

Primary Education			初中阶段 Junior Secondary Education				高中阶段 Senior Secondary Education		
四年级 Grade 4	五年级 Grade 5	六年级 Grade 6	一年级 Grade 1	二年级 Grade 2	三年级 Grade 3	四年级 Grade 4	一年级 Grade 1	二年级 Grade 2	三年级及以上 Over Grade 3
22627	**22557**	**20744**	**18030**	**17341**	**16977**	**1646**	**3474**	**2756**	**2834**
628	685	755	533	607	710	40	38	43	57
457	365	386	270	314	219	12	152	78	206
749	740	744	601	605	610	44	73	139	118
545	513	476	450	400	421	0	152	122	101
404	427	476	261	287	249	16	37	31	77
842	790	785	714	706	686	18	265	207	166
429	545	524	423	420	410	7	73	59	48
656	645	371	420	522	468	230	60	64	67
579	650	0	724	826	858	841	336	121	149
1753	1741	1699	1407	1275	1379	8	311	261	277
949	995	1186	960	873	818	0	205	153	118
695	641	601	361	384	321	0	106	92	204
1047	1046	1159	756	697	680	9	103	86	79
825	868	716	562	566	549	0	100	66	80
1522	1352	1115	1372	1224	1162	343	230	220	244
877	843	808	800	581	597	28	93	60	31
805	819	736	621	509	543	50	67	76	20
786	806	866	520	614	547	0	62	37	21
2443	2311	2248	1782	1653	1786	0	429	368	371
667	665	541	440	468	393	0	42	25	35
108	111	99	95	103	90	0	46	29	29
856	885	711	568	549	531	0	92	71	44
1447	1351	1260	959	926	907	0	111	86	58
521	507	538	469	472	345	0	111	87	68
632	818	657	778	665	673	0	19	13	13
73	134	44	44	33	34	0	0	0	0
443	399	373	392	302	265	0	22	22	23
316	365	373	256	325	290	0	59	55	45
120	104	87	95	96	102	0	17	8	10
134	141	153	186	130	172	0	41	52	47
319	295	257	211	209	162	0	22	25	28

地　区 Region	学校数 (所) Schools	班数 (个) Classes	毕业生数 Graduates	招生数 Entrants	在校生数				
					合计 Total	其中:女 of Which: Female	小学阶段		
							一年级 Grade 1	二年级 Grade 2	三年级 Grade 3
总　计 Total	**165**	**2289**	**4073**	**6335**	**35740**	**12630**	**4467**	**4472**	**5095**
北　京 Beijing	2	12	95	60	340	134	30	24	45
天　津 Tianjin	0	0	17	12	104	34	9	15	9
河　北 Hebei	18	190	158	314	1816	679	263	215	224
山　西 Shanxi	1	8	32	118	296	110	69	39	39
内蒙古 Inner Mongolia	0	0	2	9	56	22	7	20	7
辽　宁 Liaoning	3	45	40	92	580	189	83	69	59
吉　林 Jilin	6	97	67	119	949	351	100	68	223
黑龙江 Heilongjiang	4	45	44	112	580	224	103	45	49
上　海 Shanghai	2	23	85	79	418	142	42	21	35
江　苏 Jiangsu	6	76	164	169	1628	555	119	149	327
浙　江 Zhejiang	11	160	416	380	2212	752	189	211	230
安　徽 Anhui	6	99	84	140	1537	561	131	145	520
福　建 Fujian	9	152	310	345	1862	622	195	189	223
江　西 Jiangxi	3	27	124	178	855	295	124	98	132
山　东 Shandong	22	321	479	785	4080	1369	535	581	531
河　南 Henan	9	109	169	321	1724	642	259	253	195
湖　北 Hubei	5	47	112	123	751	263	104	110	83
湖　南 Hunan	4	72	132	208	1350	451	188	153	137
广　东 Guangdong	21	349	470	1097	6513	2154	831	966	979
广　西 Guangxi	5	95	118	297	1224	383	189	164	186
海　南 Hainan	0	0	2	2	19	2	2	2	3
重　庆 Chongqing	4	60	187	188	1253	501	133	118	156
四　川 Sichuan	8	90	269	239	1702	660	156	334	169
贵　州 Guizhou	4	56	54	246	959	357	194	124	197
云　南 Yunnan	6	96	326	359	1621	634	186	158	185
西　藏 Tibet	0	0	0	0	1	0	0	0	0
陕　西 Shaanxi	6	60	71	264	972	410	188	163	115
甘　肃 Gansu	0	0	28	30	159	57	15	22	16
青　海 Qinghai	0	0	8	19	54	28	4	1	1
宁　夏 Ningxia	0	0	1	10	38	12	8	5	9
新　疆 Xinjiang	0	0	9	20	87	37	11	10	11

情况(城乡结合区)
Education (Urban-rural Transitional Area)

单位:人
unit: person

Enrolment									
Primary Education			初中阶段 Junior Secondary Education				高中阶段 Senior Secondary Education		
四年级 Grade 4	五年级 Grade 5	六年级 Grade 6	一年级 Grade 1	二年级 Grade 2	三年级 Grade 3	四年级 Grade 4	一年级 Grade 1	二年级 Grade 2	三年级及以上 Over Grade 3
4281	**4219**	**3881**	**3001**	**2775**	**2658**	**192**	**240**	**237**	**222**
47	48	49	21	36	40	0	0	0	0
20	23	17	3	3	5	0	0	0	0
223	156	232	177	141	116	33	25	11	0
24	32	39	21	19	14	0	0	0	0
3	5	3	2	8	1	0	0	0	0
60	60	65	52	62	70	0	0	0	0
82	119	105	70	75	82	0	14	4	7
60	54	45	39	64	85	36	0	0	0
40	47	0	50	54	59	54	10	6	0
216	201	209	105	158	144	0	0	0	0
255	287	296	218	205	202	0	46	48	25
181	191	121	67	81	60	0	17	13	10
252	245	268	172	143	136	9	4	13	13
136	121	87	62	60	35	0	0	0	0
496	389	340	408	312	334	60	29	26	39
185	210	233	159	131	83	0	7	9	0
70	110	113	83	43	35	0	0	0	0
131	163	161	133	130	154	0	0	0	0
861	758	687	463	402	420	0	29	40	77
145	184	94	82	90	62	0	11	10	7
3	5	2	0	1	1	0	0	0	0
139	153	128	79	112	107	0	48	42	38
231	176	226	127	157	114	0	0	12	0
91	111	96	51	48	47	0	0	0	0
195	200	165	208	148	176	0	0	0	0
1	0	0	0	0	0	0	0	0	0
95	138	61	108	56	39	0	0	3	6
17	21	22	15	17	14	0	0	0	0
6	2	3	15	11	11	0	0	0	0
3	2	7	2	0	2	0	0	0	0
13	8	7	9	8	10	0	0	0	0

地 区 Region	学校数（所）Schools	班数（个）Classes	毕业生数 Graduates	招生数 Entrants	在校生数				
					合计 Total	其中:女 of Which: Female	小学阶段		
							一年级 Grade 1	二年级 Grade 2	三年级 Grade 3
总 计 Total	**947**	**9718**	**28727**	**49689**	**243519**	**88099**	**29480**	**30127**	**30815**
北 京 Beijing	1	3	117	40	362	135	8	26	31
天 津 Tianjin	0	0	27	41	159	50	15	15	15
河 北 Hebei	95	796	608	1642	7602	2763	1072	892	954
山 西 Shanxi	30	283	604	838	4716	1926	474	547	572
内蒙古 Inner Mongolia	24	240	625	1279	5789	2201	980	633	807
辽 宁 Liaoning	17	159	223	464	2618	861	352	319	250
吉 林 Jilin	14	117	255	457	2595	994	295	261	305
黑龙江 Heilongjiang	32	392	544	1193	5211	1858	988	812	409
上 海 Shanghai	2	28	231	161	862	330	10	19	59
江 苏 Jiangsu	21	301	1382	1625	9893	3417	1033	1210	1448
浙 江 Zhejiang	24	274	1144	1176	6962	2471	483	582	670
安 徽 Anhui	44	510	669	2493	12458	4466	1794	1644	2484
福 建 Fujian	31	400	1805	1821	11190	3779	936	1188	1366
江 西 Jiangxi	59	555	1744	2655	13939	5042	1641	1704	1719
山 东 Shandong	64	762	1547	2306	11914	4058	1737	1418	1489
河 南 Henan	85	779	834	3246	14116	5055	2454	2228	1927
湖 北 Hubei	33	255	364	947	5044	1720	636	623	633
湖 南 Hunan	50	486	1720	3663	16688	5836	2483	2320	2240
广 东 Guangdong	30	288	1028	2722	13089	4111	1392	1311	1692
广 西 Guangxi	49	548	794	1943	9400	3144	1150	1322	1153
海 南 Hainan	2	16	87	231	946	305	73	106	98
重 庆 Chongqing	14	146	1123	1708	8928	3166	982	1124	1084
四 川 Sichuan	59	608	5046	5502	26600	10180	2720	3220	2910
贵 州 Guizhou	49	641	1401	2893	13975	5167	1758	2111	2105
云 南 Yunnan	35	363	2427	3212	13450	5371	1338	1398	1115
西 藏 Tibet	1	13	117	392	1814	818	115	135	161
陕 西 Shaanxi	30	255	882	1867	8178	2932	1110	1073	1153
甘 肃 Gansu	24	209	522	1187	6014	2188	543	797	663
青 海 Qinghai	10	76	220	660	2582	1065	309	434	352
宁 夏 Ningxia	7	76	210	312	2021	817	162	189	445
新 疆 Xinjiang	11	139	427	1013	4404	1873	437	466	506

基本情况(镇区)
Education (Counties & Towns Area)

单位:人
unit: person

Enrolment									
Primary Education			初中阶段 Junior Secondary Education				高中阶段 Senior Secondary Education		
四年级 Grade 4	五年级 Grade 5	六年级 Grade 6	一年级 Grade 1	二年级 Grade 2	三年级 Grade 3	四年级 Grade 4	一年级 Grade 1	二年级 Grade 2	三年级及以上 Over Grade 3
27846	**28184**	**27068**	**24740**	**23154**	**21083**	**374**	**344**	**160**	**144**
35	36	90	34	45	57	0	0	0	0
15	22	17	26	19	15	0	0	0	0
896	968	829	1035	578	373	0	5	0	0
607	577	571	455	477	436	0	0	0	0
674	640	598	549	454	444	5	0	5	0
235	310	367	253	262	257	0	8	0	5
292	296	311	279	238	268	28	0	22	0
448	638	378	548	413	416	69	46	26	20
77	100	0	159	145	155	114	9	0	15
1241	1376	1287	731	740	827	0	0	0	0
773	783	1059	859	879	810	0	51	8	5
1463	1250	1102	983	936	802	0	0	0	0
1421	1411	1471	1064	1044	1207	24	19	18	21
1846	1986	1673	1337	1089	943	0	0	1	0
1364	1333	1225	1169	1087	887	109	57	32	7
1601	1443	1397	1143	1077	812	2	16	0	16
575	590	516	561	500	389	0	5	10	6
2000	2004	1549	1355	1457	1280	0	0	0	0
1414	1438	1408	1527	1411	1482	14	0	0	0
1065	1074	1220	907	830	678	1	0	0	0
127	127	147	98	93	77	0	0	0	0
1045	1145	1072	866	842	758	0	10	0	0
3003	3033	3304	2906	2893	2523	0	62	14	12
1552	1382	1549	1344	1204	970	0	0	0	0
1204	1373	1386	1915	1891	1830	0	0	0	0
203	201	190	277	255	277	0	0	0	0
1018	933	935	697	699	552	8	0	0	0
657	647	585	728	714	680	0	0	0	0
254	294	243	262	198	236	0	0	0	0
257	220	180	193	192	183	0	0	0	0
484	554	409	480	492	459	0	56	24	37

地 区 Region	学校数(所) Schools	班数(个) Classes	毕业生数 Graduates	招生数 Entrants	在校生数				
					合计 Total	其中:女 of Which: Female	小学阶段		
							一年级 Grade 1	二年级 Grade 2	三年级 Grade 3
总 计 Total	**312**	**3157**	**6819**	**13319**	**66561**	**23552**	**8966**	**9119**	**9239**
北 京 Beijing	0	0	25	13	91	30	5	9	8
天 津 Tianjin	0	0	9	18	63	20	5	5	6
河 北 Hebei	54	429	249	701	3747	1333	590	508	544
山 西 Shanxi	9	77	174	302	1501	601	208	180	159
内蒙古 Inner Mongolia	3	20	70	112	585	194	65	53	78
辽 宁 Liaoning	3	24	55	32	306	97	37	53	32
吉 林 Jilin	0	1	7	28	166	55	18	18	19
黑龙江 Heilongjiang	2	26	115	62	346	142	45	26	38
上 海 Shanghai	0	0	34	30	161	55	0	1	8
江 苏 Jiangsu	8	122	447	495	3263	1081	324	436	525
浙 江 Zhejiang	11	151	569	510	3073	1062	205	266	288
安 徽 Anhui	13	155	160	693	3337	1264	499	424	729
福 建 Fujian	13	153	564	563	3525	1170	300	372	447
江 西 Jiangxi	13	135	414	787	3704	1349	576	440	421
山 东 Shandong	29	391	630	1133	5840	1891	934	774	781
河 南 Henan	31	288	328	1404	5711	2051	1176	1039	789
湖 北 Hubei	9	59	56	213	1238	411	151	180	150
湖 南 Hunan	13	96	395	827	3857	1335	582	573	706
广 东 Guangdong	12	127	296	986	4747	1490	624	520	678
广 西 Guangxi	15	182	141	503	2824	982	369	487	426
海 南 Hainan	1	10	1	25	182	72	23	39	10
重 庆 Chongqing	4	33	177	263	1530	542	171	165	176
四 川 Sichuan	10	95	706	898	3939	1526	392	493	387
贵 州 Guizhou	14	174	230	614	3441	1219	445	705	642
云 南 Yunnan	15	142	571	858	3571	1436	456	450	332
西 藏 Tibet	0	0	4	37	142	61	4	14	17
陕 西 Shaanxi	12	86	175	506	2073	727	304	375	342
甘 肃 Gansu	10	111	131	366	1790	655	231	306	208
青 海 Qinghai	3	13	24	91	409	164	67	61	48
宁 夏 Ningxia	2	28	15	51	531	191	35	49	136
新 疆 Xinjiang	3	29	47	198	868	346	125	98	109

情况(镇乡结合区)
Education (County-town Transitional Area)

单位:人
unit: person

Enrolment									
Primary Education			初中阶段 Junior Secondary Education				高中阶段 Senior Secondary Education		
四年级 Grade 4	五年级 Grade 5	六年级 Grade 6	一年级 Grade 1	二年级 Grade 2	三年级 Grade 3	四年级 Grade 4	一年级 Grade 1	二年级 Grade 2	三年级及以上 Over Grade 3
8049	**7748**	**7580**	**5796**	**5061**	**4738**	**133**	**80**	**35**	**17**
9	9	11	10	13	17	0	0	0	0
7	9	7	13	6	5	0	0	0	0
416	485	389	383	241	191	0	0	0	0
212	192	229	113	121	87	0	0	0	0
76	106	69	44	47	47	0	0	0	0
24	31	51	18	14	41	0	0	0	5
25	23	33	10	11	9	0	0	0	0
23	60	22	74	23	34	1	0	0	0
12	14	0	30	35	27	34	0	0	0
397	462	405	204	245	265	0	0	0	0
362	318	523	377	351	339	0	31	8	5
391	336	319	239	197	203	0	0	0	0
455	443	471	318	293	384	24	9	9	0
602	483	490	256	245	190	0	0	1	0
675	728	603	518	388	356	59	10	7	7
672	593	504	373	301	264	0	0	0	0
166	142	133	112	90	99	0	5	10	0
455	492	292	263	270	224	0	0	0	0
502	505	534	440	443	487	14	0	0	0
383	263	399	175	170	151	1	0	0	0
31	34	41	2	2	0	0	0	0	0
203	213	204	135	137	126	0	0	0	0
453	477	519	499	342	352	0	25	0	0
409	293	387	227	202	131	0	0	0	0
367	394	457	422	405	288	0	0	0	0
13	5	4	33	29	23	0	0	0	0
303	210	179	166	129	65	0	0	0	0
183	171	173	196	150	172	0	0	0	0
41	48	37	25	38	44	0	0	0	0
76	62	40	48	37	48	0	0	0	0
106	147	55	73	86	69	0	0	0	0

特殊教育
Basic Statistics of Special

地　区 Region	学校数（所）Schools	班数（个）Classes	毕业生数 Graduates	招生数 Entrants	在校生数 合计 Total	其中：女 of Which: Female	小学阶段 一年级 Grade 1	二年级 Grade 2	三年级 Grade 3
总　计 Total	**133**	**1372**	**13725**	**25720**	**134278**	**47182**	**18555**	**19542**	**19600**
北　京 Beijing	3	44	119	84	699	264	51	73	76
天　津 Tianjin	0	0	27	29	206	75	17	29	32
河　北 Hebei	12	94	277	483	2765	932	395	376	414
山　西 Shanxi	12	143	294	578	3199	1209	337	482	427
内蒙古 Inner Mongolia	2	15	120	330	1316	470	262	169	184
辽　宁 Liaoning	1	6	42	141	830	258	91	126	123
吉　林 Jilin	1	17	71	217	1389	471	136	172	192
黑龙江 Heilongjiang	3	41	168	339	1051	344	260	119	117
上　海 Shanghai	1	23	86	65	363	124	13	20	32
江　苏 Jiangsu	3	48	156	347	2222	675	280	295	328
浙　江 Zhejiang	12	121	357	432	2910	1006	261	301	326
安　徽 Anhui	5	75	407	1555	8951	3048	1164	1430	1613
福　建 Fujian	5	66	759	828	5396	1842	511	640	725
江　西 Jiangxi	2	15	1462	2084	9642	3503	1567	1381	1292
山　东 Shandong	1	7	372	437	2717	955	352	495	467
河　南 Henan	3	47	387	1791	8625	2864	1345	1614	1438
湖　北 Hubei	6	51	172	371	2252	718	295	337	377
湖　南 Hunan	1	9	706	1463	7257	2381	906	1009	1029
广　东 Guangdong	15	127	454	2027	9276	2781	1685	1258	1650
广　西 Guangxi	3	56	372	1442	7051	2296	1244	1243	1006
海　南 Hainan	2	18	34	102	623	207	85	106	109
重　庆 Chongqing	1	17	262	545	3246	1166	386	461	485
四　川 Sichuan	18	155	2745	3059	15892	5823	2078	2605	2129
贵　州 Guizhou	2	20	398	1207	6512	2347	945	1015	956
云　南 Yunnan	6	66	2405	2752	14098	5502	1713	1709	1742
西　藏 Tibet	2	31	120	254	1586	671	216	264	247
陕　西 Shaanxi	6	33	174	518	2644	933	471	397	379
甘　肃 Gansu	3	10	261	795	4369	1506	541	555	586
青　海 Qinghai	1	3	77	256	1319	520	189	221	191
宁　夏 Ningxia	0	0	172	331	1677	594	234	151	344
新　疆 Xinjiang	1	14	269	858	4195	1697	525	489	584

基本情况(乡村)
Education (Rural Area)

单位:人
unit: person

Enrolment									
Primary Education			初中阶段 Junior Secondary Education				高中阶段 Senior Secondary Education		
四年级 Grade 4	五年级 Grade 5	六年级 Grade 6	一年级 Grade 1	二年级 Grade 2	三年级 Grade 3	四年级 Grade 4	一年级 Grade 1	二年级 Grade 2	三年级及以上 Over Grade 3
18285	**17885**	**17164**	**7854**	**7806**	**7167**	**73**	**165**	**92**	**90**
82	87	89	72	73	96	0	0	0	0
33	31	29	12	7	16	0	0	0	0
363	427	416	119	147	108	0	0	0	0
417	438	408	237	210	180	0	21	17	25
163	155	203	57	46	55	0	9	0	13
94	129	115	50	55	47	0	0	0	0
183	198	208	99	117	84	0	0	0	0
132	121	49	67	80	89	17	0	0	0
33	35	0	52	50	65	35	28	0	0
350	347	337	127	72	77	0	0	9	0
312	418	459	251	272	249	0	44	12	5
1302	1071	1007	462	466	413	0	12	4	7
762	816	810	360	373	388	0	0	11	0
1358	1413	1082	555	561	433	0	0	0	0
412	380	331	96	83	83	18	0	0	0
1150	1120	857	420	409	269	3	0	0	0
334	310	269	111	102	117	0	0	0	0
979	831	747	561	661	534	0	0	0	0
1405	1043	879	410	368	523	0	21	14	20
1012	960	991	222	194	179	0	0	0	0
115	107	61	17	14	9	0	0	0	0
517	488	476	181	127	125	0	0	0	0
2053	2078	2181	1010	934	785	0	12	14	13
865	878	990	283	304	276	0	0	0	0
1723	1908	2098	1047	1111	1047	0	0	0	0
236	236	220	46	44	41	0	18	11	7
385	362	319	124	127	80	0	0	0	0
599	635	616	294	275	268	0	0	0	0
161	141	167	73	83	93	0	0	0	0
248	194	257	100	75	74	0	0	0	0
507	528	493	339	366	364	0	0	0	0

地 区 Region	毕业生数 Graduates	招生数 Intakes	在校生数				
			合计 Total	小学阶段 Primary Education			
				一年级 Grade 1	二年级 Grade 2	三年级 Grade 3	四年级 Grade 4
总 计 Total	**23005**	**36854**	**196343**	**23762**	**23995**	**25378**	**23475**
北 京 Beijing	526	333	2244	154	159	204	272
天 津 Tianjin	113	194	1360	174	150	97	178
河 北 Hebei	506	1024	5953	814	656	800	735
山 西 Shanxi	647	942	4823	519	572	552	572
内蒙古 Inner Mongolia	377	747	3908	562	453	546	458
辽 宁 Liaoning	376	536	3577	487	358	359	348
吉 林 Jilin	222	503	3028	343	338	396	322
黑龙江 Heilongjiang	452	941	4329	769	612	432	449
上 海 Shanghai	562	438	2590	130	123	179	241
江 苏 Jiangsu	1179	1356	9256	1014	1085	1235	1118
浙 江 Zhejiang	930	1057	6134	503	504	596	666
安 徽 Anhui	443	1710	9121	1248	1185	1821	1150
福 建 Fujian	1272	1318	8493	725	882	1129	1057
江 西 Jiangxi	1558	1930	10389	1292	1334	1302	1431
山 东 Shandong	1367	1771	9636	1320	1087	1115	1132
河 南 Henan	715	2297	10595	1712	1651	1486	1223
湖 北 Hubei	412	729	4590	524	581	603	561
湖 南 Hunan	811	1966	10162	1407	1422	1333	1252
广 东 Guangdong	1140	2393	12233	1518	1459	1623	1470
广 西 Guangxi	573	1262	6627	868	967	938	826
海 南 Hainan	85	157	804	83	93	88	119
重 庆 Chongqing	670	1151	6471	655	811	840	844
四 川 Sichuan	3136	3517	18402	1954	2345	2261	2339
贵 州 Guizhou	829	1903	9152	1171	1273	1416	1010
云 南 Yunnan	2262	2677	12867	1402	1458	1411	1383
西 藏 Tibet	117	283	1427	192	175	173	204
陕 西 Shaanxi	505	1042	4849	717	651	680	628
甘 肃 Gansu	404	914	4866	537	572	591	551
青 海 Qinghai	157	429	1939	214	343	272	199
宁 夏 Ningxia	211	316	1862	181	154	290	227
新 疆 Xinjiang	448	1018	4656	573	542	610	510

女学生数
in Special Education

*单位：人
Unit: person

Total In-school Students

		初中阶段 Junior Secondary Education				高中阶段 Senior Secondary Education		
五年级 Grade 5	六年级 Grade 6	一年级 Grade 1	二年级 Grade 2	三年级 Grade 3	四年级 Grade 4	一年级 Grade 1	二年级 Grade 2	三年级及以上 Over Grade 3
23547	**21700**	**17326**	**16746**	**15594**	**743**	**1588**	**1231**	**1258**
286	341	220	230	313	12	12	18	23
147	155	91	121	93	4	47	26	77
793	656	488	492	388	14	28	50	39
602	542	441	418	385	0	83	76	61
431	461	332	301	280	10	23	14	37
396	397	326	337	320	4	102	68	75
383	330	275	281	252	10	43	34	21
514	268	368	359	344	104	43	35	32
280	0	336	362	361	342	123	42	71
1120	1090	730	722	779	2	129	118	114
778	843	708	698	616	0	113	51	58
976	863	601	577	513	0	49	46	92
1120	1178	746	728	778	18	47	45	40
1488	1224	820	728	668	0	38	29	35
1073	882	924	857	759	178	107	104	98
1209	1039	838	720	615	15	34	31	22
554	501	476	366	308	23	35	46	12
1154	1008	801	950	779	0	27	19	10
1343	1284	1056	937	1054	5	182	144	158
826	783	488	512	377	0	17	10	15
100	94	55	69	63	0	22	10	8
907	737	577	511	491	0	45	36	17
2247	2267	1681	1645	1486	0	85	58	34
936	1125	797	748	569	0	52	34	21
1558	1553	1389	1346	1348	0	7	6	6
211	134	117	103	107	0	4	6	1
542	528	391	370	313	2	9	6	12
589	565	449	492	449	0	28	24	19
191	180	173	166	188	0	7	3	3
218	224	192	150	166	0	14	26	20
575	448	440	450	432	0	33	16	27

特殊教育学校教职工数
Number of Educational Personnel in Special Education Schools

单位：人
unit: person

地 区 Region	教职工数 Educational Personnel					代课教师 Substitute Teachers	兼任教师 Part-time Teachers
	合计 Total	专任教师 Full-time Teachers	行政人员 Adm. Personnel	教辅人员 Supporting Staff	工勤人员 Workers		
总 计 Total	**65138**	**55979**	**3336**	**2346**	**3477**	**1546**	**246**
北 京 Beijing	1272	993	123	93	63	0	0
天 津 Tianjin	793	624	95	45	29	2	0
河 北 Hebei	3937	3319	241	163	214	27	0
山 西 Shanxi	1982	1656	88	97	141	221	28
内蒙古 Inner Mongolia	1602	1405	82	57	58	18	3
辽 宁 Liaoning	2717	2048	468	102	99	20	0
吉 林 Jilin	1869	1595	146	61	67	7	0
黑龙江 Heilongjiang	2261	1925	152	74	110	27	0
上 海 Shanghai	1623	1268	165	97	93	9	3
江 苏 Jiangsu	4043	3437	152	192	262	75	3
浙 江 Zhejiang	2853	2566	73	74	140	0	5
安 徽 Anhui	1843	1647	64	24	108	168	21
福 建 Fujian	2339	2070	87	53	129	204	5
江 西 Jiangxi	1527	1428	18	29	52	37	2
山 东 Shandong	5980	5183	196	283	318	33	12
河 南 Henan	4168	3776	141	87	164	87	3
湖 北 Hubei	2043	1765	106	71	101	83	8
湖 南 Hunan	2258	1996	119	73	70	63	15
广 东 Guangdong	5426	4451	231	343	401	55	74
广 西 Guangxi	1871	1577	63	69	162	63	15
海 南 Hainan	327	246	14	9	58	21	1
重 庆 Chongqing	1058	965	45	14	34	12	0
四 川 Sichuan	3122	2798	94	97	133	136	21
贵 州 Guizhou	1932	1728	87	17	100	5	5
云 南 Yunnan	1830	1605	50	39	136	8	18
西 藏 Tibet	237	214	14	1	8	0	0
陕 西 Shaanxi	1539	1255	133	47	104	36	0
甘 肃 Gansu	957	877	23	4	53	4	2
青 海 Qinghai	211	184	11	3	13	39	0
宁 夏 Ningxia	422	397	10	3	12	59	0
新 疆 Xinjiang	1096	981	45	25	45	27	2

特殊教育学校女教职工数
Number of Female Educational Personnel in Special Education Schools

单位：人
unit: person

地 区 Region	教职工数 Educational Personnel					代课教师 Substitute Teachers	兼任教师 Part-time Teachers
	合计 Total	专任教师 Full-time Teachers	行政人员 Adm. Personnel	教辅人员 Supporting Staff	工勤人员 Workers		
总 计 Total	**45868**	**41278**	**1599**	**1540**	**1451**	**1231**	**134**
北 京 Beijing	942	793	72	65	12	0	0
天 津 Tianjin	577	478	62	31	6	2	0
河 北 Hebei	2961	2648	112	106	95	20	0
山 西 Shanxi	1399	1274	28	47	50	175	16
内蒙古 Inner Mongolia	1049	985	26	27	11	17	1
辽 宁 Liaoning	2032	1638	310	61	23	20	0
吉 林 Jilin	1338	1233	69	29	7	6	0
黑龙江 Heilongjiang	1469	1347	80	28	14	22	0
上 海 Shanghai	1265	1046	115	74	30	8	1
江 苏 Jiangsu	2755	2496	53	119	87	69	2
浙 江 Zhejiang	2163	1988	29	57	89	0	5
安 徽 Anhui	1246	1141	28	13	64	130	8
福 建 Fujian	1754	1607	38	40	69	174	2
江 西 Jiangxi	1128	1059	12	23	34	34	1
山 东 Shandong	3715	3386	82	162	85	24	11
河 南 Henan	2975	2815	52	47	61	55	0
湖 北 Hubei	1311	1185	42	43	41	54	5
湖 南 Hunan	1573	1453	50	51	19	50	1
广 东 Guangdong	3960	3336	108	269	247	45	39
广 西 Guangxi	1456	1265	30	51	110	40	13
海 南 Hainan	232	175	7	7	43	19	1
重 庆 Chongqing	761	724	23	7	7	9	0
四 川 Sichuan	2198	2042	33	81	42	114	13
贵 州 Guizhou	1339	1239	33	10	57	3	2
云 南 Yunnan	1234	1114	17	32	71	8	10
西 藏 Tibet	138	129	7	1	1	0	0
陕 西 Shaanxi	1013	896	52	31	34	15	0
甘 肃 Gansu	622	598	1	4	19	3	1
青 海 Qinghai	130	120	1	3	6	35	0
宁 夏 Ningxia	322	316	3	2	1	57	0
新 疆 Xinjiang	811	752	24	19	16	23	2

特殊教育学校专任
Number of Full-time Teachers in Special Education

地 区 Region	合计 Total	其中：女 of Which: Female	按学历分 By Educational Attainment			
			研究生毕业 Graduate	本科毕业 Under-graduate	专科毕业 Associate Bachelor	高中阶段毕业 High School Graduate
总 计 Total	**55979**	**41278**	**1246**	**36624**	**16952**	**1130**
北 京 Beijing	993	793	67	868	56	2
天 津 Tianjin	624	478	30	476	109	9
河 北 Hebei	3319	2648	19	2067	1166	67
山 西 Shanxi	1656	1274	8	1134	471	43
内蒙古 Inner Mongolia	1405	985	25	931	419	30
辽 宁 Liaoning	2048	1638	39	1406	567	34
吉 林 Jilin	1595	1233	16	1167	358	54
黑龙江 Heilongjiang	1925	1347	6	975	867	77
上 海 Shanghai	1268	1046	124	1016	123	5
江 苏 Jiangsu	3437	2496	100	2708	603	26
浙 江 Zhejiang	2566	1988	109	1913	484	58
安 徽 Anhui	1647	1141	20	1049	542	36
福 建 Fujian	2070	1607	22	1296	699	53
江 西 Jiangxi	1428	1059	12	793	592	30
山 东 Shandong	5183	3386	133	3691	1211	148
河 南 Henan	3776	2815	27	2042	1607	100
湖 北 Hubei	1765	1185	33	976	695	60
湖 南 Hunan	1996	1453	25	1085	842	44
广 东 Guangdong	4451	3336	249	3038	1090	62
广 西 Guangxi	1577	1265	25	835	674	42
海 南 Hainan	246	175	3	128	113	2
重 庆 Chongqing	965	724	14	620	324	7
四 川 Sichuan	2798	2042	44	1577	1126	51
贵 州 Guizhou	1728	1239	10	1103	585	29
云 南 Yunnan	1605	1114	19	1115	452	19
西 藏 Tibet	214	129	2	156	54	2
陕 西 Shaanxi	1255	896	31	834	373	14
甘 肃 Gansu	877	598	12	629	228	8
青 海 Qinghai	184	120	5	114	62	3
宁 夏 Ningxia	397	316	7	250	135	5
新 疆 Xinjiang	981	752	10	632	325	10

教师学历、专业技术职务情况
Schools by Academic Qualifications and Professional Rank

单位:人
unit:person

	按专业技术职务分 By Professional Rank					
高中阶段以下毕业 Below High School Graduate	中学高级 Senior Secondary	小学高级 Senior Primary	小学一级 1st Grade Primary	小学二级 2nd Grade Primary	小学三级 3rd Grade Primary	未定职级 No-ranking
27	**6699**	**25292**	**15209**	**2579**	**294**	**5906**
0	107	500	313	20	7	46
0	77	363	150	9	0	25
0	539	1842	678	58	7	195
0	68	607	653	100	23	205
0	333	582	265	63	0	162
2	316	1351	257	45	2	77
0	297	707	446	45	0	100
0	436	1051	375	22	6	35
0	75	679	457	25	0	32
0	460	1812	787	98	8	272
2	261	1050	845	104	2	304
0	183	699	416	112	6	231
0	104	936	683	185	19	143
1	222	494	317	145	50	200
0	767	2369	1346	188	9	504
0	603	1782	1086	112	3	190
1	258	1015	330	50	13	99
0	221	812	442	120	3	398
12	269	1506	1130	409	54	1083
1	49	832	330	71	11	284
0	26	77	78	33	0	32
0	87	414	363	39	0	62
0	320	1030	1033	83	23	309
1	79	762	493	155	18	221
0	235	699	456	75	13	127
0	16	70	59	24	4	41
3	67	458	548	65	5	112
0	71	372	349	16	1	68
0	35	79	42	4	2	22
0	12	124	149	33	5	74
4	106	218	333	71	0	253

地区 Region	校舍建筑面积 Floor Space	教学及辅助用房 Teaching & Assistant Buildings				
		合计 Total	其中：of Which：			
			普通教室 General Classroom	专用教室 Special Classroom	实验室 Laboratory	微机室 PC-room
总　计 Total	**9717058.62**	**4419923.74**	**2385152.15**	**1524873.41**	**179286.05**	**151695.17**
北　京 Beijing	165974.35	67949.13	29697.88	31708.35	880.00	3332.60
天　津 Tianjin	99449.89	48674.26	26771.89	16859.68	611.00	1423.36
河　北 Hebei	499138.42	242937.28	113979.06	97189.82	9957.92	9822.66
山　西 Shanxi	231603.00	88262.03	45450.62	31141.90	2921.52	3890.94
内蒙古 Inner Mongolia	220340.45	104563.01	60741.71	33789.67	3088.90	3840.69
辽　宁 Liaoning	247460.21	119306.62	46399.29	60604.99	3167.68	4130.49
吉　林 Jilin	211937.65	100431.80	55959.46	33728.97	2767.94	3775.26
黑龙江 Heilongjiang	237016.97	112685.01	49574.71	52195.94	3611.12	3939.36
上　海 Shanghai	185755.35	93478.63	32459.31	45995.25	5585.39	3159.28
江　苏 Jiangsu	614993.74	294777.61	148162.85	108243.60	16538.15	9743.68
浙　江 Zhejiang	537931.21	204501.06	109277.76	76765.70	5634.00	5972.85
安　徽 Anhui	376531.82	187982.33	106946.68	61298.46	6238.73	5653.65
福　建 Fujian	376669.52	172068.87	86216.52	70220.61	5011.46	4081.62
江　西 Jiangxi	351427.39	165355.30	100733.95	51931.40	3206.05	4351.55
山　东 Shandong	775888.40	340664.25	154692.67	139590.94	18928.32	12757.01
河　南 Henan	599576.86	274862.08	150002.61	87152.62	13109.51	11546.42
湖　北 Hubei	355513.38	161698.63	98679.52	46429.77	4596.61	5385.29
湖　南 Hunan	392285.71	176673.25	111206.24	45846.86	5637.49	6702.32
广　东 Guangdong	739827.45	329607.38	188607.88	96811.72	22413.42	10224.46
广　西 Guangxi	363195.15	174021.80	95614.59	61685.57	5815.00	4297.84
海　南 Hainan	50807.86	19333.36	12160.70	5834.66	533.00	473.00
重　庆 Chongqing	175777.09	74243.05	52414.74	14607.95	1908.00	2900.36
四　川 Sichuan	501410.61	224776.08	139413.54	62231.21	6797.85	7609.03
贵　州 Guizhou	304599.43	139246.81	80418.83	45265.25	3908.91	5082.89
云　南 Yunnan	339747.48	170641.14	103725.75	41751.37	13656.76	5135.54
西　藏 Tibet	49987.56	11116.25	7559.14	2957.10	104.00	226.01
陕　西 Shaanxi	216218.48	96395.82	52694.92	33125.37	2847.75	3626.48
甘　肃 Gansu	186057.51	85758.02	50688.65	25965.58	2076.61	3697.47
青　海 Qinghai	57695.53	22601.27	11558.00	6378.69	2507.18	1060.20
宁　夏 Ningxia	88510.70	41779.84	31230.90	7588.35	777.52	1172.07
新　疆 Xinjiang	163729.45	73531.77	32111.78	29976.06	4448.26	2680.79

办学条件(一)
Special Education Schools (1)

单位:平方米
unit: m^2

图书室 Library	行政办公用房 Administrative 合计 Total	行政办公用房 Administrative 其中:教师办公室 of Which: for Teachers	生活用房 Residential and Welfare	其他用房 Rooms for Other Purposes	校舍面积中 of the Floor Space 危房面积 Floor Space of Dilapidated Buildings	校舍面积中 of the Floor Space 当年新增校舍 New Added in Current Year
178916.96	**951778.50**	**517054.36**	**2817182.67**	**1528173.71**	**89181.36**	**486769.69**
2330.30	16045.95	7220.70	29058.37	52920.90	0.00	161.00
3008.33	10735.45	6216.84	20243.43	19796.75	0.00	4225.13
11987.82	50220.30	28018.75	130003.34	75977.50	0.00	18554.61
4857.05	26600.84	15197.32	71260.93	45479.20	1726.00	1558.80
3102.04	21242.29	12737.39	66518.62	28016.53	0.00	4387.00
5004.17	25890.90	14893.74	53618.56	48644.13	2756.00	4379.90
4200.17	24413.49	13966.35	47458.39	39633.97	0.00	1235.40
3363.88	25486.14	15749.80	60259.19	38586.63	7510.00	14796.01
6279.40	24979.08	9991.02	32257.09	35040.55	0.00	1414.00
12089.33	60952.73	31124.87	152471.74	106791.66	8212.20	39893.00
6850.75	43573.51	24830.27	155237.07	134619.57	0.00	26160.36
7844.81	37447.21	21814.90	110632.52	40469.76	15840.00	10735.00
6538.66	35849.46	19147.34	119543.33	49207.86	5380.00	3365.20
5132.35	26539.59	12131.62	112453.74	47078.76	0.00	23705.63
14695.31	104545.35	46076.82	212384.45	118294.35	400.00	45456.32
13050.92	68845.38	44347.39	164699.71	91169.69	2883.00	12036.30
6607.44	32791.26	18266.37	115299.31	45724.18	8377.00	7169.00
7280.34	37635.88	21494.84	121244.32	56732.26	617.00	26341.90
11549.90	54743.27	32421.22	217964.93	137511.87	4627.00	75361.37
6608.80	27591.37	14041.74	119976.63	41605.35	13820.16	52438.82
332.00	2943.50	2368.50	21291.00	7240.00	0.00	0.00
2412.00	15837.77	10770.77	60656.69	25039.58	0.00	0.00
8724.45	40185.25	21057.46	173287.65	63161.63	1617.00	16685.99
4570.93	25971.54	14892.86	107813.53	31567.55	0.00	14917.64
6371.72	31259.69	13266.01	104283.69	33562.96	14093.00	11242.29
270.00	9093.86	5168.52	28856.68	920.77	0.00	19317.70
4101.30	29028.40	14068.19	62878.06	27916.20	0.00	15104.04
3329.71	16717.17	11270.73	57195.43	26386.89	1323.00	7771.00
1097.20	6067.00	4316.57	16432.62	12594.64	0.00	1670.00
1011.00	6543.11	2616.98	29292.32	10895.43	0.00	26686.28
4314.88	12001.76	7568.48	42609.33	35586.59	0.00	0.00

特殊教育学校办学条件(二)

Condition of School Buildings in Special Education Schools (2)

地区 Region	占地面积(平方米) Areas of School Sites(m^2)			图书(册) Books & Magazines in Libraries (Volume)
	合计 Total	其中:of Which:		
		绿化用地面积 Green Areas	运动场地面积 Sports Areas	
总　计 Total	**20557725.68**	**4453134.04**	**5080937.79**	**9474607**
北　京 Beijing	240761.23	31307.33	66710.92	274568
天　津 Tianjin	183954.60	20404.84	54439.20	102820
河　北 Hebei	1353976.91	214127.84	336716.90	644637
山　西 Shanxi	463913.74	61651.76	98097.08	226239
内蒙古 Inner Mongolia	537802.25	105902.00	156694.00	153582
辽　宁 Liaoning	599123.41	72829.75	166833.46	518528
吉　林 Jilin	531913.85	94271.28	157706.49	175083
黑龙江 Heilongjiang	566722.45	71630.13	198812.49	242919
上　海 Shanghai	268992.26	83277.00	65308.00	362338
江　苏 Jiangsu	1293005.70	366449.34	299958.78	736361
浙　江 Zhejiang	982275.61	305947.91	221710.87	380987
安　徽 Anhui	889058.75	201706.89	207176.28	310427
福　建 Fujian	786420.69	203900.48	215921.61	378228
江　西 Jiangxi	744014.15	169756.75	223669.84	189195
山　东 Shandong	1949082.66	429710.45	482135.92	917282
河　南 Henan	1208097.01	204922.53	245640.29	543866
湖　北 Hubei	726049.08	194871.21	173423.55	251903
湖　南 Hunan	971523.19	335073.00	154987.00	297713
广　东 Guangdong	1257962.94	322990.09	311456.69	626300
广　西 Guangxi	620553.77	106885.55	143848.14	293643
海　南 Hainan	128811.50	38033.42	25807.00	56649
重　庆 Chongqing	274835.67	54940.17	56180.07	94920
四　川 Sichuan	780762.08	148817.84	234324.23	465527
贵　州 Guizhou	721672.61	140633.37	220187.50	250574
云　南 Yunnan	742681.81	162905.95	162808.34	393459
西　藏 Tibet	125937.34	22420.01	25974.01	33418
陕　西 Shaanxi	510579.63	75435.94	91927.45	221110
甘　肃 Gansu	339741.84	60627.15	110134.48	101200
青　海 Qinghai	130697.50	23275.00	28752.00	46204
宁　夏 Ningxia	183026.47	32665.84	49917.51	60089
新　疆 Xinjiang	443774.98	95763.22	93677.69	124838

学前教育基本情况(总计)
Basic Statistics of Pre-primary Education(Total)

地　区 Region	园数(所) Kindergartens		班数(个) Classes	入园(班)人数(人) Entrants	在园(班)人数(人) Enrolment	离园(班)人数(人) Leavers
	合计 Total	其中:少数民族幼儿园 of Which:Minorities				
总　计 Total	**254950**	**7659**	**1612901**	**19379530**	**46001393**	**16526663**
北　京 Beijing	1604	9	15810	177354	445535	105651
天　津 Tianjin	1997	6	10572	94306	261535	89941
河　北 Hebei	14368	52	90571	1020380	2374688	917128
山　西 Shanxi	6937	0	44019	426423	1027546	354862
内蒙古 Inner Mongolia	3845	416	25666	234981	640024	203426
辽　宁 Liaoning	10195	54	44771	324623	953947	290407
吉　林 Jilin	4053	52	21417	217451	455305	174390
黑龙江 Heilongjiang	5888	49	25577	259411	559283	202440
上　海 Shanghai	1591	2	19319	202469	572744	174457
江　苏 Jiangsu	6982	1	78141	898199	2605312	850873
浙　江 Zhejiang	8645	1	67142	651498	1958002	618749
安　徽 Anhui	8257	8	67745	901586	2008554	734265
福　建 Fujian	8041	13	55384	638209	1654945	527661
江　西 Jiangxi	14952	3	67477	680354	1609422	597919
山　东 Shandong	19020	42	101473	1051902	2772719	1005427
河　南 Henan	20613	53	153489	1516523	4249250	1588706
湖　北 Hubei	7825	8	57607	594869	1760387	668141
湖　南 Hunan	14670	209	78509	862373	2289930	949433
广　东 Guangdong	18048	4	144808	2024707	4414144	1435015
广　西 Guangxi	11787	14	73153	1094606	2139862	811151
海　南 Hainan	2307	36	13103	160692	364338	127936
重　庆 Chongqing	5210	0	32007	412896	958667	349272
四　川 Sichuan	13243	554	86054	1339272	2625168	1033387
贵　州 Guizhou	9772	273	47450	738023	1534207	604508
云　南 Yunnan	8286	32	44467	747406	1394298	600169
西　藏 Tibet	1239	415	3952	62534	106346	49888
陕　西 Shaanxi	7810	6	50579	681277	1450523	518973
甘　肃 Gansu	7122	149	34422	372875	929708	350549
青　海 Qinghai	1735	707	7410	118047	207248	84662
宁　夏 Ningxia	1130	23	7267	114298	230515	97294
新　疆 Xinjiang	7778	4468	43540	759986	1447241	409983

学前教育基本情况(城区)
Basic Statistics of Pre-primary Education (Urban Area)

地　区 Region	园数(所) Kindergartens 合计 Total	园数(所) Kindergartens 其中:少数民族幼儿园 of Which: Minorities	班数(个) Classes	入园(班)人数(人) Entrants	在园(班)人数(人) Enrolment	离园(班)人数(人) Leavers
总　计 Total	**78961**	**348**	**593017**	**6439559**	**17068501**	**5391642**
北　京 Beijing	1232	8	13330	149872	378718	89194
天　津 Tianjin	1323	6	7630	68976	190571	60308
河　北 Hebei	2679	25	19884	219526	559038	187629
山　西 Shanxi	1663	0	12928	139412	335307	109548
内蒙古 Inner Mongolia	1217	33	9478	90381	251765	74146
辽　宁 Liaoning	5720	27	28947	175523	598746	155767
吉　林 Jilin	1853	38	10555	95798	229774	79825
黑龙江 Heilongjiang	2570	7	12800	117028	275326	96223
上　海 Shanghai	1321	2	16412	170873	486902	147338
江　苏 Jiangsu	3239	1	36882	425485	1226494	378820
浙　江 Zhejiang	3907	0	35542	352434	1034831	316879
安　徽 Anhui	1826	2	15855	183510	475426	154678
福　建 Fujian	2828	1	21609	247190	660958	202666
江　西 Jiangxi	2798	0	17345	160000	424150	137356
山　东 Shandong	5847	17	40268	416845	1148592	371519
河　南 Henan	4223	19	34014	305053	935533	292152
湖　北 Hubei	3053	0	23591	243514	715581	246971
湖　南 Hunan	4002	5	23625	235812	657012	223027
广　东 Guangdong	10216	0	85895	1028092	2629441	813211
广　西 Guangxi	2584	1	18091	232214	530850	161111
海　南 Hainan	948	0	5691	69004	153788	51904
重　庆 Chongqing	2480	0	15874	193788	476952	152511
四　川 Sichuan	3462	5	26990	339064	818092	258506
贵　州 Guizhou	1677	0	10901	135354	320009	111242
云　南 Yunnan	1459	6	11567	154038	370444	126502
西　藏 Tibet	96	5	775	14233	31238	10216
陕　西 Shaanxi	1957	5	16510	205351	500186	166477
甘　肃 Gansu	1227	25	8063	85181	242161	81234
青　海 Qinghai	236	13	1768	31281	58117	20751
宁　夏 Ningxia	344	5	2822	36519	91059	34434
新　疆 Xinjiang	974	92	7375	118208	261440	79497

学前教育基本情况(城乡结合区)
Basic Statistics of Pre-primary Education (Urban-rural Transitional Area)

地 区 Region	园数(所) Kindergartens		班数(个) Classes	入园(班)人数(人) Entrants	在园(班)人数(人) Enrolment	离园(班)人数(人) Leavers
	合计 Total	其中:少数民族幼儿园 of Which: Minorities				
总 计 Total	**15577**	**77**	**104615**	**1175733**	**3004454**	**970424**
北 京 Beijing	126	0	981	11587	26394	5878
天 津 Tianjin	237	1	770	4737	15457	7409
河 北 Hebei	826	3	5263	57899	141155	48756
山 西 Shanxi	342	0	2131	22793	51547	16538
内蒙古 Inner Mongolia	56	1	351	2843	8240	2317
辽 宁 Liaoning	558	1	2162	13442	43088	12583
吉 林 Jilin	96	1	454	3832	9750	2795
黑龙江 Heilongjiang	146	0	668	6702	13933	5314
上 海 Shanghai	134	0	1559	16754	49164	16408
江 苏 Jiangsu	459	0	4223	51915	140630	44502
浙 江 Zhejiang	1232	0	9239	88229	267445	85406
安 徽 Anhui	239	0	2127	21913	58039	19800
福 建 Fujian	567	0	4031	45999	119283	38228
江 西 Jiangxi	584	0	2794	25601	62834	21472
山 东 Shandong	1949	4	10743	101282	289417	94680
河 南 Henan	841	1	5856	50321	155407	51001
湖 北 Hubei	553	0	3760	36610	109542	38179
湖 南 Hunan	532	2	2833	29754	80627	26842
广 东 Guangdong	3361	0	27375	344343	847332	263581
广 西 Guangxi	537	1	3226	39188	89864	29570
海 南 Hainan	83	0	481	5777	13077	4229
重 庆 Chongqing	241	0	1159	13512	33423	11081
四 川 Sichuan	496	1	3415	40994	100190	30578
贵 州 Guizhou	274	0	1510	23917	44878	14564
云 南 Yunnan	377	1	2628	39964	81076	30710
西 藏 Tibet	10	2	43	759	1298	481
陕 西 Shaanxi	392	0	2657	33616	77765	26007
甘 肃 Gansu	125	2	736	8042	20735	6700
青 海 Qinghai	33	0	174	3741	5175	1591
宁 夏 Ningxia	19	0	162	2266	5163	1778
新 疆 Xinjiang	152	56	1104	27401	42526	11446

学前教育基本情况(镇区)

Basic Statistics of Pre-primary Education (Counties & Towns Area)

地　区 Region	园数(所) Kindergartens		班数(个) Classes	入园(班)人数(人) Entrants	在园(班)人数(人) Enrolment	离园(班)人数(人) Leavers
	合计 Total	其中:少数民族幼儿园 of Which: Minorities				
总　计 Total	**85807**	**1312**	**576473**	**7500240**	**17575032**	**6435136**
北　京 Beijing	140	1	1225	14118	34497	8421
天　津 Tianjin	245	0	1394	12178	35279	12550
河　北 Hebei	4902	14	32783	401152	907119	345683
山　西 Shanxi	2246	0	15908	188138	445831	154127
内蒙古 Inner Mongolia	1614	193	11331	110274	299246	98022
辽　宁 Liaoning	2331	21	9813	94187	228617	82630
吉　林 Jilin	1513	12	7514	85633	165526	65232
黑龙江 Heilongjiang	2068	12	9065	107348	211837	79097
上　海 Shanghai	212	0	2382	26124	70111	22071
江　苏 Jiangsu	2538	0	31169	361852	1057356	361067
浙　江 Zhejiang	2776	1	22032	214669	661959	215656
安　徽 Anhui	3402	3	29329	397949	903518	325657
福　建 Fujian	3161	1	20744	255679	659678	208361
江　西 Jiangxi	5821	0	30187	319036	771473	281965
山　东 Shandong	5493	11	34206	394510	1001516	376133
河　南 Henan	7283	23	54356	563549	1586833	590817
湖　北 Hubei	2781	3	21095	224759	688416	268687
湖　南 Hunan	6340	137	35314	400077	1101776	470961
广　东 Guangdong	4721	0	36646	623430	1163564	375631
广　西 Guangxi	4782	4	29509	455145	930692	332408
海　南 Hainan	998	18	5462	65556	160975	56072
重　庆 Chongqing	1837	0	11590	165370	370421	146690
四　川 Sichuan	5416	105	37534	663096	1255713	490051
贵　州 Guizhou	3536	102	21182	327291	725843	285381
云　南 Yunnan	2147	4	14113	248226	495074	190893
西　藏 Tibet	144	69	756	16024	25886	11650
陕　西 Shaanxi	3473	1	22960	340936	700105	256416
甘　肃 Gansu	1830	13	11933	154269	391818	146509
青　海 Qinghai	346	117	2166	42036	73584	30299
宁　夏 Ningxia	326	5	2458	42598	84628	34562
新　疆 Xinjiang	1385	442	10317	185031	366141	111437

学前教育基本情况(镇乡结合区)
Basic Statistics of Pre-primary Education (County-town Transitional Area)

地　区 Region	园数(所) Kindergartens 合计 Total	园数(所) Kindergartens 其中:少数民族幼儿园 of Which: Minorities	班数(个) Classes	入园(班)人数(人) Entrants	在园(班)人数(人) Enrolment	离园(班)人数(人) Leavers
总　计 Total	**25947**	**362**	**159294**	**1976286**	**4615523**	**1716483**
北　京 Beijing	38	0	336	3552	9145	2358
天　津 Tianjin	140	0	804	7616	20956	7483
河　北 Hebei	2635	5	16434	189750	442867	176163
山　西 Shanxi	834	0	5283	52700	134421	45140
内蒙古 Inner Mongolia	159	16	1050	10581	25201	9222
辽　宁 Liaoning	388	0	1305	11230	27338	10149
吉　林 Jilin	146	4	675	6519	14675	6217
黑龙江 Heilongjiang	244	2	945	9263	20817	8153
上　海 Shanghai	51	0	500	5335	15230	4828
江　苏 Jiangsu	802	0	8435	91041	278295	96450
浙　江 Zhejiang	1138	1	7659	73841	225916	74248
安　徽 Anhui	631	1	5317	73416	157105	58914
福　建 Fujian	1070	1	6386	76044	194833	61685
江　西 Jiangxi	1539	0	6432	68201	152536	58857
山　东 Shandong	2860	9	15308	172609	427100	164281
河　南 Henan	2933	8	20425	194561	560993	207677
湖　北 Hubei	733	0	5081	51213	156005	63884
湖　南 Hunan	1680	16	8437	100688	258866	114221
广　东 Guangdong	1760	0	13578	231466	417303	133140
广　西 Guangxi	1125	0	6717	107915	198754	82841
海　南 Hainan	157	0	831	9863	23762	8064
重　庆 Chongqing	400	0	2152	26883	64575	24830
四　川 Sichuan	1159	17	6339	99659	191053	77276
贵　州 Guizhou	882	45	4157	68383	139659	54498
云　南 Yunnan	616	0	3587	58948	117369	46625
西　藏 Tibet	8	3	41	1124	1805	839
陕　西 Shaanxi	882	0	5606	81912	158667	60115
甘　肃 Gansu	456	5	2467	33042	79352	28423
青　海 Qinghai	95	28	505	9243	15886	7490
宁　夏 Ningxia	51	1	352	7604	12238	4852
新　疆 Xinjiang	335	200	2150	42084	72801	17560

学前教育基本情况(乡村)
Basic Statistics of Pre-primary Education (Rural Area)

地　区 Region	园数(所) Kindergartens 合计 Total	园数(所) Kindergartens 其中:少数民族幼儿园 of Which: Minorities	班数(个) Classes	入园(班)人数(人) Entrants	在园(班)人数(人) Enrolment	离园(班)人数(人) Leavers
总　计 Total	**90182**	**5999**	**443411**	**5439731**	**11357860**	**4699885**
北　京 Beijing	232	0	1255	13364	32320	8036
天　津 Tianjin	429	0	1548	13152	35685	17083
河　北 Hebei	6787	13	37904	399702	908531	383816
山　西 Shanxi	3028	0	15183	98873	246408	91187
内蒙古 Inner Mongolia	1014	190	4857	34326	89013	31258
辽　宁 Liaoning	2144	6	6011	54913	126584	52010
吉　林 Jilin	687	2	3348	36020	60005	29333
黑龙江 Heilongjiang	1250	30	3712	35035	72120	27120
上　海 Shanghai	58	0	525	5472	15731	5048
江　苏 Jiangsu	1205	0	10090	110862	321462	110986
浙　江 Zhejiang	1962	0	9568	84395	261212	86214
安　徽 Anhui	3029	3	22561	320127	629610	253930
福　建 Fujian	2052	11	13031	135340	334309	116634
江　西 Jiangxi	6333	3	19945	201318	413799	178598
山　东 Shandong	7680	14	26999	240547	622611	257775
河　南 Henan	9107	11	65119	647921	1726884	705737
湖　北 Hubei	1991	5	12921	126596	356390	152483
湖　南 Hunan	4328	67	19570	226484	531142	255445
广　东 Guangdong	3111	4	22267	373185	621139	246173
广　西 Guangxi	4421	9	25553	407247	678320	317632
海　南 Hainan	361	18	1950	26132	49575	19960
重　庆 Chongqing	893	0	4543	53738	111294	50071
四　川 Sichuan	4365	444	21530	337112	551363	284830
贵　州 Guizhou	4559	171	15367	275378	488355	207885
云　南 Yunnan	4680	22	18787	345142	528780	282774
西　藏 Tibet	999	341	2421	32277	49222	28022
陕　西 Shaanxi	2380	0	11109	134990	250232	96080
甘　肃 Gansu	4065	111	14426	133425	295729	122806
青　海 Qinghai	1153	577	3476	44730	75547	33612
宁　夏 Ningxia	460	13	1987	35181	54828	28298
新　疆 Xinjiang	5419	3934	25848	456747	819660	219049

学前教育中女幼儿数

Number of Female Children in Pre-primary Education

单位:人
unit:person

地　区 Region	入园(班)人数 Entrants	在园(班)人数 Enrolment	离园(班)人数 Leavers
总　计 Total	**9125023**	**21490692**	**7814108**
北　京 Beijing	85396	215035	51011
天　津 Tianjin	45079	124127	42890
河　北 Hebei	483708	1119043	426953
山　西 Shanxi	205488	495647	173682
内蒙古 Inner Mongolia	112351	303953	98367
辽　宁 Liaoning	155219	449679	139446
吉　林 Jilin	104804	218294	86118
黑龙江 Heilongjiang	125320	267630	99735
上　海 Shanghai	96549	271857	82301
江　苏 Jiangsu	425910	1227414	408384
浙　江 Zhejiang	305630	911930	294941
安　徽 Anhui	421125	933852	350825
福　建 Fujian	292540	755453	246048
江　西 Jiangxi	310036	727934	270371
山　东 Shandong	485212	1275818	471064
河　南 Henan	722750	2001906	759594
湖　北 Hubei	275501	811368	311016
湖　南 Hunan	406894	1070670	458445
广　东 Guangdong	937192	2012094	622658
广　西 Guangxi	504372	972946	387216
海　南 Hainan	73835	163236	58458
重　庆 Chongqing	197078	453729	173810
四　川 Sichuan	639643	1252249	491992
贵　州 Guizhou	342506	703955	288691
云　南 Yunnan	355237	662516	290648
西　藏 Tibet	30420	51643	24676
陕　西 Shaanxi	324602	687745	245990
甘　肃 Gansu	178485	439461	171066
青　海 Qinghai	57366	99854	42246
宁　夏 Ningxia	54568	108361	46667
新　疆 Xinjiang	370207	701293	198799

幼儿园教职工数(总计)
Number of Educational Personnel in Kindergarten (Total)

单位:人
unit:person

地区 Region	教职工数 Educational Personnel						代课教师 Substitute Teachers	兼任教师 Part-time Teachers
	合计 Total	园长 Kindergarten Heads	专任教师 Full-time Teachers	保健医 Health Physician	保育员 Caretaker	其他 Other		
总 计 Total	**4192850**	**279927**	**2432138**	**101341**	**813673**	**565771**	**173360**	**41782**
北 京 Beijing	69100	2388	37903	2902	11447	14460	0	899
天 津 Tianjin	28458	2219	16713	892	4275	4359	2948	200
河 北 Hebei	175010	14728	114532	3895	24136	17719	15053	321
山 西 Shanxi	86508	6989	54796	1743	11435	11545	17259	1259
内蒙古 Inner Mongolia	69529	3766	42833	1740	10179	11011	2954	211
辽 宁 Liaoning	114466	10522	69577	1894	17524	14949	299	1038
吉 林 Jilin	55084	4705	30026	2158	11233	6962	728	364
黑龙江 Heilongjiang	66660	6571	35541	3251	11707	9590	2438	447
上 海 Shanghai	66588	2081	40106	2368	11573	10460	1584	200
江 苏 Jiangsu	255638	9855	147495	7049	61927	29312	14517	600
浙 江 Zhejiang	231543	9019	125042	7434	49602	40446	0	306
安 徽 Anhui	137141	9779	83024	3655	27015	13668	8017	884
福 建 Fujian	148157	9264	85310	3335	29704	20544	10080	287
江 西 Jiangxi	125150	12520	81868	1187	19380	10195	4504	3003
山 东 Shandong	257367	20966	173948	4332	30166	27955	20271	1604
河 南 Henan	332251	24782	197753	9083	62667	37966	22990	1652
湖 北 Hubei	165810	11295	84613	4373	39039	26490	9314	1234
湖 南 Hunan	212635	14819	103319	5634	56780	32083	4845	767
广 东 Guangdong	515112	26678	281656	13687	111825	81266	190	938
广 西 Guangxi	157053	13704	82306	3108	35311	22624	2673	2555
海 南 Hainan	41190	3137	19997	1530	9314	7212	190	292
重 庆 Chongqing	86163	6373	44327	2122	20601	12740	3477	534
四 川 Sichuan	202955	15526	117052	3419	37697	29261	8416	6927
贵 州 Guizhou	141086	8187	83376	2241	34751	12531	1612	4181
云 南 Yunnan	97635	7395	58893	1723	14662	14962	533	4090
西 藏 Tibet	5359	383	4254	25	346	351	455	11
陕 西 Shaanxi	155012	9193	90300	4239	28981	22299	3389	155
甘 肃 Gansu	62514	5422	43975	968	5918	6231	2521	4029
青 海 Qinghai	18703	1348	10663	226	3276	3190	693	74
宁 夏 Ningxia	20767	1448	11410	462	3401	4046	2134	177
新 疆 Xinjiang	92206	4865	59530	666	17801	9344	9276	2543

幼儿园教职工数(城区)

Number of Educational Personnel in Kindergarten (Urban Area)

单位:人
unit:person

地区 Region	教职工数 Educational Personnel						代课教师 Substitute Teachers	兼任教师 Part-time Teachers
	合计 Total	园长 Kindergarten Heads	专任教师 Full-time Teachers	保健医 Health Physician	保育员 Caretaker	其他 Other		
总 计 Total	**2069988**	**110954**	**1150623**	**59159**	**419270**	**329982**	**41039**	**8108**
北 京 Beijing	60979	1962	33018	2628	10379	12992	0	575
天 津 Tianjin	24925	1649	14472	793	3891	4120	1154	153
河 北 Hebei	61979	3810	37116	1659	10156	9238	2820	36
山 西 Shanxi	41833	2399	24483	1118	6393	7440	4996	904
内蒙古 Inner Mongolia	31891	1226	18935	945	5206	5579	1106	97
辽 宁 Liaoning	86158	6791	50085	1585	14968	12729	70	207
吉 林 Jilin	31431	2360	16729	1189	6760	4393	267	177
黑龙江 Heilongjiang	38153	3137	19699	1957	7017	6343	1101	234
上 海 Shanghai	56648	1742	34287	2047	9629	8943	1326	197
江 苏 Jiangsu	138531	5222	76482	4144	33586	19097	3627	79
浙 江 Zhejiang	128768	4219	70123	4231	28206	21989	0	63
安 徽 Anhui	47262	2794	27046	1374	10095	5953	1922	182
福 建 Fujian	73087	3943	40896	1997	15893	10358	2694	55
江 西 Jiangxi	43522	3272	27896	580	7761	4013	749	605
山 东 Shandong	131745	8000	84587	2769	18350	18039	4993	571
河 南 Henan	113033	6114	65852	3203	22241	15623	5160	410
湖 北 Hubei	85419	5226	42960	2581	19643	15009	2761	250
湖 南 Hunan	82311	4635	39529	2528	21969	13650	597	379
广 东 Guangdong	350491	16875	185990	10300	76290	61036	53	408
广 西 Guangxi	56575	3873	30198	1393	12443	8668	364	713
海 南 Hainan	19658	1410	9888	804	4261	3295	125	175
重 庆 Chongqing	55185	3615	28293	1576	13095	8606	986	294
四 川 Sichuan	98167	5615	53249	2262	20359	16682	904	120
贵 州 Guizhou	39936	2170	21775	984	10064	4943	113	135
云 南 Yunnan	40340	1987	23338	1006	7054	6955	72	357
西 藏 Tibet	2426	173	1552	24	337	340	9	0
陕 西 Shaanxi	63068	2899	33734	2073	12726	11636	403	22
甘 肃 Gansu	24665	1631	15377	560	3286	3811	549	630
青 海 Qinghai	6513	392	3485	107	1182	1347	101	38
宁 夏 Ningxia	11020	634	5927	248	1879	2332	522	8
新 疆 Xinjiang	24269	1179	13622	494	4151	4823	1495	34

幼儿园教职工数(城乡结合区)
Number of Educational Personnel in Kindergarten (Urban-rural Transitional Area)

单位:人
unit:person

地　区 Region	教职工数 Educational Personnel						代课教师 Substitute Teachers	兼任教师 Part-time Teachers
	合计 Total	园长 Kindergarten Heads	专任教师 Full-time Teachers	保健医 Health Physician	保育员 Caretaker	其他 Other		
总　计 Total	**333633**	**19618**	**184179**	**9220**	**68139**	**52477**	**6947**	**1237**
北　京 Beijing	3976	169	2041	173	758	835	0	79
天　津 Tianjin	1807	207	927	67	353	253	48	3
河　北 Hebei	11928	933	7329	304	1893	1469	875	8
山　西 Shanxi	5131	396	3134	124	660	817	1051	256
内蒙古 Inner Mongolia	1121	55	619	31	205	211	120	0
辽　宁 Liaoning	5211	553	3110	69	828	651	5	11
吉　林 Jilin	1362	113	711	58	287	193	2	1
黑龙江 Heilongjiang	2056	168	1049	95	341	403	98	9
上　海 Shanghai	5765	152	2906	205	1357	1145	88	12
江　苏 Jiangsu	14622	596	8190	435	3586	1815	312	5
浙　江 Zhejiang	30806	1300	16201	1133	6536	5636	0	11
安　徽 Anhui	4535	294	2667	133	948	493	163	28
福　建 Fujian	11335	691	6404	284	2390	1566	461	6
江　西 Jiangxi	5584	546	3643	54	875	466	123	132
山　东 Shandong	30024	2299	20175	527	3539	3484	1643	120
河　南 Henan	16533	1065	9229	486	3505	2248	625	56
湖　北 Hubei	12176	825	5969	365	2926	2091	411	49
湖　南 Hunan	9499	587	4456	300	2566	1590	96	54
广　东 Guangdong	107565	5209	56991	3043	23672	18650	4	141
广　西 Guangxi	8436	714	4535	177	1781	1229	33	44
海　南 Hainan	1561	121	707	69	403	261	0	7
重　庆 Chongqing	3561	291	1715	89	912	554	24	25
四　川 Sichuan	12370	766	6207	383	2760	2254	53	2
贵　州 Guizhou	4880	298	2743	126	1171	542	7	75
云　南 Yunnan	7332	436	4343	165	1209	1179	2	67
西　藏 Tibet	78	6	55	1	8	8	1	0
陕　西 Shaanxi	8847	485	4680	242	1886	1554	115	10
甘　肃 Gansu	2049	145	1416	38	219	231	39	10
青　海 Qinghai	542	44	244	5	140	109	8	4
宁　夏 Ningxia	502	35	250	9	90	118	47	0
新　疆 Xinjiang	2439	119	1533	30	335	422	493	12

幼儿园教职工数(镇区)

Number of Educational Personnel in Kindergarten (Counties & Towns Area)

单位:人
unit:person

地 区 Region	教职工数 Educational Personnel						代课教师 Substitute Teachers	兼任教师 Part-time Teachers
	合计 Total	园长 Kindergarten Heads	专任教师 Full-time Teachers	保健医 Health Physician	保育员 Caretaker	其他 Other		
总 计 Total	**1443717**	**97107**	**876958**	**29153**	**273141**	**167358**	**80893**	**16889**
北 京 Beijing	4198	198	2538	142	552	768	0	146
天 津 Tianjin	1542	224	965	44	166	143	1015	13
河 北 Hebei	71197	5563	47620	1581	10172	6261	5218	105
山 西 Shanxi	32063	2424	22204	494	3867	3074	8319	219
内蒙古 Inner Mongolia	30070	1610	19325	659	4026	4450	1277	73
辽 宁 Liaoning	18625	2304	13032	195	1677	1417	162	536
吉 林 Jilin	18504	1697	10396	738	3578	2095	396	147
黑龙江 Heilongjiang	21750	2238	12072	962	3764	2714	989	145
上 海 Shanghai	8114	266	4836	252	1548	1212	221	2
江 苏 Jiangsu	93371	3513	56854	2272	22431	8301	7625	484
浙 江 Zhejiang	73422	3006	39709	2210	15563	12934	0	182
安 徽 Anhui	62223	4202	39018	1549	11870	5584	4008	408
福 建 Fujian	55804	3586	33236	1018	10523	7441	5392	164
江 西 Jiangxi	58818	5558	39546	456	8816	4442	2144	1462
山 东 Shandong	80334	6282	57800	1047	8100	7105	8855	820
河 南 Henan	122354	8902	75138	3136	22271	12907	10480	732
湖 北 Hubei	56496	3911	29921	1189	13364	8111	4536	571
湖 南 Hunan	93298	6275	46747	2116	24936	13224	3121	275
广 东 Guangdong	118441	6511	68942	2474	25634	14880	85	293
广 西 Guangxi	68049	5611	35971	1181	15845	9441	1797	1188
海 南 Hainan	16684	1293	7908	555	3972	2956	51	79
重 庆 Chongqing	25255	2032	13370	449	6036	3368	2089	145
四 川 Sichuan	80859	6397	50300	869	13665	9628	4461	2601
贵 州 Guizhou	66977	3496	40708	899	16160	5714	875	2105
云 南 Yunnan	35173	2231	22439	496	4739	5268	230	1437
西 藏 Tibet	1260	91	1156	0	6	7	101	11
陕 西 Shaanxi	66837	4043	42430	1510	11447	7407	2333	127
甘 肃 Gansu	24118	1792	18459	304	1915	1648	1010	1936
青 海 Qinghai	6324	355	3800	65	1119	985	369	15
宁 夏 Ningxia	6857	457	3909	146	1137	1208	1131	88
新 疆 Xinjiang	24700	1039	16609	145	4242	2665	2603	380

幼儿园教职工数(镇乡结合区)
Number of Educational Personnel in Kindergarten (County-town Transitional Area)

单位:人
unit:person

地区 Region	教职工数 Educational Personnel						代课教师 Substitute Teachers	兼任教师 Part-time Teachers
	合计 Total	园长 Kindergarten Heads	专任教师 Full-time Teachers	保健医 Health Physician	保育员 Caretaker	其他 Other		
总　计 Total	**369634**	**27797**	**221470**	**7776**	**69575**	**43016**	**21886**	**3820**
北　京 Beijing	954	45	660	22	110	117	0	47
天　津 Tianjin	810	121	534	22	60	73	630	4
河　北 Hebei	32083	2795	21733	658	4331	2566	2531	91
山　西 Shanxi	9492	816	6461	148	1103	964	2512	66
内蒙古 Inner Mongolia	2519	157	1557	48	402	355	102	12
辽　宁 Liaoning	2186	355	1471	27	198	135	44	55
吉　林 Jilin	1512	151	836	63	265	197	26	13
黑龙江 Heilongjiang	2118	254	1211	100	305	248	107	12
上　海 Shanghai	1668	60	891	64	371	282	34	0
江　苏 Jiangsu	24817	1037	15050	624	5900	2206	1833	121
浙　江 Zhejiang	24211	1230	12662	807	5124	4388	0	114
安　徽 Anhui	9587	718	6034	248	1726	861	537	58
福　建 Fujian	15933	1146	9095	270	3131	2291	1512	4
江　西 Jiangxi	10538	1226	6842	81	1501	888	386	388
山　东 Shandong	33246	3025	24175	396	3170	2480	4041	273
河　南 Henan	42407	3442	24930	1148	8216	4671	2926	231
湖　北 Hubei	12439	921	6455	270	3006	1787	959	134
湖　南 Hunan	21086	1654	10057	478	5778	3119	804	42
广　东 Guangdong	42241	2365	24348	968	9247	5313	23	90
广　西 Guangxi	12870	1244	6595	238	2974	1819	226	186
海　南 Hainan	2540	192	1175	73	584	516	6	2
重　庆 Chongqing	4651	425	2325	82	1134	685	277	33
四　川 Sichuan	13863	1312	8077	192	2479	1803	455	611
贵　州 Guizhou	11949	728	7157	160	2869	1035	171	428
云　南 Yunnan	8226	627	4953	100	1238	1308	60	222
西　藏 Tibet	63	6	56	0	0	1	24	0
陕　西 Shaanxi	15278	1034	9076	391	2783	1994	453	56
甘　肃 Gansu	4501	391	3352	58	387	313	236	369
青　海 Qinghai	1245	83	744	15	225	178	82	0
宁　夏 Ningxia	686	52	376	16	126	116	213	9
新　疆 Xinjiang	3915	185	2582	9	832	307	676	149

幼儿园教职工数(乡村)
Number of Educational Personnel in Kindergarten (Rural Area)

单位:人
unit:person

地区 Region	教职工数 Educational Personnel						代课教师 Substitute Teachers	兼任教师 Part-time Teachers
	合计 Total	园长 Kindergarten Heads	专任教师 Full-time Teachers	保健医 Health Physician	保育员 Caretaker	其他 Other		
总　计 Total	**679145**	**71866**	**404557**	**13029**	**121262**	**68431**	**51428**	**16785**
北　京 Beijing	3923	228	2347	132	516	700	0	178
天　津 Tianjin	1991	346	1276	55	218	96	779	34
河　北 Hebei	41834	5355	29796	655	3808	2220	7015	180
山　西 Shanxi	12612	2166	8109	131	1175	1031	3944	136
内蒙古 Inner Mongolia	7568	930	4573	136	947	982	571	41
辽　宁 Liaoning	9683	1427	6460	114	879	803	67	295
吉　林 Jilin	5149	648	2901	231	895	474	65	40
黑龙江 Heilongjiang	6757	1196	3770	332	926	533	348	68
上　海 Shanghai	1826	73	983	69	396	305	37	1
江　苏 Jiangsu	23736	1120	14159	633	5910	1914	3265	37
浙　江 Zhejiang	29353	1794	15210	993	5833	5523	0	61
安　徽 Anhui	27656	2783	16960	732	5050	2131	2087	294
福　建 Fujian	19266	1735	11178	320	3288	2745	1994	68
江　西 Jiangxi	22810	3690	14426	151	2803	1740	1611	936
山　东 Shandong	45288	6684	31561	516	3716	2811	6423	213
河　南 Henan	96864	9766	56763	2744	18155	9436	7350	510
湖　北 Hubei	23895	2158	11732	603	6032	3370	2017	413
湖　南 Hunan	37026	3909	17043	990	9875	5209	1127	113
广　东 Guangdong	46180	3292	26724	913	9901	5350	52	237
广　西 Guangxi	32429	4220	16137	534	7023	4515	512	654
海　南 Hainan	4848	434	2201	171	1081	961	14	38
重　庆 Chongqing	5723	726	2664	97	1470	766	402	95
四　川 Sichuan	23929	3514	13503	288	3673	2951	3051	4206
贵　州 Guizhou	34173	2521	20893	358	8527	1874	624	1941
云　南 Yunnan	22122	3177	13116	221	2869	2739	231	2296
西　藏 Tibet	1673	119	1546	1	3	4	345	0
陕　西 Shaanxi	25107	2251	14136	656	4808	3256	653	6
甘　肃 Gansu	13731	1999	10139	104	717	772	962	1463
青　海 Qinghai	5866	601	3378	54	975	858	223	21
宁　夏 Ningxia	2890	357	1574	68	385	506	481	81
新　疆 Xinjiang	43237	2647	29299	27	9408	1856	5178	2129

幼儿园女
Number of Female Educational

地区 Region	教职工数		
	合计 Total	园长 Kindergarten Heads	专任教师 Full-time Teachers
总 计 Total	**3862781**	**252329**	**2378291**
北 京 Beijing	63221	2279	37029
天 津 Tianjin	26196	1979	16220
河 北 Hebei	161594	12062	111157
山 西 Shanxi	80419	6111	54053
内蒙古 Inner Mongolia	62456	3338	40899
辽 宁 Liaoning	107533	9773	68700
吉 林 Jilin	50929	4361	29490
黑龙江 Heilongjiang	61011	6003	34639
上 海 Shanghai	62812	2054	39539
江 苏 Jiangsu	240855	9482	144692
浙 江 Zhejiang	213871	8711	123515
安 徽 Anhui	127862	8592	81713
福 建 Fujian	138138	9141	84775
江 西 Jiangxi	118657	11675	80717
山 东 Shandong	236282	17831	169991
河 南 Henan	305123	21319	195465
湖 北 Hubei	150301	10073	83283
湖 南 Hunan	193204	13714	102066
广 东 Guangdong	475697	25488	277214
广 西 Guangxi	145992	12908	81307
海 南 Hainan	37607	3022	19720
重 庆 Chongqing	80488	5954	43814
四 川 Sichuan	187939	14529	115462
贵 州 Guizhou	130530	6822	79754
云 南 Yunnan	88204	6376	56209
西 藏 Tibet	4602	266	3777
陕 西 Shaanxi	139222	7397	87250
甘 肃 Gansu	55875	4485	40718
青 海 Qinghai	16152	1060	9884
宁 夏 Ningxia	18757	1158	11067
新 疆 Xinjiang	81252	4366	54172

教职工数
Personnel in Kindergarten

单位:人
unit:person

Educational Personnel			代课教师 Substitute Teachers	兼任教师 Part-time Teachers
保健医 Health Physician	保育员 Caretaker	其他 Other		
92154	**796887**	**343120**	**162586**	**34247**
2875	11379	9659	0	846
851	4144	3002	2841	179
3426	23446	11503	14462	286
1556	11106	7593	16467	1150
1534	9725	6960	2716	153
1766	17415	9879	297	907
1985	10899	4194	640	275
3008	11292	6069	2313	362
2325	11513	7381	1516	157
6881	61374	18426	13859	558
7237	49367	25041	0	279
3142	26437	7978	7505	689
3018	29370	11834	9561	240
983	19208	6074	4388	2789
3957	29140	15363	19222	1328
7579	60818	19942	21216	1222
3871	38212	14862	8919	975
4711	55439	17274	4460	434
12762	110319	49914	183	680
2705	34516	14556	2500	2279
1424	9054	4387	173	188
1948	20247	8525	3281	380
3260	37014	17674	7579	4802
1952	33494	8508	1494	3609
1593	14208	9818	447	3680
20	343	196	345	11
3696	28137	12742	3210	131
874	5681	4117	2121	3603
158	3103	1947	608	67
413	3363	2756	2068	126
644	17124	4946	8195	1862

幼儿园园长、专任教师学历、
Number of Kindergarten Heads, Full-time Teachers by

地　区 Region	合计 Total	按学历分 By Educational Attainment			
		研究生毕业 Graduate	本科毕业 Under-graduate	专科毕业 Associate Bachelor	高中阶段毕业 High School Graduate
总　计 Total	**2712065**	**7253**	**607705**	**1553973**	**497624**
北　京 Beijing	40291	564	16974	19436	3212
天　津 Tianjin	18932	341	9714	6226	2274
河　北 Hebei	129260	264	24204	72313	30973
山　西 Shanxi	61785	142	14436	34136	12160
内蒙古 Inner Mongolia	46599	228	17294	24290	4680
辽　宁 Liaoning	80099	393	14569	47032	15592
吉　林 Jilin	34731	252	9770	18455	6031
黑龙江 Heilongjiang	42112	108	11118	23968	5749
上　海 Shanghai	42187	395	30246	10274	1264
江　苏 Jiangsu	157350	526	72464	77493	6465
浙　江 Zhejiang	134061	348	51327	74039	8268
安　徽 Anhui	92803	110	17771	61865	12221
福　建 Fujian	94574	98	19350	48647	24252
江　西 Jiangxi	94388	68	9202	52476	26607
山　东 Shandong	194914	578	40541	111261	38389
河　南 Henan	222535	498	30955	131789	52803
湖　北 Hubei	95908	215	15597	51806	25991
湖　南 Hunan	118138	187	12734	73924	29239
广　东 Guangdong	308334	530	41039	197084	66069
广　西 Guangxi	96010	166	14430	55160	20998
海　南 Hainan	23134	65	3472	14050	4904
重　庆 Chongqing	50700	139	8652	32943	8449
四　川 Sichuan	132578	233	21709	88235	22185
贵　州 Guizhou	91563	55	18028	50423	22408
云　南 Yunnan	66288	139	16433	35998	12194
西　藏 Tibet	4637	9	1701	2631	257
陕　西 Shaanxi	99493	354	25294	59323	14005
甘　肃 Gansu	49397	140	18181	24965	5733
青　海 Qinghai	12011	22	2491	6821	2341
宁　夏 Ningxia	12858	49	2221	8655	1809
新　疆 Xinjiang	64395	37	15788	38255	10102

专业技术职务情况(总计)
Academic Qualifications and Professional Rank(Total)

单位:人
unit: person

	按专业技术职务分 By Professional Rank					
高中阶段以下毕业 Below High School Graduate	中学高级 Senior Secondary	小学高级 Senior Primary	小学一级 1st Grade Primary	小学二级 2nd Grade Primary	小学三级 3rd Grade Primary	未定职级 No-ranking
45510	**22736**	**209649**	**297644**	**146776**	**27636**	**2007624**
105	699	5318	7758	4240	31	22245
377	654	4148	3209	525	29	10367
1506	1546	19883	17344	3329	584	86574
911	197	6087	8572	2814	653	43462
107	2098	5523	6584	1813	117	30464
2513	1219	6945	3752	1042	641	66500
223	682	4004	3176	1019	89	25761
1169	1281	5301	4982	957	423	29168
8	755	10018	15564	3442	350	12058
402	1909	16151	26737	19212	62	93279
79	1032	13275	35805	14670	1657	67622
836	357	6962	8081	5968	801	70634
2227	397	7265	8901	6507	1272	70232
6035	653	3512	4877	2494	950	81902
4145	1680	12580	16259	8510	1391	154494
6490	1312	11330	16727	9321	35	183810
2299	783	7748	8654	4654	1406	72663
2054	468	3971	6195	3435	665	103404
3612	438	12249	18574	11921	6300	258852
5256	316	4480	5202	3713	814	81485
643	56	632	1543	1349	44	19510
517	306	1975	3204	1223	590	43402
216	1118	7199	14155	4525	1171	104410
649	174	6232	7766	8248	2418	66725
1524	903	8265	7887	4058	1243	43932
39	68	664	1325	498	304	1778
517	410	6654	12135	5981	1084	73229
378	345	6486	11287	3029	409	27841
336	99	667	520	434	305	9986
124	230	1146	907	350	23	10202
213	551	2979	9962	7495	1775	41633

幼儿园园长、专任教师学历、

Breakdown of Kindergarten Heads, Full-time Teachers by

地 区 Region	合计 Total	按学历分 By Educational Attainment			
		研究生毕业 Graduate	本科毕业 Under-graduate	专科毕业 Associate Bachelor	高中阶段毕业 High School Graduate
总 计 Total	**1261577**	**5765**	**340434**	**739089**	**167041**
北 京 Beijing	34980	527	14445	17085	2846
天 津 Tianjin	16121	333	8736	5274	1542
河 北 Hebei	40926	184	9770	24750	6100
山 西 Shanxi	26882	105	7014	15567	3926
内蒙古 Inner Mongolia	20161	161	7555	11091	1340
辽 宁 Liaoning	56876	353	11849	35373	8548
吉 林 Jilin	19089	175	5641	10230	2954
黑龙江 Heilongjiang	22836	94	6434	13723	2252
上 海 Shanghai	36029	347	25800	8898	979
江 苏 Jiangsu	81704	389	44445	35328	1476
浙 江 Zhejiang	74342	320	31932	38303	3777
安 徽 Anhui	29840	70	7336	20019	2292
福 建 Fujian	44839	85	10640	23829	9803
江 西 Jiangxi	31168	45	4381	19387	6322
山 东 Shandong	92587	431	23563	55948	11840
河 南 Henan	71966	260	14364	45409	11061
湖 北 Hubei	48186	184	10353	28030	9030
湖 南 Hunan	44164	162	6560	30001	7132
广 东 Guangdong	202865	487	31262	130568	39048
广 西 Guangxi	34071	130	7210	21377	4818
海 南 Hainan	11298	57	1643	7407	2028
重 庆 Chongqing	31908	118	6056	21613	4026
四 川 Sichuan	58864	168	11200	41105	6325
贵 州 Guizhou	23945	21	4658	13892	5286
云 南 Yunnan	25325	110	7525	14500	3014
西 藏 Tibet	1725	7	651	854	183
陕 西 Shaanxi	36633	276	8896	23741	3519
甘 肃 Gansu	17008	83	4592	10344	1909
青 海 Qinghai	3877	12	785	2329	729
宁 夏 Ningxia	6561	43	1239	4464	777
新 疆 Xinjiang	14801	28	3899	8650	2159

专业技术职务情况(城区)
Academic Qualifications and Professional Rank (Urban Area)

单位:人
unit: person

	按专业技术职务分 By Professional Rank					
高中阶段以下毕业 Below High School Graduate	中学高级 Senior Secondary	小学高级 Senior Primary	小学一级 1st Grade Primary	小学二级 2nd Grade Primary	小学三级 3rd Grade Primary	未定职级 No-ranking
9248	**12165**	**99245**	**144460**	**66865**	**13135**	**925707**
77	624	4525	6404	3538	30	19859
236	533	3452	2948	465	25	8698
122	492	5316	4674	1016	238	29190
270	109	2480	3236	1469	332	19256
14	795	2088	2396	650	35	14197
753	718	4661	2685	732	457	47623
89	333	1733	1371	473	56	15123
333	649	2683	1997	379	231	16897
5	652	8667	13095	3073	307	10235
66	1279	9725	15972	10757	45	43926
10	746	8680	21487	7147	817	35465
123	187	2435	2664	1570	452	22532
482	286	3242	4392	2731	430	33758
1033	298	1519	2474	889	200	25788
805	900	5467	7758	3914	697	73851
872	679	4816	6862	3920	30	55659
589	510	3971	4593	2397	661	36054
309	203	1553	2430	1123	220	38635
1500	359	6701	13023	9031	4900	168851
536	144	1622	2432	1746	332	27795
163	17	281	614	486	25	9875
95	208	1219	1752	610	315	27804
66	438	3045	6363	1952	547	46519
88	56	1038	1712	1224	199	19716
176	313	2657	2824	1828	441	17262
30	49	258	401	55	76	886
201	130	1919	3336	1613	360	29275
80	113	1741	2119	650	111	12274
22	33	155	242	182	146	3119
38	101	469	420	186	14	5371
65	211	1127	1784	1059	406	10214

幼儿园园长、专任教师学历、

Breakdown of Kindergarten Heads, Full-time Teachers by Academic

地　区 Region	合计 Total	按学历分 By Educational Attainment			
		研究生毕业 Graduate	本科毕业 Under-graduate	专科毕业 Associate Bachelor	高中阶段毕业 High School Graduate
总　计 Total	**203797**	**393**	**38142**	**126080**	**36888**
北　京 Beijing	2210	22	824	1121	224
天　津 Tianjin	1134	3	199	538	322
河　北 Hebei	8262	23	1616	4863	1698
山　西 Shanxi	3530	11	870	1949	626
内蒙古 Inner Mongolia	674	3	208	403	60
辽　宁 Liaoning	3663	5	591	2083	889
吉　林 Jilin	824	7	210	455	145
黑龙江 Heilongjiang	1217	4	413	618	165
上　海 Shanghai	3058	25	1560	1153	320
江　苏 Jiangsu	8786	29	3968	4462	296
浙　江 Zhejiang	17501	23	5405	10600	1468
安　徽 Anhui	2961	2	455	2197	295
福　建 Fujian	7095	7	1262	3661	2063
江　西 Jiangxi	4189	3	382	2418	1199
山　东 Shandong	22474	50	4597	13708	3808
河　南 Henan	10294	35	1361	6238	2447
湖　北 Hubei	6794	8	1063	3951	1645
湖　南 Hunan	5043	8	623	3476	903
广　东 Guangdong	62200	63	7043	41410	13105
广　西 Guangxi	5249	15	687	3279	1139
海　南 Hainan	828	1	119	503	183
重　庆 Chongqing	2006	3	246	1369	377
四　川 Sichuan	6973	12	949	5310	687
贵　州 Guizhou	3041	1	539	1825	663
云　南 Yunnan	4779	14	943	2988	760
西　藏 Tibet	61	0	16	27	18
陕　西 Shaanxi	5165	12	1170	3161	754
甘　肃 Gansu	1561	3	381	1003	173
青　海 Qinghai	288	0	31	170	87
宁　夏 Ningxia	285	0	48	195	42
新　疆 Xinjiang	1652	1	363	946	327

专业技术职务情况(城乡结合区)

Qualifications and Professional Rank (Urban-rural Transitional Area)

单位:人

unit: person

高中阶段以下毕业 Below High School Graduate	按专业技术职务分 By Professional Rank 中学高级 Senior Secondary	小学高级 Senior Primary	小学一级 1st Grade Primary	小学二级 2nd Grade Primary	小学三级 3rd Grade Primary	未定职级 No-ranking
2294	**844**	**8272**	**15670**	**8495**	**2516**	**168000**
19	35	178	342	143	0	1512
72	1	17	12	1	0	1103
62	92	1095	896	126	31	6022
74	9	272	424	223	10	2592
0	12	33	57	16	0	556
95	27	178	92	21	37	3308
7	19	46	61	8	0	690
17	45	264	181	15	11	701
0	32	333	841	112	19	1721
31	77	552	1306	1117	1	5733
5	67	1063	3821	1506	175	10869
12	9	123	144	77	34	2574
102	14	317	552	400	58	5754
187	13	58	185	55	10	3868
311	185	1024	1431	755	140	18939
213	37	327	608	370	1	8951
127	31	298	369	256	45	5795
33	12	90	169	82	13	4677
579	38	1020	2217	1976	1541	55408
129	11	99	200	169	52	4718
22	0	4	13	24	0	787
11	9	44	57	25	34	1837
15	16	118	384	156	55	6244
13	1	94	183	124	28	2611
74	27	240	282	284	77	3869
0	2	2	11	2	0	44
68	11	214	442	257	39	4202
1	4	93	166	29	22	1247
0	0	1	4	4	11	268
0	0	9	5	3	1	267
15	8	66	215	159	71	1133

幼儿园园长、专任教师学历、

Breakdown of Kindergarten Heads, Full-time Teachers by Academic

地　区 Region	合计 Total	按学历分 By Educational Attainment			
		研究生毕业 Graduate	本科毕业 Under-graduate	专科毕业 Associate Bachelor	高中阶段毕业 High School Graduate
总　计 Total	**974065**	**1191**	**198377**	**558848**	**196904**
北　京 Beijing	2736	28	1353	1197	155
天　津 Tianjin	1189	2	401	415	297
河　北 Hebei	53183	63	9386	29668	13292
山　西 Shanxi	24628	25	5927	13556	4804
内蒙古 Inner Mongolia	20935	52	8121	10373	2330
辽　宁 Liaoning	15336	25	2001	7881	4414
吉　林 Jilin	12093	64	3286	6410	2239
黑龙江 Heilongjiang	14310	13	3770	7733	2328
上　海 Shanghai	5102	38	3747	1085	229
江　苏 Jiangsu	60367	131	24029	32674	3317
浙　江 Zhejiang	42715	21	14423	25298	2935
安　徽 Anhui	43220	37	7826	29164	5808
福　建 Fujian	36822	10	7178	18545	10039
江　西 Jiangxi	45104	21	3860	24865	13602
山　东 Shandong	64082	120	12686	35767	13920
河　南 Henan	84040	196	11110	50895	19650
湖　北 Hubei	33832	20	3958	17323	11462
湖　南 Hunan	53022	23	4938	32315	14687
广　东 Guangdong	75453	39	7377	48029	18536
广　西 Guangxi	41582	29	5683	23857	9770
海　南 Hainan	9201	5	1443	5115	2296
重　庆 Chongqing	15402	19	2281	9451	3392
四　川 Sichuan	56697	51	9023	37235	10302
贵　州 Guizhou	44204	29	9375	24458	10099
云　南 Yunnan	24670	21	6455	13277	4442
西　藏 Tibet	1247	0	533	684	29
陕　西 Shaanxi	46473	60	13208	26391	6689
甘　肃 Gansu	20251	35	8565	9314	2186
青　海 Qinghai	4155	8	1062	2347	644
宁　夏 Ningxia	4366	3	750	2944	633
新　疆 Xinjiang	17648	3	4622	10582	2378

专业技术职务情况(镇区)
Qualifications and Professional Rank (Counties & Towns Area)

单位:人
unit: person

高中阶段以下毕业 Below High School Graduate	按专业技术职务分 By Professional Rank					
	中学高级 Senior Secondary	小学高级 Senior Primary	小学一级 1st Grade Primary	小学二级 2nd Grade Primary	小学三级 3rd Grade Primary	未定职级 No-ranking
18745	**7876**	**78778**	**107903**	**54760**	**9131**	**715617**
3	43	354	699	402	0	1238
74	43	232	94	21	2	797
774	593	7329	6580	1233	143	37305
316	68	2724	3966	1090	224	16556
59	993	2749	3444	922	49	12778
1015	338	1673	699	175	119	12332
94	256	1591	1264	475	33	8474
466	476	1739	2259	499	175	9162
3	77	1152	2103	321	36	1413
216	561	5585	9160	6801	16	38244
38	250	3665	10767	5425	609	21999
385	139	3215	3756	3123	281	32706
1050	104	3375	3694	2834	559	26256
2756	275	1624	1874	1145	535	39651
1589	585	4499	5358	3059	513	50068
2189	425	4625	6211	3334	5	69440
1069	223	2936	3231	1685	492	25265
1059	203	1874	2735	1653	305	46252
1472	64	3979	4184	2260	1101	63865
2243	131	2447	2196	1346	309	35153
342	18	286	746	676	12	7463
259	83	658	1197	548	234	12682
86	613	3841	6675	2029	420	43119
243	76	3487	4329	4868	1293	30151
475	444	3965	3541	1395	547	14778
1	13	202	421	230	99	282
125	252	3869	7090	3432	485	31345
151	138	2965	6078	1413	134	9523
94	50	407	208	146	77	3267
36	77	442	322	123	7	3395
63	265	1289	3022	2097	317	10658

地 区 Region	合计 Total	按学历分 By Educational Attainment			
		研究生毕业 Graduate	本科毕业 Under-graduate	专科毕业 Associate Bachelor	高中阶段毕业 High School Graduate
总 计 Total	**249267**	**285**	**41797**	**142936**	**58399**
北 京 Beijing	705	7	374	271	53
天 津 Tianjin	655	1	200	228	187
河 北 Hebei	24528	25	3659	13448	6986
山 西 Shanxi	7277	10	1489	4127	1515
内蒙古 Inner Mongolia	1714	3	593	890	222
辽 宁 Liaoning	1826	3	202	893	623
吉 林 Jilin	987	5	306	511	163
黑龙江 Heilongjiang	1465	1	251	776	367
上 海 Shanghai	951	6	546	291	108
江 苏 Jiangsu	16087	33	6198	8986	812
浙 江 Zhejiang	13892	6	3794	8808	1266
安 徽 Anhui	6752	3	1120	4539	1041
福 建 Fujian	10241	4	1705	5060	3087
江 西 Jiangxi	8068	2	543	4066	2828
山 东 Shandong	27200	36	4277	14910	7101
河 南 Henan	28372	48	2859	16857	7613
湖 北 Hubei	7376	6	674	3649	2788
湖 南 Hunan	11711	7	1067	7097	3260
广 东 Guangdong	26713	28	2319	16768	7063
广 西 Guangxi	7839	10	805	4421	2073
海 南 Hainan	1367	1	225	821	285
重 庆 Chongqing	2750	1	301	1658	722
四 川 Sichuan	9389	9	1150	6268	1942
贵 州 Guizhou	7885	7	1246	4483	2092
云 南 Yunnan	5580	5	1106	2970	1348
西 藏 Tibet	62	0	26	36	0
陕 西 Shaanxi	10110	10	2315	5925	1804
甘 肃 Gansu	3743	8	1551	1733	397
青 海 Qinghai	827	0	127	495	190
宁 夏 Ningxia	428	0	62	303	56
新 疆 Xinjiang	2767	0	707	1648	407

专业技术职务情况(镇乡结合区)
Qualifications and Professional Rank (County-town Transitional Area)

单位:人
unit: person

	按专业技术职务分 By Professional Rank					
高中阶段以下毕业 Below High School Graduate	中学高级 Senior Secondary	小学高级 Senior Primary	小学一级 1st Grade Primary	小学二级 2nd Grade Primary	小学三级 3rd Grade Primary	未定职级 No-ranking
5850	**1394**	**16074**	**22774**	**12103**	**1984**	**194938**
0	7	106	215	89	0	288
39	27	108	43	8	0	469
410	247	3513	3055	603	56	17054
136	19	690	1022	226	90	5230
6	94	183	189	66	3	1179
105	27	149	91	27	25	1507
2	28	197	130	30	0	602
70	36	133	184	41	21	1050
0	16	153	286	72	11	413
58	145	1390	2501	1929	3	10119
18	47	648	2871	1749	200	8377
49	15	396	499	420	39	5383
385	26	711	693	580	157	8074
629	17	159	267	154	85	7386
876	212	1664	1877	1051	209	22187
995	106	911	1390	977	0	24988
259	34	430	616	327	77	5892
280	34	346	613	366	63	10289
535	20	875	947	642	398	23831
530	27	251	366	256	61	6878
35	0	32	107	96	1	1131
68	3	44	101	31	20	2551
20	57	320	712	171	84	8045
57	11	494	553	650	165	6012
151	60	664	559	205	63	4029
0	0	13	25	9	3	12
56	22	747	1297	627	80	7337
54	17	573	1047	229	17	1860
15	3	15	6	5	13	785
7	10	54	23	17	0	324
5	27	105	489	450	40	1656

幼儿园园长、专任教师学历、

Breakdown of Kindergarten Heads, Full-time Teachers by

地 区 Region	合计 Total	按学历分 By Educational Attainment			
		研究生毕业 Graduate	本科毕业 Under-graduate	专科毕业 Associate Bachelor	高中阶段毕业 High School Graduate
总 计 Total	**476423**	**297**	**68894**	**256036**	**133679**
北 京 Beijing	2575	9	1176	1154	211
天 津 Tianjin	1622	6	577	537	435
河 北 Hebei	35151	17	5048	17895	11581
山 西 Shanxi	10275	12	1495	5013	3430
内蒙古 Inner Mongolia	5503	15	1618	2826	1010
辽 宁 Liaoning	7887	15	719	3778	2630
吉 林 Jilin	3549	13	843	1815	838
黑龙江 Heilongjiang	4966	1	914	2512	1169
上 海 Shanghai	1056	10	699	291	56
江 苏 Jiangsu	15279	6	3990	9491	1672
浙 江 Zhejiang	17004	7	4972	10438	1556
安 徽 Anhui	19743	3	2609	12682	4121
福 建 Fujian	12913	3	1532	6273	4410
江 西 Jiangxi	18116	2	961	8224	6683
山 东 Shandong	38245	27	4292	19546	12629
河 南 Henan	66529	42	5481	35485	22092
湖 北 Hubei	13890	11	1286	6453	5499
湖 南 Hunan	20952	2	1236	11608	7420
广 东 Guangdong	30016	4	2400	18487	8485
广 西 Guangxi	20357	7	1537	9926	6410
海 南 Hainan	2635	3	386	1528	580
重 庆 Chongqing	3390	2	315	1879	1031
四 川 Sichuan	17017	14	1486	9895	5558
贵 州 Guizhou	23414	5	3995	12073	7023
云 南 Yunnan	16293	8	2453	8221	4738
西 藏 Tibet	1665	2	517	1093	45
陕 西 Shaanxi	16387	18	3190	9191	3797
甘 肃 Gansu	12138	22	5024	5307	1638
青 海 Qinghai	3979	2	644	2145	968
宁 夏 Ningxia	1931	3	232	1247	399
新 疆 Xinjiang	31946	6	7267	19023	5565

专业技术职务情况(乡村)
Academic Qualifications and Professional Rank (Rural Area)

单位:人
unit: person

	按专业技术职务分 By Professional Rank					
高中阶段以下毕业 Below High School Graduate	中学高级 Senior Secondary	小学高级 Senior Primary	小学一级 1st Grade Primary	小学二级 2nd Grade Primary	小学三级 3rd Grade Primary	未定职级 No-ranking
17517	**2695**	**31626**	**45281**	**25151**	**5370**	**366300**
25	32	439	655	300	1	1148
67	78	464	167	39	2	872
610	461	7238	6090	1080	203	20079
325	20	883	1370	255	97	7650
34	310	686	744	241	33	3489
745	163	611	368	135	65	6545
40	93	680	541	71	0	2164
370	156	879	726	79	17	3109
0	26	199	366	48	7	410
120	69	841	1605	1654	1	11109
31	36	930	3551	2098	231	10158
328	31	1312	1661	1275	68	15396
695	7	648	815	942	283	10218
2246	80	369	529	460	215	16463
1751	195	2614	3143	1537	181	30575
3429	208	1889	3654	2067	0	58711
641	50	841	830	572	253	11344
686	62	544	1030	659	140	18517
640	15	1569	1367	630	299	26136
2477	41	411	574	621	173	18537
138	21	65	183	187	7	2172
163	15	98	255	65	41	2916
64	67	313	1117	544	204	14772
318	42	1707	1725	2156	926	16858
873	146	1643	1522	835	255	11892
8	6	204	503	213	129	610
191	28	866	1709	936	239	12609
147	94	1780	3090	966	164	6044
220	16	105	70	106	82	3600
50	52	235	165	41	2	1436
85	75	563	5156	4339	1052	20761

地区 Region	校舍建筑面积 Floor Space	教学及辅助用房 Teaching & Assistant Buildings				
		合计 Total	其中：of Which:			
			活动室 Recreational	洗手间 Toilet	睡眠室 Bed Room	保健室 Health Care
总　计 Total	**320492661.90**	**222597552.15**	**129886413.36**	**21462826.93**	**55644243.64**	**6525020.72**
北　京 Beijing	4411131.87	2626785.41	1365064.79	310152.39	804412.36	62077.07
天　津 Tianjin	1988577.12	1305611.53	770147.38	151047.70	309143.99	35737.78
河　北 Hebei	12950874.04	9226434.04	5494036.59	866993.46	2055723.09	304727.14
山　西 Shanxi	6689605.88	4488759.19	2784717.55	452212.82	929001.24	134621.95
内蒙古 Inner Mongolia	5723742.90	3738023.24	2171563.40	364465.28	958570.64	96967.93
辽　宁 Liaoning	7310155.11	5073478.52	2909124.43	504910.54	1257530.81	170968.99
吉　林 Jilin	3173216.22	2216136.24	1258019.74	198890.07	593553.50	74979.62
黑龙江 Heilongjiang	4556351.68	3057120.47	1700808.03	294965.27	792253.33	130202.35
上　海 Shanghai	6264287.81	3948406.60	2641171.00	367812.52	771447.23	78350.04
江　苏 Jiangsu	23476324.00	16043949.34	9509109.75	1610432.33	3897965.15	382243.03
浙　江 Zhejiang	17453402.32	11483206.68	6745733.15	1152268.97	3010696.17	226684.23
安　徽 Anhui	10493812.81	7654646.93	4665064.16	760897.56	1622991.91	256900.54
福　建 Fujian	11107908.23	7470554.37	4543327.98	793447.07	1761884.95	154519.68
江　西 Jiangxi	12732840.15	9410685.03	5532196.99	823861.01	2383854.14	277441.77
山　东 Shandong	21830466.39	15003750.58	9268273.09	1506647.16	3082194.70	445074.73
河　南 Henan	23082412.97	17014388.66	10134283.11	1710453.43	3835006.91	564218.36
湖　北 Hubei	11871163.58	8562114.45	4753630.02	877532.57	2257077.73	290431.54
湖　南 Hunan	16220664.00	11686455.76	6120853.89	1177511.00	3349169.91	483903.58
广　东 Guangdong	34771268.23	22984064.84	14068369.74	1865089.38	5603327.61	523904.14
广　西 Guangxi	11174048.37	8308175.66	4519210.27	779034.33	2493251.78	224399.68
海　南 Hainan	2746866.96	1940492.17	1070063.41	201686.95	530664.98	58933.45
重　庆 Chongqing	5911372.75	4342068.25	2539433.11	399035.70	1114209.33	123441.94
四　川 Sichuan	14665376.68	10707892.38	6285827.14	1005491.10	2693942.57	287877.99
贵　州 Guizhou	9712041.26	6803836.57	3605290.32	676435.01	1994603.77	233724.45
云　南 Yunnan	9019765.97	6313197.34	3492616.25	535290.22	1843364.26	195103.21
西　藏 Tibet	1106069.64	637095.21	351422.40	65191.43	174202.64	24146.81
陕　西 Shaanxi	10655608.37	7317617.03	4215775.59	744923.69	1777518.89	235907.23
甘　肃 Gansu	5205151.02	3418530.87	2079838.11	316071.98	707645.31	135112.53
青　海 Qinghai	1505722.97	991070.57	577704.36	90685.93	257954.45	29680.33
宁　夏 Ningxia	1802507.63	1232559.27	701577.11	135823.85	319903.91	33596.17
新　疆 Xinjiang	10879924.97	7590444.95	4012160.50	723566.21	2461176.38	249142.46

情况(总计)(一)
Buildings and Others (Total)(1)

单位:平方米
unit: m^2

图书室 Reading Room	行政办公用房 Administrative 合计 Total	行政办公用房 Administrative 其中:教师办公室 of Which: Office	生活用房 Residential and Welfare 合计 Total	生活用房 Residential and Welfare 其中:厨房 of Which: Kitchen	其他用房 for Other Purposes	校舍面积中 of Floor Space 危房面积 Floor Space of Dilapidated Buildings	校舍面积中 of Floor Space 当年新增校舍 New Added in Current Year
9079047. 50	**21953165. 15**	**12621817. 49**	**33366761. 11**	**15786934. 42**	**42575183. 49**	**671751. 82**	**22258393. 93**
85078. 80	358836. 85	157902. 90	549706. 28	256950. 64	875803. 33	0. 00	202097. 70
39534. 68	157555. 62	74809. 14	217941. 36	118912. 48	307468. 61	0. 00	182465. 34
504953. 76	950427. 58	551031. 93	1216527. 39	559998. 85	1557485. 03	6066. 77	1565091. 63
188205. 63	614106. 80	391819. 47	624316. 11	301293. 28	962423. 78	37334. 06	301732. 52
146455. 99	427161. 29	234691. 89	691691. 15	328864. 26	866867. 22	0. 00	394060. 35
230943. 75	491808. 50	271351. 48	762106. 23	448365. 03	982761. 86	4729. 00	152053. 41
90693. 31	202014. 97	123123. 82	294276. 75	165269. 92	460788. 26	0. 00	166798. 19
138891. 49	332020. 25	189162. 08	521324. 03	264560. 75	645886. 93	20998. 27	72131. 68
89625. 81	457636. 67	175451. 22	764024. 40	277659. 95	1094220. 14	0. 00	134906. 40
644199. 08	1542037. 77	753643. 49	2342677. 45	1042227. 25	3547659. 44	0. 00	577287. 33
347824. 16	1129572. 15	575036. 96	1717583. 55	875609. 13	3123039. 94	6637. 00	1291313. 95
348792. 76	756561. 24	468538. 69	927111. 35	478249. 10	1155493. 29	26184. 00	576402. 96
217374. 69	685333. 28	400650. 09	1043993. 16	509111. 48	1908027. 42	43237. 92	450269. 63
393331. 12	930300. 89	536859. 25	1331895. 53	485972. 98	1059958. 70	14343. 18	721244. 97
701560. 90	1578644. 90	928315. 82	2013139. 58	1012313. 38	3234931. 33	2660. 00	1815394. 69
770426. 85	1782726. 89	1122256. 10	2031531. 37	1114664. 45	2253766. 05	31873. 69	650960. 09
383442. 59	775728. 56	433753. 99	1275074. 15	616376. 94	1258246. 42	25665. 00	687637. 38
555017. 38	1096689. 57	694463. 58	1677833. 75	801724. 20	1759684. 92	22550. 00	433511. 01
923373. 97	1829339. 48	1001892. 22	4349699. 97	1656819. 61	5608163. 94	32026. 72	762959. 69
292279. 60	561778. 00	366381. 71	1202888. 04	692290. 10	1101206. 67	67175. 85	642489. 57
79143. 38	158900. 24	91243. 60	333369. 98	154749. 13	314104. 57	11609. 00	95835. 39
165948. 17	338872. 01	200475. 89	569312. 15	282314. 41	661120. 34	50005. 01	122002. 34
434753. 58	886320. 41	526176. 95	1454219. 81	723005. 28	1616944. 08	7817. 00	1701027. 31
293783. 02	675273. 46	415254. 03	1070571. 33	530111. 50	1162359. 90	0. 00	1281183. 13
246823. 40	609326. 49	358896. 42	1070077. 40	511326. 66	1027164. 74	182315. 80	749903. 24
22131. 93	92102. 12	68664. 55	256782. 18	76509. 02	120090. 13	6985. 00	172464. 78
343491. 63	1065917. 38	614392. 46	1067580. 59	497685. 89	1204493. 37	2356. 00	1509904. 39
179862. 94	518558. 55	348288. 99	495670. 51	221515. 27	772391. 09	64371. 35	642698. 85
35045. 50	102749. 58	67468. 63	201789. 78	82387. 83	210113. 04	0. 00	131911. 99
41658. 23	143168. 32	77292. 49	176331. 72	99193. 82	250448. 32	1827. 00	144902. 74
144399. 40	701695. 33	402527. 65	1115714. 06	600901. 83	1472070. 63	2984. 20	3925751. 28

幼儿园校舍及
Statistics of Kindergarten Buildings

地区 Region	校舍建筑面积 Floor Space	教学及辅助用房 Teaching & Assistant Buildings				
		合计 Total	其中：of Which：			
			活动室 Recreational	洗手间 Toilet	睡眠室 Bed Room	保健室 Health Care
总　计 Total	**138887118.67**	**95314435.89**	**55961796.18**	**9143377.21**	**24710135.82**	**2147601.65**
北　京 Beijing	3681753.14	2219631.92	1144155.10	261326.47	693356.43	49957.47
天　津 Tianjin	1536608.02	989508.83	575382.91	112899.97	247961.10	24223.39
河　北 Hebei	3710100.69	2625310.69	1465801.88	259308.41	730029.40	65809.93
山　西 Shanxi	2579183.19	1760080.39	1028447.43	178211.43	447889.07	42686.31
内蒙古 Inner Mongolia	2333434.59	1582026.41	932585.22	150026.23	411121.53	33148.66
辽　宁 Liaoning	4983425.20	3437452.55	1970812.91	350004.21	869684.32	105405.53
吉　林 Jilin	1636747.25	1165033.16	679826.88	103508.00	306021.65	33517.18
黑龙江 Heilongjiang	2261444.98	1530926.18	849653.19	146939.96	406269.89	59641.04
上　海 Shanghai	5169811.23	3309971.25	2231290.34	305919.23	632797.67	64877.85
江　苏 Jiangsu	12017860.09	7990208.14	4763783.90	793788.19	2023380.80	145785.11
浙　江 Zhejiang	9532841.48	6260190.97	3709287.56	628482.85	1637346.88	106894.33
安　徽 Anhui	2950681.14	2119111.39	1222779.18	217250.16	554295.92	48384.41
福　建 Fujian	4912883.16	3319099.68	2033160.82	341550.37	798236.53	59499.89
江　西 Jiangxi	3671317.28	2743883.75	1631543.76	219437.31	731893.90	61625.45
山　东 Shandong	9461926.85	6505947.14	3883794.65	659962.16	1536172.17	162138.60
河　南 Henan	6728510.60	4919834.58	2826549.35	476889.34	1323831.05	117670.60
湖　北 Hubei	5252323.99	3812314.77	2171057.12	378094.46	1020200.78	99685.44
湖　南 Hunan	5490732.34	4018198.61	2140904.11	405760.42	1187765.26	122323.32
广　东 Guangdong	23244636.67	15175085.29	9487091.09	1278587.46	3574960.15	293776.53
广　西 Guangxi	3521147.28	2646876.56	1469189.00	252406.74	780788.40	55277.01
海　南 Hainan	1161472.61	835040.52	476041.48	84103.07	220097.15	22626.24
重　庆 Chongqing	3324717.38	2469212.36	1418421.12	231215.74	675042.38	56248.54
四　川 Sichuan	5802976.82	4210497.73	2383130.14	394552.56	1190220.03	85611.67
贵　州 Guizhou	2313869.28	1681932.98	931031.12	150325.08	497637.50	42597.36
云　南 Yunnan	2960878.33	2057834.16	1144295.41	172124.20	619799.47	47802.66
西　藏 Tibet	282486.52	167137.64	81561.21	21752.02	53816.18	3521.20
陕　西 Shaanxi	3664631.86	2579113.00	1530321.74	257282.75	637729.19	60329.63
甘　肃 Gansu	1577652.84	1079113.03	610923.69	89805.78	300288.65	31724.76
青　海 Qinghai	363212.01	246833.65	138284.77	23739.22	70976.79	5682.87
宁　夏 Ningxia	753107.12	511393.90	292651.62	54333.90	138543.88	10029.40
新　疆 Xinjiang	2004744.73	1345634.66	738037.48	143789.52	391981.70	29099.27

其他情况(城区)(一)
and Others (Urban Area)(1)

单位:平方米
unit: m²

图书室 Reading Room	行政办公用房 Administrative 合计 Total	行政办公用房 Administrative 其中:教师办公室 of Which: Office	生活用房 Residential and Welfare 合计 Total	生活用房 Residential and Welfare 其中:厨房 of Which: Kitchen	其他用房 for Other Purposes	校舍面积中 of Floor Space 危房面积 Floor Space of Dilapidated Buildings	校舍面积中 of Floor Space 当年新增校舍 New Added in Current Year
3351525. 03	**8696880. 87**	**4322189. 74**	**14154771. 71**	**6830332. 90**	**20721030. 20**	**282792. 49**	**6360781. 51**
70836. 45	290394. 32	126498. 39	447027. 43	209535. 58	724699. 47	0. 00	164725. 54
29041. 46	123410. 58	54171. 15	165455. 65	94117. 31	258232. 96	0. 00	136901. 78
104361. 07	257749. 65	134723. 52	345343. 47	187037. 70	481696. 88	2853. 00	384637. 68
62846. 15	209139. 43	105058. 45	254304. 21	125624. 84	355659. 16	20821. 00	100982. 19
55144. 77	161460. 44	76833. 55	272747. 11	135287. 82	317200. 63	0. 00	122258. 87
141545. 58	308664. 14	155538. 01	527243. 66	309814. 22	710064. 85	3470. 00	74863. 85
42159. 45	97131. 08	54386. 00	149070. 63	86183. 81	225512. 38	0. 00	102168. 94
68422. 10	162948. 90	79984. 24	251271. 50	129983. 48	316298. 40	10514. 00	17358. 83
75086. 16	373792. 15	144748. 62	633544. 92	228311. 61	852502. 91	0. 00	99928. 36
263470. 14	727467. 63	326680. 73	1204177. 48	536107. 94	2096006. 84	0. 00	310833. 99
178179. 35	609450. 73	291621. 99	882416. 29	450174. 31	1780783. 49	42. 00	703626. 14
76401. 72	202187. 44	103889. 08	255079. 92	145568. 91	374302. 39	7342. 00	70465. 29
86652. 07	287009. 09	150550. 28	421406. 72	217646. 34	885367. 67	20149. 34	184832. 08
99383. 33	221726. 39	106768. 43	318312. 37	123271. 15	387394. 77	451. 00	127000. 64
263879. 56	637821. 99	332781. 83	885875. 22	485296. 32	1432282. 50	2660. 00	709257. 88
174894. 24	468377. 86	245347. 20	579366. 75	315672. 59	760931. 41	12650. 70	84448. 33
143276. 97	318953. 89	164156. 09	497316. 43	257551. 81	623738. 90	13640. 00	346602. 27
161445. 50	312264. 64	172764. 40	498836. 85	250986. 78	661432. 24	5645. 00	141170. 50
540670. 06	1173681. 63	592070. 72	2878454. 43	1125234. 41	4017415. 32	16697. 72	434425. 72
89215. 41	178427. 91	99768. 15	339298. 87	191883. 88	356543. 94	30840. 00	138983. 99
32172. 58	66446. 44	34424. 55	140362. 21	64486. 61	119623. 44	5780. 00	37983. 41
88284. 58	172604. 04	93541. 13	289267. 98	156224. 70	393633. 00	30941. 61	54482. 71
156983. 33	340747. 84	177750. 26	547755. 98	293864. 60	703975. 27	260. 00	582178. 52
60341. 92	145253. 28	77976. 46	204998. 47	118026. 78	281684. 55	0. 00	225771. 87
73812. 42	185272. 68	97181. 65	338212. 09	151990. 68	379559. 40	73656. 02	168369. 71
6487. 03	22655. 50	13239. 74	52492. 98	15735. 36	40200. 40	4331. 00	24690. 01
93449. 69	296608. 76	143045. 49	324768. 48	167515. 75	464141. 62	0. 00	405951. 60
46370. 15	106063. 27	59344. 36	148706. 27	84594. 42	243770. 27	18221. 10	173850. 78
8150. 00	23173. 89	12301. 84	45546. 60	19178. 36	47657. 87	0. 00	9609. 78
15835. 10	60902. 33	28445. 39	67883. 67	44168. 77	112927. 22	1827. 00	43130. 81
42726. 69	155092. 95	66598. 04	188227. 07	109256. 06	315790. 05	0. 00	179289. 44

地　区 Region	校舍建筑面　积 Floor Space	教学及辅助用房 Teaching & Assistant Buildings				
		合计 Total	其中: of Which:			
			活动室 Recreational	洗手间 Toilet	睡眠室 Bed Room	保健室 Health Care
总　计 Total	**24496136.85**	**16496390.88**	**9729613.38**	**1584583.53**	**4142988.41**	**407078.77**
北　京 Beijing	260994.75	152990.51	81133.14	18262.97	45596.49	3460.85
天　津 Tianjin	98230.99	72300.83	41858.65	7422.20	18967.99	2033.11
河　北 Hebei	801177.05	572013.82	330419.22	58528.01	140141.91	16568.44
山　西 Shanxi	363250.67	242148.71	148645.46	22415.51	54298.28	7148.59
内蒙古 Inner Mongolia	90023.79	68905.21	40298.98	5911.02	18827.68	1319.65
辽　宁 Liaoning	324154.23	227541.58	128501.39	22423.87	56823.40	8949.86
吉　林 Jilin	83348.69	54358.43	29852.73	5848.39	14518.19	1763.29
黑龙江 Heilongjiang	147225.56	88506.53	49545.12	8270.15	23258.99	3625.15
上　海 Shanghai	423788.56	279756.10	182681.95	28271.94	55689.68	6044.74
江　苏 Jiangsu	1453587.32	926303.38	542710.09	99645.59	228424.68	19855.49
浙　江 Zhejiang	2389088.03	1595320.01	953237.51	158295.12	406826.49	30064.61
安　徽 Anhui	297069.37	214964.33	128863.36	20379.10	50697.92	6447.78
福　建 Fujian	751416.09	510202.20	307868.71	53848.22	122855.27	11342.67
江　西 Jiangxi	544654.66	409130.15	242468.89	36501.72	103274.98	11203.05
山　东 Shandong	2552280.83	1721881.65	1024620.00	181299.28	388136.15	49737.45
河　南 Henan	1086433.58	788211.26	460673.18	81904.07	193942.96	20744.56
湖　北 Hubei	779841.47	571275.18	314828.36	57712.25	153707.93	18525.95
湖　南 Hunan	669932.61	481804.24	261319.37	48796.18	133491.85	17787.47
广　东 Guangdong	7709088.97	4890015.71	3009168.09	416471.98	1179639.36	102303.30
广　西 Guangxi	595818,47	444898.49	241461.28	39865.15	137257.66	10233.57
海　南 Hainan	91846.64	65857.30	35394.60	7583.50	18358.50	1843.30
重　庆 Chongqing	227864.13	170923.63	98585.57	14574.97	44259.61	5778.48
四　川 Sichuan	771949.70	564447.85	310807.53	53708.65	167031.96	11935.02
贵　州 Guizhou	319595.99	231581.04	125706.17	24607.33	66066.89	6264.90
云　南 Yunnan	584019.61	399075.56	206243.07	37071.09	123272.69	12399.17
西　藏 Tibet	8419.92	5453.20	3424.73	484.62	1255.92	92.93
陕　西 Shaanxi	586668.75	395935.15	233298.47	40703.33	94969.67	10932.65
甘　肃 Gansu	140545.77	99638.01	57824.45	8338.75	26652.93	2712.91
青　海 Qinghai	27222.85	20137.89	10720.80	1799.34	6337.20	541.25
宁　夏 Ningxia	39966.40	29732.17	19925.35	2497.37	5671.00	697.05
新　疆 Xinjiang	276631.40	201080.76	107527.16	21141.86	62734.18	4721.53

情况(城乡结合区)(一)
Others (Urban-rural Transitional Area)(1)

单位:平方米
unit: m^2

图书室 Reading Room	行政办公用房 Administrative 合计 Total	行政办公用房 Administrative 其中:教师办公室 of Which: Office	生活用房 Residential and Welfare 合计 Total	生活用房 Residential and Welfare 其中:厨房 of Which: Kitchen	其他用房 for Other Purposes	校舍面积中 of Floor Space 危房面积 Floor Space of Dilapidated Buildings	校舍面积中 of Floor Space 当年新增校舍 New Added in Current Year
632126.79	**1491112.40**	**787110.63**	**2732612.60**	**1215763.46**	**3776020.97**	**28416.01**	**1343784.58**
4537.06	21010.22	9381.09	30631.88	16448.16	56362.14	0.00	18921.00
2018.88	5939.80	2723.31	11756.76	8189.56	8233.60	0.00	12004.64
26356.24	58105.97	32262.09	77470.73	38079.42	93586.53	0.00	89239.65
9640.87	36439.24	18255.33	31166.87	16186.02	53495.85	27.00	20804.21
2547.88	4533.17	2702.17	8140.18	4873.51	8445.23	0.00	10631.19
10843.06	19747.37	10456.91	35853.25	19301.98	41012.03	0.00	2582.26
2375.83	4346.01	2535.92	7494.48	5037.90	17149.77	0.00	8231.17
3807.12	13869.73	6285.81	14740.88	8208.66	30108.42	0.00	3770.00
7067.79	28753.88	10639.93	50432.44	21141.62	64846.14	0.00	7971.00
35667.53	93171.47	41073.68	160002.54	67612.67	274109.93	0.00	21715.93
46896.28	144178.78	70404.77	230677.27	119549.83	418911.97	0.00	199309.42
8576.17	18286.72	11099.26	28001.03	14501.90	35817.29	2317.00	10615.68
14287.33	39939.94	23197.32	68454.49	35145.53	132819.46	4950.00	17819.00
15681.51	35744.07	20113.70	52693.60	17726.58	47086.84	0.00	30024.60
78088.77	174687.65	97413.34	240608.92	128768.63	415102.61	0.00	238242.88
30946.49	82241.11	47870.77	97780.05	51080.19	118201.16	4471.01	14776.64
26500.69	49388.02	25420.91	78607.61	40341.87	80570.66	0.00	46053.32
20409.37	39536.35	22453.03	78582.51	31874.11	70009.51	0.00	18273.00
182432.98	389940.00	203156.93	1048098.83	371862.58	1381034.43	3505.00	143209.82
16080.83	27618.77	17618.08	62571.86	32963.27	60729.35	8351.00	22132.81
2677.40	5827.10	3147.90	9671.48	4890.70	10490.76	0.00	4682.00
7725.00	11527.32	7384.52	25419.58	13357.14	19993.60	0.00	5890.00
20964.69	41127.48	21677.40	69035.00	41508.94	97339.37	0.00	93908.92
8935.75	22670.10	12018.29	31269.30	18329.16	34075.55	0.00	45222.39
20089.54	40378.78	22336.92	72595.47	31581.67	71969.80	3925.00	38991.13
195.00	486.80	219.61	2459.92	930.60	20.00	0.00	4313.92
16031.03	51511.87	26614.16	59641.13	29992.04	79580.60	0.00	96852.35
4108.97	9454.08	6417.86	13110.40	7441.43	18343.28	870.00	20138.37
739.30	1753.14	757.30	2555.02	1788.48	2776.80	0.00	2805.78
941.40	2500.23	1583.34	3917.00	2697.14	3817.00	0.00	13578.00
4956.03	16397.23	9888.98	29172.12	14352.17	29981.29	0.00	81073.50

幼儿园校舍及

Statistics of Kindergarten Buildings

地区 Region	校舍建筑面积 Floor Space	教学及辅助用房 Teaching & Assistant Buildings				
		合计 Total	其中：of Which： 活动室 Recreational	洗手间 Toilet	睡眠室 Bed Room	保健室 Health Care
总　计 Total	**118326052.52**	**83032955.39**	**48114434.55**	**8003467.95**	**20840275.02**	**2566163.80**
北　京 Beijing	373034.87	208273.13	112143.58	24360.84	59126.62	5475.47
天　津 Tianjin	224298.18	155696.32	92196.38	17989.58	35694.83	5103.55
河　北 Hebei	5338105.06	3813482.15	2246095.62	359238.31	889121.32	122124.78
山　西 Shanxi	2746721.71	1826585.16	1160897.97	184368.08	353943.42	54169.74
内蒙古 Inner Mongolia	2656530.32	1693176.91	976557.11	165443.33	434116.03	46962.31
辽　宁 Liaoning	1495517.28	1059616.48	604571.57	101827.67	256877.90	40920.40
吉　林 Jilin	1174914.75	804105.67	440899.98	73385.44	224080.87	29633.79
黑龙江 Heilongjiang	1690180.23	1125068.76	626251.15	109192.20	292945.93	48394.10
上　海 Shanghai	909439.99	534287.08	344350.04	51522.81	115464.32	11117.14
江　苏 Jiangsu	9219442.93	6440164.46	3822448.67	652685.28	1507557.86	171262.65
浙　江 Zhejiang	5657175.94	3722667.72	2183748.58	371855.85	979845.71	75777.50
安　徽 Anhui	4877874.74	3592470.00	2231415.30	351998.00	729012.23	120238.17
福　建 Fujian	4510832.57	3046203.37	1844748.75	327656.79	717256.88	64506.66
江　西 Jiangxi	5941751.82	4420058.05	2572150.93	383691.32	1156519.73	127584.13
山　东 Shandong	7808373.29	5250512.36	3250236.49	524850.56	1068529.88	158872.23
河　南 Henan	8889302.20	6581801.88	3970720.68	660158.10	1438884.90	215146.09
湖　北 Hubei	4532868.32	3276456.06	1801321.38	341595.76	850862.11	123212.06
湖　南 Hunan	7430940.66	5388278.32	2801323.40	534879.89	1554753.69	237697.16
广　东 Guangdong	8289214.78	5642444.66	3298371.64	429214.41	1510489.44	150186.39
广　西 Guangxi	5101468.38	3808036.47	2077000.28	349937.48	1147769.73	103985.76
海　南 Hainan	1206974.62	852528.96	460155.19	89027.90	239324.15	27276.98
重　庆 Chongqing	2069191.51	1512775.75	908448.77	133602.50	360034.98	51018.34
四　川 Sichuan	6511105.87	4790980.92	2860253.19	430771.10	1156169.21	146290.34
贵　州 Guizhou	4791089.49	3359049.76	1749015.76	332692.48	1027955.02	112560.97
云　南 Yunnan	3317175.89	2325420.73	1262968.82	201870.50	706784.41	66590.77
西　藏 Tibet	226854.71	130165.25	73950.87	10735.10	36216.12	5806.22
陕　西 Shaanxi	5024027.11	3414704.20	1937650.25	348841.13	845438.54	116966.95
甘　肃 Gansu	2129189.84	1359293.08	838139.82	126519.11	271656.45	55021.20
青　海 Qinghai	525078.59	351495.96	201481.50	35279.21	95077.63	8570.73
宁　夏 Ningxia	669371.52	465508.94	266749.73	53122.03	119418.70	11495.38
新　疆 Xinjiang	2988005.35	2081646.83	1098171.15	225155.19	659346.41	52195.84

其他情况(镇区)(一)
and Others (Counties& Towns Area)(1)

单位:平方米
unit: m^2

	行政办公用房 Administrative		生活用房 Residential and Welfare		其他用房 for Other Purposes	校舍面积中 of Floor Space	
图书室 Reading Room	合计 Total	其中:教师办公室 of Which: Office	合计 Total	其中:厨房 of Which: Kitchen		危房面积 Floor Space of Dilapidated Buildings	当年新增校舍 New Added in Current Year
3508614.07	**8372471.67**	**5028507.98**	**12107567.25**	**5576433.19**	**14813058.21**	**248016.46**	**8684885.70**
7166.62	34296.02	16548.72	52240.27	24054.41	78225.45	0.00	29951.60
4711.98	15875.42	8732.02	27877.53	12992.96	24848.91	0.00	15895.86
196902.12	376790.95	219097.12	511280.01	228128.65	636551.95	369.92	724608.57
73205.95	248830.39	169904.68	237264.76	113213.67	434041.40	12734.00	130720.62
70098.13	203465.29	117827.81	316276.91	144926.53	443611.21	0.00	215585.69
55418.94	111094.53	70475.40	148131.05	85483.93	176675.22	1000.00	60006.82
36105.59	78086.67	48933.86	111679.27	59767.85	181043.14	0.00	53107.53
48285.38	121522.78	73383.67	193109.01	97219.74	250479.68	9257.27	33680.22
11832.77	70623.65	26220.23	107166.66	41066.39	197362.60	0.00	34978.04
286210.00	649886.87	334166.43	915884.36	396425.64	1213507.24	0.00	198375.02
111440.08	369800.96	197040.40	588226.61	292823.65	976480.65	3351.00	403270.58
159806.30	350647.23	222273.44	404302.89	200834.90	530454.62	15359.00	336513.54
92034.29	285710.16	176106.97	431817.64	207081.11	747101.40	18641.58	173209.52
180111.94	428594.04	241657.48	633501.10	217525.26	459598.63	12275.18	349112.32
248023.20	570518.05	342191.82	729651.61	344965.77	1257691.27	0.00	705523.72
296892.11	692063.17	440100.82	761220.48	412185.19	854216.67	9981.11	259346.81
159464.75	306299.43	178069.63	531185.59	237473.18	418927.24	6892.00	226933.79
259624.18	521286.51	338401.76	773956.80	361060.10	747419.03	8242.00	173060.16
254182.78	454500.10	277980.43	1026232.22	374414.68	1166037.80	13194.00	249365.04
129343.22	248749.24	165888.26	531049.97	298506.32	513632.70	27537.00	353417.68
36744.74	70520.33	43121.04	142336.31	66852.32	141589.02	5317.00	48109.98
59671.16	128722.62	81223.78	210657.57	96943.84	217035.57	11581.40	48431.92
197497.08	390823.70	241730.75	635542.53	302805.90	693758.72	7312.00	842507.60
136825.53	319258.87	198145.95	521274.94	243037.73	591505.92	0.00	644943.42
87206.23	244573.40	138917.03	362472.91	179153.93	384708.85	52733.00	283301.80
3456.94	17998.68	14055.45	50854.20	12841.39	27836.58	306.00	47450.70
165807.33	542534.06	332672.95	520932.78	228544.15	545856.07	2356.00	748158.62
67956.50	217915.39	147126.57	201498.84	85251.47	350482.53	26792.80	281355.81
11086.89	36177.93	21302.89	65881.68	26354.30	71523.02	0.00	54850.35
14723.10	52670.26	29336.98	63932.03	35364.45	87260.29	0.00	61527.35
46778.24	212634.97	115873.64	300128.72	149133.78	393594.83	2784.20	897585.02

幼儿园校舍及其他

Statistics of Kindergarten Buildings

地 区 Region	校舍建筑面积 Floor Space	教学及辅助用房 Teaching & Assistant Buildings				
		合计 Total	其中：of Which：			
			活动室 Recreational	洗手间 Toilet	睡眠室 Bed Room	保健室 Health Care
总 计 Total	**30652165.29**	**21464085.73**	**12503628.59**	**2082885.26**	**5215814.26**	**690331.45**
北 京 Beijing	79880.66	46791.56	24969.83	5950.96	12790.57	1449.57
天 津 Tianjin	127903.04	91018.35	53502.53	10997.21	20845.11	3004.90
河 北 Hebei	2487122.67	1798102.63	1084261.33	162376.89	388880.31	61198.63
山 西 Shanxi	809412.99	541354.93	337318.72	59386.11	104243.25	17368.40
内蒙古 Inner Mongolia	235236.78	147343.22	85767.52	14366.18	36437.29	4594.66
辽 宁 Liaoning	177636.11	125928.71	67836.33	12214.79	33546.32	5702.38
吉 林 Jilin	112281.73	71108.15	37871.49	6193.04	20926.46	2701.76
黑龙江 Heilongjiang	164753.02	112360.61	59971.19	11284.35	29588.30	5831.87
上 海 Shanghai	162557.87	97357.47	61341.70	9278.22	22766.20	2130.04
江 苏 Jiangsu	2496216.90	1744765.06	1036047.27	179960.09	406976.28	45480.90
浙 江 Zhejiang	1807814.70	1223124.21	710547.00	120452.25	326445.16	27560.81
安 徽 Anhui	775602.69	570120.04	357036.23	58446.37	108527.67	18978.47
福 建 Fujian	1261387.58	838344.87	487645.27	90213.52	214432.36	19398.77
江 西 Jiangxi	1163333.57	857940.87	495678.58	79291.36	216668.53	25640.14
山 东 Shandong	3352319.23	2275450.60	1422472.44	222972.05	443822.35	71650.18
河 南 Henan	3134437.88	2283330.45	1353734.72	233411.56	506926.83	80760.33
湖 北 Hubei	1012193.21	740095.54	402722.04	77419.36	193524.68	29259.81
湖 南 Hunan	1760773.82	1253325.37	653254.56	121624.56	358688.65	56130.30
广 东 Guangdong	2919313.52	1976162.61	1172821.04	162208.08	493950.44	56624.85
广 西 Guangxi	954514.74	706736.65	376101.80	63686.23	218310.30	22203.14
海 南 Hainan	187001.40	130526.55	71057.93	13111.24	36326.61	4289.10
重 庆 Chongqing	395425.66	288586.84	175496.51	24705.77	68195.48	8689.80
四 川 Sichuan	1132132.86	821633.70	475065.13	74689.74	210506.64	24538.51
贵 州 Guizhou	841105.19	587009.76	301209.27	60098.39	176033.85	22655.68
云 南 Yunnan	764766.85	538898.30	295657.76	46195.38	157917.59	17615.20
西 藏 Tibet	12330.79	7570.04	3741.56	820.92	2788.88	124.54
陕 西 Shaanxi	1161711.64	788368.74	453762.38	80440.90	185990.07	27282.49
甘 肃 Gansu	407514.03	262922.72	160716.04	23577.45	51590.06	12049.32
青 海 Qinghai	112218.81	73746.41	43878.16	7621.67	18085.00	2035.78
宁 夏 Ningxia	91234.97	66122.57	35849.69	6537.42	19745.16	1622.12
新 疆 Xinjiang	552030.38	397938.20	206292.57	43353.20	130337.86	11759.00

情况(镇乡结合区)(一)
and Others (Urban-rural Transitional Area) (1)

单位:平方米
unit: m^2

	行政办公用房 Administrative		生活用房 Residential and Welfare		其他用房 for Other Purposes	校舍面积中 of the Floor Space	
图书室 Reading Room	合计 Total	其中:教师办公室 of Which: Office	合计 Total	其中:厨房 of Which: Kitchen		危房面积 Floor Space of Dilapidated Buildings	当年新增校舍 New Added in Current Year
971426.17	**2189431.78**	**1328941.31**	**3141439.01**	**1462715.11**	**3857208.77**	**51071.02**	**2470886.75**
1630.63	6905.61	3790.12	10140.00	5772.24	16043.49	0.00	4274.40
2668.60	9078.55	5060.49	16547.18	7269.71	11258.96	0.00	8136.86
101385.47	181385.73	107192.39	227767.86	99847.43	279866.45	369.92	344635.51
23038.45	73045.53	49735.16	74561.94	34408.37	120450.59	5243.00	38995.98
6177.57	19756.38	11219.41	28003.40	12521.07	40133.78	0.00	15377.96
6628.89	14363.74	8954.29	17691.90	10532.01	19651.76	0.00	5244.92
3415.40	8049.85	5144.51	11498.42	4975.54	21625.31	0.00	4590.43
5684.90	10717.59	7394.20	19132.21	9397.71	22542.61	80.00	2891.00
1841.31	11085.42	4080.47	15762.31	7852.07	38352.67	0.00	14139.04
76300.52	168048.37	87249.17	253330.96	114399.97	330072.51	0.00	68712.20
38118.99	111203.89	61628.95	188757.36	95438.25	284729.24	405.00	133295.45
27131.30	58198.50	36938.79	63268.86	31413.31	84015.29	2510.00	45786.06
26654.95	81908.46	50654.93	123941.01	59526.59	217193.24	1319.00	45404.83
40662.26	85592.59	52751.54	133259.55	41952.29	86540.56	780.00	86070.30
114533.58	240277.78	149130.64	323048.41	147666.31	513542.44	0.00	365961.83
108497.01	252279.33	160239.88	276952.74	151137.73	321875.36	5122.10	74229.29
37169.65	69477.61	39833.19	118562.53	57544.38	84057.53	100.00	60153.20
63627.30	131479.01	90229.66	185381.76	88701.34	190587.68	3070.00	43041.00
90558.20	170809.25	101587.39	361689.20	130359.46	410652.46	1920.00	97591.26
26435.18	46753.16	32351.82	102783.71	63737.64	98241.22	3867.00	55672.56
5741.67	10542.90	7040.80	23095.09	10206.59	22836.86	1640.00	15162.00
11499.28	22877.24	14473.30	36447.75	18087.18	47513.83	1796.00	17107.00
36833.68	70522.94	43310.33	111814.56	58741.37	128161.66	0.00	161559.82
27012.57	60875.80	37654.95	96104.06	43980.38	97115.57	0.00	177159.94
21512.37	59793.20	33085.90	82282.86	42660.52	83792.49	14008.00	56178.16
94.14	987.76	907.76	2223.78	894.12	1549.21	306.00	7386.90
40892.90	124376.57	72053.41	122667.64	57851.92	126298.69	400.00	203192.54
14989.85	41274.55	27315.68	43683.15	17786.77	59633.61	8135.00	49439.07
2125.80	6954.34	5294.14	15680.48	7051.90	15837.58	0.00	10906.65
2368.18	7057.68	4060.94	8323.75	4166.21	9730.97	0.00	11967.00
6195.57	33752.45	18577.10	47034.58	26834.73	73305.15	0.00	246623.59

幼儿园校舍及

Statistics of Kindergarten Buildings

地区 Region	校舍建筑面积 Floor Space	教学及辅助用房 Teaching & Assistant Buildings				
		合计 Total	其中：of Which：			
			活动室 Recreational	洗手间 Toilet	睡眠室 Bed Room	保健室 Health Care
总　计 Total	**63279490.71**	**44250160.87**	**25810182.63**	**4315981.77**	**10093832.80**	**1811255.27**
北　京 Beijing	356343.86	198880.36	108766.11	24465.08	51929.31	6644.13
天　津 Tianjin	227670.92	160406.38	102568.09	20158.15	25488.06	6410.84
河　北 Hebei	3902668.29	2787641.20	1782139.09	248446.74	436572.37	116792.43
山　西 Shanxi	1363700.98	902093.64	595372.15	89633.31	127168.75	37765.90
内蒙古 Inner Mongolia	733777.99	462819.92	262421.07	48995.72	113333.08	16856.96
辽　宁 Liaoning	831212.63	576409.49	333739.95	53078.66	130968.59	24643.06
吉　林 Jilin	361554.22	246997.41	137292.88	21996.63	63450.98	11828.65
黑龙江 Heilongjiang	604726.47	401125.53	224903.69	38833.11	93037.51	22167.21
上　海 Shanghai	185036.59	104148.27	65530.62	10370.48	23185.24	2355.05
江　苏 Jiangsu	2239020.98	1613576.74	922877.18	163958.86	367026.49	65195.27
浙　江 Zhejiang	2263384.90	1500347.99	852697.01	151930.27	393503.58	44012.40
安　徽 Anhui	2665256.93	1943065.54	1210869.68	191649.40	339683.76	88277.96
福　建 Fujian	1684192.50	1105251.32	665418.41	124239.91	246391.54	30513.13
江　西 Jiangxi	3119771.05	2246743.23	1328502.30	220732.38	495440.51	88232.19
山　东 Shandong	4560166.25	3247291.08	2134241.95	321834.44	477492.65	124063.90
河　南 Henan	7464600.17	5512752.20	3337013.08	573405.99	1072290.96	231401.67
湖　北 Hubei	2085971.27	1473343.62	781251.52	157842.35	386014.84	67534.04
湖　南 Hunan	3298991.00	2279978.83	1178626.38	236870.69	606650.96	123883.10
广　东 Guangdong	3237416.78	2166534.89	1282907.01	157287.51	517878.02	79941.22
广　西 Guangxi	2551432.71	1853262.63	973020.99	176690.11	564693.65	65136.91
海　南 Hainan	378419.73	252922.69	133866.74	28555.98	71243.68	9030.23
重　庆 Chongqing	517463.86	360080.14	212563.22	34217.46	79131.97	16175.06
四　川 Sichuan	2351293.99	1706413.73	1042443.81	180167.44	347553.33	55975.98
贵　州 Guizhou	2607082.49	1762853.83	925243.44	193417.45	469011.25	78566.12
云　南 Yunnan	2741711.75	1929942.45	1085352.02	161295.52	516780.38	80709.78
西　藏 Tibet	596728.41	339792.32	195910.32	32704.31	84170.34	14819.39
陕　西 Shaanxi	1966949.40	1323799.83	747803.60	138799.81	294351.16	58610.65
甘　肃 Gansu	1498308.34	980124.76	630774.60	99747.09	135700.21	48366.57
青　海 Qinghai	617432.37	392740.96	237938.09	31667.50	91900.03	15426.73
宁　夏 Ningxia	380028.99	255656.43	142175.76	28367.92	61941.33	12071.39
新　疆 Xinjiang	5887174.89	4163163.46	2175951.87	354621.50	1409848.27	167847.35

其他情况(乡村)(一)
and Others (Rural Area)(1)

单位:平方米
unit: m^2

图书室 Reading Room	行政办公用房 Administrative 合计 Total	行政办公用房 Administrative 其中:教师办公室 of Which: Office	生活用房 Residential and Welfare 合计 Total	生活用房 Residential and Welfare 其中:厨房 of Which: Kitchen	其他用房 for Other Purposes	校舍面积中 of the Floor Space 危房面积 Floor Space of Dilapidated Buildings	校舍面积中 of the Floor Space 当年新增校舍 New Added in Current Year
2218908.40	**4883812.61**	**3271119.77**	**7104422.15**	**3380168.33**	**7041095.08**	**140942.87**	**7212726.72**
7075.73	34146.51	14855.79	50438.58	23360.65	72878.41	0.00	7420.56
5781.24	18269.62	11905.97	24608.18	11802.21	24386.74	0.00	29667.70
203690.57	315886.98	197211.29	359903.91	144832.50	439236.20	2843.85	455845.38
52153.53	156136.98	116856.34	132747.14	62454.77	172723.22	3779.06	70029.71
21213.09	62235.56	40030.53	102667.13	48649.91	106055.38	0.00	56215.79
33979.23	72049.83	45338.07	86731.52	53066.88	96021.79	259.00	17182.74
12428.27	26797.22	19803.96	33526.85	19318.26	54232.74	0.00	11521.72
22184.01	47548.57	35794.17	76943.52	37357.53	79108.85	1227.00	21092.63
2706.88	13220.87	4482.37	23312.82	8281.95	44354.63	0.00	0.00
94518.94	164683.27	92796.33	222615.61	109693.67	238145.36	0.00	68078.32
58204.73	150320.46	86374.57	246940.65	132611.17	365775.80	3244.00	184417.23
112584.74	203726.57	142376.17	267728.54	131845.29	250736.28	3483.00	169424.13
38688.33	112614.03	73992.84	190768.80	84384.03	275558.35	4447.00	92228.03
113835.85	279980.46	188433.34	380082.06	145176.57	212965.30	1617.00	245132.01
189658.14	370304.86	253342.17	397612.75	182051.29	544957.56	0.00	400613.09
298640.50	622285.86	436808.08	690944.14	386806.67	638617.97	9241.88	307164.95
80700.87	150475.24	91528.27	246572.13	121351.95	215580.28	5133.00	114101.32
133947.70	263138.42	183297.42	405040.10	189677.32	350833.65	8663.00	119280.35
128521.13	201157.75	131841.07	445013.32	157170.52	424710.82	2135.00	79168.93
73720.97	134600.85	100725.30	332539.20	201899.90	231030.03	8798.85	150087.90
10226.06	21933.47	13698.01	50671.46	23410.20	52892.11	512.00	9742.00
17992.43	37545.35	25710.98	69386.60	29145.87	50451.77	7482.00	19087.71
80273.17	154748.87	106695.94	270921.30	126334.78	219210.09	245.00	276341.19
96615.57	210761.31	139131.62	344297.92	169046.99	289169.43	0.00	410467.84
85804.75	179480.41	122797.74	369392.40	180182.05	262896.49	55926.78	298231.73
12187.96	51447.94	41369.36	153435.00	47932.27	52053.15	2348.00	100324.07
84234.61	226774.56	138674.02	221879.33	101625.99	194495.68	0.00	355794.17
65536.29	194579.89	141818.06	145465.40	51669.38	178138.29	19357.45	187492.26
15808.61	43397.76	33863.90	90361.50	36855.17	90932.15	0.00	67451.86
11100.03	29595.73	19510.12	44516.02	19660.60	50260.81	0.00	40244.58
54894.47	333967.41	220055.97	627358.27	342511.99	762685.75	200.00	2848876.82

幼儿园办学条件(总计)(二)
Statistics of Kindergarten Buildings and Others(Total)(2)

地　区 Region	占地面积(平方米) Areas of School Sites(m^2)			图书(册) Books & Magazines in Libraries (Volume)
	合计 Total	其中:of Which:		
		绿化用地面积 Green Areas	运动场地面积 Sports Areas	
总　计 Total	**576405517.95**	**99130312.94**	**192234452.68**	**358862257**
北　京 Beijing	6862461.73	1192723.77	2348577.20	6192600
天　津 Tianjin	3610656.68	515036.68	1282880.53	2262646
河　北 Hebei	32305484.85	3771366.82	11090233.58	19369739
山　西 Shanxi	13067372.61	1587599.44	4644692.35	7109745
内蒙古 Inner Mongolia	13702286.55	2149734.19	4197942.61	5019776
辽　宁 Liaoning	13928851.51	1891484.09	5231560.42	8020577
吉　林 Jilin	6358945.15	986413.82	2197486.29	3575838
黑龙江 Heilongjiang	9244336.05	1015769.79	3206876.16	3121635
上　海 Shanghai	9042689.61	2588254.37	2266030.15	5026231
江　苏 Jiangsu	41653840.33	9154356.35	15648493.22	36804008
浙　江 Zhejiang	24686701.40	5017492.46	8773338.68	20188316
安　徽 Anhui	20277460.78	3144526.36	6105937.03	10616156
福　建 Fujian	14280271.31	2345369.77	5383779.35	8377368
江　西 Jiangxi	20245858.35	3183651.45	6804478.22	8960925
山　东 Shandong	49026842.66	8910115.66	17454202.85	24418085
河　南 Henan	45687773.48	6787393.62	14841012.34	24385171
湖　北 Hubei	20060879.37	4235247.22	5844143.36	12901073
湖　南 Hunan	25347170.42	3916238.78	7035664.33	18738496
广　东 Guangdong	45434838.79	9088023.80	16704898.48	42944440
广　西 Guangxi	14312078.49	2062790.20	5042569.28	9314345
海　南 Hainan	4280569.39	820175.58	1330040.43	2853161
重　庆 Chongqing	8112878.30	1196774.41	2923501.27	6646405
四　川 Sichuan	22328746.88	3213755.67	7500012.08	19549620
贵　州 Guizhou	18349387.34	2969273.43	6527846.88	11703419
云　南 Yunnan	15548659.69	2681358.04	4773751.66	10081110
西　藏 Tibet	3126518.07	449823.45	498363.26	619517
陕　西 Shaanxi	20540761.02	2950879.20	6424447.38	17586240
甘　肃 Gansu	12209419.71	1560239.71	4132747.87	6107127
青　海 Qinghai	4661416.26	620804.28	1256958.82	1144378
宁　夏 Ningxia	3930200.94	565204.21	1301737.15	1416556
新　疆 Xinjiang	34180160.23	8558436.32	9460249.45	3807554

幼儿园办学条件(城区)(二)
Statistics of Kindergarten Buildings and Others (Urban Area) (2)

地　区 Region	占地面积(平方米) Areas of School Sites(m^2)			图书(册) Books & Magazines in Libraries (Volume)
	合计 Total	其中:of Which: 绿化用地面积 Green Areas	运动场地面积 Sports Areas	
总　计 Total	**196306542.73**	**34711049.14**	**68125066.99**	**160966292**
北　京 Beijing	5340797.78	898640.67	1847985.89	5271453
天　津 Tianjin	2319249.44	343111.98	798025.31	1736980
河　北 Hebei	6218078.43	691347.07	2142915.46	5325040
山　西 Shanxi	3821329.94	476444.22	1346590.15	2830600
内蒙古 Inner Mongolia	3702441.04	512306.73	1292449.91	2047679
辽　宁 Liaoning	7812597.75	1111902.99	2793707.81	5363177
吉　林 Jilin	2625694.93	378141.31	920846.03	1902653
黑龙江 Heilongjiang	3677320.24	401609.87	1211037.14	1562147
上　海 Shanghai	7404044.93	2102123.01	1842089.97	4398758
江　苏 Jiangsu	18849158.58	4332544.53	7384481.69	18055715
浙　江 Zhejiang	12654642.33	2645864.34	4447609.15	10963233
安　徽 Anhui	4308143.77	711205.89	1335252.13	3018759
福　建 Fujian	5585312.25	885245.99	2131407.12	3910068
江　西 Jiangxi	4720038.62	779656.18	1506700.94	2529016
山　东 Shandong	16584190.59	2786133.22	5957592.87	11618742
河　南 Henan	10419463.28	1585337.09	3641783.94	7290137
湖　北 Hubei	7301410.40	1420974.11	2198495.62	5274836
湖　南 Hunan	7253406.54	1116919.56	2112624.97	6565137
广　东 Guangdong	27460288.69	5531525.24	10340873.23	27245471
广　西 Guangxi	4177869.62	691917.57	1509756.29	3352224
海　南 Hainan	1450908.77	238613.51	495105.54	1248478
重　庆 Chongqing	4218250.82	612695.09	1436629.68	3663759
四　川 Sichuan	8267109.41	1265619.65	2642956.14	7545496
贵　州 Guizhou	3154612.43	392640.69	1119698.60	3297551
云　南 Yunnan	3698948.98	718065.79	1243751.20	3734659
西　藏 Tibet	481411.85	83417.81	84951.54	322944
陕　西 Shaanxi	5242308.49	759911.75	1789066.62	5661156
甘　肃 Gansu	2293876.81	264310.70	766209.70	2349682
青　海 Qinghai	603365.32	89102.16	180385.16	531278
宁　夏 Ningxia	1213479.45	179352.93	435484.17	684681
新　疆 Xinjiang	3446791.25	704367.49	1168603.02	1664783

幼儿园办学条件(城乡结合区)(二)
Statistics of Kindergarten Buildings and Others (Urban-rural Transitional Area)(2)

地　区 Region	占地面积(平方米) Areas of School Sites(m^2)			图书(册) Books & Magazines in Libraries (Volume)
	合计 Total	其中:of Which:		
		绿化用地面积 Green Areas	运动场地面积 Sports Areas	
总　计 Total	**37417807.53**	**6931831.53**	**13184196.86**	**26203416**
北　京 Beijing	502122.16	102369.50	162106.67	315724
天　津 Tianjin	162066.59	20101.08	62388.61	106791
河　北 Hebei	1618449.48	209686.31	588704.31	1238088
山　西 Shanxi	629815.01	87328.81	223738.88	430731
内蒙古 Inner Mongolia	160248.71	19305.86	45589.98	64890
辽　宁 Liaoning	592953.44	72917.66	226035.28	395837
吉　林 Jilin	150448.42	25960.79	54027.88	56081
黑龙江 Heilongjiang	309962.02	52125.96	113776.26	78503
上　海 Shanghai	665007.70	186617.54	167412.50	338582
江　苏 Jiangsu	2507943.49	570432.53	950056.31	2100240
浙　江 Zhejiang	3210452.90	630295.76	1129337.56	2451157
安　徽 Anhui	484556.08	79806.71	154383.97	295114
福　建 Fujian	1025439.77	179554.77	398660.89	523522
江　西 Jiangxi	773207.07	133580.11	249755.56	388636
山　东 Shandong	5162740.63	908553.86	1876964.48	2595055
河　南 Henan	2026764.33	342135.71	689527.97	1063576
湖　北 Hubei	1214670.18	261899.64	358644.74	795587
湖　南 Hunan	884364.70	150138.02	266109.30	696265
广　东 Guangdong	9744356.45	1976449.04	3590957.79	8245628
广　西 Guangxi	666006.81	102396.15	233010.54	541666
海　南 Hainan	118865.40	21830.14	42885.59	75011
重　庆 Chongqing	331178.14	45975.88	117511.13	258584
四　川 Sichuan	1111980.53	192637.48	349892.99	860542
贵　州 Guizhou	572799.23	72901.46	205934.99	380598
云　南 Yunnan	754678.48	135205.20	260245.70	739673
西　藏 Tibet	44467.82	3364.09	4319.62	28212
陕　西 Shaanxi	991157.30	154312.32	327795.07	811139
甘　肃 Gansu	251357.38	28476.14	77455.86	156348
青　海 Qinghai	57746.93	7252.00	19441.00	31603
宁　夏 Ningxia	71350.40	13559.00	31272.00	25866
新　疆 Xinjiang	620649.98	144662.01	206253.43	114167

幼儿园办学条件(镇区)(二)
Statistics of Kindergarten Buildings and Others (Counties & Towns Area)(2)

地 区 Region	占地面积(平方米) Areas of School Sites(m^2)			图书(册) Books & Magazines in Libraries (Volume)
	合计 Total	其中:of Which: 绿化用地面积 Green Areas	运动场地面积 Sports Areas	
总 计 Total	**211349688.93**	**35422042.75**	**69938769.99**	**133466581**
北 京 Beijing	723068.30	143043.71	245428.24	542419
天 津 Tianjin	564061.52	82063.33	218539.13	248750
河 北 Hebei	11962140.05	1380337.77	3862365.10	7187053
山 西 Shanxi	5084284.96	615826.20	1771620.54	2849699
内蒙古 Inner Mongolia	5972345.13	1026692.92	1906915.38	2271603
辽 宁 Liaoning	3494591.30	458134.23	1341445.25	1679665
吉 林 Jilin	2478918.56	379503.75	830873.55	1270287
黑龙江 Heilongjiang	3447723.15	368738.09	1254182.81	1197664
上 海 Shanghai	1359389.14	401163.18	350453.45	503046
江 苏 Jiangsu	17847500.59	3838268.23	6507645.10	15110816
浙 江 Zhejiang	8306033.36	1659963.50	2961451.24	6678947
安 徽 Anhui	9136365.94	1442424.68	2795806.84	4840574
福 建 Fujian	5874097.99	960723.43	2257560.35	3391223
江 西 Jiangxi	8894947.01	1371189.73	3008561.29	4280409
山 东 Shandong	17822035.50	3365149.23	6069544.04	8147940
河 南 Henan	16840530.35	2482281.07	5384428.46	9260165
湖 北 Hubei	8247904.27	1820009.30	2350625.82	5438439
湖 南 Hunan	11490827.92	1760409.83	3155649.96	8595846
广 东 Guangdong	11921176.97	2268906.69	4221670.21	11254782
广 西 Guangxi	5998409.31	803381.32	2118309.51	4113655
海 南 Hainan	2016268.41	399932.36	597098.43	1253536
重 庆 Chongqing	2977309.17	457129.69	1121036.94	2362575
四 川 Sichuan	9888285.38	1396665.95	3385800.36	8918358
贵 州 Guizhou	8541875.84	1328792.73	3001496.42	5383120
云 南 Yunnan	5195762.73	899491.11	1614689.00	3542667
西 藏 Tibet	620557.54	82216.62	83423.14	106718
陕 西 Shaanxi	9798194.67	1369318.28	3042204.97	8657284
甘 肃 Gansu	4375983.04	572078.14	1475447.88	2421086
青 海 Qinghai	1269119.46	155122.46	327758.98	293626
宁 夏 Ningxia	1510662.37	209437.52	488530.71	517132
新 疆 Xinjiang	7689319.00	1923647.70	2188206.89	1147497

幼儿园办学条件(镇乡结合区)(二)
Statistics of Kindergarten Buildings and Others (County-town Transitional Area)(2)

地 区 Region	占地面积(平方米) Areas of School Sites(m^2)			图书(册) Books & Magazines in Libraries (Volume)
	合计 Total	其中:of Which:		
		绿化用地面积 Green Areas	运动场地面积 Sports Areas	
总 计 Total	**58955808.80**	**9853086.17**	**19702191.87**	**34637932**
北 京 Beijing	185264.22	35842.44	63862.32	113611
天 津 Tianjin	315133.92	43517.37	126017.07	148743
河 北 Hebei	6294802.13	705785.06	1992530.35	3495073
山 西 Shanxi	1631153.19	195346.86	573188.19	836936
内蒙古 Inner Mongolia	510564.76	76433.63	159815.38	191864
辽 宁 Liaoning	448154.78	51997.28	169191.71	191532
吉 林 Jilin	240066.85	32075.37	85314.00	124692
黑龙江 Heilongjiang	343505.00	37605.00	112858.93	107476
上 海 Shanghai	253096.04	68305.08	62833.29	92545
江 苏 Jiangsu	5038281.91	1106010.83	1829638.97	3915723
浙 江 Zhejiang	2715509.24	466590.55	916261.01	2286651
安 徽 Anhui	1523133.57	234191.54	492640.73	772199
福 建 Fujian	1736720.58	286881.97	651906.38	915082
江 西 Jiangxi	1867649.53	277295.85	680210.64	835518
山 东 Shandong	8097946.08	1529998.98	2787976.11	3313634
河 南 Henan	6381897.67	962143.02	2107388.10	3066714
湖 北 Hubei	2019142.69	455097.81	565450.35	1154875
湖 南 Hunan	2880297.27	454341.03	785408.66	1897348
广 东 Guangdong	4200113.79	809242.95	1519868.19	3870190
广 西 Guangxi	1231917.56	169435.58	444662.70	686509
海 南 Hainan	312130.68	61976.80	96676.35	199613
重 庆 Chongqing	557643.17	78739.97	213055.34	428444
四 川 Sichuan	1785351.24	264493.69	630008.69	1393192
贵 州 Guizhou	1618476.90	258941.08	586043.69	882040
云 南 Yunnan	1231131.26	207846.68	390784.76	982961
西 藏 Tibet	40755.76	3628.60	2901.00	3144
陕 西 Shaanxi	2325623.88	353936.78	718248.90	2020692
甘 肃 Gansu	874722.76	115536.10	321373.89	471806
青 海 Qinghai	267155.50	36785.57	74331.00	68378
宁 夏 Ningxia	265612.59	43631.23	83339.72	54964
新 疆 Xinjiang	1762854.28	429431.47	458405.45	115783

幼儿园办学条件(乡村)(二)

Statistics of Kindergarten Buildings and Others (Rural Area)(2)

地区 Region	占地面积(平方米) Areas of School Sites(m^2) 合计 Total	其中:of Which: 绿化用地面积 Green Areas	运动场地面积 Sports Areas	图书(册) Books & Magazines in Libraries (Volume)
总 计 Total	**168749286.29**	**28997221.05**	**54170615.70**	**64429384**
北 京 Beijing	798595.65	151039.39	255163.07	378728
天 津 Tianjin	727345.72	89861.37	266316.09	276916
河 北 Hebei	14125266.37	1699681.98	5084953.02	6857646
山 西 Shanxi	4161757.71	495329.02	1526481.66	1429446
内蒙古 Inner Mongolia	4027500.38	610734.54	998577.32	700494
辽 宁 Liaoning	2621662.46	321446.87	1096407.36	977735
吉 林 Jilin	1254331.66	228768.76	445766.71	402898
黑龙江 Heilongjiang	2119292.66	245421.83	741656.21	361824
上 海 Shanghai	279255.54	84968.18	73486.73	124427
江 苏 Jiangsu	4957181.16	983543.59	1756366.43	3637477
浙 江 Zhejiang	3726025.71	711664.62	1364278.29	2546136
安 徽 Anhui	6832951.07	990895.79	1974878.06	2756823
福 建 Fujian	2820861.07	499400.35	994811.88	1076077
江 西 Jiangxi	6630872.72	1032805.54	2289215.99	2151500
山 东 Shandong	14620616.57	2758833.21	5427065.94	4651403
河 南 Henan	18427779.85	2719775.46	5814799.94	7834869
湖 北 Hubei	4511564.70	994263.81	1295021.92	2187798
湖 南 Hunan	6602935.96	1038909.39	1767389.40	3577513
广 东 Guangdong	6053373.13	1287591.87	2142355.04	4444187
广 西 Guangxi	4135799.56	567491.31	1414503.48	1848466
海 南 Hainan	813392.21	181629.71	237836.46	351147
重 庆 Chongqing	917318.31	126949.63	365834.65	620071
四 川 Sichuan	4173352.09	551470.07	1471255.58	3085766
贵 州 Guizhou	6652899.07	1247840.01	2406651.86	3022748
云 南 Yunnan	6653947.98	1063801.14	1915311.46	2803784
西 藏 Tibet	2024548.68	284189.02	329988.58	189855
陕 西 Shaanxi	5500257.86	821649.17	1593175.79	3267800
甘 肃 Gansu	5539559.86	723850.87	1891090.29	1336359
青 海 Qinghai	2788931.48	376579.66	748814.68	319474
宁 夏 Ningxia	1206059.12	176413.76	377722.27	214743
新 疆 Xinjiang	23044049.98	5930421.13	6103439.54	995274

第二部分
Part Ⅱ

办 学 条 件
PHYSICAL FACILITIES

一、教育经费
Public Expenditure on Education

各类学校教育经费来源
Sources of Educational Funds and Expenditure

学校类别 Type of Schools	合　计 Total	国家财政性教育经费 Government Appropriation for Education	#公共财政教育经费 Public Expenditure for Education
全国总计 National Total	**388883850.3**	**313962518.9**	**277006325.2**
按学校类别分组 Grouped by Type of Schools			
高等学校 HEIs	101246451.3	62878522.1	52697034.6
普通高等学校 Regular HEIs	99733862.3	61988339.7	51943101.7
成人高等学校 Adult HEIs	1512589.0	890182.4	753933.0
中等职业学校 Secondary Vocational Schools	22228987.4	19487328.8	17746148.3
普通中专 Regular Specialized Secondary Schools	10384222.4	9070818.1	8229290.0
成人中专 Adult Specialized Secondary Schools	966360.5	814002.6	709207.9
职业高中 Vocational High Schools	8013672.9	7306245.0	6703765.3
技工学校 Skilled Workers Schools	2864731.5	2296263.1	2103885.0
中学 Secondary Schools	105526841.2	93475356.4	85465315.2
普通中学 Regular Secondary Schools	105457848.5	93416416.1	85408810.0
普通高中 Regular Senior Secondary Schools	39323128.1	32091070.3	29167684.1
普通初中 Regular Junior Secondary Schools	66134720.3	61325345.7	56241125.9
#农村 Rural	39276243.3	37491313.4	34522707.4
成人中学 Adult Secondary Schools	68992.7	58940.3	56505.2
小学 Primary Schools	108548494.4	103175847.4	93621422.7
普通小学 Regular Primary Schools	108546878.6	103174231.7	93619926.0
#农 村 Rural	69161972.7	67206772.3	60816564.2
成人小学 Adult Primary Schools	1615.8	1615.8	1496.6
特殊教育 Special Education	1357387.8	1326839.0	1208800.5
幼儿园 Kindergartens	28035345.6	13260717.8	12422044.2
教育行政单位 Education Administrative Department	4011660.6	3792116.8	3326169.7
教育事业单位 Education Public Institutions	8341756.2	7308604.6	6348702.7
其他 Others	9586926.0	9257185.9	4170687.2

和支出情况（2016年）
for Education in Various School (2016)

单位：万元
unit: 10,000 yuan

民办学校中举办者投入 School Funding for Private Schools	社会捐赠经费 Donor Funding for the Community	事业收入 Income from Teaching Research and Other Auxiliary Activity	学费 Tuition	其他教育经费 Other Educational Funds
2032732.6	**810447.4**	**62768291.8**	**47709339.2**	**9309859.7**
472741.7	472073.7	32238275.8	21766357.0	5184838.0
472741.7	471892.2	31680946.4	21388309.7	5119942.2
0.0	181.4	557329.3	378047.3	64895.9
79348.5	17951.2	1953247.0	1119007.5	691111.8
39845.3	8534.0	932057.8	523032.2	332967.2
5154.6	4553.3	119204.5	55504.4	23445.5
28618.2	3608.9	469299.5	278223.1	205901.3
5730.4	1255.1	432685.3	262247.9	128797.7
547999.3	156526.4	9945850.4	8003695.9	1401108.6
547999.3	156487.6	9938849.2	8002854.8	1398096.3
183138.0	89813.8	6285092.2	4895204.2	674013.8
364861.3	66673.8	3653757.0	3107650.6	724082.5
186883.9	31618.2	1246179.2	1009305.4	320248.5
0.0	38.9	7001.2	841.0	3012.3
423690.1	89879.0	3855257.0	3391133.1	1003820.8
423690.1	89879.0	3855257.0	3391133.1	1003820.8
182649.0	38144.4	1248720.5	1047046.3	485686.5
0.0	0.0	0.0	0.0	0.0
298.5	2917.9	9098.2	4622.4	18234.2
508654.5	32145.2	13845204.8	13402114.4	388623.3
0.0	5001.0	21818.0	0.0	192724.8
0.0	33113.2	677290.0	0.0	322748.4
0.0	839.8	222250.5	22408.9	106649.7

各地区教育经费来源
Sources of Educational Fund and Expenditure

地　区 Region	合　计 Total	国家财政性教育经费 Government Appropriation for Education	#公共财政教育经费 Public Expenditure for Education
中　央 Central Government	36227666.4	25351987.7	14883286.2
地　方 Local Government	352656183.9	288610531.2	262123039.0
北　京 Beijing	11934724.2	10491717.7	8822889.5
天　津 Tianjin	5365129.0	4530501.3	4257999.5
河　北 Hebei	14203833.7	11888154.1	11155774.4
山　西 Shanxi	7942195.8	6633064.8	6075868.7
内蒙古 Inner Mongolia	7624806.3	6648962.8	5432897.7
辽　宁 Liaoning	9206906.7	7421874.2	6328446.4
吉　林 Jilin	6439836.6	5403747.9	4959176.8
黑龙江 Heilongjiang	7336607.0	6385696.0	5959695.1
上　海 Shanghai	11218946.0	9237024.9	8019824.8
江　苏 Jiangsu	24020854.6	19233684.6	18419418.0
浙　江 Zhejiang	18908104.2	14235711.1	13136546.9
安　徽 Anhui	12357931.3	10304305.9	9108725.1
福　建 Fujian	10473974.9	8403251.3	7893639.9
江　西 Jiangxi	10468837.1	8816174.1	8401619.3
山　东 Shandong	22422970.0	18754459.6	18231843.2
河　南 Henan	18902582.1	14922439.2	12450079.6
湖　北 Hubei	13009263.9	10446404.3	9797918.0
湖　南 Hunan	13781958.9	10836438.7	10273884.0
广　东 Guangdong	33675375.9	24875763.5	22439023.7
广　西 Guangxi	10914240.9	9137061.2	8507844.1
海　南 Hainan	3068766.5	2496490.7	2139153.7
重　庆 Chongqing	8863208.5	7054576.5	5652592.8
四　川 Sichuan	17620946.2	14423197.4	12774498.9
贵　州 Guizhou	10335341.8	8909338.7	8402520.4
云　南 Yunnan	11886446.4	10227744.5	8641228.7
西　藏 Tibet	1857714.2	1829919.1	1758336.2
陕　西 Shaanxi	10049114.4	8086909.3	7762893.2
甘　肃 Gansu	6706136.5	6065624.3	5487834.3
青　海 Qinghai	2162972.5	1918513.1	1687874.0
宁　夏 Ningxia	2072543.8	1795089.4	1497139.2
新　疆 Xinjiang	7823914.0	7196691.0	6645852.9

和支出情况(2016 年)
for Education by Region (2016)

单位：万元
unit：10,000 yuan

民办学校中举办者投入 School Funding for Private Schools	社会捐赠经费 Donor Funding for the Community	事业收入 Income from Teaching Research and Other Auxiliary Activity	学费 Tuition	其他教育经费 Other Educational Funds
0. 0	314723. 6	8138797. 5	2846878. 6	2422157. 7
2032732. 6	495723. 8	54629494. 3	44862460. 5	6887702. 0
9260. 6	10878. 7	1299204. 9	1034188. 0	123662. 3
2167. 9	3655. 8	736267. 5	610872. 7	92536. 5
49418. 3	7216. 6	2106270. 9	1755230. 2	152773. 8
21478. 2	1349. 0	1223188. 4	998977. 8	63115. 4
16181. 5	3794. 7	597735. 1	485656. 0	358132. 1
13099. 3	3893. 3	1693886. 3	1388428. 9	74153. 6
17500. 2	3643. 5	907906. 8	786173. 7	107038. 3
7520. 6	1264. 7	903123. 4	791454. 9	39002. 3
5955. 3	8503. 5	1565521. 5	1255664. 7	401940. 8
136862. 5	92080. 9	3828459. 4	3054071. 7	729767. 2
145215. 2	34871. 8	3639753. 5	2933513. 2	852552. 6
57504. 1	9871. 1	1844677. 3	1520679. 5	141572. 9
53413. 3	55910. 0	1710075. 3	1409244. 8	251325. 1
43813. 1	13337. 2	1523412. 7	1267593. 6	72100. 0
114150. 4	19004. 4	3276471. 9	2807720. 4	258883. 6
117466. 2	6032. 1	3593113. 2	3069814. 9	263531. 4
126304. 6	6897. 8	2251450. 6	1838663. 8	178206. 6
82133. 5	6988. 4	2561467. 2	2041954. 3	294931. 0
505911. 6	93097. 8	7741252. 5	6611376. 0	459350. 5
35647. 9	9385. 9	1595245. 1	1266472. 9	136900. 9
71954. 3	2813. 9	439279. 4	357484. 1	58228. 3
117791. 5	13178. 2	1430841. 2	1135283. 3	246821. 1
126747. 9	36262. 7	2852603. 8	2276355. 4	182134. 4
44819. 2	9000. 1	1073183. 5	850507. 7	299000. 4
63875. 7	22110. 3	1226316. 1	992946. 7	346399. 7
184. 8	172. 0	22249. 8	16434. 8	5188. 3
16157. 0	7661. 4	1782643. 7	1386605. 2	155743. 1
7126. 1	6220. 7	559101. 0	439485. 5	68064. 5
4966. 5	2065. 1	103590. 8	69573. 9	133837. 0
14463. 7	3242. 1	198792. 8	157979. 8	60955. 8
3641. 7	1320. 3	342408. 9	252052. 2	279852. 2

二、教育基本建设投资
Capital Construction Investment in the Educational Sector

教育基本建设
Data on the Completion of Capital Construction

学校类别 Type of School	投资合计（万元）Total Investment Completed in the Current Year (10 Thousand Yuan)	本年完成投资按 Investment by Source of			
		国家预算内 Budgetary Allocation			
		小计 Subtotal	中央 Central	省级 Local	小计 Subtotal
总　计 Total	**41718761**	**33620140**	**6161570**	**27458570**	**7155789**
高等教育学校 Higher Education Schools	7947200	3726817	409197	3317620	4021495
中等职业学校 Secondary Vocational Schools	1673498	1460999	298238	1162761	169547
普通中学 Regular Secondary Schools	14852479	13058188	2123673	10934515	1496030
职业初中 Vocational Junior Secondary Schools	81489	80039	30556	49483	1450
小学 Primary Schools	11786327	10939586	2442686	8496900	622946
特殊教育学校 Special Education Schools	157379	142384	14178	128206	11793
幼儿园 Kindergartens	4088101	3302676	788898	2513777	616874
其他 Other	1132289	909452	54143	855308	215656

投资完成情况(总计)
Investment in the Educational Sector(Regional Aggregates)

资金来源分(万元) Fund (10 Thousand Yuan)			本年竣工建筑面积(平方米) Building Floor Area Completed (m^2)			
自筹资金 Self-raised Fund		其他 Other Sources				
其中 of Which:						
学校自筹 Raised by School	个人捐资 Individual Donations		合计 Total	教学及辅助用房 Teaching and Administrative	行政办公用房 Adm. Building Rooms for Other Purpose	其他用房 Others
6999598	**156192**	**942833**	**161147096**	**110875897**	**4883005**	**45388194**
3973583	47912	198889	23127160	12362923	606587	10157650
165795	3751	42953	6067402	3694003	224061	2149338
1413207	82823	298262	57289324	37217068	1895234	18177022
1450	0	0	227261	135790	17995	73476
618294	4652	223796	54144060	41180334	1425737	11537989
11793	0	3202	542417	356341	33580	152496
599820	17055	168551	14634479	12172229	507296	1954954
215656	0	7182	5114993	3757209	172515	1185269

教育基本建设

Data on the Completion of Capital Construction

学校类别 Type of School	投资合计（万元） Total Investment Completed in the Current Year (10 Thousand Yuan)	本年完成投资按 Investment by Source of 国家预算内 Budgetary Allocation 小计 Subtotal	中央 Central	省级 Local	小计 Subtotal
合 计 Total	**41718761**	**33620139**	**6161570**	**27458569**	**7155789**
北 京 Beijing	285359	273003	0	273003	12097
天 津 Tianjin	310955	130380	2750	127630	180075
河 北 Hebei	772528	730775	256307	474469	27702
山 西 Shanxi	612973	366323	46509	319814	242422
内蒙古 Inner Mongolia	957344	887661	157345	730316	64669
辽 宁 Liaoning	454384	375469	87587	287882	78183
大 连 Dalian	50105	49918	0	49918	187
吉 林 Jilin	467410	309743	113296	196448	157490
黑龙江 Heilongjiang	227516	218333	83558	134775	8375
上 海 Shanghai	1197411	866867	15512	851355	278833
江 苏 Jiangsu	3091703	2608746	23499	2585247	382377
浙 江 Zhejiang	3033336	2507211	44896	2462315	487364
宁 波 Ningbo	479558	452436	0	452436	27123
安 徽 Anhui	1840809	1596235	315220	1281014	225940
福 建 Fujian	837339	578548	48658	529890	197445
厦 门 Xiamen	204305	191377	0	191377	12386
江 西 Jiangxi	1163345	931550	322695	608855	216336
山 东 Shandong	4734609	3901942	175505	3726437	705620
青 岛 Qingdao	395218	388441	0	388441	400
河 南 Henan	1992786	1340665	561397	779268	640334
湖 北 Hubei	996241	977380	238314	739066	18709
湖 南 Hunan	2186779	1815194	338614	1476579	349979
广 东 Guangdong	2555746	1968595	57755	1910840	551877
深 圳 Shenzhen	764007	759571	0	759571	4435
广 西 Guangxi	2067856	1684258	496992	1187267	364428
海 南 Hainan	465610	348651	101823	246827	115114
重 庆 Chongqing	1236951	849425	218208	631217	313555
四 川 Sichuan	1980839	1599592	411570	1188022	354688
贵 州 Guizhou	1327847	1040049	517638	522412	204575
云 南 Yunnan	509596	348450	125892	222558	135135
西 藏 Tibet	195359	195359	195359	0	0
陕 西 Shaanxi	940033	702071	178767	523304	203047
甘 肃 Gansu	802936	746071	232045	514026	43115
青 海 Qinghai	220726	220726	86347	134379	0
宁 夏 Ningxia	457805	313169	168032	145137	144235
新 疆 Xinjiang	1802837	1258453	452984	805469	396442
新疆生产建设兵团 The Xinjiang Production and Construction Corps	98603	87504	86499	1005	11099

投资完成情况
Investment in the Educational Sector

资金来源分(万元) Fund (10 Thousand Yuan)			本年竣工建筑面积(平方米) Building Floor Area Completed (m^2)			
自筹资金 Self-raised Fund		其他 Other Sources				
其中 of Which:						
学校自筹 Raised by School	个人捐资 Individual Donations		合计 Total	教学及辅助用房 Teaching and Administrative	行政办公用房 Adm. Building Rooms for Other Purpose	其他用房 Others
6999598	**156192**	**942833**	**161147096**	**110875897**	**4883005**	**45388194**
12097	0	259	574117	435256	36838	102023
180075	0	500	1073093	781498	31067	260528
27702	0	14050	3702489	2402055	75884	1224550
235661	6761	4229	1072809	804785	42746	225278
64669	0	5014	3503925	2405664	119682	978579
78183	0	733	2177575	1624936	69542	483097
187	0	0	350513	301413	14561	34539
157490	0	176	2686413	1799700	164494	722219
8375	0	808	1260124	925006	47596	287522
278833	0	51711	1422883	1003899	228723	190261
380953	1424	100580	9047386	6223594	427356	2396436
472787	14577	38761	5576282	3145068	288515	2142699
27123	0	0	1184048	914936	62802	206310
225937	3	18635	9594254	7480638	177278	1936338
197445	0	61346	2405063	1977538	40892	386633
12386	0	542	471259	394605	3561	73093
201626	14710	15459	8057096	6086925	156350	1813821
705620	0	127047	19408842	14617948	692285	4098609
400	0	6377	931632	692957	32756	205919
632382	7952	11788	8927504	5622988	286566	3017950
18709	0	152	4641219	3050292	72805	1518122
312676	37303	21606	9201343	5843376	182309	3175658
513058	38818	35275	9665638	6011739	413181	3240718
4435	0	0	2014005	836559	167507	1009939
357358	7071	19170	9241242	6285490	130273	2825479
115114	0	1845	1322416	936254	40569	345593
313555	0	73972	3814978	2215465	122229	1477284
354688	0	26559	8819705	5597734	187013	3034958
204575	0	83223	9039256	6619065	112862	2307329
135135	0	26011	3136834	1495285	82294	1559255
0	0	0	501680	339557	0	162123
177896	25151	34914	4435583	3057990	86663	1290930
42274	840	13750	3362248	2560693	53253	748302
0	0	0	483133	370308	0	112825
144235	0	401	1474221	1217622	35085	221514
394860	1582	147942	6187953	4533947	194147	1459859
11099	0	0	378335	263112	3321	111902

第三部分
Part Ⅲ

科学研究活动及其他
SCIENTIFIC RESEARCH ACTIVITES & OTHER

一、自然科学与技术
Natural Science and Technology

	教学与科研人员 Personnel Engaged in S&T Activities		研究与发展人员 R & D Personnel	
	合计 Total	其中:科学家和工程师 of Which: Scientists & Engineers	合计 Total	其中:科学家和工程师 of Which: Scientists & Engineers
合计 Total	**1091319**	**1054772**	**414886**	**407824**
按学校规格分 Breakdown by Category of HEIs				
"211"及省部共建高等学校 Key HEIs	327579	315367	166939	162990
其他本科院校 Ordinary Degree Level HEIs	602202	582950	224650	221768
高等专科学校 Short-cycle HEIs	161538	156455	23297	23066
按学校隶属分 Breakdown by Control				
部委院校 HEIs under Other Central Ministries	34815	33723	17515	16981
教育部直属院校 HEIs under Ministry of Education	237568	228518	125343	122385
地方院校 HEIs under Local Governments	819079	792674	272028	268458
按学校类型分 Breakdown by Type of HEIs				
综合大学 Comprehensive Universities	330296	317519	135192	132124
工科院校 Engineering	357927	349690	140483	138963
农林院校 Agriculture	54203	52498	24459	24015
医药院校 Medicine & Pharmacy	254112	242307	78016	76430
师范院校 Teachers Training	68396	66976	29119	28755
其他院校 Others	26528	25925	7617	7537

科技人力情况
Manpower in Regular HEIs

单位：人
unit: person

研究与发展全时人员 R & D FTEs (Full-time Equivalents)		R&D 成果应用及科技服务人员 R & D Personnel		R&D 成果应用及科技服务全时人员 R & D FTEs (Full-time Equivalents)	
合计 Total	其中：科学家和工程师 of Which: Scientists & Engineers	合计 Total	其中：科学家和工程师 of Which: Scientists & Engineers	合计 Total	其中：科学家和工程师 of Which: Scientists & Engineers
248892	**244638**	**48798**	**48134**	**29263**	**28851**
100159	97787	24033	23654	14419	14188
134763	133029	21432	21215	12852	12714
13970	13822	3333	3265	1992	1949
10508	10187	4417	4391	2648	2632
75203	73430	15912	15596	9547	9357
163181	161021	28469	28147	17068	16862
81107	79255	14147	13849	8490	8308
84267	83349	26535	26320	15912	15780
14672	14405	3637	3583	2184	2148
46805	45854	1317	1263	784	749
17468	17250	2758	2717	1654	1629
4573	4525	404	402	239	237

	拨入 Revenues			
	合计 Total	政府资金 Government Funds	企事业单位委托 Contract Research Fund	其他 Others
合计 Total	**177289273**	**113368145**	**50088082**	**13833046**
按学校规格分 Breakdown by Category of HEIs				
“211”及省部共建高等学校 Key HEIs	117153576	76086714	36007850	5059012
其他本科院校 Ordinary Degree Level HEIs	57786207	36196599	13455920	8133688
高等专科学校 Short-cycle HEIs	2349490	1084832	624312	640346
按学校隶属分 Breakdown by Control				
部委院校 HEIs under Other Central Ministries	21554231	13732639	7293324	528268
教育部直属院校 HEIs under Ministry of Education	84818406	55200729	25945168	3672509
地方院校 HEIs under Local Governments	70916636	44434777	16849590	9632269
按学校类型分 Breakdown by Type of HEIs				
综合大学 Comprehensive Universities	61979587	42275715	14802287	4901585
工科院校 Engineering	82612235	45833097	31757528	5021610
农林院校 Agriculture	11239872	9272894	1368926	598052
医药院校 Medicine & Pharmacy	10910453	8702242	572295	1635916
师范院校 Teachers Training	8958885	6245363	1320726	1392796
其他院校 Others	1588241	1038834	266320	283087

科技经费情况
in Regular HEIs

单位:千元
Unit: in Thousand Yuan

支出 Expenditures				
合计 Total	劳务费 Personnel Costs	业务费 Non-Personnel Expenses	转拨外单位经费 Expenses on Extramural Services	其他 Others
155411687	**26822073**	**77551524**	**12763600**	**38274490**
100801394	17119231	51538289	10179778	21964096
52420484	9138388	25159999	2527339	15594758
2189809	564454	853236	56483	715636
17307175	2472876	8500889	1697882	4635528
73855480	13240096	38230205	7963498	14421681
64249032	11109101	30820430	3102220	19217281
54117724	9395028	26269910	4812163	13640623
72093065	12729364	36861000	5432855	17069846
9979148	1226086	5185652	1657169	1910241
9654870	1583286	5039164	535201	2497219
8220698	1625652	3488330	313749	2792967
1346182	262657	707468	12463	363594

普通高等学校研究与
Statistics of R&D Projects and

	科技课题 R & D Projects			出版科技专著(部) No. of Mono-graphs Published
	课题数(项) No. of Projects	投入人数 No. of Input of R&D Manpower	实际支出(千元) Actual Exp. (1,000 yuan)	
合计 Total	**594937**	**309036**	**100208489**	**13824**
按学校规格分 Breakdown by Category of HEIs				
"211"及省部共建高等学校 Key HEIs	282155	127309	71214882	3202
其他本科院校 Ordinary Degree Level HEIs	286143	164004	27934443	6899
高等专科学校 Short-cycle HEIs	26639	17723	1059164	3723
按学校隶属分 Breakdown by Control				
部委院校 HEIs under Other Central Ministries	35103	14619	12742898	460
教育部直属院校 HEIs under Ministry of Education	214133	94164	52184696	2326
地方院校 HEIs under Local Governments	345701	200252	35280895	11038
按学校类型分 Breakdown by Type of HEIs				
综合大学 Comprehensive Universities	186294	99547	33161290	3109
工科院校 Engineering	244308	111301	51483020	6095
农林院校 Agriculture	41428	18728	6746850	764
医药院校 Medicine & Pharmacy	68226	52878	4253979	2582
师范院校 Teachers Training	44150	21241	3996798	862
其他院校 Others	10531	5339	566552	412

发展课题、成果情况
Achievements in Regular HEIs

发表学士论文（篇） No. of Papers Published	成果获奖 Achievement Awards		技术转让 Technological Transfer		知识产权授权数 No. of Awarded	专利出售 Income from License Arrangements	
	合计 Total	其中：国家奖 of Which: National Awards	合同数 No. of Contracts	收入（千元） Actual Revenues (1,000yuan)		项数 No. of Items	实现金额（千元） Income
957332	**4787**	**280**	**12363**	**3659731**	**163157**	**5899**	**2931998**
468058	2429	223	3906	1724209	63682	2460	1737695
428387	2276	57	7760	1885565	80886	2990	1178514
60887	82	0	697	49957	18589	449	15789
65599	292	34	782	560278	8604	343	388276
341089	1741	177	2488	1009689	44850	1739	1298125
550653	2754	69	9093	2089764	109703	3817	1245597
306066	1430	112	3720	564534	46104	1848	620579
379265	1936	137	6570	2724241	87574	3296	2095555
53869	469	17	693	120245	9030	281	95257
141846	660	10	371	121231	5394	84	73843
61554	219	3	816	112753	11739	274	33630
14741	73	1	193	16727	3316	116	13134

二、社会科学
Social Science

普通高等学校人文、
Professional Manpower in Regular HEIs in the

		学校数(所) No. of HEIs	社科活动人员(人) Personnel Engaged in Social Science Research (person)				
			合计 Total	高级 Senior	中级 Middle	初级 Junior	其他人员 Others
合计 Total		**2322**	**731023**	**263017**	**338106**	**126404**	**117055**
按学校隶属关系分 Breakdown by Control	教育部直属院校 HEIs under Ministry of Education	73	65740	37007	25932	2751	35105
	其他部委院校 HEIs under Other Central Ministries	41	18244	8170	8259	1777	5951
	地方院校 HEIs under Local Governments	2208	647039	217840	303915	121876	75999
按学校规格分 Breakdown by Category of HEIs	本科院校 Regular HEIs	1180	559523	215377	259562	82380	114523
	专科院校 Short-cycle HEIs	1142	171500	47640	78544	44024	2532
按学校类型分 Breakdown by Type of HEIs	综合大学 Comprehensive Universities	562	212406	78518	96195	36937	39282
	理工农医院校 HEIs Science and Technology, Agriculture and Medicine	1055	236001	79227	115287	40515	29214
	师范院校 Teachers Training	215	113326	44486	50868	17340	19616
	语文院校 Languages	49	20288	6979	9652	3497	4459
	财经院校 Finance and Economics	242	86134	29741	39594	16435	15935
	政法院校 Political Science & Law	65	17976	7821	7740	2313	3531
	体育院校 Physical Culture	30	7735	2952	3195	1546	1003
	艺术院校 Art	87	26381	8533	11023	6423	1607
	民族院校 Minorities	17	10776	4760	4552	1398	2408

社会科学人力情况

Fields of the Humanities and Social Science

研究与发展人员(人) R & D Personnel (person)						研究与发展人员(人年) R & D Personnel (man/year)					
合计 Total	高级 Senior	中级 Middle	初级 Junior	其他人员 Others	研究生 Postgraduates	合计 Total	高级 Senior	中级 Middle	初级 Junior	其他人员 Others	研究生 Postgraduates
498616	**206183**	**194123**	**44136**	**4359**	**49815**	**105654.70**	**48586.30**	**39933.50**	**8238.80**	**617.00**	**8279.10**
85782	37904	19821	2246	728	25083	19365.40	10453.70	4422.50	387.30	90.30	4011.60
19055	8547	6710	1079	177	2542	4137.20	2009.70	1436.00	183.80	25.30	482.40
393779	159732	167592	40811	3454	22190	82152.10	36122.90	34075.00	7667.70	501.40	3785.10
430548	181825	160844	34425	3658	49796	93028.00	43869.40	33802.00	6567.50	514.70	8274.40
68068	24358	33279	9711	701	19	12626.70	4716.90	6131.50	1671.30	102.30	4.70
151670	64428	56449	12035	1576	17182	32968.30	16114.50	11810.70	2282.00	210.00	2551.10
147365	56924	62830	13622	736	13253	31146.80	13122.60	12948.60	2516.80	124.60	2434.20
86661	37389	32010	7763	815	8684	18039.50	8487.50	6510.40	1454.70	105.10	1481.80
14654	6114	5637	1233	171	1499	3012.30	1449.80	1115.30	222.50	20.90	203.80
59448	24523	23155	5564	450	5756	12229.10	5473.60	4629.00	997.50	66.20	1062.80
12368	5983	4458	1013	148	766	2476.10	1322.60	845.50	159.90	19.60	128.50
5905	2258	1660	631	43	1313	1284.40	601.00	359.80	122.20	7.70	193.70
9905	3684	4094	1376	192	559	2421.80	1005.40	968.80	314.40	34.60	98.60
10640	4880	3830	899	228	803	2076.40	1009.30	745.40	168.80	28.30	124.60

		学校数(所) No. of HEIs	拨入 Revenues						
			合计 Total	科研活动经费 Funds for R&D	科技活动人员工资 Personnel Costs	科研基建费 Capital Construction Funds for R&D	企事业单位委托项目经费 Contract Research Funds Provided by Ent. & Inst.	金融机构贷款 Loans Provided by Financial Inst.	自筹经费 Self-raised Funds
合计 Total		**2322.00**	**17973198.94**	**7529572.81**	**3226577.80**	**34387.49**	**4098049.45**	**19423.59**	**2735972.71**
按学校隶属关系分 Breakdown by Control	教育部直属院校 HEIs under Ministry of Education	73.00	5962643.43	3100103.98	526493.21	4100.00	1765070.31	0.00	344438.47
	其他部委院校 HEIs under Other Central Ministries	41.00	695439.71	347212.72	112995.85	2020.00	79029.44	0.00	147591.64
	地方院校 HEIs under Local Governments	2208.00	11315115.80	4082256.11	2587088.74	28267.49	2253949.70	19423.59	2243942.60
按学校规格分 Breakdown by Category of HEIs	本科院校 Regular HEIs	1180.00	17069162.85	7321905.38	2850113.69	32488.29	3991298.65	18086.00	2532201.31
	专科院校 Short-cycle HEIs	1142.00	904036.09	207667.43	376464.11	1899.20	106750.80	1337.59	203771.40
按学校类型分 Breakdown by Type of HEIs	综合大学 Comprehensive Universities	562.00	6536696.24	2793886.22	1006973.66	479.20	1624179.23	18000.00	937914.56
	理工农医院校 HEIs Science and Technology, Agriculture and Medicine	1055.00	3963579.11	1486100.01	898051.61	3303.30	1071631.64	1.00	408374.46
	师范院校 Teachers Training	215.00	3184009.18	1291304.13	566694.45	7990.00	699709.96	0.00	582179.07
	语文院校 Languages	49.00	605752.47	203669.25	109181.96	12437.03	82279.69	0.00	184687.05
	财经院校 Finance and Economics	242.00	2160685.84	955987.59	400126.33	6963.96	418826.82	1422.59	362091.79
	政法院校 Political Science & Law	65.00	461482.71	221250.66	80339.43	2020.00	55308.71	0.00	93304.82
	体育院校 Physical Culture	30.00	157218.83	71556.50	33578.29	680.00	22784.74	0.00	28432.30
	艺术院校 Art	87.00	633989.61	365832.02	81002.60	514.00	96728.18	0.00	87781.71
	民族院校 Minorities	17.00	269784.95	139986.43	50629.47	0.00	26600.48	0.00	51206.95

学研究与发展经费情况
Expenditure in Regular HEIs

单位：百元
unit：100 Yuan

		支出 Expenditures									
			内部支出 Intramural Expenditures								转拨给外单位经费 Extra-mural Exp.
国外资金 Foreign Funds	其他收入 Others Revenues	合计 Total	小计 Subtotal	科研人员费 Personnel Costs	业务费 Non-Personnel Expenses	科研基建费 Capital Construction Funds for R&D	仪器设备费 Instruments and Equipment	图书资料费 Books and Information	管理费 Manage-ment	其他 Others	
115923.05	**213292.04**	**16186808.02**	**16045584.75**	**4413537.63**	**7612920.94**	**35342.76**	**895262.15**	**1509723.23**	**477936.36**	**579771.13**	**141223.27**
100198.59	122238.87	5199735.14	5126329.71	886470.98	2834880.18	4100.00	253510.46	498041.73	444409.27	204917.09	73405.43
672.06	5918.00	623011.24	621298.34	134090.00	380804.73	5198.11	18039.49	32401.72	33527.09	17237.20	1712.90
15052.40	85135.17	10364061.64	10297956.70	3392976.65	4397236.03	26044.65	623712.20	979279.78		357616.84	66104.94
115677.94	207391.59	15311741.62	15175783.20	3959927.49	7356092.30	33314.56	862266.04	1438545.10	973788.82	551848.89	135958.42
245.11	5900.45	875066.40	869801.55	453610.14	256828.64	2028.20	32996.11	71178.13		27922.24	5264.85
39431.25	115832.12	5864037.65	5823700.44	1457858.49	2932162.91	2613.00	300880.07	548241.76		185396.62	40337.21
57072.80	39044.29	3623168.72	3574358.76	1155576.85	1605817.09	5820.20	128056.42	317301.87		136406.93	48809.96
10722.16	25409.41	2889277.57	2871952.64	773430.93	1228291.96	9316.65	253253.07	308307.33	179108.65	120244.05	17324.93
679.44	12818.05	507942.55	506569.34	184796.51	209545.10	1041.10	25604.65	37833.64	31491.38	16256.96	1373.21
4529.30	10737.46	1939640.81	1929850.73	526372.73	894582.27	9657.90	100560.43	192657.88		78354.04	9790.08
2699.98	6559.11	431245.52	419549.46	100498.86	223046.69	3698.11	16096.05	40276.34	8928.29	27005.12	11696.06
100.00	87.00	154217.71	153567.76	42113.29	80387.64	680.00	16086.89	4767.23	8369.58	1163.13	649.95
270.00	1861.10	546301.01	535598.14	106901.80	326814.09	1015.80	44639.94	35899.08		11557.99	10702.87
418.12	943.50	230976.48	230437.48	65988.17	112273.19	1500.00	10084.63	24438.10	12767.10	3386.29	539.00

		课题数（项）No. of Projects	当年投入人数（人年）Input of Man-year (man/year)	其中：研究生 of Which: Graduate Students	当年拨入经费（百元）Revenues (100 yuan)	当年支出经费（百元）Expenditures (100 yuan)
合 计 Total		**450028**	**105472.90**	**8278.10**	**9630172.75**	**7872766.11**
按学校隶属关系分 Breakdown by Control	教育部直属院校 HEIs under Ministry of Education	100560	19311.10	4011.60	4000185.45	3186788.80
	其他部委院校 HEIs under Other Central Ministries	15258	4131.10	482.40	433899.59	354633.20
	地方院校 HEIs under Local Governments	334210	82030.70	3784.10	5196087.71	4331344.11
按学校规格分 Breakdown by Category of HEIs	本科院校 Regular HEIs	401834	92855.40	8273.40	9355218.99	7645505.50
	专科院校 Short-cycle HEIs	48194	12617.50	4.70	274953.76	227260.61
按学校类型分 Breakdown by Type of HEIs	综合大学 Comprehensive Universities	147596	32899.20	2551.10	3716276.72	3050098.85
	理工农医院校 HEIs Science and Technology, Agriculture and Medicine	130542	31131.40	2434.20	2494978.80	2098264.51
	师范院校 Teachers Training	74044	18005.40	1481.80	1597559.78	1333329.76
	语文院校 Languages	13647	3003.60	203.80	220009.55	139512.07
	财经院校 Finance and Economics	50538	12203.00	1062.80	974700.13	746318.46
	政法院校 Political Science & Law	13133	2473.50	128.50	190162.38	140774.41
	体育院校 Physical Culture	4364	1279.20	193.70	71329.45	71210.16
	艺术院校 Art	9315	2408.00	97.60	224680.51	197537.28
	民族院校 Minorities	6849	2069.60	124.60	140475.43	95720.61

究与发展课题、成果情况
R & D and Achievements in Regular HEIs

出版专著(部) Monographs Published (titles)	发表论文(篇) No. of Papers Published				研究与咨询报告 Research and Consulting Report	
	合计 Total	国内学术刊物 In Domestic Journals	国外学术刊物 In Foreign Journals	港澳台刊物 In Hong Kong and Macao Journals	合计 Total	其中:被采纳数 of Which: Accepted Number
17584	**350769**	**336751**	**13399**	**619**	**17749**	**8613**
4302	65642	59213	6085	344	5734	3822
570	10388	9844	528	16	595	158
12712	274739	267694	6786	259	11420	4633
16543	287181	273463	13126	592	15456	7932
1041	63588	63288	273	27	2293	681
6055	112180	107046	4820	314	7006	3612
4339	98971	95032	3865	74	5935	2840
3373	58167	56617	1464	86	1603	945
513	10906	10135	724	47	525	315
1760	40890	38832	2000	58	1646	693
559	10404	10064	317	23	461	78
127	2744	2664	76	4	261	31
502	11559	11500	48	11	143	24
356	4948	4861	85	2	169	75

附　　表

Appendixes

（摘自国家统计局《2017 年中国统计年鉴》）

Data from “2017 China Statisical Yearbook”

国内生产总值

Gross Domestic Product

本表按当年价格计算。

Data in this table are calculated at current prices.

单位:亿元

unit:100 million yuan

年份 Year	国民总收入 Gross National Income	国内生产总值 Gross Domestic Product	第一产业 Primary Industry	第二产业 Secondary Industry	工业 Industry	建筑业 Construction	第三产业 Tertiary Industry	人均国内生产总值(元) Per Capita GDP (yuan)
1978	3678. 7	3678. 7	1018. 5	1755. 2	1621. 5	138. 9	905. 1	385
1979	4100. 5	4100. 5	1259. 0	1925. 4	1786. 5	144. 6	916. 1	423
1980	4587. 6	4587. 6	1359. 5	2204. 7	2014. 9	196. 3	1023. 4	468
1981	4933. 7	4935. 8	1545. 7	2269. 1	2067. 7	208. 0	1121. 1	497
1982	5380. 5	5373. 4	1761. 7	2397. 7	2183. 0	221. 6	1214. 0	533
1983	6043. 8	6020. 9	1960. 9	2663. 0	2399. 1	271. 7	1397. 0	588
1984	7314. 2	7278. 5	2295. 6	3124. 8	2815. 9	317. 9	1858. 1	702
1985	9123. 6	9098. 9	2541. 7	3886. 5	3478. 3	419. 3	2670. 7	866
1986	10375. 4	10376. 2	2764. 1	4515. 2	4000. 8	527. 3	3096. 9	973
1987	12166. 6	12174. 6	3204. 5	5274. 0	4621. 3	667. 5	3696. 2	1123
1988	15174. 4	15180. 4	3831. 2	6607. 4	5814. 1	811. 8	4741. 8	1378
1989	17188. 4	17179. 7	4228. 2	7300. 9	6525. 7	796. 1	5650. 6	1536
1990	18923. 3	18872. 9	5017. 2	7744. 3	6904. 7	861. 7	6111. 4	1663
1991	22050. 3	22005. 6	5288. 8	9129. 8	8138. 2	1017. 7	7587. 0	1912
1992	27208. 2	27194. 5	5800. 3	11725. 3	10340. 5	1417. 9	9668. 9	2334
1993	35599. 2	35673. 2	6887. 6	16473. 1	14248. 8	2269. 9	12312. 6	3027
1994	48548. 2	48637. 5	9471. 8	22453. 1	19546. 9	2968. 8	16712. 5	4081
1995	60356. 6	61339. 9	12020. 5	28677. 5	25023. 9	3733. 7	20641. 9	5091
1996	70779. 6	71813. 6	13878. 3	33828. 1	29529. 8	4393. 0	24107. 2	5898
1997	78802. 9	79715. 0	14265. 2	37546. 0	33023. 5	4628. 3	27903. 8	6481
1998	83817. 6	85195. 5	14618. 7	39018. 5	34134. 9	4993. 0	31558. 3	6860
1999	89366. 5	90564. 4	14549. 0	41080. 9	36015. 4	5180. 9	34934. 5	7229
2000	99066. 1	100280. 1	14717. 4	45664. 8	40259. 7	5534. 0	39897. 9	7942
2001	109276. 2	110863. 1	15502. 5	49660. 7	43855. 6	5945. 5	45700. 0	8717
2002	120480. 4	121717. 4	16190. 2	54105. 5	47776. 3	6482. 1	51421. 7	9506
2003	136576. 3	137422. 0	16970. 2	62697. 4	55363. 8	7510. 8	57754. 4	10666
2004	161415. 4	161840. 2	20904. 3	74286. 9	65776. 8	8720. 5	66648. 9	12487
2005	185998. 9	187318. 9	21806. 7	88084. 4	77960. 3	10400. 5	77427. 8	14368
2006	219028. 5	219438. 5	23317. 0	104361. 8	92238. 4	12450. 1	91759. 7	16738
2007	270844. 0	270232. 3	27788. 0	126633. 6	111693. 9	15348. 0	115810. 7	20505
2008	321500. 5	319515. 5	32753. 2	149956. 6	131727. 6	18807. 6	136805. 8	24121
2009	348498. 5	349081. 4	34161. 8	160171. 7	138095. 5	22681. 5	154747. 9	26222
2010	411265. 2	413030. 3	39362. 6	191629. 8	165126. 4	27259. 3	182038. 0	30876
2011	484753. 2	489300. 6	46163. 1	227038. 8	195142. 8	32926. 5	216098. 6	36403
2012	539116. 5	540367. 4	50902. 3	244643. 3	208905. 6	36896. 1	244821. 9	40007
2013	590422. 4	595244. 4	55329. 1	261956. 1	222337. 6	40896. 8	277959. 3	43852
2014	644791. 1	643974. 0	58343. 5	277571. 8	233856. 4	44880. 5	308058. 6	47203
2015	686449. 6	689052. 1	60862. 1	282040. 3	236506. 3	46626. 7	346149. 7	50251
2016	741140. 4	744127. 2	63670. 7	296236. 0	247860. 1	49522. 2	384220. 5	53980

注:1. 数据来源:摘自国家统计局《2017 中国统计年鉴》。

2. 1980 年以后国民总收入(原称国民生产总值)与国内生产总值的差额为国外净要素收入。

Note:1. Data sources:National Bureau of Statistics《2017 China Statistical Yearbook》.

2. Since 1980,the difference between the Gross Domestic Product and the Gross National Income (formerly, the Gross National Product) is the net factor income from the rest of the world.

分地区国内生产总值(2016年)

Gross Domestic Product by Region (2016)

本表绝对数按当年价格计算,指数按可比价格计算。 单位:亿元

Absolute figures in this table are calculated at current prices while indices are calculated at comparable prices. unit: 100 million yuan

地 区 Region	国内生产总值 Gross Domestic Product	三次产业增加值 Value-Added by Three Strata of Industry			分行业增加值 Value-Added by Sector		人均国内生产总值(元) Per Capita GDP (yuan)
		第一产业 Primary Industry	第二产业 Secondary Industry	第三产业 Tertiary Industry	工 业 Industry	建筑业 Construction	
北 京 Beijing	25669.13	129.79	4944.44	20594.90	4026.68	1025.50	118198
天 津 Tianjin	17885.39	220.22	7571.35	10093.82	6805.13	786.89	115053
河 北 Hebei	32070.45	3492.81	15256.93	13320.71	13387.46	1885.27	43062
山 西 Shanxi	13050.41	784.78	5028.99	7236.64	4148.91	895.63	35532
内蒙古 Inner Mongolia	18128.10	1637.39	8553.63	7937.08	7233.00	1322.50	72064
辽 宁 Liaoning	22246.90	2173.06	8606.54	11467.30	6818.32	1880.85	50791
吉 林 Jilin	14776.80	1498.52	7004.95	6273.33	6070.07	960.87	53868
黑龙江 Heilongjiang	15386.09	2670.46	4400.69	8314.94	3647.14	874.23	40432
上 海 Shanghai	28178.65	109.47	8406.28	19662.90	7555.34	879.81	116562
江 苏 Jiangsu	77388.28	4077.18	34619.50	38691.60	30455.15	4173.66	96887
浙 江 Zhejiang	47251.36	1965.18	21194.61	24091.57	18655.12	2610.72	84916
安 徽 Anhui	24407.62	2567.72	11821.58	10018.32	10076.94	1763.53	39561
福 建 Fujian	28810.58	2363.22	14093.47	12353.89	11698.36	2421.34	74707
江 西 Jiangxi	18499.00	1904.53	8829.54	7764.93	7219.11	1610.91	40400
山 东 Shandong	68024.49	4929.13	31343.67	31751.69	27588.70	3806.31	68733
河 南 Henan	40471.79	4286.21	19275.82	16909.76	17042.72	2292.04	42575
湖 北 Hubei	32665.38	3659.33	14654.38	14351.67	12536.39	2192.97	55665
湖 南 Hunan	31551.37	3578.37	13341.17	14631.83	11337.28	2016.59	46382
广 东 Guangdong	80854.91	3694.37	35109.66	42050.88	32650.89	2551.82	74016
广 西 Guangxi	18317.64	2796.80	8273.66	7247.18	6816.64	1458.41	38027
海 南 Hainan	4053.20	948.35	905.95	2198.90	482.50	424.50	44347
重 庆 Chongqing	17740.59	1303.24	7898.92	8538.43	6183.80	1715.12	58502
四 川 Sichuan	32934.54	3929.33	13448.92	15556.29	11058.79	2472.96	40003
贵 州 Guizhou	11776.73	1846.19	4669.53	5261.01	3715.64	955.44	33246
云 南 Yunnan	14788.42	2195.11	5690.16	6903.15	3891.20	1806.22	31093
西 藏 Tibet	1151.41	115.78	429.17	606.46	86.44	342.73	35184
陕 西 Shaanxi	19399.59	1693.85	9490.72	8215.02	7598.00	1943.20	51015
甘 肃 Gansu	7200.37	983.39	2515.56	3701.42	1757.53	776.35	27643
青 海 Qinghai	2572.49	221.19	1249.98	1101.32	901.68	348.67	43531
宁 夏 Ningxia	3168.59	241.60	1488.44	1438.55	1054.34	434.20	47194
新 疆 Xinjiang	9649.70	1648.97	3647.01	4353.72	2677.63	1049.93	40564

数据来源:摘自国家统计局《2017中国统计年鉴》。

Data sources: National Bureau of Statistics《2017 China Statistical Yearbook》.

国家财政收支总额及增长速度
Total Government Revenue and Expenditures and Their Increase Rate

年　份 Year	财政收入 （亿元） Total Revenue （100 million yuan）	财政支出 （亿元） Total Expenditures （100 million yuan）	增长速度（%） Increase Rate（%）	
			财政收入 Total Revenue	财政支出 Total Expenditures
1978	1132.26	1122.09	29.5	33.0
1980	1159.93	1228.83	1.2	-4.1
1985	2004.82	2004.25	22.0	17.8
1990	2937.10	3083.59	10.2	9.2
1991	3149.48	3386.62	7.2	9.8
1992	3483.37	3742.20	10.6	10.5
1993	4348.95	4642.30	24.8	24.1
1994	5218.10	5792.62	20.0	24.8
1995	6242.20	6823.72	19.6	17.8
1996	7407.99	7937.55	18.7	16.3
1997	8651.14	9233.56	16.8	16.3
1998	9875.95	10798.18	14.2	16.9
1999	11444.08	13187.67	15.9	22.1
2000	13395.23	15886.50	17.0	20.5
2001	16386.04	18902.58	22.3	19.0
2002	18903.64	22053.15	15.4	16.7
2003	21715.25	24649.95	14.9	11.8
2004	26396.47	28486.89	21.6	15.6
2005	31649.29	33930.28	19.9	19.1
2006	38760.20	40422.73	22.5	19.1
2007	51321.78	49781.35	32.4	23.2
2008	61330.35	62592.66	19.5	25.7
2009	68518.30	76299.93	11.7	21.9
2010	83101.51	89874.16	21.3	17.8
2011	103874.43	109247.79	25.0	21.6
2012	117253.52	125952.97	12.9	15.3
2013	129209.64	140212.10	10.2	11.3
2014	140370.03	151785.56	8.6	8.3
2015	152269.23	175877.77	5.8	13.2
2016	159604.97	187755.21	4.5	6.3

数据来源：摘自国家统计局《2017 中国统计年鉴》。
Data sources: National Bureau of Statistics《2017 China Statistical Yearbook》.

中央财政和地方财政收支总额

Total Revenue and Expenditures of Central and Local Governments

单位:亿元

unit: 100 million yuan

年份 Year	财政收入 Total Revenue			财政支出 Total Expenditures		
	合计 Total	中央 Central Government	地方 Local Government	合计 Total	中央 Central Government	地方 Local Government
1978	1132.26	175.77	956.49	1122.09	532.12	589.97
1980	1159.93	284.45	875.48	1228.83	666.81	562.02
1985	2004.82	769.63	1235.19	2004.25	795.25	1209.00
1990	2937.10	992.42	1944.68	3083.59	1004.47	2079.12
1991	3149.48	938.25	2211.23	3386.62	1090.81	2295.81
1992	3483.37	979.51	2503.86	3742.20	1170.44	2571.76
1993	4348.95	957.51	3391.44	4642.30	1312.06	3330.24
1994	5218.10	2906.50	2311.60	5792.62	1754.43	4038.19
1995	6242.20	3256.62	2985.58	6823.72	1995.39	4828.33
1996	7407.99	3661.07	3746.92	7937.55	2151.27	5786.28
1997	8651.14	4226.92	4424.22	9233.56	2532.50	6701.06
1998	9875.95	4892.00	4983.95	10798.18	3125.60	7672.58
1999	11444.08	5849.21	5594.87	13187.67	4152.33	9035.34
2000	13395.23	6989.17	6406.06	15886.50	5519.85	10366.65
2001	16386.04	8582.74	7803.30	18902.58	5768.02	13134.56
2002	18903.64	10388.64	8515.00	22053.15	6771.70	15281.45
2003	21715.25	11865.27	9849.98	24649.95	7420.10	17229.85
2004	26396.47	14503.10	11893.37	28486.89	7894.08	20592.81
2005	31649.29	16548.53	15100.76	33930.28	8775.97	25154.31
2006	38760.20	20456.62	18303.58	40422.73	9991.40	30431.33
2007	51321.78	27749.16	23572.62	49781.35	11442.06	38339.29
2008	61330.35	32680.56	28649.79	62592.66	13344.17	49248.49
2009	68518.30	35915.71	32602.59	76299.93	15255.79	61044.14
2010	83101.51	42488.47	40613.04	89874.16	15989.73	73884.43
2011	103874.43	51327.32	52547.11	109247.79	16514.11	92733.68
2012	117253.52	56175.23	61078.29	125952.97	18764.63	107188.34
2013	129209.64	60198.48	69011.16	140212.10	20471.76	119740.34
2014	140370.03	64493.45	75876.58	151785.56	22570.07	129215.49
2015	152269.23	69267.19	83002.04	175877.77	25542.15	150335.62
2016	159604.97	72365.62	87239.35	187755.21	27403.85	160351.36

数据来源:摘自国家统计局《2017 中国统计年鉴》。

Data sources: National Bureau of Statistics《2017 China Statistical Yearbook》.

人口数及构成

Population and Its Composition

单位：万人
unit: 10 thousand persons

年 份 Year	年底总人口 Total Population (year-end)	按性别分 By Sex				按城乡分 By Residence			
		男 Male		女 Female		城镇 Urban		乡村 Rural	
		人口数 Population	比重(%) Proportion	人口数 Population	比重(%) Proportion	人口数 Population	比重(%) Proportion	人口数 Population	比重(%) Proportion
1978	96259	49567	51.49	46692	48.51	17245	17.92	79014	82.08
1979	97542	50192	51.46	47350	48.54	18495	18.96	79047	81.04
1980	98705	50785	51.45	47920	48.55	19140	19.39	79565	80.61
1981	100072	51519	51.48	48553	48.52	20171	20.16	79901	79.84
1982	101654	52352	51.50	49302	48.50	21480	21.13	80174	78.87
1983	103008	53152	51.60	49856	48.40	22274	21.62	80734	78.38
1984	104357	53848	51.60	50509	48.40	24017	23.01	80340	76.99
1985	105851	54725	51.70	51126	48.30	25094	23.71	80757	76.29
1986	107507	55581	51.70	51926	48.30	26366	24.52	81141	75.48
1987	109300	56290	51.50	53010	48.50	27674	25.32	81626	74.68
1988	111026	57201	51.52	53825	48.48	28661	25.81	82365	74.19
1989	112704	58099	51.55	54605	48.45	29540	26.21	83164	73.79
1990	114333	58904	51.52	55429	48.48	30195	26.41	84138	73.59
1991	115823	59466	51.34	56357	48.66	31203	26.94	84620	73.06
1992	117171	59811	51.05	57360	48.95	32175	27.46	84996	72.54
1993	118517	60472	51.02	58045	48.98	33173	27.99	85344	72.01
1994	119850	61246	51.10	58604	48.90	34169	28.51	85681	71.49
1995	121121	61808	51.03	59313	48.97	35174	29.04	85947	70.96
1996	122389	62200	50.82	60189	49.18	37304	30.48	85085	69.52
1997	123626	63131	51.07	60495	48.93	39449	31.91	84177	68.09
1998	124761	63940	51.25	60821	48.75	41608	33.35	83153	66.65
1999	125786	64692	51.43	61094	48.57	43748	34.78	82038	65.22
2000	126743	65437	51.63	61306	48.37	45906	36.22	80837	63.78
2001	127627	65672	51.46	61955	48.54	48064	37.66	79563	62.34
2002	128453	66115	51.47	62338	48.53	50212	39.09	78241	60.91
2003	129227	66556	51.50	62671	48.50	52376	40.53	76851	59.47
2004	129988	66976	51.52	63012	48.48	54283	41.76	75705	58.24
2005	130756	67375	51.53	63381	48.47	56212	42.99	74544	57.01
2006	131448	67728	51.52	63720	48.48	58288	44.34	73160	55.66
2007	132129	68048	51.50	64081	48.50	60633	45.89	71496	54.11
2008	132802	68357	51.47	64445	48.53	62403	46.99	70399	53.01
2009	133450	68647	51.44	64803	48.56	64512	48.34	68938	51.66
2010	134091	68748	51.27	65343	48.73	66978	49.95	67113	50.05
2011	134735	69068	51.26	65667	48.74	69079	51.27	65656	48.73
2012	135404	69395	51.25	66009	48.75	71182	52.57	64222	47.43
2013	136072	69728	51.24	66344	48.76	73111	53.73	62961	46.27
2014	136782	70079	51.23	66703	48.77	74916	54.77	61866	45.23
2015	137462	70414	51.22	67048	48.78	77116	56.10	60346	43.90
2016	138271	70815	51.21	67456	48.79	79298	57.35	58973	42.65

注：总人口和城镇人口中包括中国人民解放军现役军人，按城乡分人口中现役军人计入城镇人口。
Note: Urban Population include the military personnel of Chinese People's Liberation Army.

分地区按性别分的15岁及以上文盲人口(2016年)
Illiterate Population Aged 15 and Over by Sex and Region(2016)

本表是2016年全国人口变动情况抽样调查样本数据,抽样比为0.837%。
Data in this table are obtained from the 2016 National Sample Survey on Population Changes, the sampling fraction is 0.837%.

地区 Region	15岁及以上人口(人) Population Aged 15 & Over			文盲人口(人) Illiterate			文盲人口占15岁及以上人口比重 Percentage to Total Population Aged 15 & Over (%)		
	合计 Total	男 Male	女 Female	合计 Total	男 Male	女 Female	合计 Total	男 Male	女 Female
合 计 Total	**965321**	**488944**	**476376**	**50980**	**13402**	**37578**	**5.28**	**2.74**	**7.89**
北 京 Beijing	16160	8275	7885	252	52	201	1.56	0.62	2.54
天 津 Tianjin	11624	6217	5407	262	66	196	2.26	1.07	3.62
河 北 Hebei	51166	25832	25334	2097	473	1623	4.10	1.83	6.41
山 西 Shanxi	26163	13383	12780	660	198	462	2.52	1.48	3.61
内蒙古 Inner Mongolia	18431	9303	9128	859	252	607	4.66	2.71	6.65
辽 宁 Liaoning	32768	16513	16254	553	144	409	1.69	0.87	2.52
吉 林 Jilin	20043	10116	9927	496	151	345	2.47	1.49	3.48
黑龙江 Heilongjiang	28670	14444	14226	1031	356	675	3.60	2.47	4.74
上 海 Shanghai	18236	9347	8889	567	114	454	3.11	1.22	5.10
江 苏 Jiangsu	57799	28713	29085	3361	790	2571	5.81	2.75	8.84
浙 江 Zhejiang	40768	21118	19650	2443	568	1875	5.99	2.69	9.54
安 徽 Anhui	42927	21710	21218	2923	810	2114	6.81	3.73	9.96
福 建 Fujian	26534	13292	13241	1628	314	1314	6.14	2.37	9.92
江 西 Jiangxi	30389	15452	14937	1469	358	1111	4.83	2.32	7.44
山 东 Shandong	69325	34752	34573	4547	1089	3458	6.56	3.13	10.00
河 南 Henan	63480	31520	31960	3586	1076	2510	5.65	3.41	7.85
湖 北 Hubei	41739	21236	20503	2352	552	1800	5.64	2.60	8.78
湖 南 Hunan	46880	23678	23201	1588	430	1158	3.39	1.82	4.99
广 东 Guangdong	76689	40344	36345	2204	429	1775	2.87	1.06	4.88
广 西 Guangxi	31991	16441	15550	1212	241	971	3.79	1.47	6.25
海 南 Hainan	6178	3228	2950	286	77	209	4.63	2.38	7.10
重 庆 Chongqing	21611	10852	10759	869	203	666	4.02	1.87	6.19
四 川 Sichuan	58371	28868	29503	4799	1336	3463	8.22	4.63	11.74
贵 州 Guizhou	23252	11848	11404	2758	742	2017	11.86	6.26	17.68
云 南 Yunnan	32301	16265	16036	2853	842	2010	8.83	5.18	12.54
西 藏 Tibet	2119	1076	1043	871	360	511	41.12	33.47	49.02
陕 西 Shaanxi	27265	13659	13606	1423	427	996	5.22	3.13	7.32
甘 肃 Gansu	18235	9127	9109	1587	460	1127	8.70	5.04	12.38
青 海 Qinghai	4004	2065	1938	538	192	347	13.45	9.27	17.90
宁 夏 Ningxia	4581	2345	2236	312	82	230	6.82	3.50	10.30
新 疆 Xinjiang	15624	7925	7699	591	219	373	3.79	2.76	4.84

注:本表"文盲人口"指15岁及15岁以上不识字及识字很少人口。
Note: Illiterate population in this table refers to the population aged 15 and over, who are unable or have difficulty in reading.

本表是 2016 年全国人口变动情况抽样调查样本数据,抽样比为 0.837%。

Data in this table are obtained from the 2016 National Sample Survey on Population Changes, the sampling fraction is 0.837%.

地 区 Region	6 岁及 6 岁以上人口 Population Aged 6 and Over			未上过学 Illiterate			小 学 Primary School			初 中 Junior Secondary School		
	合计 Total	男 Male	女 Female	合计 Total	男 Male	女 Female	合计 Total	男 Male	女 Female	合计 Total	男 Male	女 Female
全 国 National Total	**1077322**	**549723**	**527599**	**61448**	**18267**	**43181**	**275939**	**131541**	**144398**	**418395**	**225166**	**193229**
北 京 Beijing	17001	8721	8279	313	74	238	1631	741	890	4070	2156	1914
天 津 Tianjin	12401	6619	5781	333	96	239	1902	962	941	4169	2393	1776
河 北 Hebei	57884	29438	28446	2752	783	1968	14776	6989	7787	25765	13774	11991
山 西 Shanxi	29052	14883	14169	909	300	609	5620	2607	3014	12675	6648	6027
内蒙古 Inner Mongolia	19913	10053	9860	1013	332	681	4312	2011	2301	7552	4194	3359
辽 宁 Liaoning	35135	17741	17395	782	244	537	6838	3131	3708	15399	8081	7318
吉 林 Jilin	21860	11076	10784	675	234	441	5106	2436	2670	9333	4861	4472
黑龙江 Heilongjiang	30868	15574	15294	1295	482	813	6952	3302	3649	13491	7074	6417
上 海 Shanghai	19274	9910	9364	651	152	500	2528	1165	1363	6199	3304	2895
江 苏 Jiangsu	62953	31572	31381	3908	1055	2853	14012	6325	7687	22540	11931	10609
浙 江 Zhejiang	44145	22940	21204	2916	764	2153	12079	5864	6215	15554	8711	6843
安 徽 Anhui	48183	24636	23547	3549	1059	2491	13091	6056	7035	20802	11277	9526
福 建 Fujian	29688	14977	14710	1953	453	1500	9407	4307	5100	10337	5799	4538
江 西 Jiangxi	35394	18318	17076	1830	524	1306	10875	5118	5756	13502	7243	6259
山 东 Shandong	77354	39172	38183	5230	1404	3824	18766	8764	10002	30835	16546	14289
河 南 Henan	73743	37393	36351	4323	1455	2868	17933	8781	9151	32979	17355	15624
湖 北 Hubei	46004	23522	22482	2690	704	1986	10885	5115	5770	17461	9295	8166
湖 南 Hunan	53099	27041	26057	1984	618	1366	13315	6310	7004	20403	10477	9926
广 东 Guangdong	85168	45148	40020	3194	908	2286	18686	8842	9844	33330	18439	14890
广 西 Guangxi	36994	19136	17857	1697	468	1228	10350	4895	5455	16376	9019	7357
海 南 Hainan	7037	3708	3329	332	106	227	1570	751	820	3197	1715	1482
重 庆 Chongqing	24087	12182	11906	1070	287	783	7581	3667	3914	8112	4272	3839
四 川 Sichuan	65259	32466	32793	5508	1674	3835	21287	10482	10805	23637	12591	11046
贵 州 Guizhou	27172	13928	13244	3117	924	2192	9233	4698	4535	9951	5670	4281
云 南 Yunnan	36930	18655	18276	3219	1032	2186	14306	7186	7120	12135	6834	5301
西 藏 Tibet	2512	1272	1240	982	410	571	786	448	338	466	273	193
陕 西 Shaanxi	29889	15052	14837	1685	542	1143	6847	3172	3674	11835	6364	5471
甘 肃 Gansu	20445	10322	10122	1793	550	1244	6813	3264	3549	6337	3461	2876
青 海 Qinghai	4581	2359	2223	605	219	386	1602	790	812	1390	804	585
宁 夏 Ningxia	5210	2681	2529	350	99	251	1394	672	722	1821	1013	807
新 疆 Xinjiang	18087	9230	8857	790	315	475	5455	2692	2763	6743	3591	3151

注:本表数据摘自《2017 中国统计年鉴》。

Note: Data sources: National Bureau of Statistics《2017 China Statistical Yearbook》.

教育程度分的人口(2016 年)
Level and Region(2016)

单位:人
unit: person

高中 Senior Secondary School			中职 Secondary Vocational School			大学专科 College Students			大学本科 Undergraduates			研究生 Postgraduates		
合计 Total	男 Male	女 Female	合计 Total	男 Male	女 Female	合计 Total	男 Male	女 Female	合计 Total	男 Male	女 Female	合计 Total	男 Male	女 Female
137409	**77412**	**59997**	**44762**	**23914**	**20848**	**74338**	**38819**	**35519**	**59235**	**31341**	**27894**	**5797**	**3263**	**2533**
2228	1120	1108	1030	530	500	2320	1130	1190	4152	2170	1982	1257	799	458
1560	851	708	1261	713	548	1501	738	762	1517	780	737	158	86	72
6712	3731	2981	1913	1062	851	3596	1858	1737	2220	1163	1057	150	77	73
4588	2559	2029	1319	692	628	2269	1198	1071	1490	788	702	182	91	91
2701	1332	1369	694	383	312	1966	1043	923	1609	729	881	65	29	35
4161	2183	1977	1626	857	768	2974	1512	1461	3005	1552	1453	352	180	173
3020	1632	1389	633	317	316	1444	727	717	1517	803	715	132	67	65
4089	2229	1860	883	452	431	2060	1055	1005	1971	914	1057	128	65	62
2840	1570	1269	1264	690	574	2323	1214	1109	2915	1499	1416	553	315	238
8530	5018	3512	3506	1735	1770	5797	2924	2873	4190	2313	1877	471	271	200
5296	3035	2261	1594	875	720	3296	1705	1591	3186	1871	1315	223	116	107
4940	2953	1987	1286	686	600	2634	1517	1117	1771	1030	741	110	59	51
3121	1823	1298	1449	750	699	1815	979	836	1504	809	695	102	57	45
4831	2845	1986	1180	610	570	1856	1050	806	1251	887	364	70	40	30
9083	5233	3850	3942	2161	1781	5409	2757	2652	3742	2115	1628	348	192	156
10694	5911	4783	1944	1003	940	3904	1842	2061	1850	977	873	116	67	49
6345	3685	2660	2218	1205	1013	3236	1822	1414	2904	1549	1355	266	147	119
9071	5055	4016	2142	1144	997	3800	2089	1711	2201	1244	957	183	105	79
13313	7791	5522	4866	2693	2172	6197	3448	2749	5296	2869	2427	286	157	128
3932	2240	1692	1684	915	770	1879	1014	865	983	529	454	92	57	36
841	516	325	412	225	187	404	237	167	275	155	119	6	3	2
3380	1882	1498	907	478	429	1836	971	865	1135	585	550	67	40	27
6827	3756	3071	2131	1110	1022	3511	1798	1713	2243	996	1247	115	60	55
2201	1221	980	766	391	374	1060	552	509	824	465	359	21	8	13
2850	1511	1339	1210	636	574	1566	795	772	1580	629	951	64	32	32
128	71	58	18	11	6	60	29	31	71	30	41	1	0	1
4485	2521	1964	1216	697	518	2319	1067	1252	1382	628	754	121	60	61
2700	1546	1154	610	317	293	1185	643	541	938	507	431	68	34	34
428	246	183	112	59	52	244	132	112	192	104	88	8	5	4
655	364	291	189	104	84	448	240	208	333	176	157	20	12	9
1860	981	878	758	410	348	1432	732	699	989	477	512	62	31	30